Understanding Sport Organizations

Applications for Sport Managers

Third Edition

Trevor Slack, PhD
Editor

with

Terri Byers, PhD
University of New Brunswick, Canada

and

Alex Thurston, PhD
Loughborough University, UK

HUMAN KINETICS

Library of Congress Cataloging-in-Publication Data

Names: Slack, Trevor, 1948-2016, editor.
Title: Understanding sport organizations : applications for sport managers / Trevor Slack, PhD, editor, with Terri Byers, PhD, University of New Brunswick, Canada, and Alex Thurston, PhD, Loughborough University, UK.
Description: Third Edition. | Champaign, Illinois : Human Kinetics, [2021] | Second edition: 2006. | Includes bibliographical references and index.
Identifiers: LCCN 2019021138 (print) | LCCN 2019022043 (ebook) | ISBN 9781492594093 (epub) | ISBN 9781492594109 (PDF) | ISBN 9781492500803 (print)
Subjects: LCSH: Sports administration--Handbooks, manuals, etc. | Organizational sociology--Handbooks, manuals, etc.
Classification: LCC GV713 (ebook) | LCC GV713 .S576 2021 (print) | DDC 796.06--dc23
LC record available at https://lccn.loc.gov/2019021138

ISBN: 978-1-4925-0080-3 (print)

How to cite this text in APA style:

Slack, T. (Ed.), Byers, T., & Thurston, A. (2021). *Understanding sport organizations: Applications for sport managers* (3rd ed.). Champaign, IL: Human Kinetics.

The web addresses cited in this text were current as of October 2019, unless otherwise noted.

Acquisitions Editor: Andrew L. Tyler; **Senior Developmental Editor:** Christine M. Drews; **Managing Editors:** Hannah Werner and Amy Stahl; **Copyeditor:** Marissa Wold Uhrina; **Indexer:** Rebecca L. McCorkle; **Permissions Manager:** Dalene Reeder; **Graphic Designer:** Denise Lowry; **Cover Designer:** Keri Evans; **Cover Design Specialist:** Susan Rothermel Allen; **Photograph (cover):** Saicle/iStock/Getty Images; **Photographs (interior):** © Human Kinetics, unless otherwise noted; photos on page iii © Alex Thurston; **Photo Asset Manager:** Laura Fitch; **Photo Production Manager:** Jason Allen; **Senior Art Manager:** Kelly Hendren; **Illustrations:** © Human Kinetics, unless otherwise noted; **Printer:** Sheridan Books

Printed in the United States of America 10 9 8 7 6 5 4 3 2 1

The paper in this book is certified under a sustainable forestry program.

Human Kinetics
1607 N. Market St.
Champaign, IL 61820
Website: www.HumanKinetics.com

In the United States, email info@hkusa.com or call 800-747-4457.
In Canada, email info@hkcanada.com.
In the United Kingdom/Europe, email hk@hkeurope.com.

For information about Human Kinetics' coverage in other areas of the world, please visit our website: **www.HumanKinetics.com**

Tell us what you think!
Human Kinetics would love to hear what we can do to improve the customer experience. Use this QR code to take our brief survey.

E6369

This book is dedicated to the late, great Professor Trevor Slack

"May my life's work speak for me."

CONTENTS

FOREWORD

And a Reflection on My Friend Trevor Slack

It is difficult to write about a dear friend for whom one has felt such deep admiration without seeming to exaggerate. I have known Trevor Slack since 1988 when he was a member of the physical education faculty at the University of Alberta (U of A) and one of its most accomplished faculty members. He was also working on research projects on sport management with distinguished members of the U of A business faculty. Even at that first meeting, Trevor's warmth and hospitality struck me even more than his considerable scholarly wisdom and reputation.

Ever since then, Trevor has been a wonderful and supportive friend. His mastery of his research domain is well known, as was his unique ability to draw upon the best conceptual work in management and organizational theory and apply it in innovative ways to produce insights for sport management. This current edition of *Understanding Sport Organizations* is a reflection of that capacity. In it, Trevor (and the contributors that he selected) cover all of the most significant issues from the management discipline related to sport management. These include organizational goals, design, culture, power, change, conflict, leadership, strategy, and the environment. In doing so, Trevor draws judiciously upon some of the most important conceptual and empirical work in the management field, synthesizes it masterfully, and applies it to clarify and enlighten some of the most pressing and current challenges facing those in and around sport management. Thus this book will be of great value to university students at every level of study, to practitioners in the field, and to a general readership who just want to know more about the field.

Indeed, I have always been struck by the conscientiousness, practicality, and social importance of Trevor's work, the marvelous clarity of his writing and teaching, and his rich experience, both as a practitioner and scholar. This volume is a partial testimony to that.

But if I may, I would like to interject a personal note to let readers know about the kind of person Trevor was. Trevor was a generous and kind soul, always modest, and infallibly a great listener and adviser. He taught many of us by personal example what it was to be a moral and supremely courageous human being. When Trevor had his stroke in 2002, he became severely incapacitated. Some years later he also was obliged to undergo kidney dialysis. Yet despite these ever-growing hardships, Trevor never complained and never stopped soldiering on in his profession. During those 13 years of unimaginable physical challenge, he continued to work closely with students, do research, and present keynote speeches at conferences around the world. He also wrote and published important work, as attested to in part by this edition, and continued to perform many reviews. In fact, we were exchanging emails up until the week before he died, and his wife, Janet, told me that he was still reviewing a manuscript for a journal on the very day he died, knowing that he had but hours to live.

I called Trevor "the lion of England" because of his courage and his great heart. But that does not do him justice. He was to me and so many others an immensely influential but impossible-to-emulate role model and a wonderful friend who was always there to help and advise. Happily, his work and example remain to inspire us all.

Danny Miller
HEC Montreal

CONTRIBUTORS

Christos Anagnostopoulos, PhD
University of Central Lancashire - Cyprus and Molde University College, Norway

Jon Arcelus, LMS, GP(T), FRCPsych, PhD
University of Nottingham, United Kingdom

Sue Arrowsmith, QC (hon), DJur
University of Nottingham, United Kingdom

Terri Byers, PhD
University of New Brunswick, Canada

Graham Cuskelly, PhD
Griffith University, Queensland, Australia

Borja García, PhD
Loughborough University, United Kingdom

Bill Gerrard, DPhil
Leeds University Business School, United Kingdom

Marilyn Giroux, PhD
HEC Montréal, Québec, Canada

Spencer Harris, PhD
University of Colorado, Colorado Springs

James Andrew Kenyon, PhD
Loughborough University, United Kingdom

Phillip Lunga, MBA
University of New Brunswick, Canada

Lionel Maltese, PhD
Kedge Business School and Université Aix-Marseille, Marseille, France

Argyro Elisavet Manoli, PhD
Loughborough University, United Kingdom

Andy Miah, PhD
University of Salford, Manchester, United Kingdom

Frank Pons, PhD
Université Laval, Québec, Canada

Jonathan Robertson, PhD
Deakin University, Geelong, Australia

Berit Skirstad, MS
Norwegian School of Sport Sciences, Oslo, Norway

Alex Thurston, PhD
Loughborough University, United Kingdom

Meghan Thurston, DClin Psy, PhD
National Health Service, United Kingdom

PREFACE

In the early 1980s, when Trevor began his doctoral studies in the area of sport management, he started to read the books that were being written about this relatively new area of study. Although there were only a few sport management texts at that time, he became increasingly frustrated with those that did exist because, with very few exceptions, they failed to take into account the vast body of literature available in the broader field of management studies. Trevor wondered, Why did scholars in the field of sport management fail to utilize work from such areas as organizational theory, organizational behavior, strategic management, marketing, the sociology of organizations, finance, and accounting? Didn't sport organizations have cultures? Did they not expect to formulate strategies? Were their operations not influenced by technological and contextual changes? And did they not exhibit the same political and decision-making processes as other types of organizations? The answer to each of these questions was, obviously, yes!

Over the last 25 to 30 years, however, researchers in our field of sport management have developed an awareness of the contribution that the literature from the areas just cited can make to our understanding of the structure and operations of sport organizations. The formation of the North American Society of Sport Management (NASSM) in 1985 and the creation of the *Journal of Sport Management* (Trevor was the editor-in-chief from 1996 to 2000); the formation of the European Association for Sport Management (EASM) in 1993 and the creation of *European Sport Management Quarterly* (Trevor was, in fact, the founding editor of this journal); the formation of the Sport Management Association of Australia and New Zealand (SMAANZ) and the creation of *Sport Management Review*; and, more recently, the formation of other continental sport management associations, other sport-related journals, and the World Association for Sport Management (WASM) all helped tremendously in this regard. The purpose of the first edition of *Understanding Sport Organizations* was a modest attempt to demonstrate the importance of how the field of sport management should be informed by work in the broader field of management studies. The first and second editions of *Understanding Sport Organizations* became internationally recognized as the best sport management textbook by the scholarly community and beyond. This third edition once again presents seminal works on various topics applicable to sport management, which are very relevant to the field. In this edition, countless updated examples are presented to illustrate the relevance of those seminal theories in this much expanded field and, as we will see, an interdisciplinary approach—rather than a sole focus on organizational theory—is now required to make sense of a rapidly developing sport industry.

The backstory to this edition of *Understanding Sport Organizations* is that Trevor wanted to write a third edition of his groundbreaking textbook. The publisher wanted to produce a third edition. Students, academics, and practitioners alike, from all over the globe, frequently asked, "When's the next edition coming out? It's my go-to textbook." With the clear demand, the process of publishing a third edition commenced.

Although Trevor was still very active in the field of sport management—delivering keynotes (EASM 2014 and NASSM 2015), reviewing journal articles and PhD theses—he was aware that, due to his ill-health, academic work took him longer than it once did (although Trevor was lucky to have a great health-care assistant, Amy Brock, who typed his work on the computer), and he recognized that it was challenging to keep abreast with all of the very latest developments throughout the ever-expanding field of sport management. Therefore, to maintain the quality and rigor of the previous two editions, Trevor decided that it was best to make his third edition an edited textbook, bringing together experts to write several new chapters, while he updated those chapters that remained from the second edition. Once this third edition project was in motion, sadly, Trevor's health rapidly deteriorated and he passed away, surrounded by his family, in January 2016. One of Trevor's last wishes was that we would see this project through to publication. In Trevor's final keynote, his take-home message was, "Today, people who study the management of sport require knowledge in one or more of the following areas: political science, history, economics, gender studies, technology, and other subjects. . . . [We] must apply our knowledge and, in turn, help the field progress!" You will see in the table of contents of this third edition that these areas are covered. You will also notice that the book no longer places primary focus on organizational theory (as the first two editions did), because Trevor recognized the importance of interdisciplinary research and how we should broaden the literature base we use. As he explained in his penultimate keynote in 2014,

> Individuals who study the management of sport should use literature and theories that are relevant for their research. For the most part, this is found in the general management field. However, sport management academics may use, where appropriate, the literature from [other] fields. . . . They may also use the literature of sociology, the basis of organisation theory and psychology, the basis of organisational behavior, and also, the basis of many marketing studies.

With this third edition, Trevor wanted to offer one final contribution to the field of sport management to help with its continued development. We gave him our word that we would ensure this happened.

Since coming on board as coeditors, we have found this a particularly difficult and complicated process in finalizing this third edition. Clearly, we would have preferred that Trevor could have finished the project himself, but we thank him and his wife, Janet, for entrusting us with the project. In addition to producing countless journal articles, reports, reviews, and other books, Trevor provided a significant contribution to sport management with the publication of *Understanding Sport Organizations: The Application of Organization Theory*, and, as he always did, provided an opportunity for student collaboration on the second edition, in that case with his then-PhD student, Milena Parent. Hence, even after Trevor's passing, he has provided us with this opportunity to collaborate, and we have worked hard to complete this book at a standard that would make Trevor proud. We each updated several chapters for which Trevor did not get the opportunity to fully update. On the advice of the publisher, our names have been added to these chapters and we have been listed as coeditors to ensure there is no disingenuity to the readership of this book.

As you will have now come to realize, Trevor's successful approach to academic scholarship was firmly grounded in the application of mainstream management literature, as well as an appreciation of the contribution of other disciplines. This third edition contains a very detailed bibliography that includes citations from articles from the field of sport management as well as references to organizational and management literature and beyond. Citations include articles that have appeared in such major journals as *Organization Studies*, *Administrative Science Quarterly*, *Journal of Management Studies*, *Academy of Management Journal*, and *Academy of Management Review*. References to the seminal works in the field are outlined in each chapter. Our intention with this third edition is not to provide a review and update of all theoretical developments since the second edition; we have continued to use the older seminal theories found in the mainstream management literature, which remain the cornerstone of this book and are as relevant as they have always been. We have, however, also included references to key recent articles of quality that have built on these earlier concepts and frameworks. We have also updated the multitude of examples that were skillfully woven throughout each chapter (used to help explain theories) and the associated writings, offered a new contemporary opening scenario to set up each chapter, provided new Time Outs (used to further demonstrate valuable topic-related information), and concluded every chapter with a new case for analysis.

We hope that you all enjoy reading this long-awaited updated edition of *Understanding Sport Organizations*. Using a beer analogy from a Guinness UK marketing campaign (as Trevor very much enjoyed his real ales and stout): Good things come to those who wait (and work damn hard!).

Alex and Terri

ACKNOWLEDGMENTS

First and foremost, we would like to thank Trevor and his family (and raise a pint of beer, obviously!) for entrusting us to complete this project. On behalf of Trevor, we'd like to acknowledge and thank Milena Parent for all her hard work with the second edition of *Understanding Sport Organizations*. Finally, we would like to thank all the new contributors to this third edition for their support and patience throughout this project.

PART I

INTRODUCING SPORT MANAGEMENT

Like a successful sport organization, a good textbook needs an appropriate structure. The chapters in this book are arranged to provide a logical progression to understanding the various components and processes of and in sport organizations. This part introduces the reader to the field of sport management. It deals with some of the basic concepts of organizational theory and organizational behavior to help contextualize what we mean by the *sport industry*. It also describes some different ways of looking at organizations and how different perspectives and theoretical disciplines that sport managers adopt will influence what they see and how they manage. Then, various approaches of how to conduct research in sport management are provided. Within chapter 2 there are many references to specialist research methods books and journal articles that readers are encouraged to seek out to gain full understanding of the chapter.

Throughout this part, and the remainder of the textbook, the contributors have provided several examples to help illustrate the concepts and ideas discussed within each chapter. The examples are taken from a variety of organizations that collectively make up the sport industry. All examples are from real organizations. Therefore, we encourage you to take some time to search the Internet to find out more information about each organization, positioning yourself as a sport manager, then applying relevant concepts from this book.

The format of each chapter starts by listing the learning objectives and the key concepts discussed, then presents an opening scenario from an actual sport organization, illustrating the topic to be covered. The major theoretical ideas about the particular topic are then introduced and related specifically to sport organizations. Appropriate figures and tables are used to help explain the points being made. At several places in each chapter you will find Time Outs that illustrate the issues related to those being discussed by providing accounts taken from actual situations concerning sport organizations or from research findings. A section outlining key issues for sport managers brings the research presented to the level of the sport manager. Each chapter has a brief summary. A set of review questions is provided to stimulate discussion about central issues in the chapter. A section containing suggestions for further readings at the end of each chapter includes readings from general management literature and sport management literature. Finally, each chapter (except chapter 1) has a Case for Analysis, taken from an actual situation in a sport organization. Questions about the case are provided for class discussion.

CHAPTER 1

The Management of Sport Organizations

Trevor Slack, PhD
Alex Thurston, PhD

Learning Objectives

When you have read this chapter, you should be able to

1. explain why it is important for sport managers to understand organizations;
2. define what we mean when we talk about a sport organization;
3. explain the terms *organizational structure, design*, and *context;*
4. distinguish between organizational theory and organizational behavior;
5. explain the different ways of looking at sport organizations; and
6. discuss the types of research studies that can be found in the field of sport management.

Key Concepts

contingency theory
cybernetics
instruments of domination
life cycle perspective
organizational behavior
organizational context
organizational culture
organizational design
organizational structure
organizational theory
population ecology
scientific management
sport organizations
systems of political activity
systems theory

The Under Armour Story

In 1996, a 23-year-old former special teams (e.g., one of the offense, defense, or kicker squads) captain of the University of Maryland gridiron football team turned his dream into a reality. When Kevin Plank was playing college football, he used to hate wearing his heavy, sweat-soaked, cotton T-shirts when the team trained twice a day. He was determined to find a solution to this issue. Plank noticed that the base-layer compression shorts (designed to increase muscle endurance) he wore during practice stayed dry and comfortable. Interested by this fact, he visited a local textile store where he found a synthetic fabric similar to his compression shorts. He researched the athletic benefits of synthetic fabrics and created some samples to test on his teammates. The feedback was positive; the T-shirts stayed comfortable and retained very little sweat.

Plank, along with a friend, Kip Fulks, set up in his grandmother's basement developing a sample prototype. Using credit cards and savings, he launched his new company, Under Armour. The first Under Armour product was a HeatGear T-shirt that he named the #0037, which was engineered with moisture-wicking fibers (Under Armour, n.d.). Plank traveled up and down the East Coast of the United States, using his network of friends and contacts from the collegiate and professional sports leagues, selling his new product out of the back of his car. By the end of 1996 Plank had sold 500 HeatGear T-shirts and secured his first team sale, which generated US$17,000 in sales (Harrison, 2014).

In 1997 Under Armour introduced a ColdGear fabric (designed to keep athletes warm, dry, and light in cold conditions) and then a range of other lines. By the end of 1998, Under Armour outgrew Plank's grandma's basement, so Plank and Fulks (now Under Armour's vice president of production) moved to an all-new headquarters and warehouse in Baltimore (Under Armour, n.d.).

In 1999 Under Armour managed to secure a deal to supply apparel and accessories for the film *Any Given Sunday,* starring Al Pacino and Jamie Foxx. During key scenes, the gridiron football team members were seen wearing Under Armour apparel and accessories. In 2000, off the back of the success of the film, Plank jumped at the chance to further increase exposure by placing an advertisement in *ESPN The Magazine,* which depicted an athlete wearing Under Armour's performance apparel. This was an astute move that paid off: the company saw a US$750,000 increase in sales (Under Armour, n.d.), and, for the first time, Plank officially put himself on the payroll.

Over the next few years, the brand continued to develop relationships with professional sports leagues and supply apparel for other movies. In 2002 Under Armour launched its first TV campaign, moved its global headquarters to a 65,000-square-foot old soap factory in south Baltimore, and hired around 100 new staff. The following year the company launched a women's line, and the year after that they introduced boys' and girls' apparel.

On November 18, 2005, Under Armour went public. Within 10 years of its inception, Under Armour ended the year with US$281 million in revenue (Badenhausen, 2006). By the end of 2010 Under Armour surpassed US$1 billion in annual revenue, almost quadrupling revenues in a five-year period, becoming the second largest sportswear brand in the United States at the end of 2014. In 2015 Under Armour diversified its market with the purchase of fitness app companies Endomondo and MyFitnessPal, and in 2016 continued to push technology innovation.

Although Under Armour's meteoric rise demonstrates a true success story, the journey was not without its issues. Due perhaps to unwillingness, Plank had not patented his performance wear. As a result, many imitators started replicating Under Armour products. In 2001 Plank appeared to not be concerned by this, suggesting to *Sports Illustrated* that the knockoffs validated the Under Armour brand. But the imitators began to have an effect: Nike's Pro Compression, Reebok's Play Dry, and other performance apparel lines were affecting Under Armour sales. Then, to compound the situation, Reebok signed an exclusive deal with the NFL, and Nike secured the new MLB contract. The competition's bullish approach to business was eye-opening for Under Armour.

More recently, Under Armour faced fierce backlash in response to Kevin Plank's comments on CNBC praising Donald Trump. This led an industry research firm to suggest that it was "nearly impossible to effectively build a cool urban lifestyle brand in the foreseeable future" (Green, 2017b). Plank attempted to distance himself from his comments by publishing a full-page advertisement in his hometown newspaper, *The Baltimore Sun*, to clarify his previous remarks (Green, 2017a). As you will see later in this chapter, whether intended or not, all organizations are political.

What Kevin Plank created was a sport organization. As the organization grew, he found that the original informal operating structure and style of management were no longer efficient for producing the range of apparel lines and accessories for a worldwide market. This kind of volume requires a different type of organizational design, one with specialized units, complex coordinating mechanisms, and a hierarchical management structure. The success that Plank has achieved is, in large part, a result of the changes made to the structure of Under Armour as it grew and faced new and different contextual pressures. To be able to compete in the athletic apparel industry, Plank was forward thinking, which enabled him to keep ahead of changing trends and emerging competition.

Under Armour's situation is not unique: Philip Knight similarly started selling athletic footwear out of the back of his car, which was the beginning of Nike. To operate effectively and efficiently, any sport organization needs to adapt its structure and management processes to meet the demands of its contextual situation. As the contributors will show throughout this textbook, a knowledge of organizational theory, organization behavior, and other theories relevant to our field can help the sport manager in this task.

Why Sport Managers Need to Understand the Complexity of the Sport Industry

Sport is a rapidly growing and increasingly diverse industry. Increased amounts of discretionary income, a heightened awareness of the relationship between an active lifestyle and good health, a greater number of opportunities to participate in sport, and continued technological and media distribution advances have all contributed to this growth and expansion. The early proliferation of the industry can be traced back nearly 40 years when the journal *Retail Business* described the sport industry during the 1980s as "one of the most buoyant consumer markets" (Economic Intelligence Unit, 1990, p. 61) and predicted real-term growth into the 1990s. This prediction is also true for the 21st century.

Although it is difficult to estimate the monetary value of the sport industry—due to the complex nature of where the boundaries lie for the industry and, often, a lack of full access to government funding streams—several estimates have been proposed. One comprehensive attempt to estimate the gross domestic (sport) product (GD[S]P), with the intention to demonstrate the size of the sport industry in the United States, Milano and Chelladurai (2011) proposed a moderate estimate of US$189.338 billion. More recently, Pricewaterhouse-Coopers (PwC), a worldwide professional services network, publish an annual *PwC Sports Outlook* report for North America, which offers PwC's perspective on the value of the sports industry. PwC suggests that over the past 20 years North America experienced a building boom that saw more than US$55 billion spent on construction of facilities alone across professional sports and intercollegiate athletics (PWC, 2017). The 2018 report is based on four key segments of the North American sports market: media rights, gate revenues, sponsorship, and merchandising (different criteria to Milano and Chelladurai's approach). PwC suggests that sport industry in North America is worth US$71.2 billion, predicted to grow to US$80.3 billion by 2022 (PWC, 2018). On a global scale, A.T. Kearney Inc., a strategic insight global consultancy firm, estimated that in 2011 the global sport industry was worth US$620 billion. The findings of the study also suggested that sports spending was growing at a faster rate than GDP around the world, which means the sports industry has grown in both developing and developed countries (Collignon, Sultan, & Santander, 2011). One of the most recent estimates, offered by Plunkett Research, suggests that the size of the global sports industry (at year-end of 2017) has increased to an enormous US$1.3 trillion! (Plunkett Research Ltd., n.d.). Even though it is problematic to accurately measure the size of the sport industry, the following list provides some indication of its magnitude today, accompanied with some contemporary examples.

1. The average household expenditure in Canada on recreation during 2017 was Can$3,986 (US$3,013) (Statistics Canada, n.d.)
2. In 2015 Canadian households spent Can$131 (US$99) on live sporting and performing arts events, which was more than in any of the previous five years (Canadian Arts Presenting Association/l'Association canadienne des organismes artistiques [CAPACOA], 2017).
3. As of June 2017, the cost of the 2016 Rio Olympics had risen to US$13.2 billion (and continues to rise) (Reuters, 2017)
4. In 2018, boxer Floyd Mayweather was listed as the highest-paid athlete in the world, earning US$285 million (Badenhausen, 2018).
5. The combined income (consisting of earnings from prize money, salaries, and endorsements) of the 100 top-earning athletes over the 12-month period between June 2018 and June 2019 was US$4 billion (Badenhausen, 2019b).
6. In 2019, the NFL's Dallas Cowboys were reported to be the most valuable sport team in the world, worth US$5 billion, with an operating income of US$365 million. And, in July 2019, 52 teams across all sports were worth at least US$2 billion (Badenhausen, 2019a).
7. Global broadcast revenue for the 2012 London and 2016 Rio Olympic Games were US$2.569 million and US$2.868 million, respectively (IOC, 2019).
8. A 30-second commercial during the 2018 Super Bowl LII (gridiron football) cost over US$5.23 million USD. That's a 96 percent increase over the last decade. (Poggi, 2019)
9. The 30-second commercials during the 2019 Super Bowl LIII were sold for between $5.1 and $5.3 million USD. This was the first year in over a decade where the commercial price plateaued (G. Smith, 2019)
10. The Birmingham 2022 Commonwealth Games in the United Kingdom will cost £778 million (US$941 million), which will be the most expensive sports event in the United Kingdom since the 2012 London Olympic and Paralympic Games, but the figure is lower than the 2018 Gold Coast Commonwealth Games cost of £967 million (US$1.2 trillion) (Roan, 2019).

[*Note*: All currency conversions correct as of July 2019.]

A variety of types of organizations make up the sport industry, including a vast array of public, private, and voluntary organizations involved in the provision of sport products and services. Some, like Brunswick Corporation, which is heavily involved in billiards, fitness, and marine equipment, and FGL Sports Ltd., a large sporting goods retailer, both have sales in the millions and billions of dollars and employ thousands of people. Others, such as Hawkinsport (an independent family-run traditional sports equipment supplier in England), operate on a considerably smaller scale. A large number of the organizations explored in this book are designed to make a profit for their owners; others, such as Mountain Equipment Co-op (MEC) of Vancouver, operate on a cooperative basis, focusing the business structure around values (rather than being driven by profit), then offer exclusive benefits to their members (who each become an owner of MEC). Many **sport organizations** operate as voluntary or nonprofit organizations; the funds they generate are used to further activities that benefit their membership or the communities where they are based. Some sport organizations, particularly those from the public sector, have as their primary function to aid and assist other organizations in the delivery of sport. For example, Sport England (an executive nondepartmental public body, sponsored by the United Kingdom Government's Department for Digital, Culture, Media and Sport) invests funds from the government and the National Lottery to support its mandate "that everyone in England, regardless of age, background or ability, feels able to take part in sport or activity" (Sport England, n.d.). Many sport organizations are linked to educational institutions and provide recreational and competitive sport opportunities as a part of the educational process. The sport industry also includes professional sport organizations, which pay athletes to compete in their particular sport; the given event is then sold to live audiences and to television networks for its entertainment value.

Organizations and individuals (often referred to as *actors* in the literature) are, then, integral and pervasive parts of the sport industry. For those of you who hope to work in this industry, a knowledge of organizational theory and organizational behavior will help you understand the organizations with which you will interact and why they are structured and operate in a particular way. For students specializing in sport management, presumably one of the reasons for studying organizations is that someday you hope to work for or eventually manage an organization. Knowledge of organizational theory and organizational behavior that has been systematically and scientifically derived can help you better understand the problems you will face as a manager. It can help you design an appropriate structure, manage the changes that need to be made in your organization's structure as changes take place in its contextual situation, provide appropriate leadership, adopt appropriate technologies, resolve conflicts, manage human resources, and achieve the goals of your organization. *In short, it can help you become a better manager.*

Some Definitions

This chapter has already highlighted that many different types of sport organizations exist. The terms *structure*, *design*, and *context* have been used to describe aspects of these organizations, and it has been suggested that organizational theory and organizational behavior can help in the task of managing the composition of these organizations. But what exactly is meant by these terms? In the following section of this chapter some definitions are provided to help facilitate an understanding of these concepts; more detailed explanations can be found in later chapters. Although some management theorists (March & Simon, 1958) suggest that definitions do not clearly delimit the object being examined, Hall (1982) argues that definitions provide a starting point for understanding the element of interest. While the contributors of this book acknowledge that sport organizations (and their context, structure, design, and composition) are not homogeneous entities that can be exactly defined but rather are complex processes and sets of socially and historically constituted relationships, the approach taken here is consistent with Hall's argument that defining concepts can provide a basis for understanding.

What Is a Sport Organization?

While Under Armour and agencies like the San Francisco 49ers, the Canadian Olympic Committee, the Ladies Professional Golf Association, Creative Health Products Inc., the Alberta Cricket Association, Loughborough Lightning netball team, and Manchester United association football club can all be classified as sport organizations, what is it that makes them sport organizations? Certainly, it is not size—Creative Health Products Inc. sells a variety of fitness testing and assessing products, yet it has less than 10 employees. It is not the amount of money they make—a number of professional sport teams such as those in the Canadian Football League and the English Premier League (association football) consistently lose money. Nor is it the existence of employees—the Alberta Cricket Association has no full-time paid staff. The definition of a sport organization used in this book is based on definitions of an organization provided by Daft (1989, 2004, 2015) and Robbins (1990) and is as follows: *A sport organization is a social entity involved in the sport industry; it is goal directed, with a consciously structured activity system and a relatively identifiable boundary.*

There are five key elements in this definition, each of which warrant further explanation:

1. *Social entity*: All sport organizations are composed of people or groups of people who interact with each other to perform those functions essential to the organization.

2. *Involvement in the sport industry*: What differentiates sport organizations from other organizations, such as banks, pharmaceutical companies, and car dealerships, is the former's direct involvement in one or more aspects of the sport industry—for example, through the production of sport-related products or services. While agencies like banks, pharmaceutical companies, and car dealerships are regularly involved in sport (primarily through sponsorship), they are not usually directly involved with the phenomenon and hence are not included as a sport organization in this book. The aim of the book is, however, to be inclusive in explaining the nature of sport organizations. Hence, examples will be drawn from companies such as W.L. Gore & Associates, the manufacturer of Gore-Tex, a product used in a range of sportswear and equipment; the various national and state park recreation agencies that support many natural resources in which sport activities are often played and practiced. We will also examine organizations such as Yamaha and 3M (formerly known as the Minnesota Mining and Manufacturing Corporation), which, while they do not have sport products or services as their central focus, still have substantive involvement in the sport industry.

3. *Goal-directed focus*: All sport organizations exist for a purpose, whether for making a profit, encouraging participation in a given sport, or winning Olympic medals. The goals of a sport organization are not usually as easily obtainable by an individual as they are by members working together. Sport organizations may have more than one goal, and individual members may have different goals from those of the organization.

4. *Consciously structured activity system*: The interaction of people or groups of people in sport organizations does not occur through random chance; rather, activity systems such as marketing, product and service development, financial management, and human resource development are consciously structured. The main functions of the sport organization are broken down into smaller tasks or groups of tasks; the mechanisms used to coordinate and control these tasks help ensure that the goals of the sport organization are achieved.

5. *Identifiable boundary*: Sport organizations need to have a relatively identifiable boundary that distinguishes members from nonmembers. Members of a sport organization usually have an explicit or implicit agreement with the organization through which they receive money, status, or some other benefit for their involvement. For some sport organizations, particularly those in the voluntary or nonprofit sector, the boundaries may not be as easily identified as in those sport organizations concerned with making a profit or those in the public sector. Nevertheless, every sport organization must have a boundary that helps distinguish members from nonmembers, but these boundaries are not fixed and may change over time.

The elements of the definition adopted in this book are evident in Under Armour, the sport organization that Kevin Plank created. The goals of the company are to manufacture sportswear, footwear, and accessories to sell at a profit. As Under Armour has grown and more people have been hired, activity systems have been consciously structured to effectively and efficiently achieve the goals of the organization. The people hired identify themselves as employees and managers of Under Armour, which creates for them an identifiable boundary to differentiate their company from its competitors in the sportswear industry.

Organizational Structure of a Sport Organization

The term **organizational structure** is used here to define the manner in which the tasks of a sport organization are broken down and allocated to employees or volunteers, the reporting relationships among these role holders, and the coordinating and controlling mechanisms used within the sport organization. A typical organizational chart outlines, in part, the structure of an organization. (See figure 1.1.)

Identifying the dimensions that constitute the structure of any organization is, at best, a difficult exercise and one that has yielded inconsistency across studies. Yet organizational structure is an important concept to study because, as Miller (1987, p. 7) suggests, it "importantly influences the flow of interaction and the context and nature of human interactions. It channels collaboration, specifies modes of coordination, allocates power and responsibility, and prescribes levels of formality and complexity." Hall (1982), Miller and Dröge (1986), and Van de Ven (1976) all suggest that structure should be examined using three dimensions: complexity, formalization, and centralization. Each of these structural dimensions is examined in more detail in chapter 5.

Organizational Design

The concept of **organizational design** refers to the patterning of the structural elements of an organization. All managers seek to produce a design that will enhance their ability to achieve the goals of their organization. Miller (1981) argued that organizations must be constructed to ensure that there is complementary alignment or fit among their structural variables. In what is probably the best-known attempt to identify organizational designs, Mintzberg (1979) proposes five design configurations: the simple structure, the machine bureaucracy, the divisionalized form, the professional bureaucracy, and the adhocracy. Sport organizations can be found in each of these categories; these are discussed more specifically in chapter 6.

Context of a Sport Organization

The structure of a sport organization is closely related to the particular context in which the organization operates. The term **organizational context** merely refers to "the organizational setting which influences the structural dimensions" (Daft, 1989, p. 17). Variation in the structures of sport organizations are mainly found because they operate with different contextual situations. As was the case with organizational structure, different studies have identified different dimensions as characterizing an organization's context. Contextual dimensions are often referred to in the literature as determinants, imperatives, or, most frequently, contingencies. Supporters of this school of thought (i.e., contingency theory) argue that changes in an organization's structure are contingent on changes in its contextual situation. The three main contextual factors identified as influencing structure—environment, strategy, and technology—are explored in chapters 4, 8, and 21.

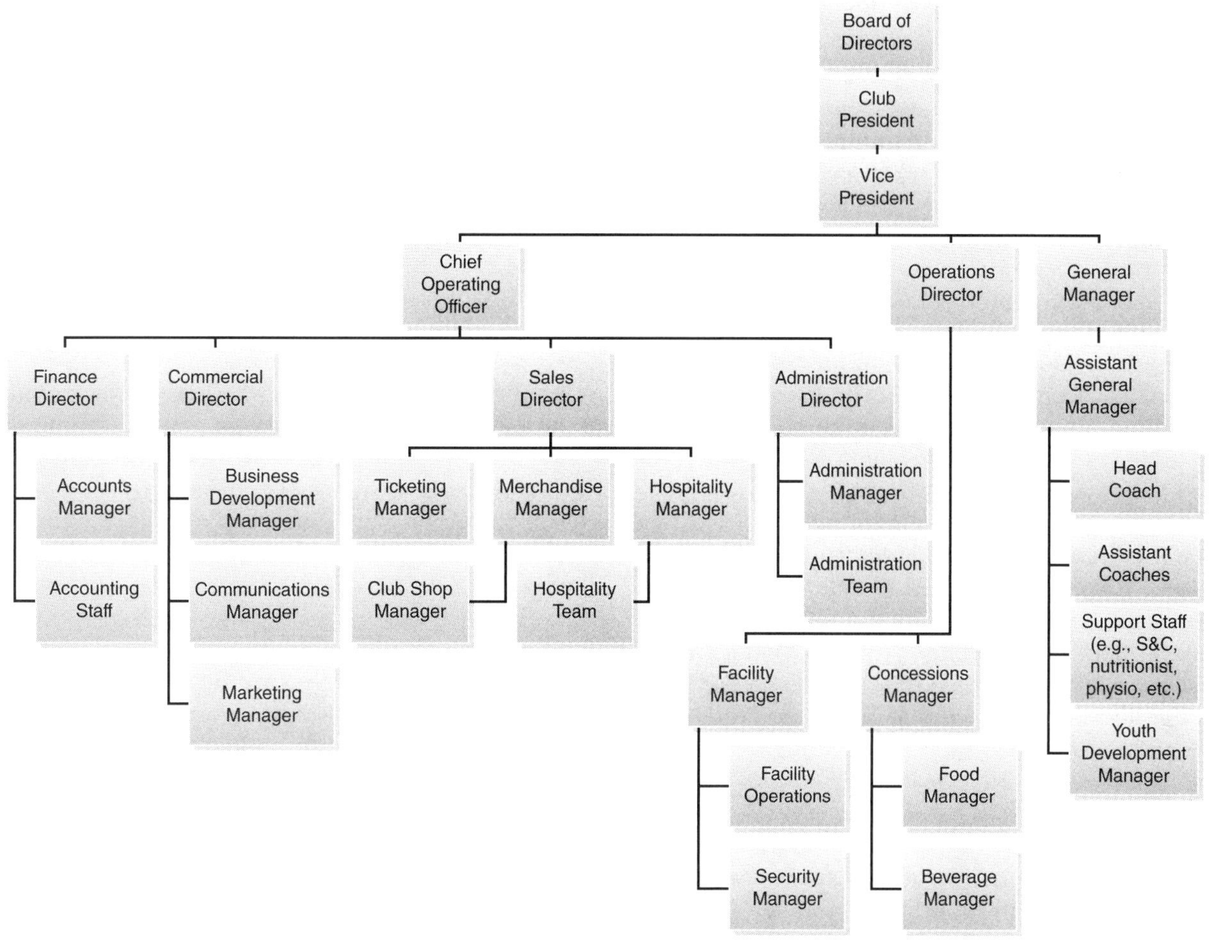

Figure 1.1 Organizational structure of a fictitious professional sport club.

Distinction Between Organizational Theory and Organizational Behavior

All organizations can be studied at different levels and in different ways; sport organizations are no exception. Within the field of sport management, students should understand what has often been referred to as the *macro and micro distinction*, or the distinction between **organizational theory** (OT) and **organizational behavior** (OB).

OT, a disciplinary area within the broader field of business and management studies, is the macro perspective concerned with the structure and design of organizations. Scholars in this field seek to identify commonly occurring patterns and regularities in organizations and understand their causes and consequences. Organizational theorists also examine the impact of contextual factors such as strategy, size, and technology on structure and design; such issues as the role of power in organizations; and how such processes as decision making and change are managed. The organization (or its primary subunits) is the unit of analysis.

To explain a sport organization from the macro perspective, it is necessary to examine its characteristics and composition (i.e., departments, groups) but also to examine the organization's environmental characteristics (Daft, 2004). Organizational theorists are concerned with the total organization's ability to achieve its goals effectively; thus, they must consider not only how it is structured but also how it is situated in a broader sociopolitical and economic context.

While organizational theorists are concerned with theoretical issues, that is, pushing back the frontiers of knowledge about organizations, sport management students should not be concerned that the subject area has no practical application. On the contrary, scholars in this area frequently work with the practicing manager (i.e., through consultancy work); the central focus of a large percentage of the research they undertake is to discover ways to help managers in their jobs. For sport managers, OT can provide a better understanding of the way sport organizations are structured and designed, how they operate, and why some are effective when others are not. This understanding can help sport managers analyze and diagnose more effectively the problems they face and enable them to respond with appropriate solutions.

In contrast to the macro perspective, in the past, researchers of OB were more concerned with individual-based issues such as job satisfaction, leadership style, communication, team-building, and motivation, all traditionally associated with the micro perspective. However, OB scholars focus on more than just the individuals and small groups within the organization; the characteristics of the environment in which they work are also important to understand. Now there is some overlap because earlier it was suggested that examining an organization's environmental characteristics adopted an OT macro perspective. In fact, Buchanan and Huczynski (2019) advise that it is often accepted in the literature that OB has become an umbrella term that covers many facets of studying an organization, from micro to macro perspectives. In their book *Organizational Behavior*, they define OB as "the study of structure and management of organizations, their environments, and the actions and interactions of their individual members and groups" (p. 3), and suggest that, in many cases, it is a combination of factors that explain the behavior in question, rather than simply one individual's personality or ability to execute tasks.

The approach for OT draws strongly from sociology, while OB draws predominantly from social psychology. This distinction between OT and OB is important for sport management students to understand because, with some exceptions, the dominant trend of the empirical work in our field has been concerned with OB topics, such as the level of job satisfaction, leadership, and motivation of sport managers. As highlighted, the OT and OB distinction is certainly not a clear one; both approaches are important to a full understanding of sport management. For example, the lack of women in senior positions in management (and sport management in particular) has often been explained by looking at the individual and her motivation, leadership ability, and skills—an OB approach. While this approach can provide useful material to start to correct some of the inequalities we see in sport organizations, it fails to address the structural conditions that constrain women's progress in these organizations, something to be considered using an OT approach. Studies from both perspectives would provide a fuller understanding of the gendered nature of sport organizations and many other important issues in management. See, for example, Sibson (2010) or Kanter (1977) for work of this nature and Hall, Cullen, and Slack (1989) for an early overview of the gender and management literature as it applied to sport. Finally, chapter 11 of this book—a new chapter—specifically focuses on gender and sport organizations.

The approach taken in the 2nd edition of this book predominantly applied work from OT to help explain how to better manage sport organizations. However, with this 3rd edition a number of chapters, such as the ones on leadership, control, volunteers, and mental health, utilize work traditionally more closely aligned with the OB perspective. The addition of the control, volunteers in sport, and mental health chapters in this edition (together with the new non-OB-focused chapters including governance, corporate social responsibility, procurement, and sports analytics), is a reflection of the continued growth of the field of sport management and is a demonstration of the breadth of perspectives and concepts now required to help us better understand the sport industry. Sport management students should not view OT and OB as opposing perspectives. Rather, each perspective emphasizes different levels of analysis that should complement the other in providing a fuller understanding of sport management.

Ways to Look at Sport Organizations

Researchers have looked at organizations in many ways; some of these approaches are complementary, some overlap, and some are conflicting, but all can be applied to the study of sport organizations and their management. The approach that has tended to dominate OT-based studies in sport management, **systems theory**, grew out of the work of the theoretical biologist Ludwig von Bertalanffy (1950, 1968) and is best exemplified in its application to organizations by the work of Katz and Kahn (1978). As you will see later, however, systems theory exhibits a number of problems, and there are other equally viable ways to look at sport organizations. One of the best works to categorize the different ways of looking at organizations is Gareth Morgan's *Images of Organization* (2006). Morgan's basic argument is that different "theories and explanations of organizational life are based on metaphors that lead us to see and understand organizations in distinctive yet partial ways" (p. 4).

By looking at these different perspectives on organizations we come to better understand them and their management. These metaphors are explained in more detail in the passages to follow, and where available, examples from the literature on sport organizations are provided.

Organizations as Machines

One of the most pervasive images we have of organizations is as machines. Originating with the classical theorists, such as Henri Fayol and, in particular, Frederick Taylor with his notions of **scientific management,** organizations are seen from this perspective as a series of interrelated parts, each performing a narrowly defined set of activities to achieve a particular end product. Like a machine, the organization is expected to operate in a rigid, repetitive, and impersonal manner.

Although heavily criticized for their impersonal nature (Braverman, 1974), ideas grounded in "Taylorism" still pervade the way in which many organizations, including some in the sport industry, operate. Sport organizations most likely to employ elements of this approach are those involved in the assembly-line production of commodities such as athletic shoes, baseball bats, hockey sticks, and bicycles. Mechanistic approaches to organization are also promoted in some elements of sport management literature. Several textbooks in the area are constructed around Henri Fayol's concepts of planning, organizing, coordinating, commanding, and controlling. In addition, many public-sector documents on the management of sport, and some sport management texts (Chelladurai, 2014; Horine, 1985; VanderZwaag, 1984), stress the usefulness and importance of the more modern mechanistic approaches to management such as management by objectives (MBO) and planning, programming, budgeting systems (PPBS). Sport teams have also often been described as machinelike in their operation (cf. Castaing, 1970; Terkel, 1972; Fielding, Miller, & Brown, 1999).

Organizations as Organisms

In large part, as a reaction to the technical emphasis of scientific management, scholars like Herzberg, Mausner, and Snyderman (1959), Maslow (1943), and McGregor (1960) started to focus on the needs of the individual, the group, and the organization. This focus, by necessity, drew attention to the environment in which the organization existed as a source of satisfaction for these needs. Thus, organizations were likened to organisms that come in a variety of forms and rely on being able to adapt to changes in their environment in order to survive. Also, like organisms, organizations were seen to exhibit different systems (usually termed the *input, throughput*, and *output systems*) that interacted with each other and their environment. Figure 1.2 shows these systems as they would apply to a sport equipment manufacturer. In each of the three systems there is a reliance on the environment for certain organizational needs. The systems theory approach to the study of organizations has frequently been used in sport management. Chelladurai, Szyszlo, and Haggerty (1987), for example, used a systems-based approach to examine the effectiveness of Canadian national sport organizations. In a more recent example, De Bosscher, De Knop, and Vertonghen (2016) analyzed policy effectiveness of elite sport schools in Flanders by evaluating the inputs, throughputs, outputs, and feedback of a system.

Within the broader field of management, a logical extension to systems theory and a more dominant approach to the study of organizations is **contingency theory**. In keeping with the metaphor of organizations as organisms, the

ANDREW HOLBROOKE/Corbis Historical/Getty Images

Manufacturers of sporting goods are among those companies that might use a mechanistic approach to organization.

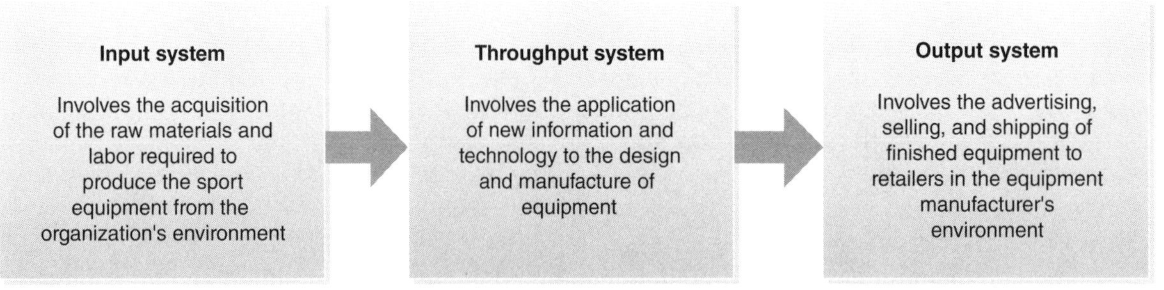

Figure 1.2 Systems of a sport equipment manufacturer.

structure of an organization is seen as contingent on contextual factors (size, strategy, and so forth). Effectiveness is seen as dependent on the proper fit between structure and context. For example, a large sport organization such as Rossignol, the ski manufacturer, will require a structure different from a small retail sporting goods store. The structure of each organization must fit with the demands that their size produces.

While work on sport organizations has often implicitly acknowledged the importance of context to structure and effectiveness, only a small number of studies have specifically focused on these relationships. The idea that organizations are products of their context and the realization that these contexts vary gave rise to the notion of variation in organizational design. Like organisms, some organizational forms are more suited to certain contextual conditions than to others. This idea has led researchers to attempt to classify different types of organization and the conditions under which they will be most effective (Mintzberg, 1979). Early attempts have been made in the field of sport management to use existing typologies to classify sport organizations (Chelladurai, 1985). Kikulis, Slack, Hinings, and Zimmermann (1989) developed the idea of classification (by type) further. Building on the ideas of scholars like Carper and Snizek (1980), McKelvey (1975, 1978, 1982), and Miller and Friesen (1984), they developed an empirical taxonomy of organizational design for voluntary sport organizations. The taxonomy illustrates the different types of organizational design with which these organizations can operate. More recently, Winand, Vos, Zintz, and Scheerder (2013) developed an explorative typology of sport federations based on attitudes and perceptions of determinants of innovation and innovation capacity.

The biological metaphor of organizations as organisms has also been adopted by researchers who approach the study of organizations from what is termed the **life cycle perspective** (Kimberly & Miles, 1980). Here, organizations, like organisms, are seen to go through distinctive life stages, their management requirements reflecting the stage of their development. Yet a further extension of the biological metaphor has given rise to an approach to studying organizations termed **population ecology**. Unlike many other approaches, population ecology focuses not on individual organizations but on populations of organizations. The idea is that organizations are dependent on their environment to acquire the necessary resources to survive, just as living organisms in nature do. To do so, they must compete with other organizations because resources are scarce, resulting in a survival of the fittest (Morgan, 1986). By plotting birth and death rates and patterns of growth and decline in organizations, population ecologists have provided important insights into organizations and their management. Though this approach has rarely been used by sport management scholars to date, sport organizations that come and go very rapidly, such as fitness centers and sporting goods stores, would provide a highly appropriate population of organizations for this type of work. Nevertheless, Cunningham (2002) offered one of the first studies that used the approach of population ecology in a sporting context with his examination of organizational change in physical education and sport programs.

Organizations as Brains

The image of organizations as brains draws attention to the information-processing capacity of organizations. While the mechanistic type of organizations advocated by Frederick Taylor may work well for performing regularized tasks in a stable environment, organizations operating under changing conditions have to be able to monitor these conditions, question the appropriateness of their actions, and, if necessary, make modifications. This necessity requires that organizations, like brains, have to exhibit information-processing capabilities and communication and decision-making systems. As such, they may also have to develop the capacity to learn in a brain-like way and eventually engage in self-management and self-organization.

This way of thinking about organizations owes much to Herbert Simon's (1945) work on decision making and his concept of bounded rationality (see chapter 14). For Simon, organizational members have limited information-processing capabilities that become institutionalized in the structure and ways of operating of organizations. Thus, organizations become understood "as kinds of institutionalized brains that fragment, routinize, and bound the decision process" in order to make it manageable (Morgan, 2006, p. 76). New ways of thinking about organizations and their design and operation have developed from this emphasis on decision making. Galbraith (1974, 1977) and Thompson (1967), for example, focused on the relationship between the information-processing capabilities of an organization and organizational design.

This interest in information processing has led organizational researchers to **cybernetics**, a field of study concerned with "the behavior, organization, and design of mechanisms, organisms, and organizations that receive, generate, and respond to information in order to attain a desired result" (Haggerty, 1988, pp. 54-55). Applied to organizations, the field of cybernetics has been concerned with designing systems that can learn, much like a brain learns, and thus can regulate themselves. A further extension of this approach is to view organizations as holographic systems, when each part of the organization has a picture of the whole, allowing learning and self-renewal. Given the rapid expansion of information processing in organizations, we may see cybernetic and holographic approaches, while still developing as ways to understand organizations, as providing the direction for future changes that will accompany these developments. In the field of sport management, it appears that it is still only Haggerty (1988) who has completed work explicitly making use of the cybernetics approach. Haggerty suggests that cybernetic strategies can be used for improving the control and information systems of sport organizations. However, an article in the *New York Times* about Vítor Frade's (a retired Portuguese university teacher) *tactical periodization* methodology (for association football) mentions that the principles of cybernetics inform part of his approach. Managers such as José Mourinho draw on Frade's work, which Frade claims is important because association football is multidimensional and not a linear process (R. Smith, 2017).

Organizations as Cultures

With the success of Japanese management and the globalization of many industries has come an increased interest in the relationship of culture to organizational life. While organizational theorists acknowledge that the culture of the society in which an organization exists will influence its modes of operation, interest has been growing in what is often called *corporate culture*. Growing out of the idea that organizations are themselves minisocieties, culture in this sense is concerned with the shared values and meanings that create the reality of organizational life. Scholars who study organizations as cultures are concerned with issues such as the way these shared values and meanings are created and maintained, the role of leadership in this process, the existence of competing cultures, and the manifestation of an organization's culture in its design and operation.

Corporate culture reveals itself in such areas of the organization as its ceremonies, stories, myths, symbols, language, and physical layout. Sport organizations are rich in these areas. Ceremonies to initiate rookie gridiron football players, stories about coaches and managers, the symbols of athletic goods companies (e.g., the Nike Swoosh, Adidas's three stripes), and the specialized language that characterizes many sports can all be examined to gain an understanding of the shared values and meanings that underpin the design and operation of sport organizations.

The 2nd edition of this textbook, in 2006, pointed out that despite the potential of utilizing a culture-based approach to understanding sport organizations, there had been virtually no work of this nature in sport management. Fast forward to today, and you can now find an expanding body of journal articles that have an explicit focus on organizational culture. One of the first studies in sport management that placed a focus on organizational culture was that of Hall, Cullen, and Slack (1989), who briefly examined the potential of a cultural approach to understanding gender issues in sport organizations but warned that it was frequently men's accounts of organizational reality, not women's, dominating most analyses of an organization's culture. The first work that came closest to a systematic analysis of the culture of a sport organization and its effects on structure and design was Fine's (1987) work on Little League Baseball. In more recent times, several sport management academics have used a cultural perspective to examine topics such as the transient nature of fitness employees (MacIntosh & Walker, 2012) and perceptions of artifacts in a local figure skating club (cf. Mills & Hoeber, 2013).

Maitland, Hills, and Rhind (2015) have presented a systematic review of organizational culture in sport, which provides a useful summary of the literature.

Organizations as Political Systems

All organizations are political. The image of organizations as political systems challenges the view that they are rational entities working for a common end. Rather, the view is one of individuals and groups loosely coupled together to more efficiently realize their own ambitions and self-interests. Scholars who work with this perspective are interested in the political activity that manifests itself in the power plays and conflicts pervading all organizations. Some would suggest this approach is particularly applicable to organizations concerned with sport!

Looking back only two decades, a scarce number of studies in sport management had specifically examined sport organizations as **systems of political activity**. Stern's (1979) analysis of the development of the National Collegiate Athletic Association (NCAA) and Sack and Staurowsky's (1998) critique of the NCAA's position on college athletes, as well as Lenskyj's (2000) analysis of the International Olympic Committee (IOC) and its Olympic Games were three of the best examples. However, there were other studies that, although it was not their primary focus, provide examples of the type of political struggles that shape sport organizations. Sack and Kidd (1985) and Kidd (1988) discussed the political struggles of athletes to gain representation in the sport organizations that control their athletic destinies. Macintosh and Whitson (1990) examined struggles between professional staff and volunteers to determine the program focus of national sport organizations in Canada. Much of the early work on gender and organizations is about political struggles between men and women (Hall, Cullen, & Slack, 1989; Hult, 1989; Lovett & Lowry, 1994; White & Brackenridge, 1985). For a contemporary understanding of gender and sport organizations, refer to chapter 11 in this textbook.

Today, in part, with the benefit of the formation of the *International Journal of Sport Policy and Politics*, we find an increasing number of studies that place primary focus on political activity in the context of the sport industry. Three recent examples include Houlihan and Zheng's (2014) analysis of sport and politics of small states; Soares, Correia, and Rosado's (2010) study examining political factors related to decision making in voluntary sports associations; and Seippel, Dalen, Sandvik, and Solstad's (2018) article that explored how and why sports issues become political and argued that cultural framing of issues is divisive. Other topics academics may include in their research agenda might be examining why countries or cities (via their National Olympic Committees) decide to bid to become host of a major or mega-event, identifying the political activities associated with bidding processes (some of these issues are highlighted in chapters 13, 15, and 24 on governance, power and politics, and procurement), or investigating the complexities of operating a community sport club (where there is often a unique mix of volunteers and paid professional staff). Although there is now greater focus on the impact of political activity, Grix (2015), in his textbook, *Sport Politics: An Introduction*, argues that a broader definition of politics is still needed—rather than placing sole focus on governments or institutions of power—due to the way political activity transcends so many forms of sport.

Organizations as Instruments of Domination

In describing organizations as **instruments of domination,** Morgan (1986, 2006) suggests that we are usually encouraged to think of organizations as positive entities created to benefit the interests of all who come in contact with them. Certainly, sport organizations are often portrayed in this manner; however, Morgan challenges this perspective. Here organizations are seen as instruments designed to benefit the interests of a privileged few at the expense of the masses; sport organizations have not been immune from this criticism. From this more critical perspective, organizations (or more accurately their dominant coalitions) are seen as exploiting their workers, their host communities, and often the environment for their own ends. Unions, work-related stresses, industrial accidents, drug and alcohol abuse, and alienation are all products of this exploitation. Until the turn of the millennium, researchers who saw themselves as working primarily in the field of sport management had, for the most part, failed to deal with these types of issues. However, Kidd and Donnelly (2000) were one of the first to examine sport and domination issues (human rights in their case). Nearly 20 years later, there's now a wealth of sport researchers who adopt a critical perspective on a wide range of domination issues. As one example, Brannagan and Giulianotti (2015) highlight how a state's use of major events can backfire, leading to forms of disempowerment rather. For example, Qatar's acquisition of the 2022 FIFA World Cup finals has drastically heightened international knowledge and awareness of the country's history of human rights abuse.

While neglected by sport management scholars in the past, this critical approach to organizations has now been used by numerous writers from both the popular press and academic literature on sport. Several authors have written in the popular press about the manner in which professional sport organizations (most notably gridiron football teams) and some colleges dominate and exploit their athletes (Huizenga, 1994; Manley & Friend, 1992; Rheenen, 2013). Government organizations have also been seen as exploiting the talents of their international athletes to meet their own ideological and policy aims (Harvey & Proulx, 1988; Kidd, 1988; Macintosh & Whitson, 1990). There is no better recent case in this regard than the state-sponsored Russian doping program (BBC Sport, 2016), which is discussed in more detail in chapter 15. Strong arguments have been made for class-, race-, and gender-based exploitation in sport organizations (Cashmore, 2000; Gruneau, 1983; Whitson & Macintosh, 1989). For a further exploration about gender and sport organizations, refer to chapter 11.

During the 1990s, companies like Nike (and other global sporting goods and apparel manufacturers) were heavily criticized for exploitative labor practices in their third world production plants (Ballinger, 1993; Clifford, 1992). Following these criticisms, Nike introduced significant reforms to improve the conditions for its factory workers, starting with the launch of their Code of Conduct in 1992 (receiving high praise from labor activists), which was recently updated in 2017. Nike states that the Code aims to "evolve our standards and programs to drive improved outcomes for the workers in the supply chain, [and] communities where our suppliers operate" (Nike, n.d., para. 1). However, in 2017, activists claimed Nike were once again exercising sweatshop practices (allegations included mass fainting, wage theft, and padlocked exits), which resulted in demonstrations outside Nike stores in America (Segran, 2017). It was reported that more than 500 (mostly female) workers in Cambodian factories supplying to Nike, Puma, Asics, and VF Corporation were hospitalized over a one-year period due to collapsing at work (McVeigh, 2017). Finally, it has been widely reported that the construction workers building stadia for association football's 2022 FIFA World Cup finals in Qatar have been treated like "slaves" (Liew, 2017) and have been "subjected to life-threatening heat" (Conn, 2017), which are all human rights issues. Organizations are under ever-increasing scrutiny, and allegations of poor practice can quickly spread around the world (often via social media). Sport managers must fully understand the responsibility of maintaining basic human rights standards of their workforce and the consequences of failing to do so.

Future Directions for Sport Management and Improving Our Understanding of Sport Organizations

As highlighted in this chapter, we can look at sport organizations in a number of ways. The central premise of Morgan's approach to understanding organizations is that they cannot be adequately described, understood, or explained using just one approach. By looking at different images of organizations, we are better able to understand their complex and paradoxical nature, and thus become better managers. As the few previous examples illustrate, in the past, sport management scholars tended to be relatively narrow in the way they looked at sport organizations. Historically, the two dominant perspectives within the literature have been to look at organizations from a mechanistic point of view or to utilize the systems theory approach.

Mechanistic approaches to the study of sport organizations, as noted earlier, have generally focused on some variant of Henri Fayol's five basic managerial functions. A number of textbooks in our field have been constructed around these concepts. However, such approaches are problematic because, as Mintzberg (1973, p. 10) notes, "these words do not in fact describe the actual work of managers at all, they describe certain vague objectives of managerial work. As such they have long served to block our search for a deeper understanding of the work of the manager." Such an approach is also limited in that it fails to recognize the ability of organizations to change as their contextual situation changes. It can also be dehumanizing for employees. Because it promotes an image of workers as cheerful robots unquestioningly going about their daily tasks, it can promote bureaucratic pathologies such as goal displacement and alienation. Finally, this approach to organizations fails to recognize the importance of power and politics in creating the reality of organizational life.

While studies based on systems theory have been more useful in providing interesting and relevant information, this approach is also limited in its explanatory abilities. Studies based on systems theory tend to be overly deterministic, ignoring the role of strategic choice in the construction of organizations. That is to say, far too much emphasis is placed on context as a determinant of structure and design, and far too little attention is given to the creative actions of individuals within the organization. Such an emphasis also presents a view of organizations as functionally unified with all the component parts working together to a common end. Consequently, as with mechanistic approaches, issues of power and politics are ignored, and conflict is dismissed as being dysfunctional.

While work of this nature is not without value, it is somewhat problematic in terms of its ability to provide a holistic understanding of sport organizations and their management. And it is for that reason the focus of this 3rd edition has been broadened—from the sole application of OT in the 2nd edition—to now encompass application of OB and other apposite disciplines (law, psychology, analytics, for example), which enables us to offer a detailed holistic perspective for better understanding the complex nature of sport organizations.

It is important that, as a sport manager or sport management student, you realize the strengths and limitations of the dominant approaches to the study of sport organizations. While the findings that emanate from the most prevalent type of studies in our field are useful and informative, they sometimes present only a partial view of sport organizations and their management. Studies based on the approaches of contingency theory and population ecology, for example, while not without their shortcomings, would certainly enhance our understanding of the impact of contextual pressures on the structure and design of sport organizations. It is also important to conduct studies to determine the nature and extent of variation in the design of sport organizations. As McKelvey (1975) suggested over 40 years ago, such classifications are in many ways one of the fundamental elements in the development of a comprehensive understanding of organizations.

The increasing importance of information processing and managing communication in organizations, and the interest generated by such popular literature as Peters and Waterman's ([1982] 2015) *In Search of Excellence* and Kanter's (1983) *The Change Masters*, prompted an interest in cybernetics and **organizational culture**. Martin (2002), for example, provided three perspectives to illustrate the numerous ways organizational culture can be conceptualized: integration, fragmentation, and differentiation. These approaches would provide useful insights if applied to sport organizations. Work that looks at sport organizations as political systems and instruments of domination would help continue our departure from the highly functional view of these organizations that had long characterized our field. These approaches would also bring issues of power and politics, something that had been missing from previous studies, to a more central position in the study of sport management. Furthermore, sport management research must start looking not only at intraorganizational relationships (e.g., power and relationships studies) but also at interorganizational relationships. As highlighted in chapter 6, with an increasing number of organizations seeking opportunities in new and emerging markets, it becomes necessary to understand how these interorganizational relationships work and what the impact is on the structural design options of sport organizations.

Nevertheless, as the field of sport management continues to flourish, a greater breadth of theories and concepts (including from other pertinent disciplines) are being applied by our scholars to help us better understand sport organizations. Hence, as noted earlier, the reason for inclusion of several new chapters throughout this 3rd edition, plus a section (part 4) dedicated to contemporary issues, which contains chapters consisting of subjects that sport managers need to come to grips with quickly to be able to effectively manage their organizations. The adoption of some of these new subject areas and perspectives will require us to employ different theoretical approaches from those currently found in sport management literature. Chapter 2 provides a first step in understanding the possible research designs in sport management.

It is impossible in one book to deal, even in a minor way, with all the approaches to sport organizations mentioned here. In fact, some of them are only in their infancy in the broader field of management. The point of discussing contemporary issues in our field is to alert readers to the potential these approaches have to enhance our understanding of sport organizations and their management. This text has been written in an effort to tap some of this potential. By focusing on a number of the central ideas in OT, OB, and pertinent disciplines, and their application to our field, it is hoped that the book will provide you with a better understanding of sport organizations and that this increased understanding will ultimately make you a better manager. You should look at each chapter of this book as a stepping-stone for that highlighted aspect of organizations. If a particular aspect interests you, the key researchers mentioned and further reading suggestions will help you delve deeper.

Review Questions

1. Pick a sport organization with which you are familiar and, using two or more of the ways to look at organizations described in the

chapter, explain how your impression of this sport organization would vary depending on the perspective you picked.

2. What problems can you see with the traditional approach to understanding sport organizations that likens them to organisms?
3. List the pros and cons of looking at organizations from a mechanistic point of view or utilizing the systems theory approach.
4. Select a research article on sport organizations. Which perspective on organizations do you think it uses?
5. Why do you think sport management scholars for many years did not focus to any great extent on issues of power and politics in sport organizations?
6. With which of the ways of looking at sport organizations are you most comfortable? Why?

Suggestions for Further Reading

To see where we as a field of study have evolved from, the first edition of the *Journal of Sport Management* (vol. 1, no. 1) contains an interesting article by Zeigler (1987) about the past, present, and future status of sport management. Also noteworthy in this edition is Paton's (1987) article on the progress that has been made in sport management research. Slack's (1991) work on future directions for our field (*Journal of Sport Management*) relates to some of the ideas found in this first chapter. Frisby's (2005) article in the *Journal of Sport Management* adds to this discussion by providing a critical perspective on the sport management field. In 2013, *Sport Management Review* offered five review articles that focused on various perspectives of theory development in sport management (Chelladurai, 2013; Cunningham, 2013; Doherty, 2013; Fink, 2013; Irwin & Ryan, 2013). Slack's (2014) article in *European Sport Management Quarterly*, based on his 2014 European Association for Sport Management (EASM) keynote, offers reflection on the role of sport management research, highlighting the importance of referring to other work (outside our field) related to the topic under investigation.

Students are of course referred to Gareth Morgan's (1986, 2006) *Images of Organization* as probably the best source of information about the different ways researchers have looked at organizations. Also see Slack's (1993) article "Morgan and the Metaphors: Implications for Sport Management," which appeared in the *Journal of Sport Management*. Alvesson and Deetz (2000), in their book *Doing Critical Management Research*, and Alvesson, Bridgman, and Willmott (2011), in their book *Critical Management Studies*, provide a much-needed critical perspective on organizations. Slack and Amis (2004) use a critical perspective to examine sport sponsorship in their article "Money for Nothing and Your Cheques for Free? A Critical Perspective on Sport Sponsorship" in Slack's (2004) *The Commercialisation of Sport*. Students are directed to read *The Corporation* by Joel Bakan (2004)—also the subject of a documentary film that features Nike—to see organizations, especially sport organizations and their management, in a critical light. Although more sociologically than managerially oriented, students may also find useful ideas in Rob Beamish's (1985) "Sport Executives and Voluntary Associations: A Review of the Literature and Introduction to Some Theoretical Issues" in *Sociology of Sport Journal*. Continuing the theme of familiarizing yourself with other fields of study (but still important for sport management), you may want to look at the textbook *Sports Law*, written by Mark James (2017); Downward, Dawson, and Dejonghe's (2009) *Sports Economics*; and Houlihan and Malcolm's (2016) sociology-focused edited textbook *Sport and Society: A Student Introduction*.

Trevor Slack, the original editor of this textbook, was a very accomplished middle-distance runner; he even won an athletics scholarship to the United States with his housemate, Alan Pascoe, when they were both studying at Borough Road College, the University of London. Alan went on to win an Olympic medal, run one of the biggest sport marketing and event management companies in the world, and join the organizing committee for the 2012 London Olympic Games. Trevor became a world-leading, world-renowned academic scholar who was fundamental in helping create the field of sport management and paved the way in developing our understanding of the field so that sport management can one day realize its full potential. For a personal memory of Trevor, his good friend, Bill Gerrard, wrote a very fitting tribute in ESMQ (Gerrard, 2016).

Finally, you should at least acquaint yourself with the three main sport management journals: *Journal of Sport Management*, *European Sport Management Quarterly*, and *Sport Management Review*, then become conversant with other sport-related, discipline-specific journals and, ultimately, read articles in the mainstream management journals. You may also want to refer to carefully selected popular press materials (such as newspaper and magazine articles, in print and online), reputable blogs, and the websites of organizations involved in sport to help inform your understanding of sport organizations. So, now, it would be prudent to adopt Trevor's take-home message from his final EASM keynote: "To be successful you should love your work and, in turn, help the field progress" (Slack, 2014, p. 462). On your marks, get set, go!

CHAPTER 2

Doing Research in Sport Management

Trevor Slack, PhD
Terri Byers, PhD

Learning Objectives

When you have read this chapter, you should be able to

1. explain the different steps of the research process,
2. provide examples of some common research designs,
3. provide examples of possible data collection and analysis techniques,
4. discuss several examples of research articles and methods employed in the sport management literature,
5. discuss your interests for topics of research in sport management,
6. evaluate the quality of an article, and
7. provide examples of research write-up options.

Key Concepts

data analysis methods
data collection methods
descriptive research
explanatory research
exploratory research
qualitative
quantitative
reliability
research design
research process
research question
theoretical framework
validity

Quality Research Does Exist in Sport Management

A typical research article will have a short abstract, an introduction, a review of the literature (or theoretical framework to be used in the research), a description of the research design, the presentation of the results, a discussion of those results, implications for researchers and managers stemming from the study's results, and a conclusion. An explanation of the limitations of the piece of research is often included. Research in sport management has developed significantly over the past two decades. Researchers have broadened both their methods used and the subject focus of their research because the industry has changed and new challenges for managers emerge. There is greater diversity in how research is presented, and students are encouraged to read widely to gain an understanding of this breadth. We focus here on a few examples to get you started.

Laurence Chalip is a well-known and respected researcher in the field of sport management. His 2003 article in the *Journal of Sport Management*, with Christine Green and Brad Hill, is an example of good sport management research. The article, "Effect of Sport Event Media on Destination Image and Intention to Visit," has a title that echoes the topic, is supported by an abstract describing the topic, explains the source of the samples (since there was a comparison of regional differences in the study), and details the main findings. The authors then provide an introduction of events and their relationship to the marketing mix and local politics and how these two issues are related. This is followed by a **theoretical framework** describing the value of media to encourage attendance of sport events through the influence of movies and television. This allows the authors to point out key problems still unanswered in the literature; problems they want to address are stated as clear research questions at the end of this section. Next, there is a methods section that includes a description of the sample, the methods used, the variables examined and how they will be measured, and data analysis techniques. The results section provides description data analysis results for each research question and whether these results are statistically significant (since data analysis is statistical in nature). The discussion section then critically looks at each result and discusses its significance in the context of the research; it analyzes the meaning of the numbers and their practical and theoretical implications. The discussion is therefore tied back to the theoretical framework. The authors conclude their article by summarizing what they believe are the key elements.

The authors found that event telecast, event advertising, and destination (location of the event) advertising have an impact on different elements of the destination's image. A wider range of effects was found in the United States sample than in the New Zealand sample. The authors concluded that if an event can be linked to the marketing strategy and communications mix of the local region, the event is in a position to provide more value and be more viable.

Lin, Chalip, and Green (2016) examined the role of sense of community in a youth sport program, using a focus group and online questionnaire, and found that parents valued coaching technique but more importantly believed a sense of community before and after the program were important in their decision to return to the program. Also, a quality piece of writing, based on years of experience and research, Chalip (2017) focuses on sport event legacy, where he presents an argument for researchers to focus on leveraging instead of the controversial concept of legacy. Readers may note that the content and format of these three references are different, but we consider all of high quality. The remainder of this chapter will help you understand and recognize quality research in sport management as well as how to identify weaknesses that can have implications for the conclusions of our research and should be addressed in future research.

Throughout this textbook, we present a range of research to help explain various concepts related to the management of sport organizations. This chapter provides an introduction to the **research process** to explain how some of the research cited in this book was conducted. The small selection of published management research in the book should give any future sport manager or researcher an idea of how to evaluate the quality of a piece and conduct research. Even if you do not plan to be involved in academia, you will undertake some kind of research during your career (e.g., a survey of your company's customers) to help your organization become more successful in one way or another. If you become a consultant, you will do research for sport organizations in order to help your clients. If you hire a consultant, as a manager you will have to judge the quality of the consultant's final report.

A cursory search of university classes and books related to the research process reveals a wealth of possibilities. Examples of books include Andrew, Pedersen, and McEvoy's (2011) *Research Methods and Design in Sport Management*; Miles, Huberman, and Saldaña's (2014) *Qualitative Data Analysis, Third Edition*; Denscombe's (2010) *The Good Research Guide for Small-Scale Social Research Projects*; Veal and Darcy's (2014) *Research Methods in Sport Studies and Sport Management: A Practical Guide*; Bauer and Gaskell's (2000) *Qualitative Researching With Text, Image, and Sound*; Bryman's (2015) *Social Research Methods*; Sparkes and Smith's (2014) *Qualitative Research Methods in Sport, Exercise and Health*. This chapter is an introduction to research and students are encouraged to read widely about how research is conducted to further their depth of understanding.

The Research Process

Before starting the actual research process, you need to understand some terms you may encounter in the chapter or other sources dealing with the research process. Research in the social sciences (sport management in our case) is both *theoretical* in nature, involving developing, exploring, testing, rejecting, or extending theories, and *empirical*, which requires observation and the measurement of a chosen setting (Trochim & Donnelly, 2001). A piece of research can be theoretical, empirical, or both.

Research is usually one of three types: exploratory, descriptive, or explanatory. **Exploratory research** uncovers facts about a certain subject or setting. The goal is to discover as much as possible about the general topic and then develop propositions or hypotheses that can be examined at a later date. A rationale for such a study could be phrased in the following qualitative way: "What can be learned from the study of local figure-skating clubs?" **Descriptive research**, as the name suggests, goes deeper into a specific topic to analyze it in greater detail. For example, if our exploratory study determined that management strategies, power structures, and volunteer commitment were the three main findings of the research, we may want to delve deeper into the management strategies. Finding this, we could decide to ask the following question: "What is the decision-making process for a volunteer board in a local figure-skating club?" Finally, **explanatory research** is causal in nature, meaning it studies the relationships of variables to explain and predict behavior. It is more about the cause-and-effect relationship. An example of an explanatory study for our local figure-skating club topic may be, "What is the effect of the volunteer board members' past experience on the decision-making process?" (Trochim & Donnelly, 2001; Yin, 2017). Of course, the three types of research are not mutually exclusive. Depending on how you set up your research, it may be both exploratory and descriptive or descriptive and explanatory. Finally, regardless of the type of research you use, you will be doing *cross-sectional* (at one point in time), *cross sectional-repeat* (same measurement taken at two intervals), or *longitudinal* (over a period of time) research. Longitudinal research is better suited for examining changes of a variable over time or for examining different processes.

We can now go deeper into the research process. Most of the time, a study starts with a research topic that interests the researcher. For example, how are large-scale sporting event organizing committees managed? The problem will usually be that the topic is too broad. In this case, what does "managed" mean? This broad topic must be narrowed down to a specific research question; the more specific the better. A good way to build a specific **research question** is to include elements of who, what, where, or when in your question. In other words, who are we going to research, what variables are we interested in, and where or when will this take place? In our example, we could pose the following research question: "What stakeholder issues must the 2024 Paris Paralympics/Olympics organizing committee deal with?" At this point we know the who (stakeholders), the what (issues), and the where or when (2024 Paris Paralympics/Olympics). The more focused your research question is, the easier it will be to actually do the study and evaluate the findings.

Once the research question is posed, the temptation is to jump into operationalizing your variables and gathering the data. Before beginning, however, you need a strong foundation in order to explore the right concepts in the right manner. This is done through the use of a *theoretical framework*. This theoretical framework is a description of the theory or theories (if you develop a framework to be tested) that will inform the research design.

The theoretical framework drives a study's **research design**, which can be described as the overall plan of action, strategy, or process that holds the choice of methods together and links that choice to the research's desired outcomes (Crotty, 1998). The *methods* mentioned are "the techniques or procedures used to gather and analyze data related to some research question or hypothesis" (Crotty, 1998, p. 3). Figure 2.1 provides a visual description of what the research process can be.

It is important that the theoretical framework, research design, and methods are consistent in what they suggest will be investigated and how the investigation will be conducted. We will now provide a brief description of the theoretical framework in social sciences. Research design and methods will be reserved for the subsequent sections, followed by quality issues, a description of key elements of the write-up of an article, and practical issues for managers.

Theoretical Framework

Doing good research starts with a strong theoretical foundation. This foundation is usually a theoretical framework, which results from an overview of key concepts and current shortcomings of a chosen theory or theories. For proper theoretical frameworks, sport management researchers can look to the management literature, as we have done throughout this book (e.g., institutional theory, stakeholder theory, population ecology, and so forth), or to other disciplines such as sociology and psychology for research focused on individual or group levels of analysis (e.g., Doyle, Filo, Lock, Funk, & McDonald, 2016).

While the theoretical framework reviews the key concepts, it is not a review of literature. A review of literature is much broader in its treatment of a theory's key concepts. In fact, a review of literature presents the state of the research in a particular area: all possible concepts, research findings, and remaining questions within that particular area of study. Researchers often conduct a review of literature and may include a concise overview of this in a research paper or report to demonstrate why they have chosen a particular theoretical framework. The theoretical framework is focused solely on presenting the essential concepts and gaps in the literature that will help drive the research design and show the importance of the research.

Sometimes the theoretical framework simply provides the key concepts for the research, but it also can include a proposed outline (already found in a theory or developed by the researcher) that will be used as the guide for data collection and analysis. Regardless, it is important to know that, in terms of the number of concepts presented or length of the theoretical framework, more is not necessarily better. In other words, it is better to focus on those concepts that are essential for the development of the data collection and analysis methods.

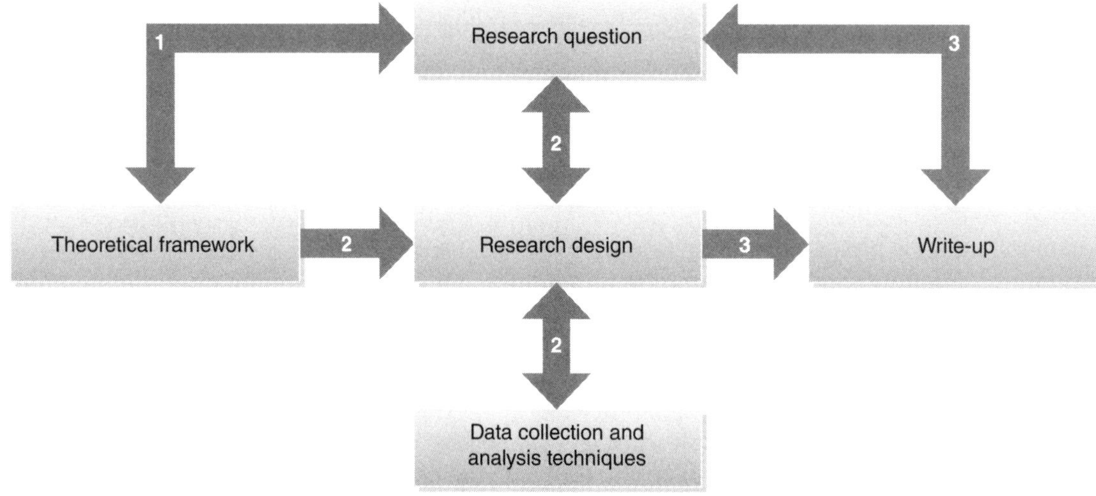

Figure 2.1 The research process.

The So-Called Debate on Qualitative-Quantitative or Mixed-Methods Research

Before describing research designs and methods, we must make one important definitional note. We have, so far, been careful to use the term *social sciences* instead of *qualitative research* to describe research done in sport management, compared with the traditional natural (physical or "pure") sciences. This is an important point, and the title speaks to the debate currently going on to prove that good research can be done with or without numbers. Many researchers still refer to the term *qualitative* to describe research done outside of the natural sciences—just look at the titles of references cited in this chapter. There is sometimes still a negative connotation to qualitative research in the sense that quantitative research is good research so qualitative research must be bad research. This is erroneous! Acceptance of qualitative research is growing in sport management research, with innovative approaches and reflexive practices encouraged to capture the complex perspectives of various actors in sport organizations.

Research outside the natural sciences can be **quantitative** (uses numbers) in nature, just as research in the natural sciences can use **qualitative** data (e.g., the smell or color of a chemical solution). Moreover, if a study relies on quantitative data, results must be interpreted to bring in a qualitative component. The main difference is how one looks at a phenomenon. What drives the type of data gathered is the research question. Therefore, social science research is more appropriate than qualitative research when describing the study's overall setting, and numerical and nonnumerical research is preferred to quantitative and qualitative research when describing the methods. Depending on the type of research done, it may be appropriate to use both qualitative and quantitative data. A researcher following this approach would be seen as using a mixed-methods research design (Creswell, 2003).

Van der Roest, Spaaij, and van Bottenburg (2015) highlight that mixed methods are underutilized, poorly legitimized, and often weakly designed in sport management research. This is not surprising given that sport management is still a relatively young field of academic inquiry, especially in relation to, for example, the social and behavioral sciences generally.

Research Design

A research design is based not only on the theoretical framework but also on the research question, context, possibility of controlling events, and the desired outcomes. The key, however, is the research question. Getting the research question right makes the research process easier. Deciding on a research question is a process that involves reading existing research, discussion with peers and advisers, and critically reflecting on your motivation for research on the topic. We will now look at some of the more popular research designs.

TIME OUT

Research Is Not Only Empirical; It Can Be Theoretical

While we talk mostly about doing research in an empirical way—in other words, obtaining some type of result from a given research design—good research can also be purely theoretical. You can see it mostly in the form of a review of literature on the state of a research topic or as a development of a theoretical model. One example of theoretical research is Mark Rosentraub and David Swindell's (2002) article "Negotiating Games: Cities, Sports, and the Winner's Curse." The article examines how professional teams in North America present bargaining demands on their communities. Rosentraub and Swindell want to know if communities can avoid subsidizing sport teams. The researchers first introduce the topic of cities bidding for teams and events. They then explain how bargaining and bidding are related to the state of information and the control of capital. These two elements join to construct a framework that large cities can follow to avoid the so-called winner's curse. This framework is based on external factors, such as league rules and the control over the supply and location of teams. It also depends on internal factors—cities' market characteristics, team owners' goals, related income potential, and public sector goals. Another example of theoretical research is Kitchin and Howe's (2013) article "How Can the Social Theory of Pierre Bourdieu Assist Sport Management Research?" in which they provide a detailed discussion of the application and benefits of theory developed by French sociologist Pierre Bourdieu. This is an insightful and detailed article that encourages researchers to embrace theory in their research.

Experiments and Quasi-Experiments

First, the research design most associated with the natural sciences is the *experiment*. An experiment seeks to answer how and why questions, so it is an explanatory type of research design. Using an experiment also requires the control of the study's events and, therefore, must be contemporary in nature (Yin, 2003), which means it is happening in real time. Pure experiments cannot truly be done in the social sciences. However, there are quasi-experiments. This research design approximates the experiment setting. It will often be used for psychological research, when subjects are asked to perform or be tested on a task. As such, it is a contemporary controlled setting.

The article by Chalip and colleagues (2003) presented in the vignette at the beginning of this chapter illustrates an experimental design with participants watching eight different videos. Kyle, Kerstetter, and Guadagnolo (2003) also used an experimental design to manipulate consumer price expectations of a 10K road race. Tarrant (1996) relied on a laboratory experiment as part of a larger study to examine outdoor recreation experiences. O'Reilly (2011) discussed the use of experimental design to investigate consumer decision making in professional sport. Finally, Swearingen and Johnson's (1995) behavioral experiment examines the impact of uniformed park employees on visitors' off-trail hiking.

Surveys

A popular research design in sport management research is the *survey*. This is a popular strategy in sport management because it can answer who, what, when, where, and how many or how much—sometimes more than one question in the same study—without needing to control the setting (Yin, 2003). Because of this quality, it can be used for exploratory, descriptive, or explanatory studies, depending on the exact question. Surveys are more accurate when done for contemporary events than for past events. Think of public opinion polls as the typical example of this strategy. The goal is to find out what people think on a certain topic. However, bigger does not mean better. More precisely, sample size must be carefully considered—it is as possible to get an equally good result with 200 participants as with 2,000, and it is cheaper and less time consuming when it comes to data entry and analysis.

An example of survey use is Chang and Chelladurai's (2003) study looking at differences in organizational commitment and citizenship behavior between part-time and full-time Korean sport organization employees. In turn, Funk, Ridinger, and Moorman (2003) show how the Sport Interest Inventory (SII) survey determines individual differences among women's professional sport consumers. Taylor (2003) relies on a national survey research design to examine the value and practice of diversity management of team-based community sport groups at sports' grassroots level.

Many examples exist of how sport management researchers can use surveys to measure a wide variety of concepts related to fans, pedagogy, volunteering, commitment, and so on. Surveys are used to get as representative a sample as possible to make generalizations of the wider population. Surveys that fail to do this or report nonrandom (nonprobability) sampling are weaker in their ability to generalize. Yoshida, Heere, and Gordon (2015) used a survey instrument to measure and predict fan loyalty. Jones, Brooks, and Mak (2008) used a random sample of 137 institutions offering undergraduate sport management programs in the United States (50 usable surveys were returned) to analyze the development of sport management programs, admission requirements, faculty profiles, and critical issues facing the field of sport management.

Case Studies

Another research design used in sport management research is the *case study*. Case studies are in-depth studies about a certain setting, organization, or event. Patton and Applebaum (2003) present an interesting argument for the use and salience of case studies in management research and organization science generally. They indicate that case studies are useful for generating hypotheses for further quantitative study and for generating and testing theories. The focus of a case can be historical or contemporary in nature. Case studies usually seek to answer *how* or *why* questions, but they can also answer *who, what, where,* or *when* questions for more exploratory or descriptive studies. Yin (2017) described case studies as an empirical inquiry investigating a real-life phenomenon whose boundaries and context are not clearly evident. Case studies have been criticized for lacking rigor, having little basis for generalization, taking too long, and resulting in too much information (and more variables than data points). However, a researcher can take certain steps to remedy these challenges, such as using multiple sources of evidence, creating a case study database (including the investigator's report), and maintaining a chain of evidence among the case study questions, protocol, evidentiary sources, database, and report (Yin, 2017). In addition, within the case study research design, you may have one or more case studies, depending on your research question. For example, if you are interested in the challenges faced by volunteer sport groups at the grassroots level, you may conduct only a single case study of a typical sport group. However, if you are interested in the impact of culture on the challenges faced by volunteer sport groups at the grassroots level, you would have to do a case study in various cultures (e.g., Canada versus United Kingdom versus China versus Brazil) and compare the results.

There are quite a few examples of case studies conducted by sport management researchers in the literature. Gladwell, Anderson, and Sellers (2003) take a case study of North Carolina to examine fiscal trends in public parks and recreation between 1986 and 2001. Mason and Slack's (2003) case study of professional hockey explores the principal–agent relationship described in agency theory. Roche (1994) finds that a case study of the 1991 Sheffield Universiade Games illustrates how research on event production should use planning, political, and urban contextual processes as a framework. Pegoraro, Scott, and Burch (2017) provide a case study of two National Sport Organizations, one in Canada and one in Australia, to illustrate the strategic use of Facebook to build brand awareness. Their study showed similarities and differences in the cases and provided practical implications for nonprofit sport organizations using Facebook to build positive brand images, promote fan engagement, and create brand ambassadors.

Ethnographies and Autoethnographies

The *ethnography* is a popular research design with anthropology-based research. A growing number of researchers are using a variety of ethnographic methods in sport management research, including autoethnography and digital ethnography. Sparkes (2002) suggested that sport researchers began to embrace ethnographic frameworks, underpinned by critical and postmodern theories, in the late 1990s. An ethnography is similar to a case study in that it is a study about a given event or setting. Ethnographic methods use participant or close-up observations of the natural world and attempt to stay away from any prior theory commitment. Conversely, case studies can and do use theory to ground their research and narrow their focus as well as incorporate other methods (Yin, 2017). Ethnographic research is definitely field research, often requiring years of commitment.

For example, Tsang's (2000) ethnographic narrative explains her perspective on one part of her personal identity, her identity as a high-performance athlete. Silk, Slack, and Amis (2000) collect ethnographic data to examine institutional pressures found in the production of televised sport for the 1998 Kuala Lumpur Commonwealth Games. Cooper, Grenier, and Macauley (2017) demonstrate the potential for autoethnography in sport management using critical theory to challenge and counter dominant ideologies that marginalize certain groups of people through sustained power structures and inequity. Schaeperkoetter (2017) uses autoethnography to reflect on and analyze her experiences as a female basketball official, providing a unique insight into a traditionally male-dominated role in sport. Kerwin and Hoeber (2015) encourage a collaborative self-ethnographic approach, drawing on a previous study of sport fans to illustrate the strengths and weaknesses of this approach.

Grounded Theory

A related research design to ethnography is *grounded theory*. This research design originated with Glaser and Strauss (1967). It can actually be seen as a particular type of ethnographic inquiry with the purpose of building theory (Crotty, 1998). Specific steps (known as the constant comparative method) are taken to have theory emerge from the data (Glaser and Strauss 2017).

Jones (2002) takes a longitudinal grounded theory approach to look at the management implications in the development of voluntary community groups in urban parks, and finds that both the community and local council must be committed for the project to succeed. Schinke, da Costa, and Andrews (2001) turn to the principles of grounded theory to build a conceptual framework of elite athletes' explanations and behaviors in relation to support-staff behavior. Whittaker and Holland-Smith (2016) use an emergent style of grounded research (Glaser and Strauss 1967), which allows issues to emerge naturally from the research process to explore the influence of social capital on parental sport volunteers salient to the delivery of UK sport initiatives. Yuksel, McDonald, Milne, and Darmody (2017) use grounded theory methodology to examine the relationship between fantasy football and NFL consumption.

Action Research

Action research, as the name suggests, is research where an applied focus of the findings enables research subjects to make improvements or some change to their organization. Unlike the previous research designs, this strategy often originates with a protagonist, or local organization, group, or individual, approaching a researcher for a specific purpose.

One of the best examples of a sport management action researcher is Wendy Frisby. In a 1997 article with Crawford and Dorer, she analyzes a participatory action research project done with low-income women to help them access local physical activity services. Frisby and her colleagues believe that action research can potentially "provide a new perspective by bringing those outside the physical activity system in contact with those who control service provision, policy development, and knowledge production in order to promote social and organizational change" (p. 9). The authors use a framework developed by Green et al. (1995) to evaluate an action research project. The framework includes elements related to participants and the nature of their involvement, the origin of the research question, the purpose of the research, its process and context, opportunities to address the issue of interest, and the nature of the research outcomes.

Frisby, Crawford, and Dorer's (1997) research and its subsequent analysis show that the local sport system can become more inclusive and the research can provide better understanding of, in this case, community involvement, collaborative decision making, resource control, power imbalances, nonhierarchical structures, and resistance to change. Chalip and Hutchinson (2017) utilize action research to understand problems associated with youth sport retention and programming. Rich and Misener (2017), in the context of a participatory action research project in rural northern Ontario, Canada, illustrate how self-reflexive practice enables greater understanding of community contexts as well as the roles and limitations of researchers.

Additional Information About Research Designs

There are many other design options that sport management researchers could consider, and we are increasingly encouraged to be innovative in designing our research (Amis & Silk, 2005; Knoppers, 2015) to push the boundaries of sport management research and critically reflect on our assumptions, give voice to underrepresented groups, and to advance knowledge of sport management practices to contribute to the field of study. In this introductory text, we cannot include all designs but other methods worth mentioning include phenomenology (Shannon, 2016; Brymer & Schweitzer, 2017), critical realism (Byers, 2013), and narrative research (Stride, Fitzgerald, & Allison, 2017)—there are many choices when designing research, each with unique implications for subsequent data collection and analysis.

Aside from the many designs to choose from, researchers can also consider developing new methodologies or designs (with support from experienced researchers) such as the one developed by Hoeber, Snelgrove, Hoeber, and Wood (2017), which serves to preserve the whole in large-scale temporal research. They present a step-by-step guide and an extensive example from social media analysis to illustrate the usefulness of the methodology to sport management research, particularly research related to fan behavior, critical incident management, and media training.

Data Collection Methods and Issues

Once the research design is chosen, the **data collection methods** and data analysis methods can be determined. Data can be primary or secondary. Primary data is collected by the researcher specifically for the purpose of answering the research question, and secondary data is existing data that can be used to answer the research question but may not have been collected for its specific purpose. An example of primary data is the results of interviews or surveys; an example of secondary data is sport participation statistics or literature in the form of journal articles or databases of information.

Before selecting your data collection method, consider the unit of analysis for your study. The *unit of analysis* is what you are studying. It is the focus of your research; it is the heart of your research. A unit of analysis can be an individual, a role, a group, an organization, a community, and so on. For example, if you are looking at volunteer commitment in a local sport club, your unit of analysis is the individual volunteer. In conjunction, the sampling procedure must be decided. Determining this and the unit of analysis is an important step because it helps to set boundaries on the research. You cannot research everything and everyone. These factors also place boundaries on the conclusions you can draw from your research and on the confidence in these conclusions (Miles & Huberman, 1994).

Sampling

Knowing the unit of analysis will help you determine your *sampling* strategy. If you are studying individuals, your sample will be made up of individuals. If you are studying organizations (e.g., a case study of organizational performance), you will be creating a sample of organizations. The key in sampling is to be representative of the population; size is *not* the most important factor. You can actually have a sample of one, whether one individual, group, or organization (e.g., a single case study). However, keep in mind sampling biases of noncoverage (missing key types of participants) and nonresponse (by having more than one planned participant per category) (Bauer & Aarts, 2000).

Methods and perspectives evolve as researchers challenge existing assumptions about what is real and how to learn about it. Case studies are a good example of how thoughts on a method and its impact change over time. While it was once widely accepted that generalizations cannot be made from case studies, research has challenged this and argued that case studies play an important role in testing theory and in generalizing research findings (Tsang, 2014).

Who you sample will depend on your research question, context, and desired outcome. For example, if you want to generalize, you will want a more random sampling for as much representation of the population as possible. However, if you are doing an exploratory study and cannot determine your exact sample in advance or if you are interviewing elites—a finicky group—you may be able to access them only through a snowball sampling (i.e., start with one, get a referral to another, and so on). However, the final size of your sample is important because it will determine whether, and to what extent, you can generalize your findings. If you are doing interviews, for example, and are unsure of how many to conduct, you will know it is time to stop when you reach saturation—the point when you aren't covering new ground because of the limited number of interpretations or versions of a reality.

Other examples of sampling strategies include

- maximum variation (units present the whole possible range of a characteristic, and patterns emerge),
- homogeneous (units are the same),
- theory-based (a fit emerges from your theoretical development),
- typical case (the average is exemplified),
- confirming or disconfirming cases (units support a pattern or variations),
- extreme or deviant case (examples represent extremes),
- random purposeful (a random sample examines a too-large population),
- stratified purposeful (subgroups of a population are examined, especially if comparisons are desired),
- criterion-based (units meet specific characteristics),
- opportunistic (an unexpected or new lead is pursued),
- combination (sampling of multiple types), and
- convenience (time or money or effort saved) (Miles & Huberman, 1994).

Sport management research uses many of the sampling strategies, although often the sampling strategy is not explicitly stated; instead details of the sample are provided. Alexandris, Dimitriadis, and Kasiara (2001) apply a random purposeful sampling to examine behavioral consequences of perceived service quality in Greek fitness clubs. Boronico and Newbert (2001) combine a typical case, criterion-based, and convenience sampling in the study of Monmouth University to empirically examine mathematical modeling analysis of play-calling strategy in gridiron football.

Questionnaires

Once the unit of analysis and sampling procedures are determined, you must establish what type of data will uncover the answer to your research question. One of the most widely used data collection methods is the *questionnaire*. There are two advantages: You can potentially reach thousands of people quickly, and data analysis can be simplified if you set up closed-response questions (that have a fixed number of possible answers) with a statistical analysis software program such as Statistical Packages for the Social Sciences (SPSS). While it may seem simple to build a questionnaire, it is actually an art form. You have to consider question wording (it must be response friendly), response categories (Likert scale, such as ranges of 1 to 7, 1 to 3, 1 to 4, 1 to 5, or 1 to 6, or numbers for salaries, such as under $10,000, $10,000-$30,000, and so forth) versus raw data, the questionnaire length, how to raise potentially difficult or objectionable questions (e.g., respondent's Social Security number), the order of the questions (one shouldn't influence those that follow), and random respondent versus the identified respondent (name is on questionnaire) (Kronberger & Wagner, 2000).

You also must decide how you will present the questions: in person, by phone or mail, or through the Internet (either by email or through a website such as Survey Monkey or Bristol online). The way the questionnaire is distributed will affect your response rate: Mailed questionnaires typically have the lowest return rate. Another large consideration is the number of respondents: You can reach more people through email than you can by visiting each person (although the quality of data through email may be lower than that of a face-to-face encounter). Data analysis of questionnaires is dictated by your response categories. Closed questions typically are analyzed quantitatively (e.g., "30 percent of respondents made less than $10,000 a year") and usually with a statistical analysis software program such as SPSS. Open-ended questions are qualitatively analyzed for emerging response patterns, usually with a qualitative data analysis software program such as ATLAS.ti or NVivo.

Questionnaires can be designed as the sole element of a study, as in the case of Kang's (2002) questionnaire to develop a decision-making process framework for participant sport consumption, a framework integrating the participant's own image congruence, attitude, and intentions. But a questionnaire is also effective in combination with other methods (e.g., interviews), as in the case of Gladden and Funk's (2002) questionnaire following a focus group method to understand brand association in team sport.

Interviews

The *interview* is an effective data collection method preceding or following the questionnaire, or on its own. Whether the interview is done in conjunction with the questionnaire (or any other method) or by itself will depend on the type of research and desired result. For example, an exploratory study on large-scale sporting events may start with interviews to determine the issues involved in such a setting and then move to observations and questionnaires as the study develops a descriptive and then explanatory focus.

Interviews can be done one on one or in groups (called focus groups), face to face, or on the phone. Modern technologies now enable Skype or FaceTime calls where researchers can see and talk to interviewees from across the globe in real time. This opens a multitude of new possibilities in cross-cultural research and in collecting data from an international network of respondents. A single interviewer usually conducts 15 to 25 personal interviews or six to eight group interviews. Another way of determining the number of interviews is to set a two-interviews-per-cell characteristic. In other words, you multiply the number of characteristics you want to study by two and end up with a rough estimate of your total sample size. Reaching saturation then indicates the end of your sampling. Of course, the number of interviews you do can depend on cost, time frame, and availability.

The purpose of interviews typically is to collect a range of opinions on the issue being studied. The interview is a joint effort between the interviewer and interviewee (Gaskell, 2000), and issues of trust and rapport can influence the depth of the interviewee's responses. These responses will also vary, depending on the type of interview guide (list of questions). The interview format may be structured (no deviation from question list; oftentimes a questionnaire), semistructured (questions are set, but others can be added), or unstructured (questions emerge as interview progresses) (Yin, 2013).

The strength of the interview is that it is highly revealing, even through perceived causal inferences, and has a clear focus (the research topic) (Yin, 2013). However, interviews do have limitations: language barriers (misinterpretations can result), omitted details (probe for more information), distorted views and response bias (compare responses to confirm veracity), reflexivity (the subject gives the response you want), bias from poorly constructed questions, and inadequate recall of the distant past (Gaskell, 2000; Yin, 2013).

The interview process can last from 20 minutes to more than two hours. However, interviews typically last one to one and a half hours. The process starts with the interview guide, which should be tied to the theoretical framework chosen for the study. Once you meet your interviewee, introduce the topic of interest (purpose of the research), thank the subject for agreeing to the interview, ensure anonymity, ask if there are questions related to the research or the process, and, if applicable, get permission to record the interview (via iPad, tablet, mobile phone, etc.) so you are free to talk without having to take notes. Depending on your questions you may not need a recorder. If your questions require short answers there is no need to record them (e.g., if you ask the gender or the age of a participant). It is best to record involved answers (longer than a paragraph) to capture accurate responses. Regardless of the use of an audiovisual recorder, interview or field notes usually supplement answers. Start an interview with nonthreatening questions, and probe first responses for more information or clarification. At the end, thank the interviewee. Finally, give the subject time to relax after the interview is officially concluded; you may get some extra information (Gaskell, 2000).

Once the interview is over, transcribe the recording verbatim, including such details as the length of pauses between responses if you are doing a conversation analysis. In a basic analysis, emphasis is on what they said, not how they said it. Interview analysis typically involves reading and rereading transcripts, constructing a matrix table for each issue studied, and looking for patterns of responses (Miles, Huberman, & Saldaña, 2014; Gaskell, 2000).

In research, interviews may be the only data source, as in the case of Chalip and Leyns' (2002) study on business leveraging in relation to a sport event. Higham and Hinch (2003) predominately use interviews in their study of sport, space, and time in relation to the effects of a New Zealand rugby team's influence on tourism. But interviews may be merged with other data sources, especially if you are doing a case study. For example, Mason and Slack (2003) combine interviews with archival material and documentation to examine principal–agent relationships in professional hockey. Researchers may also use a more structured interview as Jones, Edwards, Bocarro, Bunds, and Smith (2017) did to investigate interorganizational partnerships in youth sport nonprofit organizations.

Observations

The method of *observation* is often used in conjunction with other types of data gathering. Observation can be direct (you watch what is going on) or participant (you take part in and watch what is going on) in nature. Observation activities range from the formal protocol, which involves measuring the incidence of a particular issue over a particular time, to the more casual—for example, if you simply need to see the environment in which your research is taking place. Mackellar (2013) reviewed the techniques involved in participant observation and the strengths and weaknesses of this approach for event research, which is relevant for sport events as well as nonsporting events. One strength of observation is its real-time and contextual nature (it provides context for a phenomenon going on at that actual time). Another strong point, especially for participant observation, is that it provides a description of interpersonal behavior and motive. However, observation methods can be time consuming, costly, selective (you can't watch everything at once; you miss key elements), reflexive (individuals may modify their normal behavior or act as they think you expect they should; this is called the Hawthorne Effect), and biased, because the participant observer is manipulating the setting (Yin, 2003).

Participant observation typically is done in combination with other data collection techniques. Fairley (2003) uses participant observation in combination with interviews to answer the question of why some fans travel to follow professional sport teams. Silk, Slack, and Amis (2000) combine observations with interviews and document analysis to examine the production of televised sport. Spaaij (2013) provides an interesting ethnographic account of Somali Australians' experience of sport participation using observation, participation, and interviews. Uhrich (2014) combined observation, in-depth interviews, naturalistic observation, and netnography to examine customer-to-customer cocreation of value in the context of professional team sport.

Archival Material and Documentation

Interviews and observations are often supplemented by *archival material and documentation* data collection methods. Types of data include documents such as memoranda, bulletins, agendas, meetings minutes, letters, organizational charts, reports, proposals, announcements, formal evaluations, newspaper clippings, service records, maps, lists, and personal records. These data can be gathered from myriad places: the media, the Internet, archival organizations (including city hall), organizations, individuals, and so on. Collecting these types of data is best done first because they help clarify the research setting. Such data also support findings from other sources (e.g., interviews) because they are stable (can be examined repeatedly), not obtrusive to possible participants, exact (e.g., accurately names board members of an organization), broad in possible coverage (over time, events, or settings), and precise (and often quantitative in nature). However, they may be hard to obtain, you may have access blocked (for political reasons or because of sensitive material such as health reports), they may be selective (you may be limited to particular information), and they can have a certain reporting bias from the author (Yin, 2013).

Archival material and documentation can be the single data source, as in the case of Pedersen, Whisenant, and Schneider's (2003) study on gendering of sport newspaper personnel and newspaper coverage. However, archival material and documentation often are combined with other data sources, especially to provide a better overview of the case at hand, as is the case with Mason and Slack's (2003) study or in the case of O'Brien and Slack's (2003) use of documents and interviews to examine organizational change in the English Rugby Union. Taks, Misener, Chalip, and Green (2013) used event documents and semistructured interviews to evaluate sport development outcomes for a medium-sized, one-off international sport event. They found that these events are unlikely to cause increases in sport participation without some form of proactive strategic leveraging. Another form of document analysis is the work of Pedersen and Pitts (2001), who investigate the body of knowledge in sport management through a content analysis of the journal *Sport Marketing Quarterly*.

Advances in Data Collection

Other types of data that can be collected include physical artifacts and visual, electronic, and audio materials. Physical artifacts such as instruments, tools, works of art, and high-tech gear can provide a study with insight into either cultural features of a setting or technological operation (e.g., the quality of the production processes of a sporting goods manufacturer). However, their availability and selectivity can be a problem (Yin, 2013). Visual, electronic, and audio materials reveal various clues, such as a representation of the study participants or to discern the meaning of a phenomenon for a particular society or culture. Discerning meaning is usually done through the use of semiotics (the science of signs) by comparing the signifier (what you actually see and hear) with the signified (what the signifier refers to, a concept, an idea, a meaning) (Penn, 2000). For an example of semiotics, see Barthes' (1957) *Mythologies* or Myers' (2013) *Qualitative Research in Business and Management*. If you are using moving images or sound (e.g., a song, a sound bite), you need to transcribe what you see and hear. This can be time consuming and you must be selective, relying on theory to determine what to transcribe.

Sport management researchers have used these other types of data in their studies. Pedersen, Whisenant, and Schneider's (2003) study is such an example, combining archival material and documentation with photographs as data sources. Higgs and Weiller (1994) analyze 60 hours of taped televised coverage of the 1992 Barcelona Summer Olympics to examine gender bias in television coverage.

Hoeber and Shaw (2016) suggest that qualitative methods have become more commonplace in sport management scholarship than 20 to 30 years ago, and they produced a special issue in the journal *Sport Management Review* that illustrates some contemporary qualitative studies in sport management including the use of community-based research approaches, Indigenous methodologies, participatory action research, autoethnography, narrative, digital ethnography, and phenomenology. Even more recently, Stewart-Withers, Sewabu, and Richardson (2017) illustrate an innovative approach for sport management research that encourages inclusivity and cultural sensitivity. Technology is more commonly used in sport management research to provide innovative solutions to data collection. For example, García, Welford, and Smith (2016) discuss the use of smartphone apps in qualitative research.

Data Analysis Methods

Once you have your data, you have to manipulate it in one way or another in order to answer your research question. This is where **data analysis methods** enter. Data analysis must be tied not only to your collected data but also to your research question and theoretical framework so that you can obtain meaningful results. Complex analysis combined with poor data will lead only to poor results. Be sure to collect the right data and select the appropriate analysis. You should be aware of and plan how you will analyze your data early on in the research process, even before you actually collect the data. If you don't, you run the risk of collecting data that you don't analyze, collecting insufficient or irrelevant data, or finding that the quality of your data is lacking for the type of analysis you need to do. This can be a drain on resources of time and money. We will discuss different issues for the analysis of quantitative and qualitative data as well as mixed-methods studies, which incorporate both types of data.

Statistical Analyses

When dealing with quantitative data of any sort, you will most likely use a *statistical analysis* technique. This is usually done with a software program such as SPSS, but some analysis can also be done with basic database software such as Excel. The first thing you must know is the type of data or score you have. Nominal variables have values that differ in quality only (e.g., gender). Ordinal variables have values ordered by quantity (e.g., social class). Interval variables are ordinal variables but with equally sized intervals between each. Ratio variables are interval variables but with a true zero point (e.g., test scores) (Vieira, 2017).

The next step is to determine the statistical analysis you want to do. You have three choices: descriptive, inferential, or correlational and predictive statistics. Descriptive statistics help you to summarize, present, or organize your data set.

They are mostly for clarification purposes, and most quantitative studies will do some descriptive analysis to understand the range and characteristics of the data collected. Descriptive statistics include the mean or average, median, mode, range, frequency, variance, and standard deviation of a particular score within a group of scores (Vieira, 2017). Inferential statistics are used when you want to infer something about the population at large from the information provided by a sample of that population. Inferential statistics include chi square (to determine the probability that a discrepancy in the sample is due only to sampling error), t-test (for comparing two sample means), and ANOVAs (to determine the effect and interaction of two different treatments on a sample) (Vieira, 2017). If you have only nominal and ordinal variables, you would apply the chi square technique. If you have a nominal or ordinal and interval or ratio variables, you would rely on the t-test or ANOVA technique (Vieira, 2017). Finally, correlation and predictive statistics are used to describe a relationship between events (correlation) or to predict the outcome from one event to the next (predictive). Correlation, however, does not mean causation—you can correlate almost anything. Causation can only be done in an experimental design. Correlation statistics include the Pearson product-moment correlation (a reflection of how close two variables are to a linear relationship) and the Spearman rank-order correlation (correlation indicator for nominal or ordinal variables) (Evans, 1998; Trochim, 2001). The main predictive technique is regression analysis, which may be linear, multiple, partial, or curvilinear in nature (Vieira, 2017). The regression line is created by plotting the complete set of calculated predicted values of the dependent variable (y) for the set values of the independent variable (x) (Evans, 1998). A good, clear overview of statistical techniques with examples from sport management literature can be found in Andrew, Pedersen, and McEvoy (2011).

Many examples of statistical analysis are found in sport management research. Armstrong-Doherty (1996) used a Spearman rank-order correlation analysis to show that various stakeholders can have resource dependence-based (perceived) control over university athletic departments. Kent and Chelladurai's (2001) study found that both Pearson product-moment correlation and regression analyses indicate that there was a correlation between transformational leadership and leader–member exchange quality, as well as to show that these two elements are related to organizational commitment and organizational citizenship behavior. McGehee, Yoon, and Cárdenas (2003) use a combination of descriptive statistics, Cronbach's alpha, and cluster analysis to study involvement and travel for recreational runners. Koenigstorfer, Groeppel-Klein, and Kunkel (2010) used the partial least squares (PLS) method of structural equation modelling (smart PLS), advanced inferential statistical tools to test nine hypotheses related to fan perception of competitive balance within association football leagues and how this influences a leagues attractiveness.

Content Analysis

If you have qualitative data, you may want to do a *content analysis*. This technique is a systematic classification involving the counting of sections or units of a text. The result of the content analysis is the dependent variable (i.e., what you are looking for). Content analysis designs can be descriptive, normative (comparison between sample and a given standard), cross-sectional (e.g., different contexts), longitudinal (over time to look at changes), a cultural indicator for a certain issue, or parallel (comparison of longitudinal studies) in nature (Bauer & Gaskell, 2000).

Content analysis involves coding, or the assigning of labels to sections of text. The coding frame (set of codes) can be theory driven or emerge out of the data. Consideration must be made for the coding frame, such as the nature of the categories, the types of code variables, the organizing principal of the coding frame, the coding process, and the coder training. The coding frame must be coherent, explicit (a code book helps), reliable, and valid.

Content analysis allows for the systematic and public analysis of textual material (whether this material be originally in written, verbal, physical, audio, video, or electronic form) to make generalizations about the collective level from individual texts. It can also help construct historical data. However, separating the units analyzed may create inaccuracies in interpretation because it tends to focus on the frequency and the recurrence of codes, thereby neglecting rare or absent elements that could have a potential impact on findings. The relationship between sections in the text that are coded differently can also be lost (Bauer & Gaskell, 2000). Silk (2001) provides a description of his inductive content analysis procedure for examining the importance of the nation in media representation during the 1998 Kuala Lumpur Commonwealth Games. Other examples of content analysis in sport management research include a focus on social media sources (e.g. Filo, Lock,

& Karg, 2015; Hambrick, Simmons, Greenhalgh, & Greenwell, 2010), technology promoting physical activity (Middleweerd, Mollee, van der Wal, Brug, & te Velde, 2014), sport tourism (Van Rheenen, Cernaianu, & Sobry, 2017), and effectiveness of codes of ethics (De Waegeneer, Van De Sompele, & Willem, 2016). This method is increasingly common to create an overview and synthesis of knowledge on a particular subject.

Coding

Coding means finding patterns and identifying themes. Coding is an intrinsic part of nonnumerical data analysis. It helps to link different segments of the data, it identifies relevant concepts or themes, it helps make the data set more manageable, and it helps expand and transform the data in results that address your research question or purpose. Once concepts or themes are highlighted, examples of those phenomena can be retrieved within the data set, and an analysis of those segments can be done to find similarities, differences, patterns, and structures within the text to see the possible relationships between concepts (Coffey & Atkinson, 1996). Coding is analysis (Miles, Huberman, & Saldaña, 2014). Different methods are available to researchers to categorize and understand their data, including process coding, emotion coding, descriptive coding, dramaturgical coding, evaluation coding, holistic coding, and many others (Miles, Huberman, & Saldaña, 2014). The process of coding is often done in two stages: first cycle and second cycle (patterns). To see a full description of options available within these stages, see Saldaña (2013).

To compare the different segments of interest, Miles, Huberman, & Saldaña (2014) propose two methods: matrix and network. A *matrix* is a table showing the relationship between an independent variable and a dependent variable. It is useful for determining the flow, location, and connection of events, and for eyeballing patterns. This technique is good for exploratory studies and for comparisons of studies. A *network* is a collection of points (nodes) connected by lines (links). This technique works for dealing with many variables at one time and when trying to draw relationships among the variables. In this way, explanatory studies can benefit from this technique.

A good example of a content analysis coding method is O'Brien and Slack's (2003) article "An Analysis of Change in an Organizational Field: The Professionalization of English Rugby Union." In the article, O'Brien and Slack describe the types of data they gathered, their coding scheme, and their coding procedure. Other examples include articles such as Pedersen, Whisenant, and Schneider's (2003) study on gender in sport newspaper personnel and newspaper coverage and Mason and Slack's (2003) principal–agent study in professional hockey.

Of course, coding is also found with numerical data analysis. However, it occurs in a different way. For example, a researcher may be interested in the popularity of sport as a marketing strategy. In this case, every time a sport reference is made in an advertisement, the researcher would code that instance and then proceed to an appropriate statistical analysis.

Computer-Assisted Analysis

As alluded to earlier in this chapter, *computer-assisted analysis* is done to help with data analysis. Programs like Tableau, NVivo, Leximancer, and Atlas.ti are tools to mechanize tasks of ordering and archiving. Sotiriadou, Brouwers, and Le (2014) provide a useful comparison of these programs to illustrate their application and utility in analyzing qualitative data. The programs don't actually interpret data. Codes are used to highlight sections of text referring to a particular issue of interest. These codes can originate from theory, common sense, or the data itself if you are doing grounded theory. Creating subcategories of these codes or dimensions is called *dimensionalization*. Comparison and dimensionalization allow for deeper, more fine-tuned analyses than those done manually. This allows you to see the relationship between different highlighted concepts and helps you analyze your data. Of course, once analysis is done, you must return to the data to confirm or discount your findings.

Using computer-assisted analysis increases efficiency (you can increase your sample size and number, and decrease cost), accuracy (it is a more systematic and explicit research process), and creativity (you can play with the data to extract more results). However, it can also alienate the researcher from the data because you focus on the codes and it can reify codes (Kelle, 2000).

While most articles do not go into detail on how to use computer-assisted analysis (it is understood that for any large amount of nonnumerical data, a computer program must be used to make data analysis simpler and less time consuming), Cousens and Slack (1996) include a paragraph to explain that their data on sport sponsorship and the fast food industry was scanned for the occurrence of key words, which indicates their use of computer-assisted analysis.

TIME OUT

Research Outlets

With advances in technology and a competitive market for publications, a variety of outlets exist in which sport management researchers can publish their work. Researchers may opt to publish their research in mainstream management journals or sport-specific journals. Journals are often competitively ranked for quality, but you may choose a journal for other reasons such as a special being relevant to your research. Increasingly, sport management research is published in edited book format, such as Brittain, Boccarro, Byers, and Swart's (2017) edited volume of research on *Legacies and Mega Events: Fact or Fairy Tales?*, which contains research on sporting and nonsporting mega-event legacy. Book formats allow authors to reach a potentially larger audience and provide more details of their research, especially if they are using case studies or other qualitative methods.

Another earlier example is Burbank, Andranovich, and Heying's (2001) *Olympic Dreams: The Impact of Mega-Events on Local Politics*. The authors examine the impact of mega-events—specifically the Olympic Games—and the role of local politics using three case studies: Los Angeles, Atlanta, and Salt Lake City.

Open-access journals now exist that are free to view and a professional network site called Research Gate where authors can upload working papers as well as copies of publications. Other online spaces are devoted to disseminating research, including The Conversation, Palgrave Pivot, and Plos One.

Issues of Quality

How do you evaluate your research and other research? Two key terms that you may have heard are *validity* and *reliability*. **Validity** refers to the degree to which an instrument measures what it is supposed to measure, and **reliability** refers to consistency of measurement. If you look at different books dealing with validity, you may find differences in the number and names of validity types. However, here are the most widely used (cf. Bauer & Gaskell, 2000; Trochim, 2001; Yin, 2017):

- *Construct validity:* Is there adequate relationship between the test and the theoretical framework?
  - *Content validity*: Is the sample adequate for the concept you want to measure?
  - *Face validity*: Have you, on the surface, measured the concept you actually wanted to measure?
- *Criterion validity*: Can different elements within the test be differentiated if they are related in any way?
- *Internal validity*: Can readers have confidence in your findings through explicit telling of the coding frame?
- *External validity*: Can results be statistically (for numerical data) or analytically (linking results back to the theory, for nonnumerical data) generalizable?

Reliability has two forms: interrater and test–retest reliability. Interrater reliability is the main focus of qualitative research and refers to whether two different researchers get the same results with the same data set. The more detail that is provided during data collection and analysis, as well as the reporting of results, the higher the likelihood that interrater reliability will be high. Test–retest reliability is usually reserved for numerical data and refers to whether the same data set will provide the same findings when tested and retested using the same instrument (Bauer & Gaskell, 2000). Think of when you step on a scale to weigh yourself. If you weigh yourself once, step off the scale, then weigh yourself again, the scale should give you the same number. If it does, it has high test–retest reliability.

The Write-Up

So you've set up your research, and you've collected your data and analyzed it. Now what do you do? As a practitioner, you would write a report and present your findings to your superiors or employer (if you are under contract). Unlike the academic process described later, writing a report is usually a shorter process because (1) you may have a specific deadline, (2) you do not need to go through the peer review process, (3) you typically do not need to provide a theoretical framework or discuss validity and reliability, and (4) your superiors are more interested in the findings' bottom line. However, you still want to be as explicit—yet concise—as possible in your writing so that your readers have confidence in your results and suggestions for actions, if any. Such a report typically starts with a title page followed by a table of contents. An executive summary (about one page) of the report and its findings are then provided. This is followed by a background section that can include an introduction, history, or context for the report, and a description of the methodology used. The results are then presented. A summary with recommendations typically ends the actual report. Appendixes are included to provide additional information not essential to the basic understanding of the report but important to the process (e.g., details of respondents, action plan, and time lines). The exact format of the report should be agreed upon with your employer or supervisor at the beginning of the process.

Alternatively, you can publish the findings in a book or an article, or present your findings at a conference (although this alternative does not always require the writing of a full article). While a book can reach a broader range of readers, the article is the more popular format. The article's actual format can be traditional—title, abstract, introduction, theoretical framework, research design, results, discussion, conclusion—or instead use narratives or modifications of the traditional format.

Writing an article is a long process. You have to determine what to include and be precise while not excluding information pertinent to understanding the research process and findings. The key is to be as transparent as possible, especially if you are going to be collecting and analyzing qualitative data. Transparency means being as explicit as possible about your perspective, research design, data collection, and analysis techniques, and the range of results obtained. Your perspective is *not* simply a review of the literature—that would be like listing all possible works on a given topic. Instead, you must ensure that you build a theoretical framework, which guides your choice of research design (including data collection and analysis methods), results presentation, and discussion. In turn, the discussion is not a review of your results but a discussion of the results in relation to your theoretical framework.

Also be sure to check the required format and writing style before submitting to the intended journal. Select a journal based on its audience and the focus of your article (e.g., researcher versus practitioner, sport versus management journals). In other words, the same piece of research would be written differently if it were sent to the *Journal of Sport Management* (sport, researcher) versus the *Academy of Management Journal* (management, researcher) versus *SportBusiness International* (sport, practitioner).

The writing process does not end here because an article is typically peer-reviewed—usually three reviewers will evaluate the article in a blind review format (i.e., there is no name on the manuscript; only the editor knows the article's author). This process has one of three outcomes: accepted for publication, rejected, or returned for revisions and resubmission (with no guarantee of acceptance). Unless you are accepted for publication on the first try, which is rare, you will have to revise your article, probably more than once. From the time you begin to write to the point of acceptance for publication, you will go through many drafts—it is not unusual to have more than 10 drafts for one article—and it can take a year or more for this whole writing process. Table 2.1 provides an overview of the research process steps and their respective components.

Table 2.1 Components of the Research Process

Research designs	Data collection methods	Data analysis methods	Write-up
Experiment and quasi-experiment Survey Case study Ethnography Grounded theory Action research Phenomenology Critical realism	Questionnaire Interview Observation Participant observation Archival material and documentation Physical artifacts Visual, electronic, audio material	Statistical analysis Content analysis Computer-assisted analysis	Journal article Report Conference proceeding Book

Based on information from Miles, Huberman, and Salanda (2013); Crotty (1998); Evans (1998); Babbie (1999); Bauer and Gaskell (2000); and Yin (2013).

KEY ISSUES FOR SPORT MANAGERS

As a sport manager, you may be asked to do some research to help your company's performance (e.g., customer satisfaction survey) or evaluate research to determine the best course of action (e.g., a new test is developed for detecting a performance-enhancing drug). As a consultant, you would be asked to do research to help the employer be more effective or efficient in a certain area. For these reasons, you must be aware of the relationship between the research question, the theoretical approach, research design, methods, findings, and data interpretation. A good piece of research will be clear about each step and flow logically from one to another. However, your employer or client may not be as interested in your research design or require a detailed description of it. They are more interested in the summary of the findings and any suggestions for future action that stem from your research. Establish a writing tone consistent with your organization's vocabulary—it doesn't have to sound scientific. You need to be clear about the format of the report to be presented (i.e., ask your superior), but the presentation style should not have an impact on your actual research method.

Summary and Conclusions

Research can be exploratory, descriptive, or explanatory in nature. The research question, written properly, will dictate the appropriate theoretical framework and methods used to collect and analyze data.

Research design includes data collection and analysis techniques. Before collecting any data, you must determine your unit of analysis and sample size. Research designs include quasi-experiments, surveys, case studies, ethnographies, grounded theory, and action research. Data collection methods include questionnaires, interviews, observations, as well as the use of archival material and documentation, physical artifacts, visual, electronic, and audio material. Therefore, understanding how to conduct good quality research and analyze data to inform your manager's decision making is vital to organization success.

Review Questions

1. List the steps of the research process.
2. What is the difference between exploratory, descriptive, and explanatory research?
3. What is the difference between a theoretical framework and a review of the literature?
4. Why is a theoretical framework essential in research?
5. You are the manager of the local minor league hockey association and are asked to remedy the problem of declining participation. Pose your research question and explain how you would go about answering the association's problem through an appropriate research process.
6. What sport management research questions would you like to see answered? Why? How?

Suggestions for Further Reading

A multitude of books and articles deal with the various steps of the research process (including concepts not dealt with here such as epistemology, ontology, and theoretical perspective), especially in the management and sociology literature. While it is important to read contemporary sources for understanding current debates and perspectives, we also recommend some older sources that will start to give you an understanding of how research changes over time. This should also provide some preparation for challenging existing practices in order to contribute to changes in research methods, practices, and assumptions. Some good examples of past research methods work accessible for new researchers are Aiken, West, & Reno's (1991) *Multiple Regression: Testing and Interpreting Interactions*; Bhaskar's (1989) *Reclaiming Reality: A Critical Introduction to Contemporary Philosophy*; Burrell and Morgan's (2017) *Sociological Paradigms and Organizational Analysis: Elements of the Sociology of Corporate Life*; Creswell's (2003) *Research Design: Qualitative, Quantitative and Mixed Methods Approaches*; Denscombe's (2010) *The Good Research Guide: For Small-Scale Social*

Research Projects; Denzin and Lincoln's (2011) *The SAGE Handbook of Qualitative Research*; Eisenhardt's (1989) "Building Theories From Case Study Research" in the *Academy of Management Review*; Evans' (1998) *Using Basic Statistics in the Social Sciences*; Guba's (1990) *The Paradigm Dialog*; Miles and Huberman's (1994) *Qualitative Data Analysis, Second Edition*; Morgan's (1983) *Beyond Method: Strategies for Social Research*; Strauss' (1987) *Qualitative Analysis for Social Scientists*; and Yin's (2003) *Case Study Research: Design and Methods, Third Edition*. There are also some good readings in sport literature, such as Brannigan's (1999) *The Sport Scientists: Research Adventures* and Jackson and Burton's (1999) *Leisure Studies: Prospects for the Twenty-first Century*. Many of these authors have written updated accounts of their work such as Yin (2017) and Miles, Huberman, and Saldaña (2014). There are also a number of excellent books related to sport, recreation, and related industries that we recommend for readers to understand both how research is conducted and the topics within our field on research being conducted (e.g., Riddick & Russell, 2014; Andrew, Pedersen, & McEvoy, 2011).

Case for Analysis

Renewal of a Sport Policy for Canada

In May 2002, the Canadian government unveiled a new Canadian Sport Policy after a consultation process launched by the federal secretary of state for amateur sport in 2002. Federal, provincial, and territorial governments worked together to ensure that major stakeholders at all levels of sport would be involved. These included more than a thousand individuals, such as athletes, coaches, parents, officials, volunteers, paid staff, representatives of municipal recreation departments, provincial and national sport organizations, local school boards, businesspeople, and government officials.

These stakeholders were able to participate in six regional conferences to make their views known on the current state of sport in the country and their suggestions for the future. Working from discussion papers and the results of various surveys, the conference delegates provided their input on resources, ethics and values, leadership and partnership, participation, promotion, and development. Discussions were also held with the Aboriginal Sport Circle, Athletes CAN, sport officials, national single- and multisport organizations, and the media. Discussions focused on the issues of inclusion and equity.

In 2011, the Public Policy Forum convened 12 roundtable discussions across the country as part of the Canadian Sport Policy Renewal Process. This process brought together federal, provincial, and municipal officials as well as community representatives to determine if community capacity building could be included in a new sport policy for Canada without losing the core business of sport as outlined in the 2002 policy. Phase one of this process brought together representatives from municipal governments and community organizations from sport and nonsport sectors for roundtable sessions held in six cities: St. John, Halifax, Ottawa, Calgary, Edmonton, and Vancouver. The second phase consisted of six sessions in the five provinces where the previous roundtables were held, involving officials from provincial ministries and provincial sport organizations. This phase was to consider the findings from the community level and discuss how provincial governments viewed community building. The research was exploratory in nature and not intended to be representative of the population, but rather the start of an ongoing conversation that would inform the new policy.

The findings revealed that (1) sport has the capacity to bridge sectors, mobilize people, and contribute to a wide range of societal goals; (2) the sport community and system have the capacity to make a more robust contribution to community building than it had in the past; (3) the 2002 sport policy had done little to promote cross-sectoral partnerships between sport and nonsport stakeholders; and (4) the next sport policy should make a more intentional commitment to community building.

Questions

1. What were the research design, data collection, and data analysis methods used to develop Canada's sport policy? What additional information, if any, would you need to answer the question?
2. Evaluate the quality of this research (i.e., identify strengths and weaknesses), given the fact that this was a professional report and not an academic article.
3. Why is it important for the government to do a write-up of the findings?
4. How would you go about developing a complementary action plan for your jurisdiction?

PART II

FUNDAMENTALS OF MANAGING SPORT ORGANIZATIONS

This part presents several concepts we see as being fundamental for developing our understanding of managing sport organizations. In chapter 3 the focus is on the concept of effectiveness, which in many ways is central to the role of a sport manager. The chapter includes a review of major theoretical approaches to understanding effectiveness and a demonstration of how the concept of effectiveness is paradoxical. Chapter 4 concentrates on the environment, a source of uncertainty and opportunity for organizations, which has a major impact on the structure and processes of a sport organization. We provide methods for managers to determine the composition of the environment and how to respond to, eliminate, or minimize the impact of this uncertainty. Chapters 5 and 6 are devoted to the issues of structure and design: different structural elements result in managers adopting different organizational designs in an effort to achieve its goals. In chapter 5, three common dimensions of theorizing structure—complexity, formalization, and centralization—are introduced. Chapter 6 highlights how some designs are more effective for certain types of sport organizations than for others, so descriptions are offered for how structural elements are patterned into the various design types.

The focus of chapter 7 (new to this third edition), written by Spencer Harris, introduces different policy types and then demonstrates how organizations respond to policy requirements. In the chapter, two approaches—institutional theory and implementation theory—are used to examine the various responses of organizations to policy requirements. Chapter 8, updated by James Kenyon and Argyro Elisavet Manoli, deals with organizational strategy, which is concerned with the long-term goals and objectives of a sport organization. Strategy, one of the major determinants of organizational structure, can be deliberate or emergent, and, as a manager, you will have to formulate and implement strategies to help your organization become successful.

Chapter 9, a new chapter written by Frank Pons, Marilyn Giroux, and Lionel Maltese, looks at sport marketing. Given the exponential growth in commercialization of (and, therefore, application of marketing strategies in) the sport sector, this chapter is an important addition.

The chapter shows that, under the sport marketing umbrella, two fundamental perspectives—marketing *of* sport and marketing *through* sport—consist of a complex network of marketing activities. Throughout the chapter, insights from the different types of activities help to develop our understanding of the broad concept of sport marketing.

CHAPTER 3

Organizational Goals and Effectiveness

Trevor Slack, PhD
Terri Byers, PhD

Learning Objectives

When you have read this chapter, you should be able to

1. understand the importance of goals and effectiveness in sport organization and say why effectiveness is a difficult concept to measure,
2. explain why researchers say effectiveness is a paradoxical concept,
3. say what concepts could be used as measures of effectiveness,
4. state what type of goals a sport organization may have, and
5. explain what purpose goals serve in a sport organization.

Key Concepts

competing values approach
department or subunit goals
effectiveness
efficiency
goal attainment approach
internal process approach
long-term goals
management by objectives (MBO)
nonoperational goals
official goals
operational goals
operative goals
short-term goals
strategic constituencies approach
systems resource approach

Are Professional Sport Organizations Effective?

The financial value of a sport franchise is often thought of as an indicator of its effectiveness. After all, sport is now synonymous with "big business" and the accumulation of wealth, profit, and power, increasingly common goals in today's capitalist society. Forbes.com provides many reports of industry trends, and tracking the value of professional sport teams is one of their activities. The cutoff to qualify among the world's most valuable sport franchises is higher than ever, up 18 percent in 2016 to $1.75 billion. Thirty-six franchises worth at least $1 billion did not make the top 50. Soaring TV contracts as well as labor deals with players that almost ensure profitability (barring outrageous spending on payroll by an owner) are often behind the high values attributed to these organizations. No sport league is as profitable as the NFL, where the average team earned an operating profit (earnings before interest, taxes, depreciation, and amortization) of $91 million, and no one banked less than $26 million. The Forbes list shows North American and European teams' value as well as their percentage one-year change, with the top six indicated as follows (Badenhausen, 2018):

1. Dallas Cowboys, $4.2 billion, 5% (NFL)
2. New York Yankees, $3.7 billion, 9% (MLB)
3. Manchester United, $3.69 billion, 11% (association football)
4. Barcelona, $3.64 billion, 2% (association football)
5. Real Madrid, $3.58 billion, -2% (association football)
6. New England Patriots, $3.4 billion, 6% (NFL)

Yet in sport, all teams and organizations do not just exist to make money; they also want to win and have a large fan base. For some European association football clubs, winning is more important than financial viability, and the most valuable teams are not necessarily the most popular with fans! Statista (2018) produces reports on teams with the most Facebook followers, and as of December 2017, the top five teams were from the NBA (Los Angeles Lakers ranking first), with the Dallas Cowboys (NFL) coming in sixth place.

There is a cultural element to this as well: North American sport tends to be more commercialized with goals set on financial imperatives, whereas European professional sport has a longer history of poor financial stability and effectiveness, but a fierce culture of winning (particularly in European association football) drives goals at all costs. This chapter demonstrates how goals are important to sport organizations and highlights the difficulties for sport managers when stakeholders' goals conflict. It is important to understand various types of goals and that different stakeholders will have different expectations and goals. This opening scenario is focused on professional sport organizations, but conflicting goals can happen even in small voluntary sport clubs, so sport managers—wherever they are—should watch out for this issue.

All organizations strive to be effective. In sport organizations, multiple and often contradictory organization goals can make the concept of effectiveness difficult to measure and achieve. On the one hand, teams are increasingly valuable and therefore financially effective. However, teams also strive to win. To play, to win, to be the best in the league—indeed it can be thought of as their reason for existence. Yet there can only be one winner, so does that mean that every other team is not effective? Effectiveness is a difficult concept to define and measure, particularly for sport organizations who often have competing goals: on- and off-field success. Researchers over the years have had considerable difficulty deciding exactly what effectiveness means. In fact, some researchers (Goodman, Atkin, & Schoorman, 1983; Hannan & Freeman, 1977) have long ago suggested abandoning effectiveness as a scientific concept. In a similar vein, Connolly, Conlon, and Deutsch (1980) criticized the research literature on effectiveness for being in a state of conceptual disarray; Nord (1983) suggested the area is in a chaotic state of affairs; and Quinn and Cameron (1983) describe effectiveness as a paradoxical concept.

Robbins (1990) notes that a review of the organizational effectiveness studies that proliferated in the 1960s and 1970s identified 30 different criteria, all claiming to measure effectiveness (see Campbell, 1977; Steers, 1975). Such concepts as productivity, profit, growth, goal consensus, and stability were included. In a study of effectiveness in intercollegiate athletic programs, Chelladurai, Haggerty, Campbell, and Wall (1981) identified 11 criteria of effectiveness:

- Achieved excellence
- Spectator interest
- Adequacy of facilities
- Career opportunities
- Student recruitment potential
- Competitive opportunities
- Sharing of costs by team
- Operating costs
- Activity as a life sport
- Satisfaction of athletes
- Sport characteristics (promotes fitness)

The opening scenario highlights that professional sport organizations, being large, complex, and heavily commercialized, may need to consider a variety of measures for effectiveness, depending on what their goals may be and which stakeholders are taken into consideration. Despite the difficulties in defining and measuring effectiveness, the concept is still of relevance and interest to researchers and practitioners, policy makers, funding bodies, and managers. For instance, effectiveness research has been a continuous focus in the context of nonprofit organizations that are increasingly pressured to demonstrate their value in terms of efficiency and effectiveness (Carman, 2010; Ebrahim & Rangan, 2010; Saxton & Guo, 2011), which can be seen as a form of greater accountability to stakeholders (Liket & Maas, 2015; Sanzo-Pérez, Rey-Garcia, & Álvarez-González, 2017). Many conceptualizations of effectiveness in nonprofit organizations have relied on financial measures (Liket & Maas, 2015). Sparrow and Cooper (2014) noted that many debates around effectiveness show that contemporary and historical issues are somewhat similar. The difference is that today, performance of organizations is recognized to be contingent upon a wide variety of factors, and therefore measures of effectiveness need to be inclusive of financial and nonfinancial elements. The balanced scorecard is probably the most widely used and known tool to facilitate this and has received some attention in sport management literature as well (Dimitropoulos, Kosmas, & Douvis, 2017; Lee, Brownlee, Kim, & Lee, 2017). The basis of this method is understanding what organizational, departmental, and even individual goals actually are. The chapter covers in detail why goals are important, including how goals drive decision making, managing staff performance, and the long-term effectiveness of a sport organization. Thus, we now turn our attention to understanding the relationship between goals and effectiveness.

Importance of Understanding Organizational Goals and Effectiveness

Sport organizations are goal-seeking entities, structured to achieve a particular purpose (or purposes). Their effectiveness is assessed by how well they achieve their goals. The goals of a sport organization are extremely important for communicating its purpose and identity to both employees and external constituents. For some sport organizations, such as a professional football team or a college hockey team, their goal is to win games, and effectiveness is simply measured by the number of games won. If this were the case, we may ask, why in 1988 did Edmonton Oilers' owner Peter Pocklington trade away to Los Angeles the NHL's all-time leading goal scorer, Wayne Gretzky, at the height of his career? Was Mr. Pocklington's goal not to win games and thus own an effective organization? The answer is obviously yes! But, for a businessman like Mr. Pocklington, effectiveness was not measured solely by the number of games the Oilers won but also by the amount of money they made. European association football superstar Gareth Bale became the world's most expensive association football player, relative to the time, when he was transferred from Tottenham Hotspur to Real Madrid for £85.3 million (approximately US$135 million) in September 2013. More recently, the Brazilian player Neymar cost Qatari-owned Paris Saint-Germain around €200 million in 2017. Few sport clubs could afford such an investment, even on the player who some say will be the best in the world at his new club.

For some recreational departments who are concerned about conservation and recreational activities, effectiveness may be determined by their ability to provide opportunities for participation in outdoor sport and recreation and, at the same time, conserve natural and recreational resources, two goals that at times may prove conflicting. For the many voluntary organizations involved in sport delivery, as new executive members are elected, goals may change and thus effectiveness varies. Some amateur sport organizations (also known as voluntary sport clubs) may in fact have conflicting goals: Some members may see the organization's primary purpose as increasing the numbers participating in the sport (i.e., those members concerned with domestic development). In contrast, others may see its most important goal as producing medal-winning athletes. Others may see the club as a social entity, so increasing participation or elite performance are not of primary importance. The primary goal of some women's athletic programs at major universities may be to secure a more equitable share of resources so they can achieve other program goals. Title IX in the United States was implemented to achieve this goal.

As these brief examples illustrate, effectiveness is not a simple concept. Some organizational goals are not always readily apparent, or goals vary according to different stakeholders. For example, the athletes, parents, coaches, owners, and spectators may view effectiveness in different ways because they value different goals that the organization should achieve. Some sport organizations may have goals that conflict, and others may change their goals as their elected representatives and leadership change. In some sport organizations, the achievement of financial goals may be necessary before other important goals can be attained. To manage this type of complexity, sport managers need a clear understanding of organizational goals and the relationship of these goals to measures of organizational effectiveness.

Organizational Goals

In this section, we look at the importance of goals for a sport organization and examine the different types of goals a sport organization may set.

Importance of Organizational Goals

Goals are important in sport organizations for two main reasons. First, as pointed out earlier, all sport organizations exist for a purpose; if a sport organization does not have a purpose, there is no need for it to exist. Goals are statements that summarize and articulate the purpose of a sport organization. Second, as outlined in more detail in this chapter, goals may provide guidelines for managers and other employees in such areas as decision making, performance appraisal, the reduction of uncertainty, the direction and motivation of employees, and organizational legitimacy (Daft, 2004). The achievement of goals also determines the effectiveness of a sport organization. The extent to which organizations evaluate their effectiveness varies widely across sport and recreation services, but formulating and understanding the goals of programs and organizations is the first step to identifying their effectiveness. Some funding streams may even require organizations to evaluate their effectiveness, so both internal (organizational awareness) and external (funding) imperatives for measuring effectiveness exist. We now examine some of the management activities that rely on goals to achieve effectiveness.

Decision Making

All sport managers are required to make decisions that influence the operation of their organization and its employees. Goals provide sport managers with an understanding of the direction to take the organization. With this understanding, sport managers can then more easily make decisions about such areas as structure, product expansion, and personnel recruitment, all of which move a sport organization toward achieving its goals. As an example, the 2015 Pan American Games in Toronto set forth the following vision (mission) statement:

Our Vision

A Life-Affecting Experience

- Attract the best athletes.
- Build reliable operations and services.
- Celebrate Pan American culture and performance.
- Ensure an entertaining spectator experience.
- Integrate the Para Pan American Games into the overall Games plan.

Transforming Communities

- Inspire children to participate in sport.
- Engage local communities to embrace the Games as their own.
- Celebrate and involve Toronto's multicultural population.
- Connect the Pan American region through summits, conferences, and workshops.
- Leave a Games legacy of sustainable excellence.

Delivering on Commitments

- Build all Games infrastructure on time, on budget, and in scope.
- Create a TORONTO 2015 brand that inspires involvement.

- Enhance the outstanding legacy of previous Pan American Games hosts.
- Generate Games business revenue in excess of $150 million.

Setting a Benchmark

- Delivering the best-ever experience for all athletes and participants.

This vision and broad goals within provide guidance to sport event managers to make decisions and prioritize resources for the achievement of these goals. Large sporting events have dramatically increased in cost over recent years and are increasingly subject to scrutiny as to their effectiveness in terms of their long-term legacy for hosts (Brittain, Bocarro, Byers, & Swart, 2017). Creating a legacy plan is usually the first step, which outlines the goals in terms of what types of legacy (social, economic, environmental, cultural, etc.) an event is meant to generate. Managers then make appropriate decisions regarding budgets and resources.

Performance Appraisal

At certain intervals, the performances of both individuals and subunits (or programs) within a sport organization have to be evaluated. The guidelines or criteria that provide a standard for this assessment are the goals of the organization. Those individuals or subunits seen as contributing the most to organizational goals and thus making

TIME OUT

Grootbos Foundation: Decision Making Driven by Performance Appraisal

Photo courtesy of Grootbos Foundation.

Grootbos Foundation is a nonprofit organization established in 2003 with a mission to conserve the unique Cape Floral Kingdom and a vision of conservation and uplifting of communities in this region. The organization attempts to achieve their goals through various programs and partnerships in education, enterprise development, sport in the community, and conservation. The Foundation conducts extensive evaluations using pre- and posttesting of its programs and initiatives to inform decisions on program development with the ultimate goal of increasing its effectiveness and impact in the community. For example, through evaluation work in the community to measure awareness and community needs, Grootbos decided to develop a Food for Sport Program. They also have an award-winning Football Foundation including the following goals:

- Uplift communities by empowering individuals through skills training and leadership opportunities.
- Encourage education, health and well-being, social integration, and community participation.
- Support and initiate grassroots sports development in South Africa by providing access to education, resources, facilities, and equipment.

Through constant evaluation of its programs and activities Grootbos is able to continuously improve performance, which increases their impact in the community, meets funding requirements, and furthers its organizational mission.

Based on information from personal communication with Simone Davel, Grootbos Foundation, and http://www.grootbosfoundation.org.

the sport organization effective are usually given the biggest rewards. Performance appraisals are evaluations that lead to suggestions as to how individuals or subunits can better contribute to organizational goals. In sport, we frequently base the performance appraisals of professional athletes on their contribution to the organizational goal of winning: The players who score the most goals or points are often given the highest salaries. However, in some types of sport organizations, such as those in the voluntary sector or a sporting goods store, it is not as easy to measure objectively an employee's or subunit's performance.

Reducing Uncertainty

Uncertainty can be defined as "a lack of information about future events, so that alternatives and their outcomes are unpredictable" (Hickson, Hinings, Lee, Schneck, & Pennings, 1971, p. 219). Sport organizations, like all organizations, seek ways to reduce uncertainties; one of the ways to do this is through the setting of goals, a process that should allow the various constituents of a sport organization to discuss alternatives, reach consensus, and decide which goals are most important for the organization. Establishing goals reduces uncertainty within the organization. Goal setting can be seen as a psychological way of decreasing uncertainty when stated goals are reached (Michael, 1973) and the sport organization is seen as effective.

Directing and Motivating Employees

Goals describe a desired outcome or future state for a sport organization; they also determine whether a sport organization is seen as effective and as such they give direction to employees. They can also motivate, if employees are a part of the process of goal setting. For example, the Ottawa Senators hockey club and its parent company, Capital Sports and Entertainment, effectively use goals and goal setting to communicate goals to and motivate employees. The Ottawa Senators are divided into several departments that include but are not limited to ticketing, group sales, corporate partnerships and activations/corporate sales, in-game production, digital media, and graphics. Goals, both at the organizational and departmental level, are an important motivator and communication tool for employees. Ownership and senior management set overarching strategic goals for the entire organization and then break down these goals and communicate the relevant parts to each department to use internally. Directors are key in this process: They receive goals from senior management and must decide the best ways to break up these goals within their own departments, communicate the goals to the employees, and then ensure that these department goals are met, which helps ensure that organizational goals are met. For example, during season ticket and corporate partner renewal season, organizational goals for the amount of money renewed is communicated downward to the relevant departments (sales and corporate sales), who then break down the goals and communicate them to employees as motivation to renew season tickets and corporate partners. This often places the onus on the directors and managers to effectively communicate these goals in a way that will motivate employees. The department of corporate sales and activation has a specific goal in terms of how much renewed business should be secured going into the next season. This amount is determined through coordination between directors and senior management, specifically the vice president of corporate sales. The directors then review ongoing business and work with the coordinators, who are each responsible for a fixed number of accounts, to set out realistic goals in terms of individual renewed business to work toward the overarching goal.

Establishing Legitimacy

Sport organizations gain legitimacy through legal means such as incorporation or affiliation with an accredited body. However, they can also gain legitimacy through the goals they establish. Goals are a statement of the sport organization's purpose; they communicate what the organization stands for and provide a rationale for acceptance as a legitimate entity. Goals legitimize a sport organization to its employees, members, and external constituents such as funding bodies, alumni, and clients. Slack and Hinings (1992), for example, describe how Canadian national sport organizations who adopted the goal of producing high-performance athletes as their central focus increased their legitimacy in the eyes of the government funding agency, Sport Canada. Toohey and Beaton (2017) highlight how national anti-doping organizations have similar goals because they are all seeking to be the only legitimate lead on anti-doping education and control as regulated by WADA (World Anti-Doping Agency).

Types of Organizational Goals

Sport organizations usually have several types of goals; each type performs a particular function within the organization. Some types of goals may overlap: For example, official goals are usually nonoperative, while short-term goals are usually operative. Table 3.1 summarizes those types of goals most frequently found in sport organizations

Table 3.1 Classification of Goals: Examples From a U.S. Professional Basketball Team

Type of goal	Example
Official goal	To provide a high-quality basketball program to both entertain and benefit the community
Operative goal	To make money
Operational goal	To sell over 50,000 tickets for each home game
Nonoperational goal	To provide a fair return to shareholders
Short-term goal	To win two of the first three away games of the season
Long-term goal	To win the National Basketball Association finals
Departmental or subunit goal	To have the backcourt score at least half of the final points

and provides an example of each as it relates to a professional basketball team. Each type is then explained in more detail in the text that follows.

Official Goals

Charles Perrow (1961, p. 855) suggests that official goals are "the general purposes of the organization as put forth in the charter, annual reports, public statements by key executives, and other authoritative pronouncements." For example, Canada Basketball states that its mission is to "aspire to excellence in leading the growth and development of the game at home, and in pursuing medal performances on the international stage" (Canada Basketball 2011). **Official goals**, often subjective and usually not measurable, express the values of the organization and give it legitimacy with external constituents. They describe the reasons for the organization's existence and serve as a means for employees and members to identify with the organization.

Operative Goals

While official goals exemplify what a sport organization says it wants to achieve, **operative goals** "designate the ends sought through the operating policies of the organization; they tell us what the organization actually is trying to do, regardless of what the official goals say are the aims" (Perrow, 1961, p. 855). An indication of the operative goals of an organization, which are usually not explicitly stated, may often be obtained by examining the way resources are allocated. The late owner of the Toronto Maple Leafs, Harold Ballard, gave a good indication of his operative goals for the Leafs when shareholders at the 1985 annual general meeting inquired about the team's dismal performance on the ice. He told them, "Our shares are all right and we're making money so what the hell do we care?" (Mills, 1991, p. 11). This financial concern happened to be the crux of the 2004 to 2005 NHL lockout situation. There was such a wide gap between NHL owners and players that the NHL announced the formal cancellation of the 2004 to 2005 season on February 16, 2005—the first time a professional sport league in North America had done so. Lockouts are a modern-day example of how sport organizations' operative goals have come to focus more on commercial outcomes of sport, much to the detriment of fans.

Operational Goals

Operational goals are goals that can be measured objectively; they may be official but are more likely to be operative. One of the main ways operational goals can be developed in sport organizations is through a process known as **management by objectives (MBO)**. Growing out of the work of classical management theorists such as Fayol and Urwick, MBO is probably most often associated with the work of Peter Drucker (1954). Although it promotes a mechanistic approach to sport organizations and fails to consider many of the human and political aspects of organizations, MBO has frequently been suggested as a means of goal setting for sport organizations (cf. Jensen, 1983; Kelly, 1991; VanderZwaag, 1984). Operational goals are often seen in performance review models used to measure employee performance (Molan, Kelly, Arnold, & Mathews, 2018), where clearly defined objectives are agreed upon by both management and employees. The MBO method is a form of operational goal setting that aims to increase the effectiveness of the organization through setting, recording, and monitoring goals over a specified period of time. The process is a top-down translation of organizational goals into individual targets to achieve objectives of departments and then of the broader organization.

Nonoperational Goals

A **nonoperational goal** is one that cannot be measured objectively. Official goals, or mission statements, are usually nonoperational. For example, Ryka is a "women-only sport company" who for 30 years adopted a "made for women" mentality for their products. Although not explicitly measured or evaluated in any way, the motto is a guiding principle for creating footwear exclusively designed for a woman's unique foot shape, muscle movement, and build. While we can see their mission, they do not actually measure their achievement of it; rather, the company focuses on measuring more specific objectives such as sales, user satisfaction, or organizational performance by geographic area.

Long-Term Goals

Long-term goals are those the sport organization would like to achieve over a relatively lengthy period of time—maybe a season or a period of years. The organization may state that one of its long-term goals is to win the league championship.

Short-Term Goals

Short-term goals are those set for a relatively brief period of time. For example, the general manager of a basketball team will often set short-term goals for the team, such as winning 50 percent of its games on the next road trip.

Department and Subunit Goals

As we have seen, sport organizations formulate overall goals. They may be official or operative, operational or nonoperational, long term or short term. However, departments or subunits within a sport organization may also formulate their own goals. For example, the sales department of a company that produces sport equipment may set a goal to sell a certain amount of their product, or the defensive unit of a college hockey team may set a goal to hold opponents to under a certain number of goals. It is important that **department or subunit goals** do not work counter to overall organizational goals. Department and subunit goals should not be seen as ends in themselves but as a means of achieving the sport organization's desired end state.

Effectiveness or Efficiency

As Hannan and Freeman (1977) point out, within the tradition that emphasizes the importance of organizational goals, an important distinction needs to be made between the concepts of organizational effectiveness and organizational efficiency. **Effectiveness** refers to the extent to which an organization achieves its goals. **Efficiency**, on the other hand, takes into account the amount of resources used to produce the desired output (cf. Goodman & Pennings, 1977; Sandefur, 1983). It is often measured in economic terms, usually the ratio of inputs to outputs. However, as Mintzberg (1982, p. 104) notes, "because economic costs can usually be more easily measured than social costs, efficiency often produces an escalation in social costs." Macintosh and Whitson (1990) illustrate the occurrence of such a situation in sport when they suggest that Sport Canada's push for international sporting success has been achieved at the expense of some of the other more socially oriented goals of sport such as gender equality and regional access.

While efficiency is a goal of all sport organizations, an efficient organization is not necessarily effective. For example, a sport organization may be efficient in the way that it makes its product but, like Puma athletic shoes in the mid-1980s (Roth, 1987), if the number of people buying the product decreases, the organization will not be effective in meeting its goals. Likewise, an organization may be effective in that it achieves its goals, but it may not be efficient. For example, a professional basketball team that wins a championship but also spends large sums of money to buy established players would fall into this category. Some would argue that many professional sport organizations today are effective but few are efficient, especially those that spend and borrow large amounts of money to cover player salaries, stadium renovations incorporating advanced technology, and cater to the bespoke fan experience (Byers, 2018).

Approaches to Studying Organizational Effectiveness

As would be expected, the varying opinions of what constitutes organizational effectiveness have led to several approaches to studying the concept. Cameron (1980) identified four major approaches to evaluating effectiveness: the goal attainment approach, the systems resource approach, the internal process approach, and the strategic constituencies approach. We now look at each of these approaches and discuss their strengths and weaknesses as well as the more recently developed competing values approach (Quinn & Rohrbaugh, 1981; 1983). Researchers increasingly note concerns with these models, and multiple-constituency models have emerged as superior in capturing the many variables that contribute to effectiveness in organizations (Rojas, 2000).

The Goal Attainment Approach

As we saw earlier, all sport organizations exist to achieve one or more goals and thus be seen as effective. The **goal attainment approach** to organizational effectiveness is based on the identification of these goals and how well the sport organization attains or makes progress toward them. Effectiveness is based on the achievement of ends, not means. Operative goals are the most important goals to focus on when using this approach (Hall & Clark, 1980; Price, 1972; Steers, 1975). For the goal attainment model to be workable, the sport organization being studied must have goals that are clearly identifiable, consensual, measurable, and time-bounded (Cameron, 1984). There must be general consensus or agreement on the goals and a small enough number of them to be manageable. Campbell (1977, p. 26) suggests that MBO "represents the ultimate in a goal-oriented model of effectiveness."

In studies of sport organizations the goal attainment approach has been the most frequently used method of evaluating effectiveness. The goals "most often measured in a sport context reflect an emphasis on performance outcomes and have been operationalized in terms of win/loss records or performance rankings in comparison to other teams" (Frisby, 1986, p. 95). For example, in their study of national sport organizations, Chelladurai, Szyszlo, and Haggerty (1987) used the number of medals won at major competitions and the number of victories at dual international events as indicators of effectiveness. They suggest that the goal model may be useful for evaluating the effectiveness of elite sport programs, but they reject the use of this approach for mass sport programs, since goal attainment is not as easily measured in the latter. Former Dallas Cowboys owner H.R. "Bum" Bright shows how, in evaluating effectiveness, it is possible to reject one measure of goal effectiveness in favor of another. He noted, "The actual success or failure of our investment in the Cowboys will not be measured by the profit/loss bottom line, but will be measured by their success in their competition on the football field" (Hampton, 1984, p. 24).

Despite its popularity, the goal attainment approach to organizational effectiveness has a number of problems. The first and, according to Hannan and Freeman (1977), the most substantive of these problems arises because there is usually more than one organizational goal to achieve. While some sport organizations will have only one goal, others have more; the faculty of physical education at a university may, for example, have goals that relate to teaching, research, and service. This multiplicity of goals is compounded in organizations when operative goals are added and when subunits have their own goals, as is so often the case.

This multiplicity can also be problematic in that, as was pointed out earlier, some goals may be competing or even incompatible. For example, Sport Canada has swung between promoting grassroots sport participation, domestic development, and funding elite-level sport for more than four decades. The limited budget usually provided to sport has been spread thinly and inconsistently across the system. The Canadian sport system has suffered because it lacked a clear long-term goal. Canadians are less active, and the Canadian Olympic team has never had an overall stellar performance. It has never been first in medal rankings. Therefore, the presence of multiple and conflicting goals means that effectiveness cannot be solely determined by one single indicator.

TIME OUT

Innovations in Goal Setting: Learning Goals

While most goals focus on the outcome, some goals focus on the process of achievement as well as outcomes, which for some sport organizations, may be an innovative way to build capacity of staff and volunteers. Sport managers should consider what Redelius, Quennerstedt, and Öhman (2015, p. 643) recognize as important in the physical education sector, that "the role of the teacher has changed. Being a teacher becomes that of a facilitator of learning; someone who is in charge of setting up environments that best facilitate the achievement of the national learning goals." Their paper emphasizes the importance of how learning goals are communicated and that the process of learning takes place in a sociohistorical context; therefore, it is just as important to understand how and why people are working toward goals as it is to focus on whether they achieved the goals. This is more of a development approach to goal setting and seeks to understand and engage people in the process of learning.

A second problem with the goal attainment approach is how to identify goals and actually measure the extent to which they have been achieved. As we pointed out earlier in the chapter, official goals are usually vague and operative goals are often not written down. While it is relatively easy to argue that for some sport organizations the number of games won is a measure of goal effectiveness, it is harder to both identify and measure the goals of a high school physical education department. Likewise, profit-making sport organizations and professional sport teams may also have goals that relate to such areas as job satisfaction and player development. These goals can usually be measured only qualitatively and progress toward them is difficult to assess, further complicating the use of the goal attainment approach to effectiveness. Price (1972) suggests that one way to overcome the problem of goal clarity is to focus on the organizational decision makers because their statements and actions regarding the organization's operations reveal its priorities. However, as Chelladurai (1985) points out, although Price's suggestion has merit, it tends to ignore the fact that there may not be consensus among decision makers as to what the sport organization's goals are; in addition, their goals may change inasmuch as their power to influence decisions changes.

A third problem with the goal attainment approach relates to the temporal dimension of goals. Hannan and Freeman (1977) ask whether short term, long term, or both time frames should be considered. They suggest that most published empirical studies employing cross-sectional data focus on the short term, but whether this focus is appropriate depends on "the nature of the goals' function for each organization" (p. 113). For organizations that stress a quick return on investment, as some profit-making sport organizations do, short-term goals should be considered. Organizations oriented toward continued production, such as a university producing sport management graduates, research, and so on, the focus should be over longer periods to minimize the importance of yearly fluctuations (Hannan & Freeman, 1977). In addition, different sport organizations operating in the same environment and with the same structure may have similar goals but place a different emphasis on their rate of return on investment.

A final problem with the goal attainment approach concerns whose goals count. Even within the senior management levels of a sport organization, there will be variation in beliefs about what are appropriate organizational goals. In some sport organizations, those with power may actually be outside the senior management levels. This condition is not uncommon in voluntary sport organizations, where individuals who may have held a power position (e.g., president) in the organization remain after their tenure as a member of the rank and file. Such individuals, despite not holding an official position, may still exert considerable influence on organizational goals. The goals usually attributed to the organization are actually those of the dominant coalition. It is also possible that the goals of an organization may be considerably influenced by the contextual situation in which the sport organization exists. Macintosh and Whitson (1990), for example, have suggested that Sport Canada strongly influenced the high-performance goals of Canadian national sport organizations.

Where then, we may ask, does all this leave us? How useful is the goal attainment approach to organizational effectiveness? While it is hard to question the fact that one of the main functions of sport organizations is to achieve their goals and thus be seen as effective, the problems are identifying these goals, deciding which are important (or more important than others), and measuring whether they are achieved. Robbins (1990, p. 57) suggests five ways to increase the validity of the identified goals:

1. Ensure that input is received from all those having a major influence on formulating the official goals, even if they are not part of the senior management.
2. Include actual goals obtained by observing the behavior of organization members.
3. Recognize that organizations pursue both short- and long-term goals.
4. Insist on tangible, verifiable, and measurable goals rather than rely on vague statements that merely mirror societal expectations.
5. View goals as dynamic entities that change over time rather than as rigid or fixed statements of purpose.

Notwithstanding these suggestions and the fact that the goal attainment model of effectiveness has been used in several studies of sport organizations, those who choose to use this approach may be wise to consider Warriner's (1965, p. 140) caution that goals should be thought of "as fiction produced by an organization to account for, explain, or rationalize its existence to particular audiences rather than as valid and reliable indications of purpose." That is, goals are part of a rational approach to management. For example, Dixon, Martinez, and Martin (2015) provide a good example of the use of social media as a marketing strategy in their measure of the perceived effectiveness of such actions in accomplishing organizational objectives. A more critical perspective of goal setting would consider that the reasons they are set are not just to be achieved but to communicate legitimacy to stakeholders; present a culture or image of the organization; or, cynically, because the goal is achievable and therefore, if part of any rational performance measurement system, easily translated into some pre-agreed incentive for achieving such goals.

The Systems Resource Approach

While the goal attainment approach to effectiveness focuses on organizational outputs, the **systems resource approach** focuses on inputs. This particular approach to organizational effectiveness is based on open systems theory. Organizations are not closed to the outside. They develop exchange relationships with their environment in order to obtain resources. Consequently, effectiveness is defined as "the ability of the organization in either absolute or relative terms to exploit its environment in the acquisition of scarce and valued resources" (Yuchtman & Seashore, 1967, p. 898). The more effective organizations are those that can obtain more resources from their environments (Molnar & Rogers, 1976).

From a systems resource perspective, a sport organization like the Oakland Athletics—who in 2010 had an average attendance of 17,511 and by year 2014 had an average attendance of 24,736—would be considered effective on this criterion because of the increase. Similarly, an organization like Hockey Canada (2013-2014), with more than 600,000 minor hockey players, would, from a systems resource perspective, be considered more effective than the Canadian Weightlifting Association, Canadian Luge Association, and Cricket Canada, which each have a considerably smaller membership. It is important, however, to note that resources are not limited to financial or physical objects but can include intangibles such as reputation, influence (power), and knowledge of individuals, groups, or the organization itself (Yuchtman & Seashore, 1967). Macintosh and Whitson (1990) exemplify the use of intangible resources when they point out that national sport organizations in Canada have actively sought out board members with corporate credentials. Obviously, organizations that succeeded in placing senior management individuals on their board would, from a systems resource perspective, be seen as effective.

As Chelladurai (1985) points out, it may at first seem as though the goals model (focus on outputs) and the system resource approach (focus on inputs) are quite different. But as he goes on to point out, an organization can only secure inputs from its environment on a continuous basis if its outputs are perceived as acceptable by actors in the environment. Acquiring resources is based on the organization's attempt to achieve its goals (Hall, 1982). For example, when Virginia Tech's basketball team won the National Invitational Tournament in 1973, the university's president, T. Marshall Hahn, noted that considerable sums of money were pledged to the university. He also added that he felt alumni, corporations, and the state legislature would look more favorably on the university as a result of its success (Creamer, 1973). Clearly, here is a case where the output of the organization affected its sources of input. Frisby (1986), in her study of Canadian national sport organizations, did in fact find significant correlations between measures of goal attainment and resource acquisition. Sack and Staurowsky (1998) found that NCAA members continue to value team wins as a means of getting more resources (especially financial) to the detriment of the student-athletes.

The strengths of the systems resource approach to effectiveness are threefold. First, unlike the goal attainment approach, which considers goals as cultural entities arising outside of the organization, the systems resource approach treats the organization itself as its frame of reference. Second, it takes into account the organization's relationship to its environment. Third, it can be used to compare organizations that have differing goals (Daft, 2004). For example, all sport organizations have to obtain human, physical, and financial resources to survive (survival being the most basic measure of effectiveness); they can be compared on their ability to obtain these resources from their environment. The local association football club that is able to attract a large number of members, for example, will probably be seen by the municipal council as more effective than a badminton group with just a few members.

Despite its appealing qualities, the systems resource approach also exhibits several problems as a means of assessing effectiveness. First, and in many ways the foremost, of these problems is the fact that although this approach to organizational effectiveness is widely quoted in management literature and even within the relatively sparse literature on the effectiveness of sport organizations, it has produced "no coherent line of research" (Goodman & Pennings, 1977, p. 4). A second problem is semantic; it concerns the question of what is an input and what is an output. By way of illustration, consider the earlier example of attendance at Oakland Athletics games: Is this in fact one form of resource acquisition, or is it actually a goal of the organization to increase attendance? The same could be said of participants in minor hockey; 600,000 is actually a decrease from previous years, so does this not indicate some ineffectiveness?

The systems resource approach is also problematic in its applicability to public-sector organizations concerned with sport and to some voluntary sport organizations. The problem arises because often, for these types of organizations, a percentage of their funding is guaranteed, or at least highly certain, because it comes from a higher-level organization. For example, unlike the U.S. equivalents, many national sport organizations in Canada and Great Britain obtain a fairly large percentage of their financial resources from the government. So, using financial resources as an indicator of effectiveness is not particularly appropriate. It would, however, be legitimate to measure the effectiveness of these sport organizations by the amount of funding they obtain from other sources, such as membership fees or corporate sponsorship because these funds are not guaranteed.

A final problem with the systems resource approach is that, as Cameron (1980) points out, organizations lacking a competitive advantage in their chosen market or unsuccessful in acquiring the best resources can still be effective. Take, for example, the sport teams mentioned in the opening scenario. All 50 organizations in the list are valued in terms of billions of dollars, so given those values, all could be considered effective to some degree. Even those organizations that did not make the top 50 list, and are valued in terms of millions of dollars, are to some extent effective or they would not be valued so highly.

The systems resource approach does present an alternative perspective to assessing organizational effectiveness. It is most applicable to understanding the following types of sport organizations: those whose outputs cannot be objectively measured; those that have a clear connection between the resources (inputs) obtained and what is produced (outputs) (Cameron, 1980); and those whose supply of resources is not guaranteed by some formalized arrangement with another organization.

The Internal Process Approach

A third approach to determining organizational effectiveness is called the **internal process approach**. From this perspective, "effective organizations are those with an absence of internal strain, whose members are highly integrated into the system, whose internal functioning is smooth and typified by trust and benevolence toward individuals, where information flows smoothly both vertically and horizontally and so on" (Cameron, 1980, p. 67). While the goal attainment approach focuses on organizational outputs and the systems resource approach focuses on inputs, this approach focuses on the throughputs or transformation processes found in an organization. (Throughputs are the internal activities and processes of the organization by which inputs are converted into outputs.) These relationships are illustrated in figure 3.1.

The basis for this approach can be found in the work of writers such as Argyris (1964) and Likert

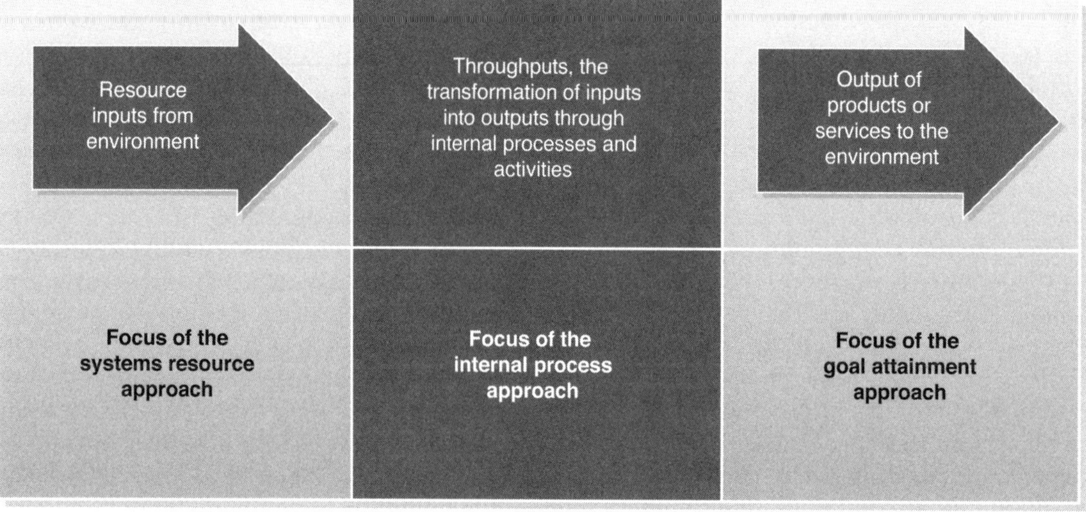

Figure 3.1 Approaches to the measurement of organizational effectiveness.

(1967), who have suggested that human resources practices are linked to organizational effectiveness. Chelladurai and Kerwin (2017) published a book on human resources in sport that may be useful for understanding this approach. Daft (2004) suggests that, from this perspective, indicators of an effective organization would include such things as the supervisors' interest and concern for their workers; a feeling of team spirit, group loyalty, and teamwork; good communications; and a compensation system that rewards managers for performance growth, the development of subordinates, and the creation of an effective working group. In a study of national sport organizations, Chelladurai and Haggerty (1991) used items such as the meaningful organization of work, information sharing among members, and concern over employee welfare and happiness as indicators of internal process effectiveness.

In contrast to an emphasis on human resources, some writers have suggested that economic efficiency should be the focus when evaluating the internal processes of an organization. Martindell (1962), for example, developed a management audit of organizations, which appraises performance on such criteria as health of earnings, fiscal policies, research and development, production efficiency, and sales. In a similar vein, Evan (1976) developed a quantitative method of looking at the economic efficiency of an organization. He suggested that it was possible to examine the inputs (I), outputs (O), and throughputs (T) of an organization; these variables could then be examined as ratios to evaluate the performance of the organization. For example, if we use the ratio of throughput to input for the local sport club or the university department as an indicator of economic effectiveness, we could get three possible results. If the cost of operations is higher than the annual budget, the ratio would be x:1 where $x > 1$. In this situation the organization would probably be seen as ineffective because it has gone over budget. If the cost of operations and the annual budget were the same, the ratio would be 1:1. If the costs of operations were less than the annual budget the ratio would be y:1 where $y < 1$. In these last two situations the organization would probably be seen as effective because it has stayed within its budget.

The major advantage of the internal process approach is that it can be used to compare organizations that have different outputs, different inputs, or little control over their environment. However, the first of a number of problems with this approach relates to the measurement of human resource variables. For example, in their study of Canadian national sport organizations, Chelladurai, Szyszlo, and Haggerty (1987) used such throughput (transformation) variables as "morale among staff members and volunteers involved in community-based programs" and "the working relationship between the NSGB [National Sport Governing Body] and its provincial branches on elite programs." While important aspects of the internal processes of these organizations, they are extremely difficult concepts to measure in any valid or reliable way.

Also, because it does not focus on organizational outputs or on an organization's relationship with its environment, the internal process approach offers only a very limited view of organizational effectiveness. As Das (1990) notes, an organization's success can be due to a unique combination of factors and conditions so that a change—whether major or minor—in these factors could result in a completely different outcome.

The internal process model also takes no account of the notion of equifinality—the ability of organizations to achieve similar ends through different means (Hrebiniak & Joyce, 1985). Two organizations with different internal processes may produce the same outputs, although two organizations with similar internal processes may produce different outputs (Das, 1990).

Finally, the internal process model is lacking in that an organization with internal problems, such as low morale, poor communication, and conflict, can still be successful. Cameron (1980, p. 69) provides a classic example—the New York Yankees of 1977 and 1978: "Lack of team discipline, fights among players and between players and coaches, threatened firings, turnover of key personnel, and lack of cohesion seemed to be the defining characteristics of that organization during the 1977 and 1978 baseball seasons. Yet the Yankees were the most effective team in baseball in terms of goal accomplishment; they won the World Series both years." The Yankees are still one of the most effective teams, in terms of winning, today having won 27 World Series in their history.

The Strategic Constituencies Approach

A fourth, and more integrative, approach to organizational effectiveness is the **strategic constituencies approach**, which emanates from the work of Connolly, Conlon, and Deutsch (1980). It may also be beneficial to look at Keeley's (1978) treatment of effectiveness for information on the origins of this perspective. Fans, the media, sponsors, and owners are all examples of groups that could be considered the strategic constituents or stakeholders of a professional baseball organization. Each has a different interest in the performance of the organization and, in turn, the organization relies on these groups for resources and support. The extent to which the team is able to satisfy the criteria used by each group to evaluate it will determine its effectiveness. Table 3.2 provides examples of the type of effectiveness criteria that might be used by selected strategic constituents of a professional basketball organization. It is important to note that constituents may be internal (e.g., players) or external (e.g., sponsors) to the organization. We will look into internal and external constituents or stakeholders in future chapters.

The strategic constituencies approach is similar to the systems resource approach but with a different emphasis. While the systems resource approach is concerned with acquiring critical resources from the environment, the strategic constituencies approach is also concerned with the actions of its stakeholders. For example, a professional baseball team like the Toronto Blue Jays does not acquire resources from members of the print media, so from a systems resource perspective they would not be considered particularly important. However, the print media are stakeholders in that they have an interest in the team and are able to exert considerable influence on its activities and success. Therefore, from a strategic constituencies perspective they are a significant group that can influence the team's goals and effectiveness.

The strategic constituencies approach takes into account the fact that managers have to work toward several goals simultaneously. Typically, they have to satisfy the interests of a number of constituents who influence the organization's ability to achieve success. Consequently, the goals selected are not value-free; each favors one constituent over another. As a result, organizations are political; they have to respond to the vested interests of their various constituents. This is a very important point for sport managers, since much of the literature in our field has presented a view of sport organizations as apolitical (Slack, 1991). Still, some researchers are showing the political nature of sport organizations (e.g. Kihl, Skinner, & Engelberg, 2017; Sage, 2015), especially in relation to Olympic Games (Lenskyj, 2000; Pound, 2004) and other mega sport events (Brittain, Bocarro, Byers, & Swart, 2017).

A strength of the strategic constituencies approach is that effectiveness is seen as a complex, multidimensional construct. It also considers factors internal and external to the organization. In addition, the issue of corporate social responsibility is taken into account (something not considered in any of the previous approaches), that is, what moral and ethical obligations the organization has to the community within which it operates. Another strength of this approach is that it forces sport managers to be cognizant of groups whose power could have an adverse effect on their operations. By knowing whose support it needs to maintain its operations, an organization can modify its goals to meet the demands of those particular constituents.

It is not always easy, however, to identify an organization's constituents and their relative importance. For example, in the case of the professional sport team, who is more important to success: the fans or the media? Another difficulty is that different people in the organization will see different constituents as important; the finance officer of a university athletic department, for example, is unlikely to see the constituents of the organization

Table 3.2 Effectiveness Criteria of Selected Strategic Constituents of a U.S. Professional Basketball Team

Constituency or stakeholder	Typical criteria of effectiveness
Owners	Profit; increased value of franchise
Players	Adequate salary and benefits; good working conditions
Fans	Entertaining games; reasonably priced tickets, concessions, and so on
Community	Visibility through team activities; economic benefits for local businesses
Media	Newsworthy coaches and players
NBA	Compliance with rules; efforts to promote a positive image of the game
Sponsors	Media exposure; high attendance

in the same way as the head basketball coach. Also problematic is the fact that the relative importance of the different constituents will change over time. For example, in the founding stages of a fitness center, financial institutions will be important constituents; the center will need access to capital for startup costs and will look to these institutions to provide this money. In later years when the center is well established and has a reliable clientele, lending institutions will be less important than strategic constituents. Finally, even if the constituents can be identified, how do sport managers identify their expectations for the organization and correctly measure this type of information?

Despite these difficulties, this approach to organizational effectiveness has proved useful (cf. Cameron, 1984; Kanter & Brinkerhoff, 1981), and it offers a more holistic approach than previous models. As mentioned earlier, the strategic constituencies approach also emphasizes the political nature of organizations. Along with the competing values approach, which we will discuss next, it provides one of the better ways of determining organizational effectiveness.

The Competing Values Approach

Like the strategic constituencies perspective, the **competing values approach** is based on the premise that there is no single best criterion of organizational effectiveness; rather, effectiveness is a subjective concept and the criteria used to assess it depend on the evaluator's value preferences. For example, in an athletic shoe manufacturing company such as Reebok, Nike, or Adidas where the primary goal is to make money, effectiveness is determined by the finance and accounting managers in terms of profitability and a balanced budget; marketing managers would look at percentage of market share; production managers would be concerned with the number and quality of shoes manufactured. Competing values takes different stakeholder goals into consideration, so measuring effectiveness becomes very complex and reliant on different perspectives. This is in part the assumption of modern performance measurement systems, which consider effectiveness to be a combination of different stakeholder groups, as Dimitropoulos, Kosmas, and Douvis (2017) illustrate in their research on implementing the balanced scorecard in a local government sport organization in Greece. Or see Shilbury and Moore's (2006) study of nonprofit Australian national Olympic sporting organization (NOSOs) effectiveness that uses a competing values approach.

The competing values approach was developed by Quinn and Rohrbaugh (1981), who used a list of criteria that Campbell (1977) claimed were indicators of organizational effectiveness. The list was analyzed using multidimensional scaling. It produced three dimensions of organizational effectiveness seen as representing competing values. The first set of values involves organizational focus; these values range from those that emphasize the well-being and development of the people in the organization (an internal focus on the organization's sociotechnical system) to a concern with the well-being and development of the organization itself (an external

TIME OUT

Increasing Participation in Swimming

The number of people swimming in Britain has dropped from 3.3 million to 2.5 million (swimming was effective because it was seen as Britain's biggest mass participation sport) (Rumsby, 2015). To counteract this decrease in effectiveness caused by the number of people participating, the Amateur Swimming Association (ASA) hired a new director of participation in 2015, Nick Caplin. Caplin was the former director of communications for Sony Computer Entertainment Europe and had helped Sony increase the number of players participating in the FIFA Interactive World Cup game (FIWC) from 25,000 to almost 3 million. Caplin suggested that swimming was 30 years behind, and his goal is to return swimming in England to what he describes as its "heyday." His five-year goals for increasing swimming's effectiveness include the following: increase swimming's visibility and relevance; improve the overall swimming environment; tailor swimming offer to different needs. In short, Caplin suggested making swimming more accessible and enjoyable, and that the ASA should engage new technology and create a digital platform. Caplin also suggested that the ASA should wean itself off of government funding and partner with private organizations.

focus on its competitive position) (Quinn & Rohrbaugh, 1983). The second set of values concerns the structure of the organization, from a structure that emphasizes flexibility (i.e., a decentralized, differentiated structure with the ability to adapt, innovate, and change) to a structure that favors control (i.e., centralized, integrated, and exhibiting stability, predictability, and order). The third set of values concerns means and ends. A focus on means stresses internal processes such as planning; a focus on ends emphasizes final outcomes such as profitability or win-and-loss record. As Quinn and Rohrbaugh (1981, p. 132) note, "these three sets of competing values are recognized dilemmas in the organizational literature." For more information on the competing values approach refer to vol. 5, no. 2 (June 1981) of *Public Productivity Review* that contains five articles (including Quinn & Rohrbaugh's work) focusing on this particular approach to organizational effectiveness.

The three sets of values can be combined, as shown in figure 3.2. The two axes—flexibility and control, and internal and external focus—produce four quadrants. Quinn (1988) suggests that each quadrant represents one of the four major perspectives in organizational theory—human relations, open systems, internal process, or rational goals. Quinn refers to these perspectives as models, but we have adapted his model to call these perspectives to indicate that the quadrants are ways of thinking about effectiveness as opposed to specific models of the effectiveness concept. He suggests that the two sets of criteria in each quadrant relate to the implicit means or ends theory that is associated with each of the models. Thus, in the human relations perspective, a focus on means would see effectiveness as represented by a cohesive workforce with high morale; a focus on ends would emphasize human resources development. Table 3.3 shows the four models and how effectiveness would be defined in each, depending on whether the focus is on means or ends. It is important to note that each model has a polar opposite. As Quinn (1988, pp. 47-48) points out, "the human relations model, which emphasizes flexibility and internal focus, stands in stark contrast to the rational goal model, which stresses control and external focus. The open systems model, which is characterized by flexibility and external focus, runs counter to the internal process model, which emphasizes control and internal focus."

Quinn goes on to point out parallels between the models. Both the human relations and open systems models emphasize flexibility; the open systems and rational goal models focus on external issues, such as responding to change. Control is a value emphasized in the rational goal and internal process models; the human relations and internal

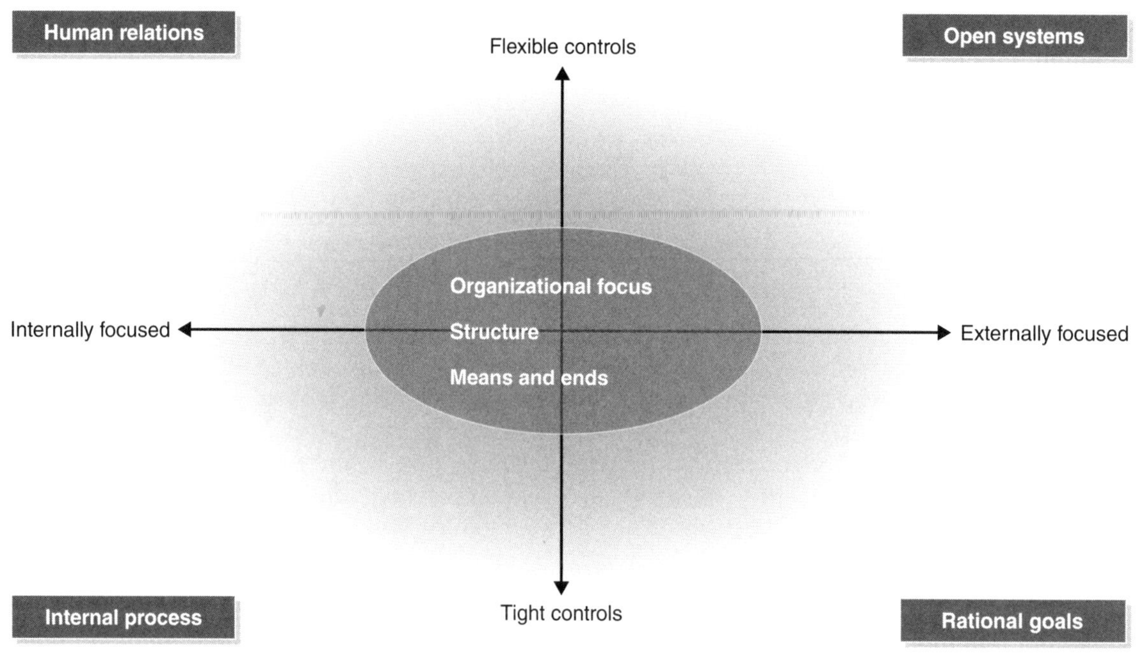

Figure 3.2 Competing values.
Based on Quinn (1988).

Table 3.3 Criteria of Effectiveness for Competing Values Models

Model	Criteria of effectiveness
Human relations	
Means	A cohesive workforce where morale is high; employees work well together
Ends	An emphasis on the training and development of human resources to perform tasks in a proper manner
Open systems	
Means	A flexible workforce able to respond well to changes in external conditions and demands
Ends	A focus on growth and the ability to acquire external resources
Internal process	
Means	A focus on communication and information management; people being well informed about issues that influence their work
Ends	A focus on stability, order, and control; operations run smoothly
Rational goal	
Means	An emphasis on planning and the setting of identifiable goals
Ends	High productivity; efficiency in terms of outputs to inputs

process models both have an internal focus that emphasizes such things as the organization's human and technical systems. Managers are faced with decisions about which of these values will direct their organization.

The competing values perspective, unlike other approaches, takes into account the paradoxical nature of effectiveness. For example, the Indiana University basketball team formerly coached by Bobby Knight was generally seen as a very effective organization, at least in terms of its win-and-loss record. Using the competing values perspective, most people would score the team high in terms of productivity (i.e., the rational goal model). However, as Feinstein (1986) indicated in his book on Knight and the Hoosiers basketball team, some of this success has been achieved at the expense of a concern with human resources. In 2001, Bobby Knight was finally fired by Indiana University after a student blew the whistle on Knight's actions. The competing values approach does not suggest that these opposing values cannot mutually exist; rather, it helps us understand the trade-offs necessary in evaluating the effectiveness of an organization.

To operationalize the competing values approach, it is first necessary for a sport manager to identify those constituents seen as necessary for the organization's survival. The next step is to determine the importance those constituents place on the various values. This task can be done by the sport managers themselves, who have to try to determine what the various constituents value in the organization; alternatively, the constituents themselves may be surveyed.

Figure 3.3 provides an example of an instrument from a research project that used the competing values approach. The purpose of this project was to examine the outcomes of employee fitness and health programs, which were valued in major corporations (cf. Wolfe, Slack, & Rose-Hearn, 1993). The instrument was administered to fitness and health professionals and to the corporation's senior management to determine the type of outcomes they valued in an effective employee fitness and health program. By plotting the cumulative scores from an instrument like this, it is possible to get a picture of how different organizations, or different groups within an organization, determine effectiveness.

Figure 3.4 shows how two sport organizations could be plotted in terms of the four models of effectiveness (see also Quinn, 1988, chapter 9). Sport Organization A could be a relatively large organization that has been in business for a number of years. It is quite likely to be structured along bureaucratic lines. Its primary emphasis is on productivity and efficiency. Planning and goal-setting are emphasized

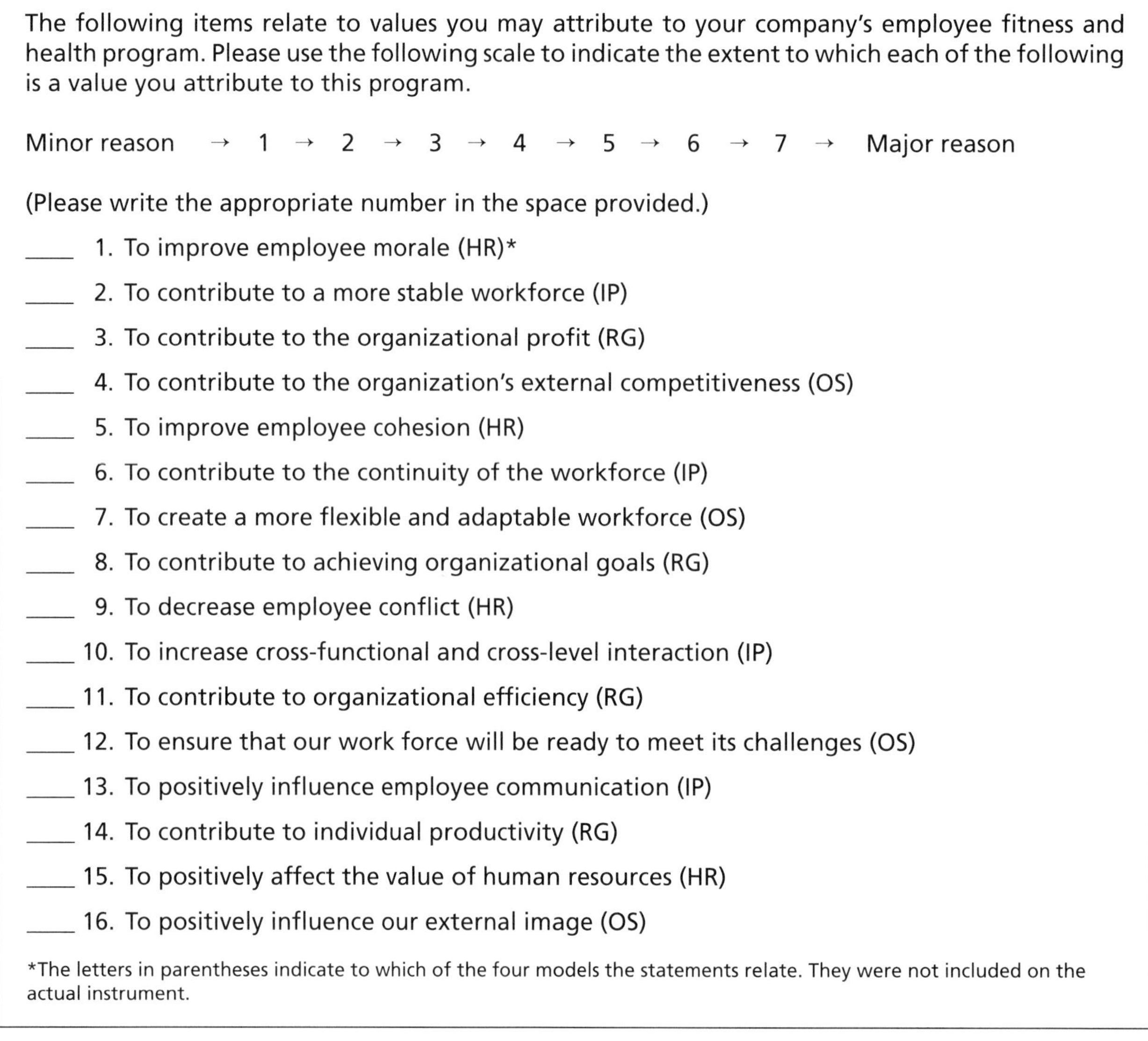
The following items relate to values you may attribute to your company's employee fitness and health program. Please use the following scale to indicate the extent to which each of the following is a value you attribute to this program.

Minor reason → 1 → 2 → 3 → 4 → 5 → 6 → 7 → Major reason

(Please write the appropriate number in the space provided.)

____ 1. To improve employee morale (HR)*

____ 2. To contribute to a more stable workforce (IP)

____ 3. To contribute to the organizational profit (RG)

____ 4. To contribute to the organization's external competitiveness (OS)

____ 5. To improve employee cohesion (HR)

____ 6. To contribute to the continuity of the workforce (IP)

____ 7. To create a more flexible and adaptable workforce (OS)

____ 8. To contribute to achieving organizational goals (RG)

____ 9. To decrease employee conflict (HR)

____ 10. To increase cross-functional and cross-level interaction (IP)

____ 11. To contribute to organizational efficiency (RG)

____ 12. To ensure that our work force will be ready to meet its challenges (OS)

____ 13. To positively influence employee communication (IP)

____ 14. To contribute to individual productivity (RG)

____ 15. To positively affect the value of human resources (HR)

____ 16. To positively influence our external image (OS)

*The letters in parentheses indicate to which of the four models the statements relate. They were not included on the actual instrument.

Figure 3.3 Measuring competing values: An example of employee fitness and health programs.

within this organization. There is little concern with flexibility, nor is there a great deal of concern with human resources development issues. In contrast, Sport Organization B could be a relatively new organization seeking to establish itself in its particular market. Consequently, adaptability and the acquisition of external resources are highly valued in this organization. There is some concern with human resource issues and with productivity and planning, but there is little value placed on stability and information management.

The type of diagram shown in figure 3.4 can help determine the organization's effectiveness. If cumulative scores from the different constituents are used to plot the diagram, it tells managers in what particular areas they are strong and where they may improve. If plots are made for each of the constituent groups, the diagram shows the type of values each constituent expects from the organization. For example, in a company that produces some type of sport equipment the workers would probably see the organization as being effective if it emphasized values related to human resources development; shareholders' values would more likely relate to productivity. Plotting how the organization scores in these areas can help managers determine how effectively constituents believe it is performing its tasks. This information can then be used to determine the relative trade-offs that have to be made to maintain overall effectiveness.

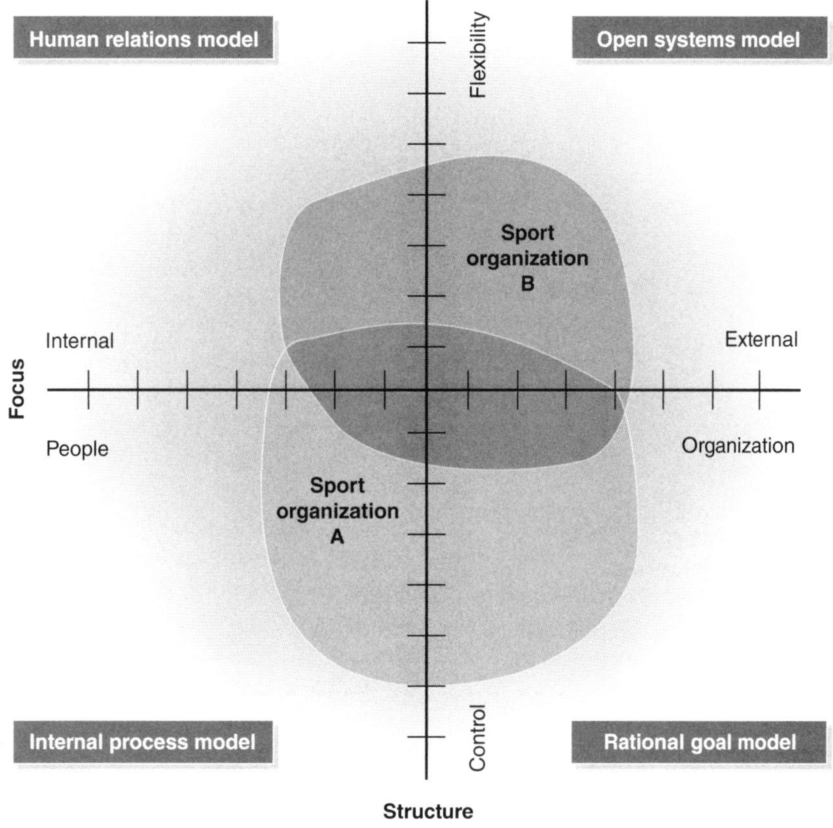

Figure 3.4 Effectiveness values of two sport organizations.
Based on information in Rohrbaugh (1981).

KEY ISSUES FOR SPORT MANAGERS

As a manager, you must be able to recognize, develop, and modify your organization's goals. As we have seen, different types of goals exist: some that overlap and some that can be named differently (e.g., mission statement, purpose). These goals must fit with your organization's environment. If the organization has different departments, they may have goals different from the overall organization. However, these goals must not be contrary to the goals of other departments or the overall organization. Be careful when establishing goals, because they will affect all the organizational members' actions and, ultimately, the organization's performance (i.e., success). For example, setting hard-to-meet goals can actually lead to unethical behavior (Schweitzer, Ordóñez, & Douma, 2004). Kihl (2017) presents many cases of unethical behavior in sport, with Roberts and Bolton (2017) specifically outlining how sport organizations are trying to reform to ensure athletes are following the rules of the game.

You also must be able to determine your organization's effectiveness and efficiency if you want it to have a competitive advantage in the marketplace and acquire the necessary resources. As we have seen, both the strategic constituencies approach and the competing values approach recognize that organizational effectiveness is a multidimensional concept. Because of the paradoxical nature of the concept of effectiveness, the various approaches for determining organizational effectiveness presented in this chapter can be useful under different circumstances.

Summary and Conclusions

This chapter has examined the concepts of organizational goals and effectiveness. Goals serve a number of purposes in a sport organization: They provide a direction for the organization, guide managers in decision making and performance appraisal, reduce uncertainty, and help the sport organization establish legitimacy both with its own personnel and with external agencies. Sport organizations usually have several types of goals: Some are formally stated, others are more implicit in the activities of the organization; some are objective, others are purposely vague and general.

If a sport organization achieves its goals, it is often considered effective. However, as we saw, there are problems with this approach, and researchers have proposed several other methods of determining organizational effectiveness. Effectiveness is paradoxical in nature. As opposed to focusing on the organization's goals or outputs, the systems resource approach focuses on the organization's ability to obtain resources from its environment. The internal process approach focuses on internal climate and efficiency as the appropriate criteria for determining effectiveness. Two more contemporary approaches take a broader view of effectiveness. The strategic constituencies approach focuses on the extent to which an organization satisfies the requirements of its stakeholders. The competing values approach emphasizes that different constituents value different organizational outcomes. Effectiveness is determined by the extent to which an organization is able to meet these often-differing value preferences.

Which of these approaches is the best? Each one in its own way is useful. Some writers have even suggested that effectiveness is better measured by integrating different approaches. Chelladurai (1987, p. 39), for example, suggests:

> When organizations are viewed as open systems inputs affect throughputs which affect outputs, which are exchanged with the environment for a return of inputs for the organization. From this perspective of an organization the goals model, system resource model, and process model focus, respectively, on the output, input, and throughput sectors of an organization. The multiple constituencies approach emphasizes the organization's dependence on its environment represented by the various interest groups and the need to satisfy their expectations. Since all of the models deal with specific elements of the system they are interrelated.

Van Puyvelde, Brown, Walker, and Tenuta (2018) suggested that board effectiveness can be political and subjective, open to influence of leader and group dynamics. From much of the research on effectiveness in sport organizations, we see that there is a wide diversity of elements that we can measure including sponsorship (Rosenberg, Lester, Maitland, & Teal, 2017), social media (Felix, Rauschnabel, & Hinsch, 2017), policy (Kihl, Read, & Skinner, 2017), and coaching (Kassim & Boardley, 2018), as well as general effectiveness of sport organizations (Dixon, Martinez, & Martin, 2015). The approach used to measure effectiveness needs careful consideration and acknowledgment of the strengths and weaknesses of that perspective. However, it is also possible to use a combination of perspectives. Sparrow and Cooper (2014, p. 2), establishing a future research agenda for effectiveness research, suggest that effectiveness research should

> adopt a broad definition of performance, and examine how the achievement of important strategic outcomes, such as innovation, customer centricity, operational excellence, globalization, become dependent on people and organization issues. It signals the need to focus on the intermediate performance outcomes that are necessary to achieve these strategic outcomes, and to examine these performance issues across several levels of analysis such as the individual, team, function, organization and societal (policy) level.

Review Questions

1. How do an organization's goals influence managerial action?
2. Pick a sport organization with which you are familiar and find out what its official goals are. How do you think these might differ from its operative goals?
3. How do the operative goals of a high school football team differ from those of a professional football team?
4. Why is effectiveness such a difficult concept to measure?
5. Discuss different perspectives of measuring effectiveness in a professional sport organization versus a community sport club.

Suggestions for Further Reading

For further reading around the concept of effectiveness, we must also consider the concept of performance (especially in the context of sport organizations). For a broad overview of effectiveness research and thoughts on future research needs, Sparrow and Cooper (2014) offer good insight. While the goal attainment approach has largely been criticized, there is merit in examining Williams, Pieper, Kellermanns, and Astrachan's (2018) paper on family firms because these differ from other types of organizations in their setting of goals. To gain understanding of the nonprofit organization's needs and challenges in measuring effectiveness, see Grazbowski, Neher, Crim, and Mathiassen's (2015) discussion of the competing values framework. Research on sport organizations varies in its choice of concepts from effectiveness (e.g. Giroux, Pons, & Maltese, 2017) to performance (Dimitropoulos, Kosmas, & Douvis, 2017; Molan, Kelly, Arnold, & Matthews, 2018). Molan et al. (2018) in particular provide a useful systematic review of processes in elite sport and other performance domains. For those interested in Olympic sport organizations, see Winand, Zintz, Bayle, and Robinson's (2010) article (journal now named *Managing Sport and Leisure*).

Case for Analysis

The 2014 Sochi Winter Olympics: Effective or Ineffective?

After any major sporting festival a debate always ensues about whether the festival was effective. The 2014 Sochi Winter Olympic Games are no exception. Having never hosted the Winter Olympics before, Russian President Vladimir Putin saw the awarding of the Olympics as a big coup for Russia. *Time* magazine (July 5, 2007) reported that "winning the right to host the 2014 Winter Olympic Games was so important to Russia and to Vladimir Putin personally, that the Russian president himself led the country's final, formal presentation before the International Olympic Committee in Guatemala City on July 4." Despite enthusiasm about their country and the city of Sochi being awarded the Winter Olympics, preparation for the events revealed some issues that would ultimately influence the effectiveness of the Olympics. The most visible and controversial of these issues was Russia's stance on lesbian, gay, bisexual, and transgender people (LBGT). The process began in 2012 when a Russian judge banned the establishment of a pride house in Sochi (Gold, 2012). He was quoted as saying "non-traditional sexual relationships" would "undermine the security of Russian society." (Gold, 2012; p.1).

An issue that will impact a city's ability to stage the Winter Olympics is snowfall. Sochi is a small resort town on the Black Sea with the Caucasus Mountains at its back, and with its subtropical climate, the city receives little snowfall (Geere, 2014). As such, Sochi was not the most obvious place to host the Winter Olympics. To ensure they had snow for the Games, Sochi installed one of the largest snowmaking systems in Europe, comprising of two huge water reservoirs that fed 400 snow cannons, which were installed along the slopes of the ski venue (Geere, 2014). If the snow cannons failed, the Sochi organizers had a store of 710,000 cubic meters of snow from previous winters. To ensure the snow did not melt the organizers had 10 separate stockpiles under insulated cover, which was kept high in the mountains to prevent melting (Geere, 2014).

One issue was the cost of the Games. Although Sochi is a resort city, it did not have adequate accommodations for the athletes, spectators, and officials. Prior to the Olympics Sochi had no winter sport facilities. Consequently, organizers had to build such facilities. These facilities included venues for the opening and closing ceremonies; rinks for figure skating and ice hockey; sheets of ice for curling; cross country and biathlon centers; bobsled, luge, and skeleton tracks; and ovals for short- and long-track speed skating (IOC, 2014). The estimated cost of the Games was $50 billion, borne by Russian taxpayers. The Games were effective in that the infrastructure and event itself was delivered on time as per the agreement with the International Olympic Committee (IOC), but the reported legacy of the Games is more controversial, calling into the question of effectiveness. While Russia was only the second candidate (next to London) to include a legacy plan in its bid, reports indicate their goals to create lasting environmental legacies have not met with success (Johnson, 2016). Azzali (2017) points out quite a few more failures of Sochi's legacy goals including those environmental, social, and physical or infrastructural in nature. While there were several outstanding performances, broken world and Olympic records, and no terrorist attacks as anticipated by the organizers (because Sochi is close to Chechnya, whose rebels had been suspected of a number of terrorist attacks in the months prior to the Games), it is difficult to measure the effectiveness of the event due to the number of different goals and stakeholders.

Questions

1. How would you evaluate the effectiveness of the Sochi Organizing Committee?
2. How would your perception vary depending on which approaches to measuring effectiveness was employed?
3. What other information about the 2014 Winter Olympic Games would help you make a better assessment of the effectiveness of the Organizing Committee?
4. What elements of this case demonstrate the political nature of organizational effectiveness?
5. How would evaluating effectiveness of the 2014 Winter Olympic Games differ if we were to focus solely on the legacy of the Games?

CHAPTER 4

Sport Organizations and Their Environments

Trevor Slack, PhD
Terri Byers, PhD

Learning Objectives

When you have read this chapter, you should be able to

1. describe the components of a sport organization's external environment;
2. discuss the major research studies that have been carried out on the influence of the environment on organizations;
3. explain the techniques that sport managers can use to manage environmental uncertainty;
4. explain the major principles of institutional theory, resource dependence theory, and population ecology;
5. explain the impact of environmental uncertainty on an organization's structure; and
6. understand the important role of environmental pressures on innovation and change in sport organizations.

Key Concepts

boundary spanners
buffering
contractual agreements
cooptation
domain
environmental complexity
environmental stability
environmental uncertainty
executive recruitment
general environment
illegal activities
innovation
institutional theory
interlocking directorate
joint venture
mechanistic
mergers and acquisitions
niche
organic
perceived environment
planning and forecasting

(continued)

Key Concepts *(continued)*

political lobbying
population density
population ecology
public relations and advertising
rationing
resource dependence
sectors
smoothing
stakeholder theory
subenvironment
task environment
trade and professional associations

Galway Women's Football Club (GWFC), Ireland

A sport organization's environment includes broad external factors, such as economic, political, and sociocultural sectors, and local external environmental factors, such as members, competitors, and regulatory agencies. The GWFC is no exception.

GWFC was born in the depths of a huge recession in Ireland in 2012. However, the environment also provided many opportunities. The National Football League men's team Galway United had gone bust, so sponsors had little competition, and GWFC was able to gain full access to the facilities in Eamonn Deacy Park. The GWFC positioned itself as a new club within a network of established clubs, making sure to cooperate as well as compete against the existing clubs. Since joining the league in 2013 two clubs within 50 miles (80 km) have left and a new club, only 60 miles (97 km) away, joined. Due to the competitive local environment, GWFC is mindful of marketing their players and monitoring potential players. GWFC participates in the Women's National League, which operates under the umbrella of the Football Association Ireland (FAI). The FAI has produced two strategic plans—one specifically for women's association football, which ended in 2016, and one general strategic plan, ending in 2020, that includes women's football as a pillar of development.

The FAI Strategic Plan identified a number of trends affecting association football participation in Ireland. Firstly, association football is the team sport with the largest rates of participation across the country, including an increase in women's participation. Within eight years, women's participation almost doubled: In 2006, 12,500 women were registered, and by 2014, 23,500 were registered. Within this time period, the number of leagues doubled, from 16 to 32, of which the Women's National League is one.

Galway gets a lot of rain year-round, which can cause issues with the state of the pitch for home matches. Eamonn Deacy Park is a grass pitch, so the wet weather can make the pitch too soft and thus unplayable, leading to the cancellation or postponement of home matches, or the cancellation of training sessions. The rest of Ireland also has very wet weather, and with climate change leading to more extreme conditions, away matches are also at risk of being cancelled or postponed. Galway City has a parks bylaw stating that association football can only be played in parks that have designated areas for the sport. This bylaw can take away from the participatory and informal nature of the sport that helps spark children's interest in it.

The current structure of GWFC is very simple. The board is entirely volunteer-run, and the only person who receives pay from the club is the manager. The seven board members are responsible for the strategic and operational duties of the club. Because the board members have full-time jobs elsewhere, they have limited time to dedicate to the governance of the club, which typically results in the prioritization of operational duties and strategic duties.

Based on personal communication with Galway Women's Football Club (GWFC).

Understanding the concept of organizational environments is essential for all managers. This chapter explains the components of an organization's external environment and how these components affect an organization, as well as the influence of the external environment on the manager's decisions and what sport managers can do to influence their environments. An important lesson of this chapter is that environments can affect organizations, but sport managers can also have an impact on their environment. In fact, as illustrated throughout the chapter, the external environment often has different levels of uncertainty that managers must attempt to control or understand in order to create efficiency and effectiveness in their organizations, thereby meeting organizational goals. The chapter also illustrates how the environment is relevant to sport managers of different types of organizations, from small voluntary sport clubs to larger, national governing bodies. No matter the size, structure, or sector of your organizations, understanding the external environment can help make your organization more successful in relation to competitors and in the eyes of stakeholders.

The Nature of the Organizational Environment

What exactly do we mean when we talk about the environment of an organization? Certainly the term has been used in a wide variety of ways (Starbuck, 1976). In one sense everything outside of the organization being studied is a part of the environment, but such a broad definition has little practical or theoretical use. Most researchers use a more focused approach to understanding the concept and suggest, as shown in figure 4.1, that organizations have two types of environment: a general environment and a task environment.

In the opening scenario, GWFC is a small, young organization that started operations in a relatively turbulent environment. Yet it also had opportunities that led to the board members' commitment to create the club. How the environment is perceived (rather than what is actually happening in the environment) plays an important factor in how organizations (more specifically, the people within them) respond, so understanding the components

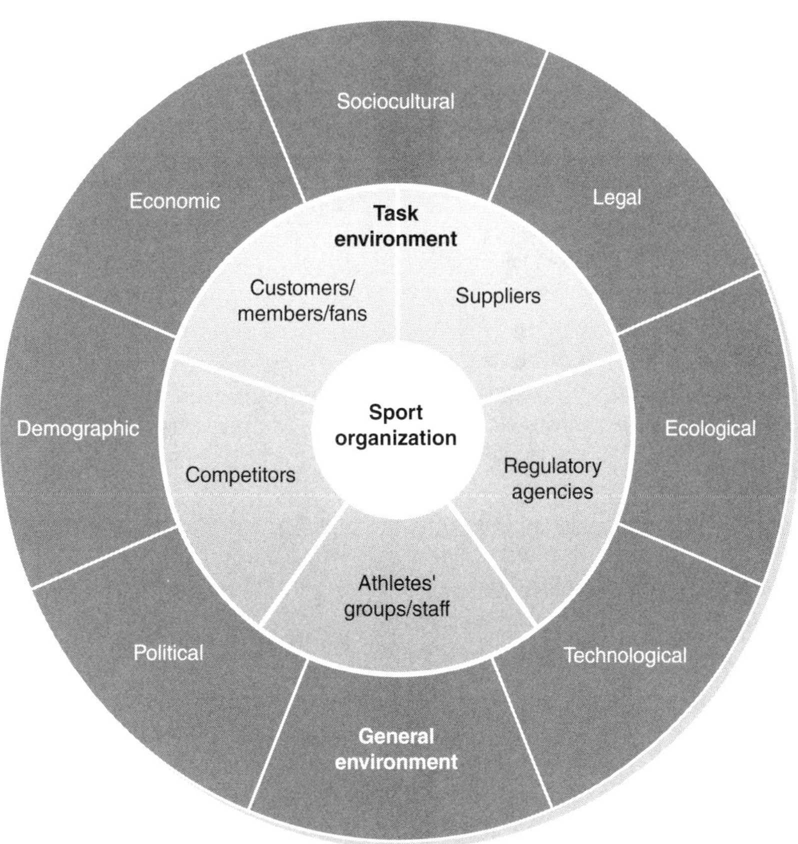

Figure 4.1 The sport organization's general and task environment.

of environment as well as how sport managers can respond to this is important.

General Environment

The **general environment** of an organization includes those **sectors** that, although they may not have a direct impact on the operations of a sport organization, can influence the industry in general ways that ultimately do have an impact on the organization (Daft, 2004). The general environment of a sport organization can be divided up into a number of sectors. Here we look briefly at the influence of each.

Economic

The general economic conditions in which a sport organization operates (whether publicly or privately owned), the system of banking in the country in which the organization operates, fiscal policies, and patterns of consumption are all components of the economic sector of a sport organization's general environment. Pugh (1989), for example, describes how austere economic conditions influenced the development of the Belfry golf complex. Economics is also the main reason for the NHL's cancellation of the 2004 to 2005 season.

Political

The prevailing political situation, the extent to which political power is concentrated, and the ideology of the party in power are all factors that can influence a sport organization. Geehern (1991), for example, describes how the dropping of trade barriers as part of the 1992 European Community reforms and the opening up of the former Soviet Bloc created considerable market potential for golf ball manufacturers such as Spalding and Acushnet. In a somewhat similar vein, bicycle manufacturers benefited considerably from the Mideast crisis of the early 1970s, when the fear of an oil embargo pushed bike sales to record levels (Charm, 1986). The political climate has also had a considerable effect on a number of Olympic Games Organizing Committees, most notably in 1980 and 1984 when, because of politically motivated rationales, a number of countries did not attend the Summer Olympic Games (Hill, 1992). More recently, we see how U.S. President Donald Trump influenced NFL owners' opinions of some players' decision to kneel in protest of social justice issues as the national anthem played before games (Rosenberg, 2018). The league eventually implemented a new policy that enabled the league to serve fines for any team with players not standing during the anthem.

Sociocultural

Sociocultural factors that can influence a sport organization include the class structure of the social system; the national, regional, and local cultures in which the sport organization exists; trends in consumer tastes; and the sporting traditions of the area in which the organization is situated. We see the impact of sociocultural conditions in the attempts to set up professional association football leagues in North America. Despite association football's popularity around the world, the sporting culture of the United States and Canada has challenged the growth of leagues such as the North American Soccer League and Major League Soccer (MLS). Manchester United even tried to open up the market more by playing games in the United States in 2003 without, unfortunately, any major impact at the time. It is also well established (Beamish, 1985; Macintosh & Whitson, 1990) that the administrative structures of many sport organizations reflect the inequalities of social life in terms of their class, race, and gender composition.

The topic of diversity and inclusion in sport organizations has received increasing attention from sport management researchers and practitioners in recent years (Cunningham, 2017). Diversity is the presence of socially meaningful differences among members of a dyad or group. There are several important elements to understanding diversity: (1) the presence of objective and subjective differences, (2) that are socially relevant, (3) for members of a particular social unit (Cunningham, 2017, p. 6). Sport is a prominent social institution where diversity is often recognized as important, but how this translates into actual practice can be challenging for some organizations, particularly community sport organizations that are more reactive to their social environment and not strategic, planned, or experienced in diversity policy implementation (Spaaij et al., 2016).

Legal

The legal conditions within the environment are an important part of an organization's general environment that is often overlooked (Hall, 1982). The type of legal system within the country in which the sport organization operates, the jurisdictions overseen by various levels of government, and the existence of laws covering such areas as taxation, unionization, and the regulation of organizations all constitute the legal conditions affecting a sport organization. In the United States, antitrust legislations (Freedman, 1987); in Canada, the Competition Act (Barnes, 1988); and in the United Kingdom, the Local Government Act of 1988 (Houlihan, 1991) all

TIME OUT

Environmental Pressures and Interorganizational Linkages

In their study on government leisure services senior managers, researchers Thibault, Frisby, and Kikulis (1999) examined the influence of economic, political, and social pressures on the development of interorganizational linkages with public, nonprofit, and private or commercial organizations. The trio found that interorganizational linkages are increasingly important for government leisure services managers. Moreover, they found that economic pressures had the largest impact on interorganizational linkage growth. More recently, Jones, Edwards, Bocarro, Bunds, and Smith (2017) demonstrate the use of partnerships by nonprofit sport organizations in response to increasing environmental pressure and the inherent difficulties they experience in doing this effectively. When considering the many parts of an organization's environment, from social to economic, and the increasing number of sport organizations trying to enter the environment, it is not surprising that some of those organizations see cooperation or partnership as one way to strengthen their position. The rationale is that through cooperation, resources are pooled, capacities are directed at a common goal, and organizations may make a bigger impact working together rather than on their own. Nonetheless, as the previously mentioned research indicates, there are challenges to this, and it is not a simple solution to environmental pressure.

provide evidence of the ways legal conditions affect sport organizations. The controversial "jock tax" imposed on professional, paid athletes in Canada and the United States as they travel and earn income is also a good example of how changes in legal requirements have an impact on sport managers and those involved in athlete management, such as accountants or agents.

Demographic

The type of people to whom a sport organization directs its products or services; changes in population distributions; and the age, gender, racial, ethnic, and class composition of the population can all influence the organization. Sparks (1992) shows, for example, how directing its programming to a primarily male audience affects The Sports Network's (TSN) operations. Richards (1986) demonstrates the influence of changing population cohorts. He suggests that Brunswick's purchase of Ray Industries, makers of Sea Ray boats, was in part inspired by the company's market research indications that baby boomers were taking an increased interest in pleasure boats. Byers, Roy, Reis, Weinstein, Lunga, and Hayday (2019) reported on the changing demographics in Canada and through an audit of how sport organizations are innovating to integrate the rising number of immigrants into sport, illustrate that this "new Canadian" population should be a consideration of sport organizations across the country.

Ecological

Because a number of sport organizations depend on their physical surroundings for success, ecological factors are an important part of their general environment. Weather conditions can affect the staging of sport events and the operation of facilities such as ski hills. Growing concerns about the total ecological system have encouraged sport organizations to pay attention to how their activities influence the natural environment. The Olympic Games are a good example: For example, for the 2008 Summer Olympics and 2022 (awarded) Winter Olympics, Beijing demonstrated plans to be ecologically responsible; however, evidence suggests that Beijing 2022 may be an environmental disaster (Leber, 2015).

Technological

All sport organizations are affected by technological developments that may improve production or service, so they must monitor constantly any technological developments that could change the nature of the industry in which the sport organization is involved. Technological developments may also lead the sport organization to engage in new activities or approach existing activities in different ways. (See also chapters 18 on change and 21 on technology.) An example of the impact of technology on the operations of a sport organization is how professional sport stadia and associated organizations such as Coca-Cola are increasingly using advances in augmented and virtual reality technology to create personalized customer experiences (Adams, 2018).

Task Environment

A sport organization's **task environment** is made up of those aspects of its general environment that can influence its ability to achieve its goals. Typically included in a sport organization's task environment are such groups as customers, members, fans, staff, suppliers, competitors, and regulatory agencies (cf. Thompson, 1967). Zeigler's (1985) study of physical education departments similarly describes the task environment, or immediate environment as he calls it, which includes clients, suppliers, controllers, advisers, adversaries, and "publics with opinions." In contrast to the general environment, which is more removed from the sport organization, the task environment is of more immediate concern to the sport manager because it contains those constituents that can strongly affect the success of the organization. Each sport organization's task environment is unique, and the constituents making up this environment may change over time. More recent research looks at environmental characteristics' influence on leadership in the context of sport for development (Jones, Wegner, Bunds, Edwards, & Bocarro, 2018). The research demonstrates the significant influence of the environment on the capacity of leadership to fully access resources, engage stakeholders, and provide inclusive, quality services in sport.

Although they are conceptually distinct, a sport organization's general environment and its task environment are related. Consider, for example, the effect of the increasing societal awareness of the inequalities of gender that exist in all types of managerial positions, including those in sport organizations—an aspect of the general environment. Legislative changes are made as more people become aware of and are actively involved in trying to eliminate such inequalities. These changes influence hiring practices in sport organizations and, consequently, its human resources practices—aspects of the sport organization's task environment.

A sport organization's task environment will vary according to the domain in which it chooses to operate. **Domain** refers to the territory that a sport organization stakes out for itself in regard to the services or products it delivers and the markets in which it operates. Different sport organizations even within the same sector of the sport industry can have different domains and therefore different task environments. MEC and the Running Room are both sporting goods stores, but they have identified different domains in which to operate: MEC focuses on outdoor gear for hiking and mountaineering; the Running Room focuses on gear specifically for runners (and walkers with the Walking Room). Consequently, they come into contact with different suppliers, customers, and competitors.

Perceived Environment

In discussing the concept of environment, it is important to distinguish between actual environment and **perceived environment**. The actual environmental conditions surrounding a sport organization may be perceived differently by different managers at the same level (Leifer & Huber, 1977). For example, the same environmental conditions may be perceived as dynamic (providing opportunities for growth) by one sport manager and in a quite different way by the manager of another sport organization operating within the same sector of the industry. The same can also be said of other stakeholders operating in the sport industry. For example, governments and bidding hosts for Olympic Games evaluate the opportunity to bid with increasing concern over costs, public opinion, and environmental factors. While cities are less likely to bid for the Olympics, some still view the Games as an opportunity, despite challenges in their environment, and spend huge sums of money just to bid.

Research on Organizational Environments

Many research studies that have contributed to our understanding of organizational environments can be applied to organizations in the sport industry. Here we focus on three of the most important of these contributions: the work of Burns and Stalker, Lawrence and Lorsch, and Duncan.

Burns and Stalker

Burns and Stalker's (1961) study of 20 British manufacturing firms was the first research to try to identify the types of organizational structures and managerial processes most appropriate under different types of environmental conditions. Burns and Stalker examined changes in scientific technology and product markets—changes in the organization's task environment. Their research identified two types of structure and managerial practices, each occurring under different environmental conditions. These were labeled **organic** and **mechanistic**. Organic structures work best in rapidly changing environments; mechanistic structures work best in stable environments.

In the sport industry, we would expect to find mechanistic structures in government agencies such as the Saskatchewan Ministry of Parks, Culture and Sport or a national sport governing body such as Sport Manitoba. These sport organizations have relatively stable environments and hence use designs such as the machine bureaucracy. These structures are what Burns and Stalker refer to as mechanistic. In contrast, organic structures are more like Mintzberg's professional bureaucracies or adhocracies and are found in rapidly changing environments. We would also find organic structures in sport physiology research labs and in short-term groups formed to stage a particular sporting event such as a basketball tournament or a road race. Table 4.1 shows the environmental, structural, and managerial characteristics associated with mechanistic and organic sport organizations.

In the most effective sport organizations there is a fit between the demands of the environment and the type of structure and managerial practice employed. Burns and Stalker recognized that organic and mechanistic structures are ideal types representing the ends of a continuum. Few if any sport organizations would be purely organic or purely mechanistic; rather, the majority show varying characteristics of each type. Burns and Stalker also did not see one type of structure as superior to the other; the environmental conditions determined which was most appropriate.

Lawrence and Lorsch

Extending the work of Burns and Stalker (1961), Lawrence and Lorsch (1967) examined companies in three industries—plastics, packaged food, and standardized containers—that were seen as having considerably different degrees of environmental diversity and uncertainty. The plastics industry was chosen because its environment was uncertain and characterized by rapid changes in technology and customer needs. In contrast, the environment of the container industry was seen as stable and predictable; growth was steady and product innovation was low. The environment of organizations in the food industry was seen as somewhere in between plastics and containers.

Essentially, Lawrence and Lorsch (1967) argued that the more complex and uncertain an organization's task environment, the more differentiated the organization would have to be to handle the uncertainty, that is, the more subunits there would be, each dealing with a particular aspect of the environment. However, to meet the demands of their environment successfully, each subunit would require specialists with different attitudes and behaviors to meet their particular subunit's goals. As a result, "differentiation" referred not only to the existence of structural differences in functionally specialized subunits within the organization but also to "differences in ways of thinking and working that develop among managers in these . . . units" (Lawrence and Lorsch, 1967, p. 9). These differences manifest themselves in variations in managerial goals, time orientation, and interpersonal orientation among the subunits. For example, applying Lawrence and Lorsch's ideas to an athletic footwear company, the goals of managers in the sales department would be different from those of production managers: Sales managers would be concerned with increasing volume and customer satisfaction; production managers would be concerned with reducing manufacturing costs and time. Similarly, production managers would more likely be concerned with the immediate problems of production, whereas the time orientation of the designers in the research and development department would focus on longer-term issues. Table 4.2 shows the type of variation that Lawrence and Lorsch found in the production, research and development, and sales departments of the organizations in their study. The greater this variation among the different organizational subunits, the more complex the organization and thus the greater need for integration through such mechanisms as rules and regulations, policies, and plans.

Lawrence and Lorsch's work was different from previous studies because they did not see the organization's environment as a unitary entity. They suggested that there were parts to the environment, just like there were parts (departments or other similar subunits) to an organization. Essentially, they believed that the ways different departments of an organization varied would reflect the variation in the subenvironment with which they interacted. Consequently, if the external environment of an organization was complex and diverse (i.e., there were a lot of parts to deal with), to be effective the internal structure of the organization would also have to be highly differentiated, leading in turn to the need for sophisticated integration mechanisms to coordinate the differentiated subunits. If an organization's environment was simple and stable, it would be less differentiated and consequently require fewer integrating mechanisms. Lawrence and Lorsch (1967) found that the production, sales, and research and development subunits showed higher levels of differentiation in those organizations that had the most diverse and uncertain environments. That is, those organizations in the plastics industry were the most differentiated, followed by organizations in the food industry, and finally those in the container industry.

However, not only did Lawrence and Lorsch look at levels of differentiation, but they also looked at a number of effectiveness criteria and the use of

Table 4.1 Comparison of Mechanistic and Organic Systems of Organization and Examples in Sport

Mechanistic	Organic
1. Tasks are highly fractionated and specialized; little regard paid to clarifying relationship between tasks and organizational objectives.	1. Tasks are more independent; emphasis on relevance of tasks and organizational objectives.
Example: Large-scale manufacturing of sports clothing, equipment such as Nike.com	*Example*: Bespoke sportswear such as EV2sportswear.com
2. Tasks tend to remain rigidly defined unless altered formally by top management.	2. Tasks are continually adjusted and redefined through interaction of organizational members.
Example: Sports retail operations of a large firm such as Sportchek.ca	*Example*: McLaughlinsports.com.au, a sports consultancy based on innovation and achieving individual client needs
3. Specific role definition (rights, obligations, and technical methods prescribed for each member).	3. Generalized role definition (members accept general responsibility for task accomplishment beyond individual role definition).
Example: Stadium operations' wide variety of roles include tickets, security, concessions, and more	*Example*: Professional service such as Sport Lawyer or Professor
4. Hierarchic structure of control, authority, and communication; sanctions derive from contract between employee and organization.	4. Network structure of control, authority, and communication; sanctions derive more from community of interest than from contractual relationship.
Example: Professional sport teams	*Example*: Voluntary sport clubs in service to their membership
5. Information relevant to situation and operations of the organization formally assumed to rest with chief executive.	5. Leader not assumed to be omniscient; knowledge centers identified were located throughout organization.
Example: Small firms where owner or operator makes most decisions	*Example*: Large multinationals like Under Armour
6. Communication is primarily vertical between superior and subordinate.	6. Communication is both vertical and horizontal depending upon where needed information resides.
Example: Equipment manufacturing	*Example*: Sports consultancy
7. Communication primarily take form of instructions and decisions issued by superiors; information and requests for decisions supplied by inferiors.	7. Communication primarily take form of information and advice.
Example: Sport market research firm, such as Mintel	*Example*: University
8. Insistence on loyalty to organization and obedience to superiors.	8. Commitment to organization's tasks and goals more highly valued than loyalty or obedience.
Example: Sports agency firm	*Example*: Professional hockey team
9. Importance and prestige attached to identification with organization and its members.	9. Importance and prestige attached to affiliations and expertise in external environment.
Example: Exclusive golf course, such as Augusta National	*Example*: University researchers on sport, needing access to research subjects

Adapted by permission from R. Steers, *Organizational Effectiveness: A Behavioral View* (Santa Monica, CA: Goodyear Publishing Company, 1977).

Table 4.2 Differences in Formality of Structure and Orientation Between Departments

Characteristic	Production	Research and development	Sales
Formality of structure	High	Low	Medium to high
Goal orientation	Cost reduction	Development of new knowledge	Customer problems
	Process efficiency	Technological improvements	Competitive activities
Time orientation	Short	Long	Short
Interpersonal orientation	Task oriented	Varied, depending on type of research	Social oriented

Based on Lawrence and Lorsch (1967).

integration mechanisms in these organizations. They found that, with one exception, the most effective organizations had a higher level of integration. It was not enough for an organization simply to have an appropriate level of internal differentiation to deal with the diversity and complexity of its environment; it also had to have the necessary integrating mechanisms if it was to ensure optimal performance.

What lessons, then, can the sport manager learn from Lawrence and Lorsch's (1967) work? First, it is important to understand that sport organizations, like other organizations, have a number of parts to their environment, each of which presents a varying level of uncertainty. For example, a collegiate gridiron football organization has, as part of its environment, the local and national media. While there may be a number of media organizations with which the football program has to interact, this aspect of the environment has a level of certainty. The number of media organizations covering the team will not usually change rapidly from one year to the next, and their demands are fairly consistent—they want information on players, coaches, future opponents, and so on. This **subenvironment,** or organizational subunit, because of its relative stability, can probably be handled by one or two people. On the other hand, in addition to the media, a college gridiron football organization also has, as a part of its environment, a number of high school gridiron football programs, a source of input in that they provide the players for the college program. Because the gridiron football program is likely to deal with far more high schools than media agencies, and because there is a higher level of uncertainty here ("blue chip" players come from different programs each year and are also recruited by other colleges), there is more diversity and uncertainty within this subenvironment, and a higher level of differentiation within the organization is needed to deal with it. That is in general why the gridiron football organization has more staff to deal with high school liaisons, scouting, and recruiting than it has to deal with the media. This illustration highlights the second lesson sport managers can learn from Lawrence and Lorsch's work: A sport organization must have an appropriate level of internal differentiation to meet the demands of its various subenvironments.

However, a third point that Lawrence and Lorsch's work should alert sport managers to is that it is not enough merely to have appropriately differentiated subunits to deal with its subenvironments. Because different managerial goals, time orientations, and interpersonal orientations exist in these subunits, there must also be the necessary level of integration to ensure that these subunits are working toward a common goal. More complex sport organizations (those in diverse and uncertain environments) will accomplish integration through formal means such as policies, cross-functional teams, and systematic planning. In sport organizations operating in simpler environments, integration will be accomplished through more informal mechanisms such as direct supervision by managers.

Duncan

Concerned, like Lawrence and Lorsch, about **environmental uncertainty** and its impact on organizations, Duncan (1972) saw that the uncertainty of an organization's environment was influenced by two factors: the extent to which the environment was simple–complex, and the extent to which it was stable–dynamic (see also Dess & Beard, 1984; Tung, 1979).

The complexity of a sport organization's environment is determined by the number and heterogeneity of external elements influencing the organization's operations. **Environmental complexity** is characterized by a large number of diverse elements interacting with or influencing the sport organization. In contrast, a simple environment has only a small number of elements, mostly homogeneous, influencing the organization. The Toronto Raptors, the USOC, the athletic department at Ohio State University, and SMG (a facility management group based in Philadelphia) all have complex environments. For example, a sport organization like the Toronto Raptors must deal with dozens of external elements: the media agencies that cover games, the NBA, the players' union, individual player's agents, companies that merchandise the team's logo, food and beverage companies that supply the concessions, equipment manufacturers, the airline companies that transport the team, and the hotels where the team stays while on the road. In contrast, a small sporting goods store, a local bowling alley, and a recreational association football team all have, for the most part, a relatively simple environment. They do not interact with a large number of external elements and those they do interact with will be quite similar.

The extent to which a sport organization's environment is stable–dynamic refers to the amount of change in those elements constituting its environment. A sport organization will be seen as having **environmental stability** if (1) its demands on the organization are relatively consistent and dependable (e.g., same types of products and services) and (2) these demands constantly come from very similar clients. A faculty of kinesiology, a publicly owned golf course, and a state high school athletic association, for example, all face relatively stable environments. That is, each face very similar demands and provide the same service to similar client groups on a year-to-year basis. Dynamic environments, on the other hand, are characterized by rapid change, caused by any number of factors, such as competitors' developing a new product line, increased imports, or a declining market. Athletic clothing manufacturers, such as Body Glove and Speedo, operate in dynamic environments, constantly facing new demands because they continually have to come up with product innovations and try to capture new market segments.

The degree of uncertainty facing a sport organization strongly influences its structure and processes. We now discuss the ways sport managers can control the environmental uncertainty facing their organizations.

Controlling Environmental Uncertainty

All sport organizations face some degree of environmental uncertainty. Uncertainty is therefore a contingency for organizational structure and behaviors (Daft, 2004). To control these uncertainties, sport organizations can either respond to the demands of their external environment (by making changes to their internal structure, processes, and behaviors), or they can attempt to change the nature of the external environment. We look now at some of the techniques sport organizations commonly use to respond to environmental pressure, focusing first on internal changes and then on actions that are externally directed. It is important to note that internal and external initiatives are not mutually exclusive; often several different actions are used at one time. Some techniques are, however, more appropriate to production companies, others to service organizations.

Internally Directed Actions

A sport organization can take internally directed actions to control environmental uncertainty by making changes to the structure and processes of the organization. Details of some options for sport organizations to employ are outlined in the following sections. The first, innovation, is a broad term that encompasses a wide variety of activities. There is some evidence that sport organizations are increasingly innovative, and this is changing the environment for all sport organizations (Byers et al., 2019). The remaining options are more traditional organizational theory–based tools, each of which is explained with examples to help sport managers understand how the internal environment can influence the external.

Innovation

Innovation at the organizational level of analysis is a form of organizational change (Damanpour & Aravind, 2012) and can be defined as the adoption of something new in an organization (Damanpour, 1996; Damanpour & Schneider, 2006). Slack and Parent (2006) suggested that sport organizations are in a constant state of change in four potential areas: technology, products or services, structures or systems, and people. The pressures for change may generate from within the organization or the external environment. Innovations may include creating strategic partnerships (Hall et al., 2003), adopting new organizational structures or forms (Fahlén, Eliasson,

& Wickman, 2015), and changing organizational environments (Eime, Payne, & Harvey, 2008).

One environmental pressure that has been creating innovations in sport organizations is the sociocultural challenge brought with increasing immigration. Immigrants' needs vary widely, and sport clubs, provincial and national governing bodies, and governments have been adopting new policies, programs, and structures to better meet the needs of immigrants in order to help integrate newcomers into sport participation and society. Byers et al. (2019) identified little attention to innovative practices in sport organizations to meet the growing complexity of immigration in England and Canada. Some innovations were present and included hiring new coaches, partnerships with community leaders, changing rules on recruitment criteria, policies on immigrant programs and taster sessions, as well as adopting new technologies (e.g., adapting Muslim women's hijabs to be a lighter, more breathable material) (Byers & Hayday, 2019). Sport clubs, however, are the least likely to innovate, which is not surprising given their limited resources and capacities. Nonprofit community sport clubs are considered the heart of the sport system (Breuer, Feiler, & Wicker, 2015; Taylor, Barrett, & Nichols, 2009) yet are characterized by considerably limited resources and capacity (Wicker & Breuer, 2011, 2013) as well as complex human resources of voluntary and paid staff (Donaldson, Leggett, & Finch, 2012), making innovation key to successfully meeting goals and objectives (Misener & Doherty, 2013). This sector has been identified as imperative to the delivery of government policy, yet research has consistently revealed the difficulties these organizations have in meeting the expectations of national and provincial or regional organizations that often hold considerable power to distribute resources and that create policy that requires top-down implementation (Byers, 2013; Fahlén, Eliasson, & Wickman, 2015; May, Harris, & Collins, 2013).

Ultimately, innovating is risky, and some sport organizations may perceive either the risk or implications of innovating as undesirable. Sport organizations that are more open to ideas (innovations) external to their organization, or even to the sport sector, are more likely to innovate and benefit from these new ideas and mitigate against uncertainty such as declining participation, reduced funding, or changes in demand for volunteers.

Buffering

The idea of **buffering** emanates from the work of J.D. Thompson (1967). The term essentially refers to attempts to protect the technical core—the part of the organization primarily responsible for production—from fluctuations in the environment. Buffering can occur on the input side by stockpiling raw materials and supplies so the organization is not affected by sudden market shortages, and on the output side by warehousing sufficient amounts of its product to allow its distribution department to meet unexpected increases in demand. Maintenance departments help buffer the technical core by ensuring that machinery is regularly serviced; personnel departments do it by ensuring the availability of the required amount of trained labor. Some buffering activities, such as stockpiling raw materials and warehousing inventory, involve tying up large amounts of capital and may not be cost effective for some smaller sport organizations. Also, these techniques are not applicable to service-oriented sport organizations since services cannot be kept in warehouses for use when needed. Buffering may occur, however, in service-oriented sport organizations through ensuring the availability of trained personnel to provide appropriate services when needed. The political environment can spur organizations to engage in this tactic, as is the suggestion by Inman (2018) that the uncertainty over a Brexit deal for Britain is causing manufacturers to stockpile raw materials for fear of rising prices and decreases in exports.

Boundary Spanners

Boundary spanners are established to obtain information about environmental changes that can affect a sport organization and to disseminate favorable information about the organization to other agencies in its environment (Aldrich & Herker, 1977; Jemison, 1984; Tushman & Scanlan, 1981a; Tushman & Scanlan, 1981b). Boundary spanners can be thought of as links between the sport organization and its environment. The more diverse the environment, the more boundary-spanning roles or units the sport organization is likely to have. Public relations, sales, market research, advertising, and personnel departments can all serve a boundary-spanning role. Staff in these departments scan the environment for information important to the company (Lenz & Engledow, 1986).

In the mid-1980s, when walking was becoming a popular fitness activity for people of many ages, the market research departments of a number of athletic footwear companies saw a potential demand for walking shoes. As a result, Nike, Converse, and Reebok all entered the walking-shoe market. By scanning their environment the market research units of these companies, acting as boundary spanners, were able to keep management informed about important new trends.

TIME OUT

Meeting the Demands of the Athletic Footwear Market

When the athletic footwear business started to boom, industry leader Reebok could not make shoes fast enough. Over a three-year period sales jumped from US$13 million to US$60 million to US$308 million. Orders were being shipped from six separate warehouses within a 30-mile (16 km) radius of each other. Basketball shoes went from one warehouse, tennis shoes from another, and running shoes from another. According to Peter McQuaid, Reebok's maintenance engineering manager at the time, each order would be shipped from different locations at different times. Customers were getting their orders at inconsistent times. Often a customer received a back-order notice, mainly because the product could not be found (Witt, 1989).

To reduce its problems Reebok acquired a new 308,000-square-foot (28,614 m) facility and consolidated its distribution. The new facility used bar codes and computers to help with shipping and billing. As a result, fluctuations in customer demand were more easily handled and environmental uncertainty was reduced. Customers are now able to order custom shoes based on foot measurements or 3D technology. Adidas has a robot-powered on-demand Speedfactory to ensure customers receive their products promptly. Under Armour, New Balance, and Nike are also in the race to meet customer demand for custom shoes in a reasonable time period of a few weeks.

Smoothing

Smoothing is very much like buffering, but it takes place only on the demand side of an organization. Smoothing attempts to reduce fluctuations in the demand for a product or service (Thompson, 1967). Sport managers who operate a facility such as a swimming pool or a hockey rink often offer lower rental or admission prices at off-peak times to encourage people to use their facilities at these times. Another example of smoothing, from Berrett, Burton, and Slack's (1993) study of entrepreneurs, involves the managers of two retail sporting goods stores, primarily retailers of hockey equipment. They found that, not surprisingly, their sales dropped off in the summer months. Consequently, they expanded their product line to include summer sport equipment in an attempt to reduce seasonal fluctuations.

Rationing

If buffering, boundary spanning, or smoothing does not work, a sport organization can try **rationing**, the practice of allocating resources on the basis of some preestablished criteria. Doctors at a university sport medicine clinic, for example, may ration their services by establishing a priority system for nonvarsity athletes. In a similar vein, many university sport studies departments ration certain classes by allowing only students with necessary prerequisites to enroll or accepting only those from certain faculties. Rationing, however, as Thompson (1967) notes, is not limited only to service organizations; when supplies are scarce many manufacturers ration allotments of their product to wholesalers or dealers. Rationing in any form is, nevertheless, an unsatisfactory technique because, while this practice may protect the technical core of the sport organization, the needs of some customers in the task environment are not being met—a problem resulting in lost revenue and the customers' loss of faith in the organization.

Planning and Forecasting

All organizations, including those in the sport industry, control environmental uncertainties by developing plans and attempting to forecast future trends (Boulton, Lindsay, Franklin, & Rue, 1982). The more turbulent the sport organization's environment, the more difficult **planning and forecasting** become; this is a necessary activity for sport organizations to identify future directions. Slack, Bentz, and Wood (1985) describe a planning process that can be used by amateur sport organizations, and Macintosh and Whitson (1990) discuss some of the problems of the rational planning program in which all Canadian sport organizations were required to participate in preparation for the 1988 Olympic Games. Slack, Berrett, and Mistry (1994) also show that, in some cases, planning can actually bring about conflict in a sport organization.

Forecasting is related to planning and involves trying to predict future environmental trends. There are a variety of forecasting techniques, such as surveys, decision-tree analysis, and stochastic modeling. Matthew Levine, then-president of the Levine Management Group, a San Francisco-based sport and entertainment marketing firm, used in-depth fan surveys (one forecasting technique) to help the Golden State Warriors' organization increase attendance ("Improving your marketing game," 1987).

Externally Directed Actions

To obtain resources from other organizations, gain legitimacy, and sell its product or service, a sport organization must depend on certain elements within its general environment. This dependence creates uncertainty for the sport organization. To reduce this uncertainty an organization can use a number of techniques. The following are the most common.

Contractual Agreements

Sport organizations can reduce environmental uncertainty by entering into long-term **contractual agreements** with firms that supply their input or those involved with the distribution and sale of their outputs. These contracts come in two forms. The first type involves one organization contracting to sell its product to another. For example, in 1984, when L.L. Bean was concerned about falling sales and losing its image as a sporting goods dealer, it entered into a contract with Cannondale, which agreed to supply it with private-label bikes (Charm, 1986; Skow, 1985).

A second form of contractual relationship, called a *licensing agreement*, involves one organization buying the rights to use an asset owned by another organization. The most common form of licensing agreement found in the sport industry involves a company buying the right to use a logo, such as the Olympic rings or a professional sport team's emblem, on its product. Between the mid-'80s and early '90s, retail sales of licensed sport merchandise rose considerably as a result of this type of contractual agreement. However, these sales hit harder times during the mid-'90s and were slow to increase again. More recently, market research suggests that innovation and improved economic conditions in developing economies like China and India are fueling a greater demand for stylish, attractive merchandise and suggests that the global sport merchandise market, valued at US$27.63 billion in 2015 could reach US$48.17 billion by 2024 (Transparency Market Research, 2016). The benefits of contracts and licensing agreements are that they reduce environmental uncertainty for a sport organization because they establish formalized links between suppliers and their customers. These links serve as a protection against any change in the relationship between the two organizations for a specified time period.

Joint Ventures

By entering into a **joint venture** (two or more companies forming a separate corporate entity), the organizations involved can achieve objectives they could not attain on their own. For example, a joint venture might be used by a sport equipment manufacturer wanting to do business in a foreign country. By getting involved with a distributor in that country the manufacturer is more easily able to deal with local regulations and modes of operation, reducing environmental uncertainty. Refer to chapter 8 for more information on such strategic alliances.

Cooptation

Cooptation occurs when a sport organization recruits influential people from important parts of its environment to be involved in the organization.

TIME OUT

Joint Venturing: Umbro, a More Fashion-Conscious Brand

Revamping its website ahead of Euro 2004 and producing coordinated Euro 2004 uniforms signaled Umbro's response to increasing pressure from competitors and social trends. Unable to compete with the marketing budgets of their rivals Nike and Adidas, Umbro embarked on a number of significant partnerships to inject expertise into its product that was simply not there previously. Umbro and famous Belgian designer Dirk Bikkembergs joined forces in 2004 at Milan Fashion Week in an effort to launch the brand of Umbro as more than just relevant to the sports star but also a highly fashionable product.

Unfortunately, it was not enough to save Umbro, which was bought out by Nike in 2007 and sold to Iconix Brand Group in 2012. An argument could be made, however, that the joint venture increased the brand's attractiveness and value to warrant Nike's interest and eventual commitment to purchase. The Umbro brand continues its joint ventures, now with retail giant Target in the United States, to provide a collection of branded apparel, footwear, and more for kids.

Macintosh and Whitson (1990), for example, note how many national sport organizations in Canada have boards made up of businesspeople so they could "open corporate doors" and thus increase the sport organizations' chances of acquiring sponsorships.

Interlocking Directorates

An **interlocking directorate** involves an individual from one company sitting on the board of directors of another. The interlock allows the individual to act as a communication channel between the two companies and to essentially represent one company on the other's board. Such representation means that policy and financial decisions can be influenced. Gruneau (1983) provides evidence of these types of links occurring between Canadian professional sport teams and organizations in both the television and food and beverage industries. Mizruchi and Stearns (1988) suggest that such interlocks are more likely when companies are facing financial uncertainty. Links between professional sport teams and television companies will likely help the team secure a television contract, and greater financial stability and less environmental uncertainty should follow. Stern (1979) also provides evidence of the utility of interorganizational linkages in understanding the evolution of the NCAA. (More on this in the opening scenario of chapter 18 on change in sport organizations.) Interorganizational linkages have, in fact, been a strong focus of research in sport management literature, with Babiak, Thibault, and Willem (2018) recently reviewing, synthesizing, and analyzing research on these linkages. They noted the increasing importance of interorganizational linkages to sport organizations and the lack of evaluations of the success or failure of linkages.

Executive Recruitment

Several studies have examined the effect that replacing a coach or manager has on a professional sport team's performance (Allen, Panian, & Lotz, 1979; Brown, 1982; Eitzen & Yetman, 1972; Gamson & Scotch, 1964; Grusky, 1963; Pfeffer & Davis-Blake, 1986). Although the general idea behind recruiting a new executive into the senior ranks is that the individual brings new contacts and ideas that can reduce environmental uncertainty and improve performance, the actual results of these studies yield mixed results. Essentially, one theory suggests that the recruitment of a new executive can improve performance, a second suggests it disrupts performance, and a third maintains that it has no effect (Allen, Panian, & Lotz, 1979). Despite these mixed findings, professional sport organizations in particular, and sport organizations in general, still continue to use **executive recruitment** as one means of controlling environmental uncertainty.

Public Relations and Advertising

Sport organizations try to influence key individuals and organizations through **public relations** (PR) programs and **advertising**. Such programs are especially important in highly competitive markets and in industrial sectors that have some variation in the demand for product. Nike has launched a variety of controversial campaigns including a celebration of "crazy" women in sport and Colin Kaepernick, all exemplified by Nike's slogan of "Believe in something. Even if it means sacrificing everything." Nike is a leader in the highly competitive apparel and footwear industry, and the PR examples illustrate how Nike aligns itself and its athletes with what the company believes to be morally superior causes such as women's right to participate in sport, racial equality, and the bravery and honor of military personnel.

Mergers and Acquisitions

If a sport organization is unable to reduce environmental uncertainty by techniques such as contractual agreements, establishing interlocking directorates, and developing public relations programs, it may choose to purchase controlling interest in an organization or acquire ownership. While **mergers and acquisitions** can be a type of growth strategy (see chapter 8), they can also be a means of reducing environmental uncertainty by helping the sport organization obtain control over necessary resources or counteract competition. Disney's acquisition of media organizations (Internet, radio, television, print, and movie) and sport teams (they owned the Anaheim Ducks hockey team until 2005) allows them to have control over content and distribution at the same time.

Changing Domains

Sport organizations, through their senior managers or owners, select the domain in which they wish to operate. Many factors, such as government regulations, a highly competitive marketplace, the increasing cost of supplies, or a declining consumer demand, can create enough uncertainty for a sport organization that it may choose to change or modify its domain. Acquiring new businesses or divesting parts of its existing business are the most frequent ways a sport organization will change its domain; another way is by adding new products or services. For example, Herman's World of Sporting Goods, a chain of sporting goods stores, expanded its offering in the area of water sports in the 1980s. H. George Walker, a vice president of the company, noted that "the water sport category is growing. More people do things at the water. No matter where you are, you find a river, a lake, or a pond. We've expanded the line to give it better presence" (Adams, 1987, p. 28). While Herman's and other sporting goods stores were moving into the water sports domain, the increased competition led to some mass merchandisers divesting themselves of any involvement in this area and focusing on their more traditional markets (Adams, 1987). Many small businesses in sport will diversify their product or service range in response to consumer demand or opportunities perceived in the environment. Likewise, professional sports leagues add domains to their portfolios, such as the NBA partnership with Nike and Top Sports to open the largest NBA retail store in China.

Trade and Professional Associations

Some sport organizations will attempt to influence their environment by joining together to form **trade** or **professional associations**. By acting collectively these associations can influence environmental issues such as government policy issues or trade regulations. The British organization the Chartered Institute for the Management of Sport and Physical Activity (CIMSPA), formerly the Institute of Leisure and Amenity Management (ILAM), is an example of this type of organization; it is "the professional body for the leisure industry and represents the interests of leisure managers across all sectors and specialisms of leisure" and has at its objective "to develop the profession and promote the value of investment in leisure services" (ILAM, 2005, p. 1). Examples of similar associations operating in North America include the American Society of Golf Course Architects, the International Association of Auditorium Managers, the National Sporting Goods Association, and the Snowsports Industries America. All have either a direct or indirect mandate to work to control environmental uncertainty for their members.

Political Lobbying

Many sport organizations lobby various levels of government in order to influence decisions about issues such as tax regulations, grant programs, and labor questions. **Political lobbying** may occur through a trade or professional association such as those discussed above, or a sport organization may engage in lobbying or other forms of political activity on its own behalf. Macintosh, Bedecki, and Franks (1987) illustrate how a number of Canadian sport organizations, such as the Canadian Sports Advisory Council, the Canadian Association for Health, Physical Education and Recreation (CAHPERD), and the Sports Federation of Canada have lobbied the Canadian government at different times for support in reaching program objectives. Burbank, Andranovich, and Heying (2001) provide many examples of the political activity that took place to ensure the smooth operation of the 1984 Los Angeles Olympics, the 1996 Atlanta Olympics, and the 2002 Salt Lake City Olympics.

Illegal Activities

In some cases, sport organizations will engage in unethical or **illegal activities** to control environmental uncertainty. These activities may include price fixing, monopoly, franchise violation, and illegal mergers and acquisitions (Staw & Szwajkowski, 1975). Also, particularly relevant for university sport organizations are recruiting violations, which are becoming commonplace in U.S. collegiate athletics. By engaging in illegal recruiting activity, the sport team is able to secure the services of a top-quality player; the team performs better, gate receipts go up, and alumni funds and television coverage increase. The net effect of these changes is that the level of environmental uncertainty facing the team is reduced (see Sack & Staurowsky, 1998).

Other Perspectives on the Organization–Environment Relationship

In addition to the work of researchers like Burns and Stalker, Lawrence and Lorsch, and Duncan, there are other ways of examining the relationship between a sport organization and its environment. Here we look briefly at the approaches of stakeholder theory, institutional theory, the resource-dependence perspective, and population ecology.

Stakeholder Theory

Earlier in the chapter, we discussed an organization's general and task environment. The groups that were mentioned, such as clients or suppliers, are called *stakeholders*. Stakeholders are groups, organizations, and individuals who can influence or be affected by an organization's actions (Freeman, 1984). They are typically classified according to their role, such as governments, clients, and media. Stakeholder theorists are concerned with studying the relationship between an organization and its stakeholders. This involves not only acknowledging stakeholders' interests but also understanding and formulating strategies to respond to these interests.

Stakeholder theory provides an easy way to classify stakeholders: those who must truly be satisfied, those who should be satisfied, and those who don't need to be satisfied in order for the organization to be successful. Mitchell, Agle, and Wood (1997) suggest that an organization's managers will want to satisfy salient stakeholders because they possess power, legitimacy, and urgency.

Harrison and St. John (1996) argue that there is a justification for appropriate stakeholder management activities. Following stakeholder theory can ultimately increase the ability to predict and control the external (stakeholder) environment, enhance product or service success, raise efficiency and flexibility, bring in contracts, and increase media power because of more (positive) interest in the corporation. It can also lead to a decrease in potential conflicts and damaging moves by the external environment. Post, Preston, and Sachs (2002) stated that both managers and scholars recognize the critical interdependencies between a firm and its stakeholders, and managing them correctly is key to the survival, competitive advantage, and wealth of an organization.

Included as a stakeholder are the organization's employees. While often forgotten in stakeholder analysis, they are a critical part of the organization's success. A whole field is dedicated to them in human resource management (HRM). HRM puts a spotlight on employee-related issues such as recruitment, selection, training, and performance appraisal. Planning for human resources means doing an environmental audit, a job analysis, projecting the supply of and demand for human resources, and matching supply and demand. Sport management literature contains a number of studies related to HRM. We have already talked about executive recruitment, but there are also studies on training sport facility staff to deal with the employee–customer interface (Martin, 1990) and on the causes of stress in physical education faculty members (Danylchuk, 1993).

Institutional Theory

The utility of institutional approaches to understanding the organization–environment relationship was first articulated by John Meyer and Brian Rowan in their 1977 article "Institutionalized Organizations: Formal Structure as Myth and Ceremony." Following Meyer and Rowan's article a number of researchers have examined the impact of the institutional environment on an organization's structure (DiMaggio & Powell, 1983; Oliver, 1988, 1991; Tolbert, 1985; Tolbert & Zucker, 1983; Zucker, 1983, 1987). The institutional environment of an organization "is conceptualized in terms of understandings and expectations of appropriate organizational form and behavior that are shared by members of society" (Tolbert, 1985, p. 1). By changing its structure to conform to the expectations of the institutional environment, "an organization demonstrates that it is acting on a collectively valued purpose in a proper and adequate manner" (Meyer & Rowan, 1977, p. 349). This conformity helps to establish the organization as a legitimate entity and in turn to ensure its long-term effectiveness.

Organizations subjected to the same institutional pressures exhibit isomorphism, that is, they tend to become structurally alike. Kikulis (2000), for example, showed how different stages and levels of institutionalization can explain continuity and change in governance and decision making in volunteer boards in national sport organizations. Silk, Slack, and Amis (2000) showed how **institutional theory** can be used to analyze televised sport production.

Resource Dependence

No sport organization exists in isolation from the other organizations in its environment, the source of the material and financial resources a sport organization needs to survive. To obtain these resources a sport organization engages in transactions with the appropriate organizations in its environment. This is called **resource dependence.** Pfeffer and Salancik (1978), in their book *The External Control of Organizations: A Resource-Dependence Perspective,* discuss the nature of these transactions. They focus specifically on the ways organizations depend on their environment for resources, the resulting uncertainty, and the techniques managers use to reduce this uncertainty.

When a sport organization engages in a resource transaction with another organization, it reduces its vulnerability to environmental fluctuations, but at the same time increases its dependence on the organization supplying the resource, thus reducing its own autonomy and ability to act independently. The extent to which a sport organization depends on another organization for resources is determined by three factors: (1) the importance of the resource (i.e., the extent to which the sport organization requires the resource for its continued operation and survival), (2) the extent to which the organization providing the resource has discretion over its allocation and use, and (3) the extent to which there are alternative sources from which the dependent organization can obtain the resource. Slack and Hinings (1992) have shown how national sport organizations in Canada are dependent for their financial resources on the federal government, and how this dependence has allowed the government to control many of the actions of these organizations, in particular the emphasis they were required to place on high-performance sport. Armstrong-Doherty (1996) uses a resource-dependence perspective to show how an athletic department is dependent on different sources, especially central administration, for survival. However, she does not go into details on this topic.

However, while the organization supplying the resource can wield considerable control over the dependent organization, it is not the dependence per se that creates problems but the uncertainty surrounding the availability of resources because the organization's environment is not reliable. The organization then has a choice: not change and possibly not survive or change to respond to the changing environment (Pfeffer & Salancik, 1978).

In order to control the uncertainties created by resource supplies, dependent organizations attempt to "enact" their environment. That is, managers use techniques such as interlocking directorates, joint ventures, and executive succession to reduce the uncertainty surrounding their supply of resources. The resource-dependence perspective has considerable potential for understanding the impact of the environment on the structure and processes of different types of sport organizations, virtually no work has been published in sport management employing this theoretical perspective.

Population Ecology

Originating with the work of Michael Hannan and John Freeman (1977), the **population ecology,** or natural selection, approach to organization–environment relations is heavily influenced by biological literature, in particular the notion of the survival of the fittest (Ulrich, 1987; Ulrich & Barney, 1984; Wholey & Brittain, 1986). The idea is that organizations, like living things, survive if they are able to exploit their environment for resources. Those that are unable to do so adequately, perish. Unlike other environmental approaches, the focus of population ecology is not on individual organizations but on populations of organizations; a population ecologist would not focus on individual sporting goods stores but on the population of these types of stores that exists in a particular community, for example, the state of California. In addition, the environment is limited to the task environment and is focused on resources, so environmental change is largely defined as fundamental changes in the resource pool.

Researchers who adopt this theoretical position look closely at the birth and death rates of particular types of organizations. New organizations attempt to establish a **niche** for themselves, that is, an area of the market from which they can obtain the resources necessary to survive. The idea is that, like living creatures, organizations must make use of the resources in their niche. If the niche is narrow, a specialist organization such as Peconic Paddler, a canoe rental and sales organization, is most likely to survive. If the niche is wider, a generalist organization is more likely. For example, narrow niches are represented by competitive cyclists' support of custom bike manufacturers such as Terry Precision Bikes for Women, whereas broad-based recreational cyclists who require a wider range of goods and services support the more general cycle manufacturers such as Huffy. Specialists are often more efficient than generalists but, because of their specialization, are more likely to suffer if the environment changes. Generalists, on the other hand, are buffered from environmental changes by the breadth of their operations. If an organization cannot locate itself in a niche, it will ultimately perish.

Each niche has a certain carrying capacity. Just as a forest can only support so many deer or similar animals, so a community can only support so many sport equipment stores or aerobics studios. The competition among these similar organizations for the limited resources means that some will be successful but others will fail (Aldrich, McKelvey, & Ulrich, 1984). In the language of population ecology, they will be selected out, just like weak animals are destined to perish. As well as niches, population ecologists are also interested in the concept of **population density** (Hannan & Freeman, 1988), the extent to which the population of organizations within a niche is able to exploit the resources available.

By using concepts like niche width, carrying capacity, and population density, scholars using the population ecology approach have been able to study the possibilities of success for new organizations entering a specific market and why entry into the niche becomes less attractive as the number of organizations in a niche grows (i.e., as population density increases). They have also been able to show how organizations pursuing "a leader strategy" (Miles and Snow's [1978] Prospectors) may be successful if they are the first to establish themselves in a niche but how, as population density increases, organizations pursuing "a follow-the-leader strategy" (Miles and Snow's [1978] Analyzers) are likely to be more successful. These findings have had a significant impact on our understanding of the way organizations operate.

Despite its utility in helping us understand many issues about the organization–environment relation, population ecology has a number of limitations (Hawley, 1981). First, it is highly deterministic in that the environment is seen as the sole factor in organizational effectiveness. Second (and related to the first limitation), population ecology takes no account of managerial action. For example, population ecologists believe that if you are the owner or manager of an aerobics studio and interest in aerobics as a form of exercise booms, you will be successful, but if interest wanes, you will not survive, regardless of what action you take; the environment has determined success or failure, not the manager. Third, survival is the only measure of organizational effectiveness. If an organization survives, it is effective; if it perishes, it is not effective. Fourth, population ecology is not well suited to the study of certain types of sport organizations, because agencies like the United State Olympic Committee (USOC), World Athletics (formerly the International Association of Athletics Federations [IAAF]), and Skate Canada are unlikely to be put out of existence; no other organization can challenge what they do because they operate under monopoly conditions. Finally, population ecologists look at changes in organizational populations over relatively long periods of time. Short-term changes are seen as aberrations, which are inconsequential to understanding change in any significant way.

Notwithstanding its limitations, the population ecology approach has considerable potential to increase our understanding of the structure and processes of sport organizations. However, to date, a limited number of studies within the field of sport management have employed the theoretical ideas contained within this approach. Cunningham (2002) is one of the very few to use population ecology, in combination with institutional theory, resource dependence, and strategic choice, to develop a model of organizational change.

The Relationship Between an Organization's Environment and Its Structure

As we have seen, all sport organizations are to some extent dependent on their environment. The more dependent an organization is on its environment, the more vulnerable it is to changes in the environment. Here we look briefly at the effect of the environment on the structural attributes of complexity, formalization, and centralization.

Environmental Conditions and Complexity

Under conditions of environmental uncertainty, a successful sport organization will exhibit a relatively high level of complexity. To respond to uncertainty, the organization has "to employ specialist staff in boundary or interface roles—in positions where they form a link with the outside world, securing and evaluating relevant information" (Child, 1984, p. 219). Consequently, an uncertain environment will require an increase in both the number of departments and in the specialist personnel required to buffer the sport organization from environmental fluctuation. Also, there may be an increase in the level of vertical differentiation within an organization (thus increasing complexity) because, under conditions of environmental uncertainty, decision making should be delegated to people who understand the local conditions and can make quick decisions.

Environmental Conditions and Formalization

The increased levels of organizational complexity found under conditions of environmental uncertainty require an appropriate means of integration. Successful organizations are more likely to use "flexible rather than highly formalized or hierarchical methods of coordination and information sharing . . ." (Child, 1984, p. 219), including face-to-face communication, the use of project teams, and the appointment of staff to liaison and negotiating roles. Under stable environmental conditions, sport organizations will tend to adopt formalized operating procedures; the organization has little need for rapid changes, so it can capitalize on the economies that result from the use of these formalized procedures.

Environmental Conditions and Centralization

Mintzberg (1979) suggests that the more complex an organization's environment is, the more likely it is to have a decentralized structure. The complexity of the environment means that one person cannot comprehend all the information needed to make appropriate decisions; consequently, the decisions are decentralized to specialists who make the

KEY ISSUES FOR SPORT MANAGERS

As you have seen in this chapter, there are different ways of looking at a sport organization's environment. As a manager, you should determine which approach seems appropriate for you and your organization, and use that approach to strategically analyze the environment.

In addition, when determining the composition of the environment (e.g., types of stakeholders) and its nature (e.g., stable–dynamic), your organization should have different structures and processes to respond appropriately to the environment. Increasingly, sport managers are adopting innovative practices, which they can learn about from within or outside their own industry. A stable environment is more accepting of low complexity, high formalization, and high centralization. An unstable or uncertain environment requires more flexibility and, most likely, organizations with high complexity, low formalization, and high decentralization. Because environmental uncertainty is undesirable for organizations, we have identified methods that help organizations reduce uncertainty: internal actions of innovation, buffering, boundary spanning, smoothing, rationing, and planning or forecasting; external actions of contracts, joint ventures, cooptation, interlocking directorates, executive recruitment, public relations and advertising, mergers and acquisitions, domain changes, trade and professional associations, political lobbying, and illegal activities. Managers must remember that responding to environmental activity or pressures and attempting to change or control environmental pressures is an ongoing process with continuous evaluation of the outcomes of managerial action.

decisions concerning the particular aspect of the environment for which they are responsible. There is, however, evidence (Mintzberg, 1979) to suggest that under conditions of extreme hostility in the environment (e.g., a threat to an organization such as the advent of a new competitor), an organization will move to centralize its structure temporarily. While this temporary centralization may pose a dilemma for those organizations that operate in complex environments, given the choice the senior managers tend to opt for a centralized structure in which everyone knows who is in control and decisions can be made quickly.

Summary and Conclusions

The environment, a source of uncertainty for the organization, has a major impact on the structure and processes of a sport organization. Managers must attempt to eliminate or minimize the impact of this uncertainty. While the environment can be broadly conceptualized as anything outside the organization, people managing sport organizations have to be concerned with those sectors of the general environment that can influence their operations and their organization's task environment. The task environment is composed of groups such as customers, suppliers, competitors, and related regulatory agencies. Also important for our understanding of the sport organization–environment relationship are the domain, the area to which the sport organization directs its products or services, and the perceived environment, which may be different from the actual environment.

We looked at three of the classic studies on the organization–environment relationship and what they mean for managers of sport organizations. Burns and Stalker's work suggests that under conditions of environmental uncertainty an organic type of structure is most effective; when the environment is stable a more mechanistic type of structure works best. Lawrence and Lorsch conceptualized an organization's environment as made up of various subenvironments. Organizational subunits are required to meet the demands of these subenvironments if the organization is to be successful. Duncan saw environmental uncertainty as influenced by the complexity of the environment and the extent to which elements within the environment are stable–dynamic. To control environmental uncertainty managers of sport organizations can use a number of techniques, some involving changes to the organization's internal structure and processes, others toward changing the external environment. Increasingly, sport managers and researchers are interested in innovations that will help them respond to environmental pressures and increase organization performance. These innovations may be in recruiting new people or in developing new structures or systems, technology, or processes.

We also looked at four more approaches to understanding the organization–environment relationship: stakeholder theory, resource-dependence theory, institutional theory, and population ecology. The latter two in particular have generated a considerable amount of literature that has contributed considerably to our understanding of the organization–environment relationship.

Review Questions

1. Pick a familiar sport organization. How do the different sectors of the general environment influence this organization?
2. Why are organic structures more appropriate for a sport organization operating in a dynamic environment?
3. Pick a familiar sport organization. What can Lawrence and Lorsch's work tell us about the relationship of this organization to its environment?
4. How do amateur sport organizations and clubs control resource uncertainty?

Suggestions for Further Reading

If you are interested in finding out more about the relationship between organizations and their environment, begin by looking at the seminal work of Burns and Stalker (1961), Lawrence and Lorsch (1967), and Duncan (1972) because, as we noted earlier in the chapter, these studies outline some of the more important findings on the organization–environment relationship and provide the basis for much of the subsequent work in this area. For those who find the resource-dependence theory an appealing approach, Pfeffer and Salancik's (1978) book *The External Control of Organizations: A Resource-Dependence Perspective* is a must. However, one of the shortcomings of the resource-dependence approach is that, despite its inherent appeal, there has been little in the way of any extension of Pfeffer and Salancik's original ideas.

Anyone interested in institutional theory should start off with Meyer and Rowan's (1977) article "Institutionalized Organizations: Formal Structure as Myth and Ceremony." Also useful and interesting is Lynne Zucker's (1988) book *Institutional Patterns and Organizations*, a collection of papers by scholars who employ the institutional perspective. Managers may also be interested in arguably the most popular tool for analyzing an organization's environment, Porter's Five Forces Model, which is described in his 1980 book *Competitive Strategy*.

If we look specifically at research on sport organizations, Slack and Hinings, in their (1992) article "Understanding Change in National Sport Organizations: An Integration of Theoretical Perspectives," use resource-dependence theory and institutional theory to explain different aspects of the change process. Also their (1994) article in *Organization Studies*, based on the arguments of institutional theory, empirically demonstrates the impact of institutional pressures on national sport organizations. Recent trends in the sport industry environment see researchers focusing on how sport organizations are adapting to these pressures. Babiak and Trendafilova (2011) provide an interesting article focused on the motives and pressures to adopt green management practices as a form of corporate social responsibility. Finally, Thibault, Frisby, and Kikulis (1999) examine different environmental pressures in relation to interorganizational linkages in their "Interorganizational Linkages in the Delivery of Local Leisure Services in Canada: Responding to Economic, Political and Social Pressures."

Understanding the changing landscape of the sport industry external environment can be challenging, but broad-based texts such as Byers's (2016) *Contemporary Issues in Sport Management: A Critical Introduction* provides a recent overview of challenges for public, private, and voluntary sector organizations.

Case for Analysis

Trends in Professional Sport and Sport Management

The sport industry is uniquely composed of organizations from the public, private, and voluntary sectors. The fastest growing sector is the commercial or private sector and, specifically, professional sport where sport is commercialized for monetary gains. This growth is primarily due to increased values from media rights and most recently the rise of egaming. Nielsen has launched an esport business to help define and quantify value for the competitive gaming market, thought to be worth over US$900 million (Beck, 2016). Esports represents considerable opportunity for further commercial gains in sport and for creating innovative products in response to environmental demand from millennial consumers.

While trends in sport present many opportunities, sport organizations face a growing number of challenges. For instance, sport teams are turning to advances in technology both within and outside the stadium to provide individualized, high-quality experiences for ticket holders. The changes in technology are rapid, it is a considerable challenge to know what technology to adopt, and the cost of new technologies can be considerable. Trends in community, grassroots sport management include decreased volunteering, declining active participation rates, and increasing pressures to provide professional services, which is very challenging given the reliance on these organizations for volunteer labor. The public sector has been experiencing challenges in funding from government and pressure to invest in elite sport over grassroots yet maintain increases in grassroots participation. The public, private, and voluntary sectors of the sport industry do not operate as silos but in fact often work together or have some impact on each other. While cross-sector partnerships and programs are important—including corporate social responsibility (CSR) initiative from professional sports, or sponsorship of voluntary sport by private sector companies—it is unclear if the benefits are felt equally by all parties.

To make sense of the interconnectivity of sport organizations across the sectors, the "wicked problems" framework is helpful.

Byers (2018), with reference to Rittel and Webber (1974) described wicked problems as problems that

- are difficult to define and often symptomatic of other problems;
- cannot be solved with a single solution, policy, or intervention but requires the collaboration of multiple stakeholders; and
- have unintended consequences that need continuous monitoring to redefine the problem as interventions are applied.

When thinking of wicked problems and considering the sport industry, the concept of environment becomes more complex than perhaps a single-sector manager (e.g., professional sport team manager) may have thought.

Questions

1. Describe the external environment of contemporary sport organizations and discuss how these environmental forces differ in their impact on public, private, and voluntary sport organizations.
2. Choose a professional sport team and find out how they seem to respond to environmental pressure to adopt new technology and cater to individual sport fans.
3. How would you describe the environmental conditions of the sport industry?
4. Apply the wicked problems framework to understanding the role of the external environment of the sport industry on management of sport at the grassroots level, and suggest some innovations for community sport organizations to respond to increasing pressure for more governance and professionalization of their operations.

CHAPTER 5

Dimensions of Organizational Structure

Trevor Slack, PhD
Alex Thurston, PhD

Learning Objectives

When you have read this chapter, you should be able to

1. explain the three most commonly cited elements of organizational structure;
2. describe the ways in which a sport organization exhibits complexity;
3. discuss the advantages and disadvantages of formalization;
4. understand the factors that influence whether a sport organization is considered centralized or decentralized; and
5. explain the interrelationship of complexity, formalization, and centralization.

Key Concepts

bureaupathic behavior
centralization
complexity
decentralization
departmentalization
division of labor
flat structure
formalization
functional specialization
goal displacement
hierarchy of authority
horizontal differentiation
minimal adherence to rules
social specialization
span of control
spatial differentiation
standardization
structure
tall structure
task differentiation
vertical differentiation

Nike Restructures

In June 2017, Nike, one of the world's largest athletic-gear manufacturers, announced that it was to perform a major restructure that would result in 1,400 employees losing their jobs, approximately 2 percent of its global workforce (Kell, 2017). Nike revealed that it was to launch a "consumer direct offense" to get fewer but more persuasive products to customers more quickly. Although the official statement from Nike's Trevor Edwards, then president of Nike, was that, "This new structure aligns all of our teams toward our ultimate goal—to deliver innovation, at speed, through more direct connections" (Nike, 2017), business analysts suggested that the announcement was not surprising because Nike had been losing its market share to Adidas and Under Armour, who were both growing at a faster rate (Manning & Rogoway, 2017).

In a written statement, Mark Parker, Nike's chairman and CEO, said, "The future of sport will be decided by the company that obsesses the needs of the evolving consumer" (Nike, 2017, para. 2), in response to Nike outlining a number of operational changes to cope with the drop in U.S. consumer traffic in its retail stores. The main priority was an attempt to drive growth by focusing on 12 key cities in 10 countries: New York, London, Shanghai, Beijing, Los Angeles, Tokyo, Paris, Berlin, Mexico City, Barcelona, Seoul, and Milan. Nike hoped that these key cities would represent over 80 percent of the company's projected growth through to 2020. Nike's other actions: a plan to scale back its structure from six regions to four (North America, Europe, Asia, and the Middle East and Africa), reduce its total product lineup by 25 percent, and cut production creation cycles in half (Nike, 2017). It appears Nike learned from its competitors: Adidas had launched its own six-city initiative two years previously in a strategic move designed to locate the company closer to its core customer and gather the emerging trends before their competitors. Industry analysts have suggested that the restructure helped Adidas' U.S. market share almost double in 2016 (Kell, 2017; Manning & Rogoway, 2017).

What Mark Parker and his executives did at Nike (and, as Adidas did two years beforehand) was respond to the environment and change the **structure** of the organization so it could more effectively achieve its goals. But what exactly does *structure* mean? For many people, organizational structure is something represented by the patterns of differentiation and the reporting relationships found on an organizational chart, and to a certain extent this view is correct. For Thompson (1967, p. 51), *structure* referred to the departments of an organization and the connections "established within and between departments." He suggested that structure was the means by which an organization was able to set limits and boundaries for efficient performance through controlling resources and defining responsibilities. The term *structure* has in fact been used by different theorists to encompass a wide variety of organizational dimensions and their interrelationships. Theorizing organizational structure dominated the research agenda in the 1960s and 1970s but experienced a decline thereafter. However, there has been recent renewed interest in the role of organizational structure to better understand organizational performance (Sandhu & Kulik, 2018).

Given the many aspects of theorizing structure (sometimes referred to as *configuration* or *architecture* in the literature), this chapter will focus in detail on three traditional, commonly used dimensions. However, the chapter will demonstrate how the terms *complexity*, *formalization*, and *centralization* may actually encompass some of the other terms (such as *span of control*, *departmentalization*, *specialization*, and *chain of command*) used to describe organizational structure. The interrelationships among the three primary dimensions are also examined.

Complexity

Complexity is, in many ways, one of the most readily apparent features of any sport organization. If you looked at an organization you would likely be aware of things such as the various job titles, the way in which the organization is departmentalized or divided into subunits, and the hierarchy of authority. Even a cursory look at a sport organization such as a university's faculty of exercise and health or of physical education and recreation will verify this observation. Individuals have job titles such as dean, chair, professor, research associate, graduate student, and administrative support. Faculties may also be divided into departments or subunits, with names such as leisure studies, health, sport management, and sport sciences. Even a sport organization such as a local judo club, which at first glance may appear relatively noncomplex, will probably have job titles, a committee structure, and a simple hierarchy of authority. In fact, in England, national governing bodies of sport (NGBs, akin to national sport organizations [NSOs] around the world) often insist that their member (voluntary) sport clubs each form a club committee, assigning individuals to roles of responsibility (or job titles), such as a welfare officer, secretary, and treasurer. In some sport organizations the level of complexity may actually vary among departments that are perceived as equally important. A large sport equipment manufacturing company, for example, may have a research and development (R&D) department with little in the way of a hierarchy of authority, no clearly defined **division of labor**, and a relatively wide span of control. In contrast, the production department is likely to have a clear chain of command, high levels of task differentiation, and a narrow span of control. If we looked at a local, independent sporting goods store, as another example, it might be viewed as having a relatively simple structure. Yet, complexity is evident in titles (such as owner, manager, assistant manager, salesclerk etc.); there is a hierarchy of authority and a division of labor.

As you can see from these brief examples, complexity is concerned with the shape of an organization's structure and the extent to which a sport organization is differentiated. This differentiation may occur in three ways: horizontally, vertically, or spatially (geographically).

Horizontal Differentiation

Horizontal differentiation, or the width of the hierarchy, occurs in two separate yet interrelated ways: specialization and departmentalization. *Specialization*, in many ways one of the central tenets of organizational theory, has its foundations in such works as Adam Smith's *The Wealth of Nations* (1776) and Emile Durkheim's *The Division of Labor in Society* (1893). There are two ways in which specialization occurs in sport organizations: first, through the division of an organization's work into simple and repetitive tasks, and second, through employing trained specialists to perform a range of organizational activities. The more a sport organization is divided up in these ways, the more complex it becomes. Complexity occurs because **task differentiation** (or **functional specialization**, as it is often called), the dividing up of work into narrow routine tasks, means there are more jobs to manage and a need to establish relationships among these jobs. The specialization of individuals rather than their work, what Robbins (1990) calls **social specialization**, also increases organizational complexity. The different training and knowledge that specialists have, such as professionals (e.g., a sport lawyer) and craft workers (e.g., a custom skate maker), create different approaches to work and thus make the coordination of their activities more difficult. They may have different ideological positions, different goals for the organization, and even different terminology for the work they do. All of these differences make interaction among these people more complex. Slack and Hinings (1992), for example, report that as a result of their training and background, the professional staff of NSOs in Canada showed greater commitment to changes brought about by a government-initiated rational planning system than did the volunteers who had traditionally operated these organizations. Furthermore, Cuskelly (2004) highlighted how hiring paid staff in community sport organizations could lead to conflict between the volunteers and paid staff, which sport managers would have to deal with and mediate, if necessary.

The task differentiation that occurs when work is broken down into simple and repetitive tasks is most often found in sport organizations that produce large quantities of a commodity in the same way. For example, when Adidas manufacture their Ultra Boost running shoe, the production process is broken down into 11 fundamental stages (such as cutting out the lining and tongue, adding labels to shoe, checking quality, lasting of the uppers, and packaging), which have numerous operations within each stage (Hypebeast, 2015). Since several of these processes are routine and uniform, this type of division of labor creates jobs that are relatively unskilled; hence, this type of work is usually high substitutable (i.e., management can usually replace workers easily). On the other hand, when the type of work to be performed is nonroutine and varied, specialization is usually based on education and training. Professionals or craft workers are employed because their skills cannot be easily routinized. In sport we find this type of specialization in organizations such as architectural firms specializing in sport facilities, custom equipment manufacturers, and university sport or physical education departments. For example, RDG Planning & Design, an architectural firm in the United States with a specialization in sport facility design and planning, not only collaborates on projects but also has in-house professionals with specialist roles such as architect, engineer, graphic designer, artist, interior designer, strategic facilities planner, lighting designer, landscape architect, and various project and construction manager roles.

While specialization creates increased complexity within a sport organization that must be managed through processes of coordination and integration, specialization has several advantages. While these advantages pertain primarily to functional specialization, some are relevant to social specialization. Specialization means that the time required to learn a job is relatively short, the chances of making errors when learning the job are reduced, and (because the task is frequently repeated) the person becomes more skillful in its execution. Specialization also means that time is not lost switching from one task to another; the chance of developing techniques to improve the way the task is carried out is improved, and individual skills are used in the most efficient manner. The dehumanizing aspects of specialization (primarily functional specialization) have been well documented by human relations theorists such as Argyris (1964) and Likert (1967). In an attempt to counter these dehumanizing aspects, many organizations employ techniques such as job rotation, job enlargement, job enrichment, quality circles (which bring small groups of employees together to solve work-related problems [Crocker, Chiu, & Charney, 1984; Lawler & Mohrman, 1985]), and, more recently, Kaizen. Kaizen, which means "improvement" and is similar to quality circles, is a business philosophy that originates from Japan and is often proposed as an underlying principle of total quality management (TQM) and a lean production approach (Brunet & New, 2003).

The specialization of individuals and their work gives rise to the second form of horizontal differentiation: **departmentalization**. Departmentalization refers to the way in which management groups differentiate activities into subunits (divisions, work groups, and so on) in order to achieve the organization's goals most effectively. As figure 5.1 shows,

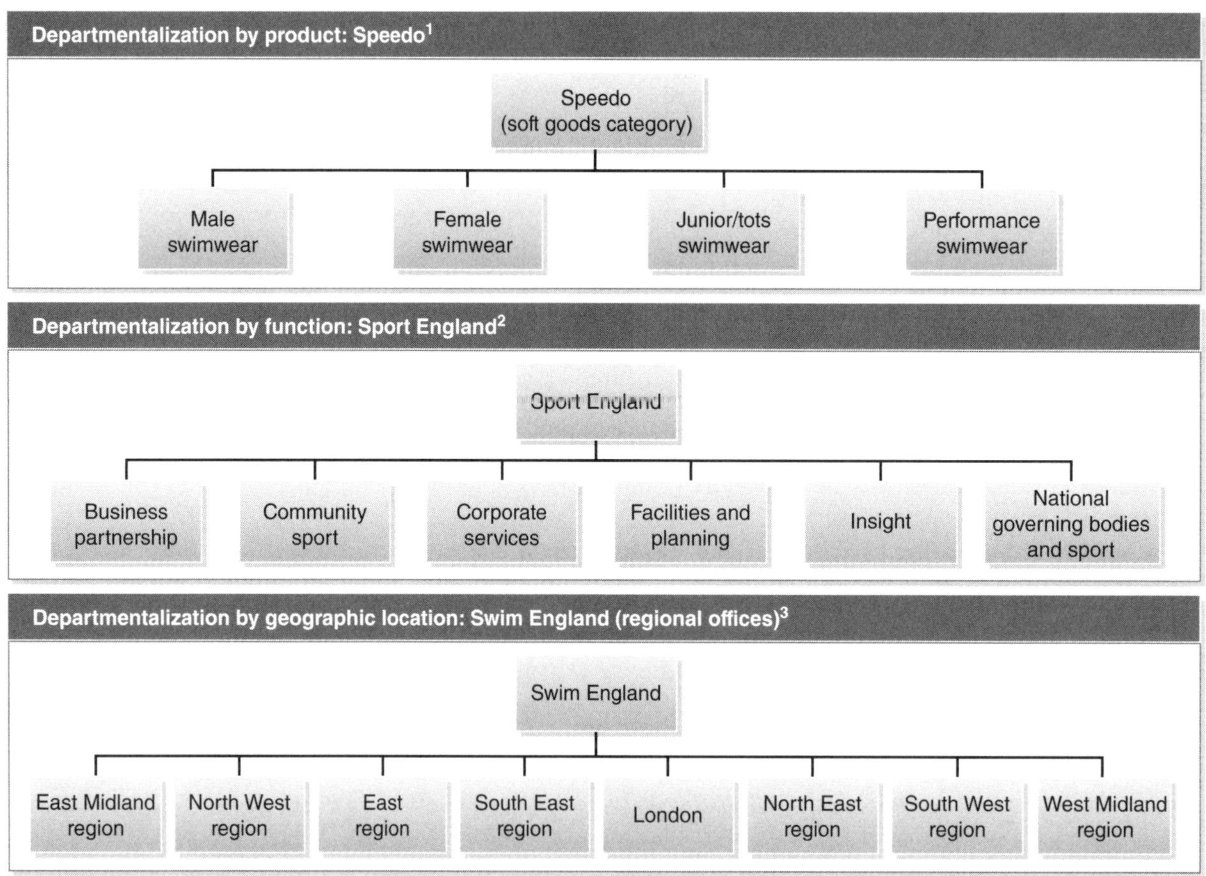

Figure 5.1 Three types of departmentalization.

[1]Based on material provided by Speedo; [2]Based on open data published by the UK central government, https://data.gov.uk/organogram/sport-england; [3]Based on information from Swim England, http://www.swimming.org/regions.

TIME OUT

Using Kaizen to Give British Cycling the Edge

Prior to the appointment of Sir Dave Brailsford in 2003 as performance director of British Cycling, the team had a very poor competition record; they had only secured two gold medals in their history (Allen, 2014). Brailsford knew that he wanted to make British Cycling successful and regularly reach the top of the Olympic podium. However, he was realistic and knew that those aspirations were a distant dream and, to begin with, too daunting (Harrell, 2015).

Using his own experience as an ex-competitive racing cyclist and the knowledge acquired during his master of business administration (MBA) degree program, he set about instilling a marginal gains philosophy with the team. While studying, he developed particular interest in Kaizen and other process improvement techniques so thought that if the team could continuously make small improvements, the accumulation could eventually lead to greater success (Harrell, 2015). In his own words, "If you broke down everything you could think of that goes into riding a bike, and then improved it by one percent, you will get a significant increase when you put them all together" (Allen, 2014, para. 2). Examples of opportunities to seek competitive advantage for British Cycling included using a wind tunnel to improve aerodynamics; painting the floor of the mechanics' area in the team truck white so dust could more easily be spotted, ensuring bike maintenance was not undermined; hiring a surgeon to teach the athletes about correct hand-washing procedures to avoid illnesses during competition (in fact, the whole of Team Great Britain were advised by the team doctor not to shake any hands during the 2012 Olympics!); precise food preparation; and taking their own mattresses and pillows to competitions so the athletes could sleep in their normal position and posture each night (Harrell, 2015).

Brailsford's instinct and shrewd approach of using Kaizen principles to focus on progression, rather than perfection, with each race proved to be a success. British Cycling rose to international dominance and at the 2016 Summer Olympic Games, Great Britain finished as the top cycling nation with six golds and 12 medals in total, double the second-place team's total.

departmentalization may occur on the basis of product or service, function, or geographic location.

Speedo is departmentalized along product lines; Sport England (a nondepartmental public body under the United Kingdom government's Department for Digital, Culture, Media and Sport [DCMS]) is departmentalized by function; and Swim England (the NGB for aquatic disciplines) is departmentalized by geographic location.

Researchers in both sport management and the broader field have defined these forms of horizontal complexity in different ways. Hage and Aiken (1967b) focused on levels of occupational specialization and professionalization. They suggested that complexity includes the number of occupational specialties, professional activity, and professional training. They then classified individuals as to their occupational specialty (e.g., teacher, coach, physiotherapist) based on their major duties. Professional activity was measured by the number of professional associations in which an individual was a member, number of meetings attended, and so on, and the variable professional training was measured by the amount of education and other professional training an individual had experienced (Hage & Aiken, 1967a; Hage & Aiken, 1970). Basically, Hage and Aiken's (1967a) argument was that the more training people have in their different specialties, the more differentiated they are (greater degree of professional activity), and hence the greater the level of organizational complexity.

Peter Blau and his colleagues, in some of their work, adopted a somewhat different definition of horizontal differentiation. Blau and Schoenherr (1971), for example, define horizontal differentiation as the number of major subdivisions in an organization and the number of sections per division. Hall, Haas, and Johnson (1967) and the Aston Group (Pugh, Hickson, Hinings, & Turner, 1968) use similar measures to those of Blau. Hall et al. (1967) focus on the number of major divisions or departments in an organization and the way they are subdivided. The Aston Group focused on functional specialization and the extent to which there are specialized roles within these functions.

In the sport literature both Frisby (1986) and Kikulis et al. (1989) have used aspects of the work of the Aston Group to examine horizontal complexity. Frisby, in her study of the organizational structure and the effectiveness of voluntary sport clubs, used measures of professionalism and specialization. Professionalism was defined as the level of education attained by both volunteers and paid staff; specialization measures were based on the number of roles for board members, executive committee members, paid staff, and support staff, as well as the number of committees in the organization. Kikulis et al. (1989) used the concept of specialization in their work. It was a composite variable defined as "the extent and pattern of differentiated tasks, units, and roles allocated to different organizational segments" (p. 132). Table 5.1 shows the items that Kikulis et al. included in their measure of specialization. Bayle and Robinson (2007) analyzed the relationship between organizational structure, strategy, and performance of French NGBs. Horizontal differentiation was used to examine the formal structures of the NGBs by looking at the number of units or departments and committees within each organization.

Vertical Differentiation

Vertical differentiation refers to the number of levels, or the height of the hierarchy, in a sport organization. The more levels there are, the greater the problems of communication, coordination, and supervision, hence the more complex the sport organization. The number of levels in an organization is usually related to the size of an organization and also to the extent to which it is horizontally differentiated. A small custom bike builder like Firefly Bicycles of Boston, Massachusetts (United States), has virtually no vertical differentiation and very little horizontal differentiation. In contrast, a large producer of bikes, equipment, and clothing like Trek Bicycle Corporation has several vertical levels and shows a high level of horizontal differentiation. Although research findings vary, horizontal differentiation is generally seen as being related to vertical differentiation because, as Mintzberg (1979, p. 72) notes, "When a job is highly specialized in the horizontal dimension, the worker's perspective is narrowed, making it difficult for him to relate his work to that of others. So, control of the work is often passed to a manager. . . . Thus, jobs must often be specialized vertically because they are specialized horizontally."

The pattern of vertical differentiation is often assumed to represent the **hierarchy of authority** in an organization and, as Hall (1982) notes, in the vast majority of cases it does. There are, nevertheless, situations in some sport organizations where this assumption may not be valid, for example, when professionals work in bureaucracies. In professional service firms in the sport industry (e.g., companies that specialize in sport law, sport medicine clinics, and architectural companies that specialize in sport facilities), professionals, because of their specialist training, are central to the firm's operations. Because the professionals require a relatively high degree of autonomy to do their jobs, management has to delegate to them a considerable amount of authority, responsibility, and, subsequently, control. Heightened by a voluntary, as opposed to for-profit, nature, this type of situation was increasingly prevalent in NSOs in Canada. Volunteers who traditionally managed these organizations lost much of their control to professionally trained sport managers who were actually positioned at a lower vertical level in the organization (Macintosh & Whitson, 1990; Thibault, Slack, & Hinings, 1991). Thompson (1961) suggests that one way to deal with such a situation is to create a dual hierarchy. However, Schriesheim, Von Glinow, and Kerr (1977) raise a number of questions about the use of dual hierarchies. A development to address this situation,

Table 5.1 Measures of Specialization in Voluntary Sport Clubs

Measure of specialization	Operationalization
Program specialization	The number of programs operated by the sport organization (e.g., national team, coaching certification)
Coaching specialization	The number of coaching roles within the sport organization (e.g., men's head coach, women's head coach, junior coach)
Specialization of professional staff	The number of professional staff roles (e.g., managing director, coach, technical director)
Specialization of volunteer administrative roles	The number of administrative roles held by volunteers on the sport organization's board of directors (e.g., vice president of administration, treasurer)
Specialization of volunteer technical roles	The number of technical roles held by volunteers on the sport organization's board of directors (e.g., vice president of coaching, director of officials)
Vertical differentiation	The number of levels in the sport organization's hierarchy

Based on Kikulis, Slack, Hinnings, and Zimmermann (1989).

and one used by a number of Canadian NSOs, is an organizational design known as the *professional bureaucracy*. Whereas the traditional bureaucracy "relies on authority of a hierarchical nature . . . the Professional Bureaucracy emphasizes authority of a professional nature—the power of expertise" (Mintzberg, 1979, p. 351). This type of organizational design is examined more fully in chapter 6 of this textbook.

As we have discussed, size influences the number of levels in an organization. It is nevertheless quite possible for two sport organizations with a similar number of nonmanagerial employees to have a different number of vertical levels. As figure 5.2 shows, some organizations like Organization A can have what is usually referred to as a **flat structure**. In contrast, Organization B has a relatively **tall structure**. The difference, as figure 5.3 shows, relates to what is termed the *span of control* (sometimes called the *span of management*). The **span of control** in an organization refers to the number of people directly supervised by a manager. In figure 5.3, although Organization X has just over 200 more first-level employees than Organization Y, it has a span of control of seven, and consequently fewer managers and a flatter structure. Organization Y, which has a span of control of three, has a tall structure and more managers.

Opinions vary as to what is an appropriate span of control. Classical theorists such as Urwick (1938, p. 8) suggest that "no superior can supervise directly the work of more than five or, at the most, six subordinates whose work interlocks." Human relations theorists favor a broader span of control that gives more autonomy to workers. A wider span of control can also enhance communication in an organization. As Simon (1945) notes, administrative efficiency increases when the number of organizational levels is minimized.

Employees may feel more secure in a taller structure because they are easily able to obtain help from a supervisor. However, tall structures with a narrow span of control may result in closer supervision than employees see as necessary. Cummings and Berger (1976) suggest that senior managers prefer tall structures whereas lower-level managers are more comfortable with a flatter structure. The nature of the work being performed also affects the size of the span of control. Some jobs require close supervision; others, particularly professional jobs, do not.

Spatial Differentiation

Spatial differentiation (or geographic differentiation) can occur as a form of either vertical or horizontal differentiation. That is to say, both levels of

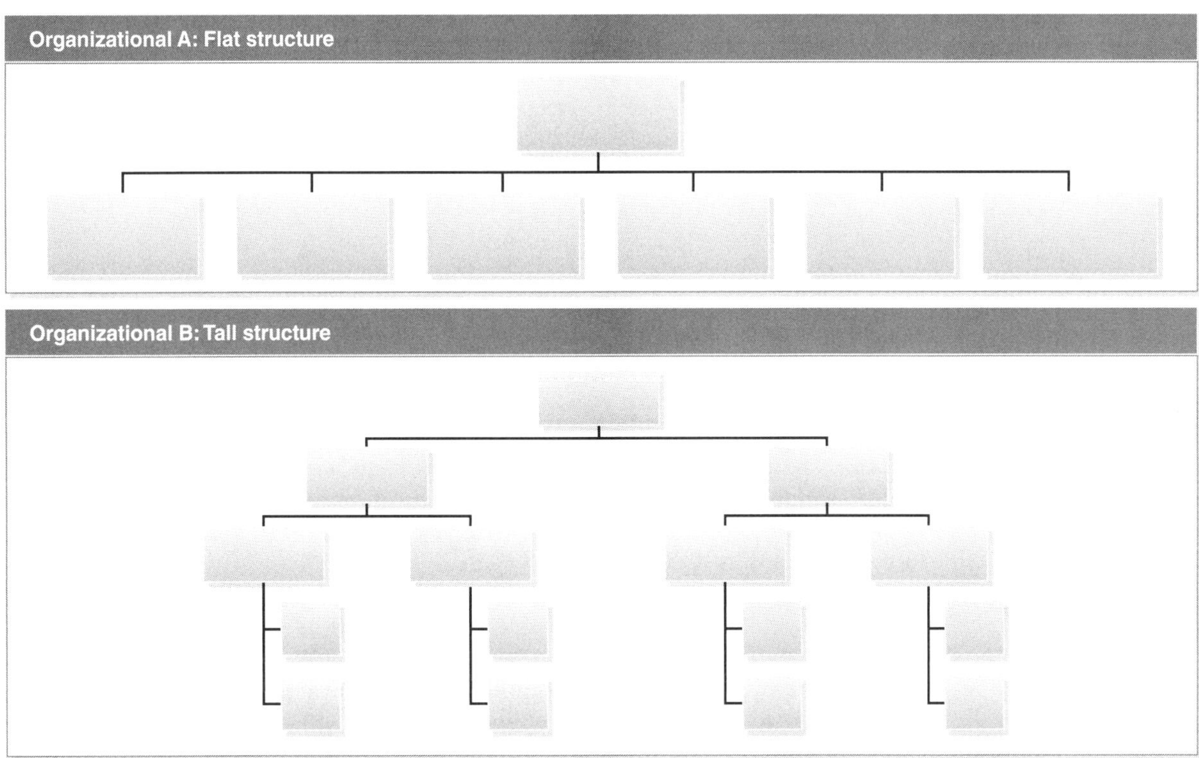

Figure 5.2 Flat and tall structures.

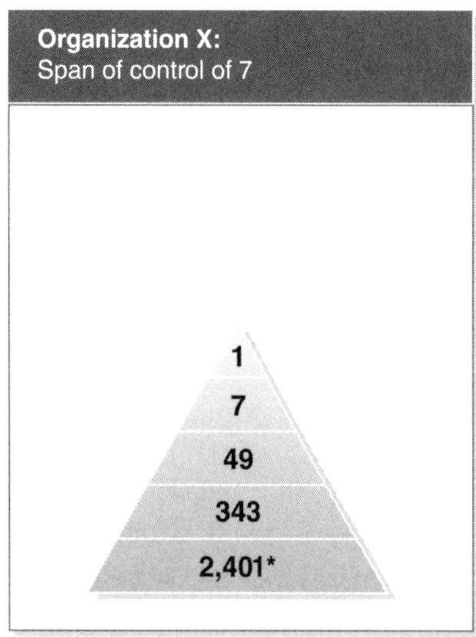

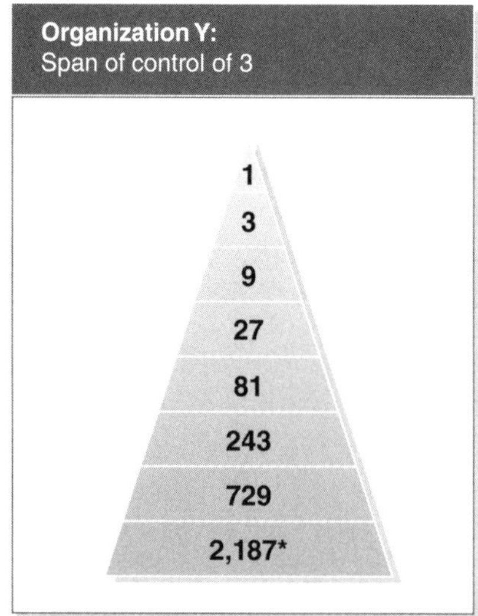

Figure 5.3 Comparing the span of control.

power and tasks can be separated geographically. For example, in the province of Saskatchewan, the department responsible for sport, the Ministry of Parks, Culture and Sport, has a number of satellite sport and recreation offices throughout the province that help facilitate the provision of opportunities for participation in sport and recreation. Power is differentiated between these satellite offices and the central government offices in the provincial capital, Regina. Because senior managers are housed in Regina and lower-level satellite managers are placed throughout the province, complexity is increased more than if they were all in one location.

Horizontally differentiated functions can also be dispersed spatially. Burton Snowboards, a company based in Vermont in the United States, shut down their manufacturing facility in 2010 to move production to Austria. The company now has offices in Australia, Austria, Canada, California, China, Japan, and Republic of Korea, and has since also started manufacturing some boards in China. The Austrian factory attempts to source the majority of materials within a 250-mile (402 km) radius. The locations of the organization's central office, various production sources, and assembly plants in different parts of the world, and the use of stores all around the globe (including online), results in increased organizational complexity.

The physical separation of an organization's operations increases its complexity, which can be further increased as a result of distance (Hall et al., 1967). For example, a sporting goods company with several retail outlets throughout London would be considered less complex than the same type of company with a similar number of outlets dispersed throughout the United States.

Interrelationship Among Elements of Complexity

Although each of the three elements of complexity have been treated separately, you may be tempted to ask if there are interrelationships among the three. The most obvious interrelationships are in very big and very small sport organizations. Companies like CCM, a major manufacturer of hockey skates; Anytime Fitness, a 24-hour health and fitness club that has over 3,000 franchised locations in 20 countries; and L.A. Gear, an athletic footwear manufacturer (and at one time one of North America's fastest-growing companies), all exhibit high levels of horizontal, vertical, and spatial differentiation. In contrast, companies such as Sports Surfaces UK, a family-run company that provides design, installation, and maintenance of sport surfaces; Shand Cycles, a small independent British bicycle company located in Scotland; and the Future Fishing Tackle shop, an angling, bait, and fishing tackle supplier in Newark, Nottinghamshire (United Kingdom), are low in all three areas.

Beyond these extremes of size, it is hard to generalize. Universities, for example, often have high levels of horizontal differentiation in terms of the number of departments that exist, a relatively low level of vertical differentiation, and usually no spatial differentiation. Gridiron football teams have high horizontal differentiation, with roles such as running back, wide receiver, and linebacker, but usually only have two levels of vertical differentiation—coaches and players (Hall, 1982). When assessing the environmental performance of the 2008 International Children's Games (a multisport event), Mallen, Stevens, Adams, and McRoberts (2010) found that the host's organizational structure hampered the Environmental Initiative, which was announced during the lead up to the Games. The structure consisted of four vertical levels and 15 horizontal units; the high level of internal complexity meant decreased cohesion between divisions. As a result, it was suggested that "the lack of integration was a major limitation for the environmental committee whose policies and programs failed to translate into the operations of functional areas" (p. 115).

The Managerial Consequences of Complexity

As sport organizations grow, which most aim to do, they generally become more differentiated. People occupying different roles, working in different departments, and having different levels of training exhibit different attitudes and behaviors; they also have different goals and expectations for the organization. This complexity leads to problems of communication, coordination, and control. Consequently, as a sport organization becomes more complex, increasing pressures are placed on managers to ensure that the organization progresses smoothly and efficiently toward achieving its goals. In short, managers have to manage complexity, so they introduce such things as committees, rules, procedures, and management information systems. The more complex the sport organization becomes, the more time and effort managers have to spend dealing with issues of communication, coordination, and control. (Organizational control is discussed in detail in chapter 10.)

Hall (1982, p. 90) describes this phenomenon as "an interesting paradox in the analysis of organizations." He notes that, although complexity is increased to help organizations economically and to improve their efficiency, it also creates pressures to add managers to maintain communication, coordination, and control and to reduce conflict. Consequently, the economies and efficiencies realized by increased complexity have to be counterbalanced by the added burden placed on managers to keep the organization together.

Formalization

The second structural dimension is formalization, a key dimension because it strongly influences the way individuals are able to behave in an organization. Just as the rules of a sport limit the way an

TIME OUT

The Emergence of Elements of Complexity in a Voluntary Sport Club (VSC)

Nottingham Leander Swimming Club was formed in 1947 as a male-only club in England. The club was formed, financed, and run by a local hotelier. In its early years the organization operated with a relatively loose and informal structure; there was little in the way of any type of role specialization because all members at various times had to assume the responsibilities of meet organizer, timekeeper, starter, and so on.

In 1952 the club restructured following the founder's departure. A committee was formed, and officers were voted into positions such as chairman and chief coach at the annual general meeting (AGM). The members of the organization, who had few professional qualifications, attained their positions in the organization because of their enthusiasm, not through any type of special training or credentials.

As the organization grew (including allowing females to join in the 1960s), the club started training at more pools around the city, making the organization more geographically dispersed. Increased size also meant that more members began to take on specialist roles; some concentrated on coaching, while others focused on organizing meets or timekeeping. Eventually, more discipline sections were added to the club, such as junior, water polo, and masters, demonstrating departmentalization, a form of horizontal differentiation. Today, the club has roughly 400 members, who train in nine pools across the city and have over 20 committee members and officers. With this level of complexity, the club has implemented a specialized management software to help deal with organization and coordination, which, over time, has become more formalized with its operations.

Based on information from the club's website (www.leandersc.com) and personal communication.

individual can behave in the playing area, formalization in organizations works to control the amount of discretion individuals or groups are allowed to exercise when performing their jobs. As Hall (1982, p. 95) notes, the focus on the way formalization controls individual behavior does not mean a move away from "the organizational level of analysis. Formalization has important consequences for the organization and its subunits in terms of such processes as communication and innovation."

What Is Formalization?

Formalization refers to the extent to which mechanisms such as rules and regulations, job descriptions, and policies and procedures govern the operation of a sport organization. If a sport organization is highly formalized it will have lots of rules and regulations, comprehensive policies and procedures, and detailed job descriptions to guide its operations. In this type of sport organization, employees have little discretion over how and when they do their work. In sport organizations with low formalization, however, employees are given the freedom to exercise discretion about their work and how and when it is carried out. In this sense, formalization is not only a structural component but also a control mechanism that has political and ethical ramifications (cf. Braverman, 1974; Clegg & Dunkerley, 1980). (See chapter 10 for more information on organization control mechanisms.)

Different types of sport organizations exhibit different levels of formalization. W.L. Gore & Associates, the manufacturer of Gore-Tex, a waterproof product used in sport equipment such as rain gear, tents, footwear, and sleeping bags, prides itself on low levels of formalization. Bill Gore adopted an organizational structure in which everyone's title is "associate," and each associate decides to follow leaders rather than be assigned a boss. In contrast, other companies that mass-produce sport equipment usually have relatively large numbers of unskilled jobs, which are likely to be highly formalized. Even sport organizations that require employees to use some degree of discretion in their work will formalize aspects of their operations. Adidas, for example, provides new retail store employees with a comprehensive *Retail Handbook* that they are expected to read and understand. The more professionals there are in a sport organization, the less likely it will have high levels of formalization. Doctors who specialize in sport medicine, university professors who teach sport management, and architects who design sport facilities are all professionals in different aspects of sport organizations that demonstrate relatively low levels of formalization.

The extent of formalization differs not only from organization to organization but also among the hierarchical levels of an organization and among departments. At the higher levels of a sport organization, jobs are generally broad and nonrepetitive, and allow more discretion over how they are carried out than at the lower-level jobs; consequently, managers' jobs are less likely to have to follow formalized procedures than those they supervise. As already noted, production departments tend to be highly formalized; in contrast, a research and development (R&D) department, because of the creative nature of the work and the fact that it is likely to be staffed by professionals, will not have high levels of formalization.

There is some question as to whether or rules, procedures, and so on have to be stated in writing for an organization to be considered "formalized." Pugh et al. (1968) used the terms *formalization* and *standardization* in their work. The two concepts are in fact highly correlated. *Formalization* refers to "the extent to which rules, procedures, instructions, and communication are written" (Pugh et al., 1968, p. 75). In the research by Pugh et al. (1968) the concept was operationalized by measuring the extent to which an organization had such written documentation as policies and procedures, job descriptions, organizational charts, and employee handbooks.

Standardization, on the other hand, refers to events that occurred regularly and were legitimated by the organization but not committed to written form. Pugh et al. (1968) rated activities such as taking inventory, ordering materials, and interviewing for their degree of standardization. Hage and Aiken (1970) used the term *formalization* to include both written and unwritten rules, by breaking formalization down into two elements: job codification (how many rules a worker is asked to follow) and rule observation (how closely workers must adhere to these rules). For their work they used both official documents and the perceptions of employees as measures of formalization. As Hall (1982) notes, the use of perceptual measures recognizes the existence of informal procedures in an organization, something that cannot be obtained from official records only. Despite the fact that both approaches purport to measure the same concept, they have been shown to produce different results (Pennings, 1973; Walton, 1981).

Studies carried out on sport organizations have tended to focus on the existence of written documentation as an indicator of formalization. Frisby (1986), in her study of organization structure and effectiveness, used three indicators: (1) publication formalization, the total number of publications produced by the sport organization; (2) constitution formalization, an estimate of the number of words in the sport organization's constitution; and (3) job description formalization, an estimate of the number of words in volunteer and paid staff job descriptions. Slack and Hinings (1987b) used the term *standardization* but note that standardized procedures are often committed to writing. Thibault et al. (1991), in their study of the impact that professional staff have on the structural arrangements of VSCs, operationalize the concept of formalization by measuring the existence of written documentation across a range of organizational activities such as personnel training, planning, marketing, and promotion. Jakobsen, Gammelsaeter, Fløysand, and Nese (2005) examined the impact of new organizational structures in Norwegian professional association football. They found that, subsequent to a transition period experienced in Norwegian association football, clubs were becoming increasingly formalized (notably, with respect to rules and procedures) with stronger role specialization. Relvas, Littlewood, Nesti, Gilbourne, and Richardson (2010) examined the organizational structures within professional association football clubs across Europe. They concluded that all of the clubs presented similar formalized structures, which they suggest aligns with DiMaggio and Powell's (1983) notion of organizational homogenization. In sport volunteering literature, the terms *formalization* and *professionalization* are often used interchangeably (Nichols & James, 2008; Nichols, Wicker, Cuskelly, & Breuer, 2015). Nagel, Schlesinger, Bayle, and Giauque (2015, p. 408) suggest that sport federations face a number of challenges and theorize that the reason many sport organizations have moved from "a volunteer-driven logic to a more formalised and business-like one, as a form of professionalisation" is because it seems to be a strategy for organizations to deal with various internal and external factors.

Reasons for Formalization

Of the reasons for formalizing the operations of a sport organization, the most central are to replace direct supervision, which would be unduly expensive, and to provide a consistent way of dealing with recurring problems. In small organizations such as a local sport equipment store, a manager can supervise employees directly because they are in close contact and there are few employees. In larger sport organizations this type of direct supervision is not possible. Although a narrow span of control can help supervision issues, it can be time consuming if a problem has to go through several hierarchical levels before a decision can be made. Formalizing procedures so that recurring problems are handled in a consistent way can alleviate supervision problems.

Formalization also helps monitor employee behavior. In many sport organizations employees are required to submit reports about what they accomplish in their jobs on a weekly, monthly, or yearly basis. Similarly, in many universities around the world, staff members must conduct an annual performance and development review (PDR). These reports help managers determine if employees are contributing to the achievement of the sport organization's goals. Companies like Tottenham Hotspur Football Club, Reebok, and Sports Direct International plc (a British retail group), because they are publicly held, all file formalized annual reports for their shareholders, who in essence own the company, to keep them informed of its accomplishments. Besides helping to monitor the behavior of employees, formalization helps ensure employees understand procedure. For example, professors who teach sport management courses often receive guidelines about how to mark student papers and what to do if students miss assignment submission deadlines because of illness or mitigating circumstances. Such procedures ensure that all students are dealt with fairly and in the same manner.

Economic aspects of formalization are also important to consider. Formalizing jobs generally means that they require less discretion and in turn can be filled by less-qualified, and hence cheaper, workers. Formalization also promotes efficiencies because organizations often spend considerable time, effort, and money to determine the best way to conduct a particular operation; once the best way is determined, formalizing the procedure induces other people who perform the operation to do so in the most cost-efficient manner.

Formalization clarifies job requirements. It is now commonplace that sport coaches at universities around the world sign a coach's agreement or coaching contract that stipulates the role, responsibilities, duration of the agreement, risk management processes, accident reporting procedures, and specific club rules and policies, for example. In addition, club handbooks are often supplied to coaching staff to provide greater in-depth information about the club. Formalizing procedures is also beneficial to determine what the organization is supposed to do. For example, Sport Canada stresses that NSOs must write down organizational structures and processes if they want to receive funds. Similarly, Sport England publishes investment guides for NGBs applying for funding (through the Whole Sport Plan process) that outlines and explains the assessment requirements that need to be satisfied for funding to be considered. As an example, governance frameworks of NGBs are assessed; NGBs must provide information about their board to demonstrate it is well balanced and that the terms of office for board members are limited.

No organization can develop formalized rules and procedures for every possible situation that can arise, but there are ways in which formalization can help. Many professional organizations develop a written code of ethics, which provides generally accepted principles based on professional values and which can be followed when unfamiliar situations are encountered. Earle Zeigler proposed such a code of professional ethics for the North American Society for Sport Management (NASSM) (Zeigler, 1989). Included in Zeigler's proposal was commitment to a high level of professional practice and service, the availability of such services to clients of all ages and conditions, and professional conduct based on sound management theory. NASSM adopted a code in 1992. Due to the increasing number of scandals in sport, De Waegeneer, Devisch, and Willem (2017) note that more organizations are starting to adopt ethical codes in attempts to achieve improved ethical behavior. Other types of code are created by organizations in efforts to minimize risk. For example, Canada West Ski Areas Association (a nonprofit organization) has written an Alpine Responsibility Code to help achieve a safe outdoor experience for users of ski areas (Canada West Ski Areas Association, n.d.).

Finally, formalizing procedures provides an indication to employees as to the purpose of the organization, its overall goals, and what they as employees can expect from their involvement. Formalization signals the organization's commitment to its employees and therefore can strengthen an employee's identification with the organization and provide a safeguard. Formalized commitments can help morale because employees have a tangible indication of their rights and responsibilities.

Methods of Formalization

There are a number of ways in which managers can formalize the operations of a sport organization. In this section, we examine the methods most frequently used.

Hiring the Right Employee

As we saw earlier, sport organizations with high numbers of professionals tend to have relatively low formalized operations. The reason is that, in many ways, professional training is a surrogate for formalization and may be considered a means of standardizing behavior prior to a job. Through their training, individuals not only learn technical skills but also the standards, norms, and accepted modes of behavior of their profession. Consequently, in staffing, organizations face what Robbins (1990) calls the "make" or "buy" decision: The organization can either control employee behavior directly through its own formalized rules and procedures, or control can be achieved indirectly by hiring trained professionals (Perrow, 1972).

Regardless of whether an organization hires professional staff or unskilled workers, candidates often deal with application forms, tests, reference letters, and interviews before employers hire the right person. The right person is someone who it is perceived will perform the job well and is willing to follow rules and regulations (Hage & Aiken, 1970). Coaches often use this logic in team selection. Because they want players who are willing to conform to rules and show consistent behavior patterns, they do not always select talented players unless they fit in with the team. You might be able to think of some examples where gridiron or association football coaches have signed a superstar player, only to find that the player does not fit with the rest of the existing team. Consequently, that player can lose form or negatively affect the performance of teammates. In basketball, there have been concerns of fit with LeBron James (often regarded as one of the best basketball players in the world) since his move to the Los Angeles Lakers; some players seem to find it hard to play in LeBron's shadow and deal with the scrutiny that surrounds him (Bucher, 2018). Selecting the right person is then a method of formalization; it helps ensure consistency in employee performance and behavior.

On-the-Job Training

Even though they go to considerable lengths to hire the right people, some sport organizations still provide on-the-job training for their employees. Training activities may be influenced by a number of factors and can include such activities as workshops, films, lectures, demonstrations, and supervised practice sessions (Slack, 1991). The idea behind all of these methods is to instill in new employees the norms and accepted patterns of behavior of the organization. Mecca Leisure, a British organization involved with ice skating rinks and billiard and snooker halls, could not find the type of staff it needed from higher education, so it developed its own in-house training program (Brown, 1990). The Organizing Committee of the 2012 Olympic Games, the London Organising Committee of the Olympic and Paralympic Games (LOCOG), provided a three-session training program for the 70,000 Games Makers (the designation for the volunteers used to help run the Games). The program provided volunteers an orientation event where volunteers were given insight into the history of the Games, sports, and venues. The second session was a role-specific training session to ensure everyone knew how to carry out their allocated responsibilities. Finally, there was venue-specific training (where each volunteer was to be stationed) to meet the rest of their team and learn the emergency procedures (Minard, 2012). Again, the idea behind the training was to standardize employee behavior.

Policies

Policies are general statements of organizational intent. They provide employees with a certain amount of discretion in making decisions in the areas covered by the policy. Policies may be internally focused; for example, Human Kinetics Publishers has policies that cover such areas as the advancement of employees and attendance at work. Policies may also be externally focused. A small sporting goods store, for example, may use them to cover situations such as accepting payment using gift cards and returning merchandise. Policies are generally written to provide some leeway in their interpretation. The City of Winnipeg (1990) Parks and Recreation Department's *Sports Services* policy states the following: "The Department will cooperate with other agencies and organizations to ensure a base level of sport programs and opportunities and encourage advanced levels of participation." The policy does not specifically state how the department will cooperate; consequently, staff is given the discretion to determine whether cooperation will merely mean endorsing a program or providing funding and other resources.

But policies can also conflict. With the return of the Olympic Games to Greece in 2004, the IOC promoted a policy of inclusion. It encouraged as many countries as possible to participate in the Olympic marathon, which would follow the exact route Pheidippides ran on his way to Athens to tell of the victory of the battle of Marathon. However, the Canadian Olympic Committee (COC) set a seemingly conflicting policy of sending only top athletes who had a chance of winning a medal. Its very tough qualifying standards ultimately meant no Canadian marathoner was in the Olympic event. For a more detailed examination of policy, refer to chapter 7 of this textbook.

Procedures

Procedures, developed for the **standardization** of particular organizational activities, are different from policies in that they are written instructions detailing how an employee should carry out an activity. These instructions, determined to be "the one best way" of operation, contribute to the efficiency of a sport organization by standardizing inputs and outputs and by abetting the optimal use of time and resources in the transformation process. Your local leisure facility will more than likely have a set of normal operating procedures, which staff should familiarize themselves with. While procedures can facilitate the smooth running of a sport organization, too many procedures, like other methods of formalization, can create difficulties for employees, customers, and clients. Good sport managers establish procedures only when they are necessary to help achieve organizational goals.

Rules

Rules are specific statements that tell employees what they may and may not do: "No smoking in the building"; "Employees are allowed an hour-long lunch break"; "All accidents must be reported immediately." Rules, unlike procedures, do not leave any leeway for employee discretion. Sport organizations will have rules for various aspects of the organization and its processes, products, and services, such as rules that apply to legal protection, public relations protocol, and employee work hours. Some sport organizations even have rules for clients as well as employees. Snow Valley Ski Club in Edmonton, Alberta, Canada, for example, has the following rule: Helmets are mandatory in both the Advanced and Beginner Terrain Parks (Snow Valley, n.d.). Rules such as these perform a public-relations function; they signal to people using the ski area that the management is concerned about public safety. They also serve a legal function in that they set limits on clients to reduce the chances of injury.

Job Descriptions

Each individual in a sport organization has a particular job to perform. Job descriptions provide written details of what a job entails. In this way they regulate employee behavior by making sure that job requirements are carried out and individuals do not impinge on other people's responsibilities. Job descriptions vary in terms of detail; some are very explicit as to responsibilities, while others are far more loosely defined. In general, the higher up the organizational hierarchy one moves, the less specific the job description (JD). Usually the JD outlines who the employee reports to and supervises, and the specific duties of the job. Job descriptions are not solely created for paid employees; volunteer positions in sport organizations often have written detail of the responsibilities. Special Olympics Oregon created a JD for sport-specific Team Oregon coaching roles for the 2018 Special Olympics USA Games held in Seattle. The coaching roles would see individuals reporting to Special Olympics Oregon Sports staff and their responsibilities would include:

Pregames

- Ensure that all athletes within your sport are training and being trained appropriately. This includes cross training during the off-season and communicating with athletes' local coaches.
- Work within the lines of communication set by Team Oregon to provide and receive information. This includes checking email daily for communication from your Sport Manager, reaching out to your assigned athletes on a regular basis, and communicating with family members/guardians with updates.
- Actively prepare for and participate in the Team Oregon Training Camp—a weekend in April 2018, location and exact dates TBD.
- Actively participate in all scheduled meetings and conference calls as needed.
- Provide an open line of communication between yourself and all members of Team Oregon. This may include, but is not limited to, daily emails, conference calls, and mailings to meet the different needs of your athletes and local coaches.
- Assist with compliance of registration and uniform procedures as needed.
- Act as a role model and conduct yourself within the Team Oregon Code of Conduct.

During USA Games (for approximately two weeks in early July 2018)

- Chaperone athletes to ensure the appropriate supervision of all athletes 24 hours a day, 7 days a week. This includes travel times as well on site in Seattle. This could also include responsibilities to athletes outside of your respective sport.
- Work with sport-specific Head Coach to ensure that during USA Games competition rules are being enforced appropriately and those Team Oregon athletes within your sport are being judged fairly.
- To ensure athletes assemble on time for all activities (competitions, special events, etc.).
- To ensure that athletes have the opportunity to participate in activities outside of the sport (Olympic Town, Healthy Athletes, etc.)
- Act as a role model and conduct yourself within the Team Oregon Code of Conduct.
- Assist with chaperoning athletes as necessary to ensure the appropriate supervision of all athletes. This could also include responsibilities outside of your respective sport.

Postgames

- Participate in an evaluation process (Special Olympics Oregon, 2018).

Committee Terms of Reference

Many sport organizations, particularly those that are volunteer-based, operate with a committee structure. Much as JDs provide individuals with direction to perform their job, so terms of reference provide committees with direction as to the areas for which they are responsible. For example, the Sport Development Committee for Swimming Natation Canada (SNC) has as part of its terms of reference the following key duties:

- At the direction of the Board of Directors, research and develop Sport Development Policy. Any policies developed will be forwarded to the SNC Board for approval.
- Review the Strategic Plan of SNC to identify policy needs. Recommend outcome-based program policy additions and revisions to the Board of Directors.
- Monitor the annual planned outcomes or milestones in Athlete Development.
- Through the Chair, enhance the quality of Board discussion on Sport Development Policy matters and facilitate effective decision making in these areas.
- Perform such additional tasks as may be delegated to the Committee by the Board of Directors (Swimming Natation Canada, 2015, p. 1).

The Dangers of Excessive Formalization

As we have seen, formalizing the operation of a sport organization can offer considerable advantages. Nevertheless, excessive amounts of formalization can produce a number of dysfunctional consequences.

Goal Displacement

In some sport organizations adherence to rules and regulations becomes so important to members of the organization that the rules and regulations themselves become more important than the goals they were designed to help achieve. As Merton (1957) explains, instead of being seen as a means, adhering to the rules can become an end in itself.

TIME OUT

John Tarrant, the Ghost Runner: The Tragic Consequences of Goal Displacement

John Tarrant was born in London in 1932. Due to the death of his mother and the absence of his father, who was away in the army, John spent much of his early life in a children's home. In his last two years of school John developed an interest in running, but when he left school at age 15 to work as a plumber's mate, he found little interest in running in the town where he lived. He did, however, meet former Royal Air Force boxing champion Tom Burton, who was keen to promote boxing. Burton approached several local young men in the town to see if they would be interested in earning a little money in a boxing tournament. In 1950 Burton promoted his first tournament; 18-year-old John Tarrant fought four two-minute rounds, for which he was paid £1 (about US$1.30). In just under two years John fought eight bouts in unlicensed rings and won a total of £17 (about US$22) (Jones, 2011). In his eighth fight John was knocked out in 55 seconds; that convinced him that boxing wasn't his sport and, for the sake of his health, he decided to return to his first love, running (Tarrant, 1979).

But when John applied to the Amateur Athletic Association (AAA) he was told that because he had boxed for money he would have to first be reinstated by the Amateur Boxing Association (ABA). John tried, but because he had broken the amateur rules he was turned down by the ABA. Despite repeated letters to both associations, John was unsuccessful in his efforts. But John's desire to run was not easily quashed; on August 12, 1956, he ran his first marathon as an unofficial competitor. Over the next year John gate-crashed several races, and in August 1957 actually received an invitation to gate-crash a 7.5-mile (12 km) race. When he arrived at the race, instead of a number John was given a piece of cardboard with the word *GHOST* on it. John ran many races as the ghost runner. In 1958, after considerable pressure from the media and fellow runners, John was reinstated by the AAA but under the rules of the International Amateur Athletic Federation (IAAF; now World Athletics). The fact that John had broken amateur rules and boxed for money meant that he could not compete internationally for his country. Despite this ruling John continued to run in England and ghosted other races throughout the world. He set world records for the 40- and 100-mile (64 and 161 km) distances and won a number of marathons and many of the classic long-distance races (Jones, 2011). But because he had won £17 boxing, John had broken the rules; rigid adherence to those rules meant that he was never allowed to realize his ambition of competing for his country (Tarrant, 1979).

This condition results in what he calls **goal displacement.**

Minimal Adherence to Rules

The purpose of rules and regulations is to indicate to employees what is considered unacceptable behavior. But they can also be seen as the minimum level of employee performance required by the organization (Gouldner, 1954). Viewing the rules in this manner promotes a **minimal adherence to rules**. If employees are not motivated by their work, the existence of rules can encourage apathy; they come to define minimum standards of behavior rather than unacceptable behavior. When employees perform at the minimum acceptable level, management attempts to control behavior even more.

Bureaupathic Behavior

As a result of the growing gap between managers (who have the right to make rules and regulations) and the specialists (the skilled workers who operate at lower levels of the organization but have the ability to solve specialized problems), superiors come to depend on subordinates. This dependence creates anxieties and insecurities in superiors, who then react with excessive controls, overreliance on rules, and insistence on the rights of their position. This tendency to overemphasize rules and follow them for their own sake is what Thompson (1961) refers to as **bureaupathic behavior**.

Formalization and Complexity

A number of researchers have identified a strong positive correlation between formalization and complexity. In a study by Pugh et al. (1968), overall role specialization correlated highly with overall standardization (0.80) and with overall formalization (0.68). Other studies have produced similar findings (Child, 1972; Donaldson & Warner, 1974), but they apply primarily to situations when employees are performing simple and routine tasks in a repetitive

TIME OUT

The Impact of Professional Practices and Staff on Formalization in VSCs

While the presence of professionally trained employees is usually associated with lower levels of formalization, Thibault et al. (1991) found in a study of VSCs that when professionals were hired in these organizations, formalization increased. They provide two possible explanations for this unexpected phenomenon. First, when the professionals entered the organizations being studied, formalization was low; consequently, the professionals created written rules, procedures, and guidelines to clarify their roles. A second explanation was that increased formalization was initiated by volunteers as a method of retaining control of the organization. Because they were not willing to give up their previously held power to these newly hired professionals, the volunteers imposed formalized behavior controls on them. By instituting formalized policies and guidelines, the volunteer executives were able to ensure that the consistency they had established was maintained in the accomplishment of tasks, that standards were kept uniform throughout the organization, and (most important for them) that they maintained the control of the organization.

Following publication of Thibault et al.'s (1991) study, the formalization of VSCs has increased exponentially. These days, it is becoming institutionalized that VSCs should formalize their operations. It has been argued that the sharp upturn of this expectation was largely as a result of former Olympic swimming coach Paul Hickson being charged in 1993 with sexual assaults of teenage swimmers in his care (Brackenridge, 2001). NGBs wanted to ensure VSCs would operate in a safer, more professional and formalized manner, so they developed new rules and policies. In England, for example, Sport England developed a quality mark framework called *Clubmark*, where clubs have to satisfy certain criteria to demonstrate a safe and sustainable environment. However, although the intentions have been to improve organizations, the challenges and impacts on volunteers need to be considered.

manner. Here, standardized rules are used to control employee behavior. In sport organizations this type of work situation is more frequent at a work site where a particular product, such as a hockey stick, is mass-produced.

In work situations that are less narrowly defined and use professionals or craft workers, the relationship does not hold true (Hage, 1965) because, as we noted earlier, professional training is a surrogate for formalization. Consequently, in situations when relatively unskilled workers perform narrow and repetitive tasks, formalization will be high, but where professional or craft workers are used, formalization will generally be low. However, as the Time Out shows, this general trend may not hold in some situations, such as this one involving VSCs.

Centralization

All sport managers make decisions. The question is: Which managers get to make which decisions and how do they make them? For example, it is unlikely that Mark Parker, the chairman and CEO of Nike, makes decisions about the purchase of paper clips and staples for his office staff; these decisions are delegated to lower-level managers. But in 2007 when Nike acquired Umbro, an association football equipment manufacturer, Parker and other members of Nike's board of directors were intimately involved in the acquisition decision. It turns out that this particular acquisition was not a success story. Parker and the board of directors would have been involved in intense discussion and decision making when they sold Umbro in 2012 for less than half of what they paid in 2008, resulting in a US$357 million loss (Brettman, 2012). We now introduce the third element of organizational structure—centralization—and the surrounding questions about the authority to make decisions and how they are made.

What Is Centralization?

Of all three dimensions of organizational structure, **centralization** is by far the most difficult to explain. It is generally accepted that if decision making takes place at the top of the organization, it is centralized; when decisions are delegated to lower levels, the organization is **decentralized**. But consider the following:

- In a large sport equipment manufacturing company the authority to make decisions has been delegated to department managers. However, the CEO of the company closely monitors these people. Because the CEO can considerably influence the career prospects of the department managers, these managers make their decisions based on what they think the CEO wants.

- In a chain of retail sporting goods stores managers have been told they can run their own show. But policy manuals and frequent communication from the head office detail how inventory must be displayed, how salespeople should deal with clients, and what type of sales promotions the store should use. In addition, a computer information system provides corporate headquarters with up-to-the-minute information in areas such as staff costs, inventory, and sales figures.
- In a national sport organization, the coach has the authority to select the players he or she thinks are the best. However, final ratification of his or her decisions have to be undertaken by the members of the organization's board of directors, many of whom have never seen the players perform together.
- In a state high school athletic association Judy Smith (a fictitious individual) served four terms as president; she then stepped down as president but still remains a member of the organization. Despite the fact that she is no longer on the board, many directors still consult Judy about the decisions they have to make.

These few hypothetical examples serve to illustrate the difficulties of determining the extent to which a sport organization is centralized or decentralized. Researchers who have studied this aspect of organizational structure have had similar difficulties in their work and as a result have produced conflicting results. Probably the most notable debate found in the literature concerns the question of whether bureaucracies are centralized (Aldrich, 1975; Blau & Schoenherr, 1971; Child, 1972; Child, 1975; Donaldson, 1975; Greenwood & Hinings, 1976; Holdaway et al., 1975; Pugh et al., 1968). Researchers have also defined the concept of centralization in a number of ways. Pugh et al. (1968, p. 76) suggest that centralization has to do with the locus of authority to make decisions affecting the organization. This point in the hierarchy was ascertained by asking, "Who was the last person whose assent must be obtained before legitimate action is taken—even if others have subsequently confirmed the decision?" This approach to centralization has been used in several studies of sport organizations (Kikulis et al., 1989; Slack & Hinings, 1987a, 1987b; Thibault et al., 1991). Van de Ven and Ferry (1980) also use the locus of decision-making authority as a central premise of their definition. They suggest, "When most decisions are made hierarchically, an organizational unit is considered to be centralized; a decentralized unit generally implies that the major source of decision making has been delegated by line managers to subordinate personnel" (p. 399). Van de Ven and Ferry (1980) further suggest that any consideration of centralization must take into account the substance of the decision. In a study of Canadian voluntary sport clubs Kikulis et al. (1995) extend this idea and suggest that decisions of less strategic importance are more likely to be decentralized.

Mintzberg (1979) focuses his definition primarily on the issues of who has the power to make decisions and the extent to which this power is concentrated. He notes that "when all power for decision making rests at a single point in the organization—ultimately in the hands of a single individual—we shall call the structure centralized; to the extent that the power is dispersed among many individuals we shall call the structure decentralized" (p. 181). Hage and Aiken (1970, p. 38) propose a similar definition: "Centralization refers to the way in which power is distributed in any organization. By power we mean the capacity of one actor to move another (or other) actors to action. The smaller the proportion of jobs and occupations that participate in decision making and the fewer the decision-making areas in which they are involved, the more centralized the organization." This approach was used by Frisby (1986) in her study of the organizational structure and effectiveness of national sport governing bodies. Mansfield and Killick (2012) looked at the impact of franchising netball in the United Kingdom (with the formation of the UK Netball Superleague) and suggested that there was a shift from a centralized hierarchical business-format franchise to a decentralized empowered franchise system. Brooke (1984) has examined the way the terms *centralization* and *decentralization* have been used in a number of empirical studies, and summarizes the differences in the connotations attached to the two concepts as shown in table 5.2.

Issues of Centralization

The question of determining the extent to which an organization is centralized is complicated by several issues; some have already been alluded to in the examples in the preceding section of this chapter. In this section we explore these issues more fully.

What Role Do Policies and Procedures Play?

While many managers delegate decisions to the lower levels of a sport organization, the amount of discretion an individual is allowed in making a decision may be severely constrained by the existence of policies and procedures. A sport manager can use them to limit the choices available to

Table 5.2 Characteristics of Centralized and Decentralized Structures

Centralized	Decentralized
Decisions made at the top of the organization	Decisions made at the lower levels of the organization
Limited participation by lower-level staff in decision making	Lower-level staff actively participate in decision making
Lower-level staff have restricted choice of decision-making alternatives	Lower-level staff given choices when making decisions
Top-down decision making	Participative decision making
Senior managers control	Senior managers coordinate
Autocratic structure	Democratic structure

Based on Brooke (1984).

lower-level decision makers. Consequently, while the organization gives the appearance of being decentralized, decisions are actually programmed by the policies and procedures, and a high degree of centralization remains (Hall, 1982). For example, if a lifeguard at a swimming pool sees someone in the pool ignoring the established procedures, the person concerned may be asked to leave the pool. While it may appear that the lifeguard is making the decision to remove this individual, the procedure to follow in this situation have been established by management; consequently, the lifeguard has little choice in this situation.

What About Informal Authority?

As we saw in the preceding section the definitions of centralization used by both Pugh et al. (1968) and Van de Ven and Ferry (1980) focused on the authority to make decisions. While not explicit in their definitions, both refer to the formal authority vested in managerial positions. But what about our example involving Judy Smith? Although Judy no longer had any formal authority, she was still able to influence the decision-making process of her state athletic association through informal channels. While most definitions of centralization focus only on formal authority, informal influences on the decision-making process should not be discounted. As another example, informal influences were found to affect formalized policies and procedures in Thurston's (2017) study of NGB policy implementation. Some VSC members (individuals at the point of delivery) transformed policy during its implementation to suit the conditions and constraints of their local environment. The varying interpretations and local-level influence were pivotal in the implementing process and significant for the success (or failure) of implementation. Consequently, some of the decision-making evidently became decentralized. In these instances, it was a NGB's lack of capacity to effectively monitor compliance of their policies and procedures that allowed for decentralized decision making, a contrast to our earlier lifeguard example. For a detailed overview of policy implementation, refer to chapter 7 in this textbook.

Do Management Information Systems Help Maintain Control?

In many sport organizations advanced computer software and information technology (IT) have become an accepted means by which managers obtain information about their organization's operations. Management information systems (MIS) are used to "collect, organize, and distribute data to managers for use in performing their management functions" (Daft, 1992, p. 288). Like policies and procedures, MIS act as a mechanism to control decision making. Even if decision making is delegated to the lower levels of the sport organization, using MIS allows managers to closely monitor these decisions. If lower-level managerial decisions are not in line with the expectations of senior managers, corrective action can quickly be taken. In these situations, although there is an appearance of decentralization, the sport organization remains centralized.

During the past decade, the use of technology within organizations has seen a significant increase, particularly in human resource management (HRM). Marler and Parry (2015) highlight how research suggests that the rapid spread of Internet-based HRM (often referred to as e-HRM) is a disruptive technology that affects the way organizations are structured. Due to the increased ability of a manager to oversee operations and decision-making processes through the use of sophisticated IT systems, the distinction between centralization and decentralization of an organization's structure is becoming increasingly blurred. Many NGBs and NGOs, for example, now use Internet-based management systems to control and monitor conformity by their members regarding various rules, policies, and procedures.

What Effects Do Professionals Have on Centralization?

The presence of professionally trained staff results in a more decentralized organization (Hage, 1980). The work of a professional is generally too complex to be supervised directly by a manager or to be standardized through the use of rules and procedures (Mintzberg, 1979). Consequently, professionals usually make many of the decisions concerning their work. In fact, Lincoln and Zeitz (1980) note that professionals seek participation in decision making, and as the number of professionals in an organization increases, all employees experience increased influence.

Centralized or Decentralized: Which Way Is Best?

The decision to centralize or decentralize the operations of a sport organization is a difficult one that involves a number of trade-offs. Both types of structure have advantages and disadvantages; the advantages claimed for one approach are often the limitations attributed to the other.

The most commonly presented argument for a centralized structure is that it is the best means of achieving coordination and control in a sport organization. It is also argued that top managers should control decision making because they typically have the most experience. They may also own the sport organization or have a large amount of their own capital invested in it. From their position at the top of an organization, senior managers get a broader perspective on its operations and thus can make decisions based on the best interest of the entire organization. They can also see the relative balance between organizational activities, putting them in the best position to make decisions to maintain this balance.

A centralized structure is also economically advantageous. It avoids the duplication of effort or resources that can occur in decentralized organizations. Economic benefits are also realized by centralizing certain activities, such as planning, personnel, and finance, which are common to a number of organizational subunits. If responsibility for these activities were dispersed to subunits, it would be difficult for them to justify such costs from their own budgets.

Given all these advantages, why do organizations decentralize? First, it is often physically impossible for one person to understand all the issues to make the decisions necessary in a sport organization. How can the CEO of a chain of retail sporting goods stores with its corporate headquarters in Chicago make day-to-day decisions about store operations in California? Even with today's sophisticated computer technology, one person simply does not have the time or capacity to absorb all the necessary information to make informed decisions. By decentralizing operations, individuals who best understand the specifics of the situation are given the power to make decisions. Senior managers are then given more freedom to devote their time to broader policy issues that may have longer-term consequences for the sport organization.

Decentralization also allows an organization to respond quickly to changes in local conditions (Mintzberg, 1979). Information does not have to pass through the various hierarchical levels of a sport organization before a decision can be made. Those people closest to the changing situation, because they have more direct access to necessary information, can respond immediately.

A third argument for decentralization is that it can help motivate employees. Involving employees in decisions about their work can help them understand that what they are doing is important to overall organizational goals. This involvement is particularly important in sport organizations staffed by professionals but governed by volunteers. As we noted earlier, professionals expect to be involved in decision making. Only by allowing these people the power to make decisions about their own work can the sport organization expect to retain their services.

A decentralized decision-making system can also motivate lower-level employees. By being involved in decisions about their work they come to understand the rationale behind decisions that affect them. Such involvement can also improve communication among the different hierarchical levels and engender a greater feeling of commitment to the organization. Filley, House, and Kerr (1976), in an examination of 38 studies on participative management, noted that such an approach to decision making is almost always related to improved employee satisfaction, productivity, or both. Miller and Monge (1986) report similar findings.

When a sport organization consists of relatively independent subunits (e.g., franchised retail sporting goods stores), decentralizing decision making to the managers of these units can result in a more effective system of control. The responsibilities of each subunit can be identified, input costs are readily determined, and the consequences of managerial action, as evidenced in performance outcomes, can be easily assessed. The use of profit centers and strategic business units are just two methods of decentralizing authority underpinned by this logic of control.

A final reason for decentralization is that it can act as an aid in management development. Involving lower-level managers in decision making can provide a good training ground for these people if they wish to progress to the more senior levels of the sport organization.

Carlisle (1974, p. 15) identifies 13 factors of importance when "determining the need for a centralized or decentralized structure." These are listed below and followed by a brief explanation:

1. *The basic purpose and goals of the organization.* Some organizations, for example a R&D company like Gore-Tex, because they seek to develop innovative new products, find it necessary to operate with a decentralized structure. In contrast, a gridiron football team requires the control that comes with centralized decision making.
2. *The knowledge and experience of top-level managers.* If senior managers have more knowledge and experience than lower-level employees, the sport organization is likely to be centralized.
3. *The skill, knowledge, and attitudes of subordinates.* If lower-level employees have specialized skills and knowledge (i.e., they are professionally trained) and are seen as being committed to the goals of the sport organization, decision making is likely to be decentralized.
4. *The scale or size of the organizational structure.* As the size of a sport organization increases so does the number and complexity of decisions that have to be made. Consequently, there is a tendency to decentralize.
5. *The geographical dispersion of the structure.* The more geographically dispersed a sport organization, the harder it is to have a centralized structure.
6. *The scientific content or the technology of the tasks being performed.* As organizational tasks become more specialized and sophisticated, decision-making responsibility for these tasks is delegated to the specialists responsible for their execution. Therefore, the organization is decentralized.
7. *The time frame of the decisions to be made.* Decisions that need to be made quickly are usually decentralized.
8. *The significance of the decisions to be made.* Decisions that are of less strategic importance to a sport organization are more likely to be decentralized.
9. *The degree to which subordinates will accept, and are motivated by, the decisions to be made.* Involving subordinates in decision making has been shown to increase their acceptance of that decision. Consequently, when it is beneficial to get subordinates' acceptance of a decision because they will be responsible for its implementation, a decentralized system should be used.
10. *Status of the organization's planning and control systems.* If decision making is highly structured as a result of organizational planning and control systems, sport managers may decentralize because they are able to determine with relative accuracy what the outcome of a particular decision will be.
11. *The status of the organization's information systems.* Decisions are often decentralized if the sport organization has a good MIS because errors can be quickly spotted and corrected.
12. *The conformity and coordination required in the tasks of the organization.* Organizational tasks requiring precise integration are best accomplished using a centralized system.
13. *External factors.* If a sport organization deals with several external organizations, it is best to centralize the point of contact for each organization.

As Carlisle (1974, p. 15) notes, not all factors are "present in all situations, and their significance will vary from situation to situation." He also stresses that it is the "composite interrelationships of the variables" that a manager must consider. All 13 factors will not necessarily always point to the same type of structure; they do, however, provide guidelines for managers in determining the need for a particular type of structure.

Centralization, Formalization, and Complexity

Pertusa-Ortega, Zaragoza-Sáez, and Claver-Cortés (2010) studied how all three common dimensions of a firm's organizational structure influenced "knowledge performance," a term they use for the extent to which internally generated knowledge is used to achieve competitive advantage. The results confirmed that "decentralizing and increasing the complexity of organizational structure have a positive, significant influence on knowledge performance. In the case of formalization, no significant

TIME OUT

Decentralizing ClubCorp

ClubCorp is an organization based in the United States that is often described as a world leader in management of private clubs. It owns or manages more than 200 facilities, including a number of golf and tennis clubs. In 1988 ClubCorp had 400,000 members, an annual revenue of over US$600 million, and a staff of 18,000. Today, there are over 20,000 peak-season employees and more than 430,000 members, and in 2017 ClubCorp expanded its operations into two new states (ClubCorp, n.d.). Much of the growth that ClubCorp has experienced has been attributed to a 1985 decision to decentralize its club operations. Management at ClubCorp determined that it could not realize the aggressive growth goals it had set for itself, nor continue to provide the necessary attention to employees and members, if it maintained its centralized power structure (Symonds, 1989). Control of operations was concentrated at the top of a pyramid-shaped organization. President Bob Johnson felt that with this type of structure they were unable to keep in touch with what was going on at the club level. He felt the company could better serve its members by delegating responsibility for decision making down the organization and having those managers who dealt with customers on a daily basis involved in the management process. Consequently, as part of an overall restructuring, the company was divided into several smaller companies. The club operations were then divided into six regions, each staffed with experts in the areas of management, finance, food and beverage services, human resources, and recreation (Symonds, 1989). Because these regional officers and managers were closer to their customers, they were better able to meet the demands of each club.

relationship with the dependent variable appeared" (p. 318). Albers, Wohlgezogen, and Zajac (2016) used three dimensions of structure in developing a framework for classifying alliances. Their five-parameter framework was based on specialization (a feature of complexity), formalization, and centralization, combined with the structural interface between partners and the structural "intraface" within partners of the alliance organization. They suggested that the framework offered new insights on the structural determinants of key alliance dynamics (e.g., interorganizational coordination, learning, and the development of interpartner trust) and found that "coordination can be enhanced by increasing specialization or formalization, how learning can be stimulated by a stronger intraface or more decentralization, and how trust can be built through a more extensive interface or through less formalization" (p. 607). In other words, what they suggest is that a plethora of ways exist in which the organizational structure of the alliance can be designed to accommodate partners' goals and preferences.

In a sporting context, Cunningham and Rivera's (2001) study aimed to identify the structural arrangements within NCAA athletic departments and used the three dimensions to examine the relationship between structure and effectiveness. Although the aim of the paper was not to examine the relationship between centralization and formalization, results demonstrated that the three structural dimensions of specialization, centralization, and formalization were conceptually distinct and were important for their analysis. They concluded that departments with a decentralized decision-making structure saw improved athletic success. Several other studies have examined the relationship of centralization to the other two structural variables. The findings of these studies are summarized next.

Centralization and Formalization

Research examining the relationship between centralization and formalization has produced conflicting results. Hage (1965, p. 297), in his "axiomatic theory," proposed that "the higher the centralization, the higher the formalization." The Aston Group (Pugh et al., 1968), however, found no strong relationship between formalization and centralization; Hinings and Lee (1971) supported this conclusion. Child (1972) replicated the Aston Group studies using a national sample rather than following the Aston approach of drawing a sample from just a single region of the country. He also focused on autonomous organizations, whereas the Aston studies included subsidiaries and branch units. Child found a strong negative correlation between formalization and centralization; that is, where formalization is high the organization will be decentralized. Donaldson (1975) reran the Aston data removing the nonautonomous organizations and concluded it made no difference to the original Aston correlations. Child (1975) responded that it may be beneficial to look at the difference between the governmental and nongovernmental organizations in the Aston study. Aldrich (1975) then removed the government organizations from the Aston sample and also found that it made little difference to the original correlations. Holdaway et al. (1975) complicated the issue even more with their study of educational organizations, finding a positive relationship between centralization and formalization. In response to these differing results, Greenwood and Hinings (1976) looked at the Aston measures of centralization once again and suggested that rather than treating centralization as a single scale, it should have been viewed as three subscales. In a subsequent attempt to solve this problem, Grinyer and Yasai-Ardekani (1980) used a different set of organizations from the Aston study and found support for the relationship between formalization and decentralized decision making. So, although we have seen contention in the literature about the relationship linking centralization and formalization, it is accepted that "formalization and centralization prevent organizational structures from devolving into chaos" (Sandhu & Kulik, 2018, p. 32). The difficulty for a manager is in finding the right balance between discretion and structure; excessive centralization and formalization limit managerial decision making and reduce a manager's ability to react to the challenges and opportunities they face (Sandhu & Kulik, 2018).

Within the sport management literature there have been very few attempts to examine the relationship between formalization and centralization. Intuitively it would seem logical to suggest that in sport organizations such as an equipment manufacturing plant, where work is relatively narrowly defined and mainly filled by unskilled workers, we would find high levels of formalization and also centralized decision making. In sport organizations, which employs a large number of professionals such as a faculty of kinesiology, there would be decentralized decision making and little formalization, at least in those areas directly related to the professionals' work. However, as the Time Out "The Impact of Professional Practices and Staff on Formalization in VSCs" (in part, detailing the work of Thibault et al. [1991]) shows, there are exceptions to this general trend. Given the diversity of organizations in the sport industry and the lack of research on this relationship in these organizations, it is hard to draw conclusions beyond general trends. There is still considerable scope to develop work of this nature on sport organizations.

Centralization and Complexity

As with centralization and formalization, very few studies have been conducted within the sport management literature that place explicit focus on the relationship between complexity and centralization. The literature from the broader field of management indicates a strong relationship between high complexity and decentralization of decision making (cf. Hage & Aiken, 1967b; Pugh et al., 1968). We could assume a similar relationship in sport organizations; that is, as the complexity of a sport organization increases either through the addition of professionals or the dividing up of work into more narrowly defined tasks, decision making ought to become decentralized. In Mansfield and Killick's (2012, p. 564) study of franchising elite women's sport, using the UK Netball Superleague (NSL) as their case study, they concluded that the "empowered franchise framework of the UK NSL is a decentralised organisational model characterised by different levels of standardisation and specialisation across the franchises." Remember that specialization relates to horizontal differentiation of an organization's structural hierarchy; the more a sport organization is divided up by specialization, the wider the organizational structure, which, in turn, increases its complexity. It is pleasing to see a study with this focus; however, further research on this relationship in a variety of sport organizations could move us beyond these scarce suggestions.

Summary and Conclusions

In this chapter, the three most common dimensions of organizational structure— complexity, formalization, and centralization—were introduced.

Complexity describes the way in which an organization is differentiated. Three types of differentiation are found in a sport organization: horizontal, vertical, and spatial (geographic). Sport organizations are horizontally differentiated when work is broken down into narrow tasks, when professionals or craft workers are employed, and when the organization is departmentalized. Vertical differentiation refers to the number of levels in the organizational hierarchy. A sport organization is spatially differentiated when tasks are separated geographically. Spatial differentiation occurs vertically when different levels of the organization are dispersed geographically, and horizontally when the functions of the organization take place in different locations. The greater the horizontal, vertical, and spatial differentiation, the more complex the sport organization.

One way to manage complexity is formalization, the second dimension of organizational structure examined in this chapter. Formalization refers to the existence of mechanisms such as rules and procedures that govern the operation of a sport organization. Formalization, whose purpose is to

KEY ISSUES FOR SPORT MANAGERS

In order to run your organization efficiently and effectively, you must have a good understanding of two aspects of your organization's structure:

1. *Characteristics.* Examine its goals (purpose, mission), size, life cycle stage (starting, growing, mature, or declining), number and type of organizational members, for-profit versus nonprofit status, local versus national versus international scope.
2. *Environment.* Examine the type of marketplace it is in and the characteristics of competitors. Changes in the environment such as technology, politics, economies, or social structures can have a large impact on sport organizations (Theodoraki & Henry, 1994).

Once you determine these elements, you can begin to set up appropriate levels of complexity, formalization, and centralization. What is even more important is the interrelationship between the structural dimensions themselves and the organization's and the environment's characteristics.

regulate employee behavior, takes place in two ways: through the existence of written documentation such as JDs and through professional training. The former approach is most common when work is narrowly defined, the latter when jobs are broader and require greater discretion.

Centralization, the last dimension of structure and the most problematic of the three to explain, is concerned with who makes decisions in a sport organization. When decisions are made at the top of an organization it is considered centralized; when decisions are made at the lower levels it is decentralized. However, several factors can complicate this general trend: the decisions to be made, the existence of policies and procedures, the use of a MIS, and the presence of professionals.

The structural elements of a sport organization provide a means of describing and comparing these types of organizations. They show how the work of the sport organization is broken down and the means used to integrate the different tasks. To manage a sport organization effectively and efficiently, it is essential that sport managers understand the various elements of structure and their interrelationships.

Review Questions

1. How do levels of complexity vary within and among sport organizations?
2. Why has functional specialization been criticized as dehumanizing, and what steps can be taken to counter its dehumanizing qualities?
3. How does the span of control affect an organization?
4. Do employees prefer working in an organization with a tall or a flat structure?
5. Select a sport organization with which you are familiar. How has it formalized its operations?
6. What is it about centralization that makes it a difficult concept to study? Organization? What influences the way they are made?
7. As the manager of a small racket or tennis club, which decisions would you centralize and which would you decentralize?
8. What are the trade-offs involved in the decision to centralize or decentralize the operations of an organization?

Suggestions for Further Reading

As you will have noticed, much of the key work on organizational structure was carried out in the 1960s and early 1970s. Of particular importance are the works of Hage and Aiken (see especially Hage, 1965; Hage & Aiken, 1967b, 1970), the Aston Group (Hinings & Lee, 1971; Pugh et al., 1968) and Child (1972). Other related and important early works that shaped much of the future work on organizational structure are Lawrence and Lorsch's (1967) *Organization and Environment* and Thompson's (1967) *Organizations in Action.*

Given the nexus between writings on bureaucracy and organizational structure, it is useful for students to read Weber's writing on bureaucracy (Gerth & Mills, 1946). Also important is Richard Hall's work in this area (Hall, 1963, 1968; Hall & Tittle, 1966).

Other works that deal with organizational structure are Henry Mintzberg's (1979) *The Structuring of Organizations*, particularly part II, and Richard Hall's (1982) *Organizations: Structure and Process*. Both provide a comprehensive treatment of the issues along with extensive referencing. Mintzberg's approach is managerial; Hall's is more sociologically informed. Ashkenas, Ulrich, Todd, and Kerr's (2002) book, *The Boundaryless Organization: Breaking the Chains of Organizational Structure*, offers a provocative framework for organizations to break through what they perceive as traditional boundaries—hierarchical (or vertical), functional (or horizontal), external, and geographic—to be more successful in today's business environment. You might notice how some of the boundaries they refer to relate to some of the dimensions of structure we have discussed in this chapter.

Both Slack and Hinings (1987b) and Frisby (1985) have developed frameworks specific to sport, based on the Aston Group's approach to organizational structure. Frisby (1986) uses her framework to examine the relationship of structure to organizational effectiveness in Canadian national sport organizations.

Other sport management studies focusing on structure include Amis and Slack's (1996) look at the size structure relationship within voluntary sport clubs; and Stotlar's (2000) study of the sport and entertainment industry's successful implementation of vertical integration.

Case for Analysis

Restructuring the Australian Olympic Committee

The Australian Olympic Committee (AOC) was formed in 1895 to develop, promote, and protect the principles of Olympism and the Olympic Movement in accordance with the Olympic Charter. In doing so, the AOC aims to encourage participation in sport to promote the benefits of exercise for everyone in Australia. It is the responsibility of the AOC to select, send, and fund Australian teams to the Summer and Winter Olympic Games, Youth Olympic Games, and Regional Games (Australian Olympic Committee, n.d.).

The AOC is a nonprofit organization independent of government and government funding and is composed of 35-member National Sport Federations, which represent each sport on the Olympic program. The AOC is financed through support of sponsors, contributions from the Australian Olympic Foundation (AOF), fundraising, and donations from the state and territory governments to the Olympic Team Appeal (Australian Olympic Committee, n.d.).

In May 2017 Matt Carroll became the new CEO of the AOC, replacing Fiona de Jong, who was CEO for two years. The AOC had grown as an organization and the new CEO wanted to ensure the organization was "fit for purpose." One month prior to the start of Carroll's tenure, an independent review found that the AOC's workplace culture was dysfunctional, with claims of bullying, favoritism, and open hostility (Harris, 2017).

Carroll announced that he planned to create two new executive positions—head of public affairs and communications and head of people and culture)—in line with the 17 recommendations of a review of the AOC's culture, which was completed by the Ethics Centre, an Australian nonprofit organization. The media director role, held by Mike Tancred, was eliminated. Tancred had in fact been on leave for a few months while he defended himself against allegations of bullying, which he was cleared of by an independent committee in August 2017. In spite of that, Tancred left the AOC, with a substantial payout, 18 years after first joining. Carroll denied that the restructuring process was used to engineer Tancred out of the organization. The Ethics Centre's report also found that bullying was not actually an issue at the AOC but recommended that the organization should be restructured and needed a human resources specialist to oversee its athlete programs, including the transition out of sport (Hytner, 2017).

Questions

1. How do you think changes to its structure could improve the AOC's workplace culture?
2. What impact would the creation of two new executive positions have on the structure of the organization and its processes?
3. What would you suggest to the AOC in its restructuring process if you were a consultant in this case?

CHAPTER 6

Design Options in Sport Organizations

Trevor Slack, PhD
Alex Thurston, PhD

Learning Objectives

When you have read this chapter, you should be able to

1. understand the difference between a typology and a taxonomy,
2. explain the five parts of an organization,
3. describe each of the five basic design types,
4. explain the advantages and disadvantages of each design type, and
5. state under what conditions each design type would be found.

Key Concepts

adhocracy
divisionalized form
hybrid structure
ideal types
ideology
machine bureaucracy
matrix design
middle line
operating core
professional bureaucracy
team-based design
simple structure
size
strategic apex
support staff
taxonomy
team-based design
technostructure
typology
virtual network design

Organizing Committees With a Difference

The 2014 XX Commonwealth Games were held in Glasgow, Scotland. The Games brought together over 7,000 athletes from 71 nations and territories within the Commonwealth, participating in 17 sports, to take part in the largest multisport event ever held in Scotland (Scottish Government, 2018a). They were organized by the Glasgow 2014 Organizing Committee (Glasgow 2014 Ltd.) who led the delivery of the Games. Glasgow 2014 Ltd. was a team of approximately 1,000 professionals, drawn from the public and private sectors for their expertise. The Organizing Committee's vision was "to stage an outstanding, athlete centred and sport focused Games of world-class competition which will be celebrated across the Commonwealth, generate enormous pride in Glasgow and Scotland, and leave a lasting legacy" (Gov.uk, 2014). To help achieve the vision, Glasgow 2014 Ltd. enlisted the help from 12,300 Games Time Volunteers known as Clyde-siders (Scottish Government, 2018b). The Games were delivered within budget and achieved the objectives.

In contrast, the 2001 XVIII Alliance London Jeux du Canada Games were held in London, Ontario. The Games saw 3,350 youth athletes competing across roughly 15 summer sports. The Games are held every two years and alternate between a winter and summer sport focus. One of the missions of the Games was to achieve "a legacy of enhanced sport development, bilingualism, facilities and volunteerism" (Doherty, 2009). With the Canada Games, planning and organizing each event is heavily reliant on the contributions of volunteers from the host community. For London, planning volunteer involvement commenced four years prior to the event. As Doherty (2009, p. 191) notes, "Planning volunteers included the Games' Co-Chairs and Vice Chairs only who were responsible for such functional areas as administration and finance, sport services, volunteer services, and the athletes' village. Associate Vice Chairs were responsible for various portfolios within each area and were assisted by sub-committees within each portfolio. Other planning volunteers included Sport Leaders and Venue Leaders who were responsible for the technical aspects of the sport competitions and logistics of the competition venues, respectively." With the hard work and dedication of the thousands of volunteers, the Games were seen as a success and resulted in significant economic benefit to the London area (Canada Games, 2001).

Despite the fact that both organizing committees had the same purpose—to host a major multisport event—they were structured differently. In fact, no two organizations within the sport industry are exactly alike, even though they may operate within the same market. The LA Galaxy management structure is different from that of Liverpool FC. Likewise, the sport and athletic departments at the University of Alberta are organized and run differently than the one at the University of Oregon. Each manager selects and manages various "aspects of structure and culture so an organization can control the activities necessary to achieve its goals" (Jones, 2013, p. 9). This process is known as *organizational design*. (You may notice that the features mentioned in Jones' definition of organizational design are the basis of other chapters in this textbook.)

Although no two sport organizations are exactly identical and follow exactly the same processes, they do have commonly occurring attributes that allow us to classify and compare them. Take, for example, custom bike builder Firefly Bicycles of Boston, Massachusetts, United States, and Triple Play Sports Cards shop; one makes bikes, the other buys and trades sport cards. But if we look closely at their structures, we find they have at least two common features: each is low in complexity and formalization, two concepts discussed in chapter 5. By identifying commonly occurring features of sport organizations we can classify them into what are called *design types* or *configurations*. In many ways, classification is one of the central tasks of organizational theorists (McKelvey, 1982; Miller & Friesen, 1984; Mintzberg, 1979). Once commonalties are identified and sport organizations are classified, it is possible to use the resultant design types for the generation of hypotheses, models, and theories. As Mills and Margulies (1980, p. 255) point out, "Typologies play an important role in theory development because valid typologies provide a general set of principles for scientifically classifying things or events. What one attempts to do in such endeavors is to generate an analytical tool or instrument, not only as a way of reducing data, but more significantly to stimulate thinking." This idea is further emphasized by McKelvey (1975, p. 523):

> Organization science, and especially the application of its findings to the problems of organizations and managers, is not likely to emerge with viable laws and principles until substantial progress is made toward an acceptable taxonomy and classification of organizations. The basic inductive-deductive process of science does not work without the phenomena under investigation being divided into sufficiently homogeneous classes. Managers cannot use the fruits of science unless they first discover which of all the scientific findings apply to their situation.

In this chapter, we first look at the approaches used to understand different configurations of organizations. Second, we review a traditional typology of organizational design, as developed by Mintzberg (1979), and offer examples of how each can be found within the sport industry. An explanation of the advantages and disadvantages of each design and a description of the conditions under which it is most likely to be found is provided. Finally, a brief section offers some contemporary perspectives on organizational design before the key issues for managers and the case for analysis conclude the chapter.

Typologies and Taxonomies

Two main approaches can be used to uncover design types (sometimes called *configurations* or *architecture* in the literature). The first of these is the creation of typologies; the second is the development of taxonomies.

> Typologies are, in a sense, of an a priori nature; they are generated mentally—not by any replicable empirical analysis—independent of experience and represent concepts. Taxonomies are derived from multivariate analyses of empirical data and measurable characteristics on organizations. Typically, organizations or aspects of their structure, strategies, environments, and processes are described along a number of variables. Attempts are then made to identify natural clusters in the data, and these clusters, rather than any a priori conceptions, serve as the basis for the configurations (Miller & Friesen, 1984, pp. 31-32, emphasis in original).

In the next few pages, we will take a brief look at the main typologies and taxonomies found in the management literature, complemented with a discussion of how they have been developed for classifying sport organizations.

Typologies

A **typology** is a theory-driven classification system based on characterizing things of a certain category or type. The first attempt to classify organizations into types can be found in Weber's (1947) writings on social domination and the attendant patrimonial, feudal, and bureaucratic forms of organization. Weber demonstrated how each type of organization "could be characterized by a number of mutually complementary or at least simultaneously occurring attributes" (Miller & Friesen, 1984, p. 32). In the 1950s Parsons (1956) followed Weber and created a typology based on the goals or functions of the organization. He identified organizations that had economic goals, political goals, integrative functions, or pattern maintenance functions. As Carper and Snizek (1980, p. 66) note, "Parsons' approach represents an early and limited form of systems theory thinking in that it attempts to tie the organization to the environment through the activities that the former performs for the latter."

Burns and Stalker (1961) suggested two types of organizational design: organic and mechanistic. The *organic* type of organization was found in changing conditions where new and unfamiliar problems had to be dealt with; it contained no rigid control systems, and employees showed high levels of commitment to the organization. In contrast, *mechanistic* organizations were found in stable conditions; tasks were narrowly defined, and there was a clear hierarchy of control, insistence on loyalty to the organization, and obedience to superiors. This form of organization is very much like Weber's legal-rational bureaucracy. Organic and mechanistic types of design were viewed as polar opposites, with organizations described according to their position on a continuum between them.

More recently, Albers, Wohlgezogen, and Zajac (2016) proposed a new organizational design typology of strategic alliance structures. Based on the classic organizational design works of Galbraith (1973) and Mintzberg (1979), this framework comprises of five dimensions: (1) *specialization* (level of involvement of organizational alliance members who focus exclusively on alliance management tasks); (2) *formalization* (codification and standardization of alliance activities); (3) *centralization* (allocation of decision-making authority in the alliance or partnership); and, the (4) *interface* and

(5) *intraface* dimensions (capturing which organizational members are involved in the alliance and how they are connected to each other within and across partnering organizations) (p. 584). They suggest that their typology facilitates "a deeper understanding of strategic alliance governance and management" (p. 607).

Blau and Scott (1962) produced a typology based on the principle of *cui bono*, or "who benefits," from the organization. Four types of structure were identified: (1) mutual benefit organizations, where the prime beneficiary is the membership; (2) business concerns, where the prime beneficiary is the owner(s) of the business; (3) service organizations, where the clients benefit; and (4) commonweal organizations, whose prime beneficiary is the public at large. Chelladurai (1987) has suggested that the prime beneficiary approach could be used in conjunction with the strategic constituents' approach to evaluate the effectiveness of sport organizations.

Several typologies have focused on the organization's technology as the criterion variable for classification. Woodward (1958, 1965) distinguished organizations as to whether they used unit or small-batch, large-batch or mass, or continuous-process types of technology. Perrow (1967, 1970) focused on whether technology was craft, routine, nonroutine, or engineering; Thompson (1967) used core technologies, which he described as either long-linked, mediated, or intensive, as his basis for classification. (See chapter 21 for more details on the work of Woodward, Perrow, and Thompson.)

Another typology is Gordon and Babchuk's (1959) tripartite classification: instrumental, expressive, instrumental-expressive. Specifically developed to classify voluntary organizations, it has been used to examine voluntary sport organizations. Instrumental organizations are designed "to maintain or create some normative condition or change" (Gordon & Babchuk, 1959, p. 25). Expressive organizations are designed to satisfy the interests of their members. Instrumental-expressive organizations show elements of both functions. In a study of the members of badminton and judo clubs, Jacoby (1965) found a very high expressive and very low instrumental orientation.

Early attempts to create typologies specifically related to sport organizations are those developed by Chelladurai (1985, 1992). In his 1985 book *Sport Management: Macro Perspectives*, he proposed a 12-cell classification system for sport and physical activity organizations. The classification was based on three dimensions: (1) whether the organization was profit-oriented or nonprofit; (2) whether it provided professional or consumer services; and (3) whether it was part of the public, private, or third sector. "Third sector" indicates an organization (e.g., some universities) is "partly or wholly funded by tax moneys and managed privately" (Chelladurai, 1992, p. 39).

Chelladurai (1985) makes no attempt to categorize sport organizations into the various cells of his model; some of the cells may actually describe few if any sport organizations. For example, it may be difficult to find public-sector sport organizations that explicitly aim to make a profit and offer consumer services. Public-sector organizations are generally not concerned with making a profit per se and usually provide professional (not consumer) services. Notwithstanding these shortcomings, which Chelladurai (1985) acknowledges when he suggests his framework requires extensive research, this classification scheme does provide a useful starting point for further discussion.

In extending his work on classification, Chelladurai (1992) does not focus on sport organizations but on the services they provide. Using two dimensions, "the type and extent of employee involvement in the production of services" and "client motives for participation in sport and physical activity," (p. 38) he produces six classes of sport and physical activity services: consumer pleasure, consumer health and fitness, human skills, human excellence, human sustenance, and human curative. Chelladurai (1992) goes on to describe each of these classes and discuss their managerial implications.

More recently, Chappelet and Parent (2015, p. 2) proposed a typology for sport events in which they placed focus on the nature of the event rather than the size. The typology is based on three dimensions:

1. *For profit-oriented or nonprofit.* Many events are now no longer organized by nonprofit sport associations. Rather, specialist firms, new important stakeholders in sport that need to make a profit in order to survive, are often appointed for the event. The example events suggested for this dimension are the Tour de France (profit-oriented) and the Olympic Games (nonprofit).
2. *Mono-sport or multisport.* This dimension determines what infrastructure and facilities are required to host the event. Event examples include the FIFA Association Football World Cup (mono-sport) and the Paralympic Games (multisport).
3. *A one-off or recurring event.* This dimension determines whether the event will be unique to the city or region, or if the event is always held in the same place. The examples pro-

vided for this dimension are a European championship, which moves to a new country every year, every two years, or every four years (one-off event) and the Royal Henley (rowing) regatta that is always at Henley-on-Thames (recurring event).

Winand, Vos, Zintz, and Scheerder (2013) developed an explorative typology of sport federations based on attitudes and perceptions of determinants of innovation and innovation capacity. Subsequently, the same group of Winand, Scheerder, Vos, and Zintz (2016) went on to examine the nonprofit sport sector, producing a typology of service innovation within regional sport federations.

It is apparent that organizations, including sport organizations, can be classified in a number of ways. Although fewer typologies have been created in sport literature than in general management literature, sport organizations can obviously be typed in many of the more general classification schema. Sport organizations, for example, could be classified on the organic or mechanistic continuum (as proposed by Burns & Stalker, 1961) or on the basis of "who benefits." Byers, Slack, and Parent (2012) suggest that *categorization* of commonly utilized terms within sport management (e.g., type of volunteer, job roles within organizations, type of club, type of fan) are more prevalent in the literature, compared with explicit typology and taxonomy analysis.

Carper and Snizek (1980, p. 70) have criticized the large number of typologies produced, suggesting that "there are virtually as many different ways to classify organizations as there are people who want to classify them." They suggest that the diversity of conceptual schemas that have been developed indicates a lack of agreement as to which variables should be used in constructing a typology. Most existing typologies have limited explanatory power because they are based on only one or two variables. Miller and Friesen (1984) support the need to focus on a broad array of variables when constructing typologies. They argue (1984, p. 33) that narrowly focused typologies "are not sufficiently encompassing to serve as a basis for reliable prediction or prescription." One typology that uses a large number and wide range of variables was developed by Mintzberg (1979). Based on an extensive survey of the literature, Mintzberg's classification scheme attempts to synthesize many of the research findings of the past two decades to produce five design types (Miller & Friesen, 1984). These design types are examined in detail a little later in this chapter and show how they apply to sport organizations.

Taxonomies

A **taxonomy** is an empirically constructed classification that identifies "clustering among organizational variables that is statistically significant and predictively useful and that reduces the variety of organizations to a small number of richly defined types" (Miller & Friesen, 1984, p. 34). McKelvey (1978, 1982) has advocated the development of taxonomies to understand a number of organizational phenomena such as environmental adaptation, structural design, and change. Nevertheless, there have been considerably fewer attempts to construct taxonomies than to construct typologies. The first empirical taxonomy of organizations was developed by Haas, Hall, and Johnson (1966). Using a sample of 75 organizations they produced 10 design types; the number of organizations found in each design type ranged from 2 to 30. Much of their work deals with the methods they used to generate their taxonomy; there is no attempt to elaborate on the nature of the design types they established or to replicate their approach on a different set of organizations to see if the same type of designs emerge.

Pugh, Hickson, and Hinings (1969), part of the Aston Group, developed a taxonomy based on structural data obtained from 52 relatively large (over 250 employees) organizations. Their analysis produced seven different types of bureaucratic structure, which led them to conclude (1969, p. 115) that the Weberian notion of a single bureaucratic type "is no longer useful, since bureaucracy takes different forms in different settings."

The most sophisticated use of taxonomy is found in the work of Miller and Friesen (1984). Using a sample of 81 organizations described along 31 variables of strategy, structure, information processing, and environment, they produced 10 common organizational design types, or what they call *archetypes*. Identifying six of these types as successful and four as unsuccessful, Miller and Friesen argue that the notion of taxonomy can be extended to study organizational transitions between these archetypes. Based on 24 variables that described changes in such areas as strategy making, structure, and environment for each transition, nine "transition archetypes" were produced. Thus, they argue that the taxonomic approach can identify common paths in organizational evolution.

Sport literature contains very few instances of using a taxonomic approach to identify organizational design types. Publications emanate from the work of Slack and Hinings and their students. Using data on the structural arrangements of 36 Canadian national-level sport organizations Hinings and Slack

(1987) developed 11 scales that addressed three aspects of organizational structure: specialization, standardization, and centralization of decision making. After a factor analysis, two factors were produced: one concerned with the extent of professional structuring in these organizations, and the other with volunteer structuring. By dividing the scores of the 36 organizations at the mean on each factor, Hinings and Slack produced nine organizational design types and were able to demonstrate the extent to which these national sport organizations (NSOs) exhibited characteristics of professional bureaucratic structuring. Sport Canada, the federal government agency that provided a large portion of the NSOs' funding, has been pushing them toward such a design.

In a somewhat similar study Kikulis, Slack, Hinings, and Zimmermann (1989) created a taxonomy using data from 59 provincial-level sport organizations. Using Ward's method of hierarchical agglomerative clustering, Kikulis et al. produced eight structural design types, ranging from sport organizations that were "implicitly structured" to those that, within this institutional sphere, showed high levels of professional bureaucratic structuring. Kikulis et al. argue the merits of their study in demonstrating the variation in structural design in these sport organizations and as a basis for understanding a range of organizational phenomena. They note (1989, p. 148) that once structural designs are identified, it is possible "to conduct in-depth studies of representative organizations and develop qualitative data bases to provide us with richer insights into the internal dynamics, formative processes, and performance implications of each structural design."

Building on this work, Theodoraki and Henry (1994) adopted a quantitative approach (for the first stage of their research), embracing a similar methodology to that of Kikulis et al. (1989), and utilizing Mintzberg's (1979) five ideal structural design configurations (a typology) of organizations to examine 34 English national governing bodies (NGBs). They proposed an organizational taxonomy to help identify six design configurations—machine bureaucracies, professional bureaucracies, professionalized simple structures, typical simple structures, simple bureaucracies, and specialized simple structure—to develop an understanding of the organizational structures and strategic management styles adopted by the NGBs. More recently, a small number of academics in the field of sport management have offered the use of taxonomies but not to help with the identification of design types (cf. Crompton, 2004, who looked at major league sports facilities benefits; Lorgnier & Su, 2014, who examined sport tourism coopetition strategies).

A final study worthy of mention is Arnold and Fletcher's (2012) taxonomic classification of organizational stressors encountered by sport performers. They suggest that organizational stressors can be classified under four main categories: leadership and personnel issues, cultural and team issues, logistical and environmental issues, and performance and personal issues. Although this study was published in the *Journal of Sport & Exercise Psychology*, you might notice that their taxonomy corresponds to concepts covered in several chapters throughout this textbook. And that's important: Drawing from (sport-related) academic literature from other disciplines will enable you to become a better sport manager. Adopting an interdisciplinary approach allows us to develop a more holistic understanding of this ever-expanding field of sport management. (This was one of the factors as to why a new chapter focusing on mental health has been included in this 3rd edition.) In sum, clearly, there is still considerable opportunity for greater application of typology and taxonomy classifications to help sport managers better understand organization design types and configurations.

Mintzberg's Configurations

One of the most sophisticated and frequently used of all organizational typologies is the one developed by Henry Mintzberg (1979). Mintzberg uses *design parameters* (e.g., specialization, formalization of positions, training of members, and the nature of decentralization, as discussed in chapter 5) combined with *contingency factors* (e.g., age, size, and environment) to produce five design types, or what he calls *configurations*: simple structure, machine bureaucracy, professional bureaucracy, divisionalized form, and adhocracy. Essentially, Mintzberg argued that there are five parts of an organization and five methods by which coordination is achieved.

Parts of the Organization

The five parts of the organization are shown graphically in figure 6.1 and explained here.

- ***Operating core***: This is where we find those employees responsible for the basic work necessary for producing the organization's products or services. At Huffy this is where we find the people who are involved in assembling the bikes. In a sport medicine clinic, the doctors and physiotherapists who treat the patients constitute the operating core.

- ***Strategic apex***: This is where we find the senior managers (e.g., CEO, director, president) of the sport organization.
- ***Middle line***: These are the managers who join the operating core to the strategic apex. In a government agency concerned with sport, for example, these people would be the middle managers (e.g., regional or provincial managers) who provide the link between staff and the senior bureaucrats.
- ***Technostructure***: This is where we find the analysts responsible for designing the systems that standardize work processes and outputs in a sport organization. In an organization that produces sport equipment, the technostructure would be made up of people such as the industrial engineers, who standardize the work process, and the planners and accountants, who standardize the organization's output.
- ***The support staff***: These are the people who provide support to the sport organization. For example, in a competitive gymnastics club, the support staff includes everyone from the athletic therapists and sport psychologists to the staff who take care of the equipment.

In sport literature, Relvas, Littlewood, Nesti, Gilbourne, and Richardson (2010, p. 175) examined organizational structures within European professional association football clubs. As part of their findings, they identified and related Mintzberg's (1979) five key parts of an organization to each of the clubs. These were: strategic apex = chief executive and chairman; middle line = sports director and the coaches; operating core = the players; and the technostructure and support staff = all the elements that work within the club and help the daily practice.

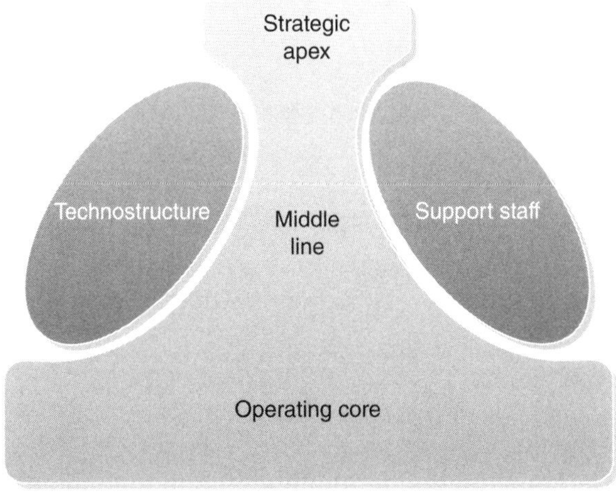

Figure 6.1 Five basic parts of organizations.

MINTZBERG, HENRY, STRUCTURING OF ORGANIZATIONS, 1ST Ed., ©1979. Reprinted by permission of Pearson Education, Inc., New York, New York.

While this chapter places its focus on Mintzberg's original ideas of a configurational approach—which have been utilized extensively in mainstream management literature—Mintzberg (2003) has more recently suggested a sixth part of an organization: an organization's **ideology**. This additional component consists of the traditions, norms, values, and beliefs that unite the organization in pursuit of a common goal, which is often referred to as *organizational culture* (Amis & Slack, 2016, p. 318). (For more information about the concept of culture and how it affects sport organizations, refer to chapter 17 in this textbook.) As Burton, Obel, and Håkonsson (2015, p. 69) note, "[A] poor choice of configuration leads to opportunity losses which can be a threat to the organization's short-term efficiency and effectiveness, as well as its long-term viability." Hence, it is crucial that managers can effectively coordinate and accomplish organizational tasks.

Methods of Coordination

Mintzberg (1979) describes the five ways in which coordination can be achieved in an organization: direct supervision, standardization of work processes, standardization of outputs, standardization of skills, and mutual adjustment. Each is explained here as they may apply to a sport organization.

- *Direct supervision*: Here one individual in the sport organization gives orders to the others to coordinate their work.
- *Standardization of work processes*: This method is used when the way in which work is to be carried out is determined by someone else. For example, the way trainers are produced in a company like Nike (as we saw in the previous chapter) is determined by the people who control the computerized design and pattern-making systems, not by the people who actually produce the jackets.
- *Standardization of outputs*: This method is used when the results of the work (i.e., the type of product or performance to be achieved) are specified. For example, output is standardized when the corporate headquarters of a sporting goods company specifies to its divisions that it wants them to increase sales by 10 percent

in the upcoming year but leaves the method of achieving this increase up to the divisional managers.

- *Standardization of skills*: Skills are standardized through programs designed to ensure the coordination and control of the work processes. Sport medicine clinics employ doctors just for this purpose. When an injured athlete enters the clinic, the doctor has been trained to assess the injury and the treatment required.
- *Mutual adjustment*: Here the coordination of work is achieved through informal communication. A group of sport management professors who plan a training workshop for local entrepreneurs in the sport industry would probably adopt this approach to coordination.

Design Types

In each of the design types (configurations) one part of the organization and one method of coordination dominates. Table 6.1 provides an overview of Mintzberg's (1984) suggested organizational and coordination combination for each design type, as well as the major reason for each combination.

We find examples of each of these design types or configurations in the sport industry. Each has strengths and weaknesses and works best under certain conditions. In the remainder of this chapter we look in detail at each design type, assess its advantages and disadvantages, and discuss when it is the most appropriate design for sport managers to use.

The Simple Structure

What do sport organizations such as a ski rental shop, the local water polo club, and a small voluntary group such as Luge Canada have in common? They all exhibit the characteristics of a simple structure.

As its name implies, the most evident characteristic of this design type is its simplicity. Typically, the **simple structure** has little or no technostructure, few support staff, no real middle line (hence no lengthy managerial hierarchy), and a loose division of labor (Mintzberg, 1979). The organization has low levels of formalization and is unlikely to rely heavily on planning and training devices. The most important parts of this organizational design are the strategic apex and the operating core. The structure is a relatively flat one and everyone reports to the strategic apex, which is usually one individual in whom power is concentrated. Coordination is achieved through direct supervision. Decision making is informal, with all important decisions being made by the CEO, who, because of proximity to the operating core, is easily able to obtain any necessary information and act accordingly.

Advantages and Disadvantages

The main advantage of the simple structure is its flexibility. Because the person at the strategic apex is in direct contact with the operating core, communication is easily achieved. Information flows directly to the person in charge, so decisions can be made quickly. The goals of the sport orga-

Table 6.1 Organizational and Coordination Tendencies in Mintzberg's Design Types

Design type	Part of the organization	Method of coordination	Reason
Simple structure	Strategic apex	Direct supervision	Strategic apex wants tight control
Machine bureaucracy	Technostructure	Standardization (especially work process)	Agrees to decentralize decisions to the technostructure
Professional bureaucracy	Operating core	Standardization of skills	Operating core wants autonomy
Divisionalized form	Middle line	Standardization of outputs	Middle line wants semi-autonomy
Adhocracy	Support staff	Mutual adjustment	Support staff wants decentralization to increase group work (collaboration)

Based on information in Mintzberg (1984).

nization are easily communicated to employees, who are able to see how their efforts contribute to achieving these goals. Since everyone reports to the strategic apex, lines of accountability are clear and straightforward. Also, decisions are made by the strategic apex with extensive knowledge of what is going on below (Mintzberg, 1979). Many people enjoy working in a simple structure because they are unencumbered by bureaucratic controls; a sense of mission often pervades this type of sport organization.

The main disadvantage of the simple structure is that it is useful only for smaller sport organizations. As a sport organization grows and its environment becomes more complex, the simple structure design type is no longer appropriate. The complexities of a large sport organization cannot be handled by a simple structure. There is also the possibility that the person who has the power to make changes, the CEO, may resist growth because it will mean increased formalization and possibly a reduction of this individual's power. The centralization of power at the top of the simple structure is in fact a double-edged sword. While it facilitates decision making, it can lead to the CEO's unwillingness to give up responsibility to others and resentment on the part of employees that one person "calls all the shots." Strategic issues may be pushed to the side if the CEO gets too involved with operational issues (Mintzberg, 1979). Finally, a simple structure is a risky design type in that, as Mintzberg (1979, p. 312) puts it, "one heart attack can literally wipe out the organization's prime coordinating mechanism." In fact, numerous NGBs of sport in England are all too aware of Mintzberg's heart attack analogy. For example, Thurston (2017, p. 266) found that England Boxing actively discourages a "one-man band" club setup due to the concern and danger of a club collapsing should anything happen to that individual.

Where Do We Find the Simple Structure?

The most common place to find a simple structure is in a sport organization that is small, in its formative years, or entrepreneurial in nature. Simple structures are also used when a sport organization's environment is simple and dynamic, when larger sport organizations face a hostile environment, and when CEOs have a high need for power or power is thrust upon them.

In a small sport organization coordination is achieved through direct supervision. It is relatively easy for one person to oversee the organization's operations and to communicate informally with employees. Many different types of smaller organizations within the sport industry have adopted the simple structure for these reasons. Figure 6.2 shows the structure of Alfred's Sports Shop, a small family-owned retail sporting goods store in New Jersey, that operates with a simple structure.

A sport organization's stage of development, as well as its size, can influence its design. Most organizations exhibit characteristics of a simple

TIME OUT

The Running Room: From Simple Structure to International Success

John Stanton started running in 1981 in an effort to get in shape. As he improved, he needed better running shoes. However, he found that the staff who typically worked on commission in sporting goods stores not only knew little about running shoes but also tried to sell the most expensive pair instead of the best pair. There was also a lack of quality shoes, even in large sporting goods stores, so Stanton decided to solve this problem.

In 1984 Stanton opened a one-room store in a renovated living room of an old house in Edmonton, Alberta. He called it "Running Room." Employees were called *team members*, and Stanton wanted the store to be run by runners for runners. The store became known for product innovation, quality service, quality products, and sport knowledge. Staff and customers are invited to give feedback about the products, providing a proven track record for products sold. The Running Room created its own label to provide customers with products that were stylish and functional, composed of innovative fabric, and affordable.

By 2018, the Running Room had more than 100 locations in Canada and the United States, with over 1,200 team members. The store offers clinics and training programs on walking, running, marathons, and personal training, and over 800,000 individuals have graduated from these clinics to date. A Running Room Running Club—no membership fees required—allows club members to work out in a social context twice a week and have access to coaching to improve their techniques and training methods. The concept has been so successful that Stanton has decided to open a similar store, the Walking Room, dedicated to gear for walkers (Running Room, n.d.).

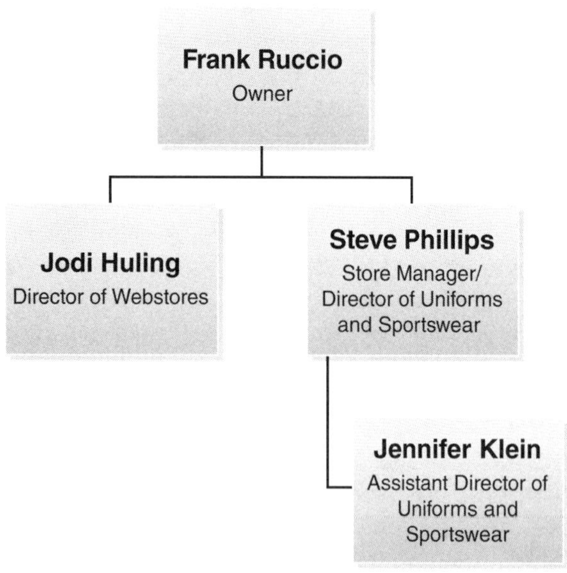

Figure 6.2 Alfred's Sports Shop: A simple structure.
Based on information from Alfred's Sports Shop (n.d.).

structure in their formative years, but some may maintain this design type beyond this stage of their development (Mintzberg, 1979). The Time Out "The Running Room: From Simple Structure to International Success" illustrates how, in its early days, the Running Room operated with a simple structure.

Entrepreneurial organizations within the sport industry often adopt the simple structure design because it allows them to be aggressive and innovative within simple and dynamic environments. This mirrors the entrepreneur's tendency to have an autocratic and charismatic leadership style (Mintzberg, 1979). Successful entrepreneurial companies often do not maintain the simple structure type of design for any length of time; as they grow, the design is replaced with a different set of structural arrangements. As we saw in chapter 1 with the Under Armour opening scenario, successful entrepreneurial sport organizations tend to operate with a simple structure in the formative years.

Even for other types of companies a simple and dynamic environment is best served by a simple structure. The simple environment is easily scanned by the person at the strategic apex, and the organic operating core found in a simple structure means a quick reaction to changes in the environment.

A crisis situation may force larger sport organizations to adopt the characteristics of a simple structure. When a sport organization's environment is hostile, the CEO may tend to centralize power and reduce bureaucratic controls to respond to the crisis. For example, in 1984 when Nike was experiencing financial problems and a serious challenge from Reebok, Philip Knight took back the presidency of Nike, which he had turned over to Bob Woodell about a year earlier.

Finally, the need for power may also precipitate the adoption of a simple structure. Given the concentration of power at the strategic apex and the lack of formalization or any type of technostructure, this type of design is ideal for those CEOs who seek to maintain power. Alternatively, this design may be found when CEOs do not necessarily seek power, but members bestow it on them. Mintzberg (1979) refers respectively to these variants of the simple structure as autocratic and charismatic organizations.

The Machine Bureaucracy

When a sport organization produces a standard output such as a hockey stick, when there is a requirement for fairness and public accountability (such as we find in a government agency), and when consistency is required in performing relatively simple tasks such as on a hockey team, the most appropriate structure to use is a machine bureaucracy. Like Weber's legal-rational bureaucracy, the **machine bureaucracy** is characterized by high levels of standardization, formalized communication procedures, the functional grouping of tasks, routine operating procedures, a clear delineation between line and staff relationships, and a centralized hierarchy of authority. In this type of design, the technostructure is the key part of the organization and contains the analysts, such as the quality control engineers, planners, and designers who standardize the work to be performed. Although their role is primarily advisory, they exercise considerable informal power because they structure everyone else's work (Mintzberg, 1979).

Advantages and Disadvantages

The main advantage of the machine bureaucracy is its efficiency because it allows "simple, repetitive tasks [to] be performed precisely and consistently by human beings" (Mintzberg, 1979, p. 333). The grouping of specialist tasks in a machine bureaucracy results in certain economies of scale and less duplication of activities. In some cases, particularly those sport organizations involved in mass production, the high levels of standardization found in a machine bureaucracy mean less qualified, and hence cheaper, employees can be used. In government agencies that use what Mintzberg (1979) calls a *public machine bureaucracy design*, the use of low-cost labor is less pronounced. That the lines of authority are clearly outlined in a machine bureaucracy means workers know their responsibilities. Plus, centralized control means that outside of the strategic apex, and to a certain extent the technostructure where the work is standardized, there is little need for creative thinking.

The three disadvantages of a machine bureaucracy identified by Mintzberg (1979) are human problems, coordinating problems, and adaptation problems at the strategic apex. Many of the human problems emanate from the narrow specialization of work found in this design type; often dehumanizing for employees, it stifles creative talents and produces feelings of alienation, making coordination difficult. Such divisions can also promote empire building within the functional areas, which in turn creates conflicts that impede communication and coordination.

Finally, while the machine bureaucracy works well in stable environments, it does not respond well to change. As Mintzberg (1979) points out, change generates nonroutine problems. When these become frequent, the strategic apex can experience work overload because these problems are passed up the hierarchy. Quick responses are difficult since managers are not in direct contact with the problem areas.

Where Do We Find the Machine Bureaucracy?

The machine bureaucracy is found in simple and stable environments. Sport organizations that adopt this design type are usually relatively large, with routine technologies in which work is easily standardized. In the sport industry companies like Head and Dunlop, which mass-produce equipment, would probably operate with this type of design. So, too, would government agencies concerned with sport and related activities, such as the Oregon Parks and Recreation Department; the Province of Newfoundland's Department of Tourism, Culture, Industry and Innovation; and Vermont's Department of Forests, Parks, and Recreation. In these organizations the treatment of clients and the hiring and promotion of employees must be seen as fair. The machine bureaucracy, with its highly regulated systems, achieves this perception best. Guttmann (1978) suggests that many of the major governing bodies of sport such as the Marylebone Cricket Club (MCC), the International Association of Athletic Federations (IAAF; now World Athletics), and the Fédération Internationale de Football Association (FIFA) exhibit a number of the characteristics of a machine bureaucracy. Amis and Slack (2016) suggest that the Rugby Football Union (RFU), England's governing body for the union code of rugby, corresponds to a machine bureaucracy design because the organization has a range of departments—including commercial; legal; finance; governance; human resources; digital, marketing, and communications; rugby development; and, professional rugby—which are all based at Twickenham Stadium, the home of England rugby.

Even a baseball team or a gridiron football team may operate as machine bureaucracies. George Allen, a former general manager of the Washington Redskins, exemplified this type of thinking when he suggested this analogy:

> A football team is a lot like a machine. It's made up of parts. I like to think of it as a Cadillac. A Cadillac's a pretty good car. All the refined parts working together make the team. If one part doesn't work, one player pulling against you and not doing his job, the whole machine fails (Terkel, 1972, p. 508).

The owner of the team represents the strategic apex, the players (the operating core), and the general manager (the middle line). The support staff is made up of team doctors, athletic therapists, strength coaches, and equipment personnel. The technostructure consists of coaches, assistant coaches, and scouts who standardize the work processes of the players in the operating core.

The Divisionalized Form

Sport organizations such as WarnerMedia, Disney Corporation, Red Bull, Brunswick Corporation, Coleman Company Inc., and Wembley National Stadium Ltd. all use some type of **divisionalized form**, effectively a set of relatively autonomous organizations coordinated by a central corporate headquarters. In some of the examples used here, not all of the company's divisions operate in the sport industry. Brunswick, for example, is a major manufacturer of power boats and is heavily involved in billiards tables and equipment, but also produces defense materials, aerospace components, and industrial products. Wembley National Stadium Ltd., in addition to staging sport events, has interests in areas such as catering and the entertainment industry (e.g., hosting music concerts). One of the characteristics of a divisionalized form is, in fact, that it operates in a diversified market.

The key part of the design is the middle line, the managers who head the various divisions and are usually given control over the strategic and operating decisions of their respective divisions. Corporate headquarters provide centralized support in areas such as finance, personnel, and legal matters. They also exercise some degree of control over divisions by monitoring and evaluating outcomes such as profit, market share, and sales growth. Essentially, division managers are given varying degrees of autonomy to operate as they see fit, provided they conform to corporate guidelines. The divisions that constitute the overall structure may exhibit a variety of designs. But the fact that corporate headquarters retains control by monitoring performance, a procedure that requires clearly defined standards, means that the divisionalized form is better suited to an organization that has machine bureaucracy–structured divisions (Mintzberg, 1979).

Advantages and Disadvantages

One of the main advantages of the divisionalized form is that its divisions are relatively autonomous. Their managers have operational and strategic control for markets falling under their responsibility (Mintzberg, 1979). This means that corporate staff does not concern itself with day-to-day operational issues and thus can pay more attention to long-term strategic planning for the entire organization. Using a divisionalized form means that corporate headquarters can allocate its financial resources more efficiently. If needed, capital can be extracted from one division and allocated to another. This type of structure also has been seen as a good training ground for senior managers. Division managers essentially run a business within a business, so they are able to gain experience in all areas. The divisionalized form is advantageous in that it allows a company to spread its risk (Mintzberg, 1979). Because it operates in diversified markets, economic fluctuations are dealt with more easily; if one part of the organization does not perform up to required expectations it can be closed down or sold off with relatively little impact on other operations.

As might be expected, the divisionalized form is not without its faults. Some of its main disadvantages revolve around the relationship among divisions as well as between divisions and corporate headquarters. Conflict may occur among divisions when they compete in similar product markets or when they vie for corporate resources. Conflict is also created when a division's goals run counter to corporate goals or when the constraints the corporation imposes on a division are seen as overly restrictive.

The existence of several divisions within the overall structure can lead to problems of coordination and control. Control in this type of design is usually achieved through quantitative performance measures, which can in turn lead to an emphasis on economic indicators and a tendency to ignore the social consequences of the division's operations. For more information about the concept of organizational control, please refer to chapter 10 of this book.

Where Do We Find the Divisionalized Form?

The divisionalized form is most frequently found in organizations operating in diversified markets. As Mintzberg (1979, p. 393) points out, this type of structure "enables the organization to manage its strategic portfolio centrally, while giving each component of the portfolio the undivided attention of one unit." For our purposes it is important to note that in most cases not every division of the overall organization will be operating within the sport industry. Some companies, such as Brunswick, have a majority of their operations in sport and sport-related products, while for others, sport may be just another product market in a company that also produces musical instruments and motorcycles.

Because it usually consists of integrated machine bureaucracies, the environment where the divisionalized form works best is relatively simple and stable, the same conditions that favor the machine bureaucracy. Size and age are also associated with the divisionalized form. As organizations grow, they tend to diversify in order to protect themselves from market fluctuations; such diversification leads to divisionalization. Likewise, with time, a company's existing product markets may face challenges from new competitors; thus, they are forced to look for new markets. Success in these markets leads to an increased number of divisions.

The Professional Bureaucracy

The last half century has seen the emergence of many new professions (Larson, 1977; Johnson, 1972; Wilkinson, Hislop, & Coupland, 2016). Sport, like other areas of social life, has not gone untouched by these developments, becoming an increasingly global, diverse marketplace (cf. Lawson, 1984; Macintosh & Whitson, 1990; Misener & Misener, 2017). Sport psychologists, athletic therapists, coaches, and sport managers have all laid claim to professional status. The rise of professionalism has led to the creation of a new organizational form. The **professional bureaucracy** combines the standardization of the machine bureaucracy with the decentralization that results from a professional's need for autonomy. The professional bureaucracy is found in a number of areas of the sport industry; faculties of kinesiology often adopt this type of design, as do sport medicine clinics, sport marketing companies, and, to an increasing extent, voluntary sport organizations and sport federations or governing bodies (Harris, Mori, & Collins, 2009; Hinings & Slack, 1987; Kikulis et al., 1989; Nagel, Schlesinger, Bayle, & Giauque, 2015; Nichols et al., 2005; Nichols & James, 2008).

The key part of the professional bureaucracy is the operating core. This is where we find the specialists, the professionals who operate relatively autonomously in this decentralized structure. The skills of the professionals are standardized through their training and their involvement in their professional association and related activities, but discretion is granted in the application of skills. For example, in a sport marketing company an individual client services manager will be expected to have some standard skills in the different areas of marketing but at the same time will be given relative discretion as to how to go about obtaining accounts. Unlike the machine bureaucracy, where work standards are developed by analysts in the technostructure and enforced by managers, the standards of the professionals emanate from their training and their involvement in their professional association. In addition to the operating core, the only other part of the professional bureaucracy developed to any extent is the support staff who assist the professionals. Because work is too complex to be supervised by a manager or standardized by analysts, there is usually only a small strategic apex and middle line (e.g., the senior partner of the sport marketing company and perhaps some managers who have a coordinating function). There is also little need for any type of technostructure.

Advantages and Disadvantages

In chapter 5 we saw how some elements of bureaucratic structuring, such as formalization and centralization, conflicted with professional values for autonomy. The advantage of the professional bureaucracy is that it minimizes these conflicts by combining the professional's need for autonomy with standardization. However, standardization is not achieved with detailed rules and procedures, but through training and other forms of professional practice (social specialization). The autonomy the professionals achieve is only acquired after lengthy education and often on-the-job training. So, when an orthopedic surgeon working in a sports medicine clinic operates on the knee of an athlete, the athlete knows the chance of a mistake has been minimized—the surgeon was trained for the procedure in medical school, and watched and helped colleagues perform the surgery many times before attempting it him- or herself.

The autonomy that a professionally trained person experiences from working in a professional bureaucracy is the major advantage of this type of design. It does, however, have disadvantages in that it can create coordination problems. Professionals, such as sport management professors, who work in a department that operates as a professional bureaucracy may have little in common with other departments, such as colleagues in exercise physiology. They have different training, different research agendas, and even a different terminology for their work. While each may prefer to be left alone to do their own thing, it is necessary for each to get along with colleagues from other areas and coordinate their efforts to produce a well-balanced physical education and sport studies program.

A further disadvantage of this type of design is that, as Mintzberg (1979, p. 373) notes, it is "appropriate for professionals who are competent and conscientious. Unfortunately, not all of them are, and the professional bureaucratic structure cannot easily deal with professionals who are either incompetent or unconscientious." This type of structure is also problematic in that allowing professionals a high level of autonomy can work against the development of any type of team approach to the problems and issues confronting the sport organization.

Where Do We Find the Professional Bureaucracy?

We find professional bureaucracies in environments that are both complex and stable. Environmental complexity means that the skills to be learned require extensive periods of training, but the stability of the environment means these skills can be well defined, and, in essence, standardized. Age and size do not play a major role in influencing the choice of a professional bureaucratic design. We find small professional bureaucracies, for example, in a law firm that specializes in contract work for professional athletes, which may operate with three or four lawyers, an office manager, and support staff. We also find the professional bureaucratic design used in relatively new sport organizations. Unlike the machine bureaucracy, which often starts out as a simple structure, the professional bureaucracy requires little start-up time.

The technology of the professional bureaucracy is important because it does not excessively regulate, it is not sophisticated, and it is not automated

TIME OUT

A Structural Taxonomy of Amateur Sport Organizations: The Professional Bureaucracy

In a study of provincial-level sport organizations Kikulis et al. (1989) produced a structural taxonomy of organizational design types. Five of the organizations in the study—figure skating, ice hockey, association football, swimming, and volleyball—exhibited the characteristics of a professional bureaucracy. These organizations had high levels of professional specialization and an extensive range of programs. Volunteer specialization, in both technical and administrative roles, was not as high as in many other organizations, indicating that program operation and management were in the hands of professionals assisted by volunteers. Coordination of programs and staff was achieved through a large number of meetings. These organizations did, however, exhibit a relatively high level of standardization, a structural characteristic not usually found in professional bureaucracies but, for these organizations, reflects their strong ties to government.

Decision making was centralized at the volunteer board level. Although in an ideal professional bureaucracy the decision making is decentralized to the professional levels, Kikulis et al. (1989) point out that in voluntary sport organizations, the situation is somewhat more complex. In these types of organizations, decisions are actually made by professionals but ratified by the board. Although decisions must go to the board level for approval, the professionals in these organizations are able to structure the flow of information to the board to get the response they want. Consequently, while there is an appearance of board control, decision making is controlled by the professional staff, as we would expect in a professional bureaucracy.

(Mintzberg, 1979). The presence of any of these characteristics in the organization's technology mitigates against the autonomy of professionals who require discretion to carry out their work.

Adhocracy

Adhocracy is a highly flexible and responsive form of sport organization, what Burns and Stalker (1961) refer to as an organic structure. Used when a high level of innovation is required in the work processes, it may be a permanent or temporary design. The adhocracy has low levels of formalization, no structured hierarchy of authority, and high levels of horizontal differentiation, with specialists grouped into functional units for organizational purposes but often deployed to project teams to do their work. Decentralization is common, standardized operating procedures are sparse if they exist at all, and coordination is achieved through mutual adjustment, as teams containing managers, operators, and support staff work together to solve unique problems. In sport we find the adhocracy used in television companies covering major sporting events, in research and development (R&D) companies such as W.L. Gore & Associates, and in some university research labs.

The adhocracy has little or no technostructure because its work cannot be standardized or formalized. The middle-line managers, the operating core, and the support staff are all professionals, so there is no clear demarcation between line and staff. Decisions are made by those who possess the expertise. The managers in the strategic apex spend their time monitoring projects, resolving the conflicts that inevitably arise in this type of free-flowing structure, and (probably most importantly) communicating with the external environment.

It is difficult to produce an organizational chart for an adhocracy because the internal structure of these organizations changes frequently as new problems require new project teams. Unlike the professional bureaucracy, the experts who work in adhocracies cannot rely on standardized skills to achieve coordination because this would move away from innovation toward standardization (Mintzberg, 1979). Rather, in the adhocracy, groups of professionals combine their efforts to build on their existing knowledge and skills to produce innovative solutions to new and different problems. For example, in order to conduct research on the contribution that sport and other forms of physical activity make to increasing an individual's well-being, a department of health, physical education, and recreation may create a research unit that houses physiologists, psychologists, and sociologists. While these people do not normally work together, they could all combine their knowledge and skills to produce innovative solutions to this type of problem. A similar type of

TIME OUT

W.L. Gore & Associates: The Lattice Organization

W.L. Gore & Associates is a material science manufacturing and research company that had a revenue of US$3.2 billion the end of the 2017 fiscal year (Forbes, n.d.). Gore manufactures a wide range of products across many industries, including their world-renowned Gore-Tex fabrics, which are used in many sport-related applications. Gore-Tex is used to make waterproof and windproof clothing such as jackets, shoes, and gloves for a range of applications that include skiing, fishing, hunting, trekking, and running. The company promotes innovation through a unique organizational design, the lattice communications structure, a type of adhocracy in which the guiding principle is described as "unmanagement." Within the lattice organization every "associate" (as employees are called) must deal with other associates one on one. There are no hierarchies, no job titles, no bosses, and no authoritative commands. The philosophy is to "collaborate and build connections without the constraints of traditional chains of command" (Gore, n.d.). When they join the organization, new associates are sponsored by an established associate. New associates pick the area to work in which they think they can make the best contribution. They are then challenged to do their best in this area. Associates are given the freedom to experiment with new ideas and to follow through on those that are potentially profitable. They must, however, consult with associates before taking any action that the company terms as being "below the waterline" (Simmons, 1987) and having the potential to cause serious damage to the organization.

adhocratic structure may be created by a municipal council developing a plan to build a new multiuse sport facility; experts would be needed from departments concerned with land-use planning, sport programming, environment, transportation, and so on.

Advantages and Disadvantages

The main advantage of the adhocracy is that it can respond rapidly to change. It promotes creativity by bringing diverse groups of professionals together to work on specific projects. Adhocracies may be permanent structures, such as the lattice type of organizational design used at W.L. Gore & Associates (Rhodes, 1982), or they may be set up on a temporary basis. For example, the PGA (Professional Golfers' Association) of America created an 11-person task force (a type of adhocracy) following the 2014 Ryder Cup defeat to Europe, which was the USA's sixth defeat from the previous seven meetings. The task force consisted of a mix of high-profile players (Tiger Woods, Phil Mickelson, Raymond Floyd, Tom Lehman, Davis Love III, Jim Furyk, Steve Stricker, and Rickie Fowler), the then-incoming PGA of America president (Derek Sprague), CEO (Pete Bevacqua), and the PGA secretary (Paul Levy). The goal was that by bringing together the range of skill sets of the individuals in the group, Team USA would be able to brainstorm solutions in an attempt to stop Team Europe's domination. Formation of the task force looks like it was a prudent move; Team USA won the subsequent 2016 Ryder Cup, and the task force was then disbanded. This type of temporary setup is not as easily achieved with other organizational design types.

The flexibility of the adhocracy is a weakness as well as a strength. High levels of flexibility mean that the adhocracy is the most politicized of the design types we have examined. There are no clear lines of authority and no formalized rules; consequently, employees may be involved in political games to achieve their goals, more than in other organizational designs. The political nature of the adhocracy means a potential for high levels of conflict, which can create stress for employees and for those who, preferring consistency in their jobs, do not like rapid change. These stresses are compounded by the flexibility of the adhocracy.

Inefficiency is also a weakness of the adhocracy. The flexibility required in this structure means high levels of face-to-face communication, frequent discussions, and meetings, all costly in time and money. Another source of inefficiency is the unbalanced workloads—periods of high activity followed by periods of slower activity—for specialists (Mintzberg, 1979).

Where Do We Find the Adhocracy?

The innovative nature of the work performed in an adhocracy means that it is found in environments that are both dynamic and complex. As Mintzberg (1979, p. 449) notes, "in effect, innovative work, being unpredictable, is associated with a dynamic environment; and the fact that the innovation must be sophisticated means that it is difficult to comprehend, in other words associated with a complex environment." For these reasons, research units such as those found in a faculty of physical education and sport studies may choose to adopt this organizational design. So, too, may the organizing committee for a temporary event such as a running or cycling road race or a basketball tournament.

Technology will also influence the decision to structure as an adhocracy. An organization with a sophisticated technical system requires "specialists who have the knowledge, power, and flexible work arrangements to cope with it" (Mintzberg, 1979, p. 458). This requirement creates a decentralized structure and considerable integration of the analysts in the technostructure, the operators, and the support staff, an integration best achieved with an adhocracy.

Other factors influencing the choice of an adhocracy are age or, as Mintzberg notes, more specifically, youth and fashion. Youth is a factor because a number of young organizations seek to be innovative with new products and markets; adhocracy facilitates this quest for innovation. Fashion is a factor because much of the pop culture management literature has critiqued notions of hierarchy and centralization in organizations and has suggested the need for more organic structures and innovations such as project teams and task forces. Again, the adhocracy is designed to meet these kinds of requirements.

Broadcasting companies such as NBC and the BBC tend to use this form of organization when it televises or streams coverage of the Olympic Games due to the operational complexities (such as geographical location and, often, language or cultural differences in host nations) and the management of workforce allocation to ensure the normal day-to-day broadcasting is not interfered with. Each country's Rights Holding Broadcaster works with the Olympic Broadcasting Services (the permanent host broadcaster, created by the IOC) to personalize their coverage for the home audiences. We also find it in research units and specialized structures such as a task force. Its strength is its flexibility and, hence, its ability to respond to change. The key part of this sport organization is the support staff of experts, on which the organization is dependent. We find this type of structure in complex and dynamic environments.

Organizational Designs as Ideal Types

It is important to note that the five design types (configurations) described here are, in fact, **ideal types**. As such, it is quite possible that very few sport organizations will be exactly like one of these designs. For example, when we look at a set of sport organizations, we may find that a number of them may be in transition between designs. In the late 1950s Coleman, a major producer of equipment for outdoor sports, had been operating with a machine bureaucracy design; management, realizing it had grown too big and diverse for this type of structure, started a process of divisionalization. Such changes take time to achieve; anyone studying this organization in its transition period would not find a neatly laid-out design type as described here. Kikulis et al. (1989) show evidence of transitional designs. In their research they found a number of amateur sport organizations that were moving toward a professional bureaucratic structure but, at the time of the study, had not reached this design; they called these organizations *nascent professional bureaucracies*. Pressures experienced by voluntary sport clubs (VSCs) to move away from a traditional ad hoc, informal organizational design toward adopting greater professional practices is becoming more prevalent. Byers (2009, p. 220) highlights how not only are VSCs expected to professionalize their operations, they now need to "focus on improving their service delivery, in line with standards experienced in the private sector." Addressing these changes in organizations such as VSCs can take many years due to the embedded institutionalized practices and cultures.

In addition to finding organizations in transitional states, it is also possible that we will find a number exhibiting what is referred to as a **hybrid structure**, where they exhibit the characteristics of more than one design type. It may be, for example, that a company producing sport equipment and operating with a machine bureaucracy design may wish to develop new products and enter new markets; it may create a small adhocracy as an appendage to its existing machine bureaucracy design. Brunswick took this type of initiative when it established venture capital groups within its divisions to nurture new products.

What does all this mean, then? Does the fact that we may not find the exact type of organizational design we have described mean that they are not useful? Of course not. As we pointed out at the start of this chapter, scholars who study organizations of all types have long considered a means of classification as one of the basic requirements of the field. As table 6.2 shows, the five designs developed by Mintzberg enable us to compare and contrast sport organizations on a number of dimensions. They also provide us with a basis for studying a wide variety of other organizational phenomena. For example, how does a sport organization change

Table 6.2 Dimensions of the Five Organizational Design Types

Dimensions	Simple structure	Machine bureaucracy	Professional bureaucracy	Divisionalized form	Adhocracy
Horizontal complexity	Low	High-functional	High-social	High-functional	High-social
Vertical complexity	Low	High	Medium	High within divisions	Low
Formalization	Low	High	Low	High within divisions	Low
Centralization	High	High	Low	High within divisions	Low
Technology	Simple	Regulating, not automated, not sophisticated	Not regulating or sophisticated	Divisible like machine bureaucracy	Sophisticated and often automated
Size	Small	Large	Varies	Large	Varies
Environment	Simple and dynamic	Simple and stable	Complex and stable	Simple and stable diversified markets	Complex and dynamic
Strategy	Intuitive and opportunistic	To maintain performance in chosen markets	Developed by individuals controlled by professional association	Portfolio	Seeks new products and new markets

from a simple structure to a machine bureaucracy to a divisionalized form? Do machine bureaucracies and professional bureaucracies formulate strategy in different ways? Are decisions made differently in a professional bureaucracy than in an adhocracy? And, how is power exercised in each of these different designs? All of these questions, and many more, are valid topics of investigation for sport management students. The design types outlined can provide a useful basis for investigation into these areas.

Notes on Organizational Size

In this chapter, with the exception of Chappelet and Parent's (2015) proposed typology that focuses on the nature of sport event, it is implicitly assumed that an organization's design is dependent, in part, on its size. Organizational **size** can be defined in many ways: total assets, return on investment, market share, sales volume, number of clients, number of employees, number of members, net profits, and so on. Kimberly (1976) suggests a combination of four aspects as a more appropriate way to operationalize the size concept: physical capacity of the organization, personnel available to the organization (the most commonly used aspect), volume of input or output, and the discretionary resources available to the organization (e.g., organizational wealth and assets).

An organization's size will determine the choice of organizational design type. For example, the local sporting goods store owner will most likely choose a simpler organizational structure than would Nike. Any increase (or decrease) in size can dictate a necessary change in organizational design type to stay efficient.

Size can have an impact on the different elements of organizational structure. Notwithstanding the nature of the organization (e.g., entrepreneurial versus manufacturing), an increase in size often goes hand in hand with an increase in the complexity and formalization of the organization (Andrews & Boyne, 2014; Miller, 1987; Rushing, 1980; Slack, 1985; Slack & Hinings, 1992). The relationship between size and centralization, however, is somewhat more difficult. On one hand it would be logical to think that growth means decentralizing to avoid overloading senior managers (Child, 1973). On the other hand, owners may be reluctant to give up their control. This can be especially true for professional sport team owners.

Contemporary Perspectives on Organizational Design

As stated at the beginning of this chapter, organizational theorists have suggested many ways of classifying organizations. We have focused on Mintzberg's (1979) classical typology of five organization design types, or configurations, throughout this chapter because, as Burton, Obel, and Håkonsson (2015) note, despite an ever-changing world, the fundamentals of organizational design remain relevant. In addition to Mintzberg's (1979) traditional typology, organizational theorists generally agree that four basic configurations exist, which can be combined to form different organizational patterns. These configurations are simple, functional, divisional, and matrix (Burton et al., 2015). The simple (akin to simple structure), functional (akin to machine bureaucracy), and divisional (akin to divisionalized form) configurations closely align with Mintzberg's typology. The **matrix design** sees product or geographical divisions intersected by functional departments, giving rise to a lattice-like arrangement. The matrix design aims to utilize advantages of divisionalized and functional forms enabling employees to work together to increase innovation and response to environmental changes while receiving functional support (Amis & Slack, 2016).

The Impact of (Advanced) Information Technology on Organizational Design

With the evolution of technology—in particular, advanced information technology (AIT)—and the digital marketplace, decentralized, team-based organizational designs are gradually replacing traditional approaches. Amis and Slack (2016) note some movement toward contemporary configurations such as the *team-based design* and a *virtual network design*. Rather than being grouped in vertical, isolated functional departments (resembling a machine bureaucracy configuration), a **team-based design** has a flat structure. This configuration enables a relatively small team (comprised of individuals with a range of complementary expertise) to rapidly respond to design and production issues and changes in the environment, important given the pace of today's fast-moving industries. The team would generally also be involved in a project from inception to completion. Hierarchy or direct supervision does not exist, so task coordination is achieved by informal communication (akin to Mintzberg's mutual adjustment) to meet needs of the team or group. Therefore, if a group leader is determined, it is important that the individual possesses excellent people management skills due to the diverse nature of the team. A team-based design contains features of Mintzberg's configurations but is not characterized as a hybrid structure in the sense that the design will not, for example, operate with a professional bureaucracy that has an adhocracy appendage added to the existing configuration. Rather, the distinct configurations amalgamate—and there are no separate parts to the organization (such as a defined strategic apex, operating core, technostructure). Everyone works together in a team as one unit, meaning individuals could adopt various roles throughout the duration of the project, spanning across the traditional definitions of design types and parts of an organization.

As a result of AIT (the merging of computer and telecommunications systems) and continued technological advances, individuals can now more easily work together on projects and not be in the same geographical location to form a **virtual network design**. It is now commonplace to have specialists, who are geographically spread, to work as part of a team, share project documents via email or online cloud-based systems, and hold online meetings. AIT enables a reduction in the levels or layers of management, allowing for decentralized decision making. Effective use of AIT systems can improve communication and coordination; information from an organization's headquarters can be easily and rapidly shared over large geographical distances. With this design, there are no relocation costs with each new project, yet it allows for a market presence. In addition, managers are able to effectively coordinate and control relationships that are both internal and external to the firm. However, it might be difficult to foster a common work ethic or culture to bind the workers together.

For a large-scale project, adopting this virtual network design often means an organization outsources many of its major functions to different specialist firms, which are all electronically connected to the organization's headquarters via the Internet. This virtual network design can give rise to what Ashkenas, Ulrich, Todd, and Kerr (2002) call a *boundaryless organization*. They suggest approaches to break down the four most common types of organizational boundaries—hierarchical (or vertical), functional (or horizontal), external, and geographic—to achieve the ability to be flexible and innovative and to respond rapidly in order to survive and thrive in today's business environment. (For a more detailed overview of technology and its impact for sport organizations, refer to chapter 21 in this textbook.)

Recently, Misener and Misener (2017, p. 125) have suggested that "we must recognize that classic structures and forms are being shaken and/or dissolved every day in favor of more flexible, responsive applications that perhaps do not fit more positivistic 'black and white, theoretical understandings." In order to progress the field of sport management, it is generally agreed that a greater understanding and development of these new forms of organizational structure and design is needed. However, that is not to say that the traditional typologies are becoming irrelevant. As Misener and Misener acknowledge, academics should not dismiss timeless concepts and should make an effort to embrace the complexity of contemporary sport management.

Summary and Conclusions

Although no two sport organizations are exactly alike, they do exhibit common features that form the basis for classifying them into design types, or configurations. Classification has been identified as one of the most important tasks for organizational theorists because it provides a basis for the generation of hypotheses, models, and theories. Organizations can be classified in two main ways: typologies (conceptually-based representations) and taxonomies (those that are empirically based).

One of the most common organizational typologies is the one developed by Mintzberg (1979), who identifies five parts (and, more recently, he has suggested a sixth part: ideology) of an organization. Depending on the part that dominates, we get one of five organizational designs: the simple

KEY ISSUES FOR SPORT MANAGERS

Organizations can be theoretically or empirically categorized in many ways. Managers must be concerned with two major aspects:

- *The parts of the organization*: What types of employees work here, and what is the overall nature of the organization (i.e., its goals, size, structural aspects, type of coordination)?
- *The type of environment*: Is it stable or unstable, and what is the nature of the market?

Determining these aspects helps narrow the best type of organizational design to fit the organization's needs and desires.

Remember that there can be a design within a design and an organization can be transitional in nature. Earlier we referred to the challenges of complexity for a country's Rights Holding Broadcaster to broadcast the Olympic Games. Ordinarily, a broadcaster is likely to operate as a machine bureaucracy, but for the Games they would also operate an adhocracy (or a team-based design), decentralizing decision making (but still being carefully coordinated by an executive producer) to facilitate the ability to respond rapidly in such a dynamic environment. That is, the broadcasters cannot plan which athletes to focus the attention on (e.g., who to interview, what the analysis will be about, creating segments about the highs and the lows) until each medal has been won.

With rapid technological advances, new design types have started to emerge, which some sport organizations have adopted. Babiak (2007) noted how governments began to embrace public–private partnerships, for-profit organizations were seen to form strategic alliances and joint ventures, and nonprofit organizations began to establish collaborations with nontraditional partners. With these new relationships and new organizational designs, a sport manager would have to select the design type they feel is best, even if it is new or unpopular. In that way, the organization's goals can be best achieved.

Practically speaking, while organizations will be similar to those in this chapter, most will not fit the ideal types because too many factors come into play at the same time. However, the design options featured here will provide you with a good starting point to develop a better understanding of an organization's configuration.

structure, the machine bureaucracy, the divisionalized form, the professional bureaucracy, or the adhocracy. We can find sport organizations representative of each of these design types.

The simple structure, most often found in small sport organizations and those in the early stages of their development, usually shows low levels of specialization and formalization. The key part of a simple structure is the strategic apex, where we find the individual who runs the sport organization and with whom power is centralized. Simple structures work best in environments that are simple and dynamic.

The machine bureaucracy is usually found in sport organizations that produce a standard output, government agencies concerned with sport, and organizations that need relatively simple tasks performed in a consistent manner. Its main attribute is its efficiency. The key part of the machine bureaucracy is the technostructure that standardizes work. We find the machine bureaucracy in simple and stable environments.

The divisionalized form is actually a group of organizations, usually machine bureaucracies, coordinated by a central headquarters. The divisions, not all of which are always involved in sport, provide product and market diversity. The key part of this organization is the presence of middle-line managers, those individuals who control the divisions. The divisionalized form is found in large organizations that have either product or market diversity; it operates in simple and stable environments.

The professional bureaucracy caters to the needs of the professional by providing the standardization of the bureaucracy but at the same time allowing professionals control of their own work. Faculties of physical education and sport studies often operate with a professional bureaucratic structure, as do sport medicine clinics and architectural firms specializing in sport facilities. The key part of the professional bureaucracy is the operating core, which contains the professionals. We find this type of design in sport organizations with complex and stable environments.

The final design of Mintzberg's (1979) typology is the adhocracy. Broadcasting companies tend to use this form of organization when they televise or stream coverage of the Olympic Games because of the operational complexities (e.g., geographical location and, often, language or cultural differences in host nations) and the need to manage workforce allocation to ensure no interference with normal day-to-day broadcasting. We also find it in research units and specialized structures such as a task force. Its strength is its flexibility and, hence, its ability to respond to change. The key part of this sport organization is the support staff of experts, on which the organization is dependent. We find this type of structure in complex and dynamic environments.

Each of the designs discussed is an ideal type, so we seldom find sport organizations that fit the pattern exactly as described. Some sport organizations may approximate one of the main designs, some may be in transitional states between designs, and others may exhibit a hybrid structure that exhibits the characteristics of more than one design.

As a result of the rapid technological advances and developments in AIT, contemporary organizational designs and configurations have started to appear. In this chapter, we have introduced a few of these design types. Over time, more organizations in the sport industry will adopt these evolving organizational designs, so now would be a good time to familiarize yourself with such typologies.

Review Questions

1. How does a typology differ from a taxonomy?
2. Pick some familiar sport organizations. What type of design do they have, according to Mintzberg?
3. Discuss how the method of coordination varies in each of the five designs.
4. What type of design did Under Armour adopt in its early years? (See chapter 1.) What type of design do you think it uses now?
5. How does an adhocracy differ from a professional bureaucracy?
6. Discuss how the role of the strategic apex varies in each of the five designs.
7. In which of the design types is formalization likely to be low? Why?
8. Can you think of a sport organization that uses a contemporary team-based design or a virtual network design?

Suggestions for Further Reading

For further reading, students are obviously referred to Mintzberg's (1979) work on organizational design. The most comprehensive treatment is found in his book *The Structuring of Organizations*. While part 4 of his book deals specifically with design, the earlier chapters lay much of the foundation for his work in this area and should have relevance for students interested in this topic. More condensed versions of Mintzberg's (1984) work on design can be found in his chapter "A Typology of Organizational Structure," and his articles (1981) "Organizational Design: Fashion or Fit?" in *Harvard Business Review* and (1980) "Structure in 5's: A Synthesis of the Research on Organization Design" in *Management Science*. Information on typologies and taxonomies can be found in Miller and Friesen's (1984) *Organizations: A Quantum View*. While this is the most sophisticated work on these topics, some of it is difficult reading, particularly chapter 2, which deals with methods of developing taxonomies. See also Carper and Snizek's (1980) "The Nature and Types of Organizational Taxonomies: An Overview," in the *Academy of Management Review*. Short, Payne, and Ketchen (2008) offer a useful review of past research on organizational configurations and suggest direction for future inquiry in the *Journal of Management*. For a progressive view of designs of organizational structure, Ashkenas et al. (2002) attempt to explain how it might be possible to overcome some of the traditional boundaries to improve business performance in their book *The Boundaryless Organization: Breaking the Chains of Organizational Structure*.

Within sport literature, Chelladurai's work (1985) on typologies in *Sport Management: Macro Perspectives* is a useful starting point for discussions on this topic. Also interesting is his 1992 article, "A Classification of Sport and Physical Activity Services: Implications for Sport Management" in the *Journal of Sport Management*. In regard to taxonomies of organizations, students should see Hinings and Slack's (1987) chapter "The Dynamics of Quadrennial Plan Implementation in National Sport Organizations" in their (Slack & Hinings, 1987) edited book *The Organization and Administration of Sport*. A more methodologically sophisticated taxonomy is developed and discussed in an extension of this work in Kikulis et al.'s (1989) article, "A Structural Taxonomy of Amateur Sport Organizations" in the *Journal of Sport Management*. As mentioned earlier in this chapter, Chappelet and Parent (2015) proposed a new typology for sport events in their edited event management textbook and, finally, Theodoraki and Henry (1994) presented an organizational taxonomy for their examination of English NGBs in the *International Review for the Sociology of Sport*.

Case for Analysis

Reshaping NSOs

Sitting in her home in the suburbs of Toronto, Susan Collinson, the volunteer president of a small Canadian sport organization, reread the material she had just received from the federal government agency, Sport Canada. *(Although the situation in this case is based on actual events, the names are fictitious.)* Susan had been the president of her organization for two years and had frequently expressed her concern about the increased involvement the government was taking in its operation. The material she just received had Susan worried.

For the past 15 to 20 years Sport Canada had provided many of the national-level amateur sport organizations with funds to operate their programs. The funds were not large, and they were given with few strings attached. Susan's organization had been fairly successful and had used their funds well, building a very strong volunteer base within the various clubs that existed throughout the country. Their provincial associations were also well organized. The national organization's board of directors was an enthusiastic group of volunteers, many of whom held managerial positions with local and national companies. Using the funds they received from Sport Canada, and other monies from membership fees and fund-raising ventures, this group of volunteers had established a wide range of developmental programs to encourage people to get involved in their sport. They had also been reasonably successful in international competition because Jim Kramer, one of the top club coaches in the country, had worked with the national team as a volunteer coach.

The organization operated in a collegial manner. Although they had the occasional dispute, members worked well together. They had no detailed policies and procedures they had to follow; they basically got on with the job. About three years ago the board had hired Katrina Torkildson, a former athlete who understood sports, to be their executive director. While she had no formal management training she was regarded as bright, enthusiastic, and well organized. Katrina worked for the board and essentially helped do the things they needed doing to make the organization run smoothly. As Susan read the material from the federal government, she wondered if all this was going to change.

Essentially, what the government was proposing was to increase significantly the amount of money they were providing to the NSOs. In large part their rationale was that this new funding would increase Canada's chances of doing well in the Olympic Games and other major international sporting events. Although no definitive figures were given, Susan roughly estimated that the funds her organization was receiving could quadruple.

However, there was a catch. To receive the funds, NSOs had to prepare a plan. The plan should outline the type of changes the sport organization would make in order to operate in a more efficient and businesslike manner. This efficiency, Sport Canada felt, was what was needed to increase Canada's medal count at major games. The plan should also contain detailed policies and procedures that documented how the organization conducted its business. One of the other changes the government appeared to be promoting was the hiring of an increased number of professionally trained staff to run the affairs of the organization, enhance its developmental programs, and coach its national teams. Funds were to be provided, up to 75 percent of their salary, to hire these people; Sport Canada would, however, have a voice in who was hired. Although it was not stated as such, implicit in the material Susan received was the idea that volunteers would play a considerably smaller role in the organization's operation, which would be turned over to the new professional staff. As Susan pondered the material, she wondered what impact all this would have on her organization and how she should deal with the information she had received.

Questions

1. What would you do if you were Susan and you had just received such material from the federal government?
2. What is the potential impact of the government's proposed initiatives on the design of this NSO?
3. How do you think Jim and Katrina will feel about the government's proposals?
4. Is there any way that Susan could take advantage of the increased funding offered by the government, yet at the same time maintain the type of organizational design that currently exists?
5. Fast-forward 15 years: Susan has followed the government's guidelines thinking it was better to do as the government said to get the money. However, the government of Canada now decides it cannot keep supporting the Canadian sport organizations given the tougher economic times. The government plans to cut its annual funding by half but still expects the same performance level from the organizations. Also, the guidelines are still in place. What would you do if you were Susan?

This Case for Analysis is not unique to Canada. In 1997, the Labour government in the United Kingdom introduced the Best Value policy, which was a strategy that aimed to modernize a range of public services. One result of this policy was that it altered funding for NGBs from an entitlement culture, enjoyed during the 1960s and 1970s, to a conditional, business approach whereby NGBs had to produce strategic plans (Whole Sport Plans). The performance outcomes were then critically evaluated, and distribution of funding became contingent on the evaluation of agreed plans (Houlihan & Lindsey, 2012). As a result, many NGBs had to make changes to their structures and operations. Therefore, the five questions just posed can also be applicable to this UK example.

CHAPTER 7

Sport Organizations and Their Responses to Policy

Spencer Harris, PhD

Learning Objectives

When you have read this chapter, you should be able to

1. discuss the policy process and its relevance and importance to sport organizations,
2. explain what is meant by the term *policy*,
3. identify and provide examples of different types of policy and provide sport-related examples of each type of policy,
4. understand the different approaches that have been used to study organizational responses to policy, and
5. examine the range of organizational responses to policy and explore the reasons for these responses.

Key Concepts

bottom-up perspective
implementation
institutional pressures
policy
policy–action continuum
policy types
power
top-down perspective

Financial Fair Play in European Association Football

The Union of European Football Associations (UEFA) Financial Fair Play (FFP) regulations are never far from the European news. Initially developed in 2011 to prevent clubs from spending beyond their means, the regulations require that clubs limit losses to €30 million (US$33 million) over each three-year period. The spending limits apply to team-specific aspects such as player transfer fees and annual wages but not broader operational matters such as stadia development or academy infrastructure. Failure to comply can lead to a number of sanctions, including warnings, financial fines, deducted points, withholding revenue, prohibition to register new players, disqualification from a current competition, and exclusion from future competitions (UEFA, 2012).

While the FFP may moderate the **power** of European soccer's financial heavyweights, notable problems are associated with implementing such policies. First, the regulations privilege wealthier clubs with the global reach to generate larger revenues than their smaller, domestically focused rivals, and, therefore, these wealthier clubs have more to spend on transfers. Second, the regulations are viewed as overly stringent. Karl-Heinz Rummenigge, chairman of the European Clubs' Association (ECA), stated that "the rigidity of the system is damaging the poorer Italian and eastern European clubs" (Herbert, 2015). Additionally, the regulations favor wealthy, established clubs in that clubs are prevented from investing significant amounts in players over short periods of time. There are also notable legal challenges to FFP on the grounds that they violate competition law. Third, the rules are open to manipulation and reinforce a culture of gaming the system, where agents learn to use the rules of the game (that were intended to protect) to manipulate the system and achieve a desired outcome. For example, clubs can artificially raise their income from substantial sponsorship deals from corporations owned by friends or relatives of club owners. Fourth, the structural context within which European association football clubs compete varies from country to country and creates inconsistencies that directly affect the revenues of clubs across Europe. For example, English clubs make substantial annual payments to the Football League and other charities. These payments are not excluded from FFP and are likely to make a significant difference, particularly for the less wealthy clubs. Another issue is the significantly different tax rates across European nations, meaning that clubs in certain countries must pay players much higher gross salaries to pay the same net salaries. The final problem relates to UEFA's willingness and ability to enforce the regulations. Until recently, UEFA has failed to take action against clubs with clear FFP infringements. At the time of writing, UEFA faces growing pressure to change the FFP system. Will they continue to maintain the regulations or buckle under the weight of criticism leveled at them? Only time will tell.

Policy represents a key pillar of the democratic process. It provides a window into government and allows others to more clearly understand what government stands for and will be measured against. It sets out priorities, provides the parameters and direction for collaborative action, allocates resources, and establishes the means of reviewing performance against objectives. However, without action, policy is merely the thoughts, words, and intentions of the policy creator. Action requires that organizations be aware of policy and respond by implementing initiatives that strive to achieve policy objectives. While this may appear a relatively straightforward proposition, the practical reality is everything but. This is a point reinforced by Skille (2008, p. 181), who advises that "the way from policy making at the national-level to the **implementation** of policy at the local level is long and uneasy," with the outcome of policy largely dependent on the disposition of local-level organizations. Thus, while creating policy may be important, the willingness and ability of organizations to implement policy is critical.

This chapter will explore the relationship between policy and organizational responses in more detail. The chapter starts with a discussion of what constitutes policy and goes on to identify different **policy types**. We discuss two approaches to studying organizational responses to sport policy: institutional theory and implementation theory. These theories are used to examine the various responses that organizations may have to policy and the reasons for such responses.

Defining Policy

What actually constitutes policy? ***Policy*** is an ambiguous and contested term in that it has a variety of definitions that are largely dependent on context (Henry, 2001; Houlihan & White, 2002). For example, Haywood and colleagues (1995) offer a view of policy as consisting primarily of outputs of the political process. Goldsmith reinforces this, stating that policy refers to "all actions of governments not just stated intentions" as well as an understanding of why governments sometimes choose to do nothing about a particular question (1980, p. 22 in Henry, 1993). In contrast, Hums and MacLean (2013, p. 51) view policy in the context of being located within organizations: "Policies are broad guidelines or procedures an organization follows as it moves toward its goals and objectives. . . . Policies are normally general, written statements providing a framework for enabling decisions while allowing employees some flexibility and discretion in problem solving." Consequently, the basic concept of policy is broad, encompassing both the outcomes of political debate, focusing on societal problems and policies that concentrate on the organization and its business interests. Despite this breadth one can identify some common characteristics. First, policy tends to focus on human action aimed at achieving certain objectives or resolving specific problems. Second, policy can be argued to be concerned with the search for effective responses to a range of problems. For Jenkins (1978, p. 15), policy is

> a set of interrelated decisions taken by an actor or group of actors concerning the selection of goals and the means of achieving them within a specified situation where those decisions should, in principle, be within the power of those actors to achieve.

This view emphasizes three common aspects to be found in policy: (1) a decision to do something, (2) a decision related to a specific problem or situation, and (3) required action through which actors achieve the desired policy outcomes. While it may be difficult to disagree with the simple insight offered by the first two characteristics, much weight is placed on the caveat attached to the third. It is this factor, in particular organizational responses to policy and their decision to act, that forms the core of this chapter.

To start, it is useful to differentiate between types of policy. In his work during the early 1970s Theodore Lowi identified four ways in which government may intervene and various types of policy that result from their intervention: (1) regulatory, (2) distributive, (3) redistributive, and (4) constituency-based. In Lowi's view (1972), regulatory policy aims to control the action of organizations and individuals by permitting or prohibiting behavior. Examples include the various eligibility rules of collegiate athletics in the United States, the requirement for schools in England to provide two hours of physical education per week, the policies that govern the movement of professional athletes in China, or the powers bestowed upon the United States Olympic Committee (USOC) as part of the Ted Stevens Amateur Sport Act of 1998.

Distributive policies involve the provision of goods and services to the masses. While in some sectors distributive policies focus on services not typically provided by the private sector, this is not the case in sport. While the public sector engages in distributive policy for sport (e.g., the provision of major participation events and the management of indoor facilities, pools, and parks), private-sector operators offer similar activities and facilities, albeit at a different cost and targeting a specific market.

Redistributive policy represents the so-called Robin Hood approach to policy, whereby benefits are passed to one group while simultaneously taking away benefits from other groups. An example of this is the requirement that 5 percent of English Premier League broadcasting income be allocated to the grassroots game (Houlihan, 2013).

The fourth type of policy, constituency-based, is the most abstract. While these policies tend to be self-regulatory, "they impose constraints upon a group, but are perceived only to increase, not decrease, the beneficial options to the group" (Salisbury, 1968, p. 158). Houlihan (2013) refers to this type of policy as "administrative structures," which means the creation or reapportionment of agencies. Examples include the creation of the United States Anti-Doping Agency (USADA), the restructuring of the National Coaching Foundation in the United Kingdom, or the growth of the General Administration for Sport (GAS) in China. Whilst this typology offers a simplistic classification, it offers a framework that helps to classify policy and "provide a criteria for policy choice in terms of predicted and desired impacts on the political system" (Lowi, 1972, p. 307).

TIME OUT

Hogwood's Four Types

In contrast to Theodore Lowi, Brian Hogwood (1978) identified four policy types: (1) matters of principle, (2) lumpy issues, (3) redistribution or cuts, and (4) budget increases. *Matters of principle* are highly polarized issues and typically involve questions of right or wrong. Examples in sport include such policy-related developments as the World Anti-Doping Agency (WADA) regulations, coach education structures, and the No Compromise funding strategies of elite sport agencies (e.g., UK Sport, USOC, etc.). *Lumpy issues* involve indivisible goods or services and contain a limited scope for bargaining. Examples in sport include the National Olympic Committee's selection of the preferred bid city and the location of the national team stadium. *Redistribution or cuts* focus attention on allocations by government (i.e., who gets what). These types of policy usually contain some bargaining. Sport-related examples include local government decisions to cut discretionary funding for sport in order to meet base budget requirements or the decision of certain authorities to address inequality in sport through targeted initiatives and funding strategies. Policy involving a *budget increase* emphasizes priorities, whether these are long-term political priorities or short-lived political concerns. This type of policy is finely divisible and bargaining is more likely. An example of budget increase might involve a future host country investing more funding into the development of elite sport programs in advance of a mega-event (e.g., UK government investment into elite sport in the years preceding the 2012 London Summer Olympics).

Studying Organizational Responses to Sport Policy

This section focuses on two specific approaches to studying organizational responses to sport policy. The first approach forms part of the much broader literature belonging to institutional theory, while the second relates to the rather dated but still highly relevant insights provided by implementation theory.

Institutional Theory

Historically, institutional theory has focused on organizations and how they respond to the environment in which they operate. In particular, theory has been concerned with institutional forces such as the law, education, social norms, and values and how these elements shape action and interaction among organizations in a given field (DiMaggio & Powell, 1983). The concept of organizations being rooted in social and political environments underpins the idea that organizations are either reflections of or responses to social norms, beliefs, and values in the wider environment (Powell, 1991). The norms and values of a given field are important determinants because they are seen to be the foundation upon which organizations' institutional environment is developed. Within this, environment policy plays a critical role in setting parameters, formalizing norms, and propagating certain beliefs. This is especially the case in fields (such as sport) where government (national, state, county, or local) commit significant public funds with some pressure to demonstrate action on the norms supported by specific policy aspirations.

In their work on institutional isomorphism, DiMaggio and Powell (1983) offer three key pressures (referred to as processes of reproduction that influence organizational action): normative, coercive, and mimetic processes. *Normative pressures* are fueled by the norms and values of the environment. These factors encourage conformity and similarity of behavior across different organizations in a given field (e.g., the increasing use of highly selective criteria upon which funding for elite-level performance is allocated from the government or the National Olympic Committee (NOC) to National Governing Bodies (NGBs) of sport. *Coercive processes* involve political pressures and the power of the state to require organizations to conform to the norms and values of the sector (e.g., the requirement for recipients of grant funding to demonstrate how they will meet the aims associated with the grant, such as increasing mass participation or addressing inequality in sport). *Mimetic forces* emphasize the point that uncertainty tends to encourage imitation. Examples of this process might involve one nation imitating mass sport participation policies that have been developed and successfully implemented in another nation even though this has been done in a different social, economic, and political context.

Powell & Colyvas (2007) also add consideration of evangelical processes, where entrepreneurial agents champion the adoption of specific practices. An example of this would be national sport organizations that promote the broader social impact of sport and advocate greater investment in sport for development projects. At a local level, evangelical processes might involve an enthusiastic club volunteer who envisions a new multi-million-dollar facility development, primarily funded by external sources, which would likely require the club to move from being an informal volunteer-run group to a more formal, professional organization with promises of delivering a return on investment in line with external funders' requirements.

While these reproductive processes may be observed in organizational responses to policy, they accentuate an overly deterministic approach whereby organizations are invariably passive and are assumed to conform to the environment based on either a normative, coercive, mimetic, or evangelical rationale (Garrett, 2004). In contrast, by emphasizing the strategic behaviors employed by organizations, it is possible to mitigate such criticism. It is here where Oliver (1991) developed her theoretical proposition regarding organizations' strategic responses to institutional processes. In particular, her ideas evolved from a combination of insights taken from institutional and resource dependence theory "to demonstrate how organizational responses may vary from passive conformity to active resistance in response to **institutional pressures**, depending on the nature and context of the pressures themselves" (p. 146). While Oliver's work addresses a broader range of institutional pressure rather than a sole focus on policy, it provides a convincing framework to examine how organizations may respond to specific institutional pressures such as policy. For example, organizations are faced with the following set of tactical options in relation to their strategic responses to institutional processes.

- *Acquiescence*: An organization might follow norms out of habit, or it might imitate, mimicking models set out by the institution. Finally, the organization might respond with compliance, simply obeying rules or accepting norms.
- *Compromise*: An organization might balance the expectations of a number of stakeholders or pacify partners by placating institutional elements. Alternatively, an organization might seek to bargain and negotiate with stakeholders.
- *Avoid*: An organization may choose to conceal or disguise nonconformity. Organizations can buffer by distancing itself or loosening the nature of relations with partners or can seek escape by changing goals or activities.
- *Defy*: Organizations may opt to dismiss by ignoring explicit norms, challenge by contesting rules, or attack the original starting point of the pressure.
- *Manipulate*: Organizations may select to co-opt by bringing influential partners on board, influence by shaping values, or control by dominating partner organizations and their processes.

In short, Oliver's (1991) integrated interorganizational relations theory offers a lens to examine the relationship between organizational behavior and institutional contexts as well as consider the conditions under which organizations resist institutionalization. Importantly, the rationale for the type of strategic response (i.e., either conformity or resistance) to institutional pressures tends to be determined by the willingness and ability of organizations to conform to the institutional environment. Organizations' willingness to conform to institutional pressures is bounded by such factors as organizational skepticism, political self-interest, and organizational control, whereas the ability of organizations to respond to institutional pressure tends to be determined by organizational capacity, conflict, and awareness (Oliver, 1991). Here, insufficient capacity (e.g., voluntary sport clubs [VSCs] with too few volunteers or volunteers with insufficient skills), conflicting pressures (e.g., NGBs focused on elite-level success and policy objectives focused on increasing mass participation), or a lack of awareness (e.g., paid professionals and volunteers understanding what the specific policy objectives are) will limit the ability of sport organizations to conform to institutional requirements. Oliver (1991) identified a total of five institutional antecedents with a key question characterizing each one.

1. *Cause*: Why are these pressures being exerted?
2. *Constituents*: Who is exerting pressure?
3. *Content*: To what norms or requirements is the organization being pressured to conform?
4. *Control*: How or by what means are the institutional pressures being exerted?
5. *Context*: What is the environmental context within which institutional pressures are being exerted?

According to Oliver, each antecedent has two predictive dimensions. It is the consideration of the organization's ability and willingness to conform that drives the predictive dimensions of strategic responses, which, in turn, determine the likelihood of resistance to institutional pressures.

- The predictive dimensions for the antecedent of *cause* are legitimacy or social fitness and efficiency or economic fitness. For example, in sport, the rise in sedentary behavior in many Western nations is an evidence-based problem requiring action.
- Related to *constituents*, the multiplicity of constituent demands and the level of dependence on institutional constituents will drive resistance or conformity. In this case, the nature of the response may largely be predicted based on the range of agencies exerting pressure, the nature of the relationship between the constituents, and the extent to which the institution is resource dependent or required to conform.
- The predictive dimension for the antecedent of *content* relates specifically to the norms or requirements to which organizations are being pressured to conform. Such norms or requirements may commonly relate to inputs such as the requirement to provide partnership funding or to meet quality assurance standards or governance codes.
- The predictive dimension relating to *control* is generally either legal coercion or enforcement (e.g., Title IX requirements for allocation of resources to sport within education) or through a voluntary diffusion of norms (e.g., the expectation that NGBs of sport will want to create and sustain comprehensive systems of coach education and development).
- In terms of *context*, the predictive dimensions are environmental uncertainty (difficulty in anticipating or predicting the future) and environmental interconnectedness (stakeholders who frequently interact and work collaboratively).

The final part of Oliver's theory considers the variation in the predictive dimensions across the five institutional factors to determine the likely choice of strategy. The five predictors of strategic responses are presented in further detail in the following section. The framework has been applied to the sport environment to illuminate the varied responses that sport organizations may have toward policy.

Cause

The cause of institutional pressure refers to the rationale, expectations, and objectives that drive external pressure for conformity (Oliver, 1991). An organization's decision to conform with or reject external policy is likely to be formed based on its assessment of the extent to which it will enhance the social or economic fitness of the organization. Institutional pressures in sport to make organizations more socially fit include developments such as club quality, accreditation standards, child protection policies, coach education programs, and environmentally conscious facility design. Efficiency and economic fitness also underpin many institutional pressures. For example, the USOC requires NGBs to be internally efficient and demonstrate effective financial decision making. Similarly, donors to sport-based nongovernmental organizations (NGOs) require them to be businesslike, accountable, and able to clearly articulate how funds have been used to effect positive social change.

In short, when an organization perceives that conformity will enhance social fitness (legitimacy) or efficiency, it will most likely conform to the institutional pressure. In contrast, some form of resistance is more likely when organizations are unsure about social legitimacy, the value of conformity, or perhaps the general view that institutional aspirations are entirely at odds with the organization's goals. In policy terms, this situation tends to reflect an environment where the expected benefits of conformity for the policy makers (e.g., the government, IOC, NOC, WADA) differ significantly from that of the policy takers (e.g., NGBs, clubs, athletes, etc.). For example, a VSC may resist pressure to formalize a club development strategy if it remains uncertain of the benefits of doing so or of the impact on its existing members. Ultimately, organizations will take their decision to conform or resist based on "the degree to which the organization agrees with and values the intentions or objectives that institutional constituents are attempting to achieve in pressuring the organization to be more socially or economically accountable" (Oliver, 1991, p. 162). Furthermore, this is a decision that will be influenced by organizational identity—the shared beliefs of members about the distinctive characteristics of the organization (Kikulis, 2000)—and the fit between this identity and the institutional pressure.

Constituents

Common institutional constituents in sport include the state, the community of Olympic organizations, interest groups of various types (leagues, clubs, and associations), and the general public. These constituents impose a number of policies and expectations on organizations, which often involve conflicting demands, particularly when the range of policies and expectations at the national, regional, and subregional level reach the local level (Scott, 1983). As a result, acquiescence to institutional pressure is likely when multiplicity (i.e., the number of conflicting policies and expectations placed on an organization) is low. Given the multifarious nature of sport, however, examples of low multiplicity are hard to come by. For example, collegiate athletics programs in the United States may be accountable to the National Collegiate Athletic Association (NCAA), the National Junior Collegiate Athletic Association (NJCAA), or the National Association of Intercollegiate Athletics (NAIA). At the same time, the program must respond to demands from their Conference, their educational institution, and the individual sports that make up their program. More common in sport are situations where agents receive multiple policy instructions from various organizations and then attempt to strategically respond to each of these pressures, as illustrated in the collegiate athletics example. Another example of this is subregional sports partnerships in England (County Sport Partnerships). These organizations receive funding from Sport England and are required to work alongside NGBs of sport to increase mass participation in sport. They must balance their strategic response to national-level policy with other demands from local authorities to develop physical activity interventions and to use sport as a vehicle for regenerating and improving local communities. Oliver (1991) argues that in such situations—where multiplicity is high—compliance, avoidance, defiance, and manipulation are the more likely strategic responses. DiMaggio and Powell (1983) argue that resource dependence plays a significant role: Organizations will conform to the demands of organizations on which they are dependent and resist those on which they are not. This does not solely apply in the case of financial resources but can be applied more broadly to include the social capital that emanates from local-level relations that have developed around a particular area of work (such as community sport development) over an extended period of time (Harris, 2013).

Content

Two factors underlie institutional pressures in relation to content. The first is the consistency of policy or pressures with organizational goals. Sport organizations will be more likely to conform to policy when it is consistent or compatible with the organization's goals. We find a clear example of this in elite sport. Many national-level governments have clear policies regarding elite sport success, and the majority of Olympic sport NGBs will readily conform to such policies given that they closely align with their own internal priorities. When there is moderate consistency between policy and organizational goals, the most likely strategic response is compromise or avoidance. Evidence of these strategies can be seen in community sport in England where larger VSCs may compromise (in return for resource support from Sport England or NGBs) or avoid national policy aspirations to increase mass sports participation (Harris, Mori, & Collins, 2009; May, Harris, & Collins, 2013). It follows, then, that when consistency between the intention of policy and the internal goals of organizations is low, organizations will defy or manipulate external policy pressures. Such strategies have been used by VSCs in receipt of lottery grants, who found themselves unable or unwilling to comply with the policies attached to the grant because the norms and values inherent in the policy were not consistent with the internal goals of the organization (Garrett, 2004). It appears that in this example, the need or desire for external funding was a more pressing concern for organizations. This led to ceremonial conformity at the funding application stage and resistance to external pressure justified by a lack of capacity once the funding was secured.

The second predictive factor associated with content focuses on constraints, in particular, the loss of autonomy associated with institutional pressures imposed on organizations. Where autonomy for organizations is preserved and the constraints are low, organizations are more likely to acquiesce to institutional pressures. An example of this can be seen in the governance of some sports whereby the International Federation retains power and influence over the global governance of the game, and the NGB retains responsibility for governing and developing the sport nationally. Here, NGBs will be more likely to respond positively to occasional institutional pressures from the International Federation so long as this pressure is focused on international concerns and does not threaten the ability of the NGB to retain control and influence over the governance and development of their sport in their country. Oliver goes on to explain that "as autonomy is seen to be threatened, organizations may move to compromise or negotiate on the extent of their permitted discretion" (1991, p. 166). For example, while NGBs such as USA Basketball may work with the International Federation on matters relating to coach education, any pressure from the Fédération Internationale de Basketball (FIBA) to impose a basketball coach education program in the United States may be perceived as overzealous, threatening the autonomy of the NGB to decide what is most appropriate for their sport within the United States, and thus lead to resistant strategic responses such as avoidance, defiance, or manipulation.

Control

Control refers to means—in other words, the way in which pressures are imposed on organizations. Oliver (1991) states that pressures are imposed in two distinct ways. The first of these is legal coercion, where regulations and policies, for example, are imposed by means of legitimate authority rather than discretionary compliance (DiMaggio & Powell, 193; Pfeffer & Salancik, 1978; Scott, 1987 in Oliver, 1991). Less organizational resistance is usually observed in cases where the law is used to embolden institutional pressure. This is primarily due to the consequences of nonconformity, which are more tangible and severe (Oliver, 1991). Such examples in sport include organizational and individual athlete requirements to abide by Anti-Doping Agency regulations. While the field is controversial, largely due to the positivist nature of the testing regimen and the protests of innocence from athletes accused of wrongdoing, tests indicating that an athlete has used a banned substance lead to lengthy bans and, in some cases, fines. However, we also see examples of legal coercion that lack robustness and, thus, do not have the same impact in terms of requiring organizational conformity. Examples of recent regulatory frameworks include UEFA's FFP Regulations and the Amateur Sport Act. With regard to the former, critics have pointed to the numerous loopholes in the FFP regulations and the ability of clubs to employ varying strategies to dodge the principles set out in the regulations. On the latter issue, USOC and NGBs have largely ignored their responsibilities for the development of grassroots, amateur sport as set out in the Amateur Sport Act, instead focusing resources on elite development with no repercussions from the U.S. Congress (Farrey, 2008).

Voluntary diffusion is another way in which institutional pressures may be acted on. In other words, certain institutional pressures may have already spread voluntarily through sport. In this way, organizational behavior across a field such as sport can help to predict the likelihood of conformity. Examples of this include the proactive and voluntary adoption of robust child protection measures or club accreditation standards without any legal requirements in place that require such measures to be taken. Thus, the action of some organizations in the field contribute to the development of new environmental norms where, in some sports, the norm is for a reputable club to have stringent child protection policies in place or to have achieved club accreditation standards. What is not addressed in any detail in such cases is the extent to which the NGB (or other governing agencies) have employed hegemonic principles to cultivate an environment where organizational conduct is consistent with the longer-term goals of the governing agent (Raco & Imrie, 2000). This can be achieved through direct means (e.g., requiring clubs to have club accreditation in order to receive grants from the NGB) or through more subtle, indirect means such as crafting an ongoing narrative via presentations, strategies, newsletters, or website information about the need for modern, high-quality clubs as represented by those clubs who aspire to achieve accreditation standards. In contrast, when voluntary diffusion is low, organizations will be less likely to conform. For example, when developing their sport's three-year strategic plan, very few NGBs consult with local-level sport development practitioners regarding the relevance of their plan or how it may be implemented in different contexts across the country. In short, diffusion is limited in this regard across the sector, and, thus, support is limited from local authorities for NGBs to engage local-level partners in the planning process.

Context

The broader environmental context within which organizations operate will also influence their response to institutional pressure. Oliver (1991) offers two predictors as significant factors in determining organizations' conformity or resistance to policy: environmental uncertainty and interconnectedness. Environmental uncertainty can best be understood as the extent to which future events cannot be anticipated or accurately predicted (Pfeffer & Salancik, 1978). When environmental uncertainty is high, organizations are far more likely to employ strategies that give the impression of conformity. For example, in uncertain times (e.g., when Sport England is in the process of renegotiating the three-year [whole sport funding] grants for NGBs of sport) NGBs are far more likely to acquiesce and compromise with Sport England pressures. This conformity not only protects NGBs from environmental turbulence (Meyer & Rowan, 1977) but also serves the purpose of presenting the NGB as a supportive and cooperating body, one that the funder would do well to invest in. As the operational environment becomes more certain, so too does organizations' confidence about future resources and legitimacy (Oliver, 1991). In this more stable environmental context, organizations more commonly defy or manipulate policy given that the benefit of pursuing organizational goals outweighs the risk of the implications associated with resisting policy goals.

The second predictor, interrelatedness, refers to the number and depth of networks across an organizational field (DiMaggio & Powell, 1983). In fields with highly interconnected organizations, cooperation with and conformity to institutional pressures are more likely.

> Because highly interconnected environments provide relational channels through which institutional norms can be diffused, this tends to create more implicit coordination and collectivization in a given environment, more consensus on diffused norms, and greater ubiquity of institutional effects (Oliver, 1991, p. 171).

On the surface, this interrelatedness can be seen in the number of networks whose primary focus is the delivery of community sport policy in England. This includes the Department of Culture, Media and Sport; Sport England; Sport Coach UK; the Sport and Recreational Alliance; NGBs of sport at the national and regional levels; county sport partnerships; county sport associations; community sport networks; local authorities; universities, sixth form and further education colleges; and schools. However, a deeper look at these networks reveals some important variation in the importance placed on values and goals as well as resentment and conflict over resources (Harris, 2013). Thus, despite there being a wide range of organizations at national, regional, and local levels and despite attempts to create the illusion of collaborative capacity (Harris & Houlihan, 2014), it is the range of organizations and their differing values and goals that makes the process of delivering community sport policy more bureaucratic and burdensome than it otherwise might be. This example then reflects a fragmented or competitive environment, which restricts conformity and leads to resistant responses such as defiance or, as is more commonly seen in community sport in England, manipulation of policy—in other words, creating the illusion of a particular reality that is in line with policy expectations but somewhat different from the actual reality of the situation. An example of this might be a NGB that spends considerable time and energy to present the impression that it invests heavily in the implementation of community sport policy when, in fact, a closer look at budget allocations reveals that the most significant funding is allocated to employing more strategists and middle managers.

Implementation Theory

This section provides a brief introduction to implementation theory and focuses on Van Meter and Van Horn's model of the implementation process to review sport organizations' responses to policy. The founding fathers of implementation theory, Pressman and Wildavsky (1984, pp. xi-xxiii), defined implementation as "the process of interaction between the setting of goals and the actions geared to achieve them." Thus, implementation theory was about more than impact in that it relates to what happened but is more about the reasons why it happened (1973). More generally, de Leon (1999, p. 134) reported that implementation was primarily concerned with "what happens between policy expectations and policy results." More specifically, Van Meter and Van Horn (1975, pp. 447-448) defined implementation as "encompassing actions by public and private individuals (or groups) that are directed at the achievement of objectives set forth in prior policy decisions." A more formal, legally bound definition of implementation has been offered by Mazmanian and Sabatier (1981, pp. 20-21).

> Implementation is the carrying out of a basic policy decision, usually incorporated in a statute but which can also take the form of important executive orders or court decisions. Ideally, that decision identifies the problem(s) to be addressed, stipulates the objective(s) to be pursued, and in a variety of ways, 'structures' the implementation process.

While these definitions help to draw common parameters around what implementation is (and is not), they fail to adequately recognize the importance of actors, specifically the interaction among actors involved in the implementation process. This is a vitally important part of the large black box that sits between what O'Toole (1995, p. 43) referred to as "government intention and actual results." Barrett and Fudge (1981, p. 4) asserted that implementation "needs to be regarded as a process on interaction and negotiation, taking place over time, between those seeking to put policy into effect and those upon whom action depends." Seen as part of a **policy–action continuum** developed by Barrett and Fudge (1981), this approach provides insight into the organic growth of the relationship between policy and action. The policy–action continuum views the state- and local-level deliverers as mutually interacting elements of an adaptive policy system. Critically, power is a central force within this model, particularly when considering "bargaining and negotiation over the control of resources" (Barrett & Fudge, 1981, p. 25). It views policy implementation as a multidimensional, multiorganizational field of interaction. Thus, policy is not viewed as constant but a property mediated

TIME OUT

Why Government Policy Fails

In 1973 Jeffrey Pressman and Aaron Wildavsky published their seminal case study *Implementation: How Great Expectations in Washington Are Dashed in Oakland.* Their study focused on a major Economic Development Administration (EDA) program to create jobs in Oakland, California. Their case illuminated a range of costly setbacks that are typically encountered in policy implementation. To support efforts to enhance future policy implementation, Pressman and Wildavsky highlighted a number of key lessons.

- *Emphasize implementation*: Implementation should not be divorced from policy.
- *Make clear the implementation infrastructure*: It is important to have a clearly structured organizational machinery in place to implement policy. This machinery requires sufficient resources and clear roles and responsibilities.
- *Reduce the number of decision points in the policy process*: The probability of successful implementation significantly decreases as the number of decision points requiring approval or clearance increases.
- *Learn the policy*: It is critical to have mechanisms in place to evaluate implementation as it happens and to disseminate intelligence.
- *Cultivate expertise among implementing agents*: This requires actors who are both knowledgeable about the policy area and have the experience, attitude, and competencies to get the job done.
- *Understand the impact of management*: It is important to create and sustain collaborative capacity between governing authorities and implementing agents; to have orderly and timely funding mechanisms; and to develop sensitive evaluation systems to track progress and identify areas for improvement.
- *Streamline decision-making processes*: Streamline processes so the principles are clearly articulated and not only command compliance but also share best practices and knowledge.
- *Expect challenge and conflict*: Pressman and Wildavsky warn agents to be aware of "hazardous rocks"—that is, the various people involved in the policy process. They especially point to the inherent features of interest group politics and how these have the potential to disrupt and derail policy implementation.

by actors and "inevitably undergoes interpretation and modification and, in some cases, subversion" (Barrett & Fudge, 1981, p. 21).

Part of the explanation for the variety of definitions of implementation is the evolutionary nature of the field, coming in and out of vogue in public administration and political science, as an area of relevant study over the past 30 years (Barrett, 2004). First-generation policy implementation theory tended to be based on the Weberian notion of a bureaucratically and rationally led society (Weber, 1947). This classical model of policy administration and the resulting metaphor of government as a machine supported the commonly held view of implementation as an automatic cog controlled by the rationalized machinery of government (Cantelon & Ingham, 2002). The second-generation implementation literature primarily focused on the relationship between policy and practice (Goggin, Bowman, Lester, & O'Toole, 1990). Empirical work revealed a number of important issues, including the importance of time periods (i.e., the time needed to implement policy) (Van Horn, 1987); the reality that policy very often does mandate what matters at the local level; the fact that values and beliefs are central to local responses; and the understanding that effective implementation relies on a careful balance of pressure and support (McLaughlin, 1987, p. 176). Much of the research in this period focused on implementation failure or implementation gaps, that is, the difference between outcome and the original policy intention. Emerging from the study of failure were two distinctive schools of thought: the **top-down** and **bottom-up perspectives**.

Top-down theorists based their work on the premise of clear national-level policies and a chain of command made up of compliant implementers (Pressman & Wildavsky, 1973). Thus, government departments and national agencies such as the National Olympic Committee and NGBs can be viewed as the policy makers at the top of the policy tree creating and passing down dictates to street-level agents such as sport clubs, local authorities, schools, coaches, and uniformed groups. Advocates

TIME OUT

The Ten Requirements for Perfect Policy Implementation

Hogwood and Gunn (1984) further developed Pressman and Wildavsky's key lessons of policy implementation and presented ten preconditions of perfect policy implementation. These preconditions can be summarized as follows.

1. External circumstances do not pose any significant constraint to the implementing agency.
2. Adequate time and sufficient resources are available for the program.
3. A combination of resources is available to support implementation.
4. The policy to be implemented is based upon a valid theory of cause and effect.
5. The relationship between cause and effect is direct with few or no intervening links.
6. There is a single (or are very few) implementing agency (or agencies).
7. There is a complete understanding of, and agreement upon, the objectives to be achieved throughout the implementation process.
8. In making progress toward the policy objectives, the tasks to be performed by each implementing agent can be specified in complete detail.
9. Communication between implementing agents is perfect.
10. Those in authority can demand and will receive perfect obedience.

of the top-down perspective point to factors that they argue result in successful implementation, including policies with clearly defined goals (Van Meter & Van Horn, 1975), a single authority responsible for the policy (Birkland, 2005), responsibility for implementation with agencies sympathetic to the policy's objectives (Sabatier, 1986), and the presence of an implementation chain that operates linearly (Birkland, 2005).

Criticisms of the top-down approach include the presupposition that policy makers can simply issue a new policy-based command and expect those below them to deliver successful outcomes. This assumes boundless rationality among implementers; fails to take account of the diverse nature of the policy process and the problematic nature of interagency collaboration; and fails to fully consider norms, behaviors, values, and attitudes of implementing agents (Barrett & Fudge, 1981; Hjern & Hull, 1982; Lipsky, 1980). The top-down perspective is also heavily criticized for ignoring the potential for service deliverers to subvert or modify the original policy decision, particularly where policies contradict local contextual matters or fail to correspond with an organization's values or purpose (Skille, 2008).

Such criticism led to the development of bottom-up models, in which a more realistic understanding of implementation emerges by analyzing it from the perspective of the service deliverer (Hill & Hupe, 2009). The bottom-up school generally sees policy implementation on two levels. Programs and initiatives are devised at the macro-implementation level and at the micro-implementation level. Local organizations respond to these macro-level plans, develop their own programs, and implement them (Berman, 1978). This model can be seen in community sport in England with initiatives such as the School Games and After School Club initiative (Sportivate) being conceived nationally and being delivered locally by County Sport Partnerships (CSPs) and NGBs.

The majority of implementation-related problems stem from the interaction of a policy with the micro-level institutional setting. Central actors have limited direct control over micro-level settings; thus, there is potential for a wide variation in how the same national policy is implemented locally. This is a reported issue within the sport policy system in England, going back to the sport development policies of the 1990s with initiatives such as TOP Play, BT Top Sport, Champion Coaching, and Girl Sport. Specifically, the challenge is that of implementing a centrally developed, one-size-fits-all program in a number of environments. This is reinforced by Matland (1995), who argued that contextual factors are critical, more so than the nationally conceived parameters governing policy. Therefore, if local-level implementers are not given the freedom to adapt programs to local conditions, implementation is likely to break down and fail (Palumbo, Maynard-Moody, & Wright, 1984).

The consideration of fit between nationally constructed policies and programs and the implementers' perception of them is the key strength of the bottom-up perspective. However, it is criticized for both normative and methodological shortcomings. The normative-based criticism is that, in a democratic society, "policy control should be exercised by actors whose power derives from their accountability to sovereign voters through their elected representatives" (Matland, 1995, p. 149). Thus, actors at the top of the top-down paradigm can be seen to possess political legitimacy. If power is to be shifted to the local level, this should only occur within the context of central authority. The second criticism focuses on a misrepresentation of the level of autonomy experienced by street-level workers (Matland, 1995). While classic organizational theory has a plentiful supply of examples of actors subordinating government or institutional goals (March & Simon, 1958; Merton, 1957; Michels, 1962; Selznick, 1949), variations in policy actions can largely be explained by local contextual differences (Matland, 1995). In these cases, policy actions fall within a relatively limited range, usually specified by centrally determined policy (Matland, 1995). In addition, bottom-up approaches simplistically overstate the intervention of central government in the policy formation process while ignoring their common function whereby they empower other special-interest groups (e.g., environmental groups) to enforce policies that are in their interests (Sabatier, 1993).

Notably, in advance of much of the literature relating to top-down and bottom-up approaches to implementation, Van Meter and Van Horn developed a systematic model of the implementation process focusing on both centralized decision making and street-level consensus, thus providing a useful sensitizing device for the analysis of policy implementation. Drawing from three strands of literature (organizational theory, public policy impact, and intergovernmental relations), Van Meter and Van Horn (1975) identified six variables as key to the policy outcome, beginning with the initial policy objectives and allocation of resources, then filtering hierarchically through interorganizational communications, characteristics of implementing agencies, and current economic and political conditions, concluding with the disposition of implementing agents (Van Meter & Van Horn, 1975).

The natural starting point in analyzing the implementation of policy is a consideration of the policy itself because this is where goals and objectives are established. Importantly, as Van Meter and Van Horn (1975) advise, the range of factors that affect implementation will vary depending on the nature of the policy to be carried out. They therefore classify policy according to two distinguishing characteristics: the amount of change involved and the extent to which goal consensus is reached among parties involved in the implementation process. The amount of change in policy is important in at least two ways. First, incremental changes in policy are more palatable and more likely to receive support than drastic ones. Second, major changes in policy will bring about major organizational and structural change, which will directly affect the implementation process. For example, the change in community sport policy in England in 2008 brought about changes in the system and structure of the delivery system. This required NGBs to lead the implementation of community sport policy and to work alongside local partnerships in the local-level delivery of their plans. The change to the structure and system of delivery means that it has taken a considerable amount of time to plan and prepare for implementation. According to some NGB and CSP representatives, it has taken as long as three to four years to plan and be clear about the goals and priorities in terms of local-level delivery (Harris, 2013), and has thus had a considerable impact on the ability and capacity of agents to work together for the purpose of actually implementing policy. Thus, major changes in structures and relationships must be considered alongside the adjustment, planning, and preparation time required so that these agencies are able to start the exercise of implementation.

The second characteristic—the degree of participatory consensus and extent of change initiated by the centrally conceived policy—must be carefully considered if successful implementation is to be achieved. The more closely aligned the centrally conceived policy objective is to that of the implementing agent, the more likely that organizations will cooperate and the original policy objective will be implemented. Thus, government departments or NSOs typically attempt to (1) consult with implementing agents and develop policy objectives that reflect the values and priorities of the majority or reflect those of specifically targeted agents, (2) use resources to incentivize agents to implement policy, (3) shape agents' preferences (Lukes, 1974) by influencing views, ensuring that they align with the aims and aspirations of the central agent, or (4) a combination of 2 and 3, whereby resources and new public management techniques (e.g., performance management, contracts, performance payments) are used to underpin the hegemony of the central agent and ensure that their values and priorities become accepted as the norm.

Sport Organizations Response to Policy

The following section applies the six variables from Van Meter and Van Horn's policy implementation model to the implementation of community sport policy in England. While neither definitive nor reflective of all policy environs, the analysis draws attention to many of the key factors that influence how and why organizations respond to policy in the way that they do.

Standards or Objectives

This variable allows for a closer explanation of the objectives to be achieved and the implications of specificity. At this crucial stage, policy moves beyond the generality of legislative documentation or headline information and into an exacting definition of the objective and the specific standards used to assess performance. For instance, while the generic community sport policy for England is to increase the number of people who play sport regularly, on closer inspection the policy standard is defined as increasing the number of people aged 14 and older who play sport on at least one occasion (for at least 30 minutes) once a week. This level of precision may, on the one hand, seem pedantic; on the other hand this level of detail is necessary to evaluate policy. To ascertain whether implementation has been successful it is necessary to count how many people aged 14 and older participate in sport at least once a week for at least 30 minutes. This figure is usually calculated during (to track progress) and after the period of policy implementation and is compared to the benchmark figure taken prior to implementation. While this process may seem relatively straightforward, the exact definition of policy can cause problems, particularly dispositional conflicts. For example, in community sport in England the precise definition of community sport, the focus on people aged 14 and older, and the decision to include and exclude certain sport-related activities have been factors that have either galvanized support from certain organizations (e.g., pure sport organizations such as NGBs of sport) or deterred would-be implementers (e.g., local authorities who are more interested in a broader strategy focusing on addressing sedentary behavior and promoting physical activity). In addition, evaluating standards can be a costly and problematic exercise. For example, the Active People survey in England is used to frequently measure changes in mass participation. This survey originally cost £5.5 million (US$6.7 million) over a five-year period. The fact that such significant funding was allocated to evaluation was itself a point of conflict across a range of stakeholders. Further, such problems were exacerbated when the results from the survey revealed that participation levels in certain sports or geographical areas were declining rather than increasing. This led to various assaults on the credibility of the measurement tool and a general pessimism of making significant gains in sports participation over a very short time period and with relatively limited funds. To be clear, of importance here is not the nature of the problems but specific policy objectives and standards of evaluation, which, while necessary, can cause deep and problematic implications for the attitude and response that organizations have to policy. In this regard, Van Meter and Van Horn's (1975) advice regarding incremental changes in policy objectives and securing consensus from implementing agents is instructive.

Policy Resources

The second variable in Van Meter and Van Horn's model relates to the resources that are available to support the policy implementation process. Funding is nearly always viewed as inadequate, and either a lack of funding or incentives are considered to be a major reason for unsuccessful implementation (Van Meter & Van Horn, 1975). This may include insufficient funds to develop the infrastructure, lack of funding to support initiatives that are required to implement policy, or funding levels that are inadequate to induce organizations to accept the burden of implementing policy. Indeed, the funding of policy carries many significant implications. For example, the funding issue raises questions of who does and does not receive funding, what happens to the funds and how this is tracked and evaluated, and what ramifications unequal funding hold for agencies that are expected to work together to implement policy. Within the English community sport system, the majority of funding is invested in NGBs (see, e.g., the NGB investment section on www.sportengland.org). Significantly smaller amounts of core funding are invested into CSPs, and no direct funding is provided to local-level implementing agencies such as local authorities and VSCs. This funding model has created considerable problems for the community sport system. In the best-case scenario, organizations have been willing to accept the decisions, reach beyond self-interest, search out areas of mutual benefit, and aspire to achieve goals. However, in the worst cases it has created a divisive and fragmented system of delivery where organizations undertake self-promotion, openly criticize other "funded" agencies, and do little, if anything, to implement policy.

A remaining question is whether greater parity across different agencies in the funding model, greater funding for local-level agencies, or funding based on existing wealth (i.e., not using public funds to invest in wealthy NGBs such as association football, tennis, cricket) would have any positive net effect on policy implementation. However, what is clear is that funding plays a significant role in shaping organizations' attitudes toward and, therefore, their response to policy. Other resource issues that have been found to play an important role in shaping organizations' response to the community sport policy include facilities (the availability of accessible, good-quality facilities), expertise (knowing what works in increasing mass sports participation and expertise in collaborative working practices), and political support (a commitment to the principle of community sport or mass participation from board members, committee members, or local councilors).

Interorganizational Communication and Enforcement Activities

This variable refers to the clarity of the policy standards, how these standards are communicated to those responsible for implementing policy, the accuracy and consistency of communication, and the range of enforcement activities used to influence behavior. Obviously, organizational responses to policy will be severely affected by a lack of clarity or awareness of policy standards. It may well be that the standards lack precision, that they are confusing, or that efforts to disseminate information about the policy have been unsuccessful or not far-reaching enough to inform local level implementers. Communication can be a complex, difficult, and time-consuming task, particularly when it involves a range of different agencies at different levels of the system. Communicators inevitably distort key messages, intentionally and unintentionally (Downs, 1967). Further, if different sources of communication provide different interpretations of policy objectives, implementers will find it difficult to carry out the intentions of policy (Van Meter & Van Horn, 1975). Such problems have been found in community sport in England, particularly among local-level club volunteers who either have a vague recollection of policy standards or maintain an out-of-date understanding of policy as being about sport for all or sport for particular target groups (Harris et al., 2009). Such problems carry significant implications. Consider, for example, a large number of the 106,000 or so VSCs in England not fully understanding or being aware of the policy objectives for community sport. For some this may be of no consequence; they would remain indifferent to policy. For others, who may well be attempting to cooperate, it may mean that despite their intentions they are actually delivering divergent policies or pursuing different strategies to national policy standards.

As indicated by the attention to enforcement, implementation requires a range of mechanisms to assess, incentivize, and enforce how implementers act and what they do to achieve policy objectives. This acknowledges that the making of policy is simply one step in the process and does little itself to assure that policy is acted upon. In single organizations the process of enforcing policy action is far clearer and centers upon a more direct organization-to-individual relationship, where if the individual fails to do what the organization requires, the organization can take appropriate action. In addition, the organization has a number of mechanisms to influence subordinate behavior, including recruitment and selection, advancement and promotion, performance-related pay and other performance incentives, and budgetary allocations that can be increased or reduced in response to performance (Van Meter & Van Horn, 1975). In contrast, when we examine the mechanisms among members of different organizations, such as in the case of community sport policy in England, many of these mechanisms are absent. Therefore, the government or other higher-level agencies (e.g., USOC, Sport Canada, Sport England) formulate alternative strategies in an attempt to facilitate, incentivize, or enforce implementation of policy. These strategies can be summarized as (1) direct payment (e.g., Sport England pay CSPs £250,000 [US$303,000] per year to support NGBs in the implementation of policy), (2) positive and negative sanctions (e.g., positive: performance payments can be made to NGBs and CSPs that exceed their performance targets; negative: future payments to poor-performing NGBs may be subject to special measures being met), and (3) technical advice (e.g., Sport England provides a range of technical guidance and support to advocate the continued provision of sport facilities by local government). Finally, the most direct and threatening form of influence is the power of the funder to withdraw or withhold funds. While this strategy was rarely used, largely because it is seen to undermine cooperative relations and create hostility at the expense of program goals (Derthick, 1972), it has been used in community sport in England including rugby union, association football, swimming, and golf. Interestingly, while the long-term effect of this change in strategy is unknown, the short-term result is that NGBs and CSPs have a clearer understanding of the consequences of nonconformity and poor performance, and NGB and CSP representatives have reported the need to be more methodological in tracking their work in order to demonstrate serious attempts to implement policy (Harris, 2013).

Characteristics of the Implementing Bodies

This part of the model involves numerous "formal structural features of the organization and the informal attributes of their personnel" (Van Meter

& Van Horn, 1975, p. 471). It also examines the relationship between implementing agents and other agencies involved in the policy process. Van Meter and Van Horn (1975) suggest six characteristics that may influence an organization's response to policy. These characteristics are shown in table 7.1 together with further details of the key agents involved in the implementation of community sport in England.

Economic, Political, and Social or Cultural Conditions

Just as the characteristics of the implementing agent affects its capacity and likely response to policy, so too do environmental conditions. Here, issues such as the economy; the local, regional, or national political conditions; or social and cultural norms will affect and be affected by the implementation of policy. For example, relating these conditions to the implementation of community sport policy in England gives rise to a range of questions.

1. Are sufficient economic resources invested in community sport to support successful implementation?
2. Are sufficient amounts of funding invested into appropriate partners to support the implementation of policy?
3. Are economic resources invested into relevant strategies, and to what extent

Table 7.1 Characteristics of Implementing Bodies Involved in Community Sport in England

Characteristics	NGBs of sport	CSPs
The competence and size of an agency's staff	Competence varies considerably, although efforts (and therefore skills) are traditionally aligned to elite and high-performance work. The size of the NGB varies from large, multi-million-pound organizations to small agencies with budgets of approx. £100,000 (US$121,000).	Competence varies considerably across the 45 CSPs. The size of the partnership also varies, although the core team (professional team of staff employed within the CSP) is typically between 6 and 20 members of staff.
The degree of hierarchical control of subunit decisions and processes within the implementing agencies	Limited control of subunits at local level (county associations). No control over local-level VSCs.	Tight control over decisions within the CSP. Very limited control over partner agencies that form a part of the partnership (local authorities, clubs).
An agency's political resources	Political resources with central government have grown in strength in recent years, particularly the power of the NGB lobby with politicians. Resources at the local level vary from sport to sport and area to area.	Limited political resources with central government, although this is improving due to the perception of being able to deliver on difficult topics. Local-level resources vary depending on the relationship between the partnership and local authorities in the area.
The vitality of an organization	The majority of NGBs have vitality. They lead the development of sport in terms of participation and excellence, and have, in most cases, governed their sport for more than 100 years.	CSPs are relatively new and still very much working to formalize themselves as a tried, tested, and respected part of the sports landscape.
The degree of open communications with persons outside the organization	Relatively guarded and closed.	Relatively open.
The agency's formal and informal linkages with the policy-making body	Well-developed links with government, Sport England, and Sport and Recreation Alliance.	Well-developed links with Sport England. Developing links with the government through creation of national CSP network.

are resources likely to be used to support divergent activities (e.g., physical activity or elite sport)?

4. How have macro-level economic conditions affected the capacity of grassroots deliverers to implement policy?
5. How will social and economic conditions be affected by the implementation of policy?
6. What level of political support (national, regional, local) exists for community sport?
7. What is the nature of public opinion toward community sport policy?
8. Is there general support or opposition for policy across key agents involved in the policy?
9. To what extent do private interest groups support or oppose the policy?

Needless to say, the way in which organizations are affected by such environmental conditions and the way in which policy may influence such conditions will affect organizational capacity and the motivation and desire of organizations to directly engage in the process of implementing policy.

Dispositions of Grassroots Implementers

The final filtering variable dictating how organizations might respond to policy relates to their perceptions of the policy. More specifically, Van Meter and Van Horn advise that organizational responses will be mediated by the willingness and ability of the organization to carry out the policy, the understanding that the organization has of the policy, and "the direction of their response to it (acceptance, neutrality, rejection) and the intensity of that response" (1975, p. 472).

Clearly, this variable is an important one in determining organizational responses to policy. To clarify, the range of filtering variables detailed in Van Meter and Van Horn's model will shape the disposition of implementers. Second, these dispositions will ultimately determine the organization's approach to policy. Obviously, widespread acceptance of the policy among key implementing agents will enhance the prospects for effective implementation. The question remains of knowing and executing exactly what is needed to bring about successful implementation. Alternatively, it is possible that implementing agents will fail to implement policies: While they wish to receive the funding attached to policy, they may

KEY ISSUES FOR SPORT MANAGERS

This chapter draws attention to two theories. In *interorganizational relations theory*, managers have a tool to examine the relationship between organizational behavior, institutional contexts, and the conditions under which organizations resist or conform to forms of institutional pressure, such as policy. This is helpful for managers because it provides a framework of variables that directly influence the extent to which organizational responses to policy may vary, from passive conformity to active resistance, subject to the nature and context within which policy is created.

With *implementation theory*, managers consider both top-down and bottom-up perspectives of policy. From a top-down perspective, the ten requirements for perfect implementation provide a useful framework for managers to reflect upon the reality of policy implementation and to assess relative areas of strength against areas for improvement.

The bottom-up perspective reminds managers of the problems of top-down policy processes, not to mention

- the problems of interagency collaboration;
- the resources, capacity, and skills of implementing agents;
- the values, norms, and behaviors of implementing agents and the possibility that policy will be subverted or modified from the original policy decision, particularly where these contradict local contextual matters or fail to correspond with an organization's values or purpose (Skille, 2008); and
- the strong probability that problems with either or both cognition and consensus with likely lead to policy failure (Barrett & Fudge, 1981; Hjern & Hull, 1982; Lipsky, 1980).

In sum, it is helpful for managers to develop insight into the interrelated and collective nature of the policy process. All stages of the policy process tend to influence others in an ongoing, cyclical manner. Such reciprocity is likely to build understanding and respect between the various parts of the policy system, thereby improving the possibility of a collective approach to policy and building a more effective policy system.

reject the goals contained in them, or perhaps their capacity is utilized to pursue activities that more closely align with their values and priorities. Finally, the intensity of an organization's disposition to policy provides an indication of the likely behavior that will follow. Those that hold intense negative attitudes will likely refuse, in forthright terms, to participate in the program of implementation. Others, who perhaps have less intense negative preferences, may revert to more discrete forms of diversion, evasion, or manipulation. Of particular importance in the implementation exercise is the need to reconcile the desire for central leadership with the reality of diffuse implementation authority (Cline, 2000). This requires a collaborative leadership approach that builds consensus around policy priorities, raises awareness of policy goals, creates a robust means of evaluating policy, and provides appropriate resources to support organizations with implementation. While developing such strategies may be practically challenging and not without limitation, they would likely help in developing a more cooperative and collective pool of policy implementers.

Summary and Conclusions

This chapter has reviewed policy from the narrower point of view of it being an explicit and stated goal rather than the broader notion of it representing all actions of organizations (or governments) (Goldsmith, 1980). The primary focus of the chapter is on policy as the outcome of political debate, with a concentration on societal-level problems and those policies that focus on the organization and its business interests. Four policy types were examined, with sport-related examples provided for clarification. These policy types were distributive (e.g., the funding of elite sport), redistributive (e.g., targeting specific underrepresented groups), constituency-based (e.g., the creation of a national coach education association), and regulatory (e.g., anti-doping regulations). While recognition of these types of policy is important, it is action, in particular the implementation of policy, that is of central concern to the chapter. The chapter utilizes two distinct bodies of literature to provide a detailed analysis of organizations that create policy and the response of others who may be expected to implement it.

Oliver's (1991) article "Strategic Responses to Institutional Processes" provides a useful framework to examine how organizational responses to policy may vary from passive conformity to active resistance depending on the nature and context within which policy is created. Oliver's model has particular utility in that it considers a range of institutional factors that influence the institutional pressure (or policy), offers predictive dimensions for each factor, and demonstrates the strategic response that most likely considers the predictive variable. For example, the model illustrates that organizations are more likely to support the implementation of policy when the legitimacy that can be gained from conformity is high. But, in contrast, if the legitimacy associated with conformity is low, implementing agents are likely to compromise, avoid, defy, or manipulate policy. Of particular importance here are the broader questions pertaining to the policy process, for example: Why has the policy been developed? Who has developed the policy? What is the implementation agent required or expected to do? How is the policy maker seeking to involve the implementation agent? What is the broader political, financial, and social context within which the policy has been developed? The model is instructive in that it underscores the willingness and ability of organizations to conform to the policy environment. An organization's willingness to conform is bounded by factors such as organizational skepticism, political self-interest, and organizational control (Oliver, 1991). Similarly, organizational capacity, conflict, and awareness tend to influence an organization's ability to cooperate with policy aspirations (Oliver, 1991).

Utilizing three strands of literature—organizational theory, policy analysis, and intergovernmental relations—Van Meter and Van Horn's (1975) policy implementation process provides a useful framework for analyzing key variables in the implementation of policy. Their framework emphasizes interaction among six variables, including the policy objectives and policy resources, three key filtering variables (interorganizational communication and enforcement activity; the characteristics of implementing bodies; and economic, political, and social or cultural conditions), and the dispositions of grassroots implementers. These variables and the interaction among them determine the response of organizations to policy and, as a result, policy performance. Consequently, the relationship between policy making and policy implementation is characterized as "a long, winding road with many possible constraints and many contingencies to take into consideration" (Skille, 2008, p. 185). Some of the more common problems include poor communication, capability problems, and dispositional conflicts as well as problems of unequal power and resource dependence (Van Meter & Van Horn, 1975). While these problems do not necessarily drive resistance or indifference toward policy goals, they do draw attention to some of the major challenges that are inherent in the policy process, not least the fundamental importance of a consensual and committed delivery system. Without this, policy is little more than rhetoric.

Review Questions

1. Why is an understanding of policy and the responses of sport organizations to policy important for sport managers?
2. Think of your home nation. In what way is the government (at various levels: national or federal, regional, state or province, county, city) involved in the formation of sport-related policy?
3. What factors have influenced the growth in sport policy across most Western nations?
4. Discuss the various strategies or ways in which policy makers can secure the consent and cooperation of implementing agents.
5. Apply Oliver's five predictions of strategic responses to a sport policy with which you are familiar.
6. Apply Van Meter and Van Horn's implementation model to a sport policy with which you are familiar.

Suggestions for Further Reading

While a wide variety of books and articles seek to illuminate the policy process, few specifically address the responses of organizations to policy. Oliver's (1991) article (presented in the first part of this chapter) provides a clear and compelling overview of organizational responses to institutional pressures and is a useful starting point in developing an understanding of the strategies that organizations use in response to institutional pressures such as policy. In terms of policy implementation, Pressman and Wildavsky's (1984) seminal text, *Implementation: How Great Expectations in Washington Are Dashed in Oakland,* provides a useful analysis of the disconnect between the formulation of policy, how implementing agents respond, and the major problems that lead to policy failure. Alongside this, Van Meter and Van Horn (1975) produced a conceptual model detailing the key variables that shape the policy implementation process. From an alternate perspective, Michael Lipksy's (1980) *Street-Level Bureaucracy* focuses on the people who work at street level and interact directly with the end user (e.g., athletic directors, coaches, teachers, youth sport coordinators) and the extent to which these individuals affect the enforcement of rules or implementation of official policy.

More specifically, a growing body of literature focuses on the application of policy analysis specific to sport and sport organizations. These texts are useful in that they analyze sport policy; however, they do not examine implementation per se, nor do they specifically consider the response of organizations to policy. First, a broad analysis of the range of political, social, and economic factors that influence the policy process is offered by Ian Henry (1993) in his book *The Politics of Leisure Policy*. Second, it is worth reviewing various works by Barrie Houlihan as well as texts published by Houlihan and his colleagues, including Anita White and Mick Green. For example, Houlihan's (1997) text *Sport, Policy and Politics: A Comparative Analysis* offers a comprehensive comparative analysis of sport policy in five countries (Australia, Canada, Ireland, the United Kingdom, and the United States). Houlihan and White's (2002) book, *The Politics of Sport Development,* also offers a detailed historical analysis of school, community, and sport policy in Great Britain. Houlihan and Green's extensive analysis of elite sport policy can be found in texts such as *Comparative Elite Sport Development* (2007) and *Elite Sport Development: Policy Learning and Political Priorities* (2008). Third, it is well worth accessing three specific academic papers that provide a helpful introduction to the various ways in which sport policy can be examined: Houlihan's (2005) "Public Sector Sport Policy: Developing a Framework for Analysis"; Skille's (2008) "Understanding Sport Clubs as Sport Policy Implementers: A Theoretical Framework for the Analysis of the Implementation of Central Sport Policy through Local and Voluntary Sport Organizations"; Harris, Mori, and Collins' (2009) "Great Expectations: Voluntary Sports Clubs and Their Role in Delivering National Policy for English Sport"; Garrett's (2004) "The Response of Voluntary Sports Clubs to Sport England's Lottery Funding: Cases of Compliance, Change and Resistance"; and Chalip's (1995) "Policy analysis in sport management." Lastly, those interested in sport policy are advised to see the *International Journal of Sport Policy and Politics*.

Case for Analysis

Implementing the London 2012 Community Sport Legacy

In June 2008 the UK government published the London 2012 Games Legacy Plan. This plan set out the pre- and post-Games legacies associated with the 2012 London Summer Olympics. It identified five broad promises. The first emphasized physical activity and, within this, contained the specific goal of getting at least two million more people in England to be more active by 2012. The aspiration was broken down into physical activity and sport, with the sport component contributing one million new frequent sport participants by 2012.

Sport England was the agency charged with leading this policy. They created a new delivery system led by NGBs. NGBs were commissioned to deliver Whole Sport Plans setting out growth targets for each sport. Funding was allocated to NGBs based on a range of criteria, including the growth potential of each sport, the growth targets of each sport, and the clarity of their plans in detailing how they would increase participation. The total investment into NGBs for the period 2008 to 2012 exceeded £380 million (US$460 million).

The annual Active People Survey, which surveys 165,000 people per year, was used to evaluate changes in sports participation. The first-round results from the 2009 to 2013 funding period were notable insofar as participation gains were primarily attributed to individual, unstructured participation (e.g., individuals choosing to go for a run or a bike ride). In contrast, 19 of 29 sports (66% of sports) witnessed decreases in participation. The net effect was that 94,300 fewer people participated in sport once a week. (See table 7.2.) This was a huge disappointment, particularly when taken into consideration the more than £400

Table 7.2 Changes in Participation and Funding Allocations, by Sport

Sport	Overall change in participation 2009-2015 (based on minimum of one 30-min session of sport per week)	Total government investment £M 2009-2016
Cricket	-0.08	66.1
Cycling	0.26	65.5
Association football	-1.01	63.9
Athletics	1.40	53.0
Swimming	-2.13	52.3
Rugby Union	-0.12	49.7
Rugby League	-0.08	48.4
Tennis	-0.16	46.2
Netball	0.07	43.3
Badminton	-0.31	40.8
Golf	-0.61	29.2
Squash and racquetball	-0.20	27.1
Hockey	-0.04	23.9
Table tennis	0.03	20.7
Sailing	-0.09	19.2
Canoeing	-0.02	18.9
Rowing	-0.01	17.7
Judo	-0.02	16.4
Basketball	-0.07	15.8
Boxing	0.12	11.3
Volleyball	-0.06	10.3
Mountaineering	-0.02	4.7
Rounders	-0.03	4.5
Bowls	-0.36	3.8
Snow sport	-0.03	3.0
Fencing	-0.01	2.7
Taekwondo	-0.01	2.1
Weightlifting	-0.07	2.0

Data from the Active People Survey.

million (US$484 million) investment into community sport.

Despite this, the government continued with its emphasis on sport-specific funding in the 2013 to 2016 period. Community sport policy was redefined, a less challenging target created (participation measured by one 30-minute session per month, and an additional £493 million (US$597 million) invested into NGBs of sport. Despite these changes and the more than £870 million (US$1 billion) of public monies being invested into NGBs of sport over the 2008 to 2016 period, participation in organized sport declined in significant numbers. (See table 7.2.)

Clearly, social trends and a new norm toward individualization are part of the explanation for these failed policies. However, it is also important to consider some of the key policy learning that flows from studies of the England community sport case (see, e.g., Harris & Houlihan, 2014). Such studies give attention to a range of factors that inhibited the effective implementation of policy, which include the following.

- *A deviant and fragmented policy system*: Community sport represents both a deviant and fragmented policy system—deviant in that it fails to genuinely reflect the central government rhetoric of decentralization and fragmented due to the disjointed structure of community sport.
- *Priority diffusion*: While NGBs and CSPs are engaged in the delivery of community sport they each have differing values and beliefs regarding sport. NGBs tend to prioritize traditional sport development whereas CSPs tend to focus attention of broader physical activity and the social outcomes attached to sport.
- *The implementation gap*: A major gap exists in the implementation of community sport policy. NGBs and CSPs are referred to as implementation agents, but they reside at the national and subregional levels and do not have the resources to deliver policies at the local level.
- *Funding bottleneck*: The problem of implementing community sport policy is further hindered by the lack of funding that makes its way down to the street level. The majority of funding invested into NGBs and CSPs is taken up by building the infrastructure and employing more staff within NGBs and CSPs. While this may be viewed as a critical investment in order for NGBs and CSPs to manage policy implementation, it is argued that the balance of investment is fundamentally flawed.
- *I before we*: The community sport policy system is made up of a number of individual units rather than being a collective or communal system, most of whom are resource dependent and therefore prioritize self-preservation.

As a final point, it is important to stress that the focus of such analyses is not the unabated criticism of government, Sport England, NGBs, or CSPs; rather, it is a contribution to the improvement and development of the community sport policy process.

Questions

1. Community sport policy in England formed part of the London 2012 Olympic and Paralympic Games Legacy. Given the data presented in this case, how you describe the community sport legacy from the 2012 Games?
2. What are the key arguments for and against directly funding NGBs of sport for the purpose of increasing participation in community sport?
3. How would you describe the overall response of NGBs of sport to the community sport policy bearing in mind the revised strategy and renewed funding of 2013 to 2016 in contrast to that of 2008 to 2012?
4. What could have been done differently in the review of policy for 2013 to 2016?

CHAPTER 8

Strategy in Sport Organizations

Trevor Slack, PhD
James Andrew Kenyon, PhD
Argyro Elisavet Manoli, PhD

Learning Objectives

When you have read this chapter, you should be able to

1. explain what we mean by the term *organizational strategy*,
2. explain the different corporate-level and business-level strategies that a sport organization can adopt,
3. describe how strategy is formulated and implemented,
4. explain Mintzberg's three modes of strategy formulation,
5. describe the strategy–structure relationship, and
6. compare Miles and Snow's four strategic types.

Key Concepts

acquisition
adaptive mode
ambush marketing
business-level strategy
cash cows
combination strategy
corporate-level strategy
cost leadership strategy
deliberate strategy
differentiation strategy
diversification
divestiture
dogs
emergent strategy
enhancers
entrepreneurial mode
explorers
focus strategy
harvesting (milking) strategy
horizontal integration
innovators

(continued)

Key Concepts *(continued)*

- joint venture
- liquidation
- merger
- mission statement
- planning mode
- portfolio analysis
- question marks
- refiners
- stars
- strategic alliance
- strategic business unit
- stuck in the middle
- SWOT analysis
- takeover
- turnaround strategy
- vertical integration

Nike's Risk-Taking Strategy

Since as early as 1984, multinational sport organization Nike has been renowned for its controversial and aggressive strategy. Since placing murals at the site of the 1984 Olympic Games in Los Angeles and constructing a highly visible store outside the Olympic village at the 1996 Games in Atlanta, despite not being a commercial partner of either event, Nike has established a reputation for being aggressive and unremorseful with their promotional strategies, with a particular preference for provocative strategies such as these **ambush marketing** examples.

More recently, in 2018 Nike launched a series of inclusive advertisements for its 30th anniversary, which featured young Muslim women, African Americans, and physically impaired athletes, all encouraging consumers to follow their dreams. One of these advertisements, featuring former National Football League (NFL) quarterback Colin Kaepernick, generated much controversy and backlash due to an incident involving the star in 2016. During the NFL preseason that year, the San Francisco 49ers quarterback was observed sitting and then later kneeling during pregame renditions of the American national anthem and would later state this was in protest to what he perceived as police brutality and racial inequality and injustice in the United States. His protest incited both support and anger in many Americans, who either saw it as patriotic or unpatriotic depending on their position, and it resulted in U.S. President Donald Trump denouncing Kaepernick's behavior (as well as those who followed his example), causing a political and media storm. In the following season, Kaepernick opted out of his contract with the San Francisco 49ers and became a free agent. After being unable to secure a

Donaldson Collection/Michael Ochs Archives/Getty Images

Nike's Kaepernick campaign.

subsequent contract with any other NFL team and accusations that he was being blackballed by the league's owners, Kaepernick, along with fellow player Eric Reid, filed a grievance against the NFL, accusing its owners of collusion to keep them out of the league.

Despite Kaepernick's challenges with employment within the game, instead of terminating his endorsement contract, Nike subsequently used his actions and image in a marketing campaign titled, "Believe in something. Even if it means sacrificing everything."

This campaign exemplifies Nike's overall strategy over the years, which has been identified as competitive, rugged, provocative, and cool. Nike's strategy has in fact centered around competitiveness, risk-taking, and passion for sport, something that has been further established through its use of sponsored athletes who value such traits (Cunningham et al., in press). The example of the recent Kaepernick campaign can give an indication to the potential outcomes of such a provocative strategy. Initially, the campaign received backlash from various quarters, and it was reported that Nike's stock dropped by 3 percent (Chadwick & Zipp, 2018). However, it was later reported that the sportswear manufacturer's online sales had increased by 31 percent following the campaign's launch and that Nike's market value has surged by nearly US$6 billion, suggesting that a potentially controversial and risk-taking strategy might have indeed proved valuable (Vizard, 2018). At the same time, such a strategy allowed Nike the opportunity to explore social issues and to continue to market their products to a different and potentially younger demographic who might be more receptive to engaging in such socially focused discussions. In other words, by adopting their risky and provocative activism strategy, Nike is seen to be delivering important social messages that resonate with younger audiences, which in turn presents an opportunity for further economic successes.

Nike has been developing their strategy to respond to changes in its environment. It concentrated on being current and relevant while reaching new markets. A number of research studies (Miles, Snow, Meyer, & Coleman, 1978; Miller, 1987a, 1987b) have suggested that, in order to be successful, organizations must respond to changes in their environment with appropriate strategies, which might mean at times adopting a more risk-taking approach, as can be seen in recent examples from professional sports, such as association football clubs in the English Premier League (EPL) (Manoli, 2016; Manoli & Hodgkinson, 2017) and gridiron football teams in the NFL (Lehman & Hahn, 2013).

In this chapter we focus on the concept of organizational strategy. We explain what we mean when we talk about strategy, and we discuss the differences between corporate-level strategies and business-level strategies. We also examine how strategy is formulated and implemented, and the relationship between strategy and structure.

What Is Organizational Strategy?

Das (1990, p. 294) likens an organization's strategy to the game plan developed by a sport team:

> [B]efore a team enters the field, an effective coach looks at the team's strengths and weaknesses and also those of its competitors. The coach carefully studies the two teams' past successes, failures, and behaviors on the field. The obvious objective is to win the game with minimal risk and personal injuries to the players. Thus, a coach may not use all the team's best players if it is not warranted (they may be kept in reserve for future games or to maintain an element of surprise). The key goal is to win the game, and the game plan itself might be modified to recognize the emerging realities.

Das goes on, however, to point out that while a gridiron football or volleyball team has a game plan for each game and each opponent, an organization's strategy is more long term and must deal with a number of issues, internal and external to the organization. Alfred Chandler (1962, p. 13), one of the first to carry out research on organizational strategy, suggested that "strategy can be defined as the determination of the basic long-term goals and objectives of an enterprise and the adoption of courses of action and the allocation of resources necessary for carrying out these goals." Mintzberg (1987) argues that strategy can be seen as a plan, ploy, pattern, position, and perspective. Sometimes the term *strategy* is used synonymously with the terms *goals* and *objectives*. But, as both Chandler's and Mintzberg's explanations make clear, strategy is more than goals and objectives; it also involves the means by which goals are to be achieved.

All sport organizations formulate strategies; they may be deliberate or emergent. **Deliberate strategies** are intended courses of action that become realized. In contrast, **emergent strategies** are those that are realized but not necessarily intended (Mintzberg, 1978). The acquisition of Bauer, the leading manufacturer of hockey products, by Nike in the mid-1990s is an example of a deliberate strategy. Nike wanted to enter the hockey market—and enter it as number one. Similarly, the agreement in 2011 between United States–based Warrior Sports and the English Premier League's Liverpool FC is also an example of a deliberate strategy. Having only been in the business of manufacturing ice hockey and lacrosse equipment for the North American market up until the agreement was announced, Warrior Sports wanted to enter the global association football market and saw the English club's stature, heritage, and worldwide supporter base as an ideal starting position. An example of a more emergent type of strategy was the one displayed by Adidas when the decision was made to acquire Reebok in 2005. Adidas paid US$3.8 billion to secure a larger slice of business in the U.S. market, while accessing discount department stores without interfering with the Adidas brand. However, the unexpected popularity of CrossFit following its acquisition allowed Adidas to access the growing and lucrative market of gym-goers through Reebok (Davies, 2005). At a more local level, Walvin (1975) describes how the strategy of some churches to use association football as a means to combat urban degeneration among the working classes in the late 19th and early 20th centuries led to the formation of association football clubs. Aston Villa, Birmingham City, Bolton Wanderers, and Fulham are all notable examples. It is, of course, possible that deliberate strategies, as they become realized, may become in part emergent, and emergent strategies in time get formalized as deliberate (Mintzberg, 1978).

In summary, strategy may then be planned and deliberate, it may emerge as a stream of significant decisions, or it may be some combination of both. In any of these situations organizational decision makers base their choice of strategy on their perceptions of the opportunities and threats in the environment, and the internal strengths and weaknesses of their organization. Then, as a result of the strategy they choose, they institute an appropriate organizational structure. This sequence is shown graphically in figure 8.1.

Levels of Strategy

Sport organizations can formulate strategies at two levels, the corporate level and the business level. **Corporate-level strategies**, which are followed by the organization as a whole, are required when a sport organization competes in a number of industries. They answer the question, What businesses should we be involved in? For example, Rogers Communications followed a corporate strategy that involved it not only in the communications industry but also in Major League Baseball, through its ownership of the Toronto Blue Jays. Obviously, there are benefits if corporate-level strategies involve "synergies among the business units and with the corporation" (Yavitz & Newman, 1982, p. 60).

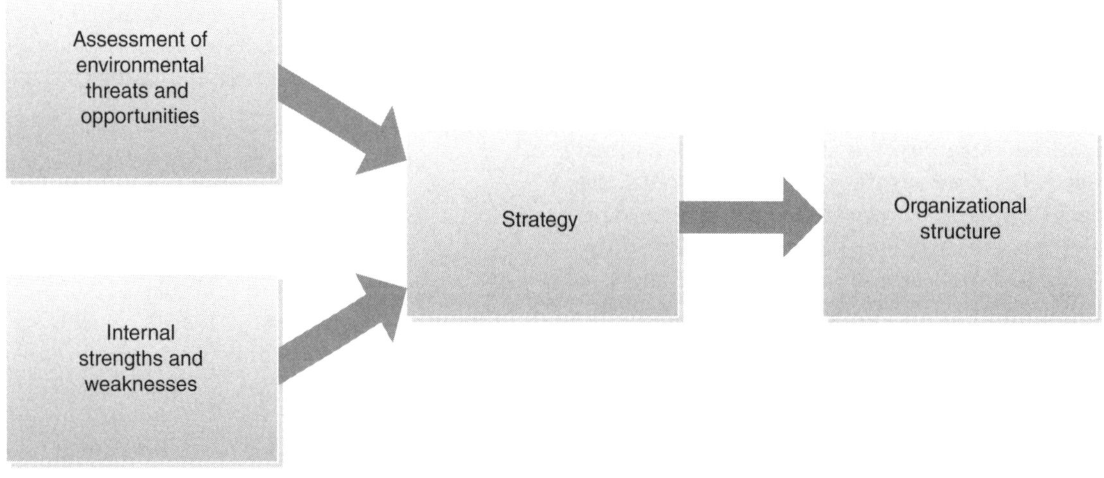

Figure 8.1 Strategy–structure relationship.

The Rogers and Blue Jays' relationship accomplished this synergy; ownership of the Blue Jays gave Rogers key sport programming content for its cable channels.

While some degree of synergy among the businesses in a corporation can be beneficial, some organizations adopt a strategy of operating in diversified markets. For example, a number of professional association football clubs in Europe have recently decided to diversify their operations by creating professional esports teams to participate in international competitions, such as Paris Saint-Germain (France), Ajax Football Club (Netherlands), Manchester City (UK), FC Schalke (Germany), and Valencia (Spain).

Business-level strategies address questions about how to compete within a particular industry; when a sport organization competes only in one industry, its business-level strategy and its corporate-level strategy will be the same. But for sport organizations competing in a number of industries, each division will formulate its own strategy. For example, a corporation like International Management Group (IMG) in all likelihood will formulate strategies for its figure-skating division (sport agents), research division, broadcasting division, academies division (sport training centers), and literary division. Figure 8.2 shows the relationship between corporate-level and business-level strategies.

A corporate strategy is usually the end result of a business-level analysis technique called **portfolio analysis** (Bates & Eldredge, 1984). We discuss this topic more fully in the next section of this chapter, where we examine corporate strategies in more detail.

Corporate-Level Strategies

An organization can engage in four types of corporate strategy. Hodge and Anthony (1991) term them *growth strategies*, *stability strategies*, *defensive strategies*, and *combination strategies*.

Growth Strategies

Almost all sport organizations seek growth as one of their goals. A growth strategy may be pursued in two major ways at the corporate level: diversification and integration. **Diversification** helps a company grow while at the same time spreading its risk. Diversification strategies may be related or unrelated. A related diversification strategy "calls for the acquired investment to have some relation to the existing businesses, such as technology, product group, managerial knowledge, or distribution channels. [It] permits a firm to spread its risk while at the same time capitalizing on its strengths" (Bates & Eldredge, 1984, p. 137). The acquisition of Reebok by Adidas, mentioned earlier in this chapter, is an example of a related diversification. Both Reebok and Adidas are in the sport industry, and Adidas wanted to enter the discount market already penetrated by Reebok. An unrelated diversification strategy means that a corporation is pursuing acquisitions in areas not necessarily related to its existing business units. The decisions of successful businesspeople such as Mike Ilitch (Little Caesar's) and Jerry Jones (oil) to acquire professional sport franchises (for Ilitch, the Detroit Red Wings and Detroit Tigers, and for Jones, the Dallas Cowboys), are all examples of an unrelated diversification strategy; Ted Turner's involvement in

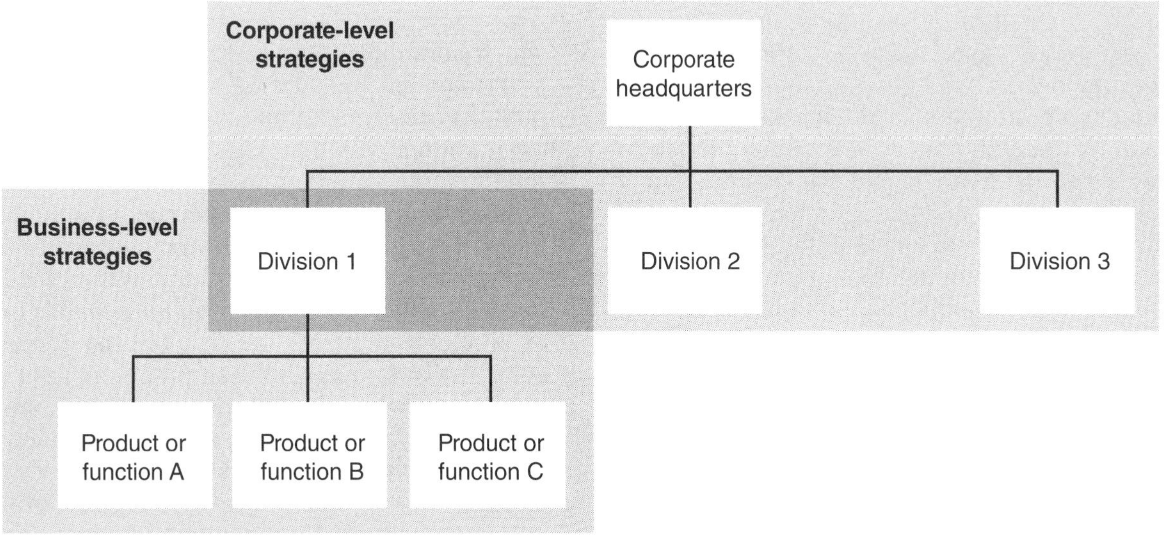

Figure 8.2 Levels of strategy.

the Atlanta Hawks and the Atlanta Braves, however, could be seen as a related diversification since both teams provide programming for his TV station.

In addition to diversification, growth can also be achieved through *integration*. Integration may be achieved horizontally or vertically. **Horizontal integration** involves adding another product, often a competitor in the same business, by buying an organization. AstroTurf manufacturer Balsam's acquisition of smaller artificial turf producers such as All Pro, Omni Turf, and Super Turf is an example of horizontal integration. **Vertical integration** occurs either when a sport organization acquires its distributors (forward integration) or its suppliers (backward integration). Vertical integration allows for more control over the production process, for potentially reduced costs by bringing the supplier in-house, and for potentially increasing higher sales margins by bringing the distributor in-house (Bates & Eldredge, 1984). An example of backward integration would be Nike purchasing Tetra Plastics, the company that produces the plastic film used in the production of Air Sole Cushioning, in 1991. In the early 1990s Nike also bought out many of its distribution operations, an example of forward integration (Yang, Oneal, Hoots, & Neff, 1994).

More recently, sport technology company Garmin announced in February 2019 the acquisition of Tacx, the Dutch maker of trainers, water bottles, and tools popular among cyclists (Tacx, 2019). While the company has not released more details about this acquisition, this vertical integration can allow the sport tech company to develop sport attire products that would feature their technology, further expanding their role in the market.

A sport organization can use a number of techniques when it adopts a growth strategy. For example, diversification may be achieved through mergers, acquisitions, takeovers, or joint ventures. A **merger** occurs when two or more companies combine to produce one. For example, a proposed merger in Welsh Rugby Union between two (fierce rival) clubs, the Scarlets and the Ospreys, would see the two teams combining to form a new team to be created in the north of Wales. However, and despite WRU's initial determination for this bold merger and its potential to help grow the sport in the region, the merger was called off following the supporters' angry backlash in early 2019 (BBC Sport, 2019). An **acquisition** involves one company buying another and absorbing it into its operations. Such is the case with Comcast's acquisition of Europe's biggest pay-TV broadcaster, Sky, in 2019. A **takeover** involves one company attempting to obtain control of another against the wishes of shareholders and management. An example of a takeover would be Walt Disney Company's takeover of 21st Century Fox Inc., which made the Walt Disney Company the owners of the popular sport channel ESPN. **Joint ventures** occur when one company joins with another to work on a specific project. The partnership between fashion designer Stella McCartney and Adidas for the creation of a fashionable sport performance line, or the one between musician Kanye West and Adidas for the creation of a fashion line, are essentially joint venture. The latter two approaches would be called **strategic alliances**, a strategy that organizations are discovering and implementing in a variety of ways in order to, among other reasons, defend themselves against stronger competitors, go on the offensive to secure a stronger position, and create new opportunities for first-mover advantage.

Strategic Alliances

Strategic alliances have alternatively been called *interfirm cooperation*, *interorganizational relationships*, and *joint ventures*. However, a joint venture is only one type of strategic alliance. Generally, a strategic alliance is a partnership between two organizations formed in response to an essential opportunity or threat in the environment (Child & Faulkner, 1998) and are an increasing phenomenon in the sport industry (Manoli, 2018). What makes them different from partnerships is that strategic alliances are based on organizational learning, as in the case of joint ventures, collaborations, and consortia. For example, the Walt Disney Company could be considered a very large consortium because it includes alliances with media organizations (e.g., 21st Century Fox, ESPN, ABC, websites, and radio stations), sport teams (e.g., the Anaheim Angels baseball team [now known as the Los Angeles Angels] and the Mighty Ducks of Anaheim hockey team [now known as the Anaheim Ducks], both of which were sold in 2003 and 2005 respectively), and entertainment organizations (e.g., movie studios, publications, a cruise line, and theme parks). These organizations within the Walt Disney Company work together to, for example, promote each other's products and decrease business costs. Partnerships based on skill-substitution arrangements, such as networks or virtual corporations, are not pure strategic alliances. However, all are possible forms of cooperative strategies, in contrast to purely competitive strategies. More precisely, joint ventures, networks, and other cooperative strategies allow organizations to compete more effectively through alliances between two organizations within or across industries. This allows organizations to go beyond simply focusing on how the organization can gain a competitive advantage within an industry or for a specific product market. Strategic

TIME OUT

City Football Group's Growth Strategies

City Football Group, founded in 2008, is a holding company under the ownership of Abu Dhabi United Group. The Group has adopted a number of growth strategies in the past decade, including investing in a number of association football clubs worldwide, making it one of the powers in the world game.

The Group was created to facilitate the takeover of English Premier League's Manchester City FC and was accompanied by significant investments toward the club's infrastructure and playing talent in both the men's and the women's squads. In 2013 the Group became the owners of the Major League Soccer's 20th team, New York City FC, whose first season in the league was 2015. The Group paid particular attention to the academies of the club, with partnerships arranged with local youth clubs around the area. In 2014 the Group acquired the Australian A-League club Melbourne Heart FC, which was quickly renamed Melbourne City FC. Once again, significant investments were made toward the club's men's, women's, and youth's squads (Bajkowski, 2016).

In 2014 the Group invested in a minority share of the Japanese team Yokohama F. Marinos, which plays in the J1 League. In 2017 the Group acquired yet another association football club, this time in Uruguay. Club Atlético Torque, which was playing at the Uruguayan Primer División at that time, reported to have received support from the Group in order to refurbish their stadium and help build their current and potential fan base in the region. At the same time, criticism was expressed regarding the motivations behind this acquisition, with critics suggesting that the Uruguayan club might be used as a means of acquiring South American players for the other football clubs of the Group. Later the same year, 2017, the Group acquired 44.3 percent of the Spanish club Girona FC. Even though the club has had a history of participating in the second tier of Spanish association football, for the last three years (at the time of writing), and partly due to the support of the Group, they have been participating in the country's first division, La Liga. Once again, critics suggested at that time that the Group developed their interest and invested in the club in an attempt to attract Pep Guardiola to the Manchester City FC. The latest acquisition of the Group was completed in 2019, with the Chinese Sichuan Jiuniu FC joining City Group's portfolio of football club investments (Financial Times, 2018).

When asked for future investments and plans, the Group chairman, Khaldoon Al Mubarak, commented, "I would say that when the opportunity arises—and we are looking at opportunities—you can expect us to add to the number of clubs we have already within that organization." This suggests that the above-mentioned growth strategies are only the beginning in City Group's plans for worldwide association football expansion (Bajkowski, 2016).

---

alliances might also occur in various contexts that are not limited to large multinational corporations. For example, a local strategic alliance might entail a collaboration between a local school that has sport facilities available, and private local clubs that can offer their expertise through their contracted coaches, in order for after-school clubs to be organized in the school facilities.

Internal growth can also occur when a sport organization is able to expand its market share. This growth may be achieved by saturating existing markets with current products or services. Alternatively, a company may take an existing product or service that has been successful in one market into a new market.

Stability Strategies

Hodge and Anthony (1991) suggest that an organization may engage in two types of stability strategies. A *neutral strategy* means that the organization continues to do what it has done in the past with no intent to grow. A **harvesting** or **milking strategy** is used when a product is becoming obsolete or if a business unit lacks potential and has little chance to turn the situation around.

This type of strategy involves management in an attempt to increase its cash flow from the product or business unit by severely reducing or eliminating the capital it puts into areas such as facility maintenance, advertising, and research (Harrigan & Porter, 1983). A harvesting strategy can have two possible consequences. First, the product or business unit may justify its existence by continuing to be successful enough, with little or no investiture, to generate cash flow that can be diverted to other units. Alternately, it may lose market share but generate an initial, albeit short-term, increase in capital that can be directed elsewhere. When the cash flow from the product or business unit starts to decline, liquidation usually follows.

TIME OUT

Philadelphia Eagles' Strategy of Stability

The NFL Philadelphia Eagles franchise won their first ever Super Bowl in 2018, rather unexpectedly, but they were able to manage their success with a long-term facing strategy in terms of their commercial development. Unlike the often-expected response of securing numerous lucrative commercial deals and thus cashing in their success, the club decided to follow a different strategy, focusing on engagement with a smaller number of sponsors and agreeing on high-value, long-term deals, a rather unusual phenomenon in the NFL. As a result, the Eagles ended up with 65 corporate partners, almost half of the league-wide average of 116. This strategy of "less is more" was advocated by the club officials, who also underlined its value in terms of risk minimization for future seasons' performance, while allowing for a closer relationship to be developed with the sponsors of the club (Nelson, 2018). This modest but long-term facing strategy of the Eagles appears to have worked for the club, with Forbes reporting that despite their lower than average number of commercial partners, their annual revenue was the eighth highest in the NFL.

Defensive Strategies

Defensive strategies, or what are sometimes termed *decline strategies*, are used when the demand for a sport organization's product or service starts to decrease. Defensive strategies try to reverse this situation or overcome a particular problem. There are three principle types of defensive strategy: turnaround, divestiture, and liquidation.

Turnaround strategies are used to counter increased costs and falling revenues and to increase cash flow and liquidity. They involve actions such as reducing or changing the products or markets served, laying off workers, replacing senior management, and cutting costs (Schendel, Patton, & Riggs, 1976). Nike, in an attempt to compete with Reebok's success in the aerobics shoe business, moved into the women's casual shoe market in the early 1980s. As Strasser and Becklund (1991, p. 506) point out, they "struggled to compete in an area in which [they] had no experience, no reputation, poor styling, and no price advantage." As their fortunes continued to decline, founder Philip Knight adopted the elements of a turnaround strategy. He stepped back into the presidency of Nike, a position he had relinquished little more than a year earlier, and told his staff he wanted to lower factory costs, control inventories, improve time lines, and increase profit margins. He also laid off 400 employees, about 10 percent of his workforce.

If a turnaround is not possible a company has the option of divestiture or liquidation. **Divestiture** involves selling off a business or some portion of the ownership of a business. For example, Walt Disney Company was reported to have had to divest of Fox Sports in Brazil and Mexico in 2019, not only because of the reduced profits from the channels but also due to their plans to take over the 21st Century Fox Inc. entertainment assets, which include the popular sport channel ESPN, as mentioned earlier (Lima & Navarro, 2019).

Liquidation involves closing down a business and selling off its assets. For example, John McCaw's Orca Bay group, who had bought an NBA franchise for Vancouver (the Grizzlies), was forced to sell the team because it was incurring too much cost and was not successful on the court. As it happens, new owner Michael Heisley promptly moved the team to Memphis in 2001, where it remains to this day. A more recent high-profile example comes from association football in Scotland. Despite relative domestic success throughout the noughties in the Scottish Premier League (SPL), as one of the league's big Old Firm clubs based in Glasgow, the Rangers (trading as The Rangers Football Club plc) experienced financial difficulties resulting in their liquidation in 2012. Subsequently, The Rangers Football Club plc business and its assets were sold to Charles Green (although a number of key players refused to transfer to the new company), who then applied for membership in the SPL to replace the old company in a straight swap. When this application was refused by the SPL's members, Rangers Football Club Ltd. (the new company) was granted Scottish Football Association (SFA) membership in 2012 and entered the Scottish Football League Third Division at the beginning of the 2012-13 season. In 2016-17, the team returned to the SPL having won the Scottish Football League Third Division in 2012-13, Scottish League One in 2013-14 (having gone unbeaten all season), and the Scottish Championship in 2015-16.

TIME OUT

Sheffield's Sport Event Strategy

Located in central England, the city of Sheffield is known as the Steel City due to its historic industrial focus on and international reputation for steel manufacturing. Through the late 1970s and into 1980s, however, the steel industry declined, contributing to the loss of 60,000 jobs in the city between 1978 and 1988. At the same time, a new trend was emerging, that of globalization, which offered international recognition for cities and corporations (Henry, 2001; Whitson & Macintosh, 1993). In 1987 the municipal government partnered with the local Chamber of Commerce and the Sheffield Economic Regeneration Committee with the goal of promoting the city, stimulating investment, and seeing it become a world-class destination. To facilitate this goal, a sport and leisure strategy was formulated in which a new image for the city, revolving around sports, was hoped would bring about the building of infrastructure, encouraging of tourism, and the generation of new capital. (This strategy was also being employed in Calgary and Edmonton, Alberta, Canada, with some success [Smith, 2001]). The central element of this strategy was obtaining the rights to host the 1991 Universiade, or World Student, Games, which it did, and although the event created a major debt for the organizers, it did leave the city with some world-class sport facilities, new infrastructure, and increased knowledge and understanding. Importantly, the Universiade jump-started Sheffield's image makeover toward a more youthful, energetic, and innovative "National City of Sport"—the first of its kind in the United Kingdom (Taylor & Gratton, 2000). On the heels of Sheffield's successful new image, other cities have started using the same strategy. For example, Manchester, England, bid for and won the rights to host the 2002 Commonwealth Games, as did Glasgow, Scotland, and Gold Coast, Australia, which were both successful in hosting the 2014 and 2018 Commonwealth Games. The most recent addition to this list is Birmingham, England, with its upcoming 2022 Commonwealth Games that are expected to help the city improve its image and appeal (BBC News, 2018).

Combination Strategies

The fourth type of corporate strategy involves a diversified sport organization using the strategies outlined above in combination. **Combination strategy** is the most popular strategy besides growth strategies (Hodge & Anthony, 1991). Rarely will a diversified sport organization have only one strategy; it may seek to expand certain parts of its operation while at the same time reduce or eliminate its involvement in other areas, depending on their performance and the environment in which it operates. In 2017 Nike revealed their strategy, called Triple Double Strategy, focusing on innovation and consumer experience through the direct communication and sales between the company and the consumer. As part of the strategy, Nike decided to put 25 percent fewer styles into the market and thus focus on the styles that would help them increase or amplify the existing sales. At the same time, Nike also decided that distribution would be streamlined to only the methods that deliver the fastest and are more profitable, suggesting a significant reduction in their distribution partners. Based on the results of their strategy so far, this risk taking has paid off for Nike, with the end of 2018 seeing a 9 percent increase in the company's revenues (Danziger, 2018).

Portfolio Analysis

In diversified companies that use combination strategies, one popular technique for analyzing the relative merits and cash flow requirements of their product or service offerings is that developed by the Boston Consulting Group (BCG). The BCG approach requires that a company identify **strategic business units** (SBUs) for each of the business areas in which it competes. The SBUs are then assessed along two dimensions: relative market share and growth rate. In assessing the first dimension, the ratio of the SBU's market share to that of its nearest competitor is used. For example, an SBU with a market share of 20 percent in an industry whose largest rival has 30 percent would have a relative market share of 20/30 (.66). A relative market share score over 1 is seen as high (i.e., it is an industry leader); a score below 1 is low. Growth rate is determined according to whether the SBU's industry is growing faster than the economy as a whole. Growth rates above average are high; those below are low (Hill & Jones, 1989).

Using the dimensions of market share and growth rate, a 2x2 matrix can be constructed as shown in figure 8.3. Each SBU can then be placed in one of the four cells. The SBUs in cell 1 are referred to as

stars; they have high growth rates and high market share. Whether they are self-sufficient depends on whether they can generate enough cash flow to support their rapid growth. Established stars are likely to be able to support themselves, while emergent stars will need cash support. Stars offer long-term profit potential when the growth rate of their market decreases; that is, they become **cash cows**. The SBUs in cell 2 are **question marks**, sometimes referred to as "problem children." They are weak in that they have a low market share, but because they are in high-growth industries they could become stars. To transform question marks into stars often requires a large infusion of cash. Strategists have to weigh the relative benefits of an increase in capital expenditure against the benefits of selling off this type of unit.

Cash cows, in cell 3, have a high market share and low growth rate; as such, they generate more profit than they need investment. Cash cows are to be "milked" and the profits they generate used for other corporate functions such as research and development and debt reduction. They can also be used to finance other SBUs such as those classified as question marks or emergent stars. In cell 4 we find **dogs**. Dogs, in low-growth industries with low market share, do not generate large amounts of cash, nor do they require large amounts. Some companies may keep these SBUs active to offer customers an entire product line; others choose to divest themselves of dogs, which offer little potential for growth.

The strategic implications of the BCG portfolio analysis involve maximizing the profitability and growth potential of an organization. The BCG recommends that managers financially support selected question marks and emerging stars, often with capital extracted from cash cows. Managers must also make decisions about selling off those question marks they do not think have potential, to avoid excessive demands on company cash. They must also consider the relative merits of retaining dogs. The manager aims to obtain a suitable balance of cash cows, stars, and question marks. If this balance is not present, the company must look at acquisitions or divestments as a means of producing a balanced portfolio.

All diversified sport organizations, regardless of whether they use the BCG matrix, use some form of portfolio analysis. Strasser and Becklund (1991), for example, describe how in 1979 more than half of Nike's business was in running shoes, 22 percent in

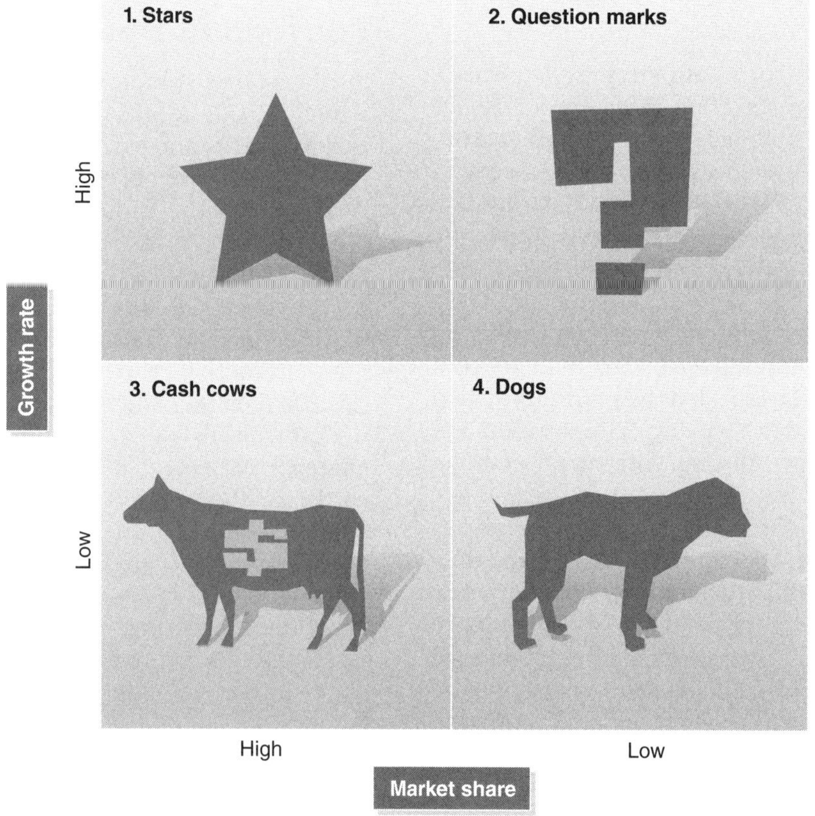

Figure 8.3 The BCG matrix.

basketball, and 16 percent in tennis. Its market share in those areas had risen 22 percent in running, 77 percent in basketball, and 37 percent in tennis. But Knight felt that tennis had already peaked, the market for running shoes was approaching saturation, and basketball was getting expensive. He "didn't like the dependence on such a narrow range of products. . . . Like a good portfolio manager, Knight was always searching to minimize risk and maximize gain by balancing the sources of revenue" (Strasser & Becklund, 1991, p. 398). Knight made a number of financial decisions to consolidate cash flow and eventually diversify more than before into product areas such as apparel and football shoes. Nowadays, Nike focuses on consumer experience and innovation, while constantly assessing their products and reaching to their customers in order to maintain their position in the market (Danziger, 2018).

The strength of the BCG matrix for diversified companies is that it forces them to focus on their cash flow requirements and plan their corporate strategy accordingly. It alerts managers to the need for acquisitions and divestitures. There are, however, as Hill and Jones (1989) point out, several problems with the BCG approach (Seeger, 1984). While the simplicity of the matrix is appealing, market share and growth are not the only two factors to consider when assessing portfolios. A company may have a low market share but establish a strong market position through differentiating its product line to serve the needs of a particular section of the market. Berrett, Burton, and Slack (1993) suggest that a number of entrepreneurs in the sport industry have established such a position by focusing on quality products and service. Hill and Jones (1989) also suggest that the relationship between market share and cost saving is not as straightforward as presented in the BCG matrix and that a high market share in a low-growth industry does not always produce a high cash yield.

Given the BCG's focus on large diversified companies, it may appear to be of limited use to some sport organizations, particularly those such as collegiate athletic departments or campus intramural departments. However, in an interesting adaptation of portfolio analysis Graham (1983) uses criteria such as cost-per-participation unit, user and community support, or level of participation compared with maximum capacity, as opposed to market share, to show how the BCG matrix could be used by sport managers to develop strategies in these types of organizations. The matrix is often used in a number of companies now, regardless of their size and portfolio of products due to its simplicity and value (Lowy & Hood, 2011; Torquati, Scarpa, Petrosillo, Ligonzo, & Paffarini, 2018).

Business-Level Strategies

Business-level strategies are those used by a sport organization to gain a competitive edge for its particular product or service. The most influential work on this topic is that of Harvard's Michael Porter (1980), who identifies three basic strategies a business-level manager can choose: cost leadership, differentiation, and focus. These strategies can be used in manufacturing, service, or voluntary sport organizations (VSOs). Sport managers can gain a competitive advantage for their organization by selecting a strategy appropriate both for the industry in which they are involved and the type of competitive position they seek to establish. Each of Porter's three strategic types are explained in more detail here.

Cost Leadership Strategy

A sport organization that adopts a **cost leadership strategy** prices its product or service lower than that of its competition by using cheaper labor (often in developing countries), efficient manufacturing processes, economies of scale, technological innovation, and low levels of product differentiation. Sport organizations that follow a cost leadership strategy do not spend large amounts on new product or service development; rather, they follow market trends and provide the product feature or service when there is an established demand. The idea is that by providing goods or services at a lower cost, a sport organization can capture a large share of the market or maintain higher profit margins.

Gore-Tex imitators such as Sympatex and Helly Hansen follow a cost leadership strategy. Dan Hansen, marketing coordinator at Helly Hansen, said of his company's product, "Our best seller was a basic warm-up suit that retailed at about $120; a Gore product would cost $150 or more. By eliminating the middlemen, we can offer a comparable product at a more competitive price" ("Give them stormy weather," 1986). UK fitness chain PureGym follows this strategy by advertising their low prices, adopting technological advances (e.g., self-check-in and check-out), and minimizing any typical running costs, such as fitness instructors and receptionists. Many public-sector providers of sport services also follow a cost leadership strategy, in large part because of their mandate of catering to a broad client base.

The main strength of this type of strategy is that a cost advantage protects a sport organization from the fluctuations of the marketplace caused by such factors as changing input costs and imitators. Problems do arise, however, when a competitor finds a way to produce the same product at a lower cost.

Cost leaders have to strive constantly to maintain their cost advantage.

Using this type of strategy involves several structural implications. Miller (1988) notes how cost leadership can be linked to control use with tighter control meaning lower costs. This control, combined with the need for economies of scale and efficient manufacturing processes, means that sport organizations that adopt a cost leadership strategy are likely to be centralized, high in complexity, and high in formalization.

Differentiation Strategy

Sport organizations that pursue a **differentiation strategy** attempt to gain a competitive advantage by presenting an image of their product or service as unique. Because the product or service is seen as unique, the sport organization is able to charge a premium price. Reebok followed a differentiation strategy in the athletic footwear industry with The Pump. Golf complexes such as the Broadmoor did it with luxury and prestige in their service provision. The main strength of a differentiation strategy is that it develops product or service loyalty, a relatively enduring phenomenon. The weaknesses of this approach are maintaining the aura of uniqueness for the product or service in a changing market, and ensuring that pricing is in accordance with what the market will bear.

Because it requires creativity to produce unique products or services, sport organizations that adopt a differentiation strategy employ "technocrats—well trained experts such as scientists and engineers—to design innovations" (Miller, 1988, p. 282). Because these people work most efficiently in flexible structures, a sport organization that adopts a differentiation strategy will most likely exhibit low levels of complexity, low levels of formalization, and decentralized decision making.

Focus Strategy

Focus strategy is directed toward serving the needs of a particular market, one defined by such criteria as geographic area, age, sex, or segment of a product or service line. Once the particular market has been chosen, the sport organization decides on a cost leadership or differentiation strategy within that market. Curves Fitness, the international fitness franchise, entered the competitive fitness industry in 1992 by adopting a focus strategy. Their focus was to offer their services to women only, a target market that they considered unexplored. This strategy proved successful for the franchise that was said to have fitness centers in over 10,000 locations and loyal customers around the world in 2006. Even though the company has downsized significantly since then, their focus strategy on the selected market allowed them significant growth, which also drew competitors in the market.

The strengths of a focus strategy are that the company develops the ability to provide products and services that others cannot and, because of a focused market, the company can stay closer to its customers and more easily respond to their changing needs. The main disadvantage is that costs may be higher because of a generally smaller product volume. Also, it is possible that the market niche the company occupies may disappear or experience a decline in popularity. The type of structure adopted by a sport organization that follows a focus strategy will depend on whether it decides to focus either through differentiation or through a low-cost approach.

Stuck in the Middle

Not all sport organizations are able to gain a competitive advantage; some do not make the right choices about their product or service and the markets in which they wish to operate. Porter (1980) describes these organizations as "**stuck in the middle**."

Sport organizations get stuck in the middle for a variety of reasons. The low-cost company may decide to use some of its profits to diversify into product markets in which it has less experience, or to invest in research and development that management thinks may bolster the prestige of the organization. Such actions are expensive and have no guarantee of success. "Consequently, bad strategic decisions can quickly erode the cost leader's above-average profitability" (Hill & Jones, 1989, p. 137).

Differentiators may get undercut by imitators who produce a cheaper or more specialized product. Those who adopt a focus strategy may not keep abreast of market trends and thus lose their market niche. Retaining a competitive advantage requires constant managerial action and attention to possible tactics: monitoring the environment for changing trends, filing patents to prevent imitations, lobbying to restrict foreign competition, establishing contracts with suppliers to limit their ability to supply competitors, and even acquiring competitors.

Strategy Formulation and Implementation

Formulating and implementing a strategic plan involves a series of interrelated steps. These steps include formulating a mission statement for the sport organization, conducting an analysis of the organization's external environment and internal operations (sometimes called a **SWOT analysis**—strengths, weaknesses, opportunities, and threats), making choices about appropriate corporate- and business-level strategies, and selecting the correct organizational structure and integration and control systems to ensure that the strategy is effective. The first three steps are primarily about strategy formulation; the fourth step is the implementation stage. The process is shown graphically in figure 8.4.

Although the process of formulating and implementing strategy is shown as a linear progression, we noted earlier in this chapter that strategy formulation could be either deliberate or emergent. The traditional point of view has been to see strategy formulation as a deliberate process following a series of sequential steps. Emergent strategies are less likely to follow this clearly defined sequence. Sport managers must evaluate the merits of emergent strategies against the organization's mission, its operating strengths, its environmental opportunities, and so on. Only by undertaking this type of comparison is a manager able to determine the fit of that strategy for the sport organization. Each stage of strategy formulation and implementation is outlined in more detail here.

Defining a Mission Statement

The senior managers' first step in the formulation of a strategic plan involves defining a **mission statement** for the sport organization. They may invite representatives from other subunits (e.g., unions, support staff, or students) to be involved in the process, or draw on the knowledge, expertise, and missions of external stakeholders. With respect to the latter, a newly formed or emerging International Federation, for example, might consult with the International Olympic Committee (IOC) or Olympic Charter in developing their own mission statement, should they harbor ambitions of having the sport they represent be included in future Games. A mission statement, or official goal (see chapter 3), defines the purpose of the sport organization, what businesses it is in, and who its principal customers, users, or clients are. The mission statement serves as a foundation for the strategic planning process by prescribing direction for the future. It can therefore affect both the inner workings of an organization (e.g., its employees) as well as its external activities (e.g., relationships and engagement with customers, users, clients, etc.). It is, according to Baker (2000), the cultural glue that enables this collective engagement. As Hill and Jones (1989, p. 9) pointed out two decades ago, a mission statement provides "the context within which intended strategies are formulated and the criteria against which emergent strategies are evaluated," a position that remains as relevant today.

Internal and External Analysis

Once the sport organization's strategic planning group has established a mission statement, the next step in the process of strategy formulation is an analysis of the organization's external environment and internal operations. This step involves what is commonly called a SWOT analysis—an examination of opportunities and threats in the external environment of the organization and the determination of its internal strengths and weaknesses. When analyzing the external environment, strategic planners must consider the industry or industries within which they are competing. This means looking at current and potential competitors, cost structures and margins, product differentiation levels, existing brand loyalties, and so on. Strategic planners must also consider the broader socioeconomic and political environment, including political issues, economic trends, globalization, and demographic shifts. All have the potential to affect a sport organization and hence must be considered. One way of achieving this is through a PESTEL analysis of the **p**olitical, **e**conomic, **s**ociocultural, **t**echnological, **e**nvironmental/ethical, and **l**egal and regulatory environments in which the organization is located. A succinct summary of this framework is offered by Kitchen (2006, p.63):

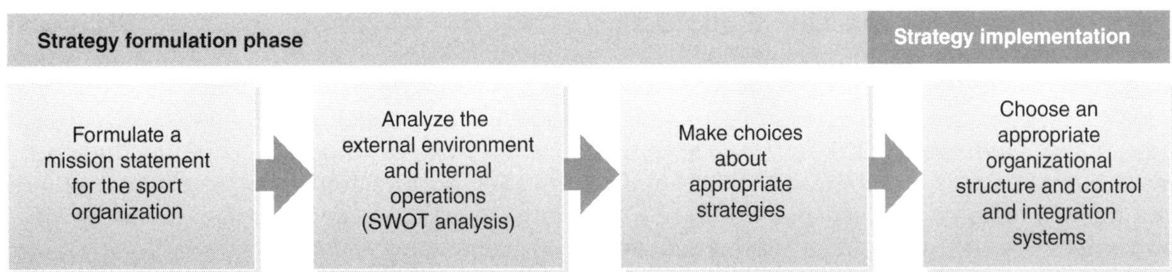

Figure 8.4 Steps in the formulation and implementation of strategy.

> . . . the political environment . . . is characterised by the ideology of the party in power and the tier (level) of government. The economic environment is dependent on macro- and micro- economic conditions that pervade organisations and the regions in which they operate. The sociocultural environment is influenced by shifts in society and consumer tastes as well as being characterised by cultural differences and their impact on the marketing process. . . . The technological environment is the impact of technology on the operations of the sport and the impact of technology on the ability of the sporting organisation to carry out its activities. . . . Impacts and decisions made in one area of the planet can have repercussions for society in another. These considerations are considered in the section on the ecological/ethical environment. Finally, the legal/regulatory environment is the final influence . . . to take into consideration [and the understanding that] [a]ll organisations operate within a regulatory environment and are subject to national, state and local legislation [with] [v]arying levels of autonomy.

From an analysis of these environments, strategic planners can identify opportunities and threats facing the sport organization.

The SWOT's internal analysis assesses strengths and weaknesses in the sport organization's operations by evaluating the available expertise and resources in areas such as research and development, manufacturing, marketing, human resources management, and new product development. In a sport organization that operates in more than one industry, the internal analysis should include an evaluation of the company's business portfolio using a technique such as the BCG matrix.

Selecting an Appropriate Strategy

The final stage in the strategy formulation phase involves making choices about the appropriate strategy for the sport organization. The choice of strategy will depend on the sport organization's mission and the match between its internal strengths and weaknesses and the external threats and opportunities. As Hill and Jones (1989, p. 12) point out, "For the single business organization, the objective is to match a company's strength to environmental opportunities in order to gain a competitive advantage and thus increase profits. For the multibusiness organization, the goal is to choose strategies for its portfolio of business that align the strengths and weaknesses of the portfolio with environmental opportunities and threats."

For example, for many years Converse was one of the strongest companies in the athletic footwear market, with a rich history that stretches back over a century to 1908; their black All Stars high-tops became standard wear on the basketball court. But the athletic footwear boom that started in the 1970s caught Converse off guard. Their black high-tops were not as appealing as the colorful and high-tech Nikes and Reeboks. Seeing the opportunities in athletic footwear, Converse's then-president J.P. O'Neil and chief executive R.B. Loynd decided to focus on this market. They wanted to try to gain in basketball while introducing strong performance shoes across their other product categories. The company decided to change its internal operations by consolidating its strengths; it dumped such product lines as hockey pucks and fishing boots to concentrate on athletic footwear. To promote its athletic footwear a strong marketing campaign was developed that included purchasing the title of "Official Athletic Shoe of the 1984 Olympics." Although sales dipped somewhat during the 1990s, the company then had such success that in 2003, Converse was purchased by Nike, and to this day, Converse All Stars still maintain global popularity and are considered a wardrobe staple by men's fashion magazine *GQ*.

Mintzberg's Three Modes of Strategy Formulation

In each stage of the process of formulating strategy, sport organizations make a number of important decisions. What we have described so far would fit within Mintzberg's (1973) planning mode of strategy formulation because of its highly rational approach prepared by an analyst or planner working with senior management. The highly structured process subjects all decision choices to systematic cost benefit analysis. In the **planning mode** the "organization's strategy is designed at essentially one point in time in a comprehensive process (all major decisions are interrelated). Because of this, planning forces the organization to think of global strategies and to develop an explicit sense of strategic direction" (Mintzberg, 1973, p. 48). The planning mode of strategy formulation is most frequently used in large established sport organizations looking for both efficiency and growth.

Although the planning mode has been the most popular method of strategy formulation, Mintzberg also identifies two other approaches: the entrepreneurial mode and the adaptive mode. In the **entrepreneurial mode**, the owner or entrepreneur makes decisions using intuition and experience to seek out growth opportunities for the organization. The early years of sport organizations such as Nike (Strasser & Becklund, 1991) were characterized by this approach to strategy formulation. The entrepreneur makes bold decisions about "where his organization can make dramatic gains" (Mintzberg, 1973, p. 45). This mode of strategy formulation is most frequently found in small and relatively new sport organizations. The process of strategy formulation involves only the owner or entrepreneur (and perhaps some close associates); it is informal in operation, and decisions are rarely committed to paper.

The main characteristic of the **adaptive mode** of strategy formulation is, as its name implies, a continual adjustment of organizational goals and the means by which they are to be achieved. The process of formulating strategy is a reactive one instead of a proactive search for new opportunities (Mintzberg, 1973). Decisions are made in an incremental and relatively disjointed manner. This approach to strategy formulation is used in established sport organizations where power is dispersed and there is no simple organizational goal. For example, we may find this approach to strategy formulation in a faculty of health, physical education, and recreation, where power is dispersed among faculty and where research, teaching, and service are all seen as important goals. Mintzberg suggests that Lindblom's (1959) phrase "the science of muddling through" is a good description of the adaptive approach to strategy formulation. Certain organizational conditions such as size, leadership, and the degree of competition and stability within the environment favor one mode of strategy formulation over another. It is, however, quite possible that an organization will operate with some combination of these three modes that reflects its particular needs.

Strategy and Structure

To implement the selected strategy, an appropriate organizational structure and the necessary control and integration systems need to be put into place. As we saw in chapters 5 and 6, a sport organization can be structured in a number of ways. An appropriate structure is selected based on decisions about how to distribute authority within a sport organization and what subunits are required to carry out its functions. Systems must be developed to integrate and control the actions of these various subunits.

Different types of structures and systems "provide strategic planners with alternative means of pursuing different strategies because they lead the company and the people within it to act in different ways" (Hill & Jones, 1989, p. 222). In this section we look in more detail at the strategy–structure relationship. We start by focusing on the landmark contribution of Alfred Chandler that has influenced much subsequent work on this relationship. We then look at the best known of the contemporary work on this issue, the writings of Miles and Snow. Finally, we conclude the section by looking at the question, Could structure determine strategy?

Chandler's Work on the Strategy–Structure Relationship

Published in 1962, Chandler's book *Strategy and Structure*, the first substantive work to examine the relationship of strategy and structure, was based on a study of large American companies such as General Motors, Du Pont, and Sears. Chandler looked at changes in these organizations over a period of approximately 50 years. The companies began by offering a limited number of product lines and exhibited a centralized structure. As they grew, they followed a diversification strategy; consequently, if they were to continue to function effectively, they needed a different type of structure. The new structure was more complex because units were added and, over time, decisions were decentralized. Chandler's (1962, p. 15) main conclusion was that a new organizational strategy "required a new or at least refashioned structure if the enlarged enterprise was to be operated efficiently." That is, structure had to follow strategy.

Chandler's research suffered from his limited conceptualization of strategy and structure. In his study, strategy was limited to growth through diversification, and structure was limited to divisionalization. Also, his results cannot be generalized because the organizations in his study were large corporations; he did not attempt to include other types and sizes of organizations. Nevertheless, despite its shortcomings, Chandler's work has been replicated by a number of other scholars (Channon, 1973; Rumelt, 1974), who have all used similar types of organizations to confirm his general findings. It would appear, at least in certain cases, that strategy does indeed influence structure. However, the concept of strategy is very broad, and contemporary work has extended and elaborated ideas about the strategy–structure relationship.

Miles and Snow's Strategic Typology

One strategic typology that continues to receive attention in sport management literature (e.g., Cunningham, 2002; Isoherranen & Kess, 2011; Yeh, Hoye, & Taylor, 2011) is Miles and Snow's four-part classification of organizations as Defenders, Prospectors, Analyzers, and Reactors.

Defenders

Organizations that adopt this type of strategy attempt to limit themselves to a narrow range of products or services offered to only "a limited segment of the total potential market, and the segment chosen is frequently one of the healthiest of the entire market" (Miles & Snow, 1978, p. 37). Organizations operating with this type of strategy carve out a niche for themselves and then work very hard to protect it. They strive for internal efficiencies and simultaneously seek to improve the quality and price of their product or service. Because they are inwardly focused, Defenders tend not to pay a lot of attention to changes outside of their immediate domain. The type of structure associated with a Defender strategy is centralized, with a high level of task specialization and a relatively high level of formalization. The centralized structure means control is in the hands of senior managers; integration is achieved through formalized policies and procedures.

An example of a sport organization that has successfully adopted a Defender strategy is the United States' largest chain of specialty running stores, Running Room, founded in Edmonton in 1984, with branches in Canada and the United States. The owner of the store quickly carved out a niche in local markets by providing quality running equipment and knowledgeable staff. Although the company experimented with aerobics gear, it found it was more successful just focusing on running. The owner felt that in trying to service a wider market, the company sacrificed focus. He noted (as quoted in a course paper by Liz Zahary at the University of Alberta), "The more we do [stick to our core market] the more successful we've been; then at least you're known for something." Similarly, Belfast, Northern Ireland–based Chain Reaction Cycles (cycling) and Portsmouth, England–based Wiggle Ltd. (triathlon) operate under similar strategies. In fact, any retailer that focuses on one particular sport or activity can be considered to be an adopter of a Defender strategy. In a similar vein, a college or university athletic department that traditionally offers (and is successful in) a limited number of intercollegiate sports, instead of offering a wide range of activities, could be seen as operating with a Defender strategy.

Prospectors

In contrast to Defenders, who stick to established products and markets, Prospectors actively seek new products and new market opportunities. These companies establish their reputation by being the first on the market with new products. Because their success depends on innovation, Prospectors must scan their environments constantly for new trends and opportunities. The need for Prospectors to respond rapidly to environmental changes means they must adopt a flexible structure. Employees require the types of skills that enable them to be moved from one project to another; consequently, task specialization is low, as is formalization; decision making is decentralized but with complex integration systems. Control is achieved largely through the professional status of the Prospector's employees. W.L. Gore & Associates, manufacturer of the well-known Gore-Tex fabric, is an example of a company operating with a Prospector strategy. Constantly looking for new applications for its products—used in running suits, skiwear, and camping equipment—the company has adopted a very informal operating structure (W.L. Gore & Associates, 2019), traditionally referred to as a lattice organization (Rhodes, 1982) but now becoming more commonly known as an open allocation management style. Other organizations have adopted this approach (e.g., video game developer Valve Corporation, and Microsoft subsidiary and web-based hosting service, GitHub [Dannen, 2013]).

Analyzers

Analyzers lie somewhere between Defenders and Prospectors. "A true Analyzer is an organization that minimizes risk while maximizing the opportunity for profit [it] combines the strength of both the Prospector and the Defender into a single system" (Miles & Snow, 1978, p. 68). The Analyzer operates with a mix of products and markets, some of which will exhibit stability, while others will be more dynamic. In stable product market areas Analyzers operate as routinely and efficiently as they possibly can. In the changing environment Analyzers watch their competitors for new, popular products and then move quickly to copy the idea so that their product arrives on the market on the heels of the developer. The idea is to maintain a base of traditional products while at the same time locating and exploiting the opportunities available in new markets and products.

The sport organization adopting an Analyzer strategy will have to develop a structure that allows them to exercise tight controls over the stable product and market areas, and looser controls over the areas in which new products are being developed. The organization adopts a more formalized and centralized structure in the former product or market areas and a more decentralized and flexible structure in the latter. Because of the presence of different types of subunits, control involves a delicate balance between systems that are "centralized and budget-oriented to encourage cost-efficient production of standard products [and systems that are] . . . decentralized and results-oriented so as to enhance the effectiveness with which new products can be adapted" (Miles & Snow, 1978, p. 77). The Analyzer label has been ascribed to companies that mass-produce imitations of popular brands, such as the major athletic footwear companies. Much more recently, it has also been a strategy adopted by many intercollegiate athletics departments in the United States. In his turn-of-the-millennium research into the organizational effectiveness of top-tier NCAA athletics departments, Cunningham (2002) found the majority of these to be employing an Analyzer strategy: "That is, while seeking to maintain a firm base within the environment (like the defender), analyzer departments also [sought] to capitalize on new opportunities that other departments (i.e. the prospector) found to be successful (Miles and Snow, 1978)" (Cunningham, 2002, p. 167). Despite this tendency, however, the Analyzer strategy wasn't the most successful in Cunningham's (2002) research, and in terms of athletic achievement, those departments adopting a prospector strategy performed best. In terms of student graduation rates, both Prospector and Defender strategies were more successful than those adopting an Analyzer strategy.

Reactors

Reactors are organizations that do not respond appropriately to their environment. Organizations find themselves operating with a Reactor strategy when "(1) management fails to articulate a viable organizational strategy; (2) a strategy is articulated but technology, structure, and process are not linked to it in an appropriate manner; or (3) management adheres to a particular strategy–structure relationship even though it is no longer relevant to environmental conditions" (Miles & Snow, 1978, p. 82). Because a Reactor strategy is an inappropriate strategy, no clear linkages exist between this type of strategy and structure.

Strategies: According to Environment and Structure

The first three of these strategic positions are each appropriate under different environmental conditions, and each requires a different type of structure. It is, of course, possible that two managers in different sport organizations within the same industry may scan their environment and respond with a different strategy. In the 1980s, Paul Fireman of Reebok saw a changing environment for the athletic footwear industry because of the aerobics boom. Consequently, he adopted a Prospector strategy, and his company aggressively pursued the aerobics market. Philip Knight and the people at Nike saw aerobics as a passing fad so adopted a Defender strategy, concentrating on its already successful running shoe business.

Managers who pursue a Prospector strategy need to adopt an organizational structure that can respond quickly to changing environmental conditions. Consequently, they cannot be encumbered by highly formalized procedures and hierarchies that have centralized control through senior managers. Defenders can function with this type of structure because their environment is stable or changing very slowly, and the highly formalized and bureaucratic structure allows them to capitalize on the efficiencies it provides. Sport organizations that choose an Analyzer strategy must balance the quest for efficiency with the need to be able to respond rapidly to change.

Could Structure Determine Strategy?

Much of the literature on the strategy–structure relationship has followed Chandler and worked from the premise that the selection of an appropriate structure follows the selection of a strategy. However, a number of writers (Bourgeois & Astley, 1979; Burgelman, 1983; Fahey, 1981) have historically suggested that it is quite possible that structure determines the choice of strategy, or that they evolve simultaneously.

One way to think about the strategy–structure relationship is that decisions on what to do next should be based, at least in part, on the organization's structure and on its capabilities. Fredrickson (1986) looked at the effect that structural dimensions of centralization, formalization, and complexity could have on strategic choice. His ideas can be summarized thus:

Centralization

As centralization increases,

- strategic decision processes are initiated only by a dominant few and result from proactive opportunity-seeking behavior;
- decision processes are aimed at achieving what are considered positive goals that will persist in spite of significant changes in means;

- strategic action is the result of intended and rational strategic choices that move significantly away from existing strategy; and
- the cognitive limitations of top management are the primary constraint on the comprehensiveness of the strategic process. Integration of decisions is relatively high.

Formalization

As formalization increases,

- strategic decision processes are initiated only in response to crises that are monitored by a formal system;
- decisions are made to achieve precise yet remedial goals, and means become more important than the ends (goals);
- strategic action is the result of standardized organizational processes and will be incremental; and
- the level of detail achieved in the standardized organizational processes is the primary constraint on the comprehensiveness of the strategic process. Integration of decisions is intermediate.

Complexity

As complexity increases,

- members initially exposed to decisions will not recognize them as being strategic or will ignore them because of their narrow-minded preferences;
- decisions need to comply with multiple parameters, which decreases the likelihood that decisions are made to achieve organization-level goals;
- strategic action results from internal political bargaining processes and will be incremental; and
- biases induced by members' narrow-minded perceptions will be the primary constraint on the comprehensiveness of the strategic process. Integration of decisions is low.

On the other hand, proponents of the Austrian School (e.g., Schumpeter, 1950; Kirzner, 1973; Jacobson, 1992) and authors such as Mintzberg (1990, p. 183) view the structure–strategy relationship as a coordinated one:

> No organization ever wipes the slate clean when it changes its strategy. The past counts, just as the environment does, and the structure is a significant part of that past. . . . We conclude, therefore, that structure follows strategy as the left foot follows the right in walking. In effect strategy and structure both support the organization. None takes precedence: each always precedes the other and follows it.

This coordinated view has started to dominate management literature. However, some questions still remain. For example, what is the impact of the organization's development stage? In newer organizations managerial choice is likely to be far less constrained than in older organizations, in which structures and modes of operation are well established and hence more likely to constrain choice on strategy issues. Or, how much lag time is there between a strategic decision and its impact on structure? Does this lag time vary within or between industries?

Researchers are also looking at other factors that can influence the strategy–structure relationship. For example, what types of changes in the environment have an impact on strategy and structure, and how? How do internal and external innovations affect the strategy–structure relationship within an organization?

The point here is that many questions still need to be answered about the strategy–structure relationship and strategy in general. Strategy is now a popular area of study in organization-management theory; most business schools offer specific courses on business strategy (or "policy," as it is called when related to public-sector organizations). Despite a growing body of literature, studies that focus specifically on strategy in sport organizations remain relatively uncommon. Since sport organizations, like all other organizations, implicitly or explicitly formulate strategy, which in turn influences many other aspects of management, more work needs to be undertaken on this topic in sport management.

Strategy in Voluntary Sport Organizations

Of the research carried out on the strategies employed by sport organizations, much has focused on the voluntary sector. In a study of Canadian national sport organizations, Thibault, Slack, and Hinings (1993) developed a theoretical framework to identify four types of strategies that could be pursued by these organizations. Using work by MacMillan (1983) on nonprofit organizations, Thibault et al. (1993) identified six strategic imperatives that must be considered when developing strategies: (1) fundability, the ability of the sport organization to secure financial resources from external sources; (2) size of client base, the number of clients the sport organization serves; (3) volunteer appeal, the organization's ability to attract human resources; (4) support group appeal, the extent to which the sport organization's programs are visible and appealing to those groups capable of providing current or future support; (5) equipment costs, the amount of money required for equipment at the introductory levels of the sport; and (6) affiliation fees, the costs associated with participating in a sport.

The first four of these imperatives were seen to constitute the organization's level of program attractiveness, that is, its ability to provide services and programs to its members while at the same time securing the necessary resources for these programs. The last two imperatives made up the sport organization's competitive position, that is, its potential to attract and retain members. By dividing the dimensions of program attractiveness and competitive position into high and low components, Thibault et al. (1993) were able to construct a 2x2 matrix as shown in figure 8.5. The four quadrants within the matrix represent the types of strategy that national sport organizations can pursue.

Enhancers were those national sport organizations that scored high on both dimensions, such as badminton and association football. These sport organizations already had well-developed strategies in place and an existing network through which to operationalize new initiatives. The sports in this category were generally popular and inexpensive to pursue; this position gave them the opportunity to experiment with new programs at little risk, thereby enhancing their already well-established strategic position. **Innovators**, such as diving and lacrosse, had a strong competitive position but low program attractiveness. That is, they were relatively cheap to pursue but had little in the way of existing programs and members, so the strategic focus of these organizations was to adopt innovative initiatives to get people involved. The strong competitive position of innovators helped these organizations because there were few cost barriers to participation in their sport. **Refiners**, such as hockey or Canadian gridiron football, already had well-established strategies but their weak competitive position, that is, the high costs associated with their sport, made expanding these programs difficult. These sport organizations were expected to follow a strategy of refining existing programs. **Explorers**, such as alpine skiing and equestrian, were in the worst strategic position since they had low levels of program attractiveness and their sport was costly. It was expected that these organizations would explore a number of strategies to create programs to enhance their sport's position. Later, Thibault, Slack, and Hinings (1994) empirically verified the dimensions of their framework and located a sample of national sport organizations according to the type of strategy they were following.

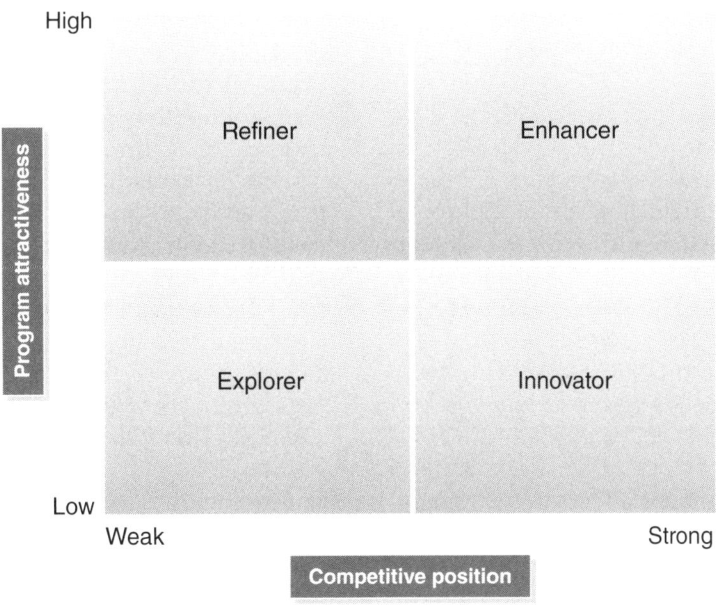

Figure 8.5 National sport organization strategic types.

Reprinted by permission from L. Thibault, T. Slack, and C.R. Hinings, "A Framework for the Analysis of Strategy in Non-Profit Sport Organizations," *Journal of Sport Management* 7 (1993): 36.

KEY ISSUES FOR SPORT MANAGERS

As a manager, you will have to formulate and implement strategies to help your organization become successful. Your hierarchical level will, however, determine whether you will be dealing more with corporate- or business-level strategies. Remember that strategies may not be clear from the outset; they may emerge over time. With this in mind, if you want to determine your organization's strategies or develop a strategy, you must consider the following elements.

- *Your organization's nature*: organizational mission, goals, internal strengths and weaknesses, structure, size, and tolerance for risk.
- *Your organization's environment*: external opportunities and threats, type of environment (stable or dynamic), and composition of the environment (see chapter 4).

These points cover the planning phase. As a manager, you must also deal with the implementation phase, which can be harder to do than the planning phase because any change within an organization can lead to resistance. To encourage implementation, you must do the following.

- *Motivate*: Establish an environment in which organizational members accept the need for the strategic change and are physically and psychologically committed to the transition.
- *Create and communicate the vision of the desired future state*: Relate the new strategy to the organization's mission and goals and set up intermediate goals that can serve as benchmarks for the transition process.
- *Mobilize political support for change from the top levels of power in the organization*: Reinforce legitimacy and access to resources to facilitate the transition.
- *Manage the transition*: Implement the management structures (e.g., task force) and processes that will set the strategy into motion.
- *Sustain the momentum*: Provide the necessary resources, build support systems, facilitate skills and competency development, and back up desired behavior through a rewards system (Cummings & Worley, 1993).

Summary and Conclusions

Organizational strategy is concerned with the long-term goals and objectives of a sport organization. Strategy, one of the major determinants of organizational structure, can be deliberate or emergent. Strategy can be formulated at two levels: the corporate level and the business level. Corporate-level strategies may focus on growth, stability, or decline (defensive strategies); companies may also adopt these strategies in combination. One technique used to determine the strategic needs of a corporation is portfolio analysis. Business-level strategies are used by individual business units to gain a competitive advantage. The most commonly used business-level strategies are cost leadership, product differentiation, and focus.

Strategy formulation and implementation involve a series of steps, including formulating a mission statement; conducting an assessment of external threats and opportunities and internal strengths and weaknesses; selecting the appropriate strategy; and designing the necessary organizational structure, control, and integration systems. Mintzberg suggests three modes of strategy formulation: the planning mode, the entrepreneurial mode, and the adaptive mode.

The relationship between strategy and structure has been a topic of considerable debate. Alfred Chandler, one of the first writers in this area, suggested that structure follows strategy; a number of other researchers replicated Chandler's work and produced similar results. Recent research, however, has suggested that strategy and structure evolve simultaneously. Work by Miles and Snow identified four strategic types: Defenders, Prospectors, Analyzers, and Reactors. Each strategic type is associated with a particular set of structural arrangements.

Review Questions

1. Strategy is more than just setting goals and objectives. What else does it involve?

2. What is the difference between a sport organization with a deliberate strategy and one with an emergent strategy?
3. When should a company within the sport industry consider a strategic alliance?
4. What type of structure do you associate with each of Porter's strategic types?
5. If you were formulating a strategy for a university athletic department, what factors do you think you would have to consider in your external analysis?
6. Why did Chandler conclude that structure followed strategy? Do you think his conclusions would have been different had he used a different sample of organizations?
7. What type of structure would you expect to find associated with each of Miles and Snow's strategic types?
8. How might the stage of a sport organization's development affect the choice of a strategy?

Suggestions for Further Reading

A fairly large body of literature within the broader field of management focuses on the topic of organizational strategy. In fact, a major publication, the *Strategic Management Journal*, deals exclusively with research on organizational strategy. Of the available literature, probably the best-known work on strategy is the Porter trilogy *Competitive Strategy: Techniques for Analyzing Industries and Competitors* (1980), *Competitive Advantage: Creating and Sustaining Superior Performance* (1985), and *The Competitive Advantage of Nations and Their Firms* (1989). Of less popular appeal but equally substantive is the work of Danny Miller. Examples of his work on strategy include his (1986) "Configurations of Strategy and Structure" and (1987b) "The Structural and Environmental Correlates of Business Strategy," both in *Strategic Management Journal*; "Strategy Making and Structure: Analysis and Implications for Performance" (1987a) and "Relating Porter's Business Strategies to Environment and Structure: Analysis and Performance Implications" (1988) appear in the *Academy of Management Journal*. You may also wish to read Miller's (1990) book *The Icarus Paradox*.

You are also recommended to read Miles and Snow's (1978) book *Organizational Strategy, Structure, and Process*; and Quinn, Mintzberg, and James' *The Strategy Process: Concepts, Contexts, and Cases* (1988), a large collection of readings about various aspects of organizational strategy, as well as Austin's *The Collaboration Challenge: How Nonprofits and Businesses Succeed through Strategic Alliances* (2010), which examines strategic alliances and how they can be used for companies and nonprofits for success.

Increasing in popularity are theories in strategy literature that deal less with the structure aspect and more with determining what will help the organization gain a sustained competitive advantage. For example, the Austrian School believes this is done through entrepreneurial discovery (Jacobson, 1992). The resource-based view focuses on the importance of the organization's resources, especially intangible resources (Barney, 1991a, 1991b; Amis, Pant, & Slack, 1997). The knowledge-based view focuses its attention on one intangible resource, knowledge, believing that this resource is the key to success (see Winter, 1987; Kogut & Zander, 1992).

Within the sport management research base there remains something of a void when it comes to strategy, although the literature is growing in varying contexts, albeit unhurriedly. Chalip and Leyns (2002) were initially one of the few with a study on business leveraging as a strategy in the context of sporting events. The aforementioned Cunningham (2002) study, published in the *International Review for the Sociology of Sport*, sought to identify different organizational strategies within intercollegiate athletics in the United States. Ferkins, Shilbury, and McDonald (2009, p. 245) later published a study in the *Journal of Sport Management* that explored "how the boards of national sport organizations might enhance their strategic capability . . . focusing on the case of New Zealand [association] Football." Since then, Yeh and colleagues have undertaken research into the relationship between strategic orientation and board roles in summer Olympic sport organizations in Taiwan, published in *Managing Leisure* (Yeh, Hoye, & Taylor, 2011). In Isoherranen and Kess' (2011) analyses of strategy in two case businesses, published in *Modern Economy*, one of these cases was the sport equipment marketer and manufacturer AMER.

Research studies aside, sport management academic literature in the form of monographs and textbooks is in a much healthier position. For example, Westerbeek and Smith's (2005) *Business Leadership and the Lessons from Sport*; Gray's (2018) *The Game Changer: How Leading Organisations in Business and Sport Changed the Rules of the Game*; and an edited collection by Dolles and Söderman (2011), *Sport as a Business: International, Professional and Commercial Aspects*, offer, among other things, insights into strategic management that are supported by real-life case studies from business and sport. Beyond academic tomes, further indication of the types of strategies pursued by sport organizations can be gained from books such as Strasser and Becklund's (1991) *Swoosh: The Story of Nike and the Men Who Played There*, and Knight's (2018) *Shoe Dog: A Memoir by the Creator of Nike*. From the world of motorsport, Brawn and Parr's (2016) *Total Competition: Lessons in Strategy from Formula One* offers various insights from within the industry.

Beyond sport, such has been the growth and popularity of business strategy and the lessons that can be learned in recent years that Amazon currently maintains a top 100 best-sellers list dedicated to the topic of strategy, with Damien Hughes's (2016) *The Winning Mindset: What Sport Can Teach Us About Great Leadership* featuring at number 2 in the list (at the time of writing).

Finally, articles on sport organizations found in business magazines such as *Fortune*, *Forbes*, *Business Week*, and *SportBusiness* will provide useful sources of knowledge with respect to topical issues and developments linked to strategy.

Case for Analysis

Roman Abramovich

Described as a "Russian oligarch," Roman Abramovich was born in Saratov, Russia, on October 24, 1966. By the age of four he was an orphan—his mother was killed when he was 18 months old, and his father later died in a construction accident. He then went on to be adopted by his paternal uncle and raised by his Jewish family in Komi, northwest Russia. Abramovich attended the Industrial Institute in Ukhta, but his academic career was interrupted when he was drafted into the Soviet Red Army. He eventually returned to school and earned a law degree from Moscow State Law Academy in 2000 (BBC News, 2004).

Abramovich's early business ventures ranged from selling plastic ducks from an apartment in Moscow to owning pig farms and ultimately to his interest in oil. His first break came in 1992 when he was befriended by Boris Berezovsky, who brought him into the inner circle of former Russian president Boris Yeltsin. Berezovsky advised him to buy shares in Sibneft (Russia's fifth-largest oil company), which had recently become privatized after the fall of communism. Later in 2001 Berezovsky moved to Britain after a falling out with new president Vladimir Putin and ongoing criminal investigations into fraud. This move opened the way for Abramovich. His business successes included the accumulation of 80 percent of Sibneft, 50 percent of Rusal (the Russian aluminum oil monopoly), and 26 percent of Aeroflot (Russia's national airline). The eventual sale of Aeroflot is said to have funded Abramovich's buyout of Chelsea Football Club (*The Guardian*, 2003; Tran, 2003; BBC News, 2004).

In addition to his business ventures Abramovich entered into politics. In 2000 he became governor of the small northeastern province of Chukotka, Russia, with a population of only 73,000 (Jarvie, 2006). Some of Abramovich's critics say that this move was merely a ploy to secure higher political office. Abramovich poured over US$200 million into the region, building everything from hotels to supermarkets and cinemas. He even brought in some of his staff from Sibneft to help run the province (Tran, 2003).

Not only did Abramovich have interests in Russian business and politics, but he also invested in the sport and entertainment industry, buying a television station and ice hockey team. But he loved association football and sought to diversify his business ventures outside of Russia by purchasing a leading British team, Chelsea. This move also capitalized on his links with Britain (i.e., Berezovsky and Millhouse Capital, the company that controlled Abramovich's assets). His purchase of Chelsea (or *Chelski* [Wagg, 2007], as it has been referred to by the British tabloids) was celebrated by the fans and staff, who saw a new infusion of money into the club. The choice of Chelsea was not random; several other clubs had been considered. Abramovich was looking for a club that was already good and had the potential to go to the top of the game. He wiped out the club's debts and reportedly made £100 million (US$132 million) of his own money available to secure star players (Giulianotti, 2005). The club saw almost immediate success, and in the time between taking over the club in 2003 and the 2017–18 EPL season, Abramovich was reported to have spent around £1.1 billion (US$1.3 billion) on the club through wages and transfers, bringing five EPL titles, five FA Cups, three Football League Cups, one UEFA Champions League, and one UEFA Europa League to the club in return for his investment. However, against the backdrop of the United Kingdom's proposed departure from the European Union (referred to as Brexit) and the poisoning of the former Russian spy Sergei Skripal and his daughter in the English city of Salisbury in 2018 (reportedly to have been the actions of two officers from the Russian military intelligence service), subsequent visa troubles have reportedly forced him to consider selling the club (Doward,

2018; Garside, 2018; Press Association, 2018). And, as you will see in chapter 15, sport mixing with politics is not uncommon.

Questions

1. How would you describe the strategy that Abramovich has followed to date?
2. Perform a PESTEL analysis of Chelsea's external environments in the present day.
3. Do a SWOT analysis of Chelsea before being bought by Abramovich, and in the present day.
4. Why, pre-2018, might Abramovich and Chelsea have been a good fit?
5. What strategy should Abramovich use in the future?

CHAPTER 9

Sport Marketing

Frank Pons, PhD
Marilyn Giroux, PhD
Lionel Maltese, PhD

Learning Objectives

When you have read this chapter you should be able to

1. understand what sport marketing is,
2. explain the two perspectives of sport marketing,
3. describe key elements of sport marketing strategies, and
4. better understand the key role played by marketing for sport organizations.

Key Concepts

activation
branding
brand personality
equivalent media advertising
fan
marketing of sport
marketing through sport
merchandising
naming
sponsorship
visibility

The Ultimate Sports Marketing Example: The Super Bowl

The Super Bowl remains one of the greatest sporting events on the planet and surely the biggest annual sporting event, not only on the field but in the business world. With an annual average of over 180 million viewers on the planet, 110 million of whom are in the United States alone, it is the most watched televised program in U.S. history. It is the best example of both a sport product marketed to passionate fans and an amazing sport tool used to market a myriad of products to consumers. This fan passion and irrational approach to consuming an amazing experience is summarized in the craze around ticket prices for this scarce and very exclusive event. For instance, the average ticket price from brokers is around US$10,000, and it keeps growing every year. In addition, the half-time show, with acts such as Katy Perry, Lady Gaga, and Justin Timberlake, adds a layer of popular entertainment that is always eagerly awaited by the audience. Another key facet of the Super Bowl is its ability to sell commercial space and to attract companies to advertise their products during the event. With costs currently around US$5 million—and rising—for a 30-second ad placement, the Super Bowl is the ultimate place to announce products. At this price and despite the huge upfront cost, companies still get an interesting deal with a cost per thousand (also called CPM), which represents the cost of 1,000 advertisement impressions, that is in line with other prime-time shows but more importantly with an unmatched level of attention for their commercial. During the Super Bowl, commercials are part of the show and not a distraction. In fact, more than 50 percent of Super Bowl TV viewers admit watching the event only for the commercials; for instance, there are four times more views of commercials (one billion views) than of game-related content. No doubt that for marketers, the Super Bowl really represents the ultimate sport business vehicle.

As the importance of sports in economic, cultural, and social fields is increasingly recognized, it is essential to gain useful insights on its nature and, in particular, which aspects of sport can spark so much passion and trigger even stronger impacts in the business and marketing world. The global sport industry is an important economic sector, with an average growth of 4 percent per year. Fullerton (2009) estimated that as global sport revenues continued to grow, it would generate more than US$185 billion in 2017. This US$185 billion mainly comes from two perspectives or streams through which sport marketing can be defined: the marketing *of* sports and marketing *through* sports (Fullerton, 2009). As highlighted in figure 9.1, sport marketing, despite its clear structure and organization, is a rather broad topic and cannot be fully detailed in one book chapter. Consequently, in this chapter we have decided to offer insights from one carefully selected component in each sport marketing perspective. These selected topics are shaded in figure 9.1, and they represent the most visible and strategic components that sport organizations have to deal with. They are the essence of what sport marketing is for sports organizations. First, for *marketing of sport*, we will focus on sporting events and spectator sports, as well as the critical issues of brand development, brand management, and merchandising in the marketing of sporting events and sports franchises. Second, for *marketing through sports*, sponsorship strategies and the latest trends in sponsorship, including activation strategies and venue-naming issues, will be detailed. Each of these components will be contextualized through case vignettes from sport properties around the world.

Marketing of Sport: Spectator Sports, Branding, and Merchandising

The **marketing of sport** perspective involves all the activities implemented to influence potential customers to consume sports products. In sports marketing literature, three categories of sport products have been identified: spectator sports, participation sports, and sporting goods (Fullerton & Merz, 2008). The first category consists of *spectator sports* that regroup minor sports leagues to professional sports leagues (e.g., NFL) to sporting events (e.g., Formula One World Championship). Spectator sports build values thanks to the synergy between the competition on the field of play and individuals off the field who buy access to attend the event. *Participation sports* are recreational sports for which the main

Figure 9.1 Sport marketing structure.
Based on Fullerton (2009).

goal for marketers is to increase the participation in terms of numbers and frequency. People who play golf or tennis every week for pleasure would be included in this category. Finally, *sporting goods* represent a vague and complex category that can include goods such as skateboards, tennis rackets, apparel, and shoes. This classification also includes sport-related products such as souvenirs or lessons that are available for purchase.

In this section, the main focus will be on the spectator sports because it represents the most prominent component of sport marketing in terms of spending as well as strategic and management decisions. In addition, spectator sports are strongly connected with two key and current trends in managing sport organizations: branding and merchandising.

Spectator Sports

In marketing, the concept of product refers to "anything that can be offered in a market for attention, acquisition, use, or consumption that might satisfy a need or want" (Kotler & Armstrong, 2014). A product can be constituted of tangible and intangible aspects. Similar to typical products, sport products include both core and extended elements. However, this is where the comparison stops. Unlike usual products, spectator sports carry a particularly strong meaning for individuals attending games, and the values and attributes they display allow consumers to express their self-identity and their belongingness to peer groups in a much stronger fashion than for typical products. In addition, sporting events also present specific characteristics that make them stand out for consumers. They are intangible, short-lived, unpredictable, and subjective in nature. They are produced and consumed at the same time, and they are often paired with a strong emotional display or commitment from consumers.

These unique characteristics and their multiple facets can fulfill a wide range of consumers' needs and motivations rarely matched by other products. Spectator sports are often the most visible and prominent aspects of sport marketing, as confirmed by economic figures. For instance, it is estimated that the gate revenues (ticketing of spectator sporting events) alone account for the largest source of income with 32.6 percent of the total sport market. This is especially true for North America and Europe, where paying higher prices for live events is part of the consumption rituals of sporting events. Sport participation also certainly contributes to spreading specific values and triggering passionate behaviors, but attending sporting events is highly significant for individuals, sport managers, and the sport industry as a whole.

Branding

In the sport marketing literature, the atypical nature of spectator sports as a product has been the center of researchers' and manager's interest. The unique features (intangible, unpredictable, and subjective) of spectator sports have underlined the need for sport organizations to better manage their offering, to make it more tangible, and to focus as much as possible on the aspects of their sport products that they are able to control. Along this line, an important stream of academic research and managerial decisions has underlined the key role that brands could play in their marketing strategies. For instance, most sport organizations aim to create a strong brand to avoid relying solely on the organization's performance during the season, to develop a manageable entity that will remain relatively consistent in the eyes of the **fans** (consumers), and with whom individuals want to associate and develop a robust and durable relationship.

A **brand** is often presented as "a name, term, sign, symbol, or design, or combination of them which is intended to identify the goods and services of one seller or group of sellers and to differentiate them from those from competitors" (Kotler, 1997, p. 443). Brands are a combination of characteristics and benefits that consumers buy and that create differentiation in the minds of consumers (Keller, 2007). Brands represent one of the most important and profitable assets of a firm (Neumeier, 2006). Brand equity represents the added value to a product or service because of its associations with a brand name (Keller, 1993). Consumers will pay a premium for a product because of its brand name. High-equity brands are normally well known by individuals and have strong, positive, and unique associations in consumers' memories (Aaker, 1991; Keller, 1993). Indeed, brand equity is often described in terms of customer-based equity measures, which express the unique set of associations that consumers create in their minds and why consumers are willing to pay this premium price.

With growing competition and increasing expenses (e.g., salaries), sport organizations have found ways to increase their sources of revenues by focusing on brand management activities that should ultimately increase their brand equity. Sport organizations stimulate this brand equity development by working on several facets of their marketing strategies. First, sport teams or events can create a stimulating and engaging experience for fans. In addition, they can sell souvenirs, which trigger nostalgic memories, in order to stimulate the emotional connection with spectators (Gladden & Funk, 2002). They can also create diverse associations with their brand. One important way to create brand associations is to develop a concrete and unique brand personality. **Brand personality** is defined as "the set of human characteristics associated with the brand" (Aaker, 1997, p. 347). The traits associated with the brand are often shaped by how the consumers perceive the brand to be (Aaker, 1997). The NFL's Oakland Raiders personify a rough, tough, and outlaw personality. Their underdog and bad-boy image and their costumed fans have strongly contributed to their outstanding personality. When a fit is created between the brand and the target market, a distinctive brand personality clearly positions the sport franchise and contributes to the creation of a strong image and therefore indirectly to the brand equity. Brand personality is taking a relatively new and prominent role in sport organizations because it offers a different perspective than the traditional image or identity.

A strong brand equity contributes strongly to the commercialization of the sport product. In general, a strong brand equity helps the sport organization develop its fan base and increase the fan base's involvement with the team. Sport brands with high equity can count on devoted supporters who consume diverse products and services directly related to their favorite team (Burton & Howard, 1999) or even with a remote connection to the sport organization (sponsor brands or brand extension to products outside of the sports industry). For instance, some teams will even use their brand names to introduce their own television network (e.g., Real Madrid) or generate revenue by spectator visits of their facilities (e.g., Boston Red Sox). In the case of super sports brands such as the Yankees or Real Madrid, one can even venture outside of the sports arena and use their brand equity to sell new products and capitalize on their brand name, awareness, and personality.

For a sport organization, a strong brand equity can provide several positive outcomes such as facilitating the integration and the extension into new product categories (Aaker & Keller, 1990). Indeed, using a current and existing brand name can considerably decrease the risks associated with launching a new product. A well-known brand can reassure consumers by signaling the quality and creating meaningful associations. In the sport industry, corporations are widely using the strategy of introducing new products and services as extensions of their current offerings. From ESPN2 to the Women's National Basketball Association (WNBA) to the Reebok Sports Club, new product offerings allow companies to create more emotional connections with fans, enhance brand strength, and acquire additional revenues.

The success of these brand extensions is often related to the perception of fit between the original and the new product, as well as the logical connection between the actual brand and its extension. For example, when the Ultimate Fighting Championship (UFC) created the UFC gym, they used their current expertise in mixed martial arts to create a product that had related characteristics to their main product. The brand consistency concept can also help the acceptance of the new product from individuals.

Brand extensions in sports can take different forms. First, the extensions can be related to sports. Organizations can create extension leagues and teams (e.g., WBNA), sport camps and clinics, youth leagues, or merchandise stores. The NHL team the Montreal Canadiens created the Canadiens Skills Clinics to teach hockey fundamentals to players from ages 7 to 14 years old as well as a hockey school to develop young players' abilities in skating,

TIME OUT

Brand Personality as a Segmentation and Strategic Tool: The Case of AS Saint-Etienne

ROMAIN LAFABREGUE/AFP/Getty Images

AS Saint-Etienne Fans: Live the passion.

In 2011 the authors of this chapter conducted a research project that aimed at better classifying and understanding fan behaviors for a French professional soccer club in Ligue 1, AS Saint-Etienne (ASSE). ASSE is a mythical club in France and remains one of the most famous soccer brands in the country, along with Marseille (OM), Paris Saint-Germain (PSG), and Lyon (OL). We administered a questionnaire through the club's website to examine the impact of brand personality and other brand variables' perceptions on consumer segmentation and on the evaluation of marketing promotional activities. A total of 2,586 questionnaires were completed and usable. Initial results were interesting in that typical psychographic segmentation of fans did not allow segmenting of the market for strategic purposes; the entire population seemed to behave rather consistently. On the contrary, when segmenting the respondents based on their perception of the brand personality of the club, a typology of four groups (the authentic, the nostalgic, the admirer, and the complainers) explained several key differences in terms of merchandising purchase differences or even negative perceptions of team management. These kinds of results allow sport organizations to target specific groups differently to address similar issues but with a different approach based on their relationship to the brand.

puck handling, shooting, and off-ice strength and conditioning. In addition, organizations can include entertainment-related products (e.g., cheerleaders), media-related extensions (e.g., broadcasting stations), and information-related extensions (e.g., websites) (Apostolopoulou, 2002). Some brand extensions, such as credit cards, fashion merchandise, and water and beverages, are less consistent (low perceived fit) with the sport organizations. In 2012 the New York Yankees introduced a fragrance for men and women. This fragrance was meant to symbolize "the winning style of the greatest team in baseball, capturing a sporty and confident attitude." (Slotnick, 2012) This new venture did not receive huge fan support, but rather a lukewarm reception. Considering the low relevance of these extensions, their success is not always guaranteed. Real Madrid proposed an idea of a soccer-themed resort in the United Arab Emirates, but this project was cancelled after lack of global interest and some financial problems from the project's organizer.

The extensions can be realized in collaboration with another brand in a cobranding strategy. Cobranding is a brand alliance strategy in which two brands appear on a single product. This situation is particularly appealing since the perceived value of the product can be increased. For example, Apple and Nike worked together by combining music and sport to create the Sports Kit, which allows shoes to talk to the music station (iPod). Nike also designed and produced the Air Jordan shoes and athletic clothing in collaboration with Michael Jordan. Nowadays, all products of this line are available for the general public. Often, brand extensions using sport organizations' high brand equity connect the branding world and the merchandising world.

Merchandising

Marketing of licensed sport merchandise represents one of the most common strategies to develop more business for sport organizations. Indeed, **merchandising** is an important source of revenues for the different leagues, and some teams are successfully capitalizing on different apparel offerings. According to Forbes, sales of sport merchandise for major sports leagues (NBA, MLB, NFL, and NHL) grew to a total of $15.2 billion in 2017. In addition, collegiate sport licensing sales also increased to a total of $4.78 billion. In comparison to gate revenues, merchandising (a subsection of sporting goods and apparel) revenues represent "only" 14.5 percent of total revenues. (This number is also heavily skewed in North America, which represents 71 percent of the global sports merchandising revenues.) However, merchandising is particularly crucial for sport organizations because it is an important part of the fans' experience by increasing the involvement of individual consumers through the widespread feeling of belongingness among spectators.

As part of their branding strategy and return on brand development, sport organizations are now directing their fans to their facilities and online stores to market team-related products. Sport team–licensed merchandise can take several forms such as clothing (e.g., gear, T-shirts, jerseys), hats, caps, souvenirs, and cards. While clothing represents the majority of sales for sport organizations, some nontraditional products are now on the market. Teams have started to commercialize animal clothing, small appliances, toothbrushes, and condiments. Furthermore, to boost their sales, teams now increasingly target female fans. Female spectators are extremely interesting for sport brands because they are extremely loyal, make an important percentage of family decisions, and are a relatively untapped segment for sponsors and media. Finally, the fashion aspect of sport apparel is crucial for certain marketing segments. Some consumers buy apparel for the fashion statement and the "cool" aspect of a team. New York Yankees hats are popular around the world and are perceived as stylish.

Licensed sport merchandise increases belongingness to a team, has a significant impact on consumers' social identity, and helps fans classify and separate themselves from other groups of people, especially fans of rival teams. However, the sales of those products are often linked to the performance and success of the team. Individuals want to be associated with positive sources to enhance their self-perception. This aspect is often referred to as the notion of basking in reflected glory, which signifies that individuals often publicize their association with successful teams. According to SportsOneSource, in 2012 the Philadelphia Phillies saw the sales of their Phillies-related products decreased by 60 percent after a disappointing season. Conversely, in 2018 the Eagles recorded a Super Bowl record for merchandising sales after their Super Bowl victory. This aspect reinforces the need for sport organizations to build a strong brand that attracts consumers in a consistent manner and reduces the impact of the win/loss record while developing their fans' identification to the team.

The previous two sections detailed the strategic aspects surrounding the marketing of sport, in particular branding issues, which currently represent the core preoccupation of sport properties, and merchandising, which also strongly affects revenue. However, branding issues also play a critical role in securing sponsorship revenues. Sponsorship is the essence of the second perspective of sport marketing, *marketing through sport*, which is presented hereafter.

Marketing Through Sport: Sponsorship, Activation, and Venue Naming

Marketing through sport represents the marketing of nonsport products using sport as a strategic and communication tool (Fullerton, 2009). Under this

KEY ISSUES FOR SPORT MANAGERS

Marketing *of* sports relates to the promotion and advertising of the sport as a product in itself. In sport marketing literature, three categories of sport products have been identified: spectator sports, participation sports, and sporting goods. The main goal of this strategy is to increase the popularity of the sport and to gain exposure in order to grow spectatorship and fan bases as well as the overall participation in the sport. By achieving this objective, sport organizations can generate more revenue through broadcasting, sponsorship, and growing memberships.

perspective, companies try to include sports as part of the marketing strategy of their products. This use can be limited to product placement or use (e.g., sports bar, energy drinks consumed during games, a simple advertising placed during a sporting event), but it may also be aimed at developing a stronger relationship and integration between the company (sponsor) and the sport organizations (sponsee). Some organizations see sponsorship activities as a way to associate their brands with sport organization and to capitalize on the level of stimulation and engagement that sports properties often trigger in carefully targeted segments.

Sponsorship

Sponsorships represent a crucial form of promotions for managers of companies around the world. Sponsorship activities are perceived as a unique marketing tool that complete a marketing communication program (Roy & Cornwell, 2004). **Sponsorship** is "an investment, in cash or in kind, in an activity in return for access to the exploitable commercial potential associated with that activity" (Meenaghan, 1991, p. 36). Sponsorships are based on the notion of exchange between the two entities, but also include the marketing of this association by the sponsor (Cornwell & Maignan, 1998). For sponsoring firms, sponsorships allow various forms of visibility and opportunities to be linked to the sport brand in exchange of financial or material support. Sponsors expect the image of the sponsored organization or event to be transferred to the brand and results in positive affection and emotions from consumers.

This industry has grown at a constant rate in the past decades around the world. Worldwide estimated sponsorship spending reached more than US$60.1 billion in 2016, representing a 4.6 percent increase over 2015 (International Events Group, 2017) and more than US$22.3 billion in North America alone. Even though sponsorships span across several categories of activities such as arts and entertainment, 70 percent of the sponsorship market is related to sports in North America (International Events Group, 2017). The sport industry clearly possesses several characteristics that make it appealing for sponsors. Indeed, the level of enthusiasm, passion, and emotional attachment triggered by sports provides a great platform to present a company's products. In addition, sponsors can profit from numerous opportunities such as merchandising, licensing, and cross promotions.

Sponsorship can deliver several communication and action objectives ranging from increased brand recall and awareness, a better brand image, stronger brand equity, and purchase intentions (Barros, Barros, Santos, & Chadwick, 2007; Cliffe & Motion, 2005; Cornwell, 2008; Koo, Quarterman, & Flynn, 2006). In addition, it can be an excellent way to differentiate the brand from other competitors (Fahy, Farrelly, & Quester, 2004). Perceived by consumers as less intrusive than advertising, sponsorships are viewed as more personal and altruist and tend to become a part of people's lives (Aaker & Joachimsthaler, 2000). Sport sponsorship represents an approved tool to concretely manage brand image, brand personality, and related aspects of the brand equity both for the sponsor and the sponsee.

Several factors can influence the effectiveness of sponsorships. One important factor is the congruence (fit) between the sponsor and the sponsee. This congruence can be perceived in terms of sponsor product relevance or functional benefit. In the case of Nike's sponsorship of the NFL, a relationship is evident between the sport company and the sport league. This pertinence can also be perceived in terms of personality or image. The accepted definition of brand image relates to "the set of associations linked to the brand that consumers hold in memory" (Keller, 1993, p. 2). In this case, the relevance is more in terms of the symbolic aspect of the brand. For example, Rolex has been an official sponsor of Wimbledon since 1978. In terms of brand image, this relationship between the luxury brand and the oldest tennis tournament makes sense since both entities target the same audience. Furthermore, geographic relevance (i.e., country of origin) can help the perceived relevance. The Hudson's Bay Company, a Canadian retail group, is the official outfitter of the Canadian Olympic Team.

Sport sponsorship includes a variety of activities by which a firm tries to take advantage of its official relationship with a sport property. Companies can sponsor a specific event, venue, organization, or individual. In terms of events, they can be either a one-off event, which is normally less expensive, or a recurrent event such as the Olympics or Super Bowl. Venue sponsorship relates to the identification of a building (e.g., TD Garden). Sport organizations can represent leagues (e.g., Major League Baseball), teams (e.g., Miami Heat), an organization (e.g., FIFA), a tournament, or an association. Athlete sponsorships are more personal but can be riskier. Several scandals concerning athletes have come up during the last few years including Tiger Woods, Ray Rice, and Michael Phelps. Nevertheless, endorsements remain a very popular type of sponsorship.

Endorsements are perceived to be personal sponsorships. A celebrity endorser is defined as "any individual who enjoys public recognition and who uses this recognition on behalf of a consumer good by appearing with it in an advertisement" (McCracken, 1989, p. 310). Companies are inclined to pay millions of dollars to be associated with top-performing athletes. Annually, corporations invest more than US$12 billion in athlete endorsements. Indeed, some professional athletes earn more money from their endorsement deals than salaries. For example, LeBron James has received more than US$100 million in salary during his career, but his endorsement deals have represented the majority of his revenues. Indeed, his numerous agreements with Nike, Coca-Cola, Upper Deck, McDonald's, and other companies represent revenues of more than US$50 million each year. Endorsement deals are considered a form of sponsorship because the company sponsors the athletes to wear its brand or use its product or service.

Overall, sponsorship deals can represent an important part of revenues for sport teams and leagues. Soccer teams benefit from their success on the field to negotiate important kit and shirt sponsorship deals. For example, Manchester United has one of the most expensive supplier kit deals with Adidas. This agreement represents an impressive US$1 billion over 10 years. In addition, the team has secured a yearly US$80 million for their shirt sponsorship deal with Chevrolet. As a testimony to the continuous increase in sponsorship spending, this impressive deal has recently been surpassed by Nike, who signed a 10-year contract (2018-2028) with Barcelona for US$140 million a year.

Traditional sponsorship deals include the recognition of the sponsor by the sports entity. Sponsorship agreements are negotiated between the company and the sport entity and normally require a written contract between the two parties. The contracts generally define the category of sponsorship and the scope of exclusivity. The exclusivity represents a crucial point of the arrangement since sponsors want to maximize their visibility and want to avoid overcrowding in the space. The contracts should also cover the benefits for the sponsor, its responsibilities and in-kind services provided by sponsors, the payment of fees, and the opt-out clause. A variety of rights can be bargained between the sponsor and the sponsee. These benefits can be related to advertising. Indeed, deals normally include the right for the sponsor to use the sponsee's logos and trademarks in different activities to capitalize on the sponsorship to reach their targeted segments of consumers (Fullerton & Merz, 2008). Corporate sponsors are encouraged to use the logo and the trademark in their advertising; for example, on their various platforms, Mobil 1 promotes that they are the Official Motor Oil of NASCAR. Traditional sponsorship can consist of title rights. Indeed, many events have sponsor names included in their titles, such as the Barclay's Premier League (association football) and the BNP Paribas Open presented in Indian Wells (tennis). In these cases, the indication of principal sponsor is pretty clear. Another strategy is to be acknowledged as the presenting sponsor, such as the Memorial Tournament presented by Nationwide (golf). Several other advantages can be included, such as pre-event materials, statements, and activities. Sponsorships normally emphasize media coverage and onsite opportunities, such as corporate entertainment booths, kiosks, signage, or exhibitions. Sponsorship contracts can also consist of brand hospitality occasions, public appearances by the sponsee, signed merchandise, product placement, contests, and ticket allocation. In classical sponsorship activities, the sponsor often evaluates its return on investment by looking at its visibility during the event and estimating its **equivalent media advertising** (i.e., how much money the same level of exposure would have cost in media placement).

In the literature and in the media, sponsorship activities have been well documented in the past decades; however, counterstrategies such as ambush marketing have also caught people's attention. Ambush marketing represents a substantial threat to the sponsoring industry. Ambush marketing happens when companies attempt to create the impression that they are associated with an event without paying the event's sponsorship fee (Sandler

TIME OUT

Measurement of the FedEx Logo During the Open 13 (ATP 250) in Marseille

In 2010 FedEx made a strategic choice to sponsor professional tennis' ATP tournaments and to be visible in the majority of tournaments across the world, including the ATP tournament in Marseille. One of the objectives was to be highly visible on the courts and all media supports during the tournament by specifically sponsoring each player and the live presentation of game statistics, maximizing the presence of the FedEx logo in the media and for the spectators (Maltese & Danglade, 2014).

In order to measure the logo **visibility** (exposure), organizers worked with a specialized agency, Vertigo, which is well known for its involvement in France in the estimation of media equivalent through its own developed tool, BIS MEDIA service.

The chosen methodology for measuring the logo visibility followed four steps:

1. Studying the media perimeter of the Open 13 tournament: The following news media sources were surveyed for a two month-period: TV (more than 40 channels), press (11,000 publications), Internet (6,000 websites), and radio (more than 100 national and local radio stations).
2. Assessment of logo visibility:
   - For the press and Internet, each logo appearance is weighted using a coefficient factor according to its visibility (1 for optimal visibility and .5 for reduced visibility).
   - For TV, five full matches are considered and used as a reference. The duration of the logo's appearance on the screen during additional matches is then measured against these initial five matches. Appearance duration is also measured during reports or highlights dealing with the tournament.
3. Overall audience size is estimated using Mediametrie National Data (equivalent to Nielsen ratings).
4. Estimate of the equivalent media advertising:
   - For the press, the average price for a quarter-page or eighth-page ad placement is used.
   - For TV and radio, the average cost for a 30-second ad placement is used.
   - For Internet, an average cost is estimated using 100 websites as reference and using the number of daily views.

FedEx's sponsorship of an ATP tournament such as Open 13 was established at €70,000 (US$78,000). In 2012 the equivalent media advertising for Open 13 was estimated around €972,386 (US$108,000) in 2012. The breakdown by media shows that there were 266 press articles on the Open 13 including 117 with a picture and four with the FedEx logo. For 143 TV reports on the tournament, the FedEx logo appeared 112 times with an overall duration of 8 hours and 23 minutes. In 117 articles on the Internet (62 with a picture), only one had a picture of FedEx logo.

It seems that FedEx got a great result for the investment because the equivalent media advertising is much higher than the initial investment. However, exposure is not everything. Sponsorship's activation (to give life to your sponsorship during the event) also plays a major role (and cost) in evaluating sponsorship success. Finally, additional consumers' measures (e.g., notoriety, recall) will help assess if FedEx made a worthwhile investment.

From Maltese and Danglade (2014).

& Shani, 1989). Major events such as the Olympic Games and the FIFA World Cup are no strangers to ambush marketing. Even with vigorous trademark protections, companies can work around the rules (e.g., hiring endorsers that are closely related to the event) to create the illusion that they are somewhat related to the event. One of the most notable examples was the strategy used by Bavaria Brewery during the 2010 FIFA World Cup, where 36 Dutch women were ejected out of the stadium in a game between the Netherlands and Denmark. The official beer sponsor for the game was Budweiser, but the fans who were ejected had dressed in the same tight and short orange dresses that were provided by and identified to a competing Dutch brewery. All major events now have anti-ambush measures before, during, and after the event. These measures include systematic monitoring of sponsorship activities around the geographical location as well as online and in key markets for the event. In addition, major events lobby to make sure that legal measures and decisions are able to respond quickly to ambush threats. It has become a key responsibility for property owners and major events to demonstrate to potential sponsors that everything is done to ensure the viability of their investment.

AFP/Getty Images

Example of daring ambush marketing.

Activation

Unlike in academic research where the concept of sponsorship activation is seldom studied, in practice, activation has become a well-developed field and a major issue. The term **activation** is often used in situations where the public has any sort of opportunity to interact with the sponsor. Partnership activation.com, a think tank on the topic, probably provides the best way of thinking about what activation is: "How to connect fans to the sponsor brand?" In fact, through activation, sponsors give a meaning to their sponsorship for fans. They engage fans with their brands and the event. Activation is therefore defined as the methods used to bring a sponsorship alive, how to bring it from a formal contract to life on the ground during the sponsored event with the objective of connecting fans (or the direct audience) to sponsors' brands. The sponsorship rights can be seen as the entry costs (the right to use the sports property name), whereas activation triggers new and additional costs, not always mentioned in the popular press but very important as they represent all the activities necessary to promote the sponsorship agreement. Recent figures suggest that for each US$1 invested in securing a sponsorship deal, sponsor will spend US$3 in activation costs.

Activation is an integrated part of communication programs designed by advertisers to develop an interaction with those who attend sporting competitions. Various tools are available to advertisers for attracting and interacting with fans (business-to-consumer [B2C]) or with companies and institutions (business-to-business [B2B]). In practice, sponsors often hire specialized agencies to design their activation programs. These agencies can pinpoint the needs of their client and negotiate the desired actions with the event organizer. Many sporting event producers, however, have started developing this kind of expertise, such as the Union of European Football Association (UEFA). The Tour de France and its caravan are also known for their activation system promoting numerous brands that interact with the public at every stage of the competition. The copyright holder and organizer, Amaury Sport Organisation (ASO), recently established an internal activation cell designed to replace agencies. Their knowledge of the offer and their capacity to anticipate the needs of partner brands help them to personalize activations.

Even though activation is currently and unequivocally the main focus in sponsorship activities, several key questions remain, mainly dealing with whether the financial and human investment in an activation program is cost effective. As the measurement of the impact of sponsorship often remains, at a practical level, limited to measuring media impact and equivalent advertising, more complex engagement operations (activation) are tougher to evaluate in terms of success and return on investment (ROI). In addition, as the choice of activation programs and their deployment integrates both internal and external actions loaded with interpersonal interactions, activation evaluations and performance assessment measurements must capture relational objectives rather than simple visibility metrics. This is the next challenge for activation strategists, and it must be at the heart of an activation strategy. More generally, sponsorship and activation measures are currently critically missing in communication strategies used by sponsors—on average only 3.2 percent of budget is spent on sponsorship and activation evaluations—and therefore it must become an essential component of any sponsorship strategy as ROI or objectives become increasingly critical for both sponsors and sponsees.

Emerging Sponsorship Strategies

Sport organizations always look for creative means to increase their profits. In recent years global sport brands have worked on creating localized sponsorship partnerships. This new trend allows sport organizations to sell commercial rights locally within a specific market. Manchester United was the first team to adopt a localized deal with Diageos' Smirnoff vodka in Asia-Pacific in 2008; several other European clubs have followed this strategy. During the 2013-14 European association football season, this income method represented additional revenues of €54 million (US$60 million). Similar to other teams, FC Barcelona pursued this path by signing profitable deals with regional or local brands such as Tecate (as their official beer in Mexico) and Chang Beer in Thailand and all around Asia.

The Internet also offers several new opportunities in sponsorships. The Internet represents an interesting vehicle for sponsors considering its

TIME OUT

Fondation La Française des Jeux: Wear Your Sneakers at the Office!

La Française des Jeux is a major European lottery actor, offering enjoyable, responsible, and safe sport games and betting for the general public. In 1993 La Française des Jeux created the first Fondation d'Entreprise (Company Foundation) dedicated to sports, whose action focused on two main areas: sports and solidarity. As such, every year, the La Française des Jeux supports over 50 projects and helps more than 350 high-level athletes (Maltese & Danglade, 2014).

In the context of its eco-citizen activation programs, La Française des Jeux partnered with Association Européenne contre les Leucodystrophies (ELA), an association of parents and patients uniting their efforts in the fight against leukodystrophies. Since 1994 ELA has been organizing a "wear your sneakers and fight disease" week in schools. La Française des Jeux subsequently involved partners from the business world in this solidarity campaign. The concept put forward by La Française des Jeux consists of inviting employees of partner companies to wear sneakers to work and measure the steps they take with pedometers. For each step, the partner contributes one centime (US$0.01) to ELA. A communication campaign bringing together all partners and sporting shows is also planned for the event.

One such day-event, which took place on May 19, 2010, in Vitrolles, Bouches du Rhône, France, engaged 690 partners of La Française des Jeux at three of the group's sites, for a participation rate of 62 percent. A total of 250 employees took part in the activities. On the national level, 14 companies joined the system (e.g., PPR, Puma, Boursorama, Allianz, Generali, Veolia, Mitsubishi). Some 19 million steps were measured, corresponding to a €163,000 (US$181,000) contribution made to ELA.

The benefit of this citizen activation operation was to raise funds for an association and to raise awareness among many employees. The internal company dynamic was also affected thanks to a friendly day of solidarity. The media coverage of this original approach earned various actors significant visibility. Finally, the positioning of La Française des Jeux was presented to current and potential commercial targets and key influencers as intrinsically suited to sports (i.e., an adult population with sufficient purchasing power for this act of consumption).

From Maltese and Danglade (2014).

active and interactive character and its numerous possibilities (e.g., streaming audio, video content). Considering the possibility of personalization and tracking devices, the Internet allows consumers to reach more effectively their target market, stimulate the engagement of consumers, and evaluate the performance of their sponsorship decisions (Drennan & Cornwell, 2004).

Corporations can use hybrid strategies that complement their offline sponsorship activities and provide additional benefits. Sponsors can take advantage of the interactivity and the bidirectional communication aspects of the Internet. Social media is increasingly used by sponsors to leverage their sponsorship activities and reach more fans. The principal advantage of social media is to reach consumers beyond the simple event. Companies can use videos, online chat groups, or other technologies to communicate with fans. The United States' Major League Soccer (MLS) posted content from the launch party for Electronic Arts Inc.'s *FIFA 13* video game on Facebook, Twitter, and other social media channels to generate enthusiasm. Social media content can be as simple as a selfies contest or using Facebook and Twitter to stimulate conversation around the brand and its sponsee. In 2011 Roger Federer asked his fans to choose the headline for the 2012 print campaign for his sponsor, Mercedes-Benz's, latest car. This campaign generated more than 38,000 likes and 5,000 comments on the Facebook page.

These strategies can fulfill the entire potential of sponsorships, especially by stimulating involvement with and experiences for the fans. These activities can stimulate consumers' attention but also allow the company to have more control over their messages and offer potential to make the brand stand out compared to its competitors. Using the Internet allows companies to expand the breadth of their sponsorship and to reach consumers at different times (pre-event, during, or post-event). Pre-event means can create anticipation and excitement to enhance passion and involvement from the consumers. Post-event strategies can stimulate vivid memories and reinforce feelings from consumers (Braun, 1999; Hall, 2002).

Venue Naming

Previously, stadia were named after a person who was important for the team or related to the town. Nowadays, almost 70 percent of the professional sport facilities in North America carry the name of a corporate sponsor. The NHL leads the way with 90 percent of its stadia having naming right agreements. For example, the Toronto Maple Leafs play their home games in the Air Canada Centre, but the name was recently changed to Scotia Bank Arena for a record-breaking $32US million a year. **Naming** rights and entitlements can be acquired in a sponsorship agreement wherein a firm obtains the right to name a facility or an event for a certain period of time. These venues' naming rights can be described as a particular type of sponsorship: building sponsorships. This practice has been utilized by teams to increase their revenues but also to finance the construction of a new stadium. Indeed, new stadia are extremely costly to build. The construction of the MetLife Stadium, home of the New York Giants and the New York Jets, cost approximately US$1.6 billion, the most expensive stadium ever built. MetLife, an insurance company, gives around $16 million a year to support the cost of this building. Among the biggest naming deals is the one between the Dallas Cowboys and AT&T, valued at between $18 and $19 million a year, or the deal between Citibank and the New York Mets for just above $20 million a year.

This strategy is interesting for sponsoring firms for several reasons. First, venues' sponsors increase their visibility toward the general public. The implementation of this strategy allows companies to sell its nonsport products through sports to acquire brand awareness and to increase their brand image and stock prices (Quester, 1997). More importantly, these sponsors are perceived as good community citizens in that they put financial support toward providing an ultramodern facility in their region. For example, United Airlines agreed to pay $5 million a year for a new 20-year naming rights contract to renew their agreement to name the United Center, home of the Chicago Bulls (NBA) and Blackhawks (NHL). In this case, the hospitality and community aspects are important because United Airlines is headquartered in Chicago. Financial corporations such as JP Morgan and Citibank can become financial partners of the sport entity. They can also integrate their own products in the stadia such as ATM machines and affiliated credit and debit cards for the fans.

Venue naming deals have been surrounded by some controversy. Traditionalist fans sometimes perceive this type of sponsorship as another step through the commercialization of sports. In North America these deals are much more accepted, while in Europe fans and media are more reluctant to naming rights. There is no doubt that naming deals are now a crucial part of sport organizations' strategies. It is, however, critical for these organizations to ensure that the deal respects team values and positioning, to try to make this association part of a long-term arrangement to keep brand consistency, and that the sponsors pay a fair price.

KEY ISSUES FOR SPORT MANAGERS

Marketing *through* sports represents the marketing and advertising of nonsports products using sports as a strategic and communication tool (Solomon, 2009). These products and services are not necessarily related to sport. Under this perspective, companies try to include an element of sport as part of the marketing strategy to promote their products or services. By using sports as an affiliation marketing strategy, companies benefit from the popularity and viewership of sport in order to gain exposure and reach a desired target market.

Summary and Conclusions

Sport marketing is omnipresent in the press because the amount of money spent on sport products, in particular spectator sports, seems sometimes unreal, irresponsible, or astronomic. However, this chapter shows that sport organizations engage in a complex network of activities under the sport marketing umbrella. All these activities are interconnected, and a successful sport organization cannot develop and thrive when making any of these decisions in a silo. A global marketing perspective, both at the strategic and tactical levels, is essential for sports organizations. Figure 9.1 summarizes the activities and forms of sport marketing that exist (marketing of sports and marketing through sports). In addition, this chapter shows that marketing in general, and sport marketing in particular, is more than simply communicating or selling tickets; it is a discipline with a strategic basis and in which accountability and performance are critical as exemplified in the sponsorship and activation sections of this chapter. Sport marketers sell a unique product in an ever-changing, multi-stakeholder, and fast-paced environment, so they must develop a clear strategic path and make sure that all elements of their marketing strategy remain consistent and complementary. Keeping this focus despite turbulence is what makes the difference between successful and failing sport businesses.

Review Questions

1. How does marketing of sports differ from marketing through sports?
2. What is branding? Why is it important for a sport organization to brand itself internally and externally?
3. Discuss how brand extensions from sports organizations can occur. What are some factors that may facilitate the success of a sport brand extension strategy? Give examples.
4. Pick some familiar sport organizations. Describe their branding strategy and their brand personality after interviewing a few of your friends.
5. What do you think of the equivalent media to assess the success of a sponsorship activity? Discuss other ways to evaluate the success of a sponsorship activity.
6. What is the rationale to use venue naming? For a sponsor? For a sports organization? Can any venue be renamed commercially?

Suggestions for Further Reading

In order to clarify what sport marketing represents, Fullerton and Merz's (2008) article provides an interesting framework related to the basic principles of sport marketing. Also noteworthy is Gladden and Funk's (2002) article, which presents interesting perspectives on the brand management in the context of sport. Ross' (2006) article "A Conceptual Framework for Understanding Spectator-Based Brand Equity" provides important contributions in terms of brand equity management by investigating the main components of brand equity for spectator sports and its repercussions on the value of the brand.

Students can refer to Trail et al.'s (2003) article "Sport Spectator Consumption Behaviour" as one of the guidelines to understand sports consumers in terms of their motivations and behaviors. Also, Pons et al.'s (2006) and Wann et al.'s (2008) papers are great sources of information for understanding the motives of various sports' fans across contexts. Students can find some interesting approaches in incorporating data in order to segment sports fans in Rohm et al.'s (2006) paper. Another engaging article on sport fans, although more oriented to sociological processes, is Cialdini et al.'s article "Basking in Reflected Glory: Three (Football) Field Studies," which examines association and dissociation mechanisms in the sport domain.

Students are encouraged to read "Understanding Sponsorship Effects" by Meenaghan (2001) for an examination of how sponsorships operate to influence and create relationships with consumers. In their article "Determinants of Sports Sponsorship Response," Speed and Thompson (2000) use classical conditioning framework to examine consumers' responses to sport sponsorships. In addition, Cornwell and Maignan (1998) provide a critical review of five important sponsorship research streams. Finally, students can find interesting ideas in terms of cultural meanings that are transferred between the celebrity, the product, and the consumer in McCracken's (1989) "Who Is the Celebrity Endorser? Cultural Foundations of the Endorsement Process."

Case for Analysis

China's Sponsorship of the 2018 FIFA World Cup

With close to one billion viewers around the world, the final of the 2018 FIFA World Cup in Russia between France and Croatia was on par with the previous final in 2014. In fact with a cumulative audience of 3.4 billion viewers during the entire tournament, the 2018 tournament edged the previous World Cup's record audience of 3.3 billion viewers. These numbers were recorded despite some key powerhouse teams (Italy and United States) missing because they failed to qualify. If we add to these figures consumers of digital content disseminated by traditional broadcasters and new players in the industry to respond to new requirements from an increasingly fragmented market, the interest for live World Cup association football cannot seem to stop growing. Therefore, and in conjunction with the broadcasting and digital rights, the associated advertising and sponsorship revenues remain an important component of the business models of major sport organizations such as FIFA. In line with these strong audience numbers, and despite strong criticisms of FIFA prior to the World Cup (leading to the departure of several major sponsors such as Castrol and Continental), several new sponsors, mainly seven Chinese sponsors including Vivo, HiSense, and Wanda, decided to partner with this major global event. These companies span across all product categories and have positioned China as one of the most prominent countries involved in sponsoring the World Cup, therefore redefining the traditional landscape of sponsoring major events.

Questions

1. What objectives are Chinese sponsors pursuing by associating themselves with the 2018 FIFA World Cup?
2. Choose one Chinese sponsor and, using additional research, describe and critique how that sponsor used their rights locally (on site in Russia and in China) as well as globally. What were the specific objectives? Also describe activation strategies that were used by this sponsor.
3. How would you measure the success of sponsorship and activation for the previously chosen sponsor and the objectives that you defined?

PART III

DYNAMICS AND COMPLEXITY OF MANAGING SPORT

This section of the book foregrounds the complexity of managing sport and, as the largest section, represents how the significant growth of the sport industry (and associated research) has revealed an increasingly complex array of issues that sport managers need to be aware of. With the rapid growth of the industry and the ever-changing environment sport managers need to be aware of how distinct contexts generate many complex issues. The concepts within this section are presented through a mix of organizational theory and organizational behavior–based chapters that demonstrate the development of sport management; the first two editions focused purely on the application of organizational theory.

Chapter 10, a new chapter written by Terri Byers, Alex Thurston, and Phillip Lunga, introduces the concept of control in sport organizations. The authors present a multilevel perspective of control and explain how recognizing the immense complexity of control can help sport managers be more effective. Chapter 11, also a new chapter written by Berit Skirstad, focuses on gender in sport organizations. This chapter is a timely addition given the increasing awareness of gender inequality in society and the beneficial effects of breaking these barriers for organizational effectiveness. Chapter 12, another new chapter written by Graham Cuskelly, presents the concept of volunteering in sport organizations. Managing volunteers has been the focus of much research on sport and recreation, and this chapter provides expert insight into the challenges of this task.

Chapter 13, a new chapter written by Borja García, pertains to governance, another concept that has received increasing attention from researchers due to its importance to organizational function and effectiveness but also due to significant problems in sport governance that have come to light frequently over the last few years. The chapter provides readers with insight into the importance, dimensions, and assessment of governance in sport organizations to enable sport managers to provide good governance. Chapter 14 focuses on decision making, a task that is fundamental in sport organizations. The chapter explains the concept, different approaches to decision making, and several major models of decision making to help guide sport managers to understanding the many ways that decisions are made in their organizations as well as how to improve decision making for increased effectiveness. Chapter 15 focuses on power and politics, and features various sources of power and some of the issues that surround the concept of power.

Chapter 16 presents an increasingly important yet largely unexplored concept in sport management: conflict. Suggestions of how to best manage conflict are considered. Chapter 17 is about organizational culture and gives readers insight into how this largely informal, intangible phenomenon can have drastic impacts on all aspects of organizational function. Chapter 18 presents the concept of organizational change, which is an inevitable feature of all sport organizations. The chapter demonstrates how change can occur in an organization's products and services, technology, structures and systems, and people. Finally, this section ends with chapter 19 on leadership. Leadership is a difficult concept to articulate and even more difficult to implement with consistent effectiveness due to the masses of conflicting research publications on the subject. This chapter clarifies what sport managers can and cannot do as leaders and how to improve leadership within their organizations, and provides many useful examples and research to help sport managers evaluate the role of leadership in their organizations.

CHAPTER 10

Control in Sport Organizations

Terri Byers, PhD
Alex Thurston, PhD
Phillip Lunga, MBA

Learning Objectives

When you have read this chapter, you should be able to

1. discuss the concept of control as it has been researched in management and sport management literature;
2. understand sport organizational control as a multilevel construct;
3. explain why the concept of control is complex in nature and the implications this has for sport managers;
4. discuss how a variety of control mechanisms operate and change in sport organizations; and
5. understand how the concept of organizational control can be useful to sport managers, researchers, and students when applied to a variety of contexts and problems.

Key Concepts

administrative control
control mechanism
emotion
language
leadership
multilevel construct
organizational control
self-controls
social control
structure
trust

Buffalo Bills' Organizational Control

The Buffalo Bills are a gridiron football team franchise based in New York. The team plays in the American Football Conference (AFC), which forms one half of the National Football League (NFL). On New Year's Day, in 2013, Bills owner Ralph Wilson announced that he had promoted Russ Brandon to the position of president and chief executive officer (CEO). Wilson was based in Detroit, and because he traveled less frequently to the stadium due to ill health, he considered it appropriate to relinquish control of the organization. The promotion provided Brandon with responsibility of the day-to-day operations and full authority over the entire organization's operations, which included maintaining government, business, and community relationships on behalf of Wilson (Brown, 2013).

In an interview, Brandon said, "I met with Mr. Wilson . . . He told me he was passing the torch to me to run this franchise in totality. He has granted me full authority to run this franchise with zero restrictions and zero limitations" (Brown, 2013).

However, when Wilson passed away in March 2014, NFL rules mandated that every club must have a single controlling (or principle) owner, so a new owner had to be appointed. As a matter of course this was his widow, Mary Wilson (Patra, 2014). Following the acquisition of the Bills by the Pegula family in September 2014, Terry Pegula assumed the role of the new owner and the CEO. Although Brandon forfeited the CEO title, he continued his role as the club's president and was also assigned president of the Buffalo Sabres (an NHL team).

The operational roles under the new Pegula ownership saw the general manager (GM) transition from Buddy Nix to Doug Whaley (who was the Assistant GM) as Nix stepped away to a special assistant role; Doug Whaley was given full control over the personnel and the 53-man roster; and Coach Marrone was given full control over the coaching staff and on-field product. Explaining the set-up, Brandon clarified, "When it comes to the football decisions, Doug Whaley and Coach Marrone have 100 percent full autonomy. They are empowered to make those decisions. We talk as a group, as an organization. But I think we're set up like most organizations where your coach and GM collaborate and make decisions that are football decisions." (The Buffalo News, 2014).

To recap, Brandon assumed full organizational control of the Bills during Wilson's decline in health. Mary Wilson automatically assumed organizational control following Wilson's death. When the Pegulas became the new owners, Terry Pegula took full control of the Bills, yet Whaley and Marrone both had full control over their respective responsibilities. Given the number of organizational actors (a term frequently used in the management literature for individuals associated with organizations) involved, who actually had control of the Bills (to what degree?) and what control does Brandon possess? Was this complexity a contributing factor to Marrone stepping down by triggering a release clause in his contract after being in charge for only a few months? Marrone resigned on December 31, 2014.

The first part of the opening scenario illustrates how most people think of organizational control: the responsibility and task of the CEO or manager. The opening scenario then also illustrates the ambiguity of who actually has the ability/autonomy to enact the desired control within a large sport organization. Where and what are the boundaries of organizational control?

Organizational control is often defined as a function of management, something that managers do through designing rules, procedures, and formal structures to guide employee behavior. The term is used synonymously with *management control*, that is, the authority a manager has over his or her subordinates. However, as we show in this chapter, control is more than a function of management; it is a complex process involving a variety of different mechanisms operating simultaneously, which is not only experienced in a large organization, like the Bills, but is also prevalent in small grassroots sport clubs where the day-to-day running of the organization is carried out by volunteers.

Understanding control can empower managers to influence the performance and strategic direction of their organization and more broadly, their sport. This chapter illustrates how control can be achieved and we highlight the various challenges faced by sport managers of different types of organizations in their attempts to manage their organizations. We also illustrate how understanding control can help sport managers achieve success in managing a range of issues, including maximizing legacy of mega-events, controlling doping in sport, managing volunteers, and increasing board engagement or participation in sport. We do this through demonstrating control as a **multilevel construct** rather than its traditional conceptualization as an activity of management alone.

It is useful to take a look back at where the concept of control has appeared in the mainstream management literature and how control (or its components) has been introduced into the sport management literature. There is over 100 years of research on control in and of organizations, and this literature is a rich source of inspiration for sport management scholars, yet it has rarely been explicitly utilized in our field.

Evolution of Control

Organizational control is perceived as integral for organizational success; control has profound effects on the emotional well-being of employees and the performance of an organization, and the satisfaction of its members are significantly influenced by patterns of control (Das & Teng, 2001). The nature of organizational control in social practices has been studied in a number of disciplines including cybernetics, engineering, sociology, psychology, and accounting (Hopwood, 1974). However, the body of literature has led scholars to criticize previous attempts to conceptualize control due to a lack of clarity and cohesion (Green & Welsh, 1988). For example, Oliga (1989) argued that in the past, social scientists have been overly absorbed with regarding control as a sacrosanct topic that must be theorized to improve our knowledge. In doing so, Oliga indicated that scholars tended to neglect their focus on the phenomenon of control itself. Sitkin, Cardinal, and Bijlsma-Frankema (2010) point out that although control is a fundamental aspect of organizing, the concept has still been somewhat neglected for the past few decades by organizational theorists.

Taylor's (1911) work on scientific management and Fayol's (1916) early definitions of control suggest the concept is an organizational process that ensures conformity, within a set of rules, achieved by employing monitoring and adjusting techniques. Graicunas (1937) highlighted issues of control between individuals from a structural approach. Weber (1947) subsequently proposed a theory of bureaucratic control and bureaucratic structure. These early definitions suggest control is a rational top-down managerial process.

During the 1960s, Tannenbaum (1962, p. 3) proposed organizational control is actually a cyclic process, arguing that control is "any process in which a person or group of persons or organization of persons determines, i.e., intentionally affects, what another person or group or organization will do." Downs (1967, p. 144) offered his proposition, in agreement with Tannenbaum, suggesting too that control follows a cyclical process, consisting of seven steps.

1. An official issues a set of orders.
2. Subordinates are given time to put each order into effect.
3. Certain orders are selected to evaluate the subordinates' performance.
4. The official seeks to discover what has actually been done at lower levels as a result of the orders being evaluated.
5. Comparison is conducted of the effects of the officials' order with original intentions.
6. The official decides whether these results are effective enough to require no more attention, ineffective but unlikely to be improved because of severe obstacles encountered, or partially effective and capable of being improved by further orders.
7. The final point, the official issues further orders, starting the cycle again.

Downs recommended that the model could include intermediate feedback loops whereby implementation would be driven by the need of the high-ranking officials to economize on certain information. This view of control is very rational and does little to consider the politics and vested interests of individuals and groups in organizations.

Cardinal, Sitkin, and Long (2004) note that the study of control gained greater prominence in the 1970s and 1980s following a number of seminal publications by Thompson (1967), Perrow (1970), Woodward (1970), and Williamson (1975). During this period, Dalton and Lawrence (1971) developed a framework identifying three categories of control: *organizational*, *individual*, and *informal* controls. Hopwood (1974) suggested three similar categories of how control can influence an organization, which he defined as *administrative*, *social*, and *self*-controls. **Administrative controls** consist of formal rules and operating procedures (e.g., disciplinary), policies, meeting agendas, and on-the-job training. **Social controls** include norms, values, and cultures negotiated by individuals and groups within organizations. **Self-controls** comprise of personal motives and acceptance by individuals of norms, administrative, and social mechanisms, which lead to self-regulation (Byers, Henry, & Slack, 2007). The category of self-controls includes mechanisms that elicit some emotional gratification or value internalization, so that actors exert control over their own behavior (Johnson & Gill, 1993).

Paving the way in the upturn of scholarly focus during the 1980s was William Ouchi (Ouchi & Johnson, 1978; Ouchi & Maguire, 1975; Ouchi, 1977, 1979, 1980). Ouchi's research defined distinct organizational typologies of control: (1) *market* (a transaction mediated by a price mechanism to ensure equitability); (2) *bureaucracies* (placing a labor value on each contribution, then compensating it fairly, assuming the bureaucratic hierarchy has the legitimacy to provide mediation [control]); (3) and *clan* (socialization, common values, and beliefs within an organization [Ouchi, 1980]). Cardinal, Sitkin, and Long (2004, p. 411) detailed that the general theme of control research in the mid-late 1980s tended to focus on identifying "specific management control mechanisms used to manage such issues as socialization, principal-agent relations, and performance evaluation" (cf. Bradach & Eccles, 1989; Eisenhardt, 1985; Merchant, 1985).

During the 1990s, control research was largely subsumed within other concepts such as strategy (Dent, 1990), strategy and board governance (Baysinger & Hoskisson, 1990), and organization culture (Lincoln & Kalleberg, 1990). Toward the end of the 1990s, more explicit attention to control in organizations could be found in manufacturing contexts (Abernethy & Lillis, 1995). In the late '90s, Jermier (1998) offered a special issue on organizational control in *Administrative Science Quarterly*. The contributors examined, one way or another, how control was asserted in contemporary organizations through a critical theorist perspective following Jermier's call that due to technological changes and managerial innovations, we had "entered a new age in which the forms of control being used are more insidious and widely misunderstood" (p. 235). The collection helped to enrich the understanding of control by looking at traditional and emerging forms of the concept (focusing on subtle forms of management practices) and also from alternative values and belief systems perspectives.

The turn of the millennium saw studies with an explicit focus on control once again develop momentum in mainstream management literature. Chenhall (2003) provided a review paper of empirical, contingency-based control research and recommended considerations of theoretical foundations that may assist in developing future research. Pfeffer and Salancik (2003) perceived that organizational activities and outcomes are accounted for by the context in which the organization is embedded. Therefore, they offered particular attention to the effects of the environment, recommending that control and influence in a social process involves an activity in which both the *influencer* and the focal *target* act to affect the conditions that govern the influence process. Berry, Broadbent, and Otley (2005) perceived control as a primary process that motivates individuals to perform activities to achieve certain organizational targets.

Traditionally, the majority of studies tended to observe the stable use of controls in mature organizations. Cardinal et al. (2004) attempted to draw on a decade-long case study of a new organization to advance understanding of the ebb and flow of early organizational control. The findings provided new data and insights about what drives shifts in the use of various types of control, that is, the role of imbalance among formal (such as official rules and procedures) and informal controls (such as norms, values, and culture) as the key driver of changes in patterns of control. Perhaps one of the most significant claims made during this period was from the opening statement of Delbridge and Ezzamel's (2005, p. 603) contemporary conceptions of control paper where they declared that "control lies at the heart of organization theory." We fully support this sentiment, although—as you will come to understand by the end of this chapter—we suggest that, to better understand organizational control, the concept is also found to be at the heart of organization behavior and, therefore, requires investigation from this perspective.

Not only have the majority of organizational control studies historically focused on examining mature organizations, but control research has predominantly been conducted in the context of large public or private organizations (Cardinal et al., 2004; Chenhall, 2003; Eisenhardt, 1985; Nieminen & Lehtonen, 2008; Otley & Berry, 1980; Sitkin et al., 2010). As a result, examining control in sport organizations has experienced comparative neglect. Contextual issues have been shown to be important for understanding control (Johnson & Gill, 1993; Pfeffer & Salancik, 2003). Das (1989) explores a modification of what he terms *the basic organizing cycle* (enactment, selection, and retention) to a hierarchical form in an attempt to understand basic control modes. He reports that control is not as simple as an organization comprising of one homogeneously distributed **control mechanism**. Rather, that there are a number of incompatible mechanisms operating within the organization.

Given the fact that context is a significant factor in how control is operationalized (or enacted) and that it is likely that multiple mechanisms are operating simultaneously, Byers, Henry, and Slack (2007) provided a holistic understanding of control in a setting other than that of a large public or private organization, focusing on voluntary sport clubs (VSCs). The research identified numerous control mechanisms (often operating simultaneously) that would not necessarily be found in the large public or private organizations (such as ignoring administrative control mechanisms to suit individuals or the group), which supports Johnson and Gill's (1993) and Pfeffer and Salancik's (2003) findings.

Elements, or Components, of Control

Research on control *in* and *of* organizations has tended to be in the form of single-factor studies that each have implications on our understanding of control, as shown in figure 10.1 (Byers, Slack, & Parent, 2012). See, for example, studies on the controlling nature of emotion in organizations (Fineman, 2000; Ouchi & Johnson, 1978), guilt (Schein, 1993), avoidance (Aquino, Tripp, & Bies, 2006), social interaction (Turner, 1989), personal motivation (Dalton & Lawrence, 1971), identification (Alvesson & Willmott, 2002), culture (Alvesson, 2002; Inzerilli & Rosen, 1983; Schein, 1990), rules and procedures (Kikulis, Slack, & Hinings, 1995; Zucker, 1987), power (Pfeffer, 1981; Pitter, 1990), environment (Pfeffer & Salancik, 2003), language (Boden, 1994; Tietze, Cohen, & Musson, 2003), trust (Das & Teng, 2001), humor (Collinson, 2002), and **leadership** (Schein, 2004).

Figure 10.1 suggests that organizations, and the people within them, are controlled by many factors—some internal and some external to the organization itself. In this textbook, some of these factors (indicated with *italics* in figure 10.1) are already covered in other chapters, and readers can refer to these to see how they may exert some control. For instance, environments, culture, power, and leadership are stand-alone chapters that illustrate

Figure 10.1 Examples of single-factor studies that illustrate elements of control.

each concept and its role in managing sport organizations. But when we consider them together, we can start to appreciate how complex understanding control can be for managers, who may have thought *they* were in control! Managers (and in some instances, leaders) are in a very influential formal position that affords them great potential to shape the direction and activity of an organization, but that does not mean they are solely responsible for victories or defeats. To explore the concept of control further, and so as not to repeat other parts of this textbook, we take three concepts from figure 10.1 that are not the focus of other chapters and elaborate on the research in mainstream and sport management literature to demonstrate the relevance of these concepts in developing the understanding of control. The three concepts covered are trust, emotion, and language; all three are emerging issues in sport management and require further research in different organizational and cultural contexts to progress our understanding.

Trust

Trust is a complex and multidisciplinary concept that is distinguishable from related concepts of trustworthiness and distrust (or mistrust). There is also a need to understand the concept of trust violation when considering how to rebuild trust. Trust and related concepts can take place at the interpersonal, group, organizational, and institutional level, and can exist in relation to a person, an organization, a particular group of people, as well as social institutions such as governments, religious groups, the media, and sport communities. We now define trust and related concepts to highlight its role in understanding control and its importance in sport management research.

McMurphy (2013, p. 1) points out that researchers have suggested various ways to define trust that include "an emotion, a behaviour, a rational decision, 'leap of faith,' neurobiological expression or some combination of the above" as opposed to the characteristics of a person (or object) being trusted, which is trustworthiness. Yet trust is also "widely recognized as a strategic, relational asset for business organizations" (Castaldo, Premazzi, & Zerbini, 2010, p. 657), indicating that trust is crucial for organizations. Castaldo et al. (2010) explored the diversity of conceptualizations of trust over a 50-year period and identified a final set of 96 definitions spanning that period. Their results suggest that researchers have often examined components of trust but have rarely taken a holistic, multilevel approach to acknowledge the complexity of trust. They proposed that trust is a "polyhedral" concept (i.e., has many aspects) consisting of an expectation (belief or confidence) that a subject (individual or organizational) displays certain characteristics such as honesty, competence, or benevolence, which indicates that they will display future actions to produce positive results for a trustor, particularly in situations of vulnerability or perceived risk.

There is much research on different types of trust such as affective-based, cognitive-based, and morality-based trust (Lahno, 2001; Olekalns & Smith, 2009). Affective trust is based on emotionality and focuses on positive expectations that the trustor will act in the best interests of the trustee or will not bring any harm to the trustee. Cognitive trust is based on rationality and focuses on the competence and integrity of the trustor as well as transparency and consistency of trustor actions. Morality-based trust can be emotional or rational and focuses on the assumption that trustee and trustor share moral standards, ethics, and principles.

Distrust

A small body of research has identified distrust (sometimes used interchangeably with *mistrust*) as a distinct concept that is more than simply being at the opposite end of a continuum from trust. Research has suggested that rather than being on the same continuum, they are on two different scales, but both are characterized by vulnerability and risk. For trust, the trustee begins with an optimistic expectation of a positive outcome or experience. In distrust, the trustee expects harmful or negative behaviors, which alters the dynamics of a relationship (Rodgers, 2009). The relationship between the two continuum scales is interesting in that once trust has been betrayed, the trustee shifts to the distrust continuum, and it may be impossible to return to a trusting relationship. Interventions to manage or increase trust may be counterproductive, only serving to increase distrust (Simons, 2002). Some research suggests that trust can be repaired but that this is a delicate and complex process, dependent on the particular type of trust violation that has occurred. For example, Kim, Dirks, Cooper, and Ferrin (2005) examined the trust repair implications of apologizing with an internal versus external attribution after a competence versus integrity-based trust violation. Their results suggested that trust was repaired more successfully when, in the case of competence-related trust violations, mistrusted parties apologized with an internal, rather than external, attribution. However, trust violations related to integrity should be managed with apologies with external attributions.

Overall, we see that trust can be distinguished from related concepts (such as mistrust and trustworthiness) and that trust research has examined these related concepts at various levels of analysis from individual to organizational and institutional. The 2015 Edelman Trust Barometer (Edelman, 2015) argues that trust is important to business, government, and a wide variety of organizations and industry sectors, including sport. They also suggest that globally, public trust in innovation, media, nonprofit organizations, and business has declined over the year (2014-2015) due to the rapid pace of change, use of new technology, and lack of transparency in product testing. The 2019 Edelman Trust Barometer (Edelman, 2019) reports that trust has changed profoundly, with people shifting "their trust to the relationships within their control, most notably their employers." Globally, their statistics indicate that 75 percent of people (of their sample) trust "my employer" to do what is right, significantly more than NGOs (57 percent), business (56 percent), and media (47 percent). The research also highlights an increasing gap between the more trusting informed public and the far-more-skeptical mass population, marking a return to record highs of trust inequality. With the proliferation and awareness of fake news, it's no surprise that the media was ranked with the lowest trust.

Research on Trust in Sport Management

Trust at the community level for sport is essential because interpersonal relationships between coaches, parents, children, administrative staff, and the community itself are core to grassroots participation. Sport management scholars have touched on some issues of trust in relation to community or grassroots sport. Jones (2001), for example, examines the fragility of trust in the context of competitive sport and the role of trust in the coaching-teaching situation, where he argues that trust has a vital purpose in the process. Shogan (1991) considered trust as a condition of paternalistic decisions, while McNamee (1998) considered the ethical perspective of trust in sport. Maxwell and Taylor (2010) highlighted the important role of trust in engaging Muslim women in community-based sport organizations.

There has been some attention to the relationship between trust and social capital in sport (Doherty & Misener, 2008; Maxwell & Taylor, 2010) and the role of trust in building capacity of VSCs (Misener & Doherty, 2009). However, this line of inquiry would benefit from attention to trends in mainstream trust literature such as defining the trust concept more fully. The studies do not distinguish between trust and trustworthiness, for instance. Nor do they define and differentiate trust from distrust as separate constructs. Fahlén's (2017) account of the trust–mistrust dynamic in the public governance of sport provides a comprehensive analysis of trust and mistrust in evaluating performance measurement systems in sport organizations. For more on governance of sport organizations, refer to chapter 13 in this textbook.

The community sport context would benefit from further investigation that specifies competence versus integrity-based trust and its development in interpersonal relations between coaches and athletes, administrators and volunteers or employees. Developments focusing on more professional community sport delivery, standardized training and accreditation for clubs, adherence to national policy, and decreasing numbers of volunteers could perhaps indicate that increasing formal mechanisms of structure and control that increase trust (Weibel et al., 2015) may not have the same effect in the VSC setting. There are endless questions related to trust that could serve to both enhance our understanding of the management of sport and further theoretical and practical knowledge of trust and related concepts. For instance, what is the role of trust in managing volunteers in sport? Volunteers traditionally had autonomy, flexibility, and a personal connection to sport. However, commercialization and professionalization of sport encourages sport mangers to adopt an increased number of formal mechanisms, such as implementing child

TIME OUT

Trust and Collaboration in Community Sport

Sport organizations are increasingly engaged in networks or some form of collaborative partnerships to achieve their goals, the importance of which was examined by Barnes, Cousens, and MacLean (2017). They argue that trust is a valuable and essential element of network stability. Specifically, they examined if organizations who reside in the same sector and organizations who indicate higher levels of trust with other organizations are more likely to collaborate. Their findings, generated through quantitative dyadic data analysis, confirm their hypothesis, providing strong evidence for the importance of developing and maintaining trust between organizations, regardless of their sector, to sustain network effectiveness.

protection policies (requiring criminal background checks) or quality assurance standards (such as the quality assurance cross-sport accreditation scheme termed Clubmark provided by Sport England). How does this formalization affect volunteer perception of trust? The scope is considerable, and we need to understand the relationship between public trust in sport (organizations and the institution) and declining participation in grassroots sport organizations, declining volunteer numbers, and changing sport organization structures.

Other sport management scholars have explored the concepts of brand trust and loyalty (Filo, Funk, & Alexandris, 2008); the role of service quality, customer satisfaction, commitment, and trust to customer loyalty in sport services (Javadein, Khanlari, & Esitri, 2008); trust and fan loyalty (Wu, Tsai, & Hung, 2012); trust in sport governance (O'Boyle & Shilbury, 2016); and trust in doping control systems (Overbye, 2016).

As we have seen from our brief review of trust literature, if a manager or leader can gain the trust of his or her employees, subordinates, or volunteer members of a VSC—or is able to go some way toward repairing distrust—it is more likely they would have greater success enacting forms of control and, therefore, achieve greater compliance.

Emotion

Fineman and Sturdy (1999) indicated that **emotion** is essential to the process of control in organizations and that emotions need to be understood in the context of the social structures in which they operate. The study of emotion in organizations has largely been under the term *emotional labor*, as discussed by Stearns (1986), who supported the notion that powerful hierarchical agents such as managers have traditionally sought to suppress or encourage particular emotions in employees. For example, many service-oriented organizations will have employee policies and training on appropriate customer management, and this often includes, implicitly or explicitly, appropriate emotions (i.e., a smile is friendly; happiness is acceptable; rudeness is unhelpful; violence is unacceptable). Yet Fineman and Sturdy (1999) noted how workers can consciously and unconsciously challenge expectations of emotion and create their own rules for self-regulation of emotion, depending too on wider social structures or expectations such as gender, historical, and ideological contexts. Callahan (2000) recognized that while emotion control may be largely driven by management in organizations with high customer interface, emotions may be more socially negotiated in nonprofit organizations.

Research on Emotion in Sport Management

Emotion in sport has been of interest for researchers for many years, primarily underpinned by psychology theories and focused on athletes, coaches, and performance (Snyder, 1990; Hanin, 2000; Botterill & Brown, 2002; Mellalieu & Hanton, 2008). More recently, the subject of emotion has appeared in sport management literature as well, with focus on brand image and fan or spectator consumption intentions (Chen, Yeh, & Huan, 2014), brand attachment (Proksch, Orth, & Cornwell, 2015), impact on product quality on fan emotion (Foroughi, Nikbin, Hyun, & Iranmanesh, 2016), and event emotions on sponsor recall and intentions to attend the event in the future (Cornwell, Jahn, Xie, & Suh, 2018).

Other research has recognized the importance of emotion in the management of sport organizations, focusing on employees of professional sport organizations (Swanson & Kent, 2017; Rodriguez-Pomeda, Casani, & Alonso-Almeida, 2017) and sport leadership of coaches (Lee & Chelladurai, 2018).

Therefore, drawing from the emotion literature, if managers or leaders are able to regulate and foster individuals' emotions (such as passion and pride), it is possible that they can develop "commitment and satisfaction, cognitive involvement, and voluntary behaviors" (Swanson & Kent, 2017, p. 362) of their employees or volunteers (i.e., experience greater success in enacting various social or informal control mechanisms) in order to achieve organizational goals.

Language

The concept of **language** is an important consideration in understanding control in sport organizations. As Boden (1994, p.1) suggested, "talk is at the heart of all organizations." This aspect of control suggests a focus on individuals and their interaction through language to help develop a greater understanding of control. However, even though language activities in organizations have been recognized as significant, the study of language has historically received little attention (Cossette, 1998) and was viewed simply as a medium of communication, resulting in minimal investigation and theorizing from scholars (Westwood & Linstead, 2001). Subsequent to Cossette's observation, several academics turned their focus to the use of language in better understanding organizations.

Oakes, Townley, and Cooper (1998) examined how the Canadian government brought business planning to museums and heritage sites in Alberta. Drawing on the work of Pierre Bourdieu (e.g., Bourdieu, 1991), they suggest that the concepts of "language and power are central to an understanding of control" (Oakes et al., 1998, p. 257). The authors demonstrate how subtle forms of symbolic control through language greatly affect business planning practices and processes. The book *Understanding Organizations through Language*, written by Tietze et al. (2003), uses semiology as a theoretical bedrock in an effort to develop a new metaphor for communication, rather than viewing communication as a something that can be unproblematically controlled and managed. Sagi and Diermeier (2017) looked at language use during negotiation processes. They found that the parties that reached agreements used gradually increasingly similar language used over the course of the negotiation. Lauring and Klitmøller (2017) examined how the use of inclusive language in multicultural organizations affected performance. They found that management that used common corporate language and were open to language diversity were able to increase an organization's output and creativity. Tietze's (2015) book, *International Management and Language*, also examines the use of language in managing organizations due to the globalization processes that have resulted in the emergence of worldwide business and management networks in which sharing knowledge is crucially important. With so many organizations operating with international structures, to have any chance of enacting control, CEOs and managers need to be sensitive to the cultures and the language used to communicate.

The majority of organizations operating in the sport sector will have to deal with multiple stakeholders, whether a VSC is negotiating a facility rental with a local authority or an international federation is disseminating a new policy or rules to its members. The language used needs to be pitched at the appropriate level: too informal of a tone may not achieve the intended outcome or compliance (and cause ambiguity); too formal or autocratic of a tone may lead to resistance, also resulting in noncompliance or failure to achieve the intended purpose of the communication.

Research on Language in Sport Management

To the best of our knowledge, no sport management researchers have addressed this concept in the context of understanding control in sport organizations, although the language of sport has received some attention through discourse analysis in reference to, for example, indigenous leadership (Chen & Mason, 2018). Although no explicit focus on language and control was included, Thurston (2017) found that when the sport national governing body (NGB), England Boxing attempted to implement various policies into their member VSCs, the NGB would often use "prescriptive language" (p. 107) in relation to serious matters. On the other hand, some NGB officials recognized "the importance of the language used to communicate with the club members" (p. 139) so as to reduce ambiguity; in an effort to achieve compliance they would attempt to engage certain individuals "by using appropriate language" (p.143), which corresponds to Sagi and Diermeier's (2017) work on negotiation. We can also see the importance of language in some phenomenology studies in, for example, sexual harassment in sport organizations (Taylor, Smith, Welch, & Hardin, 2018) and Parks and Roberton's (2002) study that looked at student attitudes toward sexist and nonsexist language used in the context of sport management education. However, no research has yet focused on the concept of language related to mainstream control literature.

Clearly, language is used all the time by managers to communicate with members of their organization and external stakeholders. The way in which language is used has a significant impact on how a message is delivered and received. If a sport manager can effectively communicate with their volunteers, employees, and stakeholders, the greater the chance they will have in gaining compliance. If a manager can use appropriate language, there is a likelihood of less ambiguity and more understanding of the manager's message, which could lead to reduced resistance and, therefore, an increased chance of achieving control.

Sport Management Research on Control

The previous section provides a comprehensive sampling from mainstream management, yet the issue of control has not received equal attention from sport management theorists. The limited amount of research on control, specifically in sport organizations, suggests that sport organizations may be affected by a unique set of factors. We therefore suggest it is important to develop the literature around control in sport to refine our understanding and advance thinking on how sport could and should be managed. We now consider studies that have explicitly addressed issues of control in sport management literature and then suggest how we can expand this thinking and provide suggestions for new concepts to be studied using the control lens.

Dynamics of Control in Sport Organizations

Byers, Slack, and Parent (2012) suggest that much of the literature on sport management is actually about control. They highlight a number of studies that implicitly address issues of control in sport organizations such as gender issues and the control of sexuality in sport (Hoeber, 2007; Shaw & Slack, 2002), and they discuss Mason, Thibault, and Misener's (2006) study that examined control of decision making in their focus on the IOC and issues of corruption within the organization.

A wide variety of issues in sport management could benefit from the adoption of a control perspective to advance knowledge and effectiveness in the field and to contribute to our understanding of control more broadly. From the complexities of sport participation to effectively tackling corruption, doping, and declining volunteerism, the concept of control focuses on both behavior and wider organization structures, internal and external environment, and historical context to understand how and why something does or does not happen.

Multilevel Perspective of Control

The limited explicit research on control in sport organizations has highlighted a limitation of the mainstream control literature, which has led academics to utilize a multilevel approach to conceptualizing control rather than focus on any one single factor. Byers, Anagnostopoulos, and Brooke-Holmes (2015), based on the work of Byers (2013), illustrate a model that allows for different levels of control to be considered in the context of voluntary organizations.

Control mechanisms and the process of control in sport organizations can be conceptualized on four levels of analysis. This conceptualization is best explained through the use of the critical realist (CR) framework. Critical realism has been widely used in management literature and in a variety of disciplines because it embraces positivist and interpretivist thought and suggests that any given situation—in a business, at an event, or perhaps within a VSC—the reality of that situation should be viewed from four perspectives (Byers, 2013):

1. *Material*: These are observable and tangible mechanisms, such as policies and operating procedures.
2. *Ideal*: This is the intangible, socially negotiated reality (e.g., the behavior of volunteers).
3. *Artifactual*: The artifactual reality is the interpretation of mechanisms over time (e.g., if a staff member or participant says of a manager, "That is just the way he does things.").
4. *Social*: These are taken-for-granted social structures and causal powers such as capital, class, and underlying mechanisms of control.

The *material reality* consists of observable or tangible phenomenon such as policies, organi-

TIME OUT

Controlling Participation in Canadian Sport

The sport system in Canada involves many stakeholders, including the Government of Canada, the private sector, provincial and territorial governments, multisport service organizations, and national sport organizations. The Government of Canada provides funding for elite athletes and promotes sport participation among all Canadians. However, despite the government's efforts, research shows an increase in nonparticipation because of various barriers. For example, children who live in unsafe neighborhoods, children of new immigrants, and children coming from low-income households are less likely to participate in sports (Sport Information Resource Centre, 2016). In the case of adults, Strashin (2016) suggests that many parents put their children's sport games and practices ahead of their own activities, which results in drop out of sports and exercise altogether.

Clearly, various factors contribute to barriers and decline in participation. Sport managers can approach these challenges by understanding the distinction of control applied to nonprofit organizations. Different control strategies are required for nonprofit organizations compared with large public or private organizations (on which most of the mainstream control research has focused) due to diverse sizes, structures, and environments in which they operate. Understanding these control variables is important for research, policy and planning, and creating a framework to overcome barriers to participation, while creating opportunities for continued physical engagement for all Canadians.

zation **structure**, or other documents that may be analyzed to aid understanding. Here, control may be seen as a function of management, to be designed and implemented. However, the design of control mechanisms or structures is often interpreted differently by individuals and groups. The *ideal reality* is how different individuals or groups perceive a phenomenon and interact to create socially negotiated rules (as opposed to the formal rules found in material reality). Therefore, if the administrative mechanisms are perceived as inefficient, workers or even volunteers may discuss this and develop ways of operating that are acceptable to them and produce the same output. *Artifactual reality* can be understood as the judgments and interpretations of socially negotiated and formal mechanisms or reality as inherently legitimate or oppressive. Over time, individuals or groups may develop judgments that are positive or negative in relation to how they feel control is exerted in an organization. Finally, the *social level of reality* consists of the taken-for-granted assumptions and norms, institutions, or identities that explain or give rise to the three preceding levels of reality. The Time Out "Control in VSCs" begins to demonstrate how these different layers of reality may be seen in, for example, VSCs.

Summary and Conclusions

A focus on control in organizations and in sport organizations is something new for sport management research. This chapter has presented the concept of control in a comprehensive fashion and illustrated how organizational control research may be useful to provide an innovative perspective on a range of issues that plague the sport arena such as doping, nonparticipation, decreasing volunteers in VSCs, and the lack of sustainable legacies from mega sporting events. Much of the current literature on control in organizations does not comprehensively recognize control as a multilevel concept or often fails to fully define control in relation to the extensive mainstream management literature.

This chapter has applied the concept of control to a variety of examples in sport management to demonstrate the utility of the concept for advancing sport management research and practice. While an explicit focus on control is not a simple research approach—which will likely require a combination of single-factor studies to inform guiding a theoretical framework—it can, for instance, help further our understanding of some long-standing problems in the sport industry.

TIME OUT

Control in VSCs

The great majority of volunteers in sport do not receive payment for their contributions. However, sporting governing bodies and governments increasingly expect community sports clubs to adopt professionalized practices (rather than follow the traditional ad hoc informal approach) and improve their service delivery, aligning with standards encountered in the private sector (Byers, 2013; Cuskelly, 2004; O'Gorman, 2012).

An example of this can be seen with Sport England's Clubmark framework. Clubmark is an accreditation program that acknowledges the quality of a club. The reason Sport England, and sport governing bodies, place so much emphasis on clubs operating in safe, effective environments is a result of historic cases of sexual abuse in the 1990s, where sport coaches took advantage of their positions of trust. Brackenridge (2001) suggested that the moment of sporting truth occurred in 1993 when former Olympic swimming coach Paul Hickson was charged with sexual assaults of teenage swimmers in his care. The Hickson case was a watershed moment that placed child abuse and sexual exploitation on the policy agenda in Britain. Subsequently, Sport England worked with NGBs and other organizations to design child protection policies.

However, most grassroots sport clubs are voluntary organizations with limited resources, so changing mechanisms of control to achieve this increased professionalization is challenging. Compliance with child protection, data protection, and other policies is difficult in small voluntary organizations that rely on individuals to give up their time and expertise each week. Although complying with such policies does increase the volunteers' workload, it is rare to find a club not implementing safeguarding policy requirements, given the potential hostile environment and ramifications of noncompliance; it is in a club's interest to show compliance with the policy. The control of VSCs has changed over the last 10 to 20 years. Can you identify the variety of mechanisms influencing these organizations mentioned in this Time Out?

KEY ISSUES FOR SPORT MANAGERS

As you have seen in this chapter, understanding control is complicated. As a manager, you will have to comprehend many facets in order to deal with (or enact) various control mechanisms in an effort to drive and influence strategic direction. Organizational control is perceived as integral for organizational success because patterns of control have profound effects upon the satisfaction and emotional well-being of individuals (e.g., employees or volunteers), and significantly influence the performance of an organization.

First and foremost, you will need to understand the context and history of control in your organization. If you are managing an informal organization (e.g., a VSC), some control processes (e.g., disciplinary procedures) might not be as effective as if you were a manager in a large public or private organization. To optimize the output of a workforce, managers should, at least, have a basic understanding of how the various single-factor concepts can influence control and thus performance. Studies have demonstrated how Hopwood's (1974) categories of control (administrative, social, and self-controls) influence an organization. But because these categories are interrelated, a change in one mechanism will cause a change in another. For example, a manger could introduce new procedures or protocols (administrative controls) or attempt to influence norms (social controls), which could be achieved by carefully selecting the language used to communicate, developing relationships, building trust, or a combination of any of the single-factor concepts we've highlighted in this chapter. If the manager has the capacity, it would be advantageous to become familiar with how the four levels of reality as control can each affect employee or volunteer behavior as well as management.

However, it is important to recognize that sport mangers are not entirely in control—that employees, volunteers, and other stakeholders play a key role in controlling the organization. Equally, a sport manager is controlled by his or her education, experience, values, and beliefs so should be aware of how his or her perceptions are constrained by these factors. A highly effective sport manager listens to a diversity of stakeholders in establishing systems and mechanisms of control and in adapting these control mechanisms over time as needed.

Within this chapter, we highlighted the utility of trust, emotion, and language concepts for control research. Many other single-factor concepts (see figure 10.1) constitute elements (and mechanisms) of control, most of which are covered in other chapters of this textbook but without explicit reference to organizational control. Now, armed with the knowledge developed from this chapter, it would be worthwhile to examine other chapters in this textbook (that we suggest have relevance to understanding organizational control) through the theoretical lens of control. For example, try to identify mechanisms that sport managers may use in attempts to enact control in their sport organization.

Review Questions

1. How do the control mechanisms operating in a small sport organization differ from those operating in a large multinational firm?
2. What is the difference between control mechanisms and the process of control in sport organizations?
3. What are some of the challenges for sport managers in exerting administrative control mechanisms in their organizations?
4. What can a sport manager do to most effectively influence people within his or her sport organization? Discuss the use of different categories of control mechanisms.
5. What is the difference between control of a sport organization and control in a sport organization?
6. How can understanding control help sport managers and students or academics understand nonparticipation in sport? Mega-event legacy failure?

Suggestions for Further Reading

To begin to understand control in sport organizations, readers may refer to some of the mainstream management literature such as Hopwood's (1974) proposal of three categories of how control can influence an organization. Another good starting point is to familiarize yourself with William Ouchi's work (Ouchi & Johnson, 1978; Ouchi & Maguire, 1975; Ouchi, 1977, 1979, 1980), a scholar who considerably helped to develop the understanding of organizational control.

Byers et al. (2007) were the first sport management academics who attempted to provide a holistic understanding of control in a setting other than that of a large public or private organization, focusing on VSCs. For a model of control to test or utilize in further research in sport management, Byers, Anagnostopoulos, and Brooke-Holmes' (2015) paper "Understanding control in nonprofit organizations: Moving governance research forward?" offers such a model. As we have made clear throughout this chapter, it would be prudent to also examine control by using any of the single-factor concepts discussed in figure 10.1.

Case for Analysis

Controlling Doping in Sport: Development of Control Mechanisms to Eradicate Doping in Sport

As high-performance sport has increasingly been commercialized through the interest of broadcasters, merchandisers, league businesses, and the use of technology, so too has the pressure to increase performances of human and animal athletes, sometimes at any cost. The use of drugs in sport is well documented (Tymowski, Byers, & Mason, 2015; Byers & Edwards, 2015), and the establishment of the World Anti-Doping Agency (WADA) signaled a significant shift to the attempt to administratively control doping. The formal mechanisms designed to control doping in sport have become so extensive and costly to administer that some question the sustainability of these efforts.

There is an extensive array of formal documents designed to influence doping behavior such as the *World Anti-Doping Code 2015 with 2019 Amendments*, list of prohibitive substances, which attempt to harmonize anti-doping policies, rules and regulations within sport organizations and among public authorities around the world (WADA, 2019). WADA works in conjunction with five International Standards, which aim to foster consistency among anti-doping organizations in various areas, including testing, laboratories, Therapeutic Use Exemptions (TUEs), the List of Prohibited Substances and Methods, and the protection of privacy and personal information. As of September 2019, there are 146 National Anti-Doping Organizations (NADOs), led by iNADO (The Institute of National Anti-Doping Organizations), to coordinate and support anti-doping education and rule enforcement, and to generally advocate for clean sport. Athletes undergo mandatory online education to discourage doping, rigorous and invasive testing procedures, and random testing before, during, or after competitions. Sanctions applied inconsistently across sports and international boundaries have been the main mechanism to deter doping and range from two-year bans to lifetime bans from sport competition (but not training).

There is also The Sports Integrity Initiative, an organization in association with Morgan Sports Law LLP, national police, and the international crime organization INTERPOL, who are all working in partnership to eradicate doping in sport. Despite these efforts, the prevalence of doping seems to have increased—whether through more advanced testing and detection procedures or through higher incidence of doping, it is difficult to identify the root cause. In this case, there are multiple stakeholders, ranging from national organizations designed to manage doping, athletes who participate in their sport voluntarily (although may receive various levels of funding from their governments for training), the public, sponsors, media, and support staff such as coaches, therapists, and medical staff who have an interest in keeping sport clean of doping.

This case focuses on the growing efforts to control doping. Central to this evolution of controls around doping is the impact on trust. The response by international and national governance organizations to increases in detection (or perhaps incidence) of doping has largely been to introduce more stringent formal control mechanisms and sanctions. Byers and Edwards (2015) revealed that athletes are failing to internalize and accept the validity and consistency of formal control mechanisms related to anti-doping, resulting in a lack of trust in sport organizations involved in administering anti-doping education and testing. Furthermore, it is not the formal control mechanisms that athletes attribute their propensity not to dope. They indicate that what prevents them from taking performance-enhancing drugs is their own personal and family values, pride in one's country, or personal achievements and the trust in their own ability. An industry of organizations and education programs, European Commission funding, and academic research has grown up around the problem of doping in sport. However, the focus of solutions has been on increasing formal mechanisms of control, which may serve to decrease trust in sport and organizations if coordinating mechanisms are not consistent.

Edelenbos and Eshuis (2012) suggested that formal controls and informal control can lead to increases in trust but that this relationship is complicated and dependent upon the specific initial situation in which the relationship between trust and control unfolds. Therefore, trust in athletes decreases as more positive doping tests are realized and new methods of cheating through the use of different performance-enhancing drugs are discovered through more advanced detection methods. As trust is lost, increases in formal control mechanisms continue but with little effectiveness. Houser, Xiao, McCabe, and Smith (2008) suggested that people can become less cooperative when threatened with sanctions. Weibel et al. (2015) highlight that formal organizational controls can serve to facilitate trust, or it can do the opposite and signal distrust in employees. Interestingly, they highlight that when talking of trust in an organization (as opposed to an individual), the associated risks are broader and more ambiguous than when talking of trust in an individual. Organizations are made up of various hierarchical levels of people with different decision-making powers, of structures and cultures, as well as multiple interpretations of who is responsible for what. In this complexity Weibel at al. (2015) found evidence that controls can serve to provide order to the complexity, reducing uncertainty through enhancement of trust by fair, consistent, and transparent processes. However, we suggest that this assumes that control can be developed and applied consistently. In the case of doping in sport, there is some evidence that this is not the case and athletes are increasingly disillusioned with a system that is not fair, consistent, or proving effective.

The fight against doping is thought to be difficult, if not impossible, to win. The setting is a fascinating context for trust researchers to examine changes in trust, the effects of mistrust, management of trust violations, and how international governance influences trust at the individual, group, organizational, and institutional levels. It would also be useful to explore the "good governance" movement (refer to chapter 13) within sport, which has served to increase professionalization and formal management of sport to ensure sport's independence from government and legal systems. However, numerous examples show governance failures in sport, and as such trust in these organizations and sport itself comes into question.

Within the context of doping in sport, there are a variety of levels at which trust researchers could explore the issues of trust, distrust, and trustworthiness. The impact of doping on trust—public trust, sport participant trust, or athlete trust—in sport governance organizations needs to be examined. It could be argued that doping, and the management of doping by international sport governance organizations, is causing a significant amount of mistrust in sport and in its management. A lack of trust in governance and in sport could have serious consequences for participation in sport, volunteering in sport, and for the consumption of sport competition. Some research suggests, given that trust and mistrust are conceptually different, that distrust in sport and its organizations and institutions cannot be repaired. Further examination of trust and distrust in international sport governance is urgently needed to understand the full implications of management practices and athlete transgressions with a focus on the role of trust and formal and informal control.

Questions

1. List the formal, administrative mechanisms of control that have been designed to eradicate doping in sport.
2. What other mechanisms does the case suggest have an influence on doping in sport?
3. Why do you think the formal mechanisms are not effective in controlling doping?
4. What suggestions would Hopwood's theory of control give to control doping in sport?
5. If control is conceptualized as a multilevel concept, explain what this means to understanding control of doping in sport.

CHAPTER 11

Gender and Sport Organizations

Berit Skirstad, MS

Learning Objectives

When you have read this chapter you should be able to

1. explain the concepts of sex and gender as well as the historical development of women in sport organizations,
2. discuss gender as a social structure of sport organizations and the barriers to women in managing sport organizations,
3. discuss various theories of gender in sport organizations, and
4. discuss female underrepresentation in sport and in sport organizations as well as how sport managers may address inequality.

Key Concepts

equal rights
gender
gender mainstreaming
gender regime
gender testing
glass ceiling
glass cliff
glass slipper
multilevel framework
positive or affirmative action
prejudice
quota
sex

Breakthrough for Women?

When Helena Costa, a 36-year old Portuguese woman, was appointed as the manager of the second division French association football club Clermont Foot the news made global headlines (Obayiuwana, 2014). She was to be the first female to head a male association football club not only in France but also in Europe. More than 100 journalists were present at the press conference announcing Costa's appointment due to skepticism of her ability to manage a male professional team. Her qualifications more than match those of the male coaches who have been appointed to similar jobs. At the press conference, Costa said, "I am not afraid. If I didn't think I'm capable of this, I wouldn't be here" (BBC Sport, 2014, para. 3).

When the players were told the decision, some laughed and wondered how she would manage a group of men. Emmanuel Imorou, the left fullback, told the French Sports Daily, *L'Équipe*, that players had spent time Googling her pictures "to see if she was pretty" (Kessel, 2014) rather than worry about her qualifications.

The appointment of Costa was seen as a great breakthrough for women. However, after a month—the day before the first training session—she quit. In a press release, the club stated she withdrew for personal reasons. The president of the club described the decision as sudden and surprising. Costa did not comment on her reasons for withdrawing but stated that she resented the situation that happened. French media speculated whether a disagreement with the male sport director had been the reason. Costa's answer on a direct question to these speculations was, "After a discussion with the president, I've decided to leave. It's my own decision" (Willsher & Martin, 2014). After some time, she revealed that the president had signed players without her knowledge.

In August 2014 Clermont Foot hired its second female coach, Corinne Diacre. She was French and became the first woman to coach a men's professional association football team in a competitive match in France. She was the coach in Clermont for three years until August 2017, when she then became the manager of the French women's national team.

It is uncommon to find equal participation opportunities for women throughout the sport world in coaching or other leadership positions at all levels of professional and voluntary sport organizations. Women often face challenges not confronted by male coaches and leaders. However, we have seen some female coaches hired to leadership positions with male leagues and teams. For example, Shelley Kerr at the University of Stirling was appointed as the first woman manager in British men's senior association football (Smith, 2014). The Scottish tennis player Andy Murray appointed the former French star Amélie Mauresmo as his coach. In August 2019, Stephanie Frappart became the first female referee, assisted by two female assistant referees, to officiate a major men's European match in the Union of European Football Associations (UEFA) Super Cup between Liverpool and Chelsea. Frappart received high praise for her performance (BBC Sport, 2019). From intercollegiate sports in the United States, on the other hand, the signals are different. Walker and Sartore-Baldwin (2013), using institutional theory as their theoretical framework, found that institutionalized practices in college basketball did not accept women as coaches for men's sports. The coaches in that study reinforced hypermasculine institutional norms, gender exclusiveness, and resistance to change in the organization.

Research examining gender and organizations, including sport organizations, is a traditionally neglected area. Gender and equality in organizations were not topics of much concern until the 1990s. Up to that time, organizations were presented as gender neutral (Acker, 1990; Alvesson, 2002). A breakthrough came with the work of Acker (1990), who emphasized that organizational structure and its theory were not gender neutral; rather, organizational theory and its concepts, models, and statement of problems were based on the problems and demands of men in dominant positions of power. Male domination had rarely been analyzed and explained, simply taken for granted. Masculinities are often taken as superior to femininities (Ely & Meyerson, 2000). Organizations were seen as gender blind, and sport organizations were no exception. This was symptomatic of the field as a whole (Hardy & Clegg 1996). In sport, male players many times made the game itself, the rules, and the arena in accordance with their specialties, skills, and interests.

This chapter will examine common areas of gender studies including concepts of sex and gender, historical development of women in sport organizations and their fight for equal rights, the use of affirmative actions, and gender mainstreaming. The barriers that women experience—described as the glass ceiling, glass cliff, and glass slipper—will be explained. Further, we will look at three major theoretical approaches that may be used to look at the underrepresentation of women in sport organizations: the multilevel approach (Burton, 2015; Cunningham, 2010; Melton & Cunningham, 2014), the gender regime approach (Connell, 2005, 2009), and the contextual approach (Pettigrew, 1987). After reviewing theoretical literature and how it is used in sport management, we will present common tools—laws, targets, quotas, and equal pay—to eliminate the gender underrepresentation in governance of sport. The end of the chapter contains suggestions for how managers can help to increase the representation of women in sport organizations and proposals for further research to be done in the field. The chapter attempts further to inspire reflection and sensitivity toward gender issues. One has to be aware that the content is influenced by Scandinavian or Western European thinking in the way one looks at gender. The situation is very different in other cultures where male domination is much greater and less challenged.

Concepts of Sex and Gender in Sport

Sex segregation is a core organizing principle of most modern sports and is deeply embedded in sport organizations. Physical education is the only school subject that is segregated in many countries. Sport is a male domain. As Meyerson and Fletcher (2000) have argued, men have generally made organizations for themselves, and this seems as truer of sport organizations as of any other kind of organization. Modern sports originate from the public schools in England in the nineteenth century. In some countries, traditional sport organizations were divided according to sex, resulting in separate male and female sport federations. The sports of shooting and sailing did not divide into classes by sex in the 1970s and '80s, but now they do. Equestrianism is the only Olympic sport that is not organized around sex segregation. In the Olympic disciplines of dressage, show jumping, and eventing, the women and men compete against each other and have done so for over 60 years (Dashper, 2012). There is formal equality in the sport situation, and they use the same equipment and clothing (Plymoth, 2012).

We must understand several key concepts in connection with gender and organizations. **Sex** is "a biological category associated with a person's chromosomes and expressed in genitals, reproductive organs, and hormones" (Ely & Padavic, 2007, p.1125). Sex is used to label the dichotomous distinction between females and males based on physiological characteristics that are genetically determined, whereas **gender** is used to label the psychological, cultural, and social dimensions of masculinity and femininity. The difference between sex and gender is meant to differentiate between the biological and the cultural (Hall, 1990). The main aim of gender studies in organizations is to fight the gender bias in practices and structures. To properly make this fight, one must understand this distinction, and that "in particular is among the most personally sensitive topics one may study" (Alvesson & Billing, 2009, p. 11).

Femininity and masculinity refer to the values, experiences, and meanings that are associated with women and men or that define a feminine or masculine image (Ely & Padavic, 2007). Concepts of femininity and masculinity change over time and across cultures (Alvesson & Billing, 1997).

In sport management research within the last decade, Adriaanse (2012), Adriaanse and Schofield (2013, 2014), and Adriaanse and Claringbould (2016) have drawn upon the sociologist Connell's conception of gender as a social structure involving a specific relationship with bodies. Connell (2009, p. 11) argues that "gender is the structure of social relations that centers on the reproductive arena, and the set of practices (governed by this structure) that bring reproductive distinctions between bodies into social processes."

Gender is a social structure that differs from culture to culture and is multidimensional. It is not only about identity, work, power, or sexuality, but rather all these things simultaneously. These points will be explored later.

Historical Development of Women in Sport and Sport Organizations

In order to fully understand gender in sport organizations, a knowledge of the situation in sport participation is necessary. Increasing participation in sport for women has occurred in many countries and also in their participation in the Olympic Games. In the 2012 London Olympics, women for the first time were able to take part in all the sports that were offered, since boxing for women was included. Three nations, Barbados, Nauru, and St. Kitts and Nevis, did not have female participants in the delegation in London, but they had included females in their delegation earlier (SHARP Center, 2013). The 2016 Rio Olympics had the highest proportion of female athletes to date (45 percent of the athletes) but still without female athletes from Nauro, Iraq, Monaco, and Tuvalu (IOC, 2016). The following paragraphs will show the different stages in the struggle for development of equality in sport as equal rights, positive or affirmative actions, and gender mainstreaming.

Equal Rights

In the beginning of the fight for equality women were fighting for **equal rights** in sport and for the assumption that women and men should be treated the same. This corresponds to a "discrimination-and-fairness paradigm" used by Thomas and Ely (1996, p. 80). The main ideas were those of gender balance, democratic equality, fairness and justice, and the fight against discrimination on the basis of gender, class, religion, ethnicity, and age. This is a liberal principle used in the national constitutions of many countries based on the idea that women should be treated the same as men (Teigen, 2002). In other words, the way men were treated was seen as the norm while women were treated like "others." Hillary Clinton declared, "There cannot be true democracy unless women's voices are heard. There cannot be true democracy unless women are given the opportunity to take responsibility for their own lives. There cannot be true democracy unless all citizens are able to participate fully in the lives of their country." (Clinton, 1997, 1).

> Gender equality means an equal visibility, empowerment and participation of both sexes in all spheres of public and private life, and it became an issue in the Scandinavian sport organizations in the 1980s (Ottesen, Skirstad, Pfister, & Habermann, 2010). Gender equality is the opposite of gender inequality, not of gender difference, and aims to promote the full participation of women and men in society (Council of Europe, 2004, p.8).

The term *equality* is used in accordance with international public policy documents as in United Nations Convention. Sport has consistently tried to establish connections to existing international documents on gender and contact with the broader global women's movement. Earlier the terms *equity* and *equality* were different, but in current use they are interchangeable. *Equality* referred to women and men having equal opportunities with the same rights and resources, while *equity* highlighted fairness and justice for women and men (Adriaanse & Claringbould, 2016).

Positive or Affirmative Action

Positive or affirmative action is taken to overcome underrepresentation of women (and minority) groups in employment or elections. To acquire a more equal gender balance, differential treatment is used. The United States and Europe have gone in opposite directions in this question. In the United States, there is great concern about the use of positive action, but in parts of Europe, this has been at the center of policies aimed at achieving equality (Teigen, 2000). An affirmative or positive action would be to prefer a woman before a man if they were equally qualified for either an elected of employed position in sport. To help underrepresented women in this way may create difficult working conditions for them. McKay (1997) did an in-depth analysis of resistance to affirmative action initiatives in sport organizations in Australia, Canada, and New Zealand. He found that most men were not in favor of affirmative action and many perceived them as a benign "women's issue."

Gender Mainstreaming

In the last phase of development of gender equality the focus shifted from the individual and the individual's rights toward the system and the structures that created the pattern of gender inequality (Rees, 2002). From now on, achieving equality should be the responsibility of both men and women in the organization and should be confronted by all in the organization.

Rees (2002, p. 29) defines **gender mainstreaming** as "the systematic integration of gender equality into all systems and structures; policies, programs, processes and projects; into cultures and their organizations, into ways of seeing and doing." For sport organizations this means both women and men have to work for gender equality. This is not any longer only a women's issue; men also have to work for a gender balance among decision makers and in other important roles in sport at all levels.

Barriers for Women to Overcome in Sport

Understanding the ways gender equality has been obstructed is key to accelerating gender equality in sport leadership.

Glass Ceiling

The metaphor of the glass ceiling has been around for about 30 years since the *Wall Street Journal* popularized the term in the mid-1980s in their special report on women and business (Hymowitz & Schellhardt, 1986). **Glass ceiling** describes the unseen and subtle barriers women face when they want to advance in management in business or in sport organizations. It is *glass* because it is not usually a visible barrier, and a woman may not be aware of its existence until she hits the barrier. The hindrance reflects the organizational culture. The glass ceiling is a way of describing whatever keeps women from achieving power and success equal to that of men. This differs from formal barriers such as requirements in education or experience.

Whiteside & Hardin (2012) studied the glass ceiling in collegiate sport and pointed out that women are hesitant in admitting the existence of the glass ceiling and they see the failure to break through the ceiling as an individual issue. Whiteside and Hardin's (2012) findings showed how women also accepted rationalized strategies for themselves. When they had children, many of the women felt they met a maternal wall, which constrained their career advancement. Based on a literature review, Baumgartner and Schneider (2010) interviewed successful businesswomen about six issues that women face in cracking the glass ceiling. Their responses give suggestions for how to overcome stereotypes, coping with the "Old Boys" network, balancing work and family, choosing mentors, understanding the queen bee syndrome (the idea that women who make it to the top find a reason not to help other women aspiring to break through the glass ceiling), developing a leadership style, and determining personal ambitions for advancement.

Double jeopardy is a term given to those women who are members of two disadvantaged groups (e.g., African American women). Additionally, sexuality is a powerful obstacle as well (Borland & Bruening, 2010). Sport management researchers have either studied gender (Adriaanse & Schofield, 2014; Inglis, Danylchyk, & Pastore, 1996; Sartore & Cunningham, 2007) or race (Bruening, 2005), but very rarely the two together, with the exception of Borland and Bruening's work (2010) in collegiate basketball. African American women have either been grouped as women as a whole or blacks as a whole. Borland and Bruening focused on black women in head coaching jobs in collegiate basketball in the United States. In this study, the suggested strategies to cope with the underrepresentation of black females were networking, more mentoring, and development programs for young black females.

Glass Cliff and Glass Slipper

A **glass cliff** is a newer form of gender discrimination and exists where women either run for or are given leadership positions in which they are likely to fail because, for example, the organization is performing poorly or, in politics, they run for a seat that will probably not be won. In other words it is no "danger" to put women there because they will not have any influence. Females are therefore often suggested as substitutes because it looks nice. Previous research on the glass cliff in politics and business suggests that women are preferred in difficult situations because they seem to have personalities that can be useful in crises (Ryan, Haslam, Hersby, & Bongiorno, 2011). One of the case studies by these authors also suggested that women were chosen during a crisis not because they would solve the situation but because they were good personal managers and would take the blame for the organizational failure. Another explanation (Bruckmüller & Branscombe, 2010; Kulich, Ryan, & Haslam, 2014) shows that choosing a nontypical leader is a way of signaling change. So far, this approach has not been used in sport organizations. Studies on glass cliffs in sport, both in the recruiting of females to high positions as well as in elections to high positions both nationally and internationally, may be investigated in order to extend the theory into sport. As social pressure increases for more diversity in sport elections on the basis of ethnicity and gender, we may see an increase in this form of discrimination. The broader the base for election will be, the harder the election will be for the minorities.

The glass slipper theory builds on the glass ceiling ideas that invisible barriers stand in the way for women. It is the newest glass metaphor used by Ashcraft (2013). She explains how the metaphor points to the fairytale in which the prince tries to find the girl—Cinderella—who fits the tiny shoe he found. The **glass slipper** indicates inherent fits for occupations and positions "suited for certain people (here the men) and impossibility for others" (Ashcraft, 2013, pp. 7-8). So far, this theory has not been used in discussing recruitment of female leaders in sport, but it seems very relevant.

Theoretical Approaches Explaining Underrepresentation of Women in Sport

Researchers have documented underrepresentation in sport organizations in Australia (Adriaanse & Schofield, 2013 & 2014; McKay, 1992, 1997), Canada

(Hall, 1996; Hall, Cullen, & Slack, 1989; Hoeber & Frisby, 2001; Shaw & Hoeber, 2003; Sibson, 2010), Germany (Hartmann-Tews & Combrink, 2005; Hartmann-Tews & Pfister, 2003; Pfister & Radtke, 2009), the Netherlands (Claringbould & Knoppers, 2007, 2008, 2012), Scandinavia (Fasting, 2000; Hovden, 2000; Ottesen et al., 2010; Sisjord, Fasting, & Sand, 2017; Skirstad, 2009), the UK (Aitchinson, 2005; Shaw, 2006; Shaw & Penney, 2003; Shaw & Slack, 2002; White & Brackenridge, 1985; White & Kay, 2006), and as an overview (Burton, 2015).

The following sections outline three theoretical approaches to explain gender in sport organizations: the multilevel approach, Connell's four-dimensional model of gender relations, and Pettigrew's contextual approach.

Multilevel Approach

Since sport organizations are multilevel entities that address factors on macro-, meso- and micro-levels, this seems to be a useful approach for looking at the underrepresentation of women in sport organizations (Cunningham, 2010). The **multilevel framework** is chosen because it enables us to reflect on the complex realities and argues for explanations of why women are underrepresented in sport organizations both as elected and employed persons. Why is this the case?

Despite an increase in female participants in the Olympic Games (up to 45 percent in Rio 2016), the underrepresentation of women in sport organizations off the field exists at all levels. Women's underrepresentation has a long history and is closely related to the traditional view of gender relations in society. In 2015 Burton provided a review of the research of underrepresentation of women in sport leadership. She used a multilevel perspective to better understand the underrepresentation in leadership roles in sport as Cunningham (2010) had done for the underrepresentation of African American head coaches in sport organizations. Burton looked at the macro-level (i.e., institutionalized practices, stakeholders' expectations, and political climate), meso-level (i.e., discrimination, prejudice, leadership stereotypes, and organizational culture), and micro-level coaching (women's expectations as leaders, occupational turnover, and career patterns). When using the multilevel approach, Burton's sub-divisions are used. The factors at each level are thought to influence each other in accordance with a system theory approach (Chelladurai, 2009). This multilevel approach will be used in this chapter to offer possible explanations. For the sake of simplicity, the factors in the multilevel model are treated separately even if they do not operate like that but are influenced by each other and also influence other factors.

Macro-Level Factors

The macro-level factors are those that function at the societal level. The dominant explanations for the underrepresentation of women in sport organizations at the macro-level are institutionalized practices and processes, political climate, and stakeholder expectations. For example, when a female is hired for a top job, this can influence all other levels such as employee satisfaction (micro-level) and the organization level (meso-level). The multilevel approach can explain which factors are active.

Institutionalized Practices and Processes Activities become institutionalized when they are standardized and categorically accepted as the way things are done (Scott, 2003). Sport is a gendered institution, and all processes operate within the masculine norm. The most important aspect of institutionalization is that the structures or the activities become imbued with values. Similar institutional practices and activities are copied by other sport organizations, a process called *institutional isomorphism* (DiMaggio & Powell, 1983; Slack & Hinings, 1995).

Through socialization of new members into the sport organizations and with the use of language and norms, members of the sport organization learn how to behave. When this behavior has a long history, it is highly resistant to change. Institutionalized masculinity is the operating principle within sport, which makes male activities preferred and protected, especially as leaders (Shaw & Frisby, 2006). These factors slow down the recruitment and career opportunities for women in sport organizations.

Political Climate The political climate both outside and inside the organization influences the institutionalized practices (Skirstad, 2009). Implementing gender equality practices or policies in certain countries is easier than in others. Norway is a country where changes in the leadership of sport are easier to make since equality is much more accepted both in the wider political system and in the organization (Strittmatter & Skirstad, 2017). The organizations must be seen as context of the changes. Changes should focus on the interplay of organizational features and individual-level processes bases for sex differences. Ely & Padavic (2007) draw on concepts from feminist theory about gender as a system, as identity, and as power, and they outline how the field will be enriched by greater attention to the links between women's identity and organizational structures and practices. The IOC has the ability to influence sport organizations under their auspices, the national Olympic committees. Government programs or others responsible for funding can require equal opportunities as a prerequisite for funding participants in sport, in part due to a perceived public demand. For instance, after the world governing bodies in golf withheld the most prestigious golf event from the private male golf club Muirfield in Britain, it resulted in the club opening up to women as members (Sawer, 2019). Legislation about equal opportunities in employment in general is another important factor that can influence the gender climate in sport as well as the political environment. With a more democratic political environment, the situation for women should be more encouraging.

Stakeholder Expectations Expectations from stakeholders are the third factor at the macro-level. The present ruling stakeholder group is generally interested in maintaining their power. The different stakeholders, such as athletes, politicians, employees in sport, sponsors, and male and female sport members, have different needs and desires. Sometimes systematic barriers are built into the system, as, for example, when a position as an athletic director in sport is linked up to be a head gridiron football coach at the same time. Normally this restricts the possibility for women to get the athletic director position since it is unlikely she has experience as a gridiron football coach as well. This is illustrated in a study of 112 school districts in the state of Texas, which showed that 17 percent of the job descriptions list the ability or experience to coach a gridiron football team as a required qualification (Whisenant, Miller, & Pedersen, 2005). The work of Schull, Shaw, and Kihl (2013, p.77), who studied an athletic department merger, show how "an alliance of women not only welcomed, but also lobbied for a male candidate" who values gender equity. The women involved felt a female would be "eaten up alive" (p.71).

Meso-Level Factors

Research at the meso-level concentrates on how factors operating in the organization, such as decisions, structures, and processes, maintain the underrepresentation of women. The decision-makers' prejudice, discrimination, leadership stereotypes, and the culture in the organization are factors at this level. For example, when a board member on the meso-level is discriminated against it can have influence on the micro-level; the board member quits (Sibson, 2010).

Prejudice and Discrimination Throughout the 1970s, 1980s, and 1990s women experienced **prejudice** if they were discriminated against when applying for positions in sport. The American researcher Rosabeth Moss Kanter's (1977) book *Men and Women of the Corporation* showed how stereotyping and discrimination influenced big organizations. She writes that groups behave differently depending on their relative size. A "uniform group" is homogeneous according to sex. A "skewed group" has a predominance of one group over the other up to 85 percent. The "tilted group" has from 65 to 85 percent and has a large majority. The "balanced group" has up to 60 percent. The role of the minority or the single person was looked upon as token. Her original concept of "critical mass," which is approximately one third of the group, continues to inform current research on gender diversity on boards. Women are often situated as "other" in sport organizations, and the presence of women in sport as athlete, coach, manager, or leader is under constant scrutiny.

Kanter (1977) points out that those in power maintain their control by allowing only those who share common characteristics to enter their circle of influence. Women were kept at dead-end jobs at the bottom of the organization by men, their own lack of aspirations, and tokenism at the top. The same picture of homologous reproduction mentioned by Kanter (1977) operates in sport organizations (Knoppers, 1987). Knoppers (1987) mentions females' underrepresentation in the coaching profession compared to men, as well as their lack of power and opportunity in the organization, as determinants of why females enter the coaching profession to a lesser degree and leave because they do not fit in. Several researchers (Claringbould & Knoppers, 2007; Hall, Cullen, & Slack, 1989; Hovden, 2000) have examined the election system for recruiting new board members as a means of preserving the existing system because men are the majority in the organization and they are expected to be more competent. The women, on the other hand, have a hard time gaining credibility and power. Hovden used the phrase "heavyweight" to describe the preferred leadership skills, which she describes to identify men. These election processes are also linked to the historical development of the sport organization where men have the most say. The same was the case in the search for athletic directors (Kihl, Shaw, & Schull, 2013; Schull, Shaw, & Kihl, 2013).

The gender process may be labeled the "us versus them" duality. Schein (1973) coined the slogan "Think manager—think male" (TMTM), which seems to be the key hurdle for women to overcome. Sport as a male domain is found in the structure (which is taken for granted), the policies, and the behaviors rooted in the sport organizations, and that makes it a gendered space. It is important to understand the practice within organizations (Martin, 2003). Ely and Meyerson (2000) emphasize that masculinity, or the behaviors, actions, and associations that are most often connected with men, are perceived to be superior to femininities, or women's behaviors. Shaw and Frisby (2006) identified that gender shapes identities and is affiliated with power.

With an increase in women's leadership in the lower echelons of management, at least in some countries, it is necessary to take a closer look at the situation under which women and men are elected or appointed to leadership positions. It must not be a numbers game, but one needs to understand women's experiences in these roles, which are often different from men's. The gender stereotypes obstruct women's attempts to reach the top positions. The context shows differentiation in the TMTM association. Female leaders are often in a lose-lose situation because when they behave like the male stereotype, they are blamed for not being female enough, and when they behave like the female stereotype, they are accused of not being leaders. The TMTM phenomenon seems to be very durable. The context is important for change, which we will see when we use the contextualist approach (Pettigrew, 1985).

Treatment and access discrimination in the hiring process is experienced by black female coaches in collegiate basketball (Borland & Bruening, 2010). They have more limited opportunities in participating in events and in important sport committees and executive boards. Black female coaches struggle to fight stereotypes and discrimination and to move up the career ladder due to white old men's network. They suffer the double burden of racism and gender.

Sex is a principle of organizing in sport, therefore, lesbians, gays, bisexuals, and transgender participants experience discriminatory treatment within heterosexist sport culture, and this produces disadvantages for those groups. All of these groups, and women in general, are the victims of marginalized coverage in the media, and they are struggling with both quantity and quality in the sport press and sexist connotations as well. An analysis of Facebook shows that Australian sportswomen face three times more negative comments online than men (Ward, 2019).

Leadership Stereotypes Because typical male attributes such as decisiveness, force, and aggression are often linked with the characteristics of leadership, men have a great advantage in how they are viewed when they run for positions or apply for jobs in sport. Feminine activity is associated with weakness, passivity, gentleness, and elegance (Hargreaves, 1986). The expectations about leaders are also formed by the people one has seen in the role through the years, and those are usually men. Research shows that even when women were judged to have the necessary masculine characteristics like being assertive, dominant, and forceful, which are perceived as necessary to be successful as an athletic director, they would still fail to get the job because they do not fit in the historically masculine domain of sport (Burton, Grappendorf, & Henderson, 2011). Since these positions have historically be reserved for men, they are looked upon as the prototypes.

Gendered Organizational Culture To say that an organization, or any other analytic unit, is gendered means that advantage and disadvantage, exploitation and control, action and emotion, meaning and identity are patterned through and in terms of a distinction (or, we would say, distinctions) between male and female, masculine and feminine. Gender is not an addition to those processes, conceived as gender neutral. Rather, it is an integral part of those processes, which cannot be properly understood without an analysis of gender (Acker, 1990).

The organizational culture in sport organizations relies on the dominant culture, and to change the culture is a long and difficult process. For further reading on culture see chapter 17. Often it is argued that the women must change in order to fit into the organization and the male world and that there is nothing wrong with the structure of the sport organization. In other words, women, instead of the sport structure, are blamed. The more hierarchical the organization is, the fewer women we find at the top, as for example in international sport federations. Many tacit assumptions and values exist in a sport organization (e.g., men are the boss and have experience and know what to do; male values prevail. Further, women lack the networks that men have and use (Hoffman, 2011).

Micro-Level Factors

Research at the micro-level of analysis focuses on individuals and how they experience the meaning of their involvement, expectations, and understanding of policies, power, and processes at the organizational level. In some cases, this leads to self-limiting behaviors because of the gendered practices in management and in coaching (Sartore & Cunningham, 2007) and because of the lack of respect they receive (Norman, 2010). Lack of time with families is another barrier women face (Bruening & Dixon, 2008; Dixon & Bruening, 2007). What is missing is analysis of qualitative data from women's leadership in sport, as well as stories about barriers they meet when they want to climb the organizational ladder and about trying to understand why their employment roles are less valued in coaching (Shaw & Hoeber, 2003).

Based on historical factors, women may assume that their competence as women in sport organizations will be challenged in such areas as management, leadership, and coaching. Women may also suffer from having few female professional role models. The social and human capital (i.e., networks and mentors) are less for women than men, and this may result in earlier turnover for women in these kinds of jobs (Hoffman, 2011).

Connell's Four-Dimensional Model of Gender Regimes Relations

Hegemony and hegemonic masculinity are theories used by many gender researchers (Connell, 1987; McKay, 1997; Sisjord & Kristiansen, 2008; Theberge, 1987) to study inequity in sport. Hegemony refers to the way ideological forces organize and structure the lives of people and their social practices (Gramsci, 1971). Connell's gender perspective is influenced by Gramsci's theory of cultural power, and Connell (2002) explored the underlying forces of hierarchical gendered power. Connell's analysis is built on the theory of gender relations.

Connell (2009) tells us how we can understand gender in the contemporary world. The first thing we must do is to move away from sex differences. She emphasizes that the theory of gender relations between males and females as created in social processes are not static in two categories. Connell focuses on the multidimensional character of gender, identifying four dimensions:

1. Gender division of labor
2. Gender relations of power
3. Emotion and human relations
4. Gender culture and symbolism

These four dimensions do not operate separately but are constantly interwoven. The particular ways in which these dimensions blend produce a specific "**gender regime**," according to Connell (2009, p. 72).

The first dimension of a gender regime is gender division of labor. First one has to know how many women and men are involved in the work in the organization and what tasks are done by males and females, including the executive board. It also includes the division between paid work and domestic work.

The second dimension of the gender regime is gender relations of power, "i.e. the way in which control, authority, and force are exercised on gender lines, including organisational hierarchy, legal power, collective and individual violence"

TIME OUT

Is Managing Association Football Still a Man's Game?

Some time has elapsed since Hannelore Ratzeburg, representing Germany in 1990, came to the first meeting of Women's Committee in International Football Association (Fédération Internationale de Football Association [FIFA]). She expressed surprise when entering the room: "I thought I was in the wrong room because only men were sitting in a meeting for a Women's Committee" (interviewed January, 2012). Association football is one of the fastest growing sports, and 118 nations out of 211 have women's teams in December 2017 (e-mail from FIFA, December 21, 2017). Still more than a hundred years passed from the founding of FIFA in 1904 to have a female, Lydia Nsekera, of Burundi, on the FIFA board in 2013. When she was elected, FIFA expanded the board from 24 to 25 since no one wanted to leave the board. In 2012 UEFA appointed the first woman, Karen Espelund, to their board. She had board experience and served ten years as the General Secretary of the Norwegian national football federation. Nsekera was elected for four years and represented Confédération Africaine de Football (CAF). Two other female candidates who were running for the seat were co-opted as members, Bien-Aime from Turks & Caicos Islands representing the Confederation of North, Central America and Caribbean Association Football (CONCACAF) and Dodd from Australia representing the Asian Football Confederation (AFC). In 2016 the statutes in FIFA were changed to provide for the election of one female representative from each continent, thus expanding the number of board members to 37. In conjunction with the FIFA congress 2017 in Bahrain, the AFC representative was elected. Experienced Dodd, co-opted member of FIFA from 2013, was beaten by 10 votes by Bangladesh's inexperienced female, Kiron. Do men prefer women without experience so they can rule as before?

(Connell, 2005, p. 7). Applied to sport organizations this means usually men's dominance and influence in decision-making and how they defend and reproduce the system that gives them privileges.

The third dimension of the gender regime is emotion and human relations, that is, the way attachment and antagonism among people and groups are organized along gender lines, including feelings of solidarity, prejudice and disdain, sexual attraction and repulsion, and so on. In sport organizations this means how they support and cooperate with each other in their work and how they are attached to each other.

The fourth dimension of the gender regime is gender culture and symbolism, that is, the way gender identities are defined in culture, the language and symbols of gender difference, and the prevailing beliefs and attitudes about gender. For sport organizations this means how they address cultural and symbolic understandings of gender equality in the organization.

This four-dimensional gender model provides a pattern for analyzing the gender regime template and helps in understanding how gender works in executive boards in sport. Connell (2005) and Schofield and Goodwin (2005) have used this framework to understand a group of Australian public sector organizations. They used it as a conceptual tool to analyze the functioning of the whole organization rather than specific policies.

Connell's theoretical framework is widely used in gender and sport research (Broch, 2011; Kristiansen, Broch, & Pedersen, 2014; Sisjord & Kristiansen, 2008). In sport management Adriaanse (2012) and Adriaanse and Schofield (2013, 2014) have used this gender model to understand the composition and operations of the boards of Australian National Sport Organizations (NSOs). They wanted to find out how gender dynamics work on sport boards. They identified three gender regimes: masculine hegemony, masculine hegemony in transition, and gender mainstreaming in process. Adriaanse and Schofield (2014) also used gender regimes when they investigated the impact of gender quotas on gender equality in sport organizations. Building on these studies Adriaanse and Claringbould (2016) investigated the construction of gender in the legacy of five world conferences on women and sport from 1994 to 2010. These researchers suggested closer collaboration with proactive men in order to further gender equality in sport; this is in line with ideas of the European Union and United Nations (Connell, 2009; Skirstad, 2009). Connell (2009) ends her key text of "Gender" by favoring what she calls *gender democracy*.

> This strategy seeks to equalize gender orders, rather than shrink them to nothing. Conceptually, this assumes that gender does not, in itself, imply inequality. The fact that there are in the world gender orders with markedly different levels of inequality is some evidence in support (Connell, 2009, p. 146).

Pettigrew's Contextual Approach

Although the contextual approach by Pettigrew is about change in general and not specifically about change in sport organizations, it may nevertheless be of value in studying gender changes in sport organizations. The contextual approach stems from Andrew Pettigrew's (1985) *The Awakening Giant*. Pettigrew focuses on the process of changing rather than the result of change, and he criticized most of the work on change for being "ahistorical, aprocessual and acontextual" (Pettigrew, 1990, p. 269). He wants to see the mechanisms and processes through which change is created. Time sets a reference to how to look at the change and how it is explained. Longitudinal data allows one to see the present in relation to the past and the future. Using Pettigrew's contextualist approach, the underrepresentation of females in sport organizations and the changes that appear as a result in the status of the sport organizations are examined in light of changes in the inner context (i.e., the structures, culture, and political make-up) and the context outside sport (i.e., the economic, political, social, and competitive environment) in which the organization is situated. All the changes are understood in the light of local time cycles (Pettigrew, Woodman, & Cameron, 2001). The process of change is described in terms of critical incidents and important key actors. Change can be a long and difficult process because it may involve a "challenge to the dominant ideology, cultures, system of meaning and power relationships in the organization" (Pettigrew, 1987, pp. 659-660). The change process happens as a result of negotiations among the key actors in relation to the proposals for change. The outer context gives legitimacy to changes in the inner context. Acker (2006) also defined the inequality within regimes as being linked to inequality in the surrounding society, its politics, history, and culture.

Pettigrew's contextual framework was used in a longitudinal study of female representation in the General Assembly in Norwegian sports (Skirstad, 2009). This framework helped to clarify how the bylaws regarding gender in the statutes of the Norwegian Confederation and Paralympic Organization and Confederation of Sports (NIF) expressed the advancement of gender equality. The study period was divided into three periods of gender development: equal rights (1971-1984), positive action (1984-1994), and gender mainstreaming (1994-2007). By using Pettigrew's contextualist approach the process of change with its key incidents and key actors became clearer. The important point is that by showing the inner context in sport as well as the outer context (the society at large), it is easier to understand and see the changes. The changes in sport are in harmony with the outer changes even if they are a little delayed.

The same contextual framework has been used in studying international sport, specifically in a comparative case study of how women move into decision-making positions in UEFA and FIFA as well as national football federations in Norway and Germany; Pettigrew's framework helps explain the difference between these scenarios. Much of the delay in Germany's football federation compared to Norway's was due to the situation in the outer context and the structures in the organization. Their male mentors supported the two pioneer females strongly in order to succeed. The executive boards of UEFA and FIFA were also studied in light of this framework (Strittmatter & Skirstad, 2017).

Gender Equity Policies in Sport

Little research has been done on gender equity policies such as sport laws, targets for gender, quotas, equal pay, and gender testing. The exception is Shaw & Penney (2003), who described the development of gender equity policies in three national governing bodies in English sport. They concluded by recommending greater organizational reflexivity and deep structure analysis. Further exceptions have come from Scandinavia (Hovden, 2006; Ottesen et al., 2010; Skirstad, 2009) and Australia (Adriaanse & Schofield, 2014). All these researchers documented the effect of the quota or target regimes that were institutionalized, especially when these measures were done in combination with other measures such as gender mainstreaming, which was then the responsibility of the whole organization.

Internationally, gender initiatives in sport equity policies such as the Brighton Declaration from 1994 have been made in order to advance the status of and opportunities for girls and women in sport. This declaration has been endorsed by more than 400 organizations (Fasting, Sand, Pike, & Matthews, 2014), and the subsequent conferences have all given inspiration and empowerment to women. The outcome of this first conference was a strategy for women and sport and the foundation of the International Working Group on Women and Sport (IWG). On a quadrennial basis the conferences have been organized in Windhoek, Namibia (1998); Montreal, Canada (2002); Kumamoto, Japan (2006); Sydney, Australia (2010); and Helsinki, Finland (2014). A legacy of the Sydney conference is the Sydney Scoreboard, an interactive online tool through which women in leadership roles within sport organizations can be tracked both nationally and internationally.

Sport Laws

The United States was one of the first countries to enhance the position of women through formal policy. They addressed the female underrepresentation in sport using Title IX of the Education Amendments Act (Kay, 2003). Title IX is federal legislation that prohibits discrimination based on sex in education programs that receive federal money. The law was enacted in 1972 and schools were given until 1978 to comply with the law. It covers only sex discrimination, but it includes all parts of education programs including athletics, intramurals, financial aid, biology, psychology, and so forth. The law applies as long as federal dollars are found within the program, whether it is public or private. This act triggered the professionalization of women's sport, but this led to men coming in and taking the posts that earlier had been administered by female amateurs. This led to a weakening of women's power in the sport establishment. Further interpretations of the law within interscholastic and intercollegiate athletics, intramural, and recreation programs were drafted (Acosta & Carpenter, 2014). Title IX has also had an impact on the American female stereotype, which has changed American views on sport from being only a male bastion. This law opened doors to participation in sport for girls and women, and now families support girls sport participation (Lopiano, 2000).

Targets

The IOC has targets, which are goals to be strived for. At the centennial conference in 1996 in Paris, the IOC decided that their aim for women was that least 10 percent of executive decision-making positions in NOCs should be held by women by December 2001, rising to at least 20 percent by December 2005. At the same time, they set up a working group on women and sport, which has now become a permanent

Commission. Almost five years after the target of 20 percent women should have been implemented by the NOCs and the international federations, the figures were respectively 17.6 percent and 18.3 percent (Henry & Robinson, 2010). In 2014 the IOC board has more female representatives than ever before, 4 out of 15 (26.6 percent), one serving one of the four vice presidents. Finally, IOC has reached their target for executive boards. Most respondents in this investigation by Henry and Robinson (2010) talked about quotas and not minimum targets upon which IOC had agreed.

Quotas

Some research has been conducted on the effect of gender quotas on gender equality in sport boards in Australia (Adriaanse & Schofield, 2014), and Norway (Ottesen et al., 2010; Skirstad 2009, 2014). **Quotas** are mandatory, in contrast to targets, which are voluntary. The aim of most quota systems is to guarantee that women constitute at least a "critical minority" of 30 percent. Kanter's (1977) concept of "critical mass" in organizations is still valid. The purpose of the quota system is to open up the closed and male-dominated recruitment patterns. When women reach this threshold they can influence the culture in the organization. The argument that there are not enough (competent) women is not accepted, and sport politicians need to start to search for women and have them on all levels in sport. In politics the establishment of quotas has been used for a long time; Dahlerup and Freidenvall (2005) stated in their article, "Quotas as a 'Fast Track' to Equal Representation for Women," that 40 countries around the world had instituted quotas for parliamentary elections either by electoral law or constitutional amendments. For many years the Nordic countries, Finland, Norway or Sweden have been among the leading countries when it comes to female representation in parliament (Dahlerup, 2013). For the Nordic countries, it took 60 years to reach 20 percent representation in politics and 70 years to reach 30 percent.

In Norway the Norwegian Olympic and Paralympic Committee and Confederation of Sports (NIF) passed a quota law in the statutes for sport in 1987 for the first time, approximately ten years after this was done in politics. The statutes of sport organizations were inspired by the Gender Equality Act of 1978. The law of NIF has been amended several times (1990, 1996, 1999, and 2007). It started with one representative of each gender, then a minimum of two candidates, then a minimum of two elected persons with an exemption for sport clubs and committees with less than three people, and finally all exemptions were abolished (Skirstad, 2009). In Norway the influence from the state has been crucial in changing men's attitudes by its public policy, for example, in connection with father's leave (Holter, 2003). Adriaanse and Schofield (2014) found that quotas were effective in order to achieve gender parity in sport organizations in Australia, at least when the quotas prescribed the minimum threshold for women.

In 2019, the president, the first vice president, and three members of NIF's board were female; when the representative of the athletes, employees, and IOC are counted, the executive board actually has 60 percent female representation. In the 54 sport federations, the average percentage of females on the board was 36.5 percent in 2014, and in the 19 sport district boards, the percentage was 47.5. Females had 18.5 percent of presidents in the sport federations and 42 percent in the districts (Skirstad, 2014). In 1974 there were no female presidents in the federations and one in the district, so changes have occurred within the last 40 years (Skirstad, 2014). The figures are high for Norway compared with other countries (Adriaanse & Schofield, 2014).

Equal Pay

The size of salaries varies in organizations. Often the differences vary with the height of the hierarchy (Acker, 2006). White men tend to earn more than any other category. In professional tennis in 2009, over a player's career, the median earnings were substantially higher for men than women (Flake, Dufur, & Moore, 2013). Prize money is equal in prestigious tournaments such as Grand Slam events, but women's prize money is noticeably lower in many of the less publicized tournaments. In 2007 Wimbledon was the last of the Grand Slam events to equalize the prize money for men and women (Flake et al, 2013). Equal pay is a tool to promote the acceptance that women and men are equal in the organization.

As another example, the United States Women's National Team (USWNT) for association football, who were winners of the 2019 FIFA Women's World Cup, launched an equal pay lawsuit against the U.S. Soccer Federation (USSF) following the tournament victory. They allege that USSF discriminates because the women receive less pay than players on the men's national team (MNT) "for substantially equal work and by denying them at least equal playing, training, and travel conditions; equal promotion of their games; equal support and development for their games; and other terms and conditions of employment equal to the MNT" (Martin, 2019, para. 18). Having highlighted a bitter high-profile association football gender equality battle, progress has been made in the sport; for the first time in history,

Liverpool Women's Football Club was invited to join the men's team on its 2019 preseason tour of the United States. The women traveled with the men's team, stayed in the same hotels, were flanked by security guards (for the first time), and trained at the same facilities. It has been suggested that the joint tour is a sign of changing status for the women's game (Sanders, 2019).

Gender Testing

From the Olympic Games in Grenoble and Mexico City (1968) and until before the 2000 Sydney Olympic Games, women had to pass a **gender test** in order to obtain a certificate of femininity to take part in the Olympic Games. Several international federations had the same requirement. These procedures were enforced by the sport organization in order to protect women. In 1968 the so-called "bucclear smear" test (Barr-test) was introduced by IOC, and in the 1992 Albertville Olympics, the IOC changed to the PCR (polymerase chain reaction) test. Both tests produced uncertain results. Many geneticists claimed such testing was not justified scientifically (Skirstad, 2000).

At the 2006 Asian Games, a 25-year-old Indian middle distance runner, Santhi Soundarajan, placed second. The day after she was asked to do a gender verification test. She was not informed about what kind of test she was taking since none of the four doctors spoke her native language of Tamil Nadu. After returning home, she learned from the newspaper that she had failed the gender test. She was then stripped of her medals and prohibited from competing again by the IAAF (now World Athletics). Soundarajan tried to commit suicide. Three years later, the women's 800-meter runner Caster Semenya from South Africa was required to undergo gender tests after winning the 2009 World Championships, which was her first international competition. Shortly before the World Championship in Berlin, Semenya unknowingly took a gender test, which the South African sports minister kept secret. She won gold in Berlin, but because her result produced so much controversy among her competitors, the IAAF required her sex to be scientifically verified. After eight months, she was cleared by the IAAF to compete. In the 2012 London Olympics, she won a silver medal in the women's 800 meters. However, she seemed to run a poor tactical race and was accused by some of holding back in order not to win and cause further controversy (Pieper, 2014). Semenya's silver medal was later upgraded to gold after the Russian winner was banned for life for doping.

Based on Semenya's case, the IAAF adopted new guidelines for gender verification in April 2011, in

The 2019 Liverpool Women's Football Club was the first women's association football club to travel with the same benefits as the men's club, but only for a preseason tour.

which the female athletes have to test below a certain threshold of testosterone. For some athletes this meant they needed compulsory hormonal therapy if they would continue competing (Pieper, 2014). For the 2012 Games, the IAAF implemented a test of testosterone levels; the gender test would only be administered if the chief medical officer of a national Olympic committee or a member of IOC medical commission requested it (Topend Sports, 2016). In 2015 the Indian sprinter Dutee Chand brought her case to Court of Arbitration for Sport (CAS) against the IAAF rule, claiming there was no scientific proof of the performance-enhancing effect of high levels of endogenous testosterone. CAS did not find the IAAF regulations scientifically supported and suspended the rule for two years to seek more evidence (Ljungqvist, 2017). In April 2018 the IAAF Council approved new eligibility regulations for female athletes; these rules were to be enforced beginning in November 2018. The regulations will apply only to track events over 400 meters to one mile. Females with testosterone levels higher than 5 nanomoles per liter had to reduce their levels by taking medicine for a period of more than six months (IAAF, 2018). Athletics South Africa (ASA) and Semenya took IAAF's new rule to CAS. On May 1, 2019, CAS announced a majority decision that supported IAAF. Even if this rule discriminates against Semenya and other women athletes in the same situation, CAS has deemed it necessary to follow the IAAF rule on testosterone in order to secure fair and equal competition among women (Court of Arbitration for Sport, 2019). Her defenders argue that hyperandrogenism, which one is born with, is just one genetic variation among many other biological differences that should not be used for classifications in sport (Kessel, 2018).

Summary and Conclusions

Gender and sport organizations is one of the most ignored topics in the field of sport management. The distinction between sex and gender has been described as well as the history of the development of gender equality through the fight for equal rights, positive and affirmative actions, and gender mainstreaming. The barriers that women meet in their quest for positions within organizations have been explained. In this chapter we have also reviewed three possible theories that can explain gender underrepresentation. The multilevel approach shows how the different levels are connected and impose on each other. Connell (2009, p. 10) emphasizes, "Gender is, above all, a matter of the social relations within which individuals and groups act." The gender regime seems to be a fruit-

KEY ISSUES FOR SPORT MANAGERS

Ways Managers Can Help Increase the Representation of Women in Sport Organizations

Better insight on gender would save many frustrations about daily activities in organizations such as how to recruit new members and get more volunteers for events. Knowledge about gender and the challenges it poses should be included in all education for coaches and leaders and in all practices and policies in an organization. For change to occur, managers need to be proactive and ensure women are elected or appointed to the board. Using targets and quotas can be effective, especially when used in combination with other facilitating efforts such as gender mainstreaming and endorsement by influential men with power (Adriaanse & Schofield, 2013). Managers should look beyond their own network and should remember that women are not a single homogenous group, since there are inequalities and differences among women. In order for change to happen, it is necessary that male presidents support females in powerful positions. Funding can also be used to further equality. Bonuses could be used as an incentive to increase the female representation (Adriaanse, 2012). There is no sense in using only men since they make up just half of the talent pool (Terjesen, Sealy, & Singh, 2009).

Managers should be aware of subtle forms of gender discrimination at work, such as the glass cliff. They can develop training programs for both men and women to make them aware of the barriers women meet in organizations (Bruckmüller et al., 2014). They should also identify role models for women in their sport organization.

ful framework in order to study the situations of females in executive boards in sport. Earlier, men were not involved in the work for more females in organizations, and they were simply seen as the ones responsible for the low number of females in governance. Therefore, men were previously a part of the problem and are now consequently a crucial part of the solution. Now there is an emerging trend to cooperate with powerful men to have more success in increasing the number of women in leadership roles (Adriaanse & Schofield, 2014; Connell, 2009; Skirstad, 2009). In this way, the pool of potential leaders and board member talents grows. Influential male directors can undo gender inequality by appointing women to prestigious and responsible tasks. To give women with competence and talent responsibility is logical. Male endorsement and support are important factors in helping achieving gender equality. For women, role models play an important part, and the male managers can help with providing them role models in their organization.

When society in general is ripe for changes, changes in sport will happen as a continued process. The single most important incident in Scandinavian politics after World War II was the increase in female representation (Karvonen & Selle, 1995). This happened in the 1970s in politics and in the late 1980s in sport in Norway (Skirstad, 2009). Pettigrew's contextual approach explains how processes outside and inside sport, key actors, and specific incidents can affect the representation of females in sport organizations.

Gender equity policies can use laws, targets, quotas, and equal pay as tools to increase female representation. Most important is that gender mainstreaming is being consolidated in organizations in tasks for men and women alike.

Review Questions

1. Why should organizations concern themselves with gender diversity?
2. Why is it necessary for sport managers to have knowledge of gender concepts in sport organizations?
3. Which three theoretical perspectives can be used to explain the situation of females in governance in sport organizations?
4. Select a sport organization with which you are familiar and explain efforts that have been made in that organization to address gender inequalities.

Suggestions for Further Reading

The following suggestions for further research on topics on gender and organizations have been formulated as questions you may ask yourself in pursuing further study on the topic.

1. How do women in higher levels of management (queen bees) in sport organizations see their special responsibility to help other women to ascend? By researching this, one can get a better understanding of what kind of help they can expect (Baumgartner & Schneider, 2010).
2. Why do the old boys' networks persist, and how do the new boys see the challenge with female managers? What effective strategies exist to fight the old boys' network and make it more gender inclusive (Walker & Sartore-Baldwin, 2013)?
3. How can we get the viewpoint of family members or work colleagues who know these successful female leaders? What might this tell us about why these women were successful (Baumgartner & Schneider, 2010)?
4. What causes glass cliff appointments or elections in sport? Can we examine the leadership selection process in sport by looking into archival studies (Burton, 2015)?
5. How can we develop awareness of recruiting and search processes in sport governance (Adriaanse & Schofield, 2014)?
6. How can we examine the public exposure of gender relations in the media (Schull, Shaw, & Kihl, 2013)? Can we use focus groups to encourage women to talk in depth about their experiences as they have climbed upward in the sport system? Would this likely have revealed a much more complex dynamic among women in the field (Whiteside & Hardin, 2012)?
7. How can we analyze the merger of gender-affiliated sport organizations in light of a gender specific process? What are the different stages of the process (Kihl, Shaw, & Schull, 2013)? What can that teach us about how females and males behave within organizations, which are highly gendered contexts (Schull, Shaw, & Kihl, 2013)?
8. Do spectators' ratings contribute to the lower pay of female tennis players in less prestigious tournaments (Fink, Parker, Cunningham, & Cuneen, 2012)?

9. How can you explain the gender situation in a sport organization you know? Alvesson and Billing's (2009) *Understanding Gender and Organizations* is a very relevant book and gives a reflective and multilevel approach to basic themes in gender and organization. Further, the book considers alternative aspects, interpretations, and approaches as well as limitations and shortcomings.
10. How do we understand quotas and equality policies in sport organizations (Dahlerup, 2013)?

In addition to sport management journals, one should also read the journals *Sex Roles* and *Gender and Society*, sociological journals, and organizational journals such as *Organizational Studies* and *Academy of Management Review*.

Case for Analysis

Gender Equity Policies in Sport

A study of women in sport shows a history of exclusion. Substantial resistance against women was voiced by Coubertin, the founder of the modern Olympic Games, who did not want women to take part. According to him, the only role women should have was to applaud and honor the medal winners. He defined the Games in 1912 in Olympic Review as "the solemn and periodic exaltation of male athleticism, with internationalism as a base, loyalty as a means, art of its setting, and female applause as reward" (DeFrantz, 1997, p. 18). The official report of the 1912 Games in Stockholm stated, with Coubertin's approval, that "an Olympiad with females would be impractical, uninteresting, unaesthetic and improper" (Boulongne, 2000, p. 23). Coubertin's view on women's participation in sports was of course marked by his upbringing, education, class, and time.

In 1960 women from Australia, the United States, and the United Socialist Soviet Republic presented a proposal about female representation to the IOC during the Olympic Games in Rome, but nothing happened. One of the first issues the IOC president Samaranch took on after having gained power in 1980 was the women's issue. Several speakers at the Baden-Baden Conference in 1981 signaled that they wanted to have female participants as IOC members. In 1981 the first women, Pirjo Hägman from Finland and Flor Isava-Fonesca from Venezuela, were co-opted (Olympic Review, 1981). At this conference, Samaranch gave the signal that women ought to get into the decision-making body. He stated, "I should mention here perhaps that the Executive Board plans to propose at our next Session the nomination of several women as members of the IOC" (Samaranch, 1981, p. 606).

These plans about involving women in the IOC as members was a wise strategic act by the newly elected president Samaranch. What the IOC did was to react to wider social trends, at least in Europe. At the 85th Session in 1982 Samaranch greeted the women with, "Welcome among us, Ladies: may I express the hope that many others will soon join you!" (Samaranch, 1982, p. 315). The Women and Sport Working Group was established in 1995 with Anita DeFrantz as chair, and its task was to advise the executive board of IOC on suitable policies in the field. In 1996 at the centennial conference IOC recommended that the female members should make up at least 10 percent of the boards in all the NOCs, international federations, and sport organizations that belong to the Olympic family by the end of year 2000. The deadline for this was extended to the end of 2001. The share should increase to 20 percent by the end of 2005. In 2004 the status of the working group was upgraded to a Commission, signaling that the work is of a more permanent character (Skirstad, 2004).

IOC president Rogge said at the international women's sport conference in Norway in 2001 that more women were needed, and his successor Bach repeated the same 13 years later in Finland. At the 6th International Women and Sport Conference in 2014, IOC president Bach, after describing the increased participation of women in the Olympic Games, insisted that the IOC "must do more" to bring women into sport leadership roles at all levels. He said, "We have seen what women can do on the field of play and now we need their intellect, energy and creativity in the administration and management of sport as well." He continued, "As a sports organisation we cannot force countries to change their legislation, but what we can do is give a shining example to the world of how a society based on the core belief of equality should operate" (Bach, 2014).

Questions

1. Discuss what the IOC has done to advance females in leading sport positions.
2. Discuss what the IOC can do to further equality in their member countries.
3. As a sport manager, what can you do to create gender equality in your organization?
4. Discuss the positive and negative aspects of gender equality politics.

CHAPTER 12

Volunteers in Sport Organizations

Graham Cuskelly, PhD

Learning Objectives

After reading this chapter you should be able to

1. understand the nature and extent of volunteerism in sport and the roles of volunteers in sport, and differentiate between core and peripheral volunteers;
2. describe the volunteer life cycle and its application to sport volunteers;
3. explain how organizational commitment and psychological contracts have been applied to understanding the relationships that develop between volunteers and sport organizations;
4. outline the processes involved in volunteer management and have an appreciation of the limitations of applying formal management principles to sport volunteers; and
5. understand interrelationships between volunteers and paid staff in sport organizations.

Key Concepts

affective commitment
continuance commitment
core volunteers
dimensions of volunteerism
free choice
human resource management (HRM)
intended beneficiaries
normative commitment
organizational commitment
peripheral volunteers
psychological contract
relational contract
remuneration
structure (formal and informal)
transactional contract
volunteerism
volunteer life cycle
volunteer management cycle
volunteer recruitment
volunteer retention

Growing Pains at Westport Football Club

Geoff Cootes is a long-standing member of Westport Youth Football Club (known as Westport FC), starting out as a coach when his child started playing association football. Over the past 15 years Geoff has held a number of committee and coaching positions and has always been willing to help out. Under the leadership of President Natasha Scott, the club developed a strategic plan and expanded rapidly over the course of three years from 320 registered players to 550. The club is performing well with all volunteer positions filled, harmonious working relationships, and a strong financial position.

At the time of Natasha's appointment, Geoff accepted the newly created position as coaching operations coordinator. In this voluntary position he is responsible for coordinating the recruitment, development, and performance management of 50 volunteer coaches as well as the allocation of team uniforms and training facilities. A little over a year ago, Geoff retired from his paid employment as a senior project manager. At Westport FC he volunteers many hours and is frequently at the club on training nights and games on both days of the weekend, more so since he retired from paid employment. Geoff enjoys his role and is well liked. Almost everyone around the club sees Geoff as the go-to guy. He rarely complains about how many hours he puts in, but about six months ago the strain started to show.

Aware that the position of coaching operations coordinator had become too large the Westport FC management committee met to consider its options. The three most viable options are to

1. separate the coaching and operations components of the position into two volunteer positions;
2. create two volunteer coaching and operations coordinator positions: one for the younger age group teams with less than 11 players (pathway association football) and the other for teams with 11 players each (competitive football); or
3. appoint a paid employee as the coaching and operations coordinator.

After a lengthy discussion the management committee decided to appoint a paid employee. The time had come to reduce the workload on volunteers and take a more professional approach to the program. With that decision made there needed to be a decision about whether to approach Geoff and offer him the position or to advertise the position. The management committee was evenly divided between appointing Geoff and openly advertising the position of director of coaching.

There is little debate about the centrality and importance of volunteers in the production and delivery of sport participation programs and sport events in communities throughout the world. Volunteers are an integral human resource in sport development and delivery systems. It would be difficult to comprehend a sport system without the involvement of volunteers at any level of sport, whether it is sport for development projects in economically underdeveloped nations, a local hockey or swim club, or a mega-event broadcast to billions of people around the globe such as the World Cup or the Olympic Games. Sport in the form of activities, programs, competitions, services, and events is delivered to players, spectators, sport club members, and the wider community largely through the time, effort, and skills of volunteers. This is not to downplay the importance of sport policy and funding bodies such as Sport Canada or Sport Australia, or the strategic role that sport national governing bodies such as Hockey Canada play in setting the overall direction and governance of sport. Without a policy framework, strategic direction and leadership, and the financial resources and infrastructure provided by all levels of government, there is little doubt that sport organizations and the sport system would be much less developed than they are today. However, the capacity and capability of the sport system to deliver sport, at the grassroots level in particular, is determined to a large extent by the passion, participation, and performance of volunteers.

Sport Volunteerism Defined

In order to understand **volunteerism** in sport it is necessary to define sport volunteering and understand the dimensionality of a widely used but sometimes ill-defined term. Individuals are often defined by their role as a volunteer in sport as a coach, team manager, committee member, or general helper. As long as they are not remunerated for their work they are generally considered to be volunteers. Such operational definitions fail to recognize the nuances and complexities of accurately defining volunteering. For example, to what extent is sport volunteering freely chosen? A parent of a young swimmer may feel obligated or even coerced into taking a volunteer role when his or her child joins a swim team for the first time. And if a direct beneficiary of volunteering is one's own family member should this activity be considered volunteering? And what if a volunteer is offered a stipend or some form of payment by their sport club to cover the costs of undertaking his or her role as a volunteer?

The International Labour Organization (ILO, 2011, p. 13) defined volunteer work as "unpaid non-compulsory work; that is time individuals give without pay to activities performed either through an organization or directly for those outside their own household." The ILO reviewed a number of international definitions of volunteering in the development of their definition and found some level of consensus of what it means to volunteer. Most definitions referred to a freely chosen and unpaid service or activity that is for the benefit of the environment, community, or people who were not living in the same household. Consensus was less evident in relation to the motives or purpose of volunteering and the question of whether volunteering includes direct help to others or only activities undertaken within a nonprofit organization. Notably, while the ILO definition does not include a motivation or purpose for volunteering, it does include reference to others outside their household.

The dimensionality of volunteering was first captured by Cnaan, Handy, and Wadsworth (1996), who developed a conceptual framework that identified four **dimensions of volunteering**. The frequently cited framework of Cnaan et al. is helpful in understanding the term *volunteering* because it recognizes that a wide variety of behaviors can categorize someone as a volunteer. The four dimensions are as follows.

- **Free choice** in which volunteering can vary between free will to relatively un-coerced to obligation to volunteer.
- **Remuneration** ranges from none at all to none expected to reimbursement of expenses to a stipend or low pay.
- **Intended beneficiaries** extends from benefiting strangers to benefiting friends or relatives to benefiting oneself.
- **Structure** accounts for both formal (organizational) and informal settings.

The dimensions of volunteering are displayed graphically in figure 12.1. The structure dimension sits outside the three other dimensions because no continuum exists for this dimension. Structure is either a formal or an informal setting. Applying this conceptual framework to sport volunteerism, volunteering is perhaps most accurately characterized as an activity in which the intended beneficiary is predominantly strangers, and it takes place in a formal setting (e.g., a sport club or event), without any expectation of remuneration, and of one's own free will. A benefit of the Cnaan et al. framework is its tolerance for categorizing a range of behaviors across several dimensions as volunteering. No clearly defined boundaries exist between what is and is not volunteering in each dimension. The further one's involvement moves away from the innermost circle in figure 12.1, the less likely one is considered to be volunteering. However, in the characterization of sport volunteering outlined here it is not necessary to exclude, for example, volunteering in which expenses are remunerated or an act of volunteering in which the beneficiaries includes one's friends or relatives.

Size, Nature, and Scope of Volunteering in Sport

It has been acknowledged that volunteers are a vital human resource in the capacity of the sport system to deliver services to members, participants, and spectators in settings as diverse as a local basketball club to a major international sport event. In order to understand the scale of volunteerism and the enormity of the volunteer management challenge in sport it is necessary to grasp the size, nature, and scope of volunteer involvement in sport. Statistics from national and international studies of volunteering help describe the numbers and rates of volunteer involvement, the scope of volunteer work, and the characteristics of volunteers themselves.

The numbers of rates of volunteering, expressed as a percentage of total volunteers or the population, suggest that sport volunteering is among the main types of organizations for which people volunteer. Based on 2010 Statistics Canada research, Vézina and Crompton (2012), reported that 12 percent

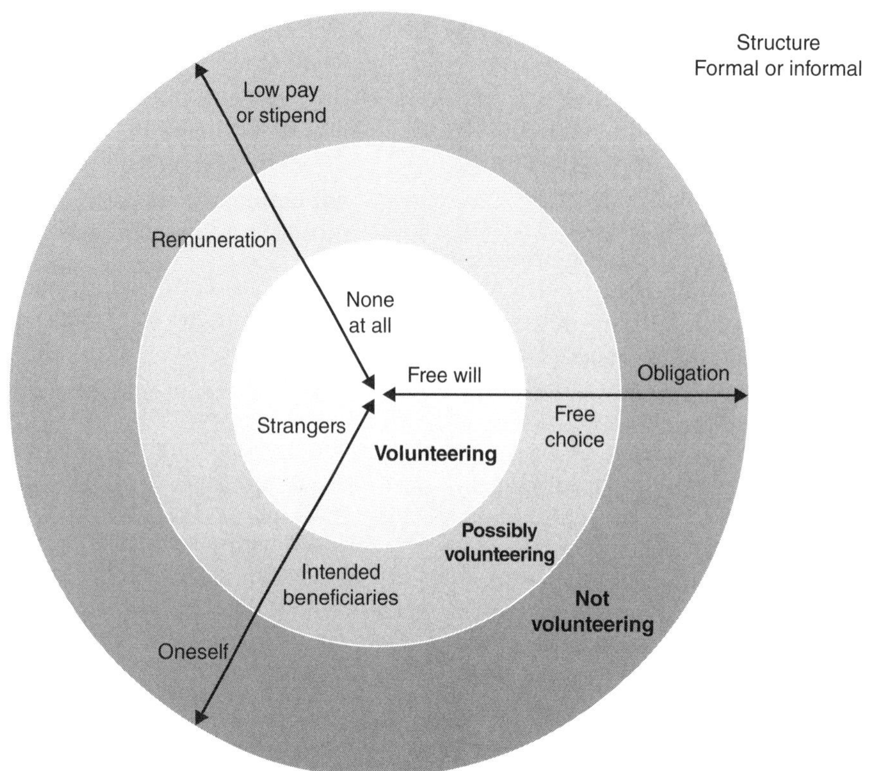

Figure 12.1 Dimensions of volunteering.

Based on Cnaan, Handy, Wadsworth, et al. (1996); and inspired by Paine, Hill, and Rochester (2010).

of Canadians aged 15 years and over volunteered for sport and recreation organizations. This was equivalent to social services and exceeded education and research (10 percent), religion (9 percent), and health (6 percent). Canadian volunteers gave the highest average number of hours to sport and recreation (120 hours per year), which was slightly higher than religion (116 hours) and social services (116 hours) but more than twice as many hours than those dedicated to education and research (66 hours) (Vézina and Crompton, 2012). Similar patterns of volunteer participation were evident in Australia (Australian Bureau of Statistics, 2010). Around 14 percent of Australians aged 18 years and over (2.3 million persons) were involved in sport and physical recreation organizations. This exceeded volunteering for religious organizations (8 percent), community and welfare organizations (8 percent), and education and training organizations (7 percent).

Volunteerism in sport appears to be associated with particular demographic variables and socioeconomic disadvantage. Among the Australian population (Australian Bureau of Statistics, 2010) sport and recreation volunteering is associated with:

- *Age and sex*: Males (15 percent) volunteer at a slightly higher rate than females (12 percent). Highest volunteer participation rates are evident amongst 25- to 34-year-olds (20 percent) and 35- to 44-year-olds (20 percent) and lowest among 18- to 24-year-olds (8 percent) and those aged 65 years and over (6 percent).
- *Family and household type*: Higher rates of volunteering are evident in households of couples with children under 15 years (23 percent) compared to all other family and household types (6 percent to 14 percent).
- *Participation in the workforce*: The rate of volunteering is 17 percent for persons employed compared to 7 percent for those who are not in the labor force and less than 4 percent of unemployed persons.
- *Socioeconomic disadvantage*: Based on Australian Bureau of Statistics (ABS) index of relative socioeconomic disadvantage, participation in volunteering rises from a rate of 9 percent for persons in the lowest quintile to 18 percent for those in the highest quintile.
- *Country of birth*: Persons born in Australia volunteer at a rate of 17 percent compared to 12 percent of those born in other main English-speaking countries (e.g., Canada, Ireland, New Zealand, South Africa, United States, and United Kingdom) and less than 5 percent for those born in other countries.

KEY ISSUES FOR SPORT MANAGERS

Volunteers tend to be viewed as a homogeneous group who volunteer in sport for similar reasons. Sport managers need to be mindful of the multidimensionality of volunteering and that volunteers come from a wide variety of sociodemographic backgrounds. This suggests that working with and managing sport volunteers is no less complex than working with paid employees.

Sport volunteers tend to stay involved in sport for a number of years. Earlier research on volunteering by the ABS (2006) reported that more than half of sport and recreation volunteers (59 percent) had been volunteering for more than 10 years and fewer than 5 percent had been volunteering for less than one year. The same ABS (2006) research reported frequency of volunteering. The majority of sport and recreation volunteers reported that they volunteered at least once per week (58 percent), 24 percent volunteered at least once per month, and the remainder volunteered less frequently. Statistics Canada (2009, p. 41) differentiated what they described as "top volunteers" or the "25% of volunteers who volunteered 171 hours or more annually and accounted for 78% of all volunteer hours." While sport and recreation volunteers were not differentiated within this group, top volunteers were described as a key resource for charitable and nonprofit organizations. The notion of top volunteers illustrates that the time that volunteers contribute to sport organizations varies widely, and without a group of core volunteers it may be difficult for organizations to function effectively.

Core and Peripheral Volunteers

The nature and extent of volunteering, particularly in terms of hours volunteered and the number of years involved in volunteering, raises questions about different patterns of volunteer participation in sport. Why do volunteers in the same organization contribute substantially more or less hours than other volunteers, and why do some volunteers stay involved for a number of years whereas others take only short-term assignments? One explanation for differential patterns of volunteer involvement is the idea that there are core and peripheral volunteers.

Pearce (1993) first distinguished and characterized core and peripheral volunteers, and Cuskelly, Hoye, and Auld (2006) applied this conceptualization to sport volunteers. **Core volunteers** tend to exhibit higher levels of involvement and commitment than those described as peripheral volunteers. Core volunteers are often seen as the leaders or coordinators and are sometimes referred to as the go-to person in a sport organization, not unlike Geoff Cootes in our opening case study. Such volunteers frequently take on roles as board or committee members, put more time into sport organizations than other volunteers, and feel that their "work is more demanding" (Pearce, 1993, p. 49). **Peripheral volunteers** have lower levels of involvement and commitment but are not necessarily languid. They often have a desire to help others and are steady contributors but want to avoid being overcommitted. While the boundary between peripheral and core volunteers is fluid (Pearce, 1993), peripheral volunteers are likely to take on casual and informally defined roles in sport organizations and may well be reliable contributors. In essence, it is the core volunteers who provide structure, direction, and stability to sport organizations, enabling programs and services to be delivered often with the assistance of less involved and committed peripheral volunteers.

Ringuet-Riot, Cuskelly, Auld, and Zakus (2014) recognized that the concepts of involvement and commitment are key to understanding core and peripheral volunteers. They used cluster analysis to classify sport volunteers as either core or peripheral volunteers and found empirical evidence of significant differences between the level of involvement and commitment of core and peripheral volunteers. Compared to peripheral volunteers, core volunteers were more highly involved and committed both to their role and to their sport organization, made greater contributions to governance (planning and decision-making), and contributed more hours to the day-to-day work of their sport organization. Ringuet-Riot et al. reported no significant differences between core and peripheral volunteers' age, sex, employment status, or level of educational attainment.

Volunteer Life Cycle

Because volunteerism in sport generally takes place in organizational settings, it is necessary to understand how connections between volunteers and sport organizations are initiated, developed, and eventually discontinued. Volunteer engagement in sport organizations varies enormously, and the concept of a volunteer life cycle may help explain some of this variability. Bussell and Forbes (2003) argued that marketing techniques are playing an ever more important role as voluntary organizations and developed the volunteer life cycle (see figure 12.2). The **volunteer life cycle** describes four stages in the volunteer journey.

- Determinants of volunteering
- Decision to volunteer
- Volunteer activity
- The committed volunteer

At the volunteering determinants stage organizations need to understand that volunteers have a wide variety of motivations for volunteering. Attracting volunteers involves a process of creating awareness and interest primarily through marketing communications tools and tapping into the motivation of volunteers, which is not always altruism. People may also volunteer to develop skills or for social or egotistical reasons. People may exit at this stage due to other commitments, because their needs are not being met, or because their needs can be met elsewhere.

The stage of deciding to volunteer is largely focused on matching the needs of the organization with that of the volunteer as part of the recruitment process. Bussell and Forbes (2003) found that organizations used a number of communication tools to recruit volunteers, the most effective method being word of mouth. Individuals who are successfully recruited enter the third stage of the volunteer life cycle—volunteer activity. Here the emphasis moves to volunteer management, discussed later in this chapter. A critical aspect of the volunteer activity stage is that the needs and motives of volunteers may change over time. What initially attracted a volunteer to a sport organization might not necessarily sustain ongoing involvement. Volunteers may also exit an organization at any time, and the factors that influence the decision to leave are often beyond the control of the organization. Family and personal circumstances, paid employment, and living arrangements, among other factors, often change and may result in a volunteer leaving the organization or reducing his or her level of engagement.

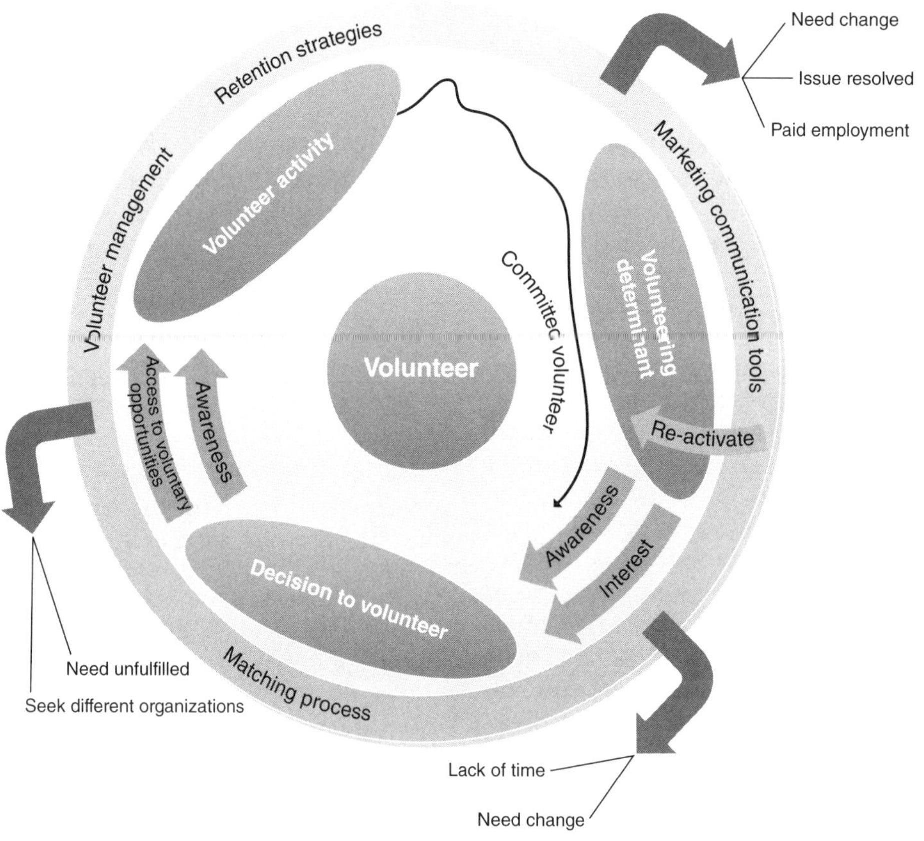

Figure 12.2 The volunteer life cycle.

Reprinted by permission from H. Bussell and D. Forbes, "The Volunteer Life Cycle: A Marketing Model for Volunteering," *Voluntary Action* 5, no. 3 (2003): 61-79.

At the fourth and final stage of the volunteer life cycle is the committed volunteer. The attraction, recruitment, and management strategies used in earlier stages of the life cycle need to switch to retention strategies that enable a volunteer to more strongly identify with and become more deeply engaged in a sport organization or sport event, particularly an event that operates on a regular basis. Committed volunteers often become advocates for sport organizations and recruit other volunteers. As discussed previously committed volunteers are more likely to make the shift from peripheral to core volunteering. The concept of commitment is introduced in the next section from the perspective of organizational commitment.

Organizational Commitment

Organizational commitment is a form of attachment to an organization that is characterized as a sense of identification, involvement, and loyalty to an organization or a role within an organization (Buchanan, 1974). In mainstream management literature, higher levels of organizational commitment have been shown to predict improved job performance and citizenship behavior, as well as lower levels of absenteeism, intention to leave, and turnover (Carbery, Garavan, O'Brien, & McDonnell, 2003; Fuller, Barnett, Hester, & Relyea, 2003; Mathieu & Zajac, 1990; Meyer & Allen, 1997). Organizational commitment among sport volunteers has received increasing attention in the literature in recent years. Studies of sport volunteers have explored links between organizational commitment and leader–member exchange, job satisfaction, work conditions, job performance, motivation, committee functioning, intention to stay or leave, retention, and proposed models to explain the development and consequences of commitment (Bang, Ross, & Reio, 2013; Cuskelly, McIntyre, & Boag, 1998; Egli, Schlesinger, & Nagel, 2014; Engelberg, Skinner, & Zakus, 2011; Engelberg, Zakus, Skinner, & Campbell, 2012; Hoye, 2007; Park & Kim, 2013; Schlesinger, Egli, & Nagel, 2013). Engelberg et al. (2011) found that commitment to a volunteer role is related to a sport volunteer's identity, which is closely linked to time devoted to organizational activities. Commitment is positively correlated with job performance for board members "who have or are serving as leaders, perform better and have higher levels of affective commitment to the board" (Stephens, Dawley, & Stephens, 2004, p. 496). Based on Meyer and Allen's (1997) three-component model of commitment and Kohlberg's (1969) moral development model, Park and Kim (2013) developed a hierarchical model of the development of organizational commitment among sport volunteers. Their model drew parallels with the six stages of Kohlberg's model of moral development, and they argued that in the higher stages, the organizational commitment of volunteers is more internalized and psychological, and they represent more favorable attitudes toward a sport organization.

Following is Park and Kim's (2013) hierarchy, along with the corresponding stages of Kohlberg's model.

1. *Primitive commitment*: This lowest level of commitment is similar to Kohlberg's stage 1, obedience and punishment orientation.
2. *Continuance commitment*: This level corresponds to Kohlberg's stage 2, naively egoistic and exchange orientation.
3. *External commitment*: This level of external commitment has parallels with Kohlberg's stages 3 and 4, orientation to approval and to pleasing others and orientation to "doing duty" and regard for earned expectations of others.
4. *Normative commitment*: This level could correspond to Kohlberg's stage 5, contractual legalistic orientation.
5. *Affective commitment*: At the most invested level, people display affective commitment, which matches Kohlberg's stage 6, conscience or principle orientation.

Mowday, Porter, and Steers (1982, p. 27) described organizational commitment as "the relative strength of an individual's identification with and involvement in a particular organization, "which is characterized by (a) a strong belief in and acceptance of the organization's goals and values; (b) a willingness to exert considerable effort on behalf of the organization; and (c) a strong desire to maintain membership in the organization." The concept of commitment has origins in several theories that attempt to explain involvement in social organizations. Theories developed a number of decades ago by Kelman (1958), Etzioni (1961), and Kanter (1968) provide a basis for understanding the development of linkages between individuals and organizations. Etzioni (1961) argued that organizations must continually recruit participants with a positive orientation to organizational power and argued that associations between power and involvement constitute categories of compliance relationships. Because voluntary organizations do not have coercive or remunerative power over volunteers, normative power is used to encourage volunteers to comply with organizational goals. Using Etzioni's terms, volunteer involvement is moral in contrast to the alienative or calculative.

Kelman (1958) postulated that although the same behavior may be observed in different individuals, three processes—compliance, identification, and internalization—lead to such behavior. In the context of a sport organization, an individual may initially decide to volunteer to be compliant with the expectation of gaining the approval of others such as friends or family members who may be participating in sport. Continuing to volunteer may lead to the development of a sense of identification with the organization and its members. Internalization is a process in which a high degree of alignment develops between the value system of a volunteer and an organization. Kanter (1968) identified three mechanisms that strengthen commitment: continuance, cohesion, and control. Continuance is about making personal sacrifices to join or stay with an organization. Cohesion describes commitment based on social relationships within an organization, and control commitment develops when an individual adopts the norms and values of an organization as his or her own, thereby deepening their sense of commitment.

Organizational commitment may develop in relation to a number of targets (Reichers, 1986), including a particular constituency (e.g., a team within a sport club), a role (e.g., volunteer coach), or the wider organization (e.g., a sport organization), and has both an attitudinal and a behavioral basis. From an employee perspective, Mowday et al. (1982) asserted that organizational commitment begins to develop prior to organizational entry (anticipation), through early employment (initiation) to mid- and later-career stages (entrenchment). They argued that behavioral and attitudinal commitment are cyclical and self-reinforcing processes. In contrast, from a behavioral perspective, Becker (1960) viewed commitment as consistent lines of activity, rejections of alternative behaviors, and the sunk costs or nontransferable benefits associated with long-term organizational membership. In other words, the act of volunteering becomes patterned or habitual.

Widely cited work by Meyer and Allen (1997) developed a comprehensive model of organizational commitment with three components: affective, continuance, and normative. **Affective commitment** is characterized as emotional attachment evident in feelings of loyalty, belongingness, and affection, and embodies the notion that individuals become committed because they *want to*. **Continuance commitment**, sometimes described as calculative

KEY ISSUES FOR SPORT MANAGERS

Commitment is an important concept in understanding volunteering particularly longer term because sport organizations do not have remunerative or coercive power over volunteers. The strength of an individual's identification with and involvement in a sport organization are positively associated with time devoted to volunteer tasks and the quality of the work they complete.

TIME OUT

Determinants of Long-Term Volunteering in Sports Clubs

In a study of volunteers in Swiss sports clubs Schlesinger, Egli, and Nagel (2013) studied whether subjective expectations, volunteer job satisfaction, and volunteer commitment influenced the tendency for long-term volunteers to continue or terminate volunteering in their sport club. They found that job satisfaction and the orientation toward collective solidarity were the strongest determinants of long-term voluntary commitment. Having children who belong to the club also had a positive influence on voluntary commitment. They argued that the opportunity costs are probably lower when one's own children are actively involved in one's club. However, length of volunteering had a negative effect on long-term commitment, which Schlesinger et al. argued may be a sign of saturation. Relating their findings to earlier research by Braun (2003) and Cuskelly, McIntyre, & Boag (1998) they concluded that "the attachment of volunteers to their club and their increasing familiarization with obligations of solidarity and reciprocity can be interpreted as an outcome of a long-term club specific socialization process" (Schlesinger et al., 2013, p. 48).

commitment, suggests that individuals become committed because they *have to*, whether as a result of a lack of alternatives or the sacrifice of a high level of sunk costs that would be incurred by leaving an organization. **Normative commitment** results from a feeling that one *ought to* be committed and is described as a sense of duty or obligation in which an individual internalizes the mission, goals, and values of an organization not unlike control commitment (Kanter, 1968) and internalization (Kelman, 1958) described earlier. Meyer and Allen (1997) postulated that each component of commitment develops simultaneously but as a result of quite different influences. Cuskelly, Boag, and McIntyre (1999) found that paid employees in sport had significantly higher levels of continuance (calculative) commitment than did volunteers and concluded that the nature and intensity of organizational commitment was qualitatively different for volunteers and paid staff in sport.

Psychological Contract and Volunteers

The concept of psychological contract provides a different perspective for understanding the relationship between volunteers and sport organizations. Unlike employees, volunteers are rarely made a formal offer of employment. When an employee joins an organization, a written formal agreement, often in the form of an employment contract, specifies the nature and extent of the rights and responsibilities of both parties to the contract. Beyond any formal contract, employees also develop a psychological contract (Rousseau, 1989). In contrast, volunteers may receive a position description but are rarely presented with any formally documented agreement when they first take up a position as a volunteer. Therefore, the relationship between a volunteer and a sport organization is, to a large extent, based on an implicit set of promises and expectations known as a **psychological contract**.

The foundation of the psychological contract is social exchange theory and can be traced back to work by Argyris (1960) and Levinson (1962). Rousseau (1989, p. 23) described psychological contract as "an individual's beliefs regarding the terms of conditions of a reciprocal exchange agreement between the focal person and another party." Psychological contract is a cognitive state that is both subjective and interpretative. It refers to the development and maintenance of the relationship between an individual and an organization and is beyond what is formally agreed. Rousseau and Tijoriwala (1998, p. 679) defined psychological contract as

> the individual's belief in mutual obligations between the person and another party such as an employer. This belief is predicated on the perception that a promise has been made (e.g. of employment or career opportunities) and a consideration offered in exchange for it (e.g. accepting a position, forgoing other job offers), binding the parties to some set of reciprocal obligations.

Two types of psychological contracts exist—transactional and relational—and both can characterize the same contract. **Transactional contracts** are based on the exchange of economic currency in which the organization provides wages or a salary, a work guarantee, and a safe workplace in exchange for specified the time, effort, and skills of an employee. **Relational contracts** are based on socioemotional currency and include job security, supportive training, and sense of community in exchange for loyalty, commitment, and involvement.

Research of the psychological contract in volunteer settings generally and in sport settings specifically is a relatively recent development. Farmer and Fedor (1999) found that the psychological contract has a limited effect on volunteer participation and no effect on withdrawal. Liao-Troth (2005, p. 512) argued that understanding the nature of psychological contracts perceived by volunteers is important because it "provides a categorization system that explains what type of relationship the volunteer believes she or he has with the organization: explicit exchange or long-term loyalty." Furthermore, fulfillment, breach, or violation of the psychological contract affects individuals' attitudes and behavior toward the organization (Conway & Briner, 2005). Taylor, Darcy, Hoye, and Cuskelly (2006) found that sport club administrators expected volunteers to adhere to professional, legal, and regulatory standards, whereas volunteers sought rewarding work in a social environment, suggesting a mismatch between the organizational and volunteer expectations. Critical of studies (e.g., Nichols, 2012; Nichols & Ojala, 2009; Vantilborgh et al., 2012) that applied employee-based frameworks to volunteer settings, Harman and Doherty (2014) conducted qualitative interviews with volunteer coaches in youth sport. They found that volunteer coaches had both relational and transactional expectations of themselves and of their organization.

TIME OUT

Psychological Contract of Youth Sport Coaches

Volunteer coaches are a vital human resource in the sport system. In Canada, for example, two million people volunteer as youth sport coaches. Having sport programs delivered by qualified coaches is highlighted in the Canadian Sport Policy. Harman and Doherty (2014) argued that it is important to understand factors in the coaching environment that may affect the development of coaches' attitudes and behavior. They investigated the factors that influenced content and variation in the development of the psychological contract among youth sport coaches in team sport settings, based on gender, level of play (recreational or competitive), and coach tenure (novice or experienced). Harman and Doherty found evidence that the development of psychological contract is both context- and role-specific, and coaches had expectations of themselves and their club. The coaches' expectations of themselves were to provide technical expertise and team administration (both transactional) as well as leadership, professionalism, and a positive experience for their athletes (relational). Coaches' expectations of their clubs were the provision of fundamental sport resources (e.g., scheduling games and practices, providing necessary equipment, arranging for referees), club administration (both transactional), and coach support (relational) in terms of guidance, communication, and autonomy. Coach tenure appeared to contribute more than gender or level of play to variations in the development of psychological contract. Harman and Doherty concluded that a coach's relationship with the club evolves over time and that the transactional and relationship elements of psychological contracts can and do vary independently of one another.

Volunteer Management

This chapter has focused largely on volunteerism in sport from the perspective of volunteers and how and why volunteers develop relationships with sport organizations. Given that volunteerism is so ubiquitous in sport, it is necessary to also consider sport volunteerism from an organizational perspective. Put simply, sport organizations need to be able to recruit, develop, and retain volunteers in order to deliver the programs, activities, and services expected by sport participants. However, Sport England (2002, p. 17) identified "shortages of volunteers; a problem in recruiting new volunteers; and consequently the loading of the required voluntary tasks on to fewer people" as three main challenges confronting sport. Agencies responsible for sport policy and development, including government and sport national governing bodies, have addressed these challenges by recommending the application of more formalized approaches to volunteer management. Resource kits and programs such as Clubmark (Sport England) advocate the application of **human resource management (HRM)** practices commonly used in the management of paid employees and what we refer to here as volunteer management.

Volunteer management is a cyclical process involving planning, recruitment, selection, induction, training, management, recognition, and retention or replacement of volunteers. The **volunteer management cycle** is displayed in figure 12.3 and briefly outlined here. Because a certain level of volunteer turnover is to be expected, sport organizations need to ensure they have sufficient capacity to be able to continue to deliver their programs, services, and activities. Planning begins by analyzing current and future needs for volunteers to establish whether the organization has a sufficient number of volunteers with appropriate skills and qualifications. Identifying capacity issues enables the organization to know where gaps and skills shortages are before entering into a process of recruiting volunteers. In sports clubs, **volunteer recruitment** is usually an informal process in which the organization tries to match the skills, qualifications, and experience of potential volunteers to a particular position. For operational level positions (e.g., coaching or managing a team) volunteers are usually appointed to their position. However, for committee or board positions, most sport organizations are bound by their constitution to run elections. Members might be invited to nominate and run for office for a particular position (e.g., chairperson), but beyond that the usual volunteer recruitment practices do not apply. Because voluntary sport organizations are democratic institutions, elected officials are not always those with the most appropriate skills and experience for the position to which they are elected. The selection process is used to appoint an individual that best meets the requirements of a position and fits with the culture, values, and goals of the organization

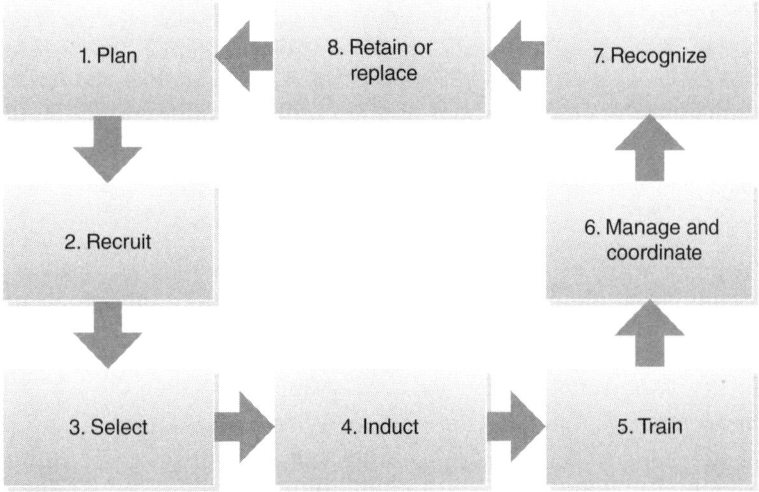

Figure 12.3 The volunteer management cycle.
Adapted from Cuskelly and Auld (1999).

(Chelladurai, 2009). It is mandatory in many jurisdictions for volunteers working with children to undergo criminal background checks. The selection process also enables an organization to identify any required training needs (e.g., coaching certification or renewal of certification) or to take the opportunity to check the currency and validity of a volunteer's current qualifications.

Induction is an important part of the volunteer management cycle, particularly for volunteers that are completely new to an organization. It is a process of familiarizing a volunteer with their role as well as the structure and operation of the organization. Even informal induction processes if conducted in an appropriate manner will help a volunteer feel welcome and a part of the organization. The induction process presents an additional opportunity to identify training needs and opportunities as a volunteer becomes more familiar with the requirements of his or her position. The management and coordination of volunteers is critical to the satisfaction and retention of volunteers. Volunteer management programs referred to earlier recommend the appointment of a volunteer coordinator. Successful sport organizations understand that motivation is a critical factor in managing volunteers. Motivation is a large and complex topic and beyond the scope of this chapter. However, sport organizations need to be aware of what different volunteers see as important and that volunteers seek to do something worthwhile and challenging. Recognizing volunteers for their time and effort is closely linked to motivation and satisfaction, but not all volunteers will respond in the same way to being recognized for their contributions.

The final stage of the volunteer management cycle is largely concerned with balancing the need for continuity in a sport organization (**volunteer retention**) with the opportunity for the organization to adapt and respond to changing circumstances (volunteer replacement). Volunteers who are retained are more likely to become part of the core group of volunteers who are more highly committed and involved and will add a sense of stability to a sport organization. Using an HRM perspective, Cuskelly, Taylor, Hoye, and Darcy (2006) developed a volunteer management inventory (VMI) and investigated the efficacy of volunteer management practices in the retention of volunteers in community rugby clubs. They found clubs that implemented planning, training, and support practices reported significantly fewer problems in the retention of volunteers. The hypothesized VMI contained seven latent HRM constructs, which were tested using confirmatory factor analysis. All 36 items are displayed in table 12.1.

Performance management is a critical component of HRM in employment settings, and it has not been left out of the volunteer management cycle because it lacks importance. Pearce (1993, p. 179) argued that volunteer performance can be managed either through informal, social, and normative controls or through more bureaucratic systems, but "no organization can be effective with neither." However, volunteer performance management is problematic because the "rewards that seem to be most important . . . [to volunteers] . . . are not under the control of the organization" (Pearce, 1993, p. 181). Performance management is subsumed into the "manage and coordinate" component of figure 12.3.

Table 12.1 Volunteer Management Inventory

Type of practice	In managing your volunteers, to what extent does your club* . . .
Planning	Identify potential volunteers before the season commences
	Target individuals for volunteer positions based on their skills
	Engage in succession planning to replace key volunteers
	Provide role or job descriptions for individual volunteers
	Actively encourage turnover of volunteers in key positions
	Maintain a database of volunteers' skills, qualifications, and experience
Recruitment	Match the skills, experience, and interests of volunteers to specific roles
	Fill key volunteer positions prior to the AGM
	Develop positions to meet the needs of individual volunteers
	Actively recruit volunteers from diverse backgrounds (e.g., minority ethnic groups, people with disabilities)
	Use advertising for volunteer recruitment (e.g., newsletters, online, local papers)
	Use word of mouth to recruit volunteers
	Actively recruit volunteers that are not directly associated with the club
Screening	Verify the accreditation of coaches and officials
	Conduct suitability checks of volunteers (e.g., child protection, responsible service of alcohol)
Orientation	Introduce new volunteers to people with whom they will work during the season
	Conduct induction sessions for specific groups of volunteers (e.g., coaches, managers, committee members)
	Encourage volunteers to operate within a code of acceptable behavior
	Organize induction meetings for new or continuing volunteers
Training and support	Mentor volunteers, particularly when starting in a new role
	Provide support to volunteers in their roles (e.g., assist with the resolution of conflicts)
	Provide sufficient resources for volunteers to effectively carry out their tasks
	Manage the workloads of individual volunteers where they are excessive
	Assist volunteers to access training outside the club (e.g., coach accreditation)
	Cover or reimburse the costs of volunteer attendance at training or accreditation courses
	Reimburse volunteers for out-of-pocket expenses
	Supply volunteers with food and beverages when volunteering
	Provide club uniforms or clothing for volunteers
Performance management	Monitor the performance of individual volunteers
	Provide feedback to individual volunteers about their performance
	Address performance problems among individual volunteers (e.g., a volunteer who fails to complete essential tasks)
Recognition	Recognize outstanding work or task performances of individual volunteers
	Plan for the recognition of volunteers
	Thank volunteers for their efforts (e.g., informal thank you)
	Publicly recognize the efforts of volunteers (e.g., in newsletters)
	Provide special awards for long-serving volunteers (e.g., life membership)

*Measured using a Likert-type scale, where 1=never, 2=rarely, 3=sometimes, 4=often, 5=always.

The application of formalized volunteer management practices is not without its critics, and the wholesale adaptation of HRM from employees to volunteers has its limitations. Drawing on earlier work that differentiated membership management from program management in voluntary organizations (Meijs & Hoogstad, 2001; Meijs & Karr, 2004), Hill and Stevens (2011) argued that volunteers who manage other volunteers (VMV) has largely been ignored in debates about the professionalization and formalization of volunteer management. Hill and Stevens (2011) developed a typology of voluntary volunteer management in which they identify primarily volunteer-led and primarily staff-led organizations. The former are either volunteer led and run or staff supported, whereas the latter are either volunteer supported or volunteer involving. In essence Hill and Stevens' (2011) typology describes four types of voluntary organizations that range from volunteer organized and managed to staff organized and managed. All four types of organizations involve volunteers; however, strategic decisions and the management of volunteers shift from volunteer centered to staff centered. They have attempted to capture the diversity of volunteer management practices and argued that good practice principles that have emerged from some types of organizations, particularly those that are led by paid staff, are unattractive and irrelevant to some VMVs and may be inappropriate and misguided.

Volunteers and Paid Staff

Two decades ago Kikulis, Hinings, and Slack (1995) recognized that the management of sport has progressed from the kitchen table to executive office and boardroom operations. This was a logical response to the increasing complexity of managing sport organizations as they searched for ways to cope with demands from and greater accountability to an expanding array of stakeholders, including government policy initiatives, the legal system, contractual obligations, sponsors, and members. Sport organizations have become increasingly professionalized, particularly at national and state or provincial levels as they employ staff to develop, implement, monitor, and report progress on strategic plans, governance reforms, and risk management protocols.

As the trend toward employing more paid staff in sport has continued unabated for more than two decades, interrelationships between volunteers and professional staff have assumed increasing importance not least because it has long been argued that volunteers do not integrate into organizational systems as completely as employees do (Simon, 1957). That volunteers do not integrate as well as employees should not be that surprising given that paid staff are often engaged on a full-time basis, whereas many if not most volunteers participate in organizational matters directly for a handful of hours per week. Amis, Slack, and Berrett (1995) found evidence that differing values, expectations, and motives between volunteers and paid staff in voluntary sport organizations are inherently conflicted. Pearce (1993, p. 177) contended that "tension can exist between volunteer and employee co-workers, which tends to undermine the legitimacy of the others'" efforts. Paid staff may feel as though they are more accountable for the achievement of strategic goals than volunteers because their employment contracts often specify expected standards of performance, including the achievement of particular outcomes such as membership retention or sponsorship revenue. The same does not apply to volunteers because they are not financially dependent on their sport organization and they are not always involved in day-to-day operational matters.

The interrelationships that develop between paid staff and volunteers and their involvement in and commitment to a sport organization are inherently complex. Paid staff in senior positions are usually directly accountable to a board that is often dominated by volunteers. Under these circumstances paid staff may be confronted with board members' demands that they view as being beyond the scope of their job or for which they have not been sufficiently resourced. From the volunteer perspective, there may be a sense of resentment when a paid staff member places demands on volunteers to undertake a task, particularly when the volunteer perceives this to be the responsibility of paid staff. From the perspective of the psychological contract, there is a clear differentiation between volunteers and paid staff, particularly with respect to the transactional contracts. The economic currency of pay and secure employment in exchange for skills, time, and effort is axiomatically important to paid staff but are not necessarily a consideration for volunteers. Relational contracts, which are based on socioemotional currency in which commitment and involvement are exchanged for a sense of community and a supportive environment, are less likely to differentiate between paid staff and volunteers.

KEY ISSUES FOR SPORT MANAGERS

Increasing professionalization of voluntary sport organizations through the employment of paid staff risks marginalizing volunteer involvement. As professional staff take on responsibility for coordinating and managing the work of volunteers, volunteers tend to become less involved in strategic decision-making as they focus more on service delivery and operational tasks.

Summary and Conclusions

In this chapter we have explored sport volunteerism from a number of perspectives and found consensus on the multidimensionality of volunteerism but less agreement about where sport volunteerism is located specifically in relation to free choice, remuneration, intended beneficiaries, and structure. The structural dimension of volunteerism in particular may be in need of further research because most research on sport volunteerism assumes that sport volunteering takes place in formal organizational settings such as sport clubs and sport events. Statistics from Canada and Australia, used to capture the size, nature, and scope of sport volunteering, reveal that more than one-tenth of the population are involved and that the rate of sport volunteering is higher than in any other sector of the economy. Sport volunteerism is also related to indicators of socioeconomic disadvantage and particular demographic groups within the population, suggesting that sport volunteerism is not as representative of diversity as might be the popularly held view.

A number of theoretical and conceptual frameworks have been used to explain the relationships that develop between volunteers and sport organizations, several of which were explored in this chapter. Sport management researchers tend to explore the dynamic nature of the links that develop and change over time between volunteers and sport organizations by adopting and adapting frameworks and models from mainstream management and marketing literatures. The overriding concern of most sport volunteerism research is to understand some aspect of the attraction, recruitment, management, retention, and productivity of volunteers not least because volunteers are critical to the capacity and capability of the sport system to develop and deliver sport services, programs, activities, and events to members of sport organizations and to the wider community. As sport continues to adapt and change in response to changing external circumstances, so too will the roles of sport volunteers, the nature of their relationship with sport organizations, and their interactions with the wider sport delivery system.

Review Questions

1. Why is volunteer involvement associated with particular demographic variables? What might sport organizations be able to do to increase volunteering from groups in the community that typically have low rates of volunteering?
2. What roles do core volunteers play in providing structure, direction, and stability in sport organizations? When might core volunteers become a hindrance to good governance?
3. Discuss Etzioni's (1961) argument that organizations must continually recruit participants with a positive orientation to organizational power. What might be the consequences if a volunteer is not positively oriented to organizational power?
4. Is it problematic if a volunteer is more highly committed to their role within an organization (e.g., as a coach) than to the wider organization?
5. What are the advantages and disadvantages of applying HRM practices to the management of volunteers in a sport club setting? At a major sport event?
6. How might the employment of paid staff tend to disenfranchise sport volunteers? How might a paid staff member reduce such feelings among volunteers in a sport club setting?

Suggestions for Further Reading

A wide array of additional reading material is available on the topic of volunteerism and a small but increasing amount of material on sport volunteering and voluntary sport organizations. Pearce's (1993) *Volunteers: The Organizational Behavior of*

Unpaid Workers is a scholarly work on volunteers from an organizational behavior perspective. Two sport-focused books on volunteers and voluntary organizations are Hoye, Cuskelly, Auld, Kappelides, and Misener (2020) *Sport Volunteering* and Robinson and Palmer's (2011) *Managing Voluntary Sport Organisations*. Hoye et al. (2020) examine the roles of volunteers in sport, and link theory and research to provide guidelines for implementing good volunteer management practice. Robinson and Palmer (2011) adapt and apply established mainstream organizational theory management strategies to voluntary sport organizations. Connors' (2012) *The Volunteer Management Handbook: Leadership Strategies for Success* offers practical guidance from a generalist perspective on volunteer programs, including volunteer demographics and motivation, analysis planning, interviewing, recruitment, and training from a leadership and management perspective.

Case for Analysis

Westport FC Appoints a New Director of Coaching

Jesse Billings, a former national team player and recent sport management graduate, took up her position as director of coaching with the Westport FC. The management committee had decided it was more transparent to openly advertise the position, and it interviewed three candidates. Among the interviewees was Geoff Cootes. He was disappointed to not be selected but was initially supportive of Jesse's appointment. As a highly committed volunteer with many years of Westport FC membership, Geoff had a lot of social connections and did not want to leave the club.

Jesse brought with her relevant and recent qualifications and a wealth of up-to-date coaching knowledge and techniques from her years on the national team. She took a professional approach as she diligently planned a three-year coaching program in her first month at Westport FC. An important component of the plan was that all coaches be required to attend a series of workshops and upgrade their coaching accreditation to a higher standard. Jesse was well accepted by the parents and players but soon realized that many of the volunteer coaches were not interested in adopting major changes to the coaching program or upgrading their accreditation. A number of the coaches, many of whom had been coaching for a number of years, were openly critical of Jesse's coaching and player development program. They questioned why they should be required to attend a series of coaching workshops given they were experienced in their roles and were already giving up a lot of time to coach their team. Behind her back, Geoff was actively undermining Jesse and fueling much of the discontent among the volunteer coaches; he suggested that everything would have been much better had he been appointed director of coaching. The football club was heading for a crisis when almost half of the volunteer coaches petitioned the management committee and said they would resign their positions.

Questions

1. Using the concept of organizational commitment explain why Geoff made the decision to stay on with Westport FC even though he was disappointed about missing out on the role of director of coaching.
2. Is a high level of organizational commitment among volunteers always a positive attribute? Why or why not?
3. Reflecting on the relationships between paid staff and volunteers explain how the Westport FC may have arrived at the present crisis situation.
4. Discuss what options might be available to the management committee and Jesse in trying to resolve the crisis situation.

CHAPTER 13

Governance of Sport Organizations

Borja García, PhD

Learning Objectives

When you have read this chapter, you should be able to

1. explain why governance is important for a sport organization,
2. identify the different dimensions of governance in sport,
3. define the most important principles of good governance, and
4. understand how governance in sport organizations can be assessed.

Key Concepts

accountability
autonomy of sport
democracy
good governance
good governance principles
systemic governance
transparency

A Governance Fight Between Athletes and Federations

The International Skating Union (ISU) is the governing body of ice skating sports, including figure skating, synchronized skating, speed skating, and short-track skating. Like most international governing bodies, the ISU organizes its own world championships, and it is in charge of the ice skating competitions in the winter Olympic Games. Since 1998 the ISU has adopted rules that regulate the eligibility of athletes to compete in the world championships. Such rules prevent skaters from taking part in out-of-season, private, independent competitions that are not part of the ISU-endorsed circuit. Skaters participating in such competitions may be subject to sanctions ranging from a warning to a lifetime ban under Rule 102.7 of ISU's constitution.

Dutch elite speed skaters Mark Tuitert (world champion in 2005 in team pursuit, and gold medalist in 1,500 meters at the 2010 Vancouver Olympic Games) and Niels Kerstholt (world champion in the 5,000-meter team relay in 2014) were planning to participate in an out-of-season competition called IceDerby, organized in Dubai. However, because Ice Derby was not recognized as an official ISU competition, the governing body reminded the skaters that, should they take part in IceDerby, they would become ineligible for the world championships and the Olympic Games.

Tuitert and Kerstholt felt the ISU was going too far in that decision. They felt the federation was simply trying to discourage private organizers from setting up skating competitions that could compete with ISU's circuit in attracting sponsorship and television revenue. Therefore, Tuitert and Kerstholt challenged the legality of ISU regulations with a complaint to the European Commission, which is supposed to protect a free market in Europe. The skaters argued that ISU was simply not allowing them to exercise their right to work freely wherever they chose to do it.

The European Commission, after an investigation, decided in favor of the skaters. The Commission ordered ISU to change its rules, which constituted an obstacle to the economic freedom of skaters and private companies that set up skating competitions.

This case calls into question ISU's governance structures. The question underlying the conflict between the Dutch skaters and the ISU is: To what extent can an international federation adopt rules that infringe athletes' fundamental freedoms? Were skaters ever consulted when ISU adopted those rules and regulations? In other words, who has the power and the legitimacy to decide in which competitions can skaters participate?

The study of governance has grown significantly over the last decades, which has led to a rather eclectic conceptual landscape. Rhodes (1997) pointed out that perhaps the term *governance* is used in too many contexts and with different meanings. Indeed, Van Kersbergen and Van Waarden (2004) identified up to nine different meanings of the term *governance*. This conceptual diversity is due to the fact that "definitions of governance depend largely on the respective research agendas of scholars or on the phenomenon that is being studied" (Geeraert, Alm, & Groll, 2014, p. 281). Governance, therefore, is highly contextual. Despite this heterogeneity, governance is a very useful concept for managers. It relates to the strategic decisions that those in power need to take to ensure proper accountability and legitimacy of decision making. Indeed, Tricker (2000) points out that while management is about running an organization, good governance is essential because it will make sure and demonstrate that the organization is properly run.

Governance is defined as being mainly concerned with "the patterns that emerge from the governing activities of social, political and administrative actors" (Kooiman, 1993, p. 2). Governance focuses, therefore, on the interaction of actors within a particular system and tends to be distinguished from the term *government*, for governance does not necessarily denote a top-down vertical regulatory relationship (Peters & Pierre, 1998). Governance is a more inclusive concept because it brings into our analysis the role of civil society and nongovernmental actors (Rosenau, 1992).

Governance, in essence, refers to the distribution of power, authority, and the legitimacy to make decisions within an organization. In addition to the decision-making structures, governance relates to the distribution of responsibilities, and the lines of management and accountability. Governance is paramount to providing legitimacy to the decisions of managers and organizations. It is important to differentiate between authority and legitimacy. The former is usually given to or invested on someone by virtue of his or her position. So, for example, a chief executive officer will have authority over senior members of his or her team, who, in turn, will have authority over the junior members of his or her department. Similarly, the International Olympic Committee (IOC) has authority over international federations, as recognized in the Olympic Charter. The federations, in turn, have power and authority over continental confederations, national federations, clubs, and athletes by virtue of the statutes and bylaws of the organization. Legitimacy, however, is a matter of perception. Legitimacy is the acceptance of the decisions and policies by those on the receiving end, and it is about ensuring that those in charge of making decisions follow proper procedures for the benefit of the organization and stakeholders. Governance is, precisely, the link between authority and legitimacy. Governance relates to all the structures and processes necessary to ensure that those with authority act in a legitimate manner and that their decisions can be understood and brought to account.

Theoretical Frameworks

Henry and Lee (2004) were among the first scholars to introduce the study of governance in sport. They argued that sport governance can be encapsulated under three headings: systemic governance, good governance, and political governance. **Systemic governance** refers to the structures that facilitate relations of stakeholders within the sports system. **Good governance** refers to the normative principles that should define those relationships within the management of sport organizations. Using a similar approach, Andre-Noel Chaker (2004, p. 5) defined sport governance as "the creation of effective networks of sport-related state agencies, sport non-governmental organizations and processes that operate jointly and independently under specific legislation, policies and private regulations to promote ethical, democratic, efficient and accountable sports activities." We can see the similarities between both definitions of sport governance. Chaker's reference to networks of state agencies and sport nongovernmental organizations links directly to Henry and Lee's concept of systemic governance. On the other hand, Chaker's emphasis of ethical, democratic, efficient, and accountable activities is clearly related to Henry and Lee's dimension of good governance.

Henry and Lee's (2004) definition of political governance refers to the specific role of the state and public authorities in regulating sport and their relationship with sport nongovernmental organizations. Building on the approaches of Chaker (2004) and Kooiman (1993), it is possible to subsume Henry and Lee's idea of political governance as one variety of the wider concept of systemic governance in which state actors are part of the governance network. Thus, we can summarize our conceptual approach to sport governance under two useful heuristic dimensions: systemic governance and good governance. Systemic governance refers here to governance as a network to structure the relationships among a large number of stakeholders (Rhodes, 1997); and good governance is defined as involving the principles of effective, transparent, and democratic management (Rhodes, 1997). Holt (2006) points out that definitions of governance can be seen as both analytical or descriptive (systemic governance) and normative (good governance). This means that we can use it to comment both on how sport is governed and on how well it is or should be governed.

Systemic Governance

Systemic governance refers to the management of a structure with a large number of stakeholders, where power, authority, and resources are diffused and distributed across the system (Henry & Lee, 2004). It is concerned with "the competition, cooperation and mutual adjustment between organizations" in sport systems (Henry & Lee, 2004, p. 26). The notion of systemic governance is based on a key shift in the way that sport is organized and controlled. Systemic governance reflects a move away from direct control and regulation of sport by the state to a more autonomous, multistakeholder, global, and self-governing industry. It is a shift from *government* to *governance* (Peters & Pierre, 1998) that has arrived in sport like so many other areas of civil society (Fioramonti & Fiori, 2010).

Systemic governance is an analytical framework that serves to simplify reality. Systemic governance facilitates our analysis of the complex structures governing the sport sector. It provides managers with the tools to understand the relationships and interactions of stakeholders within the sport sector. In a nutshell, systemic governance helps to identify the stakeholders participating in a governance system and to analyze the relations of dependency among those stakeholders. Systemic governance helps us to classify governance structures. In the sport sector, governance systems fall within two main categories: hierarchical (or vertical) governance and network governance.

Hierarchical Governance

Hierarchical governance, also known as *vertical governance*, refers to a system of governance in which the lines of power and authority are very clearly delimited and run from the top to the bottom in a decreasing hierarchical relationship. Thus, those organizations at the top will be the maximum authority of the system, whereas stakeholders situated at the bottom of the hierarchy will be rule takers with limited say in decision making. Hierarchical governance is often referred to as *pyramidal governance* (Weatherill, 2005), in reference to the so-called European model of sport (European Commission, 1998; García, 2009), which is defined as a pyramid of power with the international federation at the top, followed in a descending order by continental confederations, national governing bodies, leagues, clubs, and athletes. This is most typically exemplified by the pyramid of governance in association football, as seen in figure 13.1.

In association football, like in many other sports, the Fédération International de Football Association (FIFA) sits at the top of the pyramid as the international governing body (IGB). It is then followed by the continental confederations, such as the Union of European Football Associations (UEFA) for Europe or the Asian Football Confederation (AFC) for Asia. The national level comes next, with national federations, leagues, clubs, and players situated firmly at the bottom of the structure of power (Tomlinson, 1983). This applies to the large majority of Olympic sports. Hierarchical sport governance is characterized by having only one IGB for the sport, sitting at the top of the pyramid and acting as a de facto monopoly of power and authority in the governance structure. Its governance is also characterized by the vertical channels of authority that run from the IGB at the top all the way down to the clubs, players, and grassroots organizations at the national and local levels. So, for example, the statutes of FIFA and UEFA clearly indicate that confederations, national federations, clubs, and leagues are subject to the authority of the international federation and are required to implement and follow its policies (FIFA, 2019; UEFA, 2014). These vertical channels of authority provide clarity and efficient policy making but risk not observing elemental principles of democracy, such as consultation and stakeholder representation, if those situated at the bottom of the pyramid are not included in the decision-making process of the federations that sit at the top.

Figure 13.1 An example of pyramidal or hierarchical governance: The governance system of European association football.

Adapted by permission from B. García, "UEFA and the European Union: From Confrontation to Co-operation?" *Journal of Contemporary European Research* 3, no. 3 (2007): 202-223. This article is under the Creative Commons License 2.5.

Hierarchical governance and the classic pyramid of sport governance are now mostly considered something of the past (García, 2009; Henry & Lee, 2004) due to the transformation of sport governance structures over the last two decades. The professionalization, commercialization, and globalization of sport have put into question the ability of international sport governing bodies to effectively govern their sport. The shortcomings of hierarchical and pyramidal structures of governance have been exposed in numerous conflicts between athletes, leagues, and federations, normally caused by the emergence of commercial interests around sport. It is now generally acknowledged that sport has moved towards a more complex and horizontal systemic structure: network governance.

Network Governance

Network governance refers to a system of governance wherein power and authority are diffused across a large number of stakeholders. Governance scholars define a network as "a relatively stable horizontal articulation of interdependent, but operationally autonomous actors, who interact through negotiations, which take place within a regulative, normative, cognitive and imaginary framework" (Sørensen & Torfing, 2005, p. 197). In stark contrast to hierarchical governance, network governance is

TIME OUT

The Bosman Case: A Governance Conflict

The well-known Bosman case is a consequence of the hierarchical structures of governance in football. Jean-Marc Bosman was a Belgian association football player who wanted to sign with the French club FC Dunkerke when his contract with Belgian club RC Liège had expired. For the transfer to go ahead, FC Dunkerke was required to pay a fee to RC Liège, even when Bosman was out of contract. When Dunkerke was unable to pay the transfer fee, the Belgian federation allowed RC Liège to retain the player out of contract as long as a minimum wage was paid to him. Jean-Marc Bosman's situation was, in effect, a conflict between his fundamental rights as an association football player and the transfer regulations that clearly favored the interests of the clubs. Professional players, situated firmly at the bottom of the pyramid, had no say in the transfer rules and other employment conditions regulated by FIFA (García, 2011). Because of the vertical governance structure, Bosman's rights were not observed by the federations, and the player had to resort to a legal challenge in court, which he won. Following the Bosman ruling, the governance structures of association football changed significantly as players started to contest the legitimacy of FIFA at the top of the pyramid.

characterized by the horizontal relations among a large number of actors in the system. The nature of those relations might be dictated by a variety of factors, from regulatory authority to resource dependence. Network governance acknowledges the interdependence of the stakeholders in the system and, therefore, pays less attention to issues of vertical authority, although these are not entirely dismissed.

Network governance considers a wide variety of stakeholders within the system. Using the example of association football again, we can use a network governance analysis to map the interrelation of new stakeholders in this complex systemic structure. The traditional stakeholders, as identified in figure 13.1, are clearly still part of the system. Thus, we have FIFA, continental confederations, the national federations, the national leagues, clubs, and players as primary (or internal) stakeholders (Holt, 2006; Holt, 2007). We can add to these primary stakeholders the fans and supporters, who have now representative organizations seeking to be recognized as part of the network (García & Welford, 2015). The network is also regulated by decisions of national governments and the European Union, which need to be considered as regulatory stakeholders (García, Niemann, & Grant, 2011; Geeraert, Scheerder, & Bruyninckx, 2013). The new addition, which we can now make part of the systemic analysis through network governance, is that of the private commercial sector. Professional sport is highly dependent of the investment of TV and media companies, which are now also part of the governance network as secondary (or external) stakeholders (Chappelet & Kübler-Mabbot, 2008).

Network governance reflects a heterogeneous structure. It abandons the simplicity of hierarchical governance in favor of a more nuanced and inclusive approach that reflects the reality of most sports nowadays. Network governance is characterized by having a large number of stakeholders in the system, which are interdependent while remaining autonomous in setting their own particular interests. Network governance is also characterized by a slower process of decision making due to the increased number of stakeholders that need to be accommodated. In theory, networked systems of governance tend to be more representative and inclusive, but decision making will take more time. Policies and regulations within the system are a compromise among the stakeholders that reflect the relative degree of leverage that actors have on one another. In these negotiations, resource dependence is key. Stakeholders with more resources are able to advance their priorities. Resources are of variable nature and depend on the issue at hand, from money to knowledge or expertise.

The systemic governance of sport could be classified as hierarchical or vertical governance in the past, but it has been transformed into much more complex structures that fall within the network governance category (Geeraert et al., 2013; Chappelet & Kübler-Mabbot, 2008). The particularity of sport governance is that, despite adopting structures much more akin to a network, it still retains some traits of hierarchical governance. This refers mostly to the role of governing bodies such as the IOC or the international sport federations. The governing bodies, by virtue of their central role in the historical development of sport, still claim a degree of power and vertical authority in the governance structures of sport. This is difficult to reconcile with a reality whereby other stakeholders challenge their authority and claim their place in the network. It is not unusual to find conflicts between governing bodies and stakeholders that want to establish independent commercial competitions, as in the case of this chapter's opening scenario.

Good Governance

Good governance is the second conceptual dimension of governance. Whereas systemic governance is analytical, good governance has a normative flavor. Good governance refers to the principles and codes of behavior that all stakeholders within a governance system are expected to follow. Therefore, systemic and good governance are complementary. As Rhodes (1997) explains, good governance involves the principles of effective, transparent, and democratic management. The European Union Expert Group on Good Governance (2013, p. 5) defines good governance in sport as follows.

> The framework and culture within which a sports body sets policy, delivers its strategic objectives, engages with stakeholders, monitors performance, evaluates and manages risk and reports to its constituents on its activities and progress including the delivery of effective, sustainable and proportionate sports policy and regulation.

Conceptually, good governance is formulated around a series of normative principles that organizations are required to implement in order to earn legitimacy and to be considered well governed (Geeraert et al., 2014). Chappelet and Kübler-Mabbot (2008) argue that good governance in sport is defined by the principles of transparency, democracy, accountability, autonomy, and social responsibility. This was refined, especially as Chappelet and Mrkonjic (2013) published their Basic Indicators for Better Governance in International Sport (BIBGIS). These authors identified the principles of good governance as transparency, democracy, accountability, integrity, and solidarity (Chappelet & Mrkonjic, 2013).

One of the complexities of good governance is that many lists of **good governance principles** exist, each one with a particular spin. Lists of good governance principles have been compiled by academics, public authorities, and sport organizations alike. (See Chappelet & Mrkonjic, 2013 for a comprehensive review of good governance principles applied to sport.) One of the latest and most significant additions to this list is the UK Sport's code of good governance in sport, in which the British government makes funding conditional upon sport organizations implementing the principles of governance defined in the code. Despite some heterogeneity, we find consensus around three basic principles: accountability, which can be considered the cornerstone of good governance; transparency; and democracy. These three good governance principles are the basis of a well-governed organization. Other principles, such as integrity and solidarity, are more recent additions and respond to developments in sport such as doping or match-fixing.

Governance literature defines **accountability** as "a relationship between an actor and a forum, in which the actor has an obligation to explain and to justify his or her conduct" (Bovens, 2007, p. 450). Accountability is the most important good governance principle because it structures the relationship between decision makers and decision takers. Accountability is the principle that allows stakeholders to ask questions when policies are being designed. More importantly, proper accountability structures ensure that decision makers face the consequences of their actions. For real accountability to happen, sport organizations need to have proper procedures in which decisions and conducts are reviewed and, if necessary, rectified.

Accountability is closely linked to the principle of **transparency**, defined as the ability of stakeholders to obtain information about the management and processes of the organization (Henry & Lee, 2004). Transparency ensures that internal and external stakeholders have access to the organization's documents and information. Transparency is a precondition for accountability, but not the only one. It is impossible to have accountability without transparency, but transparency on its own does not necessarily ensure accountability. Proper accountability is only ensured if all the information obtained through transparency can then be used to put questions to the decision makers and to examine their conduct.

Democracy relates to the extent to which stakeholders may be represented in decision-making structures and influence those in office (March & Olsen, 1995). Democratic governance will ensure that members and stakeholders of a sport organization are properly consulted and represented in decision-making structures. Democracy relates, therefore, to the extent to which members and stakeholders can have a say in decision making. It also relates to the possibility to elect the leaders of the organization. In sport governing bodies it is crucial that the election process for board members and for the president are democratic; this includes the possibility of secret ballots in the elections. Another key element of democracy, which links

KEY ISSUES FOR SPORT MANAGERS

Accountability, transparency, and democracy are the three most important principles of good governance. Sport managers need to ensure that their organizations adopt processes that enable members and stakeholders to bring decision makers to account by accessing all necessary financial and performance information. Members and stakeholders need to be consulted and represented in decision-making structures. To ensure proper democracy and accountability, positions of power and authority such as presidents, general directors, or CEOs need to be reviewed at prudent intervals. Term limits for nonexecutive directors are also advised.

directly to accountability, is terms in office. Senior leadership of an organization benefits from renewal at sensible intervals in order to avoid stagnation and to provide new ideas, and long terms in office may contribute to the entrenchment of particular interests, leading to possible corruption. For these reasons, it is recommended, as part of democratic governance, that terms in office are limited to a sensible period, especially for senior board directors and presidents of sport organizations; the emerging consensus in the IOC and many international sport federations is that 12 years is an acceptable limit. This might be a problem for small organizations (e.g., local sport clubs) where the pool of available candidates is limited.

Finally, integrity and solidarity are defined as the structures that ensure a healthy development of an organization and its environment; integrity and solidarity are often linked to issues of corporate social responsibility or good corporate citizenship (Chappelet & Mrkonjic, 2013).

Good governance is a normative construct because it defines the standards that sport organizations and their managers ought to comply with in their daily work. Good governance needs to be incorporated in sport organizations at the strategic level, but it permeates executive day-to-day decisions. If an organization and its directors and senior managers are seen as observing good governance, they will be viewed as legitimate and earn the cooperation of the members and stakeholders. The extent to which a sport organization respects good governance principles will dictate whether it can self-govern effectively or if it requires external regulation.

The Autonomy of Sport and the Role of the State in Sport Governance

The role of the state is a hotly debated issue in sport governance. Governments have powers to regulate the activities of sport stakeholders. In Spain, for example, the government adopted a national sports act that set up the rights, responsibilities, and structures of national sports federations (García, Palomar Olmeda, & Pérez González, 2011). This is very common in countries with a regulatory tradition, where the government is heavily involved in the design of the economic and social structures. Other countries, mostly of Anglo-Saxon liberal tradition such as the United Kingdom or the United States, have a tradition of a small, noninterventionist state. This is naturally reflected in sport.

KEY ISSUES FOR SPORT MANAGERS

The governance of sport is increasingly complex. Sport is a multifaceted industry that covers the most commercialized leagues and sport events but also includes amateur leagues or school sport provision. All of these organizations have different demands and are situated in a different systemic environment. One of the overarching issues, of paramount importance for managers, is the role of public authorities in sport governance. The term *public authorities* relates here to governments with regulatory and distributive powers at local, regional, and national levels. It might also include supranational public bodies, such as the European Union, whose legal regulatory framework has had ample impact in sport governance (García, 2012; Geeraert et al., 2013).

The role of the state in sport governance system is related to the concept of the **autonomy of sport** (Geeraert, Mrkonjic, & Chappelet, 2015; FIFA, 2006; Vieweg, 2000; Parrish, 2002). The autonomy of sport is defined as the right of sports organizations to adopt their own policies, rules, and regulations; elect their leaders; and design their governance structures independently without excessive and unnecessary external intervention (Geeraert et al., 2015). The autonomy of sport is a key issue in governance because it assesses the extent to which sport bodies, clubs, and federations can be trusted to implement effectively good governance. In other words, the debate around the autonomy of sport is whether sport organizations are able to self-govern or if they have to be regulated and controlled by the government in order to avoid mismanagement and corruption.

Sport organizations cherish their autonomy and are willing to defend it from what they sometimes see as unnecessary intervention of governments in their own affairs (Meier & García, 2015). This often creates tensions for sport governing bodies at the national level, which are trapped between the hierarchical nature of their system of governance and the regulatory powers of the national government. In some cases, national governments want to directly regulate the structures of national sport federations, but these attempts are opposed by the international federation. In those cases, the national governing body finds itself in an awkward position because they have a statutory duty to follow the international federation's decisions, but they also are bound by the law of the land in their own country.

The autonomy of sport is heavily dependent on good governance. Initially, autonomy was included by some authors as just another good governance principle (e.g., Chappelet & Kübler-Mabbot, 2008). The consensus now, however, is that autonomy is a result of good governance rather than an active principle of it. In other words, sport organizations need to earn their autonomy through the implementation of good governance in their structures.

The Assessment of Governance

If sport organizations are asked to implement good governance to earn their autonomy in relation to the state, how can we measure how they are doing in relation to governance? Governance is a concept firmly anchored in the social sciences. It relates to strategies, processes, and mechanisms of decision making in organizations. As such, governance is by definition difficult to measure because it deals with social structures that might be perceived and interpreted in different ways. This does not mean we should not try to measure it. It only means that it is a complex exercise that will rely on both quantitative and qualitative assessments. In the last years, research into sports governance has focused heavily on measuring and assessment. Academics and sport organizations have devoted time and resources to design models that could allow for a fair and transparent assessment of governance.

Jean-Loup Chappelet and Michael Mrkonjic (2013) were the first to present a sport governance

TIME OUT

The Power of Sport Federations in Relation to the State

International sport federations make use of the autonomy of sport to resist regulation by national governments and other public authorities. The IOC suspended the Indian National Olympic Committee because it deemed the Indian government to be interfering in the election process of the NOC. IOC membership suspension means that NOCs cannot receive money from Olympic Solidarity and their athletes cannot participate in the Olympic Games. In order to protect the athletes, however, the IOC allowed Indian athletes to participate in the 2016 Rio Olympics under the Olympic flag.

FIFA has also used its powers to keep governmental intervention at bay. In 2006 FIFA intervened when the Greek parliament adopted a new national sports act that required the Greek Football Association to change a number of structures. The reaction of FIFA was to suspend the Greek FA's membership and to ask the Greek government to modify its national sports act. The Greek parliament took just 48 hours to pass an amendment in which it complied with FIFA's requirement, hence exempting association football from some of the national sports act provisions. As demonstrated in this case, the political power of some international sport federations, such as FIFA, is so strong that it can even force a change of legislation by a democratically elected parliament.

measurement tool with their Basic Indicators for Better Governance in International Sport (BIBGIS). The idea behind the BIBGIS model is relatively simple. The principles of good governance (democracy, transparency, accountability, solidarity, and integrity) are translated into seven measurable governance dimensions: organizational transparency, reporting transparency, democratic process, stakeholders' representation, control mechanisms, sport integrity, and solidarity. Both organizational and reporting transparency are the measurable definition of transparency. The democratic process and stakeholders' representation link directly to the principle of democracy. Control mechanisms are the representation of accountability.

These seven dimensions are then measured by a set of nine indicators each. So, for example, the indicators for organizational transparency are whether the organization publishes its statutes and bylaws, publishes the senior leaders' biographical information and salary, publishes the agenda and minutes of its board and committee meetings, and so on. The idea behind the BIBGIS model is that an independent assessor should be able to score each one of the nine indicators from 0 to 4, hence obtaining a numerical mark for the indicator, which is then averaged to obtain a numerical mark of each dimension. The final result is that we will be able to obtain a score from 1 to 4 (where 2 is considered the pass mark) in each of the seven governance dimensions, thereby judging the organization's success in particular areas of governance.

Building on the work of the BIBGIS model, the Danish Institute of Sport and the think tank Play the Game, in cooperation with other academics, developed the Sports Governance Observer (SGO). The SGO follows a similar structure to the BIBGIS model, but it simplifies the exercise with the definition of four, rather than seven, dimensions: transparency and public communication, democratic process, checks and balances, and solidarity (Geeraert et al., 2014; Geeraert, 2015). The idea of the SGO is similar to that of BIBGIS. The authors developed a total of 36 indicators under the four dimensions. Each indicator is scored from 1 to 5. In this case, the dimensions do not have the same number of indicators, unlike in BIBGIS.

Both BIBGIS and the SGO have been developed independently from sport organizations with the objective of helping them assess their governance structures. These models have advantages and disadvantages. Whereas BIBGIS is more comprehensive, with a bigger set of indicators and dimensions (Chappelet & Mrkonjic, 2013), the SGO model has an important advantage in that it has defined clear marking criteria for each one of the indicators (Geeraert, 2015), enhancing the reliability of the measuring instrument. Probably the main drawback of both models is that it is extremely difficult for outsiders to use them. The governance indicators rely on having access to the organizations, which means that it is quite difficult to perform a full assessment without the cooperation of the organization being assessed. (See Geeraert et al., 2014 for a description of the difficulties in applying the SGO model.)

Finally, the Association of Summer Olympic International Federations (ASOIF) has designed its own governance assessment tool to benchmark the international federations of Summer Olympic sports (ASOIF, 2016). They have designed their own governance assessment tool in cooperation with Jean-Loup Chappelet, one of the authors of the BIBGIS model. The new ASOIF model draws heavily on the BIBGIS model. This new measuring tool has five dimensions: transparency, integrity, democracy, sport development and solidarity, and checks and balances or control mechanisms (ASOIF, 2016). Each dimension has ten indicators, for a total of 50 performance indicators, that are scored from 0 to 4 (ASOIF, 2017).

The ASOIF governance assessment tool introduces a new element to the measuring of governance. It has designed an extra dimension that refers to the extent to which international federations comply with existing guiding codes and regulations, namely the Olympic Charter, the IOC's Agenda 2020 recommendations, the IOC ethics code, the Council of Europe good governance recommendations, and national and international laws. This dimension is an interesting addition because the intention is to

KEY ISSUES FOR SPORT MANAGERS

Sport organizations now have a number of governance assessment tools at their disposal. They should use these models as a starting point, in combination with any requirements that come from their local, regional, or national government. Managers, and especially senior leadership, in sport organizations should design strategic plans to improve the governance structures of their organizations in the same way they design medium- to long-term economic and human resources plans.

assess the extent to which international federations comply with hierarchical governance and the regulatory framework in which they are situated. It is a dimension that pays attention to the external environment of the federations, whereas the other dimensions are much more internally focused.

The design of an accurate governance assessment tool is of vital importance for managers in the sports sector. Governance should be an integral part of the performance of sport organizations and therefore should be assessed in a similar way as other key performance indicators. The validity and reliability of the tools that managers have at their disposal is open to debate. Most of these models are designed with international federations in mind. Adaptation of the assessment tools to national and local contexts is needed. However, the main idea behind all these tools is valid. The definition of governance dimensions, indicators, and scoring thresholds are the appropriate ways to measure governance performance reliably.

Summary and Conclusions

Governance refers to the processes and structures that ensure the transparent, efficient, and democratic management of sport organizations. It is an increasingly important issue for sport managers and should be addressed at the strategic level. The governance of sport organizations has been called into question as a result of the increasing pressure and demands by external and internal stakeholders. Governance is not directly related to the day-to-day management of sport organizations, but it sets the rules and structures for the proper day-to-day running of the organization. It is highly contextual and needs to be adapted to the demands in the context of the particular organization to which it is applied. In short, governance should allow members, stakeholders, and external interested parties to check the policies, management, and decisions of sport organizations.

The application of governance to sport can be encapsulated as two dimensions: systemic governance and good governance. The former is an analytical concept. It allows managers to understand the power, authority, and legitimacy structures in which their organization is situated. Systemic governance describes the relationships between stakeholders in a particular governance system. Traditionally, sport adopted a hierarchical systemic governance model, also called *vertical governance* or *pyramidal governance*. These models were characterized by a clear vertical channel of authority, with international federations at the top and national clubs, leagues, and athletes firmly at the bottom. The authority of the international federations under this model is almost a monopoly, and stakeholders need to comply with their rules and regulations. However, the professionalization and commercialization of sport in the last two decades has transformed sport's systemic governance. It is acknowledged that sport governance now resembles a model of network governance. The main characteristic of network systemic governance is a diffusion of power and authority horizontally among a large number of stakeholders. Relations in the network are not dictated as much by hierarchy but by the resource dependency between stakeholders. Network governance entails a certain loss of authority and power for the sport governing bodies because they now need to accommodate the demands of internal and external stakeholders, who are essential for the commercial viability of the sport.

Good governance, on the other hand, is much more of a normative concept. Good governance refers to the principles sport organizations should observe in order to be viewed as legitimate by members and stakeholders. Good governance is articulated around a list of principles that organizations are expected to implement in their day-to-day management. While some variety exists in what principles constitute good governance, it is widely agreed that democracy, transparency, and accountability are the backbone. Accountability is probably the most important principle of good governance because it allows members and stakeholders to pass judgment on the decisions of the managers and senior leaders of the organization. Good governance principles should inform sport organizations' strategy and should be applied at all levels, from top to bottom.

Compliance with good governance is paramount for sport organizations in determining to what extent they can be autonomous from external regulation. Public authorities have the power to regulate the sport sector, mostly through the public budget allocated to sport policy. In that respect, sport organizations need to demonstrate they are complying with good governance principles if they want to apply for public grants. Moreover, the confidence of the public in the sport sector is extremely low. For that reason, sport organizations are required to observe high standards of governance.

Sport managers have at their disposal a number of tools and models to assess good governance in their organizations. These assessment tools have been designed in the last few years and are normally focused on international sport federations. There is still work to be done in order to adopt those governance assessment models to national and local contexts. Managers can, however, make use of the BIBGIS, SGO, or ASOIF tools if they adapt the tool appropriately to the reality of their organization.

Review Questions

1. What are the advantages and disadvantages of hierarchical (or pyramidal) governance?
2. What are the advantages and disadvantages of network governance?
3. Why is good governance necessary in sport organizations?
4. What are the most important governance principles?
5. Is the autonomy of sport a principle of good governance? How or how not?
6. To what extent can we measure and assess governance in sport organizations?

Suggestions for Further Reading

Academic literature on sport governance is relatively young, but it is developing at a very good rate. Future sport managers need to appreciate governance in a holistic manner and to understand that governance is a multidimensional concept. To gain that holistic understanding of sport governance, the book *Sport Governance* by Russell Hoye and Graham Cuskelly (2007) is an excellent starting point in which the authors focus on the practical application of governance principles to amateur and professional sport organizations. Those links between governance and day-to-day management are fundamental for managers. In a similar vein, Neil King's (2017) introduction to governance will provide a very up-to-date account of the field with multiple practical examples. It has the advantage of its recent publication, featuring most of the recent debates in the field.

To understand the principles of good governance and their implementation in sport, the first point of call should be the work of Jean-Loup Chappelet and his colleagues leading to the BIBGIS model. Specifically, the final chapter of his book on the governance and organization of the Olympic movement (Chappelet & Kübler-Mabbot, 2008, chapter 8) has an initial definition of governance principles. It is then necessary to examine the seminal paper that published the governance dimensions and indicators of the BIBGIS model (Chappelet & Mrkonjic, 2013). Building on Chappelet's seminal work, *Sports Governance Observer* (Geeraert, 2015), and the ASOIF tool (ASOIF, 2017) also provide definitions of governance principles and dimensions. In that respect, the former is much more conceptually robust. For a more discursive approach to good governance principles, the deliverable of the European Union Expert Group on Good Governance (2013) is especially detailed. Its advantage is that it comes with an appendix in which the experts discuss which principles of good governance should be expected at different levels, from the local to the regional, national, and international.

Case for Analysis

The UK Code for Good Governance in Sport

In 2016 the UK government adopted a new code for good governance in sport. The code, *A Code for Sports Governance*, was designed by both UK Sport and Sport England, the governmental agencies in charge of elite sport policy and grassroots sports policy, respectively, in the United Kingdom. The code applies to all organizations to which UK Sport and Sport England give funding. At the heart of the code are four basic principles of good governance—structure, people, standards and conduct, and policies and processes—each of which includes a set of mandatory requirements. The code establishes three tiers of compliance with the code, and the requirements become more comprehensive and prescriptive with each tier. The basic idea behind the code is that the requirements increase with the level of funding. That is to say, the more money sport organizations want to get, the more requirements with which they must comply.

The adoption of the code forced British federations to undertake a number of reforms because they depend heavily on grants from UK Sport and Sport England. For example, British Cycling had to overhaul its decision-making structures, giving more power to the executive board to the detriment of the council, because the code prescribes that boards of governing bodies must be the ultimate decision-making body and exercise all of the powers of the organization. The reforms also included an increase in the number of openly recruited independent board members, from three to four and an independent chair. They also included a three-year term limit for directors, resulting in six of the eight elected members on the current board being forced to stand down. Finally, the reforms included a quota to ensure that at least 30 percent of the board members are female.

These reforms aim to make the governing body more independent and diverse but clashed with the wishes of the council (which was losing power in favor of the board) and the regional cycling associations (who claim they are losing representation in decision making). Had the council not endorsed the proposed reforms, British Cycling would have lost its £43 million (US$53 million) funding from UK Sport and Sport England.

Questions

1. To what extent is the UK code for good governance in sport a governmental intervention and, therefore, to what extent does it affect the autonomy of sport?
2. Which principles of good governance will be improved with the reforms at British Cycling?

CHAPTER 14

Decision Making in Sport Organizations

Trevor Slack, PhD
Alex Thurston, PhD

Learning Objectives

When you have read this chapter, you should be able to

1. explain the concept of decision making,
2. discuss the conditions under which decisions are made,
3. understand the difference between the rational approach to decision making and the concept of bounded rationality, and
4. describe the major models of organizational decision making.

Key Concepts

bounded rationality
certainty
coalitions
constricted decisions
fluid decisions
garbage can model
interrupts
management science
nonprogrammed decisions
organized anarchy
problemistic search
programmed decisions
rational decision making
risk
routines
sporadic decisions
uncertainty

Deciding on the 2018 Winter Olympic Games

On July 6, 2011, the International Olympic Committee (IOC) chose the city of PyeongChang, South Korea, to host the 2018 Winter Olympic Games. Getting to that point, however, was a lengthy process involving many decisions by many people.

In July 2009 the IOC invited National Olympic Committees (NOCs) to nominate candidate cities to host the 2018 Games. The Korean Sport and Olympic Committee decided to nominate PyeongChang. This was, in fact, PyeongChang's third attempt to win a bid for the Olympics. NOCs nominated two other cities—Munich, Germany, and Annecy, France—to host the 2018 Games.

PyeongChang 2018 launched its official campaign in September 2009, led by cochairmen—Hanjin Group Chairman, Cho Yang-ho, and Kim Jin-sun, the governor of Gangwon province (where PyeongChang is located)—along with a committee of 76 members, all whom possessed a range of expertise (GamesBids, 2009).

In June 2010 the IOC Executive Board accepted all three cities as candidates, and by January 2011 the three bid cities had submitted their candidature files to the IOC. Between February and March 2011 the IOC Evaluation Commission for the 2018 Games visited the three cities, then produced a technical appraisal report for each city. Following publication of the reports, a technical briefing for IOC members with the candidate cities was held in Lausanne, Switzerland, in May 2011 to discuss technical elements of the bids in greater detail and provide opportunity for any questions and answers (IOC, n.d.).

The final stage of the bid process involved the three candidate cities presenting their bids at the 123rd IOC Session in Durban, South Africa, after which eligible IOC members were asked to place a vote. It was announced by then-IOC president, Jacques Rogge, that PyeongChang had been elected as the host city after receiving 63 votes to Munich's 25 and Annecy's 7 votes (IOC, n.d.).

Not all decisions made in sport organizations are as long and complex as choosing a city for an Olympic Games. Mintzberg (1973), in his book *The Nature of Managerial Work*, found decision making to be one of the major tasks in which managers were involved; some people see decision making as the single most important process in an organization. The decisions made in a sport organization may range from deciding on the color and style of the company's letterhead to orchestrating a multibillion-dollar takeover bid. Some decisions prove to be successful, such as the one made by Peter Ueberroth when he decided to seek private support for the Los Angeles Olympic Games. Others, such as Nike's decision to use its name to get into the casual shoe market, have, in the past, been less than successful (Willigan, 1992). However, more recently, Nike experienced far greater success in the casual shoe market when the organization decided to collaborate with the American rapper Kanye West. The collaboration project created Nike Air Yeezy footwear, releasing Yeezy editions in 2009 and 2012, which was the brand's first nonathlete full sneaker collaboration. The US$245 Nike Air Yeezy II edition proved to be so popular, one eBay bidder purchased a pair for an eye-watering US$90,300 (Weisman, 2012), and in February 2014, a "Red October" limited-edition Yeezy II was released, which sold out within 10 minutes (Weisman, 2014). But what turned out to be an even more lucrative decision was that once Adidas recognized the success of that partnership, the brand managed to get Kanye to agree to start collaborating with them instead of Nike. The 2015 Adidas Yeezy Boost 750 was the first product to be released from the new collaboration, which also sold out within minutes, and became the most popular Yeezy sneaker to date (Halfhill, 2015). Halfhill suggested that West's marriage to Kim Kardashian (and therefore, the cultural influence of the Kardashian family) provided a drastic increase of extra exposure to a new market and demographic. In addition to the marketing strategy of using his wife, West creates social media hype, and he rolled out products in limited quantities. The decision for Adidas and Kanye to collaborate appears to have been well judged; The *New York Times* (Creswell & Draper, 2019) reported that Yeezy sales will top US$1.3 billion by the end of 2019.

In this chapter we look first at the term *decision making* and what it means. We then identify the conditions under which decisions are made. Next, we examine the different approaches to decision making, focusing first on individual decision making and then examining models of organizational decision making.

Defining Decision Making

In his book *The Effective Executive*, management guru Peter Drucker (1966, p. 143), suggests that "a decision is a judgment . . . a choice between alternatives." Sport managers use their judgment to make decisions about whether to hire or fire employees, to add new programs, to sell off a division that is losing money, or to trade a player. Simon (1960) suggests that the decisions a manager makes can be categorized into two types: programmed and nonprogrammed.

Programmed Decisions

Programmed decisions are repetitive and routine. They are made on the basis of clearly defined policies and procedures, as well as a manager's past experiences. The types of problems that can be solved using programmed decision making are usually well structured, have adequate information available, and present clear alternatives whose viability is relatively easy to assess. Examples of programmed decisions in a sport organization include the decision by a pool manager to put more lifeguards on duty when the number of swimmers increases and the decision by a university's sport information director about what to include in an online portal. If faced with a choice, managers prefer programmed to nonprogrammed decisions.

Nonprogrammed Decisions

Nonprogrammed decisions are new and unique. No guidelines or procedures are established to direct the way this type of decision should be handled. Often the sport organization has never faced decisions about this exact situation. There are no clear alternatives from which to select. Decisions such as those made by the board of governors of the NHL to grant franchises to new cities could be considered nonprogrammed; so, too, could the decisions made by association football owners and coaches about how they choose to respond to new policies that directly affect their team, such as the implementation of the Union of European Football Associations' (UEFA) Financial Fair Play (FFP) regulations, introduced to prevent a club from overspending in the pursuit of success.

Programmed decisions, because they are well structured, are generally made by the sport organization's lower-level managers and operators. Nonprogrammable decisions, because of their novel characteristics, are more likely to be handled by senior managers or highly trained professional staff. Whenever possible, sport managers attempt to program the decision making because these choices can be handled by less qualified, cheaper staff.

Conditions Under Which Decisions Are Made

Because sport organizations and the environments in which they exist change constantly, sport managers can never be exactly sure of the consequences of any decision they make. It is generally accepted that decisions are made under three types of conditions, each based on the extent to which the outcome of a decision alternative is predictable. These three conditions are discussed below.

Certainty

A decision is made under a condition of **certainty** when the manager making the decision knows exactly what the available alternatives are, and the costs and benefits of each alternative. One situation often used to illustrate decision making under certainty conditions is an investment in a bond or some other security with a guaranteed rate of return. For example, a voluntary sport club that finds itself with surplus cash on hand may choose to invest it in government bonds or treasury bills. The bonds may pay 6 percent but require a minimum investment time of five years; the treasury bills may pay only 4 percent but have a minimum investment time of one year. Here, the decision maker knows the alternatives and the benefits of each. It is simply a matter of making the most appropriate choice.

Risk

Unfortunately, very few decisions in sport organizations are made under conditions of certainty. Under a condition of **risk** (the most common condition for decision making in sport organizations), a decision maker has a basic understanding of the available alternatives, but the potential cost and benefits associated with each are uncertain. For example, a professional sport franchise owner wants to relocate her team. Three cities have offered their facilities, all fairly similar. One will charge a rental fee of $2 million per year, give the owner the rights to concessions and parking, and guarantee no change to this arrangement for the next 10 years. Another city wants only $1 million per year, will also grant the rights to concessions and parking, but will only give a 5-year guarantee. The third city will rent at a nominal $1 per year, will guarantee this rent for 5 years, but wants to retain all revenues from parking and concessions. In this situation the owner must assign probabilities to outcomes and work out the best decision, a process sometimes done objectively with available data, but often a subjective process based on past experiences.

Uncertainty

Under conditions of **uncertainty** the decision alternatives and their potential outcomes are both relatively unknown. Here no historical data or past experience exist on which to base a decision. These decisions are the most difficult to make, the kind that can make or break a manager's career. The manager of a sporting goods equipment manufacturing company entering the Eastern European market would face conditions of uncertainty; while this part of the world holds considerable potential for sporting goods, the political and economic situation is very uncertain.

Approaches to Understanding Decision Making

A large number of different models of the decision-making process can be found in management literature: Some are more applicable to the decisions made by individual sport managers; others pertain more to organizational-level decisions. In this section we look at both individual and organizational decision making.

Individual Decision Making

The two basic models of individual decision making are discussed here. The first is the rational model; the second, the administrative model, is sometimes referred to as the *bounded-rationality model.*

The Rational Model

The rational model of decision making is more a description of how decisions should be made than an account of how they actually are made. This approach focuses on a linear step-by-step analysis of the problem situation and the identification of solutions. Managers define problems and then systematically look for solutions to them; each

TIME OUT

Risky Decisions About Advertising

In 2015 Sport England, a United Kingdom government agency, launched a groundbreaking £10 million (US$12 million) multiplatform advertising campaign called *This Girl Can* (Parker, 2015). The campaign was a response to Sport England's Active People Survey data that consistently reported that significantly fewer women participated in sports compared with men in the United Kingdom. Rather than depicting stereotypical athletic individuals exercising as inspiration, the campaign portrayed ordinary women of different sizes, ages, and abilities being active, "doing their thing no matter how well they do it, how they look or even how red their face gets" (This Girl Can, n.d.) in an attempt to encourage participation. It was the first campaign of its kind to feature women sweating and jiggling as they exercised. The campaign was well received and, according to Sport England data, a year after its introduction, 2.8 million women between the ages of 14 and 40 had subsequently engaged in some or more activity (Sport England, 2016).

However, some advertising campaigns around sensitive subjects are met with controversy. For example, in 2017 Nike ran an online advertising campaign showing Arab women participating in a range of sports (boxing, ice skating, and fencing) in an attempt to dispel stereotypes about Arab women being home-bound and living docile roles. Even though the campaign empowered some individuals, others felt the advertisement was not a true representation of Arab Muslim women (Aswad, 2017). Despite the controversy, the campaign generated discussion about the brand. This is sometimes the strategy of a marketing department in an effort to "cut through the clutter" of online content and bring attention to their brand (Kadić-Maglajlić, Arslanagić-Kalajdžić, Micevski, Michaelidou, & Nemkova, 2017, p. 249). Therefore, sport managers and marketers have to be aware of potential tensions when making decisions about their advertising.

alternative is carefully weighed as to its outcomes, and the single best alternative is selected. The basic premise of this approach is that managers act in an economically rational way. In addition, managers are assumed to have the relevant information about each of the decision alternatives and to act in a nonpolitical, nonemotional manner. This rational approach is also referred to as *normative* or *prescriptive* in the literature (Bar-Eli, Plessner, & Raab, 2011). The rational model of decision making is usually depicted as a series of steps (Archer, 1980; Blai, 1986). Figure 14.1 depicts these steps, and an explanation of each follows.

- *Monitor the decision environment*: A manager scans the sport organization's internal and external environment to determine deviations from expected norms. The technique includes such activities as analyzing financial statements or sales figures, observing competitors, or talking to employees. For example, a manager of a retail sporting goods store who wants to remain competitive must monitor other stores, check what items are popular, keep up with new product availability, and so forth.
- *Define the problem about which a decision has to be made*: If a manager detects a deviation from the expected norms, a problem exists: a discrepancy between the existing state of affairs and the desired state. In our example of the sporting goods retail store, the manager may define her problem as "low profits."
- *Diagnose the problem*: Here the manager must get at the root cause of the problem so that appropriate action can be developed. It may be necessary to gather additional data. The sporting goods store may survey a number of competitors, for example, and determine that they seem to be doing a better trade because they offer a wider range of products.
- *Identify decision alternatives*: Here all the possible solutions to the problem are identified. The manager may sometimes seek the advice of others at this stage of the decision process. For the sporting goods store manager, one decision alternative may be to increase the amount of stock she carries; another may be to focus on a narrower area; another might be to increase or improve the store's online presence; and another may be to cut margins on existing stock to make it more saleable.
- *Analyze alternatives*: When the possible alternatives have been identified, the manager has to analyze each one critically, based on statistical data, personal preference, or technical ability to enact changes and past experiences. The merits of each alternative and its possible outcomes are assessed; for example, our sporting goods store manager will have to consider the costs of increasing her available stock and the probability that this decision will increase trade. This alternative has to be weighed against a choice such as focusing on a narrower market niche, which could be strongly influenced by fluctuations in this particular market.
- *Select the best alternatives*: Here, the manager picks the best alternative from all of the possibilities not eliminated in the analysis phase. Sometimes it is impossible to select just one solution. At other times two or three possible best alternatives may emerge from the analysis and more data will need

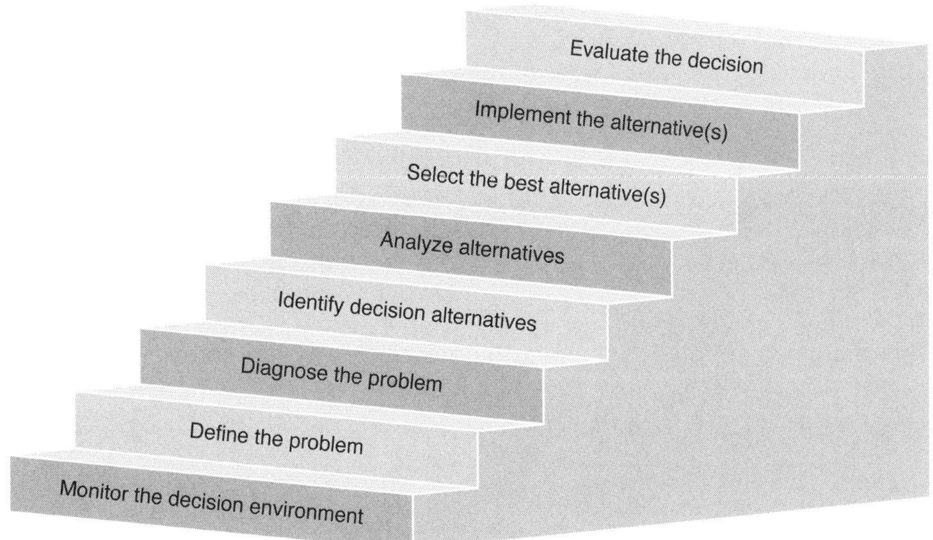

Figure 14.1 Steps in the decision-making process.

to be collected before a choice can be made. In some sport organizations it may even be possible to implement more than one of the alternatives, to see which performs the best.

• *Implement the alternative*: The chosen alternative must then be implemented. Sometimes this may be easy to do; in other cases, the manager will have to use her administrative skills, coercion, authority, and so forth, to get the decision implemented. The implementation process may be long and involved. In our example, if the manager chooses to increase stock she may need to secure a line of credit with a bank, contact suppliers, refurbish displays, and advertise her new products. All of these can present barriers to the actual implementation of a decision.

• *Evaluate the decision*: The final step in the **rational decision-making** process is to evaluate the outcome of the decision to see if the original problem has been rectified. In our sporting goods store example, the manager will have to monitor sales and cash flow to see if increasing stock is actually helping raise profits. Managers sometimes neglect this step because they don't like to find out they made a wrong decision.

The Administrative Model (Bounded Rationality)

Despite the inherent logic of the systematic approach outlined in the rational model, managers are rarely this thorough or precise in their decision making. The rational model of decision making has received frequent criticism in the literature. The limitations of the rational model were first identified by Nobel laureate Herbert Simon in his (1945) book *Administrative Behavior*. Simon drew a distinction between economic reality and what happens in everyday life. Rather than being a completely rational process, he suggested that organizational decisions were bounded by the emotions of the managers involved, by their limited cognitive ability to process information, and by factors such as time constraints and imperfect information. Hence, managers operate with what is referred to as **bounded rationality**: In any decision situation a manager has a limited perception; he or she cannot possibly understand all of the available alternatives, there is ambiguity with how to tackle the issue, and even if they do understand their options, the limits of the human mind would not allow all of that information to be processed. In addition, any attempt at rationality is constrained by the manager's emotions and experience.

As a result of these limitations, Simon argued, decision makers construct simplified models of complex decision processes. The models contain only that information that the manager feels best able to handle; consequently, only a limited number of decision alternatives and outcomes are considered. This means that managers satisfice rather than strive for the optimum solution to a decision. When this solution is found the search for other potentially better solutions stops; not all decision alternatives are considered.

An example of satisficing that is often used and can be applied to our field concerns a student who has recently graduated from a sport management program and is looking for a job. To make a rational decision this person would have to look at all the available jobs everywhere. This is obviously impossible; as a result, the student takes the first acceptable position, rather than continuing to look for one that pays more or may lead to better career opportunities.

This approach to decision making, where focus is placed on understanding what actually happens during the process (in contrast to the rational model), is also referred to in the literature as *positive* or *descriptive* (Bar-Eli et al., 2011). Table 14.1

Table 14.1 Comparison of the Rational and Administrative Models of Decision Making

Rational model	Administrative model
The decision maker is the person who knows and understands all decision alternatives and their outcomes. This individual is unaffected by time constraints, emotions, and so on.	The decision makers are limited by their mental capacity to evaluate all alternatives and their outcomes, and must respond to time constraints, emotions, and so on.
All criteria affecting a decision are considered and evaluated according to the sport organization's goals.	A limited number of criteria are identified, and these form a simple model to evaluate the problem being faced.
All possible decision alternatives are considered.	A limited number of decision alternatives that reflect the decision maker's personal preference are identified.
After careful analysis of all alternatives, the most economically viable alternative is selected.	Alternatives are considered until a suitable one is found.

summarizes and compares the basic premises of the rational and administrative models.

In sport management literature, Hill and Sotiriadou (2016), for example, looked at coach decision making on talent selection in association football. Although their main focus was utilizing an action research approach, they drew on principles of individual decision making. The discussion suggested that over time coaches' decision making deviated from a rational (normative or prescriptive) model to the administrative (positive or descriptive) model as a result of various pressures experienced by the coaches.

Organizational (Group) Decision Making

While individual managers may make decisions using both the rational and administrative models, most decisions in organizations are made by groups. The information, resources, and authority needed to make most of the decisions in complex organizations are rarely the domain of a single individual. Some decisions will require the participation of not only different managers but also sometimes representatives of different divisions, perhaps even different organizations. Studies of organizational decision making have identified a number of models and approaches for understanding the concept. Five major approaches will be now discussed in detail: the management science approach, the Carnegie model, the structuring of unstructured processes approach, the garbage can model, and the Bradford studies.

Management Science

The **management science** approach to decision making, which involves the use of complex mathematics and statistics to develop a solution to a problem (Markland, 1983), was developed during World War II to solve military problems (Leavitt, Dill, & Eyring, 1973). If, for example, Allied planes wanted to fire on enemy warships, they had to make decisions based on information about trajectories, the distance between the plane and its target, the speed at which the plane was traveling, wind speed, the altitude of the plane, and so forth. Each of these variables was modeled using mathematical equations to provide details of the best conditions under which to attack.

After the war the principles of management science were applied to industry and then further improved. Military people such as Robert McNamara, who would later become the U.S. secretary of defense, joined companies like Ford and began using management science techniques to improve the quality of decision making. Today a number of companies use these techniques, their popularity and utility being enhanced by the development of sophisticated computing systems and technology.

Linear programming, queuing theory, Monte Carlo techniques, and decision trees are all examples of management science techniques that can be used to make decisions about a problem. The management science approach works best when data relevant to the decision are easily identified and quantifiable, and problems are structured and logical. The shortcoming of management science is that it does not consider the more qualitative aspects of decision making, such as the political climate or ethical issues.

A considerable number of management science studies have looked at decisions in sport organizations (Andreu & Corominas, 1989; Farina, Kochenberger, & Obremski, 1989). Topics include such diverse issues as scheduling major league baseball games, determining batting lineups, deciding whether to go for the two-point conversion, assigning swimming order in a relay race, simulating road race finishes, and deciding when to pull the goalie in hockey.

The Carnegie Model

Richard Cyert and James March were both associated with what is now Carnegie Mellon University, in Pittsburgh, Pennsylvania, and their approach to decision making is often referred to as the Carnegie model. Their ideas are best illustrated in their (1963) book *A Behavioral Theory of the Firm*. Cyert and March's approach to decision making in some ways extends Simon's ideas of bounded rationality (Simon was also at Carnegie Mellon), and challenges the notion that an organization makes decisions rationally as a single entity. Rather, what Cyert and March show is that organizations are made up of a number of subunits, each with diverse interests. Decision making has to allow for this diversity.

Organizational-level decisions are made by **coalitions** of managers, who do not all have the time or cognitive ability to deal with all aspects of a problem. Consequently, decisions are split into subproblems. For example, in a sport equipment manufacturing company the research-and-design (R&D) department deals with design problems, the production department handles manufacturing, and so forth. This process of splitting problems leads to coalition building, where managers try to find out other managers' points of view and enlist their support for a particular decision. There is a continuous process of bargaining among the various groups in the organization, each trying to influence the decision outcome. As a result, Cyert and March suggest, managers spend more time on managing coalitions than they do on managing the problems confronting the organization itself.

Managers need to resolve the internal conflicts that result from coalition building. While they may agree with each other on organizational goals, there is often little consensus on how to achieve these goals. Decisions are therefore broken down into subproblems and allocated to subunits. But the danger is that these subunits address and solve these problems based on their own rationality and their own interests, not on what is best for the organization as a whole. Also, managers become concerned with short-term solutions rather than long-term strategies. They may involve themselves in what are called **problemistic searches**: When a problem occurs managers quickly search around for a way to handle or resolve it; as soon as one is found, the search stops. Managers tend to rely more on past experiences and procedures when problems are somewhat familiar than when they are unfamiliar, because relying on the past requires less time spent on politics and bargaining.

Cyert and March's work tells us that decision makers need to build coalitions because decision making is a political process. One of the great coalition builders in sport was Horst Dassler, the late head of Adidas. Dassler employed key figures in the world of sport on every continent, who kept him in touch with what was happening in sport in their respective areas. In this way, Dassler was able to make decisions that worked in the best interest of his company.

We see the principles of the Carnegie model in action if we look at the way in which the decision is made about the host city for the Olympic Games. Ostensibly, the IOC has as its goal to award the bid to the city that will stage the best Games. However, what happens in actuality is that various individuals within the IOC form coalitions. As explained in the opening scenario, Evaluation Commission committee members visit the bid sites to evaluate facilities, financing, security, and so forth. Each individual forms his or her preference as to what would be the

TIME OUT

Using Computer Simulation Software to Help Referees and Umpires Make Decisions

Technological development continues to advance exponentially. The use of technology has been fundamental in a wide range of sporting contexts for many years. Examples include R&D and meticulous testing of every component for a Formula 1 car in efforts to gain competitive advantage; development of performance footwear, clothing, and equipment for elite athletes; and computerized simulation and feedback systems used to improve technique. In some sports (e.g., swimming, running, cycling), electronic timing systems have been used for many years to determine the outcomes of races.

Hawk-Eye is a computer system that uses triangulation to track the trajectory of a ball, then display its path (and projected path). The system was first introduced in cricket in 2001 to help umpires with leg before wicket (LBW, i.e., batsperson's leg stopping the ball from hitting the stumps) decisions. Hawk-Eye Innovations Ltd. Equipment is now used in more than 20 sports, covering over 7,000 games or events each year in more than 65 countries around the world (Hawk-Eye, n.d.). For example, the system is used in tennis to assist umpires with line calls. More recently, in 2018, Video Assistant Referee (VAR, audio provided by Crescent Comms Ltd., and video provided by Hawk-Eye) and Goal-Line Technology (GLT, provided by Hawk-Eye) were used for the first time at a FIFA World Cup finals to help match officials make decisions. During the 2018 FIFA World Cup finals, the VAR team (four top FIFA match officials per game) supported the on-pitch referee from a centralized video operation room, located in the International Broadcast Centre in Moscow (FIFA, n.d.). VAR was also used during the 2019 FIFA Women's World Cup finals for the first time. However, the introduction of VAR at the Women's World Cup caused controversy because a record number of penalty decisions were awarded (25 total, 12 of which were with the assistance of VAR). In one instance, Nigeria's goalkeeper was adjudged to have marginally moved away from the goal line during a penalty, which meant France's player had to retake the penalty. The first penalty missed, but the second went in the back of the net, which looked like it would dump Nigeria out of the tournament. (Nigeria qualified for the next phase as a best third-placed team.) Because of the contention, FIFA—mid-tournament—applied to the International Football Association Board for a temporary rule change so that, except in a penalty shootout situation, goalkeepers would not be cautioned if they caused a retake (Pender, 2019).

best site. Coalitions are formed based on what the evaluation committee has seen or on geopolitical lines, and these groups engage in lobbying in an effort to try to make sure the committee makes the decision most favorable to them. King (1991), for example, describes how Canadian IOC member Dick Pound traveled to a number of places with the Calgary Games organizers to lobby other IOC delegates to support the Calgary bid. In sport management literature, Mason, Thibault, and Misener (2006), for example, examined consequential issues from the alleged corrupt behavior of IOC members' decision making during host city bidding processes and the impacts of attempted reforms by the IOC. However, their research used agency theory as a lens rather than explicit focus on the Carnegie model or any other of the decision-making approaches.

The Structuring of Unstructured Processes

In their research on decision making Mintzberg, Raisinghani, and Théorêt (1976) focused on decisions made at the senior levels of an organization. They argued that much of the management science approach to decision making had focused on routine operating decisions, but it is really at the top levels where an organization must make better decisions. In contrast to the concern with political factors evident in Cyert and March's (1963) work, Mintzberg and colleagues (1976) focused on identifying a structure to describe the unstructured process of strategic decision making. Data were obtained on 25 decision processes that were tracked from the initial identification of a problem to the acceptance of a decision solution. Over two thirds of the decision processes took longer than a year to complete; the majority of the decisions were nonprogrammed, that is, unique.

Mintzberg and colleagues (1976) suggest that major decisions in an organization are broken down into smaller decisions that collectively contribute to the major decision. Their research identified three major phases to the decision process. Each phase contains different **routines**, seven in total. The decision process is also characterized by what are called **interrupts**, events that result in a change in the pace or direction of the decision process. Interrupts cause delays because they force an organization to go back and modify its solution, find another one, or engage in political activity to remove an obstacle. Each of these three phases, the routines they contain, and the notion of interrupts are explained more fully in the following section.

The first phase in the decision process is the identification phase, which involves two routines. The decision recognition routine occurs when a manager recognizes a problem about which a decision must be made. A decision is required when there is "a difference between information on some actual situation and some expected standard" (Mintzberg et al., 1976, p. 253). Stimuli that signal the beginning of the need for a decision may originate both within and outside the organization. After the decision recognition routine comes the diagnosis routine; here issues around the problem are clarified and defined. Diagnosis can be explicit and formal or informal and implicit. The more crisis-like the problem to be addressed, the less likely there is to be formal diagnosis.

Following the identification phase is the development phase. Mintzberg and colleagues (1976, p. 255) describe this phase as "the heart of the decision-making process . . . the set of activities that leads to one or more solutions to a problem." This phase contains two routines. First, in the search routine, managers look for solutions to the problem situation. Initial searches are carried out by considering past experiences. If these searches fail, a more active search is carried out, involving looking in "more remote and less familiar areas."

If this search procedure is not successful, a custom-made solution is developed in the design routine. Mintzberg and colleagues (1976, p. 256) point out that this "is a complex, iterative procedure . . . designers grope along building their solution brick by brick without really knowing what it will look like until it is completed."

The final phase of the decision process is the selection phase. Here, a choice is made about a solution. The first routine in the selection phase is the screening routine, used when there are too many ready-made alternatives and a custom design is not required. During screening, certain alternatives are rejected so that a usable number can be handled. The second routine is the evaluation-choice routine. Evaluation and choice can be determined either by judgment, bargaining, or analysis: "In judgment, one individual makes a choice in his own mind with procedures that he does not, perhaps cannot explain; in bargaining, selection is made by a group of decision makers with conflicting goal systems, each exercising judgment; and in analysis . . . factual evaluation is carried out, generally by technocrats, followed by managerial choice by judgment or by bargaining" (Mintzberg et al., 1976, p. 258).

The authorization routine is the final routine in the decision-making process. Authorization occurs when the person or group making the decision does not have the necessary power to commit the organization to the particular solution. Consequently, the decision is passed up the hierarchy; in some cases, it may even have to receive the support of external bodies who could block the decision solution. Sometimes decisions are rejected when passed up to higher levels.

Figure 14.2 shows the stages of Mintzberg and colleagues' (1976) decision process and the various routines. The figure also shows the most common interrupts. The identification phase may involve internal interrupts or political interrupts because organizational members are unable to agree about the need for a strategic decision. New option interrupts occur late in the development phase or in the evaluation-choice routine, and may result in going back to the design routine, to changes in the new option, or simply to evaluation and choice, where the new option is accepted or rejected. External interrupts occur in the final phase and involve attempts by external agents to block the solution. The zigzag lines in the figure signal the possible delays from scheduling, timing, and feedback that occur at each stage of the decision process.

Although few analyses have been conducted of the major decisions made in sport organizations using the approach outlined by Mintzberg and colleagues (1976), it is quite applicable to situations in our field. Decisions such as the NFL's decision to play regular season games outside of the United States (in London, England, and Mexico City, Mexico) as part of an expansion strategy, and the

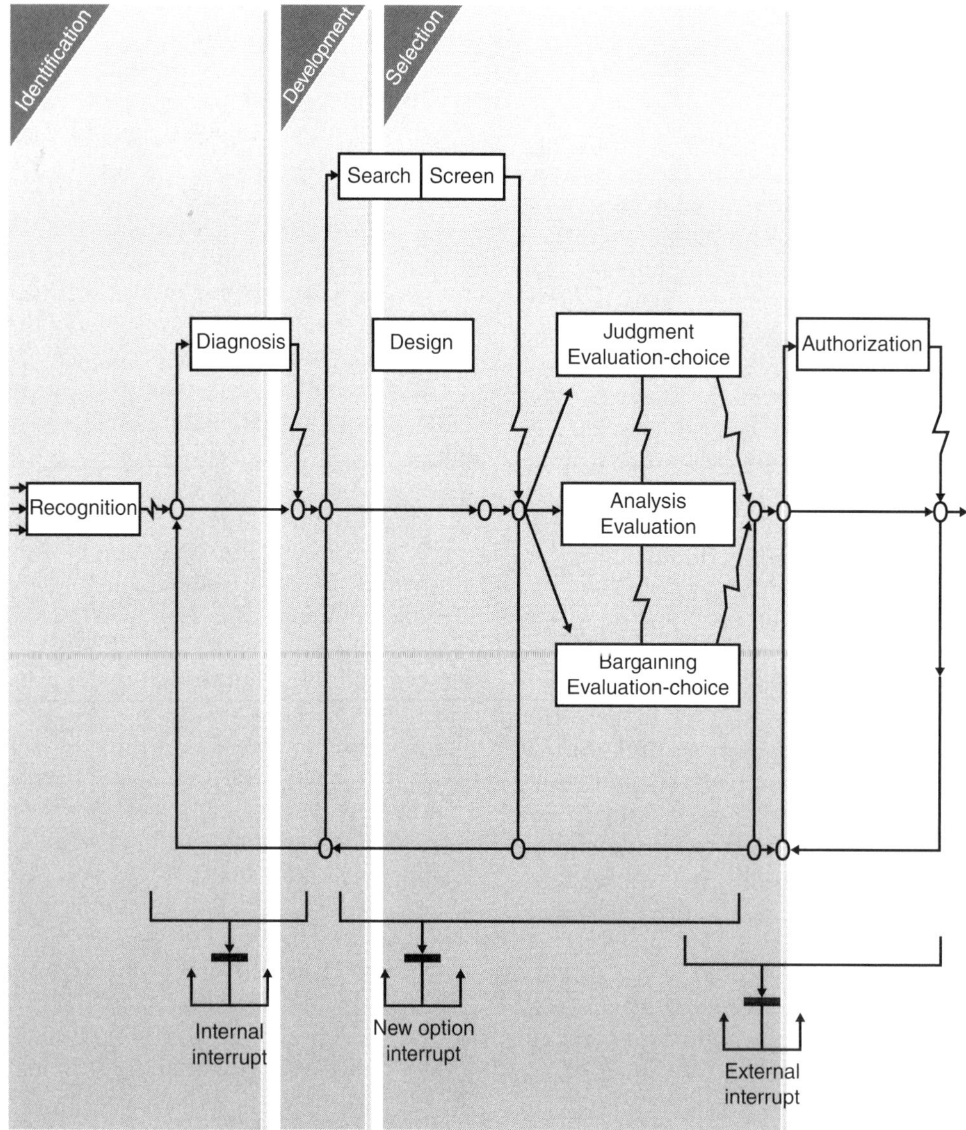

Figure 14.2 General model of the strategic decision process.

Reprinted by permission from H. Mintzberg, D. Raisinghani, and A. Théorêt, "The Structure of 'Unstructured' Decision Processes," *Administrative Science Quarterly* 21, no. 2 (1976): 266.

CFL's decision to establish franchises in the United States could all be analyzed using the "structuring of unstructured processes" approach. One study in sport management literature that has used Mintzberg and colleagues' (1976) work to inform the theoretical framework is Parent's (2010) article, which examined decision making in major sport events over time. Parent focused on the 1999 Pan American Games' organizing committee and suggested that different parameters, drivers, and strategies affected decision making, and that the model of decision making changed from administrative to garbage can to a rational approach over time.

The Garbage Can Model

Much of the work on decision making assumes that the various activities making up the process can be ordered into some logical sequence. Cohen, March, and Olsen (1972) suggest that in reality the situation is much more confusing (see also Cohen & March, 1974; March & Olsen, 1976); in the decision process of an organization many different things are going on at one time. March (1982, p. 36) notes that, "Technologies are changing and poorly understood; alliances, preferences, and perceptions are changing; problems, solutions, opportunities, ideas, people, and outcomes are mixed together in a way that makes their interpretation uncertain and their connections unclear." Cohen, March, and Olsen refer to this situation as **organized anarchy**. It is found in organizations whose structures are highly organic and that are required to change rapidly. Decision making in these organizations is an outcome of four independent streams of events.

- *A stream of problems*: Problems result from dissatisfaction with current performance. Examples include not winning enough games, declining sales, low graduation rates, or a lack of adequately trained staff.
- *A stream of choice opportunities*: This refers to the occasions when a decision is usually made in an organization. Examples include when someone is hired or fired, a budget is finalized, a new service is added, or a team is selected.
- *A stream of participants*: These are the people who make choices in an organization. They come and go as a result of hirings, firings, transfers, retirements, and so forth. Participants come from different backgrounds and have different ideas about problems and solutions.
- *A stream of solutions*: Many participants have ideas to which they are deeply committed; as a result, they may try to sell their ideas to the other members of the organization. In some organizations, people such as planners and systems analysts are actually hired to come up with solutions for situations where problems do not exist. Solutions can then exist without problems being present.

The existence of these four streams means that the process of decision making is somewhat random. The organization is described as a garbage can into which problems, choices, participants, and solutions are all placed. Managers have to act with the resultant disorder; as a result, decisions are rarely systematic and logical. Choices are made when problems come together with the right participants and solutions. As a consequence, some problems are never solved, solutions are put forward even when a problem has yet to be identified, and choices are made before problems are understood.

In sport management literature, Schlesinger, Klenk, and Nagel (2015), for example, utilized the **garbage can model** (under the assumption of bounded rationality) to analyze decision-making processes for recruiting volunteers in sport clubs. The authors acknowledged the usefulness of this theoretical framework for their study. Their findings suggest that decision-making processes were generally reactive in nature, and dominant actors attempt to handle personnel problems of recruitment in the administration; additionally, routine formal committee work and informal networks were also used to deal with other challenges. More frequently, the garbage can approach can be found in studies of policy analysis. For example, Kingdon (1995) proposed a multiple streams framework based on Cohen, March, and Olsen's (1972) garbage can theory. Kingdon (1995) suggested that public policies emerge when policy entrepreneurs capitalize on a political (opportunity) stream by coupling a problem stream with an alternative policy.

The coming together of the streams is termed *coupling*, which creates a "policy window" (of opportunity) for policy entrepreneurs to "push their pet solutions, or to push attention to their special problems" (Kingdon, 1995, p. 165). The policy window can appear and disappear unpredictably, which can result in disorderly policy making, hence the garbage can metaphor (Houlihan & Lindsey, 2012). Green (2004, p. 381) suggests that "early work on non-decision making and Kingdon's (1995) more recent multiple-streams approach . . . seek to explain why some issues make it to the political agenda and others do not."

The strength of the garbage can model is that it draws our attention to the role that chance and timing play in the decision-making process. Also, unlike other approaches, which tend to focus on single decisions, the garbage can approach is concerned with multiple decisions.

Bradford Studies

The Bradford studies, so named because they were conducted by Professor David Hickson and his research team at the University of Bradford in England, were carried out over approximately 15 years from the early 1970s to the mid-1980s (Butler, Astley, Hickson, Mallory, & Wilson, 1979; Cray, Mallory, Butler, Hickson, & Wilson, 1988, 1991; Hickson, Butler, Cray, Mallory, & Wilson, 1985, 1986; Mallory, Butler, Cray, Hickson, & Wilson, 1983; Wilson, Butler, Cray, Hickson, & Mallory, 1986). Using data from 150 decisions, Hickson and colleagues (1985) focused on the process of decision making as opposed to the outcome and implementation of a decision. His research team identified five dimensions of process, encompassing 12 variables.

The first of these dimensions, scrutiny, concerns the information sources available to the decision maker(s). Four variables were identified as making up this particular dimension. Expertise, the first variable, was assessed by the number of internal and external sources from which information about the decision was obtained. Disparity refers to the extent to which the decision makers had confidence in the sources from which information was obtained. Externality was "measured as the ratio of the confidence in external information to that placed in all information" (Cray et al., 1988, p. 16). Effort refers to the way in which the information was acquired—for example, was it merely the result of recalling personal experiences, or did it involve the use of working groups or other similar mechanisms to generate and analyze information?

The second dimension, interaction, had three variables. Informal interaction was a measure of the extent to which the decision to be made was discussed informally, such as in hallways or over coffee. Formal interaction concerns the extent to which the decision process was structured through meetings, work groups, and so forth. Scope of negotiation, the final variable, assessed the extent to which the decision was made by one individual or was subject to negotiation before a choice was made.

The third dimension, flow, relates to the delays, reconsiderations, and disruptions found in the decision process. Two variables made up this dimension. Disruptions, the first variable, concerned the length and occurrence of disruptions that took place in the decision process. Impedance concerned the extent to which the cause of delays could be controlled.

The fourth dimension, duration, was made up of two variables. Gestation time was the length of the period from the initial mention of the decision issue until specific action was taken toward making a decision. Process time was the time from the start of the specific action to when the decision was authorized.

Finally, the last dimension, authority, was a single measure of the level in the organization at which the decision was authorized.

Compiling data on each of these variables, Hickson and his colleagues analyzed 136 decisions using cluster analysis. Data on 14 of the decisions were incomplete, so they could not be used in the cluster program. Three distinct ways of making decisions were identified: sporadic processes, fluid processes, and constricted processes. The characteristics of these decisions are shown in figure 14.3 and explained in more detail in the following discussion.

Sporadic decision processes are made in a manner characterized by disruption and delay. Short periods of activity are followed by delays,

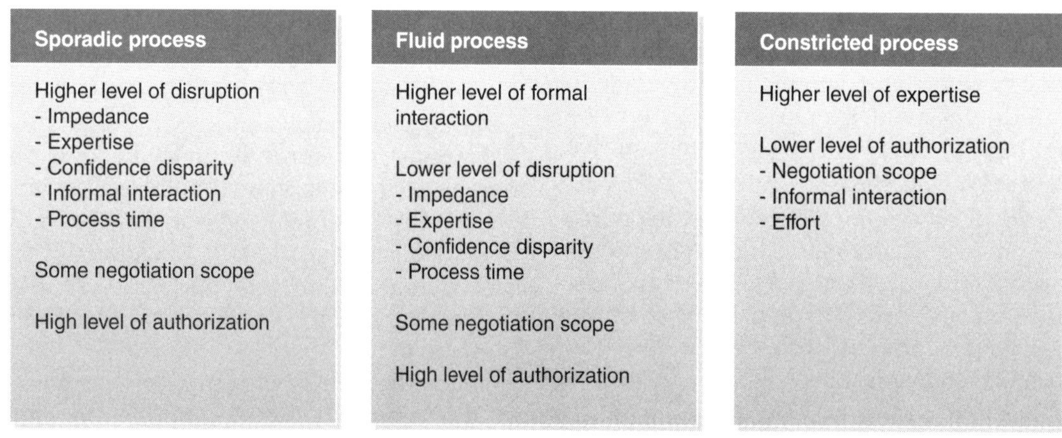

Figure 14.3 Characteristics of three types of strategic decision making.
Based on Cray et al. (1988).

KEY ISSUES FOR SPORT MANAGERS

Nutt (2004) argued that decisions fail because judgment is rushed, time and resources are unwisely allocated, and solutions are taken from stakeholder claims or current practices instead of exploring other possibilities.

In this chapter, the decisions have been presented as being made under conditions of certainty, but in truth, most decisions have a certain element of uncertainty to them—especially strategic decisions. However, the level of uncertainty can be decreased by doing a SWOT analysis.

Ford and Gioia (2000) mentioned that creativity may be a good way to deal with uncertainty and fear in decision making. However, they explained that "adopting creative choices may increase the odds of resolving the problem(s) at hand, but at the cost of leaving decision makers open to the stones and arrows of the critics should the decision fail" (p. 725). Therefore, the best solution may sometimes be the riskiest for a manager or the organization. Whether to go down that route is a decision each manager must make after weighing the pros and cons. Still, Nutt (2004) argued that a successful decision-making process should use multiple perspectives to find innovative possibilities once objectives are clearly defined.

The decision-making process, when put into practice, is rarely linear in nature, going from one clear phase to the next, as the rational model would suggest. Instead, decision making is a complex process. It involves going back and forth between phases; it is discontinuous, recursive, and reliant on incomplete information; and it even incorporates an aspect of educated guesswork, also referred to as luck, gut feeling, or intuition (Sadler-Smith & Shefy, 2004).

There are also factors that can make a decision more complex or more difficult. As a manager, you must be aware of potential ethical issues (such as Nike's use of sweatshops, in the past, to decrease production costs but to the detriment of the workers). Another concern is the power and political dynamics—issues discussed in chapter 15—that can influence whether a decision is made, how the decision-making process occurs (who's involved, which choices are examined), what decision is made, how the decision is implemented, and, ultimately, whether the result is successful.

Several recent examples of where sport and politics have mixed, resulting in policy and rule changes, highlight the complexities and consequences of decisions. One example is the introduction of the NFL's Game Day Concussion Diagnosis and Management Protocol in 2011 (which is reviewed and updated annually) as a result of the debates about player concussion (NFL, 2018). Following criticism of the NFL for not acting sooner, the policy seems to have been well received and has influenced the sport at lower levels as well as other sports. Another decision that involved sport and politics occurred when the NFL attempted to introduce a policy in May 2018 that sanctioned players if they knelt during the United States' national anthem. The anthem controversy started in 2016 when former San Francisco 49ers quarterback Colin Kaepernick began kneeling in protest about alleged racial inequalities and police brutality. (See chapter 15 for more detail.) At the time of writing, the policy is on hold due to backlash since its introduction (Maske, 2018). As a third example, decisions were made by International Federations (IFs) about female Muslim athletes wearing hijabs, a religious veil head covering, during competition. Until 2014 FIFA had banned hijabs and other head coverings due to perceived safety concerns, and it was only in late 2017 that International Basketball Federation (FIBA) changed their rules to allow players to wear the hijab during matches. Prior to FIBA lifting the ban, the Qatari women's basketball team withdrew from the 2014 Asian Games after some players were refused permission to cover their hair (BBC Sport, 2017). With an increasing number of IFs updating policies on head coverings, Nike introduced a Pro Hijab, for performance athletes, in December 2017 (Nike, 2017).

The examples above highlight how sport managers need to be mindful of how their decision-making (with rules and regulations, for example) will impact individuals. Bakan (2004) suggested that managers can only be acting morally when they act in the best interest of the shareholders and no one else.

during which information is gathered and the various constituents in the process argue over the relative merits of what has been uncovered. The scope of negotiation is fairly wide, indicating the number of individuals and groups involved in the process, but because much of the negotiation takes place in informal settings, decision making takes longer than average. There is some tendency for the decision process to require authorization by the most senior level of the organization. In short, the actual process of decision making is fairly wide-ranging and uneven, but ultimately the decision must be approved through the organization's highest level.

In contrast to sporadic decisions, **fluid decision** processes have fewer and less serious interruptions; fewer experts are involved and the whole process is quicker. The information base used to make the decision is more homogeneous, and much of the interaction during the actual making of the decision takes place in a formal setting. The search for a decision, while encompassing considerable scope for negotiation, is narrowed quickly and ultimately approved at the highest level of the organization.

Constricted decision processes are made with the use of expert information, but little effort is put into seeking data not readily obtainable. Most of the interaction around this type of decision process is informal because the relatively few people involved are in frequent contact. There is little scope for negotiation here; decisions emanate from the lower levels of senior management and will probably be ratified by the CEO (unlike sporadic and fluid decisions, which usually require board approval). Much of this process is focused on a single decision maker, in most cases the organization's CEO.

As with Mintzberg and colleagues (1976), sport management literature shows few attempts to use the Bradford approach to understand the decision-making process in sport organizations. However, the considerable number of published works emanating from this research project is one measure of its acceptance in the general field of management. The dimensions and variables identified by Hickson and colleagues are quite applicable to a variety of sport organizations. Replications and extensions of this work using sport organizations could not only enhance our understanding of the decision-making process in our field's organizations, but also extend existing theory on this topic and thus contribute to management studies in general. That said, Hill and Kikulis (1999) have utilized the Bradford studies in a study that looked at decision making in interuniversity athletic conferences. They found that using the work of Hickson et al. (1986), combined with Butler's (1991) work, to understand the dynamics of strategic decision making provided a useful theoretical framework for analysis. In addition, Parent's (2010) case study, which examined the decision making of the 1999 Pan American Games' organizing committee, also supported a number of elements of the Bradford studies.

Summary and Conclusions

All sport managers make decisions, and an understanding of how the decision-making process works can increase the effectiveness and efficiency of these decisions. In this chapter we began by explaining the concept of decision making, distinguishing between programmed and nonprogrammed decisions. We noted that managers prefer programmed decisions because they are more predictable and, because of their predictability, are most frequently found at lower levels of a sport organization. Nonprogrammed decisions are found at higher levels. We looked at the three conditions under which decisions can be made: certainty, risk, and uncertainty. Most decisions in sport organizations are made under conditions of risk and uncertainty.

We looked at the major theoretical approaches to understanding decision making. We focused on individual decision making—the rational approach and the more realistic notion of bounded rationality—and compared and contrasted the two approaches. We then examined organizational group decision making. Five major approaches to organizational group decision making were identified: the management science approach, the Carnegie model, the structuring of unstructured processes, the garbage can approach, and the Bradford studies. We noted that very little work in sport management literature had made use of any of these approaches. We examined examples of the type of sport organizations' decisions that these theoretical models could be used more frequently to understand. By understanding the decision process, and hence the factors that influence decision making, sport managers can make better decisions and become better managers.

Review Questions

1. What type of programmed decisions would you expect would be made in a local nonprofit track and field club?
2. In what type of sport organization would you expect to find a large number of nonprogrammed decisions?

3. Think of a familiar sport organization. Under what type of conditions are most of the decisions made in this organization?
4. What are the strengths and weaknesses of the management science approach to decision making?
5. What similarities can you see in Simon's idea of bounded rationality and Cyert and March's Carnegie model?

Suggestions for Further Reading

As we have noted in this chapter, little research in sport management literature has looked at the process of managerial decision making in sport organizations. While some accounts of the problems confronted by decision makers can be found in the popular press, they contain little in the way of any scholarly analysis. If you are looking for more information on this topic, you are advised to consult general organizational literature. For work on bounded rationality, begin with Simon's (1945) text *Administrative Behavior*. While this is an old book, it does form the basis for much of the future work conducted on this concept. Examples of work that builds on Simon's ideas can be found in all of the major organizational journals. For example, see Simon's (1987) article "Making Management Decisions: The Role of Intuition and Emotion" in *Academy of Management Executive*; Lyles' (1987) article "Defining Strategic Problems: Subjective Criteria of Executives" in *Organization Studies*; and Jackson and Dutton's (1988) "Discerning Threats and Opportunities" in *Administrative Science Quarterly*. If you are interested in the rational model, with a particular focus on an economic perspective (the foundation of the rational approach), read the chapter on "Individual Decision-Making" by Baucells and Katsikopoulos (2015) in the book *Experimental Economics*.

For those interested in the management science approach to decision making, we recommend the journal *Interfaces*, which sometimes contains research on sport organizations. In terms of the Carnegie model, you are advised, as with work on bounded rationality, to read the original research and then see the major management journals for extensions of this approach. Stevenson, Pearce, and Porter's (1985) "The Concept of 'Coalition' in Organization Theory and Research" in the *Academy of Management Review* is one example of how Cyert and March's original ideas can be extended. In terms of the unstructured processes approach, the garbage can model, and the Bradford approach, you are likewise advised to read the references cited in the chapter and look through management and organizational journals for extensions of this work. All of these approaches have good potential for being applied to sport organizations. The *Academy of Management Executive* published a special issue in 2004 on decision making and firm success (vol. 18, no. 4). *The Oxford Handbook of Organizational Decision Making*, edited by Hodgkinson and Starbuck (2008), provides a comprehensive overview of decision making, covering insights from the fields of (primarily) psychology, economics, political science, and sociology, and offers analysis at the individual, group, organizational, and interorganizational levels. Finally, for sport-specific contexts, Foster, O'Reilly, and Dávila (2016), in their book *Sports Business Management: Decision Making Around the Globe*, offer a useful collection of real-world situations where multiple stakeholders have made decisions, and Alamar's (2013) book, *Sports Analytics: A Guide for Coaches, Managers, and Other Decision Makers*, demonstrates how sport organizations can implement analytics into their decision-making strategies. (See also chapter 22 for a detailed discussion about sports analytics.)

Case for Analysis

Manchester United Goes Global

When David Beckham signed a deal with Adidas and his popularity soared in Asia, his team, Manchester United, saw a golden opportunity. Asian consumers, known for player loyalty, loved Beckham but not Manchester United. Though it was at the top of the European association football world, the club lacked notoriety elsewhere, but as a publicly traded organization it had a primary duty to its shareholders to make money. Manchester United saw a chance to capitalize on Beckham's fan base in Asia, an emerging market, particularly because China was to host the 2008 Summer Olympics. So, the club set a plan into motion: It would globalize into the many untapped commercial markets worldwide.

In 1999 Manchester United went to Asia to promote itself as a brand. The club played games and built megastores and Manchester United–themed cafés. The plan began to work, and as loyalty and merchandise sales grew, Manchester United's value climbed. Manchester and Beckham seemed intrinsically linked—David Beckham was a cash cow for the club that basically owned his image.

In 2002 Manchester United signed a 13-year deal with Nike for US$430 million, which conflicted with Beckham's Adidas sponsorship. In 2003 Beckham was transferred to Real Madrid—an Adidas-sponsored team—and with him went the fans. Immediately after Beckham's departure in 2003, Sir Alex Ferguson signed Cristiano Ronaldo—a Nike-sponsored footballer—from Sporting Clube de Portugal. Ronaldo became United's new superstar player, winning numerous awards before his transfer to Real Madrid in 2009.

When other teams, such as Real Madrid, tried to grab a piece of the Asian market, Manchester United entered another untapped soccer market, the United States. The club teamed up with the New York Yankees in a joint venture to help each sport penetrate the other's respective markets. Manchester United played games in the United States for two summers (2003 and 2004), increasing their popularity every time.

In 2004 Manchester United became the world's most valuable team at US$1.1 billion and became the most popular sport team in Europe, Asia, and North America, even without Beckham.

By 2005 China surpassed the United States as the largest consumer, and to keep the Asian loyalty fires burning, Manchester returned to East Asia, visiting Hong Kong and Japan. Subsequent preseason tours included visiting South Africa, Japan, China, South Korea, Australia, Malaysia, a handful of European countries, and the United States an additional five times (2011, 2014, 2015, 2017, and 2018).

In 2005 the Glazer family paid US$1.47 billion for a controlling share of Manchester United, and, as of 2018, the team was valued by Forbes as the world's most valuable association football team at US$4.12 billion (Ozanian, 2018). Possible reasons for the success include TV rights, sponsorship (in 2015 Adidas returned as the kit manufacturer for a record deal worth US$993 million over a 10-year period), and successful use of social media to grow the brand (Ozanian, 2017). Manchester United has social media accounts across many popular platforms, often in various languages, and own their own TV channel (MUTV), where games are streamed for subscribers to access. In China, for example, Sina Sports and Manchester United announced a long-term partnership in 2016 that saw Sina Sports become the club's official digital media partner in China and the exclusive broadcaster of MUTV in mainland China. Sina Sports is part of Sina Corp., which owns Weibo, often referred to as China's Twitter.

Questions

1. How would you use Cyert and March's work (the Carnegie model) to understand the decision-making processes outlined in this case?
2. Using Mintzberg, Raisinghani, and Théorêt's approach to understanding decision making, identify the different routines and interrupts that apply to Manchester United's globalization attempts over the years.
3. Which approach to organizational decision making do you think could best explain Manchester United's decision to partner with Sina Sports in China?
4. Who do you think decides where the team conducts the preseason tours? Why do you think Manchester United has visited the United States so often since 2011?

CHAPTER 15

Power and Politics in Sport Organizations

Trevor Slack, PhD
Alex Thurston, PhD

Learning Objectives

When you have read this chapter, you should be able to

1. explain what we mean when we talk about strategic choice,
2. distinguish between power and authority,
3. explain the sources of power that individuals within a sport organization can use,
4. explain how subunits come to acquire power in a sport organization,
5. understand distinctions between the various interpretations of power offered by seminal theorists, and
6. describe the types of political activity that we might find taking place in a sport organization.

Key Concepts

agency
authority
centrality
charismatic authority
coalitions
coercive power
control of resources
control over decision making
controlling information
disempowerment
empowerment
experts
expert power
hard power
legitimate power
networks
nonsubstitutability
politics
power
referent power
reward power
soft power
strategic choice
structure
uncertainty

Power, Politics, and 2022 FIFA World Cup

On December 2, 2010, Fédération Internationale de Football Association (FIFA), the global governing body for association football, shocked the world when it awarded the small state of Qatar the rights to stage the 2022 FIFA World Cup finals. Not only would Qatar be the first ever Middle Eastern country to stage the tournament, but with a population of 2.7 million (Ministry of Development Planning and Statistics, 2019), it would also be the smallest.

For Qatar, the desire to stage one of the (if not *the*) largest sport events on Earth looked to serve several political objectives, both at home and abroad. On the former, Qatar—like so many governments who stage sport events—seek, in part, to use the tournament to increase national sports participation with the hope of successfully confronting growing rates of lifestyle diseases (such as obesity and diabetes) found among the state's youth (Brannagan & Giulianotti, 2014). On the latter, Qatar looks to use its staging of the World Cup to acquire various forms of power on the international stage (Brannagan & Rookwood, 2016; Reiche, 2015). Brannagan and Giulianotti (2015), for instance, argue that Qatar's acquisition of the World Cup stems from the desire of the Qataris to showcase their nation to global audiences and, in doing so, wield "soft power," referring to the ability to acquire power through attraction rather than coercion. (See the subsection "Soft Power" later in this chapter.)

Nonetheless, while the tournament looks to serve specific sociopolitical goals for Qatar, it has also provided others with a vital opportunity to acquire various forms of power themselves, in many cases, at the expense of the host (Brannagan & Giulianotti, 2018). Indeed while, on the one hand, the World Cup looks to promote Qatar in a positive light on the world stage, on the other, it looks to be used by various global organizations to showcase the state's more negative attributes. The United Kingdom's *The Sunday Times*, for instance, has claimed Qatar unfairly acquired the rights to host the 2022 World Cup via a series of undisclosed payments-in-kind to various political and sporting officials. Most notable has been the purported role of Qatari-born and former Asian Football Confederation President and FIFA Executive Committee member, Mohamed bin Hammam, who, it is claimed, used multiple slush funds to pay in excess of £3 million (US$4 million) to FIFA officials to ensure Qatar won the rights to the tournament (Calvert & Blake, 2014). Additionally, the UK newspaper *The Guardian* produced a series of articles that claimed to reveal how many of the state's South Asian workers—the majority of whom work within Qatar's bustling construction sector—face daily cases of exploitation, mental abuse, dangerous working and living conditions, and a significant lack of pay and access to food and free drinking water (Conn, 2018). Such conditions have led to a plethora of international criticisms levied against Qatar from international nongovernmental organizations. Europe director of Human Rights Watch Jan Egeland, for example, has labeled Qatar a "crucible of exploitation and misery" (Human Rights Watch, 2013).

The opening scenario about Qatar and the 2022 association football World Cup provides a telling example of how sport and the concepts of politics and power intertwine. The hosting of major sport events such as the World Cup not only provides cities and states with opportunities for increased political capital and power acquisition, but also allows the media and various nongovernmental organizations the chance to push forward and achieve their own agendas because of such events' mass global audiences. In doing so, these organizations not only increase their international status through sport, but, in many cases, seek to successfully expand their importance and power within the wider international sphere.

In chapters 4 and 21 we look at how environment and technology influence the structure of a sport organization. Although each of these imperatives (or contingencies, as they are sometimes called) can help us explain how a sport organization should be structured, none provides a total explanation. For each imperative, questions exist about its explanatory power. Ford and Slocum (1977) suggested that more explanatory power might be obtained by combining variables. They noted that few studies of organizational structure considered more than one contingency at the same time, besides size and technology. However, Child (1972) suggests that even if this approach is employed it can still leave up to 40 percent of the structural variance in an organization as unaccounted.

Some researchers have questioned the rational approach to understanding organizations that is the basis of contingency theory. They suggest that a focus on power and politics in organizations may be a better approach and one that would help us understand much of the unexplained variance in organizational structure. Essentially, the argument made by those who subscribe to a political model of organization is that those who hold the power in the organization will choose a set of structural arrangements that will maintain or increase their power: They will engage in politically motivated behavior. Followers of this school of thought see organizations differently from those who view them as rational entities. In the rational model, organizations are seen as entities in which members share common goals, make decisions in an orderly and logical manner, and see conflict as dysfunctional to their central purpose. In the political model, it is accepted that people and groups within organizations have different goals, make decisions in their own best interests, and engage in conflictual behavior.

In this chapter we look at the issues of organizational power and politics. We look first at the concept of **strategic choice**. This "typically includes not only the establishment of structural forms but also the manipulation of environmental features and the choice of relevant performance standards" (Child, 1972, p. 1). We then look at the issue of power and how it differs from another common concept in the study of organizations: authority. We examine how power is obtained, we look at both individual and organizational sources of power, and we introduce a selection of other notable conceptualizations of power. Next, we look at political activity in sport organizations and the types of political tactics that can be employed to acquire, develop, and use power.

Strategic Choice

The notion of strategic choice was first put forward by John Child in 1972 as an argument against the emphasis that was being placed on structural imperatives. Essentially, what Child suggested was that although imperatives such as environment and technology constrain managers in the decisions they make, these people still have the power to exercise choice regarding these contingency factors, and consequently they have the power to determine the type of organizational structure they adopt. For example, Child argued that the decision makers in an organization had far more power to choose their environment, technology, and size than was commonly inferred by those who argued for the importance of these imperatives in explaining organizational structure.

In terms of environment, he suggested (1972, p. 4) that "organizational decision makers may have certain opportunities to select the type of environment in which they will operate." For example, Gymshark's founder, Ben Francis, decided in 2012 to enter the gym clothing market, adopting an online-only retail model; so, too, would the chair of a sport management department who chose to direct her department's efforts toward teaching and executive development rather than toward research. In deciding to enter a particular environmental domain, the senior managers of a sport organization are at the same time deciding the types of organizations with which they will have to interact, the type of regulations to which they will be subject, and who their competitors will be. These decisions in turn will influence their choice of structure. In short, senior managers influence structure by the choices they make about environmental domain rather than the environment itself.

Child (1972, p. 6) also maintains that technology and its relationship to structure should be "viewed as a derivative of decisions made by those in control of the organization regarding the tasks to be carried out in relation to the resources available to perform them." So, for example, when Bill Holland (Holland Cycles) chose to make custom bike frames in his small workshop in Spring Valley, California, with a group of five or six employees, he was at the same time electing to use a craft technology. It would have been very difficult for him to enter into mass production. Managers, therefore, dictate structure by their choice of domain, which in turn influences the choice of technology.

Size, too, is subject to the choices made by managers. Although having to manage many organizational members and their activities may constrain certain structural choices, numerous important choices still exist (Child, 1972). For example, managers may choose to break down large units into smaller ones that can act independently; alternatively, they may choose to limit the size of a unit. Berrett, Burton, and Slack (1993) describe how some entrepreneurs within the sport industry made a choice to limit the size of their business in order to maintain centralized control.

In addition to making choices about their organization's environment, technology, and size, Child (1972, p. 4) suggests that in some cases managers "may command sufficient power to influence the conditions prevailing within environments where they are already operating." Organizations are not always influenced by their environment; some can "enact" it (Weick, 1969). In large companies in particular, managers can create a demand for a product and take steps to limit the amount of competition within their environment. For example, the Canadian Football League (CFL) lobbied Canada's federal government to prevent the World Football League (a short-lived gridiron football league) from placing a franchise in Toronto. Another example is the 2017 merger of the R&A (an organization that jointly, with United States Golf Association, governs the sport of golf worldwide) with the Ladies' Golf Union (LGU). In both cases, the managers of sport organizations worked to enact their environment by limiting competition.

A third argument that Child (1972) makes for strategic choice concerns the difference between the actual environment of an organization and the way it is perceived by its managers. As we saw in chapter 4, managers make choices based on the way they perceive their environment to be, not necessarily the way it actually is. As such it is managerial choice rather than the actual nature of a sport organization's environment that is most likely to influence structural design. For example, a sportswear manufacturer may see Eastern Europe as a dynamic, growing environment with new market opportunities. To meet this demand new product lines may be developed, staff increased, and new manufacturing facilities acquired. Eastern Europe may or may not be a dynamic environment, but managerial perception and the choices managers make based on this perception lead to structural change, not the actual nature of the environment.

A final area where Child (1972) suggests the influence of strategic choice can be felt is the area of organizational effectiveness. Most studies of organizational effectiveness treat performance as a dependent variable. Child (1972) suggests that, in contrast, a theory concerned with organizational structure should propose structural variables as being dependent on the decisions made in reference to certain performance standards. Structure is therefore the dependent variable. Managers do not always make decisions to utilize a structure that will produce the highest level of performance because this decision may reduce their power or destabilize the organization. Rather, they select a structure that will achieve an optimal level of performance, allowing the decision group to use structural arrangements that match their preferences, which in turn allows them to increase or maintain their level of power and autonomy. An example of this type of situation is once again found in Berrett, Burton, and Slack's (1993) study of entrepreneurs in the sport and leisure industry. One of the entrepreneurs was quite willing to forego the increased profits (one of the most common measures of effectiveness) that could be achieved by expansion, in order to retain the type of structural arrangements that allowed him to maintain control of his operation. For a more in-depth discussion about the concepts of effectiveness and control, refer to chapters 3 and 10 respectively in this textbook.

Power and Authority

Power is one of the most widespread yet more problematic concepts in academic literature. The concept of power in organizations has been studied for many decades, yet notions of power are still contested (Kidd, Legge, & Harari, 2009). While some scholars have suggested that there is an overabundance of writing on power (Clark, 1967), others have indicated that the concept has not received much attention (Kotter, 1977). Martin (1971, p. 240) suggested that "theorizing about power has often been confusing, obscurantist, and banal"; he adds, "it is not surprising that March (1966) concluded that 'on the whole power is a disappointing concept.'" This is primarily due to the difficulty of observing and measuring what actually constitutes power.

Power is not something we can see within a sport organization, but its effects can be clearly felt. While organizational literature contains numerous definitions (Astley & Sachdeva, 1984; Pfeffer, 1992), the most commonly accepted conceptualization suggests that power is the ability to get someone to do something they would not have otherwise done or "the probability that one actor in a social relationship will be in a position to carry out his own will despite resistance, regardless of the basis on which this probability rests" (Weber, 1947/2012, p. 152).

Notwithstanding the widespread use of this definition, these kinds of explanations of the concept of power are not without problems. Martin (1971, p. 243), for example, suggests that this type of definition implies that power involves conflict or antagonism and ignores "the possibility that power relations may be relations of mutual convenience: [and] power may be a resource facilitating the achievement of the goals of both A and B." Martin also saw as problematic the fact that the Weberian definition of power (and others like it) view power as being personalized instead of the product of the social relationships between actors. In this regard Emerson (1962) points out that these types of relationships are not one-sided and often include mutual interdependence.

Also important to note about the use of the term *power* is that some writers use it interchangeably with, or to encompass, concepts such as coercion, influence, manipulation, and **authority** (Bachrach & Baratz, 1962; Styskal, 1980). Authority is in fact one form of power; it is the power that is formally sanctioned by a sport organization, the power that accrues to a person because of his or her role within the organization (Weber, 1947/2012). Authority is only legitimate within the sport organization that grants the authority. The power by which managers exercise strategic choice is, in essence, authority—the power they derive from the position they hold in the organization. This is not to say that people who do not have authority cannot influence these choices. Authority must be accepted by the role-holder's subordinates, and it is exercised down the organizational hierarchy. In contrast, power can be exercised vertically and horizontally within the organizational hierarchy. The examples in the following list illustrate acts that involve authority and those that entail the use of other forms of power.

Actions Based on Authority

- A sport management professor granting a student an extension to complete his or her coursework
- The owner of a sports team firing the coach following a poor run of form
- A quarterback calling the plays in a gridiron football game
- A CEO of a sporting goods company making the decision to penetrate a new market

Actions Based on Other Forms of Power

- A city governor contacting a friend who holds a high-ranking position at a sport International Federation to enlist the help of increasing the chances of that city's bid being successful during the tendering process of selecting a host city for a major sport event. (See chapters 13 and 24 for more detail about governance and procurement frameworks.)
- An athletic director asking the university's sports therapist to look at her 14-year-old son's sprained ankle
- A college basketball coach hiring a good high school player to work at the college's summer basketball camp in order to encourage her to attend the college

TIME OUT

Phil Jackson, "The Zen Master"

Phil Jackson, a retired National Basketball Association (NBA) coach, has the best win-loss percentage and holds the most championship rings (presented to the winning teams in North American sports leagues) in history (Hancock, 2016). Jackson coached an array of big-name stars—including Michael Jordan, Dennis Rodman, and Scottie Pippen when coaching the Chicago Bulls, and Kobe Bryant and Shaquille O'Neal when head coach at the Los Angeles Lakers—with great success. Many of these superstar players had egos and strong personalities, and what made Jackson so successful was his ability to effectively manage these individuals so they'd come together to share a common goal: winning. He would often use unorthodox approaches to his coaching and his leadership (see chapter 19 for a detailed overview of leadership approaches). Introducing meditation to his teams' training schedule earned him his "Zen master" moniker (Hancock, 2016). Reflecting on his coaching career, Jackson describes his coaching approach:

> After years of experimenting, I discovered that the more I tried to exert power directly the less powerful I became. I learned to dial back my ego and distribute power as widely as possible without surrendering final authority. Paradoxically, this approach strengthened my effectiveness because it freed me to focus on my job as a keeper of the team's vision. Some coaches insist on having the last word, but I always tried to foster an environment in which everyone played a leadership role. . . . If your primary objective is to bring your team into a state of harmony and oneness, it doesn't make sense for you to rigidly impose your authority. (Jackson & Delehanty, 2015)

Jackson honed his skill over time, developing power relations to be of mutual convenience and empowering his teams to become so dominant and successful.

- The president of a sport consulting company asking his secretary to buy a birthday gift for his wife

As a side note, the concept of governance, discussed in chapter 13, refers to power and authority. In the chapter, Garcia suggests that governance is concerned with the distribution of power, authority, and the legitimacy to make decisions within an organization, and relates to the decision-making structures, the distribution of responsibilities, and the lines of management and accountability.

Sources of Power

While we often think of people as being powerful, the way a sport organization is structured can lead to some subunits becoming powerful, regardless of the people within them. In this section we look first at the ways individuals acquire power. We then focus on organizational sources of power.

Sources of Individual Power

Although power is a central concept in political science, it is difficult to gather evidence of the nature and exercise of power. Hence, we see a wide range of interpretations. That said, a simple definition of power offered by Byers, Slack, and Parent (2012, p. 121) suggests power is "the ability to influence the behaviour or ideas of one or more people." That is, power can be conceptualized with a focus on how an individual gets what they want.

One of the most widely cited accounts of the sources of individual power is French and Raven's (1959) five-part typology: legitimate power, reward power, coercive power, referent power, and expert power. A description of each of these types is presented below. It is important to note that the types of power cited are not discrete and in fact may overlap. Shetty (1978, p. 177) notes, for example, that the "possession of one type of power can affect the extent and effectiveness of other types. The judicious use of reward power and coercive power can increase the effectiveness of legitimate power; inappropriate use, however, will decrease legitimate power."

Legitimate power is the same as authority. People acquire it by virtue of their position within a sport organization. Managers, athletic directors, deans, members of the board of directors of a voluntary sport organization, and coaches are all examples of people who, because of the positions they hold in their respective sport organizations, can expect compliance from their subordinates when they request that things be done. They have legitimate power. This type of power comes from a person's position and not because of any other special qualities she or he may possess. This does not mean, however, that people who occupy the same position will use the power of their office in the same way. Hill (1992), for example, describes the differing ways in which Lord Killanin and his successor Juan Antonio Samaranch utilized the power of the IOC presidency. Killanin left much of the day-to-day running of the IOC to his staff; Sama-

TIME OUT

Power in the Hands of One Man

Mario Vázquez-Raña was a Mexican furniture-store millionaire and media mogul. From 1975 until his death in 2015, he was president of the Pan American Sports Organization (PASO), as well as president of the Association of National Olympic Committees (ANOC) between 1979 and 2012 (ANOC, 2015). In fact, Vázquez-Raña was the single power figure in PASO; he was the king of kings of sport in the Americas. Anything you did in relation to the Pan American Games had to be approved by Vázquez-Raña. If he didn't like you, good luck getting anything done. If you wanted to achieve your objectives, it was essential that you got along with Vázquez-Raña because there was no one else to turn to (Pound, 2004).

His personal wealth and power allowed him to stay in charge of PASO and ANOC over the years, and he was even appointed various positions with the International Olympic Committee, including executive board member, chairman of Olympic Solidarity (2002-2012), and president of the Organizing Committee for the 114th IOC Session in Mexico City (2002). He was also a member of the following Commissions: Olympic Movement (1990-1999), Preparation of the XII Olympic Congress (1990-1994), Apartheid and Olympism (1990-1992), IOC 2000 Executive Committee (1999), Marketing (2000), IOC 2000 Reform Follow-up (2002), and 2009 Congress (2009-2010) (IOC, 2015a). Some of these were unpopular appointments but were pushed by then-IOC president (and close ally) Juan Antonio Samaranch, himself the ultimate power in amateur sports.

ranch was a "hands-on" president who was seen as less consultative in the way he operated.

Reward Power

The power that comes from one person's control of another person's rewards is termed **reward power**. The larger the reward and the greater the importance of the reward to the recipient, the more power the person who gives the reward is able to exercise. The owner of a professional sport team may offer rewards to players who perform well. Coaches can give rewards in the form of more playing time or a starting position. The volunteer president of a national sport organization can reward other volunteers by lobbying for them to be appointed to international committees or by giving them perks like naming them to honorary positions with teams traveling to major sport events.

Coercive Power

Coercive power is the power derived from the ability that one person has to punish another. The fear of punishment can be a strong motivator, and, in some ways, coercive power can be seen as the counterpart of reward power. Although many people see coercive power as dysfunctional because it alienates people and builds up resentment, it is not uncommon to see this type of power used in sport organizations. For example, the Fédération Internationale de Natation (FINA) threat of banishment for individuals supporting the International Swimming League (ISL) competition described in the Time Out later in this chapter would be considered coercive power.

Referent Power

Referent power is based on an individual's charisma and another person's identification with this quality. In many ways referent power is very much like the Weberian notion of **charismatic authority**. Referent power can occur when the members of a sport organization identify very strongly with the values espoused by their leader. Coaches like Liverpool F.C.'s Jürgen Klopp and Jon Gruden of the Oakland Raiders NFL franchise are strong personalities, seen by many people as charismatic; as such they have referent power. People with referent power are often used to promote sport teams, events, and equipment.

Expert Power

Expert power accrues because of a person's special knowledge or skill. That person does not have to be particularly high up in the sport organization's hierarchy to have expert power. For example, a computer technician in a sport organization that uses computer-aided design may wield considerable power if he or she is the only person in the company who knows how to operate the specialist computer software. Coaches, product designers, researchers, and player's agents may all be seen to have expert power because of their credibility in their specialized area. One of the ways individuals can acquire expert power is through the information they possess.

Organizational Sources of Power

As we saw in the last section, some sources of individual power are a result of holding positions of authority in a sport organization; others reflect personal qualities that are unrelated to the organization. In this section we look at the power that accrues to organizational subunits as a result of the way in which the sport organization is designed. We focus specifically on five organization-based sources of power: the acquisition and control of resources, the ability to cope with uncertainty, centrality, nonsubstitutability, and control over the decision-making process.

Acquisition and Control of Resources

One of the primary ways a subunit within a sport organization can obtain power is through its ability to acquire resources and the **control of resources**. As Pfeffer (1981, p. 101) points out, because organizations require a continuous supply of resources those subunits within the organization "that can provide the most critical and difficult-to-obtain resources come to have power in the organization." The important point to draw from Pfeffer's statement is that it is not just the ability to acquire and control resources that gives an organizational subunit power, but the fact that it can secure resources critical to the organization's operations and difficult to obtain. Resources may come in a variety of forms and can include money, people, information, and legitimacy. Burbank, Andranovich, and Heying (2001) examined the 1984 Los Angeles Olympics, the 1996 Atlanta Olympics, and the 2002 Salt Lake City Olympics and found that businesspeople dominated organizing committees because they had access to desired resources. This is likely why Mario Vázquez-Raña, discussed in the earlier Time Out, "Power in the Hands of One Man," was so successful with his committee and commission appointments; first and foremost he was a very successful business tycoon.

Money is a particularly important resource to any organization because it can be used to acquire other resources, and "it can be stored and is relatively divisible in terms of its use" (Pfeffer, 1981,

p. 101). In universities, those departments that can generate large amounts of external funding are often regarded as powerful. On many U.S. campuses the athletic department, which is often able to generate funds through its sport programs, is seen as a powerful subunit (cf. Sack & Staurowsky, 1998). People are also a valuable resource; nowhere is this more apparent than in the competition among professional and collegiate sport teams for highly skilled players. The teams that are able to secure the most talented group of players become the most powerful subunit within their respective league.

Ability to Cope With Uncertainty

Sport organizations of all types are constantly coping with **uncertainty**, arising out of changes in the task environment of the sport organization—suppliers, competitors, fans, regulatory agencies, and the like. Uncertainty can also arise as a result of the technological interdependence we discuss in chapter 21. Because uncertainty creates problems for an organization, those subunits that can reduce or control uncertainty gain increased power (Hinings, Hickson, Pennings, & Schneck, 1974). Hickson, Hinings, Lee, Schneck, and Pennings (1971) suggest three methods to help organizations cope with uncertainty. The first is by acquiring information about future trends. Market research units within sport organizations are designed exactly for this purpose. If they are successful in predicting trends such as product demand, they can become a very powerful entity within the organization. Studies of fan attendance at various sporting events (Cho, Lee, & Pyun, 2018; Gauthier & Hansen, 1993; Schofield, 1983; Storm, Nielsen, & Jakobsen, 2018) are in essence designed to identify those factors that affect attendance. Subunits that can utilize this information to maintain or increase attendance can help reduce uncertainty and thus are able to increase their own power within the organization.

The second method of coping with uncertainty is absorption. Absorption involves taking action after an event has occurred (Hickson et al., 1971). For example, if a sporting goods store that encounters a sharp drop in sales can counter with some novel selling methods, it has coped via absorption. Skechers USA Inc., for instance, is a performance and lifestyle footwear manufacturer. Skechers was the market leader in the "toning footwear" category with sales peaking in 2010 (close to US$1 billion). However, in 2012 the company settled a class action lawsuit for US$40 million as a result of deceptive advertising, exaggerating claims about their toning shoes, including the Shape-ups range (Federal Trade Commission, 2012). After this episode, sales dropped, so Sketchers redesigned their shoes, upgraded its factories and distribution centers, and improved its marketing and targeting strategies, enlisting celebrity endorsers such as singers Demi Lovato and Camila Cabello to promote lines for teenagers and pro golfer Matt Kuchar to endorse a new golf shoe. The company also targeted millennials with the so-called athleisure retail trend of sport-styled shoes and apparel, regardless of whether the consumer plans to exercise in them). As a consequence, sales have drastically increased with revenues of US$4.64 billion (as of year-end 2017), putting Skechers back as a global leading athletic-footwear company (Lutz, 2015).

Acquiring information and absorption are methods used to cope with uncertainty after it occurs. It is also possible to cope with uncertainty by preventing its occurrence, the third method suggested by Hickson and colleagues (1971). For example, in 1975 the running boom had taken off in America, and Nike (or Blue Ribbon Sports, as it was then called) was a rapidly growing company. However, sales manager Jim Moodhe and his staff could see that Blue Ribbon was going to have problems meeting the demand for its product. Its credit lines were stretched, and it did not have the money to produce the needed shoes. To solve this problem and prevent the potential uncertainty of not being able to meet the demand for the product, Moodhe developed a program he called "Futures." "The idea behind Futures was to offer major customers an opportunity to place large orders six months in advance and have them commit to that noncancellable order in writing. In exchange, customers would get a 5 to 7 percent discount and guaranteed delivery on 90 percent of their order within a two-week window of time" (Strasser & Becklund, 1991, p. 200). The plan was a success; Moodhe and his sales department were able to cope with the uncertainty facing Blue Ribbon Sports by preventing it from happening.

Centrality

A subunit's position in the work or information flow of a sport organization helps determine the amount of power that the subunit possesses. Subunits that are more central to the work or information flow will be more powerful than those on the periphery. In large part, **centrality** is determined by the sport organization's strategy and the problems it is facing at a particular time. Slack, Berrett, and Mistry (1994) show how the strategic emphasis on high-performance sport adopted by a Canadian national sport organization increased the power of a group of coaches employed by the organization. In an organization strategically oriented to the marketplace, for example, a sport equipment manufacturer, the marketing department is likely to be one of the most important functional units. If a sport organization adopts a strategy of increased efficiency and fiscal control, the finance department is likely to gain increased power merely because its activities are central to the strategic approach adopted by the organization.

Financial people are also likely to become more powerful if the sport organization faces a financial crisis. Similarly, when sales fall, the marketing and sales departments become a primary focus for the sport organization, and thus their power increases. It has even been suggested that in some organizations, subunits central to the organization's operations may sometimes create problems that they have to solve. In this way the members of the subunit can remind others in the organization of their importance (Pfeffer, 1977).

Nonsubstitutability

Nonsubstitutability (that is, being irreplaceable) is an important means of gaining power for both subunits and individuals. In their strategic contingencies theory of power, Hickson and colleagues (1971) suggest that the less a subunit's activities can be substituted, the more organizational power it has. However, to retain their power base, subunits and individuals must ensure that the particular knowledge or skills they possess are not easily replaced. As Pfeffer (1981, p. 113) points out, "if others can obtain access to the expert's information," their power base is quickly destroyed. Consequently, those with power will use strategies to maintain their status. These strategies may include "using specialized language and symbols that make the[ir] expertise look even more arcane and difficult to comprehend" (Pfeffer, 1981, p. 114), or preventing individuals with a similar expertise from being a part of the organization. In sport organizations coaches often use specialized language. Swimming coaches, for example, talk about tapering, stroke rates, shaving down, and bilateral breathing. This use of specialized language makes it difficult for others involved peripherally in swimming (particularly the parents of swimmers) to comprehend; accordingly, the power of the coaching subunit is maintained.

Control Over the Decision-Making Process

Another way that subunits and individual members of a sport organization can gain power is to have **control over decision making**. Power is gained not only by having input in the decision process but also through control of the process itself. Those subunits and individuals who can influence when decisions are made, who is involved in the decision process, and what alternatives are presented become very powerful. MacIntosh and Whitson (1990) suggest that we have seen this type of control exercised in Canada's national sport organizations. The growing number of professional administrators in these organizations, because of their location in the sport organization's structure, have been able to limit volunteer involvement in the decision-making process. As MacIntosh and Whitson point out, participation in the decision process "is restricted to those who agree on ends and [those] who are unlikely to persist in raising issues that complicate the pursuit of those ends" (p. 131). As a result, the professional administrators within these sport organizations have become very powerful.

Other Notable Interpretations of Power

It is not the intention of this chapter to present every major contribution to the literature on theorizing of power. So far, we have focused on widely cited interpretations of individual and organizational power. In the literature, you will no doubt come across many other interpretations. Following is an introduction to a select few other theories of power that you might find in sport management literature.

Mintzberg

In his writings on the structuring of organizations, Mintzberg (1979) talks about centralized and decentralized power. He focuses his definition primarily on the issues of who has the power to make decisions and the extent to which this power is concentrated. He notes (p. 181) that "when all power for decision making rests at a single point in the organization—ultimately in the hands of a single individual—we shall call the structure centralized; to the extent that the power is dispersed among many individuals we shall call the structure decentralized." Hage and Aiken (1970, p. 38) propose a similar definition:

> Centralization refers to the way in which power is distributed in any organization. By power we mean the capacity of one actor to move another (or other) actors to action. The smaller the proportion of jobs and occupations that participate in decision making and the fewer the decision-making areas in which they are involved, the more centralized the organization.

Lukes

Another prominent interpretation of power is that of Steven Lukes (1974). Lukes focused on the approaches that individuals (and groups) adopt to achieve their objectives and, therefore, how to get others to act in a particular way. He suggested that to understand power, the concept needs to be considered in a broad sense, so he offered his *Radical View*, comprising of three dimensions (or faces).

The first (overt) dimension focuses on observable conflict and decision making where the behavior or actions of individuals can be witnessed. An example of this dimension is when a coach decides that the club's athletes will not be allowed to take part in practice if they do not show up 15 minutes before the session to complete a prepractice stretching routine. Lukes (1974) argued that the work of Weber (1947/2012, 1956) is a restricted and narrow interpretation of power that only deals with the first of the three faces of power.

Criticisms of this narrow, classical pluralist, decision-making perspective recommended that power can in fact be exercised through non-decision-making, which is the second (covert) dimension (Bachrach & Baratz, 1962; Lukes, 2005). Individuals (or groups) can limit issues to be considered for decision making through exercising power. An example of this non-decision-making dimension is when a manager sets and distributes a meeting agenda, which dictates the situation by restricting and diverting potentially contentious issues away from the meeting.

Lukes (1974) considers the third (latent) dimension to be the most effective; that is, when power is least observable. This dimension has been termed *the radical view* and provides criticism of the first two dimensions, which suggests conflict is a fundamental attribute of power. This dimension suggests that an individual can fail to recognize his or her own interests (e.g., Person B only did something due to Person A's influence in shaping Person B's will). Yet importantly, this phenomenon can occur without overt conflict (Sadan, 2004). An example of this dimension would be the way that members of extremist groups are brainwashed into accepting the authority of their leaders to the point that they don't even question what they are being told to do, even though it may not be in their best interests (Kidd et al., 2009).

Foucault

Although Foucault suggests he did not explicitly develop a theory of power, Foucault's (1980, 1982) interpretation of power is another well-recognized theorization; its application is often found in the field of sociology. Rather than focusing on identifying those individuals who possess power and how they seek to get their own way (as Lukes describes), Foucault reframed the positioning of power, believing it to be spread throughout society. Foucault (1980) viewed that power is not something structural that an individual can possess or lose; actions do not stem from a locus, just from an infinite series of practices (Sadan, 2004, p. 38). For instance, a key Foucauldian concept is discourse in which he describes the way ideas or currently accepted notions of what the truth is frame the way broader power relations are played out in society.

Giddens

Continuing the idea that power comes from various sources and is played out on different levels, Giddens (1986, p. 15) develops his own interpretation of power that he terms the *duality of structure* in power relations, noting that his intention is "not to eliminate one of these types of conception [by different theorists] at the expense of the other, but to express their relation as a feature of the duality of structure." Giddens viewed power as an important integrated part of the social system, describing power as a result of the relationship between an institution's structure (e.g., rules and pattern of resource distribution) and its systematic aspects (e.g., normal social practices). The duality of structure conceptualization sees the social **structure** (which enables human activity yet also limits it, e.g., laws or resources) and human **agency** (creates, establishes, and alters the social structure) as two properties that form social relations, with power being fundamental to both.

Bourdieu

Bourdieu (1991), like Giddens, developed a concept of power that sought to balance the influence of structure and agency. However, in doing so he put relatively greater emphasis on the perspective of the individual. Thus, Swartz (2016, para. 1) defines Bourdieu's field as "arenas of production, circulation, and appropriation and exchange of goods, services, knowledge, or status, and the competitive positions held by actors [individuals] in their struggle to accumulate, exchange, and monopolize different kinds of power resources (capitals)." Bourdieu's major contribution to the discussion of power, therefore, was in describing the multiple forms of capital—economic, cultural, social, and symbolic—that people can use to influence social outcomes. Additionally, Bourdieu's theory aims to understand society's complex political environment by examining the various power relations and struggles within a field.

Hard and Soft Power

While not as directly identified with any particular theorist, a final conceptualization that is becoming more frequently used in the literature is the distinction between hard and soft power. These ideas are another way of understanding how power can be direct or indirect, materialist (in terms of physical force or economic coercion), or idealist (in terms of shaping ideas).

Hard Power

Hard power is a form of coercive power whereby the ability of states, organizations, or individuals are able to get what they want through coercion, such as, for example, through the use of force or payment. When the literature refers to "the state," it primarily refers to "a territorial unit and to a collection of institutions . . . including the military, the courts system, the police, then system of local administration and the school system" (Houlihan, 2016, p. 39). A state may, for instance, obtain the outcomes it wants using its superior military or via the ability to entice others through financial means. Furthermore, individuals may, of course, get what they want through either physical intimidation or forms of bribery and payment. Hard (and soft) power is theorized both as an organizational and an individual source of power; the concept is commonly used when discussing the state or individual leader.

Soft Power

Soft power is the opposite of hard power. It is the ability of states, organizations, and individuals to get what they want "through attraction rather than coercion or payments" (Nye, 2004, p. 256). Soft power may be gained, for example, by a state's culture, accomplishments, or police being considered by others to be attractive, or through an individual's ability to demonstrate traits of leadership, charisma, or charm.

Power in Sport Management Research

Until the turn of the millennium, power had been a neglected area of study in sport management. However, an increasing number of researchers now consider the concept of power as a central concept in their studies. In an early call to arms, Henry (2001) argued that the moral dimensions of power must be addressed when analyzing aspects of contemporary urban sport and leisure policy. Fink, Pastore, and Riemer (2001) considered power as one issue that may explain diversity in Division IA intercollegiate athletic organizations. Wolfe, Meenaghan, and O'Sullivan (2002) then developed a model that can demonstrate power relationships within a sport network context. Crompton, Howard, and Var (2003) used community power structure as one source of momentum explaining increased public investment in major league facilities. In more recent years, we have seen a growing range of sport management literature related to the political concept of soft power, most commonly used with respect to cities' and states' staging of major sport events, such as the FIFA World Cup and the Summer Olympic Games. Grix, Brannagan, and Houlihan (2015), for instance, show how Brazil's staging of the 2014 World Cup and the United Kingdom's hosting of the 2012 Olympic Games were both considered by each respective government as potent tools for soft power acquisition. A related concept here is soft disempowerment (Brannagan & Giulianotti, 2015), which reminds us how a state's use of major events can backfire, leading to forms of **disempowerment** rather than **empowerment**. See, for example, this chapter's opening scenario on how Qatar's acquisition of the 2022 World Cup finals has drastically heightened international knowledge and awareness of the country's human rights abuses at home.

Empowerment can be explained at an individual or community level. Individual empowerment is a process of personal development: a transition from a feeling of powerlessness and from a life in the shadows to an active life of real ability to act and to take initiatives in relation to the environment and the future. Community empowerment can be realized in geographically defined areas that constitute the common critical characteristic of their residents, or it can develop in groups with other common critical characteristics, such as origin, age, gender, or physical disability (Sadan, 2004).

Instances of other studies that have used power to good effect include Hoye and Cuskelly's (2003) study of board power and performance within voluntary sport organizations. Bretherton, Piggin, and Bodet (2016) examined how the 2012 London Olympic Games' pre-event sport and physical activity participation legacy targets were constructed, guided by Foucault's notion of power. Harris and Adams (2016) also utilized a Foucauldian framework to investigate power, knowledge, and discourse in processes related to political actors in a sport for development context. Steen-Johnsen and Vidar Hanstad (2008) analyzed how power was used during processes of negotiation within the Norwegian Olympic Committee and Confederation of Sport. They identified systemic power, a type of power that is taken for granted and that operates through daily practices and routines in organizations. Wangrow, Schepker, and Barker (2018) studied power, performance, and expectations in the dismissal of NBA coaches by using a power theory that suggests individuals in organizations accrue or gain power from four sources: structure, ownership, expertise, and prestige (Finkelstein, 1992). It is suggested that structural power is dependent on the individual's position in the organization and Wangrow et al.'s results provide evidence that a coach may derive power from structure, expertise, and reputation to affect ownership's decision to fire or retain the coach. With a different approach to understanding power, Sibson (2010) uses the concept of exclusionary power in her study with respect to the gendering of sport organizations. Grix, Lindsey, De Bosscher, and Bloyce (2018) provided a Special Issue to assess the theoretical and methodological trends in policy and politics research. They suggest that power is a central theme of political science. Bergsgard's (2018) article in that Special Issue combined the interpretations of power by Lukes and Bourdieu to examine power and domination in sport policy and politics in a Norwegian setting. Bergsgard suggests that adopting such an approach offered an extensive understanding of the processes and dynamics involved that lead to political outcomes. Finally, due to the increased attention on the power of athletes in the international sports debate, Play the Game's 2019 central conference theme was "athlete power on the rise." Play the Game is an integral part of the Danish Institute for Sports Studies (an independent research center set up by the Danish Ministry of Culture) that aims to improve ethical standards and promote democracy, transparency, and freedom of expression in sport (Play the Game, 2019).

Organizational Politics

As Houlihan (2016, p. 33) notes, "the difficulty of pinning down the focus of political science and its contribution to the study of sport is the diversity of fields of study that it encompasses." This may be a factor as to why in the preceding edition of this textbook it was suggested that the study of organizational politics had not received a lot of attention within sport management literature. Yet, like power, **politics** pervades all sport organizations, although it is somewhat intangible and hard to measure. However, Houlihan (2016) suggests that government and public administration, policy analysis, political theory, and international relations are fields of study all important for developing our understanding of sport and politics. Political skills are not easily taught to students or would-be managers. Politics is related to the use of power; political skills involve "the ability to use the bases of power effectively—to convince those to whom one has access; to use one's resources, information, and technical skills to their fullest in bargaining; to exercise formal power with a sensitivity to the feelings of others; to know where to concentrate one's energies; to sense what is possible; to organize the necessary alliances" (Mintzberg, 1983, p. 26).

In a study of chief executives, staff managers, and supervisors, Madison, Allen, Porter, Renwick, and Mayers (1980) found that organizational politics is seen to be both helpful and harmful to the individual members of an organization and to the operation of the organization itself. Organizational politics is helpful to the individual in that it can enable career advancement; provide recognition; enhance power, status, or ego; aid in the accomplishment of personal goals; and enable survival. It can be harmful to the individual in that it can cause a loss of power and credibility, job loss or a demotion, negative feelings toward others, and a hampered job performance. Politics can be helpful to the organization when it aids in achieving organization goals and visibility, developing teams and group functioning, and decision making. Organizational politics can be harmful to the organization when it distracts from organization goals, results in the misuse of resources, causes fights and lower coordination and communication, and damages the organization's image and reputation.

Some people see politics as involving coercion, dishonesty, and manipulative behavior by individuals seeking to further their own self-interests. Others see politics as an integral feature of organizations and a way in which differences among interest groups are resolved and tasks are accomplished. A study by Gandz and Murray (1980) found that people felt politics was a common feature of organizations, that political activity occurred more frequently at the higher levels of an organization, and that to be successful in an organization one had to be good at politics. However, like the study by Madison, Allen, Porter, Renwick, and Mayes (1980), Gandz and Murray's work also found that respondents felt there were problems and drawbacks to organizational politics.

We now examine types of political tactics used in sport organizations. While we focus specifically on four activities—building coalitions, using outside experts, building a network of contacts, and controlling information—organizations use several other political tactics such as attacking or blaming others, using information as a political tool, image building or impression management, support building for ideas, ingratiation or praising others, power coalition, developing allies, and creating obligations and reciprocity (Sussman, Adams, Kuzmits, & Raho, 2002).

TIME OUT

Power, Politics, FINA, and the ISL

"I'm incredibly disappointed next month's swim meet in Turin has been cancelled because of politics" (adam_peaty, 2018). These were the opening words of Adam Peaty's Instagram post following the news that the 2018 Energy for Swim meet in Turin, Italy, had been canceled. Peaty is Olympic, World, European, and Commonwealth Champion and multiple world record holder for breaststroke events.

FINA is the international federation recognized by the IOC for governing aquatic sport. One annual competition is the FINA Swimming World Cup, which, according to FINA's website, "gathers world-class swimmers in a series of two-day meets organized between August and November each year" (FINA, n.d.).

In 2017 ISL was formed by a group of individuals who wanted to create an innovative competition format to attract more media attention, spectatorship, and commercial growth in swimming (International Swimming League, n.d.), which would directly rival some of FINA's events. The ISL, backed by a power-sector tycoon from Ukraine, planned an inaugural meet to take place in Italy, staged by the Italian Swimming Federation, Federazione Italiana Nuoto (FIN). Part of the appeal for the top swimmers was that the prize money on offer was US$3 million for gold, US$2 million for silver, and US$1 million for bronze (Lord, 2018c), far more than they could win at any FINA event.

With news that many of the world's best swimmers were choosing to race at the ISL meet in Turin instead of FINA's World Cup, FINA wrote to FIN to inform them that the competition would not be approved by FINA (FINA, 2018). FINA then threatened sanctions against swimmers (including to ban them from the 2019 FINA World Championships) if they competed at the ISL meet.

On November 15, 2018, FIN's President, Paulo Barelli, announced that FIN was "reluctantly" cancelling the ISL Turin meet, saying that FIN "has been forced to take this decision" (Barelli, 2018) due to FINA reinterpreting one of its rules.

Cancellation of the meet resulted in an uprising from several top-level swimmers, with three of them filing an anti-competitive conduct lawsuit against FINA (Reuters, 2018), similar to a case against the International Skating Union (ISU) for monopolizing control of international competitions. (See the opening scenario in chapter 13 on governance for a detailed overview of this case.) In short, in 2017 the European Union's Competition Authority ordered the ISU to change its rules that prohibited athletes from competing at non-ISU administered events (Lord, 2018a).

This wasn't the first time a lawsuit had been filed against the ISU; a new athlete-centered nonprofit World Skating Federation (WSF) was formed in 2003, partly in reaction to the perceived unresponsiveness of the ISU to problems plaguing the sport. The WSF attempted to become the IOC-recognized international governing body for figure skating and filed an antitrust lawsuit against the ISU to fight alleged autocratic control and monopolization of the sport. It had also been suggested that FINA's rules break European Union anti-trust laws (Lord, 2018d). Peaty even challenged FINA to ban him (Hope, 2018) and stated that he was prepared to accept any potential ban, forfeiting the defense of his Olympic title in Tokyo 2020, if it helped persuade FINA to hand over 50-50 ("fair share" of) revenue generated by the sport to its athletes (Lord, 2018b).

In December 2018 the ISL hosted a summit in London where some of the world's top swimmers and law experts met to discuss the next course of action. Following the high-profile summit, FINA released a statement in January 2019 announcing that it would not sanction any swimmer competing in events beyond its jurisdiction (Anderson, 2019). Reacting to FINA's apparent relaxing of its rules, Olympic gold medalist, Cameron van der Burgh, another leading advocate of the ISL, said, "Many athletes were brave and stood together against FINA on this first front which has proven the power we have when united. This emphasizes the need for a swimmers' partnership in order to defend athletes' rights and protect against the organizations that exploit them. I urge all swimmers to join and make a better future for our sport." (Keith, 2019).

Building Coalitions

One of the main ways people in sport organizations can increase their political power is by building **coalitions** with others (cf. Pfeffer, 1981). Coalitions are built when people spend time communicating their views to others, establishing trust relationships, and building mutual respect. While these activities can occur within the formal confines of the sport organization, they often occur over dinner, in the bar, or on the golf course. Coalitions are only effective when they are tightly united around a particular issue. Sometimes political activity is directed at weakening coalitions by using a divide-and-conquer tactic. Coalitions can occur within sport organizations; for example, the coming together of the players in an organization such as the National Hockey League Players Association (NHLPA) and the swimmers joining forces discussed in the Time Out "Power, Politics, FINA, and the ISL" are forms of coalitions. Coalitions can also occur among sport organizations. For example, in Geneva, Switzerland, in 2018, the Centre for Sport and Human Rights was established by a diverse coalition that included FIFA, the IOC, the Commonwealth Games Federation, and UEFA in an effort to foster respect for human rights in the world of sport. A broad range of intergovernmental organizations, governments, athletes, hosts, sponsors, broadcasters, unions, employers' associations, and national human rights institutions also support the coalition. Recall that in the opening scenario in this chapter FIFA was heavily criticized by human rights advocates due to the poor working conditions of those building the new stadia in Qatar. By joining this coalition, is FIFA engaging in political tactics, is the organization attempting to repair or rebuild trust (discussed in chapter 10), or does the international federation now have a genuine concern about improving human rights in sport?

The Use of Outside Experts

Another common method of exercising political power used in several sport organizations is to hire outside **experts** to support or legitimize one's position. While government agencies and large companies in the sport industry often have their own in-house experts, these people often carry baggage; that is, they are seen to represent a particular constituency within the organization and favor that group's position. Hiring outside experts, perhaps a consulting company, is seen as a means of gaining an objective view. However, despite an aura of objectivity, it is often possible for those people hiring the experts to manipulate the outcome of any reports. For example, government departments such as those responsible for sport in Canada have often commissioned reports by outside experts to look at a number of aspects of the sport delivery system; these reports are usually tabled with the minister, the elected official responsible for overseeing the department. If the minister likes the report and it fits with the department's stance, it can be made public, thus supporting and legitimizing the department's position. If the report is not to the minister's liking and contrary to the department's position, it can be merely received as information, in which case its contents will not be released to the public by the minister's office. Similar tactics may be used by the CEO of a large corporation within the sport industry. The organizing committee for the 2000 Sydney Olympic Games hired individuals from Greenpeace to legitimize their position as the "Green Games." The 2014 Sochi Olympic Winter Games saw the introduction of an Olympic carbon mitigation program. It was delivered by Dow, a multinational chemical corporation, who was again appointed as the Official Carbon Partner of the 2016 Rio Olympic Games.

In addition to offering support and legitimacy, outside experts can be used for other political purposes. One vivid example in sport is the Canadian government's use of a commission headed by the associate chief justice of the province of Ontario to investigate the events surrounding Ben Johnson's positive drug test in the 1988 Olympic Games' 100-meters race. Although ostensibly set up to examine the use of performance-enhancing drugs by Canadian athletes, the Dubin Inquiry (1990), as it was known, served a number of political purposes for the Canadian government in regard to its involvement in sport, particularly track and field. As Beauchesne (cited by Hall, Slack, Smith, & Whitson, 1991, p. 224) notes, its primary purpose was "(1) to dissociate the government or government bodies from scandal; (2) to convey the impression of taking action to remedy the problem; and (3) implicit in the trial format itself, to expose the guilty and to affirm the power of sanction as the best means to deter the situation."

Building a Network of Contacts

To be politically effective in a sport organization, it is necessary to gain the support of other people. Creating a network of contacts may involve building links with people inside and outside of the organization. **Networks** are established through the formal mechanisms of the sport organization but also through informal means. Kanter (1977) suggests that within an organization three types of people are important in building a network of contacts: sponsors, peers, and subordinates.

Sponsors are those individuals at a higher level of the organization. Kanter (1977) suggests these people fulfill three important networking functions. First, they can fight for their contacts at the upper levels of the organization. Second, they can often help bypass the organizational hierarchy or at least help guide someone through it. Third, sponsors can be "an important signal to other people, a form of reflected power" (Kanter, 1977, p. 181). Peers are sometimes overlooked in the process of building contacts. However, acceptance by one's peers is often a necessary step in obtaining the favors and recognition required to acquire political power and build the type of coalition discussed above. Subordinates are also important contacts:

> The accumulation of power through alliances [is] not always upward oriented. For one thing, differential rates of hierarchical progress could mean that juniors or peers one day could become a person's boss the next. So it would be to a person's advantage to make alliances downward in the hierarchy with people who looked like they may be on the way up (Kanter, 1977, pp. 185-186).

It is also advantageous to build alliances with subordinates because they carry out the tasks necessary to acquire political power. A lack of compliance by subordinates makes the power holder powerless.

A network of contacts can often be enhanced by hiring, promoting, transferring, or firing selected individuals. Sometimes it may even be beneficial to coopt into one's network someone with a dissenting view. For example, an academic member of staff who feels the athletic teams are getting too much money from the university's central administration may, if appointed to the department's budget committee, see the athletic director's point of view and realize that athletic teams are not overfunded. Such cooptation brings the dissenting member into the athletic department's network.

In addition to building a network of contacts within the sport organization, it is also important to build outside contacts. In his book *It's How You Play the Game: The Inside Story of the Calgary Olympics*, Frank King (1991), chairman of the 1988 Olympic Games Organizing Committee, describes how he and his committee spent large amounts of time, both prior to getting the Games and in the time leading up to the Games, networking with IOC members, government bureaucrats, international sport personnel, and corporate officials. This is not an isolated incident—both McGeoch (1994) for the 2000 Sydney Olympics and Yarbrough (2000) for the 1996 Atlanta Olympics describe the same thing. However, as frequently shown in the international press, there's a fine line between developing relationships to build networks with high-ranking, powerful officials and engaging in corrupt practices. Sport corruption has been described as "a global phenomenon, that has, and continues to, threaten the integrity of the sport industry, posing a major challenge for sport managers" (Kihl, Skinner, & Engelberg, 2017, p. 1). We've seen, for example, in the opening scenario how FIFA officials, such as Mohamed bin Hammam, have been accused of using slush funds to pay bribes to ensure a tournament or competition (in this case, the 2022 World Cup finals) to be awarded to their country (Calvert & Blake, 2014). IFs are now under far greater scrutiny to ensure practices are legal and transparent. Refer to chapter 13 for a detailed overview about governance of sport organizations and chapter 24 for an introduction to understanding procurement processes and frameworks, important for transparent tendering and bidding processes of major sport events.

Controlling Information

Controlling information is a form of political activity that can be used by sport managers to influence the outcomes of the decision-making process within their organization or a decision concerning their organization. By emphasizing facts that support their position—or by hiding, limiting, or ignoring other relevant information—managers can promote their own position or discredit the points of view put forward by others. It has been argued that this tactic of controlling information tactic is frequently used by those bidding to host major sport events such as the Olympic Games (Auf de Maur, 1976; McGeoch, 1994; Pound, 2004). Essentially what happens is that those in favor of the Games emphasize the positive aspects of staging these events—the creation of new facilities, the infusion of tourist expenditure into the community, and the creation of jobs. Advocates of the Games choose not to discuss that their cost will be borne by local taxpayers, the facilities are often used by privately owned professional sport teams after the Games, low-income residents are often displaced, public funds from ethnic and cultural programs are transferred to the Games, and any long-term economic benefits to hosting them are relatively minimal (Lenskyj, 2000; Tien, Lo, & Lin, 2011). By controlling information, supporters of a Games bid hope to influence the decision process positively.

Political Tactics in Action

What you should notice in the Time Out "Power, Politics, FINA, and the ISL" is a display of how several top swimmers and other individuals—also advocates for change to the sport—utilized a combination of political tactics to substantiate their movement and legitimize power. They were seen to form a coalition (i.e., the group of swimmers actively lobbying for change and ISL representatives), use outside expertise (i.e., lawyers), and build a network of contacts (i.e., disseminating their message primarily via social media and the traditional media in an effort to get more swimmers to support and promote their interests).

The political (and power) struggles experienced in swimming are not uncommon in sport. In 2003 the World Skating Federation (WSF)—a rival group set up with the aim to replace the International Skating Union (ISU)—was established and filed an antitrust lawsuit against the ISU subsequent to threats of sanctions against supporters of the WSF. In the sport of triathlon, in the past, the International Triathlon Union (ITU) clashed with Ironman (long-distance triathlon events organized by the World Triathlon Corporation, owned by the Chinese conglomerate Wanda Group) over its role in the sport. In addition to Ironman, in 2017 Super League Triathlon (SLT)—a professional series offering new and updated race formats—added further competition for the ITU. However, rather than engaging in further clashes, the ITU signed Memorandum of Understandings with Ironman in 2017 and the SLT in 2018 to form partnerships that enable key priorities to be identified and subsequent steps set out to ensure the growth and harmonization of the sport (ASOIF, 2018).

As the Time Out highlights, political action frequently transcends sport and beyond. We've shown in the first half of this chapter how cities and states, such as Qatar, use sport (often by staging major events) to promote their country in a positive light via the political concept of soft power. However, the increased attention sometimes creates unwanted scrutiny. This scrutiny can raise international knowledge and awareness of, for example, a country's history of human rights abuse (as was the case with Qatar's acquisition of the 2022 World Cup finals). When this occurs, it is referred to as a form of disempowerment.

Occasionally, cities, states, and organizations use sport in an attempt to mask and detract from their controversial history or questionable practices, which is sometimes referred to as *sportwashing*. For example, the contentious decision that cycling's 2018 Giro d'Italia was to start in Israel provoked accusations of sportwashing given the issues of the country's war-torn image (Abraham, 2017). In addition to political concerns, organizations with questionable environmental practices involved in sport raise questions. For example, Slack (2014) notes the contradictions with some of The Olympic Partner (TOP) program sponsors, such as Coca-Cola, being classified as green. He highlights how Coca-Cola "were criticized for using chlorofluorocarbon in their refrigeration system at Olympic sites. After a series of worldwide protests, Coca-Cola adopted a new refrigeration policy and phased out their chlorofluorocarbon refrigeration units from the 2004 Olympics in Athens, Greece" (p. 459). Additionally, some have concerns that Coca-Cola's (and other fast-food companies') core product is seen to have negative health consequences. Therefore, the sponsorship arrangements and association with

TIME OUT

Colin Kaepernick Taking a Stand (Or, Rather, a Knee)

In 2016 San Francisco 49ers quarterback Colin Kaepernick sat during the national anthem during a preseason game because, in his words, "I am not going to stand up to show pride in a flag for a country that oppresses black people and people of color" (Wyche, 2016, para. 3). In a subsequent preseason game, Kaepernick once again protested against the oppression of black people and alleged police brutality but this time opted to kneel, following discussions with military veterans, because it showed veterans greater respect (Mindlock, 2019). This started more than two years of protests that involved several players, owners, athletes in other sports, and politicians (including the president of the United States, who tweeted that players who didn't stand for the national anthem should get fired and find something else to do) (Mather, 2019). In March 2017 Kaepernick opted out of his playing contract but failed to receive any new offers (and, as of July 2019, he has not played a game since). In 2018 Nike celebrated its 30th anniversary by selecting Kaepernick as the face of their Just Do It campaign (see chapter 8 for one of the images used), which ignited more controversy—literally, people started burning their Nike goods in protest of the Kaepernick association!

arguably the greatest sport spectacle on the planet are becoming increasingly problematic (Piggin et al., 2019). Notwithstanding the criticisms, the potential global reach of the Olympic Games (and other major or mega-events) audience is why these types of organizations embark on sponsorship partnerships.

As a final example, during mid-2019, Nike and Kaepernick were involved with another political situation: Kaepernick voiced his concerns about Nike's new Air Max 1 USA sneaker, created for the 2019 Fourth of July holiday, because the heel featured a U.S. flag with 13 white stars in a circle. This flag design was created during the American Revolution and commonly referred to as the *Betsy Ross flag*. However, some say the Betsy Ross flag is an offensive symbol because of its connection to an era of slavery (Safdar & Beaton, 2019). As a result of the uproar, Nike pulled its new sneaker.

Politics in Sport Management Research

In 2009 the *International Journal of Sport Policy* was established "to provide an outlet for articles that utilise political science and policy analysis theories and concepts, but also, and perhaps more importantly, to encourage more researchers to examine the role of politics in sport policy and to analyse the policy-making process and the impact of policy" (Houlihan, Bloyce, & Smith, 2009, p. 1). In March 2011 the title of the journal was altered to add "and Politics" because although the journal had established itself as the key resource for academics interested in sport policy, the editorial board were found to be turning away quality papers that did not quite fit with the original aims and scope. However, several potential authors emphasized that there was "no obvious alternative outlet for papers concerned with the intersection of sport and political science" (Houlihan, Bloyce, & Smith, 2011, p. 1). As a result of the introduction of the *International Journal of Sport Policy and Politics*, academics interested in political science and sport now had a recognized international publication outlet. The consequence was that those in the field of sport management now have the opportunity to familiarize themselves with a growing number of wide-ranging studies concerned with sport and politics. For example, Seippel, Dalen, Sandvik, and Solstad (2018) scrutinized how politicization of sports might happen and provided a better understanding as to why sports issues turn into politics. Houlihan and Zheng (2014) looked at sport and politics of small states. They suggested that "small states can be adept at operating in the political and diplomatic interstices between the major powers." Placing focus on more powerful states, Grix and Houlihan's (2014) study in *The British Journal of Politics and International Relations* observed how states are increasingly using sports mega-events as part of their soft power strategies. The research analyzed the 2012 London Olympic and Paralympic Games for a British context and the 2006 FIFA World Cup in Germany. Their findings suggest that while Germany engaged a long-term, well-planned and resourced approach to improve its poor international image, Britain was far less concerned about enhancing its (seemingly robust)

KEY ISSUES FOR SPORT MANAGERS

Organizations can be characterized by two types of elements: the basic formal elements such as its organizational structure, and the informal elements such as power and political structures. Both are equally important in understanding sport organizations. As a manager, you must be able to recognize the types of power and political activities found within your organization and promote the positive aspects of power and politics.

While managing power may be simpler under certain circumstances (e.g., a small local sporting goods store), it may be more difficult under others. For example, large publicly held sport organizations such as Nike or Under Armour not only have to deal with power issues within the organization, but they also have to deal with the outside stakeholders. The larger the organization, the harder it can be to manage this because of the increasing numbers of stakeholders. So, the question becomes, in this case, who actually controls the organization? Interestingly, Fligstein and Brantley (1992) found that it does not matter who controls the organization. Rather, organizational factors such as the CEO's background, the industry's growth, and its product or service strategies have a greater effect on performance. Shen and Cannella (2002) cautioned that the power dynamics among the senior executives influences how a CEO is dismissed and whether the result is an internal or external succession.

international image off the back of hosting the Olympics. On a much smaller scale, Soares, Correia, and Rosado (2010) analyzed the political factors related to the decision-making process in a voluntary sports association context.

Summary and Conclusions

In this chapter on power and politics in sport organizations we looked first at Child's challenge to the rational ideas of contingency theory, expressed in his notion of strategic choice. Child (1972) argued that the structure of an organization was less dependent on determinants such as size, technology, and environment, and more a product of decisions made by managers about these areas. The reconciliation of these two viewpoints is one of the major issues in the study of organizations.

The concept of strategic choice is built upon the idea that managers or the members of the dominant coalition have the power to make choices about their organization's domain of operations. Consequently, we looked at the concept of power and some of the issues that surround the concept. We specifically highlighted the difference between power and authority. We then focused on the different sources of power. Using French and Raven's five-part typology, we discussed sources of individual power. We also looked at the way in which different subunits or groups within an organization could acquire power followed by a brief introduction to other notable interpretations of power developed by several pioneering theorists.

Power is intimately related to politics; we looked at the advantages and disadvantages of the use of political activity in a sport organization. We examined some activities that people engage in to acquire political power—building coalitions, using outside experts, building a network of contacts, and controlling information.

For many years power and politics were two of the most neglected topics of study in sport management, yet they are present in every sport organization. Until the early 2000s much of the research conducted in the area of sport management adopted a rational view of organizations, which assumes that sport organizations have specific goals, that everyone agrees on these goals, and the organization's structure is a product of rational responses to changes in contingency variables such as size, technology, and environment. In contrast, a political perspective on organizations assumes diverse goals, individuals, and groups acting in their own self-interest, and organizational structure as the product of managers or the organization's dominant coalition making decisions to preserve their own privileged position.

During the last decade or so, sport management academics have realized the important role and impact that power and politics have for organizations and for the organizational actors (individuals) associated with the organizations. Consequently, we have seen an increasing number of publications that focus on these important concepts. As this chapter has demonstrated, the study of power and politics has come a long way since the publication of the second edition of this textbook in 2006. We, as a field of academics, now need to maintain the impetus of focus on these two important concepts.

Review Questions

1. Pick a familiar sport organization. Who are the powerful individuals within the organization? Why?
2. How do the use of reward power and the use of coercive power relate to the use of authority?
3. Regrettably, few women hold senior-level positions in sport organizations. Given what you have read about sources of individual power, how are women constrained in moving to senior-level management positions?
4. You are a recent graduate of a sport management program and you have just accepted a position as a marketing assistant in a professional sport franchise. What can you do to acquire power?
5. How is the use of power likely to differ in a mechanistic, as opposed to an organic, organizational structure?
6. You are the head administrator of a high school athletic department. What types of power and political activity could have an impact on you? Give examples.
7. How do the rational and political views of organizations differ? Relate these views to Morgan's metaphorical view of organizations outlined in chapter 1.
8. Pick a sport IF with which you are familiar. Can you identify any political tactics they may have used in the past?
9. In what ways might sport governing bodies acquire forms of soft power, and in what ways have they suffered from instances of soft disempowerment?

Suggestions for Further Reading

Two of the best books on power are by Jeff Pfeffer, specifically his text *Power in Organizations* (1981) and his more applied work *Managing with Power* (1992). Henry Mintzberg's (1983) *Power in and Around Organizations* is also good reading, and, although more sociologically than managerially oriented, you could benefit from Steven Lukes' (1974) classic *Power: A Radical View*.

Until fairly recently, there was somewhat of a dearth of writing on power in the sport management literature. Hill's (1992) book *Olympic Politics* (especially chapter 3) provides useful material on issues of power and authority in the Olympic movement. Also, many popular-press books give an idea of the type of power wielded by some of the major figures in sport. Auf De Maur's (1976) *The Billion-Dollar Game* shows the type of power exercised by Montreal mayor Jean Drapeau in obtaining and running the 1976 Olympic Games. Other popular books about the Olympics include Alfred Senn's (1999) book *Power, Politics, and the Olympic Games*; Helen Lenskyj's (2000) book *Inside the Olympic Industry: Power, Politics, and Activism*; Burbank, Andranovich, and Heying's (2001) book *Olympic Dreams: The Impact of Mega-Events on Local Politics*; and Dick Pound's (2004) book *Inside the Olympics: A Behind-the-Scenes Look at the Politics, the Scandals, and the Glory of the Games*. Barrie Houlihan's (2016) chapter "Politics, Power, Policy and Sport" combines the three concepts with a primary focus on the Olympic Games in Houlihan and Malcolm's (2016) edited book, *Sport and Society*.

The power of Malcolm Edwards, the former owner of Manchester United association football team, is discussed by Crick and Smith (1989) in their book *Manchester United: The Betrayal of a Legend*. Both Stephen Aris (1990) and Neil Wilson (1988), in their respective books *Sportsbiz* and *The Sports Business*, provide accounts of the power plays inherent in the sport industry. David Prouty's (1998) book, *In Spite of Us: My Education in the Big and Little Games of Amateur and Olympic Sport in the U.S.*, talk about the cycling world. Zirin's (2013) book *Game Over: How Politics Has Turned the Sports World Upside Down* reveals how important debates about class, race, religion, sex, and the raw quest for political power are played out both on and off the field. Stuart Clegg's (1989) textbook *Frameworks of Power* offers a very good introduction to the history of theorizing power. The book *Sport and Nationalism in Asia: Power, Politics and Identity*, edited by Fan and Lu (2014), provides a collection of interesting chapters about how the Olympics and other international and regional sport events have enriched an active interweaving of sport, politics, and nationalism.

In an attempt to understand power in policy analysis, in Cairney's (2012) book *Understanding Public Policy: Theories and Issues*, he suggests that the best starting point is within the decision-making process and that we should ask the following questions: Who is responsible for policy change? Who oversees the decision-makers? Who thinks they are in charge? Can policy-makers or powerful groups force or resist any opposition? Or, are hidden forms of power such as manipulation utilized? He recommends that to answer these types of question, discussions on power should include informal sources of influence as well as the general discourse that tends to focus on individuals exercising power, the role of institutions, and formal authority.

Grix's (2016) textbook *Sport Politics: An Introduction* looks at sport's relationship with politics, arguing that sport has always been political, even as far back as before the Middle Ages. Finally, the *International Journal of Sport Policy and Politics* would be a good place to start for anyone wanting to develop their understanding of the intertwined nature of sport, policy, politics, and power.

Case for Analysis

WADA, the IOC, and the Russian Doping Scandal

The Case for Analysis in chapter 10 centers on developing control mechanisms to eradicate doping in sport. One of the most high-profile cases of doping in recent years has been the alleged state-sponsored doping program in Russia.

Sochi, Russia, was the host city for the 2014 Winter Olympic Games. Subsequent to Sochi being selected as host, a number of concerns were raised, including issues related to the country's history (particularly related to the 19th-century Circassian genocide); environmental, political, and economic issues; and concerns of safety and human rights for groups of individuals as a result of Russia's stance against the lesbian, gay, bisexual, and transgender (LGBT) community. (In 2013 Russia passed a law banning the "propaganda of nontraditional sexual relations.")

With these concerns, Russia had to work hard to win over a partisan public. Furthermore, Russia wanted to improve their poor performance at the

2010 Vancouver Winter Olympics. It seemed that Russia's determination paid off: The 2014 Sochi Games had a record number of National Olympic Committees participate, it was the most expensive Games in history, and it achieved a broadcast audience record of 2.1 billion people worldwide (IOC, 2015b). Many Russian athletes also performed exceptionally well, with the host nation topping the medal table.

However, in 2016, the World Anti-Doping Agency (WADA) commissioned professor Richard McLaren to conduct an independent report to investigate allegations of Russian doping in sport. In July 2016 McLaren released Part 1 of his findings, which suggested, beyond reasonable doubt, that "Russia operated a state-sponsored doping programme for four years across the 'vast majority' of summer and winter Olympic sports" (BBC Sport, 2016b).

Following publication of the findings, tensions between the IOC and WADA were at an all-time high, when WADA recommended a blanket ban of all Russian athletes from participating in the 2016 Rio Olympic Games; however, the IOC rejected this suggestion. What was interesting about this refusal was that WADA is partially administered and funded by the IOC, so its independence was questioned (Transparency International, 2016). After weeks of legal mayhem, the IOC cleared 271 Russian athletes to compete in Rio, whereas the International Paralympic Committee (IPC) adopted a much firmer line, deciding to issue a blanket ban on Russian athletes (BBC Sport, 2016a; Gibson, 2016)—a decision upheld by the Court of Arbitration for Sport (CAS) following an appeal from Russia. The IOC's decision not to ban all Russian athletes was widely criticized.

In December 2016 Part 2 of McLaren's findings were published, confirming Russia's systematic, institutionalized doping conspiracy and centralized cover-up (McLaren, 2016). In December 2017 WADA released a statement supporting the IOC's decision to "suspend the Russian Olympic Committee with immediate effect; and, to invite individual Russian athletes to the Olympic Winter Games Pyeong-Chang 2018 under specific conditions determined by a panel" (WADA, 2017) subsequent to findings of the IOC's Schmid Commission (a follow-up to the McLaren investigation). However, in September 2018 WADA lifted the ban of Russia's anti-doping agency, resulting in worldwide outcry. WADA's stance appears to have softened (BBC Sport, 2018).

Questions

1. Can you identify the sources of power in this case?
2. How did political and power issues affect the relationship between the IOC and WADA? How did the two organizations resolve their differences?
3. Why do you think the IOC did not sanction a blanket ban (given the fact doping goes against the fundamental principles of Olympism)?
4. Why do you think Russia went to such lengths to commission an alleged state-sponsored doping program?
5. Can you identify any reasons as to why WADA lifted the suspension of Russia's anti-doping agency?

CHAPTER 16

Managing Conflict in Sport Organizations

Trevor Slack, PhD
Terri Byers, PhD

Learning Objectives

When you have read this chapter, you should be able to

1. explain the essential elements found in definitions of conflict,
2. discuss whether conflict is functional or dysfunctional to the operation of a sport organization,
3. explain why conflict should be viewed as a process and not a single incident,
4. outline the major sources of conflict in a sport organization,
5. describe the various strategies that can be used to reduce conflict, and
6. identify techniques that can be used to stimulate conflict in a sport organization.

Key Concepts

attitudinal change
behavioral change
blocking behavior
conflict aftermath
conflict management
conflict process
conflict stimulation
dysfunctional conflict
felt conflict
functional conflict
horizontal conflict
latent conflict
manifest conflict
perceived conflict
sources of conflict
vertical conflict

Lockouts in Professional Sport Leagues

Conflict in sport organizations has led to a number of lockouts in the NBA, NHL, MLB, and NFL (Esteban, 2011; CNN Library, 2019). In the NHL, when the collective agreement ended with the 2003-2004 season, talks between NHL owners, represented by Commissioner Gary Bettman, and the National Hockey League Players Association's (NHLPA) executive director and general counsel Bob Goodenow ensued over the summer. The owners wanted to fix the whole system so that the teams could be profitable. They argued that teams lost $273 million USD in the 2002-2003 season and $224 million USD in 2003-2004, with player salaries making up 75 percent of the budget. The owners proposed that the only way to make the system profitable again and keep all 30 teams is by enforcing a salary cap (maximum dollar amounts that each team can spend on player salaries) attached to revenues (CBC Sports, 2005). The players did not think the management difficulties were their problem; it was the owners, after all, who technically were increasing salary offers. They conceded to having luxury taxes on salaries, but the owners rejected the idea.

Instead of the 2004-2005 season beginning in September, the owners locked out the players because the economic problems of the league had not been reconciled. Final offers would be proposed, only to be rejected by the other side, and the process would start again.

Surveys of fans in Canada showed support was behind the owners, not the players. In the United States, little attention was paid to the lockout.

More than 150 days from the beginning of the lockout, the owners put their final offer on the table with a $40 million team salary cap, take it or leave it. Goodenow countered with, for the first time, a salary cap of $49 million—this major change in position was a surprise to the players. The owners countered with a $42.5 million salary cap. This was their final offer. Their argument was that currently only four teams (Detroit, New Jersey, Philadelphia, and Toronto) were above that amount, before factoring in free agents, and two more (Dallas and Colorado) were very close to that amount.

The NHLPA had until 11:00 a.m. the next morning, Wednesday, February 16, 2005, to accept. Having not heard from the players by that time, Gary Bettman convened a press conference at 1:00 p.m. to announce that the 2004-2005 season was officially canceled, a first for any professional North American sport leagues (Lebrun, 2005). It would be the first time since the Spanish flu of 1919 that there would be no Stanley Cup playoffs.

Both sides deeply apologized to the fans. But most fans had already moved on.

The lockout officially ended July 22, 2005, with league and player approval of a collective bargaining agreement featuring a 24 percent salary rollback on all existing contracts and a salary cap of US$34 million per team, with a minimum salary total of US$21.5 million (canada.com, 2005).

Anyone who has been involved in any type of sport organization—amateur or professional, national or local, profit or nonprofit—will have experienced the conflict that can occur in these organizations. The vignette above provides an example of the frustration, financial concerns, and bickering that can be found in many sport organizations. A 1976 study by the American Management Association found that mid- and top-level managers reported that they spent approximately 20 percent of their time dealing with conflict (Thomas & Schmidt, 1976). More recently, Ilgaz (2014), writing for *Forbes*, suggested that a typical manager can spend up to 40 percent of his or her time dealing with workplace conflict, which is often rooted in strained relationships among employees. There is no reason to believe things are different in sport organizations. Conflict is endemic to all types of organizations and has been studied by researchers from an HRM (Human Resource Management) perspective, labor process theory, organizational justice, as well as industrial relations (Currie, Gormley, Roche, & Teague (2017). The vast and diverse literature on conflict in organizations is an indication of its importance to effective organizations, and it has been suggested that the "ability to navigate through the small and large conflicts within an organization is critical to success" (Mannix, 2003, p. 543).

Other chapters in this section of the book explore a number of the processes that, like conflict, are common phenomena in understanding the dynamics of sport organizations. In addition to conflict, the focus of this chapter, we touch on the process of organizational change and the process of decision making. In this chapter, we look at what we mean by the term *conflict*. Next, we discuss horizontal and vertical forms of conflict, followed by an examination of whether conflict is **functional** or **dysfunctional** to the operation of a sport organization. Because conflict is more than just a single incident, we look at conflict as a process and also examine the sources of conflict in a sport organization. The final two sections look at ways of managing conflict and the seemingly contradictory notion of how to stimulate conflict.

What Is Conflict?

Organizational literature contains many different definitions of conflict (Schmidt & Kochan, 1972; Thomas, 1992). March and Simon (1958, p. 112) describe it as a "breakdown in the standard mechanisms of decision making so that an individual or group experiences difficulty in selecting an action alternative." Thompson (1960, p. 390) is more succinct: Conflict is "behavior by organization members which is expended in opposition to other members"; Morgan (1986, p. 155) is even more precise, suggesting that "conflict occurs whenever interests collide," indicating that conflict is often manifest between individuals and focuses on tasks or nontask aspects of organizing (Nixon, Bruk-Lee, & Spector, 2017). In the last couple decades, the rise of human resource management (HRM) has caused the view of conflict to shift from unwanted but inevitable to a sign of failure (Currie, Gormley, Roche, & Teague, 2017).

Notwithstanding the variety of explanations of what constitutes conflict, some important commonalties underpin most definitions. First, and of particular importance, the parties involved must perceive a conflict to exist. If no one perceives a conflict as existing, no conflict exists. This does not mean that all perceived conflict is real; however, perceived conflict that is not real can still result in antagonism and interference. Second, a conflict situation must involve two or more parties in opposition. Third, one or more of the parties must be involved in preventing one or more of the other parties from achieving its goal(s) by some form of **blocking behavior**. Finally, this blocking behavior must result in frustration, anger, or some other form of emotional response.

Kolb and Putnam's (1992) definition of conflict essentially encompasses these points. They suggest that "conflict may be said to exist when there are real or perceived differences that arise in specific organizational circumstances and that engender emotion as a consequence" (p. 312). These writers, however, caution against an overreliance on rigid definitions of conflict, since such explanations should always take into account the contextual circumstances in which the conflict takes place "because it is always difficult to draw a line between episodes of 'conflict' and the normal give and take of social interaction."

Horizontal and Vertical Conflict

One method of categorizing the conflicts that can occur in a sport organization is to distinguish conflicts that take place between subunits at the same level of the organization (horizontal conflict) from those that take place between different hierarchical levels (vertical conflict). Figure 16.1 shows this type of distinction as it might occur in a university athletic department.

Horizontal Conflict

Horizontal conflict occurs between subunits, or those individuals representing subunits, that are on the same level of the organizational hierarchy. Organizational behavior (OB) literature focuses on this type of conflict. Instead of trying to eliminate this type of conflict, OB researchers currently call for managing it instead (Bendersky, 2003). As figure 16.1 shows, horizontal conflict may occur in an athletic department between those individuals within the intercollegiate athletic program and those involved in the campus recreation program. The campus recreation staff may not agree with the amount of funding given to the athletic program, or conflicts may occur over scheduling or access to facilities. The two groups, because they have different roles to play in providing sport and recreational opportunities for students, tend to develop different goals and priorities. These types of conflicts are not uncommon in athletic departments or sport organizations in general. The job of the athletic director is to resolve conflicts that do occur and prevent future flare-ups by coordinating and encouraging collaboration among the units under her direction.

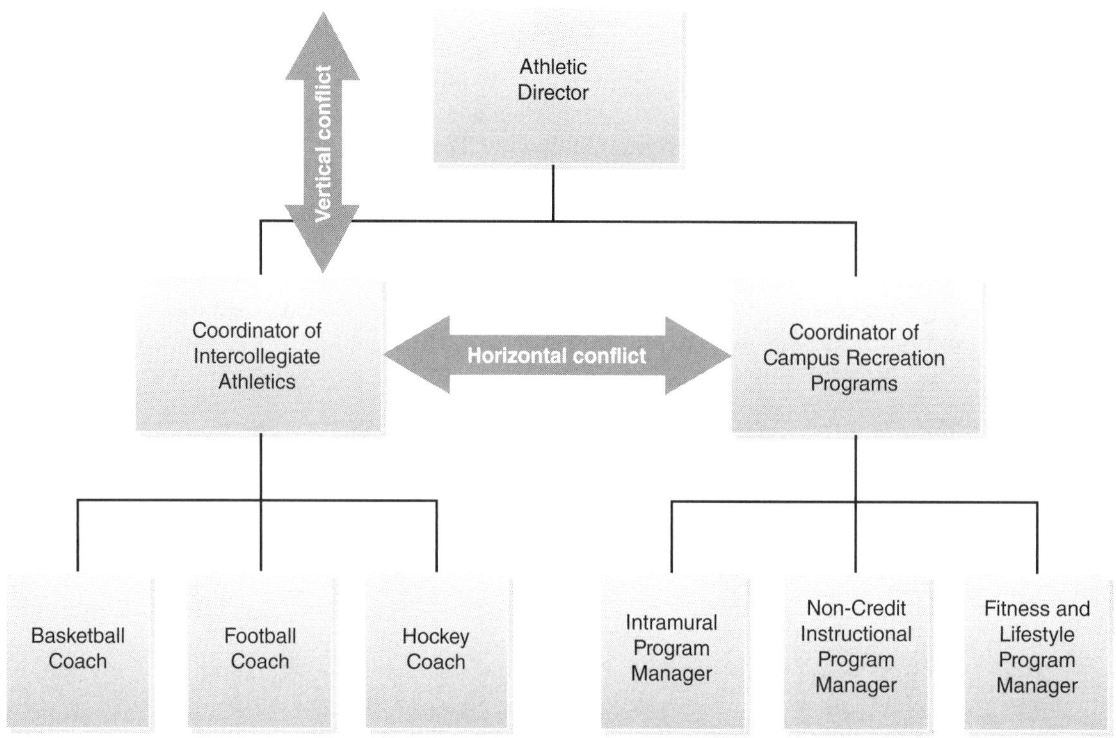

Figure 16.1 Horizontal and vertical conflict in a university athletic department.

Vertical Conflict

As figure 16.1 shows, **vertical conflict** arises between different hierarchical levels of a sport organization. Industrial relations (IR) theorists focus on this type of conflict because of the inevitable power differential found in the workplace (Bendersky, 2003). Conflict between an athletic director and a coordinator of intercollegiate athletics may occur over such issues as salary, the amount of authority the coordinator is allowed to exercise, differences over the goals of the athletic department, or the way it should operate. Much of this type of conflict stems from the need for control in a sport organization and an individual's or subunit's need for autonomy. Organizational members have to balance their own needs for personal expression and fulfillment against the demands imposed by the structure of the organization, in particular its hierarchical reporting relationships and formalized procedures.

Vertical conflicts can be avoided by appropriate leadership behavior, or techniques such as management by objectives (MBO), where there is an attempt to establish some degree of congruence between individual and organizational goals. However, none of these methods will completely eliminate vertical conflicts, and all generally involve a trade-off between the amount of control that can be exercised and an individual's or subunit's autonomy. A frequent form of vertical conflict involves managers (or owners) and workers. We see this type of conflict in professional sport organizations in struggles between team owners and players (Dworkin, 1981).

Is Conflict Dysfunctional to the Operation of a Sport Organization?

For most of us, conflict carries a negative connotation. We are brought up to believe that conflict is bad, something we should avoid. Psychologist Abraham Maslow (1965, p. 185) suggested that within North America there is "a fear of conflict, of disagreement, of hostility, antagonism, enmity" and that we place "much stress on getting along with other people, even if [we] don't like them."

These ideas about conflict are reflected in our view of sport organizations. The common perception of an effective sport organization is one where everybody gets along with each other and works toward a common goal—cooperation and collective enthusiasm or identification with the team, sport, or purpose of the organization are emphasized. Members of organizations where cooperation is high are said to interact more effectively, make better progress on tasks, and strengthen their work relationships (Tjosvold, 1988). It is also claimed that employee satisfaction is higher and the managers of these organizations are held in more esteem. In contrast, conflict is seen as dysfunctional; because it hinders the achievement of organizational goals, it is something we should avoid in our organizations. Yet some evidence shows that conflict can have beneficial impacts on performance of, for example, work groups or teams (Bradley, Anderson, Baur, & Klotz, 2015). More recently, advances in research on team conflict specifically describes the patterns of conflict that occur in teams (O'Neill, McLarnon, Hoffart, Woodley, & Allen, 2018), indicating that all teams or work groups often have multiple types of conflict occurring at once with some potential to optimize conflict for increased performance.

The view of conflict as dysfunctional can be found in both the classical approach to organization theory and the human relations school. In the former, with its emphasis on bureaucratic rationality, conflict is at best avoided and at worst managed through the imposition of rules and regulations (Taylor, 1911). Human relations theorists (Likert & Likert, 1976) and much of the HRM school of thought (Bradley, Anderson, Baur, & Klotz, 2015) also see conflict as bad. However, according to the negative view of conflict, conflict is controlled by providing people with training sessions on how to get along or by using third-party intervention when conflict arises. Both of these perspectives are limited because they fail to acknowledge the functional benefits of conflict to an organization.

Those who subscribe to the view that an optimal level of conflict can be beneficial to an organization's operation see it as a source of change and creativity. Pondy (1992, p. 259) even goes as far as to suggest that "if conflict isn't happening then the organization has no reason for being." Conflict, because it often arises over dissatisfaction with the way things are, prevents complacency and stimulates new ideas. Sport organizations that are totally free of conflict will have no reason to change and may ultimately flounder. This is not to say that all conflict in sport organizations is beneficial; the emphasis is on an optimal level of conflict. If conflict is too low, sport managers need to stimulate constructive conflict; we deal with ways of stimulating conflict later in this chapter. If conflict is too high, the manager's job is to reduce it. Figure 16.2 shows how levels of conflict that are too high or too low can influence an organization's level of effectiveness adversely.

The job of the sport manager is to recognize the situation within the organization and take the necessary steps to develop an optimal level of conflict. Obviously, managers need to adopt an attitude toward conflict that sees it as a source of innovation rather than a destructive force and to recognize when conflict is destructive so that

TIME OUT

From the Balcony to the Boardroom: Parents as a Source of Conflict

Parents are an important stakeholder in sport—they play a role in their children's experience; they volunteer, coach, and contribute to the board—and while these things can be seen as positive, parents can also be problematic and a source of conflict. Many sport organizations have taken steps to "manage" or educate parents, such as Working with Parents in Sport (WWPIS) in the United Kingdom, a website devoted to supporting parents and coaches to work together to provide positive youth experience in sport. Other organizations, such as Hockey Canada, have courses (Respect in Sport) that parents must complete to understand appropriate behaviors and communication during practices and games.

Parents often have a great passion for sport and for their child's participation, which can cause significant conflicts between a number of stakeholders. Parents servicing on boards, making decisions on team selection policy, or hiring coaches are actually in a conflict of interest between what they want for their child and what is best for the organization. Sport governance has increasingly recognized that managing conflict of interest is one way to reduce or avoid unnecessarily high levels of conflict in organizations. Good governance (transparency, accountability, responsibility) would firstly suggest that any conflict of interest be acknowledged and declared. This open, transparent expression is not admission of guilt but recognition of a situation from which a person or persons can remove themselves and, therefore, the potential for conflict to occur. Strandbu, Stefansen, Smette, & Sandvik (2017) note athletes' perceptions of parent involvement in sport can be problematic. As sport managers, we should consider whether this conflict is dysfunctional or in some way beneficial to our organizations and critically reflect on the effectiveness of our conflict management policies and practices aimed at parents.

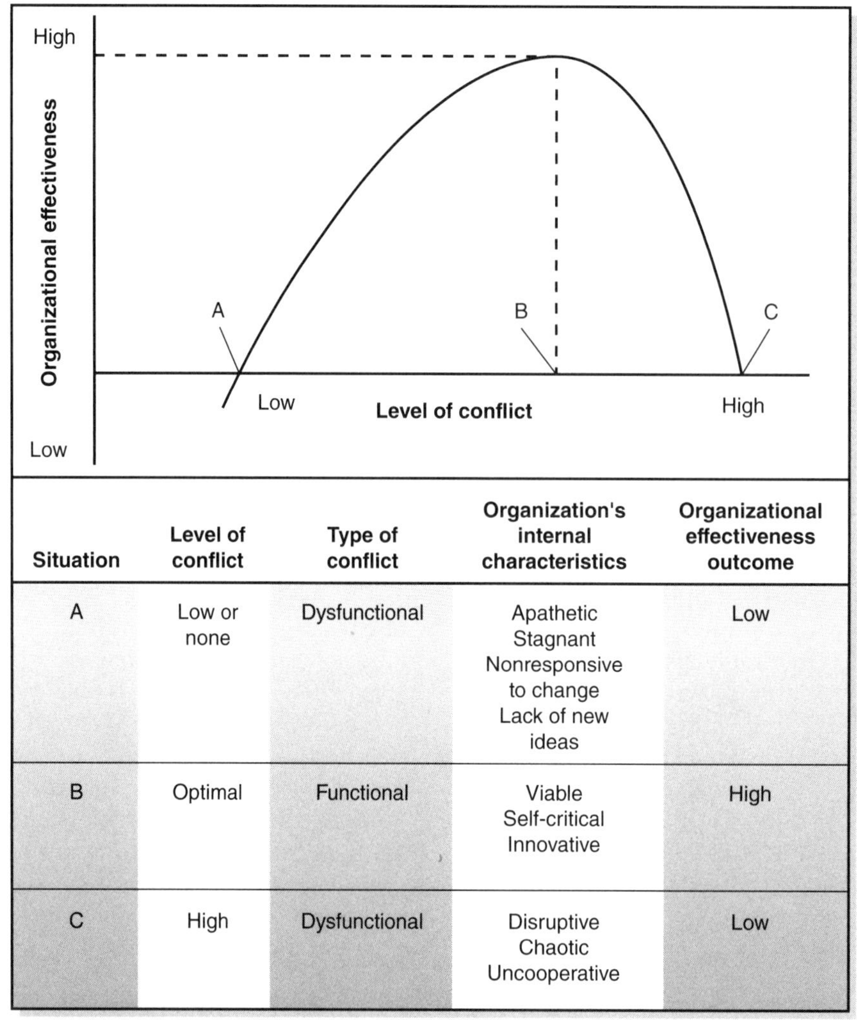

Situation	Level of conflict	Type of conflict	Organization's internal characteristics	Organizational effectiveness outcome
A	Low or none	Dysfunctional	Apathetic Stagnant Nonresponsive to change Lack of new ideas	Low
B	Optimal	Functional	Viable Self-critical Innovative	High
C	High	Dysfunctional	Disruptive Chaotic Uncooperative	Low

Figure 16.2 Conflict and organizational effectiveness.

ROBBINS, STEPHEN P., ORGANIZATION THEORY: STRUCTURES, DESIGN, AND APPLICATIONS, 3rd Edition, © 1990. Reprinted by permission of Pearson Education, Inc., Upper Saddle River, NJ.

appropriate measures can be taken to reduce or resolve problematic conflict.

The Conflict Process

We often tend to think of conflict situations as discrete events: The conflict occurs and then is resolved by some means. However, some organizational theorists (Pondy, 1967; Rahim, 1986) have suggested that a conflict situation is made up of a series of interrelated stages. By being aware of the stages of the **conflict process**, and consequently the conditions that produce conflict and the events that can trigger a conflict situation, those people responsible for the operation of a sport organization can be in a better position to manage the incident. Pondy (1967) developed the most frequently cited of the stage models of conflict. Figure 16.3 shows an adaptation of Pondy's model; each stage in the model is discussed in detail.

Pondy's Five-Stage Model of Conflict

The first stage in Pondy's model is the latent stage of conflict. Essentially what Pondy argues is that certain conditions frequently found in organizations provide the latent potential for conflict to occur. These conditions are condensed into three basic types of **latent conflict**. The first of these involves competition for scarce resources. For example, when two or more groups, such as the teams within an athletic department, are vying for a portion of the organization's financial resources, there is a latent potential for conflict.

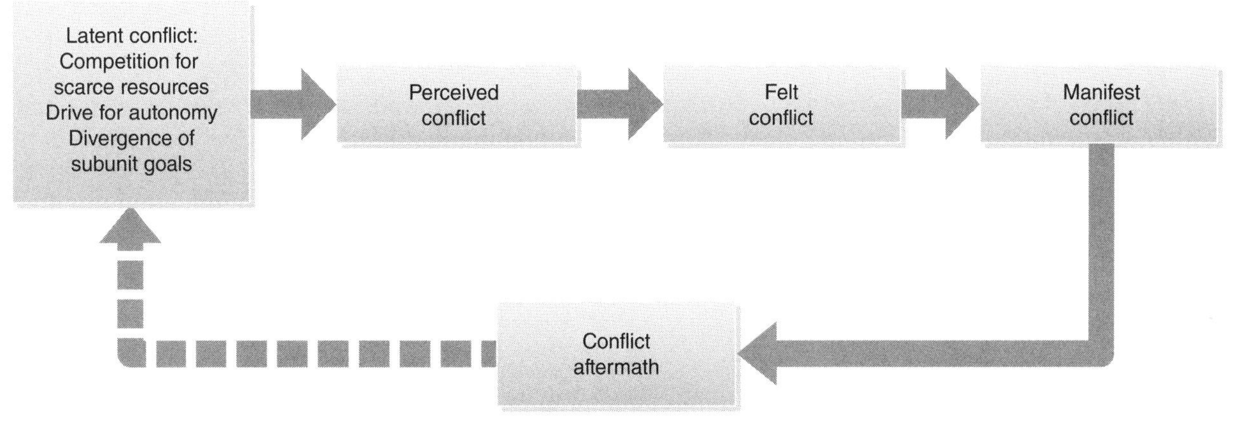

Figure 16.3 Pondy's five-stage model of conflict.
Based on Pondy (1967).

TIME OUT

Creative Tension: An Optimal Level of Conflict?

Managing the 1984 Los Angeles Olympic Games was a large and difficult task (Reich, 1986). Peter Ueberroth, the president of the Los Angeles Olympic Organizing Committee (LAOOC), knew it was not a normal business and didn't run in the customary way. These Games were unique in that they were funded entirely from private-sector money, and the goal of the Organizing Committee was to deliver the Games at no cost to the public, in a commercial, private-sector funded model (McDonald, 1991).

The regime under which the Olympic committee was managed was strict, and the formal rules and regulations reflected the brusque enforcement of these by managers (McDonald, 1991). Uberoff readily acknowledged that he intentionally created some tensions in daily operation as a means of testing his staff. Goal setting and testing of knowledge were paramount to the management style (McDonald, 1991). These games were run on a strict budget and there was little room for error, so staff were kept on alert with constant tests of their knowledge.

Examples of tensions include the "Peter test," a test administered by the president himself to all newcomers, with only 24 hours' notice before its administration (McDonald, 1991). Regardless of what the Peter test content was, the idea is that the hierarchical leader himself created tension and uncertainty by testing people when they first arrived to indicate the type of environment and expectations of the organization (Reich, 1986). Another test of sorts related to each individual being assigned a country and expected to be the resource person for that country. If the president received a delegation, for example, he would call all individuals who were supposed to know about that country and quiz them to get the desired information.

The second condition that creates a latent potential for conflict is the drive for autonomy. Individuals and subunits within sport organizations frequently attempt to operate autonomously. However, this ability is limited by the structure of the organization and the existence of similar aspirations in other individuals and subunits. For example, the owner or manager of a franchised sporting goods store may wish to undertake certain marketing activities to respond to the local conditions in his area, but he may be constrained by the company's corporate headquarters, which has a standardized approach to marketing for a consistent image of the company. Finally, latent conflict is a product of the differing goals that subunits within an organization can have. The athletic department at a university, for example, will have goals different from the physical education department, thus creating the potential for conflict.

The second stage of Pondy's model is **perceived conflict**, the stage in which one or more of the parties involved becomes aware, through some type of stimulus or information received, of the potential for a conflict. Pondy suggests that some only mildly threatening conflicts may be suppressed. Also, because organizations are often faced with more conflicts than they can handle, only a few are dealt with, usually those "for which short-run, routine solutions are available" (Pondy, 1967, pp. 301-302).

The third stage of Pondy's model is **felt conflict**. Here, emotions such as anger, hostility, and frustration are encountered. The fourth stage is **manifest conflict**. Here, some sort of adversarial behavior is exhibited, ranging from apathy and rigid adherence to rules to violence and physical abuse, although thankfully the latter is rare in sport organizations.

Pondy calls the final stage of the model the **conflict aftermath**. Here, the conflict is either resolved or becomes the basis for future conflicts, as indicated by the broken line in figure 16.3.

Sources of Conflict in Sport Organizations

Conflict in a sport organization can stem from a number of sources and take a variety of forms. Much of the work carried out on conflict in organizations has been micro in orientation (Nelson, 1989), that is, it has tended to be sociopsychology-based and to focus on conflicts at the interpersonal level. In keeping with our emphasis on the structuring of sport organizations, we focus here on structurally derived conflicts, those rooted in the way a sport organization is structured. This analysis is important to our understanding of sport organizations because, as Hall (1982, pp. 151-152) points out, "conflict in organizations involves more than simple interpersonal conflict (not that interpersonal conflict is necessarily simple) . . . the very nature of organizations themselves contribute to conflict situations." We look specifically at those structural **sources of conflict** most frequently cited in the literature (Corwin, 1969; Walton & Dutton, 1969; Walton, Dutton, & Cafferty, 1969) and the application of this literature to sport organizations (Amis, Slack, & Berrett, 1995).

Differentiation

In most sport organizations work is broken down and allocated to different subunits to achieve the goals of the organization more effectively. However, as we saw in chapter 8 the process of differentiation results in subunits exhibiting different goals, management philosophies, and time orientations (Lawrence & Lorsch, 1967). As Langhorn and Hinings (1987, p. 560) point out, although "organizations differentiate for technical reasons, these boundaries of task and expertise are reinforced by sociopsychological processes that result in technical boundaries becoming social and political boundaries." The more a sport organization differentiates (i.e., breaks down work and allocates it to different subunits), the greater the likelihood of conflict because the greater the differences created between subunits. Individuals within subunits may think differently, use different work methods, have different priorities, come from different educational backgrounds, and perhaps even use a totally different set of terminologies. While these differences are appropriate and necessary aspects of the operation of a sport organization, they do not engender tolerance and empathy for the problems that other subunits may confront.

MacIntosh and Whitson (1990) identify how the increasing differentiation of Canadian national sport organizations, which occurred with the hiring of additional professional staff during the 1984-1988 quadrennial planning period, helped precipitate conflict in these organizations. More recently, Nagel, Schlesinger, Bayle, and Giauque (2015) discussed how professionalization of sport federations led to the increasing use of professional staff and profound change in the organizations. The causes and consequences of professionalization reveal that diversification of structure has positive and negative aspects, including a strong likelihood of resistance to change and conflict through the process of negotiating change of structure and institutional logics.

Interdependence

Where there are high levels of differentiation and subsequently considerable variations in the value orientation, mode of operation, and power of the subunits within a sport organization, the potential for conflict is high. However, as Pondy (1967) points out, this potential is latent. For conflict to become manifest, some level of interdependence between the subunits is necessary. Interdependence creates the opportunity for the interference and blocking associated with conflict.

Thompson (1967) identified three types of interdependence—pooled, sequential, and reciprocal—each progressively more complex and requiring increased levels of coordination. The more complex the interdependence in a sport organization, the greater the likelihood of conflict. For example, conflict is inevitable between coaches and athletes (Wachsmuth, Jowett, & Harwood, 2017).

Low Formalization

One of the ways to manage the complexity associated with increased differentiation and reciprocal interdependence is through the use of rules, regulations, policies, and procedures. Formalization helps clarify roles, establish standard ways of operating, and reduce ambiguity. Consequently, when formalization is high, the potential for conflict in a sport organization is low; when formalization is low, the potential for conflict is high. It is important to note, however, that some writers disagree with this position and argue that rules and regulations can in fact contribute to conflict in organizations and even increased employee turnover (Katsikea, Theodosiou, & Morgan, 2015).

A lack of formalized regulatory mechanisms such as rules and regulations means that subunits come to rely more on political tactics and coercion to conduct their operations. For example, a number of Canadian national sport organizations have formalized their selection criteria for national team athletes and made the criteria known well before the selection process. This formalization reduces the subjective and political nature of the selection process, helping avoid the conflicts that sometimes occur over this issue.

Competition Over Resources

When two or more subunits within a sport organization compete for a share of limited resources, they come into conflict with each other. Because sport organizations only have so much money, space, or equipment, conflict exists over who is going to get what. Also, since these resources often help subunits accomplish their goals more easily and quickly, managers often use such strategies as inflating budgets or political maneuvers to increase their share.

Conflict over resources can occur horizontally in a sport organization, for example, when the sport studies department within a university has to compete with other departments for increased funding. It can also occur vertically, particularly between owners or managers and workers. The NHL's canceled season in 2004-2005 featured at the beginning of this chapter is a good example of conflict over resources, in this case, financial resources.

Differences in Reward Systems

The nature of the reward system used within a sport organization helps determine the extent to which subunits cooperate or are in conflict with each other (Walton & Dutton, 1969). The more frequently the managers of the various departments within an organization are rewarded for achieving the overall goals of the organization, as opposed to their own departmental goals, the higher the level of cooperation within the organization (Cliff, 1987). The more rewards are based on the performance of each individual subunit, as opposed to the overall sport organization, the greater the potential for conflict. In a sport organization that produces equipment, for example, if the sales department is rewarded for increased sales volume, it will want to establish as many new accounts as possible. Some may have risky credit ratings, and the accounting department, which is rewarded for minimizing losses, will not want to take them on as new clients. These cross-purposes will lead to conflict between these two departments. In another example, Slack, Berrett, and Mistry (1994) show how, in a national sport organization, the coaches' high salaries led to conflict with lower-paid administrators, who felt they made an equal contribution to the operation of the organization.

Power Incongruence

Even though subunits may be on the same level of a sport organization's hierarchy, some are able to wield more power because they are more central to the workflow or they can acquire and control needed resources. These differences in power can lead to conflict, particularly when the actual day-to-day interactions do not reflect perceived power. For example, in an athletic department the athletic director is higher up the organizational hierarchy than the basketball coach. However, due to the importance attributed to the basketball program on many U.S. university campuses, the basketball coach may perceive him- or herself and be perceived by others as having considerable power. If the coach then starts to give "orders" to the athletic director, conflict is likely to ensue.

Participative Decision Making

Although often promoted as an important means of getting people involved in an organization, "the opening up of organizational decisions to discussion and debate raises, or maintains, the level of conflict in the institution" (Zald, 1962, p. 47). By allowing more people to have their say, participative decision making facilitates the expression of more diverse opinions, heightening the potential for conflict. The interaction that occurs between members of a sport organization, rather than breaking down barriers, can serve to reinforce differences and thus may entrench people in their position even more.

Does this mean we should not use participative decision making in sport organizations? The answer is obviously no; participative decision making can be a very productive way of operating, even though it has the potential to precipitate conflict. Levels of participation in a sport organization's decision-making processes may range from "consultative participation," in which employees have input into the process but are not responsible for the final decision, to "employee involvement," when employees have input about work procedures and job responsibilities

(Cotton, Vollrath, Froggatt, Lengnick-Hall, & Jennings, 1988). A number of national sport organizations in Canada and the United States have successfully adopted what is termed *representative participation*; representatives from the countries' different geographic regions, the officials' organization, and the ranks of the athletes are involved in the decision-making process. The question for the sport manager in any initiative to increase the number of different viewpoints is: Does the potential for reduced alienation and improved morale outweigh the possible conflicts that could result?

Conflict Management Strategies

Conflict management strategies must be employed because conflict has both positive and negative consequences. The ideal situation for the sport manager is an organization with an optimal level of conflict. Rahim (2017, p. xi), in the third edition of his book, maintains that "diagnosis is needed to determine whether and to what extent an intervention is needed to:

1. Minimize affective and process conflicts;
2. Minimize substantive conflict in routine tasks;
3. Attain and maintain a moderate amount of substantive conflict for non-routine tasks; and
4. Enable the organizational members to learn and use the various styles of behavior, such as integrating, obliging, dominating, avoiding, and compromising for handling different conflict situations effectively."

A number of strategies are outlined below that can be used to manage conflict. Conflict can be managed by either changing behavior or changing attitudes. A **behavioral change** is superficial and does not really get at the root of the conflict; it is a short-term solution. An **attitudinal change** requires a greater commitment and usually takes longer to accomplish, but it is the basis for a more collaborative sport organization. We look at some strategies solely designed to change behavior, and others used to establish more long-term attitudinal changes.

Authority

One of the most common methods of managing conflict is for the senior managers of a sport organization to use their formal authority to resolve or suppress the conflict situation. While the parties involved may not always agree with the manager's decision, they will usually recognize and comply with whatever resolution is made. The use of authority for conflict management is also used between sport organizations as the professionalization and commercialization of sport increases. For example, as Riordan (2018) reports, the International Olympic Committee (IOC) warned the International Boxing Association (AIBA) that boxing faced exclusion from the 2020 Tokyo Olympics after the AIBA elected Gafur Rakhimov as their president. The IOC was in conflict with the AIBA (and previously suspended its funding) over their failure to comply with regulations on governance, finance, and anti-doping. The IOC had previously cautioned the AIBA on Rakhimov's links to organized crime in his native Uzbekistan and now can use their authority to ban the sport of boxing from an Olympic Games. The use of authority can be effective in reducing conflict in this situation in that it may force the AIBA to improve governance, financial management, and other such practices to avoid exclusion from the 2020 Tokyo Olympics; however, it will not resolve all conflict between the two organizations because disagreements over appropriate leadership and governance practices are likely to continue. The authority may force compliance but is not going to resolve the conflict entirely or sustainably.

Avoidance

Another commonly used technique for dealing with conflict is avoidance, that is, either directing attention away from a conflict or ignoring that it exists. If the dean of a faculty of sport studies is involved in a heated conversation with the athletic director over the resources allocated to their respective areas, he or she may, for example, change the subject to one less contentious. In a somewhat similar vein, an athletic director may choose to turn a blind eye to illegal payments to university athletes, hoping that any conflict that could ensue from such an illegal practice will be avoided. However, like the use of authority, avoidance is a short-term solution.

Separating or Merging Conflicting Units

Because conflict emanates from the interdependence between the subunits of a sport organization, one way to manage such conflict is to remove the interdependence. Where the units do not need to work together on organizational tasks, a manager could order the actual physical separation of the two groups, preventing any contact between them.

A related but opposite way of handling this type of situation is to reduce the interdependence between two subunits by merging them into one. In part, notwithstanding the economic benefits, the merging of some of the major professional sport leagues has been motivated by the desire to reduce conflict. Harris (1987, p. 16), for example, notes that after the NFL and AFL merger "peace . . . descended on the [gridiron] football business," a stark contrast to "the war that had preceded it."

Increasing Resources

As we saw earlier, resource scarcity can precipitate conflict. It follows, then, that one way to manage a conflict over resources is to increase availability. While it is not always possible to give all subunits everything they want, selected resource increases may translate into savings because wasteful conflicts are avoided. For example, in a sport management department conflict could arise between faculty and graduate students who both have to use the same photocopying machine. If use is heavy, faculty members may feel they should have priority. At the same time, graduate students who have research and teaching responsibilities feel their needs are equally important. The simple answer to avoiding or removing any conflict over this situation is to provide each group with a photocopier. However, while it is often a very satisfactory means of resolving or preventing a conflict, all too often resources for this kind of initiative are not readily available.

Integrating Devices

Integrating devices may involve the use of a small group (a committee or a task force) or an individual. Essentially, the role of these groups or individuals is to span the boundaries between subunits. If a group is used, it usually contains representatives from the subunits that are or potentially could be in conflict. Bringing these people together is seen as an effective way of solving problems because they come to see each other's perspective (Blake & Mouton, 1984). Committees are frequently used in many sport organizations to manage or prevent conflict. For example, Cross Country Canada has a high-performance committee with representatives from the coaches, athletes, and sport scientists. By having representatives from these different groups involved in decision making about high-performance sport, the incidences of conflict can be minimized. Individual sport managers themselves may sometimes fill a similar role in a committee or task force; part of every manager's job is to enhance collaboration between the subunits under managerial control. Mid-level sport managers may also act as integrators between senior managers and lower-level workers. Like those strategies that follow, the use of integrating devices is directed toward attitudinal, rather than behavioral, change.

Confrontation and Negotiation

Confrontation means that the parties involved in a conflict come together face to face and try to resolve their differences. Those involved recognize that conflict exists and that it needs to be dealt with. Confrontation as a conflict resolution technique requires a certain amount of maturity; facts have to be faced, and emotions, as much as possible, have to be put aside. Although confrontations are risky, if successful they can provide a basis for continued collaboration. Negotiations occur during the confrontation process; each subunit or their representative(s) work through the situation to try to come to an agreement. It is important to emphasize that in the negotiation process the focus should not solely be on points of difference but also on points of agreement. Negotiation skills are invaluable to owners, players, agents, and leagues because contracts and salaries are frequently the focus of conflict between stakeholders. Abreu and Spradley (2016) provide an analysis of the 2011 NFL labor dispute and identify the conflict management strategies used to decrease dysfunctional conflict between the league and players' association. Successful negotiation was underpinned by using a compromise strategy where both parties identified solutions that were of some mutual benefit and where both parties made some concessions.

Third-Party Interventions

If a conflict is particularly drawn out, a third-party intervention may be used to resolve the dispute. Here a person who is not associated with the conflict is brought in to try to resolve the situation. Although the person brought in will not be associated with either side in the conflict, the principals involved are often given the right to approve or disapprove of the person who will be the third party. The best example of this strategy in sport organizations is the situation where labor arbitrators resolve contract disputes between the owners of professional sport teams and their players. One of the best-known arbitration decisions in sport, referred to as the Seitz decision, resulted in Jim "Catfish" Hunter of the Oakland Athletics becoming baseball's first free agent in 1974 (Scully, 1989).

Resolution of conflict within a sport organization can involve third-party intervention. In 1974 a contract dispute involving pitcher Jim "Catfish" Hunter went to arbitration, with the result that Hunter became baseball's first free agent.

TIME OUT

Alternative Dispute Resolution: A System for Resolving Conflicts in Sport

At the 2000 Sydney Olympic Games, two legal battles challenged an athlete's right to participate. One case involved an equestrian athlete who wanted reinstatement, claiming he was wrongly banned from the sport for drug use, and another was a 50-meter swimmer whose coach supposedly forgot to add him to the list of participants. Cases like these are increasingly frequent or, at least, are seen more often in the media. When an athlete takes an organization to court, it can tie up the courts for weeks. Because these cases are time-sensitive, they take precedence over criminal cases, causing a backlog in the courts. In addition, it is a costly initiative for athletes who, for the most part, have little money to spare.

Canada has created an alternative dispute resolution (ADR) system called the Sport Dispute Resolution Centre of Canada to help remedy such situations in the Canadian sport system. National sport organizations are now required to refer to this organization when conflicts need resolution (Sport Dispute Resolution Centre of Canada, n.d.). The ADR system also uses the International Court of Arbitration for international matters.

ADR "has been defined as a series of processes that are alternatives to litigation . . . [and they include] prevention, negotiation, mediation, facilitation, and arbitration" (Kidd & Ouellet, 2000, p. 4). The general goals of ADR are to decrease time and costs for dispute resolution, "maintain or improve the disputants' relationship, ensure that the outcome of the system is workable, durable and implementable [and] develop a process that people can learn from" (Kidd & Ouellet, 2000, p. 5).

Superordinate Goals

Subunits within a sport organization develop their own goals. The incompatibility of these goals with those of other subunits can sometimes precipitate conflict. A strategy used to address this type of conflict is to create superordinate goals, higher-level goals that require subunits to work together. These goals must be seen as more important than the goals subunits possess individually. The creation of superordinate goals can enhance cooperation within an organization; attention is directed away from the individual subunit goals, the basis of the conflict, to the superordinate goals that must be achieved collaboratively.

A very powerful superordinate goal is survival. In good times, when resources are relatively plentiful, vigorous union lobbying for salary increases often leads to conflicts with owners and management. When a sport organization's survival is threatened, a situation that affects everyone's welfare, groups may be inclined to work together more to ensure survival.

Job Rotation

Sometimes conflict can be prevented or managed by engaging in job rotation. Very simply, a person from one subunit works in another subunit, usually on a temporary basis. Through this practice, the person who is moved comes to understand the attitudes, issues, and problems in the subunit to which she or he is moved. The individual who is moved is also in a good position to relate similar information about her own department. Although it often takes considerable time, job rotation can have a significant effect on changing some of the underlying attitudes that precipitate conflict. While some types of job rotation are not feasible, for example, having the tennis coach trade places with the football coach, the concept is applicable to a variety of sport organizations, most notably those involved in the manufacturing of sport equipment.

Issues Management

Conflict can come from internal issues but also from the environment. External issues can have a major impact on the organization's activities. One way to ensure that conflict from external sources is prevented or managed in time is to use the issues management process. According to Nigh and Cochran (1987), an organization starts with these steps:

1. Identify external issues by determining gaps between internal and external needs and expectations as well as perceived trends.
2. Analyze identified issues.
   - Examine the issue's history and forecast how it might develop over time.
   - Determine the probability of the issue's various outcomes.
   - Assess the issue's impact on the sport organization.
   - Prepare the agenda—a list or order of issues for management consideration with three categories of issues: (1) high probability of outcomes having an impact on the firm, (2) lower probability but should be tracked periodically, and (3) potential issue.
3. Formulate and implement a response to prevent or manage the issues.

The management process allows the sport organization to be proactive in its conflict resolution by identifying problems before they get out of hand. For example, the director of a high school athletics department may realize a growing discrepancy

TIME OUT

Innovation in Conflict Management in Sport

It is inevitable that university and college students experience stress. Couple a new start at college or university with playing high performance sport, and you have the varsity athlete. According to Vidic, Martin, and Oxhandler (2018), these athletes face unique challenges in that they are expected to perform their best in academics, on field, and in the community or personal areas of their lives. In recognition of this, the National Collegiate Athletic Association (NCAA) has turned its attention to innovative tools and techniques to help these athletes cope with rising pressures and stressors. One such tool that has received positive response from athletes and a mixed-methods intervention study is mindfulness meditation. Health, well-being, and athletic performance were shown to improve in a group of male association football players after a six-session mindfulness meditation intervention.

between the needs of students (physical activity, being healthy), the expectations of parents (a wide range of sports available), and the funding provided by the government (in decline). Having identified this issue, the director will look at what's been done in the past and consider possible solutions for the present. Solutions may be to decrease the number of sports, consult students about their desired sports, lobby the government for more money, or find alternative avenues of funding. Determining that the latter solution may be the most acceptable to all constituencies, given the strong sport program at the school, the director may present a proposal to the school's administration to prevent a possible conflict at budget time. The administration would then take the proposal, along with issues identified by other departments in the school, and prioritize a response according to resources available and the potential impact of the issues left unresolved.

Stimulating Conflict

Earlier in this chapter it was suggested that the effectiveness of a sport organization is influenced by the level of conflict within the organization. Because conflict can often be below an optimally desirable level, and Rahim (2011) suggests that a modern view of conflict in organizations accepts that conflict is both inevitable and an indicator of effective management, it is sometimes necessary to stimulate conflict rather than reduce it. A lack of conflict in an organization can mean a lack of change and innovation, leading to decreasing competitiveness and poor organization performance. On an individual and group level, employees may become lethargic and reliant on formal rules only to guide behavior of what they have to do rather than proactively thinking about how they can improve their contribution to their organization. Managers may recognize a variety of problems in their organizations (see table 16.1) that are indications of too little conflict among staff. Use the table as a checklist for an organization with which you are familiar and consider how increasing conflict would help alleviate the problem.

Robbins (1978) notes that while no definitive method exists for universally assessing the need for more conflict, a lack of change or new ideas or decreases in organization performance suggest that more conflict stimulation may be needed. Using some of the ideas suggested by Robbins, we briefly explore how **conflict stimulation** can be used in a sport organization.

We now look at some of the strategies presented in the table in more detail and further illustrate the essential role of conflict in sport organizations.

Introducing New Blood

Sometimes people within a sport organization become complacent; one of the ways to wake them up is to introduce one or more new people into the organization—individuals who bring new and different ideas to the sport organization, who challenge existing modes of operation, and who make staff think about new ideas. Bringing "new blood" into the organization was exactly what Reebok's Paul Fireman had in mind in 1987 when he hired C. Joseph LaBonté, a former CEO of 20th Century Fox

Table 16.1 Do You Need to Stimulate Conflict in Your Organization?

Problem	Conflict stimulation strategy	Intended result
Low innovation	Create competition	Increased innovation, improved organization performance
High resistance to change from employees	Participative decision making on strategic planning	Breaks down resistance, understands individual interpretations
Low employee or volunteer turnover	Create new position or bring in new interns	New blood creates uncertainty and less apathy in employees
	Manipulate communications (e.g. new hires)	Creates uncertainty around job roles and authority
Lack of discussion in decision making, few alternatives identified	Increase participative decision making	More perspectives will generate conflicting ideas but through discussion will lead to more reasoned decisions; increases employee satisfaction through participation

Film Corporation, to become president and CEO. Prior to LaBonté's hiring, Reebok was a one-product company. When he arrived at Reebok, LaBonté added new product lines and began a series of acquisitions designed to diversify and strengthen the company. He also cut the size of the apparel group, instituted a series of controls that created a more structured organization, and began a series of cost-cutting measures. LaBonté's initiatives created a series of conflicts: While Reebok had gained control over its internal operations, indications showed it had lost control of its external relations. Notwithstanding these problems, Reebok's profits rose 28 percent in 1989, but that same year LaBonté left the company (Jereski, 1990; Van Fleet, 1991). Introducing someone new to an organization does not have to be a formal hire but could also be a new intern, group of volunteers, or external consultant. Depending on the organization's capacity, resources, and needs, sport managers should seek ways to bring new people with new ideas into the organization on a consistent basis.

Manipulating Communications

Robbins (1978) suggests that manipulating communications can help managers stimulate conflict. Ambiguous or threatening information can create situations in which tensions run high. For example, information suggesting that certain intercollegiate athletic programs will be cut because of funding shortages can create the kind of conflict that can reduce complacency and improve the health of an athletic department. Leaving an individual or subunit out of the communication process can have the effect of signaling to them that they are not important. The confrontation resulting from this type of omission, however, can cause the individuals or subunits concerned to reexamine their role in the sport organization and their contribution to its strategic direction. There is, of course, an ethical question to consider when using this type of tactic.

Creating Competition

Creating competition between subunits or individuals is a third way managers can stimulate conflict. Coaches use this technique when they institute competitions between players on their teams. It is also used by sport organizations such as sport equipment retail stores creating competitions to see who can sell the most in a particular time period. The conflict usually resulting from these ventures is rarely hostile, as invariably everybody wins. However, if the competition results in no net gain, or if effort is duplicated, such as in a case when two groups of salespeople in the same sporting goods company compete for a large contract, the level of conflict is likely to be higher.

Current Research About Conflict in Sport Organizations

Within sport management, few researchers directly examine organizational conflict. One notable exception is the study by Burke and Collins (2000), which provides issues, approaches, and implications of work conflict for sport managers.

Mannix (2003) suggested avenues of conflict research that apply very well to the sport management field. First, she argued for research on cross-cultural conflict. Next, she proposed that conflict situations be followed over a period of time because organizational disputes are not isolated occurrences. Instead, they influence future decisions and actions. Third, she argued for the need to better understand the "links between the types of conflict and performance" (p. 544). Fourth, she argued for a detailed description of negotiation's underlying mechanisms and processes. Finally, she argued for the need to link specific types of diversity (social diversity, informational diversity, and value diversity) with specific conflict types and conflict resolution processes and outcomes.

Kerwin, Walker, and Bopp (2017), using social identity theory, examined the conflict triggering process in sport organization boards and indicated that task conflict emanates from diversity of individuals; task conflict is underpinned by interpersonal conflict and divergent priorities.

Researchers have identified several areas where too much conflict is problematic with sport. Wachsmuth, Jowett, and Harwood (2017) focus on the conflict among athletes and coaches in their review of existing theory. Their research focuses on interpersonal conflict in sport relationships and notes 80 articles in which they identified definitions of conflict, determinants of interpersonal conflict, prevention and management techniques, and consequences of conflict. They concluded that much of the research on conflict in sport relationships is perceived as negative. Our insights into the benefits of conflict are extremely limited. Research marks the role of parents in sport as a potential "stressor" in youth sport (Omli & La Voi, 2009; Smoll, Cumming, & Smith, 2011), while other research suggests the relationship between parents and young people in sport is more complex (Strandbu, Stefansen, Smette, & Sandvik, 2017).

KEY ISSUES FOR SPORT MANAGERS

The point of this chapter is that successful sport organizations and managers must be able to recognize and deal with conflict. Negative conflict can hurt a sport organization and its employees. Recognizing and dealing with conflict properly and as soon as possible, before it gets out of hand, allows the sport organization to save time, money, and other precious resources. Sport managers must also be able to choose an appropriate conflict management strategy, recognizing that the strategies we presented earlier in the chapter are not mutually exclusive. Sometimes a combination of strategies is best. The ADR example presented in the Time Out "Alternative Dispute Resolution: A System Resolving Conflicts in Sport" is, in effect, a combination of a negotiation and a third-party intervention. In addition, sport managers must look at potential conflict not only within the organization but also across the organization's boundaries. One emerging type of conflict in an increasingly globalized world is the potential differences between cultures. Expectations and needs may be very different between, say, American and Chinese counterparts, which can lead to potential conflict. Being able to recognize this possibility beforehand will save the sport organization much time and effort.

Nugent (2002) proposed four steps for managers to decide the appropriate level of involvement when faced with a conflict situation. First, managers must determine whether an intervention is even necessary. Can the protagonists be made to handle the situation themselves, or is a third party needed? Second, if an intervention is required, what is the most appropriate type of intervention: autocratic, arbitration, facilitating, bargaining, or collaborative problem solving? Third, the manager must determine whether he or she is the best person to intervene. Is someone with more power better? Finally, if the manager is the best person, does he or she need the assistance of an independent resource person (and how would this person be used)?

Successful sport organizations and managers must also be able to promote positive conflict. This can increase creativity, communication, and preparedness to help the organization gain and sustain a competitive advantage. However, most people do not see conflict as positive. As a manager, it is your responsibility to use conflict stimulation when needed and in an appropriate manner so that the exercise does not have a negative effect on employees. Increasing conflict from very low levels to an optimum amount can have benefits for sport organizations, but excessive conflict is destructive, so the sport manager must judge the appropriate level for their organization and recognize the consequences of those levels to organization effectiveness.

Summary and Conclusions

Conflict is one of the most neglected issues in the field of sport management. Research has focused more on the sporting context rather than the sport organizational context. Yet we know that conflict in sport organizations is widespread. In this chapter we addressed a number of issues related to conflict in sport organizations. Definitions of conflict drawn from the literature featured a number of common elements that delineate the occurrence of a conflict situation. However, it was noted that caution should be applied when using definitions of conflict because it is sometimes difficult to distinguish between conflict situations and the normal daily social interaction that takes place in a sport organization. Conflict was described as existing in both the horizontal and vertical levels of a sport organization. It was then shown that, contrary to what has been presented in sport management literature, conflict can in fact be functional to the operation of a sport organization. Pondy's conflict model was used to show that conflict is not a single discrete event but rather a series of interrelated stages. The most frequent sources of structurally based conflict in sport organizations were identified as differentiation, interdependence, low formalization, competition over resources, differences in reward systems, power incongruence, communication problems, participative decision making, and role conflict. Several strategies were presented to manage the conflict arising from these sources. A discussion of the more common ways to stimulate conflict in a sport organization if it drops below an optimally desirable level concluded the chapter.

Review Questions

1. What does a sport organization gain from conflict? What does it lose?
2. Using a conflict that has occurred in a sport organization you know, identify the different stages of the conflict using Pondy's model.
3. How is structurally derived conflict different from interpersonal conflict?
4. Pick a situation when you have seen a sport manager use avoidance to handle a conflict situation. Discuss what other ways the conflict could have been handled.
5. You have just been hired to be the managing director of the national governing body of one of your country's major team sports. When you arrive, you find that the board of directors, who are all volunteers, are in conflict with the national coach, who is a paid professional. The conflict essentially revolves around the fact that the board does not agree with the coach's selection of several of the players on the team. How will you go about resolving this conflict?
6. What do you think is the relationship between the structure of a sport organization and the incidence of conflict in that organization?

Suggestions for Further Reading

The field of management contains many books written about conflict. Two of the more comprehensive texts are Afzalur Rahim's (1989, 2011) book *Managing Conflict: An Interdisciplinary Approach* and *Managing Conflict in Organizations*; the latest edition of this text was published in 2011. Also interesting is Dean Tjosvold's (1991) *The Conflict-Positive Organization*. Tjosvold, unlike many writers, presents a view of conflict as a positive organizational phenomenon. His later work, including Tjosvold, Wong, and Feng Chen (2014), also advises that conflict can be positive to organization performance. Given the increasing globalization of sport, students may read Wong, Wei, Wang, and Tjosvold (2018) to explore different contexts for positive conflict management strategies. Students who want more information about conflict should also look at the major organizational journals. In particular, vol. 13, no. 3 (1992) of the *Journal of Organizational Behavior* is a special issue titled "Conflict and Negotiation in Organizations: Historical and Contemporary Perspectives." The journals *Group and Organization Management* (GOM), *International Journal of Conflict Management*, and the *Journal of Conflict Management* are dedicated to the study of conflict management and resolution.

In terms of sport literature, newspapers, magazines, and many popular-press books contain descriptive accounts of the type of conflicts that occur in sport organizations. If you are interested in conflict in professional sport and associated issues such as arbitration, you can look into books such as Gerald Scully's (1989) *The Business of Major League Baseball* and James Dworkin's (1981) *Owners Versus Players*, or the more popular-press–type books such as Jack Sands and Peter Gammons' (1993), *Coming Apart at the Seams*. A number of the articles cited in these books also provide useful insights into the issue of conflict in professional sport organizations. While the academic literature on conflict in other kinds of sport organizations is sparse, Slack, Berrett, and Mistry's (1994) article "Rational Planning Systems as a Source of Organizational Conflict" provides some interesting ideas about how planning, an exercise normally believed to eliminate disputes from organizations, can actually precipitate conflict. Also, the article by Amis, Slack, and Berrett (1995) shows how the structural antecedents of conflict operate in voluntary sport organizations. More recently, Shannon Kerwin and colleagues (2017) have produced several publications on conflict and conflict processes in sport organizations, taking primarily a negative view of conflict. Schulz (2011) produced a literature review of conflict in sport management. The increasing problems associated with corruption in sport (competition and management corruption) also point to many instances where conflict is prevalent. Students can keep informed through organizations such as Transparency International (transparency.org) or Play the Game (playthegame.org).

Case for Analysis

Conflict & Change at the USOC: Reforms to Protect Athletes From Abuse

The United States Olympic Committee (USOC) was founded in 1894 and then designated by Congress in 1978 as the principal Olympic group in the United States. To operate the organization, a 105-member board made up of representatives from the 38-member U.S. sport associations was established.

The current structure is somewhat different: the board of directors consists of 16 members and a professional staff headed by a CEO; the USOC also has three constituent councils to serve as sources of opinion and advice to the board and staff. However, despite this streamlined structure and representation from Athletes Advisory Council, National Governing Bodies Council, and Multi-Sport Organizations Council, 2018 witnessed an eruption of sexual abuse allegations, cases, and convictions across several sports. Axon (2018) discussed how sport federations were to blame for failing to acknowledge and stop the abuse, which included more than 250 athletes accusing team doctor Nassar at USA Gymnastics. Gymnastics, figure skating, speed skating, swimming, and more sport federations' athletes were involved in testifying at a U.S. Senate subcommittee investigating the allegations. Abuse reports go back decades, but the first public allegations were made in 2016. However, USOC reportedly said there was nothing they could do and that they did not have jurisdiction over Federations.

CEO of USOC, Scott Blackmun, resigned his position in February 2018 due to health issues, and was replaced by Susanne Lyons, a current board member (Murphy, 2018). She serves as acting CEO after she was selected as chair of the USOC board's working group addressing issues brought to light by the Nassar case has brought. Lyons has extensive global and Olympic experience.

The USOC announced several reforms to provide further protection to athletes (Team USA, 2018):

- New funding and resources for support and counseling and for the Center for SafeSport.
- An advisory group of survivors, advocates, child psychologists, and other medical professionals to guide on stronger safeguards.
- Review of the USOC and NGB governance structure to identify formal mechanisms to prevent abuse.
- Revisit USOC SafeSport procedures to ensure allegations of abuse are reported and follow-ups occur with relevant stakeholders.
- Increase athletes' contribution to decision making at the governing body level.
- Work with United States Artistic Gymnastics (USAG) to implement a culture change (including governance issues), and act on the results of the independent investigation once it is complete.

Questions

1. Discuss the conflict management strategies that were used by different stakeholders in this case, and suggest which of these strategies is most likely to be responsible for the decades of abuse experienced by athletes in the United States.
2. Discuss the relationship between structural and interpersonal conflict as it occurs in this case.
3. What are the sources of conflict in this case? Discuss the implications and manifestations of this conflict and your recommendations for conflict resolution.
4. What can Pondy's model of conflict teach sport managers in this case about when to manage conflict in their organization?

CHAPTER 17

Managing Culture in Sport Organizations

Trevor Slack, PhD
Terri Byers, PhD

Learning Objectives

When you have read this chapter, you should be able to

1. explain what we mean by the term *organizational culture*, as well as some of the recent developments in research on culture in sport organizations;
2. describe the manifestations of a sport organization's culture;
3. explain why some sport organizations can have more than one culture;
4. describe the relationship of culture to organizational effectiveness; and
5. discuss how a sport organization's culture is created, managed, and changed as well as the challenges of managing culture.

Key Concepts

basic assumptions
beliefs
ceremonies
language
multicultural
myths
organizational culture
physical setting
physical stimuli
physical structure
rites
rituals
shared understandings
slogans
stories
symbolic artifacts
symbols
thick culture
thin culture
values

Organizational Culture at Mountain Equipment Co-op

In 1971 in the midst of a savage mountain storm, a small group of students huddled together in a tent and discussed the need for a place to buy sophisticated mountaineering gear (MEC, 2018). The high-end gear they spoke of was unavailable at regular sporting goods stores. They decided to create a cooperative called Mountain Equipment Co-op (MEC) that asked the customers—and therefore gear users—how the company should operate. The organization has grown from these humble beginnings to its current size of five million members across the globe who still pay the same membership of $5 that they did from the beginning (MEC, 2018).

The founders took their love of the outdoors and turned it into the organization's culture. MEC's core purpose is to provide high-quality products at reasonable prices to enable everyone to lead active outdoor lifestyles (MEC, 2018). The company strives to be innovative and cooperative in producing high-quality goods and services for people with a passion for the outdoors and a healthy planet. They value ethics, integrity, respect for others and the environment, protection of the environment, community spirit and cooperation, personal growth, continual learning, and adventure.

MEC tries to live by these values from its choice of environmentally friendly material for its products to the programs it creates. In 1987 MEC started an environment fund, and each year 0.4 percent of MEC's sales and all interest made from the fund go to Canadian-based organizations working toward environmental conservation or education, and recreational projects (MEC, 2018). Currently they are a member of 1% for the Planet, a global network of individuals, nonprofits, and businesses working together for a healthy planet. Aside from the external steps it has taken, MEC has made internal changes over the last decade to make them more efficient in their use of energy, water, and materials. They were fully accredited by the Fair Labor Association (FLA) in 2013, one of only 21 brands in the world to have this status.

The description of MEC and the activities the company is involved in tell us about the culture of the organization. Culture, as we will see, is concerned with characteristics such as the type of values and beliefs found in an organization and the accepted modes of operation. At MEC the important values about protecting the environment are a central part of the organization's culture. Helping with national and local environmental projects is an accepted part of the mode of operation of the company. Everybody—employees and customers (members)—at MEC is expected to work to this end. Individuals are hired because they believe in and will work to promote this ideal. The culture of the company is reflected and reinforced by the fact that employees are encouraged to pursue outdoor activities. Their culture also values people and the environment; this is evident in their organizational structure, which includes social responsibility teams who investigate potential manufacturing partners in Asia and who regularly evaluate how those partnerships are working. They are concerned with improving the lives of people who work for them.

To begin this chapter, we provide a thorough introduction to the term *culture* and discuss what that means in organizations. We differentiate it from related topics such as organizational discourse, identity, and climate, which have emerged in recent years in mainstream management literature. The chapter does not elaborate on all the developments in research on climate, discourse, or other concepts related to culture but simply aims to make readers aware of current developments.

Despite changes in focus from culture to other concepts, the importance of culture in sport organizations is still very relevant; therefore, we look at how culture manifests itself in sport organizations including the idea of thick and thin cultures. We also discuss whether a sport organization has just one culture, and explore the relationship of culture to effectiveness in sport organizations. Finally, we look at how cultures are created, managed, and changed in sport organizations and as a result begin to identify the challenges for managers that culture presents.

Organizational Culture Compared to Climate

Organizational culture emerged as a major topic in organization studies, explicitly addressed in the 1980s and 1990s. In part, the concern with culture has grown out of the success of Japanese industry, which began in the 1970s. Increasingly, organizational theorists began to see that Japanese organizations operated in a different way from most North American and Western European organizations. Their corporate culture consisted of different values and beliefs, different norms of interaction, and a different set of collectivist understandings from their counterparts in North America and Western Europe.

The increased interest in organizational (or what is sometimes referred to as corporate) culture led several organizational theorists to attempt to define what the concept actually means. While no definition can do complete justice to the meaning of any term, looking at some of the more common definitions can give us a good understanding of what these people mean when they refer to organizational culture.

Pettigrew (1979, p. 572), for example, describes **organizational culture** as an "amalgam of beliefs, ideology, language, ritual, and myth." Schein (1985, p. 9) sees it as "a pattern of basic assumptions—invented, discovered, or developed by a given group as it learns to cope with its problems of external adaptation and internal integration—that has worked well enough to be considered valid and therefore, to be taught to new members as the correct way to perceive, think, and feel in relation to those problems." For Sathe (1983, p. 6), culture is "the set of important understandings (often unstated) that members of a community share in common." For Wilkins (1983a, p. 25), it is "the taken-for-granted and shared meanings that people assign to their social surroundings."

Some general themes emerge from these different definitions, including a concern with the **values**, **beliefs**, **basic assumptions**, **shared understandings**, and taken-for-granted meanings on which a set of individuals base the construction of their organization, group, or subgroup. These characteristics, commonly accepted as forming the basis for an organization's culture, provide stability to an organization and convey to new members the understanding that enables them to make sense of organizational activities.

The increased popularity of the concept of culture among managers and organizational theorists, Robey (1986, pp. 426-427) insightfully suggested, can be attributed to two main qualities found in this approach: "First, for many macro organization theorists, culture provides a way to bring *people* back into their analyses without using psychological models of human behavior. . . . Second, culture is widely accepted by managers, because the concept describes organizational realities that are hard to define but very relevant to running an organization" (emphasis in original).

These are important points to consider as we think about organizational culture. While they are relevant to all types of organizations, they are particularly important to the study of sport organizations. Work in sport management had traditionally employed social psychological approaches to explain the qualities and actions of sport managers. A focus on organizational culture provides a different approach to understanding patterns of action in sport organizations. This approach, if combined with traditional macroorganizational theory, could provide for richer insights into the organizations we study. An approach that focuses on organizational culture should also have considerable appeal to those of us interested in sport because the organizations in our field are rife with such characteristics as stories, myths, symbols, and rituals. These characteristics are some of the principle manifestations of an organization's culture, as we will see in the next section of this chapter. A focus on these characteristics would help shed new light on the way sport organizations operate.

Readers may also encounter related concepts in the mainstream management literature such as climate, discourse, and identity. Some would argue the concept of culture has been partly taken over by the concepts of organizational discourse and identity (Petersen, 2011), but it has been mostly confused with climate and so we differentiate these terms here. Organization climate is a concept originating from the industrial-organizational psychology literature (e.g. Litwin & Stringer, 1968; Ehrhart, Schneider, & Macey, 2014) and is now commonly defined as "the shared perceptions and meaning attached to the policies, practices and procedures employees experience and the behaviors they observe getting rewarded, and that are supported and expected" (Schneider, Ehrhart, & Macey, 2013; p. 362). Climate has been measured as a set of generic dimensions reflecting perceptions of specific aspects of the work environment such as diversity climate, safety climate, or ethics climate (Chatman & O'Reilly, 2016). While both climate and culture focus on shared meanings, climate is rooted in individual perceptions of aspects of organizational systems and structures, aggregated by researchers to form a group level measurement, and is more easily changed than culture, which is rooted in fundamental values and beliefs, more enduring, and likely to influence organization function and performance (Chatman & O'Reilly, 2016). Culture is the context in which climate operates (Chatman & O'Reilly, 2016).

Sport management research on climate is in its infancy, so plenty of ground is yet to be covered. Burton, Weltey, Peachy, and Wells (2017) recently explored the important link between leadership and ethical climate in sport. Their research is timely because they recognize the "plague" (p. 229) of scandals that have faced intercollegiate, professional, and international sport organizations in recent years. The article is more about (servant) leadership and so covered in more detail in the chapter on leadership. More broadly, Maitland, Hills, and Rhind (2015) provide a systematic review of organizational culture in sport research and suggest a body of literature is growing to examine organizational culture in sport (Girginov, 2006; Kaiser, Engel, & Keiner, 2009; Schroeder, 2010), which remains somewhat fragmented, hence their review to provide an overview of how culture has been studied, choice of paradigms, interests, perspectives, and definitions.

Given the broader importance of culture and its longer history in the field of sport management, we focus the remainder of this chapter on understanding culture and how sport management could benefit from further work on this concept.

Manifestations of a Sport Organization's Culture

Because an organization's culture is based on values, beliefs, accepted patterns of meaning, and so on, and because these features are hard to pin down, researchers who study culture have tended to focus on the way it manifests itself in organizations. In fact, scholars debate as to whether culture should be measured using qualitative or quantitative methods. Popular with cultural anthropologists, the qualitative approach to studying culture assumes culture is unique to each organization and the only way to recognize culture is to immerse oneself in it and experience it, thus developing a firsthand account of the values and meanings in culture that are intangible but powerful in shaping individual behavior. Trice and Beyer (1984) suggest a number of cultural manifestations that researchers can observe. In this section of the chapter we look at some of the most important of these manifestations. On the other hand, quantitative, functionalist views of culture define it more as something the organization *has* rather than is (Chatman & O'Reilly, 2016). Quantitative measures of culture focus on similarities across organizations rather than the unique values within an organization. Jung et al. (2009) and Denison, Nieminen, and Kotrba (2014) provide conceptual and empirical reviews in this regard.

Research on organizational culture points to a vast array of mechanisms by which we can recognize culture in an organization. Stories and myths, language, symbols, and artifacts are among the growing list of manifestations of culture that researchers are studying. We will now explain some of these manifestations and their implications for managing culture for sport managers.

Stories and Myths

Stories are narratives recounted among employees and told to new employees. **Myths** are stories, often about the origins and transformations of a company, that are not supported by fact (Trice & Beyer, 1984). Both stories and myths convey a number of important messages about a sport organization. First, they present a sense of its history. As Pettigrew (1979, p. 576) notes about myths, they "anchor the present in the past, offer explanations and, therefore legitimacy for social practices, and contain levels of meaning that deal simultaneously with the socially and psychologically significant in any culture." Stories and myths, because they help establish the organization as an enduring entity, can reduce uncertainty for employees (Martin, Feldman, Hatch, & Sitkin, 1983). If the stories are about hard times, as they sometimes are, the employees sense the ability of the organization to overcome problems. Stories also help transmit messages about organizational goals and the way employees should act. They are, as Wilkins (1983b, p. 82) notes, "important indicators of the values participants share, the social prescriptions concerning how things are done, and the consequences of compliance or deviance.

Stories can be studied through a focus on discourse (Grant, Keenoy, & Oswick, 1998) or talk (Boden, 1992; Hardy, Lawrence, & Phillips, 1992). Integral to some of this understanding is a focus on emotion in the workplace (Fineman, 2000; Ashkanasy, Härtel, & Zerbe, 2000). Sport managers should recognize that stories created by them or others in the organization are powerful indicators of the values of an organization and point to what is acceptable behavior and what is not.

Symbols

Symbols are used to convey meaning about a sport organization to its members and to the public at large. The symbol of the falcon, for example, was chosen for the Atlanta-based NFL team because "the falcon is proud and dignified with great courage and fight; it never drops its prey; it is deadly and has a great sporting tradition" (Gameday News, 2019). Nike's "swoosh" conveys speed; it is also no coincidence that Nike is the Greek goddess of victory. Other examples of symbols that serve to convey meaning about sport organizations can be found in corporate documents like organizational charts. The ski resort Nakiska inverted its organizational chart so that the employees in direct contact with customers are at the top of the chart and the general manager, president, and board of directors are at the bottom. The organization thus conveys to its first-level staff their importance to the company's success.

Closely allied to the use of symbols is the use of **slogans**. Clichés such as "When the going gets tough, the tough get going" and "No pain, no gain" are frequently used by athletic coaches to convey expectations about appropriate modes of behavior in their organizations. In a somewhat similar vein, Nike's "Just do it" slogan has taken on particular significance for the company; it conveys meaning about success in sport and about success in the Nike organization.

It has also become somewhat fashionable for company owners or CEOs to develop sayings or sets of sayings that convey the organization's culture to employees. MEC has a corporate philosophy that contains such items as "We conduct ourselves ethically and with integrity. We show respect for others in our words and actions. We act in the spirit of community and co-operation. We respect and protect our natural environment. We strive for personal growth, continual learning, and adventure" (MEC, 2005, p. 1). At W.L. Gore, Bill Gore was frequently heard asking employees "Have you had fun today? Did you make any money?" (Blank, 1986, p. 23).

Language

Different sport organizations develop their own specialized **language** or jargon to communicate with each other. Through language, members "acquire the structured 'ways' of [the] group, and along with the language, the value implications of those ways" (Pettigrew, 1979, p. 575). Basketball coaches and players talk about their 2-1-2 full court press, working the ball into the paint, or screening away from the ball. While to most people these terms mean little, to the coaches and players on the team they are part of everyday communication, and as such represent one aspect of the team's culture. They serve to strengthen the team as an organization by providing commonality, and to separate the team from others who do not communicate in this way. They highlight boundaries as to who is and who isn't part of the organization (Wilkins, 1983b). As indicated previously, research on language is often under the term *discourse*, and in sport management, this has been a popular line of inquiry into construction of gender. For example, Sanderson and Gramlich's (2016) article in the *Sociology of Sport Journal* examines Twitter conversations as a technological mechanism to change cultural norms around gender and open the conversation to the role of women in sport organizations.

TIME OUT

John Wooden and Sir Alex Ferguson

In sport, much discussion has been around what makes a successful coach because coaches often stand out for their management of the team. John Wooden is one of the most successful basketball coaches ever. While at UCLA his teams won numerous conference and NCAA titles. Wooden built his program around his Pyramid of Success, which outlined 15 values and beliefs that he saw as important to a successful team. These included loyalty, self-control, skill, confidence, and competitive greatness. Although he never used the term *culture*, the values and beliefs outlined in the pyramid were the basis for the organizational culture of the UCLA basketball teams. Davis (2017) noted that Wooden was an expert at remaining true to his core principles yet adapting to the times and a changing game.

Likewise, Sir Alex Ferguson, now retired coach of Manchester United, played a central role in a winning team and the management of the club. He created a clear structure but also worked meticulously to create and maintain a culture that supported his vision. It was not well received at first, but perseverance paid off, as Elberse (2013) notes.

Ceremonies or Rites

All sport organizations—in fact, all organizations—develop certain types of traditions that we usually refer to as **ceremonies** or **rites**. Rookie initiations, team awards nights, pregame meals, an annual Christmas party, and a pep rally are all examples of the types of ceremonies we find in sport organizations. In each, certain shared values within the organization are reinforced. These events also provide evidence of what the organization values; they are symbolic representations of the type of beliefs and activities important in the organization. Trice and Beyer (1984) identify different types of rites. A rite of passage marks a change in the role and status of the person or persons involved. For example, rookie night ceremonies are designed to initiate new members and make them part of the team. A rite of degradation dissolves the social identity and associated power of the person involved by pointing out problems with his or her work performance. The firing of coaches and general managers, a common occurrence in professional sport organizations, is a rite of degradation. Smith and Shilbury (2004) have identified 12 dimensions (and 68 subdimensions) of Australian National Sport Organization, among them rituals, symbols, size, and history or tradition.

Physical Setting

The **physical setting** in which a sport organization operates can convey meaning about the nature of its culture. Davis (1984) suggests three important parts of the physical setting useful in understanding an organization's culture: the physical structure, physical stimuli, and symbolic artifacts.

The **physical structure** can be defined as "the architect's design and physical placement of furnishings in a building that influence or regulate social interaction" (Davis, 1984, p. 272). An open floor plan instead of closed-door offices, round tables instead of rectangular ones in meeting rooms, and simply the physical location of a facility can all convey messages about a sport organization. For example, in April 1985 shortly after Doug Mitchell took over as commissioner of the CFL, he moved the league's headquarters from cramped surroundings in downtown Toronto to plush offices in the center of the city's trendy Bloor Street shopping district, an "indication he want[ed] to upgrade the league's crusty image" (Barr, 1985, p. 1). In a similar vein, the CEO of the Canadian Sport and Fitness Administration Centre, Wilf Wedmann, moved his offices from the top floor of the building to the ground floor because being at the top of the building gave the wrong impression about the role of the center's administration. In turn, **physical stimuli** include such activities as coffee breaks and mail delivery. These events can become **rituals**. They establish patterns of interaction in a sport organization and, as such, how information is channeled.

Finally, **symbolic artifacts** individually or collectively provide clues about a sport organization's culture. Banners in hockey or basketball arenas, trophies and pictures of past teams and successful individual players, and the like are artifacts that convey a message about the team as a successful organization.

Thick and Thin Cultures

The strength of a sport organization's culture will vary from one company to another. Peters and Waterman (1982, p. 75) suggest that in the organizations they studied, "the dominance and coherence of culture proved to be an essential quality of the excellent companies." Most sport organizations strive to develop strong, or what are usually referred to as thick, cultures. A **thick culture** is one in which the members of the sport organization agree about the importance of certain values and employ them in their daily routines. A thick culture helps hold an organization together by making frequent use of stories, rituals, slogans, and so on. Also, employees will be recruited into the organization because they are seen to fit with the culture that exists. This fit is further developed through the use of indoctrination ceremonies, training programs, and orientations in which new employees are expected to be involved.

Joe Montgomery built a thick culture at Cannondale with his 11-point corporate philosophy as a base. But Cannondale's culture, like any thick culture, is more than just words on paper—the words are put into practice. The company practices its credo about caring for employees by promoting from within. Ted Kutrumbos started at Cannondale loading trucks; he rose through the ranks and became company president. Cannondale also demonstrates its concern for employees by sharing profits with them. Flexibility in working conditions is encouraged by having no formal job descriptions and moving people to jobs they enjoy ("A Freewheeler," 1989).

In a **thin culture,** we do not see common values or the type of activities that Cannondale uses to build its culture. While thin cultures can be found in all types of sport organizations, one example is a university faculty that encompasses both a department of sport studies and an athletic department.

The dominant values among the staff involved in the athletic program will be ones concerned with producing the best teams, recruiting "blue chip" players, and catering to alumni. The sport studies staff will be more concerned with publishing and generating research grants. While these values are not mutually exclusive, their very presence can serve to produce a thin culture. A thin culture will also be found in sport organizations where the membership is constantly changing or has only been a part of the organization for a short period of time (Schein, 1984).

One or More Cultures

Implicit in our discussion so far is the idea that sport organizations have one single culture. This notion is implied in many of the definitions of organizational culture, which discuss shared understandings and common values. It is, however, somewhat idealistic to suggest that all members of a sport organization will think alike. The reality, that different people in different parts of the organization actually have different values and employ different norms of behavior, does not deny the possibility of "an organizational culture"; rather, it highlights the fact that sport organizations actually have a dominant culture, which reflects the core values of the majority of people in the organization (or at worst those with the most power), and a series of subcultures. Gregory (1983), for example, argues that organizations should be seen as **multicultural**. Meyerson and Martin (1987, p. 630) extend this line of thought to suggest that because "organizations reflect broader societal cultures and contain elements of occupational, hierarchical, class, racial, ethnic, and gender-based identifications [they] create overlapping, nested subcultures." Slack and Hinings' (1992) work on change in Canadian national sport organizations showed how a culture built around values for volunteer control and governance clashed with a new developing culture based on more professionally and bureaucratically oriented values. Subcultures may also develop in different departments of a sport organization. For example, the research and development department of a company producing sport equipment will most likely exhibit a somewhat different culture from the sales department. While sport managers should strive to develop unified values in the organizations they manage, it is also important for them to realize that such a goal is unlikely to be fully achieved. In actuality, as Meyerson and Martin (1987, p. 631) point out, organizations are composed of a "diverse set of subcultures that share some integrating elements of a dominant culture." It is this diversity and these common elements of culture that have to be managed. Johnson and Gill (1993) also point out that managers can attempt to control (through structures or cultures), but employees also have the ability to respond to management influence.

Organizational Culture and Effectiveness

Many writers on organizational culture have stressed the links between a strong (thick) culture and an effective organization (Deal & Kennedy, 1982; Peters & Waterman, 1982; Warrick, 2017). Arogyaswamy and Byles (1987, p. 648) suggest, however, that it is erroneous to infer "that there is one best culture, which if established in firms,

TIME OUT

Sport as a Component of Our Entertainment Culture

Sporting contests have always captivated the human imagination. From the spectacle of competition in Rome's Coliseum to Boston's Fenway Park, sport events have been and continue to be popular. Sport has infiltrated all parts of the media beyond the radio or television broadcasting of live contests. A variety of movies, such as *Bend It Like Beckham*, *Invictus*, *Girlfight*, *Million Dollar Baby*, *Remember the Titans*, *Rocky*, *Breaking Away*, and *When We Were Kings*, all have a sport as the central theme. The rising popularity of reality television also incorporates sport into shows such as *Survivor* (physical activities required), *The Amazing Race* (a footrace around the world), *Making the Cut* (hockey), and *The Contender* (boxing).

Sport is more accessible than ever in our culture. Outlets, from the traditional print media, television, and radio, to constant advances in technology including live-streaming, virtual reality (VR), and Augmented Reality (AR) allow sport fans to stay up to date with their favorite sport 24 hours a day or to consume sport in a variety of media apart from actual participation.

would lead to success." Rather, they suggest that certain types of cultural characteristics are appropriate in certain types of organizations. To understand culture and its relationship to performance in sport organizations, it is necessary to look at the various contingencies that influence the organization. To be effective such variables as strategy, environment, technology, leadership, and culture must fit.

Porter (1980), for example, emphasized that to be successful, an organization that adopts a cost-leadership strategy will be required to develop a culture that emphasizes financial efficiency and close attention to reducing costs. Skinner, Stewart, and Edwards (2004) illustrated how the changes in the Queensland Rugby Union were meant to lead to professionalism by generating and implementing policies through a government-like technology; such structural and cultural changes resulted in a managerialist culture. A company like W.L. Gore, which follows what Miles and Snow (1978) refer to as a prospector strategy, requires a culture that emphasizes creativity, high levels of horizontal communication, and some degree of risk taking.

Sport organizations that operate in stable environments should seek to develop thick cultures. However, if its environment is rapidly changing, a thick culture may actually be detrimental to the performance of a sport organization. Thick cultures by their very nature are hard to change, but dynamic environments demand that if organizations are to be successful they must change as their environment changes.

The use of different technologies also requires a different culture. In the large manufacturing plants of companies such as Nike or Adidas, mass-producing sporting goods, we would expect to find a culture where little emphasis is placed on individual initiative but where control and conformity to hierarchical communications are emphasized. In contrast, in a company like Heery, which is a professional, full-service architectural firm designing custom sport facilities, we would expect to find a culture that supports creativity, group work, and a high level of horizontal communication.

Creating, Managing, and Changing a Sport Organization's Culture

A sport organization's culture does not just happen; it is created and developed over a period of time. Some sport managers will work hard to maintain an existing culture if they feel it benefits their organization.

Creating a Culture Within a Sport Organization

While several differing opinions exist about how culture is created within an organization (Louis, 1985; Scholz, 1987), most researchers agree that the founders of an organization have a fairly significant impact on establishing its culture. There is also general agreement that the original ideas of the founder will continue to influence the organization for a long time, sometimes even after the founder is no longer with the organization (Schein, 1983). Strasser and Becklund's (1991) book shows, for example, how the informal operating codes and freewheeling atmosphere created by Philip Knight and the University of Oregon track colleagues who joined him in Nike's early years continued to influence the organization, well after it was established as a major company in the athletic footwear industry.

Peters and Waterman (1982) describe two important ways of developing culture for those who lead organizations. The first method, they suggest, operates at a high level of abstraction and involves the setting of a vision. The founder or leader of a sport organization must generate excitement and enthusiasm about the fundamental values and purpose of the organization. For Philip Knight the purpose of Nike was clear: to produce good-quality shoes at a reasonable price for U.S. athletes and to push Adidas into the number two spot in the industry. For Sheri Poe, head of Ryka, a rapidly growing athletic footwear company, her vision is to produce aerobic shoes designed especially for women and to work on behalf of women.

The second of Peters and Waterman's (1982, p. 287) suggestions is that founders or leaders can help develop culture by their attention to detail; they are to directly instill "values through deeds rather than words: No opportunity is too small." John Stanton ran to get fit and then opened a store called the Running Room. Stanton continues to promote health and exercise by hosting clinics and running with his clients. Sheri Poe has attempted to instill as part of Ryka's culture a belief that the organization should work on behalf of women. Poe enforces this by putting 7 percent of her company's profits into a fund called Ryka ROSE (Regaining One's Self-Esteem Foundation), employing a predominantly female workforce (70 percent), and speaking out on women's issues (Stodghill, 1993).

Managing a Sport Organization's Culture

Once a sport organization's culture has developed, it has to be managed. Assuming the culture is one that the company wishes to maintain, the manager of a sport organization can do a number of things to sustain and reinforce the organization's culture.

Schein (1985, pp. 224-225) suggests five primary mechanisms:

1. What leaders pay attention to, measure, and control
2. Leader reaction to critical incidents and organizational crises
3. Deliberate role modeling, teaching, and coaching by leaders
4. Criteria for allocation of rewards and status
5. Criteria for recruitment, selection, promotion, retirement, and excommunication

We look briefly at these mechanisms now. It should be noted that Schein uses the term *leaders* instead of *managers*. While there is some debate about whether the terms can be used synonymously in this book, we follow Yukl's (1998) suggestion that the two are interchangeable. For consistency, the term *managers* is used in the subheadings.

What Managers Pay Attention to, Measure, and Control

Managers can reinforce the important aspects of a sport organization's culture by paying particular attention to these areas. As Schein (1985, p. 225) notes, "paying attention" may mean "anything from what is noticed and commented on, to what is measured, controlled, rewarded, and in other ways systematically dealt with." At L.L. Bean, the outdoor equipment supplier, great stress is placed on building a culture that emphasizes customer service, a culture reinforced when Bean's own employees are treated well by their managers. Van Fleet (1991, p. 352) points out this practice:

> Employees are paid reasonable wages, are treated with dignity, and have ample opportunity for advancement. They are also given considerable freedom in how they do their job—as long as they do it well. Employees know that they can always put the needs and opinions of customers first, without fear of reprisal or rebuke from a supervisor who worries too much about the cost of something.

This attention to feelings and the dignity they are afforded by supervisors communicate to employees what the company believes in and how in turn they should treat customers. Hoeber and Frisby (2001) noted that managers can fail to see a mismatch of organizational values (gender equity, in their case) and practices if they simply rely on the dominant narrative.

Managers' Reaction to Critical Incidents and Organizational Crises

If a sport organization faces a crisis or critical incident, the way the senior managers deal with the crisis can help reinforce an organization's culture. Schein (1985, p. 230) suggests that crises aid the transmission of culture because "the heightened emotional involvement during such periods increases the intensity of learning [and] if people share intense emotional experiences . . . they are more likely to remember what they have learned." Such learning may occur, for example, in an athletic department that has built a culture based on values of fair play and an ethical approach to running an intercollegiate program. If the athletic director dismisses a coach for violating some minor recruiting regulations, it may create a crisis situation for the organization, but it provides a signal to the remaining coaches that this type of behavior is inappropriate to this organization and thus serves to reinforce the culture within which they operate. Likewise, if a sport equipment manufacturer faces declining sales, the way this crisis is dealt with may strengthen its culture. For instance, if the company had previously tried to develop a culture stressing the importance of every employee, and all staff members, including senior managers, take a salary cut to prevent layoffs of production staff, the fairness of the gesture serves to heighten this cultural dimension. Often after these crises we hear managers say things like, "We are all better for what happened" or "We are stronger because of it." The implication is that organizational learning has taken place and certain values that underpin the sport organization's culture have been reinforced.

This line of inquiry has been increasing in sport due to the many problems of athlete and management corruption (Andreff, 2016), transgressions (Westberg, Stavros, Wilson, & Smith, 2016), doping (Smith & Stewart, 2016), exploitation of sport or events for political gain (Brittain, Bocarro, Byers, & Swart, 2017), and terrorism (Galily, Yarchi, Tamir, & Samuel-Azran, 2016). As a result, we know more about managers' responses to crises and risk management (Hall, 2016) yet little research has been conducted to measure the impacts of crisis management on the culture and performance of sport organizations.

Deliberate Role Modeling, Teaching, and Coaching

Managers can stress the type of culture they are seeking to build in a sport organization through their own actions and by directly teaching and coaching staff. Bill Gore, who has been referred to several times in this book, is an excellent example of someone who used this approach to build the culture of his company. Gore would frequently wander through his production plants, meeting, talking to, and helping associates (as employees are called). He stressed that experienced associates should sponsor new associates and teach them the ways of the organization; ultimately these associates would become sponsors. In that way, the traditions and habits of cooperation and working together are managed and maintained, the essence of W.L. Gore's culture.

Criteria for Allocation of Rewards and Status

As Schein (1985, p. 234) points out, "an organization's leaders can quickly get across their own priorities, values, and assumptions by consistently linking rewards and punishments to the behavior they are concerned with." For example, the chair of a department of sport management with a culture supporting research and scholarly writing can strengthen this culture by rewarding those faculty members who engage in this type of work. A sporting goods store trying to develop a culture based on customer service would reward salesclerks on the quality of service they provide, not on sales volume.

Criteria for Recruitment, Selection, Promotion, Retirement, and Excommunication

Schein (1985) suggests that one of the subtlest yet potent ways of reinforcing an organization's culture is through the selection of new members (Schneider, 1987). These selection decisions, when coupled with the criteria used to promote, pressure into retirement, or fire, are a very powerful means of strengthening and maintaining a sport organization's culture. There is, however, a problematic dimension to this type of approach in that "organizations tend to find attractive those candidates who resemble present members in style, assumptions, values, and beliefs" (Schein, 1985, p. 235). Hall, Cullen, and Slack (1989) suggest it was one of the major reasons for the virtual exclusion of women from senior management positions in Canadian national sport organizations. Consequently, while a homogeneous group of people may strengthen a sport organization's culture (and certainly decisions about employee selection, promotion, and so on can reinforce a culture), managers must be sensitive to the fact that homogeneous groups or management can also exclude certain groups from the upper levels of management Kanter (1977).

Changing a Sport Organization's Culture

Change can involve increasing or decreasing the number of employees in a sport organization, expanding markets or product lines, and other kinds of structural modifications. However, "in a more subtle but equally important way [it also] requires a basic rethinking of the beliefs by which the company defines and carries out its business" (Lorsch, 1986, p. 97). Kanter (1984) calls this rethinking "culture change." Changing the culture of a sport organization is a long and often difficult process because it involves changing values and beliefs that have been established over a period of years.

Changes in staff behavior do not necessarily signal that cultural change has taken place. The staff of a sport organization may comply with and exhibit the newly prescribed behavioral expectations while at the same time cling to the values and beliefs that underpinned the organization's previous structure and mode of operations. When this superficial compliance occurs, change is likely to be short lived, and the sport organization involved is quite likely to revert to its former situation (Kikulis, Slack, & Hinings, 1995).

Lorsch (1986) suggests that when faced with the need for change, managers will first attempt to fix the problem with minor modifications. At times these incremental changes may be successful; however, the basic nature of the organization's culture remains the same. When environmental pressures are more severe, more substantive change is needed, calling for change in the culture of an organization.

Lorsch (1986) goes on to suggest that there are four basic stages to this change: awareness (top management gradually becomes aware that in order to ensure its survival, substantive change is needed in their organization); confusion (managers agree that existing beliefs are not working but cannot agree about the new direction); vision (often created by bringing a new manager in); and experimentation (companies experiment with new products, new markets, and new people until they arrive at a suitable situation). Slack and Hinings (1992) describe a similar process to that laid out by Lorsch (1986) occurring in Canadian national sport organizations (NSOs). As Slack and Hinings (1992, p. 127) note, to deal with pressures for cultural change, "some NSOs made fairly radical changes in their management structure." In several cases, they appointed a new CEO, and often the first task in the transformation of the culture of these organizations was to create a vision for the organization.

Other sport management scholars have used different approaches to demonstrate cultural change in different sports contexts. For instance, Cruickshank, Collins, and Minten (2015) used a grounded theory approach to add to a model of cultural change in Olympic sports teams to study best practices of management-led cultural change in professional sports teams. Culture change was led by incoming team managers and was observed as a process whereby managers' initial efforts were constantly constructed and reconstructed by stakeholders in complex and social power dynamics. Based on their model of culture change, sport managers should expect culture change to be a continuous process of responding to stakeholders' perceptions to align with new cultural norms.

Summary and Conclusions

Culture is an important variable in understanding organizational life, including sport organizations. Academics and practitioners have held an interest in how culture can affect organizational effectiveness and the relationships between culture and leadership or structure. A focus on organizational culture forces us to question some of the rational notions of the contingency perspective and start to consider sport organizations as complex patterns of human interaction. By studying a sport organization's culture, we are forced to pay attention to the somewhat intangible, but no less important, aspects of organizational life, such as the values and beliefs, the accepted modes of operation, and the shared assumptions that guide behavior within an organization. Because it is somewhat difficult to see, researchers often study culture by looking at the manifestations of culture such as stories, myths, symbols, language, ceremonies, and rites that are integral to life in an organization. The physical setting in which an organization exists, including its physical structure, physical stimuli, and the symbolic artifacts it exhibits, are also important indicators of its culture.

Some sport organizations will try to develop strong or thick cultures to enhance behavioral consistency. However, if change is required this type of culture can be constraining. In contrast, thin cultures are easily changed. While culture is often presented as a unitary entity, most sport organizations have a dominant culture and one or more subcultures. These competing cultures can lead to organizational conflict if they are not managed.

KEY ISSUES FOR SPORT MANAGERS

Key issues for sport managers in understanding organizational culture are related to the complexity of the culture concept but also its interrelatedness to an organization's structure and external environment. That is, culture (norms and values) must be consistent with the formal structure of an organization and respond to pressures from the external environment. The social and economic environment in which the sport industry operates is changing rapidly. Byers (2018) examined some of the trends in professional sport and sport management, noting that organizations face much competition for consumers' time, an increasing pace of change (especially in adopting new technologies), and the need to respond to consumer demand and increasing expectations by staff and volunteers.

Research in sport and in other industries has demonstrated that culture can be a source of competitive advantage, and sport managers should think carefully about what kind of culture to encourage in their organizations and how this relates to social norms and values. Spaaij et al. (2018) remind us that diversity is an important value to embrace but can present challenges to sport organizations that require a shift in culture. While this is a source of uncertainty for managers, it should also be a source of inspiration because change creates innovation, which can lead to improvements in operations, sustainability, and quality in management. Managing culture is never easy and sport managers should never assume it is so; there are manifestations of culture, but a simple change in physical space or policy does not mean an automatic shift in values of people in the organization. Culture change takes time, patience, and perseverance as well as some critical self-reflection at times!

Culture can contribute considerably to the effectiveness of a sport organization, but it must align with the organization's strategy, technology, and environment.

The creation of a sport organization's culture is influenced greatly by the organization's founder and by new leadership coming into an organization, but individuals and groups throughout the organization may contribute to subcultures throughout the organization as well. Culture can nevertheless be managed and, if necessary, changed through continuous attention and efforts by management.

Review Questions

1. What are the key characteristics used to define organizational culture?
2. Some organizational theorists have suggested that a strong organizational culture is a substitute for high levels of formalization. Why would they suggest this connection?
3. When would it be beneficial for a sport organization to have a thick culture? When would a thin culture be beneficial?
4. What type of culture do you think would fit best with each of the four strategic types proposed by Miles and Snow?
5. How does the founder of a sport organization influence its culture?
6. How could the manager of a sport organization go about implementing a change in the organization's culture?

Suggestions for Further Reading

To get a sense of the development of research on culture, readers should begin with Peters and Waterman's (1982) *In Search of Excellence*. This is a seminal text that was influential in generating scholarly and practitioner attention to the role of culture in organizations. Other important developments in culture research can be found by reading Schein's (1985) *Organizational Culture and Leadership*, which is an absolute must-read; Schein is considered an important contributor to our understanding of how culture develops. Paul Bate's (2010) book *Strategies for Cultural Change* presents a somewhat different and more critical view of organizational culture. A recent article by Campbell and Göritz (2014), "Culture Corrupts," provides an interesting view of the negative impacts of culture in organizations.

In addition to these texts, the editors of *Administrative Science Quarterly* produced a special issue on the topic of organizational culture (vol. 28, no. 3, 1983), and the editors of *Organization Studies* produced a special issue on organizational symbolism (vol. 7, no. 2, 1986). More recently, Giorgi, Lockwood, and Glynn (2015) presented an article in *Academy of Management Annals* titled "The Many Faces of Culture: Making Sense of 30 Years of Research on Culture in Organization Studies," and specifically in sport, where the study of culture in sport is growing, Maitland, Hills, and Rhind (2015) provided a systematic review of the field that also makes suggestions for further research and methods of studying culture in sport and organizations. For some understanding of culture, innovation, and organization performance, Hogan and Coote (2014) provide an empirical test of Schein's model. For early work on culture in sport, see Weese's (1995a, 1995b, 1996) work, which looks at leadership and organizational culture; Westerbeek's (1999) modeling of organizational culture in sport organizations; Doherty and Chelladurai's (1999) examination of cultural diversity in sport organizations; Kent and Weese's (2000) study of organizational effectiveness and culture; and Colyer's (2000) article "Organizational Culture in Selected Western Australian Sport Organizations." For cultural change in sport, see Cruickshank, Collins, and Minten (2015).

Case for Analysis

Chicago Cubs: A Strong Organizational Culture Leads to Successful Team Performance in Professional Sport

The Chicago Cubs baseball team have had their share of losing streaks. The team went 108 years without winning the coveted World Series title (Gemskie, 2018), the longest championship drought in North American sports history. However, in 2011, Theo Epstein became the new president of operations, and by 2016 the club was considered an enviable success with the league; they had the best regular season record and a roster that was richly cultivated over several years. Epstein was said to have started the Cubs' transformation by tearing it apart, then building it up slowly, including a new strategy of developing homegrown young talent and a thriving "Cubs' Way" culture (Kalman, 2016). This culture and its philosophy and values were formalized in a document that was distributed to and applied to everyone in the organization, from Epstein himself to players and summer interns. This meant that management not only produced the rules and new cultural values but demonstrated them in their own actions every day.

The next part of Epstein's plan to build a winning culture was in hiring Joe Maddon to manage the team and take responsibility for the on-field product (Gemskie, 2018). From team strategy, lineup cards, and in-game decisions, a consistent expectation was communicated that fit with the culture of the organization, which embraced winning, pride, and hard work. Maddon implemented important rituals, such as after a win, the team were said to have a 30-minute dance party in the locker room including disco ball, lights, and a fog machine. Maddon had his own language that he used consistently, such as "Embrace the target," "Never let the pressure exceed the pleasure," "Do simple better," and "Try not to suck" (Gemskie, 2018). After a loss, they commiserated for no more than 30 minutes and moved on to the next task that would help them accomplish their goals. The culture created by Epstein and Maddon established a new era and set of values for the team. In 2016, the losing streak was over: The Cubs won the World Series for the first time since 1908.

Questions

1. What are some potential problems of building a new and different culture in an organization like the Cubs?
2. How was culture built at the Cubs?
3. What actions did management take to reinforce the new culture? What else could be done to ensure the culture was strong and consistent throughout the organization?
4. What purpose did culture serve for this sport organization?

CHAPTER 18

Organizational Change in Sport

Trevor Slack, PhD
Alex Thurston, PhD

Learning Objectives

When you have read this chapter, you should be able to

1. understand what we mean when we talk about organizational change and explain why change is seen as paradoxical,
2. explain the major perspectives that are used to understand change,
3. discuss the factors that cause change,
4. explain the sources of resistance to change and how this resistance can be managed,
5. describe the stages of the change process and the concept of tracks, and
6. explain why sport organizations need to be innovative.

Key Concepts

administrative innovation
archetypes
convergent change
evolutionary change
idea champions
institutional theory
life cycle approach
paradoxical nature of change
people change
population ecology
product or service change
product or service innovation
radical change
reaction
resistance to change
resource dependence
revolutionary change
stimulus
structural and systemic change
technological change
technological innovation
tracks

Changes in the Structure and Operations of the National Collegiate Athletic Association

In 1906, 38 U.S. schools formed the first national governing body of college and university athletics. The Intercollegiate Athletic Association (IAA) was established as a result of public concern over the rampant violence in intercollegiate gridiron football. The members of the organization worked together to counter this concern. They established a standard set of rules and introduced the forward pass, which opened up play and made the game safer. In 1910 the IAA changed its name to the National Collegiate Athletic Association (NCAA) and expanded the scope of its mandate to encompass all unethical conduct in college sport. In its early years the NCAA was a loosely structured group of colleges and universities operated by seven representatives of the member institutions (Stern, 1979). Although the original intent of the organization was to regulate and control intercollegiate sport through the establishment of a set of stringent rules and strict enforcement codes, this idea was dropped in favor of accomplishing its purposes through educational means. The actual control of intercollegiate sport was placed in the hands of each individual member institution, and the NCAA had no power to sanction—its primary role was an advisory one to its membership (Wallenfeldt, n.d.).

The NCAA grew rapidly. The size of its executive board increased, and the first NCAA national championship was held in 1921 in track and field; it then gradually began to organize competitions in other sports such as swimming, wrestling, boxing, and basketball. Membership size increased from the initial 38 schools to 148 in 1926; by 1951 the NCAA included 368 member schools and 24 conferences. The organization hired its first full-time staff director in 1949.

Despite its considerable growth it was not until 1952 that the NCAA was granted any type of regulatory power over its member institutions. Public disclosures about unethical recruiting, illegally paying student athletes, point-shaving in college basketball, and tampering with student transcripts resulted in mounting pressure to do something about intercollegiate athletics. As a result, a group of college and university presidents met as members of the American Council on Education to recommend that athletics be deemphasized as a part of the college and university curriculum. Faced with the threat of external intervention in their affairs, the NCAA moved quickly to develop a system under which sanctions against member institutions could be invoked. The organization's role changed from being a passive observer and consultant on issues related to intercollegiate sport to exercising the power to penalize member institutions that violated its rules (Stern, 1979). Since 1952 the NCAA's power and the scope of its operations have continued to grow. It now controls virtually all aspects of big-time college and university sport in the United States. In 2019 the organization boasts a membership of more than 1,200, consisting of schools, colleges, universities, conferences, and affiliate organizations. This membership enables nearly half a million athletes to make up the 19,750 teams who compete against each other in 90 NCAA championships across 24 sports between three divisions (NCAA, n.d.-a).

The financial report for year-end of 2018 indicated that annual revenue during the financial year topped $1 billion USD for the second year running (Deloitte & Touche LLP, 2018). Its headquarters are centralized in Indianapolis, Indiana, and its paid staff has doubled in size since 2006 from 254 to 500 employees (NCAA, n.d.-b).

Change, such as that exhibited by the NCAA, is one of the most visible features of all sport organizations. As discussed in several chapters throughout this textbook (e.g., 4, 8, and 21), to survive and grow, a sport organization must be able to adapt to changes in environment, strategy, size, and technology. When the environment changes, such as a shift in stakeholders' needs or wants, a response may come in the form of structural changes. So, as it grew larger, the NCAA required a different operating structure from that used in its early years. As the scope of its mandate changed, so did its mode of operation.

Although university and college sport administration in the United Kingdom has yet to experience the unprecedented levels of commercialization seen with the NCAA, comparable organizational structural changes have occurred over time. In 1918 a call was made at the Presidents of University Unions conference in Manchester, England, to establish an association that would promote the development of sport at university. The Inter-Varsity Athletics Board of England and Wales was established in 1919, and the same year saw the first athletics meet take place. Over the years the administration of university sport expanded: The Women's Inter-Varsity Board was formed in 1923, and the Universities Athletic Union (formerly the Inter-Varsity Athletics Board) was established in 1930. During the 1950s, '60s, and '70s several administration boards and associations were formed, replaced, or merged. In 1994 another merger established the British Universities Sports Association (BUSA) to represent the sporting interests of students. Finally, in 2008 University and College Sport (UCS) and BUSA merged to become the British Universities & Colleges Sport (BUCS)—the new national voice for higher education sport (British Universities & Colleges Sport, n.d.). This brief history of BUCS should highlight several parallels related to the NCAA, such as how both organizations had to adapt and change in order to survive and become the national governing bodies for college and university sport in each respective country. As a proud side note, in July 2019 Loughborough University (Alex Thurston's employer) was crowned overall BUCS champions for the 40th consecutive year (Loughborough University, 2019)!

Also, in the opening scenario at the beginning of chapter 1, we saw Under Armour undergo a similar type of transformation to those experienced by the NCAA and BUCS organizations as it evolved from a company operating out of the trunk of Kevin Plank's car to one of the biggest athletic apparel and footwear manufacturers in the world.

The purpose of this chapter is to explore the multifaceted nature of change in sport organizations. We begin by looking at the concept of organizational change; we then explore the paradoxical nature of change. Next, six major theoretical approaches to understanding change are briefly outlined. We then look at what causes the need for change in sport organizations, what are the barriers to change, and how change is managed. Some theorists have suggested that change can be conceptualized as a series of stages; we look briefly at this approach but then argue that the concept of "tracks" provides a better and more realistic understanding of the change process. Finally, we look at the notion of innovation and why sport organizations need to be innovative.

The Concept of Change

Sport organizations are in a constant state of change; new people enter the organization, some leave, parts of the organization's physical layout are reorganized, and new programs or product lines are developed. In this chapter our focus is not on the day-to-day fluctuations evident in all (sport) organizations but on planned change, change that a sport organization systematically develops and implements to retain a competitive advantage in whatever market it targets. The pressures for such change may be generated externally in the sport organization's environment, or they may originate from within the organization itself. Over the past few decades, external pressures—the changing economic situation around the world, technological advances in the delivery and consumption of sport, the manufacturing of sport equipment, and increased societal interest in sport and leisure—have all contributed to changes in organizations within the sport industry. Internal factors such as an emphasis on service quality, a move to self-managed teams, and the demand for flexible operating procedures have also produced pressures for change.

As figure 18.1 shows change can occur in four areas of a sport organization: technology, products

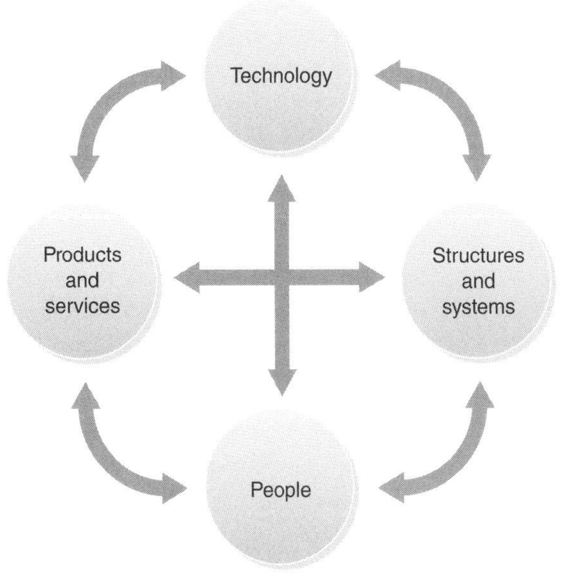

Figure 18.1 Potential areas of change in a sport organization.

and services, structures and systems, and people (McCann, 1991).

Technological change refers to the changes that occur in an organization's production process, the skills and methods it uses to deliver its services, or its knowledge base. For instance, Adidas introduced additive manufacturing (AM), also referred to as 3D printing, to speed up the time to produce prototypes. Without the use of AM, a prototype shoe would take 12 technicians four to six weeks to produce. AM reduces that production time down to only one to two days (Meier, Tan, Lim, & Chung, 2018). A **product or service change** in a sport organization may involve the addition, deletion, or modification of other areas. For example, a small independent bike shop called Butler Cycles, based in Portsmouth, United Kingdom, changed its sole focus of selling bikes (and changed its name to Wiggle) to become one of Europe's leading online sport retailers, now selling bike, run, swim, and outdoor equipment. **Structural and systemic changes** involve modifications to areas of a sport organization such as its division of labor, its authority structure, or its control systems. Such changes occurred when the NCAA increased the size of its council and added committees and professional staff. **People change** involves modifications to the way people think, act, and relate to each other. This type of change is often brought about through techniques such as sensitivity training, team-building exercises, and group planning. For instance, we now see many firms investing in corporate wellness programs as a result of an increasing awareness of the importance of supporting the mental health and well-being of a workforce (Agarwal, 2018). While we focus primarily on structural change in this chapter, these four areas are interrelated; a change in one area will often require a change in one or more of the others.

Regardless of the area of change, two types of change exist: radical and convergent. According to Greenwood and Hinings (1996), **radical change** is frame bending, completely changing orientation, while **convergent change** is more about fine-tuning a specific orientation. For example, Bombardier, the original maker of Ski-Doo and Sea-Doo, was created in 1942. Since 2000, its progressive acquisition of divisions related to other modes of transportation besides recreational-based transportation—specifically trains and planes—shows convergent change. However, Bombardier underwent a radical change in its orientation by divesting itself of its entire recreational division—its original core purpose—in 2003 to focus on the train and plane divisions. Then, in 2014 another radical change occurred when Bombardier moved from one template-in-use (i.e., an organizational arrangement or configuration designed to suit the institutional context) to another by adopting "a new leaner, more nimble organizational structure" composed of four main business segments in an effort to enhance agility (Bombardier, n.d.).

Change as Paradox

The **paradoxical nature of change** stems from the fact that a sport organization must change if it wishes to remain competitive (Peters, 1990). However, as we saw earlier, management prefers stability and predictability. A sport organization's output, costs, and workforce must remain relatively fixed if it is going to be successful. At the same time, sport managers need to look for new markets, new technology, and innovative means for service delivery. The sport organization, therefore, must find a balance between change and stability.

If sport organizations fail to change they may follow what Miller (1992, p. 24) refers to as "'trajectories' of decline." On the other hand, if an organization changes too rapidly or just for the sake of change, its operations will be disrupted.

TIME OUT

The Paradox of Sport

It's not just the concept of change that yields a paradox in sport; economists also suggest that sport is paradoxical in relation to "the peculiar economics of professional sports" (Neale, 1964, p. 1). For fans and spectators to maintain interest and continue to pay to watch contests, they need a competitive balance with uncertainty of outcome, which is why we see promotion and relegation in European leagues, and the draft system in North America. Neale (1964) explains the peculiarity using the Louis-Schmeling paradox; a case from boxing to demonstrate that in most industries the aim is to be superior to the competition, whereas in sport, governing bodies, league administrators, and event promoters endeavor to closely match the competitors (Downward & Dawson, 2000, p. 20).

If incorrectly managed, the success of previous change can become a sport organization's downfall. As Miller (1990, pp. 3-4) notes, "productive attention to detail, for instance, turns into an obsession with minutia; rewarding innovation escalates into gratuitous invention; and measured growth becomes unbridled expansion."

Achieving a balance between stability and change is not an easy task. The sport manager must recognize the need for change and understand how it can be successfully implemented and managed. Changes in environment and technology will affect the amount of change a sport organization will require. Those organizations that operate in stable environments with routine technologies will require less change than those facing dynamic environments with nonroutine technology.

Perspectives on Organizational Change

For many years the dominant models of change were based on the three strategies Chin and Benne (1985) describe as "empirical-rational," "normative reeducative," and "power-coercive." Essentially, change was seen as a linear process consisting of a series of steps that involved diagnosing problems in organizations, developing solutions to these problems, identifying resistance to the changes that would be needed to implement these solutions, formulating and implementing a change strategy, and monitoring and reviewing the change process. Particular emphasis was placed on the role of change agents, individuals who used a variety of organizational development techniques to guide the change process. For the power-coercive strategy, the change agent obtains and uses power differently from the other two strategies; political and economic power is used to create change. For more detail on the various forms of power, refer to chapter 15 in this textbook.

The political and economic fluctuations that have characterized North American and Western European societies have drawn increased attention to the process and management of change. As a result, we have seen theoretical developments in this area and hence alternative ways of looking at change. In this section we briefly examine the most popular of these perspectives. Although these perspectives are dealt with separately, they are not necessarily discrete. Some, such as **institutional theory** and **population ecology**, have been seen as converging with each other (Carroll & Hannan, 1989; Zucker, 1989), and some, for example, population ecology and the contextualist approach, are considerably different in their intellectual underpinnings and their method.

Resource Dependence

The fundamental premise of resource-dependence theory, as we saw earlier in the book, is that organizations are unable to generate internally the different types of resources they need to operate; consequently, they come to depend on their environment for resources critical to their survival. However, as Pfeffer and Salancik (1978, p. 3) point out, "environments can change, new organizations enter and exit, and the supply of resources becomes more or less scarce." Because organizations depend on resources for their operation, this potential for a reduction of resources creates uncertainty for managers. Managers can reduce this uncertainty by changing their activities in response to these environmental factors. For instance, Brown and Pappous (2017) examined the organizational performance of national disability sport organizations (NDSOs) during a time of austerity in the United Kingdom by utilizing resource-dependence theory. Their findings identified that the formation of alliances was one tactic used by some NDSOs to reduce dependency on critical resources.

Cunningham (2002) argues that **resource dependence** is part of an organization's structural change process. Managers can also act to change the nature of their organization's resource environment. The techniques used include mergers, diversification, and joint ventures. Mergers between two competing organizations help reduce uncertainty by eliminating some of the competition for resources. Diversification can be used to stabilize a sport organization's dependence on its environment by reducing the uncertainty that may result from trends in individual market areas and economic fluctuations. Joint ventures (a type of strategic alliance) reduce uncertainty by pooling resources such as capital and expertise in response to an essential opportunity or threat in the environment. All of these initiatives result in changes to an organization's structure and operations; more details of such changes can be found in chapters 4, 5, 6, and 8.

Population Ecology

As we saw in chapter 4 the population ecology approach to understanding organizations developed out of biological literature and particularly the Darwinian notion of survival of the fittest. The focus here is not on change in single organizations but on a population of like organizations in a particular geographic area or niche, for example, all sporting goods stores in the state of New York (Carroll & Hannan, 1989; Delacroix & Carroll, 1983). Population ecologists conceptualize organizational change as a three-stage process (see figure 18.2).

In the first stage of the process, considerable variation in the organizational form is found in a particular population of organizations. This variation occurs because entrepreneurs set up organizations to fill a gap in the market, or as a result of a perceived need. For example, since the early 1990s, the number of sporting goods stores in North America increased as consumers demanded a variety of sport and recreational equipment. The stores created to fill this need show variation in their structural form, the products they sell, and the way they service their customers. Some of these variants will be better equipped to meet the demands of their environment. Some will be unable to exploit this environment to obtain the resources necessary to operate or demand may be insufficient for their product or services. Those that fail to meet the demands of the environment will be "selected out," that is, they will fail. Those that are positively selected survive and are retained within the market niche. Over time the demands of the environment will change. For instance, in relation to our example of sporting goods stores (population) context, Dick's Sporting Goods (the United States' largest sporting goods retailer) announced in March 2019 that it would stop selling all assault-style weapons and other hunting equipment and replace those products with items such as licensed apparel, batting cages, and association football gear (Hsu, 2019). Ed Stack, the CEO of Dick's Sporting Goods, decided to change the organization's gun policies in the wake of the Parkland, Florida, school shooting, where 17 people were killed (Siegel, 2019). This change will likely affect other sporting goods stores; some will experience external environmental pressures to follow suit, whereas some stores might capitalize on Dick's Sporting Goods' decision and start selling firearms. Sport organizations have to change their structure, products, and services to meet these types of environmental (sometimes, politically driven) demands. Those that do will be retained; those that don't will flounder and cease to exist.

The Life Cycle Approach

Like population ecology, the **life cycle approach** is based on the idea that biology "provides certain concepts and models that . . . appear to have some relevance for understanding organizational cycles" (Kimberly, 1980, p. 6). Unlike population ecology, however, the life cycle approach is concerned with single organizations or small groups of organizations rather than entire populations. Essentially, the central theme of the life cycle approach is that organizations, like animals or people, change as they go through different life stages. These stages are described variously: creation, transformation, and decline (Kimberly, 1980); birth, growth, maturity, old age, and death (Adizes, 1979); the entrepreneurial stage, the collectivity stage, the formalization and control stage, the elaboration of structure stage, and the decline stage (Cameron & Whetten, 1983). These stages are sequential, not random, and as such they are predictable. However, the length of time that individual organizations spend in each stage may vary considerably, and every organization will not necessarily go through every stage. Some, for example, may go straight from the entrepreneurial stage to decline. Each stage has different managerial requirements. Change is seen as a developmental progression through these stages.

Certain key events in the various stages can significantly influence future changes. For example, Kimberly (1980) argues that organizations, like people, are very much influenced by the conditions of their birth. Also, like people, an organization's history will strongly influence any future changes it may make. Although it does not specifically employ the life cycle approach, Slack's (1985) study of the Alberta Section of the Canadian Amateur Swimming Association provides some indication of the stages that a sport organization may pass through. Also, Theodoraki (2001) considers the temporal aspect when examining structural configurations of Olympic Games Organizing Committees. Houlihan and

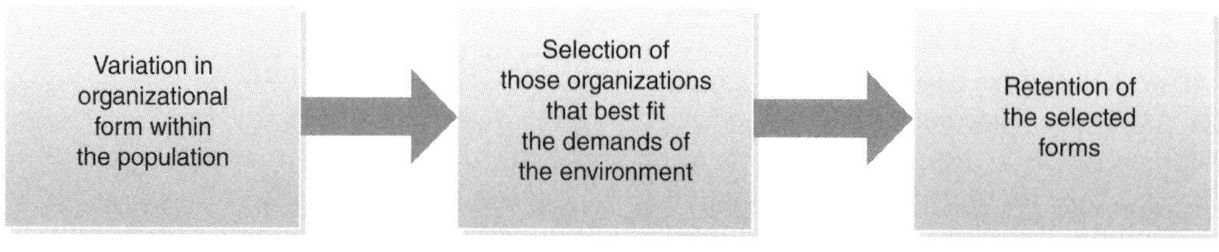

Figure 18.2 Stages of the change process: The population ecology approach.

Green (2009) traced the modernization reforms of Sport England and U.K. Sport over a period of time. Many popular press accounts of the growth of sport organizations (cf. Kogan, 1985 [Brunswick]; Geiger, 1987 [The Broadmoor]; Strasser & Becklund, 1991 [Nike]; Harrison, 2014 [Under Armour]) provide implicit indications of their various life cycle stages.

Although criticized as overly deterministic, the life cycle approach is intuitively appealing as a means of understanding change. In some ways it has also been the forerunner of work by John Kimberly, one of the original proponents of the life cycle approach, in which he adopts what he terms a "biographical" approach to understanding organizational change (Kimberly, 1987; Kimberly & Rottman, 1987).

Institutional Theory

Institutional theorists (DiMaggio & Powell, 1983; Meyer & Rowan, 1977; Meyer & Scott, 1983; Oliver, 1991; Zucker, 1983, 1987) suggest that organizations change their formal structure to conform with expectations within their institutional environment about appropriate organizational design. Usually exerted by regulatory agencies such as the state, professions, or interest groups, these institutional expectations come to define the appropriate and necessary ways to organize. As Slack and Hinings (1992, p. 123) note, "components of the structural design of an organization become widely accepted as both appropriate and necessary. In simple terms a way to organize becomes the way to organize." Organizations change and conform to the expectations of their institutional environment because by doing so they help increase their legitimacy and thus help ensure the continued flow of resources necessary for their operation (Hinings & Greenwood, 1988). Greenwood and Hinings (1996, p. 1023) go on to suggest that the application of institutional theory is useful for developing our understanding of organizational change because it helps to help explain "the similarity ('isomorphism') and stability of organizational arrangements in a given population or field of organization."

Major changes occurred in Canadian national sport organizations in the period 1984 to 1988 when the Canadian government agency Sport Canada created institutional pressures for these organizations to adopt a more professional and bureaucratic structure (MacIntosh & Whitson, 1990; Slack & Hinings, 1992). Ideas about the appropriateness of this particular organizational form were reinforced through government publications, by pressure from Sport Canada consultants, through the rewards and kudos given to conforming organizations, and through the increased employment of professional staff in national sport organizations (Slack & Hinings, 1994). Slack and Hinings (1992) show how, as a result of these pressures, these organizations changed, increasing the number of professional staff they employed and systematizing their operating procedures. At one time, national sport organizations even had their headquarters in the same building.

A similar sequence of events to those experienced in Canada also occurred in the United Kingdom. In 2000 the Labour Government published a new policy (*A Sporting Future for All*) that made it clear that the organizational infrastructure of sport was hindering national elite success and was not providing enough opportunities for young people to engage in sport. A section of the policy statement stated that studies showed "a need for a radical rethink of the way we fund and organize sport [and to this end] we offer a modernizing partnership with the governing bodies of sport" (DCMS, 2000, p. 19). Subsequently, several processes were put in place in order to change and modernize Sport England (a nondepartmental public body under the Government's Department for Digital, Culture, Media and Sport, whose responsibility is to drive up sport participation): A new CEO was appointed in 2003, and a series of reviews of Sport England were conducted, designed to help radically change its culture and management practices. In the same year, a Modernization Project Board was established, chaired by the Head of Sport Division in the DCMS, to implement the recommendations from the various reviews (Houlihan & Green, 2009). A follow-up review was conducted a few years later; the Carter Report (2005) found that Sport England had successfully implemented a radical restructure and streamlining of the organizational design. As a result of these changes at Sport England, the national governing bodies (NGBs) of sport (line managed by Sport England) had to mirror and implement similar changes. Not only did sport partnerships in Canada and the United Kingdom experience organizational change, but sport policy documents in New Zealand also shifted from the handouts or entitlement culture to a handshake or investment approach (Sam, 2009), which resulted in various conditions attached to (e.g., funding) decisions.

As another example, subsequent to a major doping scandal (the mishandling of Russian athletes' Athlete Biological Passports), which engulfed the International Association of Athletics Federations (IAAF), the federation now known as World Athletics produced a governance reform document in 2016, called *Time for Change*, as a response to the unprecedented scrutiny and loss of trust from a wide range of individuals and organizations within, and external to, its institutional environment. One of the fundamental areas that the reform document focused on was making substantial changes to the organization's structure by redefining roles and responsibilities. Constitutional changes ensured that the President had less power and could no longer make decisions alone. For more information about these reforms, see the Case for Analysis at the end of this chapter.

Evolution and Revolution

The evolution and revolution approach to organizational change is best exemplified by the work of Greenwood and Hinings (1988); Miller and Friesen (1980a, 1980b); Nadler and Tushman (1989); Tushman, Newman, and Romanelli (1986); and Tushman and Romanelli (1985). These authors suggest that organizations resist change. Even when faced with the possibility of failure, organizations will often continue to do what they have been doing in the past and not make the necessary adjustments to ensure their survival. This **resistance to change** stems from a variety of factors, including

- the reluctance to deviate from existing programs,
- the inability of organizations to accurately appraise their performance,
- the costs of facilities or equipment,
- the culture of the organization, and
- the fear by some managers that change will reduce their power.

As a result of this resistance to change the dominant organizational condition is what Miller and Friesen (1980b) refer to as *momentum*. Momentum is merely the tendency of an organization to stay within its existing structural design (e.g., a simple structure). **Evolutionary change** occurs as organizations make incremental adjustments in their strategy, structure, or processes while still remaining within this particular design. In contrast, **revolutionary change** takes place in response to a major upheaval or crisis in an organization's environment requiring a "simultaneous and sharp shift in strategy, power, structure, and controls" (Tushman, Newman, & Romanelli, 1986, p. 31). Organizations that make a change from one design type to another, that is, a move from a simple structure to a professional bureaucracy, exhibit revolutionary change. Slack and Hinings (1992) saw this type of change occurring in many of Canada's national sport organizations during the 1984 to 1988 period, and Kikulis, Slack, and Hinings (1992) provide a framework for understanding this type of change.

Similarly, as mentioned in the previous section, this type of change has occurred in the United Kingdom. After Sport England restructured its organiza-

TIME OUT

Organizational Evolution

Batuev and Robinson (2018) utilized elements of institutional theory to help guide their analysis of the processes that influenced the evolution of a modern sport, with a case study of skateboarding, due to its recent addition to the 2020 Summer Olympic Games program. The paper's findings suggested that the organization of international skateboarding has changed over time, and the authors identified three fundamental determinants of its evolution.

1. *Values of skateboarding*: The traditional noncompetitive street skateboarding had substantial influence on the development of the sport's contemporary competitive strand.
2. *Commercial interests*: Skateboarding values were traditionally anticommercialization before understanding that athletes were able to make professional careers from skateboarding (everyone's likely heard of Tony Hawk), which meant skateboarding governing bodies became commercially driven).
3. *The Olympic movement*: Many skateboarders perceive the Olympic movement or dominant culture as being against the sport's traditional values, but most elite skateboarding athletes now see Olympic participation as a step forward for the sport.

As you can see from this Time Out, contemporary sports provide sport managers with new complex issues that need to be addressed and are often faced with resistance, which we discuss later in this chapter. As a sport management student or academic, you may choose to embark on a longitudinal study of a modern sport, using either the life cycle approach or the evolution and revolution approach, for example, to help analyze organizational change.

tion, many NGBs had to follow suit to ensure Sport England's participation policy objectives could be achieved. In doing so, community-based voluntary sport clubs (VSCs) became more important and an integral part of trying to achieve participation targets (many VSCs are overseen by NGBs). Consequently, VSCs were encouraged to move toward greater contemporary and formalized operations rather than continuing a traditional ad-hoc or informal approach, which was not always well received (Nichols & James, 2008), resulting in resistance to change from several VSCs.

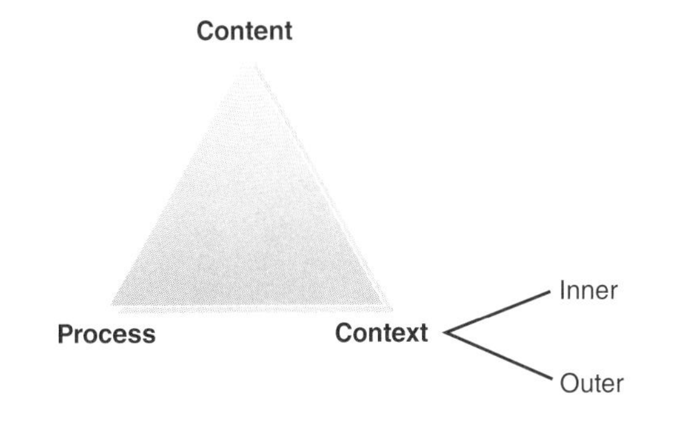

Figure 18.3 Contextualist approach to change.

Contextualist Approach

The contextualist approach to understanding organizational change emanates from the work of Andrew Pettigrew and the staff of the Centre for Corporate Strategy and Change at the University of Warwick Business School. Pettigrew (1985a, p. 15) criticizes much of the traditional work on organizational change as being "ahistorical, aprocessual, and acontextual." Much of this work, he claims, focuses on a single change event or a discrete episode of change. There are, he notes, "remarkably few studies of change that actually allow the change process to reveal itself in any kind of substantially temporal or contextual manner" and research studies are therefore concerned "with the intricacies of narrow *changes* rather than the holistic and dynamic analysis of *changing*" (Pettigrew, 1987, p. 655, emphasis in original).

To address this concern, Pettigrew suggests a multilevel analysis of change over long periods of time (Pettigrew, 1985b, 1987). This work calls for examination of three areas related to change: context (divided into inner and outer context), content, and process. Pettigrew (1987) graphically portrays an interaction among these three by placing them at the corners of a triangle (see figure 18.3). The outer context "refers to the social, economic, political, and competitive environment in which the [organization] operates" (Pettigrew, 1987, p. 657). The inner context is made up of those organizational elements that influence the change process, such as the organization's structure, culture, and political makeup. Content refers to the aspects of an organization that are being changed, and may include technology, people, products, and services. The term *process* "refers to the actions, reactions, and interactions from the varied interested parties as they seek to move the [organization] from its present to its future state" (Pettigrew, 1987, pp. 657-658).

As an example of the application of Pettigrew's (1985a) contextualist approach in the field of sport management, Girginov and Sandanski (2008) looked at Bulgarian national sport organizations as the country was undergoing fundamental political, economic, and social transformations. The authors suggested that the contextualist approach "allowed [them] to appreciate the historical, contextual and processual nature of changing and to discuss the role of managers and various forces in shaping its course and outcomes" (p. 22).

This approach to change, unlike several of the others examined here—population ecology, institutional theory, and contingency theory—does not focus solely on environmental pressures as a source of change. Rather, the work of Pettigrew and his colleagues emphasized the interrelated role over time of environment (context), structure, and human agents in shaping the change process (Pettigrew, 1985a; Pettigrew & Whipp, 1991). Unlike many studies of change, Pettigrew's methods draw heavily on the detailed construction and analysis of case studies.

The richness of data that the contextualist approach can yield makes it a very viable method for enhancing our understanding of sport organizations. Studies on organizations within our field could also be used to extend the theory. An example of the application of Pettigrew's contextualist approach is Thibault and Babiak's (2005) study exploring the changes in priorities in Canada's sport system, from the bureaucracy of sport administration to placing more focus on the high-performance athletes and their development. The authors suggest that by using the contextualist approach, it enabled them to better understand the complexity of the change process.

What Causes Organizational Change?

The impetus for change may arise externally in the environment of a sport organization or from inside the organization itself. As we have seen, many theorists (e.g., contingency theorists and population ecologists) focus on external sources of change, while others (e.g., resource-dependence theorists and those who adopt the contextualist approach) stress the interaction of external and internal factors. Externally, a wide variety of factors can cause the need for change in a sport organization. The fall of communism in the former Soviet Union has allowed many countries to be seen as emerging economies with increasing opportunities for sport. And, subsequent to athletes from North and South Korea competing under one flag at the PyeongChang 2018 Olympic Winter Games, the two Koreas have agreed to launch a joint bid to host the 2032 Summer Olympic Games.

The acquisition of new equipment and technology can also change the way a sport organization operates. For example, scanners, network-connected mobile devices, bar codes, and quick response (QR) codes have changed the way retail sporting goods stores do business. Inventory and warehousing are easier to control, so ordering can be standardized, pricing changes are easily made, and sales figures can be quickly retrieved from a store's computer network. BUCS, the organization introduced at the beginning of this chapter, started rolling out their new digital management system in February 2019, which they named BUCS Management Systems (BMS). The organization states on its website, "British Universities & Colleges Sport (BUCS) is currently transforming its digital systems. After a detailed review of existing systems and the marketplace, BUCS has elected to harness the technology of an existing sports platform, Playwaze, to deliver a web and mobile competition management solution for inter-varsity sport" (British Universities & Colleges Sport, n.d.).

Changes in government legislation may also initiate changes in the way sport organizations are structured and operated. In line with the UK government's 2015 sport strategy, Sporting Future: A New Strategy for an Active Nation, Sport England and UK Sport published the Code for Sports Governance in October 2016. The Code stipulates the governance conditions with which organizations in receipt of public investment must comply, such as having gender diversity on boards, demonstrating transparency in decision making, and exhibiting robust constitutional arrangements (HM Government/DCMS, 2018). Consequently, some organizations had to change their structures and operations to ensure receipt of funding. Another example of how a change in legislation can affect sport organizations was the implementation of the General Data Protection Regulation (GDPR) of European Union law in May 2018. Many sport organizations, ranging from small grassroots VSCs to large international corporations, within the European Union and European Economic Area had to alter the way they handled and stored personal data; the organizations had to ensure that they introduced appropriate technical and organizational measures to satisfy the data protection principles of the new regulation.

Internally, change is often initiated by change agents, people whose job it is to ensure that a sport organization makes the necessary changes to maintain or increase its effectiveness. CEOs, vice presidents, coaches, human resources development staff, union representatives, and external consultants can all act as change agents. It is important to realize that the changes these people recommend usually reflect their own interests and values. For example, the changes the Player Relations Committee may want to make to the collective bargaining agreement of Major League Baseball will likely be quite different from changes the Players Association would like to see. The types of changes senior managers want to see are different from those of the union representatives. What may be an acceptable change to some members of a sport organization will not be acceptable to others. As we noted earlier, change is a political process that may require changes not only to the structure of a sport organization but also to the dominant values expressed by its members.

One of the ways people in a sport organization try to bring some objectivity to the change process is to bring in an outside consultant. As Pfeffer (1981, p. 142) points out, these people "can serve to legitimate the decision reached and to provide an aura of rationality to the decision process." They are purportedly hired to look impartially at the problems and issues that confront the sport organization and make suggestions for change. However, it is possible for management or those doing the hiring to manipulate the results that come from this type of process, through hiring the "right" consultant and often through a consultant's realization that, even though he has been hired to be impartial, future business from those who hired him may be contingent on his coming up with the "correct recommendation" (cf. Pfeffer, 1981). That being said, with the technological advances that have allowed for the development of social media and online platforms, levels of scrutiny have increased. As a consequence, organizations have been careful to select the best outside consultant to produce a report rather than hiring the "right" individual. A high-profile example of this situation is when the World Anti-Doping Agency (WADA) commissioned professor Richard McLaren, a Canadian attorney, in 2016 to look into allegations of state-sponsored doping in Russia.

Resistance to Change

Although change is a pervasive and constant feature of sport organizations, so, too, is resistance to change. This resistance may come from within the organization itself or from external constituents. Sport managers, if they are to deal effectively with resistance to change, must understand the reasons for this opposition and realize that resistance is not always dysfunctional. Resistance is the refusal to comply or accept something but is also a means of identifying possible problems before they arise and taking action to prevent them. Resistance can force sport managers to reevaluate the appropriateness of their proposed actions and can bring forward important issues that management may not have considered. What follows is a brief discussion of four of the major sources of resistance to change.

Self-Interest

As we saw in chapter 15, subunits within a sport organization often act to maximize their own vested self-interests and help them achieve their own goals. In any change process, some groups will benefit while others may lose. As a result, individuals or groups tend to consider proposed changes in terms of their own self-interest. For example, Patti (1974) suggests that if goals relating to power, money, prestige, convenience, job security, or professional competence are threatened as a result of any potential change, the change will be resisted, even in situations where the proposed changes are beneficial to the organization as a whole, as was arguably the case for the NHL's canceled 2004-2005 season. Another example is in association football, Manchester United fans have been staging mass protests due to the current owners, Joel and Avram Glazer, siphoning more than £1 billion (US$1.25 billion) out of the club since the family took ownership in 2005 (Moore, 2019). Even with the consistent pressures of the protests (fans frequently using the #GLAZERSOUT hashtag on banners and all online platforms), the Glazers have so far resisted any change (e.g., selling the club to new owners or investing back into the club), despite the fact their ownership has caused substantial unrest among many supporters. The dissatisfaction of the Glazers' self-interest was further fueled by the knowledge that the City Football Group's Mansour bin Zayed Al Nahyan has spent more than £1.3 billion (US$1.6 billion) directly investing in rivals Manchester City since he took over in 2008 (Conn, 2018a; Manchester City Football Club, 2018). It didn't even start well for the Glazer family: With news of Malcolm Glazer's 2005 takeover, a semi-professional club, F.C. United of Manchester, was formed by disgruntled breakaway supporters. It is also frequently suggested that the Glazer family has been an important contributing factor in United's dip in form on the pitch over recent seasons (Conn, 2018b).

Lack of Trust and Understanding About the Implications of Change

Change produces a degree of uncertainty for the members of a sport organization. Employees and groups within the organization are unsure of the impact it will have on them, especially where trust is lacking between those initiating the change and those it will impact. This lack of trust may produce rumors, innuendo, and distorted information about the nature and consequences of a change, leading to defensive behavior on the part of those affected. It can also result in demotivating employees, having an impact on their performance, and, consequently, costing the business money. To minimize this resistance, management should explain—in advance—to the members of a sport organization why a change is being made and what impact it will have on them. But in sport, it is not just employees and groups within an organization that are affected by a lack of trust and understanding about implications of change; fans and spectators of sport teams—important stakeholders—also experience the emotions. As with the Glazer's takeover of Manchester United, fans of sport clubs all around the world stage protests if (new) owners implement changes without providing enough reason or information. And with the proliferation of discontent spread across the web (usually via social media), sometimes this can severely affect gate revenue when, for example, fans boycott games.

Differing Assessments of the Consequences of Change

Change will be resisted when the members of a sport organization or other significant stakeholders have differing opinions of the costs and benefits of the proposed change. This situation frequently occurs when the people affected by the change have inadequate information about the change or when they exhibit fundamentally different values regarding the proposed change.

The Cost of Change

Some groups or individuals may resist change because it is costly in terms of time, effort, and money, particularly in the short run. They do not see the benefits of the changes as being greater than the costs involved. Changes involving a significant financial investment for new facilities, technology, or machinery are often opposed on the basis of cost. For example, a sport equipment manufacturing company may wish to change to some type of computer-aided manufacturing system, but shareholders may oppose the move because of the large capital costs involved in such a change and the subsequent impact (albeit short-term) on profits.

Dealing With Resistance and Implementing Change

In the previous section we identified four of the major sources of resistance to change. Here we discuss how sport managers can deal with resistance and implement change. The approaches outlined are not independent; frequently they are used in combination to influence those who oppose change. The first six techniques identified are based on Kotter and Schlesinger's (1979) work.

Education and Communication

As we saw in the previous section, resistance to change can stem from a lack of information or inaccurate perceptions about the consequences of the change process. Sport managers responsible for initiating change often have information about the process that is not available to all members of their organization. Educating these people about the necessity for change and using communication techniques to keep them informed of how the change is progressing (e.g., group meetings, workshops, memos, and direct discussions between those initiating the change and those affected by it) can go some way to reducing resistance. This method of dealing with resistance and implementing change works best when the different groups have relatively similar goals and when the resistance to change is based on misinformation or a lack of communication. It requires a high degree of trust between the parties involved if it is to be successful.

Participation and Involvement

One of the most effective ways to deal with resistance to change and aid the implementation process is to involve those groups and individuals most likely to exhibit resistance to the planning and implementation process. The idea is that this involvement creates a commitment to the process and hence reduces opposition. By involving potential opponents to the change process, it is possible to deal with problems before they escalate and also use the skills, knowledge, and political contacts these people possess to help smooth implementation. The downside of this approach is that it is time-consuming and, as we saw in chapter 16, participative decision making can actually heighten conflict, which hinders the change process.

In Thurston's (2017) analysis of the implementation of Clubmark sport policy—developed by Sport England and NGBs, implemented into VSCs—across three sports (boxing, rugby union, and swimming), it was found that a substantial number of VSCs were initially resistant to change when directed by their respective NGBs to adopt new policies, practices, or procedures. However, over varying lengths of time and with more involvement in assisting NGBs to update iterations of policy requirements and objectives (hence, VSC members began to develop a greater understanding of why they were being

TIME OUT

Scouts Resist Changes to the Drafting of Players

For as long as baseball existed, there was one way to scout potential players. The baseball player was supposed to look a certain way; act a certain way; catch, pitch, or hit a certain way. However, when Billy Beane became general manager of the Oakland A's, he changed the whole process, starting with the minor league (farm) teams and then the Oakland A's themselves. He devised a system that used a more objective approach to scouting by examining statistics of various kinds such as on-base average, walks, and hits. When Beane's scouts found out he was looking into players who would be 19th-round draft picks or later, they vocalized their displeasure and made it clear that they weren't going to change the way they did their jobs. It was only after the team made up of oddities became successful that the scouts came around and accepted his approach (Lewis, 2003). For a detailed understanding of the change process instigated by Billy Beane, which resulted in sustained competitive advantage for the A's, refer to chapter 22 (Sports Analytics) of this textbook.

asked to implement the various policies, and the potential outcome benefits of compliance), VSC club members in all three sports became more accepting of the implementation processes.

Establishing Change Teams

One of the ways to get the support and cooperation that change requires is to establish change teams. As Kanter (1983, p. 242) points out, energizing people about change "through participation in team problem-solving has indeed produced significant results for many companies." Task forces, new venture groups, and interdepartmental committees are all excellent ways to manage resistance and implement change. These groups can undertake responsibility for training, counseling, and communicating the need for change. For example, the Professional Golfers' Association (PGA) of America created an 11-man Ryder Cup Task Force following the team's loss in 2014, which was the sixth loss in seven events. Eight then-current and former players teamed up with three PGA officials in an effort to scrutinize areas where they could improve (e.g., how players were selected, how the captain was chosen, and how he picked his wildcards) in an effort to beat the European Team (Tremlett, 2018). The process brought Team USA immediate success, with them winning the 2016 Ryder Cup on home soil in Hazeltine. However, that success was short-lived when Europe once again won the 2018, which took place on European turf in Paris.

Idea Champions

Daft (1992, p. 273) suggests that idea champions are "one of the most effective weapons in the battle for change." **Idea champions** are intensely interested and committed to the proposed changes (Chakrabarti & Hauschildt, 1989; Maidique, 1980). They play a dominant role in getting other people involved in the change process and in reducing opposition. Chakrabarti (1974) suggests that, to be successful, an idea champion must have technical competence, knowledge about the company, drive, aggressiveness, knowledge of the market, and political astuteness. Wolfe, Slack, and Rose-Hearn (1993), in their study of employee fitness programs, stressed the important role that idea champions played in getting these programs implemented in a number of major corporations.

Facilitation and Support

Some resistance to change arises from the fear and anxiety created by the uncertainty of the process. Providing a supportive atmosphere for those affected by the change can help reduce this resistance. As Zander (1950, p. 9) points out, "resistance will be prevented to the degree that the changer helps the changees to develop their own understanding of the need for change, and an explicit awareness of how they feel about it, and what can be done about those feelings." The facilitation and support provided may take the form of career counseling, job training, and therapy. This method of dealing with resistance and implementing change is particularly useful where the change can create personal problems for members of the sport organization. The biggest disadvantages of this approach are that it is time-consuming, expensive, and not accompanied by a guarantee of success. For example, employees of a large sport equipment manufacturing company that is forced to restructure its operations will be concerned that the restructuring may cost them their jobs. Consequently, some type of support during the change process, while it may not totally remove the employees' fears, may help to reduce them and thus smooth the changes that occur as a result of the restructuring.

Negotiation

Negotiation or bargaining is used when one or more powerful groups involved in a proposed change are offered some sort of incentive to comply. Negotiation is a reflection of the political reality of sport organizations. However, in many ways it is a short-term answer to suppressing resistance. If one group is given concessions, other groups may adjust their positions and begin to negotiate to get similar considerations. Such interactions are costly in both time and money and can detract from the actual change process. This type of negotiation process took place when the Seattle SuperSonics NBA franchise moved to become the Oklahoma City Thunder in the 2008-2009 basketball season. The impetus for this was the SuperSonics owners' failure to secure government funding to update their arena, KeyArena, so they sold the team to an investment group based in Oklahoma. The new investment group was also subsequently unable to persuade the Seattle government to invest millions of dollars for a new arena so notified the NBA about their intensions to move the team. A lawsuit was filed in an attempt to keep the team in Seattle. Hours before the ruling in July 2008, a settlement was agreed that the new investment group was to immediately pay the city of Seattle US$45 million for breaking the KeyArena lease, plus an additional US$30 million if Seattle did not have a replacement team within five years. As it transpired, the investment group did not have to pay the additional sum because although the team was not replaced within the set term, a stipulation in the agreement specified that the Seattle government had to approve funding to renovate KeyArena by the end of 2009, which did not happen.

Manipulation

Manipulation, although considered unethical, is frequently used as a means of bypassing potential resistance to change. Manipulation can involve such practices as distorting information or disseminating false information, splitting groups that may resist change, and influencing power brokers. Zimbalist (1992, p. 139) for example, suggests that although the Civic Center Redevelopment Corporation owned by the city of St. Louis was valued at between US$75 million and US$90 million, August Busch, owner of the St. Louis Cardinals, was able "to manipulate behind the scenes to eliminate a competitive bidder" and buy the corporation that owned what was subsequently called Busch Stadium for US$53 million.

Cooptation

Cooptation, as we saw in chapter 4, involves absorbing key resisters or influential individuals in a sport organization's decision-making structure. King (1991), for example, describes how, as the driving force behind Calgary's bid for the 1988 Winter Olympics, he secured the support of influential individuals from the city of Calgary and the province of Alberta before officially placing the bid. These people were absorbed into the organization because of their ability to influence key organizations in the bid committee's environment and as such help counter potential opposition to the bid. The Calgary example is not uncommon. Cooptation tactics are often used by mega or major sporting event local organizing bid committees in an effort to increase their chances of producing a successful bid. In another elite sporting context, Lucidarme, Babiak, and Willem (2018) identified the use of cooptation tactics in their examination of governmental power strategies (i.e., decision making and coordination) within the Flanders, Belgium, elite sport network.

Coercion

Coercion is frequently used to deal with resistance and implement change when all other methods fail. It may involve the threat of dismissal, demotion, the loss of a promotion opportunity, and transfer. Coercion is most likely to be used when a crisis situation is being faced and decisions have to be made quickly. It is problematic in that it can result in alienation and create problems in any future change attempts.

Stages of the Change Process

A number of writers have suggested that change can be conceptualized as a series of stages (Robbins, 1990; Greiner, 1967). In this section we look at one of the best-known and most widely accepted of these models. We then look at the concept of tracks, a different approach to understanding the way in which organizations change.

Greiner's Patterns of Organizational Change

Greiner (1967), surveying change literature in an attempt to distinguish successful from unsuccessful change, found that successful change processes

TIME OUT

The National Football League and Player Concussions

Heinze and Lu's (2017) longitudinal case study examined how a powerful sport governing body—the National Football League (NFL)—responded to institutional change over time in relation to the issue of player concussions. The authors suggested that organizations often adopt various strategies—such as resistance, decoupling (a type of avoidance), acquiescence (reluctantly accepting something with no protest), or becoming a change agent to exert more control over the process—at different points in time to cope with the evolution of its institutional field. Their findings (p. 509) state that "[t]he league moved from dismissing the issue [of concussions] to adopting a decoupling strategy to engaging in incremental change and finally to fundamental organizational change and gaining control of broader institutional change." Essentially, the NFL moved from a reactive strategic response toward proactive attempts to control and manage institutional change.

were characterized by six stages, each involving a **stimulus** and a **reaction** phase. The stages are now explained in more detail.

Stage 1: Pressure and Arousal

Strong pressures are placed on an organization's senior management. These pressures may arise from external environmental factors such as low sales or an innovative breakthrough by a competitor, but they can also arise internally as a result of events such as a strike or interdepartmental conflict. The pressures for change increase when internal and external forces act simultaneously. These pressures arouse top management to take action.

Stage 2: Intervention and Reorientation

Although strong pressures may arouse top management and cause them to take action, they will not necessarily respond properly. Management tends to rationalize the problems they face by blaming another group. For example, in a professional sport team the blame for low attendance may be placed on apathetic fans. Consequently, for a change to be successful, it requires the intervention of an outsider such as a new senior manager or a consultant. This person enters the organization and is able to bring some degree of objectivity to the problems it faces. The newcomer is able to encourage managers to reevaluate their past practices and current problems; they then undergo a form of reorientation to address the real problems they face.

Stage 3: Diagnosis and Recognition

Different groups within the organization join together to locate the cause of problem issues. Power is shared among the members of the organization; groups from different hierarchical levels meet to diagnose and recognize problems. Greiner (1967, p. 128) describes this as an important stage because it signals that "(a) top management is willing to change, (b) important problems are being acknowledged and faced up to, (c) ideas from lower levels are being valued by upper levels." Less successful change processes did not include this step because senior managers felt they knew what the problems were and did not need the help of other members of the organization in correcting them.

Stage 4: Invention and Commitment

Once problems have been identified, new and unique solutions have to be invented, and a commitment has to be made to a course of action. Creative solutions must be developed; the newcomer plays a role in this stage by encouraging new and creative practices. Shared power is an important feature in the development of these solutions and in securing commitment to them. Members from the lower levels of the organization show a greater commitment to solutions they helped develop.

Stage 5: Experimentation and Search

Once the solutions to problems have been decided, they are tested. The testing takes the form of a number of small-scale decisions made at different levels of the organization. This type of experimentation serves as a credibility check before the change is introduced on an organization-wide basis.

Stage 6: Reinforcement and Acceptance

The positive results obtained in stage 5 start to be reinforced and expanded to all parts of the organization. Over time they become accepted as new practice. The use of shared power as a means of introducing and implementing change is also accepted.

Tracks and the Dynamics of Change

While models such as those proposed by Greiner (1967) and others are intuitively appealing as a means of explaining the change process, they do have a number of shortcomings. For example, change is conceptualized as a linear process in which organizations clearly move from one phase to the next. As such, these models contain no provision to capture the temporal dynamic of change or to address the fact that change is rarely a smooth or sequential process. Also, no account is taken within these models for the possibility of incomplete change or change that is only partially completed and then abandoned. An alternative and somewhat more realistic method of explaining change can be found in Greenwood and Hinings' (1988) concept of tracks.

The approach of Greenwood and Hinings (1988) has its roots in the evolution and revolution theory of change. As such, it is best suited for explaining the dynamics of large-scale revolutionary change. These authors suggest that central to understanding the dynamics of the change process are the two concepts: archetypes and tracks. The concept of **archetypes** is related to Mintzberg's (1979) notion of configuration, which was addressed in chapter 6. However, it extends Mintzberg's ideas to include not only a set of structural arrangements (which is the basis of Mintzberg's work) but also the underlying values and beliefs that hold these structures in place. As Greenwood and Hinings (1988) note, design archetypes are to be identified by isolating the distinctive ideas, values, and meanings pervasively reflected in and reproduced by clusters of structures and systems. An organizational archetype in this sense is a particular composition of ideas, beliefs, and values connected with structural and systemic attributes.

In their work on Canadian national sport organizations, Kikulis et al. (1992) identified three archetypes as being present in this particular institutional sphere. The structure of these archetypes and their associated underlying values are shown in table 18.1. The kitchen table archetype is somewhat akin to Mintzberg's simple structure, and the executive office archetype parallels many of the characteristics of the professional bureaucracy. Similar archetypes to these could probably be found in national sport organizations in other countries. Also, different institutional spheres of sport organizations may contain different archetypes.

Tracks help map and explain the incidence and nature of change and the absence of change between archetypes (Greenwood & Hinings, 1988). These researchers suggest that if an organization makes a revolutionary change from one archetype (A) to another archetype (B) there is the potential for three intermediate positions. These positions, however, should be considered indicative rather than definitive since it is difficult if not impossible to establish empirically the discrete boundaries between positions. These three positions, along with two archetypal positions, are shown at the top of figure 18.4. Archetype coherence reflects a situation where an organization's structure and the underlying values held by members are consistent. For example, any of the three situations described by Kikulis et al. (1992) would reflect such coherence. Embryonic archetype coherence is a situation in which the structure of an organization nearly reflects the values of the members, but some items are discordant, for example, a kitchen-table organization that has started to hire professional staff. In a schizoid state the structure of an organization reflects the tensions between two sets of values. For example, the organization has competing groups, some of whom value the informal operating procedures and volunteer control of a kitchen-table archetype, and others who value the systematization and professional control of the executive office. Structure in these organizations will reflect the competing values: Certain elements will be like those found in the kitchen-table archetype and others will be more characteristic of the executive office. These design arrangements are incompatible.

The three positions can be used to establish the tracks that organizations follow when they make

Table 18.1 Institutionally Specific Design Archetypes for National Sport Organizations

	Kitchen table	Boardroom	Executive office
Organizational values			
Orientation	Private, volunteer, nonprofit (membership and fund-raising)	Private, volunteer, nonprofit (public and private funds)	Private, volunteer, nonprofit (government and corporate funds)
Domain	Broad: mass high performance sport	Competitive sport opportunities	Narrow: high-performance sport
Principles of organizing	Minimal coordination; decision making by volunteer executives	Volunteer hierarchy; professionally assisted	Formal planning; professionally led and volunteer assisted
Criteria of effectiveness	Membership preferences; quality service	Administrative efficiency and effectiveness	International success
Organizational structure			
Specialization	Roles based on interest and loyalty	Specialized roles and committees	Professional, technical, and administrative expertise
Standardization	Few rules, little planning	Formal roles, rules, and programs	Formal roles, rules, and programs
Centralization	Decisions made by a few volunteers	Decisions made by the volunteer boards	Decisions decentralized to the professional staff

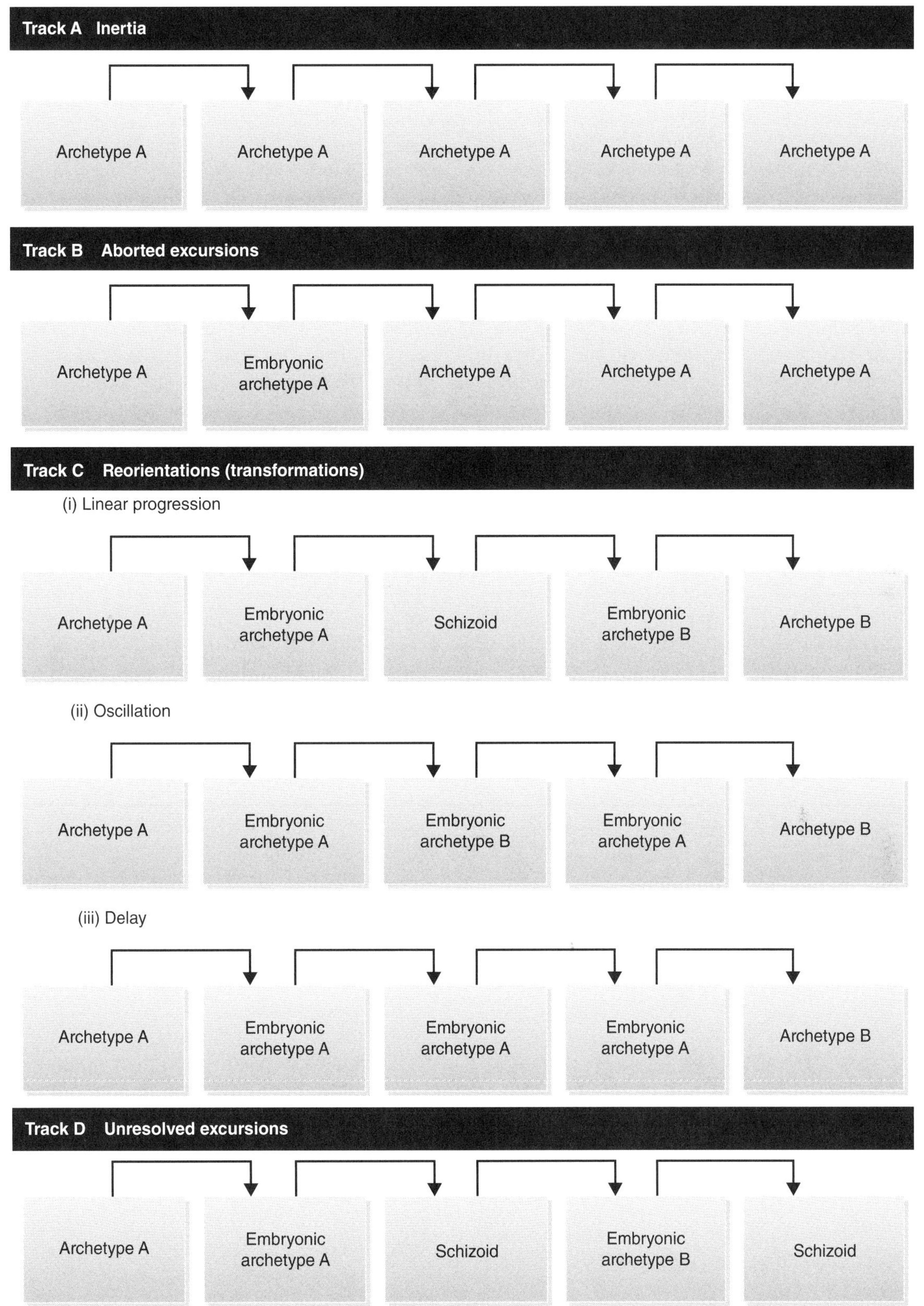

Figure 18.4 Organizational archetypes and tracks.

Reprinted by permission from R. Greenwood and C.R. Hinings, "Organizational Design Types, Tracks and Dynamics With Strategic Change," *Organization Studies* 9 (1988): 305.

revolutionary change or when they attempt such a change but fail to complete it. As shown in figure 18.4, Greenwood and Hinings (1988) identify four possible tracks. An inertial track reflects evolutionary change, the type of change that occurs when an organization is in an archetype, and the changes are small, reinforcing the archetype. An aborted excursion occurs when an organization starts to change by moving away from its existing archetype but for some reason returns to its original position. A reorientation track can take the form of a linear progression, an oscillation, or a delay; all represent successful change from one archetype to another. The linear progression is the normal sequential type of change process; the oscillation reflects the fluctuations that can occur as an organization changes; the term *delayed* is used to describe the situation when an organization resists change for some time and then makes a rapid transition to a new archetype. In an unresolved excursion an organization sets off on a change but fails to complete the change. Kikulis, Slack, and Hinings (1995), in their work on Canadian national sport organizations, have empirically verified the existence of these tracks in a change process in which these organizations were involved.

Innovation in Sport Organizations

One of the major challenges confronting all sport organizations is the need to be innovative. Rapid changes in market conditions demand more frequent innovations in product and service delivery and in administrative processes and technologies if organizational effectiveness is going to be maintained or increased. The term *innovation* refers to "the implementation of an idea—whether pertaining to a device, system, policy, program, or service—that is new to the organization at the time of adoption" (Damanpour, 1987, p. 676). Innovation involves the introduction of something new into the organization; as such it requires change. However, change does not necessarily involve innovation.

Three types of innovation can occur in a sport organization:

- Administrative innovation
- Technological innovation
- Product or service innovation

Administrative innovations involve changes to a sport organization's structure or administrative processes. For instance, the introduction of a computer-based accounting system into a municipal sport and recreation department is an administrative innovation. We saw in the Time Out "The Emergence of Elements of Complexity in a Voluntary Sport Club" in chapter 5 how a swimming VSC introduced a specialized management software system to cope with the administration tasks due to the growth of the club. And we have also seen how BUCS introduced a new management system (BMS) to develop its administration capabilities.

A **technological innovation** involves the development or use of new tools, knowledge, techniques, or systems. Hillerich and Bradsby's move to use tracer lathes in the manufacture of baseball bats and the introduction of ball-tracking technologies (such as Hawk-Eye) in sports such as tennis, cricket, and association football (used to assist match officials with line calls and decision making) are examples of technological innovations. Association football has also recently seen the implementation of another technological innovation, video assistant referee (VAR), which is a review system. Debates continue to rumble on about whether this technological innovation is positive or negative for the sport; many perceive VAR as a much-needed development, and others suggest it has disrupted the flow of the game. (During the 2019 FIFA Women's World Cup, the Cameroon team temporarily refused to play against England mid-game due to being enraged about two VAR decisions.) In addition, the Union of European Football Associations (UEFA) have recommended that any player remonstrating to a referee using a television gesture should automatically receive a yellow card (Conway, 2019).

A **product** or **service innovation** involves the development of a new product or service. With the introduction of 5G mobile technology, sport fans and spectators are now able to experience innovative consumer services. For example, Korea Baseball Organization's (KBO) defending champions, SK Wyverns, have an augmented reality mythical dragon that flew around their stadium on the opening day of the 2019 season, which was shown on the world's largest LED baseball scoreboard. To improve the experience even further, the dragon executed an interactive performance that was influenced by fans pressing a cheer button on the team's app (Hwaya, 2019).

As a result of rapid technological advances, these three types of innovation have become more interrelated and less distinct; developments in technology often enable administrative and product or service innovations. For example, Nike By You (formerly NIKEiD) allows a customer to pick a style of shoe, choose the colors, and customize the logo themselves. Nike then manufactures the product to the exact specifications and delivers it within three to five weeks. Another technological and product innovation from Nike is the Hyperadapt BB sneaker, a self-lacing basketball shoe that can tighten or loosen at the touch of a button on the sole, or by using the shoe's iPhone app, which connects via Bluetooth (Schube, 2019). A final administrative innovation (facilitated by technological developments), mentioned in chapter 8, is how the U.K. fitness chain PureGym adopted a self-check in and check-out system, which means that there is no need for receptionists, and security is also monitored via a live feed. Members sign up online (eliminating the need for administration staff at each facility), and each member enters the facility with a PIN code they receive (Cave, 2015).

A sport organization's structure influences its ability to innovate. Because of the emphasis on rigidity and control, bureaucratic organizations are seen as inhibiting innovation. In contrast, organic organizations, which are less structured, are seen as facilitating innovation. This view, however, oversimplifies the situation. Many big companies like Nike, although highly structured, are also innovative; they foster innovation through the use of such techniques as venture teams, small groups of people who are given a free hand to experiment and develop new ideas, as previously illustrated.

Other examples of sport organizations being innovative relate to the formats of competition. In today's quickly developing digital age, fans and spectators find themselves with less leisure time, and millennials and Generation Z (demographic cohorts) want immediate gratification; therefore, sports have had to alter traditional approaches. For instance, rugby introduced Rugby 7s (a fast-paced format with only seven players on the field for each team), and cricket introduced a limited 20-over Twenty20 (often, simply, referred to as T20) format and The Hundred (a further-reduced 100-ball format) rather than the traditional 50-over

KEY ISSUES FOR SPORT MANAGERS

Change will happen, whether planned or not, at some point in an organization's life cycle. Good managers use appropriate tools to facilitate the change process and overcome any form of resistance to it. Making it a positive experience for all involved will ease the process.

Change is multifaceted and complex, and affects the organization itself (e.g., its structure, core purpose), organizational members, and external stakeholders. Change can come from an inside stimulus, but more often than not, the stimulus will be external, such as the presence of an emerging market. Managers then typically have a choice whether to act (and start a change process). In this instance, change can be a tool the sport organization can use to gain a competitive advantage or simply to survive.

Whatever the stimuli for change, Amis, Slack, and Hinings (2004) argued that organizational change is dependent not only on external factors but also on the organization's own members. In a 12-year study of Canadian national sport organizations, the authors examined the impact of organizational members' values on the degree of conformance with expected changes. They found that if an organization had members whose values were close to those of the prescribed change, the organization would go through the change process successfully. If, however, an organization had members whose values opposed the change, the organization would only superficially conform—largely in response to coercive pressures—and then it would revert to an organizational form more in line with the members' values.

The key to change, however, is that it must be compatible with the organization's current characteristics. For example, you will most likely fail if you try to expand your local sporting goods stores into thousands of locations around the world. Given your small organization, you would be more successful if you started a slow expansion to a select few locations and then used the Internet to reach other areas. In this way you would minimize aspects that need to be controlled, such as organizational structure, technology, governance, human resources, and organizational culture. Having said that, the rapid development of technology has changed the way many organizations operate; the Internet allows organizations to break free of the traditional organizational structures, enabling them to reach a far greater target market or audience than ever before. However, the advances in technology mean that the external environment is also more dynamic than ever before, so sport managers must be able to keep pace and react (or, even better, be proactive) to any change to remain competitive.

one-day and (up to) five-day test match formats. The reduced formats are highly commercialized enterprises: Australia, at the time of writing, hosts the KFC [fast food] Big Bash League, England and Wales have the Vitality [health and life insurance company] Blast, and India has the Vivo [communication technology] Indian Premier League (IPL). The decision to have KP Snacks as The Hundred's main sponsor received considerable criticism from health campaigners.

Golf has also experienced changes to the format of the game in an attempt to showcase the sport to new audiences. In November 2018 Phil Mickelson and Tiger Woods competed in a head-to-head matchplay showdown called "The Match," which took place in Las Vegas. The event was a US$19.99 television pay-per-view competition that went to sudden death with Mickelson emerged victorious, taking home the US$9 million prize money. The event received a mixed response; some thought it was fun and entertaining, whereas others felt it was a pointless and indulgent activity that was steering golf in a dangerous direction due to the constant fluctuation of in-play gambling odds being heavily promoted on the screen. In fact, it was reported that the betting experts featured on the screen were "effectively promoting the idea that the only way to enjoy the golf was to have some money on it" (I. Carter, 2018, para. 6). Some also suggested that the sport of golf wanted to capitalize on the U.S. Supreme Court's ruling in May 2018, which lifted the federal ban on sports gambling; it ruled that the Professional and Amateur Sports Protection Act was in violation the 10th Amendment of the U.S. Constitution (I. Carter, 2018; Edelman, 2018).

Technology has also enabled the creation of new sports. Formula E, sanctioned by the Fédération Internationale de l'Automobile (FIA), the world governing body for motorsport, was conceived in 2011 and made its debut in Beijing in 2014 (Formula E, n.d.). Formula E is the world's first all-electric international single-seater championship, with the races taking place on city streets. Since its inception, Formula E has continued to be innovative. Formula E was the first event in the world that enables fans to influence the outcome of the race through its FANBOOST concept—fans vote for their favorite driver via the Formula E app or on the website, and during the race, drivers are awarded with extra bursts of power. During the 2018-2019 season, Attack Mode was introduced, where every driver can pick up an extra hit of power if they drive off the racing line through an activation zone (which is announced by FIA only 60 minutes prior to the race start) (BBC Sport, 2019).

Summary and Conclusions

Change is an inevitable feature of all sport organizations. It can occur in an organization's products and services, its technology, its structures and systems, and its people. Managers prefer stability, but the demands of a changing environment require that sport organizations change if they are to remain competitive. The last 30 years have seen considerable environmental uncertainty for organizations and consequently the need to change. As a result of the transformations occurring in organizations, change has become a major area of research in organizational theory. Consequently, a number of new and different approaches to studying change have been developed. Some, such as population ecology, focus on the environment as a major factor influencing change; others, such as the contextualist approach, focus more on the interaction of structure, environment, and agency.

These different foci demand different samples and methods. For example, population ecologists study large groups of organizations and usually use quantitative methods. Contextualists study much smaller groups of organizations, sometimes even a single organization, and rely on detailed case studies. The theoretical diversity in change literature offers considerable potential for the study of sport organizations.

The pressures for sport organizations to change can come from a number of sources either internal or external to the organization. Sometimes sport organizations use consultants to help initiate change. Along with pressure for change comes resistance to change—from the self-interest of those affected by the change, from a lack of trust and understanding about the change, from differing perceptions of the consequences of the change, and from the costs associated with change. We identified a number of techniques that sport managers can use to deal with resistance as they implement changes.

A number of researchers have posited different stages in the change process. One of the most common of these models, Greiner's, was outlined. However, the concept of tracks was presented as a more realistic means of explaining patterns of change. In the final section of the chapter we looked at the concept of innovation and how and why sport organizations need to be innovative.

Review Questions

1. Select a familiar sport organization that has recently undergone change. What were the

sources of resistance to this change, and how were these managed?

2. Explain how sport organizations manage the dilemma of requiring both stability and change in order to be successful.
3. Why must sport organizations change if they are to remain competitive?
4. Explain what problems you see with the life cycle approach to understanding organizational change.
5. Discuss the evolution and revolution approach to change and use it to explain how change has occurred in a sport organization with which you are familiar.
6. How do large bureaucratically structured companies promote innovation?

Suggestions for Further Reading

The body of literature on organizational change is large, so if you are interested in this area consult the major organizational journals. In addition, for those interested in population ecology, Hannan and Freeman's (1989) book *Organizational Ecology* and Singh's (1990) *Organizational Evolution* provide what is probably the most comprehensive account of work in this area. The principal work on resource-dependence theory is Pfeffer and Salancik's (1978) *The External Control of Organizations: A Resource-Dependence Perspective*. Those interested in the life cycle approach should see Kimberly and Miles's (1980) book, *The Organizational Life Cycle*. Institutional theory is best represented by Zucker's (1988) *Institutional Patterns and Organizations* and Powell and DiMaggio's (1991) *The New Institutionalism in Organizational Analysis*. However, anyone interested in this area should also read the articles by DiMaggio and Powell (1983), Meyer and Rowan (1977), Oliver (1991), and Zucker (1983, 1987, 1988, 1989). Details of the evolution and revolution approach can be found in Miller and Friesen's (1984) difficult but valuable *Organizations: A Quantum View*. Also useful and more readable is Hinings and Greenwood's (1988) *The Dynamics of Strategic Change*. Pettigrew is the main proponent of the contextualist approach, and his (1985a) book *The Awakening Giant* is a good example of this type of work. Also useful is Pettigrew and Whipp's (1991) book, *Managing Change for Competitive Success*.

In sport literature for many years the primary work on change came from the University of Alberta. Kikulis, Slack, and Hinings's (1992) article, "Institutionally Specific Design Archetypes: A Framework for Understanding Change in National Sport Organizations," provides a useful account of how the concept of archetype can be applied to our field. An extension of this work can be found in the article by these authors in the *Journal of Management Studies* (1995), where they empirically explore the notion of tracks. Slack and Hinings's *Journal of Sport Management* (1992) article is a good example of how certain theoretical perspectives of change can be integrated to give a more complete picture of the process. The *Organization Studies* article by Slack and Hinings (1994) shows how institutional theory can be applied to organizations in our field. In addition, the article by Amis, Slack, and Hinings (2002) in *The Journal of Applied Behavioral Science* looks at values in relation to organizational change. Subsequent to Trevor (Slack) posing some searching questions about the field of sport management, the *European Sport Management Quarterly* journal produced a special issue that focused on theoretical approaches to change in sports organizations. In the editorial, Waddington and Skirstad (2008) explained how papers included in the special issue represented a variety of theoretical positions, from stakeholder theory (Morrow & Idle, 2008), network theory (Steen-Johnsen, 2008), the figurational sociology of Norbert Elias (Bloyce, Smith, Mead, & Morris, 2008; Vidar Hanstad, 2008), the classical theory of Max Weber (Kelly, 2008), and Laughlin's model of organizational change and elements of postmodernism (Zakus & Skinner, 2008). Legg, Snelgrove, and Wood's (2016) article in the *Journal of Sport Management* based their study on Cunningham's (2002) Integrative Model of Organizational Change, which emanates from the works on Greenwood and Hinings's (1996) framework for understanding radical change (discussed earlier in this chapter). Legg et al. looked at youth association football clubs in Ontario, Canada, to examine the process of change by identifying the impetus for change, responses to change by stakeholders, and factors that constrained or aided the change process.

In a non-sport-specific context, several books focus on organizational change. Bradutanu's (2015) book, *Resistance to Change—A New Perspective: A Textbook for Managers Who Plan to Implement a Change*, suggests contemporary ways of thinking about how managers can deal with resistance to organizational change, and Hodges's (2016) book, *Managing and Leading People Through Organizational Change: The Theory and Practice of Sustaining Change Through People*, covers a number of the concepts discussed in this chapter.

Finally, a few popular books deal with changes in sport organizations. Michael Lewis's (2003) *Moneyball: The Art of Winning an Unfair Game* discusses changes within the Oakland A's operations (briefly mentioned in this chapter, and in greater detail in chapter 22), and Don Weiss and Chuck Day's (2003) book, *The Making of the Super Bowl: The Inside Story of the World's Greatest Sporting Event*, outlines with the evolution of the Super Bowl.

Case for Analysis

The IAAF (now World Athletics), Doping, and Corruption: Time for Change?

This case for analysis focuses on the International Association of Athletics Federations (IAAF)/World Athletics and how external environmental pressures initiated major organizational change. As mentioned earlier, the IAAF faced unprecedented backlash and scrutiny subsequent to the mishandling of Russian athletes' Athlete Biological Passports being leaked by a whistleblower in 2015. The following outlines a timeline of the IAAF's involvement and issues in relation to a selection of pertinent instances of doping and corruption (Cottrell & Carpenter, 2018; Daly & Roan, 2016; IAAF, 2006; Roan, 2015; Wagner, 2011):

- 1927 IAAF was the first international federation to ban doping
- 1988 Canadian sprinter Ben Johnson caught doping, stripped of 100-meter Olympic gold medal
- 1990 Out-of-competition doping testing introduced
- 1999 World Anti-Doping Agency (WADA) created
- 2014 Allegations of Russian doping at the Sochi Olympic and Paralympic Winter Games come to light; German broadcaster, ARD/WDR, allege several Russian athletes' positive doping tests were covered up by the IAAF
- 2014 Lamine Diack and numerous other senior IAAF officials resign
- 2015 Seb Coe is appointed IAAF President
- 2015 Whistleblower leaks more than 12,000 blood tests from 5,000 athletes taken between 2001 and 2012, where 146 samples (including 55 golds) recorded suspicious results
- 2015 Lamine Diack (former head of the IAAF) arrested as part of an investigation into corruption
- 2016 Systematic state-sponsored Russian doping program uncovered by a WADA-commissioned independent report published (in two parts) by Richard McLaren
- 2016 *Time for Change* reform document published based on four main principles: (1) redefining roles and responsibilities, including empowering Member Federations and ensuring stronger Area presentation; (2) a greater voice for athletes; (3) a better gender balance; and (4) independent anti-doping, integrity, and disciplinary functions
- 2016 Russian athletes banned by the IAAF from competing at the 2016 Rio Olympics and other international competitions
- 2017 The new Constitution outlines the roles and responsibilities of new governance approach of the IAAF; Athletics Integrity Unit created; management of IAAF's integrity programs are now managed by an independent body
- 2019 IAAF approves 41 Russian athletes to compete internationally under neutral flag
- 2019 Lamine Diack ordered to stand trial in France on charges of corruption and money laundering (including doping cover-ups, extortion, and taking bribes), e.g., Diack and five others "will be tried for their role in the case of Liliya Shobukhova, the London Marathon winner in 2010, who paid $600,000 in exchange for covering up violations in her athlete biological passport thus allowing her to compete in the London 2012 Olympic Games" (Ingle, 2019, para. 3)
- 2019 In October, the IAAF rolled out its rebrand to become World Athletics

Clearly, the publication of *Time for Change* was in direct response to the unprecedented scrutiny and loss of trust from a wide range of individuals and organizations within, and external to, the IAAF's institutional environment. (For a full explanation of governance principles and terminology, refer to chapter 13.) One of the fundamental areas that the reform document focused on was in relation to making substantial changes to the organization's structure by redefining roles and responsibilities. Constitutional changes ensured that the President now had less power and could no longer make decisions alone.

Questions

1. How and why do you think so much corruption and cover-ups were able to occur?
2. Do you think the IAAF's conduct has forced organizational change on any other international federation? If so, who and what changes?
3. Examine the relationship between the IAAF and WADA over time. Do you think it has changed?
4. Refer to the *Time for Change* document available at https://www.worldathletics.org/download/download?filename=355e5ed5-ce77-4f24-8994-a4cc1789f6a2.pdf&urlslug=Time%20For%20Change, which should be stable because transparency is one of the principles and indicators of good governance—hopefully, something that World Athletics is striving to achieve! We have highlighted how organizational structures have changed, meaning the President no longer has as much power. What other changes has the IAAF attempted to make? Have they been successful? Finally, why do you think the IAAF have changed their name to World Athletics?

CHAPTER 19

Leadership and Sport Organizations

Trevor Slack, PhD
Terri Byers, PhD

Learning Objectives

When you have read this chapter, you should be able to

1. explain the main traditional and critical approaches to the study of leadership and how these have been applied in sport management,
2. explain the major research studies that have used the contingency approach to understanding leader effectiveness,
3. understand the criticisms of leadership literature in management and sport management, and
4. discuss modern critical approaches to studying leadership and how these may apply to sport organizations.

Key Concepts

achievement leadership
assessment center approach
charismatic leadership
consideration
contingency (situational) approach
developmental interventions
employee centered
initiating structure
instrumental (directive) leadership
Leader Behavior Description Questionnaire (LBDQ)
leadership traits
Least Preferred Coworker (LPC)
managerial competencies
managerial leadership
participative leadership
path-goal theory
peer leadership
production centered
relationship behavior
situational leadership theory
style (behavioral) approach
subordinate maturity
supportive leadership
task behavior
transactional leadership
transformational leadership

The Importance of Leadership

Sam Walker, a *Wall Street Journal* editor, once attempted to determine the commonalities of the world's greatest professional sports teams. Analyzing more than 1,200 teams dating back to the 1880s, he suggested that most successful teams had a common thread: a great captain. His book *The Captain Class* (2017) summarizes his research and explains what he found by studying what he considered to be the 16 most dominant sports teams. He notes that every great, effective team has a formal or informal leader.

"The most crucial ingredient in a team that achieves and sustains historic greatness is the character of the player who leads it," Walker wrote (Feloni, 2017). Walker recognizes there are other factors that contribute to effective teams, but he gives historical evidence that a winning coach with no internal leadership does not allow for effective operations and suggests that greater importance should be placed on the quality of captains rather than coaches.

Coaches bring tactical innovations and productive cultures, yet these innovations realize the most success when a strong player-leader is on the field. Furthermore, spending millions of dollars compiling a team of the best players for each position will not be effective without cooperation and coordination of their talents. He cites Real Madrid in the early 2000s as an example; after a few years of boosting its team's success through an expensive talent acquisition strategy, management abandoned the approach in 2007, realizing that something was still missing.

The top 16 most effective teams had captains who played for their teams rather than their personal ambitions (Feloni, 2017). Players like Tim Duncan of the San Antonio Spurs sacrificed many personal rewards for the good of his team. Seven traits are thought to characterize such effective leadership for team:

- Resiliency
- Playing to the limits of the rules
- Doing thankless jobs
- Clear communication with all members of their team
- Motivating through nonverbal displays
- Possession of strong convictions but embrace diversity
- Control over emotions

Walker's ideas can also be seen in the military and the world of corporate management. Former Navy SEAL platoon leader and *Extreme Ownership* author Leif Babin believed that there is no bad team, only bad leaders, which he learned through managing a training exercise (Willink & Babin, 2017). Several teams of men engaged in repeated paddle boat races, and soon consistency emerged in the winning and losing teams. Upon switching the captains, the teams swapped first and last place within a few races. Babin believed that the team leaders were responsible through their level of communication and passion.

In big business, management consultant and author of *First, Break All the Rules* Marcus Buckingham (1999) asserts that the most important factor for a company is not its CEO, but its team managers. The role of team manager is akin to the captain of a sports team, and the role of CEO aligns well with the role of coach in Walker's theory. It is up to the person who directly leads team members doing the work to effectively communicate the directions from the top and work with them to succeed.

It seems that Walker discovered some fundamental truths about team dynamics, whether in pro sports teams or big corporations: Strong leadership from the top is crucial, but it only works when a talented leader is also on the field.

The opening scenario depicts a traditional industry approach to understanding leadership, a concept that on the face of it appears to be the most important factor in organizational effectiveness. However, as we move through this chapter you will see that leadership is not as simple as the opening scenario may suggest. Sport management has many notable leaders, including Sheri Poe, Earle Zeigler, and Donna Lopiano. Undoubtedly, the lead editor and founding author of this text, the late Trevor Slack, is considered an accomplished leader in the field of sport management. As Alvesson (2017, p. 2) notes, the study of leadership is extremely popular but can be considered "a maddening concept" because what is meant by the term is often so unclear, ranging from everything to nothing. While Bass and Stogdill's *Handbook of Leadership* (Bass, 1990a) contains over 7,500 citations (Weese, 1994), Bennis and Nanus (1985, p. 4) commented on the state of leadership research that "never have so many labored so long to say so little." But the literature can be seen as having made some progress with traditional studies being followed by more critical perspectives (Schedlitzki & Edwards, 2017). Traditional theories are thought to focus more on leadership effectiveness and include various perspectives such as trait, skills, styles, early contingency, LMX, and transactional or transformational leadership theories. Critical perspectives became more established in the mid-2000s and include poststructuralism, feminism, discursive approach, and critical management research, which sought to criticize individualistic, male-dominated, and Western assumptions embedded in the leadership mainstream, traditional studies.

The popularity of leadership research in the broader field of management is also reflected in sport management literature. Paton (1987), after a thorough review of research in the field, concluded that leadership was the topic most frequently studied by sport management scholars. More recently, Burton (2015) provided a systematic review of the literature on women in leadership in sport organizations. Another review by Welty Peachey, Zhou, Damon, and Burton (2015) examined 40 years of research on leadership in sport management. Most recently, Ferkins, Skinner, and Swanson (2018) provided a special issue on sport leadership that both brings together what we currently know and where we are in theoretical understanding of leadership in sport management and encourages broader innovative ways for leadership research and practice. In many ways, the opening scenario of this chapter reflects this recent "new generation of thinking" that Ferkins, Skinner, and Swanson (2018, p. 77) refer to in their introduction to that special issue. Leaders can be formally appointed, but they can also be socially constructed and negotiated such as the follower-centered perspective (Uhl-Bien, Riggio, Lowe, & Carsten, 2014).

Despite the proliferation of leadership studies in sport management, most of the earlier work (up to 2000) was descriptive and atheoretical, and it rarely used in any meaningful or substantive way the leadership literature that existed in the broader field of management. Exceptions during this time are works by Chelladurai and his colleagues (1978, 1980, 1983, 1987) and research by Weese (1995a, 1995b, 1996). Into the 2000s, leadership research in sport management has begun to demonstrate increasing use of critical perspectives such as feminist theories. Some attempt has been made to tie leadership to other organizational phenomena in sport organizations such as structure, power, and control.

In this chapter, we look at the topic of leadership, although any comprehensive review of all the literature in this area is beyond the scope of a textbook. We look at the major theoretical approaches to the study of leadership from the traditional and critical perspectives and how these have been studied in sport management. Traditional perspectives include the trait approach, the style (or behavioral) approach, and the contingency (or situational) approach (Bryman, 1992). In addition, we look at current popular notions of charismatic and transformational leadership. More recently, the concepts of servant leadership and authentic leadership have gained popularity among scholars (Avolio, Walumbwa, & Weber, 2009; Burton, Welty, Peachy, & Wells, 2017), and we include a discussion of these more modern approaches to leadership in this chapter. Finally, we discuss leadership research specifically in the field of sport management before examining some of the problems with work on leadership, and we make some suggestions regarding the type of leadership research that should be undertaken in our field. The traditional approaches covered are important for understanding how our knowledge of leadership has developed and to appreciate why more modern and critical approaches (discussed later in the chapter), both in sport management and mainstream management, are adopted as solutions to the weaknesses in the more dated approaches.

Traditional Approaches to Leadership

Traditional approaches to leadership provide a useful starting point to understand how scholars first viewed leadership and its importance in organizations. These approaches took a very pragmatic approach to the concept of leadership but perhaps developed a narrow view of leaders and their influence in organizations.

Trait Approach

The trait approach was one of the earliest approaches to leadership research. Its basic premise is that good leaders are born, not made. That is, leaders possess certain personal qualities that distinguish them from other members of an organization. Early researchers used psychological tests to try to identify these traits, but within this research little attention was paid to how effective these leaders were. The type of traits most frequently examined by researchers can be classified into three categories: the individual's physical characteristics, including height, physical appearance, age; intellectual qualities such as intelligence, speaking ability, and insight; and such personality features as emotional stability, dominance, and sensitivity.

One of the research themes to develop from earlier work on **leadership traits** has been concerned with the processes of managerial selection and recruitment. Commonly referred to as the **assessment center approach**, the focus of this research is to use various tests, some of which are job related, to identify traits that can predict management potential and the ability to progress to the higher levels of an organization (Gaugler, Rosenthal, Thornton, & Bentson, 1987). The assessment center approach uses projective and situational tests. One such test is the in-basket exercise, a hypothetical situation in which a candidate has a certain amount of time to act on the directives that accumulated in his or her in basket, to determine if the candidate has management traits and skills. These tests may often be accompanied by exercises to assess such skills as writing and oral communication. Many organizations, including some in the sport industry, use these kinds of tests to improve their managerial selection and promotion processes. The traits that best predict advancement can include such qualities as resistance to stress, the tolerance of uncertainty, and the candidate's level of activity (Bray, Campbell, & Grant, 1974). The assessment center approach, and much of the other work that has emanated from trait research, has one major limitation for our understanding of leadership: While it has been designed to identify those traits that predict managerial effectiveness or advancement, it does not necessarily follow that these are useful predictors of good leadership, although as Bryman (1986, p. 34) notes, "writers such as Yukl (1981) and Bass (1981) appear, at least by inference, to take assessment center studies . . . to be relevant to the study of leadership." The assessment center approach has also been criticized because results may be influenced by the gender of the assessor and the assessee (Walsh, Weinberg, & Fairfield, 1987).

Another area of research emanating from the trait studies of leadership seeks to identify **man-**

TIME OUT

Hockey and Business: The Traits of Success

Wayne Gretzky is a leader in the sport of hockey (Raphael, 2016). Most people, even those who are not hockey fans, know some of Gretzky's accomplishments. During his career, he broke records for number of goals, assists, and points, and won trophies for sportsmanship, highest scorer, and most valuable player. While in the NHL he led his team to the Stanley Cup championship. Gretzky was instrumental in the management of Team Canada (Canada's hockey team) at the 2002 Winter Olympic Games and the 2004 World Cup of Hockey, where the teams won gold medals each time (CBC.ca, 2004). Off the ice, he participates in countless charity functions. He has reached a level of renown that prompted Andy Warhol to paint his portrait. His leadership focused on bringing out the best in everyone around him, and he recognized that he could not succeed alone (Raphael, 2016).

Mark McCormack, who passed away on May 16, 2003, was a leader in the business of sport, having started his business, International Management Group (IMG), by shaking the hand of a young golfer named Arnold Palmer in 1960 (IMG, 2005). Since then IMG has grown to become the world's top sport and lifestyle marketing and management company. Acquired by WME in 2016, IMG has offices in 30 countries and represents hundreds of athletes, artists, celebrities, entertainers, writers, musicians, television properties, and prestigious organizations from around the world, including Olympic Games organizing committees. They are a global leader in entertainment, sports, and fashion (IMG, 2018).

agerial competencies, or skills. Jamieson (1987) argued for a competency-based approach to sport management. She suggested that sport managers need competence in such areas as business procedures, resource management, personnel management, planning and evaluation, and programming techniques. Unfortunately, most studies on competencies are often seriously flawed; they are often either too general and produce patently obvious findings (e.g., sport managers need good decision-making skills), or they fail to recognize that different competencies are required, to a greater or lesser extent, in the various sectors of the sport industry. For example, the skills needed by the CEO of a professional basketball franchise will be quite different from those required by the volunteer president of a community sport club. McLennan (1967) has shown that the skill requirements of managers vary depending on such factors as the nature of the organization, its size, and the extent to which decisions are centralized or decentralized.

Style or Behavioral Approach

Conducted primarily by psychologists, the two research programs that best exemplify the **style approach** are what are referred to as the Ohio State Studies and the Michigan Studies. We look briefly at the major concepts employed in both approaches and, where possible, give examples of work conducted in sport management using the ideas they contain.

The Ohio State Studies

The Ohio State researchers (Fleishman & Harris, 1962; Fleishman, Harris, & Burtt, 1955; Halpin, 1957; Halpin & Winer, 1957; Hemphill & Coons, 1957) used questionnaires to identify the types of behaviors in which leaders engaged, that is, their leadership style. From a list of about 1,800 possible leader behaviors these researchers developed a list of 130 questions. The instrument, known as the **Leader Behavior Description Questionnaire (LBDQ)**, was administered to 300 individuals, mainly people involved in the military. The resulting factor analysis of the completed questionnaires showed that subordinates conceptualized their leader's behavior as occurring primarily along two dimensions: the extent to which the leaders exhibit consideration, and what is referred to as *initiating structure*. **Consideration** is "the extent to which leaders promote camaraderie, mutual trust, liking, and respect in the relationship between themselves and their subordinates" (Bryman, 1992, p. 5). The term **initiating structure** concerns the degree to which leaders structure their own work and that of their subordinates to obtain the organization's goals. Examples of actions under initiating structure include creating job descriptions, establishing performance standards, ensuring subordinates work to maximum performance levels, and establishing deadlines.

Over the years the LBDQ has been modified and used in some capacity in many leadership studies (Katerberg & Hom, 1981; Larson, Hunt, & Osborn, 1976; Schriesheim, 1980). Bryman (1992) nevertheless suggests that despite its popularity, the Ohio State research and much of the other research characteristics of the style approach are open to a number of criticisms. First, the findings from LBDQ studies have produced inconsistent and, in some cases, statistically insignificant results (Fisher & Edwards, 1988). Second, the studies using this approach rarely take into account situational factors; when they have, most notably in the path-goal approach (House, 1971; House & Mitchell, 1974), there has been "a tendency for atheoretical investigations of particular moderating variables" (Bryman, 1992, p. 7). A third problem Bryman (1992) identifies is that because most LBDQ-type studies are cross-sectional, the direction of causality is rarely established; hence, it is wrong to conclude that leadership style influences factors such as group performance or satisfaction—quite possibly group performance and job satisfaction could influence leadership style. A fourth concern is the tendency of studies in the Ohio State tradition to focus on group-level or averaged responses, a situation by which the leader's relationship to individual organization members is masked.

Despite these shortcomings LBDQ-type studies have been used by researchers in the sport management field. Olafson and Hastings (1988) used the LBDQ-Form XII to assess administrative behavior, relating it to what they term *personal style*. Their results suggest that personal style is important in understanding a leader's decision-making behavior. Snyder (1990) used the LBDQ to examine the effect of leader behavior on intercollegiate coaches' job satisfaction. His work showed that the degree of consideration exhibited by leaders (athletic directors) was significantly correlated with coaches' satisfaction with their work and their supervision. Initiating structure did not correlate with either work satisfaction or supervision. In another study using the LBDQ, Branch (1990) looked specifically at athletic directors and the effect of their behavior on the effectiveness of intercollegiate athletic organizations.

The Michigan Studies

At approximately the same time as the Ohio State research was being conducted, researchers at the University of Michigan were also involved in an extensive program of leadership studies. The first group of these studies (Katz, Maccoby, Gurin, & Floor, 1951; Katz, Maccoby, & Morse, 1950) were directed toward determining the behaviors of effective leaders. Results showed that leaders in high-performing organizational units were more likely to

- clearly differentiate their role by spending less time doing the things that subordinates did and more time planning and supervising,
- be oriented toward their work group by being "**employee centered**" as opposed to "**production centered**,"
- not engage in close supervision of their subordinates and thus allow them more latitude in what they did,
- develop a sense of cohesiveness within their work group, and
- receive general rather than close supervision from their supervisors.

The results from the Michigan studies, along with information from the Ohio State research, were summarized by Bowers and Seashore (1966). These two researchers identified four dimensions of leadership emerging from the two sets of studies:

1. Support
2. Interaction facilitation
3. Goal emphasis
4. Work facilitation

The first two concepts focus on relationship-oriented behaviors, the second two on task-oriented behaviors. Bowers and Seashore (1966) argued that the practices they identified could be carried out by formal leaders or members of the particular work group. From this, they coined the terms **managerial leadership** and **peer leadership**.

Contingency or Situational Approach

One of the shortcomings of the Ohio State and Michigan studies, and indeed much of the work in this tradition, is its failure to take account of how contingency or situational variables moderate the relationship between the behavior of a leader and different outcomes. While it is an intuitively appealing notion that different types of leader behavior will be more appropriate than others in particular situations, not until the 1970s did we see the emergence of a significant body of research focusing in any systematic way on the impact of contingency variables—task structure, the characteristics of the environment, or subordinates' characteristics—on leadership effectiveness. Contingency theories of leadership "draw attention to the notion that there are no universally appropriate styles of leadership, [but that] particular styles have an impact on various outcomes in some situations but not in others" (Bryman, 1992, p. 11). In this section we focus on those theories of leadership that have placed contingency factors as the central focus of their analysis. We look specifically at three of the best-known **contingency approaches**: the path-goal theory of leadership, Hersey and Blanchard's situational theory, and Fiedler's LPC approach.

The Path-Goal Theory of Leadership

Developed primarily by House (1971) and his colleagues (House & Dessler, 1974; House & Mitchell, 1974) the **path-goal theory** of leadership is concerned with understanding how a leader's behavior influences the satisfaction and efforts of subordinates. Essentially the theory proposes that the influence of the leader's behavior on subordinate satisfaction and effort is contingent on situational variables such as the nature of the task being undertaken and the characteristics of the subordinates. These contingency variables "determine both the potential for increased subordinate motivation and the manner in which the leader must act to improve motivation" (Yukl, 1998, p. 266). They also influence the preferences that subordinates have for a particular type of leader behavior. House and Mitchell (1974) and Filley, House, and Kerr (1976) identify four types of leader behavior.

1. *Supportive leadership*: The leader exhibits concern about the welfare of subordinates, considers their needs, and attempts to create a work environment that is pleasant and caring.
2. *Instrumental (or directive) leadership*: The leader places a great deal of emphasis on planning, coordinating, directing, and controlling the activities of subordinates.
3. *Participative leadership*: Leaders treat subordinates almost as equals. Subordinates are encouraged to let their views be known; power is shared with subordinates.
4. *Achievement leadership*: Leaders have confidence in their subordinates. Challenging goals are set for subordinates, and they are expected to assume responsibility for meeting these goals.

The path-goal model seeks to explain what effect different types of leader behavior will have under various situational conditions. When work is stressful, frustrating, tedious, or low in autonomy, **supportive leadership** will increase the satisfaction and effort of subordinates (House, 1971; House & Dessler, 1974; Schuler, 1976; Stinson & Johnson, 1975). This style of leadership is seen to enhance the intrinsic value of the task and, by increasing subordinate self-confidence and lowering anxiety, it raises the expectancy level that tasks will be successfully completed. When tasks are not stressful, frustrating, tedious, or dissatisfying supportive, leadership does not have a major impact on the satisfaction level of subordinates or the amount of effort they put into their work. When tasks are unstructured and complex in nature, when subordinates have little experience in doing the tasks and no formalized procedures to help them complete their work, **instrumental leadership** (sometimes called directive leadership) will enhance the satisfaction and effort of subordinates. Indik (1986; cited by Yukl, 1989), in a meta-analysis, provided general support for the impact of instrumental leadership on employee satisfaction and motivation under conditions of low task structure.

While ideas about **participative leadership** are not as well developed as those about supportive or instrumental leadership, it is hypothesized that participation increases subordinate satisfaction and effort when tasks are relatively unstructured. Participative leadership, it is felt, can increase subordinates' understanding of the relationship between their efforts and goal attainment; it helps them select goals in which they are personally interested and hence toward which they are more likely to be motivated. It can also increase subordinates' control over their own work, thus increasing satisfaction. Indik's (1986) meta-analysis found support for the fact that participative leadership can in fact increase employee satisfaction when tasks are relatively unstructured.

Likc participative leadership, work on **achievement leadership** has not been extensively developed. It is generally felt that achievement leadership "will cause subordinates to strive for higher standards of performance and to have more confidence in their ability to meet challenging goals" (House & Mitchell, 1974, p. 91) when tasks are unstructured. When tasks are straightforward, achievement leadership has little effect.

Hersey and Blanchard's Situational Leadership Theory

Hersey and Blanchard's (1984) **situational leadership theory** is based on two types of leader behavior. **Task behavior**, very similar to the Ohio State concept of initiating structure, involves the leader in structuring how work is to be done. **Relationship behavior**, similar to the concept of consideration, involves providing support to employees and openly communicating with them. The mediating situational variable between task or relationship behavior and leader effectiveness is called **subordinate maturity**. Two dimensions make up this concept. The term *job maturity* describes the subordinate's technical ability; psychological maturity is the level of self-confidence and self-respect they bring to the task. Subordinates with high levels of maturity score high on both job maturity and psychological maturity. They possess the skills to do the task, will assume responsibility, and establish high aims for themselves. Subordinates with low maturity have little ability and low self-confidence. Although maturity is actually a continuum, Hersey and Blanchard divide the continuum up into four segments (see figure 19.1).

When subordinates show low levels of maturity in regard to the tasks to be performed, leaders who exhibit high task behavior are most effective; the leader provides direction by establishing clear ways of operating and standards of task accomplishment. At the medium levels of maturity (quadrants 2 and 3) leaders need to focus more on relationship behavior and gradually reduce the amount of direction they provide the subordinates as they exhibit more maturity relative to the task. At the highest level of maturity, the leader offers little direction and allows the subordinate to make decisions about how tasks

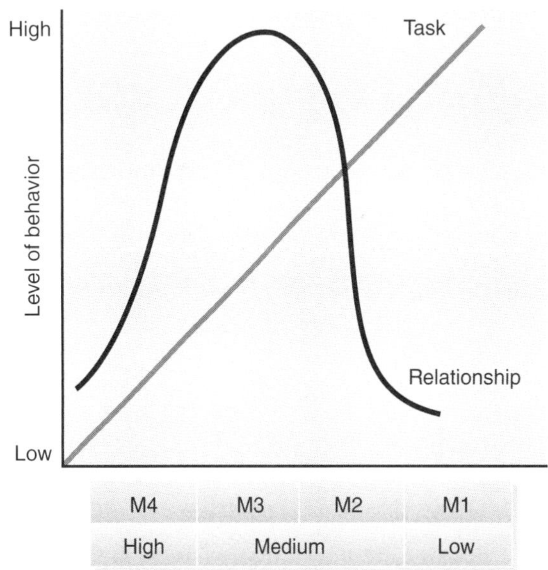

Figure 19.1 Relationship between subordinate maturity and task-oriented behavior.

are carried out.

A leader can influence the maturity level of a subordinate by using what are termed **developmental interventions**, which may involve techniques such as reducing the amount of direction given a subordinate and allowing them to take responsibility for a task. If the subordinate does well, praise and support are used to strengthen the behavior. A more complex intervention, called *contingency contracting*, involves negotiating the subordinate's tasks and responsibilities. The length of time may vary to "mature" to do the task well, depending on the nature of the task.

Hersey and Blanchard's work draws attention to the need for leaders to treat different subordinates in different ways as they progress in their work. It also draws attention to ways leaders can work with subordinates to build up their abilities and confidence level. There have been very few attempts, however, to empirically test the concepts and relationships outlined in Hersey and Blanchard's work, even in the general field of management and organization studies.

Fiedler's LPC Approach

Fiedler's (1967) approach is the oldest of the contingency theories of leadership. Unlike the path-goal approach and Hersey and Blanchard's work, both of which focus on leader behavior, Fiedler focuses on how situational variables moderate the relationship between leader traits and organizational effectiveness. The cornerstone of Fiedler's work is a measure called the **Least Preferred Coworker (LPC)** score. This score, an indicator of a leader's motivational traits, is developed using an instrument that asks leaders to think of the person with whom they can work least well and to assess that person on a series of bipolar descriptors. The 16 pairs of descriptors include adjectives such as pleasant–unpleasant, helpful–frustrating, cold–warm, supportive–hostile, and gloomy–cheerful. A leader who obtains a low LPC score is motivated by task accomplishment and will only be concerned with relationships with subordinates if the work unit is seen to be performing well. A leader who gets a high LPC score will, in contrast, be motivated to develop close interpersonal relations with subordinates; task-directed behavior is of a lesser concern, becoming important only when sound interpersonal relations have been established with subordinates and peers.

Mediating the relationship between the leader's motivational traits and group performance is a situation variable called *situational favorability*. Favorability is made up of three situational components:

1. *Leader–member relations*: The leader's personal relationship with the other members who make up the work group
2. *Position power of the leader*: The degree of formal authority the leader obtains from his or her position
3. *Task structure*: The extent to which the tasks the group have been assigned to perform are structured

The three components of situational favorability can give eight possible conditions. Fiedler suggests that task-oriented leader behavior (i.e., a low LPC

TIME OUT

Effects of Culture as a Situational Variable Influencing Leadership Effectiveness

Chelladurai, Malloy, Imamura, and Yamaguchi (1987b) suggested that one of the situational variables that could influence leadership effectiveness is culture. They defined *culture* as the attitudes, beliefs, and values of a society. Using a sample of 106 male Japanese students and 156 male Canadian students, Chelladurai and colleagues used an instrument they had developed some years earlier with Saleh (Chelladurai & Saleh, 1980), the Leadership Scale for Sports, to assess the preferred leadership of the two samples. Their results showed that Japanese students preferred more supportive leadership than Canadian students. It was also found that Japanese students in modern sports (track and field, rugby, volleyball, and so on) preferred a more participative leadership structure than Canadian students. Japanese students in traditional sports (judo, kendo, and kyuto) preferred a more authoritarian (i.e., directive) style of leadership. The researchers concluded that both the cultural background of subordinates (athletes) and the type of sport in which they were involved were situational variables that could influence leadership effectiveness. More recently, Bowers, Hall, and Srinivasan (2017) provided support for the notion that culture and leadership style may be the missing combination for selecting leaders for crisis management effectiveness. Their standard methodology for selecting appropriate leaders for crisis management was validated against six different types of crisis.

leader) is most effective in situations of high situational favorability (conditions 1, 2, or 3) or unfavorable situations (condition 8). In situations that are moderately favorable or moderately unfavorable (conditions 4 to 7), someone who is more attentive to subordinate relations (a high LPC leader) will be more effective.

Criticism of Fiedler's model has been plentiful (Kennedy, 1982; Schriesheim & Kerr, 1977), and the model has fallen out of favor within the general field of management and organizational studies. However, reviews of the large number of studies conducted using this approach (Peters, Hartke, & Pohlmann, 1985; Strube & Garcia, 1981) provide general support for the model.

Charismatic and Transformational Leadership

As Yukl (1989, p. 204) points out, the terms **transformational leadership** and **charismatic leadership** refer to the process of "influencing major change in the attitudes and assumptions of organization members and building commitment for the organization's mission or objectives. Transformational leadership is usually defined more broadly than charismatic leadership but there is considerable overlap between the two conceptions." This overlap is compounded by research that uses related terms such as "visionary leadership" (Sashkin, 1986, 1988; Westley & Mintzberg, 1989), "magic leadership" (Nadler & Tushman, 1989), and "transferential leadership" (Pauchant, 1991). Bryman (1992, pp. 104-113) provides a good overview of the difference between transformational and charismatic leadership. In this section we first look at some of the major writings on charismatic leadership and then examine transformational leadership.

Charismatic Leadership

The notion of charisma has been around for a long time, but it is Weber, in his book *Economy and Society* (1968), who is most often credited with first using the term to describe leadership in an organizational setting. Focusing primarily on religious groups and primitive tribes Weber saw leaders as gaining authority from their charisma. Charisma for Weber was "a certain quality of an individual personality by virtue of which he is considered extraordinary and treated as endowed with supernatural, superhuman, or at least specifically exceptional powers or qualities" (1968, p. 241).

Despite Weber's early writings on charisma and its links to leadership, it was not until the late 1970s and early 1980s that organizational or management researchers started to embrace the concept and examine it in any systematic way (Etzioni, 1961 and Oberg, 1972 are two notable exceptions).

House's Research on Charismatic Leadership

House's (1977) work represents one of the first substantive attempts to understand charismatic leadership. His theory seeks to explain the characteristics of charismatic leaders and their behaviors. It is suggested that charismatic leaders can be distinguished from other leaders in that they are able to establish "follower trust in the correctness of the leader's beliefs, similarity of follower's beliefs to those of the leader, unquestioning acceptance of the leader, affection for the leader, willing obedience to the leader, identification with and emulation of the leader, emotional involvement of the follower in the mission, heightened goals of the follower, and the feeling on the part of followers that they will be able to accomplish, or contribute to the accomplishment of, the mission" (p. 191). House also stresses that charismatic leaders are likely to have self-confidence, a strong conviction about their own ideals and beliefs, and a desire for the power to be able to influence others.

A charismatic leader acts as a role model for followers so that they will identify with the leader's values and beliefs. Leaders also engage in image-building to look competent and successful in the eyes of their followers. They present ideological goals that represent the types of values and beliefs they would like followers to share. Charismatic leaders have high expectations for followers to aspire to, and such leaders support and show confidence in their followers. Finally, charismatic leaders try to arouse motives relevant to the group's mission—the need to overcome a common foe, the need for excellence, affiliation, power, and the like. Phil Knight's desire to overcome Adidas and push it into second place in the athletic footwear market is an example of this type of motive.

Conger's Theory of Charismatic Leadership

Conger's initial work on charismatic leadership was conducted with Kanungo (Conger & Kanungo, 1987, 1988). Their approach is based on the idea that charisma is an attributional phenomenon. Leaders are attributed certain charismatic qualities by their followers. The focus of their research was to identify the types of leader behavior that result in these attributions.

Central to the attributional process is the leader's creation of an "idealized goal" or vision that deviates sufficiently from the existing condition of the organization. Leaders are also seen as charismatic if they involve themselves in activities that call for self-sacrifice and high personal risk to achieve the vision they have created. They use unconventional means to achieve their vision and are able to assess environmental opportunities and threats realistically. Using this information, they have to time appropriately the strategies they employ to help realize their vision. This type of leader is most likely to come to the fore when an organization is in a crisis, although crisis is not necessarily a precondition for their emergence. These people are confident in their ability to lead; they make great use of their personal power, for example, their expert knowledge, rather than their positional power, to commit others to their vision.

The concepts put forward by Conger and Kanungo (1987, 1988) were extended by Conger in his 1989 book *The Charismatic Leader: Behind the Mystique of Exceptional Leadership*. Conger essentially viewed the process of attribution that resulted in some individuals being seen as charismatic leaders as a series of stages. In the first stage, the leader senses opportunity and formulates a vision. The vision is designed to bring people in the organization together; it may be a result of dissatisfaction with the existing situation and can be a vehicle to challenge the status quo. The second stage involves the leader articulating the vision. The third stage requires the charismatic leader to build trust in the vision; he or she must be seen as having the ability to lead the organization toward achieving the vision. An emphasis on previous accomplishments and shared values with subordinates can help in building this trust. The final stage involves achieving the vision. Subordinates are empowered so that they feel they can help achieve the lofty goals that have been set. Achieving success along the way is an important factor at this stage.

Transformational Leadership

In part research on charismatic leadership in organizations has been a result of the growing interest in transformational leadership. In this section we look at the work of three of the best-known writers on transformational leadership.

Burns

The central focus of Burns' work is to contrast transformational leadership with what he refers to as *transactional leadership*. **Transactional leadership** involves the leader in some form of transaction with subordinates. Appealing to their self-interest, transactional leaders exchange pay or prestige for a subordinate's compliance with their orders. However, there is no enduring bond between the two parties.

Transformational leadership involves "leaders and followers rais[ing] one another to higher levels of motivation and morality" (Burns, 1978, p. 20). Transformational leaders work by appealing to the ideals and values of subordinates. They seek to unite subordinates as they work toward a common purpose. The bulk of early work on leadership focused on transactional leaders.

Bass

Much of the research conducted on Burns' notion of transformational leadership has been carried out by Bass and his associates (Avolio & Gibbons, 1988; Avolio & Yammarino, 1990; Bass, 1985, 1990b; Bass & Avolio, 1989, 1990a, 1990b, 1990c; Hater & Bass, 1988; Yammarino & Bass, 1990). Unlike Burns, who saw transformational and transactional leadership as being ends of a continuum, Bass saw them as separate; a leader can be both transformational and transactional (Bryman, 1992). Bass would classify leaders like Adolf Hitler and David Koresh as transformational.

Bass suggests that transformational leaders enhance their subordinates' confidence and increase awareness of selected goals and how they may be obtained. They also inspire subordinates to look beyond their own self-interests and seek to satisfy such higher-level needs as self-actualization. For Bass, transformational leaders may be charismatic; they provide personal attention to the needs of subordinates, they seek to empower them, and they provide them with a constant flow of new ideas about ways to operate.

To determine the extent to which leaders exhibit the characteristics of transformational and transactional leadership, Bass and his associates developed the Multifactor Leadership Questionnaire (MLQ). The most common version of this instrument contains 70 items asking respondents to describe the behavior of a leader in seven areas of leadership (Bass & Avolio, 1990b):

1. *Charismatic leadership*: The degree to which the leader is seen as charismatic
2. *Inspirational leadership*: The extent to which a leader inspires subordinates
3. *Individual consideration*: How much a leader gives personal attention to subordinates
4. *Intellectual stimulation*: The way in which the leader promotes new ideas and challenges

old ways of operating

5. *Contingent rewards*: The way in which a leader rewards subordinates for following specific directions
6. *Management by exception*: How leaders take action when irregularities occur
7. *Laissez-faire*: The extent to which the leader abdicates his leadership role

The first four of these measurements assess transformational leadership behaviors; contingent rewards and management by exception assess transactional leadership, and laissez-faire is a type of nonleadership assessment. The scores from the MLQ are related to organizational outcome measures such as leader effectiveness, subordinate satisfaction, and subordinate motivation. The four transformational qualities, along with contingent rewards, are more likely to be associated with positive outcomes than management by expectation and laissez-faire.

Tichy and Devanna

Tichy and Devanna (1986) identified a three-stage process that takes place when leaders transform organizations. First, the transformational leader must recognize a need to revitalize and change the organization. This recognition can be difficult, particularly when environmental changes are occurring gradually. The leader needs to convince other important people in the organization of the need for change. Tichy and Devanna (1986) suggested a number of strategies to help key organizational members recognize the need for change: encouraging people to look objectively at the organization and challenge the status quo, encouraging people from the organization to visit other organizations to see how they are managed and operated, evaluating organizational performance against that of competitors (not indicators from previous years), and creating an external network of contacts who can provide an objective assessment of the organization's performance. Once people recognize the need for change, the leader needs to establish what changes are necessary, and manage the transition process. Members of the organization will have to let go of existing values and beliefs and accept new ones, and the authority structure of the organization may change. The leader's job is to help people feel positive and confident about the transition.

One way of helping people feel better about the future is to create a vision of the way they want things to be. Vision is Tichy and Devanna's (1986) second stage. The vision cannot be one individual's ideas but must be the product of a diverse group of organization members. The final stage of the transformational process involves what Tichy and Devanna (1986) refer to as *institutionalizing the vision*. A new group of people committed to the vision may be brought on board, and new structures, strategies, and policies put in place. These changes can be facilitated through such activities as planning workshops, conducting team-building exercises, establishing new positions, changing the reward structure of the organization, and redesigning appraisal systems.

Ulrich (1987) extends Tichy and Devanna's (1986) work and applies it to the field of sport management. He suggests a six-stage process that sport managers need to adopt if they are to function as transformational leaders: creating and communicating the need for change, overcoming resistance to change, making personal commitment and sacrifices for change, articulating a vision, generating commitment to the vision, and institutionalizing the vision. Ulrich makes a number of suggestions as to how sport managers can operationalize these functions.

Before leaving this section on the traditional approaches to leadership, it is worth giving one great example of a leader in sport who demonstrates significant effectiveness: Sir Alex Ferguson. Ferguson was the manager of Manchester United (association) Football Club for 26 seasons and in that period won 13 league titles along with 25 other trophies, a feat many believe will never be matched. In a documentary, *Sir Alex Ferguson: Secrets of Success*, you can watch why Sir Alex was considered by many to be the greatest leader in sports. Hytner (2016) thought his success and ability to win was down to consistency in values and beliefs. Anita Elberse, a Harvard Business School professor featured in the documentary, also provides an in-depth view of Sir Alex in her *Harvard Business Review* article, "Ferguson's Formula." Elberse (2013) suggests that Sir Alex's approach consisted of eight leadership principles, which ranged from the importance of maintaining control over high-performing team members to the importance of observation and the inevitability of change. (See chapter 10 for details about the concept of control, and chapter 18 for more on organizational change.)

Modern Approaches to Leadership: Beyond Idealistic Views of Leaders

The previous section outlines in some detail the various approaches taken to studying and understanding leadership over the past several decades. This research has focused on the leader as more than just central to motivating and encouraging workers. The perception of leaders through focusing on what skills they have and what makes them different from others was that they were almost superhuman. The discourse around the concept of leadership focused on their charisma and unique ability to create effective environments and get work done, and made great effort to identify leadership styles and behavioral traits that were most effective (Oc, 2018). In short, research almost entirely focused on the individual leader. However, major critical views emerged (e.g., Van Dierendonck, 2011), and failure to identify universal leadership traits or styles that lead to effectiveness resulted in researchers suggesting that leaders can do nothing without their followers and that what they can accomplish varies in different situations and cultures. The more critical and modern approaches to leadership therefore recognize that leaders are one piece of the puzzle of an effective organization, and studies of leadership are widening their scope to understand how leadership affects organizations. In this section we explore some recent work in this new direction, discuss how sport management scholars have examined leadership, and provide some thoughts for future research on leadership in sport organizations. For efficiency, we identify a number of systematic and integrative reviews of each of these literatures, which reveal extensive insights into this complex concept.

Avolio et al. (2009) provide an integrative review of the current theories of leadership, noting that the field of leadership studies has evolved from the traditional approaches to focus on more than just the leader and is increasingly more concerned with "followers, peers, supervisors, work setting/context and culture" with greater diversity of public, private, and voluntary organizations examined (Avolio et al., 2009, p. 422). They note that the concept of authenticity has been of interest for a long time but was popularized in the context of leadership by George (2003) and Luthans and Avolio (2003).

From the transformational leadership perspective, a new pillar of leadership research emerged known as *authentic leadership* (Avolio et al., 2009). Authentic leadership studies address some of the most significant criticisms of the leadership literature by including leader, followers, and context in its conceptualization. Authentic leadership can be defined as

> a process that draws from both positive psychological capacities and a highly developed organizational context, which results in both greater self-awareness and self-regulated positive behaviors on the part of leaders and associates, fostering positive self-development (Luthans and Avolio, 2003, p. 243).

Four dimensions are thought to characterize authentic leadership: self-awareness, relational transparency, internalized moral perspective, and balanced processing (Gardner et al., 2005; Ilies et al., 2005). However, these have not been extensively tested or investigated in a variety of contexts and cultural settings or over time. An increasing interest is emerging in the relationship between context and leadership. Oc (2018) provides a systematic review of this line of enquiry, noting that Johns' (2006) categorical framework for context provides a useful heuristic to understand the impact of context on leadership. Johns (2017) provides his own updated thoughts and reflects upon studies that were published since his seminal and award-winning paper on context in organizational research.

Day, Fleenor, Atwater, Sturm, and McKee (2014) reviewed 25 years of leader and leadership development research, published in *Leadership Quarterly*. While this review offers an interesting summation of factors important to developing leaders and to how leaders can be developed within organizations, it is only based on knowledge produced in one journal, so conclusions should be considered limited.

Meuser et al. (2016) provide an interesting network analysis of leadership theory research published in the top 10 journals between 2000 and 2013. Of nearly 300 articles, they found that all articles identified one focal theory, integrated with two or more supporting leadership theories. Forty-nine different leadership approaches were identified, and the six leadership approaches most often appearing as the focal theory were transformational, charismatic, strategic, diversity, participative or shared, and trait approach. Their research suggests that leadership research is increasingly attempting to integrate theoretical perspectives but that the integration of supporting theories is in its infancy. Recognizing that their research is descriptive in nature, they suggest more work is needed using meta-analytic techniques to test competing combinations of leadership approaches in their relation to outcomes or consequences of leadership. Importantly, these authors propose "theoretical neighborhoods" (Meuser et al., 2016, p. 1396) as networks of leadership theories that offer great potential for researchers to develop greater integration of theory rather than creating new theories. This will add further diversity to the research rather than synthesize knowledge, which is a significant need of the current base of understanding.

Critical Leadership Studies

While the previous section highlighted advances in leadership research—including a move to more comprehensive considerations of the concept to consider context, multiple stakeholders, and integration of multiple theories in leadership—critical leadership literature may be the most inspiring avenue of research to emerge to date. Critical Leadership Studies (CLS) was born out of and is closely related to the broader Critical Management Studies (CMS) (Learmonth & Morrell, 2017), which is a diverse set of ideas that seek to reveal, challenge, and overturn power relations in organizational life and are not necessarily concerned with increasing organizational efficiency as a primary driver to knowledge creation (King & Learmonth, 2015). This is highly relevant because in modern industrialized societies, it is often through intangible social structures that people are constrained, dominated, or oppressed in some fashion. And so, CLS is concerned with how leader power and influence emerge in organizations and is attached to formal or informally constituted leaders. It also begs the question whether leaders are empowering or oppressive to certain groups in the way they conduct themselves. This perspective starts to encourage researchers to move away from the view of leaders as inherently "good" and question how broader structures such as gender, class, or race may play a role in shaping leader behavior or whether those structures restrict organization members or groups from progressing under certain leaders.

Learmonth and Morrell (2017) encourage researchers taking a critical perspective on leadership to avoid using the term *follower* in favor of *worker* to at least avoid the hierarchical assumption that leadership is a formal designation. We must also assume that workers may be leaders and may provide resistance to formal management, and this enables more critical discourse of how leadership is enacted in organizations. They suggest that to truly understand leadership perhaps we should focus on those instances where leadership is not imposed, but developed freely and socially as in music bands (Humphreys, Ucbasaran, & Lockett, 2012). Collinson (2017) provides a fascinating response to Learmonth and Morrell's (2017) suggestions by challenging what it is to be critical and encourages exploration of leadership and followers as ambiguous, paradoxical, and contradictory forms. Other debates within critical leadership studies can be found, including Leitch and Stead's (2016) special issue on gender and leadership, which challenges dominant masculinized frameworks and power structures underpinning leadership research.

Leadership Research in Sport Management

Leadership research in sport and the management of sport has been conducted for several decades. Welty Peachey, Zhou, Damon, and Burton (2015) present a systematic review of 40 years of leadership research in sport management, suggesting that progress in the field has been made. However, they suggest that the majority of sport management leadership literature has focused on coaches rather than managers of organizations in different contexts, leader behavior (specifically transformational leadership), and the traditional approaches to understanding leadership. They noted some useful research on gender and leadership and only one paper on race and leadership, with a recommendation for more diversity research including race or ethnicity and gender. Similar to mainstream literature on leadership, Welty Peachey et al. (2015) also recognize the need for multilevel research and provide a conceptual model (and associated propositions) to encourage research in this direction.

Ferkins, Skinner, and Swanson (2018) provide the most recent collection of leadership research to date focused on sport management and organizations. Their special issue, "Sport Leadership: A New Generation of Thinking," builds on the Welty Peachey et al. (2015) review to include systems in the multilevel perspective of leadership as well as the emergence of self-leadership and emotional intelligence concepts to complement developing theories of leadership. Moving beyond leaders as individuals, the special issue includes work by Jones, Wegner, Bunds, Edwards, and Bocarro (2018) demonstrating environmental characteristics of shared leadership in a sport-for-development organization. They demonstrated how the environment contributed to leadership style and highlighted the dynamic, iterative process that leaders performed in this organization context. The special issue offers a considerable advancement in sport management leadership thinking and research with evidence of leadership as constructed and occurring in professional sport, non-Western contexts, gendered perspectives, and sport for development programs.

Growing evidence suggests that sport management scholars are embracing the modern perspectives to leadership. Burton, Welty Peachey, and Wells (2017) discuss how servant leaders in sport are potentially in a good position to foster trust and an ethical climate in sport organizations. The research suggests that through servant leadership, issues of unethical behavior in sport may be addressed and ethical doubts of sport restored by cultivating an ethical climate. Billsberry et al. (2018) engage in discussion of how the social construction of leadership perspective challenges traditional hierarchical perspectives of the concept and suggests leadership can be practiced by anyone, anywhere, anytime. However, this may not be helpful in trying to synthesize and evaluate our understanding of leadership because it suggests that leadership is different according to each individual perception. This view contains the same narrow lens of leadership that the traditional theories held but in the opposite philosophical direction. Traditional theories were primarily positivistic, whereas more modern theories are essentially constructionist or interpretivist. Leadership research in sport management has yet to produce a more critical view such as Critical Realism, which accepts both positivist and interpretivist ontological views of reality. This would mean that leadership exists whether we can see it or not. Different interpretations exist of leaders and their impacts, but research has yet to fully identify why leaders are effective. Critical Realism could significantly address this problem because it attributes differences in society and in causal relationships to deeper social structures such as gender, race, and ethnicity. It is a challenging methodology but one that would make a significant contribution to resolving some of the complimentary and contradictory assertions in leadership research.

Overall, sport management scholars have been heavily engaged in leadership research and moved away from traditional approaches to more modern perspectives that see leadership as a multidimensional construct. (We still see some focus on traditional approaches, however. See, for example, Mills and Boardley, 2016.) However, two problems can be seen in sport management research on leadership. First, there is little movement beyond focusing on what leadership is, and continuously debating different forms, types, or styles of leadership is a rather fruitless exercise (Alvesson & Spicer, 2012). Second, knowledge of leadership has not moved into understanding the relationships between the many facets and types of leadership in the modern approaches, so we cannot answer with certainty yet why leaders are effective or in what contexts leaders should behave in what ways. Developing effective sport management leaders is therefore still very much a challenge. Some suggestions for research that would help develop our understanding of leadership in sport are now presented.

Critical Management and Leadership

Frisby (2005) has argued that sport management research should use a critical perspective. The argument can especially be made for leadership research. Alvesson and Deetz (2000) can be of help here by providing a framework of three overlapping tasks. First, the task of insight refers to examining and questioning taken-for-granted knowledge by focusing on "the complex relationships between local forms of domination and the broader contexts in which they are situated" (Frisby, 2005, p. 7) such as values, rules and policies, culture, and reward systems. Once this is known, the second task, critique, can occur, focusing on understanding how the various forms of domination (e.g., differences in power, information, and communication) benefit one group over another. Finally, the third task, transformative redefinition, is a description of how to change the situation—a task especially appealing to managers because it can provide new skills that can help the manager become a better leader. Leadership literature would greatly benefit from a using a critical perspective.

More research driven from the CMS literature would also aid in understanding power, oppression, and exploitation in sport leadership. Ryan and Dickson (2018) provide an excellent start to this journey by suggesting that as sport influences and is influenced by inequalities of gender, class, age, and race, it is an ideal context in which to study the underpinning nuances of what is normalized when it comes to men and the masculine subtext of leadership. They use a reflexive multilevel model to examine sport leadership in New Zealand, specifically how sport contributes to the gendering of leadership.

Leadership and Organizational Change

Linking leadership and organizational change is in many ways an obvious area for study. Leaders, after all, are supposed to direct and manage change in organizations. They mediate between the internal forces that promote stability and the external pressures that demand change if the organization is going to remain competitive. Despite these obvious linkages, little attempt has been made to look at the relationship between leadership and change within the broader field of organization studies, and even less in the field of sport management. The exception is the work of Tushman and his colleagues (Nadler & Tushman, 1990; Tushman & Romanelli, 1985; Tushman, Virany, & Romanelli, 1986). In their 1985 and 1986 articles Tushman and his colleagues argued that organizations change by going through convergent periods or by experiencing what are called *strategic reorientations* or *re-creations*. Convergent periods are times when the organization exhibits incremental change, or what Miller and Friesen (1984) call *evolutionary change*. During these relatively long periods, organizations elaborate on their strategic focus. In contrast, strategic reorientations, or re-creations, may involve changes in strategy, power, and structure, and are triggered by contextual pressures (Tushman & Romanelli, 1985). Different types of leadership are required in convergent periods from those required in re-creations: "During convergent periods executive leadership emphasizes symbolic activities and incremental change, while during recreations, executive leadership engages in major substantive as well as symbolic activities. Beyond these substantive and symbolic behaviors, executive leadership must also choose to initiate recreations" (Tushman & Romanelli, 1985, p. 214). The paradox for leaders, as Tushman and Romanelli go on to argue, is to "encourage inertial forces during convergent periods" and, when necessary, to "initiate and implement reorientations" (p. 214).

In their later work, Nadler and Tushman (1990) extend these ideas to deal with the notion of charismatic leadership. They suggest that in large-scale changes, leaders in the senior management team must drive the change process. While charismatic leadership is important in these kinds of changes, it is not enough on its own. "Charismatic leadership must be bolstered by instrumental leadership; [leaders must] build strong teams, systems, and management processes to leverage and add substance to [their] vision and energy" (Nadler & Tushman, 1990, p. 94). They must also work to institutionalize change at all levels of the management system.

Leadership and Strategy

While strategy and leadership are two central topics in the study of organizations, little consideration has been given to how these concepts are related. For some, leadership is merely the personification of an organization's strategy. However, as Leavy and Wilson (1994, p. 2) note, "the leader is just one important element in . . . strategy formulation. History and context are the other two." The interactions of these three factors in shaping an organization's strategy and growth are important considerations to pursue in sport management; researchers in our field have never empirically examined these interactions when trying to understand sport organizations. Detailed case studies that examined sport managers as leaders would help show how contextual features have influenced their actions. In addition to helping bring social, political, and economic factors into an understanding of leadership choices, work of this nature would also make clear the symbolic nature of leadership because it would direct our attention to whether the role of the leader is in fact substantive or merely symbolic. Finally, as Leavy and Wilson (1994, p. 186) point out, research that incorporated history and context with the study of leadership would "avoid the danger of developing an overly heroic and somewhat mythological view of these rare and important individuals."

The actions of sport leaders such as Peter Ueberroth, Marvin Miller, Sylvia Rempel, and David Stern could all be studied by linking their actions to the historical conditions of their respective organizations and the contexts in which they operate. This type of research would help show how strategy formulation is at times shaped by the autonomous choices made by individual leaders, but in other instances is more a product of opportunities and threats in an organization's context. Such studies would also demonstrate how leaders respond to contextual pressures and, as such, why sometimes they are effective and at other times they fail.

Leadership and Gender

Contemporary leadership theory has progressed from traditional masculine constructs to draw upon more feminist viewpoints (Fletcher, 2004). However, Leitch and Stead (2016) contend that the masculine/feminine dichotomy, in which the male is regarded as the universal neutral subject by which the female is judged, is still evident. Chapter 11 of this textbook highlights the underrepresentation of women in leadership positions in sport. Women's underrepresentation in leadership positions has been attributed in the general field of organizational studies to the internal and external barriers that women face in progressing to the senior levels of an organization (Cockburn, 1991; Powell, 1993; Terborg, 1977; Wentworth & Anderson, 1984). Hall, Cullen, and Slack (1989) and Hovden (2000) have identified the presence of similar barriers in sport organizations.

Leadership and Organizational Culture

Leaders play an important role in creating and transmitting an organization's culture. Founders, as leaders, are important in shaping culture because, as Schein (1992, p. 211) points out, they "not only choose the basic mission and the environmental context in which the new group will operate, but they choose the group members and bias the original responses that the group makes in its efforts to succeed in its environment and to integrate itself."

Leaders also play a role in embedding and transmitting the culture of an organization. At different stages of an organization's life cycle, the leader's

KEY ISSUES FOR SPORT MANAGERS

Although the study of leadership is fraught with difficulty, sport managers may consider the task as less problematic. Despite the endless amount of research and the criticisms of what is known, unknown, and undecided, we can take away some broad factors from this chapter that will help sport managers navigate their leadership role. First, leadership can be formal or informal. Just because you are the manager does not mean your employees or volunteers will feel you are their leader. Research has shown that leadership can be informal or socially constructed, meaning that individuals and groups can define and choose who is leading and what leadership means to them. Sport managers should consider their leadership qualities and style and should recognize that it is related to organizational structures and cultures but also to wider social structures, powers, and ideological beliefs. Managers who value leadership should educate themselves on mainstream management literature and what is being produced in the context of sport without relying on it for the all-encompassing solution to organization effectiveness. Many other factors and determinants exist, as evidenced by each chapter of this book.

role in managing culture takes on different forms. In its early years, culture is a force for growth; it needs to be developed and clearly articulated. Later on, as diverse subcultures form within an organization, the leader is faced with managing these subcultures by using the techniques outlined previously. When an organization reaches maturity, its culture can ensure smooth operations, but if it is not appropriate for the situation in which the organization finds itself, it can become dysfunctional. To counter this, a major internal upheaval or external crisis may be needed to change the culture to a more appropriate one. The leader plays an important role in managing this process.

Summary and Conclusions

Some researchers have suggested that leadership is a major factor in producing an effective organization (Peters & Waterman, 1982); others have been less optimistic (Pfeffer, 1977). While organizational literature displays extensive study of the topic of leadership, the question remains: Does it tell us anything? Alvesson (2017) recently suggested eight fundamental problems with our understanding and scholarly pursuit of leadership, which sport management scholars should take into consideration.

In terms of sport management, the flow of leadership literature has been relatively consistent, much of it demonstrating many of the criticisms leveled at leadership research generally. We have also seen a very recent surge of attention to leadership with systematic reviews and multilevel conceptual approaches to guide empirical analysis. We have yet to fully engage with the mainstream management's critical perspectives of leadership, and while a positive approach that attempts to figure out what constitutes leadership (by expanding our view to multidimensional) is one possibility, it also falls into the trap identified by Alvesson (2017) as inclusive of everything. He notes there is no easy solution to any of this, although he does make several thought-provoking suggestions.

In this chapter, we have reviewed the major traditional and modern or critical perspectives on leadership. Some of the criticisms of leadership research were also examined, and five potentially fruitful areas for future research were briefly outlined. While not the only areas for possible study, work on the topics suggested would help link leadership to other organizational phenomena and, given the often-abstract nature of leadership studies, would be a welcome addition to the literature. Also, studies of the type outlined would challenge the highly voluntaristic and overly rational conceptions of leadership that have pervaded the field. While we should retain a healthy skepticism about the ability of leaders as sole creators of an organization's structure and processes, we cannot ignore the role that these senior members of an organization play in integrating and directing a sport organization.

Review Questions

1. Do you think men and women exhibit similar leadership traits? Why or why not?
2. What is the relationship between leadership, organizational culture, and performance?

3. What can different approaches (traditional, modern, and critical) to understanding leadership do to help sport managers?
4. How does the research on leadership in sport management differ from the focus of mainstream management and organization studies? Using the content of this chapter, discuss why Sir Alex Ferguson is a great leader.

Suggestions for Further Reading

If you are interested in furthering your knowledge in the area of leadership, you are advised to look at the original writings of the key theorists whose works are outlined in this chapter. Some early works on leadership include Burns' (1978) book *Leadership*, Bryman's two texts *Leadership and Organizations* (1986) and *Charisma and Leadership in Organizations* (1992). McCall and Lombardo's (1978) *Leadership: Where Else Can We Go?* is a collection of essays by leading organizational theorists, people who have not necessarily focused on the topic of leadership but who attempt to answer the question in the book's title.

For an overview of traditional and critical approaches to studying leadership, see Schedlitzki & Edwards' (2017) *Studying Leadership: Traditional and Critical Approaches*. Also of relevance here is Tourish's (2013) book, *The Dark Side of Transformational Leadership*

Leavy and Wilson's (1994) *Strategy and Leadership*; Pettigrew's (1987) *Journal of Management Studies* article, "Context and Action in the Transformation of the Firm"; and Hendry and Johnson's (1993) book, *Strategic Thinking: Leadership and the Management of Change*, are insightful readings on the topic of leadership and change. In terms of leadership and gender, Calas and Smircich's (1991) article "Voicing Seduction to Silence Leadership" is a difficult but interesting read. Alimo-Metcalfe's (1994) strangely titled "Waiting for Fish to Grow Feet!" is also helpful, as is Rosener's (1990) more practical *Harvard Business Review* article, "Ways Women Lead." For those interested in culture and leadership, Schein's (1985) *Organizational Culture and Leadership* is a must. Also interesting is Bass and Avolio's (1990c) article, "Transformational Leadership and Organizational Culture." More recently, readers may examine Bowers, Hall, and Srinivasan's (2017) article on organization culture and leadership style in crisis management.

Early work on leadership in the field of sport management has been produced by Chelladurai and colleagues (Chelladurai & Carron, 1983; Chelladurai & Saleh, 1978, 1980; Chelladurai et al., 1987b). However, much of this work focuses on coaches, not on people in managerial positions in sport organizations. Inglis (1997) and Kent and Weese (2000) focused on executive leadership within sport management. Most recently, Welty Peachey et al. (2015) presented a systematic review of four decades of research on leadership in sport management and set forth a multilevel conceptual model to encourage more complex theories of leadership in sport management. Readers should also see the special issue in the *Journal of Sport Management* (Ferkins, Skinner, & Swanson, 2018, p. 77), which contains research that represents "a new generation of thinking" on leadership in sport management. This collection is focused on leadership as shared and multidimensional.

For a critical perspective of leadership studies, see Wilson's (2016) *Thinking Differently About Leadership: A Critical History of Leadership Studies*. Also recently published by a top management scholar is Alvesson's (2017) *Waiting for Godot: Eight Major Problems in the Odd Field of Leadership Studies*.

Case for Analysis

Bringing International Sport Federations Into the New Millennium: Women in Leadership Roles

Warrick (2017) contends that organizational culture is an essential component of organizational success and that effective cultures occur, to a large extent, due to effective leadership. In July 1980 Juan Antonio Samaranch became the president of the International Olympic Committee (IOC) on the first round of votes. Besides this almost unheard-of accomplishment, he managed to have his chosen executive committee members elected—and in a predetermined order—even though it was a secret ballot (Pound, 2004).

Before becoming president of the IOC, Samaranch had been the president of the Spanish Olympic Committee and a *chef de mission* (person in charge of a national team at international competition) for Spain's Olympic team. He had served as a minor governmental official under the Franco regime and then became Spain's ambassador to the Soviet Union.

His predecessor, Ireland's Lord Killanin, had been a softer and agreeable man who used a kitchen-table approach to his part-time presidency of the IOC. However, the complex international issues that faced the IOC in the 1970s (e.g., the Munich Olympic hostage crisis, Olympic boycotts) required a tougher hand at the helm. Enter Samaranch.

He was perceived to possess excellent organizational skills, a strong work ethic, and a lot of ambition. He worked behind the scenes of the IOC, never making waves or getting involved in problematic issues. He built alliances by attending all major Olympic gatherings of the various committees and "working the room," and he studiously avoided offending anyone while steadily building support for his potential candidacy as president. Samaranch understood politics and his organization's current and potential upper and lower limits.

Despite his manipulative style and the scandals that plagued the IOC near the end of Samaranch's turn as president, when he stepped down in 2001, he had achieved his vision for the IOC. However, new challenges now face the IOC and the integrity of sport itself. From 2000 until current day, the sport environment has changed significantly with increasing corruption, economic downturns, rising awareness of equality and diversity issues in sport organizations, as well as shifts in structures and business models of many sport organizations in an attempt to remain competitive and, in some cases, survive. The IOC, and arguably many other international sport federations, is no exception. In 2016 The Institute for Diversity and Ethics in Sport published the *Gender Report Card: 2016 International Sports Report Card on Women Leadership Roles in Sport* (Lapchick, 2016) in which they reported findings of a review of approximately 8,500 international sport federations. They concluded that the leadership of international sport is almost exclusively the domain of men. Furthermore, while the IOC claims to support women in sport at every level from athletes to managerial positions in international sport, the evidence does not support or demonstrate any meaningful progress in this regard. It has been demonstrated that gender balance improves governance, making the case for men and women sharing decision-making power, yet women still face significant barriers in sport management and governance.

Questions

1. How do you think men and women's leadership style may differ, or do you believe they do not differ? Explain your answer.
2. What research evidence is there that gender equality increases the effectiveness of sport governance and board performance?
3. What role do you think leadership plays in the organizational reality presented in the case?
4. What other factors aside from leadership are significant to understanding the facts of the case?

PART IV

CONTEMPORARY ISSUES IN SPORT ORGANIZATIONS

This final part of the book features several new chapters. The chapters highlight a number of emergent issues that sport managers should be aware of to effectively and progressively manage sport organizations. Three of the chapters are written by experts from outside the field of sport management. The authors have imparted their knowledge to demonstrate how we can learn from these broader contemporary issues to help contribute to the continued development of the sport management field, as Trevor always strived (and succeeded) to accomplish.

Chapter 20, a new chapter for the book written by Meghan Thurston, Jon Arcelus, and Alex Thurston, introduces the topic of mental health difficulties and how they manifest within a sport environment, and the authors recommend management strategies to deal with these situations. Chapter 21, revised and updated by Andy Miah, deals with technology. Although a technology chapter was included in the 2nd edition, that was over 10 years ago, and with the rate of the technological advances during that that period, a significant portion of the chapter is new. The way in which we organize and consume sport has seen a drastic shift. After considering traditional technologies and the relationship to organizational structure, microelectronic technologies are then discussed. Chapter 22, another new chapter written by Bill Gerrard, considers the nature of sport analytics as the use of statistical analysis to support decision making in sport organizations, placing specific emphasis on decisions related to the sporting performance of teams.

Chapter 23, written by Christos Anagnostopoulos and Jonathan Robertson, offers insight into Corporate Social Responsibility (CSR) in the context of sport organizations. CSR has now become a hotly debated issue in the study of organizations in general and professional sport teams in particular. In this new chapter, CSR is looked at from a historical, theoretical, and level-based perspective to offer sport managers and researchers a thorough understanding of how CSR is enacted and managed, as well as revealing the challenges for managers in doing so.

Finally, chapter 24, a new chapter written by Sue Arrowsmith, explains the importance of procurement to sport organizations, including for major events, provision of community sport facilities, and the running of sport federations; this is important because procurement is a neglected area of study in the field of sport. As she explains, managers in sport organizations need to understand procurement not only because it is crucial to ensuring that infrastructure, goods, and services are available on time and without exorbitant cost, but because of its relevance to CSR goals and to the need to avoid corruption and other reputation-damaging scandals. This chapter also illustrates the importance of a multidisciplinary perspective for studying sport organizations, highlighting, for example, the importance of scholarship in law, economics, and management. This new chapter is particularly timely in view of the emphasis on procurement in the work of the International Partnership against Corruption in Sport, and also links closely to the new governance and CSR chapters.

CHAPTER 20

Mental Health and Sport Organizations

Meghan Thurston, DClin Psy, PhD
Jon Arcelus, LMS, GP(T), FRCPsych, PhD
Alex Thurston, PhD

Learning Objectives

When you have read this chapter, you should be able to

1. explain what is meant by the term *mental health*,
2. understand what factors are involved in the development of a mental health difficulty,
3. understand what the most prevalent mental health difficulties are in sport and how they manifest,
4. understand how mental health difficulties are assessed and treated, and
5. understand how to manage mental health difficulties within a sport organization.

Key Concepts

anxiety
biological factors
body dysmorphia
depression
Diagnostic and Statistical Manual of Mental Disorders
disordered eating
epidemiology
etiology
identification
International Statistical Classification of Diseases and Related Health Problems
low mood
management of mental health difficulties
medication
mental health
mental health professionals

(continued)

Key Concepts *(continued)*

motivational enhancement	psychological factors	substance misuse
nonsuicidal self-injury	psychological therapy	support and management
precipitating factors	social factors	transtheoretical model

Addressing Mental Health in Sport: Team Canada's Game Plan

In late 2015 the Canadian Olympic Committee announced the launch of their Game Plan initiative. Game Plan is a program that aims to provide resources to athletes to support them beyond competition and is a collaboration between the Canadian Olympic Committee, Canadian Paralympic Committee, Canadian Olympic and Paralympic Sport Institute Network (COPSIN), Sport Canada, Deloitte, and Morneau Shepell (a consultancy firm specializing in workplace mental health). Game Plan's mission is to serve as "Canada's total athlete wellness program that strives to support national team athletes to live better and more holistic lives" (Game Plan, n.d.). Within the program are five key areas that have been identified as domains athletes may require support in: career management; networking; education; skill development; and health, with an overall emphasis on total wellness. Mental health has been highlighted as a significant area of concern. The program ensures that athletes will have access to mental health support whenever and wherever they require it. Sport organizations and athletes, such as four-time women's Olympic ice hockey gold medalist Hayley Wickenheiser have praised Game Plan, saying it "couldn't come soon enough" (Hossain, 2015). Since the launch, Canadian athletes have reflected on their mental health experiences, and many have spoken highly of the benefits Game Plan will bring to current and future Olympians. And it is not just sport organizations in Canada paying attention to mental health; sport organizations all around the world are introducing similar initiatives. For example, in 2018 UK Sport (the government's high-performance sport agency) and the English Institute of Sport (a provider of sport science and medical services) launched a new strategy that introduces various "measures to facilitate a positive mental health environment across the Olympic and Paralympic sport system" (UK Sport, 2018, para. 1).

The Game Plan initiative discussed in the opening scenario highlights the interplay between mental health, sport, and the involvement of managers and organizations when supporting athletes. This chapter provides an introduction to the topic of mental health in sport.

Although this chapter focuses on (primarily) elite athletes, anyone is susceptible to experiencing mental health difficulties. The chapter references evidence-based sources (e.g., journal articles, autobiographies, and official press releases), and so the focus is typically on (sometimes retired) elite athletes, as these are more commonly written about. Those individuals supporting athletes at any level (e.g., sport managers, including those of sport organizations that are not athlete-based such as sporting goods retailers, manufacturers, or sport organizing committees) need to be familiar with factors associated with mental health difficulties (for example, predisposing and precipitating factors—terms we explain later in this chapter), to help with early identification and to implement relevant management strategies as applicable.

An Introduction to Mental Health

What do we mean when we use the phrase **mental health**? Numerous terms are used synonymously in the field of mental health to describe emotional well-being. It is important to distinguish between them and clarify what they mean. Following are definitions of the more commonly used terms by mental health professionals and in healthcare settings.

- *Psychological well-being*: This is a multifaceted construct that encompasses affective aspects of personal experience (Warr, 1978). It includes, but is not limited to, an absence of mental health difficulty or psychiatric disorder and a good quality of life (Jahoda, 1958).

- *Mental health*: This is a state of well-being in which an individual realizes his or her potential, can cope with everyday stresses, work productively, and able to contribute to his or her community (WHO, 1992). The definition of mental health may vary according to culture.
- *Mental health problem or difficulty*: This can be described as a change in functioning in relationships, mood, behavior, or a development that may arise from any number of congenital, environmental, family, or illness-related factors. The factors include diagnosable mental health or psychiatric disorders, which are more severe and/or persistent (Health Advisory Service, 1995).
- *Mental disorder*: The term *mental disorder* is defined in the latest *Diagnostic and Statistical Manual of Mental Disorders*, 5th edition (DSM-5) as:

> a syndrome characterized by clinically significant disturbance in an individual's cognition, emotion regulation, or behavior that reflects a dysfunction in the psychological, biological, or developmental processes underlying mental functioning. Mental disorders are usually associated with significant distress or disability in social, occupational, or other important activities. An expectable or culturally approved response to a common stressor or loss, such as the death of a loved one, is not a mental disorder. (APA, 2013, p. 20)

Throughout this chapter we will use the term *mental health difficulty* to represent any mental or psychological concerns. The examples used are mainly of high-profile athletes because they are the most visible in the media and well known, but this does not exclude mental health difficulties occurring in an athlete at any level (e.g., at school or as a member of a voluntary sport club) or other individuals involved in sport.

It is important to introduce the idea that mental health exists on a continuum (Keyes, 2002). Mental health as a concept is subjective and needs to be conceptualized on a personal basis. We all experience mental health, positive and negative, and this naturally fluctuates; mental health is not static. Certain triggers may cause our mental health to vary; this is not necessarily of concern. What is of concern is the extremity of our reaction and how prolonged this is. When considering the information presented in this chapter it is essential to understand and appreciate this philosophy.

Classification Systems

Classification in mental health constitutes a means of ordering information, applying standard criteria, and providing a common language (Rutter, Shaffer, & Shepherd, 1975). The field of mental health uses two major classification systems:

1. **International Statistical Classification of Diseases and Related Health Problems**, often referred to by its short-form name, the *International Classification of Diseases* (ICD), currently in the 11th edition (WHO, 2018)
2. The **Diagnostic and Statistical Manual of Mental Disorders** (DSM), currently in the 5th edition (APA, 2013)

The classification systems and diagnostic criteria used by health professionals are constantly being updated as the understanding of illnesses and disorders increase. There are some differences and similarities between both classification systems, with the DSM being the most commonly used classification system in academia.

Factors That Contribute to Mental Health Difficulties in Sport

Certain mental health difficulties are not uncommon in the general population and in some cases, are found to be more prevalent among athletes. This section aims to outline sport-related factors that influence the manifestation of mental health difficulties.

Epidemiology

Epidemiology is the study of identifying why diseases occur in different groups of people, the incidence, and strategies for possible control. Therefore, epidemiological studies allow us to identify the frequency of certain difficulties in a specific population. The World Health Organization (WHO) reports that in the general population, one in four people are affected by mental health difficulties (WHO, 2003). However, studies investigating how common certain mental health difficulties are in athletes provide conflicting results. Variability occurs as a consequence of the population or specific mental health difficulty being studied. For example, gender influences the prevalence of eating disorders. Studies have found in the general population eating disorders occur in approximately 9 percent of females and less than 1 percent in males (Hoek & van Hoeken, 2003; Preti et al., 2009); in an elite athlete population these figures are significantly higher, with nearly a quarter (20 percent) of females and 8 percent of males identifying as having an eating disorder (Sundgot-Borgen & Torstveit, 2004). Furthermore, there is enormous variation across particular sports; within aesthetic sports such as gymnastics 42 percent of females were found to suffer from an eating disorder in contrast to 16 percent in ball games such as association football (Sundgot-Borgen & Torstveit, 2004). In comparison, 18 percent of male athletes in weight-class sports such as Judo were found to suffer from an eating disorder in contrast to 4 percent in technical sports such as golf (Sundgot-Borgen & Torstveit, 2004). These studies illustrate the complexity in providing overall prevalence rates but also highlight the relationship between specific mental health difficulties and sport.

Etiology

Etiology is the study of what factors contribute to the onset of certain disorders. Mental health difficulties are typically seen as having multifactorial origins with complex interactions between factors that make an individual vulnerable to the development of a mental health difficulty. It is important to emphasize that sport in isolation does not cause a mental health difficulty—in fact, in some circumstances, sport and exercise are recommended interventions for **low mood**—however, certain factors are specific to sport that may influence the development of certain mental health difficulties. We will first look at factors that apply to the general population and then specific sport factors.

Predisposing Factors in the General Population

Athletes are susceptible to the development of mental health difficulties for the same reasons as anyone else. **Biological factors** are one of the risk factors for the development of physical health conditions; research also implicates biological factors in the development of mental health difficulties. Biological factors may include genetic vulnerabilities, physical illness, disability, and our immunity.

For example, the children of parents that suffer from mental health difficulties (e.g., **depression**) are at a higher risk of developing depression themselves. **Social factors** that emphasize the influence of social interaction and the environment (e.g., social support, relationships, cultural beliefs, socioeconomic status) also affect the development of a mental health difficulty. For example, learning unhelpful coping skills in early childhood or growing up in an abusive environment may influence how we react to stressful events later in life. Other important factors to consider are psychological factors, which include personality, emotions, learning, memory, beliefs, and attitudes. These factors can influence how we cope with stresses and worries. Some individuals may share their thoughts and emotions with others and externalize their stresses and worries; others may internalize and engage in unhelpful coping strategies such as using substances, food, or self-harm. We have greater effect over some factors (biological, social, and psychological), but it is the combined influence and interaction between these factors that determines our mental health.

Predisposing Factors in the Sport-Specific Population

Sport-specific factors have been shown to put an individual at risk of developing a mental health difficulty. Some of the more prominent factors will now be discussed.

The Sport Environment The setting and atmosphere in sport can be associated with certain narratives and dynamics. For example, team sports such as association football have been linked with attitudes such as machismo, racism, and homophobia. Consequently, Let's Kick Racism Out of Football was launched in 1993 in the English Premier League (EPL). Since the campaign's inception, Kick it Out has developed to become association football's equality and inclusion organization, which aims to tackle all forms of discrimination. Camaraderie and rivalry are natural in both team and individual sports. It is important, to an extent, to foster a competitive atmosphere and drive in order to succeed. This can also become detrimental and cause rifts between fellow athletes, coaches, and managers. Being so closely involved with others inevitably can cause clashes of personality, particularly if there is contention about achievement, roles, or goals. Consequently, the individuals and setting that make up the sporting environment can influence the potential for mental health difficulties.

Celebrity Status Some athletes acquire (wanted or not) a celebrity status. Some prominent examples of famous sporting icons who have experienced mental health difficulties include Dame Kelly Holmes, Susie O'Neill, and Michael Phelps. An unsatisfactory performance may cause damaging and very public consequences, not least the detrimental effect to their (and their team's) reputation but also the potential loss of sponsorship deals and income. Being in the spotlight and a pressure to promote the sport through endorsement and sponsorship deals means the athlete is thrown into the fame atmosphere, whether he or she wanted this attention; with this can come a potential impact to the athlete's mental health. It is not difficult to imagine that celebrity status, even on the local level, could affect athletes in local and regional sport organizations as well.

Policy Some national governing bodies (NGBs), national sport organizations (NSOs), and sport federations set tough major competition medal targets for their athletes. Not achieving these targets can mean life-changing consequences for the individual such as being dropped from an elite program and losing up to 100 percent funding (for athletes and even a sport). In the United Kingdom, for example, there has been debate about the "no compromise" policy adopted by UK Sport in an effort to win Olympic and Paralympic medals (i.e., funding directed to sports that the organization felt had realistic chances of winning medals, and funding reduced or removed from sports that did not previously achieve targets). This cutthroat policy added increased pressures on elite athletes to perform, and it has been suggested that it has had an impact on the mental health of many athletes (BBC News, 2017a).

Sport Clothing Sport clothing can be a risk factor for the development of mental health difficulties. Revealing attire, especially in an environment of competitive thinness and aesthetic evaluations, can affect the athlete's view about his or her self. This may be particularly important for females, which is why Sport England (a non-departmental public body under the Department for Digital, Culture, Media and Sport) developed the This Girl Can campaign in 2015. The aim is to promote female sport participation "no matter how well they do it, how they look or even how red their face gets" (This Girl Can, n.d.) because many women feel self-conscious and experience reduced self-esteem when wearing sportswear. Claims of sexism surrounding sport clothing have also surfaced. For example, in 2015 it was suggested that the Manchester United women's replica home jersey's V-neck was too deep (in comparison to the men's kit), and controversy has brewed about logo placement on female tennis players' breasts. Sport clothing, as illustrated by these examples, can make athletes more body conscious and aware, and potentially contribute to the development of a mental health difficulty.

Weight Restrictions Certain sports require athletes to fall within a certain weight category in order for them to be able to participate, for example, boxing, mixed martial arts, rowing, weightlifting, judo, wrestling, and jockeying. In order to achieve the desired weight, athletes often engage in risky behavior such as food or fluid restrictions. This has implications for performance because by following any restricted eating an athlete's body would not be in peak form during the competition. The impact of this behavior on the athletes' mental health is further expanded in the "Eating Disorders and Disordered Eating" section later in this chapter.

TIME OUT

Sport as An Identity

Sport has many positive benefits, and it is important to recognize and acknowledge them. Evidence shows that exercise can help the regulation of mood and negative emotions (Berger, 2000). The routine, working towards a goal, involvement with peers, and a social structure can facilitate positive mental health (Paxton, Motl, Aylward, & Nigg, 2010). However, an individual's sense of identity has the potential to become enmeshed entirely with sport and any associated achievements. If day-to-day activity is exclusively dominated by sport and an athlete lacks other key social activities, this can become problematic. In particular, if sport is the sole coping mechanism for negative emotions, levels of self-esteem become interlinked with success. This occurs at the expense of involvement in other activities or relationships and an unhelpful vicious circle can develop. In fact, Newman, Howells, and Fletcher (2016), using narrative analysis, examined the autobiographies of 12 elite athletes. The authors found that involvement in sport initially served as a coping mechanism for mental health symptoms; however, when the demands of sport and performing became overwhelming, this exacerbated mental health symptoms. This study highlights the delicate interplay between sport and our psychological well-being. Furthermore, upon retirement, many elite athletes suffer mental health difficulties because they lose their identity and the structure or routine to their life. As a result, these individuals often face unemployment or feel a sense of underappreciation, which can lead to mental health difficulties. Runner Iwan Thomas and cyclist Victoria Pendleton have suffered with mental health difficulties following retirement from their respective sports (Sirrell, 2018).

TIME OUT

The Starter Pistol

We can use a starter pistol as an analogy for the development of a mental health difficulty. The combination of the general predisposing factors (biological, social, or psychological) load the starter pistol, the sport-related predisposing factors are the powder, and the precipitating event is the trigger. All of these are necessary for the development of a mental health difficulty. For example, an athlete with a perfectionistic personality, training in a competitive sporting environment but with no precipitating event may not develop a mental health difficulty. Also, an athlete that has developed useful coping skills, despite suffering an injury (precipitating event), may not develop a mental health difficulty.

We will illustrate this with an example: Dame Kelly Holmes has publicly discussed her depression. Although we do not have detailed information, nor is it our aim to analyze her family background, we know she is hardworking and competitive. These predisposing factors helped her become a successful athlete but also made her vulnerable to the development of a mental health difficulty. Training for the Olympics meant certain pressures to perform and from the media were placed on her. Leading up to the Olympics, she suffered multiple injuries (the precipitating event). She described "not wanting to go through all the pressures and strains of being injured and wanting to achieve the best I could as an athlete really got on top of me. Basically, it led to depression and self-harm" (Mills, 2018).

Precipitating Factors

As outlined, certain predisposing factors put us at risk for the development of a mental health difficulty, some of which are specific to sport. However, mental health difficulties do not develop without **precipitating factors**, also called a *trigger*. A trigger is typically an event that occurs prior to the onset of a mental health difficulty. How an athlete deals with this event and what his or her coping mechanisms are is fundamental to the development of a mental health difficulty and why not every athlete will develop one.

An example of a sport-related trigger might be an injury. Due to the intense demands athletes place on their bodies they are often at risk of developing health conditions (Ljungqvist et al., 2009). A significant condition may cause injury or force an athlete to take a break, having a catastrophic impact on the athlete's ability to continue in sport. Another example is physical burnout due to the extreme levels of exercise and pressure placed on an athlete's body, forcing the athlete to retire (Creswell & Eklund, 2007). Also, failing to achieve tough medal target policies, as discussed earlier, is another example of a trigger. These are some examples of sport-related instances that have the potential to prompt the development of a mental health difficulty, and the sport system needs to be aware of this. However, if an athlete has useful coping skills, not related to sport, and is able to overcome a setback such as an injury, he or she has the potential to harness this experience and return to sport in an even stronger position (Fletcher & Sarkar, 2012, 2013; Sarkar & Fletcher, 2014).

Mental Health Difficulties

Because this chapter aims to describe mental health difficulties in the field of sport, only the most prevalent mental health difficulties will be reviewed.

Depression

Individuals that experience depression, experience low mood and feel this way for the majority of the day, nearly every day. The severity and duration is the difference between experiencing an expected reaction to a distressing event, such as not winning a match, and whether the individual is suffering from depression. This can be indicated by a subjective account, for example, the individual reports feeling sad, empty, or has an irritable mood. In addition, individuals may experience other symptoms such as lack of interest in activities, weight changes, struggling to sleep, lack of energy, thoughts of worthlessness, struggling to concentrate, and potentially suicidal ideation.

Our mood naturally fluctuates, which is healthy, and periods of low mood are a natural response to distressing situations. When participating in sport, however, situations may occur that cause an overwhelming sense of low mood. The pressure to accomplish a goal, be it winning a race, maintaining a certain ranking position, ensuring funding or sponsorship continues, or being selected for the squad, can be tremendous. A desire to achieve can become a burden to perform, and failure to do so can affect the athlete's self-esteem. The ambition to succeed may never be fulfilled or the opportunity never arise to demonstrate such abilities, leaving the athlete feeling a sense of emptiness, worthlessness, and loss. These events in isolation do not cause low mood, and it is healthy and expected that an athlete may experience low mood when they occur. Coaches and managers need to be aware of the risk factors and the potential for depression to develop.

An example is Olympian Clara Hughes, who has openly discussed her struggle with low mood and depression. Hughes has successfully achieved podium status at both the winter and summer Olympic Games and has publicly disclosed how feelings of happiness and fulfillment faded following these achievements. Hughes attributes her low mood to a lack of appropriate outlet to discuss her emotions: "Nobody talked about it, nobody talked about being depressed." Hughes struggled for a long period before seeking professional support (McEwen, 2012).

In some cases, depression can be so overwhelming that the athlete may experience suicidal ideation. Suicidal behavior is defined as engaging in any behavior that could cause an individual to die. This could be thoughts or plans about how the athlete would commit suicide, for example, storing pills to use for an overdose. This is often but not always in conjunction with low mood and depression.

For example, Welsh international rugby union player Gareth Thomas has suffered several episodes of depression and suicide attempts. He disclosed his sexual orientation to the sporting environment. He was well received and applauded by the Toulouse teammates, but opposition fans subsequently shouted homophobic abuse during rugby matches. In this example, although sport organizations have attempted to reduce homophobia within their respective sports, they are far from creating a safe atmosphere, often due to spectators. He acknowledged experiencing suicidal ideation and has attempted to kill himself (Thomas, 2014). Unfortunately, homosexuality in male professional sports is seen as one of the final taboos and is the reason many sportsmen wait until retirement to reveal their sexuality. Having said that, in 2013 NBA basketball player Jason Collins and MLS association football player Robbie Rogers became the first two male athletes from the NFL, MLB, NBA, NHL, or MLS to reveal their sexuality during their playing careers. However, with Collins retiring in 2014 and Rogers retiring in November 2017, once again no openly gay male athletes participated in any of the top five North American professional leagues or in any of the top-flight professional association football leagues around the world (Buzinski, 2017). It is for this reason that nearly all teams across the five top North American leagues now host Pride or inclusion nights and are involved with various celebrations throughout LGBT Pride month. In addition, the NFL, MLB, NBA, and NHL all participated in New York's 2018 Pride march.

In another example, Corey Hirsch, a former Canadian NHL goaltender, has opened up about how his struggles with **anxiety** and a diagnosis of obsessive compulsive disorder led him to attempts to deliberately harm himself with a stick blade (to avoid playing due to anxiety) and, ultimately, to try to take his own life. Writing for the Players' Tribune, Hirsch recalled his thoughts as he stood at the top of a cliff about to commit suicide: "What if I don't die? What if I survive this crash, and I'm severely injured, and I'm stuck in bed with all these dark thoughts, on repeat, for the rest of my life? That image was so terrifying that, somehow, it seemed worse than death. It made me slam on the brakes" (Hirsch, 2017).

As well as the two case studies outlined, more recently, many athletes have disclosed dealing with mental health difficulties, including the following.

- England and Tottenham defender Danny Rose revealed he had been diagnosed with depression (BBC Sport, 2018).
- Lithuanian swimmer Ruta Meilutyte has said that she "fights depression everyday" (Hart, 2018).
- England rugby star Jonny Wilkinson battles with depression and anxiety every day (Wilkinson, 2012).
- American bobsledder Steven Holcomb disclosed that he struggled with depression and attempted to take his own life with alcohol and prescription medication (Bull, 2018).
- England badminton player Gail Emms has said she feels "ashamed" to admit she is struggling (Emms, 2017).

These names are only a few of the many athletes who have revealed mental health difficulties and spoken out about them. Importantly, coaches, too, can suffer from mental health difficulties, such as depression, as a result of the various pressures they face because of their involvement in sport (Lutton, 2019). These mental health difficulties have pushed coaches out of sport (Hanson, 2019). With the increasing awareness of the difficulties coaches can experience, the #lookafteryourcoach initiative was established in Australia. The prevalence of sportspeople who have experienced mental health difficulties highlights why it is imperative that sport managers develop a greater understanding of mental health and how best to deal with situations that may arise.

Anxiety

Low levels of anxiety accompanied by useful coping mechanisms, can be beneficial in sport because this can bolster performance (Kamm, 2005). For example, many signs of anxiety (shaking, excessive sweating, nausea, breathlessness [not in relation to physical exertion], light-headedness, tingling sensation in extremities, weakness in legs and arms, heart palpitations [again, not in relation to physical exertion]) are a natural and normal response to anxiety-provoking situations or indeed as a consequence of engaging in sport. Concerns are raised when the reaction to a perceived threat and anxious situation becomes amplified, are excessive in nature, and the athlete begins to struggle with overwhelming feelings of anxiety. These feelings may potentially occur in a sporting environment during competition.

Competing in front of an audience is an imperative part of sport. Athletes can thrive in a spectator environment, often coaxing the audience to rev up the atmosphere and foster an emulous ambiance. However, the fear of a negative judgment or evaluation from others can lead to overwhelming feelings of anxiety and often cause avoidant behavior or cause the athlete to engage in safety strategies. Avoidance can range from completely withdrawing from the situation or more subtle forms, often called *safety strategies*, such as using substances to cope or avoiding eye contact. Inadvertently, the behavior may also exacerbate the anxiety because coping strategies can impair social performance due to an inability to think clearly, shaking, sweating, the "yips" (loss of fine motor skills or wrist spasms) with golfers, for example, all of which heightens self-awareness and fear.

Susie O'Neill, an Australian Olympic swimmer, detailed in her autobiography how she was frightened of winning because that meant she would have to stand in front of crowds of people on a podium (Cuncic, 2014). NFL player Ricky Williams was diagnosed with social anxiety disorder and reported that "marijuana is ten times more helpful than **medication**" for his difficulties. Williams relied on substances to cope with his social anxiety, ultimately leading to a fine, suspension, and his retirement from professional football (George, 2002). Khalil Greene and Dontrelle Willis, both professional baseball players, have each been diagnosed with social anxiety disorder (Cuncic, 2013).

Obsessive Compulsive Behavior

Obsessive compulsive behavior, or the diagnostic term *obsessive compulsive disorder* (OCD), is characterized by the presence of obsessions, compulsions, or both. Obsessions are defined as "recurrent and persistent intrusive thoughts or urges that the individual attempts to ignore or suppress"; compulsions are defined as "repetitive behaviors that the individual feels compelled to complete in response to an obsession, often to alleviate anxiety or to prevent a negative consequence" (APA, 2013).

Athletes frequently engage in ritualistic behavior prior to or during participation in sport. The repetition of an action or performance of certain routines may signify to the individual completing them a positive outcome; examples include wearing a lucky item of clothing, practicing or warming up in a particular routine, or engaging in habitual competition preparation. In some sports, such as golf, pool or snooker, or darts, practice club swings, cue action, or arm throws immediately prior to the actual impact of the club, cue, or release of the dart are customary elements of the sport. Many people, athletes or not, engage in patterns of behavior. Predictability is important because it gives the person a feeling of safety and security, and it is not suggestive of a mental health disorder.

For example, Tiger Woods famously only wears red shirts on the final day of competition in major golf tournaments (Jackson, 2014). During the 1998 association football World Cup prior to a game the French team touched Fabien Barthez's body for good luck (Macaskill, 2009). Former rugby union player Jonny Wilkinson engaged in a meticulous kicking routine prior to taking the actual kick. In these examples a superstitious belief is attributed to an action or set of actions in order to maximize sporting achievement; this is more colloquially termed *magical thinking* or *superstition*.

The thoughts and actions in the preceding examples are harmless and form part of a normal custom and practice. They can be conceptualized as existing on an obsessive compulsive continuum. However, the potential exists for both obsessions (thoughts) and compulsions (behaviors) to manifest and ultimately be detrimental to sporting performance, culminating in the development of an obsessive compulsive fixation. The emphasis shifts from sport preparation to a compulsion to complete certain behaviors to avoid negative consequences.

For example, former association footballer David Beckham could only participate in a football match if he had a new pair of cleats (Adams, 2011). This generalized to his daily life, where Beckham had to systematically organize all of the labels in his refrigerator, realign shampoo bottles, and straighten towels in hotel rooms. Being obsessive may be an asset to an athlete; the desire to complete everything precisely and exactly may motivate an athlete to train. However, when it progresses to the point of affecting an individual's daily functioning, it has become unhelpful and can arguably be defined as obsessive compulsive behavior. In fact, some research suggests that exercise itself can be defined as a compulsive behavior (Villella et al., 2011).

Eating Disorders and Disordered Eating

The most common feeding and eating concerns that occur in athletes are related to food restriction (e.g., anorexia nervosa) and binging (e.g., bulimia nervosa). Anorexia nervosa is characterized by a restriction in energy intake leading to a significantly low body weight. Bulimia nervosa is characterized by repeated episodes of binging with a sense of feeling out of control and often engaging in compensatory behaviors such as attempting to get rid of the food consumed. **Disordered eating** occurs when eating behaviors are not typical (restrictive, compulsive, or overeating) but do not meet formal diagnostic criteria; the behaviors may also vary with regards to severity and frequency.

Any athlete strives to maintain a balanced and nutritious diet in order to maximize sporting achievement. The body functions at its optimum when fueled by the correct food and fluid. However, eating disorders and disordered eating have been found to be worryingly more frequent among athletes than nonathletes. They have been found to be particularly prevalent among females involved in aesthetic, weight category, and endurance sports and among males participating in antigravity, weight category, and endurance sports. As explained previously this does not necessarily indicate that the sporting environment causes an eating disorder but that a complex combination of factors can place athletes at risk of developing an eating disorder or disordered eating.

Other sports implicitly facilitate the desire to appear the "correct" weight and overall look; for example, in ice skating or gymnastics, athletes wear certain, often revealing and tight, clothing during competition. Furthermore, whether sporting competitions are televised, athletes' figures are on display, weigh-ins for certain sports disclose the precise weight for that athlete (such as wrestling), and the athlete can then be subject to comments or criticism, which may cause them to engage in unhealthy weight loss strategies. This can even cause further physical health complications later in life. On top of this, over the last few years athletes have become involved in modeling and advertisement campaigns, adding further pressures. All of these factors can contribute to concerns regarding an individual's food intake and their weight.

Hollie Avil, a British triathlete, retired from sport in 2012 after struggling with an eating disorder for nearly six years. Avil believes the onset of her eating disorder occurred after a coach commented that she needed to watch her weight. This triggered Avil's awareness, not only about her weight, food intake, and her overall body shape, but she would also compare herself to fellow athletes (Avil, 2012). Australian rugby star David Pocock has also revealed that he has suffered from an eating disorder. When he moved with his family from Zimbabwe in 2002 as a teenager, he noticed difficulties with his eating. Pocock has stated that he became "irrationally strict" about what food he ate and developed a "skewed idea of his body image" (Averis, 2011).

Body Dysmorphia

The clinical diagnostic definition of body dysmorphic disorder is characterized by "preoccupation with one or more perceived defects or flaws in physical appearance that are not observable or appear only slight to others, and by repetitive behaviors (e.g., mirror checking, excessive grooming, skin picking, or reassurance seeking) or mental acts (e.g., comparing one's appearance with that of other people) in response to the appearance concerns" (APA, 2013, p. 236). With **body dysmorphia**, the individual becomes obsessed about a perceived defect in a specific part of their body, for example, the nose, arms, or muscles. This can cause them to become preoccupied over the perceived defect and in some circumstances alter it through plastic surgery, controlling their eating, using steroids, or through compulsive training.

Our appearance and the way we present ourselves is an important component in many sports. The demand to achieve a desirable body shape and weight in order to compete in certain categories maintains the focus of achieving the "ideal" or "perfect" physique. In addition, with athletes often wearing revealing clothing in aquatic sports, gymnastics, or ice skating, such factors can precipitate an obsession with body image. It is therefore not unusual that for an athletic population, where self-esteem is maintained by the sense of achievement provided by the sport, that the obsession for achieving perfection can lead to a mental health difficulty such as body dissatisfaction. This in turn is linked to other mental health concerns such as low self-esteem, low mood, anxiety, and eating concerns. Athletes may feel forced to engage in extreme behaviors to achieve the ideal body image, including physically or surgically altering characteristics. In some cases, the belief that an individual (more commonly a male) feels that his body is not big enough suffers from what is called *bigorexia* (or *megarexia* and *reverse anorexia*), described as the opposite of anorexia nervosa. This *muscle dysmorphia* is a subtype of body dysmorphia (Pope, Katz, & Hudson, 1993; Mosley, 2008). Substances such as steroids are used to gain a bigger, and perceived ideal, body. The use of illegal or banned substances to achieve the perfect body is considered as harmful as anorexia nervosa. It is suggested that as many as 1 in 10 men in the United Kingdom who train in gyms could have some form of muscle dysmorphia that can lead to depression, steroid abuse, and even suicide (Ahmad, Rotherham, & Talwar, 2015). The issue is worldwide. For example, New Zealand bodybuilder Justin Rys held the titles of Junior Mr. Australasia, Mr. Gold Coast, and Mr. Oceania. Rys had talked of suffering from body dysmorphic disorder, specifically megarexia. The obsession with his appearance forced him to engage in risky, often obsessional, behavior to bulk up and increase his muscle capacity. Rys started taking the drug Gamma Hydroxybutyrate (GHB), often known as Fantasy, in an attempt to further his career. However, Rys was jailed for importing and dealing Fantasy. On his release, he became a spokesperson against the use of performance- and image-enhancing drugs (drawing on his own experiences of developing a serious heart condition and suffering heart attacks), but he passed away in 2015 at the age of just 38. The exact cause of his death is not known, but his long-term excessive drug consumption was a principle factor in his rapid decline in health prior to this death (NZ Herald, 2015).

Nonsuicidal Self-Injury

Nonsuicidal self-injury (NSSI) often occurs in the context of other mental health difficulties, particularly (but not exclusively) low mood and depression. NSSI refers to the direct and intentional injury of one's own body tissue without suicidal intent, such as cutting, burning, and hitting oneself. This functions as a way to regulate emotions and self-punishment (Claes & Vandereycken, 2007). Often individuals attempt to hide or mask signs that they engage in NSSI, for example, by wearing clothes that cover up certain areas or using makeup to minimize the appearance of any scarring.

Athletes are placed under an enormous amount of pressure to perform and achieve results. This is often alongside the daily and normal stresses and strains of life. Sporting environments do not typically lend themselves to intimate conversation about emotions and personal concerns; the focus is maintained on fitness and accomplishments. It is then conceivable that athletes may feel they have no emotional outlet, leaving them vulnerable to low mood, depression, and the potential to engage in NSSI. An athlete may use NSSI as a form of emotional release because of feeling restricted or unable to vocalize his or her thoughts or concerns about emotional well-being. Dame Kelly Holmes has commented that she was regularly cutting herself to "release the anguish" she felt (BBC News, 2017b, para. 3). As a consequence of the sporting injuries she had suffered, she started to use self-harm with scissors.

Substance Misuse

The term *substance* in this context refers to any drug. Broadly speaking, these include alcohol; caffeine; cannabis; hallucinogens; inhalants; opioids; sedatives, hypnotics, and anxiolytics; stimulants (amphetamine-type substances, cocaine, and other stimulants); tobacco; and other (or unknown) substances.

Individuals often use substances as a temporary stress relief. Use may be considered excessive when the substances are used for longer than intended, cause functional impairment, use is risky, and when the individual experiences withdrawal symptoms and requires an increasing amount to cause the same effect.

Athletes are subject to strict drug testing regimes prior to, during, and after competition. They may be suspected of using substances for a variety of reasons. Sometimes, athletes display poor judgment or conduct that results in regrettable behavior. Others purposely engage in **substance misuse** to gain an advantage over other athletes. Using prohibited substances may of course be accidental; banned substances are constantly changing and evolving as new products are introduced to the market. Athletes may not be aware if they are using a banned substance such as a nasal spray for a cold. For example, Team GB alpine skier Alain Baxter was controversially stripped of his 2002 Winter Olympic bronze medal after failing a drug test; it is argued that he was unaware that the American version of the Vicks Vapor inhaler that he purchased over the counter contained a substance on the banned list (the substance is a mood enhancer but has no significant performance-enhancing properties), whereas the UK version of the Vicks inhaler did not contain the banned substance (Hope, 2016).

As previously mentioned, some athletes use substances to cope with mental health difficulties, such as low mood or anxiety. This has a paradoxical effect in that it in fact exacerbates the difficulty. Of course, athletes and teams are known to celebrate following a victory; this could be mid-series, tournament, or competition. Many of these examples as isolated events do not cause concern. When an athlete engages in substance misuse systematically or on a regular basis the cause needs to be considered. For example, 100-meter sprinter Ben Johnson was stripped of his 1988 Olympic medal three days after claiming victory because he had tested positive for a banned substance. Johnson admitted to years of steroid abuse to further his career (Burton, 2012). This 1988 100-meter Olympic final has been coined "the dirtiest race in history" given the fact that seven out of the eight finalists have now been implicated in substance abuse (Moore, 2012).

For sport managers, another level of complexity exists around substance and medication use for athletes. The World Anti-Doping Agency (WADA), an international independent agency with the mission of creating a doping-free sporting environment, has produced a Code to systemize anti-doping policies, rules, and regulations within sport around the world. The Code lists all prohibited substances, but WADA have also developed a Therapeutic Use Exemptions (TUEs) process for athletes who may "have illnesses or conditions that require them to take particular medications" (WADA, n.d.). Although the TUE process is designed to create a level playing

TIME OUT

Neurocognitive Disorders

Although not an area of mental health, individuals who suffer brain damage may be vulnerable to developing mental health problems. During competitive sport athletes frequently experience blows or knocks to their head. This can result in significant and sometimes permanent damage. One of the world's greatest heavyweight boxing champions, Muhammad Ali, competed in his penultimate fight on October 2, 1980, against Larry Holmes. Ali lost this fight by a knockout—the only fight Ali lost this way. It is hypothesized by neurologist Dr. Stanley Fahn that a combination of this knockout fight and constant repeated blows to Ali's head contributed to the development of his Parkinson's disease (Hale, 2009). Chris Nowinski, a former World Wrestling Entertainment (WWE) star and gridiron footballer, following retirement was diagnosed with post-concussion syndrome, along with other WWE stars also suffering from concussions (e.g., The Undertaker and Fandango) (Butterly, 2014).

Evidence suggests that NFL athletes are more vulnerable to develop mild cognitive impairment than other peers of a similar age because of frequent head injuries sustained during their careers (Randolph, Karantzoulis, & Guskiewicz, 2013). As a result, five NFL players sued the union for failing to provide accurate information on the potential risks of head injury and brain damage.

All of these conditions fall under the branch of neuropsychology. Neuropsychology is the study of how certain brain structures relate to behavior and psychological processes, bridging the gap between biology and psychology. Often, **mental health professionals** work with individuals who have brain abnormalities to determine their impact behaviorally and psychologically. Examples of these include but are not exclusive to Huntington's disease, motor neuron disease, Parkinson's disease, dementia, stroke, and traumatic or acquired brain injury. Athletes who have sustained a sport-related concussion have also been linked to substance misuse and suicide (Graham, Rivara, Ford, & Spicer, 2014). Notably, three NHL enforcers (a position where players regularly incur hits to the head) have committed suicide: Wade Belak, Rick Rypien, and Derek Boogaard (Branch, 2011).

Consequently, sport organizations have been forced to reexamine their policies and procedures regarding brain injury and the impact to mental health. In association football, the world players' union, Fifpro, in collaboration with the professional football association, advocates that players should not be able to continue playing for the remainder of the game and any further care or return to play to be carefully managed following recovery from the concussion. The rugby football union (RFU) offers concussion awareness and education courses and have developed international guidelines for concussion management. Some players are trialing "smart gumshields" that monitor head impacts and send the data directly to the team's medical staff during matches or training sessions (Coles, 2019). Increasingly, this is an area that athletes, coaches, and organizations need to be concerned with because it can have potentially devastating effects.

field, some athletes and teams manipulate the system in an effort to gain competitive advantage. Overbye and Wagner (2013, p. 579) suggest that the "boundaries between the use of pharmacological substances due to a medical need and doping are sometimes blurred" and recommend "improved harmonization and increase[d] transparency" with TUE regulations.

Management of Mental Health Difficulties in Sport

Many large sports organizations have developed guidelines aimed at the early recognition and **management of mental health difficulties**. These include but are not restricted to the International Olympic Committee (IOC), National Collegiate Athletic Association (NCAA) in the United States, and NGBs in the United Kingdom. In fact, due to the prevalence and importance of understanding mental health difficulties among elite athletes in the United Kingdom, the government published a new policy paper in March 2018, named the *Mental Health and Elite Sport Action Plan*. The aim is to improve awareness and training, and by 2024 elite sport must have mental health procedures embedded in their performance plans and provide clear pathways for athletes to help them access professional mental health support (e.g., clinical psychologists) (Department for Digital, Culture, Media & Sport (DCMS) & Crouch, 2018). This section will now outline the mainstream management of mental health difficulties and discuss adaptations specifically for athletes and the sport environment. Managers of local or regional sport organizations can apply the principles on a smaller scale to their organizations.

Identification

The first step toward management of any mental health difficulty is the recognition by the athlete that he or she requires support. Although some mental health difficulties can be easier to recognize by the people around them (e.g., anorexia nervosa, where a visible decrease in body weight is visible), others can be hidden by the athlete. Research has demonstrated that athletes who disclose their mental health problems usually do so to their teammates or coach, highlighting the importance of awareness in sport environments (Plateau, Arcelus, McDermott, & Meyer, 2015). Those individuals around the athlete can play a vital role with **identification** of difficulties and increasing motivation for the athlete to accept help.

Engagement and Motivation

Motivation aims to increase focus, strength, and power, and is not an unusual concept in the sport environment. Team members are valuable facilitators of increasing motivation among peers to achieve desirable outcomes during training and competition. In this context, however, we refer to motivation in relation to seeking support or making changes to reduce distress.

The first thing to be aware of is that the athlete may worry about disclosing any difficulties because of possible implications regarding their involvement in sport. For example, he or she may be worried about being stigmatized, being asked to leave the team, having to stop training, or not being selected. He or she may also be worried about being treated differently than others. For this reason, coaches and other members of the athlete's support team need to understand the process of motivation and their role in influencing it. Table 20.1 describes each stage of the **transtheoretical model** and the behavior with a sport-related example that accompanies each stage.

An important point to understand about the transtheoretical model is that although it is generally presented as a cyclic process, individuals could progress to the next stage but suffer some form of relapse at any time throughout the change.

Motivational Enhancement

Individuals who work with athletes, such as professionals, colleagues, friends, or family members, play an important role in fostering motivation to seek support or initiate change when the individual is unmotivated to do this. In particular, they can facilitate an individual moving from one stage of change to a subsequent stage (e.g., from precontemplation to contemplation); this has been described as enhancing motivation, or **motivational enhancement** (ME).

In the first instance, it is important to assess at which stage in the transtheoretical model the individual is. The aim of ME is then to support the individual to move from one stage to another; this is done through the use of key words and phrases. For example, if an individual is in precontemplation, it is not useful to say phrases such as "Why don't you do this?" or to give them a task to do; this may be more suitable for an individual in the action stage. At the precontemplation or contemplation stage, the pros and cons of change could be explored, equally giving feedback to the individual to indicate you are listening, not forcing change to occur, not threatening them to change, giving time, and allowing them to explore the positives and negatives of

Table 20.1 Stages of the Transtheoretical Model With a Mental Health in Sport Example

Stage	Meaning	Example
1. Precontemplation	The individual does not accept that he or she has a difficulty.	A mixed martial arts fighter would like to move up to the next weight class, so he starts to take a cocktail of drugs. He does not see the harm in this and becomes defensive if athletes or coaches comment on him using them or remark on changes in his physical appearance. Managers can express concern, ask permission without forcing the athlete to discuss, be there for support, and build up trust for if they move into contemplation.
2. Contemplation	The individual starts to consider he or she may have a difficulty and that support is required. He or she will consider the advantages and disadvantages of taking any action and initiating change.	The athlete has started to experience unwanted side effects from taking the cocktail of drugs and has started to speak to others about his concerns, considering the pros and cons of change. He is open to considering how and when making changes could be possible. Managers can explore ambivalence, explore barriers, pass on relevant information, and refer to appropriate services.
3. Preparation	The individual has become aware that he or she has a difficulty and wants to make changes and seek support, but he or she is not ready yet so does not take any action.	The athlete is starting to put things in place to make some changes: determined a start date, identified the support required, considered the impact to sport or competition. Managers can discuss the training regime, competition, and any changes that need to be put in place to facilitate change.
4. Action	The individual is aware that he or she has a difficulty and starts making changes or accepting support.	The athlete has started to implement change behavior; he starts trying out new behaviors and avoiding old behaviors. Managers can support positive changes and problem solve any difficulties along the way.
5. Maintenance	The individual is ensuring that any changes made are sustained.	The athlete focuses on maintaining current behavior. Managers can support positive change, reinforce positive change, and link into other support to maintain positive change.
6. Relapse	This stage does not always occur, but it is not unusual that the individual may change his or her mind during the process of change. For example, initially he or she may be extremely motivated to make differences in his or her life or engage with support, but then he or she starts to believe he or she is coping OK and stops attending any sessions with a mental health professional. The individual then may relapse, resort to previous behaviors, and stop any positive changes that occurred.	The athlete may or may not revert to old risky behaviors. It is useful to be able to recognize signs and symptoms. Managers can support, help to identify any signs of relapse, and help the athlete learn from relapse experiences to aid prevention in the future.

Adapted from Prochaska & DiClemente (1983).

change. Not adhering to these principles may generate resistance and move the athlete back to a less motivated stage (Prochaska & DiClemente, 1983).

Role of Mental Health Professionals in Sport

Once an athlete makes the decision to seek support and has been referred to a mental health professional, the role of the coach does not end. The involvement of the coach in treatment can aid recovery and the return to sporting activities (Plateau, McDermott, Arcelus, & Meyer, 2014). A coach or manager can bring helpful insights in the causes and development of the mental health difficulty. Additionally, his or her collaboration is necessary in supporting a gradual return to sporting activities during recovery.

Typically, an athlete may be referred to a mental health professional and services if he or she has started to notice an impact on his or her daily functioning and require support. Access to such services and the specific type of mental health professional the athlete is referred to may vary according to the level of the athlete (whether professional or not), the presenting difficulty (e.g., in some countries insurance companies will pay for support regarding low mood and depression but not for bulimia nervosa), the country and health system (private or national health service), accessibility to services (geographically where services and mental health professionals are located, whether they offer visits or if the athlete has to go to their office), and the source of funding accessing services (cost of services, who pays for them, duration of funding). The different types of mental health professionals with whom an athlete may come into contact include the following.

- Psychiatrist
- Clinical psychologist
- Counseling psychologist
- Mental health nurse
- Psychotherapist
- Counselor

Although the goal for all of these professionals is to support the individual with regards to his or her mental health difficulty, there are subtle differences in their approaches. Psychiatrists and mental health nurses are medically trained, and as well as bearing in mind **psychological factors** contributing to the maintenance of the mental health difficulty, they also consider medical factors as a differential diagnosis. For example, if an individual's thyroid is not functioning properly, this could present as depression or hyperactivity. As medical doctors, psychiatrists are also able to prescribe medication such as antidepressants. Psychologists and psychotherapists are particularly involved in the psychological treatment of mental health difficulties. They tend to look at and work with a range of factors, from childhood to current functioning, and conceptualize how the difficulty has occurred and is being maintained, as well as interventions to manage the difficulties. The aim of all mental health professionals is to reduce distress, and not one approach is right for every athlete, so it is important to acknowledge and recognize the differences between individuals in order to offer suitable support.

Assessment

An assessment typically involves a clinical interview where the athlete will discuss in detail his or her current difficulties with a mental health professional. Specifically, to sport, he or she may also discuss any injuries, sickness, forced breaks

TIME OUT

The Discipline of Sport Psychology

Sport psychology is the discipline that integrates knowledge from both physiology and psychology of sport. In particular, professionals work closely with athletes, teams, coaches, referees, and volunteers across a range of sports to understand involvement and performance. They advise and develop interventions regarding preparation and participation in sport, including psychological issues such as performance-based interventions (e.g., goal setting and visualization work regarding obtaining goals); team cohesion; dealing with competition disappointment; and overcoming injury. Sport psychology is an area closely related to mental health but tends to focus on performance and how athletes can excel in sport by looking at the psychological issues underpinning involvement in sport.

or retirement, performance setbacks, and general questions about the sport environment. The athlete may also be required to complete psychometric questionnaires to provide a comprehensive overview of the presenting difficulties. Importantly, the clinical interview will also clarify any risk factors, including the risk of self-harm, suicidal ideation, or plans. The mental health professional will also bear in mind any information that relates to a differential diagnosis. This means distinguishing between difficulties that may present with similar complaints.

Assessing an athlete should not be different than assessing a nonathlete with a mental health difficulty, although as mentioned additional questions regarding sport may be asked. Clinicians should be aware and understand the athlete's attitude to exercise and consider the role this and sport in general plays in that individual's life. As part of the assessment the mental health professional will investigate the predisposing factors in the individual, the specific sport environment, the precipitating factors, and what is maintaining the difficulty. He or she will try to find out why it is occurring now and why in this particular individual.

Treatment

Treatment can be divided into two broad categories: medical (medication) and psychological (therapy). It is not the aim of the chapter to describe every single medication or **psychological therapy** that may be used by a mental health professional, but a brief overview of the two categories and more commonly used examples of each will be provided to help managers who work within sport organizations understand mental health and the support available.

KEY ISSUES FOR SPORT MANAGERS

As a manager it is important that you are aware of the potential for mental health difficulties to develop and how involvement in sport and the sporting environment may promote this. It is crucial that sport managers are mindful and alert to the signs and symptoms of mental health difficulties, including predisposing and precipitating factors, and to foster a team atmosphere where athletes support each other and are guided by each other and managers for leadership. The key issues to be mindful of are:

- *Predisposing and precipitating factors*: Predisposing factors mean the athlete is vulnerable to the development of a mental health difficulty. These can be located within the athlete or sporting context. Precipitating factors are events that typically occur immediately prior to the onset and trigger the development of a mental health difficulty. It is important for managers to be aware of any potential predisposing and precipitating factors for the athletes they manage and support.
- *Signs of mental health difficulties*: Managers need to be familiar with the signs and how mental health difficulties may present in athletes in order for them to support the athlete. They need to be aware of how these may manifest and that they may present differently in individuals.
- *Support and management*: A variety of **support and management** options are available. Support can begin within the sporting environment with athletes looking out for each other, sharing experiences, and recognizing when further professional support may be required. Each athlete will require a personalized plan of care that considers his or her motivation, preferred management choices, and training or competition regime.

If managers and organizations appreciate these factors, they can begin to increase awareness, reduce stigma, and ensure the necessary support is accessible. Furthermore, as Liddle, Deane, and Vella (2017) point out with their review of sporting organizations' websites in Australia, sport psychology aspects often receive greater attention compared with mental health difficulties; many sport organizations acknowledge the importance of certain areas of mental health (to increase competitiveness, for example) but few explicitly challenge policy and performed reviews of campaigns. Accordingly, if sport managers are able to better recognize the importance of mental health promotion, it will enable those facing difficulties to receive improved support.

Medical

A psychiatrist may use different types of medications, but the most commonly used medication for people with depression or high levels of anxiety are antidepressants. A variety of antidepressants exist, and they differ in how they work. Finding the right antidepressant for a specific individual may take time, and a trial of different antidepressants may be required. Antidepressants may take six weeks to start working, so it is important to allow enough time before assessing their efficacy. Other types of medications, such as anxiolytics, need to be used with caution and in the short term because they can become addictive. The type of medication and dose required will be dependent on the presenting mental health difficulty and severity. For example, patients with low mood may respond well to medication (antidepressants) but those with disordered eating behaviors may not.

Psychological

A vast range of psychological interventions are available. The literature is constantly being updated with novel and evidence-based models. A mental health professional will consider the formulation, goals of the athlete, and feasibility of the intervention when considering applicability. The aim and of focus of psychological interventions vary. Some specifically focus on the here and now and what is maintaining the difficulty (i.e., cognitive behavior therapy [CBT] or interpersonal psychotherapy [IPT]), whereas some others focus more on past experiences, aiming at helping the individual understand why they react in a certain way (e.g., psychodynamically informed therapy). Unfortunately, in some cases the length of time psychological interventions can be offered is dependent on funding. Practicalities, such as how often the athlete can attend or where the sessions will occur, will also need to be considered.

Summary and Conclusions

This chapter has provided a broad outline of mental health difficulties, their manifestation in sport, and management strategies available. Mental health is a complex and fluid concept, and athletes are exposed to specific sport-related factors that mean they are vulnerable to the development of certain difficulties. Certain mental health difficulties are considerably more prevalent among athletes than nonathletes, as detailed in this chapter. As outlined, this does not indicate that the sport environment precipitates a mental health difficulty. To understand why athletes develop specific mental health difficulties, we need to be aware of the predisposing factors (factors general to all individuals and those specific to sport) and the precipitating (trigger) factors. This can be more easily understood when we appreciate the role of sport in an athlete's life and how it can become dominated by achievement in sport and being the best. Athletes can access various mental health support options, but it is crucial to find an option suitable for the individual and that he or she is ready to engage. Sport organizations need to recognize athletes that are at risk and why (e.g., an athlete may be particularly vulnerable after a major event such as an injury or retirement) and understand how mental health difficulties present and how best they can support their athletes.

Review Questions

1. Mental health exists on a spectrum. What does this mean?
2. Name examples of predisposing and precipitating factors that cause the development of a mental health difficulty for the following sports:
   - Swimming
   - Rowing
   - Ballet
3. Describe how one of the mental health difficulties outlined in this chapter may present in an athlete.
4. List the stages of change outlined in the transtheoretical model. How would you recognize at what stage an athlete is? Why is it important for an individual to be motivated to engage in an intervention for a mental health difficulty?

Suggestions for Further Reading

A large body of literature exists within the wider mental health and psychology field. Some suggestions include *The Handbook of Adult Clinical Psychology: An Evidence-Based Practice Approach* by Carr and McNulty (2006), which outlines the more prevalent mental health difficulties in the general population. The book *Sport Psychiatry*, edited by Currie and Owen (2016), provides an in-depth overview of mental health problems in sport. Useful journals to consult for relevant research in this area are *Journal of Applied Sport Psychology*, *Psychology of Sport and Exercise*, *British Journal of Clinical Psychology*, or the *British Journal of Psychiatry*.

Case for Analysis

"Dance Till You Drop": The Case for Policy Change Regarding Eating Disorders in the Dance Environment

An international dance company recognized that during a two-year period, the rate of injuries had increased considerably among their dancers. The physiotherapist was concerned that this was due to eating difficulties. In the physiotherapist's view these two issues were connected.

The international dance company attracts elite dancers from all over the world. Consequently, it is not unusual that from a very early age dancers have to leave their family, friends, and country to live close to where the company is located. The dancers train for up to ten hours a day with minimal breaks; even during lunch the dancers often have appointments for massages or physiotherapy. Dancers are required to be mentally tough and committed to their training regime. A pursuit of excellence coupled with an unselfish attitude and drive to perform despite enduring pain is important in the dance world.

It is often thought that it is vital for dancers, particularly female dancers, to be thin. Male dancers need to be able to lift their female dance partners with elegance and ease. Dancers are quickly evaluated on their looks (e.g., costumes for both male and female dancers are revealing), and it is not unusual for trainers to ask them to lose weight. Eating difficulties, including food restriction and self-induced vomiting, are not uncommon among dancers, and dancers themselves acknowledge this; they see it as part of the dance world. As a result of disordered eating, dancers are at risk of injury. Dancers are aware that if they are diagnosed with an eating disorder they may not be selected to dance. In some cases, they may even be asked to take time off. It is because of this that they are unlikely to ask for help.

The company strongly believed that in order to reduce the number of injuries, eating difficulties needed to be reduced. The organization decided to develop a policy that will reduce the number of eating difficulties and consequently the number of injuries. The policy is divided into four parts:

1. The recognition of individuals who are at particular risk of developing eating problems among dancers
2. The training of staff working with dancers in the recognition and management of eating problems
3. Changes in the day-to-day structure of the dancers' training
4. Clear management of a dancer suffering from an eating problem, in particular the role of training and dancing

Questions

1. Why are eating problems more common among dancers in this company?
2. What makes particular dancers at risk of developing eating difficulties?
3. What should be included in the training of staff to help them with the management of dancers with eating difficulties?
4. What changes could the company make to training that may reduce the risk of developing eating difficulties among the dancers?
5. If a dancer was found to be suffering from an eating difficulty and is asked to stop training, how could this affect the dancer? Why?
6. What professionals would be useful to consult when considering developing the policy?
7. How could the effectiveness of the policy be evaluated?

CHAPTER 21

Technology in Sport Organizations

Trevor Slack, PhD
Andy Miah, PhD

Learning Objectives

When you have read this chapter you should be able to

1. explain what is meant by technology;
2. describe how the work of Woodward, Perrow, and Thompson has contributed to our understanding of technology;
3. discuss the major critiques of the technology imperative and the important factors to consider when studying technology;
4. explain the principal types of technology being used in sport organizations; and
5. describe how technology influences the structure of a sport organization.

Key Concepts

advanced information technology
computer-aided manufacturing
computer-assisted design
computer-integrated manufacturing
continuous-process production
craft technology
engineering technology
intensive technology
long-linked technology
mass or large-batch production
mediating technology
nonroutine technology
pooled interdependence
problem analyzability
reciprocal interdependence
routine technology
sequential interdependence
task variability
technological complexity
unit or small-batch production
workflow integration
work-group or department-level technology

The Technological Spectrum in Sport

The history of technological change in sport can be described through a number of lenses, each of which describe different regulatory and organizational structures. For example, technologies associated with doping engage the medical professions, anti-doping authorities, and the range of science and biological analytics investigators that surround such work. In contrast, the recent case of mechanical doping in cycling (i.e., hiding a motor within the bike's frame, which powers the pedals) is a matter for a sport federation's technical rule book. While these categories of technological change are often treated separately, they have critical similarities that are often overlooked. Moreover, they do not describe the entirety of such technological changes. Consider the technology behind the creation of a golf course, which combines a wide range of landscaping technologies, artificial irrigation, and ground maintenance, before one even gets into the range of equipment used by players. To clarify the different ways in which these technologies should be treated, Miah (2005) outlines a "performance policy" that could be used to govern all technologies in sport, arguing for a unified approach to assessing the merit of technological change, which takes into account a range of ethical, moral, conceptual, and practical concerns. This is necessary, especially given the rapid range of technological changes that are happening outside of sport, where, for instance, the possibility of genetic editing may change the kinds of people who exist in the world, or how digital technologies may lead to the creation of completely new audience expectations.

Technological design has a critical impact on the experience of sports, and these processes are imbued with values that affect sport's internal logic. For instance, the motivation for designing a new association football stems from a desire to diminish the influence of irrelevant inequalities that, in this case, may arise from imperfect ball design. A more perfect ball ensures that the players' ability is more truthfully reflected in the path of the ball upon each kick, ensuring then that their performance is adequately reflected. In this sense, technological innovation operates in the service of sport's pursuit of fairness. Bad design or design flaws compromise the aspiration to achieve a fair representation of an athlete's performance in the conduct of their activity, so design seeks to diminish these failings through greater, more precise and controlled technology.

For these reasons, technology has changed the way virtually all sport organizations operate since sports are also constituted by the manufacturing organizations that enable the sport to take place. Tennis needs tennis racket manufacturers, court designers, materials expertise, and so on. Equally, excellence within technological design has become synonymous with the wider values of sport. For instance, the Olympic motto of "Faster, Higher, Stronger" is embedded within the values of the technology organizations that surround the Games, which also create brands that draw on these ideas of excellence and transcending boundaries. This is made visible at the Olympic Games, where large sponsor pavilions at the Olympic park exhibit technological artifacts that speak to these values. A good example of this was the Samsung pavilion at the 2016 Rio Summer Olympic Games and 2018 PyeongChang Winter Olympic Games, which housed Samsung's latest mobile devices and virtual reality simulators. Alternatively, Intel's world record–breaking drone display in the PyeongChang 2018 Winter Olympic Games opening ceremony exhibits the innovation that is brought into the sports world and that becomes part of its ethos.

In this sense, technology is embedded in all aspects of sport, and it has become a form of currency. For instance, the sharkskin swimming suits of the 2000 Sydney Summer Olympic Games generated much publicity about their innovative properties, drawing attention to the manufacturer as an innovator. Timing technology and visual tracking have become an integrated business proposition, with such companies as GoPro working with VisLink in 2015 to provide bespoke televisual experiences for viewers who can tune in to the camera perspective of their favorite hockey player as he or she skates around the ice. Synthetic grass has spawned an entire economy of sport arena construction, while also making it possible for people to play sports in climates where grass cannot grow effectively enough to allow play all year round. Such compa-

TIME OUT

Multiple Technologies in a Single Sport

All sports rely on a multitude of technologies. Take road cycling, for example. On the lead-up to any major world event, especially the Olympic Games, riders make the news in part due to the new technologies used within their sport, whether it is their bodysuits or new helmet designs. Indeed, cyclists are regularly presented with new bike designs by world-leading engineers, and even the tracks on which they race are highly engineered surfaces. Coaches use digital systems to track training and performance in competition, while broadcast teams rely on a range of data to make sense of what is happening within the competition itself. Increasingly, biometric monitoring such as heart rate monitors or core temperature sensors track athletes' performance over their activity. Moreover, before and after competition, cyclists find themselves immersed in a technological ecosystem through social media communications and journalism. At the Olympic Games, athletes are even given their own Games-time mobile phone to access the internal information system, keeping them permanently plugged into the network. Finally, results are automatically tabulated and displayed on large digital screens for the audience to see, while the creation of connected stadia bring in elements of augmented reality, which can add new layers of content into the physical space when seen through the camera of a mobile device.

nies as Huffy use robotics in their manufacturing process, Adidas uses computer-assisted design technology to develop its sportswear, and coaches everywhere make extensive use of video analysis.

Additionally, new business partnerships are formed around new technological propositions. For instance, leading up to the 2020 Tokyo Summer Olympic Games, Chinese technology company and new Worldwide Olympic Partner, Alibaba, along with Intel announced a revolutionary new artificial intelligence platform that will use camera technology to provide real-time performance data during the Games (Impey, 2019). Additionally, technological infrastructure is also of value due to its capacity to engage additional revenue streams within an industry. For example, the Olympic Games has its own computer game, which is rereleased each time the Games occur, and one of the largest computer games worldwide is FIFA's association football game, produced by EA Sports. In this case, one can observe how FIFA, the organization charged with the development of the sport, can expand its income streams by mobilizing the games industry to reach new markets and audiences. Thus technology in its broadest sense is a major imperative that affects the structure, processes, and values of sport organizations.

This chapter examines what is meant by technology by reviewing major research studies that have analyzed the impact of technology on organizational structures. It then undertakes a critical response to these studies and of the technological imperative within sport more broadly, asking whether technology improves the sports industries. Furthermore, the chapter examines how new media technologies are changing the way that sports operate, considering the emergence of esports as a new techno-economic model for sports, which has the potential to transform television. Finally, conclusions are made about the relationship between technology and the structure of a sport organization.

Research on Technology and Organizations

Concern over the impact of technology on organizational structure and processes can be traced back to the work of Adam Smith in the 18th century. Often referred to as the founder of modern economics, Smith's concern was that technology would destroy the idea of the worker, giving rise to a reduction of fulfilling, skilled labor in exchange for a more efficient, mechanized route toward production, where each worker knows only a fraction of the entire process of crafting an object but never the whole craft. However, the 1950s and 1960s saw a heightened interest in technological labor systems, and since then, it has been an important variable in the study of organizations. This section reviews the work of three authors whose research has had a major influence on our understanding of the relationship between technology and organizational structure and provided the basis for much of the subsequent work in this area. This review focuses specifically on the work of Woodward, Perrow, and Thompson, before examining criticisms of this work. Furthermore, it examines some of the related issues to be considered when studying organizational technology.

Woodward: Technological Complexity

In the 1950s Joan Woodward and her research team in the Human Relations Research Unit at South East Essex Technical College studied 100 manufacturing organizations operating in the south of England. The organizations ranged in size from 100 employees to more than a 1,000. Woodward was interested in finding out which of their managers followed classical management principles and whether they were more effective than those who did not. Her research team collected data and established measures for a number of different aspects of an organization, including span of control, levels of management, extent of formalization, economic performance, and technology.

Woodward's (1958, 1965) initial findings were that classical management principles were not consistently used in the organizations she studied and that when they were, the application of these principles did not relate to effectiveness as measured by economic performance. However, Woodward questioned her own findings and started to look for other factors that might be influencing performance. Using the criterion "type of production technology employed," she classified the organizations into 10 groups. Based on their level of **technological complexity**, these groups were further reduced into three major categories: **unit or small-batch production**, **mass or large-batch production**, and **continuous-process production**. Unit production was seen as exhibiting the least amount of technological complexity, and continuous-process production the most. When they were grouped according to the level of technological complexity, Woodward found that she could identify a typical type of organizational structure for the group, in essence a "correct" way to organize (see table 21.1). The organizations that came closest to this structure were the most effective in terms of economic performance. Those organizations involved in unit production were less structured than those involved in mass production or continuous-process production. They tended to have a small number of managerial levels in their hierarchy, they were relatively low in formalization, and decision making was decentralized. The focus in these organizations was essentially on custom manufacturing. An example of an organization within the sport industry that employs unit production is Faulkner Brown, a British architectural company that designed Ponds Forge International and Community Sport Centre, the aquatic facility for the 1991 World University Games.

Companies that manufacture large quantities of the same product often use mass-production assembly lines. The processes employed are repetitive and routine, the span of control is high, the number of skilled workers is low, and formalization is relatively high. Examples of organizations within the sport industry involved in mass production include

Table 21.1 Relationship Between Technical Complexity and Structural Characteristics of Effective Organizations

	Technology		
Structural characteristics	**Unit production**	**Mass production**	**Continuous-process production**
Number of levels of management	Low	Low to medium	High
Number of skilled workers	High	Low	High
Supervisor's span of control	Low to medium	High	Low
Manager or supervisor to total personnel ratio	Low	Medium	High
Centralization of decision making	Low	High	Low
Amount of formalization	Low	High	Low
Type of communication			
Verbal	High	Low	High
Written	Low	High	Low

Based on Woodward (1965).

TIME OUT

Adidas Gains Market Advantage Through Technology

Adidas launched in 1949 as a family business but restructured in 1987 as a corporation. In so doing, it began by defining its three consumer groups and the apparel needs of each: sport performance, sport heritage, and sport style. Adidas' next step was to choose the latest technology to meet these product demands. Of course, Adidas had access to media-related technology (television, print, Internet) for marketing, but it also decided to use the latest technology in innovation, design, and performance. Ever since, innovation through technology has been central to its organizational values.

For example, in 2002 Adidas updated its running shoes with ClimaCool, a system designed to ventilate, and a3, an energy management technology for footwear. This design was part of a wider shift toward making technological innovation more central to the company's brand values (Adidas-Salomon, 2004). The company also launched the a3 UltraRide (a midsole that offers mechanical cushioning), as well as the Ground Control System, co-developed with Salomon, to be the first example of ground-leveling technology. The innovations all aimed and claimed to save the runner's energy, making running more efficient.

Adidas continues to improve its other product lines. In 2013 it introduced its Energy Boost running shoe, which professed to have a system of cushioning technology that returns energy back to the runner. In association football Adidas also updated its Predator shoe line with the new Predator Pulse and developed the Roteiro, the first officially approved soccer ball constructed with a thermal-bonding technique. Finally, in 2018 Adidas introduced its Futurecraft 4D shoes, which involved a personalized scanning of a customer's foot and then using 3D printing to create his or her own personal shoe. In each of these cases, new technological design meets with the desire to market the products as distinct because of their performance advantages in either comfort or efficiency.

Huffy, the bike manufacturer, and Fleer, a baseball card manufacturer that began in 1885 and filed for bankruptcy in 2005 due to rising debt.

Organizations that use continuous-process production are highly mechanized, and their production process does not stop. This type of production is not found within the sport industry; it is generally used by organizations such as oil refineries, chemical plants, and breweries.

Woodward's work demonstrated that within each of these three categories, those organizations whose scores came closest to the typical structure for the type of technology they exhibited were the most effective. She concluded that technology was the primary determinant of organizational structure. More recently, proponents of structuration theory (a theory that looks at the agent–structure relationships) have supported Woodward's work (Barley, 1986; Orlikowski, 1992).

Perrow: Task Variability and Analyzability

While Woodward's approach to understanding the impact of technology on organizations was limited to manufacturing firms, Perrow's work (1967) is more generalizable and can be applied to both manufacturing and service firms. It is also more applicable than Woodward's schema to understanding **work-group or department-level technology** (Daft, 1992). For Perrow (1967, p. 195) technology can be described as "the actions that an individual performs upon an object, with or without the aid of tools or mechanical devices, in order to make some changes in that object. The object or 'raw material' may be a living being, human or otherwise, a symbol, or an inanimate object."

To classify technology Perrow uses two dimensions. The first of these concerns the amount of variation in the tasks being performed and refers specifically to the number of exceptions encountered in the work situation. When the work being performed is routine, there will be few exceptions. For example, people assembling bikes or running shoes in factories will experience few exceptions in their work. Their jobs involve considerable repetition and few requirements for creativity. In contrast, people working in sport physiology research labs or individuals working as player agents will find a number of exceptions in their day-to-day jobs. They frequently encounter new situations and face problems they have not dealt with before.

Perrow's second dimension concerns the degree to which the exceptions encountered are analyzable. For example, if a problem occurs in some jobs, it is possible to follow a logical sequence of mechanical steps to seek a solution to the problem. The work of a sport lawyer is much like this. Although the problems sport lawyers face are complex, a fairly well-established body of literature, in the form of previous court rulings and legal precedents, usually exists that the lawyer can call on to solve the problems. In contrast, a group of architects commissioned to design a new aquatic facility with both recreational and competitive pools, along with a waterslide facility, will probably not have encountered this situation before and will find little in the way of related literature to help solve the problems. Withey, Daft, and Cooper (1983) have developed a series of questions to determine the extent of **task variability** and **problem analyzability** in a department or work group. For task variability, this includes asking about similarities between tasks from one day to the next or for descriptions over the degree to which a task is part of a routine. For problem analyzability, the questions focus on how much of the task relies on established knowledge rather than the worker's own initiative. Using the two dimensions of task variability and problem analyzability, Perrow constructed a 2x3x2 matrix (see figure 21.1). The four types of technology found in this matrix are explained here. Perrow also suggests a simplification of the construction: Because task variability and problem analyzability are often highly correlated (i.e., if a task is low in variety it is usually easily analyzable, and if a task is high in variety it is not easily analyzable), it may be possible to have a single dimension of technology. This simplification is also shown in figure 21.1 as the routine–nonroutine continuum.

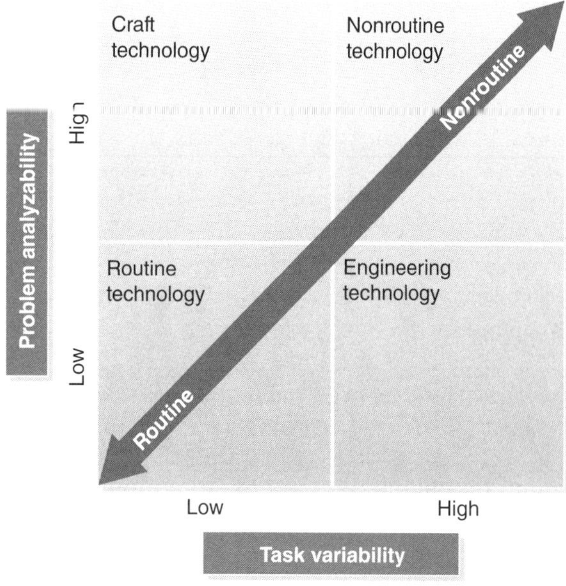

Figure 21.1 Perrow's technology classification.
Based on Perrow (1967).

Perrow's **routine technology** has few exceptions, and those that do occur are easily analyzable. A salesclerk working in a sporting goods store and a person on the assembly line making golf carts are both engaged in routine technology. Craft technologies have very few exceptions, but those that do occur are not easily analyzable; skill and experience are needed to deal with them. Someone making custom bikes, a dance instructor, or a figure-skating choreographer would be involved with a **craft technology**.

Engineering technologies have a high number of exceptions, but they are usually handled with relative ease because of established procedures. Sport lawyers usually find a number of exceptions in their work, but, as noted, because they can call on previous decisions for indications of how to proceed, these problems can be handled fairly easily. Architects who design and build traditional swimming pools and running tracks would also employ routine **engineering technology**. However, those who design more custom-built facilities will use **nonroutine technology**. Here the problems in design and construction are likely to be many, and systematic ways of solving these problems will be hard to find; the architect must count on experience and intuition. A good example of this is found within the development of media architecture as a distinct discipline, where the integration of interactive digital experiences within a building's structure is central to the visitor experience. In 2018 one of the best examples of this is found in the design of the new esports arena in Arlington, Texas, created by the renowned architectural firm Populous (2018). Researchers in a department of sport studies and sport administrators who do management consulting also exhibit nonroutine technologies.

Each of the four main technologies identified by Perrow is associated with a different type of organizational structure. Routine technology is found in bureaucratic organizations; control is achieved through high levels of formalization and centralized decision making. Workers engaged in this type of technology are generally unskilled. Craft technologies require a more organic structure; consequently, we see less formalization and centralization. Coordination is achieved through mutual adjustment and the past experience of the staff. Engineering technologies require a structure somewhat like Mintzberg's (1979) professional bureaucracy; there is a moderate level of formalization and centralization, but the people in the operating core are often professionally trained and have a certain amount of discretion in the decisions that are made. Nonroutine technology requires a very flexible structure; formalization is low, and decisions are made collectively by mutual adjustment. The staff members in these organizations are usually professionally trained. Finally, an important point is that quite possibly more than one type of technology will exist in an organization. For example, Reebok's production department has a routine technology, but its research-and-development unit uses nonroutine technology. When a structure is used that does not fit with the technology employed, the unit tends to be less effective (Gresov, 1989).

Thompson: Task Interdependence

Thompson's (1967) approach to understanding the different types of technology used in organizations is based on the concept of interdependence, a term referring to the extent to which different units or departments within an organization depend on each other for the materials or resources they need to perform their particular tasks. When departments operate independently of each other, interdependence is low; when substantive levels of communication and a frequent exchange of materials or resources among departments are required, interdependence is high. Thompson suggests that different types of interdependence require different technologies. These technologies are associated with different types of organizational uncertainty, and this uncertainty is managed using different types of strategies. This section outlines the types of interdependence Thompson identified and the technologies associated with each. It also briefly discusses the structural implications of each type of technology and the way managers cope with the associated environmental uncertainty.

Sequential Interdependence

Sequential interdependence requires high levels of coordination among the various units involved in the different stages of the production process. The requirement that the product flow from one stage to the next necessitates that the organization emphasize planning and scheduling.

In essence the output from one worker or department becomes the input for the next. The steps involved are relatively routine but must be performed in the correct sequence. This type of interdependence, which requires what Thompson (1967) calls **long-linked technology**, is most frequently found in assembly-line production. Within the sport industry one finds long-linked technology in companies producing sport equipment such as baseball bats or hockey sticks.

Structurally, organizations that employ long-linked technology to mass-produce large quantities of a product show relatively high levels of complexity, high levels of formalization, and a centralized decision-making structure. Uncertainty is usually controlled through a process of vertical integration, either forward, backward, or both. In this way, sources of input and the means of dealing with output are controlled by the manufacturing organization. Nike's purchase of Tetra Plastics (see chapter 8) demonstrates vertical integration.

Pooled Interdependence

As shown in figure 21.2, **pooled interdependence** involves linking two independent customers or clients using **mediating technology**. This process involves the organization acting as a go-between for customers and clients. Mediating technology is found mainly in service organizations. Within the sport industry, sport marketing companies such as Britain's APA use a mediating technology to link sponsors with the promoters of sport events. One also sees a mediating technology used in chains of retail sporting goods stores such as Sport Experts and Mountain Equipment Co-op, which link companies that manufacture sport equipment with those who want to buy it.

Structurally, mediating technology involves low levels of complexity because few units are involved. Coordination is achieved through rules and procedures. For example, retail stores use rules and procedures to lay out how business should be conducted, and sport marketing companies use contracts to ensure that each party understands its rights and obligations. Given this type of coordinating mechanism, formalization is relatively high. To control uncertainty, sport organizations that use a mediating technology try to increase the number of customers or clients served.

Reciprocal Interdependence

Reciprocal interdependence, the highest form of interdependence, is associated with what Thompson (1967) calls an **intensive technology**. This form of interdependence is found when people or units within an organization influence each other in a reciprocal manner. For example, the University of Alberta's Glen Sather Sports Medicine Clinic employs physicians, orthopedic surgeons, X-ray technicians, massage therapists, and physical therapists. A patient who comes to the clinic will first visit a physician, who may then refer the patient

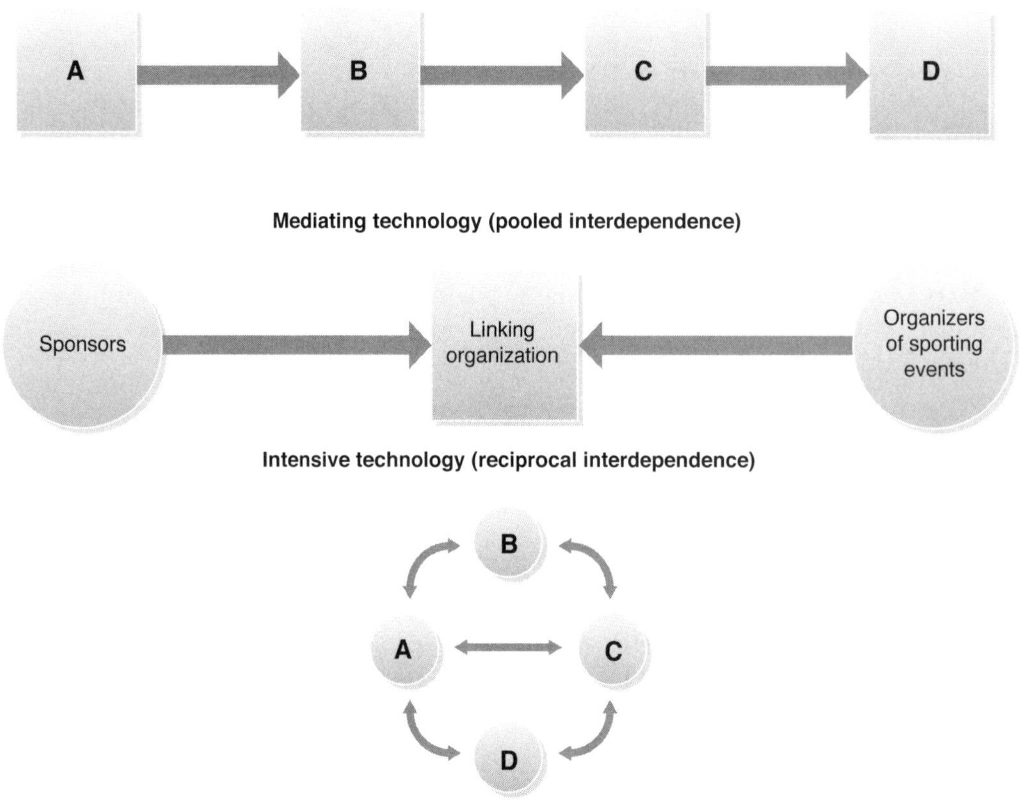

Figure 21.2 Thompson's categories of technology.

for an X-ray. The technician gives the X-ray to the physician and, based on the results of the X-ray, the physician may refer the patient to a surgeon and then physical therapist for treatment. After the treatment the patient returns to the physician, who may consult with the physical therapist and possibly instruct the patient to be X-rayed again or to return for more physical therapy. This is reciprocal interdependence: physicians, surgeons, X-ray technicians, massage therapists, and physical therapists work together; the actions of one influence the behavior of the others. There is no predetermined sequence of events as in long-linked technology; the mix and order in which the skills are used to produce the product or service are in large part a result of feedback from the person or object on which work is being performed. One would also find reciprocal interdependence and an intensive technology in some sport physiology research labs and in some types of health spas, where dietitians, fitness appraisers, and masseurs may work together with a client. Voluntary sport organizations also often exhibit reciprocal interdependence when a group of people work together cooperatively to stage a sport event.

Structurally, sport organizations that employ intensive technology are relatively organic. Coordination is achieved through frequent communication among the parties involved and by mutual adjustment on their part. Teamwork is an important aspect of this technology; decisions are often made collectively. Uncertainty arises out of the nature of the problem itself; while planning can help managers, it cannot possibly cover all the situations that arise in this type of organization. The people who work with this kind of technology are usually highly skilled and hence able to call on their training and experience to make situations more predictable.

Critiques of the Technology Imperative

The contributions of Woodward, Perrow, and Thompson, as significant as they are, have generated considerable debate within the organizational literature about technology and its impact on organizational structure. This section examines the research that has sought to critique and extend these initial studies and then looks briefly at some general problems and issues relating to work in organizational technology.

The most notable critique and extension of Woodward's work is that of the Aston group members Hickson, Pugh, and Pheysey (1969), who identified three types of technology: operations technology, materials technology, and work-flow technology. However, their work focused only on operations technology, which they define as "the techniques that [an organization] uses in its workflow activities" (1969, p. 380). Operations technology was assessed using a measure called **workflow integration**, a composite measure applicable to both manufacturing and service organizations, examining such factors as the extent to which workflow equipment was automated, the rigidity of the workflow, the level of interdependence in the workflow, and the specificity of quality evaluation of operations. Organizations scoring high on workflow integration were seen to have a complex technology; a low score meant a simple technology. Using the workflow integration measure, Hickson et al. (1969) found only a weak relationship between technology and various measures of organizational structure. However, their results showed that size could explain far more variation in structure than technology. Nevertheless, technology did have an influence on structure in smaller organizations.

One of the first to criticize the Aston findings was Aldrich (1972) (see also Kmetz, 1977; Starbuck, 1981). Aldrich reexamined the Aston data using path analysis and suggested a different causal sequence, with technology influencing size. He (1972, p. 40) suggested the Aston group's rejection of the technological imperative "to be ill-advised and premature."

At the same time that Aldrich was critiquing the Aston data, Child was replicating their work in what is known as the national study. Child and Mansfield (1972) reexamined the technology, size, and structure relationship using the Aston workflow integration measure of technology. Their work essentially confirms the Aston findings (Child, 1973a, 1973b, 1975). Although role specialization, functional specialization, and standardization showed a reasonable correlation with technology, the correlation with size was higher, leading Child and Mansfield (1972) to reject the technological imperative in favor of the size–structure relationship. However, a more recent study by Reimann and Inzerilli (1979) used a measure of technology based on Woodward's work and found significant correlations with several structural variables.

Like Woodward's work, Perrow's ideas have also been critiqued and extended. A number of studies have tested Perrow's conceptualization of technology; some have been concerned with the routine–nonroutine continuum emanating from his model, while others have focused on his fourfold classification scheme.

Van de Ven and Delbecq (1974) used measures of task difficulty, a concept similar to Perrow's problem analyzability, and task variability to examine structural variability within work units. Their results also support Perrow's predictions that organizations involved with routine-type work were more highly formalized than those involved with nonroutine activities.

Grimes and Klein (1973) used a slight variant of Perrow's four-cell matrix to examine the relationship of technology to the autonomy of management, something Perrow (1967) had alluded to in his original article. They found (1973, p. 596) "a direct although modest relationship" between technology and managerial autonomy. The influence of technology as a determinant of managerial autonomy was greatest at the work-group level; its influence became more diffuse as one moved further from this level.

Although Thompson's (1967) typology of technology is generally considered to be conceptually the richest of the three seminal works (Bedeian & Zammuto, 1991; Das, 1990), it has probably led to the least amount of subsequent research. Mahoney and Frost (1974) examined the relationship of Thompson's three types of technology to measures of organizational effectiveness. Their results support Thompson's ideas; they found that in organizations that used long-linked technology, the predominant criteria of effectiveness were smoothness of operations, output performance, and reliability of performance. In organizations using mediating technology, flexibility, smoothness of operations, output performance, supervisory control, and staff development were all cited as indicators of effectiveness. For those using intensive technologies, performance was once again important but so too were cooperation and staff quality; planning was not seen to be as important. Van de Ven, Delbecq, and Koenig (1976) used both task uncertainty (the difficulty and variability of the work undertaken), a concept from Perrow's framework, and Thompson's notion of workflow interdependence, to look at the modes of coordination at the work-unit level. They added to Thompson's types of interdependence a fourth category, "a team arrangement," and their research generally supports Thompson's idea that the use of coordinating devices would increase as interdependence increased. They also show the relative use of the different coordinating mechanisms for the different types of technology.

In addition to the findings of studies that have sought to critique and extend the work of

Woodward, Perrow, and Thompson, a number of other important issues should be mentioned in any consideration of technology as a structural imperative. The first concerns the definition of what exactly is meant when discussing “technology.” After all, different studies have used the term in different ways. As Rousseau (1983, p. 230) notes, researchers have used the term “to refer to anything from job routineness to the hardness of raw materials.” She goes on to suggest that “there is disagreement as to whether technology is an object, such as an assembly line or a computer, or a process, such as the flow of throughput within an organization.” Even recently, Scott (2000) referred to technology simply as the work that is performed by an organization. This lack of agreement as to exactly what technology is may well be a major reason for the different findings about its impact on organizational structure.

Another issue relates to the focus of the studies carried out on the technological imperative. Again, as Rousseau (1983) points out, the vast majority of work in this area has been conducted at the organizational level, with considerably less work conducted at the work-group, department, and individual levels. Studies carried out at the work-group level have generally produced stronger support for the technological imperative than research conducted at the organizational level, possibly because technology is more directly related to the work group. As Robbins (1990, p. 193) notes, when one examines the overall impact of technology, one must consider the size of the organization because “the smaller the organization the more likely it is that the whole organization will be impinged upon by the production workflow or operating core.”

Another point raised by Robbins (1990), which indirectly relates to the size issue, is the fact that the industry and the niche within that industry will affect its technology. For example, SP-Teri (figure skating) and Bauer (hockey) both make skates, but the technology they employ is very different. In Perrow’s terms, Bauer’s technology is routine, while SP-Teri uses a craft technology, a difference in technology determined in large part by the niche these sport organizations have selected for their operations. It would not be efficient for a large mass-production company like Bauer to have its customers send their specific foot casts to the production plant for modifications to their skates, as they do at SP-Teri for their custom figure skates.

A final concern about technology is the issue of manufacturing versus service technologies. The bulk of the research on organizational technology has been carried out on manufacturing organizations, but many of the organizations in the sport industry are service oriented. Consequently, in any study of a service organization, sport related or otherwise, it becomes important to take account of differences in the two types of organizations and to employ a framework that takes account of these differences (Bowen, Siehl, & Schneider, 1989). (See table 21.2.)

These insights from the technological innovation side of an organization’s work are of critical relevance for people involved in sport management. While technological innovation has always been a way of securing a competitive advantage as an organization, in more recent times one can see how this extends from simply a matter of creating better products to a world where technology is a form of currency as a lifestyle accessory. A good example of this is found in the marketing, sales, and design of mobile phones, which draw customers into the innovative aspects of the new device in order to sell more units. A simple component of this is improvements to cameras within the phone or additional memory. The earlier example of the Samsung pavilion at the Olympic Games is a case in point, but, more broadly, one can observe how sport organizations position their products around innovation. It may also include the creation of content through which innovative content can be created. For example, take the work of the International Olympic Committee’s social media team. Among their campaigns is a video project informally called Then and Now, which creates a diptych of footage from a given sport at a recent Games alongside footage from the sport from many years ago. The content creates a sense of relationship between the past and present using a novel format of video. In this respect, the content also makes a link to the longer history of media innovation that operates around the Olympic Games, an event that has pioneered many innovations in camera technology, from slow-motion replay to 360-degree film.

Technology can also influence the structure of an organization, particularly at the work-group or department level. Consequently, it is essential for managers in sport organizations to understand the impact of technology, in particular the changing technology, of their organization. Understanding the synergy between structure and variables such as technology and size is also important because it can influence the effectiveness of an organization. Finally, it is important that sport managers, if they are to create effective organizations, understand the difference between manufacturing and service technologies, and the relationship between these technologies and factors such as the size of a sport

Table 21.2 A Comparison of the Characteristics of Service and Manufacturing Organizations Within the Sport Industry

Service organizations	Manufacturing organizations
Intangible output	Tangible output
Customized output	Standardized output
Customer participation	Technical core buffered from the customer
Simultaneous production and consumption	Goods consumed at a later point in time
Labor intensive	Capital intensive
Examples of Service Organizations Within the Sport Industry	**Examples of Manufacturing Organizations Within the Sport Industry**
Department of sport studies	Athletic footwear companies
Sport medicine clinics	Baseball card companies
Sport marketing companies	Golf club manufacturers
Municipal government sport departments	Sportswear companies
Fitness clubs	Tennis racket manufacturers

Based on Bowen, Siehl, and Schneider (1989).

organization and the industrial niche in which it operates.

Microelectronic Technologies

Since 2000 many traditional manufacturing and service technologies have been replaced or augmented with microelectronic technologies, most of which are computer related. Athletic footwear manufacturers such as Nike and Reebok use advanced computer technologies to help design their shoes while also implementing in-store gait analysis technology, which can help a customer decide which of their models is best suited to their running style. Equally, mobile technology allows customers to continually reconnect with a company through mobile apps or social media communities, and it has become essential for brands to be present within these environments (Miah, 2017). This section examines the types of microelectronic technology that may be used in a sport organization, the rationale for using these technologies, and the impact they can have on organizational structure and operations.

Types of Microelectronic Technology

Two major facets of microelectronic technology are influencing the structure and operations of sport organizations: computer-integrated manufacturing (CIM) and advanced information technologies (AIT).

Computer-Integrated Manufacturing

Computer-integrated manufacturing (CIM) refers to the linking by computers of the different parts of the manufacturing process: the ordering and inventory of raw materials; the sequencing and control of the production process; and the warehousing, shipping, and servicing of the finished product (Pennings & Buitendam, 1987). The different components of computer-integrated manufacturing may include an automated materials-handling system, computer-assisted engineering, and (the two most common elements of CIM) **computer-assisted design** (CAD) and **computer-aided manufacturing** (CAM). Computer-assisted design, used to help in the design and drafting of new products, speeds up these processes by allowing designers to easily make modifications to products using the available computer technology. In this way alternative designs can be developed and tested to meet changing customer needs. Because of the ease with which changes are made, CAD is more cost effective than traditional methods of product design.

Computer-aided design is used within the sport industry to produce a wide variety of sport equipment, from running shoes to tennis rackets. Heery International, one of the leading builders of sport facilities, uses CAD in its design process. It is also a leader in the development of computer-aided design drafting software and the utilization of this software to produce construction documents.

Computer-assisted manufacturing (CAM) utilizes machines controlled by a computer to fabricate and assemble a product. This technology, because it requires fewer people to operate, can save a manufacturer money; it is also much quicker than conventional manufacturing technology. Using CAM, a manufacturer can easily change from one product to another by merely changing software. This flexibility enables the manufacturer to respond more quickly to changing customer orders and the changing demands of the marketplace. When Huffy, the bicycle manufacturer, switched to computer-assisted manufacturing, the company was able to undersell Taiwanese imports and keep its manufacturing plant in Ohio. "Computer-aided manufacturing means creating a factory of the future," according to Huffy's chairman Harry A. Shaw (Sator, n.d.).

Advanced Information Technology

Advanced information technology (AIT) is a result of the merging of computer and telecommunications technology. In the early years, it involved linking computers together via telephone systems in the creation of an Internet.

This technology is used to manage geographically dispersed operations, to place orders and control inventory, to facilitate group decision making through conference calls, and simply to enhance communications. Quicker than traditional methods of sending and receiving information, it allows for better identification of problems and facilitates broader participation in decision making. Many sport organizations make use of AIT, and the explosion of "big data" and the rising Internet of Things reinforce the utility of this organizational methodology. Sport organizations have often been at the forefront of these developments because they are intimately connected to some of the world's biggest innovation companies, namely, the media. For instance, Olympic Games rights holders have always sought to innovate with new forms of broadcast. At the 2016 Rio Olympic Games, the big experiment was with virtual reality and 360-degree film experiences. In the 2012 London Olympic Games, the focus was on the use of social media. In 1999 the Pan American Games Host Society was one of the first large-scale sport organizations to use emails to communicate, while the 1996 Atlanta Olympic Games was the first to have a website.

Benefits of Advanced Technologies

We have already briefly alluded to some of the benefits of advanced technologies. This section elaborates on the reason sport organizations are utilizing these types of manufacturing and information systems. We focus specifically on four reasons identified by Child (1984): reduced operating costs, increased flexibility, better-quality products and services, and increased control and integration.

Reduced Operating Costs

The introduction of advanced technologies like CAD, CAM, and Robotic Process Automation (RPA) is often accompanied by a reduction in the size of

TIME OUT

Cisco's Connected Athlete

In 2013 Cisco launched an Internet of Things project called Connected Athlete, which aims to draw data from the athlete's body to create a multifaceted articulation of their performance while also connecting players into their fan base (Cisco, 2013). This is part of a wider trend toward developing data-driven interactions through the use of wearable technologies. The Internet of Things describes a world in which all objects are Internet enabled and achieve efficiencies by communicating with each other. Cisco describes how the Connected Athlete uses sensors in shoes or other nonobtrusive places to collect and stream force and motion data in real time to the Cisco Intelligent Network. This wireless body area network then sends feedback to the athlete through the Cisco Mobile Packet Core network or a Cisco Stadium Wi-Fi solution. Additionally, the body sensors can feed connectivity and data to each other through Zigbee, Z-wave, 6lowpan, DASH7, or other solutions. All data can then be aggregated on the body using a device built into the athletic equipment, such as a belt, armband, or helmet, allowing a final uplink through 4G or Wi-Fi connections.

the organization's workforce. For example, application of RPA technology enables organizations to execute operations between 5 and 10 times quicker, using 37 percent fewer staff (ISG, 2017). While laying off employees or reducing their workload produces obvious significant social consequences, there is little doubt that despite the fact that an initial large outlay of capital may be required, switching to CIM or RPA can ultimately reduce workforce costs. Such a move can also lower costs through "the reduction of wasted material and time [which is] made possible by the greater precision and lack of fatigue of programmed electronic devices" (Child, 1984, p. 249). Costs are reduced because inventory information is easy to access and orders can be quickly filled, reducing wasted search time and the costs of back-ordering products not in stock. Reebok's director of distribution, Don Petersen, estimated that when they installed computers to operate their distribution center, output per hour doubled, thus generating a large saving for the company.

Increased Flexibility

Using microelectronic technologies like CAM allows a manufacturer to produce a range of products with the same equipment. Different software systems can be used to reprogram design and manufacturing equipment so modifications are easily made. With traditional methods these changes were often difficult, time consuming, and costly. Advanced information technologies also provide increased flexibility, the best example of which has been the rise of the smartphone, which has brought an unprecedented amount of mobile control for sport organizers. Indeed, at each recent Olympic Games, athletes are all given their own personal Samsung mobile phone, which is preloaded with unique applications, allowing organizers to reach out to athletes and help them remain connected throughout the Games.

Better-Quality Products and Services

Microelectronic technologies also improve the quality of products and services produced. The quality of manufactured products is improved with CIM because more design options can be considered, human errors in production are eliminated, and the completed product is more easily and rigorously tested. Sport organizations in the service sector are able to improve the quality of their service because with AIT, more comprehensive information is more readily available than with traditional methods. For example, at a fitness center that uses a computer to store information about client exercise programs, information about changes in levels of cardiovascular fitness, weight changes, and so on, is all available at the push of a button, so the fitness consultant is able to provide a more informed assessment of a client's future needs. Moreover, with the rise of mobile health apps, the habitual reinforcement of data tracking is driving a range of economic interests, which range from health care to education and entertainment. A good example of this is the Zombies, Run mobile app, which allows runners to listen to a story played out in their ears while running. Designed as a fitness app, the story is designed to optimize a workout by transforming the runner into a character within the story who must then change direction, run at different speeds, and fulfill missions to play out their role. Such an example shows how technology can transform what takes place within sports and how it is enabled by technology. Alternatively, vast networks of physical activity tracking platforms now integrate a range of immersive experiences, such as the integration of indoor cycling, multiplayer game Zwift with the fitness mobile app Strava,

Increased Control and Integration

Control and integration are important aspects of the management process, and as a result "management will therefore look to new technology to assist in meeting these requirements in ways that are more effective and less costly" (Child, 1984, p. 251). Computer-integrated manufacturing increases managerial control by allowing managers to monitor the workflow process of the sequenced jobs. The central computer controlling the manufacturing process becomes the source of information for managers, whereas when traditional manufacturing methods are used, information about the process would have to be obtained from the supervisors of the different parts of the process. Integration is enhanced because, by definition, CIM integrates the different aspects of the manufacturing process.

Information technologies improve control because they provide real-time information, which is more easily monitored and less subject to error than information supplied using retrospective reporting methods. Integration is also improved because AIT brings information from several people or units together into one place. Increasingly, such solutions are driven by data, which also explains why industry pursues the creation of data-deriving behaviors, such as fitness tracking through mobile apps.

Impact of Microelectronic Technologies on Organizational Structure

Interest in the relationship between technology and organizational structure is not restricted to a concern about traditional technologies. With the increased use of microelectronic technologies researchers have started to examine the impact of new forms of technology on organizational structure. Table 21.3 compares the kind of structural attributes typically found in a mass-production technology organization with those found in an organization that uses CIM.

As can be seen, organizations with a CIM system are more organic than the traditional mass-production company, with a narrower span of control and a smaller number of vertical levels in their hierarchy. The work to be carried out requires a higher level of skill than that needed when mass-production technology is used. Employees often work in teams that are required to be innovative in their work processes, decentralizing decision making. This type of team approach requires an emphasis on horizontal rather than vertical communication, so managers need the skills to integrate work groups. As Skinner (1983, p. 112) notes about these managers:

> Their skills feature the abilities to form up and lead effective teams for problem solving, systems design, and experimental manufacturing systems. . . They seem to thrive on change, uncertainty, and ambiguity and indeed become easily bored with routine production. They delegate easily and in fact rather loosely, relying more on trust and less on formal controls and reports.

Mintzberg's (1979) adhocracy is the type of organizational structure most suitable for a company using a CIM system.

Relationship Between Technology and Organizational Structure

While the debate over whether technology determines the structure of an organization is unresolved, some important indicators can be found in the relationship between technology and the different elements of structure. This section reviews some findings on the relationship of technology to complexity, formalization, and centralization.

Technology and Complexity

Findings about the relationship between technology and complexity yield a mixed message. Technologies such as Woodward's mass-production technology, Perrow's routine technology, and Thompson's long-linked technology are generally associated with bureaucratic structures. Therefore, one can expect this type of technology to be related to high levels of task specialization and vertical differentiation. However, specialization as measured by the amount of professional training of the workforce is likely to be low (Hage & Aiken, 1969). When technology is nonroutine, as in Perrow's classification or Woodward's unit production technology, one is likely to find a more organic structure. Here task specialization and the number of vertical levels in the organization will be low, but complexity as measured by the amount of professional training

Table 21.3 A Comparison of the Structural Characteristics of Sport Organizations

Structural characteristics	Organizations using mass-production technology	Organizations using CIM technology
Span of control	Wide	Narrow
Number of vertical levels	High	Low
Tasks	Routine or repetitive	Responsive or craftlike
Specialization	High	Low
Decision making	Centralized	Decentralized
Information flow	Vertical	Horizontal
Basis of power	Position	Knowledge
Overall design type	Machine bureaucracy	Adhocracy

Based on P.L. Nemetz and L.W. Fry, "Flexible Manufacturing Organizations: Implications for Strategy Formulation and Organizational Design," *Academy of Management Review* 13 (1988): 627-638.

KEY ISSUES FOR SPORT MANAGERS

Digital connectivity has become a dominant feature of managerial interests. Access to the Internet is the most obvious technological consideration for managers, but innovating within mobile environments is now seen as the crucial characteristic of this need, notably because of the capacity to access big data from which greater insights into client behavior can be captured. As more people access content through mobile devices first, and as more people are using them for work more often than desktops or laptops, being mobile ready is a crucial feature of today's organizations. Mobile platforms such as social media environments allow a sport organization to reach more clients from all around the world more quickly and relatively cheaply. It is also faster to conduct business by communicating through such environments; media organizations will reach out to sources directly through such environments as Twitter or WhatsApp. Moreover, customers are more likely to reach out to them through these spaces too, making client relations a public affair. The Internet also affects organizational design and size. For example, the Internet has created an increased need for IT support, thus creating more divisions within an organization. The implications of this are significant since, while it might be tempting to think that social media is secondary to more traditional formats, it is likely that the first point of contact with an organization is through its social media profiles, even before a website. Finally, it provides an additional way to get information about other organizations in the same environment. For these reasons, it is essential that managers become digitally native to develop effective strategies in organizational design.

of staff is likely to be high. These mixed results should not be construed as a product of weak or inadequate research. Rather, they serve to underscore a point made by Hrebiniak (1974, p. 408), that both structure and technology are multidimensional concepts and "that when dealing only with general categories of either concept [such as the notion of complexity] it might be unreasonable to assume clear relationships or empirical trends."

Technology and Formalization

Notwithstanding Hrebiniak's caution about the problems of trying to relate technology to broadly based concepts of organizational structure, a clearer pattern emerges in regard to technology and formalization. Gerwin (1979) reviewed five studies (Blau & Schoenherr, 1971; Child & Mansfield, 1972; Hickson et al., 1969; Hinings & Lee, 1971; Khandwalla, 1974) that showed technology to be positively related to formalization. However, when he controlled for size the relationship disappeared. What Gerwin's review suggests is that the smaller the organization, the greater the impact of technology on formalization.

Technology and Centralization

While there are exceptions (Hinings & Lee, 1971), the majority of studies (Blau & Schoenherr, 1971; Child & Mansfield, 1972; Hage & Aiken, 1969; Hickson et al., 1969; Khandwalla, 1974) have shown a relationship, albeit often small and not statistically significant, between the level of technology within an organization and the extent to which decision making is decentralized. Generally speaking, organizations that employ routine technology will be more centralized; those with nonroutine technology are likely to be decentralized.

Summary and Conclusions

The relationship between technology and organizational structure is one of the most controversial and hotly debated issues in the study of organizations. This chapter has examined what is meant by technology, theorizing it as the process by which an organization achieves a range of greater efficiencies. Subsequently, it was noted how researchers use many different definitions of technology and, in part, this may be the cause of some of the conflicting results coming from studies examining the relationship of technology to organizational structure.

Much of the work conducted on technological processes within organizations has been based on the studies of Woodward, Perrow, or Thompson. The analyses involved examining the principal arguments put forward in these studies and how the major concepts outlined in each related to sport organizations. Some of the critiques and extensions of this work were also considered, along with raising questions as to whether there is a technological imperative, that is, whether technology determines structure. It was suggested that stronger support for the technological imperative existed where studies had been conducted at the work-group, or department, level. Studies conducted at the organizational level have produced mixed results. The issue of organizational level versus work-group or department level studies raised the issue of organizational size; we also saw evidence that size may influence the technology–structure relationship. The issue of how the industry or niche within a sport industry may influence its technology was also discussed, along with the differences between manufacturing and service technologies.

After considering traditional technologies and the debates conducted about their relationship to organizational structure, the analysis moved on to consider microelectronic technologies, and suggested that CIM and AIT have had and will continue to have a significant impact on sport organizations. We looked at some of the benefits of these technologies for sport organizations, along with the impact they could have on organizational structure. The final part of the chapter examined some general relationships between technology and the structural elements of complexity, formalization, and centralization. Regardless of some of the mixed findings that research studies have produced, technology is an important variable in the study of sport organizations.

Yet, as can be seen, little theoretical or empirical work within the field of sport management has looked at the influence of technology on any type of sport organization. It is necessary to address this important omission from sport management literature, given the rapid changes occurring in technology and the impact these changes can have on sport organizations.

Review Questions

1. Explain the different ways in which technology has been defined and why it is difficult to arrive at a single definition.
2. What type of organizational structure would you expect to find associated with Woodward's unit and mass-production technologies? Relate them to familiar sport organizations.
3. The Time Out "Cisco's Connected Athlete" noted how the Internet of Things will transform how people relate to athletes. If this is the case, what can sport management professors teach students about future sport technology?
4. Think of a familiar sport organization. How has social media affected it?

Suggestions for Further Reading

If you want to understand more about the technology–structure relationship, you should begin by looking at the original work by Woodward, Perrow, and Thompson. It would also be useful to look at the work by scholars who have sought to critique and extend these original studies; a number of these are mentioned in this chapter. Excellent overviews of studies on the technology–structure relationship and details of some of the important issues to be considered in work of this nature can be found in Fry's (1982) article "Technology-Structure Research: Three Critical Issues" in the *Academy of Management Journal*; Reimann and Inzerilli's (1979) "A Comparative Analysis of Empirical Research on Technology and Structure" in the *Journal of Management*; and Rousseau's chapter "Technology in Organizations: A Constructive Review and Analytic Framework," which is in Seashore and colleagues' (1983) book *Assessing Organizational Change*.

The only work that focuses on sport is Keidel's (1984) "Baseball, Football, and Basketball: Models for Business" in *Organizational Dynamics* and his extension of the ideas (1987) contained in "Team Sports Models as a Generic Organizational Framework," in *Human Relations*. You may, however, gain some ideas about the impact of technology on sport organizations by looking for articles about companies such as Nike, Reebok, and Huffy, which sometimes appear in periodicals such as *Forbes*, *Fortune*, *Business Week*, *Sports Illustrated*, and at sportbusiness.com.

Case for Analysis

Esports in the Olympic Games

In October 2017 the International Olympic Committee with Intel announced that an esport tournament would take place ahead of the 2018 PyeongChang Winter Olympic Games, drawing together a two-year period of discussing how esports should be oriented around the Games. The esport industry has been steadily growing over the last decade as an increasing number of competitions, players, prize money, and events have been staged by games titles publishers. One of the big challenges in this relationship is the fact that computer games are often seen as oppositional to physical activity, yet the major Olympic stakeholders such as Coca Cola have already begun to occupy this space. While one may see esports as inherently technological pursuits, with computer games innovation at their heart, many other associated technological innovations take place alongside their development. For example, the company Virtually Live is using computer graphics renderings of Formula E racing to create a virtual reality live experience as the sports event is taking place. Gamers can even now "ghost race," whereby their own driving can be visualized alongside the drivers in the physical race in real time. Alternatively, stadium designers are trying to figure out how to design stadia for esports events and for this to lead to a wider embedding of digital design into the stadium, which may have value for other events. For example, windows within VIP boxes could be transparent digital screens and be used to layer onto them augmented reality content, which tracks the field of play for the spectators as they peer through it. Esport is a great example of how the organizational structure of traditional sports must be intimately connected with another innovation community to ensure that it remains relevant in times of major technological and cultural change.

A big part of this picture is the development of 5G technology, which is paving the way for enhanced mobile content experiences and enriched broadcast streaming, including the capacity to deliver high-quality 360-degree video for consumers. Sport events have already begun experimenting with these new opportunities, as with the Korean Baseball Organization opening event in 2019, which included a choreography of an augmented reality dragon, the symbol of the defending champions, SK Wyverns (Hwaya, 2019). Spectators in the stadium were guided to use a mobile phone app to generate the dragon and witness its flight across the stadium as part of the ceremony. Examples like this are made possible by the capacity to deliver more data to consumers through 5G, which signals a whole new era of connected sport.

Questions

1. Complete a SWOT analysis on the merit of integrating esports into the official Olympic program, adopting the perspectives of the International Olympic Committee, the facilities management team, and an Olympic sponsor. Take into account how technology plays a role in the decision-making process and how it can be used to drive strategic objectives from each of these perspectives.
2. How could esports change the business of a sports team?
3. If you were the manager of a sport facility, how would you respond to the rise of esports and perhaps the decline of participation numbers in your own sport?

CHAPTER 22

Sports Analytics

Bill Gerrard, DPhil

Learning Objectives

When you have read this chapter you should be able to

1. understand the nature, scope, and development of sports analytics;
2. review the *Moneyball* story of analytics in baseball and assess its transferability to other types of team sports;
3. investigate the difficulties of applying analytics in invasion team sports particularly in developing player rating systems; and
4. appreciate the practicalities of applying analytics in elite team sports.

Key Concepts

analytics
"David" strategy
invasion team sports
key performance indicators
market efficiency hypothesis
Moneyball
player rating systems
sabermetrics
traffic-lights performance management system

Analytics and the Bees

Brentford, nicknamed "The Bees," are a professional association football club based in west London and original members of Division Three of the Football League when it was founded in 1920. For most of their history Brentford have played in the lower tiers of the Football League with the exception of the years just before and after World War II, gaining promotion to Division One in 1936 and finishing in the top six in the next three seasons. However, they were relegated to Division Two in 1947, and by the beginning of February 1951 they were facing the threat of relegation to Division Three. Their manager, Jackie Gibbons, responded to the crisis by appointing an external advisor, Charles Reep, who had developed a notational system to collect and analyze data for association football (Wilson, 2008). Brentford were struggling to score goals and averaged only 1.32 goals scored per game in their first 28 league games. Reep's analysis showed that most goals are scored from moves involving three or fewer passes. He advised Gibbons to play a much more direct style of play using long passes to move the ball quickly to their forwards. The change of style paid immediate dividends. Brentford more than doubled their scoring rate, averaging 2.71 goals scored per game in their final 14 games, losing only three of these games and finishing in the top half of the table. Analytics had made a real difference.

There is a recent postscript to Brentford's early adoption of analytics. The club is now owned by Matthew Benham, a successful businessman who has made his money in the sports betting industry. Benham appointed Mark Warburton, a former financial trader, as sporting director in 2011, responsible for player recruitment. Warburton then became manager in December 2013 and, under him, Brentford gained promotion to the Football League Championship (the second tier in English association football) in 2014 and just missed out on promotion to the Premiership (the top tier in English association football) in 2015. But Benham is committed to adopting a more thoroughgoing analytical approach to coaching, particularly using **key performance indicators** (KPIs). Despite his financial background, Warburton did not support the use of analytics in the coaching function and left Brentford at the end of the 2014-2015 season. It appeared that Benham was prepared to accept the short-term pain of losing a successful manager in order to achieve long-term gains from changing the organizational culture to a more evidence-based approach. The first post-Warburton season for Brentford was not particularly successful, with three different managers in the 2015-2016 season and a ninth-place finish in the Championship, nine points away from the promotion playoffs. Warburton, by contrast, had an outstanding first season with Glasgow Rangers in Scotland, winning the Scottish Championship and promotion to the Scottish Premiership. But Warburton has suffered a reversal of fortune in subsequent seasons, leaving the Rangers to return to the Football League Championship at Nottingham Forest but then being dismissed after only nine months in charge. At the time of writing, Warburton is now coaching Queens Park Rangers in the Football League Championship. Brentford have continued to challenge for promotion to the Premiership but have failed to qualify for the end-of-season promotion playoffs since Warburton's departure in 2015.

In the 1950s Brentford were a very early trailblazer for the use of data analytics to support the sporting operation of professional teams, and now seven decades later the team is still at the forefront of the use of data analytics in association football. But other sports, particularly baseball and basketball, have streaked ahead in their use of analytical insights to support coaching and recruitment. This chapter will examine the current use of data analytics by the sporting operation of professional teams and show how experts in quants have become a source of competitive advantage for teams.

The Nature of Sports Analytics

Sports analytics is a growth area in sport organizations, attracting considerable attention in recent years and even generating Hollywood films portraying analytics as a numbers-driven approach to player recruitment that ignores the more subjective insights of scouts. The approach has met with varying results: success in the case of *Moneyball*, starring Brad Pitt, but failure in the case of *Trouble with the Curve*, starring Clint Eastwood. Indeed, *Moneyball* has had such an impact, both the film and the original book of the same title, that the term **Moneyball** has become synonymous with the use of sports analytics in the sporting operation of professional teams in any sport. So what is this thing called *sports analytics* that is generating so much interest both inside and outside sport organizations?

In *The Numbers Game* (2013, p. 5), a great account of the application of analytics in association football, Chris Anderson and David Sally use the basic Wikipedia definition of analytics as "the discovery and communication of meaningful patterns in data." Benjamin Alamar provides a more detailed definition of sports analytics as "the management of structured historical data, the application of predictive analytic models that utilise that data, and the use of information systems to inform decision makers and enable them to help their organisations in gaining a competitive advantage on the field of play" (2013, p. 4). A concise working definition of sports analytics is the use of statistical analysis and other related analytical techniques to support decision making in sport organizations.

A common theme in all three definitions is that analytics is "analysis with purpose." **Analytics** is the practical application of data analysis to real-world problems to inform the choice of decision makers in sport organizations. Analytics is about using statistical analysis to make a difference. Analytics necessarily involves the 3 D's:

1. Data analysis
2. Decision making
3. Domain knowledge

Fundamentally, analytics is data analysis, the first D of analytics. Analytics is about collecting relevant data, summarizing that data, analyzing variation, and investigating relationships in order to identify the systematic causes of the observed variation. But data analysis must be driven by a concern with decision making, the second D of analytics. Analytics is impact focused, always directed at supporting decision makers in their search to improve performance within their organizations. And in order to be effective, analytics requires the third D of analytics, domain knowledge, an understanding of the context within which the decision makers are operating. Analytics is not just about identifying generic critical success factors associated with an organization's external environment, but it must also be context specific, recognizing the objectives, resources, and culture of the specific organization as well as the uniqueness of every individual decision situation.

Although sports analytics is practiced within sports organizations, there is a very diverse set of contributors to its development. Increasingly, elite sport teams are either employing analysts or engaging external consultants to undertake data analysis. Much of their work is shrouded in secrecy, with teams and consultants concerned to protect their intellectual property and any competitive advantages gained. We only get limited insights into the analytics conducted by teams behind closed doors when analysts and consultants give media interviews or present at sports analytics conferences. Needless to say, these insights tend to be very broad and usually only indicate the types of issues being investigated and methods used.

Another group of contributors to sports analytics are academics specializing in applying data analysis to sports datasets. Originally this type of research tended to be published in sports science journals, but increasingly it can be found in academic journals in the business disciplines, either generalist journals such as *Academy of Management Journal* and *American Economic Review*, or more specialist sports-focused journals such as *Journal of Sport Management*, *European Sport Management Quarterly*, *Journal of Sports Economics*, and *Journal of Quantitative Analysis in Sports*. Academic research is highly accessible, but we have little idea of how much of this literature has actually influenced teams. Often the insights are too generic to have practical value for individual teams. One reason for this is that academic researchers typically have to work with much more limited datasets than teams who can afford to access commercial databases.

The final key group of contributors to sports analytics are the hobbyists, individuals who apply their data analytical skills to sports. In the past they published their findings in books and pamphlets but these days publish mainly in blogs and other online communities. Again, it is difficult to know just how much influence the hobbyists have on the actual practice of analytics in teams, but anecdotal evidence shows that teams scan the Internet as a source of new ideas. Of course, the hobbyist *par excellence* is Bill James, whose contributions to **sabermetrics** (i.e., baseball analytics) have revolutionized the use of data analysis not only in Major League Baseball (MLB) but in all sports.

In principle, sports analytics covers the use of analytics by all sport organizations, but most of the focus has been on the use of analytics by professional sport teams in both their sporting operations and their business operations. However, although the marketing and commercial functions of sport teams are increasingly applying the big-data techniques of consumer analytics, this is not viewed as specific to the sport business. Therefore, sports analytics has come to be identified primarily with performance analytics, that is, the application of data analysis to the sporting function. Indeed, it could be argued that sports analytics is even more specific and relates to the analysis of tactical performance data. It is this type of data analysis that is relatively new. Teams have a long history of using data analysis in the medical, strength and conditioning, and sport science functions to analyze the technical and physical (i.e., biomechanical) aspects of sporting performance. Biomechanical performance analytics plays a key role in planning workloads in training sessions to optimize the physical preparation of players while minimizing the risk of injury, particularly soft-tissue injuries. The focus of this chapter is tactical performance analytics (hereafter referred to as *tactical analytics*) rather than biomechanical performance analytics or the application of consumer or business analytics in the sport industry. Figure 22.1 provides a summary of the use of data analytics in the business and sporting operations of professional sport teams.

Tactical analytics covers data analysis to support a wide range of coaching decisions that can be influenced and potentially improved by knowing the numbers. Applications include talent identification and youth development, player recruitment and retention, player valuation, match tactics based on opposition analysis, team selection, player and team performance reviews, and planning training schedules. Tactical analytics can be seen as an extension of performance analysis beyond video analysis to investigate statistical patterns and trends across games. Tactical analytics is an application of evidence-based management (Pfeffer & Sutton, 2006) to coaching in which data analysis is combined with intuition and experience to inform decisions. Necessarily, sports analytics is coach-led analytics since the coach sets the agenda and makes the decisions, with the analyst tasked to provide the relevant analysis.

Early Developments

The statistical analysis of sports data dates back over 100 years, principally in the striking-and-fielding sports such as baseball and cricket. These sports are structured in such a way that the key performance data can be recorded during the game using paper and pencil. Scorecards for baseball and cricket have been published in newspapers since the late 19th century, so the key performance data for these sports have been widely available for analysis. Baseball is by far the most analyzed sport in statistical terms, to the point where the statistical analysis of baseball has its own nomenclature: sabermetrics, derived from the acronym, SABR, of the Society for American Baseball Research. One of the very

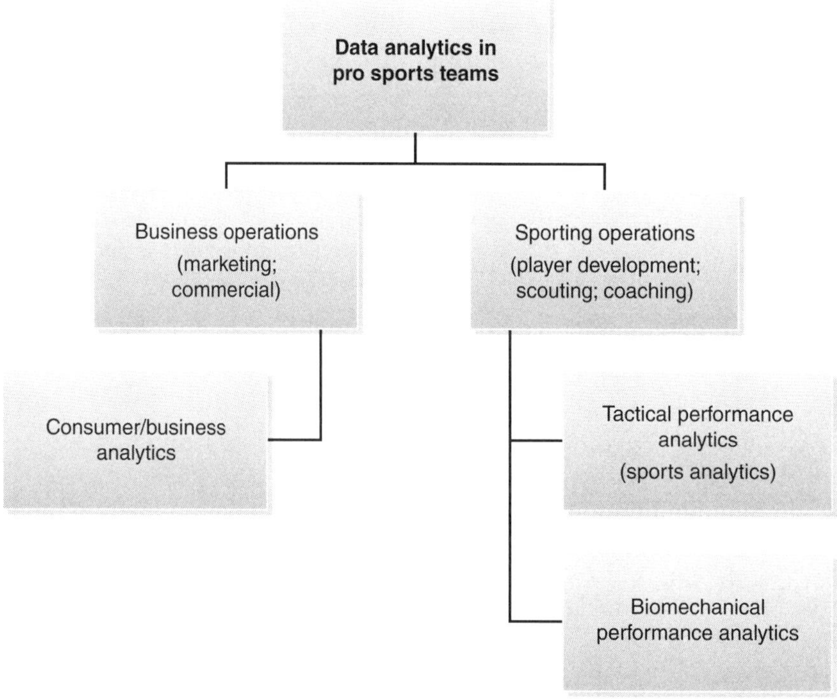

Figure 22.1 Data analytics in pro sports teams.

TIME OUT

Why Reep's Statistical Analysis Does Not Support Direct Play

Reep's analysis in support of direct play in association football has been very influential, but it is fundamentally flawed statistically. It is a classic case of biasing the results by only looking at a subset of outcomes. In Reep's case, he only considered passing sequences resulting in goals scored. If he had considered all passing sequences irrespective of whether they ended in goals scored, he would have found that most passing moves involve three or fewer passes, so it is no surprise that more goals are scored from shorter passing sequences. Once you allow for the total frequency of different lengths of passing sequences, the evidence suggests there is a proportionately lower chance of scoring from shorter passing sequences, the opposite to the conclusion made by Reep. (See Hughes & Franks, 2005 for the definitive critique of Reep's analysis.)

first attempts to systematically analyze baseball data was undertaken by the Chicago sportswriter Hugh Fullerton, in collaboration with the Chicago Cubs second baseman John Evers. They published a book, *Touching Second: The Science of Baseball* in 1910, with extracts published in *The American Magazine*. The book contains Fullerton's analysis of 1,284 ground balls in the 1909 season from which he calculated that an average ground ball took 1.15 seconds to travel 100 feet (Swanson, 2013).

Another groundbreaking step in the development of sabermetrics was "The Equation," developed by Allan Roth working with Branch Rickey at the Brooklyn Dodgers in the late 1940s and published in *Life* magazine (Rickey, 1954). Roth and Rickey produced an equation in which the number of games behind the league leader is related to a range of offensive and defensive metrics. Further important early contributions to sabermetrics included the work of Earnshaw Cook (1964), the Mills brothers (Mills & Mills, 1970), and John Thorn and Pete Palmer (1984). But the most significant development in sabermetrics was the work of Bill James, who started to publish his *Baseball Abstract* in 1977; it is his work that eventually led to the adoption of analytics by the Oakland A's in the MLB as recounted in *Moneyball* (see next section).

Analytics in the **invasion team sports** such as the various codes of football (e.g., gridiron, association, Aussie Rules, Gaelic, etc.) has developed much more slowly by comparison. These sports are more continuous in their action, and performance data are much more difficult to record. It was only with the advent of video analysis in the 1970s and the ability to replay recordings of games in a stop-start fashion that permitted systematic collection of performance data for these types of sports. Thorn and Palmer were also one of the first to apply statistical analysis to gridiron football in *The Hidden Game of Football* (Carroll et al., 1988). They analyzed the win probabilities at any point in a game based on three dimensions: pitch (field) location, score, and time remaining. In this way, they could value every play by calculating the consequent change in the win probability. One of their most contentious findings was that teams tended to kick too much on fourth down. They concluded that "you should not kick a field goal unless you have six or more yards to go on fourth down. And if you're inside your opponent's 10-yard line, you shouldn't kick no matter the distance" (p. 158).

The statistical analysis of association football began much earlier through the pioneering work of Charles Reep, a trained accountant who joined the Royal Air Force and reached the rank of Wing Commander. He developed his own notational system for association football and started recording data by paper and pencil at games he attended from 1950 on. Subsequently, he also applied his methods to televised games and video recordings. Over his lifetime he annotated nearly 2,500 games and published several papers on his research. His analysis found that most goals were scored from sequences of three passes or less (Reep & Benjamin, 1968), and this led him to advocate a direct style of play. As discussed in the Opening Scenario, Reep's work has been very influential in several teams that have adopted long-ball tactics, starting with Brentford in 1951 and including Wolves in the mid-50s, Wimbledon and Watford in the 1980s, and Norway in the 1990s (Wilson, 2008). But this seemingly close connection between analytics and a particular style of play has alienated many coaches, and Reep's research remains highly controversial in association football to this day.

Moneyball: The Game Changer

Moneyball: The Art of Winning an Unfair Game was written by Michael Lewis and published in 2003. It was subsequently released as a movie in 2011 starring Brad Pitt. It is based on the true story of the Oakland A's in the MLB and how they used sabermetrics to overcome the resource constraints of a small-market team. The book focuses on seasons 2001 and 2002, while the film starts with the last game of the 2001 season.

The key protagonist is Billy Beane, a first-round draft pick by the New York Mets in 1980. Beane signed for the Mets instead of going to Stanford on a football and baseball scholarship. Stanford wanted him to replace their departing quarterback, John Elway, who had a very successful career in the NFL with the Denver Broncos. Beane played in the MLB from 1984 to 1989 for the New York Mets, the Minnesota Twins, the Detroit Tigers, and the Oakland A's. As a player he never fulfilled the expectations that made him such a highly prized draft pick and, after being sent down to the minors at the end of spring training in 1990, Beane decided to stop playing and asked to join the A's front office as an advance scout. He was promoted to assistant general manager in 1993 and succeeded Sandy Alderson as general manager of the A's in October 1997.

Although Beane embraced sabermetrics as a potential **"David" strategy**, that is, a strategy using process innovation to achieve significant efficiency gains in order to compete more effectively against resource-richer rivals, it was his predecessor, Alderson, who first introduced sabermetric principles to the A's in response to a change in ownership in 1995 and the demand by the new owners that payroll costs be slashed. Alderson was an avid reader of Bill James and was persuaded of the importance of on-base percentage (OBP) in assessing hitter performance. Conventional wisdom treated a walk as a pitcher error rather than hitter skill, so hitter performance was assessed by the batting average (i.e., hits per at-bat) and the slugging percentage (i.e., bases per at-bat). But, as James showed, it does not matter whether you get to base by hitting or walking; the critical thing is getting to base and avoiding an out, the ultimate scarce resource in baseball. OBP attributed walks to the hitter, hence valuing the skill in pitch selection. Recognizing the potential in James's work, Alderson went out and hired a consultant, Eric Walker, in the hope of getting useful sabermetric insights that would be proprietary to the A's. Walker produced a pamphlet that Alderson passed on to Beane. It opened Beane's eyes to the possibilities of using sabermetrics to inform player recruitment decisions when operating within very tight budgetary constraints.

So when Beane became general manager, he did so in an organization already beginning to embrace sabermetrics. Beane was assisted initially by J.P. Riccardi, whom Alderson had appointed as a special assistant in 1996 and whom Beane promoted to director of player personnel. Riccardi subsequently joined the Toronto Blue Jays as their general manager. Beane also brought Paul DePodesta into the A's organization. DePodesta was a Harvard economics graduate whom Beane appointed as assistant general manager in 1999. It was DePodesta who was primarily responsible for producing the sabermetric analysis to support Beane's decisions on player recruitment. DePodesta joined the Los Angeles Dodgers as their general manager in 2004. Interestingly, DePodesta and Riccardi subsequently worked with Alderson when he became general manager at the New York Mets.

The essence of the *Moneyball* story is exploiting gain opportunities in player trading arising from the mistaken conventional wisdom of rival teams. In particular, the A's used OBP to assess hitters since it was a better predictor of winning than the batting average and the slugging percentage. Beane also started to draft more college players, taking advantage of a subjective discount in the market arising from rival teams tending to favor draft picks straight from high school (just as Billy Beane himself had been drafted). Yet in some ways college ballplayers were more predictable as MLB players because they were older and had developed both physically and emotionally as well as playing a high level of baseball during their college careers.

The use of sabermetrics by the A's is a real-world example of what researchers who study the financial aspects of sport organizations and economists call the **market efficiency hypothesis** (MEH). Asset markets are effectively informational-processing mechanisms where information about the future prospects of assets is very quickly incorporated into market prices through trading behavior. For example, new information suggesting improved future prospects will lead to increased demand for the asset, putting upward pressure on price. In the case of the MLB players' labor market, information was being used inefficiently, and the MEH would predict that eventually a trader (Beane) would exploit the opportunity to profit by trading at the "wrong" prices. It is no real surprise, then, that Michael Lewis should be attracted to the story of the A's exploiting market inefficiency. Lewis began his career as a financial trader with Salomon Brothers, working in the New York and London markets. In many ways Lewis, the financial asset trader, saw Beane, the player trader, as a kindred spirit.

Beane's achievements with the A's have been astonishing. The A's record for his first nine seasons as general manager, 1998 to 2006, is reported in table 22.1. Beane transformed a losing team to a highly efficient winning team. In the two years, on which

Table 22.1 Oakland A's Win Percentage and Payroll Expenditure, 1998 to 2006

Year	Win percentage (regular season)		Payroll expenditure	
	Win percentage	MLB ranking	Payroll	MLB ranking
1998	.457	21st=	$20.1 million	28th
1999	.537	10th	$24.2 million	26th
2000	.565	6th	$32.1 million	25th
2001	.630	2nd	$33.8 million	29th
2002	.636	2nd	$40.0 million	28th
2003	.593	4th	$50.3 million	23rd
2004	.562	9th	$59.4 million	16th
2005	.543	9th=	$55.4 million	22nd
2006	.574	5th	$62.2 million	21st

= indicates tied in the rankings with at least one other team having exactly the same win percentage
Calculations using data published over time by USA Today.

Moneyball focuses, 2001 and 2002, the A's had the second-best win percentage in the regular season yet were in the bottom three for payroll costs. So in 2002 the A's had the second-lowest payroll in the MLB with $40 million yet won 103 regular-season games. The New York Yankees won one more game but spent $125.9 million.

Gerrard (2007) reported estimates of the efficiency of MLB teams over the period 1998 to 2006, the first nine years of Beane's tenure as the A's general manager. Gerrard calculated that the A's were 59.3 percent more efficient than the MLB average, while the Yankees over the same period were 50.7 percent less efficient than the MLB average. Beane still remains with the Oakland A's, having been promoted to executive vice president of baseball operations in 2015.

Two economists, Hakes and Sauer (2006), tested what they called the *Moneyball* hypothesis that OBP is a better predictor of winning than conventional hitting metrics, but the MLB players' labor market was inefficient because it ignored this information. Using data for 1999 to 2003, Hakes and Sauer showed that OBP was a highly significant predictor of team win percentages with a weighting more than twice that of the slugging percentage. However, when Hakes and Sauer investigated hitter salaries over the period 2000 to 2003, they found that OBP had no

TIME OUT

Remember That *Moneyball* Is Not an Academic Case Study

It is important to remember that *Moneyball* is based on a true story, but neither the book nor the movie are entirely historically accurate. They certainly would not pass the academic review process. The movie in particular portrays the Oakland A's as a very dysfunctional organization with continuous conflict between the general manager and his analyst on one side and the scouting and coaching staff on the other. This makes for a much more dramatic story, but it greatly overstates the conflicts within the organization. In reality the Oakland A's use both data analysis and scouting reports as part of a thoroughgoing evidence-based approach to player recruitment.

significant impact. When teams valued hitters, they did so using slugging percentages, not OBP. All that changed when Hakes and Sauer investigated hitter salaries in 2004. They found that in 2004 OBP had become highly significant as a determinant of hitter salaries and indeed was weighted more heavily than the slugging percentage. The world had changed because the publication of *Moneyball* alerted other teams to the possibilities of sabermetrics in providing a competitive advantage. Just as the MEH predicted, as soon as the market recognized profitable opportunities could be had from using information better, traders changed their behavior and market prices adjusted. Not only was *Moneyball* a game changer in baseball, it also changed the approach in other sports by alerting teams to the possibilities of using data analysis to help improve decision making and win more.

Analytics in Invasion Team Sports

The publication of *Moneyball* and the subsequent release of the movie have generated considerable interest in the transferability of data analytics to other sports. But in order to assess the transferability, it is important to consider the specifics of the *Moneyball* experience and how these compare to other sports. One must consider three dimensions: context, data, and function.

First of all, the context of *Moneyball* is a striking-and-fielding sport, baseball, which has a very atomistic structure with a relatively low degree of tactical coordination. Consequently, individual player contributions are highly separable. As regards the second dimension, the structure of striking-and-fielding games is conducive to the collection of performance data using only human observation and in-game paper-and-pencil recording methods. Performance data for cricket and baseball have long been widely reported in the media. It follows that the performance data are effectively open source, freely available to all, which has the upside of promoting research in a wider community of enthusiasts beyond analysts within teams. The downside is that innovations have low protection from imitation by rival teams. As Hakes and Sauer (2006) showed, the publication of *Moneyball* had an immediate impact on the MLB players' market: Teams imitated the A's in using OBP to assess hitters, and OBP very quickly became a key driver of hitter salaries. The third dimension of *Moneyball* is the focus of data analytics to support the player recruitment function. The atomistic structure of the sport allows a separation-of-powers management structure in which the general manager is responsible for player recruitment independent of the field coach. This type of management structure means that analytics can be introduced into the operation of the front office without necessitating the involvement of the coaching staff, thereby avoiding a potential cultural barrier to innovation.

The transferability of *Moneyball* into the very different context of invasion team sports, such as the various codes of football and hockey as well as basketball, is highly problematic. Invasion team sports have a more complex structure particularly because of the importance of the spatial dimension and the continual need for players to make decisions to optimize their field positioning. Crucially, the field positioning of any individual player depends on the positioning decisions of other players, both teammates and opponents. It follows that invasion team sports require a high degree of tactical coordination, which puts a greater onus on coaches to produce a game plan to be implemented by the players. This implies that decision making is a key component of player performance as well as fitness and technique.

Analysis of Complex Data

Invasion team sports are complex in a number of ways. They involve a wider range of player actions, and these actions are highly interdependent. Scoring depends on creating scoring opportunities, which, in turn, requires that the ball (or puck) is moved into attacking areas of the field. But in order to build an attacking play in the first place, a team needs possession of the ball, which depends on the team's defensive play and ability to gain possession. This makes offense and defense inextricably linked. In some sports such as association football, the continuity of play is such that individual players are required to make both defensive and offensive contributions, although there can be partial specialization of playing roles, with some players allocated greater defensive responsibilities while other players may have greater offensive responsibilities. And in some sports such as rugby union some actions are joint, involving a number of players as in the case of scrums and lineouts. The high degree of complexity of invasion team sports means that individual player contributions are much less separable.

The complexity of player actions in invasion team sports leads to several problems in the collection and analysis of performance data. There is a coding problem of identifying, categorizing, and enumerating the different types of player actions. Combined with the continuity and speed of play, it is no surprise that data analytics in invasion team sports is a relatively recent phenomenon, facilitated by the development of video analysis, as well as tracking and image recognition software. Historically, performance metrics in invasion team sports were limited to appearances, scoring, and discipline. The dependency of data collection on technology has led to the provision of performance data in many team sports becoming a commercial business, with companies specializing in coding games and supplying performance data to teams. This data can be expensive and is often only available to teams playing at the elite level in high-revenue sports. It is usually not publicly available, which has limited the growth of data analysis in these sports outside of teams themselves. But within the sport itself the data from commercial providers are open source, potentially accessible to all teams with limited protection from imitation. Another issue is that this data tends to be largely tally (i.e., frequency) counts of different types of player contributions using generic definitions that are applicable across teams. Commercial data providers cannot provide expert data on player decision making or technique, which are team-specific, particularly decision making based on a team's game plan. This type of expert data can only be produced in-house by the teams themselves.

Another major data problem exists in the transferability of data analytics to invasion team sports. Baseball involves a very direct relationship between player contributions, scoring, and match outcomes so that the analytical questions have primarily focused on the choice of the best hitting, pitching, and fielding metrics. However, invasion team sports exhibit a much more indirect link between individual player contributions, scoring, and match outcomes due to potentially very extended causal chains. The core analytical issue is how to determine the weightings of individual contributions to reflect their importance to the final match outcome. Gerrard (2007) has suggested that invasion team sports are most appropriately viewed as a hierarchical structural model that captures both the causal links between different actions and match outcomes, including the interdependency of offense and defense. Offensive play, after all, is a form of defense since possession not only provides an opportunity to create a scoring opportunity but also denies the opposition the opportunity to do so.

The complexity of invasion team sports necessitates a more integrated style of management. The need for a high degree of tactical coordination on the field is mirrored by the need for a high degree of coordination between decisions on player recruitment and coaching decisions on playing style and tactics. Potential recruits need to be assessed relative to the needs of the team's specific style of play. To the extent that such judgments are perceived as subjective and need to be based more on coach knowledge and experience, it follows that the cultural barriers to the use of data analytics are more likely to be much higher in invasion team sports. On the other hand, if these barriers can be overcome, data analytics in the invasion team sports have potentially more applications beyond player recruitment, including the design of tactical plans for specific opponents, team selection, and training priorities.

Player Rating Systems

The analytical difficulties of invasion team sports are exemplified by the alternative approaches to developing **player rating systems** to summarize the overall contribution of individual players to match outcomes. Shea and Baker (2013) differentiate between top-down and bottom-up approaches. Bottom-up approaches involve combining measures of the different types of contribution into a single composite player rating using an appropriate weighting system. The problem with bottom-up approaches is that it can be very difficult statistically to estimate the weights to use in combining the various contribution metrics. One of the problems is that higher-level actions that are causally closer to match outcomes tend to be the best statistical predictors. Hence players contributing proportionately more higher-level actions tend to receive higher rankings with no allowance for the dependency on the lower-level actions of other players. It can also be difficult to estimate weightings for some actions that are closely correlated with other contributions. And sometimes the estimated weightings have the "wrong" sign. This is often the case for defensive actions such as tackles, which tend statistically to be negatively correlated to match outcomes. The reason for this is that defensive actions not only measure the amount of score-preventing actions, which will be positively related to match outcomes, but also act as a proxy for the quantity of opposition-attacking play, which is correlated to scores conceded and so negatively related to match outcomes. The latter effect tends to dominate unless the statistical model separately controls for the amount of opposition offensive play. One solution to the difficulties of the bottom-up approach to player ratings is to use a mixed-methods approach combining statistical estimation and expert judgment to determine the weightings. One example of this approach is the STARS player rating system (Gerrard, 2014) in which five different groups of actions are identified—attack, defense, negatives (i.e., errors and ill-discipline), striking, and goal-keeping—with weightings within each grouping of actions determined largely by statistical analysis, whereas the relative weightings of the five groups are imposed based on expert judgment.

An alternative approach to player ratings in invasion team sports that avoids the difficulties of combining a multitude of different types of player contributions is to use a top-down approach. The basic idea is to measure a player's contribution in terms of match outcomes, specifically the scores for and against when the player is playing. This gives what is often called the player's plus-minus statistic. It is best suited to sports in which scoring and player changes are frequent. It is no surprise, therefore, that the plus-minus statistic is widely used in basketball. Although the plus-minus statistic avoids the difficulties inherent in composite bottom-up ratings, the obvious limitation is that players are credited (and debited) with the scoring effects of the contributions of their teammates as well as their own. Thus a player can have high plus rating by virtue of being a member of a very successful team with several great players as teammates. Shea and Baker (2013) give the example of the Miami Heat's Mario Chambers in the NBA's 2012-2013 regular season. His plus-minus rating that season was 569, which ranked as the fifth highest, but Shea and Baker argue that his high rating was more a reflection of the strength of the Miami team, with stars such as LeBron James (ranked first that season with a plus-minus rating of 720) and Dwayne Wade (ranked fourth with a rating of 571).

Sports Analytics in Action: Coach-Led Analytics at Saracens

Saracens, originally founded in 1876, are one of the leading rugby union clubs in England and ever-present members of the top-tier division since the professional era began in 1996. Yet despite its long history, Saracens had won only one major trophy, the Tetley's Bitter Cup in 1998, prior to a radical restructuring of the club initiated by new investment in the club in 2008 by the South African SAIL consortium, led by the billionaire businessman Johann Rupert. One of the first consequences of SAIL's involvement in the club was the appointment of Brendan Venter, the former South African international player, 1995 Rugby World Cup winner, and qualified medical practitioner, as director of rugby in 2009. Venter initiated a major change process, starting with a radical restructuring of the playing squad. He created an evidence-based, people-centered culture that put analytics and personal development at the core of the Saracens way of doing things.

Under Venter's leadership Saracens developed a coach-led system of internal data collection on team performances. This data included not only tally counts of player contributions using the coaches' own categorization, but also included expert data on the players' decision making and technique. The data was analyzed statistically using an external consultant, and a set of player and team KPIs were identified. A **traffic-lights performance management system** was introduced to categorize performance levels of the KPIs as excellent (green), satisfactory (amber), or poor (red). The performance thresholds were based on the statistical analysis of past performances

TIME OUT

Measuring the Impact of Really Great Players

Shea and Baker are undoubtedly correct in their criticism of the plus-minus statistic as misleading for players such as Mario Chambers who are being, at least in part, assigned credit for playing with really great players such as LeBron James. These interdependencies are intrinsic to invasion team sports. (Professor Trevor Slack, a long-suffering Edmonton Oilers fan, called it the "Gretzky effect" and argued that the franchise long experienced the negative consequences of trading Wayne Gretzky to Los Angeles in 1988.) Although the plus-minus statistic may be limited as a measure of the contribution of good players playing with great players despite various attempts to create adjusted plus-minus measures, the basic plus-minus statistic can still indicate the impact of great players on their teams. So, for example, comparing the plus-minus statistic for James with the Miami Heat's plus-minus statistic when James was not on court gives an overall measure of how much James contributed to Miami, including his impact on how well Chambers played.

using win probabilities as well as the knowledge and experience of coaches. The upper threshold defining an excellent performance was also set in part as a target to which players should aspire. The KPIs were reported after every game, discussed at the coaches' game review meeting at the start of the week, and analyzed to identify weaknesses in performance that needed to be addressed in training. Player and team KPIs were also reviewed periodically during the season and formed the basis of an extensive end-of-season review to learn lessons and plan for the next season. Strategic benchmarking studies were undertaken to compare Saracens with other leading rugby union teams in Europe, South Africa, Australia, and New Zealand in order to identify how Saracens needed to develop to be competitive not only domestically but also in the premier European tournament, now known as the European Rugby Champions Cup (formerly known as the Heineken Cup).

Venter stepped down as director of rugby in January 2011 in order to return with his family to South Africa, but by then analytics had become firmly embedded into the coaching function at the club. Venter's deputy, Mark McCall, was appointed as director of rugby. McCall, like Venter, was a former international rugby player and, as a university law graduate, also committed to an evidence-based approach. Under McCall's leadership the use of analytics has been further extended, primarily in the preparation of detailed reports on opponents.

Since 2009 Saracens have been very successful (see table 22.2), featuring in seven domestic finals and ten semifinals in ten years. In addition, Saracens have reached the semifinals in Europe seven times and progressed to the final four times. Saracens won the Premiership for the first time in their history in 2011 and repeated the achievement in 2015, 2016, 2018, and 2019. In 2016 Saracens completed the double of winning both the Premiership and the European Rugby Champions Cup, retaining their European title in 2017, and completing the domestic-European double again in 2019. It is impossible to gauge just how much analytics has contributed to their success, but it is clear that Saracens consider analytics to be a key element in their competitive strategy so much so that in 2014 they engaged Deloitte, one of the leading global accounting and management consultancy companies, to provide database management services and to further develop their use of analytics. Saracens provides a powerful case study of how analytics can overcome the cultural barriers in invasion team sports and contribute effectively to an evidence-based approach to coaching.

Table 22.2 Saracens Domestic and European Record, 2009-2010 to 2018-2019

Season	Premiership	Heineken Cup/European Champions Cup/ Heineken Champions Cup
2009-2010	Finalists	Did Not Qualify
2010-2011	Winners	Group Stages
2011-2012	Semifinalists	Quarterfinalists
2012-2013	Semifinalists	Semifinalists
2013-2014	Finalists	Finalists
2014-2015	Winners	Semifinalists
2015-2016	Winners	Winners
2016-2017	Semifinalists	Winners
2017-2018	Winners	Semifinalists
2018-2019	Winners	Winners

Data sourced over time from www.premiershiprugby.com.

TIME OUT

Be Careful When Using KPIs to Set Training Priorities

It is vital when using KPIs to track performance and set training priorities that teams differentiate between systematic variation (especially a downward trend in performance) and random (or natural) variation. Training time is limited, and focusing on one area of play will mean less time for other areas, which can be counterproductive and can actually increase the variability of team performance. It is therefore important to be sure that the coaches are reacting to a systematic deterioration in a particular aspect of the team's performance rather than a one-off below-par performance. Best practice when using KPIs includes setting rules for when to intervene. If used properly, KPIs provide an early-warning system for a systematic deterioration in performance requiring coach intervention, but not every downward shift in a KPI signals a problem requiring action.

Other Applications of Analytics in Sports Organizations

As shown in figure 22.1, the use of data analytics in sport organizations is not just limited to the analysis of the sporting operation and supporting the decisions of coaches. Business analytics, broadly defined as the use of data analysis to support business decisions, is also applicable to sport teams and other sport organizations. In particular, one of the most important areas in business analytics that is relevant to the sport industry is retail analytics, which involves the analysis of customer data to support decisions on marketing strategies. The growth of retail analytics has been particularly prevalent in businesses that have embraced customer relationship marketing (CRM) and, as a consequence, possess large customer databases with detailed personal data as well as purchasing behavior. Amazon and other online retailers have been very progressive in their use of retail analytics. If you use Amazon, then you will receive regular emails suggesting possible purchases. Behind these targeted emails lies extensive data analysis to identify similar customers to you and then using their purchasing behaviors to suggest possible purchases for you.

Ticketing and other marketing decisions of teams are benefiting from the detailed analysis of fan purchasing behavior in much the same way. Many professional sport teams have adopted CRM strategies, so they have extensive information on their fans. Marketing departments of teams are using cluster analysis to segment their fanbase into groups of fans with similar personal characteristics and similar purchasing behavior. In addition a statistical technique called *logistic regression* can be used to build models to predict the likelihood of a purchase based on personal characteristics and previous purchasing behavior. Combining cluster analysis and logistic regression can provide teams with powerful tools to construct optimal marketing strategies for targeting different groups of fans with the most suitable group-specific promotions.

Summary and Conclusions

This chapter has considered the nature of sports analytics as the use of statistical analysis to support decision making in sports organizations with specific emphasis on decisions related to the sporting performance of teams. The early developments of analytics in baseball, gridiron football, and association football have been discussed before attention was focused on *Moneyball*, the story of how the Oakland A's in the MLB used analytics as a competitive strategy. The difficulties of transferring the *Moneyball* experience into invasion team sports such as the various codes of football, hockey, and basketball has been investigated particularly with regard to the development of player rating systems. The application of sports analytics has been illustrated with a discussion of coach-led analytics in action at the English rugby union club Saracens.

It seems clear that the growth in the use of data analytics in sport organizations is set to continue in both the sporting and business operations. As a consequence, sport organizations are going to have an increasing demand not only for data analysts with the skills to apply statistical analysis in both the sporting and business operations, but also for managers able to use the insights of statistical analysis to support their decision making. Therefore, it is becoming increasingly critical that sport management students understand statistical

KEY ISSUES FOR SPORT MANAGERS

The experience of pro sport teams such as the Oakland A's, Brentford, and Saracens in adopting data analytics within the sporting operation raises a number of key issues for managers in all organizations considering making greater use of data analytics.

1. *The presence of significant resource constraints is an important source of motivation for the initial adoption of data analytics.* Organizations operating in highly competitive environments while facing significant resource constraints have tended to be early adopters of data analytics. Hence data analytics has been particularly attractive to pro sport teams constrained by their location in small markets and competing in leagues with limited regulation of player salary expenditure. If these teams are to remain competitive with resource-richer rivals, they must develop a "David" strategy such as an analytics-based approach to player recruitment.

2. *The active involvement of organizational leaders committed to the generalized adoption of data analytics within the organization is crucial.* Organizations that have been most effective in their use of data analytics are characterized by a clearly articulated organizational commitment to data analytics as a sustainable source of competitive advantage, endorsed and actively promoted by the organizational leadership, and supported by the ownership. In contrast data analytics is likely to remain a localized activity within a single function or department in organizations without organizational or leadership commitment to data analytics.

3. *The development of a generalized analytics capability across the organization takes time.* The experience of pro sport teams that have made data analytics a key aspect of how they do things suggests that it can take up to ten years for the generalized adoption of data analytics across an organization. The introduction of data analytics is not a quick-fix solution.

4. *The initial adoption of data analytics is usually highly localized and becomes more generally adopted in the organization as the benefits are recognized and diffused.* The initial adoption of data analytics is usually project specific, with the projects being typically operational rather than strategic. The success of the initial applications helps generate momentum within the organization for a more generalized adoption of data analytics to support other operational decisions as well as strategic decisions.

5. *The generalized adoption of data analytics is often marked by the appointment of in-house data analysts and the creation of a centralized database.* Organizations tend to engage external consultants to undertake the initial data analytics applications. At this initial stage data is usually stored in application-specific spreadsheets, often with little integration and consistency of the data across the different users of data analytics. The move to a more organization-wide approach to data analytics is often marked by the appointment of in-house data analysts and a consequent reduction in the dependency of external consultants. This is usually associated with increased funding for the development of data analytics and the creation of a centralized database.

analysis and have the ability to work with spreadsheets in order to be able to compete effectively in the modern job market in the sport industry.

Review Questions

1. What are the 3 D's of analytics?
2. Why did sports analytics develop initially in baseball rather than in gridiron football or basketball?
3. What decisions within a sport organization are potentially amenable to an analytical approach?
4. How did Saracens use data analytics in their pursuit of sporting success in rugby union?
5. Why do sport management students need to have good statistical skills to be an effective manager in a sport organization?

Suggestions for Further Reading

If you want to learn more about sports analytics, the best place to start is Lewis's (2003) *Moneyball: The Art of Winning and Unfair Game*. This is the book that really marks the beginning of the exponential growth of interest in sports analytics. Treat the movie as an enjoyable introduction to the story of how Billy Beane and the Oakland A's embraced sabermetrics, then read the book to get a more rounded account with lots of background on the main characters and a guide to some of the main insights of Bill James and other sabermetricians. The paperback edition published in 2004 contains an afterword in which Lewis discusses the hostile reaction to *Moneyball* from many within the baseball industry.

After that, to get an understanding of how analytics can be used in other team sports, read Carroll, Palmer, and Thorn's (1988) *The Hidden Game of Football*, which was one of the first systematic applications of statistical analysis to an invasion team sport. Thorn and Palmer (1984) had previously teamed up to analyze baseball statistics in *The Hidden Game of Baseball*. They added Carroll to the team to analyze the statistics of gridiron football. Their key technical contribution is valuing each play using changes in win probabilities based on score, field position, and time remaining. The book is probably best known for questioning the effectiveness of kicking on fourth down. Anderson and Sally's (2013) *The Numbers Game: Why Everything You Know About Football Is Wrong* provides a good introduction to the types of questions being addressed by analysts in association football. Topics covered include the increasing rarity of goals in association football games, the undervaluation of defensive play, the importance of possession, and the impact on team performance of replacing the manager. Apart from reporting the results of statistical analysis, the authors also include interviews with analysts working in the professional game. And if you want to learn more about analytical methods, try Severini's (2015) *Analytic Methods in Sports*, which is a very accessible introduction to statistical methods as applied to the analysis of sports data. This is a good starting point for developing your statistical skills, from descriptive statistics to the use of Z-scores to create standardized and highly comparable metrics and ultimately the investigation of linear relationships between different metrics using correlation and regression analysis. If you want something more advanced on analytical methods employed across the business world (not just sports organizations), Camm et al.'s (2017) *Essentials of Business Analytics* (2nd edition) gives a very comprehensive coverage of the principal techniques employed by data analysts.

Case for Analysis

AZ Alkmaar: Soccer Meets *Moneyball*

AZ Alkmaar are a Dutch association football club who play in the Eredivisie, the top-tier division. Historically, the Dutch Eredivisie has been dominated by three big city clubs: Ajax Amsterdam, PSV Eindhoven, and Feyenoord Rotterdam. Alkmaar is a small provincial town, so AZ does not have the fanbase to be able to compete financially with the "Big Three." AZ has tried to be innovative, particularly in youth development, and has a good success rate in producing first-team players from their academy, with around 60 percent of its current squad having come through its own academy. AZ appointed Robert Eenhoorn as its general manager in 2014. Eenhoorn is a very experienced sport administrator, having successfully run the Dutch national baseball team for a number of years. He is a former MLB player who was a second-round draft pick by the New York Yankees in 1990. One of Eenhoorn's most interesting decisions early in his tenure at AZ was to appoint Billy Beane as an advisor to the board of AZ Alkmaar. Commenting on Beane's appointment, Eenhoorn stated

> AZ was already very interested in the Moneyball principle before I got here. I have known Billy for a while, because of my history in baseball. When we approached him for this role with AZ, he was immediately enthusiastic. He has been able to close the gap with the big market teams, by being innovative. We are very excited and look forward to work with him. Billy will give his advice from the States and he will visit Alkmaar a few times a year (AZ Alkmaar, 2015).

Questions

1. What was the main reason for AZ's appointment of Billy Beane as an advisor to the board?
2. In what specific ways do you think that Beane could contribute to the sporting operation at AZ?
3. What are likely to be the main differences that Beane will find between baseball and association football in the use of data analytics?
4. What are likely to be the main obstacles that Beane will encounter in transferring the analytics experience of the Oakland A's to AZ Alkmaar?

CHAPTER 23

Corporate Social Responsibility and Sport Organizations

Christos Anagnostopoulos, PhD
Jonathan Robertson, PhD

Learning Objectives

When you have read this chapter, you should be able to

1. explain what we mean by the term *corporate social responsibility* (CSR),
2. draw on three major theoretical perspectives and explain why sport organizations are increasingly embracing the notion of CSR,
3. explain the different levels in which CSR unfolds and discuss how each level has been approached in sport management studies, and
4. describe the manifestations of sport organizations' CSR.

Key Concepts

corporate social responsibility (CSR)
institutional theories
legitimacy theory
stakeholder theory

Philadelphia Eagles "Go Green"

The Philadelphia Eagles are a gridiron football team in the National Football League (NFL). Under the guidance of team owners Jeffrey and Christina Lurie the club has become an environmental leader in global sport. High-profile sport organizations take a significant toll on the environment. Massive spectator stadiums are resource intensive and require sufficient energy, water, and food products to service the tens of thousands of fans that attend each game. In addition to the significant construction costs of stadia, continual air travel to away games ensures that professional sport organizations (particularly in large countries such as the United States) are carbon-intensive organizations. To counter the team's environmental impact, and in keeping with the team's traditionally green team colors, the Go Green campaign was launched in 2003. The first phase of the Go Green campaign developed from small recycling efforts in the front office, to a cornerstone of the organization's brand. By 2010 the team had reduced electricity consumption by 50 percent through use of solar energy and energy-conserving initiatives within the facility; recycled over 550 tons of mixed metal, plastic, and paper; and had planted enough trees to offset 100 percent of carbon emissions caused by the team's travel (Philadelphia Eagles, n.d.). The second phase of the campaign coincided with the redevelopment of the Eagles home stadium, Lincoln Financial Field, in 2009. The redevelopment included the installation of 14 wind turbines and 11,108 solar panels. The new sustainable infrastructure enabled the organization to produce four megawatts of energy per year and purchase the remaining energy from environmentally sustainable sources. The 100 percent sustainable production of renewable energy at Lincoln Financial Field contributed to significant cost savings for the organization. In 2013 the Lincoln Financial Field was awarded the Leadership in Energy and Environmental Design (LEED) Silver certification from the U.S. Green Building Council. These actions led to the 69,000-seat stadium effectively operating off the power grid.

In an increasingly competitive business environment, the largest challenge sport organizations are faced with is the adoption of strategies that consider the social and environmental facets of their business actions. This business–society relationship, which is most commonly addressed through the notion of **corporate social responsibility (CSR)**, has borne witness to increased social involvement by sport organizations (Walker & Parent, 2010). The purpose of this chapter is to discuss the often-controversial notion of sport organizations' CSR. We begin by offering a historical background of the notion before three major theoretical approaches are briefly outlined. A multilevel approach is then specified that can help contextualize CSR within professional sport organizations.

Corporate Social Responsibility

Sport has a long history of producing social outcomes in combination with other institutions. Hargreaves (1986) described sport as facilitating social outcomes as early as the Industrial Revolution in Britain. Although social practices occurred in many organizations, it was not until the middle of the 20th century that the concept of social responsibility began to develop in the manufacturing sector. It took another 40 years until social responsibility became an issue in sport, largely through controversies in the sporting goods manufacturing sector (Klein, 1999). Since the early 20th century, when business first began donating funds for philanthropic reasons, the notion of CSR has become a priority in corporate boardrooms (Margolis & Walsh, 2003). The importance of CSR intensified after the 1960s, when corporations increasingly faced public skepticism regarding their roles, scope, and ethos. Since then, CSR has moved from being a fad, or bolt-on option, to a widespread built-in business culture (Lewis, 2001).

There is a general consensus that Bowen's (1953) publication, *Social Responsibilities of the Businessman*, inaugurated scholarly discussion about business social responsibility. As a precursor to today's CSR principles, Bowen's arguments were based on the assumption that businesses accumulate power and have a far-reaching influence on people's lives. It can be argued that sport organizations exhibit greater influence due to their media exposure and high profile. For example, in the United States the Michigan State college gridiron football team was a highly successful and racially integrated team in the 1960s, a period when public discussion around racial segregation was at its most divisive. While not classified as social responsibility, the team was influential in the public discourse and advancement of race equality due to the media exposure that came with the team's success.

Levitt (1958) mounted what Davis (1960, p. 72) described as a "powerful attack on the social responsibility of businessmen" by cautioning that the adoption of socially responsible viewpoints by business would actually have an adverse effect on society. Levitt implied what Friedman (1970) would claim outright 12 years later: The social responsibility of business is to increase its profit. Notwithstanding Levitt's standpoint, during the 1960s appeals grew for the conceptualization of the "social responsibility" movement, most notably from Davis (1960) and Frederick (1960). Davis in particular recognized that the economic functions of business are primary and the noneconomic are secondary, but stressed that "the non-economic [functions] do exist" (p. 75). Davis (1960) approached the "business and society" domain from a social power theory perspective, arguing that businesses that fail to balance social power with social responsibility will, in the long run, fail.

While Friedman's (1970) view intensified the debate, Carroll's (1979) three-dimensional conceptual framework sought to elucidate this relationship under the heading of "corporate social performance." Carroll's framework was founded on the following: (1) the entire range of social responsibilities a business has (e.g., economic, legal, ethical, discretionary); (2) the social issues involved (e.g., consumerism, environment, discrimination, product safety, occupational safety, shareholders); and (3) types of social response (e.g., reaction, defense, accommodation, pro-action). Perhaps Carroll's most important contribution was treating economic and social goals of corporations as interdependent rather than incompatible (Lee, 2008).

One general observation is that one camp (Arrow, 1997; Carr, 1996; Friedman, 1970; Jensen, 2002; Karmani, 2011) treats economic and social objectives as incompatible, while another (Donaldson & Preston, 1995; Freeman, 1984; Rivoli & Waddock, 2011) denies this within the contemporary business and society domain. More specifically, Karmani (2011, p. 70) argued that "doing well by doing good is an illusion" and that corporations "have a responsibility to their shareholders." According to Karmani (2011), while corporations must adapt their behavior to address the myriad of challenges confronting society, asking corporations to voluntarily sacrifice profits to increase public welfare will not be successful. In response to such declarations, Rivoli and Waddock (2011) argued for a time–context dynamic, whereby corporations are embedded in society and social expectations change over time. Therefore, corporations adapt their behavior in response to these changes, in the same way that public policies are modified in response to different circumstances. For them, this makes CSR "not an illusion, but an integral part of human progress" (Rivoli & Waddock, 2011, p. 115).

In essence, reasoning the significance of CSR on the grounds of "embeddedness in society," "response to social changes," or "absorbance to pressures" echoes the notion of organization legitimacy, whereby legitimacy is, as defined by Suchman (1995, p. 574), "a generalized perception or assumption that the actions of an entity are desirable, proper, or appropriate within some socially constructed system of norms, values, beliefs, and definitions." According to Baur and Palazzo (2011), organizational theory is one of the principal research strands dealing with legitimacy. Indeed, drawing on the notion of legitimacy suggests going beyond the financial performance thesis (Chen, Patten, & Roberts, 2008) and proposing that organizational survival can be ensured by the continuous flow of resources and the support of the organization's stakeholders (Freeman, 1984; Pfeffer & Salancik, 1978). Put differently, organizational survival is contingent on each corporation's social legitimacy (Shocker & Sethi, 1974).

Theoretical Perspectives of CSR

We now turn our attention to three theoretical perspectives that inform the implementation of CSR in the context of sport organizations. One should note, however, that the theoretical perspectives discussed below have no clear-cut boundaries, and all three offer a sound basis for a general understanding of why sport organizations are increasingly embracing CSR.

Institutional theory

Institutional theories broadly investigate the way social environments influence organizations (Campbell, 2007; Greenwood, Oliver, Sahlin, & Suddaby, 2008). Institutional isomorphism describes how environments pressure organizations to become more similar (Slack & Hinings, 1995) via coercive, mimetic, and normative forces (DiMaggio & Powell, 1983). Coercive forces represent the influence external regulatory agencies have on the organization. For example, the National Basketball Association (NBA) institutionalized the NBA Cares program in 2005 with the aim of providing "education; youth and family development; and, health and wellness" through a mandatory global outreach program for all NBA teams (NBA Cares, 2014). Consequently, NBA teams' social responsibility demonstrates increasing similarity by conforming to the standardized NBA Cares program promoted by the league. Mimetic forces occur when similar organizations adopt successful characteristics from competing organizations. A clear example in the association football industry is FC Barcelona's famous 2006 shirt sponsorship with United Nations International Children's Emergency Fund (UNICEF). FC Barcelona was one of the first global association football teams to donate prime advertising space on their shirt to charity, foregoing considerable sponsorship revenue (and subsequently gaining great publicity value). Mimetic forces of FC Barcelona's successful sponsorship led other clubs to mimic the successful charitable shirt sponsorship. Normative forces are pressures from various stakeholder groups (e.g., the media, interest groups, employees) to practice certain social norms. Society expects certain levels of behavior vis-à-vis race, gender, sexual orientation, and religion. When expectations are broken, for example, when an opponent racially vilifies a player, normative pressures rise.

Institutional theories also help position and track social responsibility development through different organizational fields. Scott (1995, p. 56) defined an organizational field as "a community of organizations that partakes of a common meaning system and whose participants interact more frequently and fatefully with one another than with actors outside the field." The development of CSR originated within the organizational field of industrial manufacturers and crossed over into the field of sporting goods manufacturers during highly publicized ethical crises regarding their supply chains in the 1990s. Developed from Broomhill's (2007) work, Waddington, Chelladurai, and Skirstad (2013, p. 48) argued that the transition of the social responsibility notion occurred "in a series of phases, or waves, each of which can be broadly understood as a response by corporates to criticism of what have been widely perceived as wrongful or socially irresponsibility actions on their part." If the first phase was between the corporate and sport manufacturing organizational fields, the second phase was an extension from the field of sporting goods manufacturers into the elite sport organizational field. The second phase was driven by widespread and highly publicized social irresponsibility (Hu, Lee, Wong, & Kao, 2012) such as domestic violence, gambling, illicit drug use, performance enhancement, and corruption in elite sport. (For more on each of these issues see Benson, 2017; Mazanov & Woolf, 2017; Roberts, Chadwick, & Anagnostopoulos, 2018.) The widespread irresponsibility in highly commercial sport organizations led to a relatively direct translation of the CSR notion in elite sport (Godfrey, 2009). Notwithstanding the extensive adoption of CSR theory in sport organizations, geographic and industry differences can influence the application of CSR (Godfrey, Hatch, & Hansen, 2010; Matten & Moon, 2008). The conceptualization of social responsibility for sport organizations (Sheth & Babiak, 2010) has also been shown to be different from industrial manufacturers (Pinkston & Carroll, 1996). Sport managers therefore need to carefully consider the social responsibility requirements specific to their organizational context.

Legitimacy Theory

Sport organizations' high visibility and confrontational or negative business practices have led to calls for greater transparency and accountability (Babiak & Wolfe, 2013; Breitbarth, Walzel, Anagnostopoulos, & van Eekeren, 2015), and have forced such organizations to be more socially responsible. **Legitimacy theory** helps describe why sport organizations, under growing public scrutiny, have invested in corporate social performance. In essence, what these organizations try to achieve through CSR-related involvement is to minimize any "legitimacy gaps" (Sethi, 1975). Legitimacy gaps arise when organizational goals, methods of operation, and outcomes are not aligned with the expectations of those stakeholders who confer legitimacy (Wartick & Mahon, 1994).

Early studies (Dowling & Pfeffer, 1975; Meyer & Rowan, 1977; Shocker & Sethi, 1974) suggested various organizational adaptations in order to address a legitimacy gap, such as a complete strategic and operational modification or, conversely, reframing legitimacy so that there is no conflict between social expectations and overall organizational practices. A third way entailed a less direct approach through an association with "symbols, values, or institutions that have a strong perceived image of social legitimacy" (Chen, Patten, & Roberts, 2008, p. 133; see also Bason and Anagnostopoulos, 2015) of how the corporate world is using the symbols and values associated with sport to do just that.

One could argue that sport organizations' CSR is based on mainly "pragmatic legitimacy" rather than "moral and cognitive legitimacy." Pragmatic legitimacy rests on "the self-interested calculations of an organization's most immediate audiences" (Suchman, 1995, p. 578), that is, on judgments about whether a given activity benefits the specific stakeholder groups that, in turn, legitimize the firm's operations. In this chapter's context, pragmatic legitimacy would denote a professional team's ability to respond to audience expectations (Baur & Palazzo, 2011).

Organizations legitimize their identity from multiple stakeholder groups within society (Scott & Lane, 2000). In response to the multiplicity of stakeholders, organizations possess multiple identities and logics (Kraatz & Block, 2008; Thornton & Ocasio, 2008). For instance, a single elite sport team can be legitimized through several stakeholder relationships simultaneously such as fans (performance identity), owners (financial identity), media (mass entertainment identity), leagues (member identity), spectators (fan experience identity), and players and staff (employer identity). It is therefore important to understand that organizational legitimacy accumulates from multiple stakeholders who form legitimacy perceptions that are often incongruent with other stakeholder groups. In order to effectively maintain organizational legitimacy, sport managers must manage the competing legitimacy demands of multiple stakeholder groups.

Stakeholder Theory

Stakeholder theory has enabled managers to move from an organization-based approach, in which stakeholders are seen as entities solely serving the organization, to a network-oriented vision that focuses on relationships and concepts (Ferrand & McCarthy, 2009). In other words, this perspective emphasizes a manager's primary responsibility of influencing, managing, or balancing the set of relationships that can affect an organization's purpose (Freeman & Phillips, 2002).

Since Freeman's (1984) seminal work, which developed the stakeholder concept, many sport management papers have addressed various aspects of it (Anagnostopoulos, 2011; Friedman, Parent, & Mason, 2004; Parent & Deephouse, 2007), including the definition of the concept itself. On the one hand, broad definitions specify the empirical reality that virtually anyone can affect or be affected by an organization's actions; on the other hand, narrow definitions specify that managers simply cannot attend to all actual or potential claims. These definitions obscure where a manager's responsibility begins and ends (Mitchell, Agle, & Wood, 1997). The decision, however, of whether to adopt a broad definition or a narrow one is important, since it "determines which parties are considered stakeholders" (Ferrand & McCarthy, 2009, p. 26). As is addressed later in this chapter, the term *stakeholder* is used in a rather broad sense to denote people, or other entities, that have a relationship with a sport organization.

Furthermore, according to Farquhar, Machold, and Ahmed (2005), a useful framework for looking at the stakeholder perspective is given by Donaldson and Preston (1995), who proposed three types: the normative, the instrumental, and the descriptive. This framework implies that (1) managers *should* behave in certain ways (normative); (2) certain outcomes are more likely if firms behave in certain ways (instrumental); and (3) managers *actually* behave in certain ways (descriptive). By way of example, one could argue that the professional sport organizations' normative behavior should be inclusive, meaning that ties with local businesses and public agencies should not just be maintained but continuously reinforced. Approaching matters from a more instrumental angle suggests that a socially responsible professional team will benefit from its engagement in genuine and impactful CSR programs because these practices eventually contribute to both retaining the existing clientele (e.g., various consumers or customers of the team's services and products, powerful sponsors) and, crucially, attracting new fans. Last, the descriptive type focuses on analyzing the cooperative and competing interests of the stakeholders involved in, or affected by, a team's CSR portfolio.

That said, the preferred approach in this chapter values all three perspectives equally with their interaction serving as a base for the managerial approach with regards to implementing CSR in the sport organization context.

Multilevel Approach for CSR and Sport Organizations

In a recent review on CSR, Aguinis and Glavas (2012) argued that multilevel and multidisciplinary approaches to examining CSR would offer a more complete understanding of the concept. In the following sections, we draw on this in order to structure our CSR discussion in relation to sport organizations. By so doing, the reader can form connections to the previously discussed theoretical perspectives (especially at the institutional and organizational level). In addition, we draw on sport and CSR literature with the purpose of inviting more questions rather than offering concrete answers for any of the following levels discussed. The goal for such an approach is to provide prospective sport scholars and practitioners with access points to key debates in CSR and sport literature.

Institutional Level

Scholarly activity on professional teams' social involvement has offered valuable insights into the environmental pressures that prompt organizations to engage in CSR practices. These pressures are amalgamated within both the institutional and organizational analysis levels. The institutional level addresses at least one element of Scott's (1995) three pillars of institutions, which are regulative, normative, and cultural-cognitive systems (Aguinis & Glavas, 2012; Godfrey, 2009). Hoffman (1997, cited in Scott, 2013, p. 59) described that "each pillar forms a continuum moving from the conscious and legally enforceable (for example, regulation), to the unconscious and taken for granted (for example, cultural-cognitive systems)." Guided by institutional and stakeholder perspectives, this section will focus separately on each pillar to elaborate on social responsibility systems at institutional level of analysis.

Changes in the regulative environment for sport organizations can come from a variety of sources, including governments, leagues, interest groups, unions or associations, and various other stakeholder groups. At the institutional level, changes in regulation can have significant impacts on the social responsibility of elite sport organizations. For example, in 2012 the NFL introduced new rules guiding how gridiron football teams must respond to player concussion. The change was initiated from player associations and medical groups that showed how players who had suffered severe concussions during their playing career had a higher chance of developing brain injury (chronic traumatic encephalopathy [CTE]) (Hanna & Kain, 2010). (For more information, see the Time Out "The NFL's Response to Concussion Injury.") Another example of changes coming from government was the UK government's creation of the Football Foundation charity (Taylor, 2004). The change in the institutional environment led many English association football teams to create charitable foundations following the creation of the Football Foundation charity. The institutional environment in elite sport organizations is highly complex and subject to multiple regulatory regimes

TIME OUT

The NFL's Response to Concussion Injury

American gridiron football is a traditionally physical game. For a period of time researchers have suggested that increased collisions, specifically repeated head trauma, can lead to increased risk of degenerative brain injury. In the late 2000s increased public discourse from former players and interest groups pressured the league to change its defensive position on the effect of concussion on player welfare. The tipping point came in 2009, with NFL spokesperson Greg Aiello stating, "It's quite obvious from the medical research that's been done that concussions can lead to long-term problems" (Schwarz, 2009). This was the first time that the league had publically acknowledged the link between concussion and brain injury, and marked a broader public shift in the intrinsic cultural-cognitive understanding of concussion in elite sport. Simply, the assumption that concussion was "part of the game" shifted to an understanding that if concussion leads to increased risk of brain injury for players, concussion is outside of what society expects to be legitimate and fair for players (social norms). Accordingly, it is desirable to minimize concussion within gridiron football (social values).

The need to protect players from concussion is fundamentally changing the way gridiron football is played to ensure the maximum welfare of the players, within the context of a contact sport. The increasing education of key stakeholder groups shifted society's unconscious assumptions about the health impact of player concussion. By understanding that concussion had a detrimental effect on player welfare, concussion was then perceived to breach society's normative values. The breach in normative values, and legal responsibilities to provide a safe working environment, pressured the NFL to change its regulative environment. To do so the NFL simultaneously compensated past and present NFL players (Belson, 2014) and made efforts to minimize the risk of concussion by changing the rules of the game (Breslow, 2014).

(e.g., laws of society, anti-doping, anti-corruption, governing body regulation specific to the sport). It is therefore imperative that organizations understand their external environment to avoid costly risks (noncompliance breaches) and capitalize on potential opportunities (changes in funding structures).

Normative systems occur simultaneously with regulative and cultural-cognitive elements at the institutional level. Scott (2013) described that normative systems are comprised of both values (desirable standards from which organizational behavior is assessed) and norms (the legitimate way society perceives things ought to be). Normative elements broadly conceptualize how society perceives certain obligations ought to be fulfilled. Often normative values are the precursor to society codifying laws and regulations and are therefore closely coupled with the above regulative systems (Carroll, 1979). Over the past century, several areas of institutional life have codified values and norms into laws and regulation in areas such as human rights, labor practices, fair operating practices, consumer issues, and more recently environmental issues (International Organization for Standardization [ISO] 26000, 2010). In sport organizations, a major shift has occurred in the area of environmental awareness. Trendafilova, Babiak, and Heinze (2013, p. 309) suggested that "scrutiny and regulation, and normative and associative pressures play a role in sport organizations' adoption of environmentally friendly behaviors. These forces seem to be working together and reinforcing one another, and often through the vehicle of the media, to create a broad trend around this [environmental] form of CSR." As the chapter-opening scenario on the Philadelphia Eagles demonstrated, elite sport organizations are picking up on the environmental aspect of their social responsibility and even beginning to use opportunities strategically (Porter & Kramer, 2006, 2011). The changes in social norms regarding the environment have had widespread effect on sport organizations (Babiak & Trendafilova, 2011), college sport (Trendafilova, Pfahl, & Casper, 2013), major sporting events (Zhang, Jin, Kim, & Li, 2013), consumer perceptions of sport organizations (Walker & Mercado, 2013; Walker, 2013), and sport facilities (Mercado & Walker, 2012). Normative values have also begun to give way to regulative measures such as the 1995 Kyoto protocol that outlined mandatory targets for greenhouse gas emissions, millennium development goals to meet a broad range of social issues to improve the lives of the world's poorest populations, and increasing international regulation such as the ISO 14000 standard on environmental management that regulates the environmental behavior of organizations throughout the supply chain. For sport organizations, normative values around environmental practices are becoming critical to understanding broad social expectations at the institutional level.

Cultural-cognitive systems are unconscious assumptions of an area of social life and represent "shared conceptions that constitute the nature of social reality and create the frames through which meaning is made . . . where internal interpretive processes are shaped by external cultural frameworks" (Scott, 2013, p. 67). At the institutional level, such systems help explain what makes the social responsibility of sport different from other social institutions (e.g., commerce, religion, arts). Elite sport organizations represent an identifiable cultural-cognitive system that has unique features, including instability of sport performance, a unique competitive balance between organizations, increased media exposure, and the resultant public analysis of player performance (Smith & Stewart, 2010). Consequently, sport organizations demonstrate a cultural-cognitive system of social responsibility that is unique compared to other areas of institutional life (Babiak & Wolfe, 2009, 2013). While it is taken for granted that winning, high media exposure, and a lack of direct competition (in the sense of competitive strategy) are within the remit of sport organizations, it is precisely these features that differentiate the social responsibility of the team sport cultural-cognitive system from other social and cultural systems.

Institutional, normative, and cultural-cognitive systems individually and collectively can act as a framework to guide future research directions. Institutional environments shape the manifestation of, for example, a team's responsibility to society via explicit regulative mechanisms (laws, regulations, and standards) and from multiple regulative bodies (governments, leagues, and associations). Heightened media exposure focuses normative pressures on organizations to behave in a manner that society sees fit. However, cognitive-cultural systems, or unconscious assumptions, vary significantly within a multistakeholder society. For sport organizations, the institutional level produces an environment in which the organization is required to respond to multiple actions simultaneously in order to fulfill its social responsibility.

Organizational Level

The organizational level of analysis includes research on individuals who are treated conceptually at the macro level. Such conceptualization indicates that the main focus remains on the organizations in which these individuals work rather than on personal attributes, backgrounds, values, and beliefs. As Aguinis and Glavas (2012) found while reviewing the generic CSR literature, most of the extant literature on CSR focuses on this level of analysis. At this level, instrumental drivers (e.g., long-term self-interest, public image, legitimacy) as well as theories from the strategy field such as the resource-based view (Amis, Pant, & Slack, 1997) make up the skeleton of the empirical works.

Given that sport management is a broad field, it is not surprising that scholars who examine CSR in professional sport organizations at the organizational level draw on various disciplines, including communication (Kolyperas & Sparks, 2011; Walker, Heere, Parent, & Drane, 2010), ethics (Rouvrais-Charron & Durand, 2009), finance (Inoue, Kent, & Lee, 2011), marketing (Inoue & Kent, 2012), strategy (Anagnostopoulos, Byers, & Kolyperas, 2017; Babiak & Wolfe, 2009), and governance (Anagnostopoulos & Winand, 2019; Kolyperas, Anagnostopoulos, Chadwick, & Sparks, 2016). Nevertheless, the lack of concrete answers to questions such as "What is CSR?" and "How can CSR be accomplished?" usually leads researchers to approach CSR in sport from a multidisciplinary perspective.

Three of the above-mentioned exemplar studies stand out in this regard. First, Rouvrais-Charron and Durand (2009) drew on deontological ethics to propose marketing-based strategies. Second, Inoue et al. (2011) conducted a financial analysis but argued for a general lack of awareness of the teams' CSR initiatives among fans, thereby touching on issues related to communication and strategic management. Third, Kolyperas et al. (2016) advocated charitable foundations for the strategic delivery of CSR agendas, although matters closely related to governance, ethics, and marketing also have a prominent role in their discussion. Despite an accidental or unavoidable and rather implicit multidisciplinary approach from scholars who have examined CSR in professional teams, CSR has, perhaps paradoxically, not been examined explicitly within the realms of organization theory. In view of the ever-increasing CSR activity by professional teams, a call for a closer examination of some of the key organizational theory's concepts is deemed necessary.

Husted (2003) identified three different structures that impact how organizations strategically implement CSR. The first form involves outsourcing CSR through charitable contributions. Here, an independent relationship exists between the donor and the recipient, meaning that company's involvement in the management of the project is usually minimal. An example of this is the 2006 partnership between the English association football team Aston Villa FC with the Acorns Children's Hospice. In this case, the team provided a financial contribution to cover the urgent costs of 77 days of hospice care at Selly Oak hospice. Over the past few years, Villa players have also taken the time to visit the children and families who use Acorns.

In the second form, organizations seek to internalize CSR through in-house projects. Husted (2003) wrote that through this form of CSR implementation, the company allocates financial and other resources to the project via an in-house organizational unit. Interestingly, a majority of professional teams globally have now established charitable foundations for their CSR-related agendas (Kolyperas et al., 2016; Babiak & Wolfe, 2009). Despite professional sport organizations increasingly discharging several aspects of organizational responsibility through charitable foundations, a number of issues concerning Husted's organizational dimensions remain unexplored (i.e., complexity, formalization, and centralization). This is particularly so when one considers Husted's (2003) third CSR implementation mode, that is, a collaborative or partnership model. More specifically, these charitable foundations are managed and governed by both a number of external trustees, who often play a key role in the strategic formulation of the CSR agenda, and by executives from the parent professional team, which unavoidably increases the level of organizational complexity. However, gaps exist regarding decision-making vis-à-vis the relationship between complexity and (de-)centralization in the context of CSR.

For example, where does the charitable foundation sit within the professional teams' organizational structure (Anagnostopoulos & Shilbury, 2013)? Does it take the role of an interdependent relationship between the parent team and the nonprofit organization (i.e., the charitable foundation), in which the former transfers resources to the latter? Therefore, a relevant question could deal less with why the sporting context offers great potential for CSR (Godfrey, 2009; Smith & Westerbeek, 2007) and more with what is the best modus operandi for implementing CSR in order to achieve the perceived benefits for all involved parties (Kolyperas et al., 2016). Table 23.1 offers some generic points with regards to implementing CSR through charitable foundations.

Moreover, various scholars have posited that the CSR concept itself is culturally and temporally bound and therefore carries different meanings across time and geography (Sethi, 1975). Consequently, the question is whether accurate generalizations can be made about what is the best organizational model through which CSR in professional sport organizations can achieve the best possible

Table 23.1 Advantages and Challenges of Implementing CSR Through Charitable Foundations

Advantages	Challenges
Formal management structure ensures that philanthropic activities are compliant with legal and ethical guidelines as well as with the league's "recipes" for specific theme-based programs.	These organizations are vulnerable to political change, which affects the way they are funded.
Members of the board are often executives of the founding team, which ensures a level of integration between the former and other industrial agents (i.e., public, nongovernmental, commercial).	The foundations may have different ownership structures and may require volunteer involvement for sound operation.
The organization's charitable status can mean greater accessibility to public, governmental, and commercial funds, thereby increasing the potential and capacity for community work.	These organizations are somewhat dependent on the founding company's network: • They often find it difficult to diversify their funding portfolios and seek alternative revenue sources. • Such network reliance creates tensions and constraints between the foundation and the company and may lead to disintegration, disassociation, and misalignment between the overall corporate and CSR strategies.
These organizations act as censors or antennae to collect public goodwill and criticism and advise the parent companies on CSR matters that arise in the industry.	
These organizations are tax exempt, financially interdependent entities that do not incur too much risk.	

Based on Kolyperas, Anagnostopoulos, Chadwick, and Sparks (2016).

results. In other words, does a universal model run the risk of being seen as either ahistorical or acontextual if culture, at both the institutional and organizational levels, is neglected?

These gaps represent fertile research ground for sport management scholars and could potentially lead to some clarity in the strategic and operational imperatives of the sport organizations' CSR undertakings.

Individual Level

The individual level of analysis is an overlooked area of research in sport management. Aguinis and Glavas' (2012) analysis of broad management literatures identified that only 4 percent of articles focused on socially responsible organizational practices at the individual level. From this small sample, the authors concluded the following topics could improve understanding of social responsibility motivation and determinates: (1) the influence of normative values on CSR engagement (e.g., if an individual's values align with the organizations); (2) the influence of CSR activities on employee performance; (3) whether organizational leadership and identity mediates the CSR and employee performance relationship; and (4) whether CSR activities produce greater individual outcomes under ethical and equitable management.

This problem is seemingly exacerbated within the subfield of sport management, with research on social responsibility practices and individual employment outcomes seemingly a black box. This offers several areas for future research. To what extent do social responsibility practices attract or help retain players and administrators? Do CSR activities in sport influence employee performance in the same way as corporate organizations? Are such programs a positive for players vis-à-vis their image or negative vis-à-vis increased obligations?

Moreover, gaps at the individual level inevitably invite research into topics associated with organizational behavior, such as leadership, motivation, or satisfaction. For example, who leads CSR formulation and implementation in professional teams, and what sort of leadership characteristics are required? Babiak and Wolfe (2009) argued that passion constitutes one of the inimitable resources that professional teams possess, implying that CSR-related programs' recipients comprise a target group that is not often seen in other business sectors. Furthermore, it is possible that passion carries a double meaning when it comes to CSR. That is, not only referring to what the sport product (the team, the game, the players) generates among fans and

KEY ISSUES FOR SPORT MANAGERS

It is crucial for sport managers to ensure continual social responsibility improvement and legitimacy. In the last decade, as measurement guidelines have become more ubiquitous, there has been a shift away from primarily donation-based social responsibility. In 2012 the German association football club VfL Wolfesburg became the first team sport organization to be certified as a socially responsible organization by the Global Reporting Initiative, and significant developments have been made with measuring the impact of major events such as the Olympic Games and FIFA World Cup. This trend is likely to continue and become a key pillar in maintaining a legitimate social responsibility agenda. The argument that many team sport organizations suffer from "evaluation phobia" and focus their measurement criteria within the organizational rather than societal paradigm (Walker, Heere, & Kim, 2013) is open to question. We rather see it more as an "evaluation helplessness" because at the moment, human capacity in sport organizations for CSR implementation is limited (Anagnostopoulos, Gillooly, Cook, Parganas, & Chadwick, 2017). As a result, responsible personnel may focus on doing rather than evaluating on the grounds that if an organization is constantly evaluating and not doing, any impacts found will lack substance. Having said that, both social and organizational performance can only be optimized by assessing CSR impact through rigorous evaluation. Future sport managers will therefore need to take capacity matters into consideration and ensure that appropriate monitoring, measurement, and evaluation are all embedded into their social responsibility initiatives.

consumers, but also whether working in the sport industry further motivates people to become more passionate about tackling contemporary social challenges (Anagnostopoulos, Byers, & Shilbury, 2014). For example, Anagnostopoulos, Winand, and Papadimitriou (2016) have looked at passion at work and empirically found that sport administrators who deal with CSR-related matters are more harmoniously passionate about their jobs than the personnel that oversee strictly business-related affairs.

Aguinis and Glavas' (2012) claim that it is the organizational actors themselves "who actually strategize, make decisions and execute CSR initiatives" (p. 953). Despite this, little is known about the role organizational social responsibility activities play on employee and player performance. Conversely preliminary efforts have been made to investigate athletes' social impact through model behavior and using their individual resources (financial and brand image) to establish foundations for socially beneficial causes (Kim & Walker, 2013). The individual level of analysis presents numerous opportunities for identifying and clarifying specific parameters of the effect of CSR on individuals within the organization.

Summary and Conclusions

Corporate social responsibility has now become one of the hotly debated issues in the study of organizations in general and professional sport teams in particular. In this chapter we looked at the notion of CSR from an historical, theoretical, and level-based perspective to offer sport management students the necessary access points to key debates.

Beyond the historical background that helps shape a broader appreciation of CSR development, it is necessary to understand key theoretical perspectives that explain CSR's ever-increasing adoption in sport organizations. Institutional theory gives managers insight into the environmental factors that shape their organization's social responsibilities. Legitimacy theory allows them to understand key motivations to pursue social responsibility practices. Stakeholder theory assists in identifying key constituents and relationships and how these may benefit or be compromised by socially (ir)responsible actions.

Moreover, it is important to understand the level from which social responsibility is being driven and how this affects the organization. At the institutional level, governments, regulatory agencies, leagues, and governing bodies all influence the social environment for sport organizations. These entities write the rules of the game for organizations to abide by and therefore are important for decision making. At the organizational level, different structural forms allow for greater (or otherwise) flexibility and opportunities, which in turn aim to have an impact on the organizations and the programs' recipients alike. Last, examining CSR from the individual level of analysis offers ways of exploring not only its impact on employees in sport organizations, but also how the individual can indeed shape the organizational as well as institutional context for potentially scaling up CSR practice.

All in all, the purpose of this chapter was to provide a basic perspective of the CSR notion in the context of sport organizations. After all, not only are forward-looking sport organizations spending more on their social responsibility budget than ever, but the topic of CSR has now become a mandatory subject in most sport management curricula across the globe. We hope that our modest approach to delineate this rather complex topic will assist the reader to embark on the examination and practice of CSR with a good theoretical foundation.

Review Questions

1. Pick a basketball team from the NBA, an association football team from the English Premier League, and a rugby team from Australia. Identify the CSR agendas of all three teams. What are the differences, if any? Does the cultural context, or even the nature of the sport in question, have a bearing on the nature and scope of the CSR programs these teams implement?
2. Identify legitimacy gaps in the context of sport organizations. What CSR strategies could be implemented to close these gaps?
3. What should be the case for a team sport organization when it comes to CSR implementation? A normative or an instrumental type of stakeholder theory? Justify your answer with specific examples.
4. Select a familiar sport organization with a rich CSR agenda. Discuss the content of its CSR communication. Has emphasis been given to social or business outcomes and impacts?
5. Among the three strategic CSR implementation forms or models (Husted, 2003), which one do you think is the most suitable for professional team sport organizations? Do you see your choice as appropriate for both European and U.S. professional teams, or do the structural differences between the two continents also require different CSR implementation forms or models?
6. Discuss the role athletes have in the implementation of professional teams' CSR. Does the increased establishment by individual players of charitable foundations undermine professional teams' CSR work? Should a robust institutional framework be in place for these organizations to maximize the CSR involvement of their most valuable assets? Critically discuss.

Suggestions for Further Reading

If you are interested in finding out more about the notion of CSR, you should begin by looking at the original works by Archie Carroll. It would also be useful to look at the work by scholars who have sought to either critique or extend these original studies (e.g., Friedman, 1970; Jensen, 2002; Karmani, 2011); a number of these are mentioned in this chapter. Excellent CSR overviews and details of some of the important theoretical and conceptual issues considered in work of this nature can be found in Lee's (2008) article "A Review of the Theories of Corporate Social Responsibility: Its Evolutionary Path and the Road Ahead" in the *International Journal of Management Reviews*; Garriga and Melé's (2004) "Corporate Social Responsibility Theories: Mapping the Territory" in the *Journal of Business Ethics*; and Aguinis and Glavas' (2012) "What We Know and Don't Know About Corporate Social Responsibility: A Review and Research Agenda" in the *Journal of Management*. In addition, the second edition of the textbook titled *Corporate Social Responsibility: Readings and Cases in a Global Context*, edited by Crane, Matten, and Spence (2014), compiles all the seminal works written about the topic.

In terms of sport literature, sport-focused journals (e.g., the *International Journal of Sport Management and Marketing*, guest edited by Kent, 2011; the *Journal of Sport Management*, guest edited by Bradish and Cronin, 2009; or the *European Sport Management Quarterly*, guest edited by Breitbarth, Walzel, and van Eekeren, 2019), as well as general management journals (e.g., the *Journal of Management and Organization*, guest edited by Ratten and Babiak, 2010; and *Corporate Governance: The International Journal of Business in Society*, guest edited by Breitbarth, Walzel, Anagnostopoulos, and van Eekeren, 2015) have already devoted special issues to the topic of CSR in the sporting context. Moreover, Walzel, Robertson, and Anagnostopoulos (2018) have recently reviewed the literature on professional team sport organizations' CSR in order to develop a comprehensive understanding of current and future research directions in the field (see *Journal of Sport Management*).

In addition, the topic of CSR has started penetrating the latest textbooks on sport and business management through informative chapters (e.g., in the *Routledge Handbook of Sport Management*, edited by Robinson, Chelladurai, Bodet, and Downward, 2012; or in *Managing Sport Business*, edited by Trenberth and Hassan, 2011). However, the essential read for sport management students and practitioners alike is the first textbook dedicated to the issue of CSR in the sport industry, *Routledge Handbook of Sport and Corporate Social Responsibility*, edited by Paramio-Salcines, Babiak, and Walters (2013), which brings together the most prominent scholars on the matter and through its 26 chapters offers a range of subjects, both within leisure, sport, and recreation programs and general management and corporate responsibility programs.

Case for Analysis

My Future Goal

Sport is a particularly successful avenue for corporate organizations and their community programs when trying to engage young people. Barclays provides an example of a successful community program through its partnership with Fulham FC Foundation, the charitable arm of Fulham Football Club. Barclays is an international financial services provider engaged in personal, corporate, and investment banking, and has an extensive presence in Europe, the Americas, Africa, and Asia. Barclays has five key values: respect, integrity, service, excellence, and stewardship. Community programs are very effective channels for the organization to display and communicate these core values. Through its community investment programs worldwide, including its three flagship global programs—"banking on change," "building young futures," and "Barclays spaces for sports"—the bank aims to help five million young people around the world develop the skills they need to fulfill their potential.

The Fulham Football Club Foundation (FFCF) is a leading community sport charity that aims to build better lives through sport. The foundation uses the power of sport to deliver a variety of inspiring education, health, disability, social inclusion, and association football programs. Barclays and The FFCF partnered in February 2012 to deliver a three-year association football and sport employability program. The program targets young people between the ages of 16 and 25 years who are "Not in Education, Employment or Training" (NEET), and aims to remove barriers to work and increase employment opportunities. FFCF delivered the program with the support of a £350,000 (US$431,000) investment from Barclays. Over the course of three years, 300 young people will participate in the program.

The program involves a structured 10-week course that helps participants develop skills such as communication, teamwork, work-related training, and the chance to gain national governing body (NGB)–recognized qualifications. As participants advance, employers are brought in from the local area to talk about opportunities for career progression following the completion of the course. FFCF, with the support of Barclays' staff, then mentor young people and help them in their transition toward education, employment, and training outcomes. For example, Barclays' employees run workshops on money skills, résumé writing, and job interview techniques within local branches of the bank. The success of the My Future Goal program is dependent on how effectively participants have either reduced their barriers to gaining employment or gained new employment skills. Collectively, the more unemployed young people who are able to take advantage of education, employment, or training (EET) opportunities offered to them, the greater the success of the program.

David Wheldon, head of brand, reputation, and citizenship at Barclays, commented: "Barclays plays a broader role in the communities in which we live and work beyond what we deliver through our core business activities; we do this through community investment programs and the direct efforts of our employees. By empowering young people with appropriate skills we can help them achieve economic independence and security now and in the future. We are delighted to be partnering with Fulham FC Foundation on this unique programme which brings together the independent interests and expertise of each organization to do just that" (Personal communication with author, CA, 25.03.16).

Sport is a natural link for Barclays community Programs because it links well with the commercial business sponsorships of the Barclays Premier League and Barclays ATP world tour finals. In addition, sport is a great way to engage young people, specifically those hard to reach in disadvantaged communities. Sport has a significant power that plays on people's emotions when they are involved in watching or playing sport. These emotions are used by Barclays and FFCF to draw young people into taking part in programs such as My Future Goal and are one of the main factors leading to the program's success.

Since the beginning of the project, 68 percent of participants achieved an EET outcome, and an independent research project demonstrated a significant rise in participants' perceived marketability, higher order personal skills, emotional well-being, and self-efficacy. From 2015 the findings from this project have helped inform the national rollout of the Barclays Premier League Works Programme in 20 community foundations across England. As a result the FFCF secured a further three years (2015-2018) of employability work funding through various partners, including the Premier League, and have used the learning to inform and guide the second stage of the FFCF program.

Questions

1. What long-term benefits to their brand image can Barclays expect to see from this CSR strategy?
2. At an organizational level of analysis, which CSR structure has been employed by Fulham Football Club? Discuss the advantages.
3. What sort of challenges might the Fulham FC Foundation's managers be faced with within this partnership? Explain your reasoning.
4. Discuss the impact My Future Goal may have on the Fulham Football Club itself.

Courtesy of James Jackson, Barclays Spaces for Sports Programme Officer; and Jacob Naish, former Head of Development, Fulham Football Club Foundation.

CHAPTER 24

Procurement and Sport Organizations

Sue Arrowsmith, QC (hon), DJur

Learning Objectives

When you have read this chapter, you should be able to

1. understand what procurement is and its significance for sport organizations,
2. appreciate the importance of a multidisciplinary approach to this topic,
3. outline the main phases and objectives of procurement procedures,
4. understand the role of public-sector procurement models and transparency in achieving procurement objectives,
5. appreciate the special challenges of procurement for major sporting events, and
6. explain how procurement is addressed in governance indicators for sport federations.

Key Concepts

challenge proceedings
competitive bidding
framework agreement
in-house provision
open tendering
outsourcing
partnership sourcing
procurement
professionalism
professionalization
public-private partnership
transparency

Procurement for the London 2012 Olympics

To deliver the infrastructure for the 2012 London Olympics the UK government set up the publicly funded Olympic Delivery Authority (ODA). The ODA was responsible for procuring £6 billion (US$7.7 billion) of construction works, including preparing a 400-hectare (988 acres) site for the Olympic Park, utilities infrastructure, 14 temporary and permanent sporting venues (including a stadium and aquatics center), a broadcast center and two media centers, the Athletes Village, parklands, and local transport works (ODA, 2011).

Obviously, on-time delivery was critical, but as a public body, the ODA had to achieve this within a complex legal framework that required transparent tendering of contracts.

The magnitude and complexity of its task led the ODA to adopt an innovative approach: Rather than installing a substantial internal procurement capability, it engaged an external "delivery partner" to manage and deliver the infrastructure procurement, including providing the human resources. This enabled the ODA to access the significant and expert resources needed to deliver a major program in a short timescale and also to incentivize delivery (Cornelius, Fernau, Dickinson, & Stuart, 2011; Smith, 2012a, 2012b).

The London Organising Committee (LOCOG) also undertook significant procurement for the event. LOCOG was a private company set up by the Minister for the Olympics, the Mayor of London, and the British Olympic Association, and had responsibility for venue and competition management. Its costs, including for its procurement of £1billion (US$1.2 billion) of goods and services, were almost entirely met through the revenue it generated from sponsorship, broadcast rights, and merchandise and ticket sales. Goods procured included 1.8 million items of sports equipment, 122 kilometers (76 miles) of security fencing, 5,000 medal winners' bouquets, more than 2,000 buses, 200,000 temporary seats, and nearly 9,000 Olympic and Paralympic torches, while services included security services, mobile apps for public engagement, and provision of more than 15 million meals (Cumming, Stubbs, & Walsh, 2012).

LOCOG was a private body outside the public procurement regime. However, pressures for good governance and a social legacy meant that LOCOG followed policies similar to those of the public sector, including providing transparency for procurement opportunities on the web portal CompeteFor (Cumming, Stubbs, & Walsh, 2012).

Given the financial and reputational risks, anticorruption strategy received significant attention. Following a study of how economic crime risks were addressed in previous successful Games and major UK construction projects, the police established Operation Podium in 2006 (Stanislas, 2017). Measures included setting up a Construction Industry Fraud Forum to engage with industry and embedding two crime prevention officers within the ODA (Stanislas, 2017).

An important goal for ODA and LOCOG procurement was to contribute to the sustainability commitments of the 2012 bid. Given the importance of construction, the ODA played a central role, addressing environmental issues in venue design and delivery—for example, through centralized procurement of inputs required across venues, such as concrete and timber—allowing for better monitoring of targets for sustainable transport (Cornelius et al., 2011). For LOCOG, procurement was the main vehicle for sustainability and included consideration of, for example, fair labor practices as well as environmental concerns such as use of recycled products (Cumming, Stubbs, & Walsh, 2012).

As might be expected, some problems occurred. These included an incident of fraud, in which the ODA paid significant funds to the bank account of a fraudster impersonating a supplier (the funds were, however recovered) (Stanislas, 2017); a well-publicized failure by security contractor G4S to provide LOCOG with sufficient security personnel, leading to the army and police being drafted in (Carpenter, 2016); and failing to reach renewable energy targets for the Olympic Park (Gold & Gold, 2015). It has also been alleged that the Games led the authorities to turn a blind eye to corruption by and within the host London borough in order not to tarnish the Games' image (Gillard, 2019). However, the procurement problems related directly to the Games itself were limited, the critical infrastructure was delivered in good time and within the budget set in 2007, and Transparency International praised the event for the "fair and transparent" nature of the procurement and construction activities (Barrington, 2012).

This chapter provides an introduction to **procurement** in sport organizations. The definition of procurement is considered further below, but broadly speaking, the concept refers to the activity of an organization in acquiring goods, works, and services from the marketplace.

As is apparent from the opening scenario, this activity is critical to the success of sporting events. Events depend on good procurement to ensure that relevant infrastructure, goods, and services are available in time and without exorbitant cost, to deliver sustainability goals, and to avoid corruption and other scandals that taint an event's reputation (as with the deaths of migrants working on construction for the 2022 FIFA World Cup in Qatar [Booth, 2013]). Procurement is not, though, just an issue for events. It is central in securing all kinds of sporting facilities and equipment (e.g., sports halls, gymnastic equipment) for those who need them, from professional sport teams to schools and community organizations. Further, it is important to the day-to-day running of sport federations that buy, for example, computers, insurance services, and medical services for athletes, as well as for private companies supplying the sport industry, whose procurement strategy can affect their competitive position.

The role of procurement in achieving the goals of sport organizations is therefore clear. Further, procurement is receiving increasing attention from a governance perspective: The International Partnership Against Corruption in Sport (IPACS), launched in 2017 (Council of Europe, 2017), has a significant procurement focus, while governance indicators for federations also address procurement. Familiarity with this topic is thus essential not just for those who undertake procurement but for all those involved in sport management and governance who develop policy or exercise oversight.

Despite this, sport-related procurement receives little academic attention. This new chapter helps to fill the information gap by providing a map of the field. It also contributes to the aim of the third edition of this book of highlighting the importance of a multidisciplinary perspective for studying and managing sport organizations.

After first explaining the importance of this multidisciplinary approach, this chapter examines the concept of procurement and highlights its connections with other activities, such as sale of media rights. It then outlines the objectives of procurement policy and considers the role of two key concepts, **transparency** and competitive bidding, in achieving these objectives. Finally, the chapter's themes are explored by reference to two areas, procurement for sporting events and procurement by federations, chosen because their unique features present special challenges and opportunities and also fertile ground for future research.

A Multidisciplinary Perspective

As the preface explains, one aim of this book is to highlight the importance of a multidisciplinary perspective. This is particularly pertinent to procurement. A recent literature review concluded that "it is clear that the [relevant] literature is theoretically diverse and fragmented and draws on a very wide range of underpinning disciplines" (Sanderson, Lonsdale, Mannion, & Matharu, 2015, p. 23). In an area with such a diverse and rich literature it is impossible to do more than skim the surface, but this section illustrates the above points by reference to a few key perspectives relevant to the chapter taken from classic works in several of these disciplines.

Management

First, procurement has been studied extensively from the perspective of organizational theory. For example, pioneering work of Robinson, Faris, & Wind (1967) proposed an eight-stage Model of Organizational Buying Behavior and developed a Buying Decision Grid to explain procurement decision making. The Buying Center concept of Webster and Wind (1972) identifies the actors who influence procurement and its complexities within organizations. Other work focuses on specific procurement strategies, as discussed below. While most work deals with industrial organizations, organizational differences are recognized, for example, the specificities of the public sector (Kelman, 1990), discussed below. However, public purchasing has been less studied in management literature than private-sector procurement (Mogre, Lindgreen, & Hingley, 2017) and, according to Flynn and Davis (2014), generally lacks a theoretical approach.

Studies with a sport procurement focus are even more limited in management literature. Kauppi, Moxham, & Bamford (2013), reviewing literature on operations management in sport with a category for procurement and supply chain literature, identified only a few articles, mainly on **outsourcing**. In another example, Arthur, Scott, & Woods (1997) adapted the Buying Decision Grid model for sport sponsorship acquisition, and some work also applies management theory to analyzing procurement strategy for event infrastructure (see the section "Procurement for Sporting Events") and government-provided community infrastructure (see the section "Value for Money in Acquiring the Required Goods, Works, or Services" and Propheter & Hatch, 2015). Some of this is in the "gray" literature field ignored in management literature reviews. However, work remains limited, and procurement barely merits a mention in textbooks on event management.

Law

Law is another important discipline. This is particularly so for the public sector in view of the significant and increasing regulatory dimension, described as a "global revolution" (Wallace, 1995). Arrowsmith, Linarelli, & Wallace (2000) identified three key sources of this revolution: (1) reform of national systems using a legal model, resulting from both the transformation of former socialist economies to a market-oriented approach and a push by multilateral development banks (MDBs) for national procurement reform as an aspect of good governance; (2) application of formal rules by MDBs and other aid donors to procurements of developing countries; and (3) international trade agreements. While there were once two main public procurement models in the Western and postcolonial worlds, one based on detailed and enforceable legal rules and the other (e.g., in the United Kingdom and former colonies) based mainly on administrative approaches, the latter has largely disappeared. In many jurisdictions public contract awards are so heavily regulated that the legal framework is central in shaping policy. This is important for sport organizations for two reasons. The first is that public procurement law often applies directly: As is explained later in the chapter, much sport-related procurement, including for infrastructure, is done by government bodies, and even some private sport federations are subject to these public procurement rules. The second is that public-sector models are increasingly relevant by analogy, given the emphasis on transparency as an aspect of good governance in sport federations, as described in chapter 13.

In both respects, international models for transparent procurement and related literature can provide guidance for sport managers. One model is the United Nations Commission on International Trade Law (UNCITRAL) Model Law on Public Procurement 2011 (UNCITRAL, 2011) and its accompanying guides (UNCITRAL, 2012, n.d.), providing a template law drawing on collective experience of United Nations countries (Arrowsmith, 2004). Another, although covering only major contracts, is the World Trade Organization's Agreement on Government Procurement 2012 (GPA) (Arrowsmith & Anderson, 2011), applying to 47 countries and used also as a model for numerous regional and bilateral agreements (Khorana & Garcia, 2014). In addition, the Organisation for Economic Cooperation and Development (OECD) Recommendation (OECD, 2015) and related Toolbox provide useful guidance, as do the Guidelines and related instruments for MDB-funded procurement (World Bank, 2011a & 2011b).

Doctrinal legal scholarship analyzes the law using distinctively legal techniques, for example, to interpret ambiguous words or organize regulatory material in coherent frameworks, including creating typologies or taxonomies (e.g., Arrowsmith, 2010, on the CSR dimension of procurement). This scholarship is found most often in the "doctrinal in context" form (Cownie, 2004), examining law not as a self-contained system but against its contextual background. Clearly those supervising or undertaking procurement in sport organizations must understand any legal constraints and risks. Doctrinal analysis has not looked to any significant extent at procurement in sport, reflected in its absence from textbooks on sport law (e.g., Gardiner, O'Leary, Welch, Boyes, & Naidoo, 2012; Lewis & Taylor, 2014; Sharp, Moorman, & Claussen, 2017). (Some consider briefly, for example, financing and ownership models for venues [e.g., Sharp et al., 2017, pp. 500-501] but not award and execution of venue contracts.) Legal research also often addresses the way law is perceived or applied in practice or its social impact (i.e., socio-legal studies) often involving an interdisciplinary approach, for example, work on the extent of and reasons for compliance with public procurement rules by both legal scholars (e.g., Braun, 2003; Aspey & Craven, 2018) and those working primarily in other disciplines (e.g., Telgen & de Boer, 1997; Martin, Hartley, & Cox, 1999; Madsen, 2002; Gelderman, Ghijsen, & Schoonen, 2010).

With notable exceptions, the regulatory perspective is neglected by management scholars. Flynn and Davis (2014, p. 139) concluded that public procurement research focuses on "organizational-level aspects more than regulatory-policy issues or public buyers" but examined just one management-focused journal, neglecting specialist or general journals from other disciplines and books. This partly reflects the management field's neglect of "gray" literature such as books, and a call by Adams, Smart, & Huff (2017, p. 432) for greater use of gray literature "to increase the relevance and impact of management and organization studies" is pertinent here.

Economics and Political Science

Analysis of organizational behavior and policy in procurement is also significantly informed by economics, for example, principal-agent theory (Jensen & Meckling, 1976). An agent making procurement contracts for an organization (the principal) may seek to maximize the interests of the agent's department or personal, family, or political influence (e.g., taking bribes), requiring mechanisms to align the interests (Laffont & Tirole, 1993). These mechanisms, including transparency, may vary according to the nature of the organization, as discussed below. Economic theory on market behavior also informs the design of specific procurement tools (e.g., electronic reverse auctions) and anti-collusion (bid-rigging) strategies (Dimitri, Piga, & Spagnolo, 2009). Political science, which includes the study of the processes of making and implementing policies and rules, also provides insights that are useful to managers in sport organizations seeking to understand and influence the relevant regulatory processes.

Introduction to Procurement and Its Significance for Sport Organizations

This chapter has defined procurement as the activity of an organization in acquiring goods, works, and services from the marketplace—an activity that, when carried out by individuals, is often called simply *buying* or *purchasing*.

Procurement by sport organizations covers a huge variety of transactions, requiring very different procurement systems. Goods procured include not only the kinds of office and other supplies purchased by most organizations but also sport-specific items. For example, a recent tender advertised by the Union of European Football Associations (UEFA) was for the supply of match balls for tournaments. The opening scenario indicated the variety of goods purchased by LOCOG for the 2012 Olympics, from fencing to flowers. Services include simple contracts to support day-to-day operations (e.g., office cleaning) through contracts to deliver ceremonies for sport events (another example of a recent tender from UEFA) to complex long-term arrangements for operating stadia. In the works category, facilities procured by governments for community use commonly include fields or pitches, sport halls, and sport centers (van den Hurk & Verhoest, 2015, 2017), while construction for events involves venues, accommodation facilities, and general infrastructure. Even regional events can involve significant investment: The 16th Asian Games in Guangzhou, China, involved 17 new venues and refurbishment of many more at a cost of more than US$1 billion, while investment in transport infrastructure around that time amounted to more than US$17 billion (Arrowsmith et al., 2019). Typically, as with these examples, infrastructure procurement is the responsibility of public bodies, but construction is also commissioned by private organizations, as with stadia built by professional sport teams. In fact, many models exist for financing and procuring stadia (Hoye & Nicholson, 2010).

Buying and *purchasing* have already been mentioned as terms for procurement. Other terms are *acquisition* (in the United States) and *commissioning*. These terms are often used synonymously, but some are sometimes preferred because of different connotations: *Procurement* and *commissioning* generally indicate an activity that is not simply clerical and reactive but strategic. The academic field of study is also often defined as *procurement* and *supply chain management* (Lysons & Farrington, 2016) to emphasize the need to study the whole supply chain from production to delivery including, but not limited to, procurement.

Procurement and In-House Provision

Procurement must be distinguished from internal, or **in-house, provision**. For example, sport organizations could engage their own cleaners under contracts of employment to clean their office buildings (in-house provision) or could make contracts with firms in the marketplace that offer commercial cleaning services (procurement). The strategy of choosing procurement above in-house provision is referred to as *outsourcing*. These are just main two options of many shades on a spectrum for service delivery (Sport England, 2017).

The last few decades have seen a trend toward outsourcing. For example, under successive provisions of the Local Government Act 1988 municipal leisure services were made subject to the UK government's policy of requiring proactive consideration of different options, leading to some outsourcing (Coalter, 1995). Burden and Li (2009) documented a growth of outsourcing of sport marketing, and Minis, Parashi, & Tzimourtas (2006) highlighted development of outsourcing with the Sydney Olympics. As seen in our opening scenario, a substantial part of the procurement function for infrastructure of the 2012 London Olympic Games was itself outsourced. Outsourcing has a significant impact on the complexity of procurement, requiring management of often complex services contracts and procurement procedures (UNCITRAL, 2011, 2012), as well as implications for control of policy (as highlighted in the leisure management context by Coalter, 1995); the outsourcing trend enhances the case for professional and effective procurement in sport organizations. Kauppi et al. (2013) highlighted the limited literature and suggested that this is an important area for study.

Phases of a Procurement

The eight-phase buying model of Robinson, Faris, and Wind (1967) starts with recognition of a need (phase 1), description of that need (phase 2), and draft of the specification (phase 3). It moves through the search for suppliers, solicitation of proposals, and supplier selection (phases 4 through 6); and ends with the ordering process (phase 7) and performance review (phase 8). This model has been nuanced and critiqued (Johnston & Spekman, 1982; Ćorić, Anić, Rajh, Rajh, & Kurnoga, 2017) and does not capture the whole strategic procurement function (e.g., supplier development outside individual purchases), but it still provides a starting point for analyzing industrial organizations. In an on-going contract—such as a multiyear contract for leisure center management—the performance and management phase is significant. This is an integral part of effective procurement. For example, lax enforcement or uncontrolled amendments can undermine the negotiated terms and facilitate corruption (e.g., price increases agreed between a corrupt supplier and manager).

In the legal context, a three-stage classification is sometimes employed for public procurement to reflect its legal treatment, in particular the intensity and nature of the legal constraints (Arrowsmith et al., 2000). The first stage is planning prior to formally launching an award procedure in law; this includes phases 1 and 2 above and is subject only to limited regulation since it involves policy choices unsuitable for legal review (Arrowsmith & Kunzlik, 2009), although some controls apply (e.g., on conducting consultations) to avoid specifications being geared to particular suppliers. Secondly, the award procedure stage (mainly phases 4 through 6 above) embraces the steps in choosing the supplier; this is the most heavily regulated and, for major public contracts, takes the form of competitive bidding. The third phase is the execution (performance or management) stage that, despite its importance, tends to be less governed by formal rules and is often neglected in reform efforts (Magina & McCrary, 2014).

The Boundaries of Procurement and Its Connection With Other Activities

The core of what is understood by procurement is clear, but the boundaries are sometimes fuzzy. This is the case with concessions—broadly speaking, arrangements under which a supplier is given a legal right to exploit goods, works, or services and undertakes operational risk (e.g., an agreement for a supplier to provide catering at a stadium, keeping the revenue). When the arrangement is a means to ensure the service is provided (as opposed to merely a commercial opportunity for the supplier to exploit), the transaction involves procurement as defined in this chapter. Some legal instruments, including those of the European Union (2014a), treat concessions separately. However, they are considered as procurement here since for the purposes of this chapter they present the same features as procurement in general.

An analogous transaction, sometimes considered a type of procurement, is acquisition of sponsorship. This can involve the sponsor providing services or goods such as a jersey, as well as funds. Whether that is the case, however, acquiring sponsorship has many features in common with procurement, particularly when the supply side competes to offer sponsorship, as with major events or elite teams. Here procurement can provide useful insights from the perspective of the sponsor (e.g., Arthur et al., 1997) but also the sponsored party.

Also relevant is the award of rights to host sporting events, which in part comprise acquisition of a service (providing an event). This activity has attracted significant controversy, the most high-profile illustration being the award of the FIFA World Cup 2022 to Qatar, involving corruption allegations, significant post-award changes with the event being moved from summer to winter (Szymanski, 2016; Youd, 2014), and worker safety concerns (Booth, 2013). This area of award of hosting rights involves special concerns that preclude its inclusion in this short chapter. However, lessons from procurement are relevant: when awarding procurement contracts, there is extensive experience of dealing with the same kinds of issues that arise in awarding hosting rights. The analogy between the award of procurement contracts and the award of rights to host events is recognized in the indicators for good governance, e.g., by the Association of Summer Olympic International Federations (ASOIF) by explicitly *excluding* bidding for events from general rules that apply to procurement and other commercial transactions (ASOIF, 2017a).

Another area with parallels to procurement is sale of property or rights, including media rights. Common objectives, including value for money and integrity, again mean that procurement experience can provide useful insights.

Adriaanse, van Ommeren, den Ouden, and Wolswinkel (2016) analyzed the features and legal treatment of public procurement and analogous transactions to develop a theoretical framework for regulation in a European Union (EU) context that highlights common features (e.g., their nature as commercial opportunities) and concludes that transparency is a central common element. They also conclude that while a uniform approach is not found or appropriate, there is a tendency toward harmonization and scope for further developing some transparency provisions that could be common to both public procurement and to other types of transactions in view of these common features. These can be, for example, provisions on where and how commercial opportunities are to be publicized and what exemptions from publicity apply, or on the type of reasons to be given to those whose applications for these opportunities are rejected. These insights indicate that sport managers can benefit from seeking the common element to the above activities and implementing a consistent approach, and that, where transparency is a starting point, insights from public law regulation are useful. From this perspective, it is interesting that some federations operate a single webpage providing transparency for commercial opportunities in both core procurement and other areas (e.g. UEFA, n.d.; International Cricket Council [ICC], n.d.). This approach is also reflected in some of the governance indicators for sport federations, which treat such transactions under common rules.

Procurement as a Strategic Function, Internal Organization, and Professional Development

A common definition of *strategy* is a pattern or plan that integrates an organization's major goals, policies, and action sequences into a cohesive whole. Procurement is increasingly recognized as a strategic function. Reck and Long (1988) identified four development stages, from the "passive," when procurement merely responds to requests and is clerical in nature, to the "integrative," when procurement is fully integrated into and helps formulate organizational strategy (Jones, 1999). With recognition of the potentially strategic nature of procurement, and further driving that, has come **professionalism** (i.e., development of specialist knowledge, skills, and qualifications) and **professionalization** (i.e., recognition of procurement as a profession) (Reck & Long, 1988). Closely connected with this is the internal organization of procurement, covering, for example, level of representation and report; extent of centralization or outsourcing; degree of specialization; whether procurement is organized by reference to, for example, the end product or service, spend category or profit centers, and the extent to which it operates in a cross-functional setting. This will be influenced by factors such as the stage of development and procurement's importance to the organization's mission, which with nonindustrial sport organizations will often not be profit-oriented but involve, for example, effective delivery of an event or services.

Managers in sport organizations need to understand the importance of a suitable approach to the above matters—for example, whether to engage professional procurement officers or to centralize procurement functions within the organization. Research has focused mainly on industrial organizations and, to a limited extent, the public sector (Flynn & Davis, 2014), but it would be valuable to study these issues in relation to the unique contexts of sport teams, federations, and events.

Objectives of the Procurement Process

Statements of objectives in management texts tend to focus on commercial issues, reflecting research focus on industrial organizations. Thus Baily, Farmer, Crocker, Jessop, & Jones (2015) state objectives: provide a flow of necessary material and services; ensure security of supply; buy efficiently and wisely, obtaining the best value by ethical means;

maintain sound, cooperative relationships with other departments; and develop staff, policies, and so on to achieve all this. Only the brief reference to ethical means departs from the commercial focus.

While commercial aspects are also the predominant focus of other—including public—organizations, public bodies often follow or place more emphasis on other concerns, as reflected in legal analysis. Thus Trepte (2004) states the three "most readily identifiable" objectives of public procurement as economic efficiency, social and political objectives, and trade objectives. Schooner (2002b) refers to nine (nonexhaustive) "desiderata" of regulation; however, some, such as uniformity and competition, are means to achieve objectives, rather than outcomes per se. Arrowsmith adopts an eight-fold classification (Arrowsmith, 2011), which is used below to capture all objectives of sport-related procurement, including in the public sector. Kelman (2018) suggests that the only goal, or objective, is to obtain best-value products and services and that other considerations, including integrity, are merely "constraints." This analysis offers useful insights but does not undermine the value of the eight-fold classification to illuminate the desired outcomes.

Value for Money in Acquiring the Required Goods, Works, or Services

This first objective broadly refers to commercial goals. It involves three aspects: (1) ensuring the purchase is suitable, appropriate for the purpose and not over-specified ("gold-plated"); (2) securing the best terms on price and other matters, such as quality; and (3) ensuring the supplier actually provides what was agreed. An extensive literature on this objective covers organization of procurement, plus such overlapping subjects as identifying suppliers (sourcing strategies), ongoing management of supplier relationships, negotiation techniques, pricing models, and use of electronic systems and techniques, as well as contract management. This short chapter cannot even provide a summary; it can merely be noted here that this is the "bread and butter" for those aspiring to the procurement profession, covered in texts such as Baily et al. (2015), Lysons and Farrington (2016), and (on construction) Masterman (2001) and Morledge and Smith (2013).

One point to highlight, however, is the importance of the nature of the organization. The approach of commercial organizations tends to differ from that of the public sector, especially in that supplier-purchaser relationships tend to be less transaction based. In the public sector competitive bidding is the norm for major contracts. Even arrangements for placing smaller orders for regular requirements (such as consultancy) from one or more designated suppliers (**framework agreements**) are generally openly tendered and involve regulated procedures for choosing between suppliers on the framework (Albano & Nicholas, 2016). The private sector, on the other hand, often employs relational rather than transactional approaches, focusing on building long-term relationships (**partnership sourcing**). This can, for example, allow the parties to work together to invest resources in product development (Bensaou, 1999; Lindgreen, Vanhamme, van Raaij, & Johnston, 2013; both sources provide theoretical frameworks for analyzing relationships). Parker and Hartley (1997) present such relationships as points on a continuum, the optimum approach depending on the circumstances. The reason for dominance of the transaction-based approach in public procurement lies in the role of transparency and greater significance of noncommercial objectives, as we will discuss later.

Specific issues relevant to value for money have been studied in the sport context by, for example, van den Hurk and Verhoest, evaluating use in community infrastructure of models for **public-private partnerships** (PPPs)—that is, long-term outsourcing arrangements covering (usually) the life cycle of an asset and involving private financing of the asset and risk sharing (van den Hurk & Verhoest, 2015; Long, 2013); contextual factors affecting predicted benefits from standard form contracts (van den Hurk & Verhoest, 2017); and the value of bundling smaller projects (van den Hurk, 2016). Some work also looks at value for money at specific events. However, sport-specific work is very limited.

Integrity

The second relevant objective is integrity, referring to the need to avoid corruption—"misuse of entrusted power for private gain" (Transparency International, 2009)—and collusion. Corruption operates in all procurement phases, both in the initial conception of need by undertaking unsuitable procurements to provide economic benefits to certain firms (OECD, 2007) and in the procedure, for example, by drafting specifications or misusing discretion in assessing offers in order to favor specific firms. The execution phase, as noted, also offers significant corruption opportunities. Fraud (obtaining an advantage by deception), such as siphoning off materials or diverting contractual payments, can also be considered corruption. Collusion (bid-rigging) on the supply-side, which can be assisted from within the purchasing organization, takes various forms such as cover-bidding (i.e., submitting bids to give the illusion of competition) and bid suppression (i.e., agreeing not to bid) (OECD, 2009).

Integrity and value for money are related since absence of the former negatively affects the latter. For example, at a simple level, although the relationship is complex (Rose-Ackerman & Palifka, 2016), awarding a contract because of a bribe can mean paying a higher price. There is also a relationship in that similar measures, including transparency and competitive bidding, generally address both integrity and value.

However, integrity needs to be conceived as a separate objective because it often involves considerations going beyond simply value for money (Arrowsmith et al., 2000). For example, with public-sector organizations, aims can be setting an example, tackling organized crime (Anechiarico & Jacobs, 1996), or preventing the detriment that corruption can have on general economic growth (Lanyi, 2004). In both public and private sectors there may also be concerns about the reputational effect of integrity problems, which may deter sponsors or customers or damage electoral prospects, a factor that in government may lead to anti-corruption goals being given undue attention (Branstetter, 2005). These broader considerations may mean integrity is pursued even when there is a negative impact on commercial objectives. These broader considerations, as well as the impact on value for money, make this an important issue for managers in sport organizations.

Integrity tends to be seen mostly, or even solely, as a public-sector issue (Rose-Ackerman, 1997). The existence and causes of integrity problems are difficult to measure (Lanyi, 2004; Brooks, Aleem, & Button, 2013), and greater interest in the public sector may stem from different perceptions, including because of the greater scrutiny of public projects (Jenny, 2005) as well greater concern for reputation. However, there is some indication of higher corruption levels (OECD, 2014). This could be explained by various related factors including low pay and lack of performance-related pay, absence of a profit motive, bureaucratic rules and budgets unrelated to particular goals, and political involvement (Rose-Ackerman & Palifka, 2016). Some of these features are shared by sport federations. From the perspective of industrial organizations we have seen more focus on preventing bribery *by* than *of* those organizations, particularly since the criminalization of public-sector bribery under the 1997 OECD Convention on this (OECD, 1997). Bid rigging may also be more prevalent in public procurement, in part because transparency can facilitate bid-rigging (Estevan de Quesada, 2014).

Concern over corruption is a key driver of transparency in the public sector, and this in turn explains the transactional approach since transparency is generally implemented through competitive bidding. However, as will be seen, transparency, including because of the transactional approach that it entails and because it limits the discretion that can be useful to obtaining the best deal, also has costs, creating a tension between anti-corruption objectives and other aspects of value for money, and meaning that an undue emphasis on integrity can actually hinder commercial goals.

Apart from transparency, numerous other mechanisms can enhance integrity. These include rules on disclosure and management of conflicts of interest (OECD, 2003), including those specific to procurement (OECD, 2016); rules on whistle-blowing (OECD, 2016); general regular and ad hoc audits, internal or external (Dye & Stapenhurst, 1998); codes of ethics and other professional development measures, including education; integrity pacts requiring bidders to testify to the absence of corruption; debarment of corrupt suppliers (Williams-Elegbe, 2012); supplier integrity management systems (International Federation of Consulting Engineers [FIDIC], 2011, 2015, 2019); and sanctions under law, corporate policy, or professional disciplinary procedures. Measures targeting bid-rigging include careful design of transparency measures and proactive detection through analyzing bid patterns, as well as legal sanctions. Civil society organizations also provide an important social accountability mechanism. The best known is Transparency International, which recently reported on corruption in sport (Transparency International, 2016); another is the Open Contracting Partnership, discussed later.

Corruption in sport has been under increasing focus (Brooks et al., 2013). Globalization of both sport and corruption also makes the problems more difficult to address and has led to international cooperative efforts, most recently IPACS, whose core group consists of the International Olympic Committee (IOC), Council of Europe, OECD, United Nations Office on Drugs and Crime (UNODC), and UK government. Procurement and the analogous issue of bidding for events constitute a significant element of IPACS' initial work: Task Force 1 focuses on risks of corruption in procurement relating to events and infrastructure; Task Force 2 covers integrity in selecting event hosts; while Task Force 3 is concerned with compliance with good governance principles to mitigate corruption risks.

Some literature looks at corruption in mega-events, on which UNODC has published a guide, including procurement (UNODC, 2013), but generally procurement receives little serious attention in literature on sport-related corruption. For example, Brooks et al. (2013) mention the area but do not cover this topic in their case studies, and the recent brief contribution by Matheson, Schwab, and Koval (2018) presents the topic without reference to the procurement literature.

Effective Implementation of Social Responsibility Policies (CSR)

A third objective is to support corporate social responsibility (CSR). This CSR dimension is also commonly discussed using the terminology of sustainable procurement (Sjåfjell & Wiesbrock, 2015). CSR in sport was discussed in chapter 23, and procurement is an important area through which CSR is manifested. CSR is sometimes an aspect of value for money broadly defined, where value refers not merely to the cost, quality, and so on of functional aspects of the purchase, but also of the value of the social dimension. For example, where an organization leverages procurement to create jobs for disadvantaged persons, overall value will include the number and nature of jobs delivered or the commercial value to the organization's reputation. However, it is useful to examine CSR separately.

Social responsibility is a long-established feature of public procurement, reflecting the broad welfare interests of public-sector organizations (Nagle, 1999 [United States]; Bercusson, 1978 [labor issues]; Arrowsmith, 1988 [Canada]; Turpin, 1989 [UK]). Given these interests, the debate over the legitimacy of CSR and its relationship with commercial goals takes a different form than with other organizations, for example, concerns that excluding suppliers from procurement to "regulate" behavior evades constitutional processes (Daintith, 1979, 1982; Ferguson & Page, 1978). Scholars have also examined issues relating to policy effectiveness (Bercusson, 1978; Leonard, 1985, 1990).

To the extent that sport-related procurement occurs within a public-sector framework, as with much infrastructure procurement, this regulative element of the institutional context, as discussed in chapter 23, is important, as well as the normative element that is itself affected by the public-sector environment. Such public-sector legal frameworks sometimes provide positive support as, for example, with the 2010 FIFA World Cup in South Africa, whose laws—and, indeed, Constitution—provide for systematic use of public procurement to support disadvantaged persons (Quinot, 2013; Rose, 2010). On the other hand, such frameworks also impose limitations, including resulting from trade agreements (Arrowsmith, 1995; Fernández Martín, 1996; McCrudden, 2007). For example, EU rules prohibit preference for small or local businesses, so that ODA's measures to involve small suppliers in the 2012 London Olympics focused on helping those suppliers compete in fair competition (Cornelius et al., 2011).

Outside the public sector, chapter 23 outlined how early manifestations of CSR included concern with labor conditions in manufacturing, including the sporting goods sector. This remains an important area for industrial organizations and has been extensively studied from the supply chain management perspective (Touboulic & Walker, 2015). Thus, procurement has a strategic role in industrial organizations such as Nike that procure their branded sport goods from outside suppliers; bad publicity from poor labor conditions in making branded goods for resale is one area in which CSR issues have the most significant potential to prejudice commercial performance (Vogel, 2005). Chapter 23 also explained that changing societal norms and the need to maintain legitimacy have influenced sport organizations in general, including private teams and federations, to engage in CSR. Procurement often plays a major role in CSR policies, as in the Go Green campaign of the Philadelphia Eagles gridiron football team described at the start of chapter 23, which involves sourcing green energy and other products and services on a large scale and negotiating and managing complex services arrangements, such as the Eagles' multiyear partnership with Waste Masters Solutions, recently extended to 2021, for managing the team's recycling and waste disposal activities (Waste Masters Solutions, n.d.).

The approach of 2012 London Olympics illustrates operation of CSR in procurement in both private and public organizations. Central to the 2012 bid was a commitment to zero waste, a low-carbon Games, preservation of biodiversity and promotion of environmental awareness, and social goals (Gold & Gold, 2015). The Games aimed to achieve a sustainability legacy in procurement: "Our vision is to set the benchmark for sustainability, which other organizations around the world will seek to follow" (LOCOG, 2011). A Commission for Sustainable London was created, and CSR was from the outset built into the procurement policies of both the ODA and LOCOG. The opening scenario explained the important role of both agencies. Those responsible in LOCOG have highlighted both the special opportunities for a bespoke agency to draw from best practice without baggage from past policies and to build up a new supply chain. Also highlighted were

TIME OUT

LOCOG's Social Responsibility Policy in Procurement for the 2012 London Olympics

LOCOG set out its policy framework for socially responsibility procurement in its Sustainable Sourcing Code (LOCOG, 2011). LOCOG determined priorities at the outset by analyzing key factors for each spend category, including LOCOG's ability to influence sustainability, reputational risk, and stakeholder concerns. Sustainability was built into LOCOG's Procurement Governance Model to ensure that it was embedded at every stage (Cumming, Stubbs, & Walsh, 2012).

The Code focused mainly on environmental matters, such as use of recycled content and environmentally friendly packaging and delivery. The policy operated mainly through contractual obligations for suppliers both to comply with environmental laws and to go beyond this in specified areas. The latter often involved a "best endeavours" approach rather than precise obligations, such as a requirement to "use reasonable endeavours to source products with enhanced sustainability credentials (e.g. recycled content)" combined with an obligation to report later on how this would be addressed (Cumming, Stubbs, & Walsh, 2012).

Other areas covered included fair labor practices, health and safety, diversity and inclusion, animal welfare and testing, and prompt supplier payment.

One difficulty encountered was that no formal mechanism was adopted for the sustainability team to check for inclusion in each contract of the bespoke obligations that were agreed specifically with suppliers for individual contracts (as opposed to obligations included in standard terms). However, LOCOG believed this was addressed through that team's good relationship with the legal team (Cumming, Stubbs, & Walsh, 2012). LOCOG sought to ensure compliance with contractual obligations through mechanisms including management plans, the Supplier Ethical Data Exchange (Sedex) system to manage factory disclosures and audit information, site-based supplier audits, and a complaint mechanism. The Play Fair at the Olympics campaign helped improve the robustness of the approach (Timms, 2015).

Key lessons highlighted by those responsible were the need for sustainability to be integrated from the beginning, including attention to contract management, and clarity over roles and responsibilities for supplier oversight.

---

the challenges that such an agency faces at this kind of event, including the need to gear up rapidly, the short time frame in which most deliveries take place, large number of contracts, diverse range of purchases and suppliers, and inability to offer repeat business (Cumming, Stubbs, & Walsh, 2012). CSR policies were implemented by LOCOG through procurement in a range of areas, and Timms (2015) concluded that LOCOG's policy did in fact leave a significant legacy.

In the context of public procurement, Arrowsmith (2010, 2018) has developed a taxonomy of policies that can be useful for managers in sport organizations in identifying approaches and assessing their costs and benefits, as well as for assessing legality.

Often, but not necessarily, a trade-off exists between social responsibility and other objectives; for example, facilitating small-business participation may promote other objectives by increasing competition. Trade-offs are complex (Arrowsmith, 2010), but simple examples include costs in preparing and evaluating social responsibility proposals (Wittie, 2002) and potentially higher prices where set-asides of procurement contracts for limited groups (such as companies owned by disadvantaged ethnic groups) reduce competition. LOCOG claimed to see little evidence of increased cost from its social responsibility agenda, however, although it did acknowledge higher costs in some procurements (Cumming, Stubbs, & Walsh, 2012).

Other Objectives of the Procurement Process

Other objectives can be noted more briefly. One is to achieve open trade (analyzed in economic literature by Trionfetti, 2000, 2003) under international obligations, such as the EU procurement directives and GPA. These agreements aim, among other things, to prevent discrimination in favor of domestic industry and generally apply only to public bodies. This should entail price savings for purchasers (W.S

Atkins Management Consultants, 1988). Transparency to prevent hidden discrimination and ensure competition is an important means to achieve the nondiscrimination goal. However, the costs of transparency mean that, as with anti-corruption goals, there may be trade-offs with other aspects of value for money and that open market goals can actually hinder commercial goals.

Another objective is equal opportunities for suppliers. Equal treatment is also a means to achieve other objectives, but as a separate objective it enshrines the value of giving all citizens equal chance to benefit from government business (Dekel, 2008). This can again involve trade-offs, such as higher costs in processing more applications or tenders than are needed from a value for money perspective. Similarly, fair treatment, including values such as procedural due process, may be a separate value that goes beyond what is needed to promote the public interest in terms of informed decision making.

Accountability (visibility) can also be seen as a separate objective. Arrowsmith (2011) uses this term to denote a value whereby visibility of outcomes and explanations of how they were achieved is considered as an independent value of open and democratic governance. Accountability in this sense is closely related to transparency. However, transparency is used in procurement literature to denote a concept of openness that provides a means to achieve objectives, rather than an objective per se (Arrowsmith, 2003). Chapter 13 used Bovens' (2007, p. 450) definition of accountability as "a relationship between an actor and a forum, in which the actor has an obligation to explain and to justify his or her conduct." In the present chapter on procurement, however, the concept of transparency is also tied to specific functions (including verification and enforcement) that are classified as dimensions of transparency as a means to other specific objectives, such as value and integrity, that are distinct from accountability as an objective. To avoid inconsistent terminology, the term *visibility* could be employed to denote accountability as an independent objective.

The prominence of these objectives in public procurement helps to explain the different approaches of the public and commercial sectors, including the role of transparency. While they are of limited relevance for commercial organizations, however, these objectives, or at least visibility, may be relevant to sport organizations, even in the private sector. For example, concern for visibility arguably influenced LOCOG's strategy of advertising all significant procurements through the CompeteFor web portal (Cumming, Stubbs, & Walsh, 2012).

A final objective is process efficiency, meaning that the procurement process itself does not consume unnecessary resources and costs do not exceed benefits. For example, open competitive bidding is used only when the benefits are likely to exceed the time and resource costs of running a competitive bidding procedure.

Transparency and Competitive Bidding

As already mentioned, transparency plays a role in implementing procurement objectives, particularly in the public sector. Its greater role in the public sector is in part explained by the specific objectives and priorities of the public sector, including concern with integrity and open trade and with accountability and equal treatment. It is also explained by the organizational differences mentioned earlier (Trepte, 2004), which can reduce efficiency incentives in public-sector procurement. Inclusion of transparency among good governance principles for sport federations means that this concept is also potentially important for sport procurement outside the public sector.

Using the approach of Henry and Lee (2004) chapter 13 defined transparency as the ability of stakeholders to obtain information about management and processes. This focus on information presents a common view of the core of transparency. However, transparency is a concept that has various functions and nuances according to context (Buijze, 2015) and needs to be unpacked further to understand its role in procurement. As noted, it can refer to an *objective* of procurement processes, accountability (or visibility), but is used here in line with literature to refer to a tool supporting other objectives (Arrowsmith, 2003). From this perspective, Arrowsmith et al. (2000) identified four aspects of transparency:

1. Publicity of contract opportunities.

2. Publicity of the rules governing each procedure, both the general rules of the system and the rules for the specific procurements such as evaluation criteria and their weightings.

3. Rule-based decision making that limits discretion (i.e., a reasonable degree of precision on how decisions are made). This dimension is often neglected but is fundamental to transparency, as well as having other benefits (Davis, 1969). Rule-based decision making facilitates monitoring of decisions to safeguard against abuse (e.g., for corrupt motives or to unlawfully favor national suppliers)

that may occur when the principal's and agent's interests diverge. It also enhances the quality of decisions by sharing experience and inputs with individual decision-makers and provides information relevant for action by affected parties. To illustrate, rules on exactly which evaluation criteria (e.g., price, quality) are suitable for which types of procurement can help ensure that purchasers use suitable criteria while formulating and disclosing evaluation criteria for individual procurements, and this both limits scope for decisions based on corrupt or discriminatory motives and gives bidders information to formulate bids that respond to the purchaser's needs.

4. The possibility for verifying whether desired policies have been followed and for enforcement. This is often supported by requirements to give tenderers reasons for rejection, to record and publicize decisions and reasons for them, and to give access to information on concluded contracts. Perhaps the most important enforcement mechanism is **challenge proceedings**, a formal mechanism (internal, external, or both) to hear complaints by aggrieved suppliers (e.g., United Nations Against Corruption and the UNCITRAL Model Law). Scholars have assessed the features of such mechanisms through, for example, doctrinal in context analysis (Arrowsmith et al., 2000; Gordon, 2006; Zhang, 2007) and economic theory (Marshall, Meurer, & Richard, 1994).

Transparency rules generally focus on contract award, perhaps in part because a rule-based approach is less suitable for controlling contract management. However, some detailed transparency rules (including limits on discretion) are applied in some jurisdictions, for example, the EU, requiring retendering when amendments are made other than in defined circumstances (Arrowsmith, 2014).

Extensive transparency in the first, second, and fourth dimensions (which also supports the third where limits on discretion exist) can be provided by comprehensive publication systems, and this is the goal of the Open Contracting movement.

Competitive Bidding

Transparency in all four aspects is generally implemented through **competitive bidding**, whereby the purchaser sets out requirements and suppliers formally submit their terms of supply, in competition with each other. Competitive bidding with a public solicitation was used, for example, for nearly all major infrastructure procurements for 10 international sporting events examined by Arrowsmith et al. (2019), although with notable exceptions, as discussed later. Competition generally covers price and cost (e.g., running costs) and may also cover other features. For example, the advertised criteria and weightings for the 2021 London Olympic Aquatics Centre construction project were price (30

TIME OUT

Open Contracting as a Good Governance Tool

Publishing information can be a powerful tool to help achieve procurement objectives, opening up procurement to scrutiny by interested parties such as government watchdogs, civil society, and suppliers. The Open Contracting Partnership is a program that advocates publishing full information on contracting—"open contracting"—and supports organizations in implementing this approach. The Partnership was initially developed through collaboration among stakeholders from business, civil society, and government, hosted by the World Bank Group. It became an independent program in 2014, with an advisory board drawn from various stakeholders.

Its Global Principles include a presumption of proactive disclosure of all procurement information, across all procurement phases; this entails disclosure of contracts themselves, pre-studies, bid documents, auditing reports, criteria for selection and evaluation and the results of these processes, and information on supplier performance and contract amendments. This presumption also requires governments to develop systems to "collect, manage, simplify and publish contracting data" (Open Contracting Partnership, n.d.).

For this purpose the Partnership has created the Open Contracting Data Standard (2017) a global nonproprietary standard that enables organizations to publish shareable, reusable, machine-readable data; to join that data with their own information; and to build tools to analyze or share the data.

The Partnership has offered free help to the 2024 Paris Olympic authorities to implement an open contracting approach for all contracts, suggesting that "Paris 2024 can be a landmark in integrity, effective delivery and sporting heritage and open contracting can help" (Kluttz & Hayman, 2018).

percent); acceptance of contractual terms (10 percent); quality and functionality (15 percent); project delivery (25 percent); experience and capability (10 percent); and governance (10 percent). The logic of competitive bidding is to promote competition and equal treatment through accessibility to many suppliers, who are induced by competition to offer their best terms, and to enhance transparency (Bajari & Tadelis, 2006). Under regulatory systems the default form is typically **open tendering**, allowing any supplier to bid, although subject to possible prequalification procedures for suppliers, to eliminate suppliers that do not meet conditions for participation (such as insufficient technical competence) prior to tendering (UNCITRAL Model Law on Public Procurement [2011], Art. 28). Key transparency elements of open tendering in the Model Law include a public solicitation, detailed specification providing a common basis for comparing tenders, single tendering stage with fixed deadline and requirement to award the contract to the best tender according to predisclosed criteria, and no negotiation or amendments other than limited correction of errors.

Regulated systems also provide for other competitive procedures where costs of open tendering outweigh benefits. These include flexible methods for complex procurement, allowing interaction with suppliers including negotiation where needed (e.g., to obtain supplier input into design) or to avoid bid-rigging (Bajari & Tadelis, 2006; Krueger, 1999). This approach was used, for example, for the stadium and Aquatics Centre for the 2012 London Olympics (Mead & Gruneberg, 2013; von Plessen, 2015). Different procedures also generally apply for low-value procurement to limit procedural costs. Thus the Model Law provides for "restricted tendering" or, for low-value, price-only, standard procurement, informal request for quotations. These procedures can, however, be very nontransparent and, for repeat purchases, are increasingly being replaced by framework agreements (Albano & Nicholas, 2016), as strongly advocated by UNCITRAL (UNCITRAL, 2012). Noncompetitive procurements (referred to also as *single-source* or *direct awards*) are usually permitted only in very limited cases. Under most models (e.g., the GPA and EU) this includes for extreme urgency, unless this is the purchaser's fault; however, the Model Law allows this only in situations of catastrophe, requiring competitive negotiations for other urgent procurement.

Analysis of procedures requires great care because of lack of standardized terminology and classifications. For example, framework agreement has a narrower legal meaning in EU law than in the UNCITRAL Model Law, while "restricted tendering" under the Model Law, is very different from the "restricted procedure" of EU law (which involves open solicitation).

Balancing Transparency and Discretion

A central issue in procurement governance is the third dimension of transparency, examined notably by Kelman (1990, 2002) in a case study of U.S. federal IT procurement, calling for a more discretion-based system. As Kelman explains (1990, p. 28): "As a strategy of organizational design, rules have a cautious character. When we design organizations based on rules, we guard against disaster, but at the cost of stifling excellence." Examples include the transactional focus, using competitive bidding without reference to benefits of longer-term cooperation, and limiting discussions that could lead to better product design out of a fear of abuse to favor certain suppliers (e.g., Krueger, 1999). It was mentioned above that a consequence of these costs of transparency is a tension between anti-corruption or open-market objectives and other aspects of value for money; undue emphasis on the former can thus hinder, rather than help, commercial goals. Whether specific systems provide an appropriate balance has been analyzed by scholars (Arrowsmith, 2002; Schooner, 2001; Schooner, 2002a). This may differ according to many factors such as system objectives, nature of the organization, professional skills, corruption levels (Trepte, 2004), and other controls (Kelman, 1990). Achieving it is difficult in international trade systems where these factors differ for the participating countries (Arrowsmith, 2002).

Achieving this balance is a central issue for sport organizations, both inside and outside the public sector. Sport federations may share some features of public organizations, including a commitment to transparency, but differ in other respects.

Procurement for Sporting Events

It was explained earlier that procurement has an important role in sporting events. The high-profile nature of some events provides an opportunity to showcase procurement policies and provide a legacy of good practice, as with the CSR policies of LOCOG for the 2012 London Olympics. However, procurement at such events also gives rise to significant reputational risks. Elsewhere in this chapter and book, we have discussed earlier public concern over worker safety in construction for FIFA 2022 World Cup, and event procurement has also often been afflicted by corruption scandals. However, even simple service failures cause serious embarrassment. Examples include inaccuracies in the timing system at the 2018 LEN European Aquatics Championships, affecting nine races including a potential world record by British swimmer Adam Peaty (Reuters, 2018), and the problem with G4S's security contract at the 2012 London Olympics.

Much attention has focused on the political decisions defining the needs of sport events (phase 1 and 2 of the eight-phase model), such as whether to build new stadia and siting of stadia (Schoonbee & Brümmer, 2010). Procedural strategies, on the other hand, have received less scrutiny, although some case studies exist (Cornelius et al., 2011; Mead & Gruneberg, 2013; von Plessen, 2015; Schulz Herzenberg, 2010; Cabral & Silva, 2013). This is reflected in the fact that books on event management only include a brief paragraph on this area (Parent & Smith-Swan, 2013, p. 63; Getz, 2005, p. 118), otherwise addressing it only indirectly in general chapters on risk management.

Infrastructure procurement for international events is generally undertaken by public bodies. A mapping exercise by Arrowsmith et al. (2019) covering selected procurements from twelve international events from 2010 to 2018 of various sizes and locations found that with three of the four Olympics in that period (the exception being Rio), procurement of sport-specific infrastructure was entrusted to a public or semipublic agency set up for the event, while at the other events, with one execption, it was generally carried out by existing public bodies. Generally, this infrastructure was subject to regular public procurement rules, although sometimes these were adapted for the specific event. Significant procurement, particularly outside the infrastructure context, is also often undertaken by local organizing committees that are sometimes (although not always) private entities, for example, LOCOG. Although public procurement rules may not apply, pressures for good governance and a social legacy may be manifested in similar procurement policies, as with LOCOG's approach to social responsibility and use of the CompeteFor web portal.

The reputational and other risks are heightened by the particular challenges, as catalogued by, for example, Schulz Herzenberg (2010, pp. 21-49) in relation to the 2010 FIFA World Cup. First, such events are a one-off, potentially making work more expensive, partially because the market may be affected by procurement of large volumes in a short time, which makes cost comparisons difficult. Second, the challenging nature of unique projects, combined with high visibility, may deter bidders, as with the London Olympic Stadium (von Plessen, 2015). Third, fixed deadlines make late delivery highly problematic although not uncommon (e.g., athletes for the 2014 Central American and Caribbean Games stayed in hotels because the village was not ready [Arrowsmith et al., 2019]). Time pressures can make it difficult to control costs and prevent corruption, including because of pressure to modify regular procedures.

Creating bespoke agencies also presents challenges, and even permanent authorities may need to put in place new teams and structures. However, this can also provide opportunities to do things well, as with the 2012 London Olympics. On the flip side, a transient organizational structure makes transmission of lessons more difficult (Agarwal & Selen, 2009). The bespoke nature of agencies and multiple agencies involved may also contribute to the difficulty of ensuring transparency: With all the bespoke agencies studied by Arrowsmith et al. (2019), accessing documents proved largely impossible once the agencies were wound up, while in the 2016 Rio Olympics, the central Transparency Portal that in theory covered all contracts using federal funding, omitted much information. Special considerations arise from the complexity of institutions more generally, including the mix of public and private stakeholders (including international federations) in local organizing committees and involvement of multiple levels of government, sometimes with conflicting interests (Schulz Herzenberg, 2010).

Finally, as Kauppi et al. (2013) note, drawing on analysis of the Olympics by Minis et al. (2006) and work by Beis et al. (2006), further features of some events, such as short duration with a long planning period, massive size, diversity of activities and services, and a mix of employed and volunteer workforce, all add to the special features of operational management, including procurement.

The challenges, especially with timescales, can create pressure for modifying normal rules or using urgency-based exemptions. The Delhi Commonwealth Games involved many noncompetitive awards, largely because of poor planning (although it was noted above that many international models do not allow urgency procedures in this situation), and extensive allegations of corruption and waste (Comptroller and Auditor General of India, 2011; Mishra, 2016). At the 2017 FINA World Swimming Championships, an event that also attracted media accusations of waste and cronyism (Pivarnyik, 2017), a special law exempted much event procurement from the usual laws (Law XXIII of 2015), despite nearly two years' preparation time (Arrowsmith et al., 2019).

While some modifications or exemptions are considered a necessary evil, they may also seek to avoid inadequacies in existing laws, as with the Differentiated Contracting Regime (Law No. 12462/2011) adopted by Brazil for the 2014 FIFA World Cup and 2016 Olympics infrastructure (Bereslawski, 2013; Spalding et al., 2017) and subsequently extended to some other procurements. We should note, however, that this was optional and not in the end used for the sport venues themselves (Arrowsmith et al., 2019). In fact, as UNODC (2013, p. 34) suggests, "The organization of a major event should serve as an opportunity to review and strengthen existing procurement, tendering and contracting rules." Spalding et al. (2017) concluded that various anti-corruption measures that applied to, and were to an extent prompted by, the 2014 FIFA World Cup and 2016 Rio Olympics, including the Differentiated Contracting Regime, provided an important governance legacy from these events, bringing corruption to light in a new way, even if not preventing it.

Both the unique nature of bespoke entities and the special challenges of one-off events provide opportunities for research—for example, examining the Buying Centre and organization and professionalism of procurement using organizational theory; assessing application and suitability of procurement governance models by reference to theories on transparency; and transmission of procurement lessons, including the role of the IOC, federations, and host entities.

Research could also focus on specific objectives. From the commercial perspective, management literature has studied specific events, such as the construction strategies of the 2012 London Olympics (von Plessen, 2015; Mead & Gruneberg, 2013) and approach to risk in public-private partnerships at the 2014 FIFA World Cup (Cabral & Silva, 2013) and 2000 Sydney Olympics (Jefferies, 2006; Jefferies & Chen, 2014), providing insights for future mega-events. However, Kauppi et al. (2013) found limited journal publications and highlighted this as a future research area.

Integrity is also a significant concern and explains the emphasis of IPACS. Of 12 events mapped by Arrowsmith et al. (2019), six were the subject of significant allegations of procurement corruption or cronyism from audit bodies, media, or NGOs (the 2014 Winter Olympics, 2010 Asian Games, 2016 Olympics, 2014 Central American and Caribbean Games, 2010 Commonwealth Games, and 2017 FINA World Aquatics Championships), most involving arrests, convictions, or ongoing investigations. Further, the 2010 FIFA World Cup involved significant bid-rigging, as well as allegations of other irregularities (Rose, 2010; Botha & Ntsaluba, 2010; Arrowsmith et al., 2019). Based in part on the mapping by Arrowsmith et al. (2019), IPACS has already produced recommendations for improvement, including by more strategic collection of information and better attention to planning and execution (as well as award) of contracts; and has drafted checklists for event organizers, which are to be piloted shortly (IPACS, 2019).

Issues for further study include the adequacy of local procurement rules, institutions, and culture, including integrity mechanisms; use of event-specific measures; and design of bespoke agencies from an anti-corruption perspective. Research has already provided some important perspectives and information: For example, Spalding et al. (2017) highlighted the need to address anti-corruption measures from a governance legacy perspective, and Stanislas (2017) provided a case study of a proactive anti-corruption strategy in a bespoke agency. However, as Spalding et al. (2017) highlighted, the "domestic" dimension of corruption at events, of which procurement is a major element, is neglected in comparison with work on corruption in bidding and in competitions (e.g., match-fixing) (see also Dowling, Leopkey & Smith [2018], who found that governance work on corruption focuses mainly on match-fixing and doping).

Finally, as chapter 23 observed, changed social norms have stimulated attention to CSR, especially environmental, dimensions of events (Zhang et al., 2013); this seems likely to develop in the social field with new reference in the Olympics Host City contracts to human rights and labor standards. Procurement has a significant role, both in addressing the direct social and environmental impacts of events and in creating a legacy (Timms, 2015). These points and the special challenges and opportunities for bespoke agencies were illustrated in the earlier section on CSR by reference to the 2012 London Olympics. Several studies look at the environmental legacies of specific events (Zhang et al., 2013; Gold & Gold, 2015; Müller, 2015; Cashman, 2016) and at general perspectives, such as reasons for failing to meet commitments (Geeraert & Gauthier, 2018, exploring the IOC's role from a principal-agent perspective), but few focus specifically on procurement. (For an exception, see Timms, 2015.) However, there is much scope for work on procurement dimensions of CSR in this unique context. The new Olympics Host City contract, for example, can be analyzed from a legal perspective against the backdrop of taxonomies of CSR provisions procurement. Policies for specific events can again be analyzed from a legal perspective (e.g., extent of compliance with the public procurement frameworks or influence of those frameworks on policy choices); through organizational theory (e.g., influences on policy or transmission of lessons learned in procurement, including the role of federations [Timms, 2015]); or through the procurement and supply chain literature (e.g., organization of procurement responsibilities in CSR, which LOCOG highlighted as important).

Procurement by Sport Federations

It was noted previously that federations undertake procurement for both day-to-day purposes and specific events. Federations are generally private entities and not constrained by public-sector procurement rules. However, this is not always so: For example, EU public procurement law may apply to publicly funded federations or contracts. Application of public procurement rules to and by federations could be an interesting research area for doctrinal legal scholarship and sociolegal studies.

More generally, as chapter 13 explained, federations are increasingly under pressure to be transparent, and public procurement experience and literature provides useful information. From this perspective flexible regimes that govern the more commercial government entities might be of interest, as might mechanisms focusing on information dimensions, such as Open Contracting, as an alternative to rule-based governance. Similarly, federations seeking to improve professionalism and efficiency can draw on procurement and supply chain management literature. Current interest is reflected in the fact that the IOC announced in July 2018 that its significant projects over the next two years would include contract management and procurement improvement projects (IOC, 2018); additionally, UEFA recently advertised a new procurement manager post.

Chapter 13 presented tools for assessing federation governance, in particular the Basic Indicators for Better Governance in International Sport (BIBGIS) (Chappelet & Mrkonjic, 2013), the Sports Governance Observer (SGO) (Geeraert, 2015), and the 2017 tool of ASOIF (2017a). Another tool (SIGA, n.d.-a, SIGA, n.d.-b, and SIGA n.d.-c), with more detail on procurement, is that of the Sport Integrity Global Alliance (SIGA), a nonprofit incorporated body with partnerships with an array of stakeholders, including commercial partners. Several federations have committed to pilot projects with SIGA, and a verification system commenced in January 2019 (SIGA, 2018). As noted earlier, IPACS is also working on this area.

These tools all include general integrity indicators relevant to procurement covering, in particular, audit, codes of ethics and anti-bribery provisions, conflicts of interest, risk management,

TIME OUT

EU Public Procurement Law and Sport Federations

EU Directives regulate major public procurement contracts in all 28 EU countries. These Directives apply not just to traditional public bodies such as government departments and municipalities, but also to organizations supervised or controlled by public bodies, or those that obtain most of their funding from public bodies (e.g., European Union [2014b]; Arrowsmith, 2014). This applies even if national law otherwise classifies the organization as a private organization.

Sport federations that obtain their income mainly from government grants rather than, for example, membership fees, sponsorship, or profits from events, may be covered by these rules. This is particularly relevant to federations that deal mainly with elite sport. UK Athletics, for example, solicited tenders for insurance services under these rules in 2015 (UK Athletics, 2015).

The EU provides a stringent system of challenge procedures, and consequences of noncompliance include an order rendering the contract ineffective (European Union 1989, as amended).

National legislators in the EU also sometimes define the scope of other procurement rules by reference to the EU rules. For example, the United Kingdom applies some transparency rules to contracts that are too small to be covered by EU law itself, but applies them to the same bodies that EU law covers under the Public Contracts Regulations 2015. Thus publicly funded sport federations can fall under these national rules too.

The EU procurement rules also apply to contracts for building sports, recreation and leisure, facilities whenever the specific contracts are financed mainly by a public body (e.g., European Union [2014b], Art. 14). Sport federations' contracts can also be caught on this basis.

and whistle-blowing. With respect to procurement specifically, both SIGA (in its Good Governance standards) and the SGO require federations to formulate rules: SIGA requires, even at the basic level, "clearly defined and transparent policies" for procurement (and other commercial contracts) (SIGA, n.d.-b, point 8), while SGO requires, to achieve the highest level, "rules on the selection, contracting and supervision of third parties" (Geeraert, 2015, p. 64). BIBGIS, ASOIF, and SIGA all also refer to open tenders for major procurements: BIBGIS refers to open tenders for "major marketing and procurement contracts," (Chappelet & Mrkonjic, 2013); ASOIF to "open tenders for major commercial and procurement contracts (other than events)", the latter providing that for the highest score federations should operate "state of the art open tenders for major contracts, full documentation, publication of appointments" (ASOIF, 2017a); and SIGA requires even at a basic level "open and transparent tenders for major commercial and procurement contracts, including, but not limited to, those in relation to media, sponsorship, broadcasting and construction of sporting infrastructure" (SIGA n.d.-b, point 8). The concept of open tenders is not defined or regulated, leaving adequate space for necessary flexibility. The SIGA implementation guidelines also deal specifically with the need for adequate rules for lower-value contracts; it also requires supplier review, at least through internal mechanisms. In addition, it provides at a higher level for all commercial deals and the processes leading to them to be made public and for an independent assessment of personal and institutional conflicts of interest in procurement.

Some of these organizations have collected data on procurement but have published it, if at all, only in general form. ASOIF reviews showed a low level

KEY ISSUES FOR SPORT MANAGERS

Quality procurement is important for achieving the goals of sport organizations because it potentially affects, among other things, financial performance, timely and effective delivery of sporting events and services, social responsibility objectives, and the reputation of the organization. Understanding the role of good procurement, and how to achieve it, is thus important not only for those undertaking procurement activity but also for managers of organizations and for those with governance and oversight roles. This is even more so now that procurement is being addressed in international initiatives, notably IPACS, and in governance standards for federations (such as those of SIGA, which give quite extensive attention to this). However, in the sport field, procurement has received very little attention from scholars, and anecdotal evidence suggests that the sport field lags behind other sectors in following best practices for this area.

A multidisciplinary perspective is essential because the field of procurement (in both scholarship and practice) draws on insights not just from management but from other disciplines, including law, economics, and political science. The study of procurement across other disciplines has shed light on important topics, including the professionalism of the procurement function in an organization and the design of strategies for procuring different types of product and services.

Eight key interests that the procurement process may seek to achieve are (1) value for money in acquiring the needed goods, works, and services; (2) integrity; (3) effective implementation of social responsibility policies; (4) open trade; (5) equal opportunities for suppliers; (6) accountability; (7) fair treatment of suppliers; and (8) process efficiency. These interests sometimes support each other but sometimes also require trade-offs. Managers need to carefully identify the main interests that they seek to achieve in their own procurement processes and decide how to balance those interests when they conflict.

The approach to procurement tends to differ between the public and private sectors. The public sector tends to take a more transaction-based approach governed by regulatory rules, and it emphasizes different objectives. In the public sector, there is a greater focus on transparency and on competitive bidding. A knowledge of public sector procurement practice and regulation is often relevant for managers in sport organizations, because public sector rules and policies often apply directly—for example, for the procurement of most new infrastructure for major sporting events—or are relevant by analogy when nongovernmental organizations, particularly sport federations, have similarities to public sector organizations.

of adherence to open tendering, with a mean average score in the first review of only 1.36 out of 5, the lowest of all the desirable control mechanisms examined (ASOIF, 2017b), rising to only 1.48 in the second review (ASOIF, 2018). This suggests that procurement in international federations requires significant attention.

As with procurement for sporting events, the specific environment of federations again offers scope for using the methods and findings from various disciplines to study, for example, functioning of buying centers, levels of professionalism, and strategic operation; use of public-sector governance models; and approach to specific commercial, integrity, and CSR objectives assessed through the lens of supply chain management literature. Procurement could also provide an interesting case study of implementation and compliance with standards, drawing on literature from law and political science (as discussed in the context of sport federations by Bos, van Ekkerhen, & Houihan, 2012) and on compliance with public procurement standards.

Summary and Conclusions

Procurement is an important activity for achieving the goals of sport organizations and is receiving increasing attention from a governance perspective. However, while literature on procurement in general is extensive, little work has been conducted specifically on the sport context. It was shown that it is important to study this topic from a multidisciplinary perspective, including because of its economic aspects and its increasing regulatory dimension.

This chapter has mapped the main policy issues in procurement, as identified in the literature, covering both institutional and governance aspects and procurement processes; this included the objectives of those processes—in particular, value for money, integrity, and social responsibility—and the trade-offs between them. The chapter highlighted the importance of the organizational context, explained key differences between public- and private-sector approaches (including the role of transparency), and outlined the contexts in which procurement occurs in the sport sector and the relevance of public-sector models to this sector. It was noted in particular that procurement for sporting events and procurement by federations provide interesting areas for research because their special features differentiate them from the contexts mainly studied so far in procurement literature. In this way, the chapter has sought to provide both a framework for future research and a starting point for managers in sport organizations to address the issue of effective procurement in their organizations.

Review Questions

1. To what extent is each of the eight procurement objectives identified by Arrowsmith (2011) relevant for (a) bespoke agencies set up for mega-events (whether public or private), and (b) national sport federations?
2. Select two international sport federations other than those mentioned in this chapter and find out as much as you can from publicly available information about their procurement organization and policies. Based on this information, consider the extent to which these policies provide for transparency across the four dimensions outlined in this chapter. Do they offer sufficient transparency in light of the costs and benefits of transparency? To what extent do these federations also provide the same or similar rules for other commercial transactions?
3. Find a public solicitation for a specific procurement by any sport organization. What do the documents suggest are the objectives of the particular procurement procedure? What trade-offs, if any, do you think there might be between different objectives in this procurement?
4. Should procurement for the Olympic Games be concerned only with integrity insofar as it is an aspect of value for money or also for wider reasons? If for wider reasons, what reasons?

Suggestions for Further Reading

As mentioned in several places in this chapter, little literature focuses specifically on sport and procurement in any disciplines, including management.

For an overview of current management thinking on procurement in general, mainly from the perspective of organizing and operating the procurement function to obtain value for money, readers should look at the management textbooks referred to in the chapter, namely Baily et al. (2015) and Lysons and Farrington (2016).

For an introduction to public sector models the best starting points are Arrowsmith et al. (2000), which was the first work to map the subject of public procurement regulation from a global and comparative perspective, and Trepte (2004), which adopts a multidisciplinary perspective. While many of the specific instruments referred to in these texts have been updated since they were written, the principles remain the same. The analyses by Kelman (1990, 2002) of the central rules versus discretion issue in public procurement are also well worth a read by anyone with an interest in this topic. For the details of the UNCITRAL Model Law on Public Procurement 2011, which is referred to as a model and example at many places in this chapter, a reading of the Guide to Enactment and guidance on regulations produced by UNCITRAL itself (UNCITRAL 2012, n.d.) is highly recommended.

On infrastructure procurement for sporting events, the UNODC guidance (UNODC, 2013) is well worth reading for an excellent practical overview of issues and context, as are the recent IPACS report (IPACS, 2019) and the related study in Arrowsmith et al. (2019) both for analysis of how procurement is done at these events and for ideas on how to address the integrity issues. In addition, for a flavor of the practical complexities and problems of procurement in the context of specific major events, readers should refer to, in particular, the material available on the 2012 London Olympics, in particular Mead and Gruneberg (2013), Cornelius et al. (2011), Stanislas (2017), and the section "Procurement" on the Learning Legacy website (London 2012 Olympic and Paralympic Games, n.d.) (collectively, this covers a variety of perspectives, including the three main objectives of value for money, social responsibility, and integrity); Schulz Herzenberg (2010) on procurement for the FIFA World Cup in South Africa; and the study by Spalding et al. (2017) of anti-corruption measures relating to the 2016 Rio Olympic Games. Some of these pieces make only limited reference to relevant theoretical and background literature but nonetheless offer interesting case studies.

Case for Analysis

Procurement in UEFA

UEFA is the governing body of European association football. Its objectives include dealing with matters relating to European association football, promoting association football, safeguarding the values of European association football, promoting and protecting ethical standards and good governance in European association football, maintaining relations with stakeholders, and supporting and safeguarding its 55 European member associations for the overall well-being of the European game. Its business and administrative affairs are run from its headquarters in Nyon, Switzerland. The governance of UEFA has recently undergone some significant reforms after these were approved by the UEFA Congress in 2017.

UEFA already takes a transparent approach to publicizing major procurement contracts and has a webpage on which these are advertised (UEFA, n.d.). They include, in particular, contracts in connection with events run by UEFA, which is responsible for both club tournaments such as the Champions League and international tournaments. Opportunities advertised up to August 17, 2018, included to supply official match balls to tournaments, to deliver ceremonies for major tournaments, to provide bus services for tournaments, and to provide a service for the storage and distribution of match videos.

This same page also includes information on bidding procedures for media rights to tournaments and bidding procedures to host competition finals, along with general regulations that apply to those bidding procedures and other documents.

Significantly, UEFA is now developing for the first time a formal procurement policy for the organization as a whole and in August 2018 advertised a new post of procurement manager. One of the explicit responsibilities of the post is to develop a strategic approach to procurement.

As well as undertaking its own procurement, UEFA has also taken recent steps to ensure both integrity and respect for human rights in the tournaments for which it is responsible, and this will have an impact on procurement by those hosting these UEFA tournaments.

In this respect, UEFA's Euro 2024 Tournament Requirements document now places on bidders a general obligation "to respect, protect and fulfil human rights and fundamental freedoms, with a duty to respect human, labour and child rights during the Bidding Procedure and, if appointed, until the end of the dismantling of UEFA Euro 2024." Examples provided of how this obligation might be implemented include reporting on child labor in supply chains for products and services used in the tournament, as well as monitoring of labor rights violations during the construction of stadia.

The Requirements also oblige bidders to include an anti-corruption strategy and refer in this regard to the UNODC (2013) document on safeguarding against corruption in major events.

Questions

1. What are the main risks that UEFA needs to consider and address in its procurement activity?
2. To what extent are the current provisions on procurement and on general topics relevant to procurement (such as conflict of interest) that are found in the sport governance models of BIBGIS, SGO, and SIGA valuable for organizations like UEFA?
3. What value, if any, does a study of the approach adopted to procurement by (a) commercial organizations and (b) the public sector have for an organization like UEFA?

REFERENCES

Chapter 1

Alvesson, M., & Deetz, S. (2000). *Doing critical management research.* London, UK: SAGE.

Alvesson, M., Bridgman, T., & Willmott, H. (2011). *The Oxford handbook of critical management studies.* New York, NY: Oxford University Press, USA. (Original work published 2009)

Badenhausen, K. (2006, May 26). Over the top. *Forbes*, Retrieved from www.forbes.com/global/2006/0605/048.html#30fffc-f769ee

Badenhausen, K. (2018, June 13). Full list: The world's highest-paid athletes 2018. *Forbes*, Retrieved from www.forbes.com/sites/kurtbadenhausen/2018/06/13/full-list-the-worlds-highest-paid-athletes-2018/#19b9dbe7d9f9

Badenhausen, K. (2019a, July 22). The world's 50 most valuable sports teams 2019. *Forbes*, Retrieved from www.forbes.com/sites/kurtbadenhausen/2019/07/22/the-worlds-50-most-valuable-sports-teams-2019/

Badenhausen, K. (2019b, June 11). The world's highest-paid athletes. *Forbes*, Retrieved from www.forbes.com/athletes/#19d9e03655ae

Bakan, J. (2004). *The corporation: The pathological pursuit of profit and power.* New York: Free Press.

Ballinger, J. (1993). The new free-trade heel: Nike jumps on the backs of Asian workers. In R.M. Jackson (Ed.), *Global issues 93/94* (9th ed., pp. 130-131). Guilford, CT: Dushkin.

BBC Sport. (2016). Russia state-sponsored doping across majority of Olympic sports, claims report. BBC News, Retrieved from www.bbc.co.uk/sport/36823453

Beamish, R. (1985). Sport executives and voluntary associations: A review of the literature and introduction to some theoretical issues. *Sociology of Sport Journal, 2*, 218-232.

Brannagan, P.M., & Giulianotti, R. (2015). Soft power and soft disempowerment: Qatar, global sport and football's 2022 World Cup finals. *Leisure Studies, 34*(6), 703-719. doi:10.1080/02614367.2014.964291

Braverman, H. (1974). *Labor and monopoly capital.* New York, NY: Monthly Review Press.

Buchanan, D.A., & Huczynski, A.A. (2019). *Organizational behaviour* (10th ed.). Harlow, UK: Pearson.

Canadian Arts Presenting Association/l'Association canadienne des organismes artistiques (CAPACOA). (2017). Movie attendance is declining: Is this a good or a bad news for the performing arts? Retrieved from www.capacoa.ca/en/services/arts-promotion/news/1513-movie-attendance

Carper, W.B., & Snizek, W.E. (1980). The nature and types of organizational taxonomies: An overview. *Academy of Management Review, 5*, 65-75.

Cashmore, E. (2000). *Making sense of sport* (3rd ed.). London, UK: Routledge & Kegan Paul.

Castaing, M. (1970, March 7). *Le Monde* (n.p.). Cited by Brohm, J. (1978) *Sport: A prison of measured time.* London, UK: Inks Links.

Chelladurai, P. (1985). *Sport management: Macro perspectives.* London, ON: Sports Dynamics.

Chelladurai, P. (2013). A personal journey in theorizing in sport management. *Sport Management Review, 16*(1), 22-28. doi:10.1016/j.smr.2011.12.003

Chelladurai, P. (2014). *Managing organizations for sport and physical activity: A systems perspective* (4th ed.). Abingdon, UK: Routledge.

Chelladurai, P., Szyszlo, M., & Haggerty, T.R. (1987). Systems-based dimensions of effectiveness: The case of national sport organizations. *Canadian Journal of Sport Science, 12*, 111-119.

Clifford, M. (1992, November 5). The China connection: Nike is making the most of all that cheap labour. *Far Eastern Economic Review*, 60.

Collignon, H., Sultan, N., & Santander, C. (2011). The sports market. Retrieved from https://www.atkearney.co.uk/search?q=The%20Sports%20Market&groupId=1952738&exact=true

Conn, D. (2017, September 26). Thousands of Qatar World Cup workers 'subjected to life-threatening heat.' *The Guardian*, Retrieved from https://www.theguardian.com/football/2017/sep/27/thousands-qatar-world-cup-workers-life-threatening-heat

Cunningham, G.B. (2002). Removing the blinders: Toward an intergrative model of organizational change in sport and physical activity. *Quest, 54*(4), 276-291. doi:10.1080/00336297.2002.10491779

Cunningham, G.B. (2013). Theory and theory development in sport management. *Sport Management Review, 16*(1), 1-4. doi:10.1016/j.smr.2012.01.006

Daft, R.L. (1989). *Organization theory and design* (3rd ed.). St. Paul, MN: West.

Daft, R.L. (2004). *Organization theory and design* (8th ed.). Mason, OH: Thomson/South-Western.

Daft, R.L. (2015). *Organization theory and design* (12th ed.). Mason, OH: Cengage Learning/South-Western.

De Bosscher, V., De Knop, P., & Vertonghen, J. (2016). A multidimensional approach to evaluate the policy effectiveness of elite sport schools in Flanders. *Sport in Society, 19*(10), 1596-1621. doi:10.1080/17430437.2016.1159196

Doherty, A. (2013). Investing in sport management: The value of good theory. *Sport Management Review, 16*(1), 5-11. doi:10.1016/j.smr.2011.12.006

Downward, P., Dawson, A., & Dejonghe, T. (2009). *Sports economics: Theory, evidence and policy.* London, UK: Routledge.

Economist Intelligence Unit. (1990). *The sports market overview: Research Report No. 84.* London, UK: The Economist Group.

Fielding, L.W., Miller, L.K., & Brown, J.R. (1999). Harlem Globetrotters International, Inc. *Journal of Sport Management, 13*, 45-77.

Fine, G.A. (1987). *With the boys: Little League baseball and preadolescent culture.* Chicago, IL: University of Chicago Press.

Fink, J.S. (2013). Theory development in sport management: My experience and other considerations. *Sport Management Review, 16*(1), 17-21. doi:10.1016/j.smr.2011.12.005

Frisby, W. (2005). The good, the bad, and the ugly: Critical sport management research. *Journal of Sport Management, 19*, 1-12.

Galbraith, J.R. (1974). Organization design: An information processing view. *Interfaces*, *4*, 28-36.

Galbraith, J.R. (1977). *Organization design*. Reading, MA: Addison-Wesley.

Gerrard, B. (2016). Trevor Slack: A personal memory of a great scholar and a great friend. *European Sport Management Quarterly*, *16*(2), 127-128. doi:10.1080/16184742.2016.1153279

Green, D. (2017a, February 15). Under Armour's CEO bought a full page newspaper ad to say he didn't mean to praise Trump. *Business Insider*, Retrieved from www.businessinsider.com/under-armours-ceo-newspaper-ad-2017-2?r=UK

Green, D. (2017b, February 19). Under Armour made some huge mistakes that are turning into a nightmare. *Business Insider*, Retrieved from https://www.businessinsider.com/under-armour-business-mistakes-2017-2?r=UK

Grix, J. (2015). *Sport politics: An introduction*. London, UK: Palgrave Macmillan.

Gruneau, R. (1983). *Class, sports and social development*. Amherst, MA: University of Massachusetts Press.

Haggerty, T.R. (1988). Designing control and information systems in sport organizations: A cybernetic perspective. *Journal of Sport Management*, *2*, 53-63.

Hall, M.A., Cullen, D., & Slack, T. (1989). Organizational elites recreating themselves: The gender structure of national sport organizations. *Quest*, *41*, 28-45.

Hall, R.H. (1982). *Organizations: Structure and process* (3rd. ed.). Englewood Cliffs, NJ: Prentice Hall.

Harrison, J.D. (2014, November 12). When we were small: Under Armour. *Washington Post*, Retrieved from www.washingtonpost.com/business/on-small-business/when-we-were-small-under-armour/2014/11/11/f61e8876-69ce-11e4-b053-65cea7903f2e_story.html?noredirect=on&utm_term=.4aa3d24bd73d

Harvey, J., & Proulx, R. (1988). Sport and the state in Canada. In J. Harvey & H. Cantelon (Eds.), *Not just a game: Essays in Canadian sport sociology* (pp. 93-119). Ottawa, ON: University of Ottawa Press.

Herzberg, F., Mausner, B., & Snyderman, B. (1959). *The motivation to work*. New York, NY: Wiley.

Horine, L. (1985). *Administration of physical education and sport programs*. Philadelphia, PA: Saunders.

Houlihan, D., & Malcolm, D. (Eds.). (2010). *Sport and society. A student introduction* (3rd ed.). Thousand Oaks, CA: SAGE.

Houlihan, B., & Zheng, J. (2014). Small states: Sport and politics at the margin. *International Journal of Sport Policy and Politics*, *7*(3), 329-344. doi:10.1080/19406940.2014.959032

Huizenga, R. (1994). *You're OK. It's just a bruise*. New York, NY: St. Martin's Press.

Hult, J.S. (1989). Women's struggle for governance in U.S. amateur athletics. *International Review for the Sociology of Sport*, *24*, 249-263.

IOC. (2019). *Olympic Marketing Fact File 2019 Edition*. Retrieved from https://stillmed.olympic.org/media/Document%20Library/OlympicOrg/Documents/IOC-Marketing-and-Broadcasting-General-Files/Olympic-Marketing-Fact-File-2018.pdf

Irwin, R.L., & Ryan, T.D. (2013). Get real: Using engagement with practice to advance theory transfer and production. *Sport Management Review*, *16*(1), 12-16. doi:10.1016/j.smr.2011.12.007

James, M. (2017). *Sports Law* (3rd ed.). London, UK: Red Globe Press.

Kanter, R.M. (1977). *Men and women of the corporation*. New York, NY: Basic Books.

Kanter, R.M. (1983). *The change masters*. New York, NY: Simon & Schuster.

Katz, D., & Kahn, R.L. (1978). *The social psychology of organizations* (rev. ed.). New York, NY: Wiley.

Kidd, B. (1988). The elite athlete. In J. Harvey & H. Cantelon (Eds.), *Not just a game: Essays in Canadian sport sociology* (pp. 287-307). Ottawa, ON: University of Ottawa Press.

Kidd, B., & Donnelly, P. (2000). Human rights in sport. *International Review for the Sociology of Sport*, *35*, 131-148.

Kikulis, L., Slack, T., Hinings, C.R., & Zimmermann, A. (1989). A structural taxonomy of amateur sport organizations. *Journal of Sport Management*, *3*, 129-150.

Kimberly, J.R., & Miles, R.H. (1980). *The organizational life cycle*. San Francisco, CA: Jossey-Bass.

Lenskyj, H.J. (2000). *Inside the Olympic industry: Power, politics, and activism*. Albany, NY: State University of New York Press.

Liew, J. (2017, October 3). World Cup 2022: Qatar's workers are not workers, they are slaves, and they are building mausoleums, not stadiums. *Independent*, Retrieved from www.independent.co.uk/sport/football/international/world-cup-2022-qatars-workers-slaves-building-mausoleums-stadiums-modern-slavery-kafala-a7980816.html

Lovett, D.J., & Lowry, C.D. (1994). "Good old boys" and "good old girls" clubs: Myth or reality. *Journal of Sport Management*, *8*, 27-35.

Macintosh, D., & Whitson, D.J. (1990). *The game planners: Transforming Canada's sport system*. Montreal, QC & Kingston, ON: McGill-Queen's University Press.

MacIntosh, E., & Walker, M. (2012). Chronicling the transient nature of fitness employees: An organizational culture perspective. *Journal of Sport Management*, *26*(2), 113-126.

Maitland, A., Hills, L.A., & Rhind, D.J. (2015). Organisational culture in sport: A systematic review. *Sport Management Review*, *18*(4), 501-516.

Manley, D., & Friend, T. (1992). *Educating Dexter*. Nashville, TN: Rutledge Hill Press.

March, J.G., & Simon, H.A. (1958). *Organizations*. New York, NY: Wiley.

Martin, J. (2002). *Organizational culture: Mapping the terrain*. Thousand Oaks, CA: SAGE.

Maslow, A.H. (1943). A human theory of motivation. *Psychological Review*, *50*, 370-396.

McGregor, D. (1960). *The human side of enterprise*. New York, NY: Van Nostrand.

McKelvey, B. (1975). Guidelines for the empirical classification of organizations. *Administrative Science Quarterly*, *20*, 509-525.

McKelvey, B. (1978). Organizational systematics: Taxonomic lessons from biology. *Management Science, 24,* 1428-1440.

McKelvey, B. (1982). *Organizational systematics*. Los Angeles, CA: University of California Press.

McVeigh, K. (2017, June 24). Cambodian female workers in Nike, Asics and Puma factories suffer mass faintings. *The Guardian*, Retrieved from www.theguardian.com/business/2017/jun/25/female-cambodian-garment-workers-mass-fainting

Milano & Chelladurai. (2011). Gross domestic sport product: The size of the sport industry in the United States. *Journal of Sport Management*, *25*, 1, 24-35.

Miller, D. (1981). Toward a new contingency approach: The search for organizational gestalts. *Journal of Management Studies*, *18*, 1-26.

Miller, D. (1987). Strategy making and structure: Analysis and implications for performance. *Academy of Management Journal*, *30*, 7-32.

Miller, D., & Dröge, C. (1986). Psychological and traditional determinants of structure. *Administrative Science Quarterly, 31*, 539-560.

Miller, D., & Friesen, P. (1984). *Organizations: A quantum view*. Englewood Cliffs, NJ: Prentice Hall.

Mills, C., & Hoeber, L. (2013). Exploring organizational culture through artifacts in a community figure skating club. *Journal of Sport Management, 27*, 482-496.

Mintzberg, H. (1973). *The nature of managerial work*. New York, NY: Harper & Row.

Mintzberg, H. (1979). *The structuring of organizations*. Englewood Cliffs, NJ: Prentice Hall.

Morgan, G. (1986). *Images of organization*. Thousand Oaks, CA: SAGE.

Morgan, G. (2006). *Images of organization* (Updated ed.). Thousand Oaks, CA: SAGE.

Nike. (n.d.). Code of conduct. Retrieved from https://purpose.nike.com/code-of-conduct

Paton, G. (1987). Sport management research: What progress has been made? *Journal of Sport Management, 1*, 25-31.

Peters, T.J., & Waterman, R.H. (1982). *In search of excellence*. New York, NY: Harper & Row.

Peters, T.J., & Waterman, R.H. (2015). *In search of excellence: Lessons from America's best-run companies*. London, UK: Profile Books Ltd.

Plunkett Research Ltd. (n.d.). Sports industry statistic and market size overview, business and industry statistics. Retrieved from www.plunkettresearch.com/statistics/Industry-Statistics-Sports-Industry-Statistic-and-Market-Size-Overview/

Poggi, J. (2019, January 14). Super Bowl alert: Where are all the celebrities? *AdAge*, Retrieved from https://adage.com/article/special-report-super-bowl/super-bowl-alert-celebrities/316238/

PwC. (2017). *PwC Sports Outlook: At the gate and beyond. Outlook for the sports market in North America through 2021*. Retrieved from https://files.stample.co/stample-1520259273817-pwc-sports-outlook-2017.pdf

PwC. (2018). *PwC Sports Outlook: At the gate and beyond. Outlook for the sports market in North America through 2022*. Retrieved from https://www.pwc.com/us/en/industry/entertainment-media/assets/2018-sports-outlook.pdf

Reuters. (2017, June 14). Rio 2016 price tag rises to $13.2 billion. *Reuters*, Retrieved from www.reuters.com/article/us-olympics-brazil-cost/rio-2016-price-tag-rises-to-13-2-billion-idUSKBN19539C

Rheenen, D. Van. (2013). Exploitation in college sports: Race, revenue, and educational reward. *International Review for the Sociology of Sport, 48*(5), 550-571. doi:10.1177/1012690212450218

Roan, D. (2019). Commonwealth Games 2022: Birmingham event to cost £778m. BBC News, Retrieved from www.bbc.co.uk/sport/48762084

Robbins, S.P. (1990). *Organization theory: Structure, design and applications* (3rd ed.). Englewood Cliffs, NJ: Prentice Hall.

Sack, A.L., & Kidd, B. (1985). The amateur athlete as employee. In A.T. Johnson & J.H. Frey (Eds.), *Government and sport: The public policy issues* (pp. 41-61). Totowa, NJ: Rowman & Allenheld.

Sack, A.L., & Staurowsky, E.J. (1998). *College athletes for hire: The evolution and legacy of the NCAA's amateur myth*. Westport, CT: Praeger.

Segran, E. (2017). Escalating sweatshop protests keep Nike sweating. Retrieved from www.fastcompany.com/40444836/escalating-sweatshop-protests-keep-nike-sweating

Seippel, Ø., Dalen, H.B., Sandvik, M.R., & Solstad, G.M. (2018). From political sports to sports politics: On political mobilization of sports issues. *International Journal of Sport Policy and Politics, 10*(4), 669-689. doi:10.1080/19406940.2018.1501404

Sibson, R. (2010). "I was banging my head against a brick wall": Exclusionary power and the gendering of sport organizations. *Journal of Sport Management, 24*, 379-399.

Simon, H.A. (1945). *Administrative behavior*. New York, NY: Macmillan.

Slack, T. (1991). Sport management: Some thoughts on future directions. *Journal of Sport Management, 5*, 95-99.

Slack, T. (1993). Morgan and the metaphors: Implication for sport management. *Journal of Sport Management, 7*, 189-193.

Slack, T. (Ed.). (2004). *The commercialisation of sport*. London, UK: Routledge.

Slack, T. (2014). The social and commercial impact of sport, the role of sport management. *European Sport Management Quarterly, 14*(5), 454-463. doi:10.1080/16184742.2014.974311

Slack, T., & Amis, J. (2004). "Money for nothing and your cheques for free?" A critical perspective on sport sponsorship. In T. Slack (Ed.), *The commercialisation of sport* (pp. 269-286). London, UK: Routledge.

Smith, G. (2019, January 24). Super Bowl ad prices stall after years of relentless increases. *Bloomberg*, Retrieved from www.bloomberg.com/news/articles/2019-01-24/super-bowl-ad-prices-stall-after-years-of-relentless-increases

Smith, R. (2017, April 26). Cybernetics, cesarean sections and soccer's most magnificent mind. *New York Times*, Retrieved from www.nytimes.com/2017/04/26/sports/soccer/cybernetics-cesarean-sections-and-soccers-most-magnificent-mind.html

Soares, J., Correia, A., & Rosado, A. (2010). Political factors in the decision-making process in voluntary sports associations. *European Sport Management Quarterly, 10*(1), 5-29. doi:10.1080/16184740903554033

Sport England. (n.d.). About us. Retrieved from www.sportengland.org/about-us/

Statistics Canada. (n.d.). Household spending, Canada, regions and provinces. Retrieved from www150.statcan.gc.ca/t1/tbl1/en/tv.action?pid=1110022201

Stern, R.N. (1979). The development of an interorganizational control network: The case of intercollegiate athletics. *Administrative Science Quarterly, 24*, 242-266.

Terkel, S. (1972). *Working*. New York, NY: Avon.

Thompson, J.D. (1967). *Organizations in action*. New York, NY: McGraw-Hill.

Under Armour. (n.d.). Our story. Retrieved from https://about.underarmour.com/brand/our-story

VanderZwaag, H.J. (1984). *Sport management in schools and colleges*. New York, NY: Wiley.

Van de Ven, A.H. (1976). A framework for organizational assessment. *Academy of Management Review, 1*, 64-78.

von Bertalanffy, L. (1950). The theory of open systems in physics and biology. *Science, 3*, 23-29.

von Bertalanffy, L. (1968). *General systems theory: Foundations, development, applications*. New York, NY: Braziller.

White, A., & Brackenridge, C. (1985). Who rules sport? Gender divisions in the power structure of British sport organizations from 1960. *International Review for the Sociology of Sport, 20*, 95-107.

Whitson, D.J., & Macintosh, D. (1989). Gender and power: Explanations of gender inequalities in Canadian national sport organizations. *International Review for the Sociology of Sport, 24*, 137-150.

Winand, M., Vos, S., Zintz, T., & Scheerder, J. (2013). Determinants of service innovation: A typology of sports federations. *International Journal of Sport Management and Marketing, 13*(1), 55. doi:10.1504/IJSMM.2013.055194

Zeigler, E.F. (1987). Sport management: Past, present and future. *Journal of Sport Management, 1*, 4-24.

Chapter 2

Aiken, L.S., West, S.G., & Reno, R.R. (1991). *Multiple regression: Testing and interpreting interactions*. London, UK: SAGE.

Alexandris, K., Dimitriadis, N., & Kasiara, A. (2001). The behavioural consequences of perceived service quality: An exploratory study in the context of private fitness clubs in Greece. *European Sport Management Quarterly, 4*, 280-299.

Amis, J., & Silk, M. (2005). Rupture: Promoting critical and innovative approaches to the study of sport management. *Journal of Sport Management, 19*(4), 355-366.

Andrew, D.P., Pedersen, P.M., & McEvoy, C.D. (2011). *Research methods and design in sport management*. Champaign, IL: Human Kinetics.

Armstrong-Doherty, A. (1996). Resource dependence-based perceived control: An examination of Canadian interuniversity athletics. *Journal of Sport Management,* 10(1), 49-64.

Babbie, E. (1999). *The basics of social research*. Belmont, CA: Wadsworth.

Barthes, R. (1957). *Mythologies* (A. Lavers, Trans.). London, UK: Paladin.

Bauer, M. W., & Aarts, B. (2000). Corpus construction: A principle for qualitative data collection. In M. W. Bauer & G. Gaskell (Eds.), *Qualitative researching with text, image and sound: A practical handbook* (pp. 19-37). London, UK: SAGE.

Bauer, M.W., & Gaskell, G. (Eds.). (2000). *Qualitative researching with text, image and sound: A practical handbook*. London, UK: SAGE.

Bhaskar, R. (1989). *Reclaiming reality: A critical introduction to contemporary philosophy*. London, UK: Verso.

Boronico, J.S., & Newbert S.L. (2001). An empirically driven mathematical modelling analysis for play calling strategy in American football. *European Sport Management Quarterly, 1*(1), 21-38.

Brannigan, G.G. (1999). *The sport scientists: Research adventures*. Upper Saddle River, NJ: Prentice Hall.

Brittain, I., Bocarro, J., Byers, T., & Swart, K. (Eds.). (2017). *Legacies and mega events: Fact or fairy tales?* Abingdon, UK: Routledge.

Bryman, A. (2015). *Social research methods* (5th ed.). Oxford, UK: Oxford University Press.

Brymer, E., & Schweitzer, R. (2017). *Phenomenology and the extreme sport experience*. Abingdon, UK: Routledge.

Burbank, M., Andranovich, G., & Heying, C.H. (2001). *Olympic dreams: The impact of mega-events on local politics*. Boulder, CO: Lynne Rienner Publishers.

Burden, J. (2000). Community building, volunteering and action research. *Society and Leisure, 23*(2), 353-370.

Burrell, G., & Morgan, G. (2017). *Sociological paradigms and organisational analysis: Elements of the sociology of corporate life*. Abingdon, UK: Routledge.

Byers, T. (2013). Using critical realism: A new perspective on control of volunteers in sport clubs. *European Sport Management Quarterly, 13*(1), 5-31.

Chalip, L. (2017). Trading legacy for leverage. In Brittain et al. (Eds.), *Legacies and mega events: Fact or fairy tales* (pp. 25-42). Abingdon, UK: Routledge.

Chalip, L., Green, B.C., & Hill, B. (2003). Effects of sport event media on destination image and intention to visit. *Journal of sport management, 17*(3), 214-234.

Chalip, L., & Hutchinson, R. (2017). Reinventing youth sport: Formative findings from a state-level action research project. *Sport in Society, 20*(1), 30-46.

Chalip, L., & Leyns, A. (2002). Local business leveraging of a sport event: Managing an event for economic benefit. *Journal of Sport Management, 16*, 132-158.

Chang, K., & Chelladurai, P. (2003). Comparison of part-time workers and full-time workers: Commitment and citizenship behaviors in Korean sport organizations. *Journal of Sport Management, 17*(4), 394-416.

Coffey, A., & Atkinson, P. (1996). *Making sense of qualitative data: Complementary research strategies*. Thousand Oaks, CA: SAGE.

Cooper, J.N., Grenier, R.S., & Macaulay, C. (2017). Autoethnography as a critical approach in sport management: Current applications and directions for future research. *Sport Management Review, 20*(1), 43-54.

Cousens, L., & Slack, T. (1996). Using sport sponsorship to penetrate local markets: The case of the fast food industry. *Journal of Sport Management, 10*(2), 169-187.

Creswell, J.W. (2003). *Research design: Qualitative, quantitative and mixed methods approaches*. London, UK: SAGE.

Crotty, M. (1998). *The foundations of social research: Meaning and perspective in the research process*. Thousand Oaks, CA: SAGE.

Denscombe, M. (2010). *The good research guide: For small-scale social research projects*. Berkshire, UK: Open University Press.

Denzin, N.K., & Lincoln, Y.S. (Eds.). (2011). *The Sage handbook of qualitative research*. London, UK: SAGE.

De Waegeneer, E., Van De Sompele, J., & Willem, A. (2016). Ethical codes in sports organizations: Classification framework, content analysis, and the influence of content on code effectiveness. *Journal of Business Ethics, 136*(3), 587-98.

Doyle, J.P., Filo, K., Lock, D., Funk, D.C., & McDonald, H. (2016). Exploring PERMA in spectator sport: Applying positive psychology to examine the individual-level benefits of sport consumption. *Sport Management Review, 19*(5), 506-519.

Eisenhardt, K.M. (1989). Building theories from case study research. *Academy of management review, 14*(4), 532-550.

Evans, A.N. (1998). *Using basic statistics in the social sciences* (3rd ed.). Scarborough, ON: Prentice Hall Allyn and Bacon Canada.

Fairley, S. (2003). In search of relived social experience: Group-based nostalgia sport tourism. *Journal of Sport Management, 17*(3): 284-304.

Filo, K., Lock, D., & Karg, A. (2015). Sport and social media research: A review. *Sport Management Review, 18*(2), 166-181.

Frisby, W., Crawford, S., & Dorer, T. (1997). Reflections on participatory action research: The case of low-income women accessing local physical activity services. *Journal of Sport Management, 11*(1), 8-28.

Funk, D. C., Ridinger, L. L., & Moorman, A. M. (2003). Understanding consumer support: Extending the Sport Interest Inventory (SII) to examine individual differences among women's professional sport consumers. *Sport Management Review, 6*(1), 1-31.

García, B., Welford, J., & Smith, B. (2016). Using a smartphone app in qualitative research: The good, the bad and the ugly. *Qualitative Research, 16*(5), 508-525.

Gaskell, G. (2000). Individual and group interviewing. In M.W. Bauer & G. Gaskell (Eds.), *Qualitative researching with text, image and sound: A practical handbook* (pp. 38-56). London, UK: SAGE.

Gladden, J., & Funk, D. (2002). Developing an understanding of brand associations in team sport: Empirical evidence from consumers of professional sport. *Journal of Sport Management, 16*(1), 54-81.

Gladwell, N.J., Anderson, D.M., & Sellers, J.R. (2003). An examination of fiscal trends in public parks and recreation from 1986 to 2001: A case study of North Carolina. *Journal Of Park & Recreation Administration, 21*(1): 104-116.

Glaser, B.G., & Strauss, A.L. (1967). Grounded theory: The discovery of grounded theory. *Sociology, 12*(1), 27-49.

Glaser, B.G., & Strauss, A.L. (2017). *Discovery of grounded theory: Strategies for qualitative research*. Abingdon, UK: Routledge.

Gouldner, A.W. (1954). *Patterns of industrial bureaucracy*. New York, NY: Free Press.

Green, L.W., George, M.A., Daniel, M., Frankish, C.J., Herbert, C.P., Bowie, W.R., & O'Neil, M. (1995). *Background on participatory research; study of participatory research in health promotion: Review and recommendations for the development of participatory research in health promotion in Canada*. Ottawa, The Royal Society of Canada.

Guba, E.G. (Ed.). (1990). *The paradigm dialog*. Thousand Oaks, CA: Sage Publications, Inc.

Hambrick, M.E., Simmons, J.M., Greenhalgh, G.P., & Greenwell, T.C. (2010). Understanding professional athletes' use of Twitter: A content analysis of athlete tweets. *International Journal of Sport Communication, 3*(4), 454-471.

Higgs, C.T., & Weiller, K.H. (1994). Gender bias and the 1992 Summer Olympic Games: An analysis of television coverage. *Journal of Sport and Social Issues, 18*(3), 234-246.

Higham, J.E., & Hinch, T.D. (2003). Sport, space and time: Effects of the Otago Highlanders franchise on tourism. *Journal of Sport Management, 17*, 235-257.

Hoeber, L., & Shaw, S. (2016). Contemporary qualitative research methods in sport management. *Sport Management Review, 20*(1), 4-7.

Hoeber, O., Snelgrove, R., Hoeber, L., & Wood, L. (2017). A systematic methodology for preserving the whole in large-scale qualitative-temporal research. *Journal of Sport Management, 31*(4), 1-36.

Jackson, E., and Burton, T., eds. 1999. *Leisure studies: Prospects for the twenty-first century*. State College, PA: Venture.

Jones, D.F., Brooks, D.D., & Mak, J.Y. (2008). Examining sport management programs in the United States. *Sport Management Review, 11*(1), 77-91.

Jones, G.J., Edwards, M., Bocarro, J.N., Bunds, K.S., & Smith, J.W. (2017). Collaborative advantages: The role of interorganizational partnerships for youth sport nonprofit organizations. *Journal of Sport Management, 31*(2), 148-160.

Jones, R. (2002). Partnerships in action: Strategies for the development of voluntary community groups in urban parks. *Leisure Studies, 21*(3-4), 305-325.

Kang, J.H. (2002). A structural model of image-based and utilitarian decision-making processes for participant sport consumption. *Journal of Sport Management, 16*(1), 173-189. doi:10.1123/jsm.16.3.173

Kelle, H. (2000). Gender and territoriality in games played by nine-to twelve-year-old schoolchildren. *Journal of Contemporary Ethnography, 29*(2), 164-197.

Kent, A., & Chelladurai, P. (2001). Perceived transformational leadership, organizational commitment, and citizenship behavior: A case study in intercollegiate athletes. *Journal of Sport Management, 15*(2), 135-159.

Kerwin, S., & Hoeber, L. (2015). Collaborative self-ethnography: Navigating self-reflexivity in a sport management context. *Journal of Sport Management, 29*(5), 498-509.

Kitchin, P.J., & Howe, P.D. (2013). How can the social theory of Pierre Bourdieu assist sport management research? *Sport Management Review, 16*(2), 123-134.

Knoppers, A. (2015). Assessing the sociology of sport: On critical sport sociology and sport management. *International Review for the Sociology of Sport, 50*(4-5), 496-501.

Koenigstorfer, J., Groeppel-Klein, A., & Kunkel, T. (2010). The attractiveness of national and international football leagues: Perspectives of fans of "star clubs" and "underdogs." *European Sport Management Quarterly, 10*(2), 127-163.

Kronberger, N., & Wagner, W. (2000). Statistical analysis of text features. In M.W. Bauer & G. Gaskell (Eds.), *Qualitative researching with text, image and sound: A practical handbook for social research* (pp. 299-317). London, UK: SAGE.

Kyle, G.T., Kerstetter, D.L., & Guadagnolo, F.B. (2003). Manipulating consumer price expectations for a 10K road race. *Journal of Sport Management, 17*(2), 142-155.

Lin, Y. C., Chalip, L., & Green, B.C. (2016). The essential role of sense of community in a youth sport program. *Leisure Sciences*, 38(5), 461-481.

Mackellar, J. (2013). Participant observation at events: Theory, practice and potential. *International Journal of Event and Festival Management, 4*(1), 56-65.

Mason, D.S., & Slack, T. (2003). Understanding principal–agent relationships: Evidence from professional hockey. *Journal of Sport Management, 17*(1), 37-61.

McGehee, N.G., Yoon, Y., & Cárdenas, D. (2003). Involvement and travel for recreation runners in North Carolina. *Journal of Sport Management, 7*, 305-324.

Middelweerd, A., Mollee, J.S., van der Wal, C.N., Brug, J., & te Velde, S.J. (2014). Apps to promote physical activity among adults: A review and content analysis. *International Journal of Behavioral Nutrition and Physical Activity, 11*(1), 97.

Miles, M.B., & Huberman, M.A. (1994). *Qualitative data analysis: An expanded sourcebook*. Thousand Oaks, CA: SAGE.

Miles, M.B., Huberman, M.A., & Saldaña, J. (2014). *Qualitative data analysis* (3rd ed.). Thousand Oaks, CA: SAGE.

Morgan, G. (Ed.). (1983). *Beyond method: Strategies for social research*. London, UK: SAGE.

Myers, M.D. (2013). *Qualitative research in business and management*. London, UK: SAGE.

Næss, H.E. (2017). Authenticity matters: A digital ethnography of FIA World Rally Championship fan forums. *Sport Management Review, 20*(1), 105-113.

O'Brien, D., & Slack, T. (2003). An analysis of change in an organizational field: The professionalization of English rugby union. *Journal of Sport Management, 17*, 417-448.

O'Reilly, N. (2011). Experimental design methods in sport management research: The playoff safety bias. *Journal of Sport Management, 23*(3), 217-228.

Patton, E., & Applebaum, S.H. (2003). The case for case studies in management research. *Management Research News, 26*(5), 60-71.

Pedersen, P. M., & Pitts, B. (2001). Investigating the body of knowledge in sport management: A content analysis of the Sport Marketing Quarterly. The Chronicle of Physical Education in Higher Education, *12*(3), 8-9, 22-23.

Pedersen, P.M., Whisenant, W.A., & Schneider, R.G. (2003). Using a content analysis to examine the gendering of sports newspaper personnel and their coverage. *Journal of Sport Management, 17*(4), 376-393.

Pegoraro, A., Scott, O., & Burch, L.M. (2017). Strategic use of Facebook to build brand awareness: A case study of two national sport organizations. *International Journal of Public Administration in the Digital Age, 4*(1), 69-87.

Rich, K.A., & Misener, L. (2017). Insiders, outsiders, and agents of change: First person action inquiry in community sport management. *Sport Management Review, 20*(1), 8-19.

Riddick, C.C., and Russell, R.V. (2014). *Research methods: How to conduct research in recreation, Parks, sport and tourism.* Urbana, IL: Sagamore.

Roche, M. (1994). Mega-events and urban policy. *Annals of Tourism Research, 21*(1), 1-19.

Rosentraub, M.S., & Swindell, D. (2002). Negotiating games: Cities, sports, and the winner's curse. *Journal of Sport Management, 16*(1), 18-35.

Salanda, J. (2013). *The coding manual for qualitative researchers* (2nd ed.). London, UK: SAGE.

Schaeperkoetter, C.C. (2017). Basketball officiating as a gendered arena: An autoethnography. *Sport Management Review, 20*(1), 128-141.

Schinke, R.J., da Costa, J., & Andrews, M. (2001). Considerations regarding graduate student persistence. *Alberta Journal of Educational Research, 47*(4): 341-352.

Shannon, C.S. (2016). Exploring factors influencing girls' continued participation in competitive dance. *Journal of Leisure Research, 48*(4), 285-307.

Silk, M. (2001). Together we're one? The "place" of the nation in media representations of the 1998 Kuala Lumpur Commonwealth Games. *Sociology of Sport Journal, 18*(3), 277-301.

Silk, M., Slack, T., & Amis, J. (2000). Bread, butter and gravy: An institutional approach to televised sport production. *Culture Sport Society, 3*(1), 1-21.

Sotiriadou, P., Brouwers, J., & Le, T.A. (2014). Choosing a qualitative data analysis tool: A comparison of NVivo and Leximancer. *Annals of Leisure Research, 17*(2), 218-234.

Spaaij, R. (2013). Cultural diversity in community sport: An ethnographic inquiry of Somali Australians' experiences. *Sport Management Review, 16*(1), 29-40.

Sparkes, A. (2002). *Telling tales in sport and physical activity: A qualitative journey.* Champaign, IL: Human Kinetics.

Sparkes, A.C., & Smith, B. (2014). *Qualitative research methods in sport, exercise and health. From process to product.* New York, NY: Routledge.

Stewart-Withers, R., Sewabu, K., & Richardson, S. (2017). Talanoa: A contemporary qualitative methodology for sport management. *Sport Management Review, 20*(1), 55-68.

Strauss, A.L. (1987). *Qualitative analysis for social scientists.* Cambridge, UK: Cambridge University.

Stride, A., Fitzgerald, H.F., & Allison, W. (2017). A narrative approach: The possibilities for sport management. *Sport Management Review, 20*(1), 33-42.

Swearingen, T.C., & Johnson, D.R. (1995). Visitors' responses to uniformed park employees. *Journal of Park and Recreation Administration, 13*(1), 73-85.

Taks, M., Green, B.C., Misener, L., & Chalip, L. (2018). Sport participation from sport events: why it doesn't happen? *Marketing Intelligence & Planning, 36*(2), 185-198.

Taks, M., Misener, L., Chalip, L., & Green, B.C. (2013). Leveraging sport events for participation. *Canadian Journal for Social Research, 3*(1), 12.

Tarrant, M. A. (1996). Attending to past outdoor recreation experiences: Symptom reporting and changes in affect. *Journal of Leisure Research, 28*(1), 1-17.

Taylor, T. (2003). Diversity management in a multi-cultural society: An exploratory study of cultural diversity and team sport in Australia. *Annals of Leisure Research, 6*(2), 168-188.

Trochim, W.M. (2001). The regression-discontinuity design. *International encyclopedia of the social and behavioral sciences, 19*, 12940-12945.

Trochim, W.M., & Donnelly, J.P. (2001). *Research methods knowledge base* (Vol. 2). Cincinnati, OH: Atomic Dog.

Tsang, E.W. (2014). Generalizing from research findings: The merits of case studies. *International Journal of Management Reviews, 16*(4), 369-383.

Tsang, T. (2000). Let me tell you a story: A narrative exploration of identity in high-performance sport. *Sociology of sport journal, 17*(1), 44-59.

Uhrich, S. (2014). Exploring customer-to-customer value co-creation platforms and practices in team sports. *European Sport Management Quarterly, 14*(1), 25-49.

van der Roest, J.W., Spaaij, R., & van Bottenburg, M. (2015). Mixed methods in emerging academic subdisciplines: The case of sport management. *Journal of Mixed Methods Research, 9*(1): 70-90.

Van Rheenen, D., Cernaianu, S., & Sobry, C. (2017). Defining sport tourism: A content analysis of an evolving epistemology. *Journal of Sport & Tourism, 21*(2), 75-93.

Veal, A.J., & Darcy, S. (2014). *Research methods in sport studies and sport management: A practical guide.* Abingdon, UK: Routledge.

Vieira, E.T., Jr. (2017). *Introduction to real world statistics: With step-by-step SPSS instructions.* Abingdon, UK: Routledge.

Whittaker, C.G., & Holland-Smith, D. (2016). Exposing the dark side: An exploration of the influence social capital has upon parental sports volunteers. *Sport, Education and Society, 21*(3), 356-373.

Yin, R.K. (2003). *Case study methodology.* Thousand Oaks, CA: SAGE.

Yin, R.K. (2013). Validity and generalization in future case study evaluations. *Evaluation, 19*(3), 321-332.

Yin, R. K. (2017). *Case study research and applications: Design and methods.* Thousand Oaks, CA: SAGE.

Yoshida, M., Heere, B., & Gordon, B. (2015). Predicting behavioral loyalty through community: Why other fans are more important than our own intentions, our satisfaction, and the team itself. *Journal of Sport Management, 29*(3), 318-333.

Yuksel, M., McDonald, M.A., Milne, G.R., & Darmody, A. (2017). The paradoxical relationship between fantasy football and NFL consumption: Conflict development and consumer coping mechanisms. *Sport Management Review, 20*(2), 198-210.

Chapter 3

Argyris, C. (1964). *Integrating the individual and the organization.* New York, NY: Wiley.

Azzali, S. (2017). The legacies of Sochi 2014 Winter Olympics: An evaluation of the Adler Olympic Park. *Urban Research & Practice, 10*(3), 329-349.

Badenhausen, K. (2018, July 18). Dallas Cowboys lead the world's most valuable sports teams. *Forbes*, Retrieved from https://www.forbes.com/sites/kurtbadenhausen/2018/07/18/the-worlds-most-valuable-sports-teams-2018/#5bd0157e75d1

Brittain, I., Bocarro, J., Byers, T., & Swart, K. (Eds.). (2017). *Legacies and mega events: Fact or fairy tales?* Abingdon, UK: Routledge.

Byers, T. (2018). Trends in professional sport organizations and sport management and their market impact. In M. Breuer & D. Forrest (Eds.), *The Palgrave handbook on the economics of manipulation of sport* (pp. 55-70). New York, NY: Springer.

Cameron, K.S. (1980). Critical questions in assessing organizational effectiveness. *Organizational Dynamics*, *9*, 66-80.

Cameron, K.S. (1984). The effectiveness of ineffectiveness. In B.M. Staw & L.L. Cummings (Eds.), *Research in organizational behavior* (Vol. 6, pp. 235-285). Greenwich, CT: JAI Press.

Campbell, J.P. (1977). On the nature of organizational effectiveness. In P.S. Goodman, J.M. Pennings, & Associates (Eds.), *New perspectives on organizational effectiveness* (pp. 36-41). San Francisco, CA: Jossey-Bass.

Canada Basketball (2011). Values, vision and mission. Retrieved from http://www.basketball.ca/values-vision-and-mission-s15164

Carman, J.J.G. (2010). Evaluation capacity and nonprofit organizations: Is the glass half-empty or half-full? *The American Journal of Evaluation*, *31,* 84-104.

Chelladurai, P. (1985). *Sport management: Macro perspectives*. London, ON: Sports Dynamics.

Chelladurai, P. (1987). Multidimensionality and multiple perspectives of organizational effectiveness. *Journal of Sport Management*, *1*, 37-47.

Chelladurai, P., & Haggerty, T.R. (1991). Measures of organizational effectiveness in Canadian national sport organizations. *Canadian Journal of Sport Science*, *16*, 126-133.

Chelladurai, P., Haggerty, T.R., Campbell, L., & Wall, S. (1981). A factor analytic study of effectiveness criteria in intercollegiate athletics. *Canadian Journal of Applied Sport Science*, *6*, 81-86.

Chelladurai, P., & Kerwin, S. (2017). *Human resource management in sport and recreation* (3rd ed.). Champaign, IL: Human Kinetics.

Chelladurai, P., Szyszlo, M., & Haggerty, T.R. (1987). Systems-based dimensions of effectiveness: The case of national sport organizations. *Canadian Journal of Sport Science*, *12*, 111-119.

Connolly, T., Conlon, E.M., & Deutsch, S.J. (1980). Organizational effectiveness: A multiple constituency approach. *Academy of Management Review, 5,* 211-218.

Creamer, R.W. (1973, April 16). Scorecard: More basketball business. *Sports Illustrated*, 21.

Daft, R.L. (2004). *Organization theory and design* (8th ed.). Mason, OH: Thomson/South-Western.

Das, H. (1990). *Organization theory with Canadian applications*. Toronto, ON: Gage Educational.

Dimitropoulos, P., Kosmas, I., & Douvis, I. (2017). Implementing the balanced scorecard in a local government sport organization: Evidence from Greece. *International Journal of Productivity and Performance Management*, *66*(3), 362-379.

Dixon, A.W., Martinez, J.M., & Martin, C.L. (2015). Employing social media as a marketing strategy in college sport: An examination of perceived effectiveness in accomplishing organizational objectives. *International Review on Public and Nonprofit Marketing*, *12*(2), 97-113.

Drucker, P.F. (1954). *The practice of management.* New York, NY: Harper.

Ebrahim, A.S., & Rangan, V.K. (2010, August). Putting the brakes on impact: A contingency framework for measuring social performance. Best Paper Proceedings of the Academy of Management, Montréal, Quebec, Canada.

Evan, W.M. (1976). Organizational theory and organizational effectiveness: An exploratory analysis. In S.L. Spray (Ed.), *Organizational effectiveness: Theory, research, utilization* (pp. 15-28). Kent, OH: Kent State University Press.

Feinstein, J. (1986). *A season on the brink: A year with Bob Knight and the Indiana Hoosiers*. New York, NY: Simon and Schuster.

Felix, R., Rauschnabel, P.A., & Hinsch, C. (2017). Elements of strategic social media marketing: A holistic framework. *Journal of Business Research*, *70*, 118-126.

Frisby, W. (1986). Measuring the organizational effectiveness of national sport governing bodies. *Canadian Journal of Applied Sport Science*, *11*, 94-99.

Geere, D. (2014). Freezing Sochi: How Russia turned a subtropical beach into a Winter Olympics wonderland. Retrieved from https://www.theverge.com/2014/2/4/5377356/sochi-winter-olympics-2014-subtropical-transformation

Giroux, M., Pons, F., & Maltese, L. (2017). The role of perceived brand personality in promotion effectiveness and brand equity development of professional sports teams. *International Journal of Sports Marketing and Sponsorship*, *18*(2), 180-195.

Gold, D. (2012). Judge bans Sochi 2014 gay Pride House claiming it would offend "public morality." Retrieved from https://www.insidethegames.biz/articles/16259/judge-bans-winter-olympics-gay-pride-house

Goodman, P.S., Atkin, R.S., & Schoorman, F.D. (1983). On the demise of organizational effectiveness studies. In K.S. Cameron & D.A. Whetten (Eds.), *Organizational effectiveness: A comparison of multiple models* (pp. 163-183). New York, NY: Academic Press.

Goodman, P.S., Pennings, J.M., & Associates (Eds.). (1977). *New perspectives on organizational effectiveness*. San Francisco, CA: Jossey-Bass.

Grabowski, L., Neher, C., Crim, T., & Mathiassen, L. (2015). Competing values framework application to organizational effectiveness in voluntary organizations: A case study. *Nonprofit and Voluntary Sector Quarterly*, *44*(5), 908-923.

Hall, R.H. (1982). *Organizations: Structure and process* (3rd ed.). Englewood Cliffs, NJ: Prentice Hall.

Hall, R.H., & Clark, J.P. (1980). An ineffective effectiveness study and some suggestions for future research. *Sociological Quarterly, 21,* 119-134.

Hampton, J. (1984, October). Q. and A. One-on-one with H.R. "Bum" Bright. *Dallas*, 23-25, 86.

Hannan, M.T., & Freeman, J. (1977). Obstacles to comparative studies. In P.S. Goodman & J.M. Pennings, & Associates (Eds.), *New perspectives on organizational effectiveness* (pp. 106-131). San Francisco, CA: Jossey-Bass.

Hickson, D.J., Hinings, C.R., Lee, C.A., Schneck, R.E., & Pennings, J.M. (1971). A "strategic" contingencies theory of interorganizational power. *Administrative Science Quarterly, 14,* 378-397.

Hockey Canada (2013-14). Annual Report. *Hockey Canada publication.*

Hrebiniak, L.G., & Joyce, W.F. (1985). Organizational adaptation: Strategic choice and environmental determinism. *Administrative Science Quarterly, 30,* 336-349.

IOC (2014). All about the Sochi 2014 venues. Retrieved from https://www.olympic.org/news/all-about-the-sochi-2014-venues

Jensen, C.R. (1983). *Administrative management of physical education and athletic programs*. Philadelphia, PA: Lea & Febiger.

Johnson, J. (2016). Sochi Olympics leave and environmentally damaging legacy. Retrieved from https://www.chinadialogue.net/article/show/single/en/8660-Sochi-Olympics-leave-an-environmentally-damaging-legacy

Kanter, R.M., & Brinkerhoff, D. (1981). Organizational performance: Recent developments in measurement. In R.H. Turner & J.F. Short (Eds.), *Annual Review of Sociology* (Vol. 7, pp. 321-349). Palo Alto, CA: Annual Reviews.

Kassim, A.F.M., & Boardley, I.D. (2018). Athlete perceptions of coaching effectiveness and athlete-level outcomes in team and individual sports: A cross-cultural investigation. *The Sport Psychologist*, *32*(3), 189-198.

Keeley, M. (1978). A social-justice approach to organizational evaluation. *Administrative Science Quarterly*, *23*, 272-292.

Kelly, T.W. (1991). Performance evaluation. In R.L. Boucher & W.J. Weese (Eds.), *Management of recreational sports in higher education* (pp. 153-165). Carmel, IN: Benchmark Press.

Kihl, L.A. (2017). Micro view: Individual and group explanations of sport corruption. In L.A. Kihl, J. Skinner, & T. Engelberg (Eds.), *Corruption in Sport: Understanding the complexity of corruption* (pp. 42-56). Abingdon, UK: Routledge.

Kihl, L.A., Read, D., & Skinner, J. (2017). Applying a conceptual model of policy regime effectiveness to national and international anti-doping policy in sport. In L.A. Kihl, J. Skinner & T. Engelberg (Eds.), *Corruption in Sport: Understanding the complexity of corruption* (pp. 62-78). Abingdon, UK: Routledge.

Kihl, L.A., Skinner, J., & Engelberg, T. (2017). *Corruption in sport: Understanding the complexity of corruption.* Abingdon, UK: Routledge.

Lee, S., Brownlee, E., Kim, Y., & Lee, S. (2017). Ticket sales outsourcing performance measures using balanced scorecard and analytic hierarchy process combined model. *Sport Marketing Quarterly*, *26*(2), 110.

Lenskyj, H.J. (2000). *Inside the Olympic industry: Power, politics, and activism.* Albany, NY: State University of New York Press.

Likert, R. (1967). *The human organization.* New York, NY: McGraw-Hill.

Liket, K.C., & Maas, K. (2015). Nonprofit organizational effectiveness: Analysis of best practices. *Nonprofit and Voluntary Sector Quarterly*, *44*(2), 268-296.

Macintosh, D., & Whitson, D.J. (1990). *The game planners: Transforming Canada's sport system.* Montreal, QC, and Kingston, ON: McGill-Queen's University Press.

Martindell, J. (1962). *The scientific appraisal of management.* New York, NY: Harper & Row.

Michael, D.N. (1973). *On learning to plan—and planning to learn.* San Francisco, CA: Jossey-Bass.

Mills, D. (1991). The battle of Alberta: Entrepreneurs and the business of hockey in Edmonton and Calgary, AB. *Alberta: Studies in the Arts and Sciences*, *2*, 1-25.

Mintzberg, H. (1982). A note on that dirty word "efficiency." *Interfaces*, *12*, 101-105.

Molan, C., Kelly, S., Arnold, R., & Matthews, J. (2018). Performance management: A systematic review of processes in elite sport and other performance domains. *Journal of Applied Sport Psychology*, *31*(1), 87-104.

Molnar, J.J., & Rogers, D.L. (1976). Organizational effectiveness: An empirical comparison of the goal and system resource approaches. *Sociological Quarterly*, *17*, 401-413.

Nord, W.R. (1983). A political-economic perspective on organizational effectiveness. In K.S. Cameron & D.A. Whetten (Eds.), *Organizational effectiveness: A comparison of multiple models* (pp. 95-131). New York, NY: Academic Press.

Perrow, C. (1961). The analysis of goals in complex organizations. *American Sociological Review, 26,* 854-866.

Pound, R.W. (2004). *Inside the Olympics: A behind-the-scenes look at the politics, the scandals, and the glory of the games.* Mississauga, ON: Wiley Canada.

Price, J.L. (1972). The study of organizational effectiveness. *Sociological Quarterly*, *13*, 3-15.

Quinn, R.E. (1988). *Beyond rational management.* San Francisco, CA: Jossey-Bass.

Quinn, R.E., & Cameron, K.S. (1983). Organizational life cycles and shifting criteria of effectiveness: Some preliminary evidence. *Management Science*, *9*, 33-51.

Quinn, R.E., & Rohrbaugh, J. (1981). A competing values approach to organizational effectiveness. *Public Productivity Review*, *5*, 122-140.

Quinn, R.E., & Rohrbaugh, J. (1983). A spatial model of effectiveness criteria: Towards a competing values approach to organizational analysis. *Management Science*, *29*, 363-377.

Redelius, K., Quennerstedt, M., & Öhman, M. (2015). Communicating aims and learning goals in physical education: Part of a subject for learning? *Sport, Education and Society*, *20*(5), 641-655.

Robbins, S.P. (1990). *Organization theory: Structure, design and applications* (3rd ed.). Englewood Cliffs, NJ: Prentice Hall.

Roberts, S., and Bolton, C. (2017). Approach to compliance and reform. In L.A. Kihl, J. Skinner, & T. Engelberg (Eds.), *Corruption in sport: Understanding the complexity of corruption* (pp.144-155). Abingdon, UK: Routledge.

Rohrbaugh, J. (1981). Operationalizing the competing values approach. *Public Productivity Review, 2*, 141-159.

Rojas, R. R. (2000). A review of models for measuring organizational effectiveness among for-profit and nonprofit organizations. *Nonprofit Management and Leadership, 11*, 97-104.

Rosenberg, M., Lester, L., Maitland, C., & Teal, R. (2017). A natural fit: Passion, sport and health message sponsorship effectiveness. *Journal of Science and Medicine in Sport*, *20*, 72-73.

Roth, T. (1987, February 6). Puma hopes superstar will help end U.S. slump, narrow gap with Adidas. *Wall Street Journal*, 24.

Rumsby, B. (2015, November 14). Five-year plan for us to all fall in love with swimming again. *Telegraph*, Retrieved from https://www.telegraph.co.uk/sport/olympics/swimming/11976394/Five-year-plan-for-us-to-all-fall-in-love-with-swimming-again.html, on 11/09/2019.

Sack, A.L., & Staurowsky, E.J. (1998). *College athletes for hire: The evolution and legacy of the NCAA's amateur myth.* Westport, CT: Praeger.

Sage, G.H. (2015). *Globalizing sport: How organizations, corporations, media, and politics are changing sport.* Abingdon, UK: Routledge.

Sandefur, G.D. (1983). Efficiency in social service organizations. *Administration & Society*, *14*, 449-468.

Sanzo-Pérez, M.J., Rey-Garcia, M., & Álvarez-González, L.I. (2017). The drivers of voluntary transparency in nonprofits: Professionalization and partnerships with firms as determinants. *VOLUNTAS: International Journal of Voluntary and Nonprofit Organizations*, *28*(4), 1595-1621.

Saxton, G.D., & Guo, C. (2011). Accountability online: Understanding the web-based account-ability practices of nonprofit organizations. *Nonprofit and Voluntary Sector Quarterly*, *40*, 270-295.

Schweitzer, M.E., Ordóñez, L., & Douma, B. (2004). Goal setting as a motivator of unethical behaviour. *Academy of Management Journal*, *47*, 422-432.

Shilbury, D., & Moore, K.A. (2006). A study of organizational effectiveness for national Olympic sporting organizations. *Nonprofit and Voluntary Sector Quarterly, 35*(1), 5-38.

Slack, T. (1991). Sport management: Some thoughts on future directions. *Journal of Sport Management, 5,* 95-99.

Slack, T., & Hinings, C.R. (1992). Understanding change in national sport organizations: An integration of theoretical perspectives. *Journal of Sport Management, 6,* 114-132.

Sparrow, P., & Cooper, C. (2014). Organizational effectiveness, people and performance: new challenges, new research agendas. *Journal of Organizational Effectiveness: People and Performance*, *1*(1), 2-13.

Statista (2018). Retrieved from https://www.statista.com/search/?q=twitter%20sport%20teams&qKat=search

Steers, R.M. (1975). Problems in the measurement of organizational effectiveness. *Administrative Science Quarterly*, *20*, 546-558.

Toohey, K., & Beaton, A. (2017). International cross-sector social partnerships between sport and governments: The World Anti-Doping Agency. *Sport Management Review*, *20*(5), 483-496.

VanderZwaag, H.J. (1984). *Sport management in schools and colleges*. New York, NY: Wiley.

Van Puyvelde, S., Brown, W.A., Walker, V., & Tenuta, R. (2018). Board effectiveness in nonprofit organizations: Do interactions in the boardroom matter? *Nonprofit and Voluntary Sector Quarterly, 47*(6), 1296-1310.

Warriner, C.K. (1965). The problems of organizational purpose. *Sociological Quarterly, 6*, 139-146.

Williams, R.I., Pieper, T.M., Kellermanns, F.W., & Astrachan, J.H. (2018). Family firm goals and their effects on strategy, family and organization behavior: A review and research agenda. *International Journal of Management Reviews*, *20*(S1), 63-82.

Winand, M., Zintz, T., Bayle, E., & Robinson, L. (2010). Organizational performance of Olympic sport governing bodies: Dealing with measurement and priorities. *Managing Leisure*, *15*(4), 279-307.

Wolfe, R., Slack, T., & Rose-Hearn, T. (1993). Factors influencing the adoption and maintenance of Canadian, facility-based worksite health promotion programs. *American Journal of Health Promotion*, *7*(3), 189-198.

Yuchtman, E., & Seashore, S.E. (1967). A systems resource approach to organizational effectiveness. *American Sociological Review, 32,* 891-903.

Zarakhovich, Y. (2007, July). The Sochi Olympics: A win for Putin. *Time*, Retrieved from http://content.time.com/time/world/article/0,8599,1640197,00.html

Chapter 4

Adams, M.J. (1987, July). A welcome wave hits. *Stores,* 27-35.

Adams, P. (2018). How Coke amplifies in stadium experiences via digital tech. Retrieved from https://www.marketingdive.com/news/how-coke-amplifies-in-stadium-experiences-via-digital-tech/527467/

Aldrich, H.E., & Herker, D. (1977). Boundary spanning roles and organization structure. *Academy of Management Review, 2,* 217-230.

Aldrich, H.E., McKelvey, B., & Ulrich, D. (1984). Design strategy from the population perspective. *Journal of Management*, *10*, 67-86.

Allen, M.P., Panian, S.K., & Lotz, R.E. (1979). Managerial succession and organizational performance: A recalcitrant problem revisited. *Administrative Science Quarterly*, *24*, 167-180.

Armstrong-Doherty, A.J. (1996). Resource dependence-based perceived control: An examination of Canadian interuniversity athletics. *Journal of Sport Management*, *10*, 49-64.

Babiak, K., Thibault, L., & Willem, A. (2018). Mapping research on interorganizational relationships in sport management: Current landscape and future research prospects. *Journal of Sport Management*, *32*(3), 272-294.

Babiak, K., & Trendafilova, S. (2011). CSR and environmental responsibility: Motives and pressures to adopt green management practices. *Corporate social responsibility and environmental management*, *18*(1), 11-24.

Barnes, J. (1988). *Sport and the law in Canada*. Toronto, ON: Butterworth.

Beamish, R. (1985). Sport executives and voluntary associations: A review of the literature and introduction to some theoretical issues. *Sociology of Sport Journal*, *2*, 218-232.

Beck, K. (2016). The sports industry is estimated to be worth almost $900 million. Retrieved from http://mashable.com/2016/07/20/esports-value/#d4cYB9EquEqE

Berrett, T., Burton, T.L., & Slack, T. (1993). Quality products, quality service: Factors leading to entrepreneurial success in the sport and leisure industry. *Leisure Studies*, *12*, 93-106.

Boulton, W.R., Lindsay, W.M., Franklin, S.G., & Rue, L.W. (1982). Strategic planning: Determining the impact of environmental characteristics and uncertainty. *Academy of Management Journal*, *25*(3), 500-509.

Breuer, C., Feiler, S., & Wicker, P. (2015). Sport clubs in Germany. In *Sport clubs in Europe* (pp. 187-208). New York, NY: Springer.

Brown, M.C. (1982). Administrative succession and organizational performance: The succession effect. *Administrative Science Quarterly*, *27*, 1-16.

Burbank, M.J., Andranovich, G.D., & Heying, C.H. (2001). *Olympic dreams: The impact of mega-events on local politics.* Boulder, CO: Lynne Rienner.

Burns, T., & Stalker, G.M. (1961). *The management of innovation*. London, UK: Tavistock.

Byers, T. (2013). Using critical realism: A new perspective on control of volunteers in sport clubs. *European Sport Management Quarterly*, *13*(1), 5-31.

Byers, T. (2016). *Contemporary issues in sport management: A critical introduction*. London: Sage Publications.

Byers, T. (2018). Trends in Professional Sport Organisations and Sport Management and Their Market Impact. In *The Palgrave Handbook on the Economics of Manipulation in Sport* (pp. 55-70). Cham, Switzerland: Palgrave Macmillan.

Byers, T., and Hayday, E.H. (2019). A critical realist view of integrating immigrants in sport in Canada and England: Challenges to managing diversity. Working paper, University of New Brunswick, Canada.

Byers, T., Roy, S., Reis, A., Weinstein, J., Lunga, P., & Hayday, E. (2019). *Challenges in Diversity: How Canadian Sport Organizations are Innovating to Include Newcomers.* Fredericton, NB: University of New Brunswick.

Charm, R.E. (1986, November 3). Like the company's sales, aluminum bikes of Cannondale stand out from the pack. *New England Business*, 41-43.

Child, J. (1984). *Organization: A guide to problems and practice* (2nd ed.). London, UK: Chapman.

Cunningham, G.B. (2002). Removing the blinders: Toward an integrative model of organizational change in sport and physical activity. *Quest*, *54*, 276-291.

Cunningham, G.B. (2017). *Diversity and inclusion in sport organizations*. Abingdon, UK: Routledge.

Daft, R.L. (2004). *Organization theory and design* (8th ed.). Mason, OH: Thomson/South-Western.

Damanpour, F. (1996). Organizational complexity and innovation: Developing and testing multiple contingency models. *Management Science*, *42*(5), 693-716.

Damanpour, F., & Aravind, D. (2012). Managerial innovation: Conceptions, processes and antecedents. *Management and Organization Review*, *8*(2), 423-454.

Damanpour, F., & Schneider, M. (2006). Phases of the adoption of innovation in organizations: Effects of environment, organization and top managers. *British Journal of Management*, *17*(3), 215-236.

Danylchuk, K.E. (1993). Occupational stressors in physical education faculties. *Journal of Sport Management*, *7*, 7-24.

Dess, G.G., & Beard, D.W. (1984). Dimensions of organizational task environments. *Administrative Science Quarterly*, *29*, 52-73.

DiMaggio, P.J., & Powell, W.W. (1983). The iron cage revisited: Institutional isomorphism and collective rationality in organizational field. *American Sociological Review*, *35*, 147-160.

Donaldson, A., Leggett, S., & Finch, C.F. (2012). Sports policy development and implementation in context: Researching and understanding the perceptions of community end-users. *International Review for the Sociology of Sport*, *47*(6), 743-760.

Duncan, R.B. (1972). Characteristics of organizational environments and perceived environmental uncertainty. *Administrative Science Quarterly*, *17*, 313-327.

Eime, R.M., Payne, W.R., & Harvey, J.T. (2008). Making sporting clubs healthy and welcoming environments: A strategy to increase participation. *Journal of Science and Medicine in Sport*, *11*(2), 146-154.

Eitzen, S.D., & Yetman, N.R. (1972). Managerial change, longevity, and organizational effectiveness. *Administrative Science Quarterly*, *17*, 110-116.

Fahlén, J., Eliasson, I., & Wickman, K. (2015). Resisting self-regulation: An analysis of sport policy programme making and implementation in Sweden. *International Journal of Sport Policy and Politics*, *7*(3), 391-406.

Freedman, W. (1987). *Professional sports and antitrust.* New York, NY: Quorum Books.

Freeman, R.E. (1984). *Strategic management: A stakeholder approach*. Boston, MA: Pitman.

Gamson, W.A., & Scotch, N.A. (1964). Scapegoating in baseball. *American Journal of Sociology*, *70*, 69-72.

Geehern, C. (1991, August 8). Balls. *New England Business*, 40-45, 63.

Gruneau, R. (1983). *Class, sports and social development*. Amherst, MA: University of Massachusetts Press.

Grusky, O. (1963). Managerial succession and organizational effectiveness. *American Journal of Sociology*, *69*, 21-31.

Hall, M.H., Andrukow, A., Barr, C., Brock, K., de Wit, M., Embuldeniya, D., et al. (2003). *The capacity to serve: A qualitative study of the challenges facing Canada's nonprofit and voluntary organizations.* Toronto, ON: Canadian Centre for Philanthropy.

Hall, R.H. (1982). *Organizations: Structure and process* (3rd. ed.). Englewood Cliffs, NJ: Prentice Hall.

Hannan, M.T., & Freeman, J. (1977). The population ecology of organizations. *American Journal of Sociology*, *82*, 929-964.

Hannan, M.T., & Freeman, J. (1988). Density dependence in the growth of organizational populations. In G.R. Carroll (Ed.), *Ecological models of organizations* (pp. 7-32). Cambridge, MA: Ballinger.

Harrison, J.S., & St. John, C.H. (1996). Managing and partnering with external stakeholders. *Academy of Management Executive*, *10*, 46-60.

Hawley, A.H. (1981). Human ecology: Persistence and change. *American Behavioral Scientist*, *24*, 423-444.

Hill, C.R. (1992). *Olympic politics*. Manchester, UK: Manchester University Press.

Houlihan, B. (1991). *The government and politics of sport.* London, UK: Routledge & Kegan Paul.

ILAM. (2005). About us. Retrieved from www.ilam.co.uk/aboutus.asp

Improving your marketing game. (1987, November). *Athletic Business,* 16.

Inman, P. (2018, December 3). UK manufacturers stockpile goods ahead of Brexit. *Guardian*, Retrieved from https://www.theguardian.com/business/2018/dec/03/uk-manufacturers-stockpile-goods-ahead-of-brexit

Jemison, D.B. (1984). The importance of boundary spanning roles in strategic decision making. *Journal of Management Studies, 21,* 131-152.

Jones, G.J., Edwards, M., Bocarro, J.N., Bunds, K.S., & Smith, J.W. (2017). Collaborative advantages: The role of interorganizational partnerships for youth sport nonprofit organizations. *Journal of Sport Management*, *31*(2), 148-160.

Jones, G.J., Wegner, C.E., Bunds, K.S., Edwards, M.B., & Bocarro, J.N. (2018). Examining the environmental characteristics of shared leadership in a sport-for-development organization. *Journal of Sport Management*, *32*(2), 82-95.

Kikulis, L.M. (2000). Continuity and change in governance and decision making in national sport organizations: Institutional explanations. *Journal of Sport Management*, *14*, 293-320.

Lawrence, P.R., and Lorsch, J. (1967). *Organization and environment.* Boston, MA: Harvard Graduate School of Business Administration.

Leber, R. (2015, July 31). A winter Olympics in snowless Beijing will be an environmental disaster. *The New Republic*, Retrieved from https://newrepublic.com/article/122438/winter-olympics-snowless-beijing-will-be-environmental-disaster

Leifer, R., & Huber, G.P. (1977). Relations among perceived environmental uncertainty, organizational structure, and boundary spanning behavior. *Administrative Science Quarterly, 22,* 235-247.

Lenz, R.T., & Engledow, J.L. (1986). Environmental analysis units and strategic decision making: A field study of selected "leading edge" corporations. *Strategic Management Journal*, *7*, 69-89.

Macintosh, D., Bedecki, T., & Franks, C.E.S. (1987). *Sport and politics in Canada.* Kingston, ON: McGill-Queen's University Press.

Macintosh, D., & Whitson, D.J. (1990). *The game planners: Transforming Canada's sport system*. Kingston, ON: McGill-Queen's University Press.

Martin, C.L. (1990). The employee/customer interface: An empirical investigation of employee behaviors and customer perceptions. *Journal of Sport Management*, *4*, 1-20.

May, T., Harris, S., & Collins, M. (2013). Implementing community sport policy: Understanding the variety of voluntary club types and their attitudes to policy. *International Journal of Sport Policy and Politics*, *5*(3), 397-419.

Meyer, J.W., & Rowan, B. (1977). Institutionalized organizations: Formal structure as myth and ceremony. *American Journal of Sociology*, *83*, 340-363.

Miles, R.E., & Snow, C.C. (1978). *Organizational strategy, structure, and process*. New York, NY: McGraw-Hill.

Mintzberg, H. (1979). *The structuring of organizations*. Englewood Cliffs, NJ: Prentice Hall.

Misener, K., & Doherty, A. (2013). Understanding capacity through the processes and outcomes of interorganizational relationships in nonprofit community sport organizations. *Sport Management Review*, *16*(2), 135-147.

Mitchell, R.K., Agle, B.R., & Wood, D.J. (1997). Toward a theory of stakeholder identification and salience: Defining the principle of who and what really counts. *Academy of Management Review*, *22*, 853-886.

Mizruchi, M.S., & Stearns, L.B. (1988). A longitudinal study of the formation of interlocking directorates. *Administrative Science Quarterly*, *33*, 194-210.

Oliver, C. (1988). The collective strategy framework: An application to competing predictions of isomorphism. *Administrative Science Quarterly, 33*, 543-561.

Oliver, C. (1991). Strategic responses to institutional processes. *Academy of Management Review*, *16*, 145-179.

Pfeffer, J., & Davis-Blake, A. (1986). Administrative succession and organizational performance: How administrator experience mediates the succession effect. *Academy of Management Journal*, *29*, 72-83.

Pfeffer, J., & Salancik, G. (1978). *The external control of organizations: A resource-dependence perspective*. New York, NY: Harper & Row.

Porter, M.E. (1980). *Competitive strategy*. New York, NY: Free Press.

Post, J.E., Preston, L.E., & Sachs, S. (2002). Managing the extended enterprise. The new stakeholder view. *California Management Review*, *45*, 6-28.

Pugh, P. (1989). *The Belfry: The making of a dream*. Trowbridge, Wilts, UK: Cambridge Business.

Richards, B. (1986, December 1). Brunswick Corp. plans to acquire Ray Industries. *Wall Street Journal*, 15.

Rittel, H.W., & Webber, M.M. (1974). Wicked problems. *Man-made Futures*, *26*(1), 272-280.

Rosenberg, E. (2018, May 30). "You can't win this one," Trump told NFL owners about anthem protests. They believed him. *Washington Post*, Retrieved from https://www.washingtonpost.com/news/early-lead/wp/2018/05/30/you-cant-win-this-one-trump-told-nfl-owners-about-anthem-protests-they-believed-him/?noredirect=on&utm_term=.aea1be5972e8

Sack, A.L., & Staurowsky, E.J. (1998). *College athletes for hire: The evolution and legacy of the NCAA's amateur myth*. Westport, CT: Praeger.

Silk, M.L., Slack, T., & Amis, J. (2000). Bread, butter and gravy: An institutional approach to televised sport production. *Culture, Sport, Society*, *3*, 1-21.

Skow, J. (1985, December 2). Using the old Bean. *Sports Illustrated*, 84-88, 91-96.

Slack, T., Bentz, L., & Wood, D. (1985). Planning for your organization's future. *CAHPER Journal, 51*, 13-17.

Slack, T., Berrett, T., & Mistry, K. (1994). Rational planning systems as a source of organizational conflict. *International Review for the Sociology of Sport*, *29*, 317-328.

Slack, T., & Hinings, C.R. (1992). Understanding change in national sport organizations: An integration of theoretical perspectives. *Journal of Sport Management, 6*, 114-132.

Slack, T., & Hinings, C.R. (1994). Institutional pressures and isomorphic change: An empirical test. *Organization Studies, 15,* 803-827.

Slack, T., & Parent, M.M. (2006). *Understanding sport organizations: The application of organization theory* (2nd ed.). Champaign, IL: Human Kinetics.

Spaaij, R., Magee, J., Farquharson, K., Gorman, S., Jeanes, R., Lusher, D., & Storr, R. (2016). Diversity work in community sport organizations: Commitment, resistance and institutional change. *International Review for the Sociology of Sport*, *53*(3), 278-295.

Sparks, R. (1992). "Delivering the male": Sports, Canadian television, and the making of TSN. *Canadian Journal of Communication*, *17*, 319-342.

Starbuck, W.H. (1976). Organizations and their environments. In M.D. Dunnette (Ed.), *Handbook of industrial and organizational psychology* (pp. 1069-1123). Chicago, IL: Rand McNally.

Staw, B.M., & Szwajkowski, E. (1975). The scarcity-munificence component of organizational environments and the commission of illegal acts. *Administrative Science Quarterly*, *20*, 345-354.

Steers, R.M. (1977). *Organizational effectiveness: A behavioral view*. Santa Monica, CA: Goodyear.

Stern, R.N. (1979). The development of an interorganizational control network: The case of intercollegiate athletics. *Administrative Science Quarterly*, *24*, 242-266.

Taylor, P., Barrett, D., & Nichols, G. (2009). CCPR survey of sports clubs 2009. Project Report. Central Council of Physical Recreation.

Thibault, L., Frisby, W., & Kikulis, L. (1999). Interorganizational linkages in the delivery of local leisure services in Canada: Responding to economic, political and social pressures. *Managing Leisure*, *4*, 125-141.

Thompson, J.D. (1967). *Organizations in action*. New York, NY: McGraw-Hill.

Tolbert, P.S. (1985). Institutional environments and resource dependence: Sources of administrative structure in institutions of higher education. *Administrative Science Quarterly*, *30*, 1-13.

Tolbert, P.S., & Zucker, L.G. (1983). Institutional sources of change in the formal structure of organizations: The diffusion of civil service reforms, 1880-1935. *Administrative Science Quarterly*, *23*, 22-39.

Transparency Market Research (2016). Licensed sports merchandise market to reach US $48.17 billion by 2024. *PR Newswire*, Retrieved from https://www.prnewswire.com/news-releases/licensed-sports-merchandise-market-to-reach-us4817-billion-by-2024---a-new-research-report-by-transparency-market-research-597749011.html

Tung, R.L. (1979). Dimensions of organizational environments: An exploratory study of their impact on organization structure. *Academy of Management Journal*, *22*, 672-693.

Tushman, M.L., & Scanlan, T.J. (1981a). Characteristics and external orientations of boundary spanning individuals: Part I. *Academy of Management Journal, 24,* 83-98.

Tushman, M.L., & Scanlan, T.J. (1981b). Boundary spanning individuals: Their role in information transfer and their antecedents: Part II. *Academy of Management Journal, 24,* 289-305.

Ulrich, D.R. (1987). The population perspective: Review, critique, and relevance. *Human Relations*, *40*, 137-152.

Ulrich, D.R., & Barney, J. (1984). Perspectives in organizations: Resource dependence, efficiency, and population. *Academy of Management Review*, *3*, 471-481.

Wholey, D.R., & Brittain, J.W. (1986). Organizational ecology: Findings and implications. *Academy of Management Review*, *11*, 513-533.

Wicker, P., & Breuer, C. (2011). Scarcity of resources in German non-profit sport clubs. *Sport Management Review*, *14*(2), 188-201.

Wicker, P., & Breuer, C. (2013). Understanding the importance of organizational resources to explain organizational problems: Evidence from nonprofit sport clubs in Germany. *VOLUNTAS:*

International Journal of Voluntary and Nonprofit Organizations, *24*(2), 461-484.

Witt, C.E. (1989, March). Reebok's distribution on fast track. *Material Handling Engineering*, 43-45, 48.

Zeigler, E.F. (1985). Understanding the immediate managerial environment in sport and physical education. *Quest, 37*, 166-175.

Zucker, L.G. (1983). Organizations as institutions. In S.B. Bacharach (Ed.), *Advances in organizational theory and research* (Vol. 2, pp. 1-43). Greenwich, CT: JAI Press.

Zucker, L.G. (1987). Institutional theories of organization. *Annual Review of Sociology*, *13*, 443-464.

Zucker, L.G. (1988). *Institutional patterns and organizations*. Cambridge, MA: Ballinger.

Chapter 5

Albers, S., Wohlgezogen, F., & Zajac, E.J. (2016). Strategic alliance structures: An organization design perspective. *Journal of Management*, *42*(3), 582-614. doi:10.1177/0149206313488209

Aldrich, H.E. (1975). Reaction to Donaldson's note. *Administrative Science Quarterly*, *20*, 457-460.

Allen, E. (2014). Sir Dave Brailsford at British Cycling - A Career Retrospective. Retrieved from www.britishcycling.org.uk/article/gbr20140411-British-Cycling—The-Brailsford-years-0

Amis, J., & Slack, T. (1996). The size-structure relationship in voluntary sport organizations. *Journal of Sport Management, 10,* 76-86.

Argyris, C. (1964). *Integrating the individual and the organization*. New York, NY: Wiley.

Ashkenas, R.N., Ulrich, D., Todd, J., & Kerr, S. (2002). *The boundaryless organization: Breaking the chains of organizational structure* (Revised and updated ed.). San Francisco, CA: Jossey-Bass.

Australian Olympic Committee. (n.d.). Australian Olympic Committee: Home. Retrieved from http://olympics.com.au/

Bayle, E., & Robinson, L. (2007). A framework for understanding the performance of national governing bodies of sport. *European Sport Management Quarterly*, *7*(3), 249-268. doi:10.1080/16184740701511037

Blau, P.M., & Schoenherr, R.A. (1971). *The structure of organizations*. New York, NY: Basic Books.

Brackenridge, C. (2001). *Spoilsports: Understanding and preventing sexual exploitation in sport (ethics and sport)*. London, UK: Routledge.

Braverman, H. (1974). *Labor and monopoly capital*. New York, NY: Monthly Review Press.

Brettman, A. (2012). Nike sale of Umbro could be viewed as $357 million mistake; but was it? Retrieved from www.oregonlive.com/playbooks-profits/index.ssf/2012/10/nike_sale_of_umbro_could_be_vi.html

Brooke, M.Z. (1984). *Centralization and autonomy*. London, UK: Holt, Rinehart & Winston.

Brown, R.J. (1990). The management of human resources in the leisure industry. In I.P. Henry (Ed.), *Management & planning in the leisure industries,* 70-96. Basingstoke, Hants, UK: Macmillan Educational.

Brunet, A.P., & New, S. (2003). Kaizen in Japan: An empirical study. *International Journal of Operations & Production Management*, *23*(12), 1426-1446. doi:10.1108/01443570310506704658

Bucher, R. (2018). Why doesn't anyone want to play with LeBron anymore? Retrieved from https://bleacherreport.com/articles/2808589-why-doesnt-anyone-want-to-play-with-lebron-anymore?utm_source=twitter.com&utm_medium=referral&utm_campaign=programming-national

Canada West Ski Areas Association. (n.d.). Alpine responsibility code. Retrieved from https://cwsaa.org/policy/alpine-responsibility-code/

Carlisle, H.M. (1974). A contingency approach to decentralization. *S.A.M. Advanced Management Journal*, *39*, 9-18.

Child, J. (1972). Organization structure and strategies of control: A replication of the Aston study. *Administrative Science Quarterly, 17,* 163-177.

Child, J. (1975). Comments on Donaldson's note. *Administrative Science Quarterly, 20,* 456.

City of Winnipeg. (1990). *Sports services policy*. Winnipeg, Manitoba: City of Winnipeg Parks and Recreation Department.

Clegg, S., & Dunkerley, D. (1980). *Organization, class, and control*. London, UK: Routledge & Kegan Paul.

ClubCorp. (n.d.). Who we are - history & facts. Retrieved from www.clubcorp.com/Who-We-Are/History-Facts

Crocker, O., Chiu, J., & Charney, C. (1984). *Quality circles*. New York, NY: Metheun.

Cummings, L.L., & Berger, C.J. (1976). Organization structure: How does it influence attitudes and performance? *Organizational Dynamics, 5,* 34-49.

Cunningham, G.B., & Rivera, C.A. (2001). Structural designs within American intercollegiate athletic departments. *The International Journal of Organizational Analysis, 9*(4), 369-390. doi:10.1108/eb028941

Cuskelly, G. (2004). Volunteer retention in community sport organisations. *European Sport Management Quarterly*, *4*(2), 59-76. doi:10.1080/16184740408737469

Daft, R.L. (1992). *Organization theory and design* (4th ed.). St. Paul, MN: West.

De Waegeneer, E., Devisch, I., & Willem, A. (2017). Ethical codes in sports organizations: An empirical study on determinants of effectiveness. *Ethics & Behavior*, *27*(4), 261-282. doi:10.1080/10508422.2016.1172011

DiMaggio, P.J., & Powell, W.W. (1983). The iron cage revisited: Institutional isomorphism and collective rationality in organizational fields. *American Sociological Review*, *48*(2), 147. doi:10.2307/2095101

Donaldson, L. (1975). Organizational status and the measurement of centralization. *Administrative Science Quarterly, 20,* 453-456.

Donaldson, L., & Warner, M. (1974). Structure of organizations in occupational interest associations. *Human Relations, 27,* 721-738.

Filley, A.C., House, R.J., & Kerr, S. (1976). *Managerial process and organizational behavior* (2nd ed.). Glenview, IL: Scott Foresman.

Frisby, W. (1985). A conceptual framework for measuring the organizational structure and context of voluntary leisure service organizations. *Society and Leisure, 8,* 605-613.

Frisby, W. (1986). The organizational structure and effectiveness of voluntary organizations: The case of Canadian national sport governing bodies. *Journal of Park and Recreation Administration, 4,* 61-74.

Gerth, H.H., & Mills, C.W. (1946). *From Max Weber*. New York, NY: Oxford University Press.

Gouldner, A.W. (1954). *Patterns of industrial bureaucracy*. New York, NY: Free Press.

Greenwood, R., & Hinings, C.R. (1976). Centralization revisited. *Administrative Science Quarterly, 21,* 151-155.

Grinyer, P.H., & Yasai-Ardekani, M. (1980). Dimensions of organizational structure: A critical replication. *Academy of Management Journal, 23,* 405-421.

Hage, J. (1965). An axiomatic theory of organizations. *Administrative Science Quarterly, 10,* 289-320.

Hage, J. (1980). *Theories of organizations.* New York, NY: Wiley.

Hage, J., & Aiken, M. (1967a). Program change and organizational properties: A comparative analysis. *American Journal of Sociology, 72,* 503-519.

Hage, J., & Aiken, M. (1967b). Relationship of centralization to other structural properties. *Administrative Science Quarterly, 12,* 72-91.

Hage, J., & Aiken, M. (1970). *Social change in complex organizations.* New York, NY: Random House.

Hall, R.H. (1963). The concept of bureaucracy. *American Sociological Review, 69,* 32-40.

Hall, R.H. (1968). Professionalization and bureaucratization. *American Sociological Review, 33,* 92-104.

Hall, R.H. (1982). *Organizations: Structure and process* (3rd ed.). Englewood Cliffs, NJ: Prentice Hall.

Hall, R.H., & Tittle, C.R. (1966). Bureaucracy and its correlates. *American Journal of Sociology, 72,* 267-272.

Hall, R.H., Haas, J.E., & Johnson, N.J. (1967). Organizational size, complexity, and formalization. *American Sociological Review, 32,* 903-912.

Harrell, E. (2015). How 1% performance improvements led to Olympic gold. Retrieved https://hbr.org/2015/10/how-1-performance-improvements-led-to-olympic-gold

Harris, B. (2017). Matt Carroll: The man tasked with restructuring the Australian Olympic Committee. Retrieved from www.theguardian.com/sport/2017/sep/10/matt-carroll-the-man-tasked-with-restructuring-the-australian-olympic-committee

Hinings, C.R., & Lee, G.L. (1971). Dimensions of organization structure and their context: A replication. *Sociology*, *5*, 83-93.

Holdaway, E.A., Newberry, J.F., Hickson, D.J., & Heron, R.P. (1975). Dimensions of organizations in complex societies: The educational sector. *Administrative Science Quarterly, 20,* 37-58.

Hypebeast. (2015, January 29). *Process: The Adidas Ultra Boost AKA "The World's Best Running Shoe"* [Video file]. Retrieved from www.youtube.com/watch?v=4J_kxwT9zX4

Hytner, M. (2017). AOC promises overhaul after review says it is "out of step" with Olympic ideals. Retrieved from www.theguardian.com/sport/2017/aug/24/aoc-promises-overhaul-after-review-says-it-is-out-of-step-with-olympic-ideals

Jakobsen, S.-E., Gammelsaeter, H., Fløysand, A., & Nese, G. (2005). *The formalization of club organization in Norwegian professional football.* Retrieved from brage.bibsys.no/xmlui/bitstream/handle/11250/165526/A83_05.pdf?sequence=1&isAllowed=y

Jones, B. (2011). *The ghost runner: The tragedy of the man they couldn't stop.* Edinburgh, UK: Mainstream Publishing.

Kell, J. (2017, June 15). Nike to cut about 1,400 jobs globally. *Fortune*, Retrieved from http://fortune.com/2017/06/15/nike-to-cut-1400-jobs-globally/

Kikulis, L., Slack, T., & Hinings, C.R. (1995). Does decision making make a difference: Patterns of change within Canadian national sport organizations. *Journal of Sport Management, 9,* 273-299.

Kikulis, L., Slack, T., Hinings, C.R., & Zimmermann, A. (1989). A structural taxonomy of amateur sport organizations. *Journal of Sport Management, 3,* 129-150.

Lawler, E., & Mohrman, S. (1985). Quality circles: After the fad. *Harvard Business Review, 63,* 64-71.

Lawrence, P.R., and Lorsch, J. (1967). *Organization and environment.* Boston, MA: Harvard Graduate School of Business Administration.

Likert, R. (1967). *The human organization.* New York, NY: McGraw-Hill.

Lincoln, J., & Zeitz, G. (1980). Organizational properties from aggregate data. *American Sociological Review, 45,* 391-405.

Macintosh, D., & Whitson, D.J. (1990). *The game planners: Transforming Canada's sport system.* Montreal & Kingston, ON: McGill-Queen's University Press.

Mallen, C., Stevens, J., Adams, L., & McRoberts, S. (2010). The assessment of the environmental performance of an international multi-sport event. *European Sport Management Quarterly, 10*(1), 97-122. doi:10.1080/16184740903460488

Manning, J., & Rogoway, M. (2017, June 15). Nike will eliminate 1,400 jobs, restructure. *The Oregonian*, Retrieved from www.oregonlive.com/business/index.ssf/2017/06/nike_will_eliminate_1400_jobs.html

Mansfield, L., & Killick, L. (2012). The UK Netball Superleague: A case study of franchising in elite women's sport organisations. *European Sport Management Quarterly*, *12*(5), 545-567. doi:10.1080/16184742.2012.734525

Marler, J.H., & Parry, E. (2015). Human resource management, strategic involvement and e-HRM technology. *The International Journal of Human Resource Management*, *27*, 2233-2253. doi:10.1080/09585192.2015.1091980

Merton, R.K. (1957). *Social theory and social structure*. London, UK: Free Press of Glencoe.

Miller, K.I., & Monge, P.R. (1986). Participation, satisfaction, and productivity: A meta-analytic review. *Academy of Management Journal, 29,* 727-753.

Minard, J. (2012, February 4). London 2012: Games Makers attend Wembley training event. *BBC News*. Retrieved from www.bbc.co.uk/news/uk-16874424

Mintzberg, H. (1979). *The structuring of organizations*. Englewood Cliffs, NJ: Prentice Hall.

Nagel, S., Schlesinger, T., Bayle, E., & Giauque, D. (2015). Professionalisation of sport federations – A multi-level framework for analysing forms, causes and consequences. *European Sport Management Quarterly*, *15*(4), 407-433. doi:10.1080/16184742.2015.1062990

Nichols, G., & James, M. (2008). One size does not fit all: Implications of sports club diversity for their effectiveness as a policy tool and for government support. *Managing Leisure, 13*(2), 104-114. doi:10.1080/13606710801933461

Nichols, G., Wicker, P., Cuskelly, G., & Breuer, C. (2015). Measuring the formalization of community sports clubs: Findings from the UK, Germany and Australia. *International Journal of Sport Policy and Politics*, *7*(2), 283-300. doi:10.1080/19406940.2015.1006661

Nike. (2017). NIKE, Inc. announces new consumer direct offense: A faster pipeline to serve consumers personally, at scale. Retrieved from https://news.nike.com/news/nike-consumer-direct-offense

Pennings, J.M. (1973). Measures of organizational structure: A methodological note. *American Journal of Sociology, 79,* 686-704.

Perrow, C. (1972). *Complex organizations: A critical essay*. Glenview, IL: Scott Foresman.

Pertusa-Ortega, E.M., Zaragoza-Sáez, P., & Claver-Cortés, E. (2010). Can formalization, complexity, and centralization influence knowledge performance? *Journal of Business Research*, *63*(3), 310-320. doi:10.1016/j.jbusres.2009.03.015

Pugh, D.S., Hickson, D.J., Hinings, C.R., & Turner, C. (1968). Dimensions of organizational structure. *Administrative Science Quarterly, 13,* 65-105.

Relvas, H., Littlewood, M., Nesti, M., Gilbourne, D., & Richardson, D. (2010). Organizational structures and working practices in elite European professional football clubs: Understanding the relationship between youth and professional domains. *European Sport Management Quarterly*, *10*(2), 165-187. doi:10.1080/16184740903559891

Robbins, S. (1990). *Organization theory: Structure, design and applications* (3rd ed.). Englewood Cliffs, NJ: Prentice Hall.

Sandhu, S., & Kulik, C.T. (2018). Shaping and being shaped: How organizational structure and managerial discretion co-evolve in new managerial roles. *Administrative Science Quarterly*. doi:10.1177/0001839218778018

Schriesheim, J.F., Von Glinow, M.A., & Kerr, S. (1977). Professionals in bureaucracies: A structural alternative. In P.C. Nystrom & W.H. Starbuck (Eds.), *Prescriptive models of organizations* (pp. 55-69). Amsterdam, Netherlands: North-Holland.

Simon, H.A. (1945). *Administrative behavior*. New York, NY: Macmillan.

Slack, T. (1991). The training of leisure managers. In *Proceedings of the CESU Conference* (pp. 63-83). Sheffield, UK: FISU.

Slack, T., & Hinings, C.R. (Eds.) (1987a). *The organization and administration of sport*. London, ON: Sport Dynamics.

Slack, T., & Hinings, C.R. (1987b). Planning and organizational change: A conceptual framework for the analysis of amateur sport organizations. *Canadian Journal of Sport Sciences, 12,* 185-193.

Slack, T., & Hinings, C.R. (1992). Understanding change in national sport organizations: An integration of theoretical perspectives. *Journal of Sport Management, 6,* 114-132.

Snow Valley. (n.d.). Safety on the slopes. Retrieved from www.snowvalley.ca/ski-hill/the-hill/faq.php

Special Olympics Oregon. (2018). *2018 USA games – Team Oregon coach job description & code of conduct*. Oregon. Retrieved from www.soor.org/Upload/Documents/2018_Team_Oregon_Coach_Job_Description_&_Code_of_Conduct.pdf

Stotlar, D.K. (2000). Vertical integration in sport. *Journal of Sport Management, 11,* 1-7.

Swimming Natation Canada. (2015). *Terms of reference: Sport development committee*. Retrieved from www.swimming.ca/content/uploads/2015/05/sport-development-committee11.pdf

Symonds, W. G. (1989, June). Driving to become the IBM of golf. *Business Week*, 100-101.

Tarrant, J. (1979). *The ghost runner: The autobiography of John Tarrant (1932-1975)*. Rochester, UK: Athletics Weekly.

Theodoraki, E.I., & Henry, I.P. (1994). Organizational structures and context in British national governing bodies of sport. *International Review for the Sociology of Sport, 29,* 243-263.

Thibault, L., Slack, T., & Hinings, C.R. (1991). Professionalism, structures and systems: The impact of professional staff on voluntary sport organizations. *International Review for the Sociology of Sport, 26,* 83-99.

Thompson, J.D. (1967). *Organizations in action*. New York, NY: McGraw-Hill.

Thompson, V.A. (1961). *Modern organization*. New York, NY: Knopf.

Thurston, A. (2017). *An analysis of the implementation of Clubmark and two associated policies in boxing, swimming and rugby union* (Unpublished doctoral thesis). Loughborough University, Leicestershire, UK. Retrieved from https://dspace.lboro.ac.uk/2134/25521

Urwick, L.F. (1938). *Scientific principles and organization*. New York, NY: American Management Association.

Van de Ven, A.H., & Ferry, D. (1980). *Measuring and assessing organizations*. New York, NY: Wiley.

Walton, E.J. (1981). The comparison of measures of organization structure. *Academy of Management Review, 6,* 155-160.

Zeigler, E.F. (1989). Proposed creed and code of professional ethics for the North American Society for Sport Management. *Journal of Sport Management, 3,* 2-4.

Chapter 6

Albers, S., Wohlgezogen, F., & Zajac, E.J. (2016). Strategic alliance structures: An organization design perspective. *Journal of Management*, *42*(3), 582-614. doi:10.1177/0149206313488209

Alfred's Sports Shop. (n.d.). About Alfred's. Retrieved from www.alfredssportsshop.com/about.html#

Amis, J., & Slack, T. (2016). Organisation Theory and the Management of Sport Organisations. In B. Houlihan & D. Malcolm (Eds.), *Sport and society: A student introduction* (3rd ed., pp. 312-341). London, UK: SAGE.

Andrews, R., & Boyne, G.A. (2014). Task complexity, organization size, and administrative intensity: The case of UK universities. *Public Administration*, *92*(3), 656-672. doi:10.1111/padm.12078

Arnold, R., & Fletcher, D. (2012). A research synthesis and taxonomic classification of the organizational stressors encountered by sport performers. *Journal of Sport & Exercise Psychology*, *34*, 397-429. Retrieved from https://journals.humankinetics.com/doi/pdf/10.1123/jsep.34.3.397

Ashkenas, R.N., Ulrich, D., Todd, J., & Kerr, S. (2002). *The boundaryless organization: Breaking the chains of organizational structure* (Revised and updated ed.). San Francisco, CA: Jossey-Bass.

Babiak, K. (2007). Determinants of interorganizational relationships: The case of a Canadian nonprofit sport organization. *Journal of Sport Management*, *21*, 338-376. Retrieved from https://journals.humankinetics.com/doi/pdf/10.1123/jsm.21.3.338

Blau, P.M., & Scott, W.R. (1962). *Formal organizations*. San Francisco, CA: Chandler.

Burns, T., & Stalker, G.M. (1961). *The management of innovation*. London, UK: Tavistock.

Burton, R.M., Obel, B., & Håkonsson, D.D. (2015). *Organizational design: A step-by-step approach* (3rd ed.). Cambridge, UK: Cambridge University Press.

Byers, T. (2009). Research on voluntary sport organisations: Established themes and emerging opportunities. *International Journal of Sport Management and Marketing*, *6*(2), 215. doi:10.1504/IJSMM.2009.028803

Byers, T., Slack, T., & Parent, M. (2012). *Key concepts in sport management*. London, UK: SAGE.

Canada Games. (2001). 2001 Canada Summer Games in London, ON. Retrieved from https://canadagames.ca/2001-canada-summer-games-london

Carper, W.B., & Snizek, W.E. (1980). The nature and types of organizational taxonomies: An overview. *Academy of Management Review*, *5*, 65-75.

Chappelet, J.-L., & Parent, M.M. (2015). The (wide) world of sports events. In M.M. Parent & J.-L. Chappelet (Eds.), *Routledge Handbook of Sports Event Management* (pp. 1-17). London, UK: Routledge.

Chelladurai, P. (1985). *Sport management: Macro perspectives*. London, ON: Sports Dynamics.

Chelladurai, P. (1987). Multidimensionality and multiple perspectives of organizational effectiveness. *Journal of Sport Management*, *1*, 37-47.

Chelladurai, P. (1992). A classification of sport and physical activity services: Implications for sport management. *Journal of Sport Management*, *6*, 38-51.

Child, J. (1973). Parkinson's progress: Accounting for the number of specialists in organizations. *Administrative Science Quarterly, 18*, 328-348.

Crompton, J. (2004). Beyond economic impact: An alternative rationale for the public subsidy of major league sports facilities. *Journal of Sport Management, 18*(1), 40-58. doi:10.1123/jsm.18.1.40

Doherty, A. (2009). The volunteer legacy of a major sport event. *Journal of Policy Research in Tourism, Leisure and Events*, *1*(3), 185-207. doi:10.1080/19407960903204356

Forbes. (n.d.). WL Gore & Associates. Retrieved from www.forbes.com/companies/wl-gore-associates/

Galbraith, J. (1973). *Designing complex organizations*. London, UK: Addison-Wesley.

Gordon, W.C., & Babchuk, N. (1959). A typology of voluntary organizations. *American Sociological Review*, *24*, 22-29.

Gore. (n.d.). Our culture. Retrieved from www.gore.com/about/culture

Gov.uk. (2014). Glasgow 2014: XX Commonwealth Games. Retrieved from www.gov.uk/government/news/glasgow-2014-xx-commonwealth-games

Guttmann, A. (1978). *From ritual to record*. New York, NY: Columbia University Press.

Haas, J.E., Hall, R.H., & Johnson, N.J. (1966). Towards an empirically derived taxonomy of organizations. In R.V. Bowers (Ed.), *Studies on behavior in organizations* (pp. 157-180). Athens, GA: University of Georgia Press.

Harris, S., Mori, K., & Collins, M. (2009). Great expectations: Voluntary sports clubs and their role in delivering national policy for English sport. *VOLUNTAS: International Journal of Voluntary and Nonprofit Organizations*, *20*(4), 405-423. doi:10.1007/s11266-009-9095-y

Hinings, C.R., & Slack, T. (1987). The dynamics of quadrennial plan implementation in national sport organizations. In T. Slack & C.R. Hinings (Eds.), *The organization and administration of sport*. London, ON: Sport Dynamics.

Houlihan, B., & Lindsey, I. (2012). *Sport Policy in Britain*. Abingdon, UK: Routledge.

Jacoby, A. (1965). Some correlates of instrumental and expressive orientations to associational membership. *Sociological Inquiry*, *35*, 163-175.

Johnson, T.J. (1972). *Professions and power*. Basingstoke, UK: Macmillan Education.

Jones, G.R. (2013). *Organizational theory, design, and change* (7th ed.). Boston, MA: Pearson.

Kikulis, L., Slack, T., Hinings, C.R., & Zimmermann, A. (1989). A structural taxonomy of amateur sport organizations. *Journal of Sport Management*, *3*, 129-150.

Kimberly, J.R. (1976). Organizational size and the structuralist perspective: A review critique, and proposal. *Administrative Science Quarterly, 21,* 571-597.

Larson, M. (1977). *The rise of professionalism: A sociological analysis*. Berkeley, CA: University of California Press.

Lawson, H.A. (1984). *Invitation to physical education*. Champaign, IL: Human Kinetics.

Lorgnier, N., & Su, C.-J. (2014). Considering coopetition strategies in sport tourism networks: A look at the nonprofit nautical sports clubs on the northern coast of France. *European Sport Management Quarterly*, *14*(1), 87-109. doi:10.1080/16184742.2013.876436

Macintosh, D., & Whitson, D.J. (1990). *The game planners: Transforming Canada's sport system*. Montreal & Kingston, ON: McGill-Queen's University Press.

McKelvey, B. (1975). Guidelines for the empirical classification of organizations. *Administrative Science Quarterly*, *20*, 509-525.

McKelvey, B. (1978). Organizational systematics: Taxonomic lessons from biology. *Management Science*, *24*, 1428-1440.

McKelvey, B. (1982). *Organizational systematics*. Los Angeles, CA: University of California Press.

Miller, D., & Friesen, P. (1984). *Organizations: A quantum view*. Englewood Cliffs, NJ: Prentice Hall.

Miller, G.A. (1987). Meta-analysis and the culture free hypothesis. *Organization Studies, 4,* 309-325.

Mills, P.K., & Margulies, N. (1980). Toward a core typology of service organizations. *Academy of Management Review*, *5*, 255-265.

Mintzberg, H. (1979). *The structuring of organizations*. Englewood Cliffs, NJ: Prentice Hall.

Mintzberg, H. (1980). Structure in 5's: A synthesis of the research on organization design. *Management Science 26*(3), 322-341. doi:10.1287/mnsc.26.3.322

Mintzberg, H. (1981). Organizational design: Fashion or fit? *Harvard Business Review*, *59*, 103-115.

Mintzberg, H. (1984). A typology of organizational structure. In D. Miller & P. Friesen (Eds.), *Organizations: A quantum view* (pp. 68-86). Englewood Cliffs, NJ: Prentice Hall.

Mintzberg, H. (2003). The structuring of organizations. In H. Mintzberg, J. Lampel, J.B. Quinn, & S. Ghoshal (Eds.), *The strategy process: Concepts, contexts, cases* (4th ed., pp. 209-226). Englewood Cliffs, NJ: Prentice Hall.

Misener, K.E., & Misener, L. (2017). Grey is the new black: Advancing understanding of new organizational forms and blurring sector boundaries in sport management. *Journal of Sport Management*, *31*(2), 125-132. doi:10.1123/jsm.2017-0030

Nagel, S., Schlesinger, T., Bayle, E., & Giauque, D. (2015). Professionalisation of sport federations – A multi-level framework for analysing forms, causes and consequences. *European Sport Management Quarterly*, *15*(4), 407-433. doi:10.1080/16184742.2015.1062990

Nichols, G., & James, M. (2008). One size does not fit all: Implications of sports club diversity for their effectiveness as a policy tool and for government support. *Managing Leisure*, *13*(2), 104-114. doi:10.1080/13606710801933461

Nichols, G., Taylor, P., James, M., Holmes, K., King, L., & Garrett, R. (2005). Pressures on the UK voluntary sport sector. *VOLUNTAS: International Journal of Voluntary and Nonprofit Organizations*, *16*(1), 33-50. doi:10.1007/s11266-005-3231-0

Parsons, T. (1956). Suggestions for a sociological approach to the theory of organizations. *Administrative Science Quarterly*, *1*, 63-85.

Perrow, C. (1967). A framework for the comparative analysis of organizations. *American Sociological Review*, *32*, 194-208.

Perrow, C. (1970). *Organizational analysis: A sociological view*. Belmont, CA: Brooks/Cole.

Pugh, D.S., Hickson, D.J., & Hinings, C.R. (1969). An empirical taxonomy of work organizations. *Administrative Science Quarterly*, *14*, 115-126.

Relvas, H., Littlewood, M., Nesti, M., Gilbourne, D., & Richardson, D. (2010). Organizational structures and working practices in elite European professional football clubs: Understanding the relationship between youth and professional domains. *European Sport Management Quarterly, 10*(2), 165-187. doi:10.1080/16184740903559891

Rhodes, L. (1982, August). The un-manager. *Inc.*, 34-43.

Running Room. (n.d.). About us, our story. Retrieved from www.runningroom.com/ca/inside.php?id=3036

Rushing, W.A. (1980). Organizational size, rules and surveillance. In J.A. Litterer (Ed.), *Organizations: Structure and behavior* (3rd ed., pp. 396-405). New York, NY: Wiley.

Scottish Government. (2018a). Glasgow 2014 Commonwealth Games Legacy: Final evaluation report: April 2018. Chapter 1: Background and introduction. Retrieved from https://www.gov.scot/publications/glasgow-2014-commonwealth-games-legacy-final-evaluation-report-april-2018/pages/2/

Scottish Government. (2018b). Glasgow 2014 Commonwealth Games Legacy: Final evaluation report: April 2018. Chapter 3: The economy, employment, training and volunteering. Retrieved from www.gov.scot/Publications/2018/04/5418/4

Short, J.C., Payne, G.T., & Ketchen, D.J. (2008). Research on organizational configurations: Past accomplishments and future challenges. *Journal of Management, 34*(6), 1053-1079. doi:10.1177/0149206308324324

Simmons, J. (1987). People managing themselves. *Journal for Quality and Participation, 10,* 14-19.

Slack, T. (1985). The bureaucratization of a voluntary sport organization. *International Review for the Sociology of Sport, 20,* 145-166.

Slack, T., & Hinings, C.R. (Eds.). (1987). *The organization and administration of sport.* London, ON: Sport Dynamics.

Slack, T., & Hinings, C.R. (1992). Understanding change in national sport organizations: An integration of theoretical perspectives. *Journal of Sport Management, 6,* 114-132.

Terkel, S. (1972). *Working.* New York, NY: Avon.

Theodoraki, E., & Henry, I.P. (1994). Organizational structures and context in British national governing bodies of sport. *International Review for the Sociology of Sport, 29,* 243-263.

Thompson, J.D. (1967). *Organizations in action.* New York, NY: McGraw-Hill.

Thurston, A. (2017). *An analysis of the implementation of Clubmark and two associated policies in boxing, swimming and rugby union* (Unpublished doctoral thesis). Loughborough University, Leicestershire, UK. Retrieved from https://dspace.lboro.ac.uk/2134/25521

Weber, M. (1947). *The theory of social and economic organizations* (T. Parsons, Trans.). New York, NY: Free Press.

Wilkinson, A., Hislop, D., & Coupland, C. (Eds.). (2016). *Perspectives on contemporary professional work: Challenges and experiences.* Cheltenham, UK: Edward Elgar Publishing.

Winand, M., Scheerder, J., Vos, S., & Zintz, T. (2016). Do non-profit sport organisations innovate? Types and preferences of service innovation within regional sport federations. *Innovation: Management, Policy & Practice, 18*(3), 289-308. doi:10.1080/14479338.2016.1235985

Winand, M., Vos, S., Zintz, T., & Scheerder, J. (2013). Determinants of service innovation: A typology of sports federations. *International Journal of Sport Management and Marketing, 13*(1), 55. doi:10.1504/IJSMM.2013.055194

Woodward, J. (1958). *Management and technology.* London, UK: Her Majesty's Printing Office.

Woodward, J. (1965). *Industrial organization: Theory and practice.* London, UK: Oxford University Press.

Chapter 7

Barrett, S. (2004). Implementation studies: Time for a revival? Personal reflections on 20 years of implementation studies. *Public Administration, 82*(2), 249-262.

Barrett, S., & Fudge, C. (1981). *Policy and action.* London, UK: Methuen.

Berman, P. (1978). The study of macro- and micro-implementation. *Public Policy, 26*(2), 157-184.

Birkland, T.A. (2005). *An introduction to the policy process: Theories, concepts and models of public policy making.* New York, NY: ME Sharpe.

Cantelon, H., & Ingham, A. (2002). Max Weber and the sociology of sport. In J. Maguire & K. Young (Eds.), *Theory, sport and society* (pp. 63-83). Oxford, UK: Elsevier.

Chalip, L. (1995). Policy analysis in sport management. *Journal of Sport Management, 9*(1), 1-13.

Cline, K.D. (2000). Defining the implementation problem: Organization management versus cooperation. *Journal of Public Administration Research and Theory, 10*(3), 551-571.

de Leon, P. (1999). The stages approach to the policy process: What has it done? Where is it going? In P.A. Sabatier (Ed.), *Theories of the policy process* (pp. 19-32). Boulder, CO: Westview.

Derthick, M. (1972). *New towns in-town.* Washington, DC: Urban Institute.

DiMaggio, P.J., & Powell, W. (1983) The iron cage revisited: Institutional isomorphism and collective rationality in organizational fields. *American Sociological Review, 48*, 147-160.

Downs, A. (1967). *Inside bureaucracy.* Boston, MA: Little, Brown.

Farrey, T. (2008). *Game on: The all-American race to make champions of our children.* New York, NY: ESPN.

Garrett, R. (2004). The response of voluntary sports clubs to Sport England's lottery funding: Cases of compliance, change and resistance. *Managing Leisure, 9*(1), 13-29.

Goggin, M.L., Bowman, A.O.M., Lester, J.P., & O'Toole, L.J. (1990). *Implementation theory and practice: Toward a third generation.* Glenview, IL: Scott Foresman.

Goldsmith, M. (1980). *Politics, planning and the city.* Abingdon, UK: Taylor & Francis Group.

Harris, S. (2013). *An analysis of the significance of the relationship between NGBs and CSPs in the delivery of community sport policy* (Unpublished doctoral thesis). Loughborough University, Leicestershire, UK.

Harris, S., & Houlihan, B. (2014). Delivery networks and community sport in England. *International Journal of Public Sector Management, 27*(2), 113-127.

Harris, S., Mori, K., & Collins, M.F. (2009). Great expectations: Voluntary sports clubs and their role in delivering national policy for English sport. *VOLANTUS: International Journal of Voluntary and Nonprofit Organizations, 20*(4), 405-423.

Haywood, L., Kew, F., Bramham, P., Spink, J., Capernerhurst, J., & Henry, I. (1995). *Understanding leisure.* Cheltenham, UK: Stanley Thornes.

Henry, I.P. (1993). *The politics of leisure policy.* London, UK: Palgrave.

Henry, I.P. (2001). *The politics of leisure policy* (2nd ed.). London, UK: Palgrave.

Herbert, I. (2015, May 18). FFP: How clubs put Uefa on back foot over financial fair play. *The Independent.* Retrieved from: https://www.independent.co.uk/sport/football/news-and-comment/q-and-a-how-clubs-put-uefa-on-back-foot-over-financial-fair-play-10259711.html

Hill, M., & Hupe, P. (2009). *Implementing public policy: Governance in theory and in practice* (2nd ed.). London, UK: SAGE.

Hjern, B., & Hull, C. (1982). Implementation research as empirical constitutionalism. *European Journal of Political Research, 10*(2), 105-16.

Hogwood, B.W. (1978). *The primacy of politics in the economic policy of Scottish government.* Glasgow, UK: Centre for the Study of Public Policy, University of Strathclyde.

Hogwood, B.W., & Gunn, L.A. (1984). *Policy analysis for the real world.* Oxford, UK: Oxford University Press.

Houlihan, B. (1997). *Sport, policy and politics: A comparative analysis.* London, UK: Routledge.

Houlihan, B. (2005). Public sector sport policy: Developing a framework for analysis. *International Review for the Sociology of Sport, 20*(2), 163-185.

Houlihan, B. (2013). Theorising the analysis of sport policy. In I. Henry & L.-M. Ko (Eds.), *Routledge handbook of sport policy* (pp. 11-22). London, UK: Routledge.

Houlihan, B., & Green, M. (2007). *Comparative elite sport development.* London, UK: Routledge.

Houlihan, B., & Green, M. (2008). *Elite sport development: Policy learning and political priorities.* London, UK: Routledge.

Houlihan, B., & White, A. (2002). *The politics of sport development: Development of sport or development through sport?* London, UK: Routledge.

Hums, M.A., & MacLean, J.C. (2013). *Governance and policy in sports organizations.* Scottsdale, AZ: Holcomb Hathway.

Jenkins, W.I. (1978). *Policy analysis: A political and organizational perspective.* New York, NY: St. Martin's Press.

Kikulis, L. (2000). Continuity and change in governance and decision making in national sport organizations: Institutional explanations. *Journal of Sport Management, 14*, 293-320.

Lipsky, M. (1980). *Street-level bureaucracy: Dilemmas of the individual in public services.* New York, NY: Russell Sage Foundation.

Lowi, T.J. (1972). *Nationalizing government: Public policies in America.* Thousand Oaks: CA: SAGE.

Lukes, S. (1974). *Power: A radical view.* London, UK: Macmillan.

March, J.G., & Simon, H.A. (1958). *Organizations.* New York, NY: Wiley.

Matland, R.E. (1995). Synthesizing the implementation literature: The ambiguity-conflict model of policy implementation. *Journal of Public Administration Research and Theory, 5*(2), 145-174.

May, T., Harris, S., & Collins, M. (2013). Implementing community sport policy: Understanding the variety of voluntary club types and their attitudes to policy. *International Journal of Sport Policy and Politics, 5*(3), 397-419.

Mazmanian, D.A., & Sabatier, P.A. (1981). *Effective policy implementation.* Lexington, KY: Lexington Books.

McLaughlin, M.W. (1987). Learning from experience: Lessons from policy implementation. *Educational Evaluation and Policy Analysis, 9*(2), 171-178.

Merton, R. (1957). *Social theory and social structure.* Glencoe, IL: Free Press.

Meyer, J.W., & Rowan, B. (1977). Institutional organizations: Formal structure as myth and ceremony. *American Journal of Sociology, 80*, 340-363.

Michels, R. (1962). *Political parties.* New York, NY: Free Press.

Oliver, C. (1991). Strategic responses to institutional processes. *Academy of Management Review, 18*(1), 145-179.

O'Toole, L.J.R. (1995). Rational choice and policy implementation. *American Review of Public Administration, 25*(1), 43-57.

Palumbo, D.J., Maynard-Moody, S., & Wright, P. (1984). Measuring degrees of successful implementation, achieving policy versus statutory goals. *Evaluation Review, 8*(1), 45-74.

Pfeffer, J., & Salancik, G.R. (1978). *The external control of organizations: A resource dependence perspective.* New York, NY: Harper & Row.

Powell, W. (1991). Expanding the scope of institutional analysis. In W. Powell & P.J. DiMaggio (Eds.), *The new institutionalism in organizational analysis* (pp. 183-203). Chicago, IL: University of Chicago Press.

Powell, W., & Colyvas, J.A. (2007). *The new institutionalism. The international encyclopedia of organization studies.* Thousand Oaks, CA: Sage

Pressman, J.L., & Wildavsky, A. (1973). *Implementation: How great expectations in Washington are dashed in Oakland.* Berkeley, CA: University of California Press.

Pressman, J.L., & Wildavsky, A. (1984). *Implementation: How great expectations in Washington are dashed in Oakland* (3rd ed.). Berkeley, CA: University of California Press.

Raco, M., & Imrie, R. (2000). Governmentality and rights and responsibilities in urban policy. *Environment and Planning, 32*, 2187-2204.

Sabatier, P.A. (1986). Top-down and bottom-up approaches to implementation research: A critical analysis and suggested synthesis. *Journal of Public Policy, 6*(1), 21-48.

Sabatier, P.A. (1993). Policy change over a decade or more. In P.A. Sabatier & H.C. Jenkins-Smith (Eds.), *Policy change and learning: An advocacy coalition approach* (pp. 13-39). Boulder, CO: Westview.

Salisbury, R.H. (1968). The analysis of public policy: A search for theories and roles. In A. Ramney (Ed.), *Political science and public policy* (pp. 151-175). Chicago, IL: Markham.

Scott, W.R. (1983). Reform movements and organizations: The case of ageing. In J.W. Meyer & W.R. Scott (Eds.), *Organizational environments: Ritual and rationality* (pp. 115-127). Thousand Oaks, CA: Sage.

Scott, W.R. (1987). The adolescence of institutional theory. *Administrative Science Quarterly, 32*, 493-511.

Selznick, P. (1949). *TVA and the grassroots, a study in the sociology of formal organization.* Berkeley, CA: University of California Press.

Skille, E.A. (2008). Understanding sport clubs as sport policy implementers: A theoretical framework for the analysis of the implementation of central sport policy through local and voluntary sport organizations. *International Review for the Sociology of Sport, 43*(2), 181-200.

UEFA. (2012). *UEFA club licensing and financial fair play regulations.* Nyon, Switzerland: UEFA.

Van Horn, C.E. (1987). Applied implementation research, presented at Midwest Political Science Association Meeting, Chicago, IL, 1987.

Van Meter, D., & Van Horn, C.E. (1975). The policy implementation process: A conceptual framework. *Administration and Society, 6*(4), 445-488.

Weber, M. (1947). *The theory of social and economic organization.* (A.M. Henderson & T. Parsons, Trans.). New York, NY: Free Press.

Chapter 8

Amis, J., Pant, N., & Slack, T. (1997). Achieving a sustainable competitive advantage: A resource-based view of sport sponsorship. *Journal of Sport Management, 11*, 80-96.

Austin, J.E. (2010). *The collaboration challenge: How nonprofits and businesses succeed through strategic alliances*. Hoboken, NJ: John Wiley & Sons.

Bajkowski, S. (2016, June 8). Man City bosses plot further expansion as Khaldoon Al Mubarak assures fans over future. *Manchester Evening News*. Retrieved from www.manchester-eveningnews.co.uk/sport/football/football-news/man-city-khaldoon-transcript-cfg-11443264

Baker, M. (2000). *Marketing strategy and management* (3rd ed.). London, UK: Macmillan Business.

Barney, J. (1991a). Special theory forum. The resource-based model of the firm: Origins, implications, and prospects. *Journal of Management, 17*, 97-98.

Barney, J. (1991b). Firm resources and sustained competitive advantage. *Journal of Management, 17*, 99-120.

Bates, D.L., & Eldredge, D.L. (1984). *Strategy and policy: Analysis, formulation, and implementation* (2nd ed.). Dubuque, IA: Brown.

BBC News (2004, April 17). The oil tycoon tempted by Chelsea. Retrieved from http://news.bbc.co.uk/1/hi/business/3036996.stm

BBC News (2018, October 19). Venues announced for Birmingham 2022 Commonwealth Games, BBC. Retrieved from https://www.bbc.co.uk/news/uk-england-45914588

BBC Sport (2019, March 7). Project Reset: Scarlets-Ospreys merger plans "absolute lunacy" - David Moffett. Retrieved from https://www.bbc.co.uk/sport/rugby-union/47477997

Berrett, T., Burton, T.L., & Slack, T. (1993). Quality products, quality service: Factors leading to entrepreneurial success in the sport and leisure industry. *Leisure Studies, 12*, 93-106.

Bourgeois, L.J., & Astley, W.G. (1979). A strategic model of organizational conduct and performance. *International Studies of Management and Organization, 6*, 40-66.

Brawn, R., & Parr, A. (2016). *Total competition: Lessons in strategy from Formula One*. New York, NY: Simon & Schuster.

Burgelman, R.A. (1983). A model of the interaction of strategic behaviour, corporate context, and the concept of strategy. *Academy of Management Review, 8*, 61-70.

Chadwick, S., & Zipp, S. (2018). Nike, Colin Kaepernick and the pitfalls of "woke" corporate branding, The Conversation. *The Conversation*. Retrieved from https://theconversation.com/nike-colin-kaepernick-and-the-pitfalls-of-woke-corporate-branding-102922

Chalip, L., & Leyns, A. (2002). Local business leveraging of a sport event: Managing an event for economic benefit. *Journal of Sport Management, 16*, 132-158.

Chandler, A.D., Jr. (1962). *Strategy and structure: Chapters in the history of the industrial enterprise*. Cambridge, MA: MIT Press.

Channon, D. (1973). *Strategy and structure in British enterprise*. Boston, MA: Harvard Graduate School of Business Administration.

Child, J., & Faulkner, D. (1998). *Strategies of cooperation: Managing alliances, networks, and joint ventures*. New York, NY: Oxford University Press.

Cummings, T.G., & Worley, C.G. (1993). *Organization development and change*. St. Paul, MN: West.

Cunningham, G.B. (2002). Examining the relationship among Miles and Snow's strategic types and measures of organizational effectiveness in NCAA Division I Athletic Departments. *International Review for the Sociology of Sport, 37*(2), 159-175.

Cunningham, G.B., Dixon, M.A., Singer, J.N., Oshiro, K.F., Ahn, Y., & Weems, A. (in press). A site to resist and persist: Diversity, social justice, and the unique nature of sport. *Journal of Global Sport Management*.

Dannen, C. (2013, October 18). Inside GitHub's super-lean management strategy—And how it drives innovation. FastCompany. Retrieved from www.fastcompany.com/3020181/inside-githubs-super-lean-management-strategy-and-how-it-drives-innovation

Danziger, P. (2018, December 1). Nike's new consumer experience distribution strategy hits the ground running. *Forbes*. Retrieved from www.forbes.com/sites/pamdanziger/2018/12/01/nikes-new-consumer-experience-distribution-strategy-hits-the-ground-running/#2780e545f1d0

Das, H. (1990). *Organization theory with Canadian applications*. Toronto, ON: Gage Educational.

Davies, C. (2005, August 4). Adidas buys Reebok to conquer US. *The Telegraph*. Retrieved from www.telegraph.co.uk/finance/2920095/Adidas-buys-Reebok-to-conquer-US.html

Dolles, H., & Söderman, S. (Eds.). (2011). *Sport as a business: International, professional and commercial aspects*. New York, NY: Palgrave Macmillan.

Doward, Jamie. (2018, September 9). Wealthy Russians in Britain face new visa crackdown after Salisbury. *The Observer*. Retrieved from www.theguardian.com/uk-news/2018/sep/09/home-office-review-wealthy-russian-investor-visas

Fahey, L. (1981). On strategic management decision processes. *Strategic Management Journal, 2*, 43-60.

Ferkins, L., Shilbury, D., & McDonald, G. (2009). Board involvement in strategy: Advancing the governance of sport organizations of sport organizations. *Journal of Sport Management, 23*(3), 245-277.

Financial Times (2018). Manchester City owner buys Chinese club. *Financial Times*. Retrieved from www.ft.com/content/8f90ced4-345e-11e9-bb0c-42459962a812

Fredrickson, J.W. (1986). The strategic decision process and organizational structure. *Academy of Management Journal, 11*, 280-297.

Garside, Juliette. (2018, September 25). Roman Abramovich posed threat to public security, Swiss police said. *The Guardian*. Retrieved from www.theguardian.com/world/2018/sep/25/roman-abramovich-posed-threat-to-public-security-swiss-police-said

Giulianotti, R. (2005). Playing an aerial game: The new political economy of soccer. In J. Nauright & K.S. Schimmel (Eds.), *The political economy of sport* (pp. 19-37). Basingstoke, UK: Palgrave Macmillan.

Give them stormy weather. (1986, March 24). *Forbes*, 174.

Graham, P. (1983). Strategic planning management concepts applied to team sports. In *Proceedings of the International Congress: Teaching team sports* (pp. 17-182). Rome, Italy: CONI-Scuola dello Sport.

Gray, A. (2018). *The game changer: How leading organisations in business and sport changed the rules of the game*. Abingdon, UK: Routledge.

The Guardian (2003, July 6). The deal that made a Russian oligarch. *The Guardian*. Retrieved from www.theguardian.com/business/2003/jul/06/russia.football

Harrigan, K.R., & Porter, M. (1983). End-game strategies for declining industries. *Harvard Business Review, 61*, 111-120.

Henry, I. (2001). Postmodernism and power in urban policy: Implications for sport and cultural policy in the city. *European Sport Management Quarterly, 1*, 5-20.

Hill, C.W.L., & Jones, G.R. (1989). *Strategic management: An integrated approach*. Boston, MA: Houghton Mifflin.

Hodge, B.J., & Anthony, W.P. (1991). *Organization theory: A strategic approach*. Boston, MA: Allyn & Bacon.

Hughes, D. (2016). *The winning mindset: What sport can teach us about great leadership*. London, UK: Macmillan.

Isoherranen, V., & Kess, P. (2011). Analysis of strategy by strategy typology and orientation framework. *Modern Economy, 2*(4), 575-583.

Jacobson, R. (1992). The "Austrian" school of strategy. *Academy of Management Review, 17*, 782-807.

Jarvie, G. (2006). *Sport, culture and society*. Abingdon, UK: Routledge.

Kirzner, I. (1973). *Competition and entrepreneurship*. Chicago, IL: University of Chicago Press.

Kitchen, P. (2006). Understanding the sport marketing environment. In J.G. Beech & S. Chadwick (Eds.), *The Marketing of Sport* (pp. 61-82). Harlow, UK: Pearson Education Limited.

Knight, P. (2018). *Shoe dog: A memoir by the creator of Nike*. New York, NY: Simon & Schuster.

Kogut, B., & Zander, U. (1992). Knowledge of the firm, combinative capabilities, and the replication of technology. *Organization Science, 3*, 383-397.

Lehman, D.W., & Hahn, J. (2013). Momentum and organizational risk taking: Evidence from the National Football League. *Management Science, 59*(4), 852-868.

Lima, M.S., & Navarro, A. (2019). Disney to accept divesting of Fox Sports in Brazil and Mexico. *Bloomberg*. Retrieved from www.bloomberg.com/news/articles/2019-02-21/disney-is-said-to-accept-divesting-fox-sports-in-brazil-mexico

Lindblom, C.E. (1959). The science of muddling through. *Public Administration Review, 19*, 79-88.

Lowy, A., & Hood, P. (2011). *The power of the 2 x 2 matrix: Using 2 x 2 thinking to solve business problems and make better decisions*. Hoboken, NJ: John Wiley & Sons.

MacMillan, I.C. (1983). Competitive strategies for non-profit agencies. In R.B. Lamb (Ed.), *Advances in strategic management* (Vol. 1, pp. 61-82). Greenwich, CT: JAI Press.

Manoli, A.E. (2016). Media relations in English football clubs. In J.J. Zhang & B.G. Pitts (Eds.), *Contemporary sport marketing: Global perspectives* (pp. 120-138). London, UK: Routledge.

Manoli, A.E. (2018). Sport marketing's past, present and future; an introduction to the special issue on contemporary issues in sports marketing. *Journal of Strategic Marketing, 26*(1), 6-18.

Manoli, A.E., & Hodgkinson, I.R. (2017). Marketing outsourcing in the English Premier League: The right holder/agency interface. *European Sport Management Quarterly, 17*(4), 436-456.

Miles, R.E., & Snow, C.C. (1978). *Organizational strategy, structure, and process*. New York, NY: McGraw-Hill.

Miles, R.E., Snow, C.C., Meyer, A.D., & Coleman, H.J. (1978). Organizational strategy, structure and process. *Academy of Management Review, 3*, 546-562.

Miller, D. (1986). Configurations of strategy and structure: Towards a synthesis. *Strategic Management Journal, 7*, 217-231.

Miller, D. (1987a). Strategy making and structure: Analysis and implications for performance. *Academy of Management Journal, 30*, 7-32.

Miller, D. (1987b). The structural and environmental correlates of business strategy. *Strategic Management Journal, 8*, 55-76.

Miller, D. (1988). Relating Porter's business strategies to environment and structure: Analysis and performance implications. *Academy of Management Journal, 31*, 280-308.

Miller, D. (1990). *The Icarus paradox: How exceptional companies bring about their own downfall*. New York, NY: HarperCollins.

Mintzberg, H. (1973). Strategy making in three modes. *California Management Review, 16*, 44-53.

Mintzberg, H. (1978). Patterns in strategy formulation. *Management Science, 24*, 934-948.

Mintzberg, H. (1987). The strategy concept—I: Five Ps for strategy. *California Management Review, 30*, 11-24.

Mintzberg, H. (1990). The design school: Reconsidering the basic premises of strategic management. *Strategic Management Journal, 11*, 171-195.

Nelson, A. (2018). Philadelphia Eagles opt for long-term stability, creating bespoke commercial partnerships. *Sport Business*. Retrieved from www.sportbusiness.com/2018/09/philadelphia-eagles-trade-quick-gains-for-long-term-stability-creating-bespoke-commercial-partnerships/

Porter, M.E. (1980). *Competitive strategy: Techniques for analyzing industries and competitors*. New York, NY: Free Press.

Porter, M.E. (1985). *Competitive advantage: Creating and sustaining superior performance*. New York, NY: Free Press.

Porter, M.E. (1989). *The competitive advantage of nations and their firms*. New York, NY: Free Press.

Press Association. (2018, August 26). Chelsea deny reports Roman Abramovich is considering selling club. *The Guardian*. Retrieved from www.theguardian.com/football/2018/aug/26/chelsea-roman-abramovich-deny-selling-reports

Quinn, J.B., Mintzberg, H., & James, R.M. (1988). *The strategy process: Concepts, context, and cases*. Englewood Cliffs, NJ: Prentice Hall.

Rhodes, L. (1982, August). The un-manager. *Inc.*, 34-43.

Rumelt, R.P. (1974). *Strategy, structure, and economic performance*. Boston, MA: Harvard Graduate School of Business Administration.

Schendel, D.G., Patton, R., & Riggs, J. (1976). Corporate turnaround strategies: A study of profit decline and recovery. *Journal of General Management, 3*, 3-11.

Schumpeter, J. (1950). *Capitalism, socialism, and democracy*. New York, NY: Harper & Row.

Seeger, J.A. (1984). Reversing the images of the BCG's growth share matrix. *Strategic Management Journal, 5*, 93-97.

Smith, A. (2001). Sporting a new image? Sport-based regeneration strategies as a means of enhancing the image of the city tourist destination. In C. Gratton & I. Henry (Eds.), *Sports in the city* (pp. 127-148). London, UK: Routledge.

Strasser, J.B., & Becklund, L. (1991). *Swoosh: The unauthorized story of Nike and the men who played there*. New York, NY: Harcourt Brace Jovanovich.

Tacx. (2019). Garmin® signs purchase agreement to acquire Tacx, the leading manufacturer of indoor bike trainers. Retrieved from https://tacx.com/garmin-acquires-tacx/

Taylor, P., & Gratton, C. (2000). *The economics of sport and recreation: An economic analysis*. London, UK: Routledge.

Thibault, L., Slack, T., & Hinings, C.R. (1993). A framework for the analysis of strategy in nonprofit sport organizations. *Journal of Sport Management, 7*, 25-43.

Thibault, L., Slack, T., & Hinings, C.R. (1994). Strategic planning for nonprofit sport organizations: Empirical verification of a framework. *Journal of Sport Management, 8*, 218-233.

Torquati, B., Scarpa, R., Petrosillo, I., Ligonzo, M.G., & Paffarini, C. (2018). How can consumer science help firms transform their dog (BCG Matrix) products into profitable products? In A. Cavicchi & C. Santini (Eds.), *Case studies in the traditional food sector* (pp. 255-279). Sawston, UK: Woodhead Publishing.

Tran, Mark. (2003, July 2). Roman Abramovich. *The Guardian*. Retrieved from www.theguardian.com/world/2003/jul/02/russia.football

Vizard, S. (2018). Consumers split over impact of Nike's Colin Kaepernick campaign. *Marketing Week*. Retrieved from www.marketingweek.com/2018/09/12/consumers-split-over-impact-of-nikes-colin-kaepernick-campaign/

Wagg, S. (2007). Angels of us all? Football management, globalization and the politics of celebrity. *Soccer and Society, 8*(4), 440-458.

Walvin, J. (1975). *The people's game*. Newton Abbot, UK: Readers Union.

Westerbeek, H., & Smith, A. (2005). *Business leadership and the lessons from sport*. Basingstoke, UK: Palgrave Macmillan.

Whitson, D., & Macintosh, D. (1993). Becoming a world-class city: Hallmark events and sport franchises in the growth strategies of western Canadian cities. *Sociology of Sport Journal, 10*, 221-240.

Winter, S.G. (1987). Knowledge and competence as strategic assets. In D.J. Teece (Ed.), *The competitive challenge* (pp. 159-184). Cambridge, MA: Ballinger.

W.L. Gore & Associates. (2019). Our culture. *Gore*. Retrieved from https://www.gore.com/about/culture

Yang, D.J., Oneal, M., Hoots, C., & Neff, R. (1994, April 18). Can Nike just do it? *Business Week*, 86-90.

Yavitz, B., & Newman, W.H. (1982). *Strategy in action: The execution, politics, and payoff of business planning*. New York, NY: Free Press.

Yeh, C.M., Hoye, R., & Taylor, T. (2011). Board roles and strategic orientation among Taiwanese nonprofit sport organisations. *Managing Leisure, 16*(4), 287-301.

Chapter 9

Aaker, D.A. (1991). *Managing brand equity*. San Francisco, CA: Free Press.

Aaker, D.A., & Joachimsthaler, E. (2000). The brand relationship spectrum. *California Management Review, 42*(4), 8-23.

Aaker, D.A., & Keller, K.L. (1990). Consumer evaluations of brand extensions. *Journal of Marketing, 54*(1), 27-41.

Aaker, J.L. (1997). Dimensions of brand personality. *Journal of Marketing, 35*(3), 347-356.

Apostolopoulou, A. (2002). Brand extensions by US professional sport teams: Motivations and keys to success. *Sport Marketing Quarterly, 11*(4), 205-214.

Barros, C.P., Barros, C.D., Santos, A., & Chadwick, S. (2007). Sponsorship brand recall at the Euro 2004 soccer tournament. *Sport Marketing Quarterly, 16*(3), 161-170.

Braun, K.A. (1999). Postexperience advertising effects on consumer memory. *Journal of Consumer Research, 25*(4), 319-334.

Burton, R., & Howard, D. (1999). Professional sports leagues: Marketing mix mayhem. *Marketing Management, 8*(1), 37-46.

Chalip, L., & Leyns, A. (2002). Local business leveraging of a sport event: Managing an event for economic benefit. *Journal of Sport Management, 16*(2), 132-158.

Cialdini, R.B., Borden, R.J., Thorne, A., Walker, M.R., Freeman, S., & Sloan, L.R. (1976). Basking in reflected glory: Three (football) field studies. *Journal of Personality and Social Psychology, 34*(3), 366-375.

Cliffe, S.J., & Motion, J. (2005). Building contemporary brands: A sponsorship-based strategy. *Journal of Business Research, 58*(8), 1068-1077.

Cornwell, T.B. (2008). State of the art and science in sponsorship-linked marketing. *Journal of Advertising, 37*(3), 41-55.

Cornwell, T.B., & Maignan, I. (1998). An international review of sponsorship research. *Journal of Advertising, 27*(1), 1-21.

Drennan, J.C., & Cornwell, T.B. (2004). Emerging strategies for sponsorship on the internet. *Journal of Marketing Management, 20*(9-10), 1123-1146.

Fahy, J., Farrelly, F., & Quester, P. (2004). Competitive advantage through sponsorship: A conceptual model and research propositions. *European Journal of Marketing, 38*(8), 1013-1030.

Fullerton, S. (2009). *Sports marketing* (2nd ed.). New York, NY: McGraw-Hill/Irwin Publishing.

Fullerton, S., & Merz, G.R. (2008). The four domains of sports marketing: A conceptual framework. *Sport Marketing Quarterly, 17*(2), 90-108.

Gladden, J.M., & Funk, D.C. (2002). Developing an understanding of brand associations in team sport: Empirical evidence from consumers of professional sport. *Journal of Sport Management, 16*(1), 54-81.

Hall, B. (2002). A new model for measuring advertising effectiveness. *Journal of Advertising Research, 42*(2), 23-31.

International Events Group. (2017). New year to one of growth and challenges for sponsorship industry. *IEG Sponsorship Report*. Retrieved from www.sponsorship.com/About-IEG/Press-Room/IEG-Projects-North-American-Sponsorship-Spending-t.aspx

Keller, K.L. (1993). Conceptualizing, measuring, and managing customer-based brand equity. *Journal of Marketing, 57*(1), 1-22.

Keller, K.L. (2007). Advertising and brand equity. In G.J. Tellis & T. Ambler (Eds.), *Handbook of Advertising* (pp. 54-70). Thousand Oaks, CA: SAGE.

Koo, G., Quarterman, J., & Flynn, L. (2006). Effect of perceived sport event and sponsor image fit on consumers' cognition, affect, and behavioral intentions. *Sport Marketing Quarterly, 15*(2), 80-90.

Kotler, P. (1997). *Marketing management* (7th ed.). Upper Saddle River, NJ: Prentice Hall.

Kotler, P., & Armstrong, G. (2014). *Principles of marketing*. Upper Saddle River, NJ: Prentice-Hall.

Maltese, L., & Danglade, J. (2014). *Marketing du sport et événementiel sportif* [Sports Marketing and Sports Events]. Malakoff, France: Dunod.

McCracken, G. (1989). Who is the celebrity endorser? Cultural foundations of the endorsement process. *Journal of Consumer Research, 16*(3), 310-321.

Meenaghan, T. (1991). The role of sponsorship in the marketing communications mix. *International Journal of Advertising, 10*(1), 35-47.

Meenaghan, T. (2001). Understanding sponsorship effects. *Psychology & Marketing, 18*(2), 95-122.

Neumeier, M. (2006). *The brand gap: How to bridge the distance between business strategy and design*. Berkeley, CA: New Riders Publishing.

Pons, F., Mourali, M., & Nyeck, S. (2006). Consumers' orientation toward sporting events: Scale development and validation. *Journal of Service Research, 8*, 276-287.

Quester, P.G. (1997). Awareness as a measure of sponsorship effectiveness: The Adelaide Formula One Grand Prix and evidence of incidental ambush effects. *Journal of Marketing Communications, 3*(1), 1-20.

Rohm, A.J., Milne G.R., & McDonald, M.A. (2006). A mixed-method approach for developing market segmentation typologies in the sports industry. *Sport Marketing Quarterly, 15*, 29-39.

Ross, S. D. (2006). A conceptual framework for understanding spectator-based brand equity. *Journal of Sport Management*, *20*(1), 22-38.

Roy, D.P., & Cornwell, T.B. (2004). The effects of consumer knowledge on responses to event sponsorships. *Psychology and Marketing*, *21*(3), 185-207.

Sandler, D.M., & Shani, D. (1989). Olympic sponsorship vs. "ambush" marketing: Who gets the gold? *Journal of Advertising Research*, *29*(4), 3-14.

Slotnick, D. (2012, April 23). Next up to Bat: A whiff of the Yankees. *New York Times*. Retrieved from https://cityroom.blogs.nytimes.com/2012/04/23/next-up-to-bat-a-whiff-of-the-yankees/

Solomon, M.R. (2009). *Consumer behavior: Buying, having and being*. Upper Saddle River, NJ: Prentice Hall.

Speed, R., & Thompson, P. (2000). Determinants of sports sponsorship response. *Journal of the Academy of Marketing Science*, *28*(2), 226-238.

Trail, G.T., Fink, J.S., & Anderson, D.F. (2003). Sport spectator consumption behavior. *Sport Marketing Quarterly*, *12*(1), 8-17.

Wann, D.L., Grieve, F.G., Zapalac, R.K., & Pease, D.G. (2008). Motivational profiles of sport fans of different sports. *Sport Marketing Quarterly*, *17*(1), 6-19.

Weeks, C.S., Cornwell, T.B., & Drennan, J.C. (2008). Leveraging sponsorships on the Internet: Activation, congruence, and articulation. *Psychology & Marketing*, *25*(7), 637-654.

Chapter 10

Abernethy, M.A., & Lillis, A.M. (1995). The impact of manufacturing flexibility on management control system design. *Accounting Organizations and Society*, *20*(4): 241-258.

Alvesson, M. (2002). *Understanding organizational culture*. London, UK: SAGE.

Alvesson, M., & Willmott, H. (2002). Identity regulation as organizational control: Producing the appropriate individual. *Journal of Management Studies*, *39*(5), 619-644. doi:10.1111/1467-6486.00305

Aquino, K., Tripp, T.M., & Bies, R.J. (2006). Getting even or moving on? Power, procedural justice, and types of offense as predictors of revenge, forgiveness, reconciliation, and avoidance in organizations. *American Psychological Association*, *91*(3), 653-668. doi:10.1037/0021-9010.91.3.653

Barnes, M., Cousens, L., & MacLean, J. (2017). Trust and collaborative ties in a community sport network. *Managing Sport and Leisure*, *22*(4), 310-324.

Baysinger, B., & Hoskisson, R.E. (1990). The composition of boards of directors and strategic control: Effects on corporate strategy. *Academy of Management Review*, *15*(1), 72-87.

Berry, A.J., Broadbent, J., & Otley, D. (2005). *Management control: Theories, issues and performance* (2nd ed.). London, UK: Palgrave Macmillan.

Boden, D. (1994). *Business of talk: Organizations in action*. London, UK: Polity.

Botterill, C., & Brown, M. (2002). Emotion and perspective in sport. *International Journal of Sport Psychology*, *33*(1), 38-60.

Bourdieu, P. (1991). *Language and symbolic power*. (J.B. Thompson, Ed.). Cambridge, MA: Harvard University Press.

Brackenridge, C. (2001). *Spoilsports: Understanding and preventing sexual exploitation in sport (ethics and sport)*. London, UK: Routledge.

Bradach, J.L., & Eccles, R.G. (1989). Price, authority, and trust: From ideal types to plural forms. *Annual Review of Sociology*, *15*, 97-118.

Brown, C. (2013). CEO Russ Brandon to assume organizational control of Buffalo Bills. Retrieved from https://www.buffalobills.com/news/ceo-russ-brandon-to-assume-organizational-control-of-buffalo-bills-9256418

The Buffalo News. (2014). Bills' Brandon excited about future under Pegulas' ownership. Retrieved from http://bills.buffalonews.com/2014/10/18/bills-brandon-excited-about-future-under-pegulas-ownership/

Byers, T. (2013). Using critical realism: A new perspective on control of volunteers in sport clubs. *European Sport Management Quarterly*, *13*(1), 5-31. doi:10.1080/16184742.2012.744765

Byers, T., Anagnostopoulos, C., & Brooke-Holmes, G. (2015). Understanding control in nonprofit organisations: Moving governance research forward? *Corporate Governance*, *15*(1), 134-145.

Byers, T., & Edwards, J. (2015). Why DON'T you dope?: A preliminary analysis of the factors which influence athletes decision NOT to dope in sport. *Choregia*, *11*(2), 1-20.

Byers, T., Henry, I., & Slack, T. (2007). Understanding control in voluntary sport organizations. In T. Slack & M. Parent (Eds.), *International perspectives on the management of sport* (pp. 269-283). Abingdon, UK: Routledge.

Byers, T., Slack, T., & Parent, M. (2012). *Key concepts in sport management*. London, UK: SAGE.

Callahan, J.L. (2000). Emotion management and organizational functions: A case study of patterns in a not-for-profit organization. *Human Resource Development Quarterly*, *11*(3), 245-267.

Cardinal, L.B., Sitkin, S.B., & Long, C.P. (2004). Balancing and rebalancing in the creation and evolution of organizational control. *Organization Science*, *15*(4), 411-431. doi:10.1287/orsc.1040.0084

Castaldo, S., Premazzi, K., & Zerbini, F. (2010). The meaning(s) of trust. A content analysis on the diverse conceptualizations of trust in scholarly research on business relationships. *Journal of Business Ethics*, *96*(4), 657-668.

Chen, C., & Mason, D.S. (2018). A postcolonial reading of representations of non-Western leadership in sport management studies. *Journal of Sport Management*, *32*(2), 150-169.

Chen, H.B., Yeh, S.S., & Huan, T.C. (2014). Nostalgic emotion, experiential value, brand image, and consumption intentions of customers of nostalgic-themed restaurants. *Journal of Business Research*, *67*(3), 354-360.

Chenhall, R. (2003). Management control systems design within its organizational context: Findings from contingency-based research and directions for the future. *Accounting, Organizations and Society*, *28*(2-3), 127-168. doi:10.1016/S0361-3682(01)00027-7

Collinson, D.L. (2002). Managing humour. *Journal of Management Studies*, *39*(3), 269-288. doi:10.1111/1467-6486.00292

Cornwell, T.B., Jahn, S., Xie, H., & Suh, W.S. (2018). Feeling that in-group feeling at a sponsored sporting event: Links to memory and future attendance. *Journal of Sport Management*, *32*(5), 426-437. doi:10.1123/jsm.2017-0248

Cossette, P. (1998). The study of language in organizations: A symbolic interactionist stance. *Human Relations*, *51*(11), 1355-1377. doi:10.1177/001872679805101102

Cuskelly, G. (2004). Volunteer retention in community sport organisations. *European Sport Management Quarterly*, *4*(2), 59-76. doi:10.1080/16184740408737469

Dalton, G.W., & Lawrence, P.R. (1971). *Motivation and control in organizations*. Homewood, IL: R.D. Irwin.

Das, T.K. (1989). Organizational control: An evolutionary perspective. *Journal of Management Studies*, *26*(5), 459-475.

Das, T.K., & Teng, B.-S. (2001). Trust, control, and risk in strategic alliances: An integrated framework. *Organization Studies*, *22*(2), 251-283. doi:10.1177/0170840601222004

Delbridge, R., & Ezzamel, M. (2005). The strength of difference: Contemporary conceptions of control. *Organization*, *12*(5), 603-618. doi:10.1177/1350508405055937

Dent, J.F. (1990). Strategy, organization and control: Some possibilities for accounting research. *Accounting, Organizations and Society*, *15*(1-2), 3-25.

Doherty, A., & Misener, K. (2008). Community sport networks. In M. Nicholson & R. Hoye (Eds.), *Sport and social capital* (pp. 133-162). Abingdon, UK: Routledge.

Downs, A. (1967). *Inside bureaucracy*. Boston, MA: Little, Brown and Company.

Edelenbos, J., & Eshuis, J. (2012). The interplay between trust and control in governance processes: A conceptual and empirical investigation. *Administration & Society*, *44*(6), 647-674.

Edelman. (2015). 2015 Edelman Trust Barometer. Retrieved from https://www.edelman.com/research/2015-edelman-trust-barometer

Edelman. (2019). 2019 Edelman Trust Barometer. Retrieved from https://www.edelman.com/trust-barometer

Eisenhardt, K.M. (1985). Control: Organizational and economic approaches. *Management Science*, *31*(2), 134-149. doi:10.1287/mnsc.31.2.134

Fahlén, J. (2017). The trust–mistrust dynamic in the public governance of sport: Exploring the legitimacy of performance measurement systems through end-users' perceptions. *International Journal of Sport Policy and Politics*, *9*(4), 707-722.

Fayol, H. (1916). *Administration industrielle et générale. Prévoyance, organisation, commandement, coordination, contrôle* (Vol. 10) [General and industrial management. Planning, organization, command, coordination, control]. Malakoff, France: Dunod.

Filo, K., Funk, D.C., & Alexandris, K. (2008). Exploring the role of brand trust in the relationship between brand associations and brand loyalty in sport and fitness. *International Journal of Sport Management and Marketing*, *3*(1-2), 39-57.

Fineman, S. (2000). *Emotion in organizations* (2nd ed.). London, UK: SAGE.

Fineman, S., & Sturdy, A. (1999). The emotions of control: A qualitative exploration of environmental regulation. *Human Relations*, *52*(5), 631-663.

Foroughi, B., Nikbin, D., Hyun, S.S., & Iranmanesh, M. (2016). Impact of core product quality on sport fans' emotions and behavioral intentions. *International Journal of Sports Marketing and Sponsorship*, *17*(2), 110-129.

Graicunas, V.A. (1937). Relationship in organization. In L. Gulick & L. Urwick (Eds.), *Paper on the science of administration* (pp. 182-187). New York, NY: Institution of Public Administration, Columbia University.

Green, S.G., & Welsh, M.A. (1988). Cybernetics and dependence: Reframing the control concept. *The Academy of Management Review*, *13*(2), 287. doi:10.2307/258578

Hanin, Y.L. (2000). *Emotions in sport*. Champaign, IL: Human Kinetics.

Hoeber, L. (2007). Exploring the gaps between meanings and practices of gender equity in a sport organization. *Gender, Work & Organization*, *14*(3), 259-280.

Hopwood, A. (1974). *Accounting and human behaviour*. London, UK: Haymarket.

Houser, D., Xiao, E., McCabe, K., & Smith, V. (2008). When punishment fails: Research on sanctions, intentions and non-cooperation. *Games and Economic Behavior*, *62*(2), 509-532.

Inzerilli, G., & Rosen, M. (1983). Culture and organizational control. *Journal of Business Research*, *11*(3), 281-292. doi:10.1016/0148-2963(83)90013-9

Javadein, S.R.S., Khanlari, A., & Estiri, M. (2008). Customer loyalty in the sport services industry: The role of service quality, customer satisfaction, commitment and trust. *Journal of Human Sciences*, *5*(2), 1-19.

Jermier, J. M. (1998). Introduction: Critical perspective on organizational control. *Administrative Science Quarterly*, *43*(2), 235-256.

Johnson, P., & Gill, J. (1993). *Management control and organizational behaviour*. London, UK: SAGE.

Jones, K. (2001). Trust in sport. *Journal of the Philosophy of Sport*, *28*(1), 96-102.

Kikulis, L., Slack, T., & Hinings, C.R. (1995). Toward an understanding of the role of agency and choice in the changing structure of Canada's national sport organizations. *Journal of Sport Management*, *9*(2), 135-152.

Kim, P.H., Dirks, K.T., Cooper, C.D., & Ferrin, D.L. (2006). When more blame is better than less: The implications of internal vs. external attributions for the repair of trust after a competence-vs. integrity-based trust violation. *Organizational Behavior and Human Decision Processes*, *99*(1), 49-65.

Lahno, B. (2001). On the emotional character of trust. *Ethical theory and moral practice*, *4*(2), 171-189.

Lauring, J., & Klitmøller, A. (2017). Inclusive language use in multicultural business organizations: The effect on creativity and performance. *International Journal of Business Communication*, *54*(3), 306-324. doi:10.1177/2329488415572779

Lee, Y.H., & Chelladurai, P. (2018). Emotional intelligence, emotional labor, coach burnout, job satisfaction, and turnover intention in sport leadership. *European Sport Management Quarterly*, *18*(4), 393-412.

Lincoln, J.R., & Kalleberg, A.L. (1990). *Culture, control and commitment: A study of work organization and work attitudes in the United States and Japan*. New York, NY: Cambridge University Press.

Mason, D.S., Thibault, L., & Misener, L. (2006). An agency theory perspective on corruption in sport: The case of the International Olympic Committee. *Journal of Sport Management*, *20*(1), 52-73.

Maxwell, H., & Taylor, T. (2010). A culture of trust: Engaging Muslim women in community sport organizations. *European Sport Management Quarterly*, *10*(4), 465-483.

McMurphy, S. (2013). Trust, distrust, and trustworthiness in argumentation: Virtues and fallacies. *OSSA Conference Archive. 113*. Retrieved from https://scholar.uwindsor.ca/ossaarchive/OSSA10/papersandcommentaries/113

McNamee, M. (1998). Contractualism and methodological individualism and communitarianism; Situating understandings of moral trust in the context of sport and social theory. *Sport, Education and Society*, *3*(2), 161-179.

Mellalieu, S., & Hanton, S. (Eds.). (2008). *Advances in applied sport psychology: A review*. Abingdon, UK: Routledge.

Merchant, K. (1985). *Control in business organizations*. Boston, MA: Pitman.

Misener, K., & Doherty, A. (2009). A case study of organizational capacity in nonprofit community sport. *Journal of Sport Management*, *23*(4), 457-482.

Nieminen, A., & Lehtonen, M. (2008). Organisational control in programme teams: An empirical study in change programme context. *International Journal of Project Management*, *26*(1), 63-72. doi:10.1016/j.ijproman.2007.08.001

Oakes, L.S., Townley, B., & Cooper, D.J. (1998). Business planning as pedagogy: Language and control in a changing institutional field. *Administrative Science Quarterly*, *43*(2), 257-292. doi:10.2307/2393853

O'Boyle, I., & Shilbury, D. (2016). Exploring issues of trust in collaborative sport governance. *Journal of Sport Management*, *30*(1), 52-69.

O'Gorman, J. (2012). The changing nature of sports volunteering: Modernization, policy and practice. In D. Hassan & J. Lusted (Eds.), *Managing sport: Social and cultural perspectives* (pp. 218-238). Abingdon, UK: Routledge.

Olekalns, M., & Smith, P.L. (2009). Mutually dependent: Power, trust, affect and the use of deception in negotiation. *Journal of Business Ethics*, *85*(3), 347-365.

Oliga, J.C. (1989). *Power, ideology and control*. London, UK: Plenum Press.

Otley, D., & Berry, A.J. (1980). Control, organisation and accounting. *Accounting, Organizations and Society*, *5*(2), 231-244. doi:10.1016/0361-3682(80)90012-4

Ouchi, W.G. (1977). The relationship between organizational structure and organizational control. *Administrative Science Quarterly*, *22*(1), 95-113.

Ouchi, W.G. (1979). A conceptual framework for the design of organizational control mechanisms. *Management Science*, *25*(9), 833-848. doi:10.1287/mnsc.25.9.833

Ouchi, W.G. (1980). Markets, bureaucracies, and clans. *Administrative Science Quarterly*, *25*(1), 129-141.

Ouchi, W.G., & Johnson, J.B. (1978). Types of organizational control and their relationship to emotional well-being. *Administrative Science Quarterly*, *23*(2), 293-317. doi:10.2307/2392566

Ouchi, W.G., & Maguire, M.A. (1975). Organizational control: Two functions. *Administrative Science Quarterly*, *20*(4), 559-569.

Overbye, M. (2016). Doping control in sport: An investigation of how elite athletes perceive and trust the functioning of the doping testing system in their sport. *Sport Management Review*, *19*(1), 6-22.

Parks, J.B., & Roberton, M.A. (2002). The gender gap in student attitudes toward sexist/nonsexist language: Implications for sport management education. *Journal of Sport Management*, *16*(3), 190-208. doi:10.1123/jsm.16.3.190

Patra, K. (2014). Mary Wilson becomes controlling owner of Buffalo Bills. Retrieved from http://www.nfl.com/news/story/0ap2000000339260/article/mary-wilson-becomes-controlling-owner-of-buffalo-bills

Perrow, C. (1970). *Organizational analysis: A sociological view*. Belmont, CA: Wadsworth.

Pfeffer, J. (1981). *Power in organizations*. New York, NY: HarperCollins.

Pfeffer, J., & Salancik, G.R. (2003). *The external control of organizations: A resource dependence perspective* (2nd ed.). Redwood City, CA: Stanford University Press.

Pitter, R. (1990). Power and control in an amateur sport organization. *International Review for the Sociology of Sport*, *25*(4), 309-321. doi:10.1177/101269029002500404

Proksch, M., Orth, U.R., & Cornwell, T.B. (2015). Competence enhancement and anticipated emotion as motivational drivers of brand attachment. *Psychology & Marketing*, *32*(9), 934-949.

Rodgers, W. (2009). Three primary trust pathways underlying ethical considerations. *Journal of Business Ethics, 91*, 83-93.

Rodriguez-Pomeda, J., Casani, F., & Alonso-Almeida, M.D.M. (2017). Emotions' management within the Real Madrid football club business model. *Soccer & Society*, *18*(4), 431-444.

Sagi, E., & Diermeier, D. (2017). Language use and coalition formation in multiparty negotiations. *Cognitive Science*, *41*(1), 259-271. doi:10.1111/cogs.12325

Schein, E.H. (1990). Organizational culture. *American Psychologist*, *45*(2), 109-119. doi:10.1037/0003-066X.45.2.109

Schein, E.H. (1993). How can organizations learn faster? The challenge of entering the green room. *Sloan Management Review*, *34*(2), 85-92.

Schein, E.H. (2004). *Organizational culture and leadership* (3rd ed.). San Francisco, CA: John Wiley & Sons.

Shaw, S., & Slack, T. (2002). "It's been like that for donkey's years": The construction of gender relations and the cultures of sports organizations. *Sport in Society*, *5*(1), 86-106.

Shogan, D. (1991). Trusting paternalism? Trust as a condition for paternalistic decisions. *Journal of the Philosophy of Sport, 18*(1), 49-58. doi: 10.1080/00948705.1991.9714485

Simons, T. (2002). Behavioral integrity: The perceived alignment between managers' words and deeds as a research focus. *Organization Science*, *13*(1), 18-35.

Sitkin, S.B., Cardinal, L.B., & Bijlsma-Frankema, K.M. (2010). *Organizational control* (Reissue ed.). Cambridge, UK: Cambridge University Press.

Snyder, E.E. (1990). Emotion and sport: A case study of collegiate women gymnasts. *Sociology of Sport Journal*, *7*(3), 254-270.

Sport Information Resource Centre. (2016). Underserviced youth: Sports participation barriers and best practices. Retrieved from http://sircuit.ca/underserviced-youth/

Stearns, P. N. (1986). Historical analysis in the study of emotion. *Motivation and Emotion*, *10*(2), 185-193.

Strashin, J. (2016). Why your kids' sports may be bad for your health. Retrieved from www.cbc.ca/sports/sports-participation-canada-adults-1.3577244

Swanson, S., & Kent, A. (2017). Passion and pride in professional sports: Investigating the role of workplace emotion. *Sport Management Review*, *20*(4), 352-364. doi:10.1016/J.SMR.2016.10.004

Tannenbaum, A.S. (1962). Control in organizations: Individual adjustment and organizational performance. *Administrative Science Quarterly*, 7(2), 236-257.

Taylor, E.A., Smith, A.B., Welch, N.M., & Hardin, R. (2018). "You should be flattered!": Female sport management faculty experiences of sexual harassment and sexism. *Women in Sport and Physical Activity Journal*, *26*(1), 43-53.

Taylor, F.W. (1911). *The principles of scientific management*. New York, NY: Harper.

Thompson, J.D. (1967). *Organizations in action: Social science bases of administrative theory*. New York, NY: McGraw-Hill.

Thurston, A. (2017). *An analysis of the implementation of Clubmark and two associated policies in boxing, swimming and rugby union* (Unpublished doctoral thesis). Leicestershire, UK: Loughborough University. Retrieved from https://dspace.lboro.ac.uk/2134/25521

Tietze, S. (2015). *International management and language*. Abingdon, UK: Routledge.

Tietze, S., Cohen, L., & Musson, G. (2003). *Understanding organizations through language*. London, UK: SAGE.

Turner, J.H. (1989). *A theory of social interaction*. Redwood City, CA: Stanford University Press.

Tymowski, G., Byers, T., & Mason, F. (2015). Ethical behavior and values in sport. In T. Byers (Ed.), *Contemporary issues in sport management: A critical introduction*. London, UK: SAGE.

WADA. (2019). World anti-doping code 2015 with 2019 amendments. Retrieved from https://www.wada-ama.org/sites/default/files/resources/files/wada_anti-doping_code_2019_english_final_revised_v1_linked.pdf

Weber, M. (1947). *The theory of social and economic organization* (Reprint ed.). New York, NY: Martino Fine Books.

Weibel, A., Den Hartog, D.N., Gillespie, N., Searle, R., Six, F. & Skinner, D. (2015). How do controls impact employee trust in the employer? *Human Resources Management, 55*, 437-462. doi:10.1002/hrm.21733

Westwood, R.I., & Linstead, S. (2001). *The language of organization*. London, UK: SAGE.

Williamson, O. (1975). *Markets and hierarchies: Antitrust analysis and implications*. New York, NY: Free Press.

Woodward, J. (1970). *Industrial organisation: Behaviour and control*. Oxford, UK: Oxford University Press.

Wu, S.H., Tsai, C.Y.D., & Hung, C.C. (2012). Toward team or player? How trust, vicarious achievement motive, and identification affect fan loyalty. *Journal of Sport Management, 26*(2), 177-191.

Zucker, L.G. (1987). Institutional theories of organization. *Annual Review of Sociology, 13*, 443-464.

Chapter 11

Acker, J. (1990). Hierarchies, jobs, bodies: A theory of gendered organizations. *Gender & Society, 4*(2), 139-158.

Acker, J. (2006). Inequality regimes: Gender, class, and race in organizations. *Gender & Society, 20*(4), 441-464.

Acosta, R.V., & Carpenter, L.J. (2014). Women in intercollegiate sport. A longitudinal, national study thirty-seven year update. Retrieved from http://www.acostacarpenter.org/

Adriaanse, J.A. (2012). *Gender dynamics on boards of national sport organisations in Australia.* (Unpublished doctoral dissertation). University of Sydney, Sydney, Australia.

Adriaanse, J.A., & Claringbould, I. (2016). Gender equality in sport leadership: From the Brighton declaration to the Sydney scoreboard. *International Review of the Sociology of Sport, 51*(5), 547-566.

Adriaanse, J.A., & Schofield, T. (2013). Analysing gender dynamics in sport governance: A new regimes-based approach. *Sport Management Review, 16*(4), 498-513.

Adriaanse, J.A., & Schofield, T. (2014). The impact of gender quotas on gender equality in sport governance. *Journal of Sport Management, 28*(5), 485-497.

Aitchinson, C.C. (2005). Feminist and gender research in sport and leisure management: Understanding the social-cultural nexus of gender-power relations. *Journal of Sport Management, 19*, 422-441.

Alvesson, M. (2002). *Understanding organizational culture*. London, UK: SAGE.

Alvesson, M., & Billing, Y.D. (1997). *Understanding gender and organizations*. London, UK: SAGE.

Alvesson, M., & Billing, Y.D. (2009). *Understanding gender and organizations*. London, UK: SAGE.

Ashcraft, K. (2013). The glass slipper: Incorporating occupational identity in management studies. *Academy of Management Review, 38*(1), 6-31.

Bach, T. (2014). Opening speech at 6th IWG Conference on Women and Sport. Retrieved from https://iwg–gti-org.directo.fi/@Bin/372463/Thomas+Bach+IWG+Opening+Ceremony+-speech+12+June.pdf

Baumgartner, M.S., & Schneider, D.E. (2010). Perceptions of women in management: A thematic analysis of razing the glass ceiling. *Journal of Career Development, 37*(2), 559-576.

BBC Sport. (2014, May 22). Helena Costa has "no fear" of coaching men's team. BBC Sport, Retrieved from www.bbc.co.uk/sport/football/27526264

BBC Sport. (2019, August 15). Stephanie Frappart: History-making referee praised for Super Cup performance. BBC Sport, Retrieved from www.bbc.com/sport/football/49352647

Borland, J.F., & Bruening, J.E. (2010). Navigating barriers: A qualitative examination of the under-representation of black females as head coaches in collegiate basketball. *Sport Management Review, 13*(4), 407-420.

Boulongne, Y.-P. (2000). Pierre de Coubertin and women's sport. *Olympic Review*, February-March, 23-26.

Broch, T.B. (2011). Norwegian big bang theory: Production of gendered sound during team handball broadcasts. *International Journal of Sport Communication, 4*(3), 344-358.

Bruckmüller, S., & Branscombe, N.R. (2010). The glass cliff: When and why women are selected as leaders in crisis contexts. *British Journal of Social Psychology, 49*, 433-451.

Bruckmüller, S., Ryan, M.K., Rink, F., & Haslam, S.A. (2014). Beyond the glass ceiling: The glass cliff and its lessons for organizational policy. *Social Issues and Policy Review, 8*(1), 202-232.

Bruening, J.E. (2005). Gender and racial analysis in sport: Are all the women White and all the Blacks men? *Quest, 57*(4), 330-349.

Bruening, J.E., & Dixon, M.A. (2008). Situating work–family negotiations within a life course perspective: Insights on the gendered experiences of NCAA Division I head coaching mothers. *Sex Roles, 58*, 10-23.

Burton, L.J. (2015). Underrepresentation of women in sport leadership: A review of research. *Sport Management Review, 18*(2), 155-165.

Burton, L.J., Grappendorf, H., & Henderson, A. (2011). Perceptions of gender in athletic administration: Utilizing role congruity to examine (potential) prejudice against women. *Journal of Sport Management, 25*, 36-45.

Chelladurai, P. (2009). *Managing organizations for sport and physical activity: A systems perspective* (3rd ed.). Scottsdale, AZ: Holcomb-Hathaway.

Claringbould, I., & Knoppers, A. (2007). Finding a 'normal' woman: Selection processes for board membership. *Sex Roles, 56*, 495-507.

Claringbould, I., & Knoppers, A. (2008). Doing and undoing gender in sport governance. *Sex Roles, 58*, 81-92.

Claringbould, I., & Knoppers, A. (2012). Paradoxical practices of gender in sport-related organisations. *Journal of Sport Management, 26*, 404-416.

Clinton, H.R. (1997). *Remarks and commentary by First Lady Hillary Rodham Clinton: Vital voices, 1997-1999*. Washington, D.C.: U.S. GPO.

Connell, R.W. (1987). *Gender and power*. Sydney, Australia: Allan & Unwin.

Connell, R.W. (2002). *Gender*. Cambridge, UK: Polity Press

Connell, R.W. (2005). Advancing gender reform in large-scale organisations: A new approach for practitioners and researchers. *Policy and Society, 24*(4), 5-24.

Connell, R.W. (2009). *Gender*. Cambridge, UK: Polity Press.

Council of Europe (2004). *Gender mainstreaming: Conceptual framework, methodology and presentation of good practice: Final report of activities of the Group of Specialists on Mainstreaming (EG-S-MS)*. Strasbourg, France: Directorate General of Human Rights.

Court of Arbitration for Sport. (2019, May 1). *CAS arbitration: Caster Semenya, Athletics South Africa (ASA) and International Association of Athletics Federation (IAAF)* [Press release]. Retrieved from www.tas-cas.org/fileadmin/user_upload/Media_Release_Semenya_ASA_IAAF_decision.pdf

Cunningham, G.B. (2010). Understanding the under-representation of African American coaches: A multilevel perspective. *Sport Management Review*, *13*(4), 395-406.

Dahlerup, D. (Ed.). (2013). *Women, quotas and politics*. Abingdon, UK: Routledge.

Dahlerup, D., & Freidenvall, L. (2005). Quotas as a 'fast track' to equal representation for women: Why Scandinavia is no longer the model. *International Feminist Journal of Politics*, *7*(1), 26-48.

Dashper, K. (2012). Together, yet still not equal? Sex integration in equestrian sport. *Asia-Pacific Journal of Health, Sport and Physical Education*, *3*(3), 213-225.

DeFrantz, A.L. (1997). The changing role of women in the Olympic Games. *Olympic Review 26*(15), 18-21.

DiMaggio, P.J., & Powell, W.W. (1983). The iron cage revisited: Institutional isomorphism and collective rationality in organizational fields. *American Sociological Review*, *48*(2), 147-160.

Dixon, M.A., & Bruening, J.E. (2007). Work–family conflict in coaching I: A top-down perspective. *Journal of Sport Management*, *21*(3), 377-406.

Ely, R.J., & Meyerson, D.E. (2000). Theories of gender in organizations: A new approach to organizational analysis and change. *Research in Organizational Behavior*, *22*, 103-151.

Ely, R.J., & Padavic, I. (2007). A feminist analysis of organizational research on sex differences. *Academy of Management Review*, *32*, 1121-1143.

Fasting, K. (2000). Women's role in national and international sport governing bodies. In B.L. Drinkwater (Ed.), *Women in sport: Volume XIII of the encyclopaedia of sports medicine.* (pp. 441-451). Oxford, UK: Blackwell Science.

Fasting, K., Sand, T.S., Pike, E., & Matthews, J. (2014). *From Brighton to Helsinki. Women and sport progress report 1994-2014.* Helsinki, Finland: Finnish Sports Confederation Valo.

Fink, J.S., Parker, H.M., Cunningham, G.B., & Cuneen, J. (2012). Female athlete endorsers: Determinants of effectiveness. *Sport Management Review*, *15*(1), 13-22.

Flake, C.R., Dufur, M.J., & Moore, E.L. (2013). Advantage men: The sex pay gap in professional tennis. *International Review for the Sociology of Sport*, *48*(3), 366-376.

Gramsci, A. (1971). *Selections from the prison notebooks of Antonio Gramsci* (Q. Hoare & GN Smith, Eds. & Trans.). New York, NY: International.

Hall, M.A. (1990). How should we theorize gender in the context of sport. In M. Messner (Ed.), *Sport, men, and the gender order: Critical feminist perspectives* (pp. 223-239). Champaign, IL: Human Kinetics.

Hall, M.A. (1996). *Feminism and sporting bodies: Essays on theory and practice*. Champaign, IL: Human Kinetics.

Hall, M.A., Cullen, D., & Slack, T. (1989) Organisational elites recreating themselves: The gender structure of national sports organisations. *Quest*, *41*, 28-45.

Hardy, C., & Clegg, S.R. (1996). Some dare call it power. In S.R. Clegg, C. Hardy, & W.R. Nord (Eds.), *Handbook of organization studies* (pp. 622-641). London, UK: SAGE.

Hargreaves, J.A. (1986). Where's the virtue? Where's the grace? A discussion of the social production of gender relations in and through sport. *Theory, Culture and Society*, *3*(1), 109-121.

Hartmann-Tews, I., & Combrink, C. (2005). Under-representation of women in governing bodies of sport. In G. Doll-Tepper, G. Pfister, D. Scoretz, & C. Bilan (Eds.), *Sport, women & leadership* (pp. 71-78). Berlin, Germany: Sport and Buch Strauss.

Hartmann-Tews, I., & Pfister, G. (Eds.). (2003). *Sport and women: Social issues in international perspective.* London, UK: Routledge.

Henry, I., & Robinson, L. (2010). *Gender equality and leadership in Olympic bodies*. Loughborough, UK: Centre for Olympic Studies and Research, Loughborough University and International Olympic Committee.

Hoeber, L., & Frisby, W. (2001). Gender equity for athletes: Rewriting the narrative for this organizational value. *European Sport Management Quarterly*, *1*(3), 179-209.

Hoffman, J. (2011). The old boys' network. *Journal for the Study of Sports and Athletes in Education*, *5*(1), 9-28. doi:10.1179/ssa.2011.5.1.9

Holter, Ø.G. (2003). *Can men do it?: Men and gender equality—the Nordic experience*. Copenhagen, Denmark: Nordic Council of Ministers.

Hovden, J. (2000). 'Heavyweight' men and younger women? The gendering of selection processes in Norwegian sports organisations. *NORA: Nordic Journal of Women's Studies*, *8*, 17-32.

Hovden, J. (2006). The gender order as a policy issue in sport: A study of Norwegian sports organizations. *Nordic Journal of Women's Studies*, *14*(1), 41-53.

Hovden, J. (2010). Female top leaders–prisoners of gender? The gendering of leadership discourses in Norwegian sports organizations. *International Journal of Sport Policy*, *2*(2), 189-203.

Hymowitz, C., & Schellhardt, T.D. (1986, March 24). Special report on the corporate woman: The glass ceiling: Why women can't seem to break the invisible barrier that blocks them from the top jobs. *The Wall Street Journal*.

IAAF. (2018). *IAAF introduces new eligibility regulations for female classification* [Press release]. Retrieved from www.iaaf.org/news/press-release/eligibility-regulations-for-female-classifica

Inglis, S., Danylchuk, K.E., & Pastore, D. (1996). Understanding retention factors in coaching and athletic management positions. *Journal of Sport Management*, *10*(3), 237-249.

IOC. (2016). Annual report. IOC. Retrieved from https://www.olympic.org/news/the-ioc-publishes-its-2016-annual-report-and-financial-statements

Kanter, R.M. (1977). *Men and women of the corporation*. New York, NY: Basic Books.

Karvonen, L., & Selle, P. (1995). *Women in Nordic politics: Closing the gap.* Aldershot, UK: Dartmouth.

Kay, T. (2003). Sport and gender. In B. Houlihan (Ed.), *Sport and society: A student introduction* (pp. 89-104). London, UK: SAGE.

Kessel, A. (2014, May 8). Helena Costa will have to be a master tactician off the football field. *The Guardian*, Retrieved from www.theguardian.com/commentisfree/2014/may/08/helena-costa-master-tactician-football-field-managing-clermont-foot

Kessel, A. (2018, February 18). The future of the Commonwealth. The unequal battle: Privilege, genes, gender and power. *The Guardian*, Retrieved from https://www.theguardian.com/world/2018/feb/18/the-unequal-battle-privilege-genes-gender-and-power

Kihl, L., Shaw, S., & Schull, V. (2013). Fear, anxiety, and loss of control: Analyzing an athletic department merger as a gendered political process. *Journal of Sport Management*, *27*(2), 146-157.

Knoppers, A. (1987). Gender and the coaching profession. *Quest*, *39*(1), 9-22.

Kristiansen, E., Broch, T.B., & Pedersen, P.M. (2014). Negotiating gender in professional soccer: An analysis of female footballers in the United States. *Choregia*, *10*(1), 5-27.

Kulich, C., Ryan, M.K., & Haslam, S.A. (2014). The political glass cliff: Understanding how seat selection contributes to the underperformance of ethnic minority candidates. *Political Research Quarterly*, *67*(1), 84-95.

Ljungqvist, A. (2017). Sex segregation and sport. *British Journal of Sports Medicine*, *52*(1), doi:10.1136/bjsports-2017-098511

Lopiano, D.A. (2000). Modern history of women in sports: Twenty-five years of Title IX. *Clinics in Sports Medicine*, *19*(2), 163-173.

Martin, J. (2019). "It's a ruse": USWNT and US soccer fight for moral high ground on equal pay battle. CNN, Retrieved from https://edition.cnn.com/2019/07/30/football/uswnt-players-respond-to-us-soccer-president-open-letter-spt-intl/index.html

Martin, P.Y. (2003). Said and done versus saying and doing gendering practices, practicing gender at work. *Gender & Society*, *17*(3), 342-366.

McKay, J. (1992). *Why so few? Women executives in Australian sport.* Canberra, Australia: National Sports Research Centre.

McKay, J. (1997). *Managing gender: Affirmative action and organizational power in Australian, Canadian, and New Zealand sport.* Albany, NY: SUNY Press.

Melton, E.N., & Cunningham, G.B. (2014). Who are the champions? Using a multilevel model to examine perceptions of employee support for LGBT inclusion in sport organizations. *Journal of Sport Management*, *28*, 189-206.

Meyerson, D.E., & Fletcher, J.K. (2000). A modest manifesto for shattering the glass ceiling. *Harvard Business Review*, *78*(1), 126-136.

Norman, L. (2010). Bearing the burden of doubt. *Research Quarterly for Exercise and Sport*, *81*(4), 506-517.

Obayiuwana, O. (2014, May 12). *Osasu Obayiuwana*: Crossing the gender frontier. Inside World Football, Retrieved from .www.insideworldfootball.com/osasu-obayiuwana/14614-osasu-obayiuwana-crossing-the-gender-frontier?acm=4715_757

Olympic Review. (1981). New members. *Olympic Review*, *169*, 632-633.

Ottesen, L., Skirstad, B., Pfister, G., & Habermann, U. (2010). Gender relations in Scandinavian sport organizations: A comparison of the situation and the policies in Denmark, Norway and Sweden. *Sport in Society*, *13*(4), 657-675.

Pettigrew, A.M. (1985). *The awakening giant.* Oxford, UK: Basil Blackwell.

Pettigrew, A.M. (1987). Context and action in the transformation of the firm. *Journal of Management Studies*, *24*(6), 649-668.

Pettigrew, A.M. (1990). Longitudinal field research on change: Theory and practice. *Organization Science*, *1*(3), 267-292.

Pettigrew, A.M., Woodman, R.W., & Cameron, K.S. (2001). Studying organizational change and development: Challenges for future research. *Academy of Management Journal*, *44*(4), 697-713.

Pfister, G., & Radtke, S. (2009). Sport, women and leadership: Results of a project on executives in German sports organizations. *European Journal of Sport Science*, *9*, 229-243.

Pieper, L.P. (2014). Sex testing and the maintenance of western femininity in international sport. *The International Journal of the History of Sport*, *31*(13), 1557-1576.

Plymoth, B. (2012). Gender in equestrian sports: An issue of difference and equality. *Sport in Society*, *15*(3), 335-348.

Rees, T. (2002, April 18-21). A new strategy: Gender mainstreaming. European women and sport, presented at 5th EWS Conference on Women, Sport and Innovation, Berlin. Berlin, Germany: Deutscher Sportbund.

Ryan, M.K., Haslam, S.A. Hersby, M.D., & Bongiorno, R. (2011). Think crisis–think female: Glass cliffs and contextual variation in the think manager–think male stereotype. *Journal of Applied Psychology*, *96*, 470-484.

Samaranch, J.A. (1981). Speech by Mr. Juan Antonio Samaranch. *Olympic Review*, *169*, 603-607.

Samaranch, J.A. (1982). Speech delivered by IOC President. *Olympic Review*, *170*, 315-318.

Sanders, E. (2019). Liverpool Women's pre-season tour with men's team a sign of changing status. BBC Sport, Retrieved from www.bbc.co.uk/sport/football/49152793

Sartore, M.L., & Cunningham, G.B. (2007). Explaining the under-representation of women in leadership positions of sport organizations: A symbolic interactionist perspective. *Quest*, *59*(2), 244-265.

Sawer, P. (2019, June 27). Muirfield Golf Club finally admits its first women members 275 years after it opened. Retrieved from https://www.telegraph.co.uk/news/2019/06/27/muirfield-golf-club-finally-admits-first-women-members-275-years/

Schein, V.E. (1973). The relationship between sex role stereotypes and requisite management characteristics. *Journal of Applied Psychology*, *57*(2), 95.

Schofield, T., & Goodwin, S. (2005). Gender politics and public policy making: Prospects for advancing gender equality. *Policy and Society*, *24*(4), 25-44.

Schull, V., Shaw, S., & Kihl, L.A. (2013). "If a woman came in . . . she would have been eaten up alive": Analyzing gendered political processes in the search for an athletic director. *Gender & Society*, *27*(1), 56-81.

Scott, W. (2003). *Organizations: Rational, natural and open systems* (5th ed.). Englewood Cliffs, NJ: Prentice-Hall.

SHARP Center. (2013). Women in the Olympic and Paralympic games. Research report. Retrieved from http://sharp.research.umich.edu/wp-content/uploads/2017/03/olympic_report_2012_final-4-11-13.pdf

Shaw, S. (2006). Scratching the back of Mr. X: Analyzing gendered social processes in sport organizations. *Journal of Sport Management*, *20*, 510-534.

Shaw, S., & Frisby, W. (2006). Can gender equity be more equitable? Promoting an alternative frame for sport management research, education, and practice. *Journal of Sport Management*, *20*, 483-509.

Shaw, S., & Hoeber, L. (2003). "A strong man is direct and a direct woman is a bitch": Gendered discourses and their influence on employment roles in sport organisations. *Journal of Sport Management*, *17*, 347-375.

Shaw, S., & Penney, D. (2003). Gender equity policies in national governing bodies: An oxymoron or a vehicle for change? *European Sport Management Quarterly*, *3*, 78-102.

Shaw, S., & Slack, T. (2002). "It's been like that for Donkey's Years": The construction of gender relations and the cultures of sports organizations. *Sport in Society*, *5*(1), 86-106.

Sibson, R. (2010). "I was banging my head against a brick wall": Exclusionary power and the gendering of sport organizations. *Journal of Sport Management*, *24*, 379-399.

Sisjord, M.K., Fasting, K., & Sand, T.S. (2017). The impact of gender quotas in leadership in Norwegian organised sport. *International Journal of Sport Policy and Politics*, *9*(3), 505-519.

Sisjord, M.K., & Kristiansen, E. (2008). Serious athletes or media clowns? Female and male wrestlers' perceptions of media constructions. *Sociology of Sport Journal*, *25*, 350-368.

Skirstad, B. (2000). Gender verification in competitive sport: turning from research to action. In T. Tännsjö & C. Tamburrini

(Eds.), *Values in sport: Elitism, nationalism, gender equality and the scientific manufacture of winners* (pp. 116-122). Oxfordshire, UK: Taylor & Francis.

Skirstad, B. (2004). Democratisation of access to sport activities and sport organisations, presented at 6th European Women and Sport Conference, Paris, April 22-23, 2014. Paris, France: Comité National Olympique et Sportif Français (CNOSF).

Skirstad, B. (2009). Gender policy and organizational change: A contextual approach. *Sport Management Review*, *12*(4), 202-216.

Skirstad, B. (2014). Er kvinner under-representert i norsk idrettsledelse? Utviklingen de siste 30 år. [Are women under-represented in Norwegian sport leadership? Developments in the last 30 years.] In G. von der Lippe & H. Hognestad (Eds.), *Kjønnsmakt i idrett og friluftsliv* [Gender power in sport and outdoor activities] (pp.215-237). Oslo, Norway: Novus forlag.

Slack, T., & Hinings, C.R. (1995). Institutional pressures and isomorphic change: An empirical test. *Organization Studies*, *15*(6), 803-827.

Smith, A. (2014, October 4). Interview: Shelley Kerr, Stirling University Coach. *The Scotsman*, Retrieved from www.scotsman.com/sport/football/interview-shelley-kerr-stirling-university-coach-1-3562550

Strittmatter, A.-M., & Skirstad, B. (2017). Managing football organizations: A man's world? Comparing women in decision making positions in Germany and Norway and their international influence: A Contextual Approach. *Soccer & Society*, *18*(1), 81-101.

Teigen, M. (2000). *Likestilling som legitimeringsstrategi: Rekrutteringsnormer og likestillingspolitikk ved NTNU.* [Equality legitimation strategy and recruitment norms and gender policy at NTNU.] *Sosiologisk tidsskrift*, *2*(125), 47.

Teigen, M. (2002). The universe of gender quotas. *NIKK magasin*, *3*, 4-8.

Terjesen, S., Sealy, R., & Singh, V. (2009). Women directors on corporate boards: A review and research agenda. *Corporate Governance: An International Review*, *17*(3), 320-337.

Theberge, N. (1987). Sport and women's empowerment. *Women's Studies International Forum*, *10*, 387-393.

Thomas, D.A., & Ely, R.J. (1996). Making differences matter: A new paradigm for managing diversity. *Harvard Business Review*, September-October, 79-90.

Topend Sports. (2016). Gender testing at the Olympic Games. Topend Sports, Retrieved from www.topendsports.com/events/summer/gender-testing.htm

Walker, N.A., & Sartore-Baldwin, M.L. (2013). Hegemonic masculinity and the institutionalized bias toward women in men's collegiate basketball: What do men think? *Journal of Sport Management*, *27*(4), 303-315.

Ward, M. (2019, April 24). "Get women back in the kitchen": Women in sport suffer more online abuse. *The Sunday Morning Herald*, Retrieved from www.smh.com.au/lifestyle/gender/get-back-in-the-kitchen-women-in-sport-suffer-more-online-abuse-20190423-p51gie.html

Whisenant, W., Miller, J., & Pedersen, P.M. (2005). Systemic barriers in athletic administration: An analysis of job descriptions for interscholastic athletic directors. *Sex Roles*, *53*(11-12), 911-918.

White, A., & Brackenridge, C. (1985). Who rules sport? Gender divisions in the power structure of British sports organisations from 1960. *International Review for the Sociology of Sport*, *20*(1-2), 95-107.

White, M., & Kay, J. (2006). Who rules sport now? White and Brackenridge revisited. *International Review for the Sociology of Sport*, *41*(3-4), 465-473.

Whiteside, E., & Hardin, M. (2012). On being a "good sport" in the workplace: Women, the glass ceiling and negotiated resignation in sports information. *International Journal of Sport Communication*, *5*(1), 51-68.

Willsher, K., & Martin, M.-H. (2014). Helena Costa: I walked from Clermont Foot 63 after being sidelined by men. *The Guardian*, Retrieved from https://www.theguardian.com/football/2014/jun/25/helena-costa-male-colleagues-football-france

Chapter 12

Amis, J., Slack, T., & Berrett, T. (1995). The structural antecedents of conflict in voluntary sport organizations. *Leisure Studies*, *14*, 1-16.

Argyris, C. (1960). *Understanding organizational behavior*. Homewood, IL: Dorsey.

Australian Bureau of Statistics. (2006). Volunteers in Sport, Cat. No. 4440.0.55.001. Canberra: Commonwealth of Australia.

Australian Bureau of Statistics. (2010). Volunteers in Sport, Cat. No. 4440.0.55.001. Canberra: Commonwealth of Australia.

Bang, H., Ross, S., & Reio, T. (2013). From motivation to organizational commitment of volunteers in non-profit sports organizations. *Journal of Management Development*, *32*(1), 96-112.

Becker, H.S. (1960). Notes on the concept of commitment. *American Journal of Sociology*, *66*, 32-40.

Braun, S. (2003). Delivering services in voluntary associations: Collective work and the volunteer crisis. In J. Baur & S. Braun (Eds.), *Integration efforts of sports clubs as voluntary organizations* (pp. 191-241). Aachen, Germany: Meyer & Meyer.

Buchanan, B., II. (1974). Building organizational commitment: The socialization of managers in work organizations. *Administrative Science Quarterly*, *19*, 533-546.

Bussell, H., & Forbes, D. (2003). The volunteer life cycle: A marketing model for volunteering. *Voluntary Action*, *5*(3), 61-79.

Carbery, R., Garavan, T.H., O'Brien, F., & McDonnell, J. (2003). Predicting hotel managers' turnover cognitions. *Journal of Managerial Psychology*, *18*, 649-679.

Chelladurai, P. (2009). *Managing organizations for sport and physical activity: A systems perspective* (3rd Ed.). Scottsdale, AZ: Holcomb Hathaway.

Cnaan, R.A., Handy, F., & Wadsworth, M. (1996). Defining who is a volunteer: Conceptual and empirical considerations. *Nonprofit and Voluntary Sector Quarterly*, *25*(3), 364-383.

Connors, T. (2012). *The volunteer management handbook: Leadership strategies for success*. Hoboken, NJ: Wiley.

Conway, N., & Briner, R.B. (2005). *Understanding psychological contracts at work: A critical evaluation of theory and research*. New York, NY: Oxford University Press.

Cuskelly, G., & Auld, C.J. (1999). People management: The key to business success. In L. Trenberth and C. Collins (Eds.), *Sport business management in New Zealand* (pp. 164-183). Palmerston North, New Zealand: Dunmore Press.

Cuskelly, G., Boag, A., & McIntyre, N. (1999). Differences in organizational commitment between paid and volunteer administrators in sport. *European Journal of Sport Management*, *6*, 39-61.

Cuskelly, G., Hoye, R., & Auld, C. (2006). *Working with volunteers in sport: Theory and practice*. London, UK: Routledge.

Cuskelly, G., McIntyre, N., & Boag, A. (1998). A longitudinal study of the development of organizational commitment amongst volunteer sport administrators. *Journal of Sport Management*, *12*(3), 181-202.

Cuskelly, G., Taylor, T., Hoye, R., & Darcy, S. (2006). The relationship between volunteer management practices and volunteer retention in community sport organisations. *Sport Management Review*, *9*(2), 141-163.

Egli, B., Schlesinger, T., & Nagel, S. (2014). Expectation-based types of volunteers in Swiss sports clubs. *Managing Leisure*, *19*(5), 359-375. doi:10.1080/13606719.2014.885714

Engelberg, T., Skinner, J., & Zakus, D. (2011). Exploring the relationship between commitment, experience, and self-assessed performance in youth sport organisations. *Sport Management Review*, *14*, 117-125.

Engelberg, T., Zakus, D., Skinner, J., & Campbell, A. (2012). Defining and measuring dimensionality and targets of the commitment of sport volunteers. *Journal of Sport Management*, *26*(2), 192-205.

Etzioni, A. (1961). *A comparative analysis of complex organizations*. New York, NY: Free Press.

Farmer, S.M., & Fedor, D.B. (1999). Volunteer participation and withdrawal: A psychological contract perspective on the role of expectations and organizational support. *Nonprofit Management & Leadership*, *9*(4), 349-367.

Fuller, J.B., Barnett, T., Hester, K., & Relyea, C. (2003). A social identity perspective on the relationship between perceived organizational support and organizational commitment. *Journal of Social Psychology*, *143*, 789-791.

Harman, A., & Doherty, A. (2014). The psychological contract of volunteer youth coaches. *Journal of Sport Management*, *28*(6), 687-699. doi:10.1123/jsm.2013-0146

Hill, M., & Stevens, D. (2011). Volunteers who manage other volunteers and the professionalization of volunteer management: Implications for practice. *Voluntary Sector Review*, *2*(1), 107-114.

Hoye, R. (2007). Commitment, involvement and performance of voluntary sport organization board members. *European Sport Management Quarterly*, *7*(1), 109-121.

Hoye, R., Cuskelly, G., Auld, C., Kappelides, P., & Misener, K. (2020). *Sport volunteering*. London, UK: Routledge.

International Labour Organization (ILO). (2011). *Manual on the measurement of volunteer work*. Geneva, Switzerland: International Labour Office.

Kanter, R.M. (1968). Commitment and social organization: A study of commitment mechanisms in utopian communities. *American Sociological Review*, *33*, 499-517.

Kelman, H.C. (1958). Compliance, identification, and internalization: Three processes of attitude change. *Journal of Conflict Resolution*, *2*(1), 51-60.

Kikulis, L.M., Slack, T., and Hinings, B. (1995). Does decision making make a difference? Patterns of change within Canadian national sporting organizations. *Journal of Sport Management*, *9*, 273-299.

Kohlberg, L. (1969). Stage and sequence: The cognitive-developmental approach to socialization. In D.A. Goslin (Ed.), *Handbook of socialization theory and research* (pp. 347-480). Chicago, IL: Rand McNally.

Levinson, H. (1962). *Men, management and mental health*. Cambridge, MA: Harvard University Press.

Liao-Troth, M.A. (2005). Are they here for the long haul? The effects of functional motives and personality factors on the psychological contracts of volunteers. *Nonprofit and Voluntary Sector Quarterly*, *34*(4), 510-530.

Mathieu, J.E., & Zajac, D.M. (1990). A review and meta-analysis of the antecedents, correlates, and consequences of organizational commitment. *Psychological Bulletin*, *108*(2), 171-194.

Meijs, L.C.P.M., and Hoogstad, E. (2001). New ways of managing volunteers: Combining membership management and programme management. *Voluntary Action*, 3(3), 41-61.

Meijs, L.C.P.M., and Karr, L.B. (2004). Managing volunteers in different settings: Membership and programme management. In R. Stebbins and M. Graham (Eds.), *Volunteering as leisure/leisure as volunteering* (pp. 177-193). Wallingford, UK: CABI Publishers.

Meyer, J., & Allen, N. (1997). *Commitment in the workplace. Theory, research, and application*. Thousand Oaks, CA: SAGE.

Mowday, R.T., Porter, L.W., & Steers, R.M. (1982). *Employee-organization linkages: The psychology of commitment, absenteeism, and turnover*. New York, NY: Academic Press.

Nichols, G. (2012). The psychological contract of volunteers: A new research agenda. *VOLUNTAS: International Journal of Voluntary and Nonprofit Organizations*, *24*(4), 986-1005.

Nichols, G., & Ojala, E. (2009). Understanding the management of sports events volunteers through psychological contract theory. *VOLUNTAS: International Journal of Voluntary and Nonprofit Organizations*, *20*, 369-387.

Paine, A.E., Hill, M., & Rochester, C. (2010). *"A rose by any other name . . ." Revisiting the question: "what exactly is volunteering?"* London, UK: Institute for Volunteering Research.

Park, S., & Kim, M. (2013). Development of a hierarchical model of sport volunteer's organizational commitment. *European Sport Management Quarterly*, *13*(1), 94-109.

Pearce, J.L. (1993). *Volunteers: The organizational behavior of unpaid workers*. London, UK: Routledge.

Reichers, A.E. (1986). Conflict and organizational commitments. *Journal of Applied Psychology*, *71*(3), 508-514.

Ringuet-Riot, C., Cuskelly, G., Auld, C., & Zakus, D.H. (2014). Volunteer roles, involvement and commitment in voluntary sport organizations: Evidence of core and peripheral volunteers. *Sport in Society: Cultures, Commerce, Media, Politics*, *17*(1), 116-133.

Robinson, L., & Palmer, D. (2011). *Managing voluntary sport organisations*. London, UK: Routledge.

Rousseau, D.M. (1989). Psychological and implied contracts in organizations. *Employee Responsibilities and Rights Journal*, *2*, 121-139.

Rousseau, D.M., & Tijoriwala, S.A. (1998). Assessing psychological contracts: Issues, alternatives and measures. *Journal of Organizational Behavior*, *19*, 679-695.

Schlesinger, T., Egli, B., & Nagel, S. (2013). "Continue or terminate?" Determinants of long-term volunteering in sports clubs. *European Sport Management Quarterly*, *13*(1), 32-53.

Simon, H.A. (1957). *Administrative Behavior* (2nd ed.). New York, NY: Free Press.

Sport England. (2002). *Sports volunteering in England in 2002*. London, UK: Sport England.

Statistics Canada. (2009). *Caring Canadians, involved Canadians: Highlights from the 2007 Canada survey of giving, volunteering and participating*. Ottawa, Canada: Ministry of Industry.

Stephens, R.D., Dawley, D.D., & Stephens, D.B. (2004). Commitment on the board: A model of volunteer directors' levels of organizational commitment and self-reported performance. *Journal of Managerial Studies*, 16, 483-504.

Taylor, T., Darcy, S., Hoye, R., & Cuskelly, G. (2006). Using psychological contract theory to explore issues in effective volunteer management. *European Sport Management Quarterly*, *6*(2), 123-147.

Vantilborgh, T., Bidee, J., Pepermans, R., Willems, J., Huybrechts, G., & Jegers, M. (2012). Volunteers' psychological contracts: Extending traditional views. *Nonprofit and Voluntary Sector Quarterly*, 41(6), 1072-1091.

Vézina, M., & Crompton, S. (2012). *Volunteering in Canada*. Cat. No. 11-008. Ottawa, Canada: Statistics Canada.

Chapter 13

The Association of Summer Olympic International Federations. (2016). *ASOIF Governance Task Force Report*. Retrieved from https://www.asoif.com/sites/default/files/download/asoif_governance_task_force_report.pdf

The Association of Summer Olympic International Federations. (2017). *ASOIF International Federation self-assessment questionnaire*. Retrieved from https://www.asoif.com/sites/default/files/download/if_governance_questionnaire-stage_2.pdf

Bovens, M. (2007). Analysing and assessing accountability: A conceptual framework. *European Law Journal*, *13*, 447-468.

Chaker, A.-N. (2004). *Good governance in sport, a European Survey*, Strasbourg, France: Council of Europe Publishing.

Chappelet, J.-L. & Kübler-Mabbot, B. (2008). *The International Olympic Committee and the Olympic system: The governance of world sport*. London, UK: Routledge.

Chappelet, J.-L. & Mrkonjic, M. (2013). Basic indicators for better governance in international sport (BIBGIS): An assessment tool for international sport governing bodies. *IDHEAP Online Working Papers*. Retrieved from https://serval.unil.ch/resource/serval:BIB_7BDD210D3643.P001/REF

European Commission. (1998). *The European model of sport: Consultation document of DG X*, Brussels, Belgium: European Commission.

European Union Expert Group on Good Governance. (2013). Deliverable 2: Principles of good governance in sport. Retrieved from http://ec.europa.eu/assets/eac/sport/library/policy_documents/xg-gg-201307-dlvrbl2-sept2013.pdf

FIFA. (2006). FIFA and UEFA stress the vital importance of football autonomy. Retrieved from https://www.fifa.com/about-fifa/who-we-are/news/fifa-and-uefa-stress-the-vital-importance-football-autonomy-106979

FIFA. (2019). FIFA Statutes. *June 2019 Edition*. Retrieved from https://resources.fifa.com/image/upload/fifa-statutes-5-august-2019-en.pdf?cloudid=ggyamhxxv8jrdfbekrrm

Fioramonti, L., & Fiori, A. (2010). Civil society after democracy: The evolution of civic activism in South Africa and Korea. *Journal of Civil Society*, *6*(1), 23-38.

García, B. (2009). Sport governance after the White Paper: The demise of the European model? *International Journal of Sport Policy*, *1*(3), 267-284.

García, B. (2011). The 2001 informal agreement on the international transfer system. *European Sports Law and Policy Bulletin*, *I-2011*, 17-29.

García, B. (2012). The EU and sport governance: Between economic and social values. In M. Groeneveld, B. Houlihan, & F. Ohl (Eds.), *Social capital and sport governance in Europe* (pp. 33-52). Oxon, UK: Routledge.

García, B., Niemann, A., & Grant, W. (2011). Conclusion: A Europeanised game? In A. Niemann, B. García, & W. Grant (Eds.), *The transformation of European football: Towards the Europeanisation of the national game* (pp. 239-262). Manchester, UK: Manchester University Press.

García, B., Palomar Olmeda, A., & Pérez González, C. (2011). Spain: Parochialism or innovation? In A. Niemann, B. García, & W. Grant (Eds.), *The transformation of European football: Towards the Europeanisation of the national game* (pp. 134-150). Manchester, UK: Manchester University Press.

García, B., & Welford, J. (2015). Supporters and football governance, from customers to stakeholders: A literature review and agenda for research. *Sport Management Review*, *18*(4), 517-528.

Geeraert, A. (2015). *Sports Governance Observer*. Copenhagen, Denmark: Play the Game. Retrieved from playthegame.org/media/5786679/sgo_report_final_3.pdf

Geeraert, A., Alm, J., & Groll, M. (2014). Good governance in international sport organizations: An analysis of the 35 Olympic sport governing bodies. *International Journal of Sport Policy and Politics*, *6*(3), 281-306. doi:10.1080/19406940.2013.825874

Geeraert, A., Mrkonjic, M., & Chappelet, J.-L. (2015). A rationalist perspective on the autonomy of international sport governing bodies: Towards a pragmatic autonomy in the steering of sports. *International Journal of Sport Policy and Politics*, *7*(4), 473-488. doi:10.1080/19406940.2014.925953

Geeraert, A., Scheerder, J., & Bruyninckx, H. (2013). The governance network of European football: Introducing new governance approaches to steer football at the EU level. *International Journal of Sport Policy and Politics*, *5*, 113-132. doi:10.1080/19406940.2012.659750

Henry, I., & Lee, P.C. (2004). Governance and ethics in sport. In S. Chadwick & J. Beech (Eds.), *The business of sport management* (pp. 25-41). Harlow, UK: Pearson Education.

Holt, M. (2006). *UEFA, governance and the control of club competition in European football*. London, UK: Football Governance Research Centre, Birkbeck, University of London.

Holt, M. (2007). The ownership and control of elite club competition in European football. *Soccer and Society*, *8*(1), 50-67.

Hoye, R., & Cuskelly, G. (2007). *Sport governance*. London, UK: Elsevier.

King, N.A. (2017). *Sport governance: An introduction*. London, UK: Routledge.

Kooiman, J. (1993). Social-political governance: Introduction. In J. Kooiman (Ed.), *Modern governance: New government-society interactions* (pp. 1-8). London, UK: SAGE.

March, J.G., & Olsen, J.P. (1995). *Democratic governance*. New York, NY: Free Press.

Meier, H.E., & García, B. (2015). Protecting private transnational authority against public intervention: FIFA's power over national governments. *Public Administration*, *93*(4), 890-906. doi:10.1111/padm.12208

Parrish, R. (2002). Judicial intervention and sporting autonomy: Defining the territories of EU involvement in sport. *European Sport Management Quarterly*, *2*(4), 296-307.

Peters, B.G., & Pierre, J. (1998). Governance without government? Rethinking public administration. *Journal of Public Administration Research and Theory*, *8*, 223-243.

Rhodes, R. (1997). *Understanding governance: Policy networks, governance, reflexivity and accountability*. Buckingham, UK: Open University Press.

Rosenau, J. (1992). Governance, order and change in world politics. In J. Rosenau & E.O. Czempiel (Eds.), *Governance without government* (pp. 1-29). Cambridge, UK: Cambridge University Press.

Sørensen, E., & Torfing, J. (2005). The democratic anchorage of governance networks. *Scandinavian Political Studies*, *28*, 195-218.

Tomlinson, A. (1983). Tuck up tight lads: Structures of control within football culture. In A. Tomlinson (Ed.), *Explorations in football culture* (pp. 165-186). Eastbourne, UK: Leisure Studies Association Publications.

Tricker, R.I. (2000). *Corporate governance (history of management thought)*. London, UK: Ashgate.

UEFA. (2014). *UEFA statutes: Edition 2014*. Retrieved from www.uefa.org/MultimediaFiles/Download/OfficialDocument/uefaorg/WhatUEFAis/02/09/93/25/2099325_DOWNLOAD.pdf

Van Kersbergen, K., & Van Waarden, F. (2004). "Governance" as a bridge between disciplines. *European Journal of Political Research, 43*, 143-171.

Vieweg, K. (2000). The legal autonomy of sport organisations and the restrictions of European law. In A. Caiger & S. Gardiner (Eds.), *Professional sport in the European Union: Regulation and re-regulation* (pp. 83-107). The Hague, Netherlands: TMC Asser.

Weatherill, S. (2005). Is the pyramid compatible with EC law? *International Sports Law Journal, 3*, 3-4.

Chapter 14

Alamar, B. (2013). *Sports analytics: A guide for coaches, managers, and other decision makers*. New York, NY: Columbia University Press.

Andreu, R., & Corominas, A. (1989). SUCCCES92: A DSS for scheduling the Olympic Games. *Interfaces, 19*, 1-12.

Archer, E.A. (1980). How to make a business decision: An analysis of theory and practice. *Management Review, 69*, 54-61.

Aswad, C. (2017, February 23). Women in sports ad strikes nerve in Arab world. *Reuters*, Retrieved from www.reuters.com/article/us-arab-women-nike/women-in-sports-ad-strikes-nerve-in-arab-world-idUSKBN162017?feedType=RSS&feedName=lifestyleMolt

Bakan, J. (2004). *The Corporation: The pathological pursuit of profit and power.* Toronto, ON: Penguin Group.

Bar-Eli, M., Plessner, H., & Raab, M. (2011). *Judgment, decision-making and success in sport*. West Sussex, UK: John Wiley & Sons.

Baucells, M., & Katsikopoulos, K.V. (2015). Individual decision-making. In P. Branas-Garza & A. Cabrales (Eds.), *Experimental economics* (pp. 17-33). London, UK: Palgrave Macmillan UK. doi:10.1057/9781137538192_2

BBC Sport. (2017, May 4). Basketball's governing body Fiba changes headgear rules to allow hijab. *BBC Sport*, Retrieved from www.bbc.co.uk/sport/basketball/39802099

Blai, B. (1986, January). Eight steps to successful problem solving. *Supervisory Management*, 7-9.

Butler, R. (1991). *Designing organizations. A decision-making perspective*. New York, NY: Taylor & Francis.

Butler, R.J., Astley, W.G., Hickson, D.J., Mallory, G.R., & Wilson, D.C. (1979). Strategic decision making: Concepts of content and process. *International Studies of Management and Organization, 9*, 5-36.

Cohen, M.D., & March, J.G. (1974). *Leadership and ambiguity: The American college president*. New York, NY: McGraw-Hill.

Cohen, M.D., March, J.G., & Olsen, J.P. (1972). A garbage can model of organizational choice. *Administrative Science Quarterly, 17*, 1-25.

Cray, D., Mallory, G.R., Butler, R.J., Hickson, D.J., & Wilson, D.C. (1988). Sporadic, constricted, and fluid processes: Three types of strategic decision making in organizations. *Journal of Management Studies, 25*, 13-39.

Cray, D., Mallory, G.R., Butler, R.J., Hickson, D.J., & Wilson, D.C. (1991). Explaining decision processes. *Journal of Management Studies, 28*, 227-251.

Creswell, J., & Draper, K. (2019). Black superstars pitch Adidas shoes. Its black workers say they're sidelined. *New York Times*, Retrieved from www.nytimes.com/2019/06/19/business/adidas-diversity-employees.html

Cyert, R.M., & March, J.G. (1963). *A behavioral theory of the firm*. Englewood Cliffs, NJ: Prentice Hall.

Drucker, P. (1966). *The effective executive*. New York, NY: Harper & Row.

Farina, R., Kochenberger, G.A., & Obremski, T. (1989). The computer runs the Bolder Boulder: A simulation of a major running race. *Interfaces, 19*, 48-55.

FIFA. (n.d.). VAR at the 2018 FIFA World Cup. Retrieved from https://football-technology.fifa.com/en/innovations/var-at-the-world-cup/#thevarteam

Ford, C.M., & Gioia, D. (2000). Factors influencing creativity in the domain of managerial decision making. *Journal of Management, 26*, 705-732.

Foster, G., O'Reilly, N., & Dávila, A. (2016). *Sports business management: Decision making around the globe*. Abingdon, UK: Routledge.

GamesBids. (2009). Pyeongchang 2018 launches official campaign with co-chairmen. Retrieved from https://gamesbids.com/eng/winter-olympic-bids/pyeongchang-2018/pyeongchang-2018-launches-official-campaign-with-co-chairmen/

Green, M. (2004). Changing policy priorities for sport in England: The emergence of elite sport development as a key policy concern. *Leisure Studies, 23*(4), 365-385. doi:10.1080/0261436042000231646

Halfhill, M. (2015). Yeezy is more popular with Adidas than with Nike. Retrieved from https://www.nicekicks.com/yeezy-is-more-popular-with-adidas-than-with-nike/

Hawk-Eye. (n.d.). About. Retrieved from www.hawkeyeinnovations.com/about

Hickson, D.J., Butler, R.J., Cray, D., Mallory, G.R., & Wilson, D.C. (1985). Comparing one hundred fifty decision processes. In J.M. Pennings (Ed.), *Organizational strategy and change* (pp. 114-142). San Francisco, CA: Jossey-Bass.

Hickson, D.J., Butler, R.J., Cray, D., Mallory, G.R., & Wilson, D.C. (1986). *Top decisions: Strategic decision making in organizations*. San Francisco, CA: Jossey-Bass.

Hill, B., & Sotiriadou, P. (2016). Coach decision-making and the relative age effect on talent selection in football. *European Sport Management Quarterly, 16*(3), 292-315. doi:10.1080/16184742.2015.1131730

Hill, L., & Kikulis, L.M. (1999). Contemplating restructuring: A case study of strategic decision making in interuniversity athletic conferences. *Journal of Sport Management, 13*(1), 18-44. doi:10.1123/jsm.13.1.18

Hodgkinson, G.P., & Starbuck, W.H. (2008). *The Oxford handbook of organizational decision making*. Oxford, UK: Oxford University Press.

Houlihan, B., & Lindsey, I. (2012). *Sport policy in Britain*. Abingdon, UK: Routledge.

IOC. (n.d.). 2018 host city election. Retrieved from https://www.olympic.org/2018-host-city-election

Jackson, S.E., & Dutton, J.E. (1988). Discerning threats and opportunities. *Administrative Science Quarterly, 33*, 370-387.

Kadić-Maglajlić, S., Arslanagić-Kalajdžić, M., Micevski, M., Michaelidou, N., & Nemkova, E. (2017). Controversial advert perceptions in SNS advertising: The role of ethical judgement and religious commitment. *Journal of Business Ethics, 141*(2), 249-265. doi:10.1007/s10551-015-2755-5

King, F.W. (1991). *It's how you play the game: The inside story of the Calgary Olympics*. Calgary, AB: Writers' Group.

Kingdon, J.W. (1995). *Agendas, alternatives, and public policies* (2nd ed.). New York, NY: HarperCollins.

Leavitt, H.J., Dill, W.R., & Eyring, H.B. (1973). *The organizational world*. New York, NY: Harcourt Brace Jovanovich.

Lyles, M. (1987). Defining strategic problems: Subjective criteria of executives. *Organization Studies, 8,* 263-280.

Mallory, G.R., Butler, R.J., Cray, D., Hickson, D.J., & Wilson, D.C. (1983). Implanted decision making: American-owned firms in Britain. *Journal of Management Studies*, *20*, 192-211.

March, J.G. (1982). Theories of choice and making decisions. *Society*, *20*, 29-39.

March, J.G., & Olsen, J.P. (Eds.). (1976). *Ambiguity and choice in organizations*. Bergen, Norway: Universitetsforlaget.

Markland, R.E. (1983). *Topics in management science* (1st ed.). New York, NY: Wiley.

Maske, M. (2018). NFL puts national anthem policy on hold under agreement with NFLPA. *The Washington Post*. Retrieved from https://www.washingtonpost.com/news/sports/wp/2018/07/19/nfl-puts-national-anthem-policy-on-hold-under-agreement-with-nflpa/

Mason, D.S., Thibault, L., & Misener, L. (2006). An agency theory perspective on corruption in sport: The case of the International Olympic Committee. *Journal of Sport Management*, *20*(1), 52-73. doi:10.1123/jsm.20.1.52

Mintzberg, H. (1973). *The nature of managerial work*. New York, NY: Harper & Row.

Mintzberg, H., Raisinghani, D., & Théorêt, A. (1976). The structure of "unstructured" decision processes. *Administrative Science Quarterly*, *21*, 246-275.

NFL. (2018). NFL Head, Neck and Spine Committee's concussion protocol overview. NFL Play Smart, Play Safe. Retrieved from www.playsmartplaysafe.com/newsroom/videos/nfl-head-neck-spine-committees-concussion-protocol-overview/

Nike. (2017). The Nike Pro Hijab goes global. Nike News. Retrieved from https://news.nike.com/news/nike-pro-hijab

Nutt, P.C. (2004). Expanding the search for alternatives during strategic decision-making. *Academy of Management Executive*, *18*, 13-28.

Ozanian, M. (2017, June 17). Why Manchester United is the world's most valuable soccer team. *Forbes*, Retrieved from www.forbes.com/sites/mikeozanian/2017/06/17/why-manchester-united-is-the-worlds-most-valuable-soccer-team/#5d20562d50f4

Ozanian, M. (2018, June 12). The world's most valuable soccer teams 2018. *Forbes*, Retrieved from www.forbes.com/sites/mikeozanian/2018/06/12/the-worlds-most-valuable-soccer-teams-2018/#6776fad645c8

Parent, M.M. (2010). Decision making in major sport events over time: Parameters, drivers, and strategies. *Journal of Sport Management*, *24*, 291-318.

Parker, O. (2015). #ThisGirlCan is sweeping the nation: Are you on board yet? *Telegraph*, Retrieved from www.telegraph.co.uk/women/womens-life/11347840/ThisGirlCan-is-sweeping-the-nation-are-you-on-board-yet.html

Pender, K. (2019, July 5). From VAR drama to a viral video: Six key Women's World Cup moments. *Guardian*, Retrieved from www.theguardian.com/football/2019/jul/05/var-viral-video-womens-world-cup-key-moments-

Sadler-Smith, E., & Shefy, E. (2004). The intuitive executive: Understanding and applying "gut feel" in decision-making. *Academy of Management Executive*, *18*, 76-91.

Schlesinger, T., Klenk, C., & Nagel, S. (2015). How do sport clubs recruit volunteers? Analyzing and developing a typology of decision-making processes on recruiting volunteers in sport clubs. *Sport Management Review*, *18*(2), 193-206. doi:10.1016/j.smr.2014.04.003

Simon, H.A. (1945). *Administrative behavior*. New York, NY: Macmillan.

Simon, H.A. (1960). *The new science of management decision*. Englewood Cliffs, NJ: Prentice Hall.

Simon, H.A. (1987). Making management decisions: The role of intuition and emotion. *Academy of Management Executive, 1,* 57-64.

Sport England. (2016). This Girl Can delivers results one year on. Retrieved from www.sportengland.org/news-and-features/news/2016/january/12/thisgirlcanbirthday/

Stevenson, W.B., Pearce, J.L., & Porter, L.W. (1985). The concept of "coalition" in organization theory and research. *Academy of Management Review, 10,* 256-268.

This Girl Can. (n.d.). Home. Retrieved from http://www.thisgirlcan.co.uk/

Weisman, A. (2012, June 13). Kanye West's Nike Air Yeezy 2 sneakers are selling for over $90,000. *Business Insider*, Retrieved July 5, 2018, from www.businessinsider.com/kanye-wests-nike-air-yeezy-2-sneakers-are-selling-for-over-90000-2012-6?IR=T

Weisman, A. (2014, February 11). Kanye West's last "Air Yeezy" Nike sneakers are selling for $15,000 on eBay. *Business Insider*, Retrieved July 5, 2018, from www.businessinsider.com/kanye-wests-last-nike-shoes-are-selling-for-thousands-2014-2?IR=T

Willigan, G.E. (1992, July-August). High performance marketing: An interview with Nike's Phil Knight. *Harvard Business Review*, *70*, 91-101.

Wilson, D.C., Butler, R.J., Cray, D., Hickson, D.J., & Mallory, G.R. (1986). Breaking the bounds of organization in strategic decision making. *Human Relations*, *39*, 309-332.

Chapter 15

Abraham, R. (2017, September 24). Giro d'Italia's start in Israel provokes accusations of "sport-washing." *The Guardian*, Retrieved from www.theguardian.com/sport/2017/sep/24/israel-giro-ditalia-race-conflict-2018-start-cycling

adam_peaty. (2018, November 15). I'm incredibly disappointed next month's swim meet in Turin has been cancelled because of politics. Retrieved from www.instagram.com/p/BqM2k-hl-5W0/?utm_source=ig_embed

Anderson, J. (2019). *ISL statement: FINA move is "implicit admission of guilt."* Retrieved from swimswam.com/isl-statement-fina-move-is-implicit-admission-of-guilt/

ANOC. (2015). *ANOC mourns loss of former ANOC president, Mr Mario Vâzquez Raña*. Retrieved from www.anocolympic.org/anoc-new/anoc-mourns-loss-of-former-anoc-president-mr-mario-vazquez-rana/

Aris, S. (1990). *Sportsbiz: Inside the sports business*. London, UK: Hutchinson.

ASOIF. (2018). *ITU and Super League Triathlon sign MoU to avoid clashes*. Retrieved from www.asoif.com/news/itu-and-super-league-triathlon-sign-mou-avoid-clashes

Astley, W.G., & Sachdeva, P.S. (1984). Structural sources of interorganizational power: A theoretical synthesis. *Academy of Management Review*, *9*, 104-113.

Auf de Maur, N. (1976). *The billion-dollar game*. Toronto, ON: James Lorimer.

Bachrach, P., & Baratz, M.S. (1962). The two faces of power. *American Political Science Review*, *56*(4), 947-952.

Barelli, P. (2018). Energy for swim—Letter to the federations. Retrieved from www.federnuoto.it

BBC Sport. (2016a). Rio Olympics 2016: Which Russian athletes have been cleared to compete? *BBC Sport*, Retrieved from www.bbc.co.uk/sport/olympics/36881326

BBC Sport. (2016b). Russia state-sponsored doping across majority of Olympic Sports, claims report. *BBC Sport*, Retrieved from www.bbc.co.uk/sport/36823453

BBC Sport. (2018). Russia reinstated by Wada after doping scandal suspension. *BBC Sport*, Retrieved from www.bbc.co.uk/sport/45565273

Bergsgard, N.A. (2018). Power and domination in sport policy and politics—Three intertwined levels of exercising power. *International Journal of Sport Policy and Politics*, *10*(4), 653-667. doi:10.1080/19406940.2018.1490335

Berrett, T., Burton, T.L., & Slack, T. (1993). Quality products, quality service: Factors leading to entrepreneurial success in the sport and leisure industry. *Leisure Studies*, *12*, 93-106.

Bourdieu, P. (1991). *Language and symbolic power*. (J.B. Thompson, Ed.). Cambridge, MA: Harvard University Press.

Brannagan, P.M., & Giulianotti, R. (2014). Qatar, global sport and the 2022 FIFA World Cup. In J. Grix (Ed.), *Leveraging legacies from sports mega-events* (pp. 154-165). London, UK: Palgrave Macmillan UK. doi:10.1057/9781137371188_14

Brannagan, P.M., & Giulianotti, R. (2015). Soft power and soft disempowerment: Qatar, global sport and football's 2022 World Cup finals. *Leisure Studies*, *34*(6), 703-719. doi:10.1080/02614367.2014.964291

Brannagan, P.M., & Giulianotti, R. (2018). The soft power–soft disempowerment nexus: The case of Qatar. *International Affairs*, *94*(5), 1139-1157. doi:10.1093/ia/iiy125

Brannagan, P.M., & Rookwood, J. (2016). Sports mega-events, soft power and soft disempowerment: International supporters' perspectives on Qatar's Acquisition of the 2022 FIFA World Cup finals. *International Journal of Sport Policy and Politics*, *8*(2), 173-188. doi:10.1080/19406940.2016.1150868

Bretherton, P., Piggin, J., & Bodet, G. (2016). Olympic sport and physical activity promotion: The rise and fall of the London 2012 pre-event mass participation "legacy." *International Journal of Sport Policy and Politics*, *8*(4), 609-624. doi:10.1080/19406940.2016.1229686

Burbank, M.J., Andranovich, G.D., & Heying, C.H. (2001). *Olympic dreams: The impact of mega-events on local politics*. Boulder, CO: Lynne Rienner.

Byers, T., Slack, T., & Parent, M. (2012). *Key concepts in sport management*. Thousand Oaks, CA: SAGE.

Cairney, P. (2012). *Understanding public policy: Theories and issues*. London, UK: Palgrave Macmillan.

Calvert, J., & Blake, H. (2014, June 1). Plot to buy the World Cup. *The Times*, Retrieved from www.thetimes.co.uk/article/plot-to-buy-the-world-cup-lvxdg2v7l7w

Child, J. (1972). Organizational structure, environment and performance: The role of strategic choice. *Sociology*, *6*, 1-22.

Cho, H., Lee, H.-W., & Pyun, D. Y. (2018). The influence of stadium environment on attendance intentions in spectator sport: The moderating role of team loyalty. *International Journal of Sports Marketing and Sponsorship*, *20*(2), 276-290 doi:10.1108/IJSMS-04-2017-0025

Clark, T.N. (1967). The concept of power: Some overemphasized and underrecognized dimensions. *The Southwestern Social Science Quarterly*, *48*, 271-286.

Clegg, S. (1989). *Frameworks of power*. London, UK: SAGE.

Conn, D. (2018, September 26). Qatar migrant workers are still being exploited, says Amnesty report. *The Guardian*, Retrieved from www.theguardian.com/football/2018/sep/26/qatar-world-cup-workers-still-exploited-says-amnesty-report

Crick, M., & Smith, D. (1989). *Manchester United: The betrayal of a legend*. London, UK: Pan Books.

Crompton, J.L., Howard, D.R., & Var, T. (2003). Financing major league facilities: Status, evolution and conflicting forces. *Journal of Sport Management, 17,* 156-184.

Dubin, C.L. (1990). *Commission of inquiry into the use of drugs and banned practices intended to increase athletic performance*. Ottawa, ON: Canadian Government Publishing Centre.

Emerson, R.E. (1962). Power-dependence relations. *American Sociological Review*, *27*, 31-41.

Fan, H., & Lu, Z. (Eds.). (2014). *Sport and nationalism in Asia: Power, politics and identity*. London, UK: Routledge.

Federal Trade Commission. (2012). *Skechers will pay $40 million to settle FTC charges that it deceived consumers with ads for "toning shoes."* Retrieved from www.ftc.gov/news-events/press-releases/2012/05/skechers-will-pay-40-million-settle-ftc-charges-it-deceived

FINA. (n.d.). *FINA Swimming World Cup 2018*. Retrieved from www.fina.org/event/fina-swimming-world-cup-2018/home

FINA. (2018). *Annex 1—Non-approved event—Unauthorised Relationships*. Lusanne, Switzerland. Retrieved from https://cdn.swimswam.com/wp-content/uploads/2018/11/Annex-1-ITA_Energy-For-Swim-30.10.2018.pdf

Fink, J.S., Pastore, D.L., & Riemer, H.A. (2001). Do differences make a difference? Managing diversity in Division IA intercollegiate athletics. *Journal of Sport Management, 15,* 10-50.

Finkelstein, S. (1992). Power in top management teams: Dimensions, measurement, and validation. *Academy of Management Journal*, *35*(3), 505-538.

Fligstein, N., & Brantley, P. (1992). Bank control, owner control, or organizational dynamics: Who controls the large modern corporation? *American Journal of Sociology*, *98*, 280-307.

Ford, J.D., & Slocum, J.W., Jr. (1977). Size, technology, and environment and the structure of organizations. *Academy of Management Review*, *2*, 561-575.

Foucault, M. (1980). *Power/knowledge: Selected interviews and other writings, 1972-1977*. New York, NY: Random House.

Foucault, M. (1982). The subject and power. *Critical Inquiry*, *8*(4), 777-795.

French, J.R.P., Jr., & Raven, B. (1959). The bases of social power. In D. Cartwright (Ed.), *Studies in social power* (pp. 150-167). Ann Arbor, MI: University of Michigan Press.

Gandz, J., & Murray, V.V. (1980). The experience of workplace politics. *Academy of Management Journal*, *23*, 237-251.

Gauthier, R., & Hansen, H. (1993). Female spectators: Marketing implications for professional golf events. *Sport Marketing Quarterly, 2,* 21-28.

Gibson, O. (2016, August 8). Russia given blanket Paralympic ban amid "medals over morals" criticism. *The Guardian*, Retrieved from www.theguardian.com/sport/2016/aug/08/russia-blanket-paralympic-ban-medals-over-morals-rio-2016

Giddens, A. (1986). *The constitution of society*. Berkeley, CA: University of California Press

Grix, J. (2016). *Sport politics: An introduction*. London, UK: Palgrave Macmillan.

Grix, J., Brannagan, P.M., & Houlihan, B. (2015). Interrogating states' soft power strategies: A case study of sports mega-events in Brazil and the UK. *Global Society*, *29*(3), 463-479. doi:10.1080/13600826.2015.1047743

Grix, J., & Houlihan, B. (2014). Sports mega-events as part of a nation's soft power strategy: The cases of Germany (2006) and the UK (2012). *The British Journal of Politics and International Relations*, *16*, 572-596. doi:10.1111/1467-856X.12017

Grix, J., Lindsey, I., De Bosscher, V., & Bloyce, D. (2018). Theory and methods in sport policy and politics research. *International Journal of Sport Policy and Politics*, *10*(4), 615-620. doi:10.1080/19406940.2018.1537217

Hage, J., & Aiken, M. (1970). *Social change in complex organizations*. New York, NY: Random House.

Hall, M.A., Slack, T., Smith, G., & Whitson, D. (1991). *Sport in Canadian society*. Toronto, ON: McClelland & Stewart.

Hancock, D. (2016). *The Zen master*. Retrieved from https://leadersinsport.com/performance/coaching-and-development/zen-master-phil-jackson/

Harris, K., & Adams, A. (2016). Power and discourse in the politics of evidence in sport for development. *Sport Management Review*, *19*, 97-106. doi:10.1016/j.smr.2015.05.001

Henry, I. (2001). Postmodernism and power in urban policy: Implications for sport and cultural policy in the city. *European Sport Management Quarterly, 1,* 5-20.

Hickson, D.J., Hinings, C.R., Lee, C.A., Schneck, R.E., & Pennings, J.M. (1971). A "strategic" contingencies theory of interorganizational power. *Administrative Science Quarterly*, *14*, 378-397.

Hill, C.R. (1992). *Olympic politics*. Manchester, UK: Manchester University Press.

Hinings, C.R., Hickson, D.J., Pennings, J.M., & Schneck, R.E. (1974). Structural conditions of interorganizational power. *Administrative Science Quarterly*, *17*, 22-44.

Hope, N. (2018, December 19). Adam Peaty: World record holder challenges Fina to ban him. *BBC Sport*, Retrieved from www.bbc.co.uk/sport/swimming/46625942

Houlihan, B. (2016). Politics, power, policy and sport. In B. Houlihan & D. Malcolm (Eds.), *Sport and society* (3rd ed., p. 582). London, UK: SAGE.

Houlihan, B., Bloyce, D., & Smith, A. (2009). Developing the research agenda in sport policy. *International Journal of Sport Policy*, *1*(1), 1-12. doi:10.1080/19406940802681186

Houlihan, B., Bloyce, D., & Smith, A. (2011). Change made to the title of the journal. *International Journal of Sport Policy and Politics*, *3*(1), 1. doi:10.1080/19406940.2011.547723

Houlihan, B., & Malcolm, D. (2016). *Sport and society: A student introduction* (3rd ed.). London, UK: SAGE.

Houlihan, B., & Zheng, J. (2014). Small states: Sport and politics at the margin. *International Journal of Sport Policy and Politics*, *7*(3), 329-344. doi:10.1080/19406940.2014.959032

Hoye, R., & Cuskelly, G. (2003). Board power and performance within voluntary sport organisations. *European Sport Management Quarterly*, *3*(2), 103-119. doi:10.1080/16184740308721943

Human Rights Watch. (2013). *Qatar: Promises, little action on migrant workers' rights*. Retrieved from www.hrw.org/news/2013/02/07/qatar-promises-little-action-migrant-workers-rights

International Swimming League. (n.d.). *About International Swimming League*. Retrieved from https://isl.global/about/

IOC. (2015a). *Death of Mario Vázquez Raña, former IOC member*. Retrieved from www.olympic.org/news/death-of-mario-vazquez-rana-former-ioc-member

IOC. (2015b). *Factsheet: Sochi 2014 Facts & Figures*. Retrieved from https://stillmed.olympic.org/media/Document Library/OlympicOrg/Games/Winter-Games/Games-Sochi-2014-Winter-Olympic-Games/Facts-and-Figures/Factsheet-Facts-and-Figures-Sochi-2014.pdf

Jackson, P., & Delehanty, H. (2015). *Eleven rings: The soul of success* (Kindle ed.). London, UK: Virgin Digital.

Kanter, R.M. (1977). *Men and women of the corporation*. New York, NY: Basic Books.

Keith, B. (2019). *FINA relaxes rules, won't ban athletes for competing in non-FINA meets*. Retrieved from https://swimswam.com/fina-relaxes-rules-wont-ban-athletes-for-competing-in-non-fina-meets/

Kidd, W., Legge, K., & Harari, P. (2009). *Politics & power (skills-based sociology)*. London, UK: Palgrave Macmillan.

Kihl, L.A., Skinner, J., & Engelberg, T. (2017). Corruption in sport: Understanding the complexity of corruption. *European Sport Management Quarterly*, *17*(1), 15. doi:10.1080/16184742.2016.1257553

King, F.W. (1991). *It's how you play the game: The inside story of the Calgary Olympics*. Calgary, AB: Writers' Group.

Kotter, J.P. (1977). Power, dependence and effective management. *Harvard Business Review*, *55*, 125-136.

Lenskyj, H.J. (2000). *Inside the Olympic industry: Power, politics, and activism*. Albany, NY: State University of New York Press.

Lord, C. (2018a, November 6). Adam Peaty faces threat of ban. *The Times*, Retrieved from www.thetimes.co.uk/article/adam-peaty-faces-threat-of-ban-9wz5v5h8d

Lord, C. (2018b, December 20). Adam Peaty threatens boycott of Tokyo 2020 Olympics. *The Times*, Retrieved from www.thetimes.co.uk/article/adam-peaty-threatens-boycott-of-tokyo-2020-olympics-jh76s32wz

Lord, C. (2018c, November 18). Proposed new swimming competition is making waves. *The Times*, Retrieved from www.thetimes.co.uk/article/proposed-new-swimming-competition-is-making-waves-s86fcxfhz

Lord, C. (2018d, November 18). Swimming revolution could net Peaty $5 million. *The Times*, Retrieved from www.thetimes.co.uk/article/peaty-backs-billionaires-swimming-revolution-9xqc9mx9c

Lukes, S. (1974). *Power: A radical view*. London, UK: Macmillan.

Lukes, S. (2005). *Power: A radical view*. *Philosophy* (2nd ed., Vol. 9). Basingstoke, UK: Palgrave Macmillan.

Lutz, A. (2015, August 29). A shoe company that was once widely scorned has executed an incredible turnaround. *Business Insider*, Retrieved from www.businessinsider.com/skechers-posts-36-sales-increase-2015-8?r=US&IR=T

MacIntosh, D., & Whitson, D.J. (1990). *The game planners: Transforming Canada's sport system*. Montreal, QB: McGill-Queen's University Press.

Madison, D.L., Allen, R.W., Porter, L.W., Renwick, P.A., & Mayers, B.T. (1980). Organizational politics: An exploration of managers' perceptions. *Human Relations*, *33*(2), 79-100. doi:10.1177/001872678003300201

March, J.G. (1966). The power of power. In D. Easton (Ed.), *Varieties of political theory* (pp. 39-70). Englewood Cliffs, NJ: Prentice Hall.

Martin, R. (1971). The concept of power: A critical defense. *British Journal of Sociology*, *22*, 240-256.

Mather, V. (2019, February 15). A timeline of Colin Kaepernick vs. the N.F.L. *New York Times*, Retrieved from www.nytimes.com/2019/02/15/sports/nfl-colin-kaepernick-protests-timeline.html

McGeoch, R. (1994). *The bid: How Australia won the 2000 Games*. Port Melbourne, Australia: William Heinemann Australia.

McLaren, R.H. (2016). *The independent person 2nd report*. Retrieved from www.wada-ama.org/sites/default/files/resources/files/mclaren_report_part_ii_2.pdf

Mindlock, C. (2019, February 4). Taking a knee: Why are NFL players protesting and when did they start to kneel? *Independent*, Retrieved from www.independent.co.uk/news/world/americas/us-politics/taking-a-knee-national-anthem-nfl-trump-why-meaning-origins-racism-us-colin-kaepernick-a8521741.html

Ministry of Development Planning and Statistics. (2019). *Monthly figures on total population*. Retrieved from www.mdps.gov.qa/en/statistics1/StatisticsSite/pages/population.aspx

Mintzberg, H. (1979). *The structuring of organizations*. Englewood Cliffs, NJ: Prentice Hall.

Mintzberg, H. (1983). *Power in and around organizations*. Englewood Cliffs, NJ: Prentice Hall.

Nye, J.S. (2004). Soft power and American foreign policy. *Political Science Quarterly*, *119*(2), 255-270.

Pfeffer, J. (1977). Power and resource allocation in organizations. In B.M. Staw & G.R. Salancik (Eds.), *New directions in organizational behavior* (pp. 235-265). Chicago, IL: St. Clair Press.

Pfeffer, J. (1981). *Power in organizations*. Marshfield, MA: Pitman.

Pfeffer, J. (1992). *Managing with power: Politics and influence in organizations*. Boston, MA: Harvard Business School Press.

Piggin, J., Lange De Souza, D., Furtado, S., Milanez, M., Cunha, G., Louzada, B. H., Graeff, B., & Tlili, H. (2019). Do the Olympic Games promote dietary health for spectators? An interdisciplinary study of health promotion through sport. *European Sport Management Quarterly*, *19*(4), 481-501. doi.org:10.1080/16184742.2018.1562484

Play the Game. (2019). *Play the Game 2019. Athlete power on the rise*. Retrieved from https://playthegame.org/conferences/play-the-game-2019/

Pound, R.W. (2004). *Inside the Olympics: A behind-the-scenes look at the politics, the scandals, and the glory of the games*. Toronto, ON: J. Wiley & Sons Canada.

Prouty, D.F. (1988). *In spite of us: My education in the big and little games of amateur and Olympic sport in the U.S.* Brattleboro, VT: Vitesse Press.

Reiche, D. (2015). Investing in sporting success as a domestic and foreign policy tool: The case of Qatar. *International Journal of Sport Policy and Politics*, *7*(4), 489-504. doi:10.1080/19406940.2014.966135

Reuters. (2018, December 8). Top swimmers challenge FINA with lawsuit. *Reuters*, Retrieved from https://uk.reuters.com/article/uk-swimming-fina-competitions-lawsuit/top-swimmers-challenge-fina-with-lawsuit-idUKKBN1O70UK

Sadan, E. (2004). *Empowerment and community planning* (R. Flantz, Trans.). Tel Aviv, Israel: Hakibbutz Hameuchad.

Sack, A.L., & Staurowsky, E.J. (1998). *College athletes for hire: The evolution and legacy of the NCAA's amateur myth*. Westport, CT: Praeger.

Safdar, K., & Beaton, A. (2019, July 1). Nike nixes "Betsy Ross flag" sneaker after Colin Kaepernick intervenes. *Wall Street Journal*, Retrieved from www.wsj.com/articles/nike-nixes-betsy-ross-flag-sneaker-after-colin-kaepernick-intervenes-11562024126

Schofield, J.A. (1983). Performance and attendance at professional team sports. *Journal of Sport Behavior, 6,* 196-206.

Seippel, Ø., Dalen, H.B., Sandvik, M.R., & Solstad, G.M. (2018). From political sports to sports politics: On political mobilization of sports issues. *International Journal of Sport Policy and Politics*, *10*(4), 669-689. doi:10.1080/19406940.2018.1501404

Senn, A.E. (1999). *Power, politics, and the Olympic Games*. Champaign, IL: Human Kinetics.

Shen, W., & Cannella, A.A., Jr. (2002). Power dynamics within top management and their impacts on CEO dismissal followed by inside succession. *Academy of Management Journal*, *45*, 1195-1206.

Shetty, Y.K. (1978). Managerial power and organizational effectiveness: A contingency analysis. *Journal of Management Studies*, *15*, 176-186.

Sibson, R. (2010). "I was banging my head against a brick wall": Exclusionary power and the gendering of sport organizations. *Journal of Sport Management*, *24*, 379-399. Retrieved from https://journals.humankinetics.com/doi/pdf/10.1123/jsm.24.4.379

Slack, T. (2014). The social and commercial impact of sport, the role of sport management. *European Sport Management Quarterly*, *14*(5), 454-463. doi:10.1080/16184742.2014.974311

Slack, T., Berrett, T., & Mistry, K. (1994). Rational planning systems as a source of organizational conflict. *International Review for the Sociology of Sport*, *29*, 317-328.

Soares, J., Correia, A., & Rosado, A. (2010). Political factors in the decision-making process in voluntary sports associations. *European Sport Management Quarterly*, *10*(1), 5-29. doi:10.1080/16184740903554033

Steen-Johnsen, K., & Vidar Hanstad, D. (2008). Change and power in complex democratic organizations. The case of Norwegian elite sports. *European Sport Management Quarterly*, *8*(2), 123-143. doi:10.1080/16184740802024393

Storm, R.K., Nielsen, C.G., & Jakobsen, T.G. (2018). The complex challenge of spectator demand: Attendance drivers in the Danish men's handball league. *European Sport Management Quarterly*, *18*(5), 652-670. doi:10.1080/16184742.2018.1470195

Strasser, J.B., & Becklund, L. (1991). *Swoosh: The unauthorized story of Nike and the men who played there*. New York, NY: Harcourt Brace Jovanovich.

Styskal, R.A. (1980). Power and commitment in organizations: A test of the participation thesis. *Social Forces*, *58*, 925-943.

Sussman, L., Adams, A.J., Kuzmits, F.E., & Raho, L.E. (2002). Organizational politics: Tactics, channels, and hierarchical roles. *Journal of Business Ethics*, *40*, 313-329. Retrieved from http://web.b.ebscohost.com/ehost/pdfviewer/pdfviewer?vid=2&sid=4867c261-498f-4124-b5cc-900633546063%40pdc-v-sessmgr05

Swartz, D.L. (2016). Bourdieu's concept of field. *Oxford Bibliographies* in Sociology. https://dx.doi.org/10.1093/obo/9780199756384-0164

Tien, C., Lo, H.-C., & Lin, H.-W. (2011). The economic benefits of mega events: A myth or a reality? A longitudinal study on the Olympic Games. *Journal of Sport Management*, *25*(1), pp. 11-23. Retrieved from https://journals.humankinetics.com/doi/pdf/10.1123/jsm.25.1.11

Transparency International. (2016). *Cleaning up sport: Conflicts of interest at the top*. Retrieved from http://blog.transparency.org/2016/12/09/cleaning-up-sport-conflicts-of-interest-at-the-top/

WADA. (2017). *WADA statement regarding the IOC's decision concerning Russia*. Retrieved from www.wada-ama.org/en/media/news/2017-12/wada-statement-regarding-the-iocs-decision-concerning-russia

Wangrow, D.B., Schepker, D.J., & Barker, V.L. (2018). Power, performance, and expectations in the dismissal of NBA coaches: A survival analysis study. *Sport Management Review*, *21*(4), 333-346. doi:10.1016/j.smr.2017.08.002

Weber, M. (1956). *The protestant ethic and the spirit of capitalism* (5th ed.). New York, NY: Scribner.

Weber, M. (2012). *The theory of social and economic organization* (Original work published 1947). New York, NY: Martino Fine Books.

Weick, K.E. (1969). *The social psychology of organizing*. Reading, MA: Addison-Wesley.

Wilson, N. (1988). *The sports business*. London, UK: Piatkus.

Wolfe, R., Meenaghan, T., & O'Sullivan, P. (2002). The sports network: Insights into the shifting balance of power. *Journal of Business Research, 55,* 611-622.

Wyche, S. (2016). *Colin Kaepernick explains why he sat during national anthem*. Retrieved from www.nfl.com/news/story/0ap3000000691077/article/colin-kaepernick-explains-protest-of-national-anthem

Yarbrough, C.R. (2000). *And they call them games: An inside view of the 1996 Olympics*. Macon, GA: Mercer University Press.

Zirin, D. (2013). *Game over: How politics has turned the sports world upside down*. New York, NY: The New Press.

Chapter 16

Abreu, M.A., & Spradley, B.D. (2016). The 2011 National Football League labor dispute. *The Sport Journal*, Retrieved from https://thesportjournal.org/article/the-2011-national-football-league-labor-dispute/

Amis, J., Slack, T., & Berrett, T. (1995). The structural antecedents of conflict in national sport organizations. *Leisure Studies*, *14*, 1-16.

Axon, R. (2018, April 18). Athletes critical of USOC, sports federations in failing to prevent, stop sexual abuse. *USA Today*, Retrieved from www.usatoday.com/story/sports/olympics/2018/04/18/athletes-critical-usoc-federations-failing-stop-sexual-abuse/529749002/

Bendersky, C. (2003). Organizational dispute resolution systems: A complementarities model. *Academy of Management Review*, *28*, 643-656.

Blake, R.B., & Mouton, J.S. (1984). Overcoming group warfare. *Harvard Business Review*, *62*, 98-108.

Bradley, B.H., Anderson, H.J., Baur, J.E., & Klotz, A.C. (2015). When conflict helps: Integrating evidence for beneficial conflict in groups and teams under three perspectives. *Group Dynamics: Theory, Research, and Practice*, *19*(4), 243-272.

Burke, V., & Collins, D. (2000). Dealing with work conflict: Issues, approaches and implications for sport managers. *European Journal for Sport Management*, *7*, 44-64.

Canada.com. (2005). *Ice breaker: NHL, NHLPA finally come to an agreement*. Retrieved from www.canada.com/sports/hockey/labourdispute/index.html

CBC Sports. (2005). Lingo of the hockey biz: Defining common terms in hockey negotiations. Retrieved May 18, 2005 from http://www.cbc.ca/sports/indepth/cba/glossary/.

Cliff, G. (1987). Managing organizational conflict. *Management Review*, *76*, 51-53.

CNN Library. (2019). Pro sports lockouts and strikes fast facts. CNN, Retrieved from www.cnn.com/2013/09/03/us/pro-sports-lockouts-and-strikes-fast-facts/index.html

Cotton, J.L., Vollrath, D.A., Froggatt, K.L., Lengnick-Hall, M.L., & Jennings, K.R. (1988). Employee participation: Diverse forms and different outcomes. *Academy of Management Review*, *13*, 8-22.

Corwin, R. (1969). Patterns of organizational conflict. *Administrative Science Quarterly*, *14*, 507-520.

Currie, D., Gormley, T., Roche, B., & Teague, P. (2017). The management of workplace conflict: Contrasting pathways in the HRM literature. *International Journal of Management Reviews*, *19*(4), 492-509.

Dworkin, J.B. (1981). *Owners versus players: Baseball and collective bargaining*. Boston, MA: Auburn House.

Esteban (2011, November 3). Most significant strikes and lockouts in pro sports history. Retrieved from www.totalprosports.com/2011/11/03/9-most-significant-strikes-and-lockouts-in-pro-sports-history/

Hall, R.H. (1982). *Organizations: Structure and process* (3rd. ed.). Englewood Cliffs, NJ: Prentice Hall.

Harris, D. (1987). *The league, the rise and decline of the NFL*. Toronto, ON: Bantam Books.

Ilgaz, Z. (2014, May 15). Conflict resolution: When should leaders step in? *Forbes*, Retrieved from www.forbes.com/sites/85broads/2014/05/15/conflict-resolution-when-should-leaders-step-in/#43bada623357

Jereski, L. (1990, June 18). Can Paul Fireman put the bounce back in Reebok*? Business Week,* 181-182.

Katsikea, E., Theodosiou, M., & Morgan, R.E. (2015). Why people quit: Explaining employee turnover intentions among export sales managers. *International Business Review*, *24*(3), 367-379.

Kerwin, S., Walker, M.B., & Bopp, T. (2017). When faultlines are created: Exploring the conflict triggering process in sport. *Sport Management Review*, *20*(3), 252-260.

Kidd, B., & Ouellet, J.-G. (2000). *A win-win solution: Creating a national alternate dispute resolution system for amateur sport in Canada*. Retrieved from www.pch.gc.ca/coderre/report-rapport/ADR-2000.pdf

Kolb, D.M., & Putnam, L.L. (1992). The multiple faces of conflict in organizations. *Journal of Organizational Behavior*, *13*, 311-324.

Langhorn, K., & Hinings, C.R. (1987). Integrated planning and organizational conflict. *Canadian Public Administration*, *30*, 550-565.

Lawrence, P.R., & Lorsch, J. (1967). *Organization and environment*. Boston, MA: Harvard Graduate School of Business Administration.

Lebrun, P. (2005). *NHL commissioner Bettman says it's lights out on the 2004-05 NHL season*. Retrieved from www.canada.com/sports

Likert, R., & Likert, J.G. (1976). *New ways of managing conflict*. New York, NY: McGraw-Hill.

Macintosh, D., & Whitson, D.J. (1990). *The game planners: Transforming Canada's sport system*. Montreal, QC: McGill-Queen's University Press.

Mannix, E. (2003). Editor's comments: Conflict and conflict resolution—a return to theorizing. *Academy of Management Review*, *28*, 543-546.

March, J.G., & Simon, H. (1958). *Organizations*. New York, NY: Wiley.

Maslow, A.H. (1965). *Eupsychian management*. Homewood, IL: Irwin.

McDonald, P. (1991). The Los Angeles Olympic Organizing Committee: Developing organizational culture in the short run. In P.J. Frost, L.F. Moore, M.L. Reis, C.C. Lundberg, & J. Martin (Eds.), *Reframing organizational culture* (pp. 26-38). Newbury Park, CA: SAGE.

Morgan, G. (1986). *Images of organization*. Beverly Hills, CA: SAGE.

Murphy, D. (2018). USOC leader admits to failures in protecting athletes. Retrieved from www.espn.com/olympics/story/_/id/23584572/united-states-olympic-committee-leader-admits-failure-protecting-athletes

Nagel, S., Schlesinger, T., Bayle, E., & Giauque, D. (2015). Professionalisation of sport federations—A multi-level framework for analysing forms, causes and consequences. *European Sport Management Quarterly*, *15*(4), 407-433.

Nelson, R.E. (1989). The strength of strong ties: Social networks and intergroup conflict in organizations. *Academy of Management Journal, 32,* 377-401.

Nigh, D., & Cochran, P.L. (1987). Issues management and the multinational enterprise. *Management International Review*, *27*, 4-12.

Nixon, A.E., Bruk-Lee, V., & Spector, P.E. (2017). Grin and bear it?: Employees' use of surface acting during coworker conflict. *Stress and Health*, *33*(2), 129-142.

Nugent, P.S. (2002). Managing conflict: Third-party interventions for managers. *Academy of Management Executive*, *16*, 139-155.

Omli, J., & La Voi, N.M. (2009). Background anger in youth sport: A perfect storm?. *Journal of Sport Behavior*, *32*(2), 242.

O'Neill, T.A., McLarnon, M.J., Hoffart, G.C., Woodley, H.J., & Allen, N.J. (2018). The structure and function of team conflict state profiles. *Journal of Management*, *44*(2), 811-836.

Pondy, L.R. (1967). Organizational conflict: Concepts and models. *Administrative Science Quarterly*, *12*, 296-320.

Pondy, L.R. (1992). Reflections on organizational conflict. *Journal of Organizational Behavior, 13*, 257-261.

Rahim, M.A. (1986). *Managing conflict in organizations*. New York, NY: Praeger.

Rahim, M.A. (Ed.) (1989). *Managing conflict: An interdisciplinary approach*. New York, NY: Praeger.

Rahim, M.A. (2011). *Managing conflict in organizations* (4th ed.). New York, NY: Routledge.

Rahim, M.A. (2017). *Managing conflict in organizations* (3rd ed.). London, UK: Routledge.

Reich, K. (1986). *Making it happen: Peter Ueberroth and the 1984 Olympics*. Santa Barbara, CA: Capra Press.

Riordan, I. (2018). Olympic boxing faces fresh treat of exclusion after AIBA election: Gafur Rakhimov elected new president of AIBA in defiance of Olympic Council. *The Irish Times*, Retrieved from www.irishtimes.com/sport/other-sports/olympic-boxing-facing-fresh-threat-of-exclusion-after-aiba-election-1.3685631

Robbins, S.P. (1978). Conflict management and "conflict resolution" are not synonymous terms. *California Management Review*, *21*, 67-75.

Robbins, S.P. (1990). *Organization theory: Structure, design and applications* (3rd ed.). Englewood Cliffs, NJ: Prentice Hall.

Sands, J., & Gammons, P. (1993). BOOK EXCERPT: Coming apart at the seams. *The Journal of Business Strategy*, *14*(4), 58.

Schmidt, S.M., & Kochan, T.A. (1972). Conflict: Towards conceptual clarity. *Administrative Science Quarterly*, *17*, 359-370.

Schulz, J. (2011). Sport organisations, professionalisation and organisational conflict: A review of the literature. In H. Dolles & S. Söderman (Eds.), *Sport as a business: International, professional and commercial aspects* (pp. 137-152). Hampshire, UK: Palgrave MacMillan.

Scully, G.W. (1989). *The business of major league baseball*. Chicago, IL: University of Chicago Press.

Slack, T., Berrett, T., & Mistry, K. (1994). Rational planning systems as a source of organizational conflict. *International Review for the Sociology of Sport*, *29*, 317-328.

Smoll, F.L., Cumming, S.P., & Smith, R.E. (2011). Enhancing coach-parent relationships in youth sports: Increasing harmony and minimizing hassle. *International Journal of Sports Science & Coaching*, *6*(1), 13-26.

Sport Dispute Resolution Center of Canada (n.d.). Retrieved from www.crdsc-sdrcc.ca/eng/about-history

Strandbu, Å., Stefansen, K., Smette, I., & Sandvik, M.R. (2017). Young people's experiences of parental involvement in youth sport. *Sport, Education and Society*, *24*(1), 66-77.

Taylor, F.W. (1911). *The principles of scientific management*. New York, NY: Harper & Row.

Team USA. (2018). U.S. Olympic Committee announces significant changes to further protect athletes. Retrieved from www.teamusa.org/News/2018/February/28/US-Olympic-Committee-Announces-Significant-Changes-To-Further-Protect-Athletes

Thomas, K.W. (1992). Conflict and conflict management: Reflections and update. *Journal of Organizational Behavior*, *13*, 265-274.

Thomas, K.W., & Schmidt, W.H. (1976). A survey of managerial interests with respect to conflict. *Academy of Management Journal*, *19*, 315-318.

Thompson, J.D. (1960). Organizational management of conflict. *Administrative Science Quarterly*, *4*, 389-409.

Thompson, J.D. (1967). *Organizations in action*. New York, NY: McGraw-Hill.

Tjosvold, D. (1988). Cooperative and competitive interdependence: Collaboration between departments to serve customers. *Group and Organization Studies*, *13*, 274-289.

Tjosvold, D. (1991). *The conflict-positive organization: Stimulate diversity and create unity* (Vol. 51485). Reading, MA: Addison-Wesley.

Tjosvold, D., Wong, A.S., & Feng Chen, N.Y. (2014). Constructively managing conflicts in organizations. *Annual Review of Organizational Psychology and Organizational Behavior*, *1*(1), 545-568.

Van Fleet, D.D. (1991). *Contemporary management* (2nd ed.). Boston, MA: Houghton Mifflin.

Vidic, Z., Martin, M.S., & Oxhandler, R. (2018). Mindfulness meditation intervention with male collegiate soccer players: Effect on stress and various aspects of life. *Sport Journal*, Retrieved from http://thesportjournal.org/article/mindfulness-meditation-intervention-with-male-collegiate-soccer-players-effect-on-stress-and-various-aspects-of-life/

Wachsmuth, S., Jowett, S., & Harwood, C.G. (2017). Conflict among athletes and their coaches: What is the theory and research so far? *International Review of Sport and Exercise Psychology*, *10*(1), 84-107.

Walton, R.E., & Dutton, J.M. (1969). The management of interdepartmental conflict: A model and review. *Administrative Science Quarterly*, *14*, 73-84.

Walton, R.E., Dutton, J.M., & Cafferty, T.P. (1969). Organizational context and interdepartmental conflict. *Administrative Science Quarterly*, *14*, 522-542.

Wong, A., Wei, L., Wang, X., & Tjosvold, D. (2018). Collectivist values for constructive conflict management in international joint venture effectiveness. *International Journal of Conflict Management*, *29*(1), 126-143.

Zald, M. (1962). Power balance and staff conflict in correctional institutions. *Administrative Science Quarterly*, *7*, 22-49.

Chapter 17

Andreff, W. (2016). Corruption in sport. In T. Byers (Ed.), *Contemporary Issues in Sport Management: A Critical Introduction* (pp. 46-66). London, UK: SAGE.

Arogyaswamy, B., & Byles, C.M. (1987). Organizational culture: Internal and external fits. *Journal of Management*, *13*, 647-659.

Ashkanasy, N.M., Härtel, C.E., & Zerbe, W.J. (2000). *Emotions in the workplace: Research, theory, and practice*. Westport, CN: Quorum Books.

Barr, G. (1985, July 1). The daunting challenge of selling the CFL. *Financial Times*, *1*, 18.

Bate, S.P. (2010). *Strategies for cultural change*. Abingdon, UK: Routledge.

Blank, S. (1986). The future workplace. *Management Review*, *75*, 22-25.

Boden, D. (1992). *The business of talk*. Cambridge, UK: Polity Press.

Brittain, I., Bocarro, J., Byers, T., & Swart, K. (Eds.). (2017). *Legacies and mega events: Fact or fairy tales?*. London, UK: Routledge.

Burton, L.J., Welty Peachey, J., & Wells, J.E. (2017). The role of servant leadership in developing an ethical climate in sport organizations. *Journal of Sport Management*, *31*(3), 229-240.

Byers, T. (2018). Trends in professional sport organizations and their market impact. In M. Breuer & D. Forrest (Eds.), *The Palgrave handbook on the economics of the manipulation of sport* (pp. 55-70). London, UK: Palgrave MacMillan.

Campbell, J.L., & Göritz, A.S. (2014). Culture corrupts! A qualitative study of organizational culture in corrupt organizations. *Journal of Business Ethics*, *120*(3), 291-311.

Chatman, J.A., & O'Reilly, C.A. (2016). Paradigm lost: Reinvigorating the study of organizational culture. *Research in Organizational Behavior*, *36*, 199-224.

Colyer, S. (2000). Organizational culture in selected Western Australian sport organizations. *Journal of Sport Management*, *14*(4), 321-341.

Cruickshank, A., Collins, D., & Minten, S. (2015). Driving and sustaining culture change in professional sport performance teams: A grounded theory. *Psychology of Sport and Exercise*, *20*, 40-50.

Davis, S. (2017, March 8). Revisiting the remarkable legacy of John Wooden, the greatest coach of them all. *Sports Illustrated*, Retrieved from https://www.si.com/college-basketball/2017/03/08/john-wooden-greatest-basketball-coaches

Davis, T.R.V. (1984). The influence of the physical environment in offices. *Academy of Management Review*, *9*, 271-283.

Deal, T.E., & Kennedy, A.A. (1982). *Corporate cultures: The rites and rituals of corporate life*. Reading, MA: Addison-Wesley.

Denison, D., Nieminen, L., & Kotrba, L. (2014). Diagnosing organizational cultures: A conceptual and empirical review of culture effectiveness surveys. *European Journal of Work and Organizational Psychology*, *23*(1), 145-161.

Doherty, A.J., & Chelladurai, P. (1999). Managing cultural diversity in sport organizations: A theoretical perspective. *Journal of Sport Management*, *13*(4), 280-297.

Ehrhart, M.G., Schneider, B., & Macey, W.H. (2014). *Organizational climate and culture: An introduction to theory, research, and practice*. London, UK: Routledge.

Elberse, A. (2013). Ferguson's formula. *Harvard Business Review*, *91*(10), 116-125.

Fineman, S. (Ed.). (2000). *Emotion in organizations*. London, UK: SAGE.

Freewheeler on Firm Ground, A. (1989, March 22). *New England Business*, 34-39, 80-81.

Frost, P. J., Moore, L. F., Louis, M. R. E., Lundberg, C. C., & Martin, J. E. (1985). *Organizational culture*. Thousand Oaks, CA: SAGE.

Galily, Y., Yarchi, M., Tamir, I., & Samuel-Azran, T. (2016). Terrorism and sport: A global perspective. *American Behavioral Scientist*, *60*(9), doi:10.1177/0002764216632839

Gameday News (2019). *How every NFL team got their name*. Retrieved from www.gamedaynews.com/football/how-every-nfl-team-got-their-name/?firefox=1

Gemskie, M. (2018). The Chicago Clubs: A case study in aligning strategy, structure and culture. Gagen MacDonald, Retrieved from www.gagenmacdonald.com/2017/chicago-cubs-case-study-aligning-strategy-structure-culture/

Giorgi, S., Lockwood, C., & Glynn, M.A. (2015). The many faces of culture: Making sense of 30 years of research on culture in organization studies. *The Academy of Management Annals*, *9*(1), 1-54.

Girginov, V. (2006). Creating a corporate anti-doping culture: The role of Bulgarian sports governing bodies. *Sport in Society*, *9*(2), 252-268.

Grant, D., Keenoy, T.W., & Oswick, C. (Eds.). (1998). *Discourse and organization*. London, UK: SAGE.

Gregory, K.L. (1983). Native-view paradigms: Multiple cultures and culture conflicts in organizations. *Administrative Science Quarterly*, *28*, 359-376.

Hall, M. A. (2016). *The girl and the game: A history of women's sport in Canada*. Toronto, ON: University of Toronto Press.

Hall, M.A., Cullen, D., & Slack, T. (1989). Organizational elites recreating themselves: The gender structure of national sport organizations. *Quest*, *41*, 28-45.

Hardy, C., Lawrence, T.B., & Phillips, N. (1992). Talk and action: Conversations and narrative in inter-organizational collaboration. In D. Grant, T.W. Keenoy, & C. Oswick, *Discourse and organization* (pp. 65-83). London, UK: SAGE.

Hoeber, L., & Frisby, W. (2001). Gender equity for athletes: Rewriting the narrative for this organizational value. *European Sport Management Quarterly*, *1*, 179-209.

Hogan, S.J., & Coote, L.V. (2014). Organizational culture, innovation, and performance: A test of Schein's model. *Journal of Business Research*, *67*(8), 1609-1621.

Johnson, P., & J. Gill (1993). *Management control and organizational behaviour*. London, UK: Paul Chapman.

Jung, T., Scott, T., Davies, H.T., Bower, P., Whalley, D., McNally, R., & Mannion, R. (2009). Instruments for exploring organizational culture: A review of the literature. *Public Administration Review*, *69*(6), 1087-1096.

Kaiser, S., Engel, F., & Keiner, R. (2009). Structure-dimensional analysis—An experimental approach to culture in sport organisations. *European Sport Management Quarterly*, *9*(3), 295-310.

Kalman, F. (2016). *Lessons from the Cubs' success: Culture matters*. Talent Economy, Retrieved from www.talenteconomy.io/2016/10/12/chicago-cubs-success-culture-matters/

Kanter, R.M. (1977). *Men and women of the corporation*. New York, NY: Basic Books.

Kanter, R.M. (1984). Managing transitions in organizational culture: The case of participative management at Honeywell. In J.R. Kimberly & R.E. Quinn (Eds.), *Managing organizational transitions* (pp. 195-217). Homewood, IL: Irwin.

Kent, A., & Weese, W.J. (2000). Do effective organizations have better executive leaders and/or organizational cultures? A study of selected sport organizations in Canada. *European Journal for Sport Management*, *7*, 4-21.

Kikulis, L., Slack, T., & Hinings, C.R. (1995). Sector specific patterns of organizational design change. *Journal of Management Studies*, *32*, 67-100.

Litwin, G.H., & Stringer, R.A. (1968). *Motivation and organizational climate*. Cambridge, MA: Harvard Business School, Division of Research.

Lorsch, J. (1986). Managing culture: The invisible barrier to strategic change. *California Management Review, 28*, 95-109.

Louis, M.R. (1985). An investigator's guide to workplace culture. In P.J. Frost, L.F. Moore, M.R. Louis, C.C. Lundberg, & J. Martin (Eds.), *Organizational culture* (pp. 73-93). Beverly Hills, CA: SAGE.

Maitland, A., Hills, L.A., & Rhind, D.J. (2015). Organisational culture in sport–A systematic review. *Sport Management Review, 18*(4), 501-516.

Martin, J., Feldman, M.S., Hatch, M.J., & Sitkin, S.B. (1983). The uniqueness paradox in organizational stories. *Administrative Science Quarterly, 28*, 438-453.

MEC. (2005). *Mountain Equipment Co-op. About our Co-op: Mission and values.* Retrieved from www.mec.ca/Main/content_text.jsp? CONTENT%3C%3Ecnt_id=8987&FOLDER%3C%3Efolder_id=619263&bmUID=1109650617041

MEC. (2018). *About us.* Retrieved from www.mec.ca/en/explore/our-roots

Meyerson, D., & Martin, J. (1987). Cultural change: An integration of three different views. *Journal of Management Studies, 24*, 623-647.

Miles, R.E., & Snow, C.C. (1978). Organizational strategy, structure, and process. New York, NY: McGraw-Hill.

Peters, T.J., & Waterman, R.H. (1982). *In search of excellence.* New York, NY: Harper & Row.

Peterson, M.F. (2011). Organizational culture and organization theory. In N.M. Ashkanasy, C.P.M. Wilderom, & M.F. Peterson (Eds.), *Handbook of organizational culture and climate* (pp. 415-422). London, UK: SAGE.

Pettigrew, A.M. (1979). On studying organizational cultures. *Administrative Science Quarterly, 24*, 570-581.

Pondy, L, Frost, P., Morgan, G., & Dandridge, T. (1982). *Organizational symbolism.* Greenwich, CT: JAI Press.

Porter, M.E. (1980). *Competitive strategies: Techniques for analyzing industries and competitors.* New York, NY: Free Press.

Robey, D. (1986). *Designing organizations* (2nd ed.). Homewood, IL: Irwin.

Sanderson, J., & Gramlich, K. (2016). "You go girl!": Twitter and conversations about sport culture and gender. *Sociology of Sport Journal, 33*(2), 113-123.

Sathe, V. (1983). Implications of a corporate culture: A manager's guide to action. *Organizational Dynamics, 12*, 5-23.

Schein, E.H. (1983). The role of the founder in creating organizational culture. *Organizational dynamics, 12*(1), 13-28.

Schein, E.H. (1984). Culture as an environmental context for careers. *Journal of Organizational Behavior, 5*(1), 71-81.

Schein, E.H. (1985). *Organizational culture and leadership.* San Francisco, CA: Jossey-Bass.

Schneider, B. (1987). The people make the place. *Personnel Psychology, 40*, 437-453.

Schneider, B., Ehrhart, M. G., & Macey, W. H. (2013). Organizational climate and culture. *Annual Review of Psychology, 64*, 361-388.

Scholz, C. (1987). Corporate culture and strategy: The problem of strategic fit. *Long Range Planning, 20*, 78-87.

Schroeder, P.J. 2010. Changing team culture: The perspectives of ten successful head coaches. *Journal of Sport Behavior, 32*(4): 63-88.

Skinner, J., Stewart, B., & Edwards, A. (2004). Interpreting policy language and managing organisational change: The case of Queensland Rugby Union. *European Sport Management Quarterly, 4*(2), 77-94.

Slack, T., & Hinings, C.R. (1992). Understanding change in national sport organizations: An integration of theoretical perspectives. *Journal of Sport Management, 6*, 114-132.

Smith, A.C., & Shilbury, D. (2004). Mapping cultural dimensions in Australian sporting organisations. *Sport Management Review, 7*(2), 133-165.

Smith, A., & Stewart, B. (2016). Doping in sport. In T. Byers (Ed.), *Contemporary Issues in Sport Management: A Critical Introduction* (pp. 256-66). London, UK: SAGE.

Spaaij, R., Magee, J., Farquharson, K., Gorman, S., Jeanes, R., Lusher, D., & Storr, R. (2018). Diversity work in community sport organizations: Commitment, resistance and institutional change. *International Review for the Sociology of Sport, 53*(3), 278-295.

Stodghill, R. (1993, June 14). What makes Ryka run? Sheri Poe and her story. *Business Week*, 82, 84.

Strasser, J.B., & Becklund, L. (1991). *Swoosh: The unauthorized story of Nike and the men who played there.* New York, NY: Harcourt Brace Jovanovich.

Trice, H.M., & Beyer, J.M. (1984). Studying organizational cultures through rites and ceremonials. *Academy of Management Review, 9*, 653-669.

Van Fleet, D.D. (1991). *Contemporary management* (2nd ed.). Boston, MA: Houghton Mifflin.

Warrick, D.D. (2017). What leaders need to know about organizational culture. *Business Horizons, 60*(3), 395-404.

Weese, W.J. (1995a). Leadership and organizational culture: An investigation of Big-Ten and Mid-American Conference campus recreation administrators. *Journal of Sport Management, 9*, 119-134.

Weese, W.J. (1995b). Leadership, organizational culture, and job satisfaction in Canadian YMCA organizations. *Journal of Sport Management, 9*, 182-193.

Weese, W.J. (1996). Do leadership and organizational culture really matter? *Journal of Sport Management, 10*, 197-206.

Westberg, K., Stavros, C., Wilson, B., & Smith, A. (2016). Athlete transgressions: Implications for sport manager. In T. Byers (Ed.), *Contemporary issues in sport management: A critical introduction* (pp. 259-72). London, UK: SAGE.

Westerbeek, H.M. (1999). A research classification model and some (marketing oriented) reasons for studying the culture of sport organizations. *European Journal for Sport Management, 6*, 69-87.

Wilkins, A.L. (1983a). The culture audit: A tool for understanding organizations. *Organizational Dynamics, 12*, 24-38.

Wilkins, A.L. (1983b). Organizational stories as symbols which control the organization. In L.R. Pondy, P.J. Frost, G. Morgan, & T.C. Dandridge (Eds.), *Organizational symbolism* (pp. 81-92). Greenwich, CT: JAI Press.

Yukl, G.A. (1998). *Leadership in organizations* (4th ed.). Englewood Cliffs, NJ: Prentice Hall.

Chapter 18

Adizes, I. (1979). Organizational passages: Diagnosing and treating life cycle problems of organizations. *Organizational Dynamics, 8*, 3-25.

Agarwal, P. (2018, June 24). How do we design workplaces that support mental health and well-being. *Forbes*, Retrieved from www.forbes.com/sites/pragyaagarwaleurope/2018/06/24/how-can-workplace-design-help-mental-health/#59156f214dc1

Amis, J. Slack, T., & Hinings, C.R. (2002). Values and organizational change. *The Journal of Applied Behavioral Science, 38*, 436-465.

Amis, J., Slack, T., & Hinings, C. (2004). Strategic change and the role of interests, power, and organizational capacity. *Journal of Sport Management, 18*(2), 158-198.

Batuev, M., & Robinson, L. (2018). What influences organisational evolution of modern sport: The case of skateboarding. *Sport, Business and Management: An International Journal, 8*(5), 492-510. doi:10.1108/SBM-10-2017-0052

BBC Sport. (2019, March 8). "Unpredictable, astonishing"—The Formula E season so far. *BBC Sports*, Retrieved from www.bbc.co.uk/sport/av/motorsport/47496096

Bloyce, D., Smith, A., Mead, R., & Morris, J. (2008). "Playing the game (plan)": A figurational analysis of organizational change in sports development in England. *European Sport Management Quarterly, 8*(4), 359-378. doi:10.1080/16184740802461637

Bombardier. (n.d.). History of Bombardier. Retrieved from www.bombardier.com/en/about-us/history.html

Bradutanu, D. (2015). *Resistance to change—A new perspective: A textbook for managers who plan to implement a change*. Scotts Valley, CA: CreateSpace.

British Universities & Colleges Sport. (n.d.). Our history. Retrieved from www.bucs.org.uk/page.asp?section=17396§ionTitle=Our+History

Brown, C., & Pappous, A. (2017). The organisational performance of national disability sport organisations during a time of austerity: A resource dependence theory perspective. *International Journal of Sport Policy and Politics, 10*(1), 63-78. doi:10.1080/19406940.2017.1381635

Cameron, K.S., & Whetten, D.A. (1983). Models of the organizational life cycle: Application to higher education. *Review of Higher Education, 6*, 269-299.

Carroll, G.R., & Hannan, M.T. (1989). Density dependence in the evolution of populations of newspaper organizations. *American Sociological Review, 54*, 524-541.

Carter, I. (2018, November 26). The Match: $9m Event Indicates Dangerous Direction Golf is Heading. *BBC Sports*, Retrieved from www.bbc.co.uk/sport/golf/46347935

Carter, P. (2005). *Review of national sport: Effort & resources*. London, UK: Sport England.

Cave, A. (2015, January 10). Pure Gym founder on how he built Britain's biggest gym chain. *Telegraph*, Retrieved from www.telegraph.co.uk/finance/newsbysector/retailandconsumer/11337645/Pure-Gym-founder-on-how-he-built-Britains-biggest-gym-chain.html

Chakrabarti, A.K. (1974). The role of champion in product innovation. *California Management Review, 17*(2), 58-62.

Chakrabarti, A.K., & Hauschildt, J. (1989). The division of labour in innovation management. *R & D Management (UK), 19*, 161-171.

Chin, R., & Benne, K.D. (1985). General strategies for effecting change in human systems. In W.G. Bennis, K.D. Benne, & R. Chin (Eds.), *The planning of change* (pp. 22-45). New York, NY: Holt, Rinehart & Winston.

Conn, D. (2018a, September 13). Manchester City accounts show Sheikh Mansour has put £1.3bn into club. *The Guardian*, Retrieved from www.theguardian.com/football/2018/sep/13/manchester-city-accounts-sheikh-mansour

Conn, D. (2018b, October 4). Manchester United have been owned by the Glazers for 13 years. No wonder they're struggling. *The Guardian*, Retrieved from www.theguardian.com/football/2018/oct/04/glazers-manchester-united

Conway, R. (2019, February 6). Video assistant referee: Uefa says "TV gesture" a bookable offence. *BBC Sports*, Retrieved from www.bbc.co.uk/sport/football/47149484

Cottrell, S., & Carpenter, K. (2018). A detailed review of the IAAF governance reforms. Retrieved from www.lawinsport.com/topics/sports/item/a-detailed-review-of-the-iaaf-governance-reforms

Cunningham, G.B. (2002). Removing the blinders: Toward an integrative model of organizational change in sport and physical activity. *Quest, 54*(4), 276-291. doi:10.1080/00336297.2002.10491779

Daft, R.L. (1992). *Organization theory and design* (4th ed.). St. Paul, MN: West.

Daly, M., & Roan, D. (2016, January 25). Adidas to end IAAF sponsorship deal early in wake of doping crisis. *BBC Sport*, Retrieved from www.bbc.com/sport/athletics/35385415

Damanpour, F. (1987). The adoption of technological, administrative, and ancillary innovations: Impact of organizational factors. *Journal of Management, 13*, 675-688.

DCMS. (2000). *A sporting future for all*. London, UK: DCMS.

Delacroix, J., & Carroll, G.R. (1983). Organizational foundings: An ecological study of the newspaper industries in Argentina and Ireland. *Administrative Science Quarterly, 28*, 274-291.

Deloitte & Touche LLP. (2018). *National Collegiate Athletic Association and subsidiaries*. Indianapolis, IN: Deloitte & Touche LLP. Retrieved from https://ncaaorg.s3.amazonaws.com/ncaa/finance/2017-18NCAAFin_NCAAFinancialStatement.pdf

DiMaggio, P.J., & Powell, W.W. (1983). The iron cage revisited: Institutional isomorphism and collective rationality in organizational field. *American Sociological Review, 35*, 147-160.

Downward, P., & Dawson, A. (2000). *The economics of professional team sports*. Abingdon, UK: Routledge.

Edelman, M. (2018). Explaining the Supreme Court's recent sports betting decision. *Forbes*, Retrieved from www.forbes.com/sites/marcedelman/2018/05/16/explaining-the-supreme-courts-recent-sports-betting-decision/#ea2f211537cb

Formula E. (n.d.). History: The Formula E story. Retrieved from www.fiaformulae.com/en/discover/history

Geiger, H.M. (1987). *The Broadmoor story* (Rev. ed.). Denver, CO: Hirschfeld Press.

Girginov, V., & Sandanski, I. (2008). Understanding the changing nature of sports organisations in transforming societies. *Sport Management Review, 11*(1), 21-50. doi:10.1016/S1441-3523(08)70102-5

Greenwood, R., & Hinings, C.R. (1988). Organizational design types, tracks, and the dynamics of strategic change. *Organization Studies, 9*, 293-316.

Greenwood, R., & Hinings, C.R. (1996). Understanding radical organizational change: Bringing together the old and the new. *The Academy of Management Review, 21*(4), 1022-1054.

Greiner, L.E. (1967). Patterns of organizational change. *Harvard Business Review, 45*, 119-130.

Hannan, M.T., & Freeman, J. (1989). *Organizational ecology*. Cambridge, MA: Harvard University Press.

Harrison, J.D. (2014, November 12). When we were small: Under Armour. *Washington Post*, Retrieved from www.washingtonpost.com/business/on-small-business/when-we-were-small-under-armour/2014/11/11/f61e8876-69ce-11e4-b053-65cea7903f2e_story.html?noredirect=on&utm_term=.4aa3d24bd73d

Heinze, K.L., & Lu, D. (2017). Shifting responses to institutional change: The National Football League and player concussions. *Journal of Sport Management, 31*(5), 497-513. doi:10.1123/jsm.2016-0309

Hinings, C.R., & Greenwood, R. (1988). *The dynamics of strategic change*. Oxford, UK: Basil Blackwell.

HM Government/DCMS. (2018). *Sporting future second annual report*. London, UK: HM Government/DCMS.

Hodges, J. (2016). *Managing and leading people through organizational change: The theory and practice of sustaining change through people*. London, UK: KoganPage Limited.

Houlihan, B., & Green, M. (2009). Modernization and sport: The reform of Sport England and UK Sport. *Public Administration, 87*(3), 678-698. doi:10.1111/j.1467-9299.2008.01733.x

Hsu, T. (2019, March 12). Dick's Sporting Goods shifts from guns even as sales suffer. *New York Times*, Retrieved from www.nytimes.com/2019/03/12/business/dicks-sporting-goods-stock-gun-control.html

Hwaya, K. (2019). Augmented reality dragon wows baseball fans on opening day. Retrieved from www.korea.net/NewsFocus/Sci-Tech/view?articleId=169492

IAAF. (2006). A piece of anti-doping history: IAAF Handbook 1927-1928. Retrieved from www.iaaf.org/news/news/a-piece-of-anti-doping-history-iaaf-handbook

Ingle, S. (2019, June 24). Lamine Diack to stand trial for money laundering and corruption. *The Guardian*, Retrieved from https://www.theguardian.com/sport/2019/jun/24/lamine-diack-trial-money-laundering-corruption-iaaf

Kanter, R.M. (1983). *The change masters*. New York, NY: Simon & Schuster.

Kelly, S. (2008). Understanding the role of the football manager in Britain and Ireland: A Weberian approach. *European Journal for Sport Management, 8*(4), 399-419. doi:10.1080/16184740802461652

Kikulis, L., Slack, T., & Hinings, C.R. (1992). Institutionally specific design archetypes: A framework for understanding change in national sport organizations. *International Review for the Sociology of Sport, 27*, 343-370.

Kikulis, L., Slack, T., & Hinings, C.R. (1995). Sector specific patterns of organizational design change. *Journal of Management Studies, 32*, 67-100.

Kimberly, J.R. (1980). The life cycle analogy and the study of organizations: Introduction. In J.R. Kimberly & R.H. Miles (Eds.), *The organizational life cycle* (pp. 1-14). San Francisco, CA: Jossey-Bass.

Kimberly, J.R. (1987). The study of organizations: Toward a biographical perspective. In J.W. Lorsch (Ed.), *Handbook of organizational behavior* (pp. 223-237). Englewood Cliffs, NJ: Prentice Hall.

Kimberly, J.R., & Miles, R.H. (1980). *The organizational life cycle*. San Francisco, CA: Jossey-Bass.

Kimberly, J.R., & Rottman, D.B. (1987). Environment, organization and effectiveness: A biographical approach. *Journal of Management Studies, 24*, 595-622.

King, F.W. (1991). *It's how you play the game: The inside story of the Calgary Olympics*. Calgary, AB: Writers' Group.

Kogan, R. (1985). *Brunswick: The story of an American company from 1845 to 1985*. Skokie, IL: Brunswick Corporation.

Kotter, J.P., & Schlesinger, L.A. (1979). Choosing strategies for change. *Harvard Business Review, 57*, 106-124.

Legg, J., Snelgrove, R., & Wood, L. (2016). Modifying tradition: Examining organizational change in youth sport. *Journal of Sport Management, 30*, 369-381. doi:10.1123/jsm.2015-0075

Lewis, M. (2003). *Moneyball: The art of winning an unfair game*. New York, NY: WW Norton & Co.

Loughborough University. (2019). Loughborough University secures unprecedented 40th consecutive BUCS crown. Retrieved from www.lboro.ac.uk/media-centre/press-releases/2019/july/loughborough-university-secures-40th-bucs-crown/

Lucidarme, S., Babiak, K., & Willem, A. (2018). Governmental power in elite sport networks: A resource-dependency perspective. *European Sport Management Quarterly, 18*(3), 348-372. doi:10.1080/16184742.2017.1405998

MacIntosh, D., & Whitson, D.J. (1990). *The game planners: Transforming Canada's sport system*. Montreal & Kingston, ON: McGill-Queen's University Press.

Maidique, M.A. (1980). Entrepreneurs, champions, and technological innovation. *Sloan Management Review, 21*, 59-76.

Manchester City Football Club. (2018). *Financial report: For the year ended 30 June 2018*. Manchester, UK: Manchester City Football Club. Retrieved from https://annualreport2018.mancity.com/downloads/ManCity_AR17-18_Financials.pdf

McCann, J.E. (1991). Design principles for an innovating company. *Academy of Management Executive, 5*, 76-93.

Meier, M., Tan, K.H., Lim, M.K., & Chung, L. (2018). Unlocking innovation in the sport industry through additive manufacturing Article information. *Business Process Management Journal, 25*(3), 456-475. doi:10.1108/BPMJ-10-2017-0285

Meyer, J.W., & Rowan, B. (1977). Institutionalized organizations: Formal structure as myth and ceremony. *American Journal of Sociology, 83*, 340-363.

Meyer, J.W., & Scott, R. (1983) *Organizational environments: Rituals and rationality*. Beverly Hills, CA: SAGE.

Miller, D. (1990). *The Icarus paradox: How exceptional companies bring about their own downfall*. New York, NY: HarperCollins.

Miller, D. (1992). The Icarus paradox: How exceptional companies bring about their own downfall. *Business Horizons, 35*(1), 24-35.

Miller, D., & Friesen, P. (1980a). Archetypes of organizational transition. *Administrative Science Quarterly, 25*, 268-292.

Miller, D., & Friesen, P. (1980b). Momentum and revolution in organizational adaptation. *Academy of Management Journal, 23*, 591-614.

Miller, D., & Friesen, P. (1984). *Organizations: A quantum view*. Englewood Cliffs, NJ: Prentice Hall.

Mintzberg, H. (1979). *The structuring of organizations*. Englewood Cliffs, NJ: Prentice Hall.

Moore, J. (2019). Manchester United fan protests: Darren Gough blasts Glazers for siphoning £1 BILLION out of club since 2003 takeover. Retrieved from https://talksport.com/football/564117/manchester-united-darren-gough-glazers-1billion/

Morrow, S., & Idle, C. (2008). Understanding change in professional road cycling. *European Sport Management Quarterly, 8*(4), 315-335. doi:10.1080/16184740802461603

Nadler, D.A., & Tushman, M.L. (1989). Organizational frame bending: Principles for managing reorientation. *The Academy of Management Executive, 3*, 194-204.

NCAA. (n.d.-a). Membership. Retrieved from www.ncaa.org/about/membership

NCAA. (n.d.-b). What is the NCAA? Retrieved from www.ncaa.org/about/resources/media-center/ncaa-101/what-ncaa

Neale, W.C. (1964). The peculiar economics of professional sports: A contribution to the theory of the firm in sporting competition and in market competition. *The Quarterly Journal of Economics, 78*(1), 1-14.

Nichols, G., & James, M. (2008). One size does not fit all: Implications of sports club diversity for their effectiveness as a policy tool and for government support. *Managing Leisure, 13*(2), 104-114. doi:10.1080/13606710801933461

Oliver, C. (1991). Strategic responses to institutional processes. *Academy of Management Review*, *16*, 145-179.

Patti, R.J. (1974). Organizational resistance and change: The view from below. *Social Service Review*, *48*, 367-383.

Peters, T. (1990). Get innovative or get dead. *California Management Review*, *33*, 9-26.

Pettigrew, A.M. (1985a). *The awakening giant*. Oxford, UK: Blackwell.

Pettigrew, A.M. (1985b). Contextualist research: A natural way to link theory and practice. In E. Lawler (Ed.), *Doing research that is useful in theory and practice* (pp. 222-248). San Francisco, CA: Jossey-Bass.

Pettigrew, A.M. (1987). Context and action in the transformation of the firm. *Journal of Management Studies*, *24*, 649-670.

Pettigrew, A.M., & Whipp, R. (1991). *Managing change for competitive success*. Oxford, UK: Basil Blackwell.

Pfeffer, J. (1981). *Power in organizations*. Marshfield, MA: Pitman.

Pfeffer, J., & Salancik, G. (1978). *The external control of organizations: A resource-dependence perspective*. New York, NY: Harper & Row.

Powell, W.W., & DiMaggio, P.J. (1991). *The new institutionalism in organizational analysis*. Chicago, IL: University of Chicago Press.

Roan, D. (2015, August 2). Leaked IAAF doping files: Wada "very alarmed" by allegations. *BBC Sports*, Retrieved from www.bbc.co.uk/sport/0/athletics/33749208

Robbins, S.P. (1990). *Organization theory: Structure, design and applications* (3rd ed.). Englewood Cliffs, NJ: Prentice Hall.

Sam, M.P. (2009). The public management of sport. *Public Management Review*, *11*(4), 499-514. doi:10.1080/14719030902989565

Schube, S. (2019). The Nike Hyperadapt BB Is laceless, reasonably priced, and sent here directly from the future. *GQ*, Retrieved from www.gq.com/story/nike-hyperadapt-bb-self-lacing

Siegel, R. (2019, May 31). Dick's Sporting Goods overhauled its gun policies after Parkland. The CEO didn't stop there. *Washington Post*, Retrieved from www.washingtonpost.com/business/economy/dicks-sporting-goods-overhauled-its-gun-policies-after-parkland-the-ceo-didnt-stop-there/2019/05/31/9faa6a08-7d8f-11e9-a5b3-34f3edf1351e_story.html?utm_term=.d09ee7cc3e84

Singh, J. (Ed.) (1990). *Organizational evolution: New directions*. Beverly Hills, CA: SAGE.

Slack, T. (1985). The bureaucratization of a voluntary sport organization. *International Review for the Sociology of Sport*, *20*, 145-166.

Slack, T., & Hinings, C.R. (1992). Understanding change in national sport organizations: An integration of theoretical perspectives. *Journal of Sport Management*, *6*, 114-132.

Slack, T., & Hinings, C.R. (1994). Institutional pressures and isomorphic change: An empirical test. *Organization Studies*, *15*, 803-827.

Steen-Johnsen, K. (2008). Networks and the organization of identity: The case of Norwegian snowboarding. *European Sport Management Quarterly*, *8*(4), 337-358. doi:10.1080/16184740802461629

Stern, R.N. (1979). The development of an interorganizational control network: The case of intercollegiate athletics. *Administrative Science Quarterly*, *24*(2), 242-266. doi:10.2307/2392496

Strasser, J.B., & Becklund, L. (1991). *Swoosh: The unauthorized story of Nike and the men who played there*. New York, NY: Harcourt Brace Jovanovich.

Theodoraki, E.I. (2001). A conceptual framework for the study of structural configurations of organizing committees for the Olympic Games (OCOGs). *European Journal for Sport Management*, *8*, 106-124.

Thibault, L., & Babiak, K. (2005). Organizational changes in Canada's sport system: Toward an athlete-centred approach. *European Sport Management Quarterly*, *5*(2), 105-132. doi:10.1080/16184740500188623

Thurston, A. (2017). *An analysis of the implementation of Clubmark and two associated policies in boxing, swimming and rugby union* (Unpublished doctoral thesis). Loughborough University). Loughborough, UK. Retrieved from https://dspace.lboro.ac.uk/2134/25521

Tremlett, S. (2018, September 25). Team USA Ryder Cup task force explained. *Golf Monthly*, Retrieved from www.golf-monthly.co.uk/ryder-cup/ryder-cup-blog/team-usa-ryder-cup-task-force-explained-165661

Tushman, M.L., Newman, W.H., & Romanelli, E. (1986). Convergence and upheaval: Managing the unsteady pace of organizational evolution. *California Management Review*, *29*, 29-44.

Tushman, M.L., & Romanelli, E. (1985). Organizational evolution: A metamorphosis model of convergence and reorientation. In L.L. Cummings & B.M. Staw (Eds.), *Research in organizational behavior* (Vol. 7, pp. 171-222). Greenwich, CT: JAI Press.

Vidar Hanstad, D. (2008). Drug scandal and organizational change within the International Ski Federation: A figurational approach. *European Journal for Sport Management*, *8*(4), 379-398. doi:10.1080/16184740802461645

Waddington, I., & Skirstad, B. (2008). Theoretical approaches to change in sports organizations. *European Sport Management Quarterly*, *8*(4), 311-313. doi:10.1080/16184740802461595

Wagner, U. (2011). Towards the construction of the World Anti-Doping Agency: Analyzing the approaches of FIFA and the IAAF to doping in sport. *European Sport Management Quarterly*, *11*(5), 445-470. doi:10.1080/16184742.2011.624107

Wallenfeldt, J. (n.d.). National Collegiate Athletic Association. In *Encyclopaedia Britannica*. Retrieved from www.britannica.com/topic/National-Collegiate-Athletic-Association

Weiss, D., & Day, C. (2003). *The making of the Super Bowl: The inside story of the world's greatest sporting event*. New York, NY: Contemporary Books.

Wolfe, R., Slack, T., & Rose-Hearn, T. (1993). Factors influencing the adoption and maintenance of Canadian, facility-based worksite health promotion programs. *American Journal of Health Promotion*, *7*, 189-198.

Zakus, D.H., & Skinner, J. (2008). Modelling organizational change in the International Olympic Committee. *European Sport Management Quarterly*, *8*(4), 421-442. doi:10.1080/16184740802461660

Zander, A. (1950). Resistance to change: Its analysis and prevention. *Advanced Management*, *15*(1), 9-10.

Zimbalist, A. (1992). *Baseball and billions*. New York, NY: Basic Books.

Zucker, L.G. (1983). Organizations as institutions. In S.B. Bacharach (Ed.), *Advances in organizational theory and research* (Vol. 2, pp. 1-43). Greenwich, CT: JAI Press.

Zucker, L.G. (1987). Institutional theories of organization. *Annual Review of Sociology*, *13*, 443-464.

Zucker, L.G. (1988). *Institutional patterns and organizations*. Cambridge, MA: Ballinger.

Zucker, L.G. (1989). Combining institutional theory and population ecology: No legitimacy, no history. *American Sociological Review*, *54*, 542-545.

Chapter 19

Alimo-Metcalfe, B. (1994). Waiting for fish to grow feet!: Removing organizational barriers to women's entry into leadership positions. In M. Tanton (Ed.), *Women in management* (pp. 27-45). London, UK: Routledge & Kegan Paul.

Alvesson, M. (2017). Waiting for Godot: Eight major problems in the odd field of leadership studies. *Leadership, 15*(6), 27-43.

Alvesson, M., & Deetz, S. (2000). *Doing critical management research*. London, UK: Sage.

Alvesson, M., & Spicer, A. (2012). A stupidity-based theory of organizations. *Journal of Management Studies, 49*(7), 1194-1220.

Avolio, B.J., & Gibbons, T.C. (1988). Developing transformational leaders: A life span approach. In J.A. Conger & R.N. Kanungo (Eds.), *Charismatic leadership: The elusive factor in organizational effectiveness* (pp. 276-308). San Francisco, CA: Jossey-Bass.

Avolio, B.J., & Yammarino, F.J. (1990). Operationalizing charismatic leadership using a levels of analysis framework. *Leadership Quarterly, 1*, 193-208.

Avolio, B.J., Walumbwa, F.O., & Weber, T.J. (2009). Leadership: Current theories, research, and future directions. *Annual Review of Psychology, 60*, 421-449.

Bass, B.M. (1981). *Stogdill's handbook of leadership*. New York, NY: Free Press.

Bass, B.M. (1985). *Leadership and performance beyond expectations*. New York, NY: Free Press.

Bass, B.M. (1990a). *Bass and Stogdill's handbook of leadership: Theory, research, and managerial application* (3rd ed.). New York, NY: Free Press.

Bass, B.M. (1990b). From transactional to transformational leadership: Learning to share the vision. *Organizational Dynamics, 18*, 19-31.

Bass, B.M., & Avolio, B.J. (1989). Potential biases in leadership measures: How prototypes, leniency, and general satisfaction relate to ratings and rankings of transformational and transactional leadership constructs. *Educational and Psychological Measurements, 49*, 509-527.

Bass, B.M., & Avolio, B.J. (1990a). Developing transformational leadership: 1992 and beyond. *Journal of European Industrial Training, 14*, 21-27.

Bass, B.M., & Avolio, B.J. (1990b). The implications of transactional and transformational leadership, team, and organizational development. *Research in Organizational Change and Development, 4*, 231-272.

Bass, B.M., & Avolio, B.J. (1990c). Transformational leadership and organizational culture. *International Journal of Public Administration, 17*, 541-554.

Bennis, W.G., & Nanus, B. (1985). *Leaders: The strategies for taking charge*. New York, NY: Harper & Row.

Billsberry, J., Mueller, J., Skinner, J., Swanson, S., Corbett, B., & Ferkins, L. (2018). Reimagining leadership in sport management: Lessons from the social construction of leadership. *Journal of Sport Management, 32*(2), 170-182.

Bowers, D.G., & Seashore, S.E. (1966). Predicting organizational effectiveness with a four-factor theory of leadership. *Administrative Science Quarterly, 11*, 238-263.

Bowers, M.R., Hall, J.R., & Srinivasan, M.M. (2017). Organizational culture and leadership style: The missing combination for selecting the right leader for effective crisis management. *Business Horizons, 60*(4), 551-563.

Branch, D. (1990). Athletic director leader behavior as a predictor of intercollegiate athletic organizational effectiveness. *Journal of Sport Management, 4*, 161-173.

Bray, D.W., Campbell, R.J., & Grant, D.L. (1974). *Formative years in business: A long-term AT&T study of managerial lives*. New York, NY: Wiley.

Bryman, A. (1986). *Leadership and organizations*. London, UK: Routledge & Kegan Paul.

Bryman, A. (1992). *Charisma and leadership in organizations*. London, UK: SAGE.

Buckingham, M, & Coffman, C. (1999). *First, break all the rules*. New York, NY: Simon & Schuster.

Burns, J.M. (1978). *Leadership*. New York, NY: Harper & Row.

Burton, L.J. (2015). Underrepresentation of women in sport leadership: A review of research. *Sport Management Review, 18*(2), 155-165.

Burton, L.J., Welty Peachey, J., & Wells, J.E. (2017). The role of servant leadership in developing an ethical climate in sport organizations. *Journal of Sport Management, 31*(3), 229-240.

Calas, M.B., & Smircich, L. (1991). Voicing seduction to silence leadership. *Organization Studies, 12*, 567-602.

CBC.ca. (2004). Top ten greatest Canadians: Wayne Gretzky. Retrieved February 28, 2005, from www.cbc.ca/greatest/top_ten/nominee/gretzky-wayne.html

Chelladurai, P., & Carron, A.V. (1983). Athletic maturity and preferred leadership. *Journal of Sports Psychology, 5*, 371-380.

Chelladurai, P., & Saleh, S.D. (1978). Preferred leadership in sports. *Canadian Journal of Applied Sport Sciences, 3*, 85-92.

Chelladurai, P., & Saleh, S.D. (1980). Dimensions of leader behavior in sports: Development of a leadership scale. *Journal of Sport Psychology, 2*, 43-45.

Chelladurai, P., Szyszlo, M., & Haggerty, T.R. (1987a). Systems-based dimensions of effectiveness: The case of national sport organizations. *Canadian Journal of Sport Science, 12*, 111-119.

Chelladurai, P., Malloy, D., Imamura, H., & Yamaguchi, Y. (1987b). A cross-cultural study of preferred leadership in sports. *Canadian Journal of Sport Sciences, 12*, 106-110.

Cockburn, C. (1991). *In the way of women: Men's resistance to sex equality in organizations*. Houndmills, UK: Macmillan.

Collinson, D. (2017). Critical leadership studies: A response to Learmonth and Morrell. *Leadership, 13*(3), 272-284.

Conger, J.A. (1989). *The charismatic leader: Behind the mystique of exceptional leadership*. San Francisco, CA: Jossey-Bass.

Conger, J.A., & Kanungo, R.N. (1987). Towards a behavioral theory of charismatic leadership in organizational settings. *Academy of Management Review, 12*, 637-647

Conger, J.A., & Kanungo, R.N. (1988). Behavioral dimensions of charismatic leadership. In J.A. Conger & R.N. Kanungo (Eds.), *Charismatic leadership: The elusive factor in organizational effectiveness,* 78-97. San Francisco, CA: Jossey-Bass.

Day, D.V., Fleenor, J.W., Atwater, L.E., Sturm, R.E., & McKee, R.A. (2014). Advances in leader and leadership development: A review of 25 years of research and theory. *The Leadership Quarterly, 25*(1), 63-82.

Elberse, A. (2013). Ferguson's formula. *Harvard Business Review, 91*(10), 116-125.

Etzioni, A. (1961). *A comparative analysis of complex organizations*. New York, NY: Free Press.

Feloni, R. (2017, August 5). An analysis of the 16 best sports teams in history shows the most important person on the team isn't its coach or best athlete. *Business Insider*, Retrieved from www.businessinsider.com/the-most-important-person-on-a-team-isnt-its-coach-or-best-athlete-2017-8

Ferkins, L., Skinner, J., & Swanson, S. (2018). Sport leadership: A new generation of thinking. *Journal of Sport Management*, 32(2): 77-81.

Fiedler, F.E. (1967). *A theory of leadership effectiveness*. New York, NY: McGraw-Hill.

Filley, A.C., House, R.J., & Kerr, S. (1976). *Managerial process and organizational behavior* (2nd ed.). Glenview, IL: Scott Foresman.

Fisher, B.M., & Edwards, J.E. (1988). Consideration and initiating structure and their relationships with leaders' effectiveness: A meta-analysis, presented at Best Paper Proceedings, Academy of Management, Anaheim, 2014. Anaheim, CA: Academy of Management.

Fleishman, E.A., & Harris, E.F. (1962). Patterns of leader behavior related to employee grievances and turnover. *Personnel Psychology, 15*, 43-56.

Fleishman, E.A., Harris, E.F., & Burtt, H.E. (1955). *Leadership and supervision in industry*. Columbus, OH: Ohio State University, Bureau of Educational Research.

Fletcher, J.K. (2004). The paradox of postheroic leadership: An essay on gender, power, and transformational change. *The Leadership Quarterly, 15*(5), 647-661.

Frisby, W. (2005). The good, the bad, and the ugly: Critical sport management research. *Journal of Sport Management, 19,* 1-12.

Gardner, W.L., Avolio, B.J., Luthans, F., May, D.R., & Walumbwa, F. (2005). "Can you see the real me?" A self-based model of authentic leader and follower development. *The Leadership Quarterly, 16*(3), 343-372.

Gaugler, B.B., Rosenthal, D.B., Thornton, G.C., & Bentson, C. (1987). Meta-analysis of assessment center validity. *Journal of Applied Psychology, 72,* 493-511.

George, B. (2003). *Authentic leadership: Rediscovering the secrets to creating lasting value*. Hoboken, NJ: John Wiley & Sons.

Hall, M.A., Cullen, D., & Slack, T. (1989). Organizational elites recreating themselves: The gender structure of national sport organizations. *Quest, 41*, 28-45.

Halpin, A.W. (1957). The observed behavior and ideal behavior of aircraft commanders and school superintendents. In R.M. Stogdill & A.E. Coons (Eds.), *Leader behaviors: Its description and measurement* (pp. 65-68). Columbus, OH: Ohio State University, Bureau of Business Research.

Halpin, A.W., & Winer, B.J. (1957). A factorial study of the leader behavior descriptions. In R.M. Stogdill & A.E. Coons (Eds.), *Leader behaviors: It's description and measurement,* 39-51. Columbus, OH: Ohio State University, Bureau of Business Research.

Hater, J.J., & Bass, B.M. (1988). Superiors' evaluations and subordinates' perceptions of transformational and transactional leadership. *Journal of Applied Psychology, 73,* 695-702.

Hemphill, J.K., & Coons, A.E. (1957). Development of the leader behavior description questionnaire. In R.M. Stogdill & A.E. Coons (Eds.), *Leader behaviors: Its description and measurement,* 6-38. Columbus, OH: Ohio State University, Bureau of Business Research.

Hendry, J., and Johnson, G., with Newton, J. (Eds.). (1993). *Strategic thinking: Leadership and the management of change*. Chichester, UK: Wiley.

Hersey, P., & Blanchard, K.H. (1984). *Management of organizational behavior* (4th ed.). Englewood Cliffs, NJ: Prentice Hall.

House, R.J. (1971). A path-goal theory of leader effectiveness. *Administrative Science Quarterly, 16*, 321-339.

House, R.J. (1977). A 1976 theory of charismatic leadership. In J.G. Hunt & L.L. Larson (Eds.), *Leadership: The cutting edge* (pp. 189-207). Carbondale, IL: Southern Illinois University Press.

House, R.J., & Dessler, G. (1974). The path-goal theory of leadership: Some post hoc and a priori tests. In J. Hunt & L. Larson (Eds.), *Contingency approaches to leadership* (pp. 29-55). Carbondale, IL: Southern Illinois Press.

House, R.J., & Mitchell, T.R. (1974). Path-goal theory of leadership. *Contemporary Business, 3*, 81-98.

Hovden, J. (2000). Gender and leadership selection processes in Norwegian sporting organizations. *International Review for the Sociology of Sport, 35*, 75-82.

Humphreys, M., Ucbasaran, D., & Lockett, A. (2012). Sensemaking and sensegiving stories of jazz leadership. *Human Relations, 65*(1), 41-62.

Hytner, R. (2016). Sir Alex Ferguson on how to win. Retrieved from www.london.edu/lbsr/sir-alex-ferguson-on-how-to-win

Ilies, R., Morgeson, F.P., & Nahrgang, J.D. (2005). Authentic leadership and eudaemonic well-being: Understanding leader–follower outcomes. *The Leadership Quarterly, 16*(3), 373-394.

IMG. (2005). History. Retrieved from www.imgworld.com/history/default.sps?itype=5415&icustompageid=8811

IMG. (2018). Our Story. Retrieved from at http://img.com/story/

Indik, J. (1986). Path-goal theory of leadership: A meta-analysis. Best paper proceedings, Academy of Management. Anaheim, CA: Academy of Management. (Cited by Yukl, 1989.)

Inglis, S. (1997). Shared leadership in the governance of amateur sport: Perceptions of executive directors and volunteer board members. *Avante, 3,* 14-33.

Jamieson, L.J. (1987). Competency-based approaches to sport management. *Journal of Sport Management, 1*, 48-56.

Johns, G. (2006). The essential impact of context on organizational behavior. *Academy of Management Review*, 3, 386-408.

Johns, G. (2017). Reflections on the 2016 decade award: Incorporating context in organizational research. *Academy of Management Review, 42*(4), 577-595.

Jones, G.J., Wegner, C.E., Bunds, K.S., Edwards, M.B., & Bocarro, J.N. (2018). Examining the environmental characteristics of shared leadership in a sport-for-development organization. *Journal of Sport Management, 32*(2), 82-95.

Katerberg, R., & Hom, P.W. (1981). Effects of within-group and between-groups variations in leadership. *Journal of Applied Psychology, 66*, 218-222.

Katz, D., Maccoby, N., Gurin, G., & Floor, L. (1951). *Productivity, supervision, and morale among railroad workers*. Ann Arbor, MI: Survey Research Center, University of Michigan.

Katz, D., Maccoby, N., & Morse, N. (1950). *Productivity, supervision, and morale in an office situation*. Ann Arbor, MI: Institute for Social Research, University of Michigan.

Kennedy, J.K. (1982). Middle LPC leaders and the contingency model of leadership effectiveness. *Organizational Behavior and Human Performance, 30*, 1-14.

Kent, A., & Weese, W.J. (2000). Do effective organizations have better executive leaders and/or organizational cultures? A study of selected sport organizations in Canada. *European Journal for Sport Management, 7,* 4-21.

King, D., & Learmonth, M. (2015). Can critical management studies ever be "practical"? A case study in engaged scholarship. *Human Relations, 68*(3), 353-375.

Lapchick, R.E. (2016). Gender report card: 2016 international sports report card on women leadership roles in sport. Retrieved from http://nebula.wsimg.com/0e5c5c3e23367795e9ec9e5ec49fc9b2?AccessKeyId=DAC3A56D8FB782449D2A&disposition=0&alloworigin=1

Larson, L.L., Hunt, J.G., & Osborn, R.N. (1976). The great hi-hi leader behavior myth: A lesson from Occam's razor. *Academy of Management Journal, 19*, 628-641.

Learmonth, M., & Morrell, K. (2017). Is critical leadership studies "critical"?. *Leadership, 13*(3), 257-271.

Leavy, B., & Wilson, D.C. (1994). *Strategy and leadership*. London, UK: Routledge & Kegan Paul.

Leitch, C., & Stead, V. (2016). Gender and leadership. *Leadership, 12*(1), 127-128.

Luthans, F., & Avolio, B.J. (2003). Authentic leadership: A positive development approach. In K.S. Cameron, J.E. Dutton, & R.E. Quinn (Eds.), *Positive organizational behavior* (pp. 241-258). San Francisco, CA: Barrett-Koehler.

McCall, M.W. Jr., & Lombardo, M.M. (1978). *Leadership: Where else can we go?* Durham, NC: Duke University Press.

McLennan, K. (1967). The manager and his job skills. *Academy of Management Journal, 3*, 235-245.

Meuser, J.D., Gardner, W.L., Dinh, J.E., Hu, J., Liden, R.C., & Lord, R.G. (2016). A network analysis of leadership theory: The infancy of integration. *Journal of Management, 42*(5), 1374-1403.

Miller, D., & Friesen, P. (1984). *Organizations: A quantum view*. Englewood Cliffs, NJ: Prentice Hall.

Mills, J.P., & Boardley, I.D. (2016). Expert Premier League soccer managers' use of transformational leadership behaviours and attitude towards sport integrity: An intrinsic case study. *International Journal of Sports Science & Coaching, 11*(3), 382-394.

Nadler, D.A., & Tushman, M.L. (1989). What makes for magic leadership? In W.E. Rosenbach & R.L. Taylor (Eds.), *Contemporary issues in leadership* (pp. 135-138). Boulder, CO: Westview.

Nadler, D.A., & Tushman, M.L. (1990). Beyond the charismatic leader: Leadership and organizational change. *California Management Review, 32*, 77-97.

Oberg, W. (1972). Charisma, commitment, and contemporary organization theory. *MSU Business Topics, 20*, 18-32.

Oc, B. (2018). Contextual leadership: A systematic review of how contextual factors shape leadership and its outcomes. *The Leadership Quarterly, 29*(1), 218-235.

Olafson, G.A., & Hastings, D.W. (1988). Personal style and administrative behavior in amateur sport organizations. *Journal of Sport Management, 2*, 26-39.

Paton, G. (1987). Sport management research: What progress has been made? *Journal of Sport Management, 1*, 25-31.

Pauchant, T.C. (1991). Transferential leadership: Towards a more complex understanding of charisma in organizations. *Organization Studies, 12*, 507-527.

Peters, L.H., Hartke, D.D., & Pohlmann, J.T. (1985). Fiedler's contingency theory of leadership: An application of the meta-analytic procedures of Schmidt and Hunter. *Psychological Bulletin, 97*, 274-285.

Peters, T.J., & Waterman, R.H. (1982). *In search of excellence*. New York, NY: Harper & Row.

Pettigrew, A.M. (1987). Context and action in the transformation of the firm. *Journal of Management Studies, 24*, 649-670.

Pfeffer, J. (1977). The ambiguity of leadership. *Academy of Management Review, 2*, 104-112.

Pound, R.W. (2004). *Inside the Olympics: A behind-the-scenes look at the politics, the scandals, and the glory of the games*. Mississauga, ON: Wiley Canada.

Powell, G.N. (1993). *Women and men in management* (2nd ed.). Newbury Park, CA: Sage.

Raphael, A. (2016). The enduring legacy of "The Great One" is his leadership. Entrepreneur, Retrieved from www.entrepreneur.com/article/279098

Rosener, J. (1990). Ways women lead. *Harvard Business Review, 68*, 119-125.

Ryan, I., & Dickson, G. (2018). The invisible norm: An exploration of the intersections of sport, gender and leadership. *Leadership, 14*(3), 329-346.

Sashkin, M. (1986). True vision in leadership. *Training and Development Journal, 40*, 58-61.

Sashkin, M. (1988). The visionary leader. In J.A. Conger & R.N. Kanungo (Eds.), *Charismatic leadership: The elusive factor in organizational effectiveness* (pp. 122-160). San Francisco, CA: Jossey-Bass.

Schedlitzki, D., & Edwards, G. (2017). *Studying leadership: Traditional and critical approaches*. London, UK: SAGE.

Schein, E.H. (1985). *Organizational culture and leadership*. San Francisco, CA: Jossey-Bass.

Schein, E.H. (1992). *Organizational culture and leadership* (2nd ed.). San Francisco, CA: Jossey-Bass.

Schriesheim, J.F. (1980). The social context of leader-subordinate relations: An investigation of the effects of group cohesiveness. *Journal of Applied Psychology, 65*, 183-194.

Schuler, R.S. (1976). Participation with supervisor and subordinate authoritarianism: A path-goal reconciliation. *Administrative Science Quarterly, 21*, 320-325.

Schriesheim, J.F., & Kerr, S. (1977). Theories and measures of leadership: A critical appraisal. In J.G. Hunt and L.L. Larson (Eds.), *Leadership: The cutting edge* (pp. 9-45). Carbondale, IL: Southern Illinois University Press.

Snyder, C.J. (1990). The effects of leader behavior and organizational climate on intercollegiate coaches' job satisfaction. *Journal of Sport Management, 4*, 59-70.

Stinson, J.E., & Johnson, T.W. (1975). The path goal theory of leadership: A partial test and suggested refinement. *Academy of Management Journal, 18*, 242-252.

Stogdill & A.E. Coons (Eds.). (1957). *Leader behaviors: It's description and measurement*. Columbus, OH: Ohio State University, Bureau of Business Research.

Strube, M.J., & Garcia, J.E. (1981). A meta-analytic investigation of Fiedler's contingency model of leadership effectiveness. *Psychological Bulletin, 90*, 307-321.

Terborg, J.R. (1977). Women in management: A research review. *Journal of Applied Psychology, 62*, 647-664.

Tichy, N.M., & Devanna, M.A. (1986). *The transformational leader*. New York, NY: Wiley.

Tourish, D. (2013). *The dark side of transformational leadership: A critical perspective*. London, UK: Routledge.

Tushman, M.L., & Romanelli, E. (1985). Organizational evolution: A metamorphosis model of convergence and reorientation. In L.L. Cummings & B.M. Staw (Eds.), *Research in organizational behavior* (Vol. 7, pp. 171-222). Greenwich, CT: JAI Press.

Tushman, M.L., Virany, B., & Romanelli, E. (1986). Executive succession, strategic reorientations, and organizational evolution: The microcomputer industry as a case in point. *Technology in Society, 7*, 297-313.

Uhl-Bien, M., Riggio, R.E., Lowe, K.B., & Carsten, M.K. (2014). Followership theory: A review and research agenda. *The leadership quarterly, 25*(1), 83-104.

Ulrich, D.R. (1987). The role of transformational leaders in changing sport arenas. In T. Slack & C.R. Hinings (Eds.), *The organization and administration of sport*. London, ON: Sport Dynamics.

Van Dierendonck, D. (2011). Servant leadership: A review and synthesis. *Journal of management, 37*(4), 1228-1261.

Walker, S. (2017). *The captain class*. New York, NY: Penguin Random House LLC.

Walsh, J.P., Weinberg, R.M., & Fairfield, M.L. (1987). The effects of gender on assessment centre evaluations. *Journal of Occupational Psychology*, *60*(4), 305-309.

Warrick, D.D. (2017). What leaders need to know about organizational culture. *Business Horizons*, *60*(3), 395-404.

Weber, M. (1968). *Economy and society* (Vol. 1) (G. Roth & C. Wittich, Trans.). Berkeley, CA: University of California Press.

Weese, W.J. (1994). A leadership discussion with Dr. Bernard Bass. *Journal of Sport Management*, *8*, 179-189.

Weese, W.J. (1995a). Leadership and organizational culture: An investigation of Big-Ten and Mid-American Conference campus recreation administrators. *Journal of Sport Management*, *9*, 119-134.

Weese, W.J. (1995b). Leadership, organizational culture, and job satisfaction in Canadian YMCA organizations. *Journal of Sport Management*, *9*, 182-193.

Weese, W.J. (1996). Do leadership and organizational culture really matter? *Journal of Sport Management*, *10*, 197-206.

Welty Peachey, J., Zhou, Y., Damon, Z.J., & Burton, L.J. (2015). Forty years of leadership research in sport management: A review, synthesis, and conceptual framework. *Journal of Sport Management*, *29*(5), 570-587.

Wentworth, D.K., & Anderson, L.R. (1984). Emergent leadership as a function of sex and task type. *Sex Roles*, *11*, 513-523.

Westley, F.R., & Mintzberg, H. (1989). Profiles of strategic vision: Levesque and Iacocca. In J.A. Conger & R.N. Kanungo (Eds.), *Charismatic leadership: The elusive factor in organizational effectiveness* (pp. 161-212). San Francisco, CA: Jossey-Bass.

Willink, J., & Babin, L. (2017). *Extreme ownership*. New York, NY: St. Martin's Press.

Wilson, S. (2016). *Thinking differently about leadership: A critical history of leadership studies*. Cheltenham, UK: Edward Elgar Publishing.

Yammarino, F.J., & Bass, B.M. (1990). Transformational leadership and multiple levels of analysis. *Human Relations*, *43*, 975-995.

Yukl, G.A. (1981). *Leadership in organizations*. Englewood Cliffs, NJ: Prentice Hall.

Yukl, G.A. (1989). *Leadership in organizations* (2nd ed.). Englewood Cliffs, NJ: Prentice Hall.

Yukl, G.A. (1998). *Leadership in organizations* (4th ed.). Englewood Cliffs, NJ: Prentice Hall.

Chapter 20

Adams, S. (2011, February 6). OCD: David Beckham has it—as do over a million other Britons. *Telegraph*. Retrieved from www.telegraph.co.uk/news/health/news/8306947/OCD-David-Beckham-has-it-as-do-over-a-million-other-Britons.html

Ahmad, A. Rotherham, N., & Talwar, D. (2015, September 21). Muscle dysmorphia: One in 10 men in gyms believed to have "bigorexia." *BBC News*. Retrieved from www.bbc.co.uk/newsbeat/article/34307044/muscle-dysmorphia-one-in-10-men-in-gyms-believed-to-have-bigorexia

APA. (2013). *Diagnostic and statistical manual of mental disorders V*. Washington, DC: American Psychiatric Association.

Averis, M. (2011, November 13). Up & under: Australia flanker David Pocock reveals eating disorder. *The Guardian*. Retrieved from www.theguardian.com/sport/2011/nov/13/up-under-david-pocock

Avil, H. (2012, May 22). London 2012 Olympics: Triathlete Hollie Avil reveals why she has decided to bring an end to her promising career. *Telegraph*. Retrieved from www.telegraph.co.uk/sport/olympics/triathlon/9280566/London-2012-Olympics-triathlete-Hollie-Avil-reveals-why-she-has-decided-to-bring-an-end-to-her-promising-career.html

BBC News. (2017a, February 28). Michael Jamieson: Depression goes unrecognised in elite sport. *BBC News*. Retrieved from www.bbc.co.uk/news/uk-scotland-39114128

BBC News. (2017b, September 24). Olympic champion Dame Kelly Holmes "cut herself daily." *BBC News*. Retrieved from www.bbc.co.uk/news/uk-england-kent-41372189

BBC Sport. (2018, June 6). World Cup 2018: England's Danny Rose reveals depression diagnosis. *BBC Sport*. Retrieved from www.bbc.co.uk/sport/football/44392337

Berger, B.G., & Motl, R.W. (2000). Exercise and mood: A selective review and synthesis of research employing the Profile of Mood States. *Journal of Applied Sport Psychology*, *12*, 69-92.

Branch, J. (2011, September 1). Hockey players' deaths pose a tragic riddle. *New York Times*. Retrieved from www.nytimes.com/2011/09/02/sports/hockey/deaths-of-three-nhl-players-raises-a-deadly-riddle.html

Bull, A. (2018, February 6). The life and death of Steve Holcomb, forever seeking that perfect line. *The Guardian*. Retrieved from www.theguardian.com/sport/2018/feb/06/steve-holcomb-blind-bobsled-winter-olympics

Burton, S. (2012). 50 stunning Olympic moments No33: Ben Johnson wins gold . . . tests positive. *The Guardian*. Retrieved from www.theguardian.com/sport/2012/may/25/ben-johnson-seoul-olympics-1988

Butterly, A. (2014, April 8). WWE WrestleMania star The Undertaker has head injury. *BBC News*. Retrieved from www.bbc.co.uk/newsbeat/article/26934095/wwe-wrestlemania-star-the-undertaker-has-head-injury

Buzinski, J. (2017). There aren't any out gay male athletes in major professional sports. SBNation. Retrieved from www.outsports.com/2017/11/15/16620066/out-gay-sport-robbie-rogers

Carr, A., & McNulty, M. (2006). *The handbook of adult clinical psychology: An evidence-based practice approach*. London, UK and New York, NY: Routledge Taylor & Francis Group.

Coles, B. (2019). New mouthguards that help monitor concussion to be worn by Ospreys and Cardiff Blues. Telegraph. Retrieved from https://www.telegraph.co.uk/rugby-union/2019/04/26/new-mouthguards-help-monitor-concussion-worn-ospreys-cardiff/

Claes, L., & Vandereycken, W. (2007). Self-injurious behavior: Differential diagnosis and functional differentiation. *Comprehensive Psychiatry*, *48*, 137-144.

Creswell, S.L., & Eklund, R.C. (2007). Athlete burnout: A longitudinal qualitative investigation. *Sport Psychology*, *21*, 1-20.

Cuncic, A. (2013). Khalil Greene's experience with social anxiety. Verywell. Retrieved from http://socialanxietydisorder.about.com/od/celebritieswithsad/p/khalilgreene.htm

Cuncic, A. (2014). What is Susie O'Neill's Experience with Social Anxiety? Verywell. Retrieved from http://socialanxietydisorder.about.com/od/celebritieswithsad/p/susieoneill.htm

Currie, A., & Owen, B. (Eds.). (2016). *Sport psychiatry*. Oxford, UK: Oxford University Press.

Department for Digital, Culture, Media & Sport (DCMS), & Crouch, T. (2018, March 21). *Government unveils mental health action plan to improve support for elite sportspeople* [Press release]. Retrieved from www.gov.uk/government/news/government-unveils-mental-health-action-plan-to-improve-support-for-elite-sportspeople

Emms, G. (2017). I'm ashamed to admit I'm struggling. The Mixed Zone. Retrieved from www.themixedzone.co.uk/im-ashamed-admit-im-struggling/

Fletcher, D., & Sarkar, M. (2012). A grounded theory of psychological resilience in Olympic champions. *Psychology of Sport and Exercise*, *5*, 669-678.

Fletcher, D., & Sarkar, M. (2013). Psychological resilience: A review and critique of definitions, concepts and theory. *European Psychologist*, *18*, 12-23.

Game Plan. (n.d.). *Our mission*. Retrieved from https://mygameplan.ca/about/#mission-block

George, T. (2002, July 24). Pro football; emerging from the shadows. *New York Times*. Retrieved from www.nytimes.com/2002/07/24/sports/pro-football-emerging-from-the-shadows.html

Graham, M., Rivara, F.P., Ford, M.A., & Spicer, C.M. (2014). *Sports-related concussions in youth: Improving the science, changing the culture*. Washington, DC: National Academies Press.

Hale, M. (2009, October 26). Boxing king casts his shadow, even at time of defeat. *New York Times*. Retrieved from www.nytimes.com/2009/10/27/arts/television/27muhammad.html?mtrref=undefined&gwh=AFE8F468275B604DCA027420D-BE0F639&gwt=pay&assetType=REGIWALL

Hanson, I. (2019). Mental health issues driving coaches out of sport, says Olympic mentor Leigh Nugent. Retrieved from https://www.swimmingworldmagazine.com/news/mental-health-issues-driving-coaches-out-of-sport-says-olympic-mentor-leigh-nugent/

Hart, T. (2018). Ruta Meilutyte: "I fight against depression everyday." Swim Swam. Retrieved from https://swimswam.com/ruta-meilutyte-i-fight-against-depression-everyday/

Health Advisory Service (HAS). (1995). *Child and adolescent mental health service. Together we stand*. London, UK: HMSO.

Hirsch, C. (2017). Dark, dark, dark, dark, dark, dark, dark, dark. The Players' Tribune. Retrieved from www.theplayerstribune.com/en-us/articles/corey-hirsch-dark-dark-dark

Hoek, H.W., & van Hoeken, D. (2003). Review of the prevalence and incidence of eating disorders. *International Journal of Eating Disorders*, *34*, 383-396.

Hope, N. (2016, January 15). GB alpine skiers still affected by Alain Baxter's stripped medal. *BBC News*. Retrieved from www.bbc.co.uk/sport/winter-sports/35292538

Hossain, A. (2015). Team Canada and partners announce Game Plan to help athletes. Retrieved from https://olympic.ca/2015/09/24/team-canada-and-partners-announce-game-plan-to-help-athletes/

Jackson, R. (2014, August 11). The joy of six: Athletes' superstitions. *The Guardian*. Retrieved from www.theguardian.com/sport/blog/2014/aug/12/the-joy-of-six-athletes-superstitions

Jahoda, M. (1958). *Current concepts of positive mental health*. New York, NY: Basic Books.

Kamm, L. (2005). Interviewing principles for the psychiatrically aware sports medicine physician. *Clinical Sport Medicine*, *24*, 745.

Keyes, C. (2002). The mental health continuum: From languishing to flourishing in life. *Journal of Health and Social Behaviour*, *43*(2). doi.org/10.2307/3090197

Liddle, S.K., Deane, F.P., & Vella, S.A. (2017). Addressing mental health through sport: A review of sporting organizations' websites. *Early Intervention in Psychiatry*, *11*(2), 93-103. doi:10.1111/eip.12337

Ljungqvist, A., Jenoure, P., Engebretsen, L., Alonso, J.M., Bahr, R., Clough, A., et al. (2009). The International Olympic Committee (IOC) consensus statement on periodic health evaluation of elite athletes. *British Journal Sports Medicine*, *43*, 631-643.

Lutton, P. (2019). 'It takes a toll': Campaign shines light on mental health of coaches. *The Sydney Morning Herald*. Retrieved from https://www.smh.com.au/sport/it-takes-a-toll-campaign-shines-light-on-mental-health-of-coaches-20191015-p530wg.html

Macaskill, S. (2009, February 25). Top 10: Football superstitions to rival Arsenal's Kolo Toure. *The Telegraph*. Retrieved from www.telegraph.co.uk/sport/football/teams/arsenal/4805924/Top-10-Football-superstitions-to-rival-Arsenals-Kolo-Toure.html

McEwen, T. (2012). Olympian Clara Hughes shares her tale of depression. Retrieved from http://clara-hughes.com/olympian-clara-hughes-shares-her-tale-of-depression/

Mills, J. (2018, June 7). England footballer Danny Rose praised for opening up about depression battle. *The Metro*. Retrieved from metro.co.uk/2018/06/07/england-footballer-danny-rose-opens-depression-battle-7614623/

Moore, R. (2012). *The dirtiest race in history: Ben Johnson, Carl Lewis and the Olympic 100m final*. London, UK: Wisden.

Mosley, P.E. (2008). Bigorexia: Bodybuilding and muscle dysmorphia. *European Eating Disorders Review*, *17*(3), 191-198. doi:10.1002/erv.897

Newman, H.J., Howells, K.L., & Fletcher, D. (2016). The dark side of top level sport: An autobiographic study of depressive experiences in elite sport performers. *Frontiers in Psychology*, *7*, 868.

NZ Herald. (2015, June 5). Troubled Kiwi bodybuilder Mr Big dies. *New Zealand Herald*. Retrieved from www.nzherald.co.nz/nz/news/article.cfm?c_id=1&objectid=11460327

Overbye, M., & Wagner, U. (2013). Between medical treatment and performance enhancement: An investigation of how elite athletes experience Therapeutic Use Exemptions. *International Journal of Drug Policy*, *24*(6), 579-588.

Paxton, R.J, Motl, R.W., Aylward, A., & Nigg, C.R. (2010). Physical activity and quality of life—The complementary influence of self-efficacy for physical activity and mental health difficulties. *International Journal of Behavioral Medicine*, *17*(4), 255-263. doi:10.1007/s12529-010-9086-9.

Plateau, C., Arcelus, J., McDermott, H., & Meyer, C. (2015). Responses of track and field coaches to athletes with eating problems. *Scandinavian Journal of Medicine and Science in Sport*, *25*(2), e240-250.

Plateau, C., McDermott, H., Arcelus, J., & Meyer, C. (2014). Identifying and preventing disordered eating among athletes: Perceptions of track and field coaches. *Psychology of Sport and Exercise*, *15*(6), 721-728.

Pope, H.G. Jr., Katz, D.L., & Hudson, J.I. (1993). Anorexia nervosa and "reverse anorexia" among 108 male bodybuilders. *Comprehensive Psychiatry*, *34*(6), 406-409.

Preti, A., Girolamo, G., Vilagut, G., Alonso, J., Graaf, R., Bruffaerts, R., Demyttenaere, K., Pinto-Meza, A., Haro, J.M., & Morosini, P. (2009). The epidemiology of eating disorders in six European countries: Results of the ESEMeD-WMH project. *Journal of Psychiatry Research*, *43*(14), 1125-1132.

Prochaska, J.O., & DiClemente, C.C. (1983). Stages and processes of self-change of smoking: Toward an integrative model of change. *Journal of Consulting Clinical Psychology*, *51*(3), 390-395.

Prochaska, J.O., DiClemente, C.C., & Norcross, J.C. (1992). In search of how people change. Applications to addictive behaviors. *American Psychologist*, *47*(9), 1102-1114.

Randolph, C., Karantzoulis, S., & Guskiewicz, K. (2013). Prevalence and characterization of mild cognitive impairment in retired National Football League players. *Journal of the International Neuropsychological Society*, *19*, 1-8.

Rutter, M., Shaffer, D., & Shepherd, M. (1975). *A multiaxial classification of child psychiatric disorders*. Geneva, Switzerland: World Health Organization.

Sarkar, M., & Fletcher, D. (2014). Psychological resilience in sport performers: A narrative review of stressors and protective factors. *Journal of Sports Sciences*, *32*, 1419-1434.

Sirrell, O. (2018). Lost in transition: The Team GB stars who struggle with retirement after Olympic Games glory. Retrieved from http://buzz.bournemouth.ac.uk/2018/01/lost-in-transition/

Sundgot-Borgen, J., & Torstveit, M.K. (2004). Prevalence of eating disorders in elite athletes is higher than in the general population. *Clinical Journal of Sport Medicine*, *14*, 25-32.

This Girl Can. (n.d.). *Homepage*. Retrieved from www.thisgirlcan.co.uk

Thomas, G. (2014). *Proud: My autobiography*. London, UK: Ebury Press.

UK Sport. (2018). UK Sport and EIS working to deliver a positive mental health environment across Olympic and Paralympic sport. Retrieved from www.uksport.gov.uk/news/2018/10/10/positive-mental-health-environment-across-olympic-and-paralympic-sport

Villella, C., Martinotti, G., Di Nicola, M., Cassano, M., La Torre, G., Gliubizzi, M.D., Messeri, I., Petruccelli, F., Bria, P., Janiri, L., & Conte, G. (2011). Behavioural addictions in adolescents and young adults: Results from a prevalence study. *Journal of Gambling Studies*, *2*(2), 203-214.

WADA. (n.d.). Therapeutic use exemptions. Retrieved from www.wada-ama.org/en/what-we-do/science-medical/therapeutic-use-exemptions

Warr, P. (1978). A study of psychological well-being. *British Journal of Psychology*, *69*(1), 111-121.

Wilkinson, J. (2012). *Jonny: My autobiography*. London, UK: Headline.

WHO. (1992). *The ICD-10 classification of mental and behavioural disorders: Clinical descriptions and diagnostic guidelines*. Geneva, Switzerland: World Health Organization.

WHO. (2003). *Investing in mental health*. Geneva, Switzerland: WHO.

WHO. (2018). *Classifications*. Retrieved from www.who.int/classifications/icd/en/

Chapter 21

Adidas-Salomon. (2004). Adidas. Retrieved from www.adidas-salomon.com/en/investor/strategy/adidas/default.asp

Aldrich, H.E. (1972). Technology and organization structure: A re-examination of the findings of the Aston group. *Administrative Science Quarterly*, *17*, 26-43.

Barley, S. (1986). Technology as an occasion for structuring: Evidence from observation of CT scanners and the social order of radiology departments. *Administrative Science Quarterly*, 31, 78-109.

Bedeian, A.G., & Zammuto, R.F. (1991). *Organizations: Theory and design*. Chicago, IL: Dryden Press.

Blau, P.M., & Schoenherr, R.A. (1971). *The structure of organizations*. New York, NY: Basic Books.

Bowen, D.E., Siehl, C., & Schneider, B. (1989). A framework for analyzing customer service orientations in manufacturing. *Academy of Management Review*, *14*, 75-95.

Child, J. (1973a). Parkinson's progress: Accounting for the number of specialists in organizations. *Administrative Science Quarterly*, *18*, 328-348.

Child, J. (1973b). Predicting and understanding organization structure. *Administrative Science Quarterly*, *18*, 168-185.

Child, J. (1975). Managerial and organizational factors associated with company performance (Part II): A contingency analysis. *Journal of Management Studies*, *12*, 12-27.

Child, J. (1984). *Organization: A guide to problems and practice* (2nd ed.). London, UK: Chapman.

Child, J., & Mansfield, R. (1972). Technology, size, and organization structure. *Sociology*, *6*, 369-393.

Cisco. (2013, December 19). The Internet of everything and the connected athlete: This changes . . . everything. Retrieved from www.cisco.com/c/en/us/solutions/collateral/service-provider/mobile-internet/white_paper_c11-711705.html

Daft, R.L. (1992). *Organizational theory and design*. St. Paul, MN: West Publishing Company.

Das, H. (1990). *Organization theory with Canadian applications*. Toronto, ON: Gage Educational.

Fry, L.W. (1982). Technology-structure research: Three critical issues. *Academy of Management Journal*, *25*, 532-552.

Gerwin, D. (1979). Relationships between structure and technology at the organizational and job levels. *Journal of Management*, *16*, 70-79.

Gresov, C. (1989). Exploring fit and misfit with multiple contingencies. *Administrative Science Quarterly*, *34*(3), 431-453. http://dx.doi.org/10.2307/2393152

Grimes, A.J., & Klein, S.M. (1973). The technological imperative: The relative impact of task unit, modal technology, and hierarchy on structure. *Academy of Management Journal*, *16*, 583-597.

Hage, J., & Aiken, M. (1969). Routine technology, social structure, and organization goals. *Administrative Science Quarterly*, *14*(3), 366-376.

Hickson, D.J., Pugh, D.S., & Pheysey, D.C. (1969). Operations, technology and organization structure: An empirical reappraisal. *Administrative Science Quarterly*, *14*, 378-397.

Hinings, C.R., & Lee, G.L. (1971). Dimensions of organization structure and their context: A replication. *Sociology*, *5*, 83-93.

Hrebiniak, L.G. (1974). Job technology, supervision, and work-group structure. *Administrative Science Quarterly*, *19*(3), 395-410.

Hwaya, K. (2019, March 27). Augmented reality dragon wows baseball fans on opening day. Korea.net, Retrieved from www.korea.net/NewsFocus/Sci-Tech/view?articleId=169492

Impey, S. (2019, January 8). Alibaba and Intel launch AI-driven athlete-tracking tool: Technology's Olympics debut will be "game-changer" for audience engagement. Sports Pro Media, Retrieved from www.sportspromedia.com/news/alibaba-intel-ai-athlete-tracking-olympics

ISG. (2017). An ISG research report: ISG Automation Index™ April 2017. Retrieved from http://info.isg-one.com/rs/257-STB-379/images/2118-ISG%20Automation%20Index%20Report-26April2017.pdf

Keidel, R. (1984). Baseball, football, and basketball: Models for business. *Organizational Dynamics*, *12*(3), 5-18.

Keidel, R. (1987). Team sports models as a generic organizational framework. *Human Relations*, *40*(9), 591-612.

Khandwalla, P.N. (1974). Mass output orientation of operations technology and organizational structure. *Administrative Science Quarterly*, *19*, 74-97.

Kmetz, J.L. (1977). A critique of the Aston studies and results with a new measure of technology. *Organization and Administrative Sciences*, 8, 123-144.

Mahoney, T.A., & Frost, P.J. (1974). The role of technology in models of organizational effectiveness. *Organizational Behavior and Human Performance*, *11*, 122-138.

Miah, A. (2005). From anti-doping to a "performance policy" sport technology, being human, and doing ethics." *European Journal of Sport Science*, 5(1), 51-57. doi:10.1080/17461390500077285

Miah, A. (2017). *Sport 2.0*. Cambridge, MA: The MIT Press.

Mintzberg, H. (1979). *The structuring of organizations*. Englewood Cliffs, NJ: Prentice Hall.

Orlikowski, W.J. (1992). The duality of technology: Rethinking the concept of technology in the organization. *Organization Science*, *3*, 398-427.

Pennings, J., & A. Buitendam (1987). *New technology as organizational innovation: The development and diffusion of microelectronics*. Cambridge, MA: Ballinger Pub. Co.

Perrow, C. (1967). A framework for the comparative analysis of organizations. *American Sociological Review*, *32*, 194-208.

Populous. (2018). Esports Stadium Arlington. Populous, Retrieved from https://populous.com/project/esports-stadium-arlington

Reimann, B.C., & Inzerilli, G. (1979). A comparative analysis of empirical research on technology and structure. *Journal of Management*, *5*(2), 167-192.

Robbins, S.P. (1990). *Organization theory: Structure, design and applications* (3rd ed.). Englewood Cliffs, NJ: Prentice Hall.

Rousseau, D.M. (1983). Technology in organizations: A constructive review and analytic framework. In S.E. Seashore, E.E. Lawler III, P.H. Mirvis, & C. Cammann (Eds.), *Assessing organizational change* (pp. 229-255). New York, NY: Wiley.

Sator, D. (n.d.). Huffy bikes will remain Ohio-built. *Dayton Daily News and Journal Herald*, 1.

Scott, W.R. (2000). *Organizations: Rational, natural and open systems* (5th ed.). Englewood Cliffs, NJ: Prentice Hall.

Skinner, W. (1983). Wanted: Managers for the factory of the future. *Annals of the American Academy of Political and Social Science*, *470*, 102-114.

Starbuck, W.H. (1981). A trip to view the elephants and rattlesnakes in the garden of Aston. In A.H. Van de Ven & W.J. Joyce (Eds.), *Perspectives on organization design* (pp. 167-198). New York, NY: Wiley.

Thompson, J.D. (1967). *Organizations in action*. New York, NY: McGraw-Hill.

Van de Ven, A.H., & Delbecq, A.L. (1974). A task contingent model of work unit structure. *Administrative Science Quarterly*, *19*, 183-197.

Van de Ven, A.H., Delbecq, A.L., & Koenig, R. (1976). Determinants of coordination modes within organizations. *American Sociological Review*, *41*(2), 322-338.

Withey, M., Daft, R.L., & Cooper, W.H. (1983). Measures of Perrow's work unit technology: An empirical assessment and a new scale. *Academy of Management Journal*, *26*, 45-63.

Woodward, J. (1958). *Management and technology*. London, UK: Her Majesty's Printing Office.

Woodward, J. (1965). *Industrial organization: Theory and practice*. London, UK: Oxford University Press.

Chapter 22

Alamar, B.C. (2013). *Sports analytics: A guide for coaches, managers and other decision makers*. New York, NY: Columbia University Press.

Anderson, C., & Sally, D. (2013). *The numbers game: Why everything you know about football is wrong*. London, UK: Viking.

AZ Alkmaar. (2015). AZ excited to welcome Beane as club advisor. Retrieved from www.az.nl/en/nieuws/az-excited-to-welcome-beane-as-club-advisor

Camm, J.D., Cochran, J.J., Fry, M.J., Ohlmann, J.W., Anderson, D.R., Sweeny, D.J., & Williams, T.A. (2017). *Essentials of business analytics* (2nd ed.). Boston, MA: Cengage Learning.

Carroll, B., Palmer, P., & Thorn, T. (1988). *The hidden game of football*. New York, NY: Warner Books.

Cook, E. (1964). *Percentage baseball*. Cambridge, MA: MIT Press.

Evers, J.J., & Fullerton, H.S. (1910). *Touching second: The science of baseball*. Chicago, IL: Reilly & Britton.

Gerrard, B. (2007). Is the Moneyball approach transferable to complex invasion team sports? *International Journal of Sport Finance*, *2*, 214-230.

Gerrard, B. (2014). Achieving transactional efficiency in professional team sports: The theory and practice of player valuation. In J. Goddard & P.J. Sloane (Eds.), *Handbook on the economics of football* (pp. 189-202). Aldershot, UK: Edward Elgar.

Hakes, J.K., & Sauer, R.D. (2006). An economic evaluation of the *Moneyball* hypothesis. *Journal of Economic Perspectives*, *20*, 173-185.

Hughes, M., & Franks, I. (2005). Analysis of passing sequences, shots and goals in soccer. *Journal of Sports Sciences*, *23*, 509-514.

James, B. (1977). 1977 *Baseball abstract: Featuring 18 categories of statistical information that you can't just find anywhere else*. Holton, KS: Self-published.

Lewis, M. (2003). *Moneyball: The art of winning and unfair game*. New York, NY: Norton.

Mills, E.G., & Mills, H.D. (1970). *Player win averages: A computer guide to winning baseball players*. New York, NY: A.S. Barnes.

Pfeffer, J., & Sutton, R.I. (2006). Evidence-based management. *Harvard Business Review*, January issue, 62-74.

Reep, C., & Benjamin, B. (1968). Skill and chance in association football. *Journal of the Royal Statistical Society Series A (General)*, *131*, 581-585.

Rickey, B. (1954, August 2). Goodbye to some old baseball ideas. *Life*, 79-89.

Severini, T.A. (2015). *Analytic methods in sports*. Boca Baton, FL: CRC Press.

Shea, S., & Baker, C.E. (2013). *Basketball analytics: Objective and efficient strategies for understanding how teams win*. St. Louis, MO: Advanced Metrics.

Swanson, R. (2013). The science of baseball 100 years later. Retrieved from http://60ft6in.com/2013/02/07/the-science-of-baseball-100-years-later/

Thorn, T., & Palmer, P. (1984). *The hidden game of baseball*. New York, NY: Doubleday & Company.

Wilson, J. (2008). *Inverting the pyramid: A history of football tactics*. London, UK: Orion Books.

Chapter 23

Aguinis, H., & Glavas, A. (2012). What we know and don't know about corporate social responsibility: A review and research agenda. *Journal of Management*, *38*(4), 932-968.

Amis, J., Pant, N., & Slack, T. (1997). Achieving a sustainable competitive advantage: A resource-based view of sport sponsorship. *Journal of Sport Management*, *11*(1), 80-96.

Anagnostopoulos, C. (2011). From corporate social responsibility to club stakeholder relationship: The case of football. *Social Responsibility Review*, *3*, 14-17.

Anagnostopoulos, C., & Shilbury, D. (2013). Implementing corporate social responsibility in English football: Towards multi-theoretical integration. *Sport, Business, and Management: An International Journal, 3*(4), 268-284.

Anagnostopoulos, C., Byers, T., & Shilbury, D. (2014). Corporate social responsibility in professional team sport organisations: Toward a theory of decision-making. *European Sport Management Quarterly, 14*(3), 259-281.

Anagnostopoulos, C., Byers, T., & Kolyperas, D. (2017). Understanding strategic decision-making through a multi-paradigm perspective: The case of charitable foundations in English football. *Sport, Business and Management: An International Journal, 7*(1), 2-20.

Anagnostopoulos, C., Winand, M., & Papadimitriou, D. (2016). Passion in the workplace: Empirical insights from team sport organisations. *European Sport Management Quarterly, 16*(4), 385-412.

Anagnostopoulos, C., Gillooly, L., Cook, D., Parganas, P., & Chadwick, S. (2017). Stakeholder communication in 140 characters or less: A study of community sport foundations. *VOLUNTAS International Journal of Voluntary and Nonprofit Organizations*, 28(5), 2224-2250.

Anagnostopoulos, C., & Winand, M. (2019). The board–executive relationship in team sport charitable foundations: Unpacking trust building through 'exchange currencies'. In M. Winand & C. Anagnostopoulos (Eds.), *Research handbook on sport governance* (pp. 236-256). Cheltenham, UK: Edward Elgar.

Arrow, K. (1997). Social responsibility and economic efficiency. In T. Donaldson & T. Dunfee, (Eds.), *Ethics in business and economics* (Vol. 1, pp. 137-151). Aldershot, UK: Ashgate/Dartmouth.

Babiak, K., & Trendafilova, S. (2011). CSR and environmental responsibility: Motives and pressures to adopt green management practices. *Corporate Social Responsibility and Environmental Management, 18*(1), 11-24.

Babiak, K., & Wolfe, R. (2009). Determinants of corporate social responsibility in professional sport: Internal and external factors. *Journal of Sport Management, 23*(6), 717-743.

Babiak, K., & Wolfe, R. (2013). Perspectives on social responsibility in sport. In J.L. Paramio-Salcines, K. Babiak, & G. Walters (Eds.), *Routledge handbook of sport and corporate social responsibility* (pp. 17-34). New York, NY: Routledge.

Bason, T., & Anagnostopoulos, C. (2015). Corporate social responsibility through sport: A longitudinal study of the FTSE100 companies. *Sport, Business and Management, 5*(3), 218-241.

Baur, D., & Palazzo, G. (2011). The moral legitimacy of NGOs as partners of corporations. *Business Ethics Quarterly, 21*(4), 579-604.

Belson, K. (2014, July 7). Altered N.F.L. settlement wins judge's approval. *New York Times*, Retrieved from www.nytimes.com/2014/07/08/sports/football/judge-approves-preliminary-nfl-settlement.html

Benson, P. (2017). Big football: Corporate social responsibility and the culture and color of injury in America's most popular sport. *Journal of Sport and Social Issues, 41*(4) 307-334.

Bowen, H. (1953). *Social responsibilities of the businessman*. New York, NY: Harper and Row.

Bradish, C., & Cronin, J. (2009). Corporate social responsibility in sport. *Journal of Sport Management, 23*(6), 691-699.

Breitbarth, T., Walzel, S., Anagnostopoulos, C., & van Eekeren, F. (2015). Corporate social responsibility and governance in sport: "Oh, the things you can find, if you don't stay behind!" *Corporate Governance, 15*(2), 254-273.

Breitbarth, T., Walzel, S., & van Eekeren, F. (2019). European-ness' in social responsibility and sport management research: Anchors and avenues. *European Sport Management Quarterly, 19*(1), 1-14.

Breslow, J.M. (2014, February 4). What we've learned from two years of tracking NFL concussions. PBS, Retrieved from www.pbs.org/wgbh/pages/frontline/sports/concussion-watch/what-weve-learned-from-two-years-of-tracking-nfl-concussions/

Broomhill, R. (2007). *Corporate social responsibility: Key issues and debates*. Dunstan paper no. 1/2007. Adelaide, Australia: Don Dunstan Foundation, University of Adelaide.

Campbell, J. (2007). Why would corporations behave in socially responsible ways? An institutional theory of corporate social responsibility. *Academy of Management Review, 32*(3), 946-967.

Carr, A. (1996). Is business bluffing ethical? In S. Rae & K. Wong (Eds.), *Beyond integrity: A Judeo-Christian approach* (pp. 55-62). Grand Rapids, MI: Zondervan Publishing House.

Carroll, A. (1979). A three-dimensional conceptual model of corporate performance. *Academy of Management Review, 4*(4), 497-505.

Chen, J., Patten, D., & Roberts, R. (2008). Corporate charitable contributions: A corporate social performance or legitimacy strategy? *Journal of Business Ethics, 82*(1), 131-144.

Crane, A., Matten, D., & Spence, L. (2014). *Corporate social responsibility: Readings and cases in a global context* (2nd ed.). London, UK: Routledge.

Davis, K. (1960). Can business afford to ignore social responsibilities? *California Management Review, 2*, 70-76.

DiMaggio, P., & Powell, W. (1983). The iron cage revisited: Institutional isomorphism and collective rationality in organizational fields. *American Sociological Review, 48*(2), 147-160.

Donaldson, T., & Preston, L. (1995). The stakeholder theory of the corporation: Concepts, evidence, and implications. *Academy of Management Review, 20*(10), 65-91.

Dowling, J., & Pfeffer, J. (1975). Organizational legitimacy: Social values and organizational behaviour. *Pacific Sociological Review, 18*(1), 122-136.

Farquhar, S., Machold, S., & Ahmed, K. (2005). Governance and football: An examination of the relevance of corporate governance regulations for the sports sector. *International Journal of Business Governance and Ethics, 1*(4), 329-349.

Ferrand, A., & McCarthy, S. (2009). *Marketing the sports organisation*. London, UK: Routledge.

Frederick, W. (1960). The growing concern over business responsibility. *California Management Review, 2*(4), 54-61.

Freeman, E. (1984). *Strategic management: A stakeholder approach*. Boston, MA: Pitman Publishing.

Freeman, E., & Phillips, A. (2002). Stakeholder theory: A libertarian defense. *Business Ethics Quarterly, 12*(3), 331-349.

Friedman, M. (1970, September 13). The social responsibility of business is to increase its profits. *New York Times Magazine*, 32-33.

Friedman, M.T., Parent, M., & Mason, D. (2004). Building a framework for issues management in sport through stakeholder theory. *European Sport Management Quarterly, 4*(3), 170-190.

Garriga, E., & Melé, D. (2004). Corporate social responsibility theories: Mapping the territory. *Journal of Business Ethics, 53*(1-2), 51-71.

Godfrey, P. (2009). Corporate social responsibility in sport: An overview and key issues. *Journal of Sport Management, 23*(6), 698-716.

Godfrey, P., Hatch, N., & Hansen, J. (2010). Toward a general theory of CSR's: The roles of beneficence, profitability, insurance, and industry heterogeneity. *Business and Society, 49*(2), 316-344.

Greenwood, R., Oliver, C., Sahlin, K., & Suddaby, R. (2008). *The SAGE handbook of organisational institutionalism.* London, UK: SAGE.

Hanna, J., & Kain, D. (2010). The NFL's shaky concussion policy exposes the league to potential liability headaches. *Entertainment and Sports Lawyer, 28*(3), 9-16.

Hargreaves, J. (1986). *Sport, power and culture: A social and historical analysis of popular sports in Britain.* Cambridge, UK: Blackwell Publishers Ltd.

Hoffman, A. (1997). *From heresy to dogma: An institutional history of corporate environmentalism.* San Francisco, CA: New Lexington Press.

Hu, J., Lee, C., Wong, H., & Kao, T. (2012). Understanding corporate social irresponsibility on sports organizations. *International Business Research, 5*(12), 46-58.

Husted, B.W. (2003). Governance choices for corporate social responsibility: To contribute, collaborate or internalize? *Long Range Planning, 36*(5), 481-498.

Inoue, Y., & Kent, A. (2012). Investigating the role of corporate credibility in corporate social marketing: A case study of environmental initiatives by professional sport organizations. *Sport Management Review, 15*(3), 330-344.

Inoue, Y., Kent, A., & Lee, S. (2011). CSR and the bottom line: Analyzing the link between CSR and financial performance for professional teams. *Journal of Sport Management, 25*(6), 531-549.

International Organisation for Standardisation. (2010). *ISO 26000: Guidance on social responsibility.* Geneva, Switzerland: International Organisation for Standardisation.

Jensen, M. (2002). Value maximisation, stakeholder theory, and the corporate objective function. *Business Ethics Quarterly, 12*(2), 235-264.

Karmani, A. (2011). "Doing well by doing good": The grand illusion. *California Management Review, 53*(2), 69-86.

Kent, A. (2011). Special issue on corporate responsibility, sustainability and stewardship within sport. *International Journal of Sport Management and Marketing, 10*(1-2).

Kim, W., & Walker, M. (2013). The influence of professional athlete philanthropy on donation intentions. *European Sport Management Quarterly, 13*(5), 579-601.

Klein, N. (1999). *No logo: Taking on the brand bullies.* New York, NY: Picador.

Kolyperas, D., & Sparks, L. (2011). Corporate social responsibility (CSR) communications in the G-25 football clubs. *International Journal of Sport Management and Marketing, 10*(1-2), 83-103.

Kolyperas, D., Anagnostopoulos, C., Chadwick, S., & Sparks, L. (2016). Applying a communicating vessels framework to CSR value co-creation: Empirical evidence from professional team sport organizations. *Journal of Sport Management, 30*(6), 702-719.

Kraatz, M., & Block, E. (2008). Organizational implications of institutional pluralism. In R. Greenwood, C. Oliver, K. Sahlin, & R. Suddaby (Eds.), *The SAGE handbook of organizational institutionalism* (pp. 243-275). London, UK: SAGE.

Lee, M.P. (2008). A review of the theories of corporate social responsibility: Its evolutionary path and the road ahead. *International Journal of Management Reviews, 10*(1), 53-73.

Levitt, T. (1958). The dangers of social responsibility. *Harvard Business Review, 36*(5), 41-50.

Lewis, S. (2001). Measuring corporate reputation. *Corporate Communication: An International Journal, 6*(1), 31-35.

Margolis, J., & Walsh, J. (2003). Misery loves companies: Rethinking social initiatives by business. *Administrative Science Quarterly, 48*(2), 268-305.

Matten, D., & Moon, J. (2008). "Implicit" and "explicit" CSR: A conceptual framework for a comparative understanding of corporate social responsibility. *Academy of Management Review, 33*(2), 404-424.

Mazanov, J., & Woolf, J. (2017). Corporate social responsibility and managing drugs in sport. *Journal of Global Sport Management, 2*(2) 96-110.

Mercado, H., & Walker, M. (2012). The value of environmental social responsibility to facility managers: Revealing the perceptions and motives for adopting ESR. *Journal of Business Ethics, 110*(3), 269-284.

Meyer, J.W., & Rowan, B. (1977). Institutional organizations: Formal structure as myth and ceremony. *American Journal of Sociology, 83*(2), 340-363.

Mitchell, K., Agle, R., & Wood, J. (1997). Toward a theory of stakeholder identification and salience: Defining the principle of who and what really counts. *Academy of Management Review, 22*(4), 853-886.

NBA Cares. (2014). Mission. National Basketball Association, Retrieved from http://cares.nba.com/

Paramio-Salcines, J., Babiak, K., & Walters, G. (Eds.). (2013). *Routledge handbook of sport and corporate social responsibility.* New York, NY: Routledge.

Parent, M., & Deephouse, D. (2007). A case study of stakeholder identification and prioritization by managers. *Journal of Business Ethics, 75*(1), 1-23.

Pfeffer, J., & Salancik, R. (1978). *The external control of organisations: A resource dependence perspective.* New York, NY: Harper and Row.

Philadelphia Eagles. (n.d.). Community mission. Retrieved from www.philadelphiaeagles.com/community/

Pinkston, T., & Carroll, A. (1996). A retrospective examination of CSR orientations: Have they changed? *Journal of Business Ethics, 15*(2), 199-206.

Porter, M., & Kramer, M. (2006). Strategy and society: The link between competitive advantage and corporate social responsibility. *Harvard Business Review, 84*(12), 78-93.

Porter, M., & Kramer, M. (2011). Creating shared value. *Harvard Business Review, 89*(1), 1-17.

Ratten, V., & Babiak, K. (2010). The role of social responsibility, philanthropy and entrepreneurship in the sport industry. *Journal of Management and Organization, 16*(4), 482-487.

Rivoli, P., & Waddock, S. (2011). "First they ignore you . . .": The time-context dynamic and corporate responsibility. *California Management Review, 53*(2), 69-96.

Roberts, S., Chadwick, S. & Anagnostopoulos, C. (2018). Sponsorship programmes and corruption in sport: Management responses to a growing threat. *Journal of Strategic Marketing, 26*(1), 19-36.

Robinson, L., Chelladurai, P., Bodet, G., & Downward, P. (Eds.). (2012). *Routledge handbook of sport management.* Abingdon, UK: Routledge.

Rouvrais-Charron, C., & Durand, C. (2009). European football under close scrutiny. *International Journal of Sports Marketing and Sponsorship, 10*(3), 33-46.

Schwarz, A. (2009, December 20). N.F.L. acknowledges long-term concussion effects." *New York Times,* Retrieved from www.nytimes.com/2009/12/21/sports/football/21concussions.html

Scott, S., & Lane, V. (2000). A stakeholder approach to organizational identity. *Academy of Management Review*, *25*(1), 43-62.

Scott, W. (1995). *Institutions and organizations* (1st ed.). Thousand Oaks, CA: SAGE.

Scott, W. (2013). *Institutions and organizations* (4th ed.). Thousand Oaks, CA: SAGE.

Sethi, S. (1975). Dimensions of corporate social performance: An analytical framework. *California Management Review*, *19*(3), 58-64.

Sheth, H., & Babiak, K. (2010). Beyond the game: Perceptions and practices of corporate social responsibility in the professional sport industry. *Journal of Business Ethics*, *91*(3), 433-450.

Shocker, A., & Sethi, S. (1974). An approach to incorporating social preferences in developing corporate action strategies. In S.P. Sethi (ed.), *The unstable ground: Corporate social policy in a dynamic society* (pp. 67-80). Los Angeles, CA: Melville Publishing Company.

Slack, T., & Hinings, C. (1995). Institutional pressures and isomorphic change: An empirical test. *Organization Studies*, *15*(6), 803-827.

Smith, A., & Stewart, B. (2010). The special features of sport: A critical revisit. *Sport Management Review*, *13*(1), 1-13.

Smith, A., & Westerbeek, H. (2007). Sport as a vehicle for deploying corporate social responsibility. *The Journal of Corporate Citizenship*, *25*, 43-54.

Suchman, M. (1995). Managing legitimacy: Strategic and institutional approaches. *Academy of Management Review*, *20*(3), 571-610.

Taylor, N. (2004). Giving something back: Can football clubs and their communities co-exist? In S. Wagg (Ed.), *British football and social exclusion* (pp. 47-66). London, UK: Routledge.

Thornton, P., & Ocasio, W. (2008). Institutional logics. In R. Greenwood, C. Oliver, K. Sahlin, & R. Suddaby (Eds.), *The SAGE handbook of organizational institutionalism* (pp. 99-129). London, UK: SAGE.

Trenberth, L., & Hassan, D. (2011). *Managing sport business: An introduction*. London, UK: Routledge.

Trendafilova, S., Babiak, K., & Heinze, K. (2013). Corporate social responsibility and environmental sustainability: Why professional sport is greening the playing field. *Sport Management Review*, *16*(3), 298-313.

Trendafilova, S., Pfahl, M., & Casper, J. (2013). CSR and environmental sustainability: The case of NCAA athletic departments. In J. L. Paramio-Salcines, K. Babiak, & G. Walters (Eds.), *Routledge handbook of sport and corporate social responsibility* (pp. 105-118). New York, NY: Routledge.

Waddington, I., Chelladurai, P. & Skirstad, B. (2013). CSR in sport: Who benefits?. In J.L. Paramio-Salcines, K. Babiak, & G. Walters (Eds.), *Routledge handbook of sport and corporate social responsibility* (pp. 35-51). New York, NY: Routledge.

Walker, M. (2013). Does green management matter for donation intentions? The influence of environmental consciousness and environmental importance. *Management Decision*, *51*(8), 1716-1732.

Walker, M., & Mercado, H. (2013). The resource-worthiness of environmental responsibility: A resource-based perspective. *Corporate Social Responsibility and Environmental Management*, *22*(4), 208-221.

Walker, M., & Parent, M. (2010). Toward an integrated framework of corporate social responsibility, responsiveness, and citizenship in sport. *Sport Management Review*, *13*(3), 198-213.

Walker, M., Heere, B., & Kim, C. (2013). The paradox of CSR measurement: Putting the "responsibility" back in CSR through program evaluation. In J.L. Paramio-Salcines, K. Babiak, & G. Walters (Eds.), *Routledge Handbook of Sport and Corporate Social Responsibility* (pp. 309-316). New York, NY: Routledge.

Walker, M., Heere, B., Parent, M.M., & Drane, D. (2010). Social responsibility and the Olympic Games: The mediating role of consumer attributions. *Journal of Business Ethics*, *95*(4), 659-680.

Walzel, S., Robertson, J., & Anagnostopoulos, C. (2018). Corporate social responsibility in professional team sport organisations. *Journal of Sport Management*, *32*(6), 511-530.

Wartick, S., & Mahon, J. (1994). Toward a substantive definition of the corporate issue construct: A review and synthesis of the literature. *Business and Society*, *33*(3), 293-311.

Zhang, J., Jin, L., Kim, M., & Li, H. (2013). Environmental CSR practices within the Asian sport event industry: A case study of the Beijing Olympics. In J.L. Paramio-Salcines, K. Babiak, & G. Walters (Eds.), *Routledge Handbook of Sport and Corporate Social Responsibility* (pp. 119-134). New York, NY: Routledge.

Chapter 24

Adams, R.J., Smart, P., & Huff, A.S. (2017). Shades of grey: Guidelines for working with the grey literature in systematic reviews for management and organizational studies. *International Journal of Management Reviews*, *19*, 432-454. doi:10.1111/ijmr.12102

Adriaanse, P., van Ommeren, F., den Ouden, W., & Wolswinkel, J. (2016). The allocation of limited rights by the administration: A quest for a general legal theory. In P. Adriaanse, F. van Ommeren, W. den Ouden, & J. Wolswinkel (Eds.), *Scarcity and the state I: The allocation of limited rights by the administration* (pp. 3-25). Cambridge, UK: Intersentia.

Agarwal, R., & Selen, W. (2009). Dynamic capability building in service value networks for achieving service innovation. *Decision Sciences*, *40*(3), 431-475. doi:10.1111/j.1540-5915.2009.00236.x

Albano, G.L., & Nicholas, C. (2016). *The law and economics of framework agreements: Designing flexible solutions for public procurement*. Cambridge, UK: Cambridge University Press.

Anechiarico, F., & Jacobs, J. (1996). *The pursuit of absolute integrity: How corruption control makes government ineffective*. Chicago, IL: University of Chicago Press.

Arrowsmith, S. (1988). *Government procurement and judicial review*. Toronto, ON: Carswell.

Arrowsmith, S. (1995). Public procurement as a tool of policy and the impact of market liberalisation. *Law Quarterly Review*, *111*(2), 235-284.

Arrowsmith, S. (2002). The EC procurement directives, national procurement policies and better governance: The case for a new approach. *European Law Review*, *27*(1), 3-24.

Arrowsmith, S. (2003). Transparency in government procurement: The objectives of regulation and the boundaries of the World Trade Organization. *Journal of World Trade*, *37*(2), 283-303.

Arrowsmith, S. (2004). Public procurement: An appraisal of the UNCITRAL model law as a global standard. *International and Comparative Law Quarterly*, *53*(1), 17-46. doi:10.1093/iclq/53.1.17

Arrowsmith, S. (2010). Horizontal policies in public procurement: A taxonomy. *Journal of Public Procurement*, *10*(2), 149-186.

Arrowsmith, S. (Ed.). (2011). *Public procurement regulation: An introduction*. EU Asia Inter University Network for Teaching and Research in Public Procurement Regulation, Retrieved from www.nottingham.ac.uk/pprg/documentsarchive/asialinkmaterials/publicprocurementregulationintroduction.pdf

Arrowsmith, S. (2014). *The law of public and utilities procurement, volume 1* (3rd ed.). London, UK: Sweet & Maxwell.

Arrowsmith, S. (2018). *The law of public and utilities procurement, volume 2* (3rd ed.). London, UK: Sweet & Maxwell.

Arrowsmith, S., & Anderson, R.D. (Eds.). (2011). *The WTO regime on government procurement: Challenge and reform.* Cambridge, UK: Cambridge University Press.

Arrowsmith, S., Bayley, R., Gorzczynska, A., Idoko, J., Kay, S., Faria Lopes, J., Barreto Cifuentes, C.S., Quinot, G., Ren, K., Nobel, A., Solomanya, A., Sobieraj, I., Soos, G., and Thurston, A. (2019). Procuring infrastructure for international sporting events: Mapping the field for IPACS and Beyond. *Public Procurement Law Review, 28*(6), 257-318.

Arrowsmith, S., & Kunzlik, P. (2009). EC regulation of public procurement. In S. Arrowsmith & P. Kunzlik (Eds.), *Social and environmental policies in EC procurement law: New directives and new directions* (pp. 55-107). Cambridge, UK: Cambridge University Press.

Arrowsmith, S., Linarelli, J., & Wallace, D. (2000). *Regulating public procurement: National and international perspectives.* The Hague, Netherlands: Kluwer Law International.

Arthur, D., Scott, D., & Woods, T. (1997). A conceptual model of the corporate decision-making process of sport sponsorship acquisition. *Journal of Sport Management, 11*(3), 223-233. doi:10.1123/jsm.11.3.223

Aspey, E., & Craven, R. (2018). Regulating complex contracting: A socio-legal study of decision-making under EU and UK law. *Modern Law Review, 18*(2), 191-221. doi:10.1111/1468-2230.12326

ASOIF. (2017a). *ASOIF governance task force (GTF) international federation (IF) self-assessment questionnaire.* Retrieved from www.asoif.com/sites/default/files/download/if_governance_questionnaire-stage_2.pdf

ASOIF. (2017b). *First review of international federation governance: 2017 ASOIF General Assembly.* Retrieved from https://asoif.my.salesforce.com/sfc/p/#D0000000lcuP/a/570000004ZoI/440hi-JwYRu9Ub7KRUGPWbfAfw4A8T1cFVflinsATOqg

ASOIF. (2018). *Second review of international federation governance: 2018 ASOIF General Assembly.* Retrieved from www.asoif.com/sites/default/files/download/asoif_2018_second_review_v4_interactive.pdf

Baily, P., Farmer, D., Crocker, B., Jessop, D., & Jones, D. (2015). *Procurement principles and management* (11th ed.). Harlow, UK: Pearson.

Bajari, P., & Tadelis, S. (2006). Incentives and award procedures: Competitive tendering vs. negotiations in procurement. In N. Dimitri, G. Piga, & G. Spagnolo (Eds.), *Handbook of Procurement* (pp. 121-142). Cambridge, UK: Cambridge University Press.

Barrington, R. (2012). *Corruption and the Olympics.* Transparency International, Retrieved from www.transparency.org.uk/corruption-and-the-olympics/#.W3B5MegzbIU

Beis, D.A., Loucopoulos, P., Pyrgiotis, Y., & Zografos, K.G. (2006). PLATO helps Athens win gold: Olympic Games knowledge modelling for organizational change and resource management. *Interfaces, 36*(1), 26-42. doi:10.1287/inte.1060.0189

Bensaou, M. (1999). Portfolios of buyer-supplier relationships. *Sloan Management Review, 40*(4), 35-44.

Bercusson, B. (1978). *The fair wages resolutions.* London, UK: Mansell.

Bereslawski, E. (2013). *A critical analysis of the procedures of the differentiated contracting regimen (RDC) of Brazil: The impact of the disclosure or not of the estimated budget and the use of the estimated budget as a ceiling and contract awarding factor* (Unpublished LL.M. dissertation). The University of Nottingham, Nottingham, UK.

Booth, R. (2013, October 1). Qatar World Cup 2022: 70 Nepalese workers die on building sites. *The Guardian*, Retrieved from www.theguardian.com/world/2013/oct/01/qatar-world-cup-2022-nepalese-die-building-sites

Bos, A., van Ekkerhen, F., & Houihan, B. (2012). *AGGIS: Implementation and compliance of good governance in International Sport Federations.* Action for Good Governance in International Sports Organisations, Retrieved from www.playthegame.org/fileadmin/documents/AGGIS_Conditions_for_good_governance__Eekeren_.pdf

Botha, E., & Ntsaluba, G. (2010). Tendering irregularities in the East Cape. In C.S. Schulz Herzenberg (Ed.), *Player and referee: Conflicting interests and the 2010 FIFA World Cup* (pp. 51-71). Pretoria, South Africa: Institute for Security Studies, Retrieved from http://ccs.ukzn.ac.za/files/ISS%20Player%20and%20Referee.pdf

Bovens, M., (2007). Analysing and assessing accountability: A conceptual framework. *European Law Journal, 13*, 447-468.

Branstetter, J. (2005). Darleen Druyun: An evolving case study in corruption, power, and procurement. *Public Contracts Law Journal, 34*(3), 443-468.

Braun, P. (2003). Strict compliance versus commercial reality: The practical application of EC public procurement law to the UK's private finance initiative. *European Law Journal, 9*(5), 575-598. doi:10.1046/j.1468-0386.2003.00193.x

Brooks, G., Aleem, A., & Button, M. (2013). The extent of fraud and corruption in sport. In G. Brooks, A. Aleem, & M. Button (Eds.), *Fraud, corruption and sport* (pp. 30-44). London, UK: Palgrave MacMillan.

Buijze, A.W.G.J. (2015). Transparency: The Swiss knife of EU law. *European Review of Public Law, 26*(3), 1123-1161.

Burden, W., & Li, M. (2009). Minor league baseball: Exploring the growing interest in outsourced sport marketing. *Sport Marketing Quarterly, 18*(3), 139-149.

Cabral, S., & Silva Jr, A.F. (2013). An approach for evaluating the risk management role of governments in public-private partnerships for mega-event stadiums. *European Sport Management Quarterly, 13*(4), 472-490.

Carpenter, K. (2016). Preventing corruption ahead of major sports events: Learning from the 2012 London Games. In *Transparency International, Global Corruption Report: Sport* (pp. 178-182). Oxford, UK: Routledge, Retrieved from www.transparency.org/whatwedo/publication/global_corruption_report_sport

Cashman, R. (2016). Legacy and sustainability aims and outcomes at the Olympic Games and the football World Cup. In S. Frawley (Ed.), *Managing Sport Mega-Events* (pp. 165-177). London, UK: Routledge.

Chappelet, J.-L. & Mrkonjic, M., 2013. Basic Indicators for Better Governance in International Sport (BIBGIS): An assessment tool for international sport governing bodies. IDHEAP Online Working Papers. Available at: https://serval.unil.ch/resource/serval:BIB_7BDD210D3643.P001/REF

Coalter, F. (1995). Compulsory competitive leisure management: A lost opportunity? *Managing Leisure, 1*(1), 3-15. doi:10.1080/136067195376538

Comptroller and Auditor General of India. (2011). *Audit Report of XIXth Commonwealth Games: Report No. 6 of 2011.* Retrieved from www.cag.gov.in/content/report-no-6-2011-%E2%80%93-performance-audit-xixth-commonwealth-games

Ćorić, D.S., Anić, I., Rajh, S.P., Rajh, E., & Kurnoga, N., (2017). Organizational buying decision approaches in manufacturing industry: Developing measures and typology. *Journal of Business & Industrial Marketing*, *32*(2), 227-237. doi:10.1108/JBIM-10-2014-0214

Cornelius, M., Fernau, J., Dickinson, P., & Stuart, M. (2011). Delivering London 2012: Procurement. *Proceedings of the Institution of Civil Engineers—Civil Engineering*, *164*(5), 34-39. doi:10.1680/cien.2011.164.5.34

Council of Europe. (2017). *First meeting of the informal working group on the "International Sports Integrity Partnership report.* Retrieved from https://rm.coe.int/report-of-the-first-meeting-of-the-informal-working-group-on-the-inter/168073e07b

Cownie, F. (2004). *Legal academics: Culture and identities*. Oxford, UK: Hart Publishing.

Cumming, P., Stubbs, D., & Walsh, G. (2012). *Sustainable procurement—the London 2012 Olympic Games and Paralympic Games*. Retrieved from http://learninglegacy.independent.gov.uk/documents/pdfs/sustainability/cs-games-sustainable-procurement.pdf

Daintith, T. (1979). Regulation by contract: The new prerogative. *Current Legal Problems*, *32*(1), 41-64. doi:10.1093/clp/32.1.41

Daintith, T. (1982). Legal analysis of economic policy. *Journal of Law and Society*, *9*(2), 191-224. doi:10.2307/1410175

Davis, K.C. (1969). *Discretionary justice: A preliminary inquiry*. Baton Rouge, LA: Louisiana State University Press.

Dekel, O. (2008). The legal theory of competitive bidding for government contracts. *Public Contract Law Journal*, *37*, 237-268.

Dimitri, N., Piga, G., & Spagnolo, G. (Eds.). (2009). *Handbook of procurement*. Cambridge, UK: Cambridge University Press.

Dowling, M., Leopkey, B., & Smith, L. (2018). Governance in sport: A scoping review. *Journal of Sport Management*, *32*, 438-451.

Dye, K.M., & Stapenhurst, R. (1998). *Pillars of integrity: The importance of Supreme Audit Institutions in curbing corruption*. WBI working papers. Washington, DC: World Bank, Retrieved from http://documents.worldbank.org/curated/en/199721468739213038/Pillars-of-integrity-the-importance-of-Supreme-Audit-Institutions-in-curbing-corruption

Estevan de Quesada, C. (2014). Competition and transparency in public procurement markets. *Public Procurement Law Review*, *5*, 229-244.

European Union. (1989). Council Directive 89/665/EEC on the coordination of the laws, regulations and administrative provisions relating to the application of review procedures to the award of public supply and public works contracts. Official Journal J L 395 p. 33.

European Union. (2014a). European Parliament and Council Directive 2014/23/EU on the award of concession contracts. Official Journal L 94, p. 1.

European Union. (2014b). European Parliament and Council Directive 2014/24/EU on public procurement and repealing Directive 2004/18/EC. Official Journal L 94, p. 65.

Ferguson, R.B., & Page, A.C. (1978). Pay restraint: The legal constraints. *New Law Journal*, *127*, 515. doi:10.1177/001139285033001009

Fernández Martín, J.M. (1996). *The EC public procurement rules: A critical analysis*. Oxford, UK: Oxford University Press.

Flynn, A., & Davis, P. (2014). Theory in public procurement research. *Journal of Public Procurement*, *14*(2), 139-180. doi:10.1108/JOPP-14-02-2014-B001

Gardiner, S., O'Leary, J., Welch, R., Boyes, S., & Naidoo, U. (2012). *Sports law* (4th ed.). London, UK: Routledge.

Geeraert, A. (2015). *Sports governance observer 2015: The legitimacy crisis in international sports governance* (1st ed.). Aarhus, Denmark: Play the Game—Danish Institute for Sports Studies. Retrieved from http://playthegame.org/media/5786679/sgo_report_final_3.pdf

Geeraert, A., & Gauthier, R. (2018). Out-of-control Olympics: Why the IOC is unable to ensure an environmentally sustainable Olympic Games. *Journal of Environmental Policy and Planning*, *20*(1), 16. doi:10.1080/1523908X.2017.1302322

Gelderman, K., Ghijsen, P., & Schoonen, J. (2010). Explaining non-compliance with European Union procurement directives: A multidisciplinary perspective. *Journal of Common Market Studies*, *48*(2), 243-264. doi:10.1111/j.1468-5965.2009.02051.x

Getz, D. (2005). *Event management & event tourism* (2nd ed.). New York, NY: Cognizant Communication Corp.

Gillard, M. (2019). *Legacy: Gangsters, corruption and the London Olympics*. London, UK: Bloomsbury.

Gold, J.R., & Gold, M.M. (2015). Framing the future: Sustainability, legacy and the 2012 London Games. In R. Holt & D. Ruta (Eds.), *Routledge handbook of sport and legacy: Meeting the challenge of major sports events* (pp. 142-158). London, UK: Routledge.

Gordon, D. (2006). Constructing a bid protest system: The choices that every procurement challenge system must make. *Public Contracts Law Journal*, *35*, 427-446.

Henry, I., & Lee, P.C., 2004. Governance and ethics in sport. In S. Chadwick & J. Beech (Eds), *The business of sport management* (pp. 25-41). Harlow, UK: Pearson Education.

Hoye, R., & Nicholson, M. (2010). Sport stadia governance. *Sport Management Review*, *13*(2), 171-178. doi:10.1016/j.smr.2009.07.003

ICC. (n.d.). Retrieved from www.icc-cricket.com/about/partners/commercial-opportunities

International Federation of Consulting Engineers (FIDIC). (2011). *Guidelines for integrity management in the consulting industry, Part I—Policies and principles* (1st ed.). Geneva, Switzerland: International Federation of Consulting Engineers

International Federation of Consulting Engineers (FIDIC). (2015). *Guidelines for integrity management in the consulting industry, Part II—Procedures* (1st ed.). Geneva, Switzerland: International Federation of Consulting Engineers

International Federation of Consulting Engineers (FIDIC). (2019). *Guidelines for integrity management in the consulting industry, Part III—FIMS and ISO37001 procedures* (1st ed.) Geneva, Switzerland: International Federation of Consulting Engineers

IOC. (2018, July 18). *IOC Executive Board reviews progress of governance reforms, decides on further action*. Retrieved from www.olympic.org/news/ioc-executive-board-reviews-progress-of-governance-reforms-decides-on-further-action

International Partnership Against Corruption in Sport (IPACS). (2019). *Task Force 1, Report, Mapping of procurement standards and risk management activities in the construction of infrastructure for sporting events*.

Jefferies, M. (2006). Critical success factors of public private sector partnerships: A case study of the Sydney SuperDome. *Engineering Construction & Architectural Management*, *13*(5), 451-462. doi:10.1108/09699980610690738

Jefferies, M., & Chen, S.E. (2014). Identifying risk factors of boot procurement: A case study of Stadium Australia. *Australian Journal of Construction Economics and Building*, *4*(1), 11-20. doi:10.5130/AJCEB.v4i1.2935

Jenny, F. (2005). Competition and anti-corruption considerations in public procurement. In OECD, *Fighting corruption and promoting integrity in public procurement* (pp. 29-35). OECD Publishing.

Jensen, M.C., & Meckling, W.H. (1976). Theory of the firm: Managerial behavior, agency costs and ownership structure. *Journal of Financial Economics*, *3*(4), 305-360. doi:10.1016/0304-405X(76)90026-X

Johnston, W.J., & Spekman, R.E. (1982). Industrial buying behavior: A need for an integrative approach. *Journal of Business Research*, *10*(2), 135-146.

Jones, D.M. (1999, March 18). Development models. *4 Supply Management*

Kauppi, K., Moxham, C., & Bamford, D. (2013). Should we try out for the major leagues? A call for research in sport operations management. *International Journal of Operations and Production Management*, *33*(10), 1368-1399. doi:10.1108/IJOPM-11-2011-0418

Kelman, S. (1990). *Procurement and public management: The fear of discretion and the quality of government performance*. Washington, DC: The AEI Press.

Kelman, S. (2002). Remaking the federal procurement. *Public Contract Law Journal*, *31*, 581-622.

Kelman, S. (2018). Reinventing government, 25 years on: Has the procurement system improved? *Public Procurement Law Review*, *3*, 101-108.

Khorana, S., & Garcia, M. (2014). Procurement liberalization diffusion in EU agreements: Signalling stewardship? *Journal of World Trade*, *48*(3), 481-500.

Kluttz, C., & Hayman, G. (2018, February 15). Digital transparency of the Paris 2024 Olympics contracts to build public trust, improve competition & deliver value for money [Blog post]. Retrieved from www.open-contracting.org/2018/02/15/digital-transparency-paris-2024-olympics-contracts-build-public-trust-improve-competition-deliver-value-money/

Krueger, K. (1999). The scope for post-tender negotiations in international tendering procedures. In S. Arrowsmith & A. Davies, *Public procurement: Global revolution*. London, UK: Kluwer Law International.

Laffont, J., & Tirole, J. (1993). *A theory of incentives in procurement and regulation*. Cambridge, MA: MIT Press.

Lanyi, A. (2004). *Measuring the economic impact of corruption: A survey*. The Iris Discussion Papers on Institutions and Development: The IRIS Center, Retrieved from http://unpan1.un.org/intradoc/groups/public/documents/apcity/unpan024055.pdf

Leonard, J.S. (1985). What promises are worth: The impact of affirmative action goals. *Journal of Human Resources*, *20*(1), 3-20. doi:10.3386/w1346

Leonard, J.S. (1990). The impact of affirmative action regulation and equal employment law on black employment. *Journal of Economic Perspectives*, *4*(4), 47-63. doi:10.1257/jep.4.4.47

Lewis, A., & Taylor, J. (2014). *Sport: Law and practice* (3rd ed.). Haywards Heath, UK: Bloomsbury.

Lindgreen, A., Vanhamme, J., van Raaij, E.M., & Johnston, W.J. (2013). Go configure: The mix of purchasing practices to choose for your supply base. *California Management Review*, *55*(2), 72-96. doi:10.1525/cmr.2013.55.2.72

LOCOG. (2011). *LOCOG sustainable sourcing code*. Retrieved from http://learninglegacy.independent.gov.uk/documents/pdfs/sustainability/cp-locog-sustainable-sourcing-code.pdf

London 2012 Olympic and Paralympic Games. (n.d.). Learning legacy. Retrieved from https://webarchive.nationalarchives.gov.uk/20180426101359/http://learninglegacy.independent.gov.uk/

Long, J.G. (2013). *Public/private partnerships for major league sports facilities*. New York, NY: Routledge.

Lysons, K, & Farrington, B. (2016). *Procurement and supply chain management* (9th ed.) Harlow, UK: Pearson Education.

Madsen, P.T. (2002). Re-opening the debate on the lack of impact of EU tenders on the opening of public procurement. *Public Procurement Law Review*, *19*(5), 265-281.

Magina, P., & McCrary, R. (2014). Applying OECD public procurement principles. In G.M. Racca & C.R. Yukins (Eds.), *Integrity and efficiency in sustainable public contracts: Balancing corruption concerns in public procurement internationally* (pp. 11-20). Brussels, Belgium: Bruylant.

Marshall, R., Meurer, M., & Richard, J-F. (1994). Curbing agency problems in the procurement process by protest oversight. *Rand Journal of Economics*, *25*(2), 297-318. doi:10.2307/2555832

Martin, S., Hartley, K., & Cox, A. (1999). Public procurement directives in the European Union: A study of local authority purchasing. *Public Administration*, *77*(2), 387-406. doi:10.1111/1467-9299.00159

Masterman, J. (2001). *Introduction to building procurement systems* (2nd ed.). Oxford, UK: Routledge.

Matheson, V.A., Schwab, D., & Koval, P. (2018). Corruption in the bidding, construction and organisation of mega-events: An analysis of the Olympics and World Cup. In M. Breuer & D. Forest (Eds.), *The Palgrave handbook on the economics of manipulation in sport* (pp. 257-278). New York, NY: Cham Springer International Publishing.

McCrudden, C. (2007). *Buying social justice: Equality, government procurement and legal change*. Oxford, UK: Oxford University Press

Mead, J.M., & Gruneberg, S. (2013). *Programme procurement in construction: Learning from London 2012*. Oxford, UK: Wiley-Blackwell.

Minis, I., Parashi, M., Tzimourtas, A. (2006). The design of logistics operations for the Olympic Games. *International Journal of Physical Distribution and Logistics Management*, *36*(8), 621-642. doi:10.1108/09600030610702899

Mishra, K.A. (2016). Malpractice in the 2010 Delhi Commonwealth Games and the renovation of Shivaji Stadium. In Transparency International, *Global corruption report: Sport* (pp. 174-177). Oxford, UK: Routledge, Retrieved from www.transparency.org/whatwedo/publication/global_corruption_report_sport

Mogre, R., Lindgreen, A., & Hingley, M. (2017). Tracing the evolution of purchasing research: Future trends and directions for purchasing practices. *Journal of Business and Industrial Marketing*, *32*(2), 251-257. doi:10.1108/JBIM-01-2016-0004

Morledge, R., & Smith, A. (2013). *Building procurement* (2nd ed.). West Sussex, UK: Wiley-Blackwell.

Müller, M. (2015). (Im-)Mobile policies: Why sustainability went wrong in the 2014 Olympics in Sochi. *European Urban and Regional Studies*, *22*(2), 191-209. doi:10.1177/0969776414523801

Nagle, J.E. (1999). *The history of government contracting* (2nd ed.). Washington, DC: George Washington University Press.

ODA. (2011). *Learning legacy: Lessons learned from the London 2012 construction project*. Retrieved from http://learninglegacy.independent.gov.uk/documents/pdfs/supporting-documents/learning-legacy.pdf

OECD. (1997). *Convention on combatting bribery of foreign public officials in international business transactions.* Retrieved from www.oecd.org/daf/anti-bribery/ConvCombatBribery_ENG.pdf

OECD. (2003). *Managing conflict of interest in the public service: A toolkit.* Retrieved from www.oecd.org/gov/ethics/49107986.pdf

OECD. (2007). *Integrity in public procurement: Good practice from A-Z.* Retrieved from www.oecd.org/gov/ethics/integrityinpublicprocurementgoodpracticefromatoz.htm

OECD. (2009). *OECD guidelines for fighting bid rigging in public procurement.* Retrieved from www.oecd.org/daf/competition/cartels/42851044.pdf

OECD. (2014). *2014 OECD survey on managing conflict of interest in the executive branch and whistleblower protection.* Retrieved from www.oecd.org/gov/ethics/2014-survey-managing-conflict-of-interest.pdf

OECD. (2015). *OECD recommendation of the Council on Public Procurement.* Retrieved from www.oecd.org/gov/public-procurement/recommendation/OECD-Recommendation-on-Public-Procurement.pdf

OECD. (2016). *Preventing corruption in public procurement.* Retrieved from www.oecd.org/gov/ethics/Corruption-Public-Procurement-Brochure.pdf

Open Contracting Partnership. (n.d.). *Global principles.* Retrieved from www.open-contracting.org/implement/global-principles/

Open Contracting Partnership. (2017). *Open contracting data standard.* Retrieved from www.open-contracting.org/data-standard/

Parent, M.M., & Smith-Swan, S. (2013). *Managing major sports events: Theory and practice.* London, UK: Routledge.

Parker, D., & Hartley, K. (1997). The economics of partnership sourcing versus adversarial competition: A critique. *European Journal of Purchasing & Supply Management, 3*(2), 115-125. doi:10.1016/S0969-7012(97)00004-X

Pivarnyik, B. (2017, July 14). FINA 2017—The story behind the biggest and most expensive sports event in Hungary's history. *The Budapest Beacon*, Retrieved from https://budapestbeacon.com/fina-2017-story-behind-biggest-expensive-sports-event-hungarys-history/

Propheter, G., & Hatch, M.E. (2015). Evaluating lease-purchase financing for professional sports facilities. *Urban Affairs Review, 51*(6), 905-925. doi:10.1177/1078087414563990

Quinot, G. (2013). Promotion of social policy through public procurement in Africa. In G. Quinot & S. Arrowsmith (Eds.), *Public procurement regulation in Africa* (pp. 393-401). Cambridge, UK: Cambridge University Press.

Reck, R.F., & Long, B. (1988). Purchasing a competitive weapon. *Journal of Purchasing and Materials Management, 24*(3), 2-8. doi:10.1111/j.1745-493X.1988.tb00631.x

Reuters. (2018). *Swimming—Peaty's world record amended after timing problem at Euros. Reuters*, Retrieved from https://uk.reuters.com/article/uk-european-championships-aquatics/swimming-peatys-world-record-amended-after-timing-problem-at-euros-idUKKBN1KQ0LD

Robinson, P.J., Faris, C.W., and Wind, Y. (1967). *Industrial buying and creative marketing.* Boston, MA: Allyn & Bacon.

Rose, R. (2010). Soccer City: What it says about the murky world of government tenders. In C.S. Herzenberg (Ed.), *Player and referee: Conflicting interests and the 2010 FIFA World Cup* (pp. 21-49). Pretoria, South Africa: Institute for Security Studies, Retrieved from http://ccs.ukzn.ac.za/files/ISS%20Player%20and%20Referee.pdf

Rose-Ackerman, S. (1997). The political economy of corruption. In K.A. Elliott (Ed.), *Corruption and the global economy* (pp. 31-60). Washington, DC: Institute for International Economics.

Rose-Ackerman, S., & Palifka, B.J. (2016). *Corruption and government: Causes, consequences, and Reform* (2nd ed.). Cambridge, UK: Cambridge University Press, 2016.

Sanderson, J., Lonsdale, C., Mannion, R., & Matharu, T. (2015). Theories about procurement and supply chain management. In J. Sanderson, C. Lonsdale, R. Mannion, & T. Matharu (Eds.), *Towards a framework for enhancing procurement and supply chain management practice in the NHS: Lessons for managers and clinicians from a synthesis of the theoretical and empirical literature* (pp. 21-38). Health Services and Delivery Research, No. 3.18. Southampton, UK: NIHR Journals Library. Retrieved from www.ncbi.nlm.nih.gov/books/NBK286079/pdf/Bookshelf_NBK286079.pdf

Schoonbee, K., & Brümmer, S. (2010). Public loss, FIFA's gain: How Cape Town got its white elephant. In C.S. Herzenberg (Ed.), *Player and referee: Conflicting interests and the 2010 FIFA World Cup* (pp. 133-168). Pretoria, South Africa: Institute for Security Studies, Retrieved from http://ccs.ukzn.ac.za/files/ISS%20Player%20and%20Referee.pdf

Schooner, S.L. (2001). Fear of oversight: The fundamental failure of businesslike government. *American University Law Review, 50*(3), 627-723. doi:10.2139/ssrn.283369

Schooner, S.L. (2002a). Commercial purchasing: The chasm between the United States government's evolving policy and practice. In S. Arrowsmith & M. Trybus (Eds.), *Public procurement: The continuing revolution.* London, UK: Kluwer Law International.

Schooner, S.L. (2002b). Desiderata: Objectives for a system of government contract law. *Public Procurement Law Review, 21*, 103-110.

Schulz Herzenberg, C.S. (Ed.). (2010). *Player and referee: Conflicting interests and the 2010 FIFA World Cup.* Pretoria, South Africa: Institute for Security Studies, Retrieved from http://ccs.ukzn.ac.za/files/ISS%20Player%20and%20Referee.pdf

Sharp, L., Moorman, A., & Claussen, C. (2017). *Sport law: A managerial approach* (3rd ed.). London, UK, and New York, NY: Routledge.

SIGA. (n.d.-a). *Universal standards: Financial integrity in sport.* Retrieved from https://siga-sport.com/universal-standards-on-financial-integrity/

SIGA. (n.d.-b). *Universal standards: Good governance in sport.* Retrieved from https://siga-sport.com/universal-standards-on-goog-good-governance-in-sporting-organisations/

SIGA. (n.d.-c). *Universal standards: Sports betting integrity.* Retrieved from https://siga-sport.net/universal-standards-on-sports-betting-integrity/

SIGA. (2018). *SIGA launches tender process for sport integrity rating and verification system (SIRVS)* [Press release]. Retrieved from http://siga-sport.net/press-releases/siga-launches-tender-process-for-sport-integrity-rating-and-verification-system-sirvs/

Sjåfjell, B., & Wiesbrock, A. (2015). Why should public procurement be about sustainability? In B. Sjåfjell & A. Wiesbrock (Eds.), *Sustainable public procurement under EU law—New perspectives on the state as stakeholder* (pp. 1-22). Cambridge, UK: Cambridge University Press.

Smith, P. (2012a). The Olympics "Delivery Partner" model—A precedent worth following? (Part 1). Retrieved from http://spendmatters.com/uk/olympics-delivery-partner-model-precedent-worth-following-part-1/

Smith, P. (2012b). The Olympics "Delivery Partner" model—A precedent worth following? (Part 2). Retrieved from http://spendmatters.com/uk/oda-2/

Spalding, A., & University of Richmond Law School Anti-Corruption Team. 2017. *Olympic anti-corruption report: Brazil and the Rio 2016 Games* (pp. 51-96). Richmond, VA: University of Richmond School of Law, Retrieved from https://law.richmond.edu/olympics/archive-brazil.html

Sport England. (2017). *Leisure management options guidance.* Retrieved from www.sportengland.org/media/12348/se-management-options-guidance.pdf

Stanislas, P. (2017). Tackling corruption and crime in public procurement in the 2012 London Olympics and Paralympics Games: The role of Operation Podium, the Specialist Organized and Economic Crime Unit of the Metropolitan Police. In P. Gottschalk & P. Stanislas (Eds.), *Public corruption: Regional and national perspectives on procurement fraud* (pp. 107-127). Boca Raton, FL: CRC Press.

Szymanski, S. (2016). Compromise or compromised? The bidding process for the award of the Olympic Games and the FIFA World Cup. In Transparency International, *Global corruption report: Sport* (pp. 157-162). Oxford, UK: Routledge.

Telgen, J., & de Boer, L. (1997). Experience with the EC directives on public procurement: A survey of Dutch municipalities. *Public Procurement Law Review, 6*(3), 121-127

Timms, J. (2015). A socially responsible business legacy. Raising standards in procurement, supply chains and employment at the London Olympics of 2012. In R. Holt & D. Ruta (Eds.), *Routledge handbook of sport and legacy: Meeting the challenge of major sports events* (pp. 217-228). London, UK: Routledge.

Touboulic, A., & Walker, H. (2015). Theories in sustainable supply chain management: A structured literature review. *International Journal of Physical Distribution and Logistics Management, 45*(1/2), 16-42. doi:10.1108/IJPDLM-05-2013-0106

Transparency International. (2009). *The anti-corruption plain language guide.* Retrieved from www.transparency.org/whatwedo/publication/the_anti_corruption_plain_language_guide

Transparency International. (2016). *Global corruption report: Sport.* Oxford, UK: Routledge. Retrieved from www.transparency.org/whatwedo/publication/global_corruption_report_sport

Trepte, P. (2004). *Regulating procurement: Understanding the ends and means of public procurement regulation.* Oxford, UK: Oxford University Press.

Trionfetti, F. (2000). Discriminatory procurement and international trade. *The World Economy, 23*(1), 57-76. doi:10.1111/1467-9701.00262

Trionfetti, F. (2003). Home-biased government procurement and international trade: Descriptive statistics, theory and empirical evidence. In S. Arrowsmith & M. Trybus (Eds.), *Public procurement: The continuing revolution.* London, UK: Kluwer Law International.

Turpin, C. (1989). *Government procurement and contracts.* Harlow, UK: Longman.

UEFA. (n.d.). Library. Retrieved from www.uefa.com/insideuefa/documentlibrary/tenders/index.html

UK Athletics. (2015). Contract notice: "Services - 180163-2015." Official Journal-S 099-180163.

UNCITRAL. (n.d.). *Guidance on procurement regulations to be promulgated in accordance with article 4 of the UNCITRAL model law on public procurement.* Retrieved from www.uncitral.org/pdf/english/texts/procurem/ml-procurement-2011/Guidance-on-procurement-regulations-e.pdf

UNCITRAL. (2004). *UNCITRAL model legislative provisions on privately financed infrastructure projects.* Retrieved from www.uncitral.org/pdf/english/texts/procurem/pfip/model/03-90621_Ebook.pdf

UNCITRAL. (2011). *UNCITRAL model law on public procurement.* Retrieved from www.uncitral.org/pdf/english/texts/procurem/ml-procurement-2011/2011-Model-Law-on-Public-Procurement-e.pdf

UNCITRAL. (2012, June 28). *Guide to enactment of the UNCITRAL model law on public procurement.* Retrieved from www.uncitral.org/pdf/english/texts/procurem/ml-procurement-2011/Guide-Enactment-Model-Law-Public-Procurement-e.pdf

UNODC. (2013). *A strategy for safeguarding against corruption in major public events.* Retrieved from www.unodc.org/documents/corruption/Publications/2013/13-84527_Ebook.pdf

van den Hurk, M. (2016). Bundling the procurement of sports infrastructure projects: How neither public nor private actors really benefit. *Environment and Planning C: Government and Policy, 34*(8), 1369-1386.

van den Hurk, M., & Verhoest, K. (2015). The governance of public–private partnerships in sports infrastructure: Interfering complexities in Belgium. *International Journal of Project Management, 33*(1), 201-211. doi:10.1016/j.ijproman.2014.05.005

van den Hurk, M., & Verhoest, K. (2017). On the fast track? Using standard contracts in public–private partnerships for sports facilities: A case study. *Sport Management Review, 20*(2), 226-239. doi:10.1016/j.smr.2016.07.004

Vogel, D. (2005). *The market for virtue: The potential and limits of corporate social responsibility.* Washington, DC: Brookings Institution Press.

von Plessen, D. (2015). *The procurement strategies for the Olympic Stadium and the Aquatic Centre for the London 2012 Olympic Games.* Hamburg, Germany: Anchor Academic Publishing.

Wallace, D. (1995). The changing world of national procurement systems: Global reformation. *Public Procurement Law Review, 4*, 57-62.

Waste Masters Solutions. (n.d.). *Philadelphia Eagles, Waste Masters Solutions agree on multi-year partnership extension.* Retrieved from https://wastemasters.com/news/

Webster, F.E. Jr. and Wind, Y (1972). A general model for understanding organisational buying behaviour. *Journal of Marketing*, 36, 12-19.

Williams-Elegbe, S. (2012). *Fighting corruption in public procurement: A comparative analysis of disqualification or debarment measures.* Oxford, UK: Hart Publishing.

Wittie, P. (2002). Transnational concerns: Domestic preferences. *Public Procurement Law Review, 9*, 145-148.

World Bank. (2011a). *Guidelines: Procurement of goods, works, and non-consulting services under IBRD loans and IDA credits and grants by World Bank borrowers.* Retrieved from http://pubdocs.worldbank.org/en/492221459454433323/Procurement-GuidelinesEnglishJuly12014.pdf

World Bank. (2011b). *Guidelines: Selection and employment of consultants under IBRD loans and IDA credits and grants by World Bank borrowers.* Retrieved from http://siteresources.worldbank.org/INTPROCUREMENT/Resources/Consultant_GLs_English_Final_Jan2011_Revised_July1_2014.pdf

W.S. Atkins Management Consultants. (1988). *The "cost of Non-Europe" in public-sector procurement*. Brussels, Belgium: Office for Official Publications of the European Communities.

Youd, K. (2014). The winter's tale of corruption: The 2022 FIFA World Cup in Qatar, the impending shift to winter, and potential legal actions against FIFA. *Northwestern Journal of International Law and Business, 35(1),* 167-197.

Zhang, J.J., Jin, L., Kim, M., & Li, H. (2013). Environmental CSR practices within the Asian sport event industry: A case study of the Beijing Olympics. In J.L. Paramio-Salcines, K. Babiak, G. Walters (Eds.), *Routledge handbook of sport and corporate social responsibility* (pp. 119-134). New York, NY: Routledge.

Zhang, X. (2007). Supplier review as a mechanism for securing compliance with public procurement rules: A critical perspective. *Public Procurement Law Review, 16(5)*, 325-351.

INDEX

Note: The italicized *f* and *t* following page numbers refer to figures and tables, respectively.

P

ABOUT THE EDITORS

Alex Thurston

Trevor Slack, PhD, was the Canada research chair of the International Institute for the Study of Sport Management at the University of Alberta in Edmonton. He was widely published in major sport and organization journals and was a keynote speaker at conferences on sport organizations around the world. He was editor of the *Journal of Sport Management* and the *European Journal of Sport Management,* and he served on the editorial board of several journals related to sport management. Slack was awarded numerous grants for social science and humanities research projects. In 1995, he presented the Zeigler Lecture, the leading lecture in sport management, and in 2001, he was awarded a Canada research chair for his work in sport management. Trevor Slack passed away in January 2016.

Terri Byers, PhD, is an associate professor at the University of New Brunswick, Canada. She was previously a principal lecturer at Coventry University, and she has taught in higher education in the United Kingdom for almost 20 years. She is widely published in journals, books, and online forums. She is currently working on projects related to managing innovation in sport organizations, using innovation (virtual reality) to create positive legacy from Paralympic Games, and managing diversity in sport organizations. Byers has collaborated with colleagues from around the globe and has been granted research funding from the European Union and Canada for her research in sport management. She takes an innovative and creative approach to projects and believes that students of sport management should always challenge existing practices to constantly improve the sport environment for diverse populations.

Terri Byers

Alex Thurston

Alex Thurston, PhD, completed his PhD in analysis of sport policy implementation and is currently teaching several modules across the sport management degrees at Loughborough University in the United Kingdom. He leads the Introduction to Sport Management module and supervises undergraduate and postgraduate dissertation project students. In 2019, Loughborough was ranked number one in the QS World University Rankings for sports-related subjects for the third consecutive year, receiving a 5-star rating. Thurston has a growing list of publications and has presented at conferences all around the world. He also delivered Trevor Slack's final two keynote speeches: one at the EASM conference in Coventry, England (2014), and the other at the NASSM conference in Ottawa, Canada (2015). Outside of academia, Thurston has more than 10 years of swimming coaching experience. He completed a two-way English Channel relay swim, became a double European champion in 2016, and holds an age-group world record.